Frommer's 96

Mexico

by Marita Adair

Assisted by Herb Felsted,
Carla Martindell Felsted,
and Maribeth Mellin

Macmillan • USA

About the Author

Marita Adair's lifelong passion for Mexico's culture, people, and history began at age 11 on her first trip across the border to Nogales. An award-winning travel writer, she logs about 10,000 miles a year traveling in Mexico—by all means of conveyance—and is the author of six Frommer guides to that country. Her freelance photographs and articles about Mexico have appeared in numerous newspapers and magazines.

MACMILLAN TRAVEL

A Simon & Schuster Macmillan Company
1633 Broadway
New York, NY 10019

Copyright © 1996 by Simon & Schuster, Inc.

ISBN: 0-02-860499-7
ISSN: 1084-418X

Editor: Ian Wilker
Assistant Editor: Blythe Grossberg
Map Editor: Douglas Stallings
Design by Michele Laseau
Digital cartography by James Moore & Ortelius Design

Special Sales

Bulk purchases (10+ copies) of Frommer's travel guides are available to corporations at special discounts. The Special Sales Department can produce custom editions to be used as premiums and/or for sales promotion to suit individual needs. Existing editions can be produced with custom cover imprints such as corporate logos. For more information write to Special Sales, Simon & Schuster, 1633 Broadway, New York, NY 10019.

Manufactured in the United States of America

Contents

List of Maps

An Invitation To The Reader

In researching this book, I discovered many wonderful places. I'm sure you'll find others. Please tell us about them, so we can share the information with your fellow travelers in upcoming editions. If you were disappointed with a recommendation, I'd love to know that, too. Please write to:

Marita Adair
Frommer's Mexico '96
Macmillan Travel
1633 Broadway
New York, NY 10019

An Additional Note

Please be advised that travel information is subject to change at any time—and this is especially true of prices. We therefore suggest that you write or call ahead for confirmation when making your travel plans. The authors, editors, and publisher cannot be held responsible for the experiences of readers while traveling. Your safety is important to us, however, so we encourage you to stay alert and be aware of your surroundins. Keep a close eye on cameras, purses, and wallets, all favorite targets of thieves and pickpockets.

A Few Words About Prices

In December 1994, the Mexican government devalued its currency, the peso. Over the ensuing months, the peso's value against the dollar plummeted from 3.35 pesos against U.S. $1 to nearly 7 pesos against U.S. $1; the peso's value continues to fluctuate—at press time it was slightly more than 6 to the dollar. Inflation in Mexico for 1995 and 1996 is predicted to be between 40% and 60%. Therefore to allow for inflation, prices in this book (which are always given in U.S. dollars) have been converted to U.S. dollars at a rate of 4.5 pesos to the dollar. Many moderate-priced and expensive hotels, which often have U.S. toll-free reservation numbers and have many expenses in U.S. dollars, did not lower rates in keeping with the sinking peso.

Mexico has a Value-Added Tax of 15% (*Impuesto de Valor Agregado,* or IVA, pronounced "*ee*-bah") on almost everything, including hotel rooms, restaurant meals, bus tickets, and souvenirs. (Exceptions are Cancún, Cozumel, and Los Cabos, where the IVA is 10%.) This tax will not necessarily be included in the prices quoted by hotels and restaurants. In addition, prices charged by hotels and restaurants have been deregulated. Mexico's new pricing freedom may cause some price variations from those quoted in this book; always ask to see a printed price sheet and ask if the tax is included.

What The Symbols Mean

✪ Frommer's Favorites

Hotels, restaurants, attractions, and entertainment you should not miss.

⑤ Super-Special Values

Hotels and restaurants that offer great value for your money.

The Best of Mexico

With hair amuss, wearing the plush hotel robe I've hastily donned, I open my hotel room's door at the sound of the early morning knock I'm expecting. A nattily dressed waiter flourishes a tray loaded with a pot of coffee and orange juice—my complimentary treat for requesting a wake-up call at the Presidente Inter-Continental in Mexico City.

At the Casa Que Canta in Zihuatanejo, I'm shown the ins and outs of my lavishly large suite, its spacious terrace overlooking the bay, *and* the small refrigerator stocked with complimentary beverages—and this last was a plus I'd never seen anywhere. I'm accustomed to paying for every bottle I touch—but not here, not from that little fridge. I luxuriate during my stay, knowing that the maid will never wake me to clean the room—she waits until I'm up and out for the day to create a spotless territory for my return.

Not every traveler knows to expect this kind of luxury when traveling south of the border, but within the last 20 years the country we're used to thinking of as a cheap, rough-it destination has lavished a number of fine hostelries and restaurants on its landscape that rival the world's best.

Even if deluxe digs are in almost every corner of Mexico now, don't worry; you'll still find many comfortable, much less expensive, and charming places to stay—on the beach, in the heart of colonial cities, in the jungles, and mountains. This book is for everyone going to Mexico, from those who want the flavor of everyday life for the average Mexicans (the budget inns that abound throughout the country make great bases for such explorations) to those who want to kick back at the top luxury resorts.

Travel services in Mexico have seen a lot of progress over the last 20 years—many fine establishments, new freeways, and expanded air access—but it would be Pollyannaish to say that the broader life of the nation hasn't seen its share of grief, especially this year and last. Mexico's problems—political assassinations, the devaluation of the peso, curtailed international business, volcanic ash spewing from Popocatepetl, violence in Chiapas, and a cloud of suspicion hovering over a once-revered president—have been such prominent news in the United States that it has perhaps skewed our perception of what it really means to travel there.

You won't see the grim face of depression when in Mexico—the country bustles with commerce as much as ever, and ready smiles greet as they always have.

If you are so brazen as to ask people, as I have, "How difficult has the devaluation been for you," you may catch glimpse of a sad sense of resignation, but it's quickly followed by a look of set-jawed determination and a vow to work harder and get through it—and that most often in a tone that makes light of the problem. Mexicans have a deep reservoir of personal strength. Bringing up the subject of devaluation, however, is about as polite and fun to talk about as a blemish on someone's face. Besides, it touches Mexicans' deep sense of personal and national pride, both of which are best left alone.

Another thing Mexico is blessedly free of is depressing news from home. Yes, you can buy U.S. newspapers or catch CNN news, but you can avoid them, too, and forget your own thorny set of local and national problems. This is a country that asks "O.J. who? Newt who?"—absorbed as we are in our own world, we forget that our dramas aren't news in Mexico. One of the best perks of my job, and one available to any foreigner traveling in Mexico, is to be free for a while from problems that afflict life outside of Mexico. How wonderful to leave it all behind and to awaken to pampering—hot coffee at my fingertips, a terrace and balcony overlooking the ocean and a panorama of sailboats. Or, when traveling in a way that puts me right in the heart of a small village, to awaken to the sounds of children playing and chattering in Spanish, to the maid gossiping while slapping the laundry on an old-fashioned scrub board, to a rooster crowing from a nearby rooftop, and to the *pat-pat* of the cook forming fresh tortillas, all while anticipating the energizing zest of a sundae-size glass of freshly squeezed orange juice.

And then there are the bargains. It's been 10 years since prices were this good. As I write this, inflation has yet to spiral prices out of sight, and Mexico is a true travel bargain. Food was so inexpensive, for example, that I found myself tipping more than necessary, aware that wages have not kept pace with the cost of feeding families. All over the country, I muzzled my tongue and resisted the urge to crow aloud about the fabulous windfalls I was finding (a lot of people really are suffering with the devaluation), but I sure did enjoy them. Alone in my room, I smiled while looking over my new purchases—the folk tapestries that I bought in Pátzcuaro, the set of Picassoesque dishes I found in Dolores Hidalgo, the silver earrings from Zacatecas, the Casas Grande anthropomorphic pottery reproduction that I bought in Morelia. And the savings I enjoyed? All the while I was plotting to use them to return to Mexico as soon as this year's round of books were off to the publisher. It's all waiting south of the border.

The Best Cultural Experiences

There are moments in Mexico that visitors vainly wish they could shelve away intact, to be brought out and savored again and again at home. But even though such experiences are fleeting, they leave an indelible mark in the memory.

The Callejoneada, in Zacatecas   Nothing compares to the exhilaration of following a band of horns and drums, a burro laden with barrels of fiery mezcal (from which you imbibe frequently using a cup hung around your neck), and a group of merry people swinging hands and dancing through the narrow streets (*callejons*) of Zacatecas until the wee hours—legally disturbing the peace. (Contact Cantera Tours, ☎ 2-9065.)

The Estudiantinas, in Guanajuato   When University students (*estudiantes*) dressed in medieval garb sing their way through the streets of Guanajuato accompanied by crowds and a burro laden with tequila (from which you take liberal cups of the intoxicating liquor), it's an unforgettable experience. Crowds follow along, dancing and singing until exhaustion sets in. Often, especially during the Cervantino Festival, the estudiantinas appear spontaneously in restaurants. Their mixed voices are so wonderful you wish for a recording.

Hanging Out in the Plaza de Armas, in Veracruz   Few plazas compare to this one—there's nearly nonstop music provided by marimbas, strolling trios, and harpists singing spontaneous poems to diners. All this for the price of a tip—you'll probably want to leave a large one.

Mariachi Serenades   On the Plaza Garibaldi in Mexico City and under the portals of El Parian in Tlaquepaque near Guadalajara, numerous groups of elegantly clad musicians play their lustrous horn and string instruments and belt out their songs. Anytime you hear mariachis in Mexico, this dreamy yet intensely alive feeling settles over you and you say, "Now *this* is Mexico."

Fireworks   Pyrotechnic displays are seen so frequently in Mexico that it's easy to take them for granted. Their creativity bests any laser show—I'm convinced fireworks are a kind of national genius. They appear somewhere almost nightly in Acapulco and at almost every festival countrywide.

Regional Folk Dancing   From the Ballet Folklórico in Mexico City or Guadalajara to the almost nightly park performances in Mérida to hotel fiesta nights countrywide, folk dancing in Mexico never becomes tiresome, no matter how many performances you've seen.

The Best Archaeological Sites

Palenque   In a dense jungle setting, the long-ago makers of these powerful Chiapan ruins carved histories in stone that allow them to speak through the centuries to us. Just imagine the ceremony that must have taken place the day King Pacal was buried below ground in a secret pyramidal tomb, which remained untouched from A.D. 683 to its discovery in 1952.

Teotihuacán   So close to Mexico City, this site is still centuries away. You feel the majesty of the past in a stroll from the Pyramid of the Sun to the Pyramid of the Moon down the pyramid-lined the Avenue of the Dead. Imagine what a fabulous place this must have been when the walls were stuccoed and painted in brilliant colors. Unlike at Palenque, where important personages were honored with their likenesses carved in stone the builders of Teotihuacán did not leave behind self-portraits.

Monte Alban   A grand ceremonial city built on a mountaintop overlooking the city of Oaxaca, Monte Alban leaves visitors with more questions than answers. We still wonder who they were and why they were obsessed with deformed humans.

Uxmal   No matter how many times you see Uxmal, the splendor of its stone carvings is awesome. A stone rattlesnake undulates across the facade of the Nunnery complex here, and 103 masks of Chaac, the rain god, project from the Governor's Palace.

Chichén-Itzá Stand beside the giant serpent head at the foot of El Castillo pyramid and marvel at the mastermind who conspired to position the building precisely so shadow and light would form a serpent's body slithering all the way to the giant head each March 21 and September 21.

The Best Beach Vacations

Almost as valuable as knowing the best beaches is knowing which beaches are not so inviting—such as San Blas, north of Puerto Vallarta, and most of the coast of Veracruz. In both places, the hard-packed sand is as appealing as a concrete parking lot.

Barra de Navidad The golden sands of Barra de Navidad Bay spread from this village to its neighbor, Melaque. Inexpensive hotels are right on the beach or very nearby.

Ixtapa/Zihuatanejo This resort duo packs a lot of good beaches into a relatively small area. The best and most beautiful of those close to Zihuatanejo is Playa La Ropa. The wide, beautiful beach at Playa Las Gatas, with its beachside eateries and snorkeling sites, is also a great place to play. The luxury hotels in Ixtapa, on the next bay over from Zihuatanejo, front Playa Palmar, a fine, wide strip of beach. Just offshore, Isla Ixtapa boasts a good beach and snorkeling area and lots of palapa restaurants serving incredible fresh fish.

Manzanillo Beaches spread out all along Bahía Manzanillo and Bahía Santiago, the two big bays on which Manzanillo is built. One of the best beaches—and certainly the most accessible—is Playa Las Brisas, fronted by small hotels and condominiums.

Mazatlán The waterfront is lined with wide, golden-yellow beaches where such water sports as parasailing and banana boats are big draws. The best stretch is known as Playa Sábalo, but beaches line the ocean, especially northward beyond the marina, all the way to Los Cerritos. On the oceanside of the small village on Isla de las Piedras (Stone Island), a pale-sand beach bordered by coconut groves stretches for miles. On Sunday afternoons, the palapa restaurants there host music and dancing, attracting families and young people; on other days, the beach is almost empty.

Puerto Vallarta The spectacularly wide Bandera Bay is lined with fine beaches and with many economical places to stay. Boat excursions take you to other nearby beaches to spend the day and dine on fresh fish beneath a woven palm umbrella.

Playa del Carmen The town beach, fronted by small hotels and little restaurants, is beautiful and wide. Topless sunbathing, while illegal, seems to be permitted here. From here you're just a ferry ride away to the island of Cozumel, not far from the ruins of Tulum and Cobá, and near the snorkeling lagoons of Xcaret and Xel-Ha.

Puerto Angel The town beaches are beautiful on the small bay here, and townsfolk clean up the trash deposited by coastal currents. Nearby, there are a number of almost uninhabited beaches accessible by taxi or bus; discovering them is one of the treats of a leisurely Puerto Angel vacation.

Puerto Escondido Some people love this spot for the enormous breakers that roll into Playa Zicatela, a world-class surfing beach. Others love sharing the beauty of the town beach with fishermen who pull their colorful *pangas* under the shade of palms leaning so far over they almost touch the ground.

The Yucatán's Quintana Roo Coast   The best beaches in the country are in Cancún and to its south, almost all the way to Chetumal on the border with Belize. All along the coast, there are extraordinarily inexpensive places to stay right on the powdery, nearly white-sand beaches. The palm-lined beach at Xpuja is among the most beautiful stretches here.

Isla Mujeres   There's only one small best beach here—Playa Norte—but it's a dandy. From this island, you can dive in the cave of the sleeping sharks, snorkel right off shore, and take a fascinating boat excursion to the Isla Contoy National Park, which features great birdlife and a fabulous, uninhabited beach.

The Best Active Vacations

Biking   Several outlets in Puerto Vallarta now feature mountain-bike trips into the mountains surrounding this picturesque village.

Spelunking   The mountains of Baja California are riddled with more than 100 caves painted with bold prehistoric pictures and petroglyphs. Reaching them, an adventure in itself, requires horses, mules, or Jeeps, usually from Santa Rosalía but also from Guerrero Negro. Although the trips can be made year-round, the most pleasant months are October through December.

Scuba Diving   The coral reefs off the island of Cozumel are Mexico's premier diving destinations. On the Yucatán mainland, diving into the deep, dark *cenotes* (sinkholes or natural wells) is an interesting twist on underwater exploration. There are also fascinating dive sites at Cabo Pulmo off Los Cabos in the Sea of Cortez; around the islands off Loreto; and at Ixtapa/Zihuatanejo, Puerto Vallarta, and Manzanillo.

Sportfishing   Billfishing for graceful marlin and sailfish is among the popular sports in Los Cabos, La Paz, Mazatlán, Manzanillo, Cozumel, Playa del Carmen, and Zihuatanejo, but you may hook any number of edible fish in these waters. Serious fishers will find bonefish near Punta Allen, south of Tulum, where they can stay at the Cuzan Guest House. Most of the major fishing towns have annual contests.

Hiking and Mountaineering   Tough challenges await you on the slopes of volcanoes in central Mexico—Paricutín, Orizaba, Popocatépetl, and Ixtaccíhihuatl. In the Copper Canyon, hiking the deep canyons and lofty ridges requires a good guide and plenty of stamina.

Sea Kayaking   Bahía Concepción, south of Mulege, is one of Baja's most beautiful kayaking spots. Its islands and remote coves make for interesting exploration.

Boating the Maya Canals   Ancient narrow canals made by the Maya travel inland from the Caribbean through the jungle to a place near the ruins of Muyil. You can journey along the canals from the Punta Allen Peninsula.

River Rafting   The Usumacinta River, which divides Mexico from Guatamala, offers an extraordinary opportunity to steep yourself in jungle scenery and to visit the almost inaccessible Maya ruins of Yaxchilán.

Surfing   Surfers congregate on Puerto Escondido's Zicatela Beach, where large curling waves challenge the best in the sport.

The Best Places to Get Away from It All

A few places in Mexico come to mind as total escapes for a moment, a day, a week, or more of sublime tranquility. Some of these could double as romantic escapes if you're not expecting posh digs.

Costa Alegre, Pacific Coast   Between Puerto Vallarta and Manzanillo, three super exclusive hotels cater to those with both time and money, including celebrities who want to vacation in peace. These stylish resorts, including Las Alamandas, the Hotel Bel-Air El Tamarindo, and Hotel Bel-Air Costa Careyes, are miles from civilization and boast their own private beaches.

Bacalar, Quintana Roo   Once you see the manicured grounds with hammocks hanging between the trees and the handsomely crafted casitas of the Hotel Rancho Encantada, you'll know you've arrived at *the* place to unwind. The hotel is on the shores of the placid lake Bacalar, and there's nothing around for miles. But if you want adventure, you can take excursions to Belize and to the obscure but highly intriguing Maya ruins on the Río Bec ruin route.

Batopilas, Copper Canyon   After seven hours of passing nary a soul on a twisty, narrow, dirt mountain road, you enter a near ghost town from 18th- and 19-century silver-mining booms. Preserved as though someone sealed it for safekeeping last century, the town has feel of yesteryear indelibly imprinted on its stucco walls and cobbled streets. This outpost has no telephones or newspapers. Electricity, a recent installation, makes the one or two televisions operable.

Casa de la Tortuga and El Burro Boracho, Ixtapa   Six miles north of Ixtapa, this Pacific-Coast hideaway started out as a simple-but-wonderful place to have a delicious lobster or shrimp lunch, a swim in the ocean, and a stroll along the beach without bumping into a soul. With rooms for a few guests, now it's a complete getaway that's hard to beat for simplicity and tranquility, without phones or other worldly interruptions.

Todos Santos, Baja California Sur   Just 85 miles north of Cabo San Lucas but a world apart from that town's resort atmosphere is Todos Santos. The ride up the Pacific Coast passes gorgeous wild beaches, isolated campgrounds, and a few solitary homes and farms. Housed in one of the old mansions around the town plaza is the Café Santa Fe, a superb place to dine and reason alone to come to Todos Santos.

The Yucatán's Costa Turquesa, south of Cancún   Away from the busy resort of Cancún, a string of heavenly quiet getaways, including Pamul, Xcalacoco, and Xpuja, offer tranquility on beautiful palm-lined beaches.

The Yucatán's Punta Allen Peninsula   South of the Tulum ruins, a string of beachside budget inns offers some of the most peaceful getaways in the country. Life here among the birds and coconut palms has never been anything but leisurely.

Isla Mujeres, near Cancún   If there's one island in Mexico that encourages relaxation, this is it. Though the island has plenty of hotels and restaurants, there are no crowds. Guests here bring laziness to new heights, stretching out and dozing beneath shady palms or languidly strolling about, "dressed up" in flip flops, tee shirts, and shorts.

The Best Cities in which to Learn Spanish

Every year, particularly in the summer, thousands of foreigners head to Mexico to study Spanish. They find schools with intensive study programs; some are geared to businesspeople, while others focus on more casual, conversational use of the language. Schools employ a variety of teaching styles, often using history, culture, food, and literature as vehicles into the language, along with classroom study and streetside language use. Most schools are flexible enough to take students at any level of proficiency for as little as a week to more than a month of instruction.

San Miguel de Allende and **Cuernavaca** have the most language schools and are probably the best known among foreigners for Spanish language instruction. Schools in **Oaxaca, Guanajuato,** and **San Cristóbal de las Casas** also win a lot of praise from former students.

The Best Shopping

Hardly a tourist returns from Mexico without at least one craft. Some people bring an empty bag for purchases, and some haul their loot by the trunk. Sure bets for superior shopping are found in more than a half-dozen cities and villages.

Dolores Hidalgo   A few miles north of San Miguel de Allende, this village is fast becoming the best-known pottery-producing village in Mexico. Almost every block has factories or store outlets devoted to the colorful Talavera-style pottery.

Mexico City   Shopping highlights include the Fonart stores; the Museo de Artes y Industrias Populares; the Avalos Brothers glass factory; and the Bazar Sábado, Lagunilla Market, and La Ciudadela Market.

Oaxaca   A colonial city with good shops and crafts markets, it's also ringed by villages specializing in pottery, textiles, and colorful, imaginative wood carving.

Pátzcuaro   Deep in the Sierra Madres, this village, and the smaller ones surrounding it, feature beautiful cotton textiles; wood carving; pottery; lacquerware; and straw weaving. One nearby village is Santa Clara del Cobre, Mexico's "Copper Capital," where shops glimmer with copper.

Puebla   A pottery center even before the conquest of Mexico, it's Talavera-style tile adorns building facades and church domes throughout the area. Factories produce highly collectible tile and colorful tableware with unique motifs.

San Cristóbal de las Casas   Deep in the heart of the Maya highlands, San Cristóbal's shops, open plazas, and markets feature the distinctive waist-loomed wool and cotton textiles of the region, as well as leather shoes, handsomely crude pottery, genre dolls, and Guatemalan textiles.

San Miguel de Allende   Street after street of shops carrying textiles, brass, tin, iron, pottery, glass, and much more are housed here in colonial-era mansions.

Taxco   Mexico's "Silver Capital," Taxco features more than 200 stores selling the metal worked into fine jewelry and decorative objects.

Toluca   The Friday Toluca Market is one of the grandest in the country; its enormity is exhausting and its contents fascinating. The huge Casart, the state-owned crafts shop, is one of the best in Mexico; it features locally made baskets, pottery, glass, Persian-style carpets from Temoaya, and more.

Tonala and Tlaquepaque Two villages near Guadalajara, they are renowned for pottery, papier-mâché, and hand-blown glass. More than 400 artisans have workshops in Tonala.

The Best Sunsets & Margaritas

Many visitors to Mexico plan their days around the perfect place to gaze upon Mexico's magnificent sunsets (*puestas del sol*), which are extraordinarily good on the Pacific Coast.

Acapulco Pie de la Cuesta, a beach north of Acapulco, has long been famous for its sunsets, which you can see any time of year. In Acapulco, sunsets aren't visible all year, but when they are, the best place to be is Su Casa, an open-patio restaurant set high on a hill with a stupendous view of the whole bay. The giant-size margaritas send off the sun admirably.

Barra de Navidad Beachfront restaurants in this laid-back village host sunset happy hours that bring in resident North Americans and locals alike.

Cabo San Lucas Here, the place to be when the sun meets the horizon is on the slender point that leads to Land's End, where the two seas meet. At El Trebol, in the Solimar Hotel, mariachis play while the setting sun gilds the high outcropping of sienna rocks behind the hotel. The high terrace of the Whale Watcher's Bar, in the Hotel Finisterra, affords a splendid view of the sea.

Ixtapa/Zihuatanejo Stake out a place anywhere on the sand to enjoy the sunset, but to loll about with class, take a cushy seat in the lobby bar of the Westin Brisas Hotel. There, an open-air window frames the sunset perfectly while a trio croons romantic ballads.

La Paz A favorite ringside seat at dusk is a table at La Terraza, next to the Hotel Perla, which makes good schooner-size margaritas. Pelicanos Bar in the second story of the Hotel Los Arcos has a good view of the waterfront and a clubby, cozy feel. An inexpensive alternative is to stroll along the Malecón, where just about everyone stops to pay homage to the setting sun while people watching, drinking, snacking, and listening for the sound of wandering troubadours.

Manzanillo When the sun starts to set, the place to be is the outdoor patio of the cozy La Posada hotel on the Las Brisas Peninsula. Here, you join guests in the daily sunset ritual honoring the last rays with margaritas.

Puerto Angel From Zipolite beach or the viewing hill above the Posada Cañyon de Vata, the sunsets here are gorgeous.

Puerto Vallarta Anywhere along the beach facing the magnificent Banderas Bay, you'll see people pausing for the last orange-gold rays of light. From the rooftop of the Hotel Los Cuatro Vientos, the whole town is silhouetted against the entire bay as visitors nurse some of the best margaritas in town and the sun drops beyond the horizon.

The Hottest Nightlife

In Mexico nightlife runs the gamut from quiet supper clubs with dance floors (although there aren't many of these) to beachside dance floors with live bands to extended "happy hours" in seaside bars to some of the flashiest discos in the world.

Yes, *discos*. These flamboyant seventies-style clubs may be passé in the rest of the world, but in Mexico "*dees-cohs*" are more than alive and well, they have a thriving life of their own. Most nightspots start up around 9:30 or 10pm and close somewhere between 2am and sunrise.

Acapulco   For hot nightlife, this city is tops in the country, with lots of the latest discos, several of which have a wall of windows overlooking the bay. Establishments blaring pulsating Caribbean and salsa sounds can be just as crowded as the most "in" disco.

Puerto Vallarta   Here, you can find mariachi hotspots that rollick until the wee hours or work yourself into a dancing frenzy at one of several almost all-night discos.

Cancún   From live music in hotel-lobby bars to the most sophisticated discos around, there are a lot of options in Cancún for staying out until the sun comes up.

Baja California   Cabo San Lucas is the nightlife capital of Baja, though after-dark fun is centered around the party ambience and camaraderie found in the casual bars and restaurants rather than a flashy disco scene—but you'll find discos too.

Mazatlán   Though this clean beachside city doesn't have the breadth of nightlife of other resorts, it does have Valentinos, one of the best known and most popular discos in the country. Dramatically perched on a rocky outcropping overlooking the sea, this white, Moorish-looking building has a high-tech light show with green laser beams.

The Most Luxurious Hotels

Mexico offers a long list of special places where the service is as polished as the quality of the establishment. Below are a few that should be on your short list of posh accommodations, but there are many others (see also "The Costa Alegre" under "The Best Places to Get Away from It All," above).

Las Mañanitas, Cuernavaca   This small hotel, with decades of experience, is the standard-bearer for luxury hotels in Mexico. Though elegant in every way, it offers exclusivity without snobbery. Everything here is polished, from the brass and mahogany to the top-notch service. Even the strolling peacocks in the garden are well groomed.

Hotel Marqués Reforma, Mexico City   Few hotels have gone as far as this one to cater to your every need, from rental cellular phones to in-room connections for fax and computer, voice mail, and even a choice of feather or polyester pillows. Each evening a harpist or quartet of musicians playing stringed instruments provides soft sounds in the lobby.

Four Seasons, Mexico City   The first foray of this chain into Mexico, this hotel manages to capture the serenity of the countryside and the elegance of colonial architecture to create a cool oasis in the midst of the biggest city in the world.

Casa de Sierra Nevada, San Miguel de Allende   A collection of six elegantly outfitted manor houses make up this luxury hotel in one of the country's most appealing colonial-era villages.

Villa Montaña, Morelia   The Villa Montaña defines perfection. There's so much attention to detail here that everything gleams as though it's been polished for a presidential visit. Rooms, each of which is completely different, are furnished with priceless antiques. Terraces have fabulous views from the hotel's perch on a mountain overlooking the city, and the casually beautiful restaurant is one of the city's best.

Camino Real, Oaxaca   Fashioned from a colonial convent, this hotel exudes all that is special about colonial Oaxaca—well-preserved structures hundreds of years old showcase Mexican history and mystery. We still know nothing about the people who painted the faded religious murals on the hotel's walls that blend so eloquently with the Gregorian chant echoing through the stony halls. Rooms are as lovely as the hotel is historic.

Hotel Bel-Air, Puerto Vallarta   A stay here is akin to falling deep into the lap of luxury. This hotel boasts spacious, beautifully furnished rooms, gleaming marble floors, and excellent service, all right on a golf course.

Avandaro Golf and Spa Resort, Valle de Bravo   It's worth a trip here just to absorb the hotel's setting beside the rolling lawns of the 18-hole golf course against a mountain backdrop that's justifiably compared to Switzerland. The large suites feature spacious sitting areas and balconies. The full spa is on a par with the best spas in the world.

La Casa Que Canta, Zihuatanejo   Architecturally dramatic, this hotel harmonizes all that is wonderful about Mexican art, including adobe and folk art, in the grandly scaled rooms. It's delightful to think of staying here—reading books on the terrace overlooking the bay and ordering room service.

Westin Brisas Resort, Ixtapa   Few hotels manage grandness of scale while maintaining their intimacy, but this one has achieved a perfect balance. Rooms, elegantly Spartan, come with large private terraces overlooking the ocean and the hotel's private beach.

Hotel Krystal, Puerto Vallarta   Built like a self-contained village, this hotel is a low-rise oasis in a line of high-rise hotels. Rooms, all of which are large, often have balconies overlooking the palm-filled lawns. Seven restaurants mean you'll never be hungry and never be compelled to head off to town for a meal.

The Best Budget Inns

Some inns stand out for their combination of hospitality and simple-but-colorful surroundings. These are places guests return to again and again.

Posada Terranova, San José del Cabo   The best budget inn in town, this posada offers invitingly bright and clean rooms. The patio restaurant serves good American- and Mexican-style meals.

Los Cuatro Vientos, Puerto Vallarta   A quiet, cozy inn set on a hillside overlooking Banderas Bay, this hotel features colorfully decorated rooms built around a small pool and central patio, daily continental breakfast, the best place to watch the sunset in Puerto Vallarta. It is run by two fine hostesses: owner Gloria Whiting and the equally helpful manager, Lola Bravo.

Hotel Flor de María, Puerto Escondido   This place is charming in every detail, from the hospitable owners Lino and María Francato; to the rooms, which are individually decorated with Lino's fine artistic touches; to the restaurant, which is the best in town.

Hotel Mansión Iturbe Bed and Breakfast, Pátzcuaro   Few budget hotels offer more free perks for guests, including welcome drinks; hot water for instant coffee in the lobby early each morning; full breakfasts in Doña Paca, the hotel's great little restaurant; free daily paper; two hours of free bicycle rental; and the fourth night free. The hotel is in a 17th-century town house on Pátzcuaro's Plaza Grande.

Hotel Posada de la Basílica, Pátzcuaro   A mansion-turned-hotel, this appealing colonial-style inn has comfortable rooms with fireplaces built around a lovely patio with a view of the village.

Hotel Rancho Taxco Victoria, Taxco   With a fabulous hillside setting overlooking all of Taxco and its pristine 1940s decor, this hotel gets special marks as an inexpensive inn that exudes all the charm of old-fashioned Mexico.

Posada del Cafeto, Jalapa   Travelers are delighted to discover this comfortable town house-turned-hotel with its colorful rooms and Mexican tile accents. Coffee is available for guests mornings and evenings.

Casa Mexilio Guest House, Mérida   Host Roger Lynn has created the atmosphere of a private home rather than that of a hotel in this 19th-century town house, and he offers some of the most unusual guided tours of the area.

Hotel Mucuy, Mérida   Owners of one of the most hospitable budget hotels in the country, Alfredo and Ofelia Comin strive to make guests feel at home with cheery, clean rooms; comfortable outdoor tables and chairs; a communal refrigerator in the lobby; and laundry and clothesline facilities.

Cabañas Pamul, Cancún-Tulum Highway   Seven coral-colored bungalows face a beautiful, small cove and a wide, beautiful, cream-colored beach and the cerulean Caribbean. Reef diving and snorkeling sites are within a five-minute walk, but the nearest civilization is at Puerto Aventuras, $2^{1}/_{2}$ miles away.

Villas Xpuja and Restaurant, Cancún-Tulum Highway   The rooms here are sparsely furnished and inexpensive, but the setting is priceless. Tall, luscious coconut palms lean over the wide, clean, nearly empty beach that seems to stretch forever in both directions, with no sign of other development. You still feel as if you were on a nearly uninhabited island here rather than on some of the hottest real estate on the Yucatán Peninsula. Get here before it disappears.

Cuzan Guest House, the Yucatán's Punta Allen Peninsula   Getting to the isolated lobster-fishing village of Punta Allen is half the adventure, after which you can nest in one of the tipi-shaped thatched roof cottages, swing in a hammock, dine on lobster and stone crabs, and absolutely forget there's an outside world. There are no phones, televisions, or newspapers, and "town" is 35 miles away. You can engage in nature trips and bone fishing if you wish to move.

The Most Authentic Culinary Experiences

Fonda Don Chon, Mexico City   Ever had a hankering for armadillo *en chimole*, a heap of toasted grasshoppers, chrysanthemums stuffed with tuna, or perhaps a pile of ant eggs sautéed in butter and wine sauce? Don Chon gets back to the basics of authentic Mexican cuisine at his restaurant, billed as the "Cathedral of Pre-Hispanic Cooking." More traditional fare is served too, but even if you don't eat here, it's worth a trip just to read the menu and examine the walls of articles and accolades written about this famous place.

Fonda del Refugio, Mexico City   Elegantly casual, this place prepares specialties from all over the country, including manchamanteles (tablecloth stainer) on Tuesday and albondigas en chile chipotle (meatballs in chipotle sauce) on Saturday.

Fonda de Santa Clara, Puebla   The menu here features such local dishes as pollo mole poblano, mixiotes, and tinga (a great beef stew). There are seasonal specialties as well, like fried grasshoppers in October and November, maguey worms in April and May, chiles enogada in July through September, and huitlacoche in June.

Casa Puntarenas, Zihuatanejo   A modest spot with a tin roof and nine wooden tables, Puntarenas is one of the best places in town to try one of Mexico's finest culinary treats—fried whole fish served with toasted bolillos, sliced tomatoes, onions, and avocado.

El Fogón de Jovel, San Cristóbal de las Casas   Chiapan food is served at this handsome old townhouse, with dining under the portals and rooms built around a central courtyard. The waiters wear local indigenous costumes. The scrumptious food highlights the specialties of Chiapas.

Las Pichanchas, Tuxtla Gutiérrez   Chiapan variations on sausages, tamales, and beef are featured in this festively decorated restaurant named after the holy pot used to make nixtamal masa dough.

Los Almendros, Merida, Cancún, Ticul and Mexico City   This family-owned restaurant chain features Yucatecan specialties. Their famous poc-chuc, a marinated and grilled pork dish, was created at the original restaurant in Ticul some years ago.

2

Getting to Know Mexico

Everyone north of the Río Grande has at least some idea—usually an old-fashioned one—about what Mexico is like, but only those who go there can know the real Mexico. The country is undergoing fast-paced and far-reaching change, as are most countries touched by modern technology. Mexico is so forcefully affected by what goes on in its neighbor to the north, the United States, that the old Mexico of cowboy songs and the movies was long ago replaced by a land full of the familiar signs of 20th-century life.

1 The Land & Its People

Mexico includes seemingly trackless desert in the north, thousands of miles of lush seacoast, tropical lowland jungle, volcanic peaks, and the snowcapped mountains of the Sierra Madre. From the breathtaking gorges of Chihuahua to the jungle coastal plain of Yucatán, from the Pacific at Baja California to the Caribbean at Quintana Roo, Mexico stretches across nearly 2,000 miles from east to west and more than 1,000 miles from north to south. Four times the size of Texas, it's bordered to the north by the United States and to the southeast by Belize, Guatemala, and the Caribbean; to the east by the Gulf of Mexico; and to the west by the Sea of Cortez and the Pacific Ocean.

THE REGIONS IN BRIEF
BAJA CALIFORNIA

A peninsula longer than Italy, the Baja stretches 876 miles from its border with California, and northernmost city of Tijuana, to **Cabo San Lucas** at its southern tip where the Sea of Cortes meets the Pacific Ocean. Formed by volcanoes that left multicolored mountains and mysterious caves later painted by Indians, today this craggy desertscape is framed on both sides by deep blue waters. Culturally and geographically set apart from mainland Mexico, it achieved statehood only in 1974. Development has been slow. Even now only a few roads penetrate Baja California, but for centuries a few intrepid souls have staked their lives on its promise. Slowly the peninsula has evolved into a vacation haven noted for its fishing, diving, leaping dolphins, sea lions, colonies of migrating whales, and posh resorts. Though much of Baja is expensive, with planning, there are still

Mexico

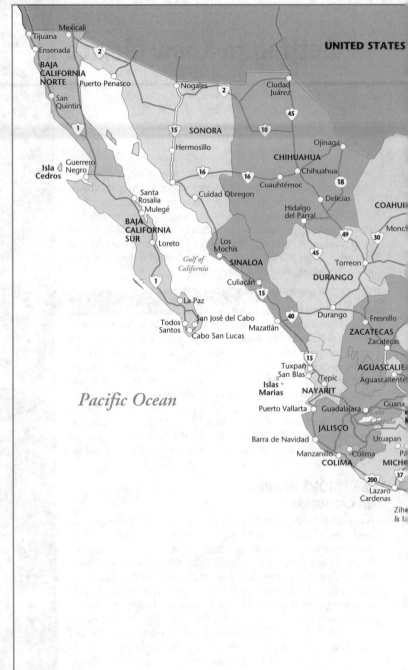

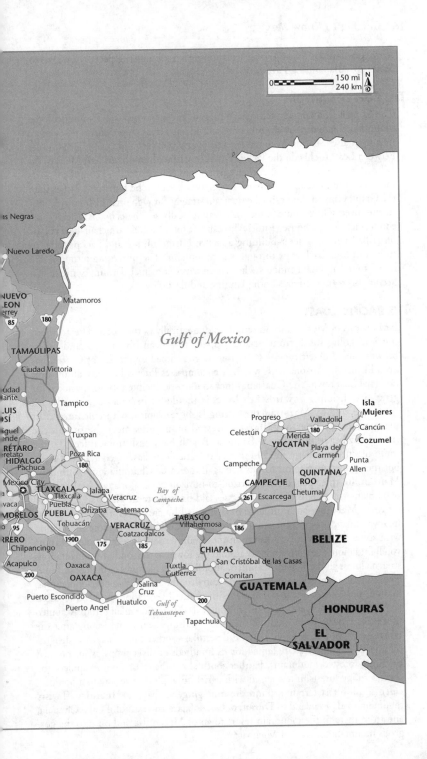

many possibilities for enjoyable vacationing on a budget, especially in **Loreto, Santa Rosalia,** and **La Paz.**

THE COPPER CANYON

The Copper Canyon is so remote, so rugged, and so gorgeous in its multicolored mountain grandeur that few other areas in Mexico create more curiosity, or more dreamy praise. Soaring from sea level to over 9,000 feet and covering 390 miles between **Los Mochis** on the Pacific Coast to **Chihuahua** in northern Mexico, the railroad, which took several entrepreneurs from 1863 to 1928 to complete, skirts the edge of more than 20 canyons in a network said to be four times larger than the Grand Canyon. You can take the train straight through on a 15-hour ride, but staying overnight enroute is the only way to really see the canyons. Rustic-but-comfortable lodges house visitors who can opt for a leisurely armchair-type trip or one filled with character-building adventure from hiking and backpacking to strenuous horseback trips through the mountains. The intriguing terrain is the home to Tarahumara Indians who live in caves and small farming settlements. Seeing this region requires both planning and flexibility.

THE PACIFIC COAST

Few regions in Mexico vary in terrain as dramatically as this coast. The northern portion, going south from Arizona, opens to a beautiful sienna- and milky brown-colored desertscape that, with its edge rimmed by the Sea of Cortéz, has been likened to Arizona with water. It encompasses Puerto Penasco, an off-beat holiday beach town, and Guayamas (not so touristically interesting, but noted for giant-size shrimp). Towards **Los Mochis** the desert becomes cultivated with sugarcane, and by **Mazatlán** the setting is more tropical with cultivated fruit plantations. At **Puerto Vallarta,** forested mountains meet the sea on the smashingly beautiful and wide Banderas Bay; it has a lush tropical feel. To the south of Puerto Vallarta for 50 miles or so agriculture has largely replaced trees, but then gorgeous tropical forests rise again north of **Chamula** and continue to **Manzanillo,** interspersed with horizon-to-horizon banana, mango, and coconut palm plantations. This area encompasses laid-back **Barra de Navidad** and its sister town **Melaque,** both on large bays rimmed by cream-colored beaches. The highway inland from Manzanillo to the city of **Colima** covers more mountains, with some fairly beautiful scenery in mountain passes. At **Zihuatanejo/Ixtapa** you'll find more deep-green forests around the town; to the south, fruit plantations stretch almost all the way to **Acapulco,** affording brief glimpses of the ocean. Tree-covered mountains still remain around Acapulco, though hillside development has marred them some, but in some places the natural vegetation has been replaced with tropical gardens around plush hillside villas. Traveling inland from Acapulco to **Taxco,** the thinly covered mountainous landscape can be refreshing after the rainy season, but blisteringly hot and desertlike at other times. Taxco, a delightful hillside colonial-era city famed for its hundreds of silver shops, is surrounded by thinly forested mountains. Farther south along the coast from Acapulco, the short scrubby forests, interspersed with agricultural plots, give way to a boulder-laden scrub forest terrain around the nine gorgeous bays of **Huatulco.** Twisty mountain roads go inland to **Durango, Guadalajara** and beautiful **Lake Chapala,** and from there to the mountain resort town of **Mazamitla** and on into the gorgeous mountainous state of Michoacán.

Of all these destinations the least budget friendly is Acapulco, where economical lodgings are a step down compared to what you get for the same price almost anywhere along this coast. Puerto Vallarta and Mazatlán combine the most to do with the best economical lodgings, especially in their downtown areas, while Barra de Navidad and Puerto Angel offer the most relaxation for the least money.

THE CENTRAL REGION

This region encompasses the area from the Texas border as far south as **Mexico City,** and includes the heaviest concentration of population and beautiful colonial cities, many of which were founded during Mexico's early silver mining centuries. The rugged mountain terrain proved a tough obstacle when bringing silver out of the mines, so many of the towns were established both to refine the metal and to provide safety for its transport on the way to the capital and to coastal ports. From the almost barren, cactus-filled desert of the Texas border all the way to **San Luis Potosí,** in north-central Mexico, the hint of the Sierra Madre Oriental to the east and the Sierra Madre Occidental to the west is visible in unending barriers of hazy mountains in the distance. These two ranges, along with the Sierra Madre del Sur on the southern Pacific Coast, begin to merge in the middle as the country narrows into the tail of its cornucopia shape. It's flat from **Saltillo** to the pristinely preserved colonial city of **Zacatecas.** Veering to the west, you enter mountains slightly going to **Guanajuato,** and twist through them east of **Querétaro** heading along the Fray Junipero Serra Mission Route, or farther southeast to the silver mining region around **Pachuca.** South of Saltillo, dozens of hopeful roadside vendors sell strands of rattlesnake skins and ground snakeskin powder. At major crossroads where vehicles slow down, vendors proffer armloads of leather and fleece-lined vests, hubcaps, cheese, strawberries and cream, or perhaps caged parrots.

From Mexico City northward, the region is made up of seven high mountain valleys, all with natural drainage except Mexico City. Except for immediately around the capital, the valleys are known for their agricultural produce, namely cattle, goats, cheese, and grain. Around Querétaro, Guanajuato and **Dolores Hidalgo** vineyards in vast tracts produce grapes to feed the country's wine industry. Except for **Monterrey,** the budget traveler can expect excellent value for the travel dollar, even in the country's capital.

THE MID-EAST REGION

The northern part of this region—eastward from **Monterrey** to **Ciudad Victoria**—passes fertile flatlands with distant mountains to the west. Between **Ciudad Mante** and the mountain town of **Tamazunchale** is some of the Mexico's most incredible mountain scenery. Tropical forests threaten to overgrow the roadway, and humble huts have immense hedges of giant variegated croton, cactus, and red hibiscus. Mango, orange, and lime trees shade these minimal abodes in an almost edenic scene. This region is traversed by Highway 85; between Ciudad Mante and Tamazunchale it's a twisty two-lane paved road with white-knuckle hairpin curves. You're torn between devouring the fabulous vistas and attending to the road, which is the kind where oncoming trucks speed around curves traveling in your lane. When the road rises to the top of the mountain ridges (as it does many times) you see ripples of seemingly uninhabited forests and mountains completely to the horizon. It's as though no other Mexico exists beyond the purple hue of these mountains.

Occasionally, Huastec Indians trudge up from the valleys to the highway, some of them wearing regional clothing and a few women wearing their hair twisted around bulky yarn in elaborate traditional hairdos. Roadside stands sell honey, cone-shaped brown sugar (*piloncillo*), and huge squash cooked in the sweet brew. After such a drive, the scenery beyond Tamazunchale is almost anticlimactic until you reach the colonial mountain city of **Pachuca,** capital of the state of Hidalgo. Around Pachuca, numerous mountain villages grew up around silver mines during the colonial era.

Throughout this region you have the pleasure of seeing Mexico as it was 40 or more years ago—except for bustling Pachuca, the area is becomingly rural and rustic with no vestiges of the hectic, commercial, resort-heavy Mexico of the present day. Enjoy this region at a slow pace and bring a flexible spirit.

THE GULF COAST

Rarely traveled by tourists, this whole coast has marvelous pockets of scenery and culture and encompasses the long, skinny state of Veracruz. Highway 180 leads down from **Matamoros** at the Texas border, providing a few glimpses of the Gulf, which in some places is the same cerulean blue as the Caribbean. Roads are not always in the best shape, since torrential rains can leave vast stretches of potholes. But the mostly two-lane road is paved and flat almost until you reach **Lake Catemaco.** There it undulates gently among almost flat grassy fields humped strangely with unexplored mounds left by the Olmecs more than 3,000 years ago. Four highlights make this region worth seeing: The ruins of **El Tajín** near the mountain village of **Papantla; Jalapa** and the magnificent Museo de Antropología there; lively colorful **Veracruz,** the colonial port city with a terrific Latin beat; and the region around the placid Lake Catemaco, known for its beautiful setting and splendid collection of birds and other wildlife, and for a surprising number of *curanderos* (healers who use chants, herbs, and magic), who advertise with signs outside their homes. Coffee and sugarcane are grown around Jalapa, but you'll see sugarcane fields along most of the coast. Near **Santiago Tuxtla** and Lake Catemaco the produce of abundant fruit tree plantations spills over into roadside stands with pyramidal mounds of fruit in colorful displays. Cattle raising, however, has made this area one of the wealthiest in the nation. This is another region to choose if you're longing for the Mexico of yesteryear, for another cultural face of Mexico, and for some of the most economic hotels and restaurants. It's easily traveled by bus.

TARASCAN COUNTRY

This region, in the state of Michoacan, encompasses two completely different colonial-era towns—**Pátzcuaro,** with its rural colonial architecture, and stately **Morelia,** where rich colonial citizens built handsome mansions. Isolated by mountains from the rest of the country, Michoacan's forests provide raw inventory for an enormous furniture industry, and the state is the country's leading producer of avocados. The area's living Indian culture—the Tarascan, or Purépecha, people—is disappearing as the indigenous groups shed their regional costumes, but the language still dominates in markets. An enormous number of craft communities produce pottery, textiles, and colorful furniture, and all are easily reached by local bus. Monarch butterflies winter in the eastern part of the state in a forest of omeyel fir trees. This is one of the most economical regions to visit and one not overrun with tourists.

SOUTHERNMOST MEXICO: OAXACA, CHIAPAS, AND TABASCO STATES

This ruggedly mountainous region steeps travelers in the living color and texture of Zapotec, Mixtec, and Maya cultures. Most people don't drive from one area to the other (they usually fly), but the mountain terrain is stupendous. Nevertheless, a new toll highway from near Puebla to **Oaxaca** makes Oaxaca more accessible by car. The climate is hotter and more arid in Oaxaca than in **San Cristóbal de las Casas,** where high altitudes and lush, vegetation-covered mountains provide the cool mountain air. As you approach San Cristóbal from any direction, you see small plots of corn tended by colorfully clad Maya, many of whom are seen along the highways with loads of firewood on their backs. Oaxaca and Chiapas are both rich in crafts from wood carvers to potters and weavers. Of the three, Tabasco is the least interesting, and both Chiapas and Oaxaca offer fine accommodations and dining for budget travelers.

THE YUCATÁN PENINSULA

Traveling this remote peninsula is an opportunity to see pre-Hispanic ruins— **Chichén-Itzá, Uxmal, Tulum,** etc.—and the living descendants of the cultures who built them, as well as the ultimate in resort Mexico—**Cancún**.

Edged by the rough deep-aquamarine Gulf of Mexico on the west and north and the clear cerulean-blue Caribbean Sea on the east, the peninsula covers almost 84,000 square miles, with nearly 1,000 miles of shoreline. Covered with dense jungle, the porous limestone peninsula is mostly flat, with thin soil supporting a low, scrubby jungle that contains almost no surface rivers. Rainwater is filtered by the limestone into underground rivers. *Cenotes*, or collapsed caves, are natural wells dotting the region. The only sense of height comes from the curvaceous terrain rising from the western shores of Campeche inland to the border with Yucatán state. This rise, called the Puuc hills, is the Maya "Alps," a staggering 980 feet high. Locally the hills are known as the Sierra de Ticul or Sierra Alta. The highways undulate a little as you go inland, and south of Ticul, there's a rise in the highway that provides a marvelous view of the "valley" and misty Puuc hills lining the horizon. Maya towns near the Puuc hills developed a decorative style that incorporated geometric patterns and masks of Chaac, thus giving the style its name—Puuc.

The interior is dotted with lovely rock-walled villages inhabited by the kind, living Maya of today along with crumbling henequén haciendas surrounded by fields of maguey. Henequén, a yucca-like plant with tough fiber ideal for binder twine was the king crop in the Yucatán in the 19th century, and the industry is still going strong, making rope, packing material, shoes, and purses from the spiny plant. Besides henequén, other crops in the mostly agricultural peninsula are corn, coconuts, oranges, mangoes, and bananas.

The Yucatán's interior stands in strange contrast to the hubbub of the touristed 20th-century Caribbean Coast. From Cancún south to Chetumal the jungle coastline is interrupted by development of all kinds from posh to budget, but also hosts an enormous array of wildlife including hundreds of species of birds. Beaches from Cancún south to Chetumal are almost uniform in their powdery, drifting beauty. The western side of peninsula fronts the Gulf Coast and is the complete opposite of the Caribbean Coast. The beaches, while good enough, don't compare to those on the Caribbean. But nowhere else can you see flocks of flamingos as you can at national parks near **Celestún** and **Río Lagartos.**

This peninsula is excellent for a driving trip, since roads are generally flat, well-kept and not heavily trafficked. Outside the resorts, the Maya continue life as they did before the invasion of tourists began in 1974. Besides the friendly Maya faces you can meet in any village where you stop, you see men on bicycles with a rifle and cork-capped water gourd on the shoulder turning from the highway down bumpy, narrow dirt tracks into the thick jungle.

Even in Cancún you can plot an economical vacation, but your bucks will go much farther on the islands of **Isla Mujeres** and **Cozumel** and farther still down the coast south of Cancún.

THE MEXICAN PEOPLE

The population of Mexico is 85 million; 15% are ethnically European (most of Spanish descent), 60% are *mestizo* (mixed Spanish and Indian), and 25% are pure Indian (descendants of the Maya, Aztecs, Huastecs, Otomies, Totonacs, and other peoples). Added to this ethnic mix are Africans brought as slaves (this group has been so thoroughly assimilated that it is barely discernible); a French presence that lingers on from the time of Maximilian's abortive empire; and other Europeans.

Although Spanish is the official language, about 50 Indian languages are still spoken, mostly in the Yucatán peninsula, Oaxaca, Chiapas, Chihuahua, Nayarit, Puebla, Sonora and Veracruz, Michoacán, and Guerrero.

Modern Mexico clings to its identity while embracing outside cultures; Mexicans enjoy the Bolshoi Ballet as easily as a family picnic or village festival. Mexicans have a knack for knowing how to enjoy life, and families, weekends, holidays, and festivities are given priority. They also enjoy stretching a weekend holiday into four days called a *puente* (bridge) and, with the whole family in tow, fleeing the cities en masse to visit relatives in the country, picnic, or relax at resorts.

The Mexican work day is a long one: Laborers begin around 7am and get off at dusk; office workers go in around 9am, take a two- to three-hour lunch, and get off at 7 or 8pm. Once a working career is started, there is little time for additional study. School is supposedly mandatory and free through the sixth grade, but many youngsters quit long before that or never go at all.

Sociologists and others have written volumes trying to explain the Mexican's special relationship with death. Death and the dead are at once mocked and mourned. The Day of the Dead, November 1–2, a cross between Halloween and All Saints' Day, is a good opportunity to observe Mexico's relationship with the concept of death.

Mexico's social complexity is such that that it's difficult to characterize the Mexican people as a whole, but some broad generalizations that can be drawn.

CLASS DIVISIONS

There are vast differences in the culture and values of Mexico's various economic classes, and these gulfs have grown even wider over the last 10 years. On the one hand there are the fabulously rich; according to *Forbes* magazine, Mexico has the fourth-most billionaires in the world, with at least 24. Upper-class Mexicans are extremely well-educated and well-mannered; they are culturally sophisticated and often speak several languages. Many of Mexico's recent presidents have been educated in the United States.

The Mexican middle class—merchants, small-restaurant and souvenir-shop owners, taxi drivers, and tour guides, etc.—swelled from the 1950s through the

1980s but is struggling to stay afloat after a decade of incredible inflation. And yet these middle-class Mexicans are educating their children to higher standards—many young people now complete technical school or college. The middle-class standard of living includes trappings of life many take for granted in the States—maybe a phone in the home (a luxury that costs the equivalent of U.S. $1,000 to install), fancy tennis shoes for the children, occasional vacations, an economy car, and a tiny home or even smaller apartment in a modest neighborhood or high-rise.

Mexico's poorer classes have expanded. Their hopes for a decent future are dim and the daily goal for many is simple survival.

MACHISMO & MACHISMA

Sorting through the world of machismo and machisma in Mexico is fraught with subtleties better suited to sociological studies. Suffice to say that in Mexico, and especially Mexico City, the roles of men and women are changing both slowly and rapidly. Both sexes cling to old sex roles—women in the home and men in the workplace—but they are relinquishing traditional ideas too. More women are being educated and working than ever before. And men are learning to work side by side with women of equal education and power.

Though women function in many professional positions, they encounter what they call the "adobe ceiling" (as opposed to the see-through "glass ceiling" in the United States): The male grip on upper-level positions in Mexico is so firm that women aren't able to even glimpse the top. Strong-willed women opt for setting up their own businesses as a result. Anyone used to a more liberated world may be frustrated by the extent to which Mexico is still a man's world—not uncommon are women who pander to old-fashioned negative stereotypes and flirtatious Mexican men who have difficulty sticking to business when dealing with a woman, even a serious businessperson who is dressed accordingly. Typically the Mexican man is charmingly polite, and affronted or embarrassed by the woman who won't permit him to open doors, seat her, and in every way put her on a respectful pedestal.

THE FAMILY

As a rule, Mexicans are very family-oriented. Family takes priority over work. Whole extended families routinely spend weekends and holidays together, filling parks and recreational spots until the last minute of the holiday. During those times men are often seen playing with, tending to, and enjoying the children as readily as women. In the home, girls are supervised closely until they are married. But the untethering of boys begins around age 15, when they are given more

Impressions

Considering the variety of nations, tongues, cultures, and artistic styles, the unity of these peoples comes as a surprise. They all share certain ideas and beliefs. Thus it is not inaccurate to call this group of nations and cultures a Mexoamerican civilization. Unity in space and continuity in time; from the first millennium before Christ to the sixteenth century, these distinct Mexoamerican peoples evolve, reelaborate, and re-create a nucleus of basic concepts as well as social and political techniques and institutions. There were changes and variation . . . but never was the continuity broken.

—Octavio Paz, 1990

freedoms than their sisters. It's customary, however, for all children to remain in the home until they marry, although there are more young people breaking the mold nowadays.

Family roles among indigenous people are clear-cut. Women tend the babies, the home, the hearth, and often the fields. Men do the heavy work, tilling the soil, but women often join them for planting and harvesting. Theirs is a joint life focused on survival. Though not so much an unbendable custom now among these cultures, it's common to see women walking behind her spouse, carrying a child on her back and heavy bundles on her shoulders. When these people reach Mexico City, these roles shift somewhat; for example, a husband and wife will take turns tending their street stall with a child sleeping in a box or playing nearby. But always she will prepare the food.

Generally speaking, children are coddled and loved and are very obedient. Misbehaving children are seldom rebuked in public, since Mexican parenting style seems to favor gentle prodding, comforting, or nurturing instead.

2 A Look at the Past

Dateline

- 13000–2300 B.C. Pre-Historic Period.
- 1500 Preclassic Period begins: Olmec culture develops and spreads.
- 1000–900 Olmec San Lorenzo center destroyed; Olmecs regroup at La Venta.
- 600 La Venta Olmec cultural zenith; Cholula begins 2,000-year history as ceremonial center.
- 500–100 B.C. Zapotecs flourish; Olmec culture disintegrates.
- A.D. 100 Building begins on Sun and Moon pyramids at Teotihuacán; Palenque dynasty emerges in Yucatán.
- 300 Classic Period begins: Xochicalco established; Maya civilization develops in Yucatán and Chiapas.
- 650 Teotihuacán burns and by 700 is deserted. Cacaxtla begins to flourish.
- 750 Zapotecs conquer valley of Oaxaca; Casas Grandes culture begins on northern desert.

continues

PREHISPANIC CIVILIZATIONS   The earliest "Mexicans" were Stone Age men and women, descendants of a people who had crossed the Bering Strait and reached North America before 10,000 B.C. These were *Homo sapiens* who hunted mastodons and bison and gathered other food as they could. Later, during the Archaic Period (5200–1500 B.C.), signs of agriculture and domestication appeared: baskets were woven; corn, beans, squash, and tomatoes were grown; turkeys and dogs were kept for food. By 2400 B.C., the art of pot making had been discovered (the use of pottery was a significant advance). Though life in these times was still very primitive, there were "artists" who made clay figurines for use as votive offerings or household "gods." Many symbolized Mother Earth or Fertility. (Use of these figurines predates any belief in well-defined gods.)

It was in the **Preclassic Period** (1500 B.C.–A.D. 300) that the area known by archaeologists as Mesoamerica (running from the northern Mexico Valley to Costa Rica) began to show signs of a farming culture. The inhabitants farmed either by the "slash-and-burn" method of cutting grass and trees and then setting fire to the area to clear it for planting or by constructing terraces and irrigation ducts. The latter method was used principally in the highlands around Mexico City, where the first large towns developed. At some time during this period, religion became an institution as certain men took the role of shaman, or guardian of magical and religious secrets. These were the predecessors of the folk healers and nature priests still found in modern Mexico.

The most highly developed culture of this Preclassic Period was that of the Olmecs, which flourished from 1500 to 100 B.C. They lived in what are today the states of Veracruz and Tabasco, where they used river rafts to transport the colossal multiton blocks of basalt out of which they carved roundish heads that are the best-known legacy of their culture. These sculptures still present problems to archaeologists: What do they signify? The heads seem infantile in their roundness, but all have the peculiar "jaguar mouth" with a high-arched upper lip. Those with open eyes are slightly cross-eyed. The artists seemed obsessed with deformity, and many smaller carved or clay figures represent monstrosities or misshapen forms. Besides their achievements in sculpture, the Olmecs were the first in Mexico to use a calendar and to develop a written language, both of which were later perfected by the Maya.

The link between the Olmecs and the Maya has not been clearly established, but Izapa (400 B.C.– A.D. 400), a ceremonial site in the Chiapan cacao-growing region near the Pacific coast, appears to be one of several places where transition between the two cultures took place. When discovered, its monuments and stelae were intact, having escaped the destruction wrought on so many sites. El Pital, a large site being excavated in northern Veracruz state, may illuminate more links between the Olmec and other cultures.

Most of pre-Columbian Mexico's artistic and cultural achievement came during the **Classic Period** (A.D. 300–900), when life centered in cities. Class distinctions arose as a military and religious aristocracy took control; a class of merchants and artisans grew, with the independent farmer falling under a landlord's control. The cultural centers of the Classic Period were Yucatán and Guatemala (also home of the Maya), the Mexican Highlands at Teotihuacán, the Zapotec cities of Monte Albán and Mitla (near Oaxaca), and the cities of El Tajín and Zempoala on the Gulf Coast.

The Maya represented the apex of pre-Columbian cultures. Besides their superior artistic achievements, the Maya made significant discoveries in science, including the use of the zero

- 900 Post-Classic Period begins: Toltec culture emerges at Tula. Cacaxtla begins to decline.
- 978 Toltec culture spreads to Chichén-Itzá.
- 1156–1230 Toltecs abandon Tula and El Tajín. Aztecs trickle in to the Valley of Mexico.
- 1290 Zapotecs decline and Mixtecs emerge at Monte Albán; Mitla becomes refuge of Zapotecs.
- 1325–45 Aztec capital Tenochtitlán founded. Aztecs dominate Mexico until 1521, when they are defeated by Spaniards.
- 1519–21 Conquest of Mexico: Hernán Cortés and troops arrive near present-day Veracruz; Spanish gain final victory over Aztecs at Tlaltelolco near Tenochtitlán in 1521. Diseases brought by Spaniards begin to decimate native population.
- 1521–24 Cortés organizes Spanish empire in Mexico and begins building Mexico City atop ruins of Tenochtitlán; Spanish bring first cattle to Mexico; first Franciscan friars arrive from Spain.
- 1530 King Charles V of Spain declares Mexico City the capital of New Spain.
- 1535–1821 Viceregal Period: Mexico governed by 61 viceroys appointed by King of Spain. Landed aristocracy, a small elite owning huge portions of land (haciendas) emerges.
- 1810–21 Independence War: Miguel Hidalgo's grito starts independence movement; after a decade of war, Augustín Iturbide

continues

achieves compromise between monarchy and a republic. Mexico becomes independent nation.

- 1822–24 First Empire: Iturbide enjoys brief reign as emperor; is expelled; returns; and is executed by firing squad.
- 1824–55 Federal Republic Period: In 1824, Guadalupe Victoria elected first president of Mexico; 26 presidents and interim presidents follow during next three decades, among them José António Lopez de Santa Anna, who is president of Mexico off and on 11 times.
- 1835 Texas declares independence from Mexico.
- 1838 France invades Mexico at Veracruz.
- 1845 United States annexes Texas.
- 1846–48 War with United States concludes with U.S. paying Mexico $15 million for half of its national territory under terms of Treaty of Guadalupe Hidalgo.
- 1855–72 Era of Benito Juárez, literal or de facto president through Reform Wars and usurpation of Mexican leadership by foreign Emperor Maximilian. Juárez nationalizes church property and declares separation of church and state. Dies in Mexico City in 1872.
- 1872–84 Post-Reform Period: Only four presidents hold office but country is nearly bankrupt.
- 1880 Electric lights go on in Mexico City for the first time.

continues

in mathematics and a complex calendar with which priests were able to predict eclipses and the movements of the stars for centuries to come. The Maya were warlike, raiding their neighbors to gain land and subjects as well as to take captives for their many blood-centered rituals. Recent studies, notably Blood of Kings (Braziller, 1986) by Linda Schele and Mary Ellen Miller, debunked the long-held theory that the Maya were a peaceful people. Scholars continue to decipher the Maya hieroglyphs, murals, and relief carvings, revealing a world tied to the belief that blood sacrifice was necessary to communicate with celestial gods and ancestors and to revere the dynasties of earthly blood kin. Through bloodletting and sacrifice the Maya nourished their gods and ancestors and honored royal births, deaths, marriages, and accessions during a calendar full of special occasions. Numerous carvings and murals show that members of the ruling class, too, ritualistically mutilated themselves to draw sacrificial blood.

The identity of the people of Teotihuacán (100 B.C.– A.D. 700—near present-day Mexico City) isn't known, but it is thought to have been a city of 200,000 or more inhabitants covering 9 square miles. At its height, Teotihuacán was the greatest cultural center in Mexico; its influence extended as far southeast as Guatemala. Its layout has religious significance: High priests' rituals occurred on the tops of pyramids consecrated to the sun and moon, and these were attended, but not observed, by the masses of people at the foot of the pyramid. Some of the magnificent reliefs and frescoes that decorated the religious monuments can be seen in Mexico City's museums.

The Zapotecs, influenced by the Olmecs, raised an impressive culture in the region of Oaxaca. Their two principal cities were Monte Albán (500 B.C.–A.D. 800), inhabited by an elite of merchants and artisans, and Mitla, reserved for the high priests. Both cities exhibit the artistic and mathematical genius of the people; highlights include characteristic geometric designs, long-nosed gods with feathered masks, hieroglyph stelae, a bar-and-dot numerical system, and a 52-cycle calendar. Like the Olmecs, the Zapotecs favored grotesque art, of which the frieze of the "Danzantes" at Monte Albán—naked figures of distorted form and contorted position—is an outstanding example.

El Tajín (A.D. 300–1100), covering at least 2,600 acres on the upper Gulf coast of Veracruz, continues to stump scholars. The Pyramid of the Niches there is unique, and recent excavations have uncovered a total of 17 ball courts and Teotihuacán-influenced murals. Although Huastec Indians inhabited the region, the identity of those who built the site and occupied it remains a mystery. Death and sacrifice are recurring themes depicted in relief carvings. Pulque (pre-Hispanic fermented drink), cacao (chocolate) growing, and the ball game figured heavily into Tajín society.

In the **Postclassic Period** (A.D. 900–1500), warlike cultures developed impressive societies of their own, although they never surpassed the Classic peoples. All paintings and hieroglyphs of this period show war, migration, and disruption. Somehow the glue of society became unstuck; people wandered from their homes, and the religious hierarchy lost influence. Finally, in the 1300s, the warlike Aztecs settled in the Mexico Valley on Lake Texcoco (site of Mexico City), with the island city of Tenochtitlán as their capital. Legend has it that as the wandering Aztecs were passing the lake, they saw a sign predicted by their prophets: an eagle perched on a cactus plant with a snake in its mouth. They built their city there, and it became a huge (pop. 300,000) and impressive capital. The Aztec empire was a more or less loosely united territory of great size. The high lords of the capital became fabulously rich in gold, stores of food, cotton, and perfumes; skilled artisans were prosperous; state events were elaborately ceremonial. Victorious Aztecs returning from battle sacrificed thousands of captives on the altars atop the pyramids, cutting their chests open with stone knives and ripping out their still-beating hearts to offer to the gods.

The legend of **Quetzalcoatl,** a holy man who appeared during the time of troubles at the end of the Classic Period, is one of the most important tales in Mexican history and folklore and contributed to the overthrow of the Aztec empire by the Spaniards. Quetzalcoatl means "feathered serpent." Learned beyond his years, he became the high priest and leader of the Toltecs at Tula and put an end to human sacrifice. His influence completely changed the Toltecs from a group of warriors to peaceful and productive farmers, artisans, and craftsmen. But his successes upset the old priests,

- **1876–1911** Porfiriato: With one four-year exception, Porfirio Díaz is president/dictator of Mexico for 35 years, leading country through rapid modernization.
- **1911** Mexican Revolution begins; Díaz resigns; Francisco Madero becomes president.
- **1913** Madero assassinated.
- **1914, 1916** United States invades Mexico.
- **1917–40** Reconstruction: Present constitution of Mexico signed in 1917. Land and education reforms are initiated and labor unions strengthened. Mexico expels U.S. oil companies and nationalizes all natural resources and railroads. Presidential term limited to one term of six years. Presidents Obregón and Carranza are assassinated as are Pancho Villa and Emiliano Zapata.
- **1940** President Lázaro Cárdenas leaves office; Mexico enters period of political stability, tremendous economic progress, and rising quality of life that continues to this day, though not without many continuing problems.
- **1942** Mexico enters World War II when Germans sink two Mexican oil tankers in the Caribbean.
- **1946** 10,000 year old "Tepexpan Man" is unearthed near Mexico City.
- **1955** Women given full voting rights.
- **1957** Major earthquake rocks the capital.
- **1960** Mexico nationalizes electrical industry.

continues

- 1968 President Díaz
  Ordaz orders army to fire
  on protesters at Tlaltelolco
  Plaza meeting, killing
  hundreds of spectators
  and participants.
  Olympic games are
  held in the capital.
- 1982 President Echeverria
  nationalizes the country's
  banks.
- 1985 Deadly earthquake
  crumbles buildings in
  the capital and takes
  thousands of lives.
- 1988 Mexico enters
  the General Agreement
  on Tariffs and Trade
  (GATT).
- 1992 Sale of *ejido* land
  (peasant communal
  property) to private
  citizens is allowed.
  Mexico and the Vatican
  establish diplomatic
  relations after an
  interruption of 100 years.
- 1993 Mexico deregulates
  hotel and restaurant
  prices; New Peso
  currency begins circulation.
- 1994 An Indian uprising
  in Chiapas sparks protests
  countrywide over
  government policies
  concerning land
  distribution, bank loans,
  health, education, and
  voting and human rights.
  In an unrelated incident
  PRI candidate Luis
  Donaldo Colossio is
  assassinated five months
  before the election;
  replacement candidate
  Ernesto Zedillo Ponce
  de Leon is elected and
  inaugurated as president
  in December. Within
  weeks, the peso is
  devalued, throwing the
  nation into turmoil.

continues

and they called on their ancient god of darkness, Texcatlipoca, to degrade Quetzalcoatl in the eyes of the people. One night the priests conspired to dress Quetzalcoatl in ridiculous garb, get him drunk, and tempt him to break his vow of chastity. The next morning the shame of this night of debauchery drove him out of his own land and into the wilderness, where he lived for 20 years. He emerged in Coatzacoalcos, in the Isthmus of Tehuantepec, bade his few followers farewell, and sailed away, having promised to return in a future age. Toltec artistic influences noted at Chichén-Itzá in the Yucatán seem to suggest that he in fact landed there and, among the Maya, began his "ministry" again, this time called Kukulkán. He supposedly died there, but the legend of his return in a future age remained.

THE CONQUEST OF MEXICO When Hernán Cortés and his fellow conquistadores landed in 1519, in what would become Veracruz, the enormous Aztec empire was ruled by Moctezuma (a name often misspelled Montezuma) in great splendor. It was thought that these strange visitors might be Quetzalcoatl and his followers, returning at last. Moctezuma was not certain what course to pursue; if this was in fact the god returning, no resistance must be offered; on the other hand, if the leader was not Quetzalcoatl, he and his men might be a threat to his empire. Moctezuma tried to bribe them with gold to go away, but this only whetted the Spaniards' appetites. Along the way from Veracruz to Tenochtitlán, Cortés made allies of Moctezuma's enemies, most notably the Tlaxcaltecans.

Though the Spaniards were outnumbered by the hundreds of thousands of Aztecs, they skillfully kept things under their control (with the help of their Tlaxcalan allies) until a revolt threatened Cortés's entire enterprise. He retreated to the countryside, made alliances with non-Aztec tribes, and finally marched on the empire when it was governed by the last Aztec emperor, Cuauhtémoc. Cuauhtémoc defended himself and his people valiantly for almost three months, but was finally captured, tortured, and ultimately executed.

What began as an adventure by Cortés and his men, unauthorized by the Spanish Crown or its governor in Cuba, turned out to be the undoing of a continent's worth of people and cultures. Soon

Christianity was being spread through "New Spain." Guatemala and Honduras were explored and conquered, and by 1540 the territory of New Spain included Spanish possessions from Vancouver to Panama. In the two centuries that followed, Franciscan, Augustinian, and Dominican friars converted great numbers of Indians to Christianity, and the Spanish lords built up huge feudal estates on which the Indian farmers were little more than serfs. The silver and gold that Cortés had sought and found made Spain the richest country in Europe.

THE VICEREGAL ERA   Hernán Cortés set about building a new city and the seat of government of New Spain upon the ruins of the old Aztec capital. Spain's influence was immediate. For indigenous peoples (besides the Tlaxcaltecans, Cortés's Indian allies), heavy tributes once paid to the Aztecs were now rendered in forced labor to the Spanish. In many cases they were made to provide the materials for the building of New Spain as well. Diseases carried by the Spaniards, against which the Indian populations had no natural immunity, killed millions.

■ **1995** The peso loses half its value within the first three months of the year. The government raises prices on oil and utilities. Interest on debt soars to 140 percent; businesses begin to fail; unemployment rises. The Chiapan rebels threaten another rebellion, which is quickly quashed by the government. Former President Carlos Salinas de Gortari, with the devaluation having left his reputation for economic leadership in a shambles, leaves Mexico for the United States. And Salinas's brother is accused of plotting the assassination of their brother-in-law, the head of the PRI.

Over the three centuries of the Viceregal Period (1535–1821), Mexico was governed by 61 viceroys appointed by the king of Spain. From the beginning, more Spaniards arrived as overseers, merchants, craftsmen, architects, silversmiths, etc., and eventually negro slaves were brought in as well. Spain became rich from New World gold and silver, chiseled out by backbreaking Indian labor. The colonial elite built lavish homes both in Mexico City and in the countryside. They filled their homes with ornate furniture, had many servants, and adorned themselves in velvets, satins, and jewels imported from abroad. A new class system developed: the *gauchupines* (Spaniards born in Spain), considered themselves superior to the *criollos* (Spaniards born in Mexico). Those of other races, the *castas* or castes, the pure Indians and Negros, and mixtures of Spanish and Indian, Spanish and Negro, Indian and Negro, all took the last place in society.

It took great cunning to stay a step ahead of the money-hungry Spanish crown, which demanded increasingly higher taxes and contributions from its well-endowed faraway colony. Still, the wealthy prospered grandly enough to develop an extravagant society.

However, discontent with the mother country simmered for years over issues such as the Spanish-born citizen's advantages over a Mexican-born subject; taxes; the Spanish bureaucracy; and restrictions on commerce with Spain and other countries. Dissatisfaction with Spain boiled to the surface in 1808 when, under the weak leadership of King Charles IV, it was invaded by Napoleón Bonaparte of France, who placed his brother Joseph in the Spanish throne. To many in Mexico, allegiance to France was out of the question. Mexico seemed left without leadership. After nearly 300 years of restrictive Spanish rule, Mexican discontent with the mother country reached the level of revolution.

INDEPENDENCE   The independence movement began in 1810 when a priest, Father Miguel Hidalgo, gave the cry for independence from his pulpit in the town of Dolores, Guanajuato. The revolt soon became a revolution, and Hidalgo, Ignacio Allende, and another priest, José María Morelos, gathered an "army" of citizens and threatened Mexico City. Battle lines were drawn between those who sided with the Spanish crown and those who wanted Mexico to be a free and sovereign nation. Ultimately Hidalgo was executed, but he is honored as "the Father of Mexican Independence." Morelos kept the revolt alive until 1815, when he too was executed.

The nation endured a decade of upheaval (1810 until 1821), and then the warring factions finally agreed on a compromise, Augustín Iturbide's *Plan de Iguala.* It made three guarantees: Mexico would be a constitutional monarchy headed by a European prince; the Catholic church would have a monopoly on religion; and Mexican-born citizens would have the same rights as those born in Spain. He thoughtfully tagged on another proviso allowing for a Mexican emperor, should no European prince step forward to take the role of king. When the agreement was signed, Iturbide was positioned to take over. No suitable European monarch was located and the new Mexican congress named him emperor. His empire proved short-lived: the very next year his administration fell. The new nation became a republic, but endured a succession of presidents and military dictators, as well as invasions, a war, and devastating losses of territory to its neighbor to the north, the United States.

Characteristic of the Republic's turbulent history during the half-century following independence was the French Intervention, in which three old colonial powers—England, France, and Spain—and the United States demonstrated continued interest in meddling with Mexico's internal affairs, and found, in the fractured world of mid-19th-century Mexican politics, plenty of help in carrying out their intrigues. Before it was over, Mexico had seen troops from the three European powers occupy Veracruz (the English and Spanish withdrew before long, but the French remained and declared war on Mexico); had enjoyed a glorious, if hollow, victory over the French at Puebla (the event that birthed the nation's Cinco de Mayo celebrations); had watched the Mexican president, Benito Juárez, retreat to the countryside to bide his time while the French marched on Mexico City and, with the help of anti-Juárez factions, installed a naive young Austrian, Archduke Maximilian of Hapsburg, as king of Mexico; and finally had rolled its collective eyes at the three-year-long spectacle of Maximilian trying to "rule" a country effectively in the midst of civil war, only to be left in the lurch when the French troops that supported him withdrew at the behest of the United States and then summarily executed by Juárez upon his triumphant return. Juárez, who would be remembered as one of the nation's great heroes, did his best to strengthen and unify the country before dying of a heart attack in 1872.

THE PORFIRIATO & THE REVOLUTION   From 1877 to 1911, a period now called the "Porfiriato," center stage in Mexico was occupied by Porfirio Díaz, a Juárez general who was president for 30 years and lived in the Castillo de (Castle of) Chapultepec in Mexico City. He was a terror to his enemies—that is, anyone who dared to challenge his absolute power. Nevertheless, he is credited with bringing Mexico into the industrial age and for his patronage of architecture and the arts, the fruits of which are still enjoyed today. Public opinion forced him from office in 1911; he was succeeded by Francisco Madero.

Impressions

Without more chin than Maximilian ever had, one can be neither handsome nor a successful emperor.

—Charles Flandrau, *Viva Mexico* (1908)

After the fall of the Porfirist dictatorship, several factions split the country, including those led by "Pancho Villa" (whose real name was Doroteo Arango), Alvaro Obregón, Venustiano Carranza, and Emiliano Zapata. A famous photograph shows Zapata and Villa taking turns trying out Díaz's presidential chair in Mexico City. The decade that followed is referred to as the Mexican Revolution. Around 2 million Mexicans died for the cause. Drastic reforms occurred in this period, and the surge of vitality and progress from this exciting, if turbulent, time has inspired Mexicans to the present. Succeeding presidents have invoked the spirit of the Revolution, which lives in the hearts and minds of Mexicans as though it happened yesterday.

BEYOND THE REVOLUTION The decades from the beginning of the revolution in 1911 to stabilization in the 1940s and 1950s were tumultuous. Great strides were made during these years in distributing land to the peasant populations, irrigation, development of mineral resources, and the establishment of education, health, and sanitation programs. However, the tremendous economic pressure Mexico faced from its own internal problems and the world depression of the 1930s did little for political stability. From 1911 to 1940 sixteen men were president of Mexico. Some stayed in power a year or less.

The longest-lasting (1934–40), and one of the most significant leaders of the period, was Lázaro Cárdenas. He helped diminish the role of Mexico's military in national politics by dismantling the machine of Gen. Plutarco Calles and exiling him from the country. He is remembered fondly as a president who listened to and cared about commoners. He made good on a number of the revolution's promises, distributing nearly 50 million acres of land, primarily to *ejidos*, or communal farming groups; plowing money into education; and encouraging organized labor. And in one of his most memorable and controversial decisions, he nationalized Mexico's oil industry in 1938, sending foreign oil companies packing. Although Mexicans still view this act with great pride, it did considerable damage to Mexico's standing with the international business community.

Despite many steps forward during the Cárdenas era, jobs could not keep pace with population growth, and with foreign investors shy of Mexico, and the world mired in the Great Depression, the Cárdenas era ended in 1940 with the nation in dark economic circumstances.

From the 1930s through the 1970s, socialism had a strong voice in Mexico; its impact was most marked in the state's attempts to run the country's businesses—not just oil, but railroads, mining, utilities, hotels, motion pictures, the telephone company, supermarkets, etc. Miguel Aleman, president from 1946 to 1958, continued progress by building dams, improving highways and railways, encouraging trade, and building the Ciudad Universitario (University City) in Mexico City, home of Mexico's national university. Americans began to invest in Mexico again. Yet problems remained, many of which still plague the country today: the country's booming population created unemployment, wages of the common people were appallingly low, and Aleman's administration was plagued by corruption and graft.

In 1970, Luis Echeverria came to power, followed in 1976 by José López Portillo. During their presidencies there emerged a studied coolness in relations with the United States and an activist role in international affairs. This period also saw an increase in charges of large-scale corruption in the upper echelons of Mexican society. The corruption, though endemic to the system, was encouraged by the river of money from the rise in oil prices. When oil income skyrocketed, Mexican borrowing and spending did likewise. The reduction of oil prices in the 1980s left Mexico with an enormous foreign bank debt and serious infrastructure deficiencies.

The country inherited by Pres. Miguel de la Madríd Hurtado in 1982 was one without King Oil, and with new challenges to build agriculture, cut expenditures, tame corruption, and keep creditors at bay. He began the process of privatizing government-held businesses (airlines, hotels, banks, etc.) and led the country into membership in GATT (the General Agreement on Tariffs and Trade), an important preparation for entering NAFTA (the North American Free Trade Agreement), which was accomplished during his successor's presidency. Nevertheless, a soaring inflation of 200% faced Carlos Salinas de Gortari as he took office in 1989. Salinas's accomplishments included, decreasing inflation to 15% annually by adeptly gaining the necessary agreement of industry and labor leaders to hold wages and prices, continuing the privatization of government-held businesses, and leading the country into NAFTA, which over a 15-year period would reduce trade barriers and allow business to flourish more freely between Mexico, the United States, and Canada. During Salinas's six-year term, Mexico's world position as a country poised for great prosperity strengthened, and Mexican public opinion held his administration in high esteem. But a cloud arose over the country towards the end of the Salinas era when disgruntled Maya Indians staged an armed uprising after the NAFTA agreement was signed, and assassins' bullets felled both the PRI presidential candidate and the head of the PRI party. The presidential elections, while automated for the first time and more honest than previous ones, were still marred by allegations of corruption. Still, these incidents failed to dampen Mexico's hope for continued progress when Ernesto Zedillo assumed office in December 1994.

TOWARD THE FUTURE   From the time of the revolution to the present, political parties and their role have changed tremendously in Mexico. Although one political party, the **Partido Revolucionario Institucional** (PRI, called "el pree") has been in control under that name since 1946, opposition to it has become increasingly vocal and effective in recent years. In the beginning, the forerunner of the PRI the Partido Revolucionario Mexicano, established by Lázaro Cárdenas, had four equal constituent groups—popular, agrarian, labor, and the military. At the risk of greatly oversimplifying a complex history and attendant issues, the

Impressions

[Porfirio Díaz] looks what he is—a Man of Iron, the most forceful character in Mexico. Whatever was done in the sixteenth century was the work of Cortez . . . who was responsible for everything but the climate. Whatever is effected in Mexico to-day is the work of Porfirio Díaz.

—Stanton Davis Kirkham, *Mexican Trails* (1909)

widespread perception that the party is out of touch with the common Mexican, and its current problems retaining leadership, are the result of a change in focus away from those groups. The PRI today is heavily backed by, and in turn run by, business and industry leaders.

The crisis in Chiapas has become a focal point for many of the nation's problems. Opposition parties such as the **Partido Accion Nacional** (PAN) had taken up the cause of the seemingly disenfranchised masses, but no one had spoken for or paid much attention to Mexico's millions of poor indigenous people for some time. And on New Year's Day in 1994, when militant Maya Indians attacked Chiapan towns, killing many, attention was drawn to the plight of neglected indigenous groups and others in rural society, which the PRI-led government seemed to relegate to the bottom of the agenda. These groups are still clamoring for land they never received after the Revolution. That population growth has outstripped the availability of distributable land, that Mexico needs large-scale, modern agribusiness to keep up with the country's food needs—these are realities not understood by the millions of rural Mexicans who depend on their small family fields to feed the family. President Carlos Salinas de Gortari's bold, controversial decision in the early 1990s to allow sale of *ejido* land may reflect Mexico's 21st-century needs, but it is at odds with firmly entrenched farm- and land-use traditions born before the 16th-century Conquest. These issues of agrarian reform and the lack of other basics of life (roads, electricity, running water, education, health care, etc.) are being raised in areas besides Chiapas, most notably Oaxaca, Chihuahua, Guerrero, and Michoacán. This is a grave and festering problem, made all the more serious now that Mexico is reeling from the devaluation of the peso. The surprise decision to devalue the currency threw domestic and international confidence in Mexico into turmoil. The peso had already been in a fairly rapid, but controlled, daily devaluation process just prior to the government intervention, and it had been obvious for at least three years that a devaluation was overdue. But the Zedillo government erred in not involving industry and labor in the decision, in shocking the population with an overnight devaluation, and in not anticipating national and international repercussions. Within three months of the devaluation, the peso lost half its value and Mexico's buying power was reduced by half. After the government issued its harsh economic recovery program, interest rates on credit cards and loans (which have variable, not fixed rates in Mexico), soared 80% to 140%. Overnight the cost of gasoline increased 35% and gas and electricity 20%. As a partial solution, the United States offered Mexico a 40 million dollar loan package to ease the peso crisis, using the country's sacred petroleum revenue as collateral—a staggering blow to Mexico's national pride. The effect so far has been a loudly expressed lack of confidence in Zedillo and in the PRI, a dramatically slowed and cautious international investment climate, and a feeling among the citizenry of betrayal by the government. Responsibility for paying for governmental mismanagement of the economy has been shifted to ordinary Mexican citizens who were blindsided by this unexpected financial burden. Ordinary costs of daily living exceed the ability of average people to pay; businesses are closing and jobs are being eliminated.

Meanwhile as the effects of the peso crisis worsened, the Chiapan rebels threatened another uprising, the volcano Popocatepetl began spitting smoke and flames, and inflation predictions of 45% to 60% were heard. Former president Carlos Salinas de Gortari's brother was jailed and accused of involvement in the

Where to Find Mexico's Folk Art & Crafts

The charm of Mexico is no better expressed than in the arts and crafts. Hardly a tourist will leave this country without having bought at least one handcrafted item. Mexico is famous for textiles, ceramics, baskets, and onyx and silver jewelry, to mention only a few.

Prices for the crafts are really dependent on your bargaining ability. It's very helpful to visit a government fixed-price shop (usually called the Artes Populares of FONART) before attempting to bargain. This will give you an idea of the cost versus quality of the various crafts.

Following are the various crafts, in alphabetical order. The best towns in which to seek each craft are listed as well.

Baskets   Woven of reed or straw—Oaxaca, Copper Canyon, Toluca, Yucatán, Puebla, Mexico City.

Blankets   Saltillo, Toluca, Santa Ana Chiautempan, north of Puebla, Oaxaca, and Mitla (made of soft wool with some synthetic dyes; they use a lot of bird and geometric motifs). Make sure the blanket you pick out is in fact the one you take because often the "same" blanket in the wrapper is not the same.

Glass   Hand-blown and molded—Monterrey and Tlaquepaque; Mexico City at the Avalos Brothers glass factory, Carretones 5 (Metro Pino Suárez).

Guitars   Made in Paracho, 25 miles north of Uruapan on Highway 37.

Hammocks and Mosquito Netting   Mérida, Campeche, Mazatlán. See the market section in Mérida (Chapter 16) for details on buying.

Hats   Mérida (Panama), made of sisal from the maguey cactus; finest quality weaving; easy to pack and wash—San Cristóbal de las Casas, Chiapas, is a good place for varied regional hats.

Huaraches   Leather sandals, often with rubber-tire soles—San Blas, Mérida, Mexico City, Guadalajara, Hermosillo, San Cristóbal de las Casas, and in fact most states.

Huipils   Embroidered or brocaded handwoven overblouses indigenous to almost all Mexican states but especially to Yucatán, Chiapas, Oaxaca, Puebla, Guerrero, and Veracruz. Most of the better huipils are used ones bought from the village women. Huipils can be distinguished by villages; look around before buying—you'll be amazed at the variety.

Lacquer Goods   Olinala, Guerrero, northeast of Acapulco, is known for ornate lacquered chests and other lacquered decorative and furniture items.

assassination of their brother-in-law, the head of the PRI party. Carlos Salinas de Gortari and his family left Mexico quickly for the United States, after Salinas threatened a hunger strike unless his name was cleared regarding the assassination of his brother-in-law, and after he spoke publicly (an unheard-of breech of conduct by a past president) against the present government's handling of the peso crisis.

It seems incredulous that a country so poised for prosperity should career backwards so rapidly, and that such an admired president should so quickly fall from

Pátzcuaro and Uruapan, west of Mexico City, are also known for gold-leafed lacquered trays.

Leather Goods   Monterrey, Saltillo, León, Mexico City, San Cristóbal de las Casas, and Oaxaca.

Masks   Wherever there is locally observed regional dancing you'll find mask makers. The tradition is especially strong in the states of Guerrero, Chiapas, Puebla, Oaxaca, and Michoacán.

Onyx   Puebla (where onyx is carved), Querétaro, Matehuala, Mexico City.

Pottery   Tlaquepaque, Tonala, Oaxaca, Puebla, Michoacán, Coyotepec, Izúcar de Matamoras, Veracruz, Copper Canyon, Dolores Hidalgo, and Guanajuato.

Rebozos   Woman's or man's rectangular woven cloth to be worn around the shoulders, similar to a shawl—Oaxaca, Mitla, San Cristóbal de las Casas, Mexico City, and Pátzcuaro. Rebozos are generally made of wool or a blend of wool and cotton, but synthetic fibers are creeping in, so check the material carefully before buying. Also, compare the weave from different cloths since the fineness of the weave is proportional to the cost.

Serapes   Heavy woolen or cotton blankets with a slit for the head, to be worn as a poncho—Santa Ana Chiautempan (30 miles north of Pueblo near Tlaxcala), San Luis Potosí, Santa María del Río (25 miles south of San Luis Potosí), Chiconcoac (an hour's drive northeast from Mexico City, near Texcoco), Saltillo, Toluca, and Mexico City.

Silver   Taxco, Mexico City, Zacatecas, Guadalajara. Sterling silver is indicated by "925" on the silver, which certifies that there are 925 grams of pure silver per kilogram, or that the silver is 92.5% pure. A spread-eagle hallmark is also used to indicate sterling. Look for these marks or you may pay a high price for an inferior quality that's mostly nickel, or even silverplate called alpaca.

Stones   Chalcedony, turquoise, lapis lazuli, amethyst—Querétaro, San Miguel de Allende, Durango, Saltillo, San Luis Potosí. The cost of turquoise is computed by weight, so many pesos per carat.

Textiles   Oaxaca, Chiapas, Santa Ana near Puebla, Guerrero, and Nayarit are known for their excellent weaving, each culturally distinct and different.

Tortoiseshell   It's illegal to bring it into the United States, so save your money.

grace. However, as grim as all this seems, using Mexico's history just this century as a rule, the country bounces back from adversity to become even stronger. A strong popular will to progress undergirds the Mexican spirit, and despite recent sobering events, the country still bustles with commercial activity. Meanwhile, as long as inflation doesn't outpace the effect of the devaluation, the country is quite a bargain; prices are better than they've been since 1985.

Economically, Mexico, though still a third world country, is by no means a poor country. Only about a sixth of the economy is in agriculture. Mining is still fairly important. Gold, silver, and many other important minerals are still mined, but the big industry today is oil. Mexico is also well-industrialized, manufacturing textiles, food products, and everything from cassette tapes to automobiles.

3 Margaritas, Tortillas & *Poc-Chuc*: Food & Drink in Mexico

Mexican food served in the United States or almost anywhere else in the world is almost never truly Mexican. The farther you get from the source the more the authenticity is lost in translation. True Mexican food usually isn't fiery hot, for example; hot spices are added from sauces and garnishes at the table.

While there are certain staples like tortillas and beans that appear almost universally around the country, Mexican food and drink varies considerably from region to region; even the beans and tortillas will sidestep the usual in different locales.

MEALS & RESTAURANTS À LA MEXICANA

BREAKFAST Traditionally, businesspeople in Mexico may start their day with a cup of coffee or *atole* and a piece of sweet bread just before heading for work around 8am; they won't sit down for a real breakfast until around 10 or 11am, when restaurants fill with men (usually) eating hearty breakfasts that may look more like lunch with steak, eggs, beans, and tortillas. Things are slowly changing as some executives are beginning to favor an earlier breakfast hour, beginning between 7 and 8am, during which business and the morning meal are combined.

Foreigners searching for an early breakfast will often find that nothing gets going in restaurants until around 9am; however, markets are bustling by 7am (they are a great place to get an early breakfast) and the capital's hotel restaurants often open as early as 7am to accommodate business travelers and those leaving on early flights. If you like to stoke the fires first thing, you might also bring your own portable coffee pot and coffee and buy bakery goodies the night before and make breakfast yourself.

LUNCH The main meal of the day, lunch, has traditionally been a two- to three-hour break, occurring between 1 and 5pm. But in the capital at least an abbreviated midday break is beginning to take hold. Short or long, the typical Mexican lunch begins with soup, then rice, then a main course with beans and tortillas and a bit of vegetable, and lastly dessert and coffee. But here too you'll see one-plate meals and fast food beginning to encroach on the multicourse meal. Workers return to their jobs until 7 or 8pm.

DINNER The evening meal is taken late, usually around 9 or 10pm. Although you may see many Mexicans eating in restaurants at night, big evening meals aren't traditional; a typical meal at home would be a light one with leftovers from breakfast or lunch, perhaps soup or tortillas and jam, or a little meat and rice.

RESTAURANT TIPS & ETIQUETTE Some of the foreigner's greatest frustrations in Mexico occur in restaurants, when they need to hail and retain the waiter or get their check. To summon the waiter, waive or raise your hand, but don't motion with your index finger, a demeaning gesture that may even cause the waiter to ignore you. To gesture someone to them, Mexicans will stand up, extend an arm straight out at shoulder level, and make a straight-armed, downward, diving motion with their hand cupped. A more discreet version, good to use when seated, has the elbow bent and perpendicular to the shoulder; with hand cupped, make a quick, diving motion out a bit from the armpit. (Both of these motions may make you feel silly until you practice. The latter one looks rather like the motion Americans make to signify "be still" or "shut up.")

If the waiter arrives to take your order before you are ready, you may have trouble getting him again. Once an order is in, however, the food usually arrives in steady sequence. Frequently, just before you've finished, when your plate is nearly empty, the waiter appears out of nowhere to whisk it away—unwary diners have seen their plates disappear mid-bite.

Finding your waiter when you're ready for the check can also be difficult. While waiters may hover too much while you're dining, they tend to disappear entirely by meal's end. It's considered rude for the waiter to bring the check before it's requested, so you have to ask for it, sometimes more than once. (To find a missing waiter, get up as if to leave and scrape the chairs loudly; if that fails, you'll probably find him chatting in the kitchen.) If you want the check and the waiter is simply across the room, a smile and a scribbling motion into the palm of your hand will send the message. In many budget restaurants, waiters don't clear the table of finished plates or soft drink bottles because they use them to figure the tab. Always double-check the addition.

FOOD AROUND THE COUNTRY

You won't have to confine yourself to Mexican food during a visit to Mexico—you'll find restaurants that prepare world-class French, Italian, Swiss, German, and other international cuisines. But you can also delve into the variety of Mexico's traditional foods, which derive from pre-Hispanic, Spanish, and French cuisines. At its best, Mexican food is among the most delicious in the world. Visitors can fairly easily find hearty, filling meals on a budget, but finding truly delicious food is not so easy—one positive is that some of the country's best food is found in small inexpensive restaurants where regional specialties are made to please discerning locals. Explanations of specific dishes are found in the appendix.

Recipes such as mole poblano—developed by nuns during colonial times to please priests and visiting dignitaries—have become part of the national patrimony, but the basics of Mexico's cuisine have endured since pre-Hispanic times. Corn, considered holy, was the foundation staple food of pre-Hispanic peoples. These people used corn leaves to bake and wrap food and ground corn to make the *atole* drink in many flavors (bitter, picante, or sweet) as well as tortillas and tamales (stuffed with meat).

When the Spanish arrived they found a bounty of edibles never seen in the Old World, including turkey, chocolate, tomatoes, squash, beans, avocados, peanuts, and vanilla (in addition to corn). All of these ingredients were integral parts of pre-Hispanic foods, and remain at the heart of today's Mexican cooking. Also central to the Indian peoples' cuisines were chiles, nopal cactus, amaranth, eggs of ants, turtles and iguanas, corn and maguey worms, bee and fly larvae, flowers of the maguey and squash, grasshoppers, jumiles (similar to stinkbugs), armadillos, rattlesnake, hairless dogs, deer, squirrels, monkeys, rats, frogs, ducks, parrots, quail, shrimp, fish, crabs, and crawfish. Exotic fruits such as sapodilla, guava, mamey, chirimoya, and pitahuayas rounded out the diet. Some of these are mainstream foods today; others are considered delicacies and may be seen on specialty menus.

But much of what we consider Mexican food wouldn't exist without the contributions of the Spanish. They introduced sugar cane, cattle, sheep, wheat, grapes, barley, and rice. The French influence is best seen in the extensive variety of baked goods available in the capital.

MEXICO'S REGIONAL CUISINES   Tamales are a traditional food all around Mexico, but there are many regional differences. In Mexico City you can often find the traditional Oaxaca tamales, which are steamed in a banana leaf. The zacahuil of coastal Veracruz is the size of a pig's leg (and that's what's in the center) and is pit-baked in a banana leaf; it can be sampled from street vendors on Sunday at the Lagunilla market.

Tortillas, another Mexican basic, are also not made or used equally. In Northern Mexico flour tortillas are served more often than corn tortillas. Blue corn tortillas, once a market food, have found their way to gourmet tables throughout the country. Tortillas are fried and used as a garnish in tortilla and Tarascan soup. Filled with meat they become, of course, tacos. A tortilla stuffed, rolled, or covered in a sauce and garnished results in an enchilada. A tortilla filled with cheese and lightly fried is a quesadilla. Rolled into a narrow tube stuffed with chicken, then deep fried, they become a flauta. Leftover tortillas cut in wedges and crispy fried are called totopos and used to scoop beans and guacamole salad. Yesterday's tortillas mixed with eggs, chicken, peppers, and other spices are called chilaquiles. Small fried corn tortillas are delicious with ceviche, or when topped with fresh lettuce, tomatoes, sauce, onions, and chicken they become tostadas. Each region has a variation of these tortilla-based dishes and most can be found in Mexico City.

Since a variety of Mexico's cuisines appear on menus in the capital, its useful to know some of the best to try.

Puebla is known for the many dishes created by colonial-era nuns, among them traditional *mole poblano* (a rich sauce with more than 20 ingredients served over turkey), the eggnoglike rompope, and bunuelos (a kind of puff pastry dipped in sugar). Puebla is also known for its Mexican-style barbecue, lamb *mixiotes* (cooked in spicy sauce and wrapped in maguey paper), and tinga (a delicious beef stew). And *chiles enogada,* the national dish of Mexico, was created in Puebla in honor of Emperor Agustín Iturbide. The national colors of red, white, and green appear in this dish, in which large green poblano peppers are stuffed with spicy beef, topped with white almond sauce, and sprinkled with red pomegranate seeds. It's served around Independence Day in September.

Tamales wrapped in banana leaves and a number of different mole sauces are hallmarks of **Oaxacan** cuisine.

The **Yucatán** is noted for its rich (but not *picante*) sauces and pit-baked meat. Mild but flavorful achiote-based paste is one of the main flavorings for Yucatecan sauces.

The states of **Guerrero, Nayarit,** and **Jalisco** produce *pozole,* a soup of hominy and chicken or pork make in a clear broth or one from tomatoes or green chiles (depending on the state), and topped with a variety of garnishes.

Michoacán comes forth with a triangular-shaped tamal called *corunda,* and *uchepo,* a rectangular tamal that is either sweet or has meat inside. The state is also known for its soups, among them the delicious *Tarascan* soup, made with a bean-broth base.

And **Veracruz,** of course, is famous for seafood dishes, especially red snapper Veracruz-style, smothered in tomatoes, onions, garlic, and olives.

MEXICAN BEVERAGES

Though Mexico grows flavorful **coffee** in Chiapas, Veracruz, and Oaxaca, a jar of instant coffee is often all that's offered, especially in budget restaurants. Decaffeinated coffee appears on some menus, but often it's the instant variety, even in the best restaurants.

Specialty drinks are almost as varied as the food in Mexico. **Tequila** comes from the blue agave grown near Guadalajara and its the intoxicating ingredient in the famed Margarita. Hot *ponche* (punch) is found often at festivals and is usually made with fresh fruit and spiked with tequila or rum.

Domestic wine and beer are excellent choices in Mexico, and in the past have been cheaper than any imported variety. However, NAFTA has lowered trade barriers against U.S.-made alcoholic drinks, and prices for them are becoming lower as well.

Baja California and the region around Querétaro is prime grape growing land for Mexico's **wine** production. Excellent **beer** is produced in Monterrey, the Yucatán and Veracruz. The best *pulque,* a pre-Hispanic drink derived from the juice of the maguey plant, supposedly comes from Hidalgo state. Mexicans prefer freshly fermented pulque and generally avoid the canned variety, saying it's just not the real thing. Visitors to the capital can sample it at restaurants around Garibaldi square. Delicious **fruit-flavored waters** appear on tables countrywide; they are made from hibiscus flowers, ground rice and melon seeds, watermelon, and other fresh fruits. Be sure to ask if they are made with purified water. **Sangria** is a spicy tomato-, orange juice-, and pepper-based chaser for tequila shots.

Though the rich, eggnoglike *rompope* was invented in Puebla, now other regions such as San Juan de los Lagos, Jalisco, produce it. It's sold in liquor and grocery stores countrywide.

4 Recommended Books

Mexico Insight, published by Excelsior in Mexico City (Bucarelli No. 1, 5 Piso, Mexico, D.F. Mexico 06600), is a hard-hitting news magazine published twice monthly in English. It's the best way to keep on top of what's happening, from economics, to politics, to day-to-day issues on such recent topics as police reform, Mexico City's earthquake warning system, border agents, developers, business, free trade, the Chiapas uprising . . . well, you name it. Subscriptions cost $46 for 24 issues.

There are an endless number of books written on the history, culture, and archeology of Mexico and Central America. I have listed those I especially enjoyed.

HISTORY   Dennis Tedlock produced an elegant translation of the *Popul Vuh,* a collection of ancient Maya mythological tales (Simon & Schuster, 1985). *A Short History of Mexico* (Doubleday, 1962) by J. Patrick McHenry is a concise historical account. A remarkably readable and thorough college textbook is *The Course of Mexican History* (Oxford University Press, 1987) by Michael C. Meyer and William L. Sherman. Bernal Díaz's *The Conquest of New Spain* (Shoe String, 1988) is the famous story of the Mexican Conquest written by Cortés's lieutenant. *The Crown of Mexico* (Holt, Rinehart & Winston, 1971) by Joan Haslip, a biography of Maximilian and Carlotta, reads like a novel. Eric Wolf's *Sons of the Shaking Earth* (University of Chicago Press) is the best single-volume introduction to Mexican history and culture that I know. *Ancient Mexico; An Overview* (University of

New Mexico Press, 1985) by Jaime Litvak, is a short, very readable history of pre-Hispanic Mexico.

The Wind That Swept Mexico (University of Texas Press, 1971) by Anita Brenner, is a classic illustrated account of the Mexican Revolution. Charles Flandrau wrote the classic *Viva Mexico; A Traveller's Account of Life in Mexico* (Eland Books, 1985) early this century; it's a blunt and humorous description of Mexico. Most people can't put down Gary Jenning's *Aztec* (Avon, 1981), a superbly researched and colorfully written fictionalized account of Aztec life before and after the Conquest.

CULTURE   *Five Families* (Basic Books, 1979) and *Children of Sanchez* (Random House, 1979), both by Oscar Lewis, are sociological studies written in the late 1950s about typical Mexican families. Irene Nicholson's *Mexican and Central American Mythology* (Peter Bedrick Books, 1983) is a concise illustrated book that simplifies the subject.

A good but controversial all-around introduction to contemporary Mexico and its people is *Distant Neighbors: A Portrait of the Mexicans* (Random House, 1984) by Alan Riding. In a more personal vein is Patrick Oster's *The Mexicans: A Personal Portrait of the Mexican People* (HarperCollins 1989), a reporter's insightful account of ordinary Mexican people. A book with valuable insights into the Mexican character is *The Labyrinth of Solitude* (Grove Press, 1985) by Octavio Paz.

Anyone going to San Cristóbal de las Casas, Chiapas, should first read *Living Maya* (Harry N. Abrams, 1987) by Walter F. Morris, with excellent photographs by Jeffrey J. Foxx, all about the Maya living today in the state of Chiapas. For some fascinating background on northern Mexico and the Copper Canyon, read *Unknown Mexico* (Dover Press, 1987) by Carl Lumholtz, an intrepid writer and photographer around the turn of the century.

The best single source of information on Mexican music, dance, and mythology is Frances Toor's *A Treasury of Mexican Folkways* (Crown, 1967). *Life in Mexico: Letters of Fanny Calderón de la Barca* (Doubleday, 1966), edited and annotated by Howard T. Fisher and Marion Hall Fisher, is as lively and entertaining today as when it first appeared in 1843, but the editor's illustrated and annotated update makes it even more contemporary. Scottish-born Fanny was married to the Spanish ambassador to Mexico, and the letters are the accounts of her experiences. *My Heart Lies South* by Elizabeth Borton de Treviño (1953) is a humorous, tender, and insightful autobiographical account of the life of an American woman married to a Mexican in Monterrey; it begins in the 1930s.

ART, ARCHAEOLOGY & ARCHITECTURE   Anyone heading for Yucatán should first read the wonderfully entertaining accounts of travel in that region by the 19th-century traveler, New York lawyer, and amateur archaeologist John L. Stephens. His books Incidents of *Travel in Central America, Chiapas and Yucatán* and also the account of his second trip, *Incidents of Travel in Yucatán*, have been reprinted by Dover. The series also includes Diego de Landa's *Yucatán Before and After the Conquest* (Dover, 1978), written in the 1560s. Friar Diego's account is a detailed description of Maya daily life, much of which has remained the same from his time until today. Another must is *The Maya* (Thames and Hudson, 1987) by Michael Coe, which is helpful in relating to the different Maya periods. *A Forest of Kings: The Untold Story of the Ancient Maya* (William Morrow, 1990) by Linda Schele and David Freidel, uses the written history of Maya hieroglyphs to tell the dynastic history of selected Maya sites. *The Blood of Kings: Dynasty and Ritual in*

Maya Art (George Braziller, 1986) by Linda Schele and Mary Ellen Miller, is a pioneer work and unlocks the bloody history of the Maya. The most comprehensive guide to Maya ruins is Joyce Kelly's *An Archeological Guide to Mexico's Yucatán Peninsula* (University of Oklahoma, 1993).

A book that tells the story of the Indians' "painted books" is *The Mexican Codices and Their Extraordinary History* (Ediciones Lara, 1985) by María Sten. *Mexico Splendors of Thirty Centuries* (Metropolitan Museum of Art, 1990), the catalog of the 1991 traveling exhibition, is a wonderful resource on Mexico's art from 1500 B.C. through the 1950s. Another superb catalog, *Images of Mexico: The Contribution of Mexico to 20th Century Art* (Dallas Museum of Art, 1987) is a fabulously illustrated and detailed account of Mexican art gathered from collections around the world. Elizabeth Wilder Weismann's *Art and Time in Mexico: From the Conquest to the Revolution* (HarperCollins, 1985), illustrated with 351 photographs, covers Mexican religious, public, and private architecture with excellent photos and text. *Casa Mexicana* (Steward, Tabori & Chang, 1989) by Tim Street-Porter, takes readers through the interiors of some of Mexico's finest homes-turned-museums or public buildings and private homes using color photographs. *Mexican Interiors* (Architectural Book Publishing Co., 1962) by Verna Cook Shipway and Warren Shipway, uses black-and-white photographs to highlight architectural details from homes all over Mexico.

FOLK ART   Chloè Sayer's *Costumes of Mexico* (University of Texas Press, 1985) is a beautifully illustrated and written work. *Mexican Masks* (University of Texas Press, 1980) by Donald Cordry, based on the author's collection and travels, remains the definitive work on Mexican masks. Cordry's *Mexican Indian Costumes* (University of Texas Press, 1968) is another classic on the subject. Carlos Espejel wrote both *Mexican Folk Ceramics* and *Mexican Folk Crafts* (Editorial Blume, 1975 and 1978), two comprehensive books that explore crafts state by state. *Folk Treasures of Mexico* (Harry N. Abrams, 1990) by Marion Oettinger, curator of Folk and Latin American Art at the San Antonio Museum of Art, is the fascinating illustrated story behind the 3,000-piece Mexican folk-art collection amassed by Nelson Rockefeller over a 50-year period, and also includes much information about individual folk artists.

NATURE   *Peterson Field Guides: Mexican Birds* (Houghton Mifflin) by Roger Tory Peterson and Edward L. Chalif, is an excellent guide to the country's birds. *Birds of the Yucatán* (Amigos de Sian Ka'an) has color illustrations and descriptions of 100 birds found primarily in the Yucatán peninsula. *A Guide to Mexican Mammals and Reptiles* (Minutiae Mexicana) by Norman Pelham Wright and Dr. Bernardo Villa Ramírez, is a small but useful guide to some of the country's wildlife.

3

Planning a Trip to Mexico

In this chapter, the where, when, and how of your trip are discussed—the advance planning that gets your trip together and takes it on the road.

After deciding where to go, most people have two fundamental questions: What will it cost and how do I get there? This chapter not only answers those questions but also addresses such important issues as when to go, whether or not to take a tour, what pretrip health precautions should be taken, what insurance coverage to investigate, where to obtain additional information, and more.

1 Visitor Information, Entry Requirements & Money

SOURCES OF INFORMATION

The **Mexico Hotline** (☎ 800/44-MEXICO in the U.S.) is a good source for very general informational brochures on the country and for answers to the most commonly asked questions.

MEXICAN GOVERNMENT TOURIST OFFICES

Mexico has tourist offices throughout the world, including the following:

United States: 70 E. Lake St., Suite 1413, Chicago, IL 60601 (☎ 312/565-2778); 2702 N. Loop W., Suite 450, Houston, TX 77008 (☎ 713/880-5153); 10100 Santa Monica Blvd., Suite 224, Los Angeles, CA 90067 (☎ 310/203-8191); 233 Ponce de Leon Blvd., Suite 710, Coral Gables, FL 33134 (☎ 305/443-9160); 405 Park Ave., Suite 1401, New York, NY 10022 (☎ 212/755-7261); and 1911 Pennsylvania Ave. NW, Washington, DC 20006 (☎ 202/728-1750).

Canada: One Place Ville-Marie, Suite 1526, Montréal, PQ H3B 2B5 (☎ 514/871-1052); 2 Bloor St. W., Suite 1801, Toronto, ON M4W 3E2 (☎ 416/925-0704).

Europe: Weisenhüttenplatz 26, 6000 Frankfurt-am-Main 1, Germany (☎ 4969/25-3413); 60-61 Trafalgar Sq., London WC2 N5DS, United Kingdom (☎ 441/734-1058); Calle de Velázquez 126, Madrid 28006, Spain (☎ 341/261-1827); 4 rue Notre-Dame-des-Victoires, 75002 Paris, France (☎ 331/40-20-07-34); and via Barberini 3, 00187 Rome, Italy (☎ 396/482-7160).

Asia: 2.15.1 Nagato-Cho, Chiyoda-Ku, Tokyo 100, Japan (☎ 813/580-2962).

STATE TOURISM DEVELOPMENT OFFICES

Two Mexican states have tourism and trade development offices in the United States: **Casa Guerrero State Promotion Office,** 5075 Westheimer, Suite 980 West, Houston, TX 77056 (☎ 713/552-0930; fax 713/552-0207); **Casa Nuevo León State Promotion Office,** 100 W. Houston St., Suite 1400, San Antonio, TX 78205 (☎ 210/225-0732, fax 210/225-0736).

OTHER SOURCES

The following newsletter may be of interest to readers:

Mexico Meanderings, P.O. Box 33057, Austin, TX 78764, is a new six- to eight-page newsletter with photographs featuring off-the-beaten-track destinations in Mexico. It's aimed at readers who travel by car, bus, or train and is published six times annually. A subscription costs $18.

For other newsletters, see "For Seniors" under "Tips for Special Travelers," below.

ENTRY REQUIREMENTS

DOCUMENTS   All travelers to Mexico are required to present **proof of citizenship,** such as an original birth certificate with a raised seal, a valid passport, or naturalization papers. Those using a birth certificate should also have a current photo identification such as a driver's license. And those whose last name on the birth certificate is different from their current name (women using a married name, for example) should also bring a photo identification card *and* legal proof of the name change such as the *original* marriage license or certificate. This proof of citizenship may also be requested when you want to reenter either the United States or Mexico. Note that photocopies are *not* acceptable.

You must also carry a **Mexican Tourist Permit,** which is issued free of charge by Mexican border officials after proof of citizenship is accepted. The Tourist Permit is more important than a passport in Mexico, so guard it carefully. If you lose it, you may not be permitted to leave the country until you can replace it—a bureaucratic hassle that takes several days to a week at least.

A Tourist Permit can be issued for up to 180 days, and although your stay south of the border may be shorter than that, you should ask for the maximum time, just in case. Sometimes officials don't ask—they just stamp a time limit, so be sure to say "six months" (or at least twice as long as you intend to stay). If you should decide to extend your stay, you'll eliminate hassle by not needing to renew your papers.

This is especially important for people who take a car into Mexico. Additional documentation is required for driving a personal vehicle in Mexico (see "By Car" under "Getting There," below).

Note that children under age 18 traveling without parents or with only one parent must have a notarized letter from the absent parent or parents authorizing the travel.

Lost Documents   To replace a **lost passport,** contact your embassy or nearest consular agent, listed in "Fast Facts: Mexico," below. You must establish a record of your citizenship and also fill out a form requesting another Mexican tourist card. Without the **Tourist Permit** you can't leave the country, and without an affidavit affirming your passport request and citizenship, you may have hassles at customs when you get home. So it's important to clear everything up *before* trying to leave. Mexican customs may, however, accept the police report of the loss of the tourist card and allow you to leave.

CUSTOMS   When you enter Mexico, customs officials will be tolerant as long as you have no illegal drugs or firearms. You're allowed to bring in two cartons of cigarettes, or 50 cigars, plus a kilogram (2.2 lb.) of smoking tobacco; the liquor allowance is two bottles of anything, wine or hard liquor.

When you're reentering the United States, federal law allows you to bring in duty free up to $400 in purchases every 30 days. The first $1,000 over the $400 allowance is taxed at 10%. You may bring in a carton (200) of cigarettes or 50 cigars or 2kg (4.4 lb.) of smoking tobacco, plus 1 liter of an alcoholic beverage (wine, beer, or spirits).

Canadian citizens are allowed $20 in purchases after a 24-hour absence from the country or $100 after a stay of 48 hours or more.

MONEY

CASH/CURRENCY   In 1993, the Mexican government dropped three zeroes from its currency. The new currency is called the *Nuevo Peso,* or New Peso. The purpose was to simplify accounting; all those zeroes were becoming too difficult to manage. Old Peso notes will be valid at least until 1996. Paper currency comes in denominations of 2, 5, 10, 20, 50, and 100 New Pesos. Coins come in denominations of 1, 2, 5, and 10 pesos and 20 and 50 centavos (100 centavos make one New Peso). The coins are somewhat confusing because different denominations have a similar appearance. New Peso prices appear written with *N* or *NP* beside them; and for a while the Old Peso prices will appear as well. Currently the U.S. dollar equals around NP$6; at that rate an item costing NP$5, for example, would be equivalent to U.S. 83¢.

These changes are likely to cause confusion among U.S. and Canadian travelers to Mexico in several ways. Before the New Peso was instituted, merchants and others skipped the small change, now they don't. Small change isn't always available so cashiers often offer gum or candy to make up the difference. Also, small change appears on restaurant bills and credit cards. On restaurant bills that you pay in cash, for example, the change will be rounded up or down to the nearest five centavos. Credit-card bills, however, will show the exact amount and will have *N* written before the amount to denote that the bill is in New Pesos. Be sure to double-check any credit-card vouchers to be sure the *N* or *NP* appears on the total line.

Getting change continues to be a problem in Mexico. Small-denomination bills and coins are hard to come by, so start collecting them early in your trip and continue as you travel. Shopkeepers everywhere seem to always be out of change and small bills; that's doubly true in a market.

Note: The dollar sign ($) is used to indicate pesos in Mexico. To avoid confusion, I will use the dollar sign in this book *only* to denote U.S. currency.

Only dollar prices are listed in this book; they are a more reliable indication than peso prices. Many establishments dealing with tourists quote prices in dollars. To avoid confusion, they use the abbreviations "Dlls." for dollars and "m.n." (*moneda nacional*—national currency) for pesos.

Mexico's predicted inflation rate for 1995 is 45%. Every effort has been made to provide the most accurate and up-to-date information in this guide, but price changes are inevitable.

EXCHANGING MONEY   The 1994 devaluation of the peso has had a varied effect on tourists. First, the rate of exchange fluctuates daily, so be careful not to exchange too much of your currency at once. Don't forget, however, to allow enough to carry you over a weekend or Mexican holiday, when banks are closed. Cash can sometimes be difficult to exchange because counterfeit U.S. dollars have been circulating recently in Mexico; merchants and banks are wary, and many, especially in small towns, refuse to accept dollars in cash. In general, avoid carrying the U.S. $100 bill, the one most commonly counterfeited. Since small bills and coins in pesos are hard to come by in Mexico, the U.S. $1 bill is very useful for tipping bellboys and chambermaids.

Banks in Mexico often give a rate of exchange below the official daily rate, and hotels usually exchange below the banks' daily rate. Exchange houses are generally more convenient than banks since they have more locations and longer hours, but the rate of exchange will be slightly lower. Personal checks may be cashed but will delay you for weeks since a bank will wait for your check to clear before giving you your money. Canadian dollars seem to be most easily exchanged for pesos at branches of Banamex and Bancomer. *Before leaving a bank or exchange house window, always count your change in front of the teller before the next client steps up.*

Banks are open Monday through Friday from 9am to 1:30pm; a few banks in large cities offer extended afternoon hours. You'll save time at the bank or currency-exchange booths by arriving no earlier than 10am, about the time the official daily rate is received. Usually they won't exchange money until they have the official rate. Large airports have currency-exchange counters that sometimes stay open as long as flights are arriving or departing, but don't exchange money at the first one you see in an airport—there's usually more than one and you'll often find a better exchange rate farther along the concourse.

TRAVELER'S CHECKS   Traveler's checks are readily accepted nearly everywhere, but they can be difficult to cash on a weekend or holiday or in an out-of-the-way place. Their best value is in replacement in case of theft. I usually carry half of my money in cash ($1, $20, $50) and half in traveler's checks ($20 and $50). Mexican banks pay more for traveler's checks than for dollars in cash, but *casas de cambio* (exchange houses) pay more for cash than for traveler's checks. Some banks, but not all, charge a service fee as high as 5% to exchange either traveler's checks or dollars. Sometimes banks post the service charge amount so you can see it, but they might not, so it pays to ask first and shop around for a bank without a fee.

CREDIT CARDS & ATMS   You'll be able to charge some hotel and restaurant bills, almost all airline tickets, and many store purchases on your credit cards. You can get cash advances of several hundred dollars on your card, but there may be a wait of 20 minutes to two hours. You can't charge gasoline purchases in Mexico.

VISA ("Bancomer" in Mexico), MasterCard ("Carnet" in Mexico), and, less widely, American Express are the most accepted cards. The Bancomer bank, with branches throughout the country, has inaugurated a system of **automatic-teller machines (ATMs)** linked to VISA International's network. If you are a VISA customer, you may be able to get peso cash from one of the Bancomer ATMs.

WIRE FUNDS   If you need cash in a hurry, **Dineros en Minutos** (Money in Minutes) is affiliated with Western Union and makes wire cash transactions at Electrika furniture/electronic stores in Mexico. Your contact on the other end presents money to Western Union, which is received by Electrika, then presented in pesos to you. The service only recently got off the ground in Mexico, but 500 outlets are planned.

BRIBES & SCAMS

BRIBES   Referred to in Mexico as *propinas* (tips), *mordidas* (bites), or worse, customary bribes and kickbacks are probably almost as old as humankind. Bribes exist in every country, but in developing countries, the amounts tend to be smaller and collected more often. You will most likely find yourself in situations where bribes are expected, so you should know how to deal with it.

Border officials have become more courteous, less bureaucratic, and less inclined to ask/hint for a bribe. I'm still wary, however; just so you're prepared, here are a few hints based on my previous experiences.

Some border officials will do what they're supposed to do (stamp your passport or birth certificate and inspect your luggage) and then wave you on through. If you don't offer a tip of a few dollars to the man who inspects your car (if you're driving), he may ask for it, as in "Give me a tip (*propina*)." If you're charged for the stamping or inspection, ask for a receipt. If you don't get a receipt, you've paid a bribe.

Officials don't ask for bribes from everybody. Travelers dressed in a formal suit and tie, with pitch-black sunglasses and a scowl on the face are rarely asked to pay a bribe. Those who are dressed for vacation fun or seem good-natured and accommodating are targets. Ignore the request. Pretend not to understand. Don't speak Spanish. Whatever you do, avoid impoliteness, and absolutely *never* insult a Latin American official! When an official's sense of machismo is roused, he can and will throw the book at you, and you may be in trouble. Stand your ground, but do it politely.

SCAMS   As you travel in Mexico, you may encounter several types of scams. The **shoeshine scam** is an old trick, used most often in Mexico City. Here's how it works. A tourist agrees to a shine for, say, 15 pesos. When the work is complete, the vendor says "That'll be 50 pesos" and insists that the shocked tourist misunderstood. A big brouhaha ensues involving bystanders who side with the shoeshine vendor. The object is to get the bewildered tourist to succumb to the howling crowd and embarrassing scene and fork over the money. A variation of the scam has the vendor saying the price quoted is per shoe. To avoid this scam, ask around about the price of a shine, and when the vendor quotes his price, write it down and show it to him *before* the shine.

Tourists are suckered daily into the **iguana scam**, especially in Puerto Vallarta and nearby Yelapa beach. Someone, often a child, strolls by carrying a huge iguana and says "Wanna take my peekchur?" Photo-happy tourists seize the opportunity. Just as the camera is angled properly, the holder of the iguana says (more like mumbles) "One dollar." That means a dollar per shot. Sometimes they wait until the shutter clicks to mention money.

Because hotel desk clerks are usually so helpful, I hesitate to mention the **lost objects scam** for fear of tainting them all. But here's how it works. You "lose" your wallet after cashing money at the desk, or you leave something valuable such as a purse or camera in the lobby. You report it. The clerk has it, but instead of telling you he does, he says he will see what he can do; meanwhile, he suggests you offer a high reward. This scam has all kinds of variations. In one story a reader wrote about, a desk clerk in Los Mochis was in cahoots with a bystander in the lobby who lifted the reader's wallet in the elevator.

Another scam readers have mentioned might be called the **infraction scam.** Officials, or men presenting themselves as officials, demand money for some supposed infraction. Never get into a car with them. I avoided one begun by a bona fide policeman-on-the-take in Chetumal when my traveling companion feigned illness and began writhing, moaning, and pretending to have the dry heaves. It was more than the policeman could handle.

Legal and necessary car searches by military personnel looking for drugs are mentioned elsewhere in this book. Every now and then, however, there are police-controlled illegal roadblocks where motorists are forced to pay before continuing on their way.

Along these lines, if you are stopped by the police, I also suggest you avoid handing your driver's license to a policeman. Hold it so that it can be read but don't give it up.

Then there's the **taxi ticket scam.** This usually happens at taxi ticket booths in airports and bus stations. You're vulnerable because you may be a new arrival to the country and not yet have your peso legs, your Spanish may not be up to par, or you're preoccupied with getting where you're going. You give the ticket seller a 50-peso bill and the seller returns change for 20 pesos. I'll say this elsewhere: *Count your change before leaving the booth!* Better yet, when you hand the seller the bill, say out loud the amount of the ticket and the amount of the bill and say *cambio* (change).

Although you should be aware of such hazards and how to deal with them, I log thousands of miles and many months in Mexico each year without serious incident, and I feel safer there than at home in the U.S. (see also "Emergencies" and "Safety" under "Fast Facts: Mexico" later in this chapter).

2 When to Go

From **Puerto Vallarta south to Huatulco,** Pacific Mexico offers one of the world's most perfect winter climates—dry and balmy with temperatures ranging from the 80s by day to the 60s at night. (Although geographically within the tropic zone, Mazatlán is excluded from this perfect weather belt.) From Puerto Vallarta south you can swim year-round.

The winter climate on the **Gulf Coast** is very different. While high mountains shield Pacific beaches from *nortes* (northers—freezing blasts out of Canada), the gulf enjoys no such immunity. They strike so suddenly that within an hour, temperatures can drop by as much as 40°. Here's an interesting twist: While *nortes* hit Veracruz (latitude 19°) with vicious intensity, their sting is far less severe in the most northerly Yucatán Peninsula fronting the Gulf of Mexico. Gales hit Veracruz over land and Mérida over water; the gulf has a warming effect.

In summer the difference between West Coast and Gulf Coast temperatures is much less pronounced. Both areas become warm and rainy. Of the two regions, the Gulf is far rainier, particularly in the states of Tabasco and Campeche.

On national holidays, banks, stores, and businesses are closed; hotels fill up quickly; and transportation is crowded. Mexico celebrates the following national holidays: **January 1,** New Year's Day; **February 5,** Constitution Day; **March 21,** Birthday of Benito Juárez; March–April (movable), **Holy Week** (Good Friday through Easter Sunday); **May 1,** Labor Day; **May 5,** Battle of Puebla, 1862 (Cinco de Mayo); **September 1,** President's Message to Congress; **September 16,** Independence Day; **October 12,** Day of the Race (Columbus Day in the U.S.);

November 1–2, All Saints' and All Souls' days (Day of the Dead); **November 20,** Anniversary of the Mexican Revolution; **December 11–12,** Feast Day of the Virgin of Guadalupe (Mexico's patron saint); **December 24–25,** Christmas Eve and Christmas Day.

MEXICO CALENDAR OF EVENTS

January

- **Three Kings Day.** Commemorates the Three Kings' bringing of gifts to the Christ Child. On this day the Three Kings "bring" gifts to children. January 6.
- **Feast of San Antonio Abad,** Mexico City. Blessing of the Animals at the Santiago Tlatelolco Church on the Plaza of Three Cultures, at San Juan Bautista Church in Coyoacán, and at the Church of San Fernando, two blocks north of the Juárez/Reforma intersection. January 17.

February

- **Candlemas.** On January 6, Rosca de Reyes, a round cake with a hole in the middle, is baked with a tiny doll inside representing the Christ Child. Whoever gets the slice with the doll must give a party on February 2.
- ✪ **Carnaval.** This celebration resembles New Orleans's Mardi Gras, with a festive atmosphere and parades. In Chamula, however, the event harks back to pre-Hispanic times with ritualistic running on flaming branches. On the Tuesday before Ash Wednesday in Tepoztlán and Huejotzingo, masked and brilliantly clad dancers fill the streets. In some towns there will be no special celebration, in others a few parades.

  Where: Especially celebrated in Tepoztlán, Morelos; Huejotzingo, Puebla; Chamula, Chiapas; Veracruz, Veracruz; Cozumel, Quintana Roo; and Mazatlán, Sinaloa. **When:** Date is variable but always the three days preceding Ash Wednesday and the beginning of Lent. **How:** Transportation and hotels will be clogged, so it's best to make reservations six months in advance and arrive a couple of days ahead of the beginning of celebrations.

- **Ash Wednesday.** The start of Lent and time of abstinence. It's a day of reverence nationwide, but some towns honor it with folk dancing and fairs. Movable date.

March

- **Benito Juárez's Birthday.** Small hometown celebrations countrywide, especially in Juárez's birthplace—Gelatao, Oaxaca.
- ✪ **Holy Week.** Celebrates the last week in the life of Christ from Good Friday through Easter Sunday with somber religious processions almost nightly, spoofing of Judas, and reenactments of specific biblical events, plus food and craft fairs. Among the Tarahumara in the Copper Canyon, celebrations have pre-Hispanic overtones. Businesses close and Mexicans travel far and wide during this week.

  Where: Special in Pátzcuaro, Taxco, Malinalco, and among the Tarahumara villages in the Copper Canyon. **When:** March or April. **How:** Reserve early with a deposit. Airline seats on flights into and out of the country will be reserved months in advance. Buses to these towns or to almost anywhere in Mexico will be full, so try arriving on the Wednesday or Thursday before Good Friday. Easter Sunday is quiet.

May
- **Labor Day.** Workers' parades countrywide and everything closes. May 1.
- **Holy Cross Day,** Día de la Santa Cruz. Workers place a cross on top of unfinished buildings and celebrate with food, bands, folk dancing, and fireworks around the worksite. Celebrations are particularly colorful in Valle de Bravo, in the state of Mexico, and Paracho, Michoacán. May 3.
- **Cinco de Mayo.** A national holiday that celebrates the defeat of the French at the Battle of Puebla. May 5.
- **Feast of San Isidro.** The patron saint of farmers is honored with a blessing of seeds and work animals. May 15.

June
- **Navy Day.** Celebrated by all port cities. June 1.
- ✪ **Corpus Christi.** Honors the Body of Christ—the Eucharist—with religious processions, masses, and food. Celebrated nationwide. Festivities include numerous demonstrations of the Roman *voladores* (flying pole dancers) beside the church and at the ruins of El Tajín. In Mexico City children, dressed as Indians, and their parents gather before the National Cathedral on the Zócalo, carrying decorated baskets of fruit for the priest's blessing. *Mulitas* (mules), handmade from dried corn husks and painted, often with a corn-husk rider, and sometimes accompanied by pairs of corn-husk dolls, are traditionally sold there on that day.

    Where: Particularly special in Papantla, Veracruz. **When:** Variable date, 66 days after Easter. **How:** By bus from Tampico, Tuxpan, or Poza Rica. Make reservations well in advance.
- **Saint Peter's Day,** Día de San Pedro. Celebrated wherever St. Peter is the patron saint and honors anyone named Pedro or Peter. It's especially festive at San Pedro Tlaquepaque, near Guadalajara, with numerous mariachi bands, folk dancers, and parades with floats. June 29.

July
- **Virgin of Carmen.** A nationally celebrated religious festival centered in churches nationwide. July 16.
- **Saint James Day,** Día de Santiago. Observed countrywide wherever St. James is the patron saint and for anyone named Jaime or James or any village with Santiago in its name. Often celebrated with rodeos, fireworks, dancing, and food. July 25.

August
- **Fall of Tenochtitlán,** Mexico City. The last battle of the conquest took place at Tlatelolco, ruins that are now a part of the Plaza of Three Cultures. Wreath-laying ceremonies there and at the Cuauhtémoc monument on Reforma commemorate the event when thousands lost their lives and the last Aztec king, Cuauhtémoc, surrendered to Hernán Cortés. August 13.
- ✪ **Assumption Of The Virgin Mary.** Celebrated throughout the country with special masses and in some places with processions. Streets are carpeted in flower petals and colored sawdust. At midnight on the 15th a statue of the Virgin is carried through the streets; the 16th is a running of the bulls. On August 15 in Santa Clara del Cobre, near Pátzcuaro, Our Lady of Santa Clara de Asis and the Virgen de la Sagrado Patrona are honored with a parade of floats, dancers on the main square, and an exposition of regional crafts, especially copper.

Where: Special in Huamantla, Tlaxcala, and Santa Clara del Cobre, Michoacán. **When:** August 15–16. **How:** Buses to Huamantla from Puebla or Mexico City will be full, and there are few hotels in Huamantla. Plan to stay in Puebla and commute to the festivities.

September

- **Independence Day.** Celebrates Mexico's independence from Spain. A day of parades, picnics, and family reunions throughout the country. At 11pm on September 15 the president of Mexico gives the famous independence *grito* (shout) from the National Palace in Mexico City. At least half a million people are crowded into the Zócalo, and the rest of the country watches the event on television. The enormous military parade on September 16 starts at the Zócalo and ends at the Independence Monument on Reforma. Tall buildings downtown are draped in the national colors of red, green, and white, and the Zócalo is ablaze with lights; it's popular to drive downtown at night to see the lights—truly spectacular. It's also elaborately celebrated in Querétaro and San Miguel de Allende, where Independence conspirators lived and met. September 16 (parade day).

October

- **Cervantino Festival.** Begun in the 1970s as a cultural event bringing performing artists from all over the world to the Guanajuato, a picturesque village northeast of Mexico City. Now the artists travel all over the republic after appearing in Guanajuato. Check local calendars for appearances. Early to mid October.
- **Feast of San Francisco de Asis.** Anyone named Frances, Francis, or Francisco and towns whose patron saint is Francisco celebrate with barbecue parties, regional dancing, and religious observances. October 4.
- **Día de la Raza,** Day of the Race, or Columbus Day (the day Columbus landed in America). Commemorates the fusion of the Spanish and Mexican peoples. October 12.

November

- ✪ **Day of the Dead.** What's commonly called the Day of the Dead is actually two days: All Saints' Day, honoring saints and deceased children, and All Souls' Day, honoring deceased adults. Relatives gather at cemeteries countrywide, carrying candles and food, often spending the night beside graves of loved ones. Weeks before, bakers begin producing bread formed in the shape of mummies or round loaves decorated with bread "bones." Decorated sugar skulls emblazoned with glittery names are sold everywhere. Many days ahead, homes and churches erect special altars laden with Day of the Dead bread, fruit, flowers, candles, and favorite foods and photographs of saints and of the deceased. On the two nights of the Day of the Dead, children dress in costumes and masks, often carrying mock coffins through the streets and pumpkin lanterns into which they expect money will be dropped.

  Where: The most famous celebration is on Janitzio, an island on Lake Pátzcuaro, Michoacán, west of Mexico City, but it has become almost too well known. Mixquic, a mountain village south of Mexico City, hosts an elaborate street fair, and around 11pm on both nights, solemn processions lead to the cemetery in the center of town where villagers are already settled in with candles, flowers, and food. **When:** November 1–2.

- **Revolution Day.** Commemorates the start of the Mexican Revolution in 1910 with parades, speeches, rodeos, and patriotic events. November 20.

December

✪ **Feast of the Virgin of Guadalupe.** Throughout the country the Patroness of Mexico is honored with religious processions, street fairs, dancing, fireworks, and masses. The Virgin of Guadalupe appeared to a young man, Juan Diego, in December 1531 on a hill near Mexico City. He convinced the bishop that the apparition had appeared by revealing his cloak, upon which the Virgin was emblazoned. It's customary for children to dress up as Juan Diego, wearing mustaches and red bandanas. The most famous and elaborate celebration takes place at the Basílica of Guadalupe, north of Mexico City, where the Virgin appeared. But every village celebrates this day, often with processions of children carrying banners of the Virgin and with *charreadas* (rodeos), bicycle races, dancing, and fireworks. December 12.

    Where: Basílica de Guadalupe. **When:** The week preceding December 12. **How:** Public transportation will be packed, so your best bet is a taxi, which will let you off several blocks from the basílica.

- **Christmas Posadas.** On each of the 12 nights before Christmas it's customary to reenact the Holy Family's search for an inn, with door-to-door candlelit processions in cities and villages nationwide. You may see them especially in Querétaro and Taxco.

- **Christmas.** Mexicans extend this celebration and leave their jobs often beginning two weeks before Christmas all the way through New Year's. Many businesses close, and resorts and hotels fill up. On December 23 there are significant celebrations. Querétaro has a huge parade. In Oaxaca it's the "Night of the Radishes," with displays of huge carved radishes. On December 24 in Oaxaca processions culminate on the central plaza. On the same night Santiago Tuxtla, Veracruz celebrates with dancing the *huapango* and with *jarocho* bands in the beautiful town square. In Quiroga, Michoacán, villagers present Nativity plays (*Pastorelas*) at churches around the city on the evenings of December 24 and 25.

- **New Year's Eve.** As in the United States, New Year's Eve in Mexico is the time to gather for private parties and to explode fireworks and sound noisemakers. Places with special festivities include Santa Clara del Cobre, with its candlelit procession of Christs, and Tlacolula near Oaxaca, with commemorative mock battles for good luck in the new year.

3 Outdoor Sports, Adventure Travel & Wilderness Trips

Mexico has numerous **golf** courses, especially in the resort areas, and there are excellent ones in Mexico city and Guadalajara. It is sometimes easier in Mexico to rent a **horse** than a car, since horseback riding is a pastime enjoyed by many people at beach resorts as well as in the country. Sport **bicycling** has grown in popularity, so it isn't unusual to see young men (usually) making the grind of steep mountain passes during cycling club marathons.

    Tennis, racquetball, squash, waterskiing, surfing, and **scuba diving** are all sports visitors can enjoy in Mexico. While it's possible to scuba dive in the Pacific and the Sea of Cortez, the best place for that sport is Mexico's Yucatán Caribbean coast. **Mountain climbing** and **hiking volcanoes** is a rugged sport where you'll meet like-minded folks from around the world.

Mexico is behind the times with regard to ecological adventure and wilderness travel. As a result, most of the national parks and nature reserves are understaffed and/or not staffed by knowledgeable people. Most companies offering this kind of travel are U.S. operated, with trips led by specialists. The following companies offer a variety of off-the-beaten-path travel experiences:

The American Wilderness Experience, P.O. Box 1486, Boulder, CO 80306 (☎ 303/444-2622, or 800/444-0099), leads catered camping, kayaking, biking, and hiking trips in Baja California and the Copper Canyon.

ATC Tours and Travel, Calle 5 de Febrero no. 15, San Cristóbal de las Casas, Chiapas 29200 (☎ 967/8-2550; fax 967/8-3145), a Mexico-based tour operator with an excellent reputation, offers specialist-led trips primarily in southern Mexico. In addition to trips to the ruins of Palenque and Yaxchilán (extending into Belize and Guatemala by river, plane, and bus if desired), they also offer horseback tours and day-trips to the ruins of Toniná around San Cristóbal de las Casas, Chiapas; birding in the rain forests of Chiapas and Guatemala (including in the El Triunfo Reserve of Chiapas where you can see the rare quetzal bird and orchids); hikes out to the shops and homes of native textile artists of the Chiapas highlands; and walks from the Lagos de Montebello in the Montes Azules Biosphere Reserve, with camping and canoeing.

Baja Expeditions, 2625 Garnet Ave., San Diego, CA 92109 (☎ 619/518-3311, or 800/843-6967 in the U.S.), offers whale-watching, sailing, sea kayaking, and scuba-diving trips out of La Paz, Baja California.

Biological Journeys, 1696 F Ocean Dr., McKinleyville, CA 95521 (☎ 707/839-0178, or 800/548-7555), offers naturalist-led natural-history and whale-watching cruises off Baja California.

Columbus Travel, Route 12, Box 382B, New Braunfels, TX 78132-9701 (☎ 210/885-2000, or 800/843-1060 in the U.S. and Canada), has a variety of easy to challenging adventures, primarily in the Copper Canyon. They can design trips for special-interest groups of agriculturalists, geologists, rockhounds, and birdwatchers. The company also arranges trips to see the monarch butterflies in Michoacán.

Far Flung Adventures, P.O. Box 377, Terlingua, TX 79852 (☎ 915/371-2489, or 800/359-4138), takes clients on specialist-led Mexico river trips in Veracruz, Río Usumacinta, and other places that combine rafting and camping at Yucatán's archaeological sites.

Foundation for Field Research, P.O. Box 771, Mornejaloux, St. George's, Grenada, West Indies (☎ 809/440-8854), accepts volunteers who contribute a tax-deductible share to project costs doing scientific work at Bajia de Los Angeles and Isla de Cedros in Baja California, Mexiquillo Beach in Michoacán state, Alamos in the state of Sonora, and in the state of Chiapas.

Off the Gringo Trail, 1526 NW 23rd Ave., Portland, OR 97210, Attn: Chris Hanlon (☎ 503/226-7200, or 800/344-8890 in the U.S.), leads week-long trips by donkey into the central sierras of the Baja Peninsula from November through April.

Pacific Sea Fari Tours, 2803 Emerson St., San Diego, CA 92106 (☎ 619/226-8224), has weekly whale-watching cruises to Baja from San Diego during February and March.

Rancho El Cielo, c/o Fred S. Webster, Jr., 4926 Strass Dr., Austin, TX 78731 (☎ 512/451-1669), offers once- or twice-a-year, weeklong trips (usually in June) to the Rancho El Cielo in the remote mountain El Cielo Biosphere Reserve. The trips are sponsored by the Gorgas Science Foundation of Texas Southmost College, to the region which is 50 miles south of Ciudad Victoria, Tamaulipas. The area is rich in birds, orchids, and bromeliads and is home to endangered black bear, jaguar, and ocelot.

Remarkable Journeys, P.O. Box 31855, Houston, TX 77231-1855 (☎ 713/721-2517, or 800/856-1993 in the U.S.; fax 713/728-8334), offers unusual trips such as a rugged crossing of the Copper Canyon, spending Easter in the Copper Canyon, seeing the monarch butterflies in Michoacán, and experiencing Carnaval and Day of the Dead in Mérida.

San Juan Kayak Expeditions, P.O. Box 2041, San Juan Harbor, WA 98250 (☎ 206/378-4436), takes travelers kayaking between Loreto and Mulege from November through April.

Sobek Mountain Travel, 6420 Fairmount Ave., El Cerrito, CA 94530 (☎ 510/527-8100, or 800/227-2384), leads groups into the Copper Canyon and kayaking in the Sea of Cortez.

Victor Emanuel Tours, P.O. Box 33008, Austin, TX 78764 (☎ 512/328-5221, or 800/328-8368), is an established leader in birding and natural-history tours.

Wings, Inc., P.O. Box 31930, Tucson, AZ 85751 (☎ 602/749-1967), has a wide assortment of trips, including birding in Oaxaca, Chiapas, Colima, and Jalisco.

Zapotec Tours, 500 N. Michigan Ave., Chicago, IL 60611 (☎ 312/973-2444 or, outside Ill., 800/326-7251; fax 312/248-5245), offers an intriguing variety of specialist-led, eight-day trips to Oaxaca. Highlights include introductions to local experts whose knowledge of architecture, archaeology, art, weaving, wood carving, and food provide cultural experiences unavailable to the casual tourist.

4 Learning Vacations

SPANISH LESSONS   A dozen towns south of the border are famous for their Spanish-language programs. Mexican Government Tourist Offices may have information about schools in Cholula, Cuernavaca, Guadalajara, Guanajuato, Mérida, Morelia, Oaxaca, San Cristóbal de las Casas, and San Miguel de Allende. I also mention specific schools in these cities. Go any time of year—you needn't really wait for a "semester" or course year to start. It's best to begin on a Monday, however.

Don't expect the best and latest in terms of language texts and materials; many are well out-of-date. Teachers tend to be underpaid and perhaps undertrained but very friendly and extremely patient.

The **National Registration Center for Studies Abroad (NRCSA),** 823 N. Second St., Milwaukee, WI 53203 (☎ 414/278-0631), has a catalog ($5) of schools in Mexico. They will register you at the school of your choice, arrange for room and board with a Mexican family, and make your airline reservations. Charge for their service is reflected in a fee that's included in the price quoted to you for the course you select.

5 Health & Insurance

STAYING HEALTHY

Of course, the very best way to avoid illness or to mitigate its effects is to make sure you're in top health when you travel and you don't overdo it. Eat three wholesome meals a day, and get more rest than you normally do; also, don't push yourself if you're not feeling in top form.

COMMON AILMENTS

TURISTA *Turista* is the name given to the persistent diarrhea, often accompanied by fever, nausea, and vomiting, that attacks so many travelers to Mexico. Doctors, who call it travelers' diarrhea, say it's not caused by just one "bug," or factor, but by a combination of consuming different food and water, upsetting your schedule, being overtiring, and experiencing the stresses of travel. Being tired and careless about food and drink is a sure ticket to turista. A good high-potency (or "therapeutic") vitamin supplement, and even extra vitamin C, is a help; yogurt is good for healthy digestion is becoming much more available in Mexico than in the past.

Preventing Turista: The U.S. Public Health Service recommends the following measures for prevention of travelers' diarrhea:

* *Drink only purified water.* This means tea, coffee, and other beverages made with boiled water; canned or bottled carbonated beverages and water; beer and wine; or water you yourself have brought to a rolling boil or otherwise purified. Avoid ice, which may be made with untreated water. However, most restaurants with a large tourist clientele use only purified water and ice.
* *Choose food carefully.* In general, avoid salads, uncooked vegetables, and unpasteurized milk or milk products (including cheese). Choose food that is freshly cooked and still hot. Peel fruit yourself. Don't eat undercooked meat, fish, or shellfish.

The Public Health Service does not recommend you take any medicines as preventatives. All the applicable medicines can have nasty side effects if taken for several weeks. In addition, something so simple as clean hands can go a long way toward preventing "turista." I carry packages of antiseptic towelettes for those times when wash facilities aren't available and to avoid using a communal bar of soap—a real germ carrier.

How to Get Well: If you get sick, there are lots of medicines available in Mexico that can harm more than help. Ask your doctor before you leave home what medicine he or she recommends for travelers' diarrhea.

The Public Health Service guidelines are the following: If there are three or more loose stools in an eight-hour period, especially with other symptoms (such as nausea, vomiting, abdominal cramps, and fever), see a doctor.

The first thing to do is go to bed and don't move until the condition runs its course. Traveling makes it last longer. Drink lots of liquids: Tea without milk or sugar or the Mexican *té de manzanilla* (chamomile tea) is best. Eat only *pan tostada* (dry toast). Keep to this diet for at least 24 hours, and you'll be well over the worst of it. If you fool yourself into thinking a plate of enchiladas can't hurt or beer or liquor will kill the germs, you'll have a total relapse.

The Public Health Service advises that you be especially careful to replace fluids and electrolytes (potassium, sodium, and the like) during a bout of diarrhea.

Do this by drinking Pedialyte, a rehydration solution available at most Mexican pharmacies, or glasses of fruit juice (high in potassium) with honey and a pinch of salt added, or you can also try a glass of boiled pure water with a quarter teaspoon of sodium bicarbonate (baking soda) added.

ALTITUDE SICKNESS   At high altitudes it takes about 10 days to acquire the extra red blood corpuscles you need to adjust to the scarcity of oxygen. At very high-altitude places, such as Ixta-Popo Park outside Mexico City (13,000 ft.), your car won't run very well, you may have trouble starting it, and you may not even sleep well at night.

Altitude sickness results from the relative lack of oxygen and the decrease in barometric pressure that characterizes high altitudes (over 5,000 ft./1,500m). Mexico City is at an altitude of more than 7,000 feet, as are a number of other central Mexican cities, so discomfort is possible. Symptoms include shortness of breath, fatigue, headache, and even nausea.

Avoid altitude sickness by taking it easy for the first few days after you arrive at a high altitude. Drink extra fluids but avoid alcoholic beverages, which not only tend to dehydrate you but also are more potent in a low-oxygen environment. If you have heart or lung problems, talk to your doctor before going above 8,000 feet.

BUGS & BITES   Mosquitoes and gnats are prevalent along the coast and in the Yucatán lowlands. Insect repellent (*rapellante contra insectos*) is a must, and it's not always available in Mexico. If you're sensitive to bites, pick up some antihistamine cream from a drugstore at home. Rubbed on a fresh mosquito bite, the cream keeps the swelling down and reduces the itch.

Most readers won't ever see a scorpion (*alacrán*), but if you're stung, go to a doctor.

MORE SERIOUS DISEASES

You don't have to worry about tropical diseases, such as malaria, dengue fever, dysentery, cholera, and schistosomiasis, if you stay on the normal tourist routes. Talk to your doctor, or a medical specialist in tropical diseases, about any precautions you should take. You can protect yourself by taking some simple precautions. In addition to being careful about what you eat and drink, don't go swimming in polluted waters. This includes any stagnant water, such as ponds, slow-moving rivers, and Yucatecan *cenotes* (wells). Mosquitoes can carry malaria, dengue fever, and other serious illnesses. Cover up, avoid going out when mosquitoes are active, use repellent, sleep under mosquito netting, and stay away from places that seem to have a lot of mosquitoes. The most dangerous areas seem to be on Mexico's west coast away from the big resorts (which are relatively safe).

To prevent malaria if you go to a malarial area, you must get a prescription for antimalarial drugs and begin taking them before you enter the area. You must also continue to take them for a certain amount of time after you leave the malarial area. Talk to your doctor about this and ask about any risks in taking the drugs; for example, people with psoriasis, or a family history of it, may not wish to take antimalarial drugs. It's a good idea to be inoculated against tetanus, typhoid, and diphtheria, but this isn't a guarantee against contracting the diseases.

EMERGENCY EVACUATION   For extreme medical emergencies there's a service from the United States that will fly people to American hospitals: **Air-Evac,** a 24-hour air ambulance (☎ 800/854-2569 in the U.S. or call collect: 713/880-9767 in Houston, 619/278-3822 in San Diego, and 305/772-0003 in Miami, 24 hours daily).

INSURANCE

HEALTH/ACCIDENT/LOSS   Even the most careful of us can experience the Murphy's Law of travel—you discover you've lost your wallet, your passport, your airline ticket, or your Tourist Permit. Always keep a photocopy of these documents in your luggage—it makes replacing them easier. To be reimbursed for insured items once you return, you'll need to report the loss to the Mexican police and get a written report. If you don't speak Spanish, take along someone who does. If you lose official documents, you'll need to contact both Mexican and U.S. officials in Mexico before you leave the country.

Health Care Abroad, 107 W. Federal St. (P.O. Box 480), Middleburg, VA 22117 (☎ 703/687-3166, or 800/237-6615), and **Access America,** 6600 W. Broad St., Richmond, VA 23230 (☎ 804/285-3300, or 800/628-4908), offer medical and accident insurance as well as coverage for luggage loss and trip cancellation. Always read the fine print on the policy to be sure that you're getting the coverage you want.

6 Tips for Special Travelers

FOR SENIORS   Handrails are often missing. Unmarked or unguarded holes in sidewalks countrywide present problems for all visitors.

Retiring   Mexico is a popular country for retirees, although their income doesn't go nearly as far as it once did. How much it costs to live depends on your lifestyle and where you choose to live. Car upkeep and insurance, as well as clothing and health costs, are important variables to consider.

The Mexican government requires foreign residents to prove they have a specific amount of income before permanent residence is granted, but you can visit for six months on a tourist visa. For decades, North Americans have been living indefinitely in Mexico by returning to the border and recrossing with a new tourist card every six months. Recently, but not uniformly at every border crossing, Mexico has begun to crack down on this practice by refusing readmittance to someone they remember just crossed over. So if you've been there six months and haven't decided on permanent residency yet and want to return immediately for another stay on a Tourist Permit, you'll have to exercise caution about where and when you recross.

Mexican health care is surprisingly inexpensive. You can save money by living on the local economy: Buy food at the local market, not imported items from specialty stores; use local transportation and save the car for long-distance trips. Some of the most popular places for long-term stays include Guadalajara, Lake Chapala, Ajijic, and Puerto Vallarta—all in the state of Jalisco; San Miguel de Allende and Guanajuato in the state of Guanajuato; Cuernavaca, Morelos; Alamos, Sinaloa; and to a lesser extent Manzanillo, Colima, and Morelia in Michoacán. Crowds don't necessarily mean there are no other good places: Oaxaca, Querétaro, Puebla, Guanajuato, Tepoztlán, and Valle de Bravo have much to offer, even though Americans have yet to collect there in large numbers.

The following newsletters are written for prospective retirees: *AIM,* Apdo. Postal 31-70, Guadalajara 45050, Jal., Mexico, is a well-written, candid, and very informative newsletter on retirement in Mexico. Recent issues reported on evaulated retirement in Lake Chapala, Aguascalientes, Alamos, Zacatecas, west coast beaches, Acapulco, and San Miguel de Allende. Subscriptions cost $16 to the United States and $19 to Canada. Back issues are three for $5.

The annual *Retiring in Mexico,* Apdo. Postal 50409, Guadalajara, Jal., Mexico (☎ 36/21-2348 or 47-9924), comes in three editions—a large January issue and smaller spring and fall supplements—all for $12. Each newsletter is packed with information about retiring in Guadalajara. It's written by Fran and Judy Furton, who also sell other packets of information as well as host an open house in their home every Tuesday for $12.

Finally, **Sanborn Tours,** 1007 Main St., Bastrop, TX 78602 (☎ 800/531-5440), offers a "Retire in Mexico" Guadalajara orientation tour.

FOR SINGLES   Mexico may be the land for romantic honeymoons, but it's also a great place to travel on your own without really being or feeling alone. Although combined single and double rates is a slow-growing trend in Mexico, most of the hotels mentioned in this book still offer singles at lower rates.

Mexicans are very friendly, and it's easy to meet other foreigners. Certain cities such as Acapulco, Manzanillo, and Huatulco have such a preponderance of twosomes that single travelers may feel as though an appendage is missing. On the other hand, singles can feel quite comfortable in Isla Mujeres, Puerto Vallarta, San Blas, Cancún, Zihuatanejo, Ixtapa, Puerto Angel, Celestún, La Paz, and Cabo San Lucas. In those places you'll find a good combination of beachlife, nightlife, and tranquility, whichever is your pleasure.

If you don't like the idea of traveling alone, then try **Travel Companion Exchange,** P.O. Box 833, Amityville, NY 11701 (☎ 516/454-0880; fax 516/454-0170), which brings prospective travelers together. Members complete a profile, then place an anonymous listing of their travel interests in the newsletter. Prospective traveling companions then make contact through the Exchange. Membership costs $66 for six months or $120 for a year.

For Women   As a frequent female visitor to Mexico, mostly traveling alone, I can tell you firsthand that I feel safer traveling in Mexico than in the United States. Mexicans are very warm and welcoming people, and I'm not afraid to be friendly wherever I go. But I use the same common-sense precautions I use traveling anywhere else in the world—I'm alert to what's going on around me.

Mexicans in general, and men in particular, are nosy about single travelers, especially women. They want to know with whom you're traveling, whether you're married or have a boyfriend, and how many children you have. My advice to anyone asked these details by taxi drivers or other people with whom you don't want to become friendly is to make up a set of answers (regardless of the truth): I'm married, traveling with friends, and I have three children. Divorce may send out a wrong message about availability. Drunks are a particular nuisance to the lone female traveler. Don't try to be polite—just leave or duck into a public place.

Generally women alone will feel comfortable going to a hotel lobby bar yet are asking for trouble by going into a pulquería or cantina. In restaurants, as a general rule, single women are offered the worst table and service. You'll have to be vocal about your preference and insist on service. Don't tip if service is bad.

Finally, remember that Mexican men learn charm early. The chase is as important as the conquest (maybe more so). Despite whatever charms you may possess, think twice before taking personally or seriously all the adoring, admiring words you'll hear.

For Men   I'm not sure why, but non-Spanish-speaking foreign men seem to be special targets for scams and pickpockets. So if you fit this description, whether traveling alone or in a pair, exercise special vigilance.

FOR FAMILIES Mexicans travel extensively with their families, so your child will feel very welcome. Hotels will often arrange for a babysitter. Several hotels in the mid-to-upper range have small playgrounds and pools for children and hire caretakers on weekends to oversee them. Few budget hotels offer these amenities.

Before leaving, you should check with your doctor to get advice on medications to take along. Bring along a supply just to be sure. Disposable diapers are made and sold in Mexico. The price is about the same as that in the United States, but the quality is poorer. Gerber's baby foods are sold in many stores. Dry cereals, powdered formulas, baby bottles, and purified water are all easily available in mid-size and large cities.

Cribs, however, may present a problem. Except for the largest and most luxurious hotels, few Mexican hotels provide cribs. However, rollaway beds to accommodate children staying in the room with parents are often available.

Many of the hotels I mention, even in noncoastal regions, have swimming pools, which can be a treat at the end of a day of traveling with a child who has had it with sightseeing.

FOR PEOPLE WITH DISABILITIES Travelers who are unable to walk or who are in wheelchairs or on crutches discover quickly that Mexico is one giant obstacle course. Beginning at the airport on arrival, you may encounter steep stairs before finding a well-hidden elevator or escalator—if one exists. Airlines will often arrange wheelchair assistance for passengers to the baggage area. Porters are generally available to help with luggage at airports and large bus stations, once you've cleared baggage claim.

In addition, escalators (there aren't many in the country) are often not operating. Few handicapped-equipped restrooms exist, or when one is available, access to it may be via a narrow passage that won't accommodate a wheelchair or someone on crutches. Many deluxe hotels (the most expensive) now have rooms with baths for the handicapped and handicapped access to the hotel. Those traveling on a budget should stick with one-story hotels or those with elevators. Even so, there will probably still be obstacles somewhere. Stairs without handrails abound in Mexico. Intracity bus drivers generally don't bother with the courtesy step on boarding or disembarking. On city buses, the height between the street and the bus step can require considerable force to board. Generally speaking, no matter where you are, someone will lend a hand, although you may have to ask for it.

7 Getting There

BY PLANE

The airline situation in Mexico is changing rapidly, with many new regional carriers offering scheduled service to areas previously not served. In addition to regularly scheduled service, charter service direct from U.S. cities to resorts is making Mexico more accessible from the U.S.

THE MAJOR INTERNATIONAL AIRLINES

The main airlines operating direct or nonstop flights from the United States to points in Mexico include **Aero California** (☎ 800/237-6225), **Aeroméxico** (☎ 800/237-6639), **Air France** (☎ 800/237-2747), **Alaska Airlines** (☎ 800/426-0333), **American** (☎ 800/433-7300), **Continental** (☎ 800/231-0856), **Delta** (☎ 800/221-1212), **Lacsa** (☎ 800/225-2272), **Lufthansa** (☎ 800/

645-3880), **Mexicana** (☎ 800/531-7921), **Northwest** (☎ 800/225-2525), **United** (☎ 800/241-6522), and **USAir** (☎ 800/428-4322).

Southwest Airlines (☎ 800/435-9792) serves the U.S. border. The main departure points in the United States for international airlines are Chicago, Dallas/Fort Worth, Denver, Houston, Los Angeles, Miami, New Orleans, New York, Orlando, Philadelphia, Raleigh/Durham, San Antonio, San Francisco, Seattle, Toronto, Tucson, and Washington, D.C.

Bargain hunters rejoice! Excursion and package plans proliferate, especially in the off-season. A good travel agent will be able to give you all the latest schedules, details, and prices, but you may have to investigate regional airlines for yourself (see "By Plane" under "Getting Around," below).

CHARTERS

Charter service is growing, especially during winter months and usually is sold as a package combination of air and hotel. Charter airlines, however, may sell air packages only, without hotel. Charter airlines include **Taesa Airlines,** which has service from several U.S. cities. **Latur** offers charters from New York to Cancún, Puerto Vallarta, and Acapulco; Chicago to Cancún; and Boston to Cancún.

Tour companies operating charters include **Club America Vacations, Apple Vacations, Friendly Holidays,** and **Gogo Tours**. You can make arrangements with these companies through your travel agent.

BY BUS

Greyhound-Trailways (or its affiliates) offers service from around the U.S. to the Mexican border, where passengers disembark, cross the border, and buy a ticket for travel into the interior of Mexico. At many border crossings there are scheduled buses from the U.S. bus station to the Mexican bus station.

BY CAR

Driving is certainly not the cheapest way to get to Mexico, but it is the best way to see the country. Even so, you may think twice about taking your own car south of the border once you've pondered Mexico's many bureaucratic requirements involved in doing so.

In 1994, Mexico's Ministry of Tourism published its own *Official Guide: Traveling to Mexico by Car.* Don't depend on it—its information can be inconsistent, unclear, or inaccurate. Of possible use, however, is the list it includes of the times at which you'll find government officials on-duty at border crossings to review your car documents and issue Temporary Car Importation Permits. To get a copy, inquire at a regional branch of the Mexican Government Tourism Office.

It's wise to check and double-check all the requirements before setting out for a driving tour of Mexico. Read through the rest of this section, and then address any additional questions you have or confirm the current rules by calling your nearest Mexican consulate, Mexican Government Tourist Office, AAA, Sanborn's (☎ 210/686-3601), or the above-mentioned Mexican Vehicle Import Information line. At the latter, the person who answered the phone when I called seemed to have accurate information.

CAR DOCUMENTS

To drive a personal car into Mexico, you'll need a Temporary Car Importation Permit, granted upon completion of a long and strictly required list of documents (see below). The permit can be obtained either through Banco del Ejército

(Banjercito) officals, who have a desk, booth, or office at the Mexican Customs (*Aduana*) building immediately upon crossing the border into Mexico. You can obtain the permit before you travel through Sanborn's Insurance and the American Automobile Association (AAA), each of which maintains border offices in Texas, New Mexico, Arizona, and California. These companies may charge a fee for this service, but it will be worth it to avoid the uncertain prospect of traveling all the way to the border without proper documents for crossing. However, even if you go through Sanborn's or AAA, your credentials *may* be reviewed again by Mexican officials at the border—you must have them all with you since they are still subject to questions of validity.

The following requirements for border crossing were accurate at press time:

- *A valid driver's license*, issued outside of Mexico.
- *Current, original car registration and a copy of the original car title*. If the registration or title is in more than one name and not all the named people are traveling with you, then a notarized letter from the absent person(s) authorizing use of the vehicle for the trip may be required; have it ready just in case. The car registration and your credit card (see below) must be in the same name.
- *An original notarized letter from the lien holder*, if your registration shows a lien, giving you permission to take the vehicle into Mexico.
- *A valid international major credit card*. Using only your credit card, you are required to pay a $12 car-importation fee. The credit card must be in the same name as the car registration.

  Note: Those without credit cards will forego the $12 importation fee and instead will be required to post a cash bond based on the value of the car. The rules and procedures are complicated, so contact AAA or Sanborn's for details.
- *A signed declaration* promising to return to your country of origin with the vehicle. This form is provided by AAA or Sanborn's before you go or by Banjercito officials at the border. There's no charge. The form does not stipulate that you return through the same border entry you came through on your way south.

You must carry your Temporary Car Importation Permit, Tourist Permit, and, if you purchased it, your proof of Mexican car insurance in the car at all times.

Important reminder: Someone else may drive the car, but the person (or relative of the person) whose name appears on the Car Importation Permit must *always* be in the car at the same time. (If stopped by police, a nonregistered family member driver, driving without the registered driver, must be prepared to prove familial relationship to the registered driver.) Violation of this rule makes the car subject to impoundment and the driver to imprisonment and/or a fine.

Only under certain circumstances will the driver of the car be allowed to leave the country without the car. If it's undrivable, you can leave it at a mechanic's shop if you get a letter to that effect from the mechanic and present it to the nearest Secretaria de Hacienda y Credito Público (a treasury department official) for further documentation, which you then present to a Banjercito offical upon leaving the country. Then you must return personally to retrieve the car. If the driver of the car has to leave the country without the car due to an emergency, the car must be put under Customs seal at the airport and the driver's Tourist Permit must be stamped to that effect. There may be storage fees. If the car is wrecked or stolen, your Mexican insurance adjuster will provide the necessary paperwork for presentation to Hacienda officals.

If you receive your documentation at the border (rather than through Sanborn's or AAA), Mexican border officials will make two copies of everything and charge you for the copies.

The Temporary Car Importation Permit papers will be issued for six months and the Tourist Permit is usually issued for 180 days, but they might stamp it for half that, so check. It's a good idea also to overestimate the time you'll spend in Mexico, so that if something unforeseen happens and you have—or want to—stay longer, you'll have avoided the long hassle of getting your papers renewed.

Important note: Whatever you do, don't overstay either permit. Doing so invites heavy fines and/or confiscation of your vehicle, which will not be returned. Remember also that six months does not necessarily work out to be 180 days— be sure that you return before whichever expiration date comes first.

Other documentation is required for an individual's permit to enter Mexico— see "Entry Requirements," above.

MEXICAN AUTO INSURANCE

Although auto insurance is not legally required in Mexico, driving without it is foolish. U.S. insurance is invalid in Mexico; to be insured there, you must purchase Mexican insurance. Any party involved in an accident who has no insurance is automatically sent to jail and his or her car is impounded until all claims are settled. This is true even if you just drive across the border to spend the day, and it may be true even if you're injured.

All agencies selling Mexican insurance will show you a full table of current rates and recommend the coverage they think is adequate. The policies are written along lines similar to those north of the border, with the following exception: The contents of your vehicle aren't covered. It's no longer necessary to overestimate the amount of time you plan to be in Mexico because it's now possible to get your policy term lengthened by fax from the insurer. However, if you are staying longer than 48 days, it's more economical to buy a nonrefundable annual policy. For example, a car (registered to an individual, not a business) with a value of $10,000 can be insured for $132.50 for two weeks or $71.25 for one week. An annual policy for a car valued between $10,000 and $15,000 would be a reduced rate of $519 which you get by joining Sanborn's Amigo Club for $30. (The Amigo Club membership offers hotel discounts and a newsletter). Be sure the policy you buy will pay for repairs in either the United States or Mexico and will pay out in dollars, not pesos.

One of the best insurance companies for south of the border travel is **Sanborn's Mexico Insurance,** with offices at all of the border crossings in the United States. I never drive across the border without Sanborn's insurance. It costs the same as the competition and you get a *Travelog* that's like a mile-by-mile guide along your proposed route. With the ongoing changes in Mexico's highway system it's inevitable that the log occasionally is a bit out-dated, but for the most part, it's like having a knowledgeable friend in the car telling you how to get in and out of town, where to buy gas (and which stations to avoid), what the highway conditions are, and what scams you need to watch out for. It's especially helpful in remote places. Most of Sanborn's border offices are open Monday through Friday, and a few are staffed on Saturday and Sunday. You can purchase your auto liability and collision coverage by phone in advance and have it waiting at a 24-hour location if you are crossing when the office is closed. The annual insurance includes a type of evacuation assistance in case of emergency, and emergency evacuation insurance for shorter policies is available for a small daily fee. They also offer a medical policy. For information, contact Sanborn's Mexico Insurance, P.O. Box 310, Dept. FR, 2009 S. 10th, McAllen, TX 78505-0310 (☎ 210/686-0711; fax 210/686-0732 in Texas or 800/222-0158 in the U.S.). **AAA** auto club also sells insurance.

PREPARING YOUR CAR

Check the condition of your car thoroughly before you cross the border. Parts made in Mexico may be inferior, but service generally is quite good and relatively inexpensive. Carry a spare radiator hose and belts for the engine fan and air-conditioner. Be sure your car is in tune to handle Mexican gasoline. Also, can your tires last a few thousand miles on Mexican roads?

Take simple tools along if you're handy with them; also take a flashlight or spot-light, a cloth to wipe the windshield, toilet paper, and a tire gauge—Mexican filling stations generally have air to fill tires but no gauge to check the pressure. When I am driving, I always bring along a combination gauge/air compressor sold at U.S. automotive stores; it plugs into the car cigarette lighter, making it a simple pro-cedure to check the tires every morning and pump them up at the same time.

Not that many Mexican cars comply, but Mexican law requires that every car have **seat belts** and a **fire extinguisher.** Be prepared!

CROSSING THE BORDER WITH YOUR CAR

After you cross the border into Mexico from the United States and you've stopped to get your Tourist Card and Car Permit, somewhere between 12 and 16 miles down the road you'll come to a Mexican customs post. In the past, all motorists had to stop and present travel documents and possibly have their cars inspected. Now there is a new system under which some motorists are inspected at random. All car papers are examined, however, so you must stop. If the light is green, go on through; if it's red, stop for inspection. In the Baja Peninsula the procedures may differ slightly—first you get your Tourist Permit then further down the road you may not be stopped for the car inspection.

RETURNING TO THE U.S. WITH YOUR CAR

The car papers you obtained when you entered Mexico *must* be returned when you cross back with your car or at some point within the time limit of 180 days. (You can cross as many times as you wish within the 180 days.) If the documents aren't returned, heavy fines are imposed ($250 for each 15 days late), and your car may be impounded and confiscated or you may be jailed if you return to Mexico. You can only return the car documents to a Banjercito official on duty at the Mexican Customs (*Aduana*) building *before* you cross back into the United States. Some border cities have Banjercito officials on duty 24 hours a day, but others do not; some also do not have Sunday hours. On the U.S. side, customs agents may or may not inspect your car from stem to stern.

PACKAGE TOURS

Package tours offer some of the best values to the coastal resorts, especially dur-ing high season—from December until after Easter. Off-season packages can be real bargains. However, to know for sure if the package will save you money, you must price the package yourself by calling the airline for round-trip flight costs and the hotel for rates. Add in the cost of transfers to and from the airport (which pack-ages usually include) and see if it's a deal.

Packages are usually per person, and single travelers pay a supplement. In the high season a package may be the only way of getting to certain places in Mexico because wholesalers have all the airline seats. The cheapest package rates will be those in hotels in the lower range, always without as many amenities as higher-priced hotels. You can still use the public areas and beaches of more costly hotels without being a guest.

Travel agents have information on specific packages.

8 Getting Around

BY PLANE

To fly from point to point within Mexico, you'll rely on Mexican airlines. Mexico has two privately owned large national carriers: **Mexicana** (☎ 800/531-7921 in the U.S.) and **Aeroméxico** (☎ 800/237-6639 in the U.S.), in addition to several up-and-coming regional carriers. Mexicana and Aeroméxico both offer extensive connections to the United States as well as within Mexico.

Several of the new regional carriers are operated by or can be booked through Mexicana or Aeroméxico. Regional carriers are **Aero Cancún** (see Mexicana), **Aero Caribe** (see Mexicana), **Aero Leo López** (☎ 915/778-1022 in El Paso; fax 915/779-3534), **Aerolitoral** (see Aeroméxico), **Aero Monterrey** (see Mexicana), **Aero Morelos** (☎ 73/17-5588 in Cuernavaca; fax 73/17-2320), and **Aerovias Oaxaqueñas** (☎ 951/6-3824 in Oaxaca). The regional carriers are expensive, but they go to places that are difficult to reach. In each applicable section of this book, I've mentioned regional carriers with all pertinent telephone numbers.

Because major airlines can book some regional carriers, read your ticket carefully to see if your connecting flight is on one of these smaller carriers—they may leave from a different airport or check in at a different counter.

AIRPORT TAXES   Mexico charges an airport tax on all departures. Passengers leaving the country on an international departure pay $12 in cash—dollars or the peso equivalent. Each domestic departure you make within Mexico costs around $6, unless you're on a connecting flight and have already paid at the start of the flight; you shouldn't be charged again if you have to change planes for a connecting flight.

RECONFIRMING FLIGHTS   Although airlines in Mexico say it's not necessary to reconfirm a flight, I always do. Also, be aware that airlines routinely overbook. To avoid getting bumped, check in for an international flight the required hour and a half in advance of travel. That will put you near the head of the line.

BY BUS

Except for the Baja and Yucatán peninsulas, where bus service is not well developed, Mexican buses are frequent and readily accessible and can get you to almost anywhere you want to go. Buses are an excellent way to get around, and they're often the only way to get from large cities to other nearby cities and small villages. There's little English spoken at bus stations, so come prepared with your destination written down, then double check the departure several times just to make sure you get to the right departing lane on time. Ticket agents can be quite brusque or indifferent, especially if there's a line; in general, however, people are willing to help, so never hesitate to ask questions if you're confused about anything.

Dozens of Mexican companies operate large, air-conditioned, Greyhound-type buses between most cities. Travel class is generally labeled first, second, and deluxe, referred to by a variety of names—*plus, de lujo, ejecutivo, primera plus* and so on. The deluxe buses often have fewer seats than regular buses, show video movies en route, are air-conditioned, and have few stops; many run express from origin to the final destination. They are well worth the few dollars more you'll pay than you would for first-class buses. Second-class buses have many stops and cost only slightly less than first-class or deluxe buses. In rural areas, buses are often of the school-bus variety, with lots of local color.

Whenever possible, it's best to buy your reserved-seat ticket, often via a computerized system, a day in advance on many long-distance routes. Schedules are fairly dependable, so be at the terminal on time for departure.

Many Mexican cities have replaced the bewildering array of tiny private company offices scattered all over town with new central bus stations, much like sophisticated airport terminals.

Keep in mind that routes and times change, and as there is no central directory of schedules for the whole country, current information must be obtained from local bus stations.

For long trips, *always* carry food, water, toilet paper, and a sweater (in case the air-conditioning is too strong).

See the Appendix for a list of helpful bus terms in Spanish.

BY CAR

Most Mexican roads are not up to U.S. standards of smoothness, hardness, width of curve, grade of hill, or safety marking.

Important note: Never drive at night if you can avoid it—the roads aren't good enough; the trucks, carts, pedestrians, and bicycles usually have no lights; and you can hit potholes, animals, rocks, dead ends, or bridges out with no warning. Enough said!

You will also have to get used to the spirited Mexican driving styles, which require other drivers to possess superior vision and reflexes. Be prepared for new procedures, as when a truck driver flips on his left-turn signal when there's not a crossroad for miles. He's probably telling you the road's clear ahead for you to pass—after all, he's in a better position to see than you are. It's difficult to know, however, whether he really means that he intends to pull over on the left-hand shoulder. You may have to follow trucks without mufflers and pollution-control devices for miles. Under these conditions, drop back and be patient, take a side road, or stop for a break when you feel tense or tired.

Be prepared to pay tolls on some of Mexico's expressways and bridges. Tolls are among the highest in the world. The word for "toll" in Spanish is *cuota*.

GASOLINE   There's one government-owned brand of gas and one gasoline station name throughout the country—**Pemex** (Petroleras Mexicanas). Each station has a franchise owner who buys everything from Pemex. There are two types of gas in Mexico: **nova,** an 82-octane leaded gas, and **magna sin,** an 87-octane unleaded gas. Magna sin is sold from brilliantly colored pumps and costs around $2.15 a gallon; nova costs slightly less. In Mexico, fuel and oil are sold by the liter, which is slightly more than a quart (40 liters equals about $10^1/_2$ gallons). Nova is readily available. Magna sin is now available in most areas of Mexico, along major highways, and in the larger cities. Even in areas where it should be available, you may have to hunt around. The usual station may be out of Magna sin for a couple of days, especially on weekends, or you may be told that none is available in the area, just to get your business. Plan ahead; fill up every chance you get, and keep your tank topped off. No credit cards are accepted for gas purchases.

Here's what to do when you have to fuel up. Drive up to the pump, close enough so you'll be able to watch the pump run as your tank is being filled. Check that the pump is turned back to zero, go to your fuel filler cap and unlock it yourself, and watch the pump and the attendant as the gas goes in. Though many service-station attendants are honest, many are not. It's good to ask for a specific peso amount rather than saying "full." This is because the attendants tend to over-fill, splashing gas on the car and anything within range.

As there are always lines at the gas pumps, attendants often finish fueling one vehicle, turn the pump back quickly (or don't turn it back at all), and start on another vehicle. You've got to be looking at the pump when the fueling is finished because it may show the amount you owe for only a few seconds. This "quick draw" from car to car is another good reason to ask for a certain peso amount of gas. If you've asked for a certain amount, the attendant can't charge you more for it.

Once the fueling is complete, let the attendant check the oil or radiator or put air in the tires. Do only one thing at a time, be with him as he does it, and don't let him rush you. Get into these habits, or it'll cost you.

If you get oil, make sure the can that is tipped into your engine is a full one. If in doubt, have the attendant check the dipstick again after the oil has supposedly been put in. Check your change and, again, don't let them rush you. Check that your locking gas cap is back in place.

DRIVING RULES   If you park illegally or commit some other infraction and are not around to discuss it, police are authorized to remove your license plates (*placas*). You must then trundle over to the police station and pay a fine to get them back. Mexican car-rental agencies have begun to weld the license tag to the tag frame; you may want to devise a method of your own to make the tags more difficult to remove. Theoretically, this will make the policeman move on to another set of tags which are easier to confiscate. On the other hand, he could get his hackles up and decide to have your car towed. To weld or not to weld is up to you.

Be attentive to road signs. A drawing of a row of little bumps means there are speed bumps (*topes*) across the road to warn you to reduce your speed while driving through towns or villages. Slow down when coming to a village whether you see the sign or not—sometimes they install the bumps but not the sign!

There is always a shortage of directional signs, so check frequently to be sure that you're on the right road. Don't count on plenty of notice of where to turn, even on major interchanges; more often than not, the directional sign appears without prior notice exactly at the spot where you need to make a decison—a turn, take a spaghetti bowl loop, a lane ending, and the like. Common road signs include these:

Camino en Reparación	Road Repairs
Conserva Su Derecha	Keep Right
Cuidado con el Ganado, el Tren	Watch Out for Cattle, Trains
Curva Peligrosa	Dangerous Curve
Derrumbes	Falling Rocks

Deslave	Caved-in Roadbed
Despacio	Slow
Desviación	Detour
Disminuya Su Velocidad	Slow Down
Entronque	Highway Junction
Escuela	School (Zone)
Grava Suelta	Loose Gravel
Hombres Trabajando	Men Working
No Hay Paso	Road Closed
Peligro	Danger
Puente Angosto	Narrow Bridge
Raya Continua	Continuous (Solid) White Line
Tramo en Reparación	Road Under Construction
Un Solo Carril a 100 m.	One-Lane Road 100 Meters Ahead
Zone Escolar	School Zone

TOLL ROADS   Mexico charges among the highest tolls in the world to use its network of new toll roads. As a result, they are comparatively little used. Generally speaking, using the toll roads will cut your travel time between destinations. The old roads, on which no tolls are charged, are generally in good condition, but overall, mean longer trips since they usually pass through more mountains and are usually clotted with an abundance of slow-moving trucks.

MAPS   Guía Rojo, AAA, and International Travel Map Productions have good maps to Mexico. In Mexico, maps are sold at large drugstores like Sanborn's, at bookstores, and in hotel gift shops.

BREAKDOWNS   Your best guide to repair shops is the yellow pages. For specific makes and shops that repair them, look under "Automoviles y Camiones: Talleres de Reparación y Servicio"; auto-parts stores are listed under "Refacciones y Accesorios para Automoviles." On the road, often the sign of a mechanic simply says TALLER MECÁNICO.

I've found that the Ford and Volkswagen dealerships in Mexico give prompt, courteous attention to my car problems, and prices for repairs are, in general, much lower than those in the United States or Canada. I suspect other big-name dealerships give similar satisfactory service. Often they will take your car right away and make repairs in just a few hours, sometimes minutes.

If your car breaks down on the road, help might already be on the way. Radio-equipped green repair trucks manned by uniformed English-speaking officers patrol the major highways during daylight hours to aid motorists in trouble. The **"Green Angels"** will perform minor repairs and adjustments for free, but you pay for parts and materials.

MINOR ACCIDENTS   When possible, many Mexicans drive away from minor accidents to avoid hassles with police. If the police arrive while the involved persons are still at the scene, everyone may be locked in jail until blame is assessed. In any case you have to settle up immediately, which may take days of red tape. Foreigners who don't speak fluent Spanish are at a distinct disadvantage when trying to explain their side of the event. Three steps may help the foreigner who doesn't wish to do as the Mexicans do: If you're in your own car, notify your Mexican insurance company, whose job is to intervene on your behalf. If you're in a rental car, notify the rental company immediately and ask how to contact the nearest adjuster. (You did buy insurance with the rental—right?) Finally, if all else fails, ask to contact the nearest Green Angels.

See also "Mexican Auto Insurance" in "By Car" under "Getting There," above.

PARKING   When you park your car on the street, lock it up and leave nothing within view inside (day or night). I use guarded parking lots, especially at night, to avoid vandalism and break-ins. This way you also avoid parking violations. When pay lots are not available, dozens of small boys will surround you as you stop, wanting to watch your car for you. Pick the leader of the group, let him know you want him to guard it, and give him a peso or two when you leave.

CAR RENTALS   With some trepidation I wander into the subject of car-rental rules, which change often in Mexico. The best prices are obtained by reserving your car a week in advance in the United States. Mexico City and most other large Mexican cities have rental offices representing the various big firms and some local ones. You'll find rental desks at airports, all major hotels, and many travel agencies. The large firms like Avis, Hertz, National, and Budget have rental offices on main streets as well. Renting a car during a major holiday may prove difficult if all the cars are booked or not returned on time. To avoid being stranded without a vehicle, plan your arrival before the anticipated rush of travelers.

I don't recommend renting a car in Mexico City for one-day excursions from the city. It can be a real hassle, and parking is also a problem.

Cars are easy to rent if you have a charge or credit card (American Express, VISA, MasterCard, and the like), are 25 or over, and have a valid driver's license and passport with you. Without a credit card, you must leave a cash deposit, usually a big one. Rent-here/leave-there arrangements are usually simple to make but very costly.

Costs   Don't underestimate the cost of renting a car. When I checked recently for rental on May 15 (after Easter when rates go down) the basic cost of a one-day rental of a Volkswagen Beetle, with unlimited mileage (but before 15 % tax and $15 daily insurance) was $44 in Cancun, $45 in Mexico City, $38 in Puerto Vallarta, and $25 in Mérida. Renting by the week gives you a lower daily rate. For renting from Avis during the week of May 15, the basic seven-day weekly rate for a VW Beetle (without tax or insurance) was $180 in Cancún and Puerto Vallarta, $150 in Mérida, and $216 in Mexico City.

So you can see that it makes a difference where you rent, for how long, and when. If you have a choice of renting in Mérida and driving to Cancún, you could save considerably more money than if you rent in Cancún. Mileage-added rates can run the bill up considerably; I recommend renting with mileage included rather than with mileage added.

Rental Confirmation   Make your reservation directly with the car-rental company using its toll-free number. Write down your confirmation number and request that a copy of the confirmation be mailed to you (rent at least a week in advance so the confirmation has time to reach you). Present that confirmation slip when you appear to collect your car. If you're dealing with a U.S. company, the confirmation must be honored, even if the company has to upgrade you to another class of car—don't allow them to send you to another agency. The rental confirmation also has the agreed-on price that prevents you from being charged more, in case there is a price change before you arrive. Insist on the rate printed on the confirmation slip.

Deductibles   Be careful—deductibles vary greatly; some are as high as $2,500, which comes out of your pocket immediately in case of car damage. Don't fail to get information about deductibles.

Insurance   Many credit-card companies offer their cardholders free rental-car insurance. *Don't use it in Mexico,* for several reasons. Even though insurance policies that specifically cover rental cars are supposedly optional in Mexico, there may be major consequences if you don't have one. First, if you buy insurance, you pay only the deductible, which limits your liability. Second, if you have an accident or your car is vandalized or stolen and you don't have insurance, you'll have to pay for everything before you can leave the rental-car office. This includes the full value of the car if it is unrepairable—a determination made only by the rental-car company. While your credit card may eventually pay your costs, you will have to lay out the money in the meantime. Third, if an accident occurs, everyone may wind up in jail until guilt is determined, and if you are the guilty party, you may not be released from jail until restitution is paid in full to the rental-car owners and to injured persons—made doubly difficult if you have no rental-car insurance.

Insurance is offered in two parts. **Collision and damage** insurance covers your car and others if the accident is your fault, and **personal accident** insurance covers you and anyone in your car. I always take both.

Damage   Always inspect your car carefully, and mark all problem areas using this checklist:

- Hubcaps
- Windshield (for nicks and cracks)
- Tire tread
- Body (for dents, nicks, etc.)
- Fenders (for dents, etc.)
- Muffler (is it smashed?)
- Trim (loose or damaged?)
- Head and taillights
- Fire extinguisher (it should be under the driver's seat, as required by law)
- Spare tire and tools (in the trunk)
- Seat belts (required by law)
- Gas cap
- Outside mirror
- Floor mats

Note every damaged or missing area, no matter how minute, on your rental agreement or you will be charged for all missing or damaged parts, including missing car tags, should the police confiscate your tags for a parking infraction (which is very costly). I can't stress enough how important it is to check your car carefully. Car companies have attempted to rent me cars with bald tires and tires with bulges; a car with a license plate that would expire before I returned the car; and cars with missing trim, floor mats, or fire extinguishers. They've also attempted to charge me for dings that were on the auto when I rented it, which they were unable to do because the dings were marked on the agreement.

Fine Print   Read the fine print on the back of your rental agreement and note that insurance is invalid if you have an accident while driving on an unpaved road.

Trouble Number   One last recommendation: Before starting out with a rental car, be sure you know the rental company's trouble number. Get the direct number to the agency where you rented the car and write down its office hours. The large firms have toll-free numbers, but they may not be well staffed on weekends.

Problems, Perils, Deals   At present, I find the best prices are through Avis, and that's the company I use; generally I am a satisfied customer, though I sometimes have to dig in my heels and insist on proper service. I have had even more difficult problems with other agencies. I have encountered certain kinds of situations within the past four years that could occur with any company. These problems have included an attempt to push me off to a no-name company rather than upgrade me to a more expensive car when a VW Beetle wasn't available; poorly staffed offices with no extra cars, parts, or mechanics in case of a breakdown; and a demand I sign a credit-card voucher for 75% of the value of the car in case of an accident even though I had purchased insurance (I refused and still rented the car). Since potential problems are varied, I'd rather deal with a company based in the States so at least I have recourse if I am not satisfied.

Signing the Rental Agreement   Once you've agreed on everything, the rental clerk will tally the bill before you leave and you will sign an open credit-card voucher that will be filled in when you return the car. Read the agreement and double-check all the addition. The time to catch mistakes is before you leave, not when you return.

Picking Up/Returning the Car   When you rent the car, you agree to pick it up at a certain time and return it at a certain time. If you're late in picking it up or if you cancel the reservation, there are usually penalties—ask what they are when you make the reservation. If you return the car more than an hour late, an expensive hourly rate kicks in. Also, you must return the car with the same amount of gas in the tank it had when you drove out. If you don't, the charge added to your bill for the difference is much more than for gas bought at a public station.

FAST FACTS: Mexico

Abbreviations   Dept.=apartments; Apdo.=post office box; Av.=Avenida; Calz.=Calzada (boulevard). "C" on faucets stands for *caliente* (hot), and "F" stands for *fría* (cold). PB (*planta baja*) means ground floor.

Business Hours   In general, Mexican businesses in larger cities are open between 9am and 7pm; in smaller towns many close between 2 and 4pm. Most are closed on Sunday. Bank hours are Monday through Friday from 9 or 9:30am to 1pm. A few banks in large cities have extended hours.

Camera/Film   Buying a camera can be inconvenient and expensive in Mexico, but film costs about the same as that in the United States. Take full advantage of your 12-roll film allowance by bringing 36-exposure rolls. Also bring extra batteries: AA batteries are generally available, but AAA and small disk batteries for cameras and watches are rare. A few places in resort areas advertise color film developing, but it might be cheaper to wait until you get home.

Important note about camera use: Tourists wishing to use a video or still camera at any archaeological site in Mexico and at many museums operated by the Instituto de Historia y Antropología (INAH) may be required to pay $8.50 per video and/or still camera at each site or museum visited. (In some museums camera use is not permitted.) If you want to use either kind of camera or both, the fee must be paid for each piece of equipment. When you pay the fee, your camera will be tagged and you are permitted to use the equipment. Watchmen are often posted to see that untagged cameras are not used. Such fees are noted in the listings for specific sites and museums.

Complaints Tourists experiencing difficulties with public officials such as police officers can call 91-800/0-0148 toll free in Mexico to report incidents.

Customs Mexican customs inspection has been streamlined. At most points of entry tourists are requested to punch a button. If the resulting light is green, you go through without inspection; if it's red, your luggage or car may be inspected thoroughly or briefly.

Doctors/Dentists Every embassy and consulate is prepared to recommend local doctors and dentists with good training and modern equipment; some of the doctors and dentists even speak English. See the list of embassies and consulates under "Embassies/Consulates," below, and remember that at the larger ones, a duty officer is on call at all times. Hotels with a large foreign clientele are often prepared to recommend English-speaking doctors. Almost all first-class hotels in Mexico have a doctor on call.

Drug Laws Briefly, don't use or possess illegal drugs in Mexico. Mexicans have no tolerance for drug users, and jail is their solution, with very little hope of getting out until the sentence (usually a long one) is completed or heavy fines or bribes are paid. (*Important note:* It isn't uncommon to be befriended by a fellow user only to be turned in by that "friend," who then collects a bounty for turning you in. It's a no-win situation!) Bring prescription drugs in their original containers. If possible, pack a copy of the original prescription with the generic name of the drug.

I don't need to go into detail about the penalties for illegal drug possession upon return to the United States. Customs officials are also on the lookout for diet drugs sold in Mexico, possession of which could also land you in a U.S. jail because they are illegal here. If you buy antibiotics over the counter (which you can do in Mexico)—say, for a sinus infection—and still have some left, you probably won't be hassled by U.S. customs.

Drugstores Drugstores (*farmacías*) will sell you just about anything you want, with a prescription or without one. However, over-the-counter medicines such as aspirin, decongestants, or antihistamines are rarely sold. Most drugstores are open Monday through Saturday from 8am to 8pm. If you need to buy medicines after normal hours, ask for the *farmacía de turno*—pharmacies take turns staying open during off-hours. Find any drugstore, and in its window may be a card showing the schedule of which drugstore will be open at what time.

Electricity The electrical system in Mexico is 110 volts, 60 cycles, as in the United States and Canada. However, in reality it may cycle more slowly and overheat your appliances. To compensate, select a medium or low speed for hairdryers, though they may still overheat. Older hotels still have electrical outlets for flat two-prong plugs; you'll need an adapter for using any modern electrical apparatus that has an enlarged end on one prong or that has three prongs to insert. Many first-class and deluxe hotels have the three-holed outlets (*trifacicos* in Spanish). Those that don't may loan adapters, but to be sure, it's always better to carry your own.

Embassies/Consulates They provide valuable lists of doctors and lawyers, as well as regulations concerning marriages in Mexico. Contrary to popular belief, your embassy cannot get you out of a Mexican jail, provide postal or banking services, or fly you home when you run out of money. Consular officers can provide you with advice on most matters and problems, however. Most countries have a representative embassy in Mexico City and many have consular offices or representatives in the provinces.

The Embassy of **Australia** in Mexico City is at Jaime Balmes 11, Plaza Polanco, Torre B (☎ 5/395-9988 or 566-3053); it's open Monday through Friday from 8am to 1pm.

The Embassy of **Canada** in Mexico City is at Schiller 529, in Polanco (☎ 5/724-7900); it's open Monday through Friday from 9am to 1pm and 2 to 5pm (at other times the name of a duty officer is posted on the embassy door). In Acapulco, the Canadian consulate is in the Hotel Club del Sol, Costera Miguel Alemán, at the corner of Reyes Católicos (☎ 74/85-6621); it's open Monday through Friday from 8am to 3pm.

The Embassy of **New Zealand** in Mexico City is at Homero 229, 8th floor (☎ 5/250-5999 or 250-5777); it's open Monday through Thursday from 9am to 2pm and 3 to 5pm and Friday from 9am to 2pm.

The Embassy of the **United Kingdom** in Mexico City is at Lerma 71, at Río Sena (☎ 5/207-2569 or 207-2593); it's open Monday through Friday from 9am to 2pm. There are honorary consuls in the following cities: Acapulco, Hotel Las Brisas, Carretera Escénica (☎ 74/84-6605 or 84-1580); Ciudad Juarez, Calle Fresno 185 (☎ 16/7-5791); Guadalajara, Paulino Navarro 1165 (☎ 3/611-1678); Mérida, Calle 58 no. 450 (☎ 99/28-6152 or 28-3962); Monterrey, Privada de Tamazunchale 104 (☎ 83/78-2565); Oaxaca, Ev. Hidalgo 817 (☎ 951/6-5600); Tampico, 2 de Enero 102-A-Sur (☎ 12/12-9784 or 12-9817); Tijuana, Blvd. Salinas 1500 (☎ 66/81-7323); and Veracruz, Emparan 200 PB (☎ 29/31-0955).

The Embassy of the **United States** in Mexico City is next to the Hotel María Isabel Sheraton at Paseo de la Reforma 305, at the corner of Rió Danubio (☎ 5/211-0042). There are U.S. consulates in Ciudad Juárez, López Mateos 924-N (☎ 16/13-4048); Guadalajara, Progreso 175 (☎ 3/625-2998); Hermosillo, Calle Monterrey 141 (☎ 621/7-2375 or 7-2382); Matamoros, Av. Primera 2002 (☎ 88/12-4402); Mérida, Paseo Montejo 453 (☎ 99/25-6366); Monterrey, Av. Constitución 411 Poniente (☎ 83/45-2120); Nueuvo Laredo, Calle Allende 3330 (☎ 871/4-0512); and Tijuana, Tapachula 96 (☎ 66/81-7400). In addition, consular agents reside in Acapulco (☎ 74/85-6600 or 5-7207); Cabo San Lucas (☎ 114/3-3566); Cancún (☎ 98/84-2411 or 4-6399); Mazatlán (☎ 69/13-4444, ext. 285); Oaxaca (☎ 951/4-3054); Puerto Vallarta (☎ 322/2-0069); San Luis Potosí (☎ 481/2-1528); San Miguel de Allende (☎ 465/2-2357 or 2-0068); Tampico (☎ 12/13-2217); and Veracruz (☎ 29/31-5821).

Emergencies   The 24-hour Tourist Help Line in Mexico City is 5/250-0151.

Guides   Most guides in Mexico are men. Many speak English (and occasionally other languages) and are formally trained in history and culture to qualify for a federally approved tourism license. Hiring a guide for a day at ruins or to squire you around Mexico City may be a worthwhile luxury if you establish boundaries in the beginning. Be specific about what you want to do and how long you want the service. The guide will quote a price. Discussion may reduce the initial quote. If your guide is using his own car, is licensed (something he can prove with a credential), and speaks English, the price will be higher and is generally worth it. If you are together at lunch, it's customary to buy the guide's meal. When bus tours from the United States diminished a few years ago, many licensed English-speaking guides became taxi drivers, so it isn't unusual to find incredibly knowledgeable taxi drivers who are experienced guides. In Mexico City these licensed guides/taxi drivers often have a permanent spot outside the better hotels and are available for private duty. If the service has been out of the ordinary, a tip is in order—perhaps 10% of the daily rate. On tours, the recommended client tip is $1.50 to $2 per day per person to each guide.

Hitchhiking Generally speaking, hitchhiking is not a good idea in Mexico. Take a bus instead—they're cheap and go everywhere.

Legal Aid International Legal Defense Counsel, 111 S. 15th St., 24th Floor, Packard Building, Philadelphia, PA 19102 (☎ 215/977-9982), is a law firm specializing in legal difficulties of Americans abroad. See also "Embassies/Consulates" and "Emergencies," above.

Mail Mail service south of the border tends to be slow (sometimes glacial in its movements) and erratic. If you're on a two-week vacation, it's not a bad idea to buy and mail your postcards in the arrivals lounge at the airport to give them maximum time to get home before you do.

For the most reliable and convenient mail service, have your letters sent to you c/o the American Express offices in major cities, which will receive and forward mail for you if you are one of its clients (a travel-club card or an American Express traveler's check is proof). They charge a fee if you wish to have your mail forwarded.

If you don't use American Express, have your mail sent to you care of Lista de Correos (General Delivery), followed by the Mexican city, state, and country. In Mexican post offices there may actually be a "lista" posted near the Lista de Correos window bearing the names of all those for whom mail has been received. If there's no list, ask and show them your passport so they can riffle through and look for your letters. If the city has more than one office, you'll have to go to the central post office—not a branch—to get your mail. By the way, in many post offices they return mail to the sender if it has been there for more than 10 days. Make sure people don't send you letters too early.

In major Mexican cities there are also branches of such U.S. express mail companies as Federal Express and DHL, as well as private mail boxes such as Mail Boxes Etc.

Newspapers/Magazines The English-language newspaper *The News*, published in Mexico City, carries world news and commentaries, plus a calendar of the day's events including concerts, art shows, and plays. Newspaper kiosks in larger Mexican cities will carry a selection of English-language magazines.

Police Police in general in Mexico are to be suspected rather than trusted; however, you'll find many who are quite helpful with directions, even going so far as to lead you where you want to go.

Restrooms The best bet in Mexico is to use restrooms in restaurants and hotel public areas. Always carry your own toilet paper and hand soap, neither of which is in great supply in Mexican restrooms. Public facilities, usually near the central market, vary in cleanliness and usually have an attendant who charges a few pesos for toilet use and a few squares of toilet paper. Pemex gas stations have improved the maintenance of their restrooms along major highways. No matter where you are, even if the toilet flushes with paper, there'll be a waste basket for paper disposal. Many people come from homes without plumbing and are not accustomed to toilets that will take paper and will throw paper on the floor rather than put it in the toilet; thus, you'll see the basket no matter what quality of place you are in. On the other hand, the water pressure in many establishments is so low that paper won't go down. There's often a sign telling you whether or not to flush paper.

Safety   Crime is more of a problem in Mexico than it used to be. Although you will feel physically safer in most Mexican cities than in comparable big cities at home, you must take some basic, sensible precautions.

First, remember that you're a tourist and an obvious target for crime. Beware of pickpockets on crowded buses, on the Metro, and in markets. Guard your possessions very carefully at all times; don't let packs or bags out of your sight even for a second. The big first-class bus lines will store your bag in the luggage compartment under the bus, and that's generally all right; however, keep your things with you on the less responsible village buses and some second-class buses on country routes.

Next, if you have a car, park it in an enclosed or guarded lot at night. Vans are a special mark. Don't depend on "major downtown streets" to protect your car—park it in a private lot with a guard or at least a fence.

Women must be careful in cities when walking alone, night or day. Busy streets are no problem, but empty streets are lonely places.

Important warning: Agreeing to carry a package back to the States for an acquaintance or a stranger could land you in jail for years if it contains drugs or some other contraband. Never do it, no matter how friendly, honest, or sincere the request. Perpetrators of this illegal activity prey on innocent-looking single travelers and especially senior citizens.

Allowing anyone into your room whom you don't know could invite an instant robbery. This includes someone announcing him or herself (by phone or at your hotel room door) as room service bringing a "free" meal or drinks as compliments of the house—or anything you didn't order. When you open the door expectantly, robbers burst in. Always use caution before opening your door to anyone. When in doubt call hotel security or the reception desk.

Women travelers should see "For Women" in "Tips for Special Travelers," above, in this chapter for more specific safety information.

Taxes   There's a 10% tax on goods and services in Mexico, and it's supposed to be included in the posted price.

Telephone/Fax   Telephone area codes are gradually being changed all over the country. The change may affect the area code and first digit or only the area code. Some cities are even adding exchanges and changing whole numbers. Often a personal or business telephone number will be changed without notification to the subscriber. Telephone courtesy messages announcing a phone number change are nonexistent in Mexico. You can try operator assistance for difficult-to-reach numbers, but often the phone company doesn't inform its operators of recent changes. People who have fax machines often turn them off when their offices are closed. Many fax numbers are also regular telephone numbers; you have to ask whoever answers your call for the fax tone (*Por favor darme el tono por fax*). Telephone etiquette in Mexico does not prompt the answerer to offer to take a message or to have someone return your call; you'll have to make these suggestions yourself. In addition, etiquette doesn't necessarily demand that a business answer its phone by saying its name; often you'll have to ask if you have the right place.

Time   Central standard time prevails throughout most of Mexico. The west-coast states of Sonora, Sinaloa, and parts of Nayarit are on mountain standard time. The state of Baja California Norte is on Pacific time, but Baja California Sur is on mountain time.

Water   Most hotels have decanters or bottles of purified water in the rooms, and the better hotels have either purified water from regular taps or special taps marked AGUA PURIFICADA. In the resort areas, especially the Yucatán, hoteliers are beginning to charge for in-room bottled water. Virtually any hotel, restaurant, or bar will bring you purified water if you specifically request it, but you'll usually be charged for it. Bottled purified water is sold widely at drugstores and grocery stores.

Mexico City 4

Mexico City glitters with all the fascination and excitement of a world capital. It's a vital, romantic place of monuments, palaces, parks, broad boulevards, tall buildings, and smart boutiques. It's the fountainhead of government and in every way the center of Mexican life. It's not even "Mexico City" but simply "Mexico" in the lexicon of every Mexican who talks about it.

The region of Mexico City (alt. 7,240 ft.; pop. 23,000,000) has held the most important place in the country's history since the rise of Teotihuacán in 300 B.C.

According to legend, (a rewrite of actual history), in A.D. 1300, the Aztecs built their great capital of Tenochtitlán on an island in the middle of Lake Texcoco, following a legendary prophecy they should build where they saw a "sign": an eagle perched on a cactus with a serpent in its beak. Historical research however, shows that the Aztecs were a servant/worker class, who, through intermarriage, rose to power over several centuries. Lake Texcoco, now shrunken, once filled the valley to the base of Chapultepec ("Grasshopper Hill" in the Aztec language), and broad causeways connected the island to the shore. Little remains of this magnificent city of 300,000 inhabitants. What we know of Tenochtitlán is from the 16th-century chronicles of the Spanish conquerors, especially of Bernal Díaz del Castillo, who saw "the great towers and temples and buildings rising from the water—it was like the enchantments."

After the Aztec defeat, the Spanish made the city their capital, and in the centuries that followed the lake was filled in and the city limits were greatly extended. Maximilian of Hapsburg did much to beautify the city during his short and stormy tenure. He remodeled Chapultepec Palace, built by a Spanish viceroy in 1783, and established the grand boulevard now named the Paseo de la Reforma.

You can see many signs of Mexico City's varied history: The pyramids of Teotihuacán are a short ride from downtown; Xochimilco, a reminder of the Aztec Floating Gardens in Lake Texcoco, is close by; the Zócalo with its cathedral and Palacio Nacional is Spain's standard contribution to colonial town planning. And the Mexican Republic has made the city what it is today.

In more ways than these the city is still a creature of its history. In fact, it's literally sinking into it, for the soft lake bottom gives easily under the weight of such formidable structures as the marble palace of the Bellas Artes or the skyscraping Latin American Tower. But it gives only an inch a year, so you needn't worry—take your time in visiting one of the most fascinating capital cities in the world.

You've undoubtedly heard about Mexico City's pollution problem: It is as immense as the city itself. Major steps to improve the air quality (restricted driving, factory closings, new emission-controlled buses and taxis) have worked wonders, but the problem continues. For the visitor, dealing with the pollution is a matter of luck. On some days you won't notice it; on other days it will make your nose run, eyes water, and throat rasp. One positive note: The air in the evenings is usually deliciously cool and relatively clean. (See also "Pollution" under "Fast Facts: Mexico City" later in this chapter.)

If you have respiratory problems, be very careful; being at an altitude of 7,240 feet makes things even worse. Minimize your exposure to the fumes by refraining from walking busy streets during rush hour. Make Sunday, when many factories are closed and many cars escape the city, your prime sightseeing day.

1 Orientation

The thought of tackling one of the world's most enormous cities is enough to give the most experienced traveler nightmares, but fortunately Mexico City is quite well organized for the arriving traveler. Almost all touristically important sites are grouped in several areas that are easily walkable and easy to reach.

ARRIVING & DEPARTING
BY PLANE

For information on carriers serving Mexico City from the United States, reconfirmation of flights, etc., see Chapter 3.

Mexico City's **Benito Juárez International Airport** is something of a small city, where you can grab a bite or buy a wardrobe, books, gifts, and insurance, as well as exchange money or arrange a hotel room.

Near Gate A is a guarded **baggage-storage area.** The key-locked metal storage lockers measure about 2 feet by 2 feet by 18 inches and cost $5 daily. Larger items are stored in a warehouse; cost for the first 24 hours is $6 to $16, depending on the size, and $10 each additional day; they'll hold your items up to a month—but be sure to double check that they haven't changed that policy.

The Mexico City Hotel and Motel Association offers a **hotel-reservation service** at their member hotels. Look for their booths before you leave the baggage-claim area and near Gate A on the concourse. They'll make the call according to your specifications for location and price. If they book the hotel, they require one night's advance payment and will give you a voucher showing payment, which you present at the hotel. Ask about hotels with specials, which can substantially reduce the rate. Special low-cost **long-distance telephones** (Ladatel) are strategically placed all along the public concourse (for instructions on how to use them, see the Appendix).

When you're getting ready to leave Mexico City and need local information on flights, times, and prices, contact the airlines directly. Although airline numbers seem to change every year, the following numbers may be useful: **Aero California** (☎ 207-1378 or 207-1392 for reservations, or 785-1101 or 785-1162 at the airport), **Aeroméxico** (☎ 207-8233 or 228-9910 for reservations, or 571-3267 at the airport), **American** (☎ 203-9444 for reservations, or 571-3219 at the airport), Aviacsa (☎ 559-1955), **Continental** (☎ 280-3434 for reservations, or 762-3539 or 571-4271 at the airport), **Delta** (☎ 202-1608 for reservations, or

762-0258 at the airport), **Mexicana** (☎ 325-0980 or 325-0984 for reservations, or 325-0990 at the airport), **Saro** (☎ 273-1766 or 273-1521 for reservations, or 726-0157 at the airport), **Taesa** (☎ 227-0700, 705-0880 or 566-5991 for reservations), and **United** (☎ 627-0222 for reservations).

Note: Telephoning an airline in Mexico City can be frustrating because the city's telephone system is old, and in certain sections of the city it's downright nonfunctional. Besides, the airlines often don't have enough telephone lines to handle calls—keep trying. Also check the latest telephone directories for new or additional numbers.

Be sure to allow at least 45 minutes' travel time from either the Zona Rosa or the Zócalo area to the airport. Check in at least 90 minutes before international flights and 60 minutes before domestic flights.

GETTING INTO TOWN   The **authorized airport taxis** provide good, fast service but are relatively expensive. Here's how to use them: After exiting the baggage-claim area and entering the public concourse, you'll see yellow booths marked "Taxi." These authorized taxi booths are staffed by personnel wearing bright-yellow jackets or bibs emblazoned with "Taxi Autorizado" (authorized taxi). Tell the ticket-seller your hotel or destination, as the price is based on a zone system. Expect to pay around $10 for a ticket to the Zona Rosa. *Count your change! Taxi-ticket sellers have attempted to shortchange me countless times here.* A yellow-shirted escort will then show you to an available taxi in front or to the end of a line if there is one. Present your ticket to the driver. Avoid turning your luggage over to an unauthorized taxi "assistant" who does nothing but lift your luggage into the waiting taxi—naturally he will want a tip. Putting your luggage in the taxi is the driver's job, and these "assistants" seem to whiz in and out of nowhere to do the job.

Ignore those who approach you in the arrivals hall offering taxis; they are usually nonlicensed and unauthorized. Take only an authorized cab with all the familiar markings: yellow car, white taxi light on the roof, and TRANPORTACIÓN TERRESTRE painted on the doors.

The authorized cabbies maintain a monopoly of the airport business. You can try to beat the system by first seeing what authorized taxis charge, then walking to the Terminal Area Metro station (see below), at the intersection of the busy Bulevar Aeropuerto and the airport entrance, and look for a **regular city taxi.** When you see a yellow-and-white or green-and-gray VW Beetle or little Datsun cab, flag it down. You may save at least 25%.

To make sure you get a proper, trustworthy cab, be sure to read the information on taxis in "Getting Around," below.

The **Metro,** Mexico City's modern subway system, is cheaper and faster than a taxi. As you come from your plane into the arrivals hall, turn left toward Gate A and walk all the way through the long terminal, out the doors, and along a covered sidewalk. Soon you'll see the distinctive Metro logo that identifies the Terminal Area station, down a flight of stairs. The station is on Metro Line 5. Follow the signs for trains to Pantitlán. At Pantitlán, change for Line 1 ("Observatorio"), which will take you to stations that are just a few blocks south of the Zócalo and the Alameda Central: Pino Suárez, Isabel la Católica, Salto del Agua, Balderas. The fare is astoundingly low—only a few cents. But wait! You may not be able to go by Metro if you have luggage. Read carefully the Metro information in "Getting Around." If you decide to go by Metro with luggage, don't plan to take a Metro route that requires you to change trains at La Raza station.

Downtown Mexico City

1238

Cuitláhuac Circle

COLONIA MORELOS

Guerrero Ⓜ

COLONIA GUERRERO

Santa María Redonda

Allende

Comfort

Brasil

Rep de Argentina

Rayon

20

Héroe de Granaditas

Paseo de la Reforma

Lázaro Cárdenas

Simón Bolivar Circle

19

Allende

Chile

Rep de Ecuador

Rep de Paraguay

Rep de Honduras

Zarco

Rep de Peru

Rep de Bolivia

Hidalgo Ⓜ

Av Hidalgo

10

2 de Abril

B Dominguez

Rep de Cuba

21

Rep de Colombia

Rep de Venezuela

San Ildefonso

C del Carmen

Bellas Artes Ⓜ

18

Donceles

22

Tacuba

Justo Sierra

Rep de Guatemala

Av Juárez

13

Allende

Juárez Ⓜ

11

Independencia

14

Bolívar

5 de Mayo

23

Moneda

E Zapata

Victoria

15

17

Madero

24

Zócalo Ⓜ

25

Ayuntamiento

16

16 de Septiembre

COLONIA CENTRO

Revillagigedo

Luis Moya

Buen Tono

12

V Carranza

Rep de Uruguay

Rep de El Salvador

Corregidora

Dolores

San Juan de Letrán

5 de Febrero

20 de Noviembre

Jesús María

Anillo de Circunvalación

alderas Ⓜ

Isabel la Católica

Regina

26

Arcos de Belén Ⓜ

Salto del Agua Ⓜ

Isabel la Católica Ⓜ

José María Izazaga

27

San Pablo

28 **29**

Merced Ⓜ

30

Dr Río de la Loza

Piño Suárez Ⓜ

Fray Servando Teresa de Mier

Chimalpopoca

31

Dr Liceaga

Bolívar

Ción San Antonio Abad

COLONIA DOCTORES

Diag 20 de Noviembre

Isabel la Católica

San Antonio Abad

Clavijero

Calz de la Vica

Dr J Terres

COLONIA OBRERA

Lorenzo Boturini

The walk between lines there is 10 to 15 minutes, and you'll be carrying your luggage.

By Bus

Mexico City has a bus terminal for each of the four points of the compass: north, east, south, and west. You can't necessarily tell which terminal serves which area of the country by looking at a map, however. All stations have restaurants, book and magazine stands, money-exchange booths or banks, post offices, and long-distance telephone booths.

Note: Each station has a taxi system based on fixed-price tickets to various zones within the city, operated from a booth or kiosk in or near the entry foyer of the terminal. Locate your destination on a zone map or tell the seller where you want to go, buy a *boleto* (ticket), and most important, count your change—more travelers are shortchanged at this moment than at any other point—and present your ticket to the driver out front. For bus rider's terms and translations, see the Appendix.

You'll find a **Greyhound** office at Amores 707 no. 102 (☎ 536-4702), where you can buy tickets on its buses and on Mexican connecting lines into the United States. Office hours are Monday through Friday from 8am to 4pm.

TERMINAL CENTRAL DE AUTOBUSES DEL NORTE   Called by shorter names as "Camiones Norte," "Terminal Norte," "Central del Norte," or even just "C.N.," this is Mexico's largest bus station, on Avenida de los 100 ("Cien") Metros. It handles most buses coming from the U.S.–Mexico border. All buses to/from the Pacific coast as far south as Puerto Vallarta and Manzanillo; to/from the Gulf coast as far south as Tampico and Veracruz; and to/from such cities as Guadalajara, San Luis Potosí, Durango, Zacatecas, Morelia, and Colima arrive and depart from here. You can also get to the pyramids of San Juan Teotihuacán and Tula from here.

The Central del Norte is a mammoth place where you can change money (during normal banking hours), have a meal or a drink, take out insurance, or rent a car. You'll even find a post office and a long-distance phone installation. A tourism information booth is set up at the center of the terminal's crescent-shaped facade, and nearby is a hotel-reservation booth. Both can be very helpful.

To get downtown from the Terminal Norte, you have a choice: The Metro has a station (Estación Terminal de Autobuses del Norte, or T.A.N.) right here, so it's easy to hop a train and connect for all points. Walk to the center of the terminal, go out the front door, straight ahead, down the steps, and to the Metro station. This is Línea 5. Follow the signs that say DIRECCIÓN PANTITLÁN. For downtown, you can change trains at either La Raza or Consulado (see the Mexico City Metro map on the inside back cover). Be aware that if you change at La Raza, you'll have to walk for 10 to 15 minutes and will encounter stairs. The walk is through a marble-lined underground corridor, but it's a long way with heavy luggage.

Another way to get downtown is by trolleybus. The stop is on Avenida de los Cien Metros, in front of the terminal. The trolleybus runs right down Avenida Lázaro Cárdenas, the "Eje Central" (Central Artery). Or try the "Central Camionera del Norte–Villa Olímpica" buses, which go down Avenida Insurgentes, past the university.

TERMINAL DE AUTOBUSES DE PASAJEROS DE ORIENTE (TAPO)   The terminal is known by all as **TAPO.** Buses from the east (Puebla, Cholula, Amecameca, the Yucatán Peninsula, Veracruz, San Cristóbal de las Casas, and others) arrive here. Buses originating in Oaxaca arrive here as well, since they pass through Puebla, which is east of Mexico City. Underneath the station's broad green dome are ticket counters, toilets, a post office, a cafeteria, bookstalls, and snack shops. Taxi tickets to anywhere in the city are sold inside on the main concourse near the exit doors; they are priced by zone. Count your change!

For those departing, this is the place to go if you are looking for a bus to Oaxaca, Puebla, Tlaxcala, Pachuca, Amecameca, Jalapa, Yucatán, or Guatemala. Companies that sell tickets here include Autobuses Unidos (AU), Autobuses de Oriente, ADO, Pullman Plus, Estrella Roja, ATAH, and Cristóbal Colón. AU buses have the most frequent departures for Tehuacán, Veracruz, and Jalapa. Deluxe Pullman Plus buses are the most comfortable for a trip to Puebla. ADO has "Lujo" (luxury) service to Oaxaca, Cancún, Villahermosa, and Catemaco. ATAH buses go directly to Tlaxcala.

To get to TAPO, take a "Hipodromo-Pantitlán" bus east along Alvarado, Hidalgo, or Donceles; if you take the Metro, go to the San Lázaro station on the eastern portion of Line 1 ("Dirección Pantitlán").

TERMINAL CENTRAL DE AUTOBUSES DEL SUR   Mexico City's southern bus terminal is the "Terminal Central de Autobuses del Sur," Avenida Taxqueña 1320, right next to the Taxqueña Metro stop, the last stop on that line. The Central del Sur handles buses to/from Cuernavaca, Taxco, Acapulco, Zihuatanejo, and intermediate points. The easiest way to get to or from the Central del Sur is on the Metro. The station for the terminal is Taxqueña (or Tasqueña, as it's also spelled). For the signs that say DIRECCIÓN PANTITLÁN to get downtown. Or take a trolleybus on Avenida Lázaro Cárdenas.

If you're here to get a bus out of the city, this terminal is fairly easy to figure out. If you're going to Cuernavaca, head straight for the ticket counters of Autobuses Pullman de Morelos, as its buses depart every 10 or 15 minutes throughout the day for that destination; there's hardly ever a problem getting a seat. If, however, you're headed for Acapulco or Zihuatanejo, go to the first-class line named Estrella de Oro; at its ticket counter, you can choose your bus seat on a computer screen. The best service to Taxco is on Estrella Blanca/Flecha Roja. Second-class lines will save you a minuscule sum of money over first-class lines, so I recommend going first class.

TERMINAL PONIENTE DE AUTOBUSES   The western bus terminal is conveniently located right next to the Observatorio Metro station at Sur 122 and Río Tacubaya. This is the station you'll arrive at if you're coming from Acapulco, Cuernavaca, Ixtapa, Taxco, Zihuatanejo and Morelia.

This is the smallest of the terminals, and its main reason for being is to serve the route between Mexico City and Toluca. But other cities to the west and northwest are served also, including Ixtapan de la Sal, Valle de Bravo, Morelia, Uruapan, and Guadalajara. In general, if your chosen destination is also served from the Terminal Norte, you'd be better off going there. The Terminal Norte simply has more buses and better bus lines.

BY CAR

If you are brave enough to drive in Mexico City here are a few tips. Arrive and depart before dawn, when there is very little traffic. This way you can arrive at your destination without the added distraction of a zillion cars all coming at you from as many directions. Then park the car in a guarded lot and don't drive it again until you are ready to leave the city—at dawn. Driving in this city is best left to those who know it.

Here are the chief thoroughfares for getting out of the city: Insurgentes Sur becomes Highway 95 to Taxco and Cuernavaca. Insurgentes Norte leads to Teotihuacán and Pachuca. Highway 57, the Periférico (loop around the city), is called Camacho as it goes north and leads out of the city north to Tula and Querétaro. Constituyentes leads west out of the city past Chapultepec Park and connects with Highway 15 to Toluca, Morelia, and Pátzcuaro. Zaragoza leads east to Highway 150 to Puebla and Veracruz.

VISITOR INFORMATION

The Departamento de Distrito Federal (Federal District Department), provides several information services for visitors. First of all, there are **Infotur** offices, the most convenient of which is in the Zona Rosa at Amberes 54, at the corner of Londres (☎ 525-9380 or 525-9384). Others are at the bus terminals, airport, and railroad station. They're open daily from 9am to 9pm.

The **Secretaría de Turismo (SECTUR),** Avenida Presidente Mazaryk 172 (☎ 250-0151 or 250-0123), north of Chapultepec Park in the district known as Polanco, is a bit out of the way, but any telephone will serve to get you information 24 hours daily. The staff speaks English.

The **Mexico City Chamber of Commerce** (☎ 566-0457) maintains an information office with a very friendly, helpful staff who can provide you with a detailed map of the city (or country) and answer your questions. It's conveniently located at Reforma 42—look for the *Cámara Nacional de Comercio de la Ciudad de México,* open Monday through Thursday from 9am to 2pm and 3 to 6pm; and Friday from 9am to 2pm and 3 to 5:30pm.

CITY LAYOUT

FINDING AN ADDRESS　Despite its size, Mexico City is not outrageously hard to understand. The city is divided into 350 *colonias,* or neighborhoods. But unless you are venturing out of the Colonia Centro (city center), you'll rarely need to know the colonia names. However, when you're trying to find an obscure address, such as a shop or a restaurant that may be unfamiliar to a taxi driver, it may be helpful to have these handy. A few to know are Colonia Polanco, a fashionable neighborhood immediately north of Chapultepec park, and all the Lomas—Lomas de Chapultepec, Lomas Tecamachalco, etc.—which are very exclusive neighborhoods west of Chapultepec Park, the "in" addresses so to speak. In addresses the word is abbreviated *Col.*; the full colonia name is vital in addressing correspondence.

Taxi drivers are notoriously ignorant of the city, including the major tourist sights and popular restaurants. Before getting in the taxi, always give them, in addition to a street address and colonia, cross streets as a reference and locate your destination on a map that you carry with you.

A LANDMARK　Probably the most frequently used and noticed landmark in Mexico City is the Monumento a la Independencia, often referred to as the Angel of Independence Monument, at the intersection of Reforma, Florencia, and Río Tiber. Set upon a tall marble shaft, the golden angel is an important and easily discerned guidepost for travelers. A creation of Antonio Rivas Mercado, the 22-foot-high gold-plated bronze angel—cast in Florence, Italy—was completed in 1906 at a cost of $2.5 million. With its base of marble and Italian granite, the monument's total height is 150 feet.

⭐ Frommer's Favorite Mexico City Experiences

Breakfast, Lunch or Dinner at the Hotel Majestic Rooftop Restaurant. Enjoy at least one meal under one of the colorful umbrellas overlooking the historic downtown and Zócalo. If you arrive just before sunset, you can watch soldiers file out of the Palacio Nacional and perform the flag-lowering ceremony on the Zócalo.

The Ethnography Section of the Museo Nacional de Antropología. Overlooked by many visitors, the second-floor Ethnography Section is the perfect introduction to Mexican life away from the beaches, resorts, and cities. Fine, unusual weavings, pottery, handcrafts, furniture, huts, plows, and canoes are presented in the context of everyday life. It's a must for those about to visit the interior of the country, those who are curious about the villagers seen on the capital's streets, and those who expect their Mexico journeys to be off the well-worn path.

The Sunday Lagunilla Market. The best flea market in Mexico, this one spreads out for blocks with vendors selling santos, jewelry, antiques, pottery, miniatures, brass, glass, and oddities such as old locks and keys, an armadillo purse complete with head and feet, a piece of Spanish armor, a 16th-century religious sculpture, an elkhorn earring, and much more.

Shopping in the Zona Rosa and Polanco. The dozens of fashionable shops lining the streets of these attractive areas sell designer clothing, jewelry, and antiques; there are lots of tempting restaurants in between.

The Saturday Bazaar in San Angel. Only on Saturdays (thus Bazar Sábado) is this colonial-era suburb of mansions near Parque San Jacinto invigorated with hundreds of artists, antiques dealers, street vendors, and sellers of popular art; the area restaurants consequently are mobbed.

Afternoon Tea at the Salón de Thé Duca d'Este. In Mexico, tea and coffee breaks are taken seriously. This cheerful Zona Rosa restaurant/pastry shop is great for sipping a frothy cappuccino and whiling away some time watching passersby through the huge windows facing the street.

The Ballet Folklórico de México. Among the best folkloric ballet groups in Mexico are those that perform in Mexico City either at the Teatro Bellas Artes or at the Teatro de la Ciudad. At the Bellas Artes you'll get to see the famed Tiffany glass curtain, which is usually (but not always) shown before each performance.

An Evening in the Zona Rosa. The popular Zona Rosa sidewalk cafes and pedestrian streets are ideal for a night of hopping from place to place, without cover charges and taxis, and all to see and be seen. Arrive before dusk to get a good seat for a relaxing drink and to watch the zone come alive for the evening. Copenhague, between Reforma and Ham–burgo, is among the best streets for an entire evening or just for drinks. It's a narrow, trafficless artery with awning-covered dining, bustling waiters, and food that's usually good enough to keep the places packed—though it's overpriced for the quality and quantity.

The Ruins of Teotihuacán. There's nothing to compare with walking down the wide Avenue of the Dead, with the Pyramid of the Moon at one end and pyramidal structures on both sides, imagining what it must have looked like when the walls were embellished with murals on brilliantly colored stucco.

STREET MAPS Should you want more detailed maps of Mexico City than the ones included in this guide, you can obtain them easily. Most bookstores (including Sanborn's) and many newsstands carry a local map-guide entitled *Mexico City Trillas Tourist Guide,* a softbound book of gorgeous block-by-block pictorial maps covering most areas of the city that are of interest to visitors. The English text includes interesting facts and statistics on Mexico City and its sights.

NEIGHBORHOODS IN BRIEF

Centro Centro refers to the heart of Mexico City, its business, banking, and historic center, including the areas in and around the Parque Alameda and Zócalo.

Chapultepec A huge area west of the city center, it mainly includes Chapultepec park—with its numerous museums—and its immediate environs.

Coyoacán Thirteen miles from the city center, south of San Angel and east of the Ciudad Universitario, Coyoacán is another colonial-era suburb noted for its beautiful town square, cobblestone streets lined with fine old mansions, and several of the city's most interesting museums.

Polanco A district immediately north of Chapultepec Park, Polanco is one of the city's trendiest neighborhoods. It's dotted with glitzy boutiques, luxury hotels, interesting antique shops, and some of the city's best restaurants. President Mazaryk is the main artery running through it.

San Angel Nine miles south of the city center, San Angel was once a distinct village but is now surrounded by the city. Yet the neighborhood remains a beautiful suburb of cobbled streets and beautiful colonial-era homes.

Xochimilco Fifteen miles south of town center, Xochimilco is noted for its famed canals and "floating gardens," which date from pre-Hispanic times.

Zona Rosa West of the Centro, the "Pink Zone" is a trendy area noted for its pedestrian-only streets, shops, restaurants, and hotels.

2 Getting Around

Luckily for budget travelers, Mexico City has a highly developed and remarkably cheap public transportation system. The Metro, first- and second-class buses, minibuses (colectivos), and yellow-and-white or green-and-gray VW taxis will take you anywhere you want to go for very little money.

BY METRO The subway system in Mexico City offers a smooth ride for one of the lowest fares anywhere in the world. Nine lines canvas the sprawling city.

As you enter the station, buy a *boleto* (ticket) at the glass *caja* (ticket booth). Insert your ticket into the slot at the turnstile and pass through; inside you'll see two large signs showing the line's destination (for example, for Line 1, it's Observatorio and Pantitlán). Follow the signs in the direction you want and *know where you're going,* since there is usually only one map of the routes, at the entrance to the station. There are, however, two signs you'll see everywhere: *Salida,* which means "exit," and *Andenes,* which means "platforms." Once inside the train, you'll see above each door a map of the station stops for that line, with symbols and names.

Transfer of lines is indicated by *Correspondencias.* The ride is smooth, fast, and efficient (although hot and crowded during rush hours). The stations are clean and beautifully designed and have the added attraction of several archaeological ruins unearthed during construction. There is also a subterranean passage that goes between the Pino Suárez and Zócalo stations so you can avoid the crowds and the rain along Pino Suárez. The Zócalo station features dioramas and large photographs of the different periods in the history of the Valley of Mexico, and at Pino Suárez is the foundation of a pyramid from the Aztec empire.

Important notes: The Metro system runs Monday through Friday from 6am to 1am; and Saturday and Sunday from 7am to midnight. Large baggage is not allowed into the system and signs are duly posted. In practice, this means that bulky suitcases or backpacks sometimes make you persona non grata (but a large shoulder bag such as I use is not classed as luggage, nor is an attaché case or even a case that's slightly bigger). The reason is that on an average day Mexico City's Metro handles over 5 million riders and that leaves precious little room for bags! But, in effect, if no one stops you as you enter, you're in. *Pickpockets are very crafty—they'll even pilfer a fanny pack from the front—be careful.*

Metro travel is crowded during daylight hours on weekdays and consequently pretty hot and muggy in summer. In fact, you may find that between 4 and 7pm on weekdays, the Metro is virtually unusable downtown because of sardine-can conditions. At some stations, there are even separate lanes roped off for women and children because the press of the crowd is so great someone might get molested. Buses, colectivos, and taxis are all heavily used during these hours. On weekends and holidays, the Metro is a joy to ride.

BY BUS   Moving millions of people through this sprawling urban mass is a gargantuan task, but the city officials do a pretty good job of it, though they tend to change bus numbers and routes frequently. Maps of the entire system are impossible to find. However, bus stops on the major tourist streets usually have a map posted with the full route description.

The large buses that ran on the major tourist routes (Reforma and Insurgentes) tended to become suffocatingly overpacked and have been phased out in favor of small buses, and more of them. Thus, crowding is uncommon except perhaps during peak hours. The cost in pesos is usually the U.S. equivalent of around 17¢ to 25¢. Although the driver usually has change, try to have the exact fare when you board.

One of the most important bus routes is the one that runs between the Zócalo and the Auditorio (National Auditorium in Chapultepec Park) or the Observatorio Metro station. The route is via Avenida Madero or Cinco (5) de Mayo, Avenida Juárez, Paseo de la Reforma. Buses marked "Zócalo" run this route.

Another important route is **"Indios Verdes-Tlalpan,"** which runs along Avenida Insurgentes connecting the northern bus terminal (Terminal Norte), Buenavista railroad station, Reforma, the Zona Rosa, and—far to the south—San Angel and University City.

BY TAXI   Mexico City is pretty easy to negotiate by Metro and bus, and these methods bring you few hassles. Taxis are another matter, but there are times when nothing else will do. Cabs operate under several distinct sets of rules, established in early 1991 and *may* make using one less of a combat zone situation than in the past.

Metered Taxis   Yellow and white or green and grey Volkswagen Beetle and "sitio" (radio-operated) Datsun cabs are your best bet for low cost and good service. Though you will often encounter a gouging driver ("Ah, the meter just broke yesterday; I'll have it fixed tomorrow!"), or one who advances the meter (yes, I've seen it), or drives farther than necessary to run up the tab, most of the service will be quick and adequate. As of early 1991, these taxis began operating strictly by the meter. If the driver says his meter isn't working, find another taxi. Also, don't get in a taxi that doesn't have the driver's taxi permit prominently displayed. It's a laminated license, about 5" x 7", and it's often above the rearview mirror or attached to a string near the glove box. It's illegal for a taxi to operate without the license in view. A taxi operating without it usually means the person driving the taxi is not a registered driver. These drivers are most often the ones that will try to cheat the passenger and you have no recourse if something goes wrong with the service.

"Turismo" taxis These cabs are unmarked, have special license plates, bags covering their meters, are usually well-kept big cars, and are assigned to specific hotels. The drivers negotiate rates with individual passengers for sightseeing etc. but rates to and from the airport are established, although higher than the Datsun or VW taxis. Ask the bell captain what the airport rate should be and establish the rate before taking off. These drivers are often licensed English-speaking guides and can provide exceptional service.

Don't use a car that is not an official taxi. All official taxis (except those expensive "Turismo" cabs) are painted yellow or green and grey. Except the "Turismo" cabs, they have white plastic roof signs bearing the word "Taxi" and they have "Taxi" or "Sitio" painted on the doors and they have meters. Look for all of these indications, not just one or two of them.

There is no need to tip any taxi driver in Mexico, unless the driver has performed a special service, such as carrying your luggage inside a hotel.

BY COLECTIVO Also called *peseros,* these are sedans or minibuses, usually green and gray, that run along major arteries. They pick up and discharge passengers along the route, charge established fares, and provide more comfort and speed than the bus. Routes are displayed on cards in the windshield; often a Metro station will be the destination. One of the most useful routes for tourists runs from the **Zócalo** along **Avenida Juárez,** along **Reforma** to **Chapultepec,** and back again. Get a colectivo with a sign saying "Zócalo," not "Villa." A "Villa" bus or pesero goes to the Basílica de Guadalupe.

Note that some of the minibuses on this route have automatic sliding doors—you don't have to shut them, a motor does.

As the driver approaches a stop, he may put his hand out the window and hold up one or more fingers. This is the number of passengers he's willing to take on (vacant seats are difficult to see if you're outside the car).

FAST FACTS: Mexico City

In "Fast Facts: Mexico" in Chapter 3 you'll find the answers to all sorts of questions about daily life in Mexico City. But here are a few essentials for getting along in this charming, enormous metropolis:

Altitude Remember you are now at an altitude of 7,240 feet—almost a mile and a half in the sky—where there's a lot less oxygen in the air than you're used to. If you run for a bus and feel dizzy when you sit down, it's the altitude; if you think you're in shape but huff and puff getting up Chapultepec hill, again it's the altitude. It takes about 10 days or so to adjust to the scarcity of oxygen. Go easy on food and alcohol the first few days in the city.

American Express   The Mexico City office is at Reforma 234 (☎ 5/207-7282 or 514-0629) in the Zona Rosa. It's open for banking, the pickup of American Express clients' mail, and travel advice Monday through Friday from 9am to 6pm and Saturday from 9am to 1pm.

Area Code   The telephone area code for Mexico City is 5.

Banks   Banks are usually open Monday through Friday from 9am to 5pm. Banamex is open Monday through Friday from 9am to 5:50pm. Bank branches at the airport are open whenever the airport is busy, including weekends. They usually offer ATM machines and very good rates of exchange.

Bookstores   In Mexico City, Sanborn's always has books in English, as well as magazines and newspapers. So does the American Bookstore, Madero 25 off Bolívar (☎ 512-7284); it's open Monday through Saturday from 9:30am to 7pm.

French and English books and magazines, especially those dealing with Mexico and its history, archaeology, and people, are the specialty of Librería de Porrua y CIA. One of its branches is located across from the Palacio de Bellas Artes at Juárez 16.

About the most convenient foreign- and Spanish-language bookstore in Mexico City, with a good selection of guidebooks and texts on Mexico, is Central de Publicaciones–Librería Mizrachi, Juárez 14, near Avenida Lázaro Cárdenas (☎ 510-4231), right across from the Bellas Artes. Another shop, nearby, is the Librería Británica, Madero 30-1, in the Hotel Ritz building (☎ 521-0180). The Museo Nacional de Antropología, in Chapultepec Park (☎ 553-6266), also has an excellent shop with a good selection of books on Mexico, particularly special-interest guides (birds, flowers, geology, mineralogy, archaeology, cuisine, folk art, and so forth).

Currency Exchange   The alternative to a bank is a currency-exchange booth, or *casa de cambio*. These are often open Monday through Friday from 8:30am to 5:30pm, and some are open Saturday from 8:30am to 2:30pm as well; many stay open until 6pm. The exchange rates offered by casas de cambio are sometimes better—and sometimes worse—than those offered by banks. Usually, their rates are much better than the rates offered by most hotels.

Drugstores   The drug departments at Sanborn's stay open late. Check the phone directory for the location nearest you. After hours, check with your hotel staff, who can usually contact the drugstore *de turno* (on call).

Emergencies   A government-operated service, **Locatel** (☎ 658-1111) is most often associated with finding missing persons anywhere in the country. With a good description of a car and its occupants, they'll search for motorists who have an emergency back home. **SECTUR** (Secretaría de Turismo) staffs telephones 24 hours daily (☎ 250-0123 or 250-0150) to help tourists in difficulty. The police number is hard to reach, so have a local help you.

Hospitals   Catering to foreigners, the American-British Cowdray (A.B.C.) Hospital is located at Calle Sur. 132 no. 136, at the corner of Avenida Observatorio, Colonia Las Américas (Sur 132 is the name of the street) (☎ 272-8500, or for emergencies 515-8359 or 516-8077).

Luggage Storage/Lockers   There are *guarda equipaje* rooms at the airport and bus stations. Most hotels have a key-locked storage area for guests who want to leave possessions for a few days.

Newspapers/Magazines   *The News* is the country's only English-language daily. See also "Bookstores," above.

Photographic Needs   Try Foto Regis, Juárez 80 at Balderas, near the Alameda.

Pollution   September and October seem to be light months for pollution, while mid- to late November, as well as December and January, are months noted for heavy pollution. During January, schools are often closed because of it, and restrictions on driving usually imposed only on weekdays may be imposed on weekends during heavy pollution; be sure to check before driving into or around the city (see below). Be careful if you have respiratory problems; being at an altitude of 7,240 feet will make your problems even worse. Just before your planned visit, call the Mexican Government Tourist Office nearest you (see "Visitor Information, Entry Requirements & Money" in Chapter 3 for the address) and ask for the latest information on pollution in the capital. Minimize your exposure to the fumes by refraining from walking busy streets during rush hour. Make Sunday, when many factories are closed and many cars escape the city, your prime sightseeing day.

Prohibited Driving Days

	Mon.	Tues.	Wed.	Thurs.	Fri.
Tag color	Yellow	Pink	Red	Green	Blue
Tag ends in	5 or 6	7 or 8	3 or 4	1 or 2	9 or 0

This means that if your car tag is yellow and ends in a 5 or 6, you are prohibited from driving in Mexico City on Monday, but you can drive any other day of the week. Note that this applies to rental cars and to tourist cars, but it is not in effect on Saturday or Sunday. There's a stiff fine for violating this regulation.

Post Office   The city's main post office, the Correos Mayor, is a block north of the Palacio de Bellas Artes on Avenida Lázaro Cárdenas, at the corner of Tacuba.

Although I don't recommend mailing a package in Mexico, since it may never get to its intended destination, if you must mail one in Mexico City, here's what to do: Take it to the post office called Correos Internacional no. 2, Calle Dr. Andrade and Río de la Loza (Metro: Balderas or Salto del Agua), open Monday through Friday from 8am to noon. Don't wrap up your package securely until an inspector examines it. (For a glossary of mail terms, see the Appendix.)

Safety   Read the "Safety" section under "Fast Facts: Mexico" in Chapter 3. Watch for pickpockets. Mexico City is unique in many ways, but in one matter it resembles any big city anywhere—pickpockets. Crowded subway cars and buses provide the perfect workplace for petty thieves, as do major museums (inside and out), thronged outdoor markets and bullfights, and indoor theaters. The "touch" can range from light-fingered wallet lifting or purse opening to a fairly rough shoving by two or three petty thieves. Sometimes the ploy is this: Someone drops a coin, and while everyone is looking, pushing, and shoving, your wallet disappears. Another trick is a child who takes your hand on a crowded bus or the Metro. While you kindly steady this child, someone else is pilfering your fanny pack, wallet, purse, etc. Watch out for any place tourists go in numbers: on the Metro, in Reforma buses, in crowded hotel elevators, at the Ballet Folklórico, and at the Museo de Antropología.

Luckily, violent muggings are pretty infrequent in Mexico City. But if you find yourself up against a handful of these guys in a crowded spot, the best thing to do is to raise a fuss—no matter whether you do it in Spanish or in English. Just a few shouts of "¡Ladrón!" ("Thief!") should put them off.

Taxes Mexico's 15% sales tax may be included in posted prices, or it may be added to a posted price. It's wise to ask "¿Más IVA?" (plus tax?) or "¿Con IVA?" (with tax?). There are also airport taxes for domestic and international flights. (See "Getting Around" in Chapter 3.)

Telephones Generally speaking, Mexico City's telephone system is in terrible shape. A number you reached five seconds ago may not be reachable again for days. As elsewhere in the country, the telephone company changes numbers without informing the telephone owners or the information operators. Telephone numbers are registered in the name of the corporation, which may be different than the name of a hotel or restaurant owned by the corporation. A telephone number is accessed by the operator under the corporate name unless the corporation pays for separate listing. Changes of telephone numbers are ongoing in the capital—numbers that were correct at the time this edition was updated may have changed by the time you visit. So you never know if the number you have is an operating one or not. The local number for information is 04, and you are allowed to request three numbers with each information call. However, reaching the information operator can be difficult, so make every call count. Most coin-operated phones have been replaced by Ladatel phones, which usually accept both coins and Ladatel cards. Ladatel cards are usually available for purchase at pharmacies and newsstands near public phones. They come in denominations of 10, 30, 50, and 100 New Pesos. If you expect to do much calling, buy at least a 30-peso card—the 10-peso card lasts for about 10 minutes' worth of talking. Long-distance calls within Mexico and to foreign points are surprisingly expensive. Consult "Telephones & Mail" in the Appendix for how to use phones. Hotels are beginning to charge for local calls, but budget-priced hotels are less likely to do this because they lack the equipment to track calls from individual rooms.

Weather/Clothing Mexico City's high altitude means you'll need a warm jacket and sweater in winter. The southern parts of the city, such as the university area and Xochimilco, are much colder than the central part of the city. In summer, it gets warm during the day and cool, but not cold, at night. The rainy season runs between May and October (this is common all over Mexico)—take a raincoat or rain poncho. The showers may last all day or for only an hour or two.

3 Accommodations

Luxury hotels in Mexico City can be every bit as plush and expensive as deluxe hotels in the world's other great cities. But you can also stay here in perfectly adequate and comfortable hotels for far less. It costs less to stay in Mexico City than it does in most European capitals or almost any U.S. city of any size. The city is a bargain when you consider that for $20 to $60 you can find a double room in a fairly central hotel complete with a bath and often such extras as air conditioning and TV. Many hotels have their own garages where guests can park free. Most new construction in the last decade has been luxurious hotels with central air conditioning, elevators, restaurants, and the like; these are usually at the top of our range. Cheaper hotels tend to be the older ones, well kept and with a restaurant, but without all the extras that inflate prices.

My recommendations for lodging and dining in Mexico City are grouped around the city's major landmarks, places that are easily found and explored by first-time visitors.

Important note: Hotels catering to business travelers often lower rates Friday through Sunday.

The **Zona Rosa** is Mexico City's Mayfair, Faubourg-St-Honoré, or Central Park West: the status address. The chic boutiques, fancy restaurants and cafes, and expensive hotels are here. **Sullivan Park** (Jardín del Arte) is a wedge-shaped park extending west from the intersection of Paseo de la Reforma and Avenida Insurgentes. It has a good range of hotels, old and new, colonial and modern, flashy and humble. Many are on quiet streets, some have views of the park, and all are close to the Zona Rosa and to transportation.

The **Monumento a la Revolución** is in the large Plaza de la República, at the very western end of Avenida Juárez. Here you're centrally located, about equidistant from the Zona Rosa and the Zócalo, close to the Alameda and major transportation routes, but most of the hotel streets are quiet. The **Alameda Central,** next to the Palacio de Bellas Artes, is closer to the downtown shopping district, a bit farther from the Zona Rosa. Transportation is still good. Most of the hotels are well-used structures on streets to the south of the Alameda. The **Zócalo** is the heart of the historic Mexico City, surrounded by colonial buildings and Aztec ruins. It's also the heart of the downtown shopping district, with interesting small stores to the west and the gigantic Mercado Merced to the east.

CHAPULTEPEC PARK & POLANCO

Hotel Camino Real

Mariano Escobedo 700, México, D.F. 11590. ☎ **5/203-2121,** or 203-3113 or 800/ 722-6466 in the U.S. and Canada. Fax 5/250-6935 or 250-6897. 710 rms. A/C MINIBAR TV TEL. $245–$285 single or double; $300 Executive Club rooms.

Long one of the capital's leading hotels, the Camino Real continues to be so popular that often every room is booked. A Rufino Tamayo mural, "Man Facing Eternity," greets visitors as they enter the front doors, and a mural by José Luis Covarrubias graces the hotel's La Huerta restaurant. No expense is spared as the Camino Real vies to remain one of the capital's hot spots for business and social entertaining. The spacious rooms, all with pastel-colored modern furnishings and a sitting and desk area, come with armoires concealing the television and minibar, in-room safety boxes, hairdryers, remote-control TVs, electronic card door locks, fax connections, and direct dial phones with voice mail. There are only 30 rooms for non-smokers, however, and other rooms are afflicted with the lingering, powerful odor of tobacco smoke. Book early if you need to avoid this. Two rooms are handicap equipped. Executive Club rooms come with bathrobes, continental breakfast and evening cocktail hour, and daily newspaper.

Dining/Entertainment: Fouquet's de Paris is the hotel's best restaurant and one of the capital's top dining establishments (see section 4, "Dining," below). The hotel has other more informal restaurants.

Services: Laundry and dry cleaning, car rental, travel agency, barber and beauty shop, concierge, boutiques, book and gift shop, jewelry store.

Facilities: Full service business center, private conference rooms, complete gym, massage, sauna, steam room, four tennis courts, pool.

Hotel Four Seasons

Reforma 500, Col. Juárez, México, D.F. 06600. ☎ **5/230-1818,** or 800/332-3442 in the U.S., 800/268-6282 in Canada. Fax 5/230-1808. 248 rms and suites. A/C MINIBAR TV TEL. $230–$1,200.

This hotel, built in the style of an elegant Mexican hacienda surrounding a beautiful interior courtyard, is a veritable sanctuary in this busy city. Though you're only steps from the busy Paseo de la Reforma, the grounds inside the eight-story hotel seem more like the quiet countryside around a gracious manor house. On one side of the large and inviting outdoor courtyard there's umbrella-covered al fresco dining with colonnaded walkways all around; other dining rooms and bars face this pleasant scene. Gracious manners are the hallmark of the staff here; rather than point you to an elevator or restaurant, someone will escort you. The airy, huge rooms have high ceilings and are sumptuous to the ultimate degree. Each has plush, thick bedspreads, pastel walls, beautiful talavera pottery lamps and talavera coordinated bathroom accessories, Indonesian tapestries, and rich dark wood furnishings. All rooms have twice-daily maid service (with ice refills), hairdryer, remote-control TV, safety deposit box, fax outlet, separate shower and tub, robes, and illuminated makeup mirrors. Most rooms face the interior courtyard, two deluxe suites have patios facing the courtyard, and most Executive Suites (with one or two separate bedrooms) overlook Reforma. Thirty rooms are reserved for nonsmokers and there are two handicap-equipped rooms. The Four Seasons is located at the western end of the Zona Rosa, near Chapultepec Park and Polanco and opposite the Hotel Marquis Reforma.

Dining/Entertainment: The fine-dining spot here features low-key live entertainment. A more informal dining option is open for all three meals. El Salón is a cozy bar, and the Lobby Lounge, open from 4pm to midnight, is like a series of gracious living rooms with comfortable couch-and-chair groupings and an excellent atmosphere for conversation.

Services: Laundry, dry cleaning, room service, private specialist-led tours to the capital's museums, concierge, boutiques, beauty and barber shop.

Facilities: Spa with completely equipped gym, sauna, massage, whirlpool, swimming pool, complete business center with private meeting rooms.

Hotel Marquis Reforma

Reforma 465, Col. Cuauhtémoc, México, D.F. 06500. ☎ **5/211-3600,** 211-0577, or 800/525-4800 in the U.S. Fax 5/211-5561. 116 rms, 84 suites. MINIBAR TV TEL. $260 single or double; $435–$460 suites.

With an art deco exterior and elegant combinations of glass, marble, and rich dark mahogany within, the Marquis Reforma opened in 1991 as one of the city's state-of-the-art luxury hotels. For its quality it's also a member of Small Luxury Hotels of the World. Excellently located, it's at the eastern end of Chapultepec Park opposite the Four Seasons—Regent and western end of the Zona Rosa, and it's almost equidistant between the U.S. Embassy and the Chapultepec/Polanco area. Among the standard amenities in each luxuriously furnished room are full-length mirrors, lighted makeup mirror, bathrobe, fax outlet, remote-control TV with U.S. channels, and an in-room safe large enough for a camera, laptop computer, and more. Rooms are quite varied in shape and size. Some have terraces; some have separate living-, dining-, and bedrooms; some have an attached meeting room; and standard double rooms have a king-size bed and small sitting area. The Suite Reforma has a view of the Castillo de Chapultepec. The fourth floor is for non-smokers and there's one handicap-equipped room. Guests staying in first or second floor Diamond floor rooms have separate check-in and check-out and receive complimentary continental breakfast as well as late afternoon cocktails and appetizers. When I checked, the hotel reserved Diamond floor rooms directly, rather than through its toll-free number.

Dining/Entertainment: There are two restaurants, one of which specializes in northern Italian food. An elegant musical quartet entertains nightly in the lobby Caviar Bar where tea, drinks, and light meals are served.

Services: Laundry and room service, hair salon, newsstand with small drug section, concierge, car rental, travel agency, bookstore, florist, video recorders, computers and fax machines for rent, electric adapters and converters on request. Golf privileges at a local course.

Facilities: Complete business center, fitness center with workout equipment, massage service, three whirlpools and sauna and steam rooms, parking adjacent to hotel.

Hotel Nikko

Campos Elíseos 204, Col. Polanco, México, D.F. 11560. ☎ **5/280-1111,** or 800/NIKKO-US in the U.S. Fax 5/280-8965 or 280-9191. 750 rms. A/C MINIBAR TV TEL. $265 deluxe; $300 Executive floors; $575–$1400 suites.

One of the best hotels in the city, with 38 floors and plushly decorated rooms, the Nikko is located opposite Chapultepec Park and the Auditorio Nacional, near all the Chapultepec Park museums. It blends modern comfort and convenience with traditional Asian decorating styles, making for a world-class hotel with a hint of the Far East. Rooms, which are quiet and spacious, are accessed with electronic keys. When I visited, some amenities standard in other hotels of this class were lacking—in-room security boxes, voice mail, purified tap water. (Security boxes and remote control for the television are available at the front desk, and electric plug adapters are found at the concierge.) These deficiencies may all disappear during the life of this book, since the Nikko is a top hotel. Nonsmokers have two floors reserved for them. Handicapped clients will find four specially equipped rooms. Two floors are "Nikko Floors," with special check-in and checkout, concierge service, and a lounge for continental breakfast and evening cocktails.

Dining/Entertainment: Of the hotel's four restaurants two offer Japanese cuisine, one offers French, and another is international with a Mexican and American slant. Shelty Bar, with an English theme, often features live music; there's also a lobby bar and a disco.

Services: Laundry and dry cleaning, room service, beauty and barber shop, boutiques, art gallery, jewelry shop, car rental, and travel agency.

Facilities: Indoor glass-topped pool, three tennis courts, practice court, fitness center, steam and sauna, whirlpool, massage, jogging track.

Hotel Presidente Inter-Continental

Campos Elíseos 218, Col. Polanco, México, D.F. 11560. ☎ **5/327-7700,** or 800/327-0200 in the U.S. and Canada. Fax 5/327-7737. 635 rms, 34 suites. A/C MINIBAR TV TEL. $325–$335 single or double; $370 Club floor.

Opposite Chapultepec Park, next to the Nikko Hotel, this 42-story hotel was the first luxury hotel in the area and has been admirably kept up. The enormous lobby, with its sitting areas and off-lobby bars and restaurants, holds some of the capital's most popular meeting places. Rooms at this distinguished hotel are spacious, quiet, and nicely furnished, with many talavera pottery accents. All have remote control televisions, magnified and lighted makeup mirrors, hairdryers, and purified tap water. One of the best perks of staying here is the complimentary coffee or tea that arrives at the door just after a wake-up call (if you request it in advance). All suites have fax machines. Three-pronged and European electrical outlets were being added. Safety deposit boxes are at the front desk. Phones have direct access to international operators, but there's no voice mail. Rooms on the 28th and 29th floors are reserved for nonsmokers and 24 rooms on the 14th floor are equipped for the handicapped. Parking is available but costs $20 daily.

Dining/Entertainment: Maxim's de Paris is an elegant French restaurant. The hotel also has an elegant tea room, a 24-hour coffee shop, a seafood restaurant, a bar/grill, and a cafe with al fresco dining.

Services: Laundry, dry cleaning, beauty and barber shops, boutiques, bookstore, gift shop, art gallery, florist, travel agency, car rental.

Facilities: Full service business center with meeting rooms on the 12th floor, complete gym on the 10th floor.

ZONA ROSA
VERY EXPENSIVE

Hotel María Isabel Sheraton
Reforma 325, at Río Tiber, México, D.F. 06500. ☎ **5/207-3933,** or 800/325-3535 in the U.S. Fax 5/207-0684. 750 rms, 64 suites. A/C MINIBAR TV TEL. $125–$190 single or double; $190–$230 Tower suites (these are "super saver" rates, which are the lowest rates).

The María Isabel Sheraton set the original standard for luxury hotels in Mexico City, and it continues to hold its own against newer competition. Its location in front of the Monumento a la Independencia is ideal, next to the U.S. Embassy and across Reforma from the heart of the Zona Rosa. The plush marble lobby hums with the comings and goings of foreign guests and the efficient activity of hotel personnel. In all its rooms the hotel offers amenities such as hairdryers and magnified makeup mirrors, purified tap water, three-pronged electrical outlets, and telephone voice mail. Three floors are reserved for non-smokers, and seven rooms are outfitted for handicapped guests. Tower suites, the most deluxe in the hotel, occupy the fourth floor and have private check-in, butler service, continental breakfast and evening canapés, remote control TV, and robes.

Dining/Entertainment: The hotel's three restaurants, serving Italian and international foods, are very popular. There's a Fiesta Mexicana Monday through Friday from 7 to 10pm. The Jorongo Bar offers live entertainment nightly. (See section 7, "Mexico City After Dark," below, for more on the Jorongo.)

Services: Laundry, dry cleaning, room service, travel agency, beauty and barber shop, concierge, boutiques, art galleries, jewelry stores, first-floor business center.

Facilities: Complete business center with computers, workout facilities, two tennis courts, pool.

EXPENSIVE

Hotel Krystal
Liverpool 155, México, D.F. 06600. ☎ **5/228-9928,** or 800/231-9860 in the U.S. Fax 5/511-3480. 288 rms, 14 suites. A/C MINIBAR TV TEL. $155 single or double; $285–$328 junior suite; $220 Club room.

Foreigners have tended to overlook the stylish Krystal among the Zona Rosa's numerous posh accommodations. There's really no good reason—located in the heart of the Zona Rosa at the corner of Liverpool and Amberes, the Krystal belongs to one of the best Mexican-owned chains, with a reputation for quality and service. In the enormous yet cozy lobby, a lake of white marble floors is covered with oriental carpets and potted plant groupings, which help separate the comfortable seating areas. Rooms, which are large and bright, have neutral-colored wood furniture and pastel fabrics on beds and drapes. All rooms come with direct-dial phones, voice mail, purified tap water, electronic card door lock, and in-room safety box. Electrical adapters are available from the concierge. Floors 5 and 16 are no-smoking floors, and there's one handicap-equipped room. Rooms in the three floors of the Krystal Club have separate check-in and checkout, hairdryers, robes and magnified makeup mirrors, complimentary daily newspaper, continental breakfast and afternoon canapés and cocktails.

Dining/Entertainment: Of the hotel's two restaurants, the finest is Kamakura, featuring the best foods of Japan (see section 4, "Dining," below). Maquiavelo, the hotel's entertainment club, features taped music from 1pm to 5pm and live jazz at night.

Services: Laundry and dry cleaning, room service, ice machines on each floor, travel agency, car rental, boutiques.

Facilities: First-floor business center, heated swimming pool.

Hotel Westin Galeria Plaza

Hamburgo 195, Col. Juárez, México, D.F. 06600. ☎ 5/230-1717, or 800/228-3000 in the U.S. Fax 5/207-5867. 415 rms, 19 suites. A/C MINIBAR TV. $201 standard double; $230 Executive Club; $300 Premier suite; $362 junior suite.

This Westin-operated hotel is excellent for its location and top-quality amenities. The lobby bar is one of the capital's most popular meeting places. Standard rooms and suites are stylishly furnished in soft pastels and natural wood. All rooms have electronic key cards, remote control TV, illuminated magnified makeup mirror, hairdryer, purified tap water, and in-room safety deposit box. Premier Suites are equipped with a computer, laser printer, and fax machine. Executive Club rooms on the 10th and 11th floors have 24-hour concierge service, robes, hairdryers, continental breakfast, coffee, tea, and cookies all day, and late-afternoon drinks and hot refreshments. On the 5th floor, 42 rooms have been reserved for nonsmokers. Two rooms are reserved for handicapped guests. It's two blocks from the Monumento a la Independencia near the corner of Florencia. Parking is available for $10 daily.

Dining/Entertainment: There's a fine-dining restaurant, a more casual spot, and a breakfast restaurant; the lobby bar has live music in the evenings.

Services: Laundry and dry cleaning, room service, business center, voice mail, boutiques, beauty and barber shop, bookstore, flower and gift shop, car rental, cellular phone rental, travel agency, 24-hour money exchange.

Facilities: Full business center; pool with fully equipped gym, sauna, and whirlpool; golf privileges at nearby country club.

Hotel Calinda Geneve Quality Inn

Londres 130, México, D.F. 06600. ☎ 5/211-0071, or 800/228-5151 in the U.S. Fax 5/208-7422. 337 rms. A/C MINIBAR TV TEL. $156 double.

Probably one of the capital's most popular hotels, the Geneve has been receiving guests for more than 50 years. The lobby is always teeming with travelers who've chosen it for its comfort and convenience—the location is top-notch. It's just steps from all the Zona Rosa restaurants and shops. Rooms are fresh and modern with colonial-style furniture, though you may want to request one on the upper floors; lobby noise has a way of traveling in this hotel. Problems with the new phones installed a few years ago haven't been ironed out; the old interior system continues to cross lines and the like, and you can't count on your phone working. There's a casual restaurant to the left of the lobby after you enter, but the hot spot here is El Jardín, a restaurant/bar with gorgeous stained-glass walls. The hotel is at the corner of Londres and Genova.

AROUND THE ZONA ROSA

Casa González

Río Sena 69, México, D.F. 06500. ☎ **5/514-3302.** 21 rms, 1 suite (all with bath). $23–$27 double; $40 suite for four. Metro: Insurgentes (four blocks away.)

Casa González is a two-story hostelry made up of two mansions that have been converted to hold guest rooms, each of which is unique. The houses, with little grassy patios out back and a huge shade tree, make a pleasant and quiet oasis in the middle of the city. Meals (optional) are taken in a dining room bright with stained glass. The price for a single is exceptionally low, but there are only two. There's limited parking in the driveway. Casa González is especially good for women traveling alone. The hotel is between Río Lerma and Río Panuco.

Hotel Regente

Paris 9, México, D.F. 06030. ☎ **5/566-8933.** Fax 5/593-5794. 132 rms (all with bath). TV TEL. $40–$47 double. Free parking. Metro: Revolución or Insurgentes.

This remodeled hotel is within walking distance of Sullivan Park, the Alameda, and the Zona Rosa. Once a frumpy hotel with mismatched furnishings and a horrible phone system, today it's state-of-the-art. Rooms have matching bedspreads and drapes; carpeted floors themed around pastel green, gray and blue; overbed reading lights; full-length mirrors; and new tile baths. The hotel's excellent Restaurant Corinto, open daily from 7am to 11pm, is off the lobby. The hotel is in the triangle formed by Insurgentes Centro, Antonio Caso, and Reforma.

NEAR SULLIVAN PARK

Ⓢ Hotel Mallorca

Serapio Rendon 119, Mexico, D. F. 06470. ☎ **5/566-4833.** Fax 5/566-1789. 150 rms. TV TEL. $31–$35 double. Free parking.

Almost catercorner from the Hotel Compostela and opposite the western end of the Jardín del Arte, the nine-story (with elevator) Mallorca is an excellent budget choice. Rooms are freshly painted and bedspreads coordinate with the drapes. Single rooms with a twin or double bed are small, however. The hotel is at the corner of Sullivan and Rendon.

NEAR THE MONUMENTO A LA REVOLUCIÓN
VERY EXPENSIVE

Hotel Fiesta Americana Reforma

Reforma 80, México D.F., 06600. ☎ **5/705-1515,** or 800/223-2332 in the U.S. Fax 5/705-1313. 628 rms. A/C MINIBAR TV TEL. $185–$210 double; $205 Executive Suites floor.

The Fiesta America Reforma is one of the city's premier hotels, and you can always be assured of a comfortable stay here. Its location between the Alameda and the Zona Rosa is a good one, and the hotel caters to both vacationers and business travelers, with 25 floors of stylish, sizeable rooms that overlook Columbus Circle on Reforma and one of the most efficient telephone systems in town. All rooms come equipped with remote-control TV, robes, electronic card locks, voice mail and purified tap water. Security boxes are at the front desk. The 20th floor is a no-smoking floor; there's a handicap-equipped room on this floor as well. The three floors of Executive Suites have a private, express, key-operated elevator, and rooms on these floors have hairdryers and magnified makeup mirrors; the price for these suites includes continental breakfast, afternoon canapés, and 24-hour concierge.

Dining/Entertainment: Of the hotel's three restaurants, two are standouts even with locals: Maximilian's (see listing in "Dining," below) and La Hacienda Steak House and Bar. The Lobby Bar offers jazz and other live entertainment daily from 11am to 1am. The hotel has three nightclubs: Caballo Negro, Barbarela, and Las Sillas.

Services: Laundry and dry cleaning, room service, beauty and barber shop, travel agency, car rental, babysitting, florist.

Facilities: Business center; gym, with sauna, massage, and beauty shop.

EXPENSIVE

Hotel Sevilla Palace

Reforma 105, México, D.F. 06030. ☎ **5/566-8877,** or 800/732-9488 in the U.S. Fax 5/703-1521. 413 rms and suites. A/C MINIBAR TV TEL. $132 double; $200–$330 suite.

Although the Sevilla Palace is top quality in every way, it's another of those hotels overlooked by foreigners that deserves more attention. Its soaring lobby is embellished with teak-stained wood and burgundy marble and has four glass elevators whizzing up and down. Rooms are large, handsomely furnished, and all have remote-control TV, direct dial phones with voice mail, in-room safety boxes, electronic card locks, and hairdryers. Most rooms have large showers and a couch with a sitting/table area. Three-prong electrical adapters are available at the reception desk. The 21st floor is reserved for nonsmokers. The toll-free number listed above answers in Mexico and *may* only be answered Monday through Friday from 9am to 6pm. Free parking is available.

Dining/Entertainment: There's a fine-dining restaurant (El Lepanto), a more casual spot (Los Naranjos), and a lobby bar with evening piano entertainment.

Services: Laundry and room service, ice machines on each floor, travel agency, beauty and barber shop, gift shop, newsstand.

Facilities: Business center, workout room with enclosed swimming pool and whirlpool.

MODERATE

Hotel Casa Blanca

Lafragua 7, México, D.F. 06030. ☎ **5/566-3211,** or 800/972-2162 in the U.S. Fax 5/705-4197. 248 rms, 22 suites. A/C TV TEL. $64–$103 double. Metro: "Revolución" or "Hidalgo" (5 long blocks away); the hotel is between Antonio Caso and Plaza de la República.

Just a few steps off the Plaza de la República, Hotel Casa Blanca is located on a quiet street only a block or so from Reforma and Avenida Juárez. It's been a dependably comfortable, friendly, and efficient place to stay for many years. Amenities found in much more expensive hotels are found here at a fraction of the price. Renovation is giving the rooms a light and airy feel. The lower rates quoted are for rooms that have not been remodeled. They're fine rooms, but the wood accents are dark, making the room seem more somber than the refurbished ones. All rooms have purified tap water, full-length mirrors, in-room safety deposit boxes, over-bed reading lights with bedside switches, remote-control TV (with U.S. channels), and direct-dial phones. Several rooms are equipped for the handicapped and several are reserved for nonsmokers. Single rooms, with one double or one twin-size bed, are small, but other rooms are substantially larger. Several suites have saunas and separate living/conference rooms. The small kidney-shaped swimming pool and sun deck on the hotel's top floor goes undiscovered by most guests, making it a wonderfully quiet—almost private—getaway. Free parking is available.

The hotel offers laundry and dry cleaning, room service, concierge, car rental, travel agency, beauty and barber shop, ice machines on each floor, babysitting. There's a rooftop pool. Hotel office fax and copier are available to guests.

INEXPENSIVE

ⓢ Hotel Edison

Edison 106, México, D.F. 06030. ☎ **5/566-0933.** 45 rms (all with bath). TV TEL. $23–$25 double. Metro: Revolución (two blocks away).

The Hotel Edison, a block from the Monumento a la Revolución, is a real find. Its odd three-story construction around a narrow court with grass and trees gives a sense of sanctuary from the city's noise and bustle. Some rooms are built in tiers overlooking the court, and even larger ones are hidden away down hallways. These latter rooms tend to be dark but big and comfortable with huge king-size beds. Blond wood and light colors, piped-in music, and sunlight make this a cheerful place. All rooms include baths with separate washbasin areas, and some have bidets, plus tub/shower combinations. The hotel is between Iglesias and Arriaga.

Hotel Mayaland

António Caso 23, México, D.F. 06030. ☎ **5/566-6066.** Fax 5/535-1273. 91 rms (all with bath). TV TEL. $32–$34 double. Metro: Juárez (3¹/₂ blocks away).

This conveniently located six-story hotel features coordinated drapes and spreads in its pleasant rooms. Baths have an additional faucet for purified water. You can't miss the Maya mural on one lobby wall, and another stained-glass wall separate the lobby from the hotel's small restaurant. The hotel is between González and Bucareli.

NEAR THE ALAMEDA CENTRAL

Hotel Capitol

Uruguay 12, México, D.F. 06050. ☎ **5/518-1750.** Fax 5/521-1149. 76 rms, 3 suites (all with bath). TV TEL. $29–$34 double; $62 suite. Metro: Bellas Artes or Salto de Agua (five blocks away).

A welcome addition to the lineup of Alameda/Zócalo area hotels is the four-story Capitol, which opened in late 1989. Rooms open to the lobby atrium, and there's a restaurant in back. You'll find such extras as carpeting and reading lights. Each double room is furnished with either a king-size bed or two doubles. Rooms and baths are large, except for the three "suites," which are tiny but have enormous whirlpool tubs big enough for two. Rooms along the front have small balconies opening to Uruguay, while others have interior windows opening to the lobby atrium. It's within walking distance of the Alameda, Bellas Artes, and historic Zócalo. The hotel is between Cárdenas and Bolívar.

✪ Hotel El Salvador

República Del Salvador 16, México, D.F. 06000. ☎ and fax **5/521-1247,** or 521-2160. 94 rms (all with bath). TV TEL. $28 double. Free parking. Metro: Salto de Agua (six blocks away).

The five-story El Salvador, half a block off Lázaro Cárdenas, completed a total remodeling in 1994. The impressive new lobby, aswirl in beige marble, is up a wide staircase from the sidewalk. Rooms have natural-colored pine furniture, fresh stucco and paint, carpeting, overbed reading lights, and coordinated pastel drapes and spreads. Baths are small, but there's plenty of room for luggage storage, either in the closets or on built-in benches. Halls are narrow and dark, with only a few lights visible during the day. A small restaurant is adjacent. It's a very nice and convenient place to stay at budget prices. The hotel is between Cárdenas and Bolívar.

✪ Hotel Fleming

Revillagigedo 35, México, D.F. 06050. ☎ **5/510-4530.** 75 rms (all with bath). TV TEL. $35 double; $45 room with whirlpool tub. Free parking. Metro: Juárez.

If you stayed at the Fleming in the past, you won't recognize it now. In 1992, the mismatched ancient furnishings gave way to soft cool colors, coordinated carpeting and textiles, mirrored closet doors, and updated baths—even some with whirlpool tubs. Each room comes with either one king-size bed, two doubles, or two twin-size beds. The hotel's clean, dependable restaurant is off the lobby. It's excellently located near the Alameda and within walking distance of the Zócalo. The hotel is between Articulo 123 and Victoria.

Hotel Metropol

Luís Moya 39, México, D.F. 06050. ☎ **5/521-4901,** or 510-8660. Fax 5/512-1273. 165 rms (all with bath). A/C TV TEL. $45 double. Parking $1.75 per hour. Metro: Juárez (two blocks away).

After a total facelift, each room at the Metropol is beautifully furnished and carpeted, with a safety deposit box, a color TV broadcasting U.S. channels, and purified water from a special tap. If the essence of luxury is what you want at relatively low prices, this is the place. The location is choice—within walking distance of both the Zócalo and the Alameda. The hotel is between Articulo 123 and Independencia.

NEAR THE ZÓCALO
MODERATE

Best Western Hotel Majestic

Av. Madero 73, México, D.F. 06000. ☎ **5/521-8600,** or 800/528-1234 in the U.S. Fax 5/518-3466. 85 rms (all with bath). A/C TV TEL. $88 or double. Metro: Zócalo.

You can save a quite a few dollars by booking direct with the hotel, and by asking for promotional rates or current discounts. Otherwise you're paying a lot for location. Still, the Majestic is somewhat of a Mexico City institution that everyone should experience at least once, precisely because of it's location on the Zócalo. The Majestic has rooms that look onto Mexico City's main square, Avenida Madero, or the hotel's own inner court. From the lobby, a place of stone arches, beautiful tiles, and stone fountains, take the elevator to the second floor and its courtyard, with a floor of glass blocks set with sofas, tables, and chairs great for gazing all the way up to the glass roof six stories above. Each doorway has a border of blue-and-white tiles.

The adequately furnished rooms have dated furniture, and tile baths with tubs. In lower-floor rooms facing Avenida Madero noise from the street may be a problem—you may not go for the quieter rooms that look out onto the interior court (people look in on you!)—but on the upper floors and in the rooms that front on the Zócalo you needn't worry about voyeurs. On the other hand, occupants of rooms facing the Zócalo will have the unexpected jolt of the early-morning flag-raising ceremony, complete with marching feet, drums, and bugle. The finishing touch to the Majestic is a popular rooftop cafe/restaurant with umbrella-shaded tables for all three meals.

INEXPENSIVE

✪ Hotel Canada

Av. Cinco de Mayo No. 47, México, D.F. 06000. ☎ **5/518-2106.** Fax 5/512-9310. 85 rms, (all with bath). TV TEL. $26–$28 double. Metro: Zócalo (1¹/₂ blocks away).

The Hotel Canada, opened in 1984, has an up-to-date decor, Formica furnishings, double or king beds, and showers. It's comfortable and so different from the rest of the downtown hotels, which tend to be older and somewhat worn. The hotel is between Isabel la Católica and Palma.

Hotel Catedral

Calle Donceles 95, México, D.F. 06010. ☎ **5/518-5232.** Fax 5/512-4344. 116 rms (all with bath). TV TEL. $37 double. Parking available. Metro: Zócalo.

One block north of Tacuba is Calle Donceles, a street noted for its bookstores, stationery stores, and gunsmith shops. Here, set back from the street by a shopping arcade, is the six-story (with elevator) Hotel Catedral, half a block from the Templo Mayor and very popular with Mexico's middle class. In front of the big cool lobby is the restaurant/bar, bustling with white-jacketed waiters. Rooms are well kept, and some have tub/shower combinations. Bonuses are a bar, a parking garage next door, good housekeeping standards, and rooms on the upper floors with views of Mexico City's mammoth cathedral. The hotel is between Brasil and Argentina.

✪ Hotel Gillow

Isabel la Católica 17, México, D.F. 06000. ☎ **5/518-1440.** Fax 5/512-2078. 110 rms (all with bath). TV TEL. $34 double. Metro: Zócalo.

Personal friends and many readers give this hotel high praise. From the lobby, the six-story Gillow appears to be among the simple but dignified older downtown Mexico City hotels. But take one of the two elevators up to the guest rooms and you'll discover behind the dignified facade a modern hotel with five stories of rooms grouped around a long glass-canopied rectangular courtyard with a colonial fountain. The clean rooms boast new tile-and-marble baths and a feeling of cheery comfort. Interior windows open to an airshaft. There's a restaurant on the first floor. The hotel is at the corner of 5 de Mayo. The hotel is between 5 de Mayo and Madero.

NEAR THE AIRPORT
EXPENSIVE

Ramada Inn Aeropuerto

Blv. Aeropuerto 502, México, D.F. 15620. ☎ **5/785-8522,** or 800/228-9898. Fax 5/762-9934. 324 rms. A/C MINIBAR TV TEL. $135–$170 double. Transportation: Wait for the courtesy van under the white Ramada Inn shelter in front of the airport.

This Ramada Inn is close to the airport; to get there, call from the Holiday Inn phone in the airport terminal and the courtesy van will take you on a circuitous block-long ride to the hotel. Recently revamped, the hotel has taken great steps toward improving its sagging image. The staff is attentive and the rooms are fashionably furnished, each with color TV with U.S. channels and purified water from the tap. You'll find several restaurants, a bar, a disco, and a pool and workout facilities. The hotel also provides a courtesy van to the airport, but those with early flights should leave in plenty of time since the demand for transportation may be greater than the vans can handle.

INEXPENSIVE

Hotel Riazor

Viaducto Miguel Alemán 297, México, D.F. 08310. ☎ **5/726-9998.** Fax 5/654-3840. 175 rms (all with bath). TV TEL. $38–$47 double. Transportation: Take a taxi from the airport.

The six-story Riazor is only a short cab ride from the airport. You can take shelter in any one of the modern, comfy rooms, each complete with king-size bed, shower, and perhaps even a view of the city. There are a pool, restaurant, and bar. The hotel fills up by nightfall, but if you arrive early there's a good chance to get a room.

4 Dining

The capital of Mexico is also the dining capital of the country. Some of the country's top restaurants are here. And you can expect to find the cuisines of the world—German, Japanese, Italian, French, pre-Hispanic—you name it. Cantinas, until not so long ago the privilege of men only, offer some of the best food and colorful local atmosphere. Some of the best cantinas are mentioned in this chapter. Other cantinas may be too local for touristic taste—women may get hassled and men cajoled to fight.

Everybody eats out in Mexico City—from the wealthy executive to the peasant. Consequently, you can find restaurants of every type, size, and price range scattered across the city. Mexicans take their food and dining seriously too, so wherever you see a full house that's generally recommendation enough. But those same places may be entirely empty if you arrive early.

I have not described American-type chains such as McDonald's, Subway, Burger King, Pizza Hut, Vip's, Denny's and Lyni's—but you'll see them frequently. The latter three—which have branches all over the city—have familiar fare at reasonable prices.

In the more expensive restaurants, particularly in the Zona Rosa, you'll be able to pay with a major credit card.

CHAPULTEPEC & POLANCO
VERY EXPENSIVE

✪ Fouquets de Paris

In the Hotel Camino Real, Mariano Escobedo 700. ☎ **5/203-2121**, ext. 8500. Reservations recommended for dinner. Main courses $18.50–$26.50. Daily 7–10:30am, 2–4:30pm, and 7–11:30pm. Metro: "Chapultepec." INTERNATIONAL.

Polanco/Chapultepec Area

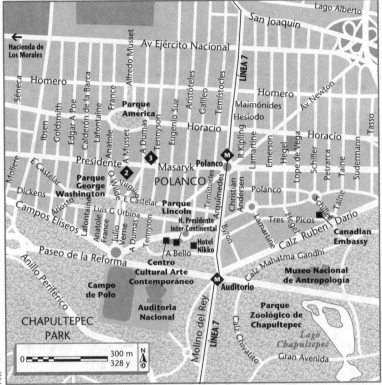

Dining at Fouquets de Paris is a culinary experience of the first order, made all the better by the elegant atmosphere and refined service. Government ministers, senators and visiting dignitaries often dine here. And this is a popular place for those trendy power breakfasts; the morning menu mixes creative combinations of Mexican and international cuisines—for example, crêpes with machaca (dried beef) and eggs, huitlacoche omelettes, or omelettes with morel mushrooms and artichokes—with traditional breakfast fare such as hotcakes. For other meals you might consider lobster bisque, asparagus and crawfish in a puff pastry, rack of lamb, beef tenderloin, or veal in morel mushrooms. For men, a jacket and tie is required. Highly recommended.

Hacienda de Los Morales

Vazquez de Mella 525. ☎ **540-3225,** or 202-1973. Reservations required. Main courses $15–$65. Mon–Sat 1pm–midnight. MEXICAN/AMERICAN/CONTINENTAL.

The Hacienda de los Morales, which resides in a great Spanish colonial house not far from Chapultepec Park, has been a favorite of visitors and locals for years. Within the house are a cocktail lounge with entertainment, numerous richly decorated dining rooms, and a plant-filled inner courtyard. The service is polished, the food delicious. In the evenings men are required to wear jackets and ties. The restaurant is northwest of Chapultepec Park at the corner of Avenida Ejercito Nacional.

EXPENSIVE

✪ Fonda del Recuerdo

Bahía de las Palmas 39. ☎ **545-7260.** Reservations not accepted. Main courses $8.50–$25.50. Mon–Sat 1pm–midnight. MEXICAN/SEAFOOD.

For an all-out good time, no other restaurant in the city compares to this one. Diners at Fonda del Recuerdo enjoy their platters of Mexican food amid a glorious din created by *jarocho* musicians from Veracruz (there will be several groups roving around the restaurant at once). Come here if you want to immerse yourself in Mexico and join people eating, drinking, and singing, having the time of their lives. The menu is authentically Mexican, with an emphasis on seafood; specials match the culinary traditions of whichever Mexican holiday is closest on the calendar. Arrive before 1:30pm for lunch or you'll have to wait in a long line—which will nonetheless be worth it if you have all afternoon for lunch. At night it's just as festive, but try to make it before 9pm, when it begins to get crowded.

IN & AROUND THE ZONA ROSA
VERY EXPENSIVE

✪ Cicero Centenario

Londres 195. ☎ **533-3800.** Reservations recommended. Main courses $18–$42. Mon–Sat 7pm–2am. Metro: "Insurgentes." INTERNATIONAL/NOUVELLE MEXICAN.

Cicero Centenario is the epitome of the capital's elegant cafe society. Tables in the intimate nooks of the restaurant's leafy salons look out on a dim backdrop of stained glass and flickering candlelight. There are two menus here: among the heights of the main menu are a delectable cream of morrel mushroom soup, an excellent Caesar salad, and main dishes like chicken in a rich almond sauce and red snapper in green sauce. The second and smaller menu features recipes developed for the restaurant by noted chef and author Patricia Quintana. The restaurant is between Florencia and Amberes.

Restaurant Angus

Copenhague 21, near the corner of Hamburgo. ☎ **207-3747,** or 522-8633. Reservations recommended. Main courses $16–$23; steaks $8.50–$25. Daily 1pm–12:45am. Metro: "Insurgentes." STEAKS.

Restaurant Angus is the place to go in the D.F. when you want nothing so much as a good, juicy steak. The refined interior features lots of dark wood and brass, there's outdoor dining under a green awning with brass rails on cafe-lined Copenhague (recently expanded, it's as popular as ever). The clientele is a mix of business types clad in suits and others dressed a bit more casually. All variety of steaks are served here, and there's prime rib and fajitas as well. A few shrimp selections may satisfy those who don't want beef.

EXPENSIVE

Kamakura Japanese Restaurant and Sushi Bar

At the Hotel Krystal, Liverpool 155, corner of Amberes. ☎ **511-8308.** Reservations recommended for dinner. Main courses $7–$30. Daily 1–11:30pm. Metro: "Insurgentes." JAPANESE.

This streetside restaurant of the Hotel Krystal's garden is a serene retreat any time of day. Select your Japanese favorite—teppanyaki, shabu shabu, sushi, and others are offered—then watch the meal as it's prepared. If you aren't familiar with all a Japanese meal offers, the menu has full descriptions in Spanish and English.

Restaurant Passy

Amberes 10. ☎ **511-0257.** Reservations recommended. Main courses $10–$20. Mon–Sat 1–11pm. Metro: Insurgentes. INTERNATIONAL.

The Restaurant Passy is an elegant old favorite of locals and tourists alike. The attractive, classic, and restrained decor features low lights, antiques, linen, and candles. The service is polished and polite, and the menu is traditional French: Oysters Rockefeller, onion or oyster soup, chicken Cordon Bleu, canard (duck) à l'orange, and coq au vin are among the continental favorites. There's also a good selection of fish. Passy is opposite the Honfleur restaurant. It's between Reforma and Hamburgo.

MODERATE

Café Konditori

Genova 61. ☎ **208-1846.** Main courses $6–$12; coffee and dessert $5–$7. Daily 8am–midnight. Metro: "Insurgentes"; it's between Hamburgo and Londres. DANISH.

Located in the Zona Rosa, the Café Konditori advertises itself as a Danish restaurant, bar, and coffee shop. It's not what you'd call aggressively Danish, but it does have a very pleasant sidewalk-cafe section. You can sit out in the open air in good weather (which is nearly always) or by a window in the restaurant proper anytime. Choose from 11 different coffees. The cappuccino is the perfect accompaniment for one of the Konditori's luscious cakes or tarts. Be sure to inspect the dessert display before you sit. The cafe is open for breakfast, lunch, and dinner.

✪ Chalet Suizo

Niza 37. ☎ **511-7529.** Main courses $6–$20. Daily 12:30pm–midnight. INTERNATIONAL.

One of the most dependable and cozy restaurants around, Chalet Suizo features Swiss decor, of course: checkered tablecloths, pine walls, beamed ceilings, and alpine landscapes. The menu features hearty French onion soup and a wide range of interesting entrees, some of which are changed daily. Among these are veal with morel mushrooms, smoked pork chops, German-style pot roast, chicken tarragon, veal goulash, sauerbraten, and excellent fondue. The food is delicious, the portions are large, and the service is friendly and quick.One caveat: The bread and butter placed on your table is not included in the price of the meal and cost extra. It's between Hamburgo and Londres.

✪ Fonda El Refugio

Liverpool 166. ☎ **207-2732,** or 525-8128. Main courses $9–$12. Mon–Sat 1pm–midnight. Metro: Insurgentes. MEXICAN.

Fonda El Refugio, with service, food, and an atmosphere shaped by more than 40 years of tradition, is a very special place to dine a la mexicana. Although small, it's unusually congenial, with a large fireplace decorated with gleaming copper pots and pans; rows and rows of culinary awards and citations hang behind the desk. The restaurant manages the almost impossible task of being elegant and informal at the same time. The menu runs the gamut of Mexican cuisine—arroz con platanos (rice with fried bananas) to enchiladas con mole poblano, topped with the rich, thick, spicy chocolate sauce of Puebla. There's a daily specialty; for example, on Tuesday it's manchamanteles (tablecloth stainer) and on Saturday it's albondigas en chile chipotle (meatballs in chipotle sauce). Fonda El Refugio is very popular, especially on Saturday night, so get there early. It's between Florencia and Amberes.

NEAR THE MONUMENTO A LA REVOLUCIÓN

✪ Maximilians

Hotel Fiesta Americana Reforma, Reforma 80. ☎ **705-1515.** Reservations recommended. Main courses $17–$51. Mon–Fri 8–11am and 1–11:30pm, Sat 7:30–11:30pm. INTERNATIONAL.

Taking in Maximilians from the street, you'll notice the distinctive accordion sheers covering a wall of windows. Inside the small serene restaurant, tables are situated in intimate groupings on several minilevels. Muted lighting and a pianist's soft tickling of the ivory contributes to the atmosphere. A large selection of starters, including a pannequete of smoked salmon and deliciously fresh spinach salad, will pique appetites. Fish, chicken, and beef entrees include such stand-bys as fillet of sole and (most days) roast duckling. For dessert it's worth the wait to try pears with toffee, an artistic creation of pastry and pears swimming in a delicious yellow and red sauce.

NEAR THE ALAMEDA

✪ Restaurant Danúbio

Uruguay 3. ☎ **512-0912.** Main courses $6–$15; comida corrida $9. Daily 1pm–midnight (comida corrida served 1–4pm). Metro: Bellas Artes or Salto de Agua. INTERNATIONAL.

Elbow your way past the crowds for a gigantic fixed-price comida corrida that's practically an institution—it's plenty for two. A typical lunch consists of a shrimp or oyster cocktail, maybe Valencia soup or tomato consommé, boiled lentils, a choice of hot or cold fish dish, a choice of three main courses, custard or fruit, and coffee or tea. The à la carte menu is extensive, but you get better service during the busy time if you stick to the fixed-price meal. An upstairs room accommodates the lunchtime overflow. The house specialty, langostinos (baby crayfish), are well worth the splurge! The restauant is south of the Alameda at the corner of Lázaro Cárdenas.

Sanborn's Casa de Azulejos

Madero 4. ☎ **518-6676.** Main courses $4.50–$10; dessert and coffee $2–$4. Daily 7:30am–11pm. Metro: Bellas Artes. MEXICAN/AMERICAN.

Located in Sanborn's House of Tiles, this gorgeous antique building was once the palace of the counts of the Valley of Orizaba. For many years now it has housed a branch of the Sanborn's restaurant and variety-store chain. Dining tables are set in an elaborate courtyard complete with carved pillars, tiles, and peacock frescoes. It's a lovely place for a rest. It's on the corner of Correo, the alleyway that runs along the main post office.

AROUND THE ZÓCALO
MODERATE

✪ Café de Tacuba

Tacuba 28. ☎ **512-8482.** Main courses $4.50–$11.50; comida corrida $14–$18. Daily 8am–11:30pm. Metro: Allende. MEXICAN.

One of the city's best established and popular restaurants, the Café de Tacuba has a handsome colonial-era look but dates from 1912. A stately atmosphere welcomes guests to the two long dining rooms, with brass lamps, dark and brooding oil paintings, a large mural of several nuns working in a kitchen. The customary fixed-price comida corrida offers a selection of daily lunch plates served with soup. In the front window and pastry case is a tempting selection of homemade cakes and pies and candied fruit. On Thursday through Sunday, from 6pm until closing, a wonderful group of medieval-costumed singers entertains; their sound is like the melodious estudiantina groups of Guanajuato accompanied by mandolins and guitars. It's between República de Chile and Bolívar.

Hostería de Santo Domingo
Domínguez 72. ☎ **510-1434.** Breakfast $3–$4; main courses $5–$8; specialties of the day $5–$8. Daily 9am–11pm. Metro: Allende. MEXICAN.

Established in 1860, the Hostería de Santo Domingo is said to be the oldest restaurant in the city still in operation. A mural at one end of the main dining room shows the Plaza Domingo during colonial times. The player piano will fool you into thinking a pianist is playing nonstop. The food is excellent, with large portions. At lunchtime the place is generally packed, so come early. Try the stuffed peppers with cheese, the pork loin, or the unusual bread soup. Note: The bread placed on your table costs extra. The restaurant is north of the Zócalo, between República de Brazil and República de Chile.

INEXPENSIVE

Café Cinco de Mayo ✪
Cinco de Mayo No. 57. ☎ **510-1995.** Breakfast $1.75–$3; main courses $3.50–$8; comida corrida $4–$7. Daily 7am–11pm. Metro: Zócalo. MEXICAN.

A real money-saver near the Zócalo, the Café Cinco de Mayo is the very picture of a Mexican lunchroom. Less than a block west of the cathedral on the south side of the street, it's bright with fluorescent lights and loud with conversation. The walls bear fake-stone wallcovering and mirrors, and its long lunch counter is filled with regulars. Waiters scurry here and there bearing enormous glasses of fresh orange juice, cups of hot coffee, baskets of pan dulce, sandwiches, pork chops—just about anything you can imagine. If you order café con leche, a waiter will approach with a big copper coffee pot, pour an inch of thick, bitter coffee into the bottom of your glass, then fill it up with hot milk. The restaurant is between the Zócalo and Palma.

A TEA HOUSE

✪ Salón de Thé Duca D'este
Hamburgo 164b. ☎ **525-6374.** Breakfast $3–$6; ice cream or pastry $2–$4; salads and soups $2.50–$5. Sun–Thurs 8am–11pm, Fri–Sat 8am–midnight. Metro: Insurgentes. CONTINENTAL.

This is another favorite of mine, opposite the above-mentioned Auseba. Small tea tables draped in apricot cloths look out onto the bustle of pedestrian traffic. But many of the customers are absorbed in gazing at the Duca d'Este's refrigerated display cases, which shelter many kinds of pastries, fresh and candied fruits, ice creams, and other fare. There's a good selection of coffees, teas, and hot chocolates. You can have a light lunch or supper by ordering soup, salad, or salmon. It's at the corner of Florencia and Hamburgo.

A CANTINA

La Opera Bar

Cinco de Mayo 10. ☎ **512-8959.** Reservations recommended at lunch. Main courses $5–$12; mixed drinks $3–$5. Mon–Sat 1pm–midnight. Metro: Bellas Artes. INTERNATIONAL.

La Opera Bar, three blocks east of the Alameda, is the most opulent of the city's cantinas. Below gilded baroque ceilings, slide into one of the darkwood booths with patches of beveled mirror and exquisite small oil paintings of pastoral scenes or grab a linen-covered table with a basket of fresh bread. La Opera is the Mexican equivalent of a London club, although it has become so popular for dining that fewer and fewer men play dominoes. In fact, you see more and more people enjoying romantic interludes in one of the cavernous booths, but tables of any kind are hard to find. Service is best if you arrive for lunch when it opens or go after 5pm when the throngs have diminished. The menu is sophisticated and extensive. While you wait for one of the jacketed waiters to bring your meal, look on the ceiling for the bullet hole that legend says Pancho Villa left when he galloped in on a horse. It's half a block from Sanborn's Casa de Azulejos, between Mata and Correo.

5 Exploring Mexico City

You'll find that in Mexico City such a routine activity as walking in the park can bring delightful surprises, and even an ordinary stroll in the city's markets presents the opportunity to admire exotic items unavailable at home.

Mexico City was built on the ruins of the ancient city of Tenochtitlán. A downtown portion of the city comprising almost 700 blocks and 1,500 buildings has been designated a **Historical Zone (Centro Historico).** The area is being reclaimed from years of neglect and restored to its former colonial charm.

In summer, always be prepared for rain, which comes daily. In winter, carry a jacket or sweater—stone museums are cold inside, and when the sun goes down, the outside air gets chilly.

THE TOP ATTRACTIONS

✪ Museo Nacional de Antropología

Chapultepec Park. ☎ **553-6266.** Admission $5.50; free Sun. Tues–Sat 9am–7pm, Sun 10am–6pm. Metro: Auditorio.

Occupying 44,000 square feet, Mexico City's anthropology museum is regarded as one of the top museums in the world. First-floor rooms are devoted to the pre-Hispanic cultures of Mexico. Second-floor rooms cover contemporary rural cultures through their crafts and everyday life. This museum offers the single best introduction to Mexico.

There are three sections. First is the entrance hall to the museum proper, with a checkroom and the museum bookstore on the left. The bookstore has a superior collection of guides to cultural, culinary, and archaeological attractions in Mexico. A good book to buy is *The Mexican National Museum of Anthropology*, written by three museum curators and published by Panorama Books. The room-by-room background provides invaluable information for understanding the thousands of artifacts on display. It's especially useful if you don't read Spanish and don't take a guided tour in English.

Inside the museum proper is an open courtyard (containing the Chávez Morado fountain) with beautifully designed spacious rooms running around three sides on two levels. The ground-floor rooms are theoretically the most significant, and they are the most popular among studious visitors, devoted as they are to history and prehistoric days all the way up the most recently explored archaeological sites. These rooms include dioramas of the way Mexico City looked when the Spaniards first arrived and reproductions of part of a pyramid at Teotihuacán. The Aztec calendar stone "wheel" takes a proud place here.

Save some of your time and energy, though, for the livelier and more readily understandable **ethnographic rooms** upstairs. This portion is a "living museum," devoted to the way people throughout Mexico live today, complete with straw-covered huts, tape recordings of songs and dances, crafts, clothing, and lifelike models of village activities. To me, both floors are equally interesting, one dealing with the past and the other dealing with the living past so to speak, because much of Mexican village life still retains vestiges of pre-Hispanic customs.

There is a lovely restaurant in the museum with moderate prices, air conditioning, and cheerful patio tables.

Note: Most of the museum is wheelchair accessible; however, assistance will be needed in places. Signs are in Spanish only.

✪ Museo del Templo Mayor (Great Temple)

Off the Zócalo. ☎ **542-1717.** Admission $4.50; free Sun. Tues–Sun 9am–6pm. Metro: Zócalo.

Opened in 1987 at the site of the newly excavated Aztec Templo Mayor, this quickly became one of the city's top museums. At the time of the 1521 Conquest the site was the center of religious life for the city of 300,000. No other museum shows the variety and splendor of the Aztec Empire the way this one does. All 6,000 pieces came from the relatively small plot of excavated ruins just in front of the museum. (See "Walking Tour 1—Near the Zócalo" later in this chapter.)

✪ The Historic District

Metro: Zócalo or Bellas Artes.

At least 1,500 buildings and an area of almost 700 acres of historic downtown Mexico City around the Alameda and Zócalo have been earmarked for preservation. Much of the history of Mexico from the 16th to the 20th century is reflected in the grand palaces and buildings in these two areas. (See the walking tours of the Zócalo and the Alameda later in this chapter.)

Diego Rivera Murals

Diego Rivera, one of Mexico's top muralists, left an indelible stamp on Mexico City's walls and, through his painted political themes, affected the way millions view Mexican history. See his stunning and provocative interpretations at the Palacio Nacional, the Bellas Artes, the National Preparatory School (his first ones), the Department of Public Education, the National School of Agriculture at Chapingo, the National Institute of Cardiology, and the Museo de la Alameda (formerly in the Hotel Del Prado). (See the walking tours of the Alameda and the Zócalo later in this chapter.)

✪ Museo Franz Mayer

Hidalgo 45, facing the Alameda. ☎ **518-2265.** Admission $2 adults, $1 students; free Sun. Tues–Sun 10am–5pm. Metro: Hidalgo or Bellas Artes.

German immigrant Franz Mayer spent a lifetime collecting rare furniture and other utilitarian decorative pieces dating from the 16th to the 19th century. When he died in 1975, he bequeathed them to the Mexican people with a trust fund for their care and display. (See "Walking Tour 2—Near the Alameda" later in this chapter.)

MORE ATTRACTIONS
NEAR THE ALAMEDA

North, west, and south of the Alameda proper are other attractions worthy of note. For the major highlights, see "Walking Tour 2—Near the Alameda" later in this chapter.

Plaza and Cemetery of San Fernando

Puente de Alvarado and Vicente Guerrero. Admission free. Daily dawn–dusk.

At one end of the plaza is the 18th-century San Fernando Church and behind it, $2^{1}/_{2}$ blocks west of the Alameda, is a small cemetery by the same name where a few of Mexico's elite families are buried. It's the only cemetery remaining in the city from the 19th century, and President Benito Juárez was the last person buried here, on July 23, 1872.

Museo de San Carlos

Puente de Alvarado 50. ☎ **535-4848**, or 592-3721. Admission $2.75; free Sun. Tues–Sun 10am–6pm. Walk $5^{1}/_{2}$ blocks west of the Alameda and $2^{1}/_{2}$ blocks west of San Fernando Plaza; it's at the corner of Arizpe.

The San Carlos Museum shows works from students of the Academy of San Carlos. Most of the country's great painters—Diego Rivera among them—count it as their alma mater. The beautiful converted mansion that houses the museum was built in the early 1800s by architect Manuel Tolsá for the Marqués de Buenavista.

☯ Monumento a la Revolución & Museo Nacional de la Revolución

Av. Juárez and La Fragua. ☎ **546-2115**, or 566-1902. Admission free. Tues–Sun 9am–5pm. From the Colón Monument on Reforma, walk one block north on either La Fragua or I. Ramírez; the monument will loom ahead.

The stocky art deco Monument to the Revolution, set in the large **Plaza de la República,** has a curious and ironic history. The government of Porfirio Díaz, perennially "reelected" as president of Mexico, began construction of what was intended to be a new legislative chamber. However, only the dome was raised by the time the Mexican Revolution (1910) put an end to his plans—not to mention his dictatorship. In the 1930s, after the turmoil of the revolution had died down, the dome was finished as a monument: The mortal remains of two revolutionary presidents, Francisco Madero and Venustiano Carranza, were entombed in two of its pillars, and it was dedicated to the revolution. Later, the bodies of Presidents Plutarco Elías Calles and Lázaro Cárdenas were buried there, as was that of revolutionary leader Francisco Villa (Pancho Villa).

Beneath the Monument to the Revolution is the Museo Nacional de la Revolución. The tumultuous years from 1867 through the revolution (which started in 1911) to 1917, when the present constitution was signed, are chronicled in excellent exhibits of documents, newspaper stories, photographs, drawings, clothing, costumes, uniforms, weapons, and furnishings. The museum is well worth a visit if you're at all interested in the period or the revolution.

Plaza de las Tres Culturas

At the corner of Lázaro Cárdenas and Flores Magón. Admission free. Daily dawn–dusk. Walk six long blocks north on Lázaro Cárdenas; turn right on Rayón two blocks to the Lagunilla Market; turn left and follow street to traffic circle with Cuitláhuac Monument; plaza is on other side of circle. Metro: Line 3 to Tlatelolco; use Manuel González exit; turn right; walk two blocks to Lázaro Cárdenas; turn right; plaza is about half a block south, on the left, just past the Clínico Hospital.

Here three cultures converge—Aztec, Spanish, and contemporary. Surrounded by modern office and apartment buildings are large remains of the **Aztec city of Tlatelolco,** site of the last battle of the Conquest of Mexico, and off to one side is the **Cathedral of Santiago Tlatelolco.** During the Aztec Empire, Tlatelolco was on the edge of Lake Texcoco, linked to the Aztec capital by a causeway. Bernal Díaz de Castillo, in his *True Story of the Conquest of New Spain*, described the roar from the dazzling market there. Later, he described the incredible scene after the last battle of the Conquest in Tlatelolco on August 13, 1521—the dead bodies were piled so deep that walking there was impossible. That night determined the fate of the country and completed the Spanish Conquest of Mexico.

View the pyramidal remains from raised walkways over the site. The cathedral, off to one side, was built in the 16th century entirely of volcanic stone. The interior has been tastefully restored, preserving little patches of fresco in stark-white plaster walls, with a few deep-blue stained-glass windows and an unadorned stone altar. Sunday is a good day to combine a visit here with one to the Sunday Lagunilla street market (for details, see "Shopping" later in this chapter) which is within walking distance south across Reforma.

IN CHAPULTEPEC PARK

One of the biggest city parks in the world, Chapultepec Park is more than a playground. Besides accommodating picnickers on worn-away grass under centuries-old trees, it boasts canoes on the lake (now dirty, though); vendors selling balloons, trinkets, and food; a garden for senior citizens only; a miniature train; an auditorium; and Los Pinos, home of Mexico's president. Most importantly for tourists, it contains a number of interesting museums.

Chapultepec Park has become quite run-down and is no longer the pleasant place it was in years past. Enter the park from a main entrance and head directly toward your sightseeing goal rather than doing a lot of wandering through the park.

To reach the park, take any "Auditorio" or "Reforma/Chapultepec" bus on Reforma; these will drop you within a block of the Museo Rufino Tamayo and the Museo de Arte Moderno or within two blocks of the Museo Nacional de Antropología. All these are situated off Reforma, about half a mile past the Diana Statue, near the Chapultepec Park zoo. If you'd rather take the Metro, Line 1 will take you to the Chapultepec station, outside the park. Line 7 will take you to Auditorio, which is even closer.

Castillo de Chapultepec/Museo Nacional de Historia

Chapultepec Park. ☎ **553-6224,** or 553-6396. Admission $4.50; free Sun. Tues–Sat 9am–5pm; Sun 10am–4pm.

Houses a variety of historical artifacts covering the period between 1521 and 1917. You'll see murals by Orozco, Siqueros, and others; elaborate European furnishings brought here by Maximilian and Carlota; and jewelry and colonial art objects. *Note:* Hold onto your ticket the entire time you're on the hill—you may be asked to show it.

Galería de la Museo de Historia

Chapultepec Park. Admission $4.50; free Sun. Tues–Sun 10am–5pm.

About 200 yards below Chapultepec Castle is this circular glass building, also known as the Museo Caracol (Snail Museum) because of its spiral shape, and as the Museo de la Lucha del Pueblo Mexicano por su Libertad (Museum of the Mexican People's Fight for Their Liberty) because of its content. It's a condensed chronological history of Mexico from 1800 to 1917, complete with portraits, reproductions of documents, and dramatic montages. In many ways, this museum is more riveting than the Museo Nacional de Historia on the hill above.

✪ Museo de Arte Moderno

Chapultepec Park. ☎ 553-6233. Admission $4; free Sun. Tues–Sun 10am–5:30pm.

The museum is actually in two buildings set together, with two entrances: one on Reforma, the other across from the Niños Héroes monument. The museum features both Mexican and foreign artists, including such greats as Kahlo, Rivera, Orozco, Montenegro, Tamayo, Coronel, and Magritte.

Museo Nacional de Historia Natural

Chapultepec Park. ☎ 556-2848, or 515-6304. Admission 50¢; free Sun. Tues–Sun 10am–5pm.

The 10 interconnecting domes that form the Museum of Natural History contain nature dioramas, exhibits on geology, astronomy, biology, the origin of life, and more. It's totally absorbing for youngsters.

✪ El Papalote, Museo del Niño (Children's Museum)

Avenida de los Constituyentes, Chapultepec Park. ☎ 273-0774. Admission $5 adults ($7.50 including IMAX show); $3.50 children ($5 including IMAX show). Tues–Fri 9am–6pm, Sat–Sun 9am–1pm and 2–6pm.

This interactive children's museum opened in 1993 in three separate buildings. The Building of the Pyramids holds most of the exhibits, while the IMAX building shows a film twice daily. There's virtually nothing here that children can't touch; once they discover this, they'll want to stay a long time. Children must be accompanied by an adult.

Rotonda de los Hombres Ilustres

Dolores Cemetery, Section 3 of Chapultepec Park, Constituyentes and Av. Civil Dolores. Admission free. Daily 6am–6pm.

The resting place of Mexico's illustrious military, political, and artistic elite. It's more like an outdoor museum of monuments than a cemetery; the stone markers are grouped in a double circle around an eternal flame. A stroll here will enliven a conversation about who's who in Mexican history. Among the famous buried here are artists Diego Rivera, Alfredo Siqueros, José Clemente Orozco, and Gerardo Murillo; presidents Sebastian Lerdo de Tejada, Valentín Gómez Farías, and Plutarco Calles; musicians Jaime Nuño (author of the Mexican national anthem), Juventino Rosas, and Augustín Lara; and outstanding citizens such as Carlos Pellicer. Stop in the entrance building and the guard will give you a map with a list of those buried here, which includes biographical information.

✪ Museo Rufino Tamayo

Chapultepec Park. ☎ 286-6599, or 286-3572. Admission $3.50; free Sun. Usually Tues–Sun 10am–6pm. Free guided tours Sat–Sun 10am–2pm.

Oaxaca-born painter Rufino Tamayo not only contributed a great deal to modern Mexican painting, but also collected pre-Hispanic, Mexican, and foreign

Chapultepec Park

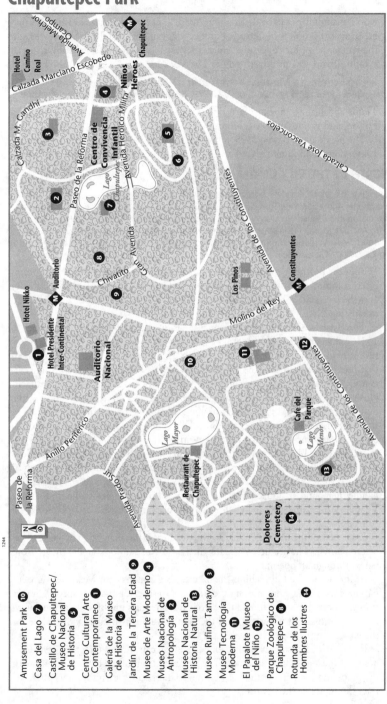

Amusement Park ⑩

Casa del Lago ⑦

Castillo de Chapultepec/
Museo Nacional
de Historia ⑤

Centro Cultural Arte
Contemporáneo ①

Galería de la Museo
de Historia ⑥

Jardín de la Tercera Edad ⑨

Museo de Arte Moderno ④

Museo Nacional de
Antropología ②

Museo Nacional de
Historia Natural ⑬

Museo Rufino Tamayo ③

Museo Tecnología
Moderna ⑪

El Papalote Museo
del Niño ⑫

Parque Zoológico de
Chapultepec ⑧

Rotunda de los
Hombres Ilustres ⑭

1244

works, including pieces by de Kooning, Warhol, Dalí, and Magritte. Tamayo's pre-Hispanic collection is in Oaxaca, but here you can see a number of his works and the remainder of his collection, unless they are temporarily displaced by a special exhibit. If you see one advertised (in *The News*, for instance), don't miss it.

Museo Tecnología Moderno (Museum of Technology)

Chapultepec Park. ☎ **516-0964,** or 277-5779. Admission free. Tues–Sun 9am–4:45pm.

Trains and planes, mockup factories, displays on the experiments of Morse and Edison, and various energy exhibits.

The polyhedral dome outside is the planetarium, which has scheduled shows at 10am, noon, and 2pm daily.

NORTH OF THE CITY CENTER

Basilica of Our Lady of Guadalupe

No phone. Admission free. Tues–Sun 10am–6pm. Metro: Line 3 to the "Basílica" station; take the exit marked SALIDA AV. MONTIEL. Half a block or so north of the Metro station, turn right onto Avenida Montiel (the street is crowded with food and trinket vendors); after about 15 minutes' walk, you'll see the great church looming ahead. From La Villa station, walk north on Calzada de Guadalupe.

Within the northern city limits is the famous Basilica of Guadalupe. Tour groups often combine a trip to the basilica with the Plaza of Three Cultures (see above) and the Pyramids of Teotihuacán (see Chapter 5), which makes a rushed and exhausting day.

The Basilica of Our Lady of Guadalupe is on the site where, on December 9, 1531, a poor Indian named Juan Diego is reputed to have seen a vision of a beautiful lady in a blue mantle. The local bishop, Zumarraga, was reluctant to confirm that Juan had indeed seen the Virgin Mary, so he asked the peasant for some evidence. Juan saw the vision a second time, on December 12, and it became miraculously emblazoned on the peasant's cloak. The bishop immediately ordered the building of a church on the spot, and upon its completion the image was hung in the place of honor, framed in gold. Since that time millions of the devout and the curious have come to view the miraculous image that experts, it is said, are at a loss to explain. The blue-mantled Virgin of Guadalupe is the patron saint of Mexico.

So heavy was the flow of visitors—many of whom approached for hundreds of yards on their knees—that the old church, already fragile, was insufficient to handle them, and an audacious new basilica was built, designed by Pedro Ramírez Vazquez, the same architect who did the breathtaking Museo Nacional de Antropología.

For a view of the miraculous cloak, which hangs at the altar, go to the lower level of the church. The architect has designed it so you can look at the image from below through an opening.

At the top of the hill, behind the basilica, is a cemetery for Mexico's more infamous folk (Santa Anna among them) and also several gift shops specializing in trinkets encased in seashells and other folk art. The steps up this hill are lined with flowers, shrubs, and waterfalls, and the climb, although tiring, is worthwhile for the view from the top.

If you visit Mexico City on December 12, you can witness the grand festival in honor of the Virgin of Guadalupe. The square in front of the basilica fills up with the pious and the party-minded as prayers, dances, and a carnival atmosphere attract thousands of the devout.

Coyoacán

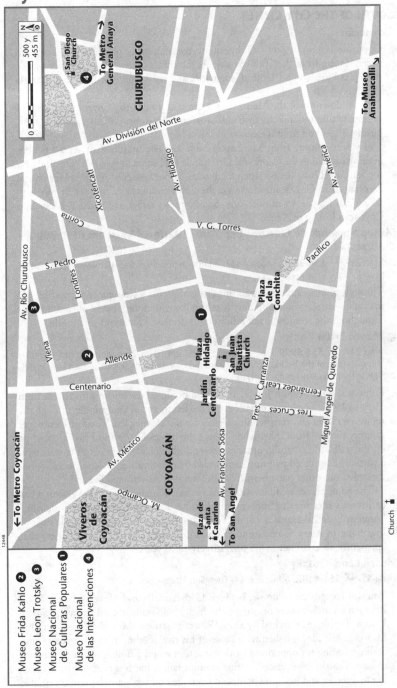

Museo Frida Kahlo **2**

Museo Leon Trotsky **3**

Museo Nacional
de Culturas Populares **1**

Museo Nacional
de las Intervenciones **4**

Church ✝️■

12448

SOUTH OF THE CITY CENTER

Coyoacán

Coyoacán is a pretty and wealthy suburb boasting many old houses and cobbled streets dating from the 16th century. At the center are two graceful large plazas, the Plaza Hidalgo and Jardín Centenario, and the Church of San Juan Bautista (1583).

From downtown, the Metro Line 3 can take you to the Coyoacán or Viveros station, within walking distance of Coyoacán's museums. Or "Iztacala-Coyoacán" buses will get you from the center to this suburb.

If you're coming from San Angel, catch the "Alcantarilla–Col. Agrarista" bus heading east along the Camino al Desierto de los Leones or Avenida Altavista, near the San Angel Inn. Get off when the bus gets to the corner of Avenida Mexico and Xicotencatl in Coyoacán. However, the simplest, quickest, and easiest way is to take a cab for the 15-minute ride. Sosa, a pretty street, is the main artery into Coyoacán from San Angel.

Museo Nacional de Culturas Populares (National Museum of Popular Cultures)

Hidalgo 289. ☎ **554-3800,** or 554-8882. Admission free. Tues–Sat 10am–6pm, Sun 10am–5pm.

Through photographs and paintings, this museum—housed in a beautiful old mansion—displays contemporary Mexican life within the context of communities throughout the country. Each exhibition is displayed for about six months.

✪ Museo Frida Kahlo

Londres 247. ☎ **554-5999**. Free admission. Tues–Sun 10am–2pm; however, the caretaker has his own idea of the hours. He's usually around even if the door is closed, so keep knocking. Note that no cameras are allowed.

Kahlo was born here on July 7, 1910, and occupied the house with Rivera from 1929 to 1954. The house is basically as she left it, and as you wander through the rooms you'll get an overwhelming feeling for the life they led. Their mementos are in every room—from the kitchen, where the names Diego and Frida are written on the walls, to the studio upstairs, where a wheelchair sits next to the easel with a partially completed painting surrounded by paintbrushes, palettes, books, photographs, and other paraphernalia of the couple's art-centered lives.

The bookshelves are filled with books in many languages, nestled against a few of Rivera's files bearing such inscriptions as "Protect Rockefeller Vandalism," "Amigos Diego Personales," and "Vários Interesantes y Curiosos." Frida's paintings hang in every room, some of them dominated by the gory imagery that apparently obsessed her in her final surgery-filled years.

Museo Leon Trotsky

Viena 45. ☎ **554-4482**. Admission $4. Tues–Sun 10am–5pm.

You will recognize this house, between Gómez Farías and Morelos, by the brick riflemen's watch-towers on top of the high stone walls. Exiled from the Soviet Union, Trotsky was invited by Diego Rivera to settle in Mexico City to continue his work. His ideas clashed with those of his rival, Stalin, in many respects, and Stalin, wanting no opposition or dissension in world Communist ranks, set out to have Trotsky assassinated. A first attempt failed, but it served to give a warning to Trotsky and his household, and from then on the house became a veritable fortress, with the watchtowers' steel doors (Trotsky's bedroom was entered only by thick steel doors), and round-the-clock guards, several of whom were Americans who sympathized with Trotsky's philosophies. Finally a man thought to have been paid, cajoled, or blackmailed by Stalin, directly or indirectly, was able to get himself admitted to the house by posing as a friend of Trotsky's and of his political views. On August 20, 1940, he put a mountaineer's ax into the philosopher's head. He was caught, but Trotsky died of his wounds shortly afterward. Not long after Trotsky arrived, he and Diego Rivera had a falling out. When Trotsky was murdered, both Rivera and Kahlo were suspects for a short while.

The museum is divided into two parts. In the first section you pass through displays of newspaper clippings chronicling the life of Trotsky and his wife in Mexico and the assassination. Then you enter the home, which is much more meager in its furnishings than you might expect for such a famous person.

The set of the film *The Death of Trotsky* was a very good replica of the house and gardens. Some of the walls still bear the bullet holes left from the first attempt on his life. Trotsky's tomb, designed by Juan O'Gorman, is in the garden.

Museo Nacional de las Intervenciones (National Museum of Interventions)

20 de Agosto y General Anaya, Churubusco. ☎ **604-0699.** Admission $4; free Sun. Tues–Sun 9am–6pm.

If your country has been invaded as many times as Mexico has, and for some of the most unusual reasons, there would be a museum about it, too. Housed in a beautiful old convent, the well-done displays chronicle each foreign intervention into Mexico's affairs. Visitors from France or the States, rather than being in for some American or French bashing, discover just the facts—very well displayed.

San Angel

San Angel is a fashionable colonial-era suburb of cobblestone streets with several worthwhile museums. The nearest Metro station is M.A. Quevedo. From downtown, take a colectivo ("San Angel") or bus ("Indios Verdes–Tlalpan" or "Central Norte–Villa Olímpica") south along Insurgentes near the Zona Rosa. Ask to get off at La Paz. To the east is a pretty park, the Plaza del Carmen, and on the west side of Insurgentes is a Sanborn's store/restaurant, good for a quick, moderately priced meal.

Museo Centro Cultura Isidro Fabela

Plaza San Angel 15. Free admission. Tues–Sun 10am–5pm.

Formerly a mansion known as the Casa del Risco, this is now an art museum. Contemporary works are downstairs, with a changing collection that often includes photographs. Upstairs are paintings from the 16th to 18th century by artists from around the world. The focal point of the house is the open courtyard with its central fountain made of thousands of pieces of broken pottery.

Museo Colonial del Carmen

Avenida de la Revolución 4 and Monasterio. ☎ **548-9849,** 548-2838, or 548-5312. Admission $1; free Sun. Tues–Sun 10am–4:45pm.

This former Carmelite convent, now filled with religious paintings and other ancient artifacts, keeps in its cellar a batch of naturally mummified men and women in glass cases. The museum is a maze of interlocking halls, corridors, stairways, chapels, and pretty flower-filled patios.

Museo de Arte Alvaro y Carmen T. Carrillo Gil

Revolución 1608, at the corner of Desierto de los Leones. ☎ **550-4018** or 550-3983. Admission $2; free Sun. Tues–Sun 10am–6pm.

Sometimes called the Museo de la Esquina (Museum of the Corner) since it's at a major intersection on Avenida de la Revolución, this modern gallery features a collection that includes rooms dedicated to the works of Orozco, Rivera, Siqueiros, and other Mexican painters.

✪ Museo Estudio Diego Rivera

Calle Diego Rivera and Avenida Altavista. ☎ **548-3032**. Admission $2.75; free Sun. Tues–Sun 10am–6pm.

It was here, in the studio designed and built by Juan O'Gorman in 1928, that Rivera drew sketches for his wonderful murals and painted smaller works. He died here in 1957. Now a museum, the Rivera studio holds some of the artist's personal effects and mementos, and there are changing exhibits relating to his life and work.

San Pablo Tepetlapán

✪ The Anahuacalli (Diego Rivera Museum)

Calle Museo 150, Col. Tepetlapa. ☎ **677-2984**. Admission free. Tues–Sun 10am–2pm and 3–6pm. Take the Metro (Line 2) to the Tasqueña terminal and change to SARO bus ("Tasqueña–Peña Pobre") west, which passes the museum. Another way to get there is on buses labeled "Zacatenco-Tlalpan" south along Balderas, or "El Rosario–Xochimilco" south along Avenidas Vasconcelos, Nuevo León, and Division del Norte; hop off at the Calle del Museo stop.

Not to be confused with Rivera's Studio Museum near the San Angel Inn, this is probably the most unusual museum in the city. Designed by Rivera before his death in 1957, it's devoted to his works as well as to his extensive collection of pre-Columbian art. Called the Anahuacalli ("House of Mexico") Museum and constructed of pedregal (the lava rock in which the area abounds), it resembles Maya and Aztec architecture. The name *Anahuac* was the old name for the ancient Valley of Mexico.

In front of the museum is a reproduction of a Toltec ball court, and the entrance to the museum itself is via a coffin-shaped door. Light filters in through translucent onyx slabs and is supplemented by lights inside niches and wall cases containing the exhibits. Rivera collected nearly 60,000 pre-Columbian artifacts, and the museum showcases thousands of them, in 23 rooms in chronological order, stashed on the shelves, tucked away in corners, and peeking from behind glass cases.

Upstairs, a replica of Rivera's studio has been constructed, and there you'll find the original sketches for some of his murals and two in-progress canvases. His first sketch (of a train) was done at the age of three, and there's a photo of it, plus a color photograph of him at work later in life in a pair of baggy pants and a blue denim jacket. Rivera (1886–1957) studied in Europe for 15 years and spent much of his life as a devoted Marxist. Yet he came through political scrapes and personal tragedies with no apparent diminution of creative energy, and a plaque in the museum proclaims him "A man of genius who is among the greatest painters of all time."

It's in the southern outskirts of the city in the suburb of San Pablo Tepetlapán, south of the Museo Frida Kahlo.

San Angel

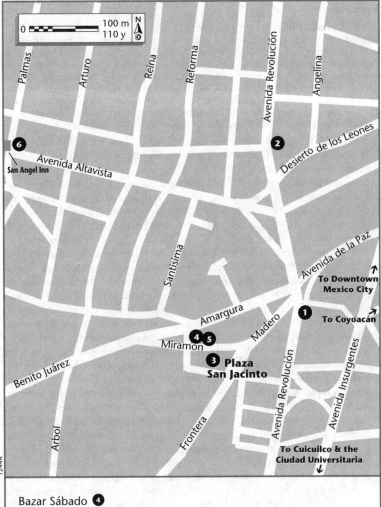

Bazar Sábado ④
Museo Centro Cultura Isidro Fabela ⑤
Museo Colonial del Carmen ①
Museo de Arte Alvaro y Carmen T. Carrillo Gil ②
Museo Estudio Diego Rivera ⑥
Plaza San Jacinto ③

Xochimilco

✪ The Canals and "Floating Gardens"

Admission to the area is free; charge for boat rides is $17 per boat; boats can be shared by up to 8 to 10 people. Daily, morning to dusk. Metro: Take the metro to the Tasqueña stop, then the *tren ligero* (light train) which stops at the outskirts of Xochimilco. From there take a taxi to the main plaza of the town of Xochimilco. Buses run all the way across the city from north to south to end up at Xochimilco, but they take longer than the Metro. Of the buses coming from the center, the most convenient is "La Villa-Xochimilco," which you catch going south on Correo Mayor and Pino Suárez near the Zócalo; or near Chapultepec on Avenida Vasconcelos, Avenida Nuevo Leon, and Avenida Division del Norte.

The canals of Xochimilco (pronounced "so-chee-MEEL-co"), about 15 miles south of the historic center, have survived from the civilization of the Aztecs; the name means "flower cultivators." They built *chinampas* (gardens/cultivated fields) on a lake by filling them with fertile lake bottom mud and anchoring them in a shallow part of the lake, first with poles and then by tall, vertical *ahuehuete* trees around the edges. The lake eventually filled in with *chinampas* and, contrary to popular thought, they don't float. They are narrow, rectangular-shaped islands flanked on all sides by canals. In fact there are at least 50 miles of canals in Xochimilco.

If you've not been to Xochimilco in a while, you'll see a big difference. The long-announced revival and cleanup of Xochimilco has finally happened.

There are two main parts to Xochimilco, the **tourism-oriented area** in the historic center of town, where colorful boats take loads of tourists (some of them picnicking along the way) through a portion of the canals. Lively music is a staple, some of it provided by mariachi and trio musicians for hire who board the boats. The area is flanked by historic buildings, restaurants, souvenir stands, curio sellers and boat vendors who pester you to take one boat over another. The other section, north of the center of town, is the **ecology oriented area—Parque Natural Xochimilco.** Colorful boats also take tourists through the latter canals to see farming of the chinampas, and abundant bird life. Food and drink, however, are not allowed on boats in this section, though there are food, drink, and curio vendors where you board the boats. The chinampas have been used agriculturally for more than 500 years, and after almost 30 years of neglect are being reclaimed and put to use again as farmland. Descendents of the families that worked them in the past can be seen planting the fertile rectangular-shaped fields with flowers, as well as broccoli, corn, cabbage, squash and other vegetables. Among the more than 170 species of birds is the rare Martín pescador. A water treatment plant cleans the water in the canals and a man-made lake has been created to funnel fresh water into them and is stocked with carp for fishing. Fronting the lake is a huge **modern visitors center** with a restaurant, book and gift shop, boat rentals (for the lake) and picnicking area. Beside it, a **botanical garden** grows species of plants native to different areas around the city—Tlalpan, Texcoco, the Pedregal, Mixquic, and Xochimilco. The ecologically oriented section is calmly pastoral compared to the lively atmosphere of the more tourist-oriented area. Though the two are connected by canal, boats from one aren't allowed to travel to the other.

On Sunday, Xochimilco (especially the tourist-oriented section) is jammed with foreign tourists and Mexican families with babies and picnic hampers; on weekdays, it's nearly deserted.

When you get to the town of Xochimilco, you'll find a busy market in operation, specializing in rugs, ethnic clothing and brightly decorated pottery. As you enter Xochimilco proper you will see many places to board boats. Should you miss

Xochimilco

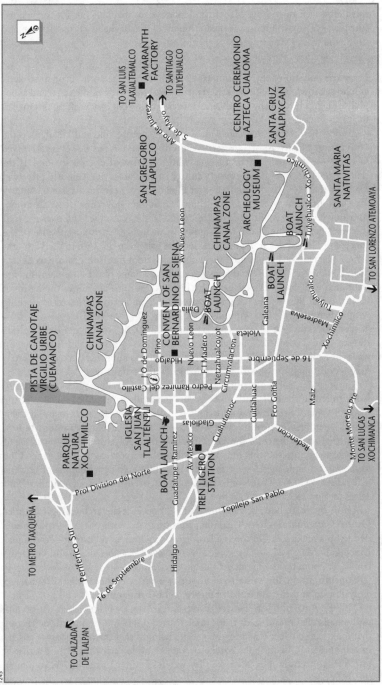

them, however, turn along Madero and follow signs that say "Los Embarcaderos" (the piers). If you can resist the blandishment of the inevitable curio salesmen and shills, you will eventually arrive at the docks.

The Village of Xochimilco

Leave the hubbub of the colorful canals behind and take an hour or so to stroll around the town of Xochimilco. Restaurants are at the edge of the canal and shopping area, and historically significant churches are within easy walking distance of the main square.

Among these, facing the main square (at the corner of Pino and Hidalgo), is the **16th century Convent of San Bernardino de Siena,** with its flower petals carved in stone—a signature of the Indians who did most of the work—and 16th-century retables, one of the country's three such retables miraculously preserved for more than 400 years. (Another is at Huejotzingo, near Puebla; see Chapter 5 "Excursions from Mexico City.") The last Indian governor of Xochimilco, Apoxquiyohuatzin, is buried here. Inside and to the right, the skull over the font is from a pre-Hispanic skull rack signifying an Indian/Christian mixture of the concept of life and death. Eight lateral retables date from the 16th to the 18th centuries. The fabulous gold-gilted main altar, also from the 16th century, is like an open book with sculpture and religious paintings. Some of the altar paintings are attributed to Baltasar Echave Orio the Elder. Over the altar, above the figure of Christ, is San Bernardino with the *caciques* (local authorities) dressed in clothing with Indian elements and without shoes.

Five blocks away at the corner of Sabino and J. O. de Dominguez is the **Iglesia de San Juan Tlaltentli.** Quetzalcoatl is symbolized by a snail and Aztec face on walls. The enormous ahuehuete tree across the street is hundreds of years old. From February through October the tree is loaded with nesting cranes.

A mile and a half south of the central plaza is the **Archeological Museum of Xochimilco,** at the crossroads of Avenida Tenochtitlán and Calle La Planta in the town of Santa Cruz Acalpixcan. It houses artifacts from the area, many of them found when residents built their homes—10,000-year-old mammoth bones, mythic figures dating from the Teotihuacán period, polychromed pottery, carved abalone, and tombs showing funerary practices of 23 Teotihuacán inhabitants. One of the most unique pieces is a clay figure of a child holding a bouquet of flowers. The museum (☎ 675-0168 or 675-0426), is open Tuesday through Sunday from 10am to 5pm and admission is free.

Across the road, but not within walking distance, is the **archaeological zone/ Centro Ceremonial Azteca Cualama,** consisting of a series of petroglyphs meandering up a rocky hill. On top is a large clearing which is still used for ceremonial dancing on March 21, for Fiesta de la Primavera Tlacaxipeualiztli, and on October 12, at noon, for the Fiesta del Pueblo Altepeilhuitl.

Continuing on the same road about two miles is the village of Santiago Tulyehualco and the **amaranth factory/Tehutl-Amaranto** (☎ 842-0752 and 842-2778). Amaranth was the sacred crop of the Aztecs, a plant yielding tiny whitish lysine-loaded round seeds that can be toasted or ground, and nutritious leaves that look like spinach. (Lysine is an essential amino acid that's sometimes absent in plant protein). Because the Aztecs used amaranth in their rituals, the Spaniards forbid its cultivation, but as we see they weren't entirely successful. As you enter the front door, amaranth plants are on the left. Ask permission to see the process in back, of separating, grading, toasting, and packaging of products. To the right of the entrance is a store selling amaranth products, with include amaranth mixed with powdered chocolate for a hot drink, flour, cereal, pasta for soup, cookies, and granola. During the Days of the Dead amaranth skulls are sold at street markets countrywide. Amaranth is grown commercially in Puebla and Morelos states and locally on family plots. Green and black olives and olive oil are also sold, made from trees grown in the area. Each February the village hosts an **Olive and Amaranth fair.** The factory is open daily from 7am to 8pm.

Xochimilco celebrates with at least 422 **festivals** annually, the most famous of which is for the **Niñopa,** a figure of the Christ child that since 1875 is believed to possess miraculous powers. The figure is venerated on **January 6** (Three Kings Day), **February 2** (changing of the Niñopa's custodian), **December 16–24** (posadas for the Niñopa), and **April 30** (Day of the Child). Caring for the Niñopa is a coveted privilege which lasts a year, and the schedule of approved caretakers is filled through the year 2031.

WALKING TOUR 1
The Zócalo

Start: The Palacio Nacional, on the east end of the Zócalo (Metro: Zócalo).
Finish: Burial vault of Hernán Cortés at the Hospital de Jesús Nazareno.
Time: One or two days, depending on the length of time you spend at each stop.
Best Times: Sunday, when the streets are relatively uncrowded, or the week before or after September 15 (Mexican Independence Day), when the Zócalo and surrounding streets are festooned in ribbons and lights.
Worst Times: Monday, when the museums are closed.

1. **The Zócalo.** Every Spanish colonial city in North America was laid out according to a textbook plan, with a plaza at the center surrounded by a church, government buildings, and military headquarters. Since Mexico City was the capital of New Spain, its Zócalo is one of the grandest and is graced on all sides by stately 17th-century buildings.

   Zócalo actually means "pedestal," or "plinth." A grand monument to Mexico's independence was planned and the pedestal built, but the project was never completed. Nevertheless, the pedestal became a landmark for visitors, and soon everyone was calling the square after the pedestal, even though the pedestal was later removed. Its official name is Plaza de la Constitución. It covers almost 10 acres and is bounded on the north by Cinco de Mayo, on the east by Pino Suárez, on the south by 16 de Septiembre, and on the west by Monte de Piedad. Occupying the entire east side of the Zócalo is the majestic, red tezontle stone:

2. **Palacio Nacional,** begun in 1692 on the site of Moctezuma's "new" palace, which became the site of Hernán Cortés's home and the residence of colonial viceroys. It has changed much in 300 years, taking on its present form in the late 1920s when the top floor was added. The complex of countless rooms, wide stone stairways, and numerous courtyards adorned with carved brass balconies is also where the president of Mexico works. But to most visitors it's better known for the fabulous second-floor Diego Rivera murals depicting the history of Mexico. Just 30 minutes here with an English-speaking guide will provide a good background for your understanding of Mexico's history. The cost of a guide is negotiable, $12 or less, depending on your negotiating ability.

Enter by the central door. Over it hangs the bell from Dolores Hidalgo rung by Padre Miguel Hidalgo when he proclaimed Mexico's independence in 1810. Each September 15, Mexican Independence Day, the president of Mexico stands on the balcony above the door to echo Hidalgo's cry to thousands of spectators filling the Zócalo. Take the stairs to the Rivera murals, which were painted over a 25-year period. If you know something of the history of Mexico their content is easy to understand. *The Legend of Quetzalcoatl* depicts the famous legend of the flying serpent bringing a blond-bearded white man to the country. When Cortés arrived, many of the Aztecs remembered this legend and believed him to be Quetzalcoatl. Another mural tells of the American Intervention when American invaders marched into Mexico City during the War of 1847. It was on this occasion that the military cadets of Chapultepec Castle (then a military school) fought bravely to the last man. The most notable of Rivera's murals is the *Great City of Tenochtitlán,* a pictorial study of the original settlement in the Valley of Mexico. The city takes up only a small part of the mural, and the remainder is filled with what appears to be four million extras left over from a Hollywood epic. In fact, no matter what their themes, most of the murals incorporate a piece of ancient Mexican history, usually featuring Cortés and a cast of thousands. It's open daily from 9am to 5:30pm. Admission is free.

Inside the corridors of the Palacio Nacional, at the northern end, is the comparatively little known:

3. **Museo Benito Juárez** (☎ 522-5646). Walk north inside the palace, to the statue of Benito Juárez and then up the stairs. To the left is the Juárez Museum and the well-preserved apartments where the former president of Mexico died. It's usually bustling with schoolchildren studying the handwritten letters and papers kept in glass cases around the room. The last room at the rear is Juárez's bedroom, which gives one the eerie feeling that the former president might walk in at any moment: His dressing gown is laid out on the four-poster bed, and a chamber pot peeks from under the bed. The museum is supposedly open Monday through Friday from 9am to 7pm, but it was closed for remodeling when I checked. Admission is free.

Before heading north, you may want to take a look at La Acequia Real (Royal Canal) on the south side of the building at the corner of Corregidora. It was the most important canal in colonial times, carrying commerce from the southern outskirts of the city. A portion of it was recently restored.

From the Palacio Nacional, go to the northern edge of the Zócalo and the:

4. **Catedral Metropolitano.** An impressive, towering cathedral, begun in 1573 and finished in 1667, it blends Greek and Mexican *churrigueresque* (baroque) architecture. In your look around the cathedral and the Sagrario next to it, note the sinkage of the building into the soft lake bottom beneath. The base of the facade is far from being level and straight, and when one considers the weight of the immense towers, it's no surprise.

In Mexico, the sacred ground of one religion often becomes the sacred ground of its successor. Cortés and his Spanish missionaries converted the Aztecs, tore down their temples, and used much of the stone to construct a church on this spot. The church they built was pulled down in 1573 so the present Catedral Metropolitana could be built. The building of today has 5 naves and 14 chapels. As you wander past the small chapels, you may hear guides describing some

Walking Tour—The Zócalo

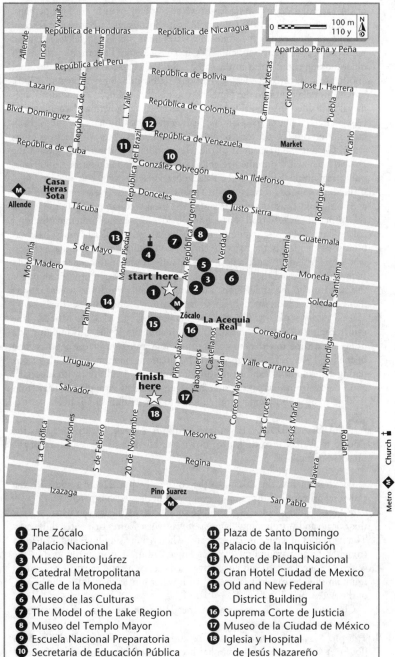

1. The Zócalo
2. Palacio Nacional
3. Museo Benito Juárez
4. Catedral Metropolitana
5. Calle de la Moneda
6. Museo de las Culturas
7. The Model of the Lake Region
8. Museo del Templo Mayor
9. Escuela Nacional Preparatoria
10. Secretaria de Educación Pública
11. Plaza de Santo Domingo
12. Palacio de la Inquisición
13. Monte de Piedad Nacional
14. Gran Hotel Ciudad de Mexico
15. Old and New Federal
    District Building
16. Suprema Corte de Justicia
17. Museo de la Ciudad de México
18. Iglesia y Hospital
    de Jesús Nazareno

of the cathedral's outstanding features: the tomb of Agustín Iturbide perhaps, placed here in 1838, or the paintings by the Spanish artist Bartolomé Esteban Murillo, or the fact that the stone holy-water fonts ring like metal when tapped with a coin. Like many huge churches, it has catacombs underneath. The much older looking church next to the cathedral is the chapel known as El Sagrario, another tour de force of Mexican baroque architecture built in the mid-1700s.

As you walked around the cathedral you no doubt noticed a reminder of medieval trade life. The west side of the cathedral is the gathering place of carpenters, plasterers, plumbers, painters, and electricians who have no shops. Each craftsperson displays the tools of his trade, sometimes along with pictures of his work. Go out the front door of the Metropolitano and turn left toward the Palacio Nacional. Continue straight ahead across Seminario to the pedestrians-only street on the left side of the Palacio Nacional:

5. **Calle de la Moneda (Street of the Treasury or Mint).** The street is lined with aged buildings constructed of tezontle, the local volcanic rock. On the left, at the corner of Calle Verdad, is the Edificio Arzobispal, the former archbishop's palace. True to Spanish tradition, the chief ecclesiastical official's power base was built smack on top of the Aztecs' Temple of Tezcatlipoca, the multifaceted god who gave life and governed a host of lesser gods. It was on this site that the child Juan Diego revealed the cloak with the figure of the Virgin of Guadalupe for the first time to the archbishop. The building from which the street takes its name is at no. 13, on the right about halfway down, and it houses the:

6. **Museo de las Culturas** (☎ 512-7452). Formerly La Casa de Moneda (the mint), built as a part of the Palacio Nacional in the 1500s, this building was home for a time to the national anthropology museum before the new one opened in 1964 in Chapultepec Park. It remains a museum, and holds a fascinating assortment of exhibits relating to other world cultures, with especially good pieces from Asia and Africa. It's open Tuesday through Saturday from 9:30am to 6pm and Sunday from 9:30am to 4pm. Admission is free.

☕ **TAKE A BREAK**   If you are ready for a break, backtrack across the Zócalo to Cafe Cinco de Mayo, down the block, past the entrance of the Hotel Majestic.

Backtrack across the Zócalo to the corner of Moneda and stand with the cathedral on your left. At ground level you'll notice pigeons perched on:

7. **The Model of the Lake Region.** The model shows the area in what today is the Zócalo and surrounding region as it was when Cortés first entered the city. The two cities of Tenochtitlán (the area where you're standing) and Tlatelolco (roughly the area around the Plaza of Three Cultures) were surrounded by the waters of Lake Texcoco and linked by raised causeways and canals. The model's fountain fills the canal-like "streets" with water just as they did in the heyday of the Aztec capital.

Continue on Seminario. Straight ahead and on the right are remnants of pre-Conquest Mexico at the:

8. **Templo Mayor Archaeological Site and Museum** (☎ 542-1717 or 542-0606). A small corner of the site has been exposed for years, but it was never excavated. In 1978, a workman digging on the east side of the Catedral Metropolitana, next to what is now the Palacio Nacional, unearthed an exquisite Aztec stone of the moon goddess Coyolxauhqui. Mexican archaeologists

followed up the discovery with major excavations, and what they uncovered were interior remains of the Pyramid of Huitzilopochtli, also called the Templo Mayor (Great Temple), the most important religious structure in the Aztec capital. What you see are actually remains of pyramids that were covered by the great pyramid the Spaniards saw on their arrival in the 16th century.

Strolling along the walkways built over the site, you pass a water-collection conduit constructed during the presidency of Porfirio Díaz (1877–1911), as well as far-earlier constructions. Building dates are on explanatory plaques (in Spanish), which give the time frames in which the building took place. Shelters cover the ruins to protect traces of original paintwork and carving. Note especially the Tzompantli, or Altar of Skulls, a common Aztec and Maya design.

To enter the Museo del Templo Mayor (Museum of the Great Temple), which opened in 1987, take the walkway to the large building in the back portion of the site, which contains the fabulous artifacts from on-site excavations.

Inside the door, a model of Tenochtitlán will give you a good idea of the scale of the vast city of the Aztecs, which flourished in the century before Cortés arrived (1519). The rooms and exhibits are organized by subject on many levels around a central open space. You'll see some marvelous displays of masks, figurines, tools, jewelry, and other artifacts, including the huge stone wheel of the moon goddess Coyolxauhqui, "she with bells painted upon her face," on the second floor. The goddess ruled the night, so the Aztecs believed, but died at the dawning of every day, slain and dismembered by her brother Xiuhcoatl, the Serpent of Fire.

Look also for the striking jade-and-obsidian mask and the full-size terra-cotta figures of the guerreros aguilas, or "eagle warriors." A cutaway model of the Templo Mayor shows the layers and methods of construction.

Here's a quick guide to the exhibit rooms: Sala 1, "Antecedentes," contains exhibits about the early days of Tenochtitlán. Sala 2, "Guerra y Sacrificio," goes into the details of the Aztec religious duties of war and human sacrifice. Sala 3, "Tributo y Comercio," deals with Aztec government and its alliances and commerce with tributary states. Sala 4, "Huitzilopochtli," treats this most important of Aztec gods, a triumphant warrior, the son of Coatlicue, who bore him without losing her virginity. Huitzilopochtli, the "hummingbird god," was the one who demanded that human sacrifices be made to sustain him. In Sala 5, "Tlaloc," are exhibits explaining the role of the Aztec rain god in daily and religious life. Sala 6, "Faunas," deals with the wild and domesticated animals common in the Aztec Empire at the time when the capital flourished. Sala 7, "Religion," explains Aztec religious beliefs, which are amazingly complex and sometimes confusing because they are so different from the familiar religions of Europe and the Middle East. Sala 8, "Caida de Tenochtitlán," recounts the fall of the great city and its last emperors, Moctezuma and Cuauhtémoc, to Hernán Cortés and his conquistadores. The museum is open Tuesday through Sunday from 9am to 6pm. The entry fee is $4.50; free for children under 12 and free for all on Sunday. Use of your camera is an additional $3.50. The admission is for both the ruins and the museum.

When you're finished at the museum, exit and return to the entrance on Seminario opposite the cathedral. The street changes to República de Argentina in front of the archaeological site. Continue north half a block, to the corner of Argentina and Donceles, and then turn right; half a block ahead on the left is the:

9. **Escuela Nacional Preparatoria,** an 18th-century building of red tezontle stone with murals by three Mexican greats: Rivera, Orozco, and Siqueiros. It was closed for renovation on my last visit and may not be open when you travel.

Continue north on Argentina, cross Calle González Obregón, and turn left; on the right will be the entrance to the:

10. **Secretaría de Educación Pública,** built in 1922 and decorated with a great series of more than 200 Diego Rivera murals dating from 1923 and 1924. Other artists did a panel here and there, but it's the Rivera murals that are superb. The building is usually open Monday through Saturday from 9:30am to 5:30pm, but the interior was closed for renovation on my last visit.

From the front door of the Secretaría, turn right and walk half a block to the corner of República de Brasil; across the street on the right is the:

11. **Plaza de Santo Domingo,** featuring a wonderful slice of Mexican life. A fascinating plaza with arcades on one side, a Dominican church on the other, it's dominated by a statue of the corregidora of Querétaro, Josefa Ortiz de Domínguez. The plaza is best known for the scribes who compose and type letters for clients unable to do so for themselves. Years ago, it was full of professional public writers clacking away on ancient typewriters, and a few still ply their trade on ancient electric typewriters among a proliferation of small print shops. Emperor Cuauhtémoc's palace once occupied this land, then Dominicans built their monastery there.

Catercorner across the street, at the corner of Venezuela and Brasil, is the:

12. **Palacio de la Inquisición** (Inquisition Palace), built in 1732. For more than 200 years (1571–1820), accused Mexican heretics and other religious criminals were strangled and/or burned at the stake; for almost 100 years this was the building in which they were held prisoner and their fates decided. The last accused heretic to be executed was José María Morelos, hero of the Mexican Independence. Today the palace houses several rooms devoted to the very interesting Museum of the History of the Mexican Medicine, with displays of modern and pre-Hispanic medicine. Informational signs are in Spanish only. To the left of the palace as you enter is a small bookstore/historical library of art, medicine, and culture. Outside the bookstore is a small restaurant serving light refreshments. The building and museum are open daily from 10am to 6pm.

☕ **TAKE A BREAK** From the front door of the palacio, angle to the right (but do not turn the corner) for one block on Domínguez; on the right is the **Hostería de Santo Domingo,** Domínguez 72 (☎ 510-1434), established in 1860 and reportedly the oldest restaurant in Mexico City. Meals and drinks are a little expensive, but it's lively at midday, and the service and atmosphere are delightful. It's open daily from 9am to 11pm.

From the Hostería de Santo Domingo, double-back to the corner of Domínguez and Brasil and turn right in the direction of the Zócalo, walking 2½ blocks. On the right is the:

13. **Monte de Piedad Nacional,** or national pawn shop (☎ 597-3455), at the corner of Monte de Piedad and Cinco de Mayo. Whoever heard of touring a pawn shop? In Mexico City it's done all the time in what could be described as the world's largest and most elegant Goodwill/Morgan Memorial thrift store. Electric power tools, jewelry, antique furniture, heavy machine tools, sofa beds, and a bewildering array of other things from trash to treasure are all on display.

Buying is not required, but taking a look is recommended. Be sure to see the "Sala de Arte y Regalos" (art and gift shop); it's a hodgepodge of items ranging from the ridiculous to the exquisite. The building is on the site of Moctezuma's old Axayácatl palace (his "new" palace occupied the site of the present Palacio Nacional, across the street), the site where the captive Emperor Moctezuma was accidentally killed, and the site later occupied by a viceregal palace constructed by Cortés. The present building was given by Pedro Romero de Terreros, the Count of Regla, an 18th-century silver magnate from Pachuca, so that Mexican people might obtain low-interest loans. It's open Monday through Friday from 8:30am to 6pm and Saturday from 8:30am to 3pm.

☕ **TAKE A BREAK**   For a pause in your walking tour, continue south half a block and cross Cinco de Mayo; on the corner is one of the city's most popular hotels and rooftop restaurants, the **Hotel Majestic.** From the seventh-floor indoor/outdoor rooftop restaurant is a wonderful view of the Zócalo. For the best seat in town for the flag-lowering ceremonies, get there before sunset. On a clear day you can even see the Ixta and Popo volcanoes. It's great to begin your Zócalo tour here, to stop at midday, or to pay a late visit to the bar adjoining the restaurant, where there's a live singer nightly. It's open daily from 7:30am to 10:30pm.

Continue south to Monte de Piedad, with the Majestic Hotel on your right and the Zócalo on your left, to the next corner, 16 de Septiembre; turn right a few steps to the:

14. Gran Hotel Ciudad de México. Originally a department store and later converted to a hotel, it is now operated by the Howard Johnson chain. It boasts one of the most splendid interiors of any downtown building. Step inside to see the lavish lobby, topped with its breathtaking Tiffany stained-glass canopy, and gilded open elevators on both sides.

Backtrack half a block east on 16 de Septiembre toward the Zócalo. Across Cinco de Febrero (Monte de Piedad) on the right are the:

15. Arcades of the 16th-century Old Federal District Building and the New Federal District Building, which dates from 1935 but looks like the older building. Both are on the south side of the Zócalo.

Continue east across the next street, Pino Suárez, with the Palacio Nacional on the left. On your right is the:

16. Suprema Corte de Justicia (Supreme Court of Justice), built in the mid-1930s. Inside, on the main staircase and its landings are José Clemente Orozco murals, following a theme of justice that he was given the liberty to interpret.

Some $2^1/_2$ blocks farther south on Pino Suárez, on the left at the corner of República del Salvador, is the:

17. Museo de la Ciudad de México, Pino Suárez 30 (☎ 542-8356 or 542-0487). Before you enter, go to the corner of República del Salvador and look at the enormous stone serpent head, a corner support at the building's base. The stone was once part of an Aztec pyramid. At the entrance, a stone doorway opens to the courtyard of this mansion built in 1528 as the House of the Counts of Santiago de Calimaya. This classic old building was converted into the Museum of the City of Mexico in 1964 and should be visited by anyone interested in the country's past. Dealing solely with the Mexico Valley, where the first people arrived in 8000 B.C., the museum contains some fine maps and pictographic presentations of the initial settlements, outlines of the social organization as it developed, and a huge mockup of Tenochtitlán, the city of the Aztecs. The Conquest and destruction of Tenochtitlán by the Spaniards is wonderfully portrayed in a Capdevila mural that appears to have been painted in fire.

Unfortunately, most of the space upstairs has become either offices, meeting rooms, or areas blocked off for remodeling. Do go up, though; you might get a peak at some beautiful religious paintings. The third floor has a sun-drenched studio of Mexican impressionist Joaquin Clausell, but when I was last there, this too, was closed.

The museum is open Tuesday through Sunday from 9:30am to 6:30pm; admission is free. However, it was closed for remodeling when I checked.

Catercorner from the museum, at the corner of Suárez and Salvador, is the:

18. Iglesia y Hospital de Jesús Nazareno, founded by Hernán Cortés soon after the Conquest. A stone marker outside marks it as the spot where Cortés and Moctezuma reportedly met for the first time. Cortés died in Spain in 1547, but his remains are in a vault inside the chapel (entered by a side door on República del Salvador). Vaults on the opposite wall store the remains of Cortés's relatives. Notice the Orozco mural *The Apocalypse* on the choir ceiling. The chapel is open Monday through Saturday from 7am to 8pm and Sunday from 7am to 1pm and 5 to 8pm.

At the end of your tour here, the nearest Metro station is Pino Suárez or Zócalo (equal distance).

WALKING TOUR 2
Near the Alameda

Start: The Alameda Central (Metro: Bellas Artes).
Finish: Museo de Artes e Industrías Populares.
Time: One or two days, depending on the time spent at each location.
Best Times: Saturday, when museums and shops are open, and around Christmas and Independence Day (Sept 15), when the area is festooned in holiday color.
Worst Times: Monday, when the museums are closed.

Today, the lovely tree-filled Alameda Central is a magnet for pedestrians, cotton-candy vendors, lovers, organ grinders—everyone enjoying a daily repast in the park. Long ago, the site of the Alameda was an Aztec marketplace. When the conquistadores took over in the mid-1500s, heretics were burned at the stake there under the Spanish Inquisition. In 1592, the governor of New Spain, Viceroy Luís de Velasco, converted it to a public park.

As you wander around the Alameda Central, you're bound to notice the:

1. Juárez Monument, sometimes called the **Hemiciclo** (hemicycle or half-circle), facing Avenida Juárez. Enthroned as the hero he was, Juárez assumes his proper place here in the pantheon of Mexican patriots. Most of the other statuary in the park was done by European sculptors (particularly French) in the late 19th and early 20th centuries.

On the west side of the Alameda, along Avenida Juárez, where the old Hotel Regis once stood, is the:

2. Jardín de la Solidaridad, or Solidarity Garden, built in 1986 in remembrance of those who died during the terrible 1985 earthquake.

Walking Tour—Near the Alameda

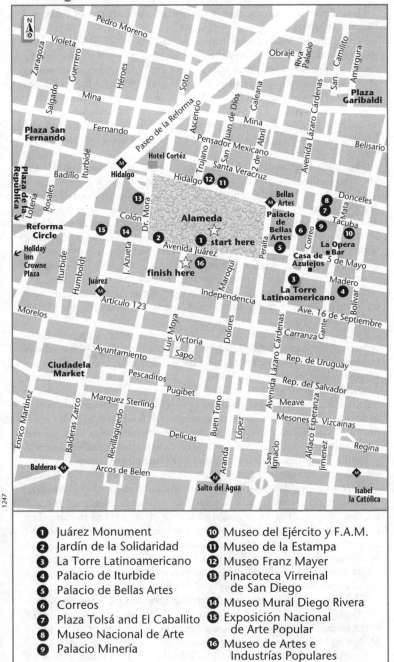

1 Juárez Monument
2 Jardín de la Solidaridad
3 La Torre Latinoamericano
4 Palacio de Iturbide
5 Palacio de Bellas Artes
6 Correos
7 Plaza Tolsá and El Caballito
8 Museo Nacional de Arte
9 Palacio Minería

10 Museo del Ejército y F.A.M.
11 Museo de la Estampa
12 Museo Franz Mayer
13 Pinacoteca Virreinal de San Diego
14 Museo Mural Diego Rivera
15 Exposición Nacional de Arte Popular
16 Museo de Artes e Industrías Populares

Opposite the southeastern edge of the Alameda, at the corner of Juárez and Lázaro Cárdenas, is:

3. La Torre Latino Americano, or Latin American Tower (☎ 510-2545). Here you can see the fabulous views of the whole city and the route of your walking tour from the observation deck on the 42nd floor of this skyscraper soaring above the intersection of Juárez and Cárdenas. Buy a ticket for the deck (open daily from 10am to 11pm) at the booth as you approach the elevators—admission is $4.50 for adults, $3.75 for children. Tokens for the telescope up top are on sale here, too. You then take an elevator to the 37th floor, cross the hall, and take another elevator to the 42nd floor. An employee will ask for your ticket as you get off.

The view is magnificent, with mountains surrounding the capital on all sides, but those to the north are the nearest and Avenida Lázaro Cárdenas seems to head straight for them. To the north, just below, is the white-marble Bellas Artes, and west of it is the green patch of the Alameda. Due west is the Monument to the Revolution, just beyond the intersection of Juárez and Reforma. You can't see Reforma too well because it's hidden by the buildings that line it, but the green swath of Chapultepec Park and its palace on the hilltop are easy to spot. To the east is the Zócalo, dominated by the cathedral. To the south is an area densely packed with homes, factories, and tall apartment buildings.

From the front door of the tower, turn right to the corner and right (west) on Madero (the street name changes from Juárez) 1 1/2 blocks past the Church of San Francisco to the magnificent:

4. Palacio de Iturbide, at Madero 17. This ornate stone palace with huge hand-carved wooden doors and a wildly baroque 40-foot-high carved-stone archway was built in the 1780s for the Marqués de Jaral de Berrio, but by 1821 it belonged to Don Agustín de Iturbide, who later became the self-proclaimed Agustín I, Emperor of Mexico (1822–23). His reign lasted only a matter of months, for although he was a partisan of Mexican independence, his political outlook was basically royalist and conservative. The future of Mexico lay in the liberal social reforms advocated by the great revolutionaries Hidalgo and Morelos. Iturbide was exiled and, later, on his unauthorized return, was executed in Padillo, Tamualipas, and buried there. Years later his contribution to Mexican independence was recognized, and his body was reburied in the Catedral Metropolitana (see "Walking Tour 1—The Zócalo"), where it remains today.

Banamex, the present owner of the building, restored the palace in 1972, and the result is beautiful. Enter a courtyard with three tiers of balconies: The ground floor is a banking office and has a temporary art-exhibition area; the upper floors have executive offices. Period paintings and statues grace walls and corners, and the second-floor chapel has been beautifully restored. Banamex has a brief (but free) printed guide to the building; ask the guard for one and come in and have a look at any time daily from 10am to 7pm.

While you're here you may want to stop in a few doors down at the American Book Store or take a look at the exterior of the Casa Borda that belonged to the silver baron from Taxco, on the same side of the street at the corner of Madero and Allende, across from the bookstore.

Now cross the street to the opposite side of Madero and double-back on Madero toward the Alameda.

☕ **TAKE A BREAK**   On the way back from the Iturbide Palace toward the Alameda you must stop in, however briefly, at a downtown institution: The **Casa de Azulejos** (House of Tiles), Madero 4 (☎ 518-6676).

Continuing back toward the Alameda, turn right at the next corner, the busy Avenida Lázaro Cárdenas, and cross it to the beautiful white marble:

5. **Palacio de Bellas Artes** (pronounced "BEY-ahs ARR-tess"), at the east end of the Alameda (☎ 510-1388). The building is a supreme achievement of art deco lyricism. In addition to being the concert hall, it houses permanent and traveling art shows. Inside is the fabulous art nouveau glass curtain of Mexican painter Gerardo Murillo ("Doctor Atl"); it was constructed by Louis Comfort Tiffany in the Tiffany Studios of New York. Made from nearly a million iridescent pieces of colored glass, the curtain portrays the Valley of Mexico with its two great volcanoes. You can see the curtain before important performances at the theater and on Sunday mornings.

On the third level are the famous murals by Rivera, Orozco, and Siqueiros. The controversial Rivera mural *Man in Control of His Universe* was commissioned in 1933 for Rockefeller Center in New York City. He completed the work there just as you see it: A giant vacuum sucks up the riches of the earth to feed the factories of callous, card-playing, hard-drinking white capitalist bullies, while the noble workers of the earth, of all races, rally behind the red flag of socialism and its standard-bearer, Lenin. Needless to say, the Rockefellers didn't enjoy their new purchase. Much to their discredit, however, they had it painted over—destroyed. Rivera duplicated the mural here as *Man at the Crossing of the Ways* to preserve it.

You can look around in the building Tuesday through Sunday from 10am to 6pm. For information on tickets to performances of the Ballet Folklórico, see "Mexico City After Dark" later in this chapter.

Go back across Cárdenas. The huge building at the corner of Guardiola and Cárdenas is the:

6. **Correos** (post office). The beautiful white stone building, built between 1902 and 1907, was designed by Italian architect Adamo Boari, who also contributed to the Bellas Artes.

From the front of the Correos, go right (north) barely half a block to the corner of Tacuba and turn right again. On the left is the:

7. **Plaza Tolsá** and **El Caballito,** a huge equestrian statue in front of the Museo Nacional de Arte. The gallant statue of King Carlos IV of Spain (1788–1808) atop a high-stepping horse was crafted by Mexican sculptor Manuel Tolsá. Mexicans call the statue *El Caballito* ("The Little Horse"), and the name reveals a lot: They prefer not to mention Carlos, who was king shortly before Mexico's Independence movement from Spain began in 1810.

Just behind the statue is the entrance to one of the city's best, but least-visited, museums, the:

8. **Museo Nacional de Arte** (☎ 512-3224 or 521-7320). The palacelike building, designed by Italian architect Silvio Contri and completed in 1911, another legacy of the years of Europe-loving Porfirio Díaz, was built to house the government's offices of Communications and Public Works. The National Museum of Art took over the building in 1982. Wander through the immense

rooms with polished wooden floors as you view the wealth of paintings showing Mexico's art development, primarily covering the period from 1810 to 1950. It's open Tuesday through Sunday from 10am to 5:30pm. Admission is $4; free on Sunday.

The beautiful building across from the Museo Nacional de Arte is the:

9. **Palacio de Minería,** built in the 1800s, one of architect Manuel Tolsá's finest works. If it's open, step inside for a look at the several patios and fabulous stone work.

☕ **TAKE A BREAK** An indoor/outdoor restaurant with colorful umbrellas, **La Mansión,** next to the museum (turn left out the front door) is a good place to recharge. Or try **La Gran Torta,** next door but around the corner at Tacuba 10, for great fruit, juices, and inexpensive sandwiches.

Cross the street and backtrack east on Tacuba for half a block to the corner of Mata and you'll find the:

10. **Museo del Ejército y F.A.M.,** Calle de Tacuba and Filomeno Mata 6 (☎ 512-7586 or 512-3215), a rather new museum. Ejército means "army," and delicately and artistically displayed inside these high-ceilinged, serene rooms are select instruments used in warfare—from coats of armor and swords to modern weapons. Blood and suffering seem like they could never have been a part of anything so tastefully designed and presented. It's open Monday through Saturday from 10am to 6pm and Sunday from 10am to 4pm.

Once more on Tacuba, cross Cárdenas and walk 1½ blocks west. Opposite the north side of the Alameda, near the corner of Hidalgo and Trujano, is the:

11. **Museo de la Estampa,** Hidalgo 39 (☎ 521-2244), next door to the Museo Franz Mayer (see below). Estampa means "engraving" or "printing," and the museum is devoted to understanding and preserving the graphic arts. The museum has permanent displays on the second floor and changing exhibits on the first. The most famous works here are probably those of José Guadalupe Posada, Mexico's famous printmaker, who poked fun at death and politicians through his skeleton figure drawings. If your interest in this subject is deep, ask to see the video programs on graphic techniques—woodcuts, lithography, etching, and the like. It's open Tuesday through Sunday from 10am to 6pm. Admission is $2.75; free on Sunday.

From here, go right a few steps across the plaza to the entrance of the:

12. **Museo Franz Mayer,** Hidalgo 45 (☎ 518-2265), one of the capital's foremost museums, which opened in 1986 in a beautifully restored 16th-century building on Plaza de la Santa Veracruz. It's opposite the north side of the Alameda. The extraordinary 10,000-piece collection of antiques, mostly from Mexico's 16th through 19th centuries, was amassed by one man, Franz Mayer. A German immigrant, he adopted Mexico as his home in 1905 and grew rich there. Before his death in 1975, Mayer bequeathed the collection to the country and arranged for its permanent display through a trust with the Banco Nacional. The pieces, all utilitarian objects (as opposed to pure art objects), include inlaid and richly carved furniture; an enormous collection of Talavera pottery; gold and silver religious pieces; rare watches and clocks (the oldest is a 1680 lantern clock); and 770 El Quijote volumes, many of which are rare editions or typographically unique. There's so much it may take two visits to absorb it. The museum is open Tuesday through Sunday from 10am to 5pm. Admission is $2.75 for adults, $2 for students; free on Sunday. There are guided tours Monday through Saturday at 10:30 and 11:30am and 12:30pm. Tours cost $1.75.

☕ **TAKE A BREAK**   If a break is in order at this point, try a light snack at the **Cafeteria** of the Museo Franz Mayer, at its marble-top tables in a pleasant courtyard. Or take in another ancient religious structure: Continue one block farther west of the Franz Mayer on Hidalgo to the corner of Reforma, where you'll find the **Hotel de Cortés,** converted to a hotel from an 18th-century building that has been both an insane asylum and a hospice for Augustinian monks. Drinks in the open courtyard dripping with pink bougainvillea and outfitted in umbrella-shaded tables are inexpensive.

From the Hotel de Cortés, cross Hidalgo toward the park and, just at the corner on your right, opposite the Alameda, passing the Centro Cultural José Martí, is the:

13. **Pinacoteca Virreinal de San Diego**, Dr. Mora 7 (☎ 510-2793 or 512-2079). This former church is now a gallery of paintings, most from the 16th and 17th centuries and ecclesiastical in theme. Highlights are apparent immediately as you walk around: In the wing to the right of where the altar would have been is a room featuring a gorgeous blue-and-gilt ceiling with gleaming rosettes and a striking mural by Frederico Canto, one of the few modern works. Upstairs in a cloister are many small paintings by Hipolito de Rioja, Baltazar de Echave Ibia, and others. By the way, the tremendous painting on the cloister wall, *Glorificación de la Inmaculada* by Francisco Antonio Vallejo, should be viewed from upstairs—the lighting is better. The Pinacoteca is open Tuesday through Sunday from 10am to 5pm; admission is $2.75; free on Sunday.

Turn right out the front door and right again on Colón, a short street facing the Plaza de la Solidaridad; walk to the entrance to the:

14. **Museo Mural Diego Rivera** (☎ 510-2329), housing Rivera's famous mural *Dream of a Sunday Afternoon in Alameda Park*, which was painted on a wall of the Hotel Prado in 1947. The hotel was demolished after the 1985 earthquake, but the precious mural, perhaps the best known of Rivera's works, was saved and transferred to its new location in 1986. The mural, 50 feet long and 13 feet high, chronicles the history of the park from the time of Cortés onward. Among the historical figures who have made their mark in Mexican history are, portrayed more or less from left to right (but not in chronological order): Cortés; a heretic suffering under the Spanish Inquisition; Sor Juana Inés de la Cruz, a brilliant and progressive woman who became a nun to help those in need; Benito Juárez, putting forth the laws of Mexico's great Reforma; the conservative Gen. António López de Santa Anna, handing the keys to Mexico to the invading American Gen. Winfield Scott; Emperor Maximilian and Empress Carlota; José Martí, the Cuban revolutionary; Death, with the plumed serpent (Quetzalcoatl) entwined about his neck; Gen. Porfirio Díaz, great with age and medals, asleep; a police officer keeping the Alameda free of "riffraff" by ordering a poor family out of the elitists' park; and Francisco Madero, the martyred democratic president who caused the downfall of Díaz, whose betrayal and alleged murder by Gen. Victoriano Huerta (pictured on the right) resulted in years of civil turmoil in Mexico. The museum is open Tuesday through Sunday from 10am to 2pm and 3 to 6pm; admission is $3; free on Sunday.

Folk-art enthusiasts will delight in two excellent government-operated craft shops. For the first, turn right out of the front door of the Museo de la Alameda; at the corner; turn left one block, then right onto Juárez. On the right is the:

15. **Exposición Nacional de Arte Popular,** Juárez 89 (☎ 518-3058), described in detail under "Shopping" later in this chapter.

An even-larger crafts shop is reached by backtracking on Juárez for 2¹/₂ blocks. On the right is the:

16. **Museo de Artes e Industrías Populares,** at Juárez 44 (☎ 521-6679). The building was once the Corpus Christi Convent, built during the 17th century. You can see the upstairs museum portion Tues–Fri 9am–6pm; its entrance is in the rear of the building. The showrooms are packed with good-quality regional crafts. The store is open daily 9am–6pm.

☕ **WINDING DOWN**   A good place to finish an Alameda tour is the **Fonda Santa Anita,** Humboldt 48 (☎ 518-4609). Serving good traditional Mexican food, this place is good for kicking back and reviewing the day amid colorful banners and painted chairs. It's open Monday through Friday from noon to 10pm and Saturday and Sunday from 1:30 to 9pm.

SPECTATOR SPORTS

JAI ALAI   The strike that closed the **Fronton de México,** Plaza de la República (☎ 546-5369, 546-1479, or 546-3240), is over, and jai alai (pronounced "hi-lie") is once again being played. It must be the fastest game in the world and is exciting to watch even without prior knowledge of the sport. It doesn't much matter when you arrive, as there are several games on each night's schedule. As you walk into the fronton, the ticket office is to your left: There you pay and pick up a program, then take a seat.

Jai alai players wear on their right arms small baskets with which they catch and sling a fantastically resilient ball against the wall to the right of where you're sitting. In the best game, four players, two with blue armbands and two with red ones, compete against each other in a fashion similar to tennis, but even more similar to squash. The member of one team throws the ball against the wall, and the other team has to return it. The whole thing is done at an incredible speed—how they manage to see, much less catch, a ball traveling at about 80 miles per hour is marvelous.

The most fun is in the betting; a game just seems more exciting when you have money riding on the result. Wait until the program announces a game of 30 points (*partido a treinta tantos*) and watch the bookies. These colorful gentlemen, wearing burgundy vests, carry little pads of betting slips edged in red (*rojo*) or blue (*azul*), and when the game begins they'll be offering only a slight edge on one team or another. Bets are placed inside of slashed tennis balls and thrown to bookies during the game. When the scoring starts, however, the odds will change. If you're as good a mathematician as most jai alai aficionados, you'll be able to bet with impunity on both sides at different points of the game—and still finish ahead.

Note: This has become a game for elite spectators, meaning that for men coats and ties are required. Women must be similarly nicely dressed.

Admission is $18. The box office opens at 6:30pm, and games are held on Tuesday through Sunday at 5pm year-round. To get there, head for the northeast corner of Plaza de la República (at the corner of Calle Ramos Arizpe, a few blocks along Juárez west of Reforma). Any bus going west along Juárez will take you to the Juárez-Reforma intersection, and it's a short walk from there. Or you can take the Metro to the Revolución station and walk three blocks down Arriaga (south) to the plaza.

BULLFIGHTS   The capital's **Plaza de Toros Monumental México** is among the largest bullrings in the world. It seats 64,000 people, and on Sunday during the professional season (usually December through April, but no fixed dates) most seats are taken. On other Sundays through the year the arena is given over to the beginners (nouvilleros), most of whom are as bad as the beginners in any other sport. Six fights make up a corrida, which begins precisely at 4pm and is one of the few things in Mexico that's always on time.

There are several ways to reach Plaza de Toros, which is situated 2 or 3 miles south along Insurgentes. Any big hotel or tour agency will be happy to book you onto a tour with transportation. In about 25 minutes, the bus will pass the bullring on the right. Most of the people on the bus will alight here, so you'll know you're at the bullring, which is just around the corner ahead.

Dozens of men and women sell nuts, hats, and all kinds of whatnots. Look for a woman, or *muchacha,* selling chewing gum and waving small "programs." If you buy the chewing gum, she'll give you (free) the one-page sheet that lists the names of the day's toreros.

Unless you want to pay more, take your place in the line at one of the windows marked SOL GENERAL. It will be in the sun and it will be high up, but the sun isn't too strong (it sets soon, anyway) and you won't see many other tourists that way. (Try to avoid the seats numbered 1 to 100; for some reason, the roughnecks prefer to gather in this section.) Seats in *la sombra* (shade) are more expensive, of course. Tickets cost between $3 and $26. Fights start at 4pm, but get there well in advance for a good seat.

Usually, there are six separate bulls to be fought (two by each matador) in a corrida, but I'd suggest you leave just before the last bull—to avoid the crowds. Outside, around two sides of the bullring is a scene of frantic activity. Hundreds of tiny stalls have masses of food frying, cold beer stacked high, and radios blaring with a commentary on the action inside the ring.

To get there, take the Metro (to the San António station on Line 7) or a colectivo; the number of colectivos that normally roam Insurgentes is supplemented by Sunday-afternoon taxis headed for the plaza, and they'll often pick up extra passengers going their way. Or you can catch one of the buses marked PLAZA MÉXICO that travels down Insurgentes on Sunday afternoon.

6 Shopping

Mexico City is a marvelous place to buy crafts of all types. You'll come across numerous places displaying fascinating native products, and you're certain to find something you want as a souvenir. Here's the rundown on the best places to shop, from small, selective crafts shops to vast general markets.

Today it often costs only a little more money to buy these things in the capital than at the source, if one knows a good shop. Several government-run shops and a few excellent privately run shops have exceptionally good collections of Mexico's arts and crafts. As fascinating as a fine-art gallery, these shops deserve a visit regardless of whether or not you intend to buy.

The two best districts for browsing are on and off Avenida Juárez facing the Alameda, Avenida Madero and the streets parallel to it, and in the Zona Rosa (for jewelry, Calle Amberes is the place, for instance). A few unique shops deserve particular mention.

SHOPPING A TO Z
CRAFTS
Artesanías Michoacán
Londres 117. ☎ **514-2025** or 514-7455.

This shop, in the Zona Rosa, brings crafts from the state of Michoacán. It isn't large, but it's a good place to see a wide selection of that state's pottery, textiles, and copper. Open Monday through Friday from 10am to 7pm and Saturday from 10am to 6pm.

Exposición Nacional De Arte Popular (FONART)
Juárez 89. ☎ **521-6681.** Metro: Hidalgo or Juárez.

This government-operated store is usually loaded with crafts. It is operated by the Fonda Nacional para el Fomento de las Artes (FONART), a government organization that helps village craftspeople. It's open daily from 10am to 6pm.

FONART
Londres 136A. ☎ **525-2026.** Metro: Hidalgo or Juárez.

Another branch of the government-operated store (see above) is in the heart of the Zona Rosa. Though in a small, narrow upstairs quarters, it is absolutely packed with folk art, much of it not duplicated at the larger store on Juárez. Open Monday through Saturday from 10am to 7pm.

Museo Nacional de Artes e Industrias Populares
Juárez 44. ☎ **521-6679.** Metro: Hidalgo or Juárez.

The museum store here, located across from the Benito Juárez statue in Alameda Park, has an enormous selection of high-quality Mexican crafts for sale. Because the prices are fixed, you can get an idea of quality versus cost for later use in market bargaining. (Upstairs, with the entrance in back is the museum.) Open daily from 9am to 6pm; the museum is open Monday through Friday from 9am to 6pm.

GLASS
Avalos Brothers
Carretones 5. ☎ **522-5311.** Fax 522-6420.

For more than 100 years, blown glass has been issuing forth from this location in the old section of town. You can watch men and women scurry around with red-hot glass in various stages of shaping until it cools. A sales showroom to the left of the entrance holds shelves full of glass objects in various colors. Among locals this is the store of choice for selection and price. One block from San Pablo at Tapacio and Carretones, it's open Monday through Friday from 10:30am to 3pm and Saturday from 10:30am to 2pm.

MARKETS
Bazar Sábado
San Angel

The Bazar Sábado is held every Saturday, as its name indicates, in an expensive colonial-era suburb of cobbled streets, mansions, and parks a few miles south of the city. This is the only day the actual bazaar building (a fine two-story mansion built around a courtyard) is open. It showcases dozens of permanent stalls offering high-quality decorative art. On adjacent plazas, hundreds of easel artists display their paintings, and members of indigenous groups from Puebla and elsewhere bring their folk art—baskets, masks, pottery, textiles, and so on. Restaurants (some in mansions) lining the streets play host to leisurely diners seated at umbrella-shaded tables. Plan to spend all Saturday touring the attractions on the southern outskirts of the city. (See also "San Angel" earlier in this chapter.)

Centro Artesanal (Mercado de Curiosidades)
At the corner of Ayuntamiento and Dolores. Metro: Salto del Agua.

This rather modern building set back off a plaza is composed of a number of stalls on two levels, selling everything from leather to tiles. They have some lovely silver jewelry and, as in most non-fixed-price stores, the asking price is high but the bargained result is often very reasonable.

Lagunilla Market
A few blocks north of Plaza de Garibaldi. Metro: Allende.

This is another market well worth visiting. The best day is Sunday, when the Lagunilla becomes a colorful outdoor market filling the streets for blocks. Vendors sell everything from axes to antiques. Be careful about pickpockets. The two enclosed sections are open all week and are separated by a short street, Calle Juan Alvarez. They have different specialties: The one to the north is noted for clothes, rebozos, and blankets; the one to the south for tools, pottery, and household goods, such as attractive hanging copper lamps. This is also the area to find old and rare books, many at a ridiculously low cost, if you're willing to hunt and bargain. Most, however, are in Spanish.

Mercado de Artesanías "La Ciudadela"
Plaza de la Ciudadela. Metro: Juárez.

An interesting market that's large and clean, the Mercado de Artensanías rambles on forever just off Balderas and Ayuntamiento in the Plaza de la Ciudadela. The merchandise is of good quality and well displayed, and bartering is a must.

Mercado Insurgentes
On Londres between Florencia and Amberes.

Mercado Insurgentes is a full-fledged crafts market tucked in the Zona Rosa. Because of its address you might expect exorbitant prices, but vendors in the maze of stalls are eager to bargain, and good buys aren't hard to come by.

Merced Market

This is the biggest market in the city and it's among the most fascinating in the country, with intense activity and an energy level akin to the Abastos market in Oaxaca and the Friday Ocotlán market south of there. Shops line tidy-but-people-filled streets all the way to the Zócalo. Near the market, street vendors hawk their wares as well. The first building is mainly for fruits and vegetables; the others contain just about everything you would find if a department store joined forces with a discount warehouse—a good place to shop especially for housewares such as hand-held lemon, lime and orange juicers of all sizes, tinware, colorful spoons, decorative oil cloth, etc. The main market is east of the Zócalo on Circunvalación between General Anaya and Adolfo Gurrión. To get here from the Zócalo take Corregidor, the street to the right of the Palacio Nacional, and follow it five blocks to Circunvalación and turn right. Walk for two long blocks and you'll see the entrance to the market on the left.

7 Mexico City After Dark

If you have any energy left after sightseeing at this high altitude, the capital of Mexico offers up quite a variety of nighttime entertainment from mariachis and reggae to the opera, regional folkloric dancing to classic ballet, and dinner shows to drinking establishments, the choice is enormous. Mostly you can enjoy them in Mexico City at a price that is less than comparable entertainment in another of the world's major cities. On the other hand, if you're willing to let *la vida Mexicana* put on its own fascinating show for you, the bill will be much less. People-watching, cafe-sitting, music, even a dozen mariachi bands all playing at once, can be yours for next to nothing.

THE ENTERTAINMENT SCENE

For current information on cultural offerings at all of the establishements listed below, the best source is the Sunday edition of *The News,* which has a full listing of cultural events. A limited number of events are printed other days. *Donde,* a free magazine found in hotels is another good source for locating the newest places, but it doesn't list changing entertainment or current exhibits. For performances of major attractions tickets can usually be obtained through **Ticketmaster** (☎ 325-9000).

Lobby bars tend to have live entertainment of the low-key type in the late afternoon and on into the evening. Disco dancing is alive and well in Mexico with flashy light shows and megadecible music. Discos and dinner dance establishments tend to get going around 9 or 10:30pm and last until at least 3am. Most discos operate only Thursday through Saturday. Fiesta nights give visitors a chance to dine on typical Mexican food and see Mexico's wonderful regional dancing, which seems to always be a treat no matter how many times you've seen them.

Much of the city's night life takes place around the **Zona Rosa,** a traditional place to stroll, sip and eat at several places if you want—appetizers one place, dinner another and dessert somewhere else, winding up at a nearby disco or dancing establishment, hotel lobby bar, or cozy coffee house. Outdoor cafes on **Copenhague street** are among the liveliest for being in the thick of the Zona Rosa scene, but with one or two exceptions, it has become more expensive than it is good. Another tradition is Garibaldi Square, where mariachis tune up and wait to be hired. Restaurants and drinking establishments there feature them in a typical Mexican atmosphere. It's a slice of Mexican life that every traveler must experience at least once.

FOLKLORIC BALLET

Palacio de Bellas Artes

Lázaro Cárdenas, on the east side of the Alameda. ☎ **709-3111,** ext. 173. Tickets $30–$42. Metro: Bellas Artes.

Besides hosting traveling ballet and opera companies from around the world, performances of Mexico's famed **Ballet Folklorico de Mexico** are held here several times weekly.

The Ballet Folkloric is a celebration of pre-and post-Hispanic dancing in Mexico. A typical program will include Aztec ritual dances, agricultural dances from Jalisco, a fiesta in Veracruz, a Christmas celebration—all welded together with mariachis, marimba players, singers, and dancers. Since many other events are held in the Bellas Artes—visits by foreign opera companies, for instance—there are times when the Ballet Folklórico is moved. Usually, it reappears in the National Auditorium in Chapultepec Park. Check at the Bellas Artes box office. Three are two companies—three, if you count the one usually on tour. The show is popular and tickets are bought up rapidly (especially by a tour agency at twice the cost). The box office is on the ground floor of the Bellas Artes, main entrance. Note: The theater tends to very cold so you may want to bring a sweater. The box office is open Mon–Sat 11am–7pm, Sun 8:30–9am; Ballet Folklórico performances, Sun 9:30am and 9pm; Wed 9pm.

Teatro de La Ciudad

Donceles 36. ☎ **521-2355.** Tickets $10.50 to the Ballet Folklórico; call about other perfor-mances. Shows Sun 9:30am, 2:30pm; Tues 8:30pm. Metro: Bellas Artes.

An alternative to the Ballet Folklórico de Mexico is the **Ballet Folklorico Nacional Aztlán,** in the beautiful turn-of-the-century Teatro de La Cuidad, a block northeast of the Bellas Artes between Xicotencatl and Allende. Performances here are as good as the better-known ones in the Bellas Artes, but tickets are a lot cheaper and much easier to obtain. Other major performances of ballet, concerts etc. also appear here.

THE CLUB & MUSIC SCENE
MARIACHIS

At some time or other, everybody—Mexicans and *turistas* alike—goes to see and hear the mariachi players. The mariachis are strolling musicians who wear distinc-tive costumes, which make them look like Mexican cowboys dressed up for a special occasion. Their costume—tight spangled trousers, fancy jackets, and big floppy bow ties—dates back to the French occupation of Mexico in the mid-19th century, as indeed, does their name. *Mariachi* is believed to be the Mexican mis-pronunciation of the French word for marriage, which is where they were often on call for music.

In Mexico City, the mariachis make their headquarters around the **Plaza de Garibaldi,** which is a ten-minute stroll north of the Palacio de Bellas Artes up Avenida Lázaro Cárdenas, at Avenida República de Honduras. You will pass dozens of stores and a couple of burlesque houses.

In the Plaza de Garibaldi itself, mariachi players are everywhere. At every cor-ner, guitars are stacked together like rifles in an army training camp. Young mu-sicians strut proudly in their flashy outfits, on the lookout for señoritas to impress. They play when they feel like it, when there's a good chance to gather in some tips, or when someone orders a song—the going rate seems to be around $5 or $10 per song. The best time to hear music in the square itself is after 9 or 10pm, especially on Sunday.

In any of the eating and drinking establishments around the plaza you can en-joy the mariachi music that swirls through the air. **Tlaquepaque,** across the square, is a well-known tourist-oriented restaurant where you can dine to strolling mariachis. But remember—if you give a bandleader the sign, you're the one who pays for the song, just like outside in the square.

Another popular place on the square is **Plaza Santa Cecilia,** Amaragura 30 (☎ 526-2455 or 529-1102). Monday through Saturday shows are at 9 and 10:30pm, midnight, and 1:30am, for a cost of $12.

Pulquería Hermana Hortensia, Amargura 4 (☎ 529-7828), is perhaps the most adventurous spot for newcomers to Mexico City. It's on the Plaza Garibaldi near the northeast corner at Amargura and República de Honduras. Unlike most pulque bars, La Hermana Hortensia is a *pulquera familiar* (a "family" bar, that is, you can bring your wife—but not your kids). Pulque (that's "POOL-keh") is a thick and flavorsome drink made by fermenting the juice of a maguey (century) plant. Invented by the ancient Toltecs and shared with the Aztecs, pulque was a sacred drink forbidden to the common people for centuries. One of the effects of the Spanish Conquest was to liberate pulque for the masses. Was this good or bad? Ask your neighbor in La Hermana Hortensia as you quaff the thick brew. Pulque packs a wallop, although it's not nearly so strong as those other maguey-based drinks, tequila and mezcal. By the way, the pulque here can be ordered with nuts blended in for a different flavor.

Don't get the idea that you'll see only your countryfolk in the Plaza Garibaldi, for it is indeed a Mexican phenomenon. As evening falls, lots of people from the neighborhood come to stroll or sit. (See also Jorongo Bar, below.)

TRIO MUSIC, JAZZ & FIESTAS

El Chato la Posta
Londres 25. Col. Juárez. ☎ **546-1199** or 705-1457. Cover $35.

This popular bar features great trio music and botanas (snacks) with the drinks. Several different groups entertain. Open Thurs–Sat 10:30–3am.

Jorongo Bar
Hotel María Isabel Sheraton, Reforma 325. ☎ **207-3933.**

For wonderful Mexican trio music in plush surroundings, make your way to Jorongo Bar at the María Isabel-Sheraton Hotel, facing the Angel Monument. The reputation for this bar's good trio/mariachi music has been good for decades—it's an institution. From 7pm to 2am, you can enjoy the smooth and joyous sounds for the price of a drink ($4–7) and a cover charge of about $15.

Maquiavelo
Hotel Krystal, Liverpool 155. ☎ **211-0092** or 211-3460. Cover $15 5pm–midnight.

This little known nightclub, in the heart of the Zona Rosa, changes from an informal bar during the day to a jazz center in the evenings. Open 1pm–midnight; jazz 5pm–midnight.

El Patio
Atenas 9, Col. Juárez. ☎ **566-1743.** Call for current charge.

Some of Mexico's most famous singers, and entertainers perform in an lengthy after dinner show. It's at the far eastern edge of the Zona Rosa. Open Tues–Sat 10pm–3am.

Hotel de Cortes
Avenida Hidalgo 85. ☎ **518-2182.** Cover $20–$30.

Unless it rains, there's a Mexican Fiesta every Saturday on the open patio of this colonial-era convent-turned-hotel on the Alameda. (See also" Walking Tour—Near the Alameda," above.) The price of admission includes drinks, dinner, and the show.

La Veranda

Hotel María Isabel Sheraton, Reforma 325, at Río Tiber. ☎ **5/207-3933.** Cover $30–$40.

The elaborate Fiesta Mexicana dinner and show here has also been a staple of capital entertainment for years, featuring good dinner and a lively show of Mexican regional dancers in colorful attire. Open Mon–Fri 7–10pm.

NIGHTCLUBS & DISCOS

Dynasty Disco

Hotel Nikko, Campos Elíseos 204, Polanco. ☎ **280-1111.** Cover $7 Mon–Thurs; $10 Fri, Sat, Sun.

An upscale disco in one of the capital's top hotels. Besides the disco there are two nightly live shows of mariachi or trio music which last about 45 minutes each, all for the price of admission. Drinks, of course, are extra. Open Mon–Thurs 9pm–1:30am, Fri–Sun 9pm–3am.

Hotel Majestic

Av. Madero 73, México, D.F. 06000. ☎ **5/521-8600.** No cover.

The popular rooftop bar of this hotel overlooks the Zócalo and the Catedral Metropolitana. A variety of good singers (usually) entertains, although there could be a trio crooning romantic Mexican favorites. Open daily noon–1am; entertainment 7pm–1am.

LOBBY BARS

Caviar Bar

Hotel Marquís Reforma, Reforma 465, Col. Cuauhtémoc. ☎ **5/211-3600.**

While guests enjoy light meals and drinks, a string quartet plays in the evening hours. It's totally elegant and wonderfully soothing.

Hotel Camino Real

Mariano Escobedo 700, Col. Nueva Anzures. ☎ **203-2121.** No cover.

You'll be surrounded by people enjoying the piano music at this very popular lobby bar. Order a drink and kick back for a relaxing respite. Open daily noon–1am.

Hotel Galeria Plaza

Hamburgo 195, at Varsovia. ☎ **211-0014.** No cover.

Ever since this luxury hotel opened in the early 1980s it's been known for its inviting lobby-bar entertainment. The type of music varies, but often includes jazz. Open 11am–1am; live music 7pm–1am.

5 Excursions from Mexico City

Just as Paris has its Versailles and Rome its Villa d'Este, so Mexico City is surrounded by suburban areas that are every bit as fascinating as the city itself—and all can be reached by a bus ride that is inexpensive and comfortable. In addition, two spa hotels can arrange for a private car to transport guests from the Mexico City airport.

This chapter focuses on the main attractions of these excursions. The ruins of Teotihuacán, the Viceregal Museum at Tepotzotlán, and Toluca are suitable for day-trips that are short enough to have you back in Mexico City by evening. Tlaxcala and Puebla are also good choices for day-trips, but you may find these cities' attractions worthy of more than one day. Taxco, known for its silver shops, museums, and picturesque hillside colonial-era charm, is worthy of at least an overnight (or more if you can spare the time). Valle de Bravo and Ixtapan de la Sal, known for their spas and golf courses, are only about 2¹/₂ to 3¹/₂ hours from Mexico City, but they are best thought of as two- or three-day (or longer) getaways.

1 The Pyramids of San Juan Teotihuacán

30 miles NE of Mexico City

The ruins of Teotihuacán are among the most remarkable in Mexico, and you shouldn't miss them. The name means "place where gods were born." Occupation of the area of Teotihuacán began around 500 B.C., but it wasn't until the 100 B.C. that construction of the enormous Pyramid of the Sun at Teotihuacán was begun. Teotihuacán's rise corresponds to the time when the Classical Greeks were building their great monuments on the other side of the world, and with the beginning of cultures in Mexico's Yucatán Peninsula, Oaxaca, and Puebla. Teotihuacán was the dominant city in Mesoamerica during the Classical Period, covering eight square miles with its magnificent pyramids and palaces. At its zenith around A.D. 500 there were at least 200,000 inhabitants, more than in contemporary Rome. Through trade and other contact, its influence was known in other parts of Mexico and as far south as Mexico's Yucatán peninsula and Guatemala. But little is known about the city's inhabitants, what language they spoke, where they came from, or why they abandoned the place in A.D. 700. It is known that at the beginning of the first century A.D. the Xitle volcano erupted near Cuicuilco (south of Mexico City) and decimated that city, which was the most dominant city of the time. Those inhabitants migrated to Teotihuacán. Scholars believe that Teotihuacán's decline was gradual, and perhaps occurred over a 250-year period; overpopulation and depletion of natural resources may have been the problems. In the end it appears that the people were poorly nourished and that the city was deliberately burned.

Ongoing excavations have revealed something of the culture. According to archaeoastronomer John B. Carlson, the cult of Venus that determined wars and human sacrifices elsewhere in Mesoamerica was prominent at Teotihuacán as well. Ceremonial rituals were timed with the appearance of Venus as the morning and evening star. The symbol of Venus at Teotihuacán (as at Cacaxtla, 50 miles away, near Tlaxcala) appears as a star or half star with a full or half circle. Carlson also suggests the possibility that Teotihuacán was conquered by people from Cacaxtla, since name glyphs of conquered peoples at Cacaxtla show Teotihuacán-like pyramids. Numerous tombs with human remains (many of them either sacrificial inhabitants of the city or perhaps war captives) and objects of jewelry, pottery, and daily life have been uncovered along the foundations of buildings. It appears that the primary deity at Teotihuacán was a female called "Great Goddess" for lack of any other known name. Today what remains are the rough stone structures of the three pyramids and sacrificial altars, and some of the grand houses, all of which were once covered in stucco and painted with brilliant frescos (mainly in red). The Toltecs, who rose in power after the decline of Teotihuacán, were fascinated with Teotihuacán and incorporated Teotihuacán symbols into their own cultural motifs. The Aztecs, who came after the Toltecs, were likewise fascinated with the Toltecs and ruins of Teotihuacán, and adopted many of *their* symbols and motifs. (For more information on Teotihuacán and it's influence in Mesoamerica see also Chapter 2, "Getting to Know Mexico").

ESSENTIALS

GETTING THERE & DEPARTING   By Bus   Buses leave every half hour (from 5am to 10pm) every day of the week from the Terminal Central de Autobuses del Norte, and the trip takes one hour. When you reach the Terminal Norte, look for the **Autobuses Sahagun** sign located at the far northwest end all the way down to the sign "8 ESPERA."

Since entrances to the archaeological zone were changing when this book was written, be sure to ask the driver where you should wait for returning buses, how frequently buses run, and especially the time of the last bus back.

By Car   Driving to San Juan Teotihuacán on either the toll Highway 85D or free Highway 132D will take about an hour. Head north on Insurgentes to get out of the city. Highway 132D passes through picturesque villages and the like, but is excruciatingly slow, due to the surfeit of trucks and buses; Highway 85D, the toll road, is duller but faster.

If you do take Highway 132D through the villages, about 15 miles from Mexico City the village of **San Cristóbal Ecatepec** looms off to the left. Note also on the left an old wall built centuries ago to keep what was then a lake from flooding the area. When the road forks a mile or so farther north, take the road to the right. About 3 miles farther along this road is the Convent of **San Agustín Acolman** (1539–60). Not long ago the fortresslike monastery was in ruins: The only sounds were the ticking of a modern clock, the faint bleating of sheep from the fields outside, and the chatter of birds building nests on the roof. At one time it was even flooded with mud. Now, however, the monastery and church are restored, and you

Excursions from Mexico City

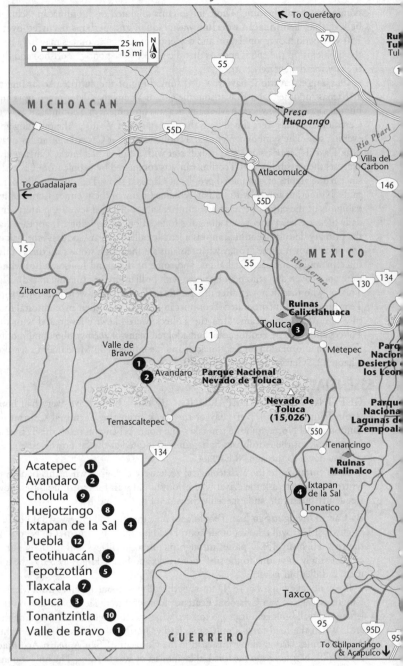

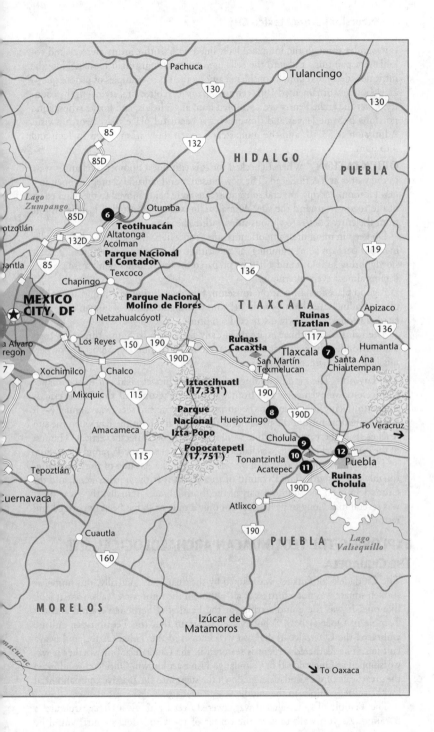

can wander through the immense halls lined with 16th-century frescoes and colonial-era paintings and into the cells used by the Augustinian monks. Note the
intricately decorated portal, considered among the finest examples of plateresque—
an elaborately ornamented 16th-century Spanish architectural style—in the country. Over the arched entry are a sculpted lion, angel heads, and horses whose hind
portions become leaves and flowers. It's a beautiful place that's worth a visit.
Admission is $3.50, and the monastery is open daily from 10am to 1pm and
3 to 6pm.

ORIENTATION   When I checked for this edition, a number of changes were
in the works at Teotihuacán. The new museum and cultural center are open in a
new location. Parking lots and souvenir stands were being moved to the outer edges
of the roadway around the site. A small train was to be installed to take visitors
from the entry booths to various stops within the site.

Do keep in mind these important points: You will be doing a great deal of walking, and perhaps some climbing, at an altitude of more than 7,000 feet. Take it
slowly; bring sunblock and a hat; be prepared for the summer rainy season, when
it rains almost every afternoon.

A good place to start is at the **museum.** Findings during recent digs are on display including several tombs with skeletons wearing necklaces of human and simu-
lated jawbones, and newly discovered sculpture.

The ruins of Teotihuacán are open daily from 8am to 5pm. Admission costs
$5.50 Monday through Friday and it's free to all on Sunday; $8.50 fee for permission to use a video camera.

The Layout   The grand buildings of Teotihuacán were laid out in accordance
with celestial movements. The front wall of the **Pyramid of the Sun** is exactly
square to (facing) the point on the horizon where the sun sets twice annually—if
a line were drawn from the pyramid to the sun at noon on the day when the sun
reaches its highest point, the line would in theory be perfectly vertical. The rest
of the ceremonial buildings were laid out at right angles to the Pyramid of the Sun.

The main thoroughfare, called by archaeologists the **Avenue of the Dead,** runs
roughly north-south. The **Pyramid of the Moon** is at the northern end, and the
Ciudadela is on the southern part of the thoroughfare. Actually, the great street
was several miles long in its heyday, but only a mile or so has been uncovered and
restored.

EXPLORING THE TEOTIHUACÁN ARCHAEOLOGICAL SITE
THE CIUDADELA

The Ciudadela, or Citadel, was named by the Spaniards. Actually, this immense
sunken square was not a fortress at all, although the impressive walls make it look
like one. It was the grand setting for the Feathered Serpent Pyramid and the
Temple of Quetzalcoatl. Scholars aren't certain that the Teotihuacán culture
embraced the Quetzalcoatl deity so well known in the Toltec, Aztec, and Maya
cultures. The feathered serpent is featured in the Ciudadela, but whether it was
worshipped as Quetzalcoatl or a similar god isn't yet known. Once you've admired
the great scale of the Ciudadela, go down the steps into the massive court and head
for the ruined temple, in the middle.

The Temple of Quetzalcoatl was covered over by an even larger structure, a
pyramid. As you walk toward the center of the Ciudadela's court, you'll be

approaching the pyramid. The Feathered Serpent Pyramid will be on your left. Walk around to the right of it, and soon you'll see the reconstructed temple close behind the pyramid. There's a narrow passage between the two structures, and traffic is supposed to be one way—which is why I directed you to the right.

Early temples were often covered over by later ones in Mexico and Central America. The Pyramid of the Sun may have been built up in this way. Archaeologists have tunneled deep inside the Feathered Serpent Pyramid and found several ceremonially buried human remains, interred with precise detail and position, but as yet no person of royalty. Drawings of how the building once looked show that every level was covered with faces of a feathered serpent. As for the Temple of Quetzalcoatl, you'll notice at once the fine big carved serpents' heads jutting out from collars of feathers carved in the stone walls. Other feathered serpents are carved in relief low on the walls. You can get a good idea of the glory of Mexico's ancient cities from this temple.

AVENUE OF THE DEAD

The Avenue of the Dead got its strange and forbidding name from the Aztecs, who mistook the little temples that line both sides of the avenue for tombs of kings or priests.

As you stroll north along the Avenue of the Dead toward the Pyramid of the Moon, look on the right for a bit of wall sheltered by a modern corrugated roof. Beneath the shelter, the wall still bears a painting of a jaguar. From this fragment, you might be able to build a picture of the breathtaking spectacle that must have met the eye when all the paintings along the avenue were intact.

PYRAMID OF THE SUN

The Pyramid of the Sun is located on the east side of the Avenue of the Dead. As pyramids go, this is the third largest in the world. The Great Pyramid of Cholula, near Puebla, is the largest structure ever built. Second largest is the Pyramid of Cheops on the outskirts of Cairo, Egypt. Teotihuacán's Pyramid of the Sun is, at the base, 730 feet per side—almost as large as Cheops. But at 210 feet high, the Sun pyramid is only about half as high as its Egyptian rival. No matter. It's still the biggest restored pyramid in the Western Hemisphere, and an awesome sight. Although the Pyramid of the Sun was not built as a great king's tomb, it does have secret tunnels and chambers beneath it, but they aren't open to the public.

The first structure of the pyramid was probably built a century before Christ, and the temple that used to crown the pyramid was finished about 400 years later (A.D. 300). By the time the pyramid was discovered and restoration was begun (early in our century), the temple had completely disappeared, and the pyramid was just a mass of rubble covered with bushes and trees.

If you're game, trudge up the 248 steps to the top. The view is marvelous, if the smog's not too thick.

PYRAMID OF THE MOON

The Pyramid of the Moon faces an interesting plaza at the northern end of the avenue. The plaza is surrounded by little temples, and by the Palace of Quetzal-Mariposa (or Quetzal-Butterfly), on the left (west) side. You get about the same range of view from the top of the Pyramid of the Moon as you do from its larger neighbor, because the moon pyramid is built on higher ground. The perspective straight down the Avenue of the Dead is magnificent.

PALACE OF QUETZAL-MARIPOSA

The Palace of Quetzal-Mariposa lay in ruins until the 1960s, when restoration work began. Today it echoes wonderfully with its former glory, as figures of Quetzal-Mariposa (a mythical exotic bird-butterfly) appear painted on walls or carved in the pillars of the inner court.

Behind the Palace of Quetzal-Mariposa is the Palace of the Jaguars, complete with murals showing a lively jaguar musical combo, and some frescoes.

DINING

You may want to pack a box lunch to take to the ruins—doing so will save you a long walk to any of the restaurants. Almost any hotel or restaurant in the city can prepare it for you. Vendors at the ruins also sell drinks and snacks.

La Gruta

☎ **595/6-0127**; 6-0104. Main courses $5–$11. Daily 11am–7pm. Ask for the most direct way from where you exit the ruins. MEXICAN.

La Gruta is a huge, delightfully cool natural grotto filled with natty waiters and the sound of clinking glasses. Soft drinks and beer are served until the full bar opens. You have the option of ordering a five-course set-price lunch or choosing your own combination—perhaps a hamburger and a soft drink.

2 Ixta-Popo National Park

135 miles SE of Mexico City

Amecameca, a town of 37,000 situated at a height of 7,500 feet, is blessed with a big square, a 200-year-old parish church constructed in the 16th century for priests of the Dominican order, and fresh, clear air. But the reason you're here is to see or perhaps to hike or climb in the Ixta-Popo National Park, whose raison d'être is the volcanoes Popocatépetl and Ixtaccíhihuatl. Popocatépetl last erupted in December 1994.

ESSENTIALS

GETTING THERE & DEPARTING By Bus Take Metro Line 1 east (toward Pantitlán) to the San Lázaro stop. As you come to the surface, you'll see the green-domed **TAPO** (Terminal de Autobuses de Pasajeros de Oriente), Mexico City's eastern bus terminal. Walk along Tunnel 1, the corridor to the central domed area, and look for **Líneas Unidas–Cristóbal Colón** buses to Amecameca and Popo Park. Buses leave every half hour every day. The bus will let you off a block and a half from the central square in Amecameca.

To get to Ixta-Popo National Park and the mountain lodge, about 8 miles from Amecameca, you'll have to hire a taxi for about $24 one way. Check at the Hotel San Carlos, on the square, for other passengers and perhaps you'll be able to split the cost. Make a deal with the taxi driver to pick you up later since there's no telephone at the lodge; or you can take a chance and try to thumb a ride down the mountain, which is often easily done. Hitchhiking from Amecameca to the lodge isn't recommended because there's little traffic.

By Car Take the Puebla road (Route 190) out of Mexico City, turning off to the right on Route 115 to the village of Chalco. A few miles father on is Amecameca. From there, ask directions for the road to the park, 8 miles farther up the mountain on a good paved road that twists through alpine beauty.

Teotihuacán

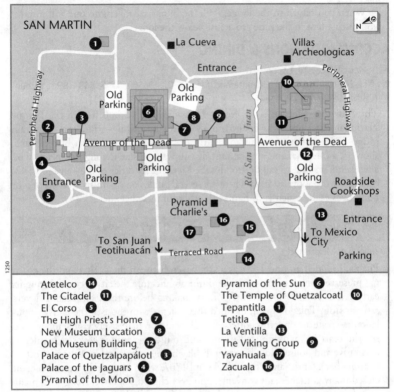

SAN MARTIN

N

La Cueva

Villas Archeologicas

Entrance

Peripheral Highway

Peripheral Highway

Old Parking

Old Parking

Old Parking

Rio San Juan

Avenue of the Dead

Avenue of the Dead

Old Parking

Old Parking

Entrance

Old Parking

Roadside Cookshops

Entrance

Pyramid Charlie's

Entrance

To San Juan Teotihuacán

To Mexico City

Parking

Terraced Road

1250

Atetelco ⑭		Pyramid of the Sun ⑥
The Citadel ⑪		The Temple of Quetzalcoatl ⑩
El Corso ⑤		Tepantitla ①
The High Priest's Home ⑦		Tetitla ⑮
New Museum Location ⑧		La Ventilla ⑬
Old Museum Building ⑫		The Viking Group ⑨
Palace of Quetzalpapálotl ③		Yayahuala ⑰
Palace of the Jaguars ④		Zacuala ⑯
Pyramid of the Moon ②		

HIKING & CLIMBING IN THE PARK

Outside the Albergue lodge (see below) is the snow-covered summit of **Popocatépetl,** 18,177 feet high at the rim. In the morning the clouds may drift away for an hour, yielding an incomparable close-up view. Across the valley, Popo's sister volcano, **Ixtaccíhihuatl,** may be exposed as well. When you see them gleaming in the morning sun, surrounded by the chilly morning air, you'll remember the moment for a lifetime.

THE TRAILS   Popocatépetl is no mountain for rookie climbers or for any expert climber who's not in top shape. At the lodge trailhead the air is so thin that even walking makes a normal, healthy person dizzy—and the air's considerably thinner at 17,887 feet! Besides, it's cold up here, even in the sweltering heat of summer. But if you're an expert climber, check in at the lodge reception or the rescue hut next to the lodge. You may be asked to pass an equipment check and sign your name in the hiker's register before you set out.

Maps of the various trails to the summit, showing the several huts and shelters, are on view in the lodge hut. The trek to the summit takes two days or longer, depending on what shape you're in and which trail you choose. You camp below the summit and return the next day. Despite the name RESCUE HUT on one of the buildings, there is no staff rescue team on hand. You climb at your own risk, and rescue—if any—will come from those on hand who pitch in to help.

When you return to the lodge, if all the bunks are taken, no one will mind if you pitch a tent in the pine grove just below the lodge.

ACCOMMODATIONS & DINING

Albergue Vicente Guerrero

Río Elba 20, 10th Floor, Col. Cuauhtémoc, México, D.F. 06500. ☎ 5/553-5896. $5 bunk with sheet, pillow case, and blanket.

The Albergue Vicente Guerrero at Tlamacas (alt. 12,800 ft.), in the Parque Nacional Ixta-Popo, was opened in 1978. It's beautiful—a modern mountain lodge done in native stone and natural wood, complete with bunkrooms, showers, a cafeteria, and a restaurant. If you want to stay the night, especially on a weekend, it's best to call or drop by the Mexico City office of the lodge for a reservation at the above address. There are several bunkrooms with six sections of four bunk beds each, which you share with others of mixed gender.

3 Puebla: Museums & Architecture

80 miles E of Mexico City

Puebla, founded around 1531 as a safe haven between the capital and the coast, has preserved much of the wealth and fine architecture the city accrued during its early years. Already known for pottery making before the Conquest, Talavera artisans from Toledo, Spain, blended their talents with those of the native population to create a wonderful pottery and tile tradition that is very visible today. You see the craft in many church domes and building facades covered in tile, as decorative and household objects on display in museums, and in Talavera pottery factories here. Christianity flourished until 1767, when an antireligious movement closed many churches and convents. Some 99 churches survive, along with many grand monasteries, convents, and a magnificent Bishop's Palace next to the cathedral.

ESSENTIALS

GETTING THERE & DEPARTING   By Bus   The bus trip from Mexico City to Puebla takes about two hours. From Mexico City's TAPO bus station, **Pullman Plus** runs deluxe service to Puebla every half hour. **ADO** buses depart every 15 minutes, and **Autobuses Unidos** provides service every 5 to 10 minutes.

If you're going on from Puebla to Tlaxcala or Pachuca from Puebla, **Flecha Azul** or **ERCO** (☎ 49-7177) has the most direct service. ERCO also goes to Izúcar de Matamoros every 10 minutes, and the trip takes about 90 minutes. **Autobuses Surianos** goes directly to Huamantla every 10 minutes, as does **ATAH**.

To get to downtown Puebla, go out the front door and look for the lineup of taxis or take a city bus marked "CAPU Central Camionera-Centro."

By Car   There are two roads to Puebla from the capital: Highway 190, an old, winding one that you'll drive with great frustration, following strings of lumbering trucks with no chance to pass; and Highway 150D, a new toll road that's faster. The bus usually follows the new highway.

ORIENTATION   Arriving   Buses arrive at a modern **bus terminal,** known by its acronym CAPU; it's located on the outskirts of the city. A taxi to the city center costs $2.50–$3. City buses ("Centro" or "Zócalo") travel to the downtown area.

Information   The **State Tourist Office** (☎ 46-1285 or 46-2044; fax 22/ 34-1224) is at Av. 5 Oriente no. 3, next to the cathedral and the Biblioteca Palafoxiana; the office is open Monday through Friday from 8am to 8:30pm, Saturday from 9am to 8:30pm, and Sunday from 9am to 2pm—closed on holidays. The friendly staff can give you a good map of the city. The **City Tourist Office** faces the main plaza at Portal Hidalgo 14 (☎ 32-0357 or 42-1099; fax 22/ 32-1399), and its staff seems very eager to please. On the same side of the plaza as the Royalty Hotel, it's open daily from 9am to 9pm.

City Layout   Touristically speaking, the heart of town is the shady zócalo, known as the **Plaza de la Constitución,** a beautiful place with a central bandstand and tile-covered benches. On one side are the cathedral and Calle 3 Oriente, and the other sides are flanked by the portales of colonial-era buildings that today house restaurants, hotels, and shops. These are on Calle del 16 de Septiembre, Calle 2 Sur, and Avenida de la Reforma where it meets Avenida Camacho. Most of the museums, shops, and hotels mentioned here are within walking distance of the zócalo.

Most streets running east and west are avenidas, and those running north and south are calles. **Avenida de la Reforma** divides the city north and south, with even-numbered avenues to the north and odd-numbered avenues to the south. **Calle del 16 de Septiembre,** which changes its name to **Calle del 5 de Mayo** north of Reforma, is the east-west dividing line, even-numbered streets to the east. City streets are further divided by direction: North "Norte" (Nte.), South "Sur," West "Poniente" (Pte.), and East "Oriente" (Ote.)

FAST FACTS: PUEBLA

American Express   The American Express office is on Calle 5 de Mayo, at Plaza Dorada 2 (☎ 37-5558).

Area Code   The telephone area code is 22.

Post Office   The Correos (post office) is in the Archbishop's Palace next to the cathedral, at the corner of Avenida 5 Oriente and Calle del 16 de Septiembre, but there is no sign.

EXPLORING PUEBLA
A STROLL THROUGH THE DOWNTOWN AREA

The heart of town is the shady zócalo, known as the Plaza de la Constitución, a beautiful place with a central fountain and painted iron benches. On one side is the **cathedral**, completed in 1649. The cathedral towers are the tallest in Mexico. Bells hang in the tower closer to the zócalo (the other tower is empty). The other sides of the zócalo are flanked by the *portales* (arcades) of colonial-era buildings, which today house restaurants, hotels, and shops. Most of the museums, shops, and hotels mentioned here are within walking distance of the zócalo.

Across the street from the cathedral, on the corner of Avenida 5 Oriente and Calle del 16 de Septiembre, is the old Archbishop's Palace, which now houses the **Casa de la Cultura** and the **Biblioteca Palafoxiana.** This library, the oldest in the Americas (also the most beautiful), was built in 1646 by Juan de Palafoxe y Mendoza, then archbishop and founder of the College of Saints Peter and Paul. It bespeaks the glory of this period with its elegant tile floor, hand-carved wood walls and ceiling, inlaid tables, and gilded wooden statues. Bookcases are filled with 17th-century books and manuscripts in Spanish, Creole, French, and English.

Be sure to stop in for a look at the **Iglesia de Santo Domingo,** on the corner of 5 de Mayo and 4 Poniente. Finished in 1611, the church was originally part of a monastery. Don't miss the **Capilla del Rosario,** a fantastic symphony of gilt and beautiful stone dedicated to the Virgin of the Rosary and built in 1690. Puebla has many other beautiful churches and convents that date from the 17th and 18th centuries.

MUSEUMS

✪ Museo Amparo
Calle 2 Sur 708. ☎ **22/46-4200.** Admission $3.50 adults; $1.75 students; free Mon. Wed–Mon 10am–6pm.

Opened in 1991, this is among the top archaeological museums in the country. It's housed in a colonial-era building that was first a hospital in 1534, then a college for women founded by Juan de Palafoxe y Mendoza, later the Colegio San José de Gracia for married women, and lastly the Colegio Esparza before its adaptation as a museum. You can rent audio phones to guide you through or simply pass on your own. There are seven *salas* (rooms) on the first floor and five on the second. Sala "Arte Rupestre" contains examples of cave paintings throughout the world, and in the Sala "Codice del Tiempo" a wonderful wall-size timeline marks important world cultures and events from 2500 B.C. to A.D. 1500. Viewing benches in front of it provide a place to ponder the development of the world's civilizations. Other first-floor salas include information on the discovery of corn and its importance to Mexican culture, techniques for the production of art, and the function of art in society. Upstairs is a fabulous collection of pre-Hispanic art covering the pre- to post-Classic periods. Some of the clay figures from Nayarit are especially amazing. Signs are in Spanish and English. No cameras are permitted.

✪ Museo Bello (Museum of Art)
Av. 3 Pte. No. 302. ☎ **22/41-9475.** Admission $1.50; free Tues. Tues–Sun 10am–4:30pm.

Located near the corner of Calle 3 Sur and Avenida 3 Poniente, this museum is definitely worth a visit. The collection includes some of the finest 17th-, 18th-, and 19th-century art I've seen anywhere. Señor Bello made his fortune in tobacco and began to collect art from all over the world. He never traveled, but he hired art dealers who did. Later, Señor Bello, who was a fine artist and an accomplished organist, founded a museum, which he left to the state when he died. His taste is evident throughout the house: velvet curtains, French porcelain, beautiful hand-carved furniture, several very fine organs, and numerous paintings. The mandatory guided tour (in English or Spanish) is included in the price of admission.

✪ State Regional Museum
Calle 4 Ote. no. 416. ☎ **22/41-4296.** Admission $1.50 adults; 65¢ children and students. Tues–Sun 10am–4:30pm.

One of the most interesting parts of this museum is the building itself, called the Casa de Alfenique. The 18th-century house resembles an elaborate wedding cake; in fact, the name means "sugar-cake house." Inside, it's architecturally embellished with an elaborate plaster doorway and brick-and-beam ceilings. The exhibits include a good collection of pre-Hispanic artifacts and pottery, displays of regional crafts, colonial-era furniture, and a sizable collection of china poblana costumes. The museum is 3¹/₂ blocks northwest of the zócalo, between Calle 7 and Calle 6 Norte.

Puebla

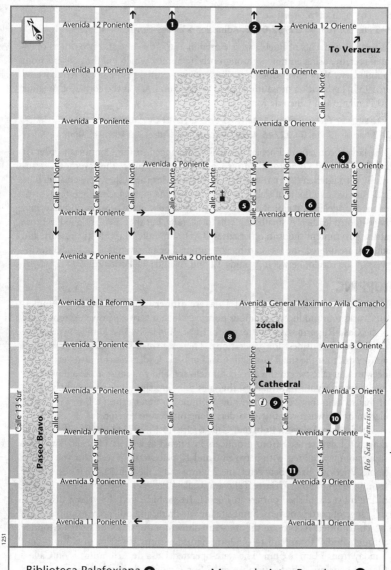

Avenida 12 Poniente — Avenida 12 Oriente

To Veracruz

Avenida 10 Poniente — Avenida 10 Oriente

Avenida 8 Poniente — Avenida 8 Oriente

Avenida 6 Poniente — Avenida 6 Oriente

Avenida 4 Poniente — Avenida 4 Oriente

Avenida 2 Poniente — Avenida 2 Oriente

Avenida de la Reforma — Avenida General Maximino Avila Camacho

zócalo

Avenida 3 Poniente — Avenida 3 Oriente

Cathedral

Avenida 5 Poniente — Avenida 5 Oriente

Avenida 7 Poniente — Avenida 7 Oriente

Avenida 9 Poniente — Avenida 9 Oriente

Avenida 11 Poniente — Avenida 11 Oriente

Calle 11 Norte · Calle 9 Norte · Calle 7 Norte · Calle 5 Norte · Calle 3 Norte · Calle del 5 de Mayo · Calle 2 Norte · Calle 4 Norte · Calle 6 Norte

Calle 13 Sur · Calle 11 Sur · Calle 9 Sur · Calle 7 Sur · Calle 5 Sur · Calle 3 Sur · Calle 16 de Septiembre · Calle 2 Sur · Calle 4 Sur

Paseo Bravo

Rio San Francisco

Information ⓘ   Church ✝■

Biblioteca Palafoxiana ⑨
Callejon de los Sapos ⑩
Convent of Santa Monica ②
Iglesia de Santo Domingo ⑤
Mercado El Parian ⑦
Museo Amparo ⑪
Museo Bello ⑧

Museo de Artes Populares ①
Principal Theater ④
Regional Mexican
  RevolutionaryMuseum ③
State Regional Museum/
  Casa de Alfenique ⑥

1251

Convent of Santa Monica
Av. 18 Pte. no. 103. ☎ **22/32-0178.** Admission $3. Tues–Sun 10am–4:30pm.

When the convents of Puebla were closed in 1767, this one and two others operated secretly, using entrances through private homes, which hid the convent from
public view. Very few people knew this convent existed before it was rediscovered
in 1935. Today it's a museum, kept as it was found. It's at the corner of Avenida
18 Poniente and Cinco de Mayo.

✪ Museo de Artes Populares and the Cocina de Santa Rosa
Calle 3 Nte. at 12 Pte. ☎ **22/46-4526.** Admission $1. Tues–Sun 10am–4:30pm.

The largest convent in Puebla, Santa Rosa belonged to the Dominican order. It
has been beautifully restored and is worth a visit just to see the cavernous, beautifully tiled kitchen (cocina) where many native Mexican dishes were created. The
museum has two floors of elaborate Mexican arts and crafts, including 6-foot earthenware candelabra, regional costumes, minute scenes made of straw and clay, and
hand-tooled leather. A small shop sells local crafts, but they aren't as good as those
at the government shops in other cities. Twenty-minute tours of the museum and
kitchen are offered, the last starting at 4:30pm. The museum is eight blocks northwest of the zócalo, between Avenida 12 and Avenida 14 Poniente.

SHOPPING

If you're in the market for a set of **Talavera dinnerware,** this is the city. Numerous workshops produce this famous pottery, which is very expensive. Among them
is the **Casa Rugerio,** Av. 18 Pte. no. 111 (☎ 22/41-3843), a family-owned shop
that's been in business for generations. There's a small showroom in front, and
visitors can tour the small production area in back. Orders for complete sets of dinnerware can take two to three years for delivery, and you must make a down payment. Just for your information, the sales folks are family members who've been
at this so long they've forgotten how to smile, so don't expect a flurry of appreciation or joy when you buy or order. Hang on to your receipt.

The **Centro Talavera Poblana,** Calle 6 Ote. 11 (☎ 22/42-0848), offers a wide
range of Talavera ware from producers in Puebla as well as Tlaxcala. The huge
showroom has full sets with between 6 and 12 place settings ready for you to take
home. Prices are fixed. Between Calle 2 Norte and Calle 5 de Mayo, it's open daily
from 9:30am to 8pm. **Uriarte Talavera,** Calle 4 Pte. 911 (☎ 22/32-1598), is one
of the most established potters in Puebla. Its sophisticated showroom displays a
full range of pottery designs. Some are for sale there, and others are examples from
which to order. Ask to see the museum showroom upstairs. It's open Monday
through Friday from 9am to 6:30pm, Saturday from 10:30am to 6:30pm, and
Sunday from 11am to 3pm. The state-operated **Casa de Artesanías** is on Calle 5
Oriente between 16 de Septiembre and 2 Sur. Crafts made in the state fill the room
and include fine pottery from Acatlán and Izúcar de Matamoros; pottery from
these two villages southwest of Puebla is nothing like the Talavera pottery so readily
seen in Puebla. The Casa de Artesanías is open Monday through Saturday 10am
to 6pm.

The **Mercado de Artistas,** or **El Parian** as it's also called, is a pedestrian-only
open-air shopping area on Calle 8 Norte between Avenidas 2 and 6 Oriente. You'll
see rows of neat brick shops selling crafts and souvenirs. Don't judge all Talavera
pottery by what you see here, though. Artists seem to have gone overboard with

design. The shops are open daily from 10am to 8pm. Bargain to get a good price. While you're in this area, you can take a look at the Principal Theater.

For some good antiques browsing, go to **Callejon de los Sapos** (Frog Street), about five blocks south of the zócalo near Calle 4 Sur and Avenida 7 Oriente. Wander in and out, for there's good stuff both large and small. Shops are generally open daily from 10am to 2pm and 4 to 6pm. Bargain to get a good price.

ACCOMMODATIONS

Puebla has many hotels, but I haven't found a single well-run inexpensive establishment among them. However, the peso devaluation has brought several downtown hotels into the reasonable range.

Hotel Colonial

Calle 4 Sur no. 105, Puebla, Pue. 72000. ☎ **22/46-4199.** Fax 22/46-0818. 70 rms (all with bath). TEL. $30 double.

The six-story hotel (with elevator) is charming in an old way, with arches and lots of tiles on the interior public areas. The rooms, too, have tile floors and are neatly furnished. It's comfortable and close to all the sights. The restaurant is popular with locals. Expensive garage parking is around the corner. The Colonial is one block east of the zócalo, between Camacho and Avenida 3 Oriente.

Hotel San Angel

Av. 4 Pte. no. 504, Puebla, Pue. 72000. ☎ and fax **22/32-3845.** 37 rms (all with bath). TV TEL. $45 double. Rates include breakfast.

This cheery little hotel, which opened in 1993, is a welcome addition to the downtown scene. Created from a large three-story 19th-century town house (with an elevator), it's centered on a covered interior patio. The hotel's welcoming little restaurant occupies the central patio, where guests take the complimentary breakfast or other meals. The carpeted rooms are exceedingly cheerful, with matching bedspreads and drapes and overbed reading lights. The baths are small, but the sinks are conveniently outside the toilet/shower area. It's near the corner of Calle 5 Norte.

DINING

Puebla is known throughout Mexico for the famous *mole poblano,* a sauce with more than 20 ingredients, as well as *mixiotes*—beef, pork, or lamb in a spicy red sauce baked in maguey paper. *Dulces* (sweets) shops are scattered about, with display windows brim-full of marzipan crafted into various shapes and designs, candied figs, guava paste, and camotes, which are little cylinders of a fruity sweet-potato paste wrapped in waxed paper.

There are more small, cheap Puebla-style eateries on **Calle 6 Norte,** all doing their part to uphold the reputation Puebla bears as a culinary fount. Great pots of boiling mole and other mysteriously delectable regional sauces bubble temptingly. Find something you like by peeking into the kitchens right in front. Most restaurants are open daily, but several are closed on Wednesday.

✪ El Cortijo

Calle 16 de Septiembre no. 506. ☎ **22/42-0503.** Main courses $5.50–$14; comida corrida $7. Daily 10am–7pm (comida corrida served 1–3pm). MEXICAN.

This enclosed patio restaurant has a comfortable atmosphere and tasty food. Dishes range from pork chops to delicious jumbo shrimp or paella. The cubierto (or comida corrida) starts with a fruit cocktail; followed by a choice of two soups; a mid-course of perhaps paella or spaghetti; then the main course, which might include a choice of pork leg, mole, fish, or chicken. This is a good place for that large afternoon meal and a bottle of wine. The restaurant is $2^1/_2$ blocks south of the zócalo, between Calles 16 de Septiembre and 2 Sur.

✪ Fonda de Santa Clara

Av. 3 Pte. no. 307. ☎ **22/42-2659.** Lunch $7–$9; dinner $3.50–$7. Tues–Sat noon– 9:30pm, Sun 11am–9:30pm. REGIONAL.

This is one of the city's most popular and traditional restaurants, serving regional food. It's busy but cozy and slightly formal. The menu includes such local dishes as pollo mole poblano, mixiotes, and tinga (a great beef stew). There are seasonal specialties as well, like fried grasshoppers in October and November, maguey worms in April and May, chiles enogada in July through September, and huitlacoche in June. The light dinner menu features such specials as tacos, tamales, pozole, mole de panza (mole with stomach meat), and atole. The restaurant is $1^1/_2$ blocks west of the zócalo, opposite the Bello Museum.

Sanborn's

Av. 2 Ote. no. 6. ☎ **22/42-9436.** Breakfast $3–$5; main courses $3.25–$8. Sun–Fri 7:30am–11pm, Sat 7:30am–midnight. MEXICAN.

The dining room, in a fine colonial courtyard has tables set around a stone fountain. The menu, as at others at this reliable chain, covers the culinary spectrum form chicken, fajitas, fish, to enchiladas, chilaquiles, and sandwiches. Apart from the restaurant a large section of the store is devoted to the sale of books magazines, cameras, jewelry, gifts, luggage, etc. It's $1^1/_2$ blocks north of the zócalo, between Avenidas 2 and 4 Oriente.

PUEBLA AFTER DARK

Mariachis play daily, beginning at 6pm, on **Plaza de Santa Inés,** at Avenida 11 Poniente and Calle 3 Sur. They stroll through the crowds that gather at the sidewalk cafes. Another square that attracts mariachis is **Plaza de los Sapos,** Avenida 7 Oriente near Calle 6 Sur. To get there, walk two blocks from the zócalo and take a left onto Avenida 7 Oriente, toward the river. To find the plaza, follow the sound of music. A third place to hear mariachis nightly is the **Plazuela del Alto,** Calle 14 Oriente and Avenida 12 Sur.

   Teorema, Reforma 540 near Calle 7 Norte (☎ 22/42-1014), is a wonderful coffee shop/bookstore that features guitarists and folksingers every evening. This is a good place to meet young local residents. It's open daily from 9:30am to 2:30pm and 4:30pm to midnight.

SIDE TRIPS FROM PUEBLA
CHOLULA: CITY OF CHURCHES

Six miles northwest of Puebla along Highway 190 (not the toll road, 190D), the colonial town of Cholula (pop. 45,000) is one of the holiest places in Mexico. It was here that Quetzalcoatl, the famed feathered serpent, is thought to have lived in exile after he was forced to leave his city of Tula, capital of the Toltecs, in A.D. 900. During pre-Hispanic days pilgrims came here to pay their respects to this great leader. Today it's very easy to get to Cholula from Puebla by taking one of the small white vans marked "Cholula," at the corner of Avenida 10 Poniente and Calle 11 Norte or on Avenida 6 Norte at the corner of Calle 13 Norte.

The Cholulans strongly resisted Cortés and his men. When the Spaniards discovered the residents of this town were plotting to overthrow them, at least 3,000 Cholulans were killed.

Cholula boasts so many churches it's often said there's one for every day of the year. It's also the home of the **University of the Americas**—popular with American students. From Cholula's main plaza, you can see a large yellow church. Behind it, atop what looks like an enormous hill, you'll see the white **Los Remedios Church** etched against the sky. The "hill," however, is the **Great Tepanapa Pyramid,** only a five-minute walk away. To get there from the plaza, walk on Morelos and across the railroad tracks. On the right, about a football field's length from the tracks, is the entrance. The pyramid is actually several pyramids built one on top of the other. Around the perimeter reconstructed portions show what parts of the pyramid once looked like, and other areas show excavations. The famous frescoes deep inside date back to the Classic Period, but they are closed from public access for the time being while a mold problem is studied. The lighted interior tunnels were dug by archaeologists and are easy to follow by yourself, but a hired guide can provide interesting details and show where one pyramid stops and another begins. Listed prices for guides are $12 for a tour inside and out and $6 for a tour inside only.

The ruins are open daily from 10am to 5pm. Admission is $5.25; free on Sunday and holidays; $8.50 for use of your video.

If you take the stone walkway up the hill (to the top of the pyramid), you'll reach the lovely chapel of the Virgen de los Remedios. The gilded interior of this little gem is as pretty as its exterior. While regaining your breath, you'll enjoy the spectacular view of the town's steeples and plaza.

HUEJOTZINGO'S MARKET & MONASTERY

Huejotzingo, Puebla (alt 7,550 ft.; pop. 30,000), is a pleasant town with a large main square 9 miles northwest of Cholula. Fine woolen goods, especially serapes and blankets, are sold at the open-air market on Saturday. Even if you don't come for market day, you can stop and enjoy a glass or two of the sparkling (alcoholic) cider, a local specialty.

While in town, be sure to visit the **Franciscan monastery,** right across the main road from the town plaza. It was built between 1529 and 1570 and is one of the oldest in Mexico. As you walk up the stairs from the main road and enter the monastery compound, stop to admire the little square chapels (posas) topped by pyramidal roofs at each corner of the enclosure. The cross mounted on a pedestal in the courtyard dates from the 1500s as well.

The church, very austere on the outside, has a wonderfully lacy Gothic vault inside, plus a dazzling altar in the plateresque style. The monastery building next door, entered through the double-arch doorway, has a few excellent friezes in black and white painted by Fray António de Roldan in 1558. There are a lovely chapel, a cloister for the monks, kitchens, and a dining room. The monastery is open Tuesday through Sunday from 10am to 4:30pm; there is a small admission fee.

From Puebla, ask about current transportation; bus schedules were changing at press time. From Cholula, take a taxi from the central plaza for around $8.

A SPECIAL EVENT   The colorful story of a bandit, Augustín Lorenzo, and the kidnapping of a beautiful young girl is reenacted in Huejotzingo the Tuesday before Ash Wednesday with a colorful firecracker-filled **Carnaval** featuring a cast of

Two Indian Baroque Churches

If you go to Cholula, try to visit the churches of **Santa María Tonanzintla** and **San Francisco Acatepec,** three miles southeast of Cholula. Called Indian baroque because the Indians used pre-Hispanic ideas to present Christian concepts, the churches are elaborately decorated with beautifully colored Puebla tiles and wood carved by local artisans. Saints are swaddled in stylized quetzal bird feathers, once used to depict the god Quetzalcoatl, and faces protrude from a headdress of corn leaves, in the same way they did in pre-Christian times. The interior of the Tonanzintla church is covered floor to ceiling in fabulous gilded and polychrome faces, cherubs, and foliage—an unforgettable sight. The facade of the Acatepec church is a fantasy of tile, though it has a less elaborate interior than the Tonanzintla church.

The churches are only 8 miles outside Cholula and are easy to reach from there: Take one of the buses marked "Chipito," which go by the entrance to the ruins. Hours are unpredictable, but the caretaker is usually not far away; ask around for him and chances are he'll appear.

thousands wearing brilliantly colored costumes. The story goes that during the colonial era in Huejotzingo, Lorenzo kidnapped the daughter of a rich landowner and spirited her away into the mountains in order to wed her. During the wedding celebration local soldiers came to her rescue. It's one of the most colorful Carnaval celebrations in Mexico; the carnaval market is at least 10 blocks square.

COLONIAL TLAXCALA & THE NEARBY CACAXTLA RUINS

Located 25 miles north of Puebla and 75 miles east of Mexico City, Tlaxcala is the capital of Mexico's smallest state (same name) and is a pretty colonial-era city with several unique claims to fame. Tlaxcalan warriors, who allied with Cortés against the Aztecs, were essential in Cortés's defeat of the Aztecs. Tlaxcalan chiefs were the first to be baptized by the Spaniards; the baptismal font used for them is found in the **Monastery of San Francisco,** located two blocks from the main plaza and noted for its elaborately inlaid Moorish ceiling below the choir loft. A painting inside the Chapel of the Third Order shows the baptism of the chiefs. Less than a mile from the town center is the famed **Ocotlán Sanctuary,** constructed after Juan Diego Bernardino claimed to have seen an apparition of the Virgin Mary on that site in 1541. Baroque inside and out, the elaborate interior decorations of carved figures and curling gilded wood date from the 1700s. These carvings are attributed to Francisco Miguel Tlayotehuanitzin, an Indian sculptor who labored for more than 20 years to create them. The **Government Palace,** on the handsome tree-shaded central zócalo, is painted inside with vivid murals of Tlaxcala history by a local artist, Desiderio Hernández Xochitiotzin.

The newly reopened and expanded **Museo de Artesanías** at Sanchez Piedras and 1 de Mayo, near Tlaxcala's zócalo, showcases the state's wide-ranging crafts and customs. Every day except Monday, when the museum is closed, local artisans give visitors demonstrations in such crafts as embroidery, weaving, and pulque making. **Santa Ana,** a wool-weaving village, is only 1¹/₂ miles east of Tlaxcala. Shops selling large rugs, serapes, and sweaters woven locally line the main street.

Huamantla, 30 miles southeast of Tlaxcala, is a small village noted for its commemoration of the Assumption of the Virgin on August 12 (see below). Tlaxcala's main attraction, however, is **Cacaxtla** (pronounced Kah-*kahsh*-tlah), a unique pre-Hispanic hilltop site 12 miles southwest of the city of Tlaxcala. In general, this wonderfully pleasant city hosts few tourists and because of that retains its small-town atmosphere and overall low prices. It's worthy of a day—perhaps several days—of your journey.

Exploring the Cacaxtla Archaeological Site

Scholars were startled by the discovery of vivid murals, unearthed in 1975, in red, blue, black, yellow, and white, showing Maya warriors (from the Mexican Yucatán Peninsula 500 miles south). Since then more murals, more history, and at least eight construction phases have been uncovered. Presently, scholars attribute the influence of the site to a little-known group, the Olmec-Xicalanca, from Mexico's Gulf Coast. Among the translations of its name, one—merchant's trade pack— seems most revealing. Like Casas Grandes north of Chihuahua City and Xochicalco (also with distinctive Maya influence) between Cuernavaca and Taxco, Cacaxtla apparently was an important crossroads for merchants, astronomers, and others in the Mesoamerican world. Its apogee, between A.D. 650 and 900, corresponds with the abandonment of Teotihuacán (near Mexico City), the beginning of Casas Grandes culture, and in the final phase, the decline of the Maya in Yucatán, the emergence of the Toltec culture at Tula (also near Mexico City), and the spread of Toltec influence to Yucatán. How, or even if, those events affected Cacaxtla isn't known yet. Apparently the mural is a victory scene with warrior figures clothed magnificently in jaguar skins and seemingly victorious over figures dressed in feathers who were to be sacrificial victims. Some of the victims are even depicted lying on the floor, where they will undergo the ultimate humiliation of being walked on by the victors. Numerous symbols of Venus (a half star with five points) found painted at the site have led archaeoastronomy scholar John Carlson to link historical events such as wars, captive taking, and ritual sacrifice with the appearance of Venus; all of this was likely undertaken in hopes of assuring the continued fertility of crops. These symbols of blood, along with toads and turtles (all water symbols), sacrifice, and Venus, together with others of corn stalks and cacao (chocolate) trees (symbolizing fertility), were to appease the gods to assure a productive cycle of rains, crops, and trade. The latest mural discoveries show a wall of corn and cacao trees leading to a merchant whose trade pack is laden with these symbolic crops. The murals flank a grand acropolis with unusual architectural motifs. For a lavishly illustrated account of the site, read "Mural Masterpieces of Ancient Cacaxtla" (National Geographic, September 1992). The grand plaza and murals are now protected by a giant steel roof. *Important notes:* It's about a mile from the parking lot to the hillside entrance to the site. Be careful of the weak and crudely made wooden steps, which become slippery with the accumulation of dust. Since neither a flash nor a tripod is allowed, the site is difficult to photograph from the inside because of dust and low light caused by shading from the giant roof. I recommend you pay to photograph the site only when you've determined it's worth it to you. When you pay, the attendant tags your camera and you are permitted to use it.

Admission is $5.50 plus $8.50 per either still or video camera; free Sundays and holidays. It's open Tuesday through Sunday from 9am to 5pm.

To get to Cacaxtla from Tlaxcala, take a combi (collective minivan) or city bus to the village of San Miguel Milagro or Nativitas (nearest the ruins). From there, walk or take a taxi to the ruins. If you're driving from Tlaxcala, take the road south to Tetlatlahuaca and turn (right) there to Nativitas, where there are signs to Cacaxtla. From Puebla, take Highway 119 north to the crossroads near Zacualpan and turn left passing Tetlatlahuaca; turn right when you see signs to Nativitas and Cacaxtla. From Mexico City, take Highway 190 to San Martín Texmelucan, where you should ask directions for the road leading directly to the ruins, which are about 6 miles ahead. (This is the southern road you can use without going to Tlaxcala.)

Exploring the Village of Huamantla

On the evening preceding the **Assumption of the Virgin** event, the streets are decorated in murals made of flower petals and colored sawdust, all of which are destroyed when a figure of the virgin is carried through downtown streets. The following weekend a running of the bulls takes place through the downtown streets. Just as colorful and fascinating is the **Museo Nacional del Titere Rosete Aranda** (Rosete Aranda National Puppet Museum), a rare collection of handmade puppets from the Aranda family, who lived in Huamantla. As early as 1835 the family toured the state and went to the capital with their puppet plays—poking fun at politics and history, and performing dances, parades, cockfights, bullfights, and circus acts, complete with marching bands playing instruments—all with puppets. The idea for the character of Cantinflas (a Mexican comedian played by Mario Moreno) came from an Aranda puppet called Vale Coyote. The museum also houses puppets from around the world and from several centuries. Just in case you develop a love affair with this family of puppets, there's another huge collection of them at the Museo Rafael Coronel in Zacatecas (see Chapter 6). The Huamantla museum is near the main plaza; ask for directions to it from there. Admission is $3.50, and the museum is open Tuesday through Sunday from 10am to 4pm.

Accommodations & Dining in Tlaxcala

Besides the hotel listed below, Tlaxcala has several restaurants and inexpensive hotels near the zócalo and along the road to Apizaco.

Posada San Francisco Villas Arqueológicas

Plaza de la Constitución 17, Tlaxcala, Tlax. 9000. ☎ **256/2-6402**, or 2-6022, or 800/258-2633 in the U.S., or 91-800/9-0170 in Mexico. Fax 256/2-6818. 62 rms, 6 suites (all with bath). TV TEL. $102 double; $147 suite. Free parking.

Operated by Club Med as one of its Villas Arqueológicas, this posada opened in 1992 on Tlaxcala's zócalo. The new hotel occupies a turn-of-the-century building known locally as the Casa de las Piedras (House of Stones) because its gray-stone facade stands apart from the stucco used elsewhere around the zócalo. Two stories of beautifully furnished rooms are built around a pool and patio beyond the central entrance patio. The parking lot is entered one street behind the hotel's front entrance, which faces the zócalo. Even if you don't stay, stop in for a look around or a meal at La Trasquila, the elegant fine-dining restaurant on the second story overlooking the plaza and lobby; it's open daily from 7am to 11pm. The cozy first-floor Cafetería offers Mexican specialties daily from 11am to 7pm. Bar Rancho Seco, just off the lobby, is a popular place in the evenings, when a soloist entertains; it's open daily from 10am to 11pm.

Tlaxcala

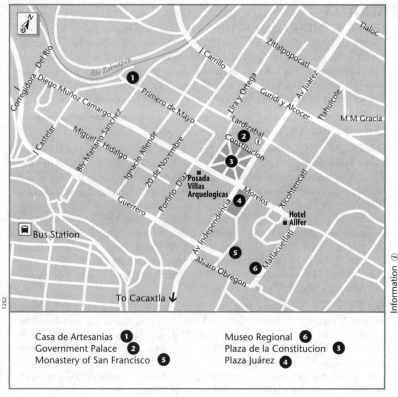

Information ⓘ

Casa de Artesanias ❶
Government Palace ❷
Monastery of San Francisco ❺

Museo Regional ❻
Plaza de la Constitucion ❸
Plaza Juárez ❹

4 Toluca: Museums, a Bustling Market & Nearby Ruins & Crafts Villages

45 miles W of Mexico City

The capital of the state of México, Toluca (pop. 200,000) is at 8,760 feet the highest city in Mexico. The hour-long trip here from Mexico City offers spectacular scenic views: Pine trees and icy-looking blue lakes dot the landscape, and only an occasional cactus plant or brightly colored painting, drying in the sun, will remind you that you're in Mexico.

Toluca's Friday market was once so popular that a parade of buses loaded up tourists every hour from Chapultepec Park in Mexico City. Toluca declined in popular tourism in the 1970s after its famous Friday market moved from its downtown location to its present one, nearer the outskirts of town by the bus station. Though tourism dropped, business boomed. Today Toluca is a thriving industrial center; you'll see the plants lining the highway as you drive into town. With healthy business growth came city beautification, as well as new museums and restaurants. In short, with city sights and excellent shopping in Toluca, and easily reached nearby villages, there's good reason to put Toluca back on the tourist itinerary.

ESSENTIALS

GETTING THERE & DEPARTING   By Bus   It's easy to get to Toluca and the market by bus from Mexico City. Take the Metro to the Observatorio station which is also called the **Terminal Poniente** bus station. Reserved-seat buses ("Toluca-Directo") of various companies depart every 5 or 10 minutes for the hour-long trip. **ETN,** at the far end of the concourse, offers deluxe service to Toluca and is well worth the little extra cost over that for standard buses.

By Car   From Mexico City, follow Paseo de la Reforma west until it merges with Carretera a Toluca (Highway 15).

ORIENTATION   Arriving   From Mexico City you'll enter town on the broad **Paseo Tollocán,** a four-lane highway lined with industrial plants like Chrysler and Pfizer. The bus will discharge passengers at the central bus station in front of the famed Friday market. Both are on **Isidro Fabela** near the intersection of Tollocán. If you're going directly to the market, it's behind the bus station. If you're going to a hotel first and have luggage, you'll want to get a taxi. They line up on a side street opposite the bus station's front exits. Slash the quoted price by half or a third and you may strike a reasonable bargain. If you're traveling light, use the city buses ("Centro") that go to the city center and are also lined up in front.

From the bus station, the center of town is northwest between Lerdo de Tejada and Avenida Hidalgo. It's too far to walk.

Fast Facts   The **telephone area code** is 72. The well-staffed and helpful **State Tourist Office** is in the central city at Lerdo Poniente 101 in the Edificio Plaza Toluca, second floor (☎ 72/14-1342; fax 13-3142). Hours are Monday through Friday from 9am to 3pm and 4 to 9:30pm. It stocks a wide variety of booklets with maps outlining the state's regions, as well as Toluca maps and museum information. The **American Express** representative is Viajes Corona, Villada no. 445 (☎ 72/12-4189; fax 14-2655), at the corner of Ramón Corona.

EXPLORING TOLUCA

Plan your Toluca foray for a Friday, just so you can say you saw the **market,** even if you don't stay long. The crowds and hubbub are taxing, and an hour or two should do it, even for a die-hard market lover. Follow that with a trip to **CASART,** the state crafts store a long block from the market. Then catch a bus ("Centro") for downtown. The first two should take the better part of the morning. After lunch, you'll have time to see some of the city's terrific museums and walk around the historic town center. A trip to nearby archaeological sites and the craft villages takes another day.

THE MARKET

The gigantic **Mercado Juárez,** at the edge of town on the highway to Mexico City, has both market buildings and open-air grounds. Shops in the buildings are open all week, but it's on Friday that the people from surrounding villages come and crowd the plaza. The bus from Mexico City pulls into a terminal right across the street from the Mercado Juárez. You'll recognize the market by the pair of slender concrete slabs that tower above it to serve as a landmark.

Because of the natives' bargaining powers, a peaceful walk around the market is not easy. Every time you pause to admire such unfamiliar sights as a boxful of chattering chickens, a two-foot-high pile of assorted shoelaces, or an array of framed saints' pictures, some man or boy will accost you with cries of "Serapes, rebozos, señor, very cheap." Some sights will make you pause—a marimba band banging away cheerfully between the stalls or a little open-fronted bakery where chains of tortillas can be seen pouring off a conveyor belt into a basket. But sooner or later the heat and crowdedness of the market will begin to get you down; the man with the pig under his arm or the woman with a turkey sticking out its head from the back of her shawl brushing past probably won't even cause you to bat an eye.

THE HISTORIC CENTER

This area in the heart of Toluca is bounded by Avenidas Hidalgo, Juárez, and Sebastián Lerdo de Tejada. Here you'll see the housing for the heart of state government in stately buildings framing the square—the Palace of Justice, Chamber of Deputies, Government Palace, Municipal Palace, Cosmovitral Botánico, and the cathedral, which was established by the Franciscans in the mid-1800s.

The famous **portales** (arcades) of Toluca, begun in 1832, are one block east of the main plaza. They are a popular meeting, shopping, and dining place. From the Days of the Dead (November 1 and 2) through Christmas, they're filled with temporary vendors selling the candy for which the state is famous.

Located at the corner of Juárez and Lerdo, off Plaza de los Martires between the Chamber of Deputies and the Government Palace, the **Cosmovitral Botánico** (Botanical Garden) (☎ 72/14-6785) is an indoor garden inside the walls of a 19th-century art nouveau building and is one of the city's greatest creations. It was the site of the famed Toluca market until 1975. In 1980, it reopened to house the botanical gardens. The upper half of the building is emblazoned with 54 bold stained-glass panels telling the story of humanity in relation to the cosmos. All the elements of a good tale are there—good and evil, happiness and sadness, freedom and imprisonment. From design to completion, it took local artists three years. The stained glass, however, is only the frame for the gardens showing plants native to the state of México and other countries. The gardens are open Tuesday through Sunday from 9am to 5pm; admission is $2.

Velasco was one of the state's favorite sons, so it's only fitting that the man known as Mexico's foremost 19th-century landscape painter should have a museum here in his honor. The ❂ **Museo José María Velasco,** Lerdo de Tejada 400, at the corner of N. Bravo (☎ 72/13-2814), is a showcase for Velasco's vast landscapes that feature enormous Mexican valleys, usually with a volcano in the background. Viewers of his work may feel as though they are standing on the same mountaintop as the painter himself. Some of these works are on display, and it's well worth the short time it takes to see them. The museum is opposite the main plaza, across from the Palacio del Gobierno and a block from the Cosmovitral Botánico. It's open Tuesday through Sunday from 10am to 6pm; admission is free.

In a grand mansion connected and next door to the Velasco Museum, the **Museo Santiago Gutiérrez,** at Nicolas Bravo Nte. 303 (☎ 72/13-2814), pays homage to another of the state's famous painters. Gutiérrez and Velasco were friends, and both studied at the San Carlos Museum. Gutiérrez was the country's foremost 19th-century portrait, figure, and *costumbrista* artist. (Costumbrista paintings used Mexican themes with figures clad in Mexican attire.) He traveled and studied widely, eventually founding the Academia de Artes de Bogotá, Colombia, during his years there. The Museo Gutiérrez in Toluca houses the largest collection of his works, one of which was included in the spectacular "Thirty Centuries of Mexican Art" exhibit that toured the United States in 1990. The museum is open Tuesday through Sunday from 10am to 6pm; admission is free.

You may never have heard of this master painter, but you won't forget him once you see his work housed on two floors here in the ✪ **Museo-Taller Luis Nishizawa** at Nicolas Bravo Nte. 305 (☎ 72/13-2647): His oil portraits and skilled use of color are unforgettable. Born to a Japanese father and a Mexican mother, he moved with his parents from Toluca to Mexico City in 1925. At 24 he entered the San Carlos Academy and within three years was given the title "Master of Plastic Arts." In his long career he has won hundreds of awards. Now in his 70s, he divides his time between residing in Mexico City and teaching at the museum between 10am and 2pm each Saturday. The stained-glass ceiling over the patio is a Nishizawa creation. The beautifully restored house dates from 1781 and boasts a colorful history, including tales of ghosts that are said to appear even today. The Instituto Mexiquense de Cultura published in 1993 an illustrated history of the house, "La Vieja Casona de Nicolas Bravo Norte 305." The museum is located farther up the street from the Museo Santiago Gutiérrez (see above); it's one block north of the main plaza between Lerdo de Tejada and Santo Degollado. This is a top museum you should not miss. It's open Tuesday through Sunday from 10am to 6pm.

The new ✪ **Museo de la Acuarela,** Pedro Ascencio at Nigromante (☎ 72/14-7304), housed in a mansion built early this century and restored recently, is devoted entirely to watercolor paintings. Featured here are the works of state-born artists and paintings about the state by artists from around the world. Since the state of México is so large and almost surrounds the Federal District, the subject matter—from archaeological sites to landscapes and village streets—is vast. The work, too, is wonderful, and you may find yourself lingering to admire it or to identify recognizable places artists have captured in watercolor. The museum is only $1^1/_2$ blocks west of the central square. To find it from the northwest corner of the main plaza (where Bravo meets Independencia), turn left onto Independencia (which becomes Serdan) and walk straight one block, then turn left on Pedro Ascencio de Alquisiras; the museum is on the right about half a block. It's open Tuesday through Sunday from 10am to 6pm; admission is free.

Also new is the **Museo de Numismatica,** Av. Hidalgo Pte. 506 (☎ 72/13-1927), housed in a grand turn-of-the-century stone mansion. It features Mexican currency from pre-Hispanic times to the present. Among the most interesting are the pre-Hispanic beads and cacao (chocolate beans), once used as currency among various tribes, and the regional money printed during the tumultuous years of the Mexican Revolution. To find it from the southwest corner of the main plaza, walk west on Hidalgo, crossing 5 de Febrero and Pedro Ascencio de Alquisiras; it's in the middle of the next block on the right. If you're coming from the Museo de la Acuarela (see above), turn right out the front door and walk two blocks to Hidalgo. Turn right; it's on the right. The museum is open Tuesday through Saturday from 10am to 6pm and Sunday from 10am to 4pm; admission is free.

✪ Centro Cultural Mexequense

Seeing this cultural center is reason enough to stay on in Toluca. In 1987, the Centro Cultural Mexequense (☎ 72/12-4113 or 72/12-4738) opened on the sprawling grounds of the former Hacienda de la Pila, in a southeastern suburb of the city. The ambitious and beautiful museum incorporates four cultural entities and a library that were once scattered throughout Toluca. The various buildings

Toluca

Museo Bellas Artes ❶
Museo de la Acuarela ❺
Museo José María Velasco ❹
Museo Numismatica ❻
Museo Santiago Gutiérrez ❸
Museo-Taller Luis Nishizawa ❷

form a one-story U shape around an enormous central yard where orchestras and dancers sometimes entertain.

English-speaking guides are often available for the asking at the library, on your left as you approach the cluster of buildings. Or you are free to wander at your leisure, but all signs are in Spanish.

The center and all its museums are open Tuesday through Sunday from 9am to 5pm; the restaurant is closed on Sunday. The $7.75 admission price includes all the buildings and museums at the Centro. Admission is paid at the kiosk in the parking lot—not in the museums. It's free for all on Sunday.

Especially worthwhile is the **Popular Arts Museum,** on the right, in the original hacienda building, if you plan to visit any of the state's crafts villages. You'll get not only a great overview of what the state has to offer and where but also an idea of quality. As you enter, you can't miss the spectacular, building-size polychrome-clay "trees of life" from the artisans of Metepec. They would have been too huge to bring into the building, so the artists made and fired them inside before the museum opened. As you walk through the salons you'll find exhibits of regional costumes, Persian-like tapestries from Temoaya, leather-covered chests from San Mateo Atenco, and embroidery from Ameyalco among the thousands of objects. In the **Charro Museum** you'll see lariats and swords, a great sombrero display, spurs, bits, and saddles. There's even a 16th-century stirrup and a charro wedding suit. A cozy restaurant (inexpensive), bookstore, and sales shop are in this building.

Opposite the Popular Arts Museum and next to the **library** is the **Museum of Modern Art** in a building originally intended as an observatory. Here you can study paintings by Rufino Tamayo, Juan O'Gorman, José Chávez Morado, Orozco, and Diego Rivera, all of whom were better known for their murals. The works are quite good, and you'll likely discover other lesser-known artists whose efforts rival their better-known contemporaries.

In the middle, straight ahead from the entrance, between the Popular Arts and Modern Art museums, is the **Museum of Anthropology.** The massive number of artifacts are well displayed in a broad and spacious building. Objects from the state's 10 most important archaeological sites include beautiful pottery and mural fragments from Teotihuacán and the famous wood drum from Malinalco, showing carved jaguars and eagles. Other excellent displays show the forests and animals by region, insects, butterflies, and a considerable collection of stuffed animals. Memorabilia from colonial days to the present include a bust of Emperor Maximilian, a fan and lace gloves that belonged to Empress Carlota, French dresses from the time of Porfirio Díaz, photographs, and the first soft-drink machine in the state of México.

SHOPPING

Besides the famous Mercado Juárez mentioned above, Toluca and environs offer several good options for shopping, especially for regionally made crafts. The Centro Cultural Mexequense and the Toluca Market give you two insights into regional crafts; ✪ **CASART,** Paseo Tollocán and Urawa (☎ 72/17-5144 or 72/17-5108), gives another. You can't miss the showy building on the main road by the central market and bus station. Inside is an enormous showroom and sales outlet for a majority of the state's crafts—blown glass; dinnerware; textiles; wood carving; Persian-style rugs from nearby Temoaya; hand-woven sweaters, rugs, and serapes from Guaulapita; baskets of all kinds; silver jewelry from San Felipe el Progreso; and pottery from Metepec. A few crafts from other regions in Mexico are for sale as well, such as lacquer chests from Olinala, Guerrero. Local women demonstrate textile and basket weaving and sell their wares. Upstairs are more crafts and excellent photographs of artisans at work, with labels describing the regions and crafts. CASART is open daily from 10am to 7pm.

A SIDE TRIP TO METEPEC

Approximately 5 miles from the edge of Toluca, **Metepec** is probably the most famous of the crafts villages, known for its pottery and polychrome "trees of life." A trip here is worth the little time it takes: Frequent buses leave the central bus station in Toluca, and the trip takes less than 30 minutes. Avoid arriving between 2 and 4pm when shops are closed. Pottery shops line the main street into town. Potters generally have their workshops away from the city center, so if you want to see them at work, ask around for directions.

ACCOMMODATIONS & DINING

If you should decide to spend the night, good choices near the portales and main plaza include the inexpensive but very nice **Hotel Colonial**, Hidalgo Oriente 103, Toluca, Edo. de México 50000 (☎ 72/15-9700 or 72/14-7066); the even less expensive **Hotel San Carlos**, Portal Madero 210, Toluca, Edo. de México 50000 (☎ 72/14-9422; fax 72/14-9704); or the best hotel downtown, the moderately

Ixtapan de la Sal

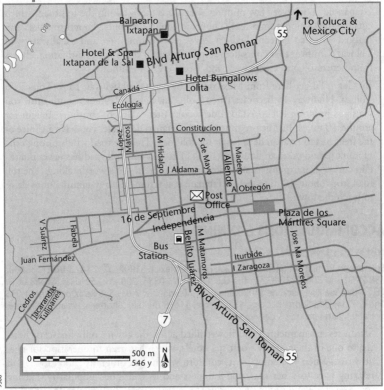

priced **Hotel San Francisco**, Rayon 104, Toluca, Edo. de México 50000 (☎ 72/13-3114; fax 72/13-2482). Restaurants are along Hidalgo and inside the portales just off the main square.

5 Ixtapan de la Sal: Thermal Spa Town

75 miles SW of Mexico City

Southwest of Mexico City, the whitewashed town of Ixtapan de la Sal (not to be confused with Ixtapa on the Pacific coast) caters to pleasures based on thermal mud baths. The Balneario Ixtapan, next to the Hotel Spa Ixtapan, is the town's public spa and bathhouse. Here, you can take private thermal water baths or have a massage, facial, hair treatment, paraffin wrap, pedicure, and manicure—all of which cost between $10 and $20 each. It's open daily from 8am to 6pm.

Hotels in Ixtapan de la Sal are packed on weekends and Mexican holidays. There's little to do but relax in the town. Cuernavaca, Taxco, and Toluca are all easy side trips.

ESSENTIALS

GETTING THERE & DEPARTING   By Bus   From Mexico City's Terminal Poniente, **Omnibus Azteca de Oro** and **Tres Estrella de Oro** buses leave for

Ixtapan de la Sal every few minutes. Get a bus that's taking the toll road, which cuts the travel time from 3 to 3¹/₂ hours to about 2¹/₂ hours. To return, take a bus marked "Mexico Directo," which leaves every 10 minutes and usually stops in Toluca. (Confirm that yours does stop in Toluca if that's your destination.) Buses from here also go to Cuernavaca and Taxco every 40 minutes.

By Car   To get here from Mexico City by car, take Highway 15 to Toluca. In Toluca, Highway 15 becomes Paseo Tollucan. Follow Tollucan south until you see signs pointing left to Ixtapan de la Sal. After the turn, continue straight for around 10 miles. Just before the town of Tenango del Valle, you have a choice of the free road to Ixtapan de la Sal or the toll road. The free road winds through the mountains and takes an hour and a half. The two-lane toll road has fewer mountain curves, is inexpensive, and takes around an hour—it's worth taking. The toll road stops about 10 miles before Ixtapan; you resume a curvy mountainous drive to reach the town.

ACCOMMODATIONS & DINING

Hotel Spa Ixtapan

Bulevar San Roman s/n Ixtapan de la Sal, Edo. de México 51900. ☎ **714/3-0021,** or 800/638-7950 and 800/223-9832 in the U.S. Fax 714/3-0856. 200 rms, 50 villas. MINIBAR TV TEL. 7-day Spa Diet package $1090 single, $1,805 double; 7-day Spa Relax package $1,035 single; 7-day Spa Sports package $880 single, $1668 double. (Shorter stays and daily rates available). Rates include 3 daily meals.

Set on several manicured and flower-filled acres, the town's only first-class hotel is also one of the country's best spa hotels, which has been in operation for over 40 years. When you compare its comfort, weight loss programs, good food, and relaxing pace to other spas, you'll understand its continued popularity. Having spent several wonderful weeks at this spa over the years, I can vouch for its value, and it seems to get better with each visit. A typical day starts with an hour's hike into the surrounding hills, followed by an hour of aerobics or yoga and water exercise. A personalized treatment schedule follows which includes massages, facials, and hair treatments; herbal wraps and salt-glow loofa scrubs; saunas, steam baths, and whirlpool tubs; and perhaps a tennis or golf lesson. A reflexologist is also available. Programs are separate for men and women, but everyone eats together. The spa week goes from Monday through Friday, with Sunday arrival preferred. Spa facilities are closed on Sunday. Hotel guests not on the spa program can use the spa facilities on a per-treatment pay plan, and there's no daily admission charge.

Food in the main (non-spa) dining room (also included in the room prices) is excellent and graciously served. Rooms, which are large, comfortable, and stylishly furnished, also come with cable TV with U.S. channels.

Services: Laundry, room service, tour desk. You must provide your own workout clothes and bathrobe. Round-trip transportation from the Mexico City airport can be arranged at the time of your reservation, but it's expensive. Consider the public bus (see "Getting There & Departing," above) instead.

Facilities: Challenging nine-hole golf course, fully equipped gym, aerobics room, three indoor whirlpools, two outdoor pools (one thermal and one freshwater), rooftop sun lounge, two tennis courts, spa dining room and hotel dining room, horseback riding.

Valle de Bravo & Avandaro

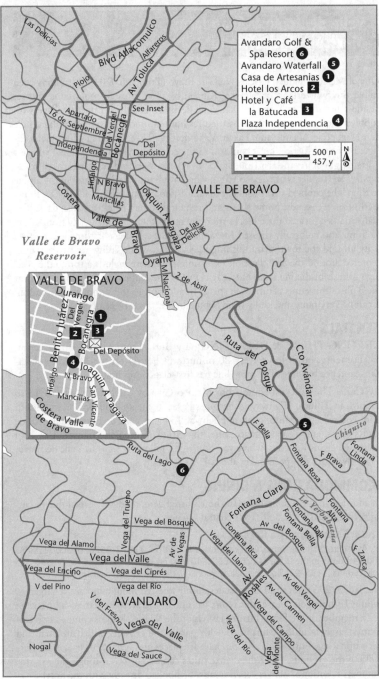

Avandaro Golf &
 Spa Resort ⑥
Avandaro Waterfall ⑤
Casa de Artesanias ①
Hotel los Arcos ②
Hotel y Café
 la Batucada ③
Plaza Independencia ④

0 — 500 m
457 y

N

Las Delicias

Blvd Atlacomulco

Av Toluca

Alfareros

Piojo

Apartado
16 de Septiembre

Del Vergel

Bocanegra

See Inset

Del
Depósito

Independencia

Hidalgo

N Bravo

Mancillas

Costera

Valle de

Bravo

Joaquin A Pagaza

VALLE DE BRAVO

De las
Delicias

*Valle de Bravo
Reservoir*

Oyamel

M Nacional

2 de Abril

VALLE DE BRAVO

Durango

Del Vergel

Benito Juárez

Bocanegra

Hidalgo

①

②

③

Del Depósito

④

Joaquin A Pagaza

N Bravo

San Vicente

Mancillas

Costera Valle
de Bravo

Ruta del Bosque

Cto Avándaro

Chiquito

⑤

F Bella

Fontana Rosa

F Brava

Fontana
Linda

Ruta del Lago

⑥

Fontana Clara

La Yerbabuena

Fontana
Alta

Fontana
Baja

Fontana Bella

Av del Bosque

F Zarca

Vega del Trueno

Vega del Bosque

Av de
las Vegas

Fontana Rica

Vega del Llano

Vega del Alamo

Vega del Valle

Vega del Ciprés

Vega del Encino

V del Pino

Vega del Río

AVANDARO

V del Fresno

Vega del Valle

Nogal

Vega del Sauce

Vega del Río

Av
Rosales

Av del Carmen

Av del Vergel

Vega del Campo

Vega
del Monte

9507

6 Valle de Bravo & Avandaro: Mexico's "Switzerland"

95 miles SW of Mexico City

One of Mexico's hidden retreats, Valle de Bravo (altitude 6,070 feet) has aptly been called the Switzerland of Mexico. Ringed by pine-forested mountains and set beside a beautiful man-made lake, Valle de Bravo is a 16th-century village with cobblestone streets and colonial structures built around a pretty town plaza. Like San Miguel de Allende and Taxco, Valle de Bravo is a National Monument village; new construction must conform to the colonial style of the original village.

Its neighbor **Avandaro** (four miles away) is a weekend retreat for well-to-do *capitalinos* (residents of Mexico City), who have built palatial estates in the alpine setting. The cobbled streets, small restaurants, hotels, and shops of Valle de Bravo are full on weekends. Some shops and restaurants may be closed weekdays. The crafts market, located three blocks from the main square, is open daily from 10 am to 5pm, and colorfully dressed Mazahua Indians sell their handmade tapestries daily around the town plaza. Fishing for bass and water skiing are two activities centered around the lake. Possible excursions from here include a trip to the nesting grounds of the monarch butterfly between November and February. A day at the Toluca museums is time well spent. In addition to the summer rainy season, it can be very rainy and chilly from September through December.

ESSENTIALS

GETTING THERE & DEPARTING   By Bus   From Mexico City's Terminal Poniente, buses leave every 20 minutes (3 hours) on the Mexico-Toluca-Zinacantepec bus line. The same line has first-class buses hourly.

By Car   The quickest route from Mexico City by car is via Highway 15 to Toluca. In Toluca, Highway 15 becomes Paseo Tollucan. Follow Tollucan south until you see signs pointing left to Highway 134 and Valle de Bravo, Francisco de los Ranchos, and Temascaltepec. After the turn, continue on Highway 142 until Francisco de los Ranchos, where you bear right, following signs to Valle de Bravo. The drive from this point takes about $1^1/_2$ to 2 hours.

ACCOMMODATIONS & DINING

In addition to the restaurants at the hotels listed here, there are several fine restaurants on or near Valle de Bravo's central square.

Avandaro Golf and Spa Resorts

Fracc. Avándaro, Valle de Bravo, Edo. de México 51200. ☎ **726/2-0626,** or 800/ALL SPAS or 800/448-8355 in the U.S. Fax 726/2-0626. 40 rms, 60 suites. A/C MINIBAR TV. $65–$85 double cabaña; $135–$215 double deluxe room. (7-day spa or golf package available.)

Nestled on 296 acres amid large estates, lushly forested mountains, and a gorgeous, rolling 18-hole golf course, this resort has one of the prettiest settings in Mexico. It's a member of the Small Luxury Hotels of the World. Rooms come in two categories: large, beautifully furnished deluxe suites and cabañas, which are small and need updating. Both kinds of room have fireplaces and terraces or balconies overlooking the grounds. Only the deluxe suites can be booked through the toll-free numbers mentioned above; cabañas must be booked directly with the hotel.

Services: Massages, wraps, facials, aerobics, exercise classes, numerous special treatments for cellulite and facial lines. Spa attire is provided. Transportation can be arranged from Mexico City.

Facilities: The ultra-modern spa compares to the best in the U.S., with a well-trained staff. A full range of services includes sauna and steam rooms, hot and cold whirlpools, and state-of-the-art weight training equipment. A 25-meter junior-olympic size pool overlooks the 18-hole golf course and 7 tennis courts. Two restaurants. Daily staff-led walks.

Hotel Los Arcos

Bocanegra 310, Valle de Bravo, Edo. de México 51200. ☎ **726/2-0042.** Fax 726/2-2878. 25 rms. $40–$50 double Sun–Thurs; $65–$75 double Fri–Sat.

Close to the main square, the Hotel Los Arcos has views of the village and mountains. Two stories of rooms on one side and three stories on the other are all built around a swimming pool. Rooms 13, 14, and 15 each have a fireplace, an important feature in winter here. Some rooms have balconies, and most have glass walls with views. Eleven of the highest-priced rooms have televisions. The restaurant is open on weekends.

7 Cuernavaca

64 miles S of Mexico City, 50 miles N of Taxco

Cuernavaca (alt. 5,058 ft.; pop. 800,000), capital of the state of Morelos, has been popular as a resort for people from Mexico City ever since the time of Moctezuma. Emperor Maximilian built a retreat here over a century ago. Mexicans say the town has a climate of "eternal spring," and on weekends the city is crowded with day-trippers from surrounding cities, especially the capital. On weekends the roads between Mexico City and Cuernavaca are jammed, and restaurants and hotels may be full as well. Cuernavaca has a large American colony, plus students attending the myriad language and cultural institutes that crowd the city.

Emperor Charles V gave Cuernavaca to Cortés as a fief, and the conquistador built a palace here in 1532 (now the Museo Cuauhnahuac) and lived there on and off for half a dozen years before returning to Spain. Cortés introduced sugarcane cultivation to the area, and Caribbean slaves were brought in to work in the cane fields. His sugar hacienda at the edge of town is now the luxurious Hotel de Cortés. The economics of large sugarcane growers failed to serve the interests of the indigenous farmers and there were numerous uprisings in colonial times.

After independence, mighty landowners from Mexico City gradually dispossessed the remaining small landholders, converting them to virtual serfdom. It was this condition that led to the rise of Emiliano Zapata, the great champion of agrarian reform, who battled the forces of wealth and power, defending the small farmer with the cry of *"Tierra y Libertad!"* (Land and Liberty!) during the Mexican Revolution following 1910.

In this century, Cuernavaca has seen the influx of wealthy foreigners and of industrial capital. The giant CIVAC industrial complex on the outskirts has brought wealth to the city but also the curse of increased traffic, noise, and air pollution.

ESSENTIALS

GETTING THERE & DEPARTING **By Bus** The Mexico City **Central de Autobuses del Sur**'s reason for being is the route Mexico City–Cuernavaca–Taxco–Acapulco–Zihuatanejo, so you'll have little trouble getting a bus. **Autobuses Pullman de Morelos** is the line with the most frequent departures (every 10 minutes) and the most convenient downtown terminal in Cuernavaca, at the corner of Abasolo and Netzahualcoyotl, four blocks south of the center of town. The trip takes one hour.

Lineas Unidas del Sur/Flecha Roja offers 17 buses daily from Mexico City to Cuernavaca. Its new terminal in Cuernavaca, at Morelos 505 (6 blocks north of town center), is also convenient to Cuernavaca's downtown. Here you'll find frequent buses to Toluca, Chalma, Ixtapan de la Sal, Taxco, Acapulco, the Cacahuamilpa Caves, and Querétaro.

The **Autobuses Estrella de Oro** terminal in Cuernavaca is at Morelos Sur 900, at the corner of Veracruz, about 15 blocks south of the center of town. This is the terminal with buses to Taxco (three per day); Zihuatanejo (two per day); Acapulco, Iguala, and Chilpancingo (five per day); and Mexico City (six per day).

By Car From Mexico City, take Paseo de la Reforma to Chapultepec Park and merge with the Periférico, which will take you to Highway 95D, the toll road on the far south of town that goes to Cuernavaca. From the Periférico, take the Insurgentes exit and continue until you come to signs for Cuernavaca/Tlalpan. Choose either the Cuernavaca Cuota (toll) or the old Cuernavaca Libre (free) road on the right.

ORIENTATION **Arriving** Bus stations are close to the town center, and most are within walking distance of several of my hotel recommendations.

Information Cuernavaca's **State Tourist Office** is at Av. Morelos Sur 802, between Jalisco and Veracruz (☎ 73/14-3860 or 14-3920), half a block north of the Estrella de Oro bus station and about a 10- or 15-minute walk south of the cathedral. There's little information there, however, and it's usually staffed by students who don't know much. It's open Monday through Friday from 9am to 8pm and Saturday and Sunday from 9am to 5pm.

City Layout In the center of the city are two contiguous plazas. The small and more formal of the two is square, with a Victorian gazebo (designed by Gustave Eiffel of Eiffel Tower fame) at its center. This is the **Jardín Juárez**. The larger, rectangular plaza planted with trees, shrubs, and benches is the **Plaza de Armas**. These two tree-filled plazas are known as the zócalo and are the hub for strolling vendors selling balloons, baskets, bracelets, and other crafts from surrounding villages. It's all easygoing, and one of the pleasures is grabbing a park bench or a table in a nearby restaurant just to watch. On Sunday afternoons orchestras play from the gazebo. At the eastern end of the Alameda is the **Cortés Palace,** the conquistador's residence that now serves as the Museo de Cuauhnahuac.

You should be aware that this city's street-numbering systems are extremely confusing. It appears that the city fathers, during the past century or so, became dissatisfied with the street numbers every 10 or 20 years and imposed a new numbering system each time. Thus you may find an address given as "no. 5" only to find that the building itself bears the number "506." One grand gateway I know bears no fewer than five different street numbers, ranging from 2 to 567! In my descriptions of hotels, restaurants, and sights, I'll note the nearest cross street so you can find your way to your chosen destination with a minimum of fuss.

Cuernavaca

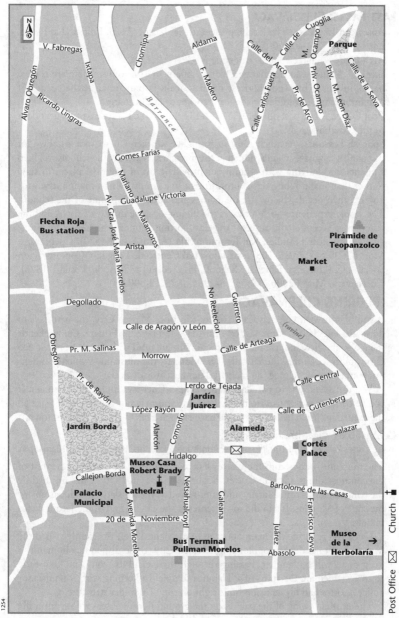

Getting Around Frequent **buses** go from downtown to all the outlying centers. Just tell a local where you want to go, and most will go out of their way to help you. **Taxis** are relatively inexpensive in Cuernavaca; $3 to $4 should get you from downtown to the outlying herb museum, for example. Determine the fare before taking off.

FAST FACTS: CUERNAVACA

American Express   The local representative is Viajes Marin, Edificio Las Plazas, Loc. 13 (☎ 73/14-2266; fax 73/12-9297).

Area Code   The telephone area code is 73.

Banks   Money can be changed from 9:30am to 1pm only. There are several banks in town, but the handiest to the zócalo is Bancomer at the corner of Matamoros and Lerdo de Tejada, catercorner to Jardín Juárez.

Post Office   The post office (☎ 73/12-4379) is on the Plaza de Armas, next door to the Café Los Arcos.

Spanish Lessons   As much as for its springlike weather, Cuernavaca is known for its Spanish-language schools, aimed at the foreigner. Generally the schools will help students find lodging with a family or provide a list of potential places to stay. Rather than make a long-term commitment in a family living situation, try it for a week, then decide. Below are the names and addresses of some of the schools. The whole experience—from classes to lodging—can be quite expensive, and the school may accept credit cards for the class portion. Contact the Center for Bilingual Multicultural Studies, San Jeronimo 304 (Apdo. Postal 1520), Cuernavaca, Mor. 62000 (☎ 73/17-1087); or Universal Centro de Lengua y Comunicacion Social A.C. (Universal Language School), H. Preciado 332 (Apdo. Postal 1-1826), Cuernavaca, Mor. 62000 (☎ 73/18-2904 or 73/12-4902).

EXPLORING CUERNAVACA

If you plan to visit Cuernavaca on a day-trip from Mexico City, the best days to do so are Tuesday, Wednesday, or Thursday (and perhaps Friday). On weekends the roads, the city, and its hotels and restaurants are filled with people from Mexico City, and prices jump dramatically. On Monday, the museum—which you definitely must see—is closed. So make it Tuesday through Friday.

You can spend one to two days sightseeing in Cuernavaca pleasantly enough. If you've come on a day-trip from Mexico City, you may not have time to make all the excursions listed below, but you'll have enough time to see the sights in town.

✪ Museo de Cuauhnahuac

In the Cortés Palace, Levya 100. No phone. Admission $4.50; free Sun. Tues–Sun 10am–5pm.

The museum is housed in the Cortés Palace, the former home of the greatest of the conquistadores, Hernán Cortés. Begun by Cortés in 1530, it was finished by the conquistador's son, Martín, and later served as the legislative headquarters for the state of Morelos. It's in the town center at the eastern end of the Jardín de los Héroes.

Once you're inside the main door, go to the right. If you've recently visited the Museo Nacional de Antropología in Mexico City, these displays of humanity's early times will be familiar. Passing through these exhibits, you come to a little court in which are the ruins of a Tlahuica temple. In keeping with conquistador policy, Cortés had his mansion built right on top of an older structure.

The northern wing of the palace, on the ground floor, houses exhibits from the colonial era: suits of armor juxtaposed with the arrows, spears, and maces used by the Indians. Upstairs in the northern wings are costumes, domestic furnishings, carriages, and farm implements from Mexico of the 1800s, mostly from *haciendas azucareras* (sugar plantations). There are also mementos of the great revolutionaries Francisco Madero and Emiliano Zapata.

Through the door on the right are more exhibits from colonial times, including several fascinating pages from "painted books," or Indian codices, which survived the book burnings of the Spaniards. There's also a clock mechanism *(reloj)* from Cuernavaca's cathedral, thought to be the first public clock on the American continent.

When you get to the east portico on the upper floor, you're in for a treat. A large Diego Rivera mural commissioned by Dwight Morrow, U.S. ambassador to Mexico in the 1920s, depicts the history of Cuernavaca from the coming of the Spaniards to the rise of Zapata (1910). It's fascinating to examine this magnificent mural in all its epic detail.

Catedral de la Asunción

At the corner of Hidalgo and Morelos. Admission free. Daily 8am–2pm and 4–10pm. Walk three blocks southwest of the Plaza de Armas.

As you enter the church precincts and pass down the walk, try to imagine what life in Mexico was like in the old days. Construction on the church was begun in 1533, a mere 12 years after Cortés conquered Tenochtitlán (Mexico City) from the Aztecs. The churchmen could hardly trust their safety to the tenuous allegiance of their new converts, so they built a fortress as a church. The skull-and-crossbones above the main door is not a comment on their feelings about the future, however, but a symbol for the Franciscan order, which had its monastery here in the church precincts.

Inside, the church is stark, even severe, having been refurbished in the 1960s. The most curious aspect of the interior is the mystery of the frescoes. Discovered during the refurbishing, they depict Christian missionary activity and persecution in Japan and are painted in Japanese style. No one is certain who painted them or why.

Museo Casa Robert Brady

Calle Netzahualcoyotl 4. ☎ **73/18-8554.** Admission $5.50. Thurs–Fri 10am–2pm and 4–6pm, Sat 10am–2pm.

This museum in a private home contains more than 1,300 works of art. Among them are pre-Hispanic and colonial pieces; oil paintings by Frida Kahlo and Rufino Tamayo; and handcrafts from America, Africa, Asia, and India. Admission includes a guide in Spanish; English and French guides are available if requested at the time of your reservation.

Visits can be arranged during other days at a special price.

Jardín Borda

Morelos 103, at Hidalgo. ☎ **73/14-0282,** or 18-6372. Admission 80¢. Tues–Sun 10am–5pm.

Half a block from the cathedral is the Jardín Borda (Borda Gardens). One of the many wealthy builders to choose Cuernavaca was José de la Borda, the Taxco silver magnate, who ordered a sumptuous vacation house built here in the late 1700s. The large enclosed garden next to the house was actually a huge private park, laid out in Andalusian style with little kiosks and an artificial pond. Maximilian found it worthy of an emperor and took it over as his private preserve in the mid-1800s. After Maximilian, the Borda Gardens fell on hard times; decades of neglect followed.

The paintings of the French Intervention enhance a stroll through the gardens. Here are the scenes you'll see: Emperor Maximilian and Empress Carlota arrive in Cuernavaca for the first time; then, Maximilian, while out for a ride, gets his first glimpse of La India Bonita, who was to become his lover. The next scene is of court festivities in the Borda Gardens, with courtiers taking turns rowing little boats.

Finally, Maximilian's niece pleads with President Benito Juárez, after the siege of Querétaro, to spare the emperor's life. (At that time, Carlota was off in Europe, trying to round up support for her husband's cause, without result.) Juárez refused her request, and Maximilian, along with two of his generals, was executed by firing squad on the Hill of Bells in Querétaro a few days thereafter.

On your stroll through the gardens you'll see the same little artificial lake on which Austrian, French, and Mexican nobility rowed in little boats beneath the moonlight. Ducks have taken the place of dukes, however, and there are rowboats for rent. The lake is now artfully adapted as an outdoor theater, with seats for the audience on one side and the stage on the other.

The Borda Gardens have been completely restored and were reopened in October 1987 as the Jardín Borda Centro de Artes. In the gateway buildings are several galleries for changing exhibits, a cafe for refreshments and light meals, and several large paintings showing scenes from the life of Maximilian and from the history of the Borda Gardens.

Museo de la Herbolaría

Matamoros 200, Acapantzingo. ☎ **12-5956.** Admission $4.50. Daily 10am–5pm.

This museum of traditional herbal medicine, in the southern Cuernavaca suburb of Acapantzingo, has been set up in a former resort residence built by Maximilian, the Casa del Olindo, or Casa del Olvido. It was here, during his brief reign, that the Austrian-born emperor would come for trysts with La India Bonita, his Cuernavacan lover. Restored in 1960, the house and gardens now preserve the local wisdom in folk medicine. The shady gardens are lovely to wander through, and you shouldn't miss the 200 orchids growing near the rear of the property. However, the lovers' actual house, the little dark-pink building in the back, is closed. Catch combi no. 6 at the mercado on Degollado. Ask to be dropped off at Matamoros near the museum. Turn right on Matamoros and walk 1 1/2 blocks; the museum will be on your right.

ACCOMMODATIONS

Because so many *capitalinos* come down from Mexico City for the day or for the weekend, the hotel trade here may be heavy on weekends and holidays, light at other times. A few local hoteliers adapt their policies and prices to these shifts.

VERY EXPENSIVE

Camino Real Sumiya

Interior Fracc. Sumiya s/n, Col. José Parres, Jiutepec, Mor. ☎ **73/20-9199,** or 800/7-CAMINO in the U.S. Fax 73/20-9155. 163 rms, 6 suites. A/C MINIBAR TV TEL. High season $185–$255; low season $190–$250. Low-season packages and discounts available.

About 7 miles south of Cuernavaca, this unusual resort, whose name means "the House on the Corner," was once the exclusive home of Woolworth heiress Barbara Hutton. Using materials and craftsmen from Japan, she constructed the $3.2 million estate in 1959 on 30 beautifully wooded acres. The main house, a series of large interconnected rooms and decks, overlooks the grounds and contains restaurants and the lobby.

The guest houses, which are clustered in three-storied buildings flanking manicured lawns, are plain in comparison to the striking Japanese architecture of the main house. Rooms, however, have nice Japanese accents, with austere but comfortable furnishings, scrolled wood doors, and round pulls on the armoire and closet. Each room has direct-dial long-distance phones, fax connections, three-prong electrical outlets, ceiling fans, and in-room wall safes. A kabuki-style theater on the grounds is used for special events, and beyond it lies a Japanese garden with stones placed in the same positions as the Japanese islands.

Cuernavaca is a $5 taxi ride away. Sumiya's charm is its relaxing atmosphere, which is best midweek since escapees from Mexico City tend to fill it on weekends. Sightseeing suggestions are the same as for Cocoyoc. From the freeway, take the Atlacomulco exit and follow Sumiya signs. Ask directions in Cuernavaca if you're coming from there since the route to the resort is complicated.

Dining/Entertainment: There's La Arboleda, an outdoor restaurant shaded by enormous Indian laurel trees; Sumiya, with both terrace and indoor dining; and a snack bar by the pool.

Services: Room service, business center.

Facilities: Pool, 10 tennis courts.

Las Mañanitas

Ricardo Linares 107, Cuernavaca, Mor. 62000. ☎ **73/14-1466,** or 12-4646. Fax 73/18-3672. 22 rms (all with bath). TEL. $80–$92 double; $130–$280 suite. No credit cards. Valet parking. Buses going north on Morelos stop within half a block of the hotel.

Among Cuernavaca's best-known luxury lodgings is Las Mañanitas, $5^{1}/_{2}$ long blocks north of the Jardín Borda. Antique headboards, heavy brass candlesticks, authentic period furniture and decoration, and large baths make each room charming. Many have verdant, vine-encumbered balconies big enough for sitting and sipping while overlooking the emerald lawns where peacocks and other exotic birds strut and preen and fountains tinkle musically. Thirteen rooms have fireplaces, and the hotel also has a heated pool. Accommodations come in four types, all doubles, but the standard rooms are by far the best value. The terrace, patio, and garden suites cost a great deal more.

Dining/Entertainment: The restaurant, overlooking the gardens, is one of the premier dining places in the country. The restaurant serves breakfast but is open to nonguests for lunch and dinner only.

Services: Laundry and room service, concierge.

EXPENSIVE

Hotel Hacienda de Cortés

90 Plaza Kennedy (Apdo. Postal 430), Cuernavaca, Mor. 62240. ☎ **73/15-8844,** or 16-0867. Fax 73/15-0035. 22 suites. TEL. $100–$120 double; $130 double suite; $250 imperial suite for six people. Free parking.

This hotel lies in the suburb of Atlacolmulco, just off the Cuernavaca/Acapulco highway. Formerly the Hacienda de San Antonio Atlacomulco, it was used to process sugarcane during the 1600s. After several incarnations, in the 1970s it was converted into one of the country's most splendid hacienda hotels. Towering chimneys from the sugar-processing era still loom above the beautiful suites, which are all in original hacienda rooms edging the immaculate interior gardens. Each room is furnished with carefully chosen antiques, area rugs, and Mexican textiles. This is a true getaway—its only drawback is its distance from town.

Dining/Entertainment: The vine-covered, stone-walled former grinding room is the dining room, where trios strum romantic tunes during meals. There's also outside dining.

Services: Room and laundry service.

Facilities: A small secluded pool.

MODERATE

Hotel María Cristina

Leyva 200 (Apdo. Postal 203), Cuernavaca, Mor. 62000. ☎ **73/18-5767.** 14 rms (all with bath). TV TEL. $60–$70 double; $95 suite. Free parking. Walk 3 long blocks to the right of the Cortés Palace or walk 2 blocks east (right) of Pullman Morelos bus station.

The María Cristina's beauty justifies its price. Formerly La Posada de Xochiquetzal, its high walls conceal many delights: a small swimming pool, lush gardens with fountains, tasteful colonial-style furnishings, a good restaurant, patios, and large and small guest rooms. Even if you don't stay here, come for a meal.

INEXPENSIVE

✪ Hotel Cadiz

Alvaro Obregón 329, Cuernavaca, Mor. 62000. ☎ **73/18-9204.** 17 rms (all with bath). FAN. $29 double.

Every now and then I discover a hotel with the kind of homey charm that makes me want to return. Such is the Hotel Cadiz, run by the gracious Aguilar family. You may have known it as the Hotel María Cristina. Each of the fresh, simple rooms is furnished uniquely, and there's a lot of old-fashioned tile and big, old (but well-kept) freestanding sinks. The grounds, set back from the street, make a pleasant respite. There are a pool and a small inexpensive restaurant open from 9am to 4pm. From Morelos, turn left on Ricardo Linares and go past Las Mañanitas. Turn left at the first street, Obregón; the hotel is a block ahead on the right.

DINING

VERY EXPENSIVE

Casa de Campo

Abasolo 101. ☎ **73/12-4947,** or 18-2635. Breakfast buffet $10; main courses $19–$25; Sun brunch $30. INTERNATIONAL

The elegant Casa de Campo has become a rival of longtime favorite Las Mañanitas (see below). Like Las Mañanitas, it boasts strolling peacocks and blue-and-red parrots. A converted one-story townhouse built in a U shape around beautiful grounds, Casa de Campo spares no expense in its decor and food. Dining rooms open onto the terrace and grounds. Main courses include red snapper in créole sauce, fresh salmon, chateaubriand, and daily specials. Throughout the serving hours there's some kind of live entertainment such as a crooning trio, marimbas in the garden, or soft piano music in the bar.

✪ Restaurant Las Mañanitas

Ricardo Linares 107. ☎ **73/14-1466,** or 12-4646. Reservations recommended. Main courses $12.50–$18. Daily noon–5pm, 7–11pm. Buses going north on Morelos stop within half a block of the restaurant. MEXICAN/INTERNATIONAL.

Las Mañanitas sets the standard for sumptuous dining in Cuernavaca. Tables are set on a shaded terrace with a view of gardens, strolling peacocks, and softly playing violinists or a romantic trio. The decor and ambience are lightly colonial, and the service is extremely attentive. When you arrive, you can enjoy cocktails in the cozy sala; when you're ready to dine, a waiter will present you with a menu listing at least half a dozen daily specials. The cuisine is Mexican with an international flair; the dishes include seasonal fruits and vegetables and a full selection of fresh seafood, beef, pork, veal, and fowl. Las Mañanitas is 5$^1/_2$ long blocks north of the Jardín Borda.

MODERATE

○ Restaurant La India Bonita

Morrow 1066B. ☎ **73/18-6967.** Breakfast $3–$7.70; main courses $4–$9. Tues–Sat 8:30am–8pm, Sun 8:30am–6pm. MEXICAN.

This new location of La India Bonita may well be its best. Housed among the interior patios and portals of the restored home of former U.S. Ambassador Dwight Morrow (1920s), it's gracious, sophisticated, and definitely a Cuernavaca haven where you can enjoy the setting as well as the food. Specialties include mole poblano (chicken with a sauce of bitter chocolate and fiery chilies) and filet a la parrilla (charcoal-grilled steak). There are also several daily specials. A breakfast mainstay is the gigantic desayuno Maximiliano—a huge platter featuring enchiladas. The restaurant is two blocks north of the Jardín Juárez between Matamoros and Morelos.

○ Restaurant Vienes

Lerdo de Tejada 4. ☎ **73/18-4044,** or 14-3404. Breakfast $1.25–$3.75; main courses $5.50–$9. Daily 8am–10pm. VIENNESE.

A legacy of this city's Viennese immigrant heritage is the Restaurant Vienes, a tidy and somewhat Viennese-looking place a block from the Jardín Juárez between Lerdo de Tejada and Morrow. The menu also has Old World specialties such as grilled trout with vegetables and German potato salad; for dessert there's apfelstrudel followed by Viennese coffee. Next door, the restaurant runs a pastry/coffee shop called Los Pasteles de Vienes, where the pastries are temptingly displayed atop a long counter. Although the menu is identical, the atmosphere in the coffee shop is much more leisurely.

INEXPENSIVE

La Parroquía

Guerrero 102. ☎ **73/18-5820.** Breakfast $2–$4; main courses $4.50–$8; comida corrida $6. Daily 8am–10:30pm. MEXICAN/PASTRIES.

This place does a brisk business, partly because of its great location (half a block north of the Alameda opposite Parque Juárez and almost next to Los Pasteles de Vienes) and partly because it has fairly reasonable prices for Cuernavaca. It's open to the street with a few outdoor cafe tables—perfect for watching the changing parade of street vendors and park life.

CUERNAVACA AFTER DARK

Cuernavaca has a number of cafes right off the Jardín Juárez where people gather to sip coffee or drinks till the wee hours of the morning, the best of which are Los Arcos, La Parroquía, and the Los Pasteles de Vienes (see "Dining," above). There are band concerts in the Jardín Juárez on Thursday and Sunday evenings.

Harry's Grill, Gutenberg 3, at Salazar, just off the main square (☎ 73/12-7639), is another addition to the Carlos Anderson chain and includes its usual good food and craziness with Mexican revolutionary posters and jaunty waiters. Although it serves full dinners, I'd recommend you go for drinks ($3 to $5). It's open daily from 1:30 to 11:30pm.

EXCURSIONS FROM CUERNAVACA

If you have enough time, you should try to make some side trips around Cuernavaca. To the north you'll find pine trees and an alpine setting; to the east, lush hills and valleys. On the road north to Mexico City you will climb several thousand feet within half an hour into some gorgeous mountain air. If you have a car, you can go for a brisk morning hike (it's cold up there) or a lazy afternoon picnic.

TEPOZTLÁN: STREET MARKET & A MONASTERY   Less than 20 miles northeast of Cuernavaca, this Tlahuica village nearly surrounded by mountains (not to be confused with Tepozotlán, north of Mexico City) predates the Conquest. On weekends, it's a popular retreat for *capitalinos.*

The best times to go are Saturdays and Mexican holidays when there's a sprawling outdoor **crafts market** around the central square. Tepoztlán's folk healers (*curanderos*), for which the village is well known, are often there selling medicinal herbs and other magical cures. The market is especially good during **Carnaval** (three days before Ash Wednesday), a moveable date usually in February, and around **Days of the Dead**, November 1 and 2. During Carnaval, colorfully costumed and masked dancers perform. Since outsiders flock to the town during Carnaval, plan to arrive early in the day to stake out a good observation point before things get too congested. **September 8** is the festival honoring the god of pulque (a fermented drink), another occasion on which there are dancers and the market is especially large.

The ruins of an **Aztec temple,** Tepozteco, honoring the god of pulque, are on a sheer rock outcropping 1,200 feet above the town. The town itself is built around a 16th-century Dominican monastery. On the street behind the monastery (actually in the back of the monastery) is the **Museo Arqueología Carlos Pellicer,** which exhibits a fine collection of pre-Hispanic artifacts. It's open Tuesday through Sunday from 9am to 5pm. Admission is $1.25.

There are several restaurants around the square, as well as a couple of good inns. To get here take one of the frequent buses or minivans by the Cuernavaca market. Tourists don't use these much, and other passengers generally go out of their way to be helpful and will let you know when to get off.

XOCHICALCO RUINS   About 16 miles south of Cuernavaca along Highway 95 (the "Libre"—no-toll—road to Taxco) is the town of Alpuyeca, and 9¹/₂ miles northeast of Alpuyeca are the ruins of Xochicalco, the "House of Flowers." High on a mountaintop, Xochicalco boasts a magnificent situation and an interesting complex of buildings dating from about A.D. 600 through 900. Most interesting is the **Temple of the Feathered Serpents,** with beautiful bas-reliefs. There are also a ball court, some underground passages, and other temples. Xochicalco is of interest to archaeologists because it seems to have been the point at which the Teotihuacán, Toltec, Zapotec, and Maya cultures met and interacted. You can visit the ruins from 8am to 5pm daily. Catch a bus to the crucero (crossing) from the Pullman de Morelos station. Buses run frequently. From the crucero take a combi to the ruins for $4. Admission is $4.50; additional $8.50 for use of a personal video camera.

8 Taxco

111 miles S of Mexico City, 50 miles S of Cuernavaca, 185 miles N of Acapulco

Taxco (pronounced "TAHS-ko"), famous for its silverwork, sits at nearly 6,000 feet on a hill among hills, and almost everywhere you walk in the city there are fantastic views.

Taxco's renowned silver mines, first worked in the time of Cortés, four centuries ago, were revived, for all practical purposes, by an American, William Spratling, in the 1930s. Today its fame rests more on the over 200 silver shops, most little one-man factories, that line the cobbled streets all the way up into the hills. Whether you'll find bargains depends on how much you know about the quality and price of silver. But there is no doubt that nowhere else in the country will you find the quantity and variety of silver. The artistry and imagination of the local silversmiths are evident in each piece.

You can get the idea of what Taxco's like by spending an afternoon, but there's much more to this picturesque town of 87,000 than just Plaza Borda and the shops surrounding it. You'll have to stay overnight if you want more time to climb up and down its steep cobblestone streets, discovering little plazas and fine churches. The main part of town is relatively flat. It stretches up the hillside from the highway, and although it's a steep walk, it's not a particularly long one. But you don't have to walk up and down all the hills: Vehicles make the circuit through and around the town picking up and dropping off passengers along the route. There are *burritos*, white VW minibuses that run the route from about 7am until 9pm. Taxis in town are around $1.50 to $2.

Warning: Self-appointed guides will undoubtedly approach you in the zócalo (Plaza Borda) and offer their services—they get a cut (up to 25%) of all you buy in the shops they take you to. Before hiring a **guide,** ask to see his Departamento de Turismo credentials. The Department of Tourism office on the highway at the north end of town can recommend a licensed guide for about $5 to $8 per hour.

ESSENTIALS

GETTING THERE & DEPARTING   By Bus   From Mexico City, buses to Taxco depart from the Central de Autobuses del Sur station (Metro: Tasqueña) and take two to three hours. **Estrella Blanca** and its **Líneas Unidas del Sur/Flecha Roja** lines have service to Taxco every 30 minutes with a variety of bus types. Your best bet is their "Plus" service for $8.75. These buses have air-conditioning, a TV, soft drinks, and bathrooms. **Estrella de Oro** has seven direct no-frills buses a day to Taxco for $6.75. **From Cuernavaca,** see details in "Excursions from Cuernavaca," above.

By Car   From Mexico City, take Paseo de la Reforma to Chapultepec Park and merge with the Periférico, which will take you to Highway 95D on the south end of town. From the Periférico, take the Insurgentes exit and merge until you come to the sign to Cuernavaca/Tlalpan. Choose either CUERNAVACA CUOTA (toll) or CUERNAVACA LIBRE (free). Continue south around Cuernavaca to the Amacuzac interchange and proceed straight ahead for Taxco. The drive from Mexico City takes about 3^1/2 hours. Fill up with gas at Cuernavaca.

From Acapulco you have two options. Highway 95D is the new toll road through Iguala to Taxco; almost all of the road is open now. Or you can take the old two-lane road (95) that winds through villages and is slower, but it's in good condition.

ORIENTATION   Arriving   Taxco has two **bus** stations. **Estrella de Oro** buses arrive at their own station on the southern edge of town. **Flecha Rojo** buses arrive at the station on the eastern edge of town on Avenida Kennedy. Both stations present a hard walk to town. If you have only a small suitcase, take a white minivan marked "Santa Prisca" or "Zócalo" from the front of either station to get to the town center. Taxis cost around $2 to the zócalo.

Information   The **State of Guerrero Dirección de Turismo** (☎ and fax 762/2-2274, 2-2079, or 2-1525) has offices at the arches on the main highway at the north end of town, useful if you're driving into town. The office is open daily from 9am to 3pm and 6 to 9pm. To get there from Plaza Borda, take a combi ("Zócalo Arcos") and get off at the arch over the highway. As you face the arches, the tourism office is on your right, upstairs.

City Layout   The center of town is the tiny **Plaza Borda,** shaded by perfectly manicured Indian laurel trees. On one side is the imposing twin-towered, pink-stone **Santa Prisca Church,** and the other sides are lined with whitewashed red-tile buildings housing the famous **silver shops** and a restaurant or two. Beside the church, deep in a crevice of the mountain, is the **city market.** Brick-paved streets fill out from here in a helter-skelter fashion up and down the hillsides. Besides the silver-filled shops, the plaza swirls with vendors of everything from hammocks to cotton candy and from bark paintings to balloons.

FAST FACTS: TAXCO

Area Code   The telephone area code is 762.

Long-Distance Phone   Farmacia Oscarin, Av. Kennedy 47 (☎ 762/2-1847), opposite the Flecha Roja bus station, serves as the community long-distance telephone center. For a small service fee (around $4), one of its staff will dial the number you want, then you step into a private booth to take your call. If you call collect, the service fee is the only charge; otherwise, you pay both the service fee and cost of the call. It's open Monday through Saturday from 8:30am to 9pm and Saturday from 8:30am to 2pm.

Post Office   The post office moved to the outskirts of Taxco on the highway heading toward Acapulco. It's in a row of shops with a black-and-white sign reading CORREO.

Scam   Some taxi drivers at the bus station and tour guides who greet you on arrival in town receive a payoff to take you to certain hotels in Taxco. They'll even go so far as to tell you the hotel at which you have reservations is closed or in horrible disrepair in order to take you to a hotel for which they get a kickback. Proceed with your own plans and leave these guys to their dirty tricks.

Spanish/Art Classes   In 1993, the Universidad Anonima de Mexico (UNAM) opened its doors in the buildings and grounds of the Hacienda del Chorillo, formerly part of the Cortés land grant. Here students can study silversmithing, Spanish, drawing, composition, and history under the supervision of UNAM instructors. Classes contain between 10 and 15 students, and courses are generally for three months at a time. The school will provide a list of prospective town accommodations that consist primarily of hotels. As an alternative, I suggest you select an inexpensive hotel for the first several nights, then search for something more reasonable for a lengthy stay. At locations all over town are notices of furnished apartments or rooms for rent at reasonable prices. For information about the school, contact either the Dirección de Turismo (tourist office) in Taxco (see "Information," above) or write the school directly: UNAM, Hacienda del Chorillo, Taxco, Gro. 40200 (☎ 762/2-3690).

EXPLORING TAXCO

Since Taxco boasts more than 200 shops selling silver, shopping for the brilliant metal is the major pastime—and the main reason most tourists come. But Taxco's cultural show is on an upward move. Besides the opulent, world-renowned **Santa**

Prisca y San Sebastián Church, the Spratling Archaeology Museum, the Silver Museum, and the Museo Gráfica, there's the recently opened von Humboldt House/Museo Virreynal de Taxco. In Taxco, museums seem to have "official" hours and "real" hours, so you may find some are closed when they should be open.

You also might consider taking a look at Juan O'Gorman's mosaic tile mural beside the pool at the Hotel Posada de la Misión (on the highway; go via minibus).

SPECIAL EVENTS

Taxco's **Silver Fair** starts the last Saturday in November and continues for one week. It includes a competition for silver sculptures from among the top silversmiths. **Holy Week** in Taxco is one of the most compelling in the country, beginning the Friday a week before Easter with nightly processions and several during the day. The most riveting procession, on Thursday evening, lasts almost four hours and includes villagers from the surrounding area carrying statues of saints, followed by hooded members of a society of self-flagellating penitents chained at the ankles and carrying huge wooden crosses and bundles of penetrating thorny branches. On the Saturday morning before Easter, the Plaza Borda fills for the procession of three falls, reenacting the three times Christ stumbled and fell while carrying his cross. From the middle of May to April 1 are the **Jornadas Alarcon-ianas,** featuring plays and literary events in honor of Juan Ruíz de Alarcón (1572–1639), a world-famous dramatist who was born in Taxco.

SIGHTS IN TOWN

✪ Santa Prisca y San Sebastián Church
Plaza Borda. No phone. Admission free. Daily 8am–11pm.

This is Taxco's centerpiece parish church, around which village life takes place. Facing the pleasant Plaza Borda, it was built with funds provided by José de la Borda, a French miner who struck it rich in Taxco's silver mines. Completed in 1758 after eight years of labor, it's one of Mexico's most impressive baroque churches. Outside, the ultracarved facade is flanked by two elaborately embellished steeples and a colorful tile dome. Inside, the intricacy of the gold-leafed saints and cherubic angels is positively breathtaking. The paintings by Miguel Cabrera, one of Mexico's most famous colonial-era artist, are the pride of Taxco. A long-overdue restoration and cleaning of the interior walls has been completed, but they have become dusty again. The room behind the altar is now open and contains even more Cabrera paintings.

Guides, both boys and adults, will approach you outside the church offering to give a tour, and it's worth the small price to get a full rendition of what you're seeing. Make sure the guide's English is good, however, and establish whether the price is per person or per tour. Give him 75¢ to $1.

✪ Silver Museum
Plaza Borda. ☎ 762/2-0558. Admission $1.25. Daily 10am–5pm.

A recent addition is the Silver Museum, operated by a local silversmith. After entering the building next to Santa Prisca (it's also the site of the Sr. Costilla's restaurant), look for a sign on the left; the museum is downstairs. It's not a traditional public-sponsored museum. Nevertheless, it does a much-needed job of describing the history of silver in Mexico and Taxco, as well as displaying some historic and contemporary award-winning pieces. Time spent here seeing quality silverwork will make you a more discerning shopper in Taxco's dazzling silver shops.

✪ Museo de Taxco Guillermo Spratling

Calle Veracruz. ☎ **762/2-1660**. Admission $4; free Sun. Tues–Sun 10am–5pm.

A plaque (in Spanish) explains that most of the collection of pre-Columbian art displayed here, as well as the funds for the museum, came from William Spratling, an American born in 1900 who studied architecture in the United States, later settled in Taxco, and organized the first workshops to turn out high-quality silver jewelry. From this first effort in 1931 the town's reputation as a center of artistic silverwork grew to what it is today. In a real sense, Spratling "put Taxco on the map." He died in 1967 in a car accident. You'd expect this to be a silver museum, but it's not—for Spratling silver, go to the Spratling Ranch Workshop (see "Nearby Attractions," below). The entrance floor of this museum and the one above display a good collection of pre-Columbian statues and implements in clay, stone, and jade. The lower floor has changing exhibits.

To find the museum, turn left out of the Santa Prisca Church and left again at the corner; it's on the left at the end of the street.

✪ Von Humboldt House/Museo Virreyenal De Taxco

Calle Juan Ruíz de Alarcón. ☎ **762/2-5501**. Admission $3.50. Tues–Sat 10am–5pm, Sun 9am–3pm.

Stroll along Ruíz de Alarcón (the street behind the Casa Borda) and look for the richly decorated facade of the von Humboldt House, where the renowned German scientist/explorer Baron Alexander von Humboldt (1769–1859) visited Taxco and stayed one night in 1803. The new museum houses 18th-century memorabilia pertinent to Taxco, most of which came from a secret room discovered during the recent restoration of the Santa Prisca y San Sebastián Church. It's a fascinating museum, especially if you take a guided tour; however, signs with detailed information are in both Spanish and English. The von Humboldt House has known many uses, including 40 years as a guesthouse run until the mid-1970s by the von Wuthenau family. To the right as you enter are two huge and very rare *tumelos* (three-tiered funerary paintings). The bottom two were painted in honor of the death of Carlos III of Spain; the top one, with a carved phoenix on top, was supposedly painted for the funeral of José de la Borda.

The three stories of the museum are divided by eras and persons famous in Taxco's history. In the *sala* (room) dedicated to José de la Borda is a copy of a painting (which hangs in the church) showing him dressed in the finery of his times, with samples of such garments in other cases. In a room of photographs are pictures of Taxco's 10 principal churches. Another room shows paintings of what workshops must have been like during the construction of Santa Prisca y San Sebastián. Another section is devoted to historical information about Don Miguel Cabrera, Mexico's foremost 18th-century artist. Fine examples of clerical garments decorated with gold and silver thread hang in glass cases. More excellently restored Cabrera paintings are hung throughout the museum; some were found in the frames you see, others were haphazardly rolled up. And, of course, a small room devoted to von Humboldt shows what this young explorer looked like and gives a short history of his sojourns through South America and Mexico.

Taxco

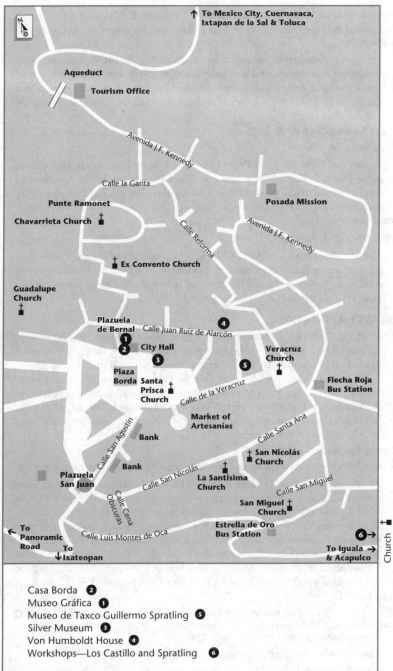

To Mexico City, Cuernavaca, Ixtapan de la Sal & Toluca

Aqueduct
Tourism Office

Avenida J.F. Kennedy

Calle la Garita

Punte Ramonet

Chavarrieta Church

Posada Mission

Avenida J.F. Kennedy

Calle Reforma

Ex Convento Church

Guadalupe Church

Plazuela de Bernal

Calle Juan Ruiz de Alarcón

City Hall

Veracruz Church

Plaza Borda

Santa Prisca Church

Calle de la Veracruz

Flecha Roja Bus Station

Market of Artesanías

Calle San Agustín

Bank

Calle Santa Ana

San Nicolás Church

Bank

Calle San Nicolás

La Santisima Church

Calle San Miguel

Plazuela San Juan

Calle Cena Obscuras

San Miguel Church

To Panoramic Road

Calle Luis Montes de Oca

To Ixateopan

Estrella de Oro Bus Station

To Iguala & Acapulco

Church

Casa Borda ❷
Museo Gráfica ❶
Museo de Taxco Guillermo Spratling ❺
Silver Museum ❸
Von Humboldt House ❹
Workshops—Los Castillo and Spratling ❻

Museo Gráfica de la Historia Social de Taxco en El Siglo XX

Plaza Bernal. No phone. Admission free. Tues–Fri 9am–3pm and 6–8pm, Sat–Sun 10am–2pm and 4–6pm.

Using great photographs and engravings produced over the last 90 years, this small, interesting museum shows Taxco's metamorphosis into a major touristic center. You'll recognize many existing streets and buildings and their changing uses over the years. It faces the Plaza Bernal, behind the Casa Borda and opposite Los Castillo silver store.

Casa Borda/Casa de la Cultura

Plaza Borda. No phone.

Catercorner from the Santa Prisca Church and facing Plaza Borda, this was the home José de la Borda built for his son. When I checked, it was to be converted from office use to a city cultural center with performing arts and changing exhibits. Check to see the progress when you travel.

Mercado Central

Plaza Borda. Daily 7am–6pm.

To the right of the Santa Prisca Church, behind and below Berta's, Taxco's central market meanders deep inside the mountain. Take the stairs off the street. Among the curio stores you'll find the food stalls and cook shops, always the best place for a cheap meal.

NEARBY ATTRACTIONS

The large **Grutas De Cacahuamilpa** (Cacahuamilpa Caves) are 20 minutes north of Taxco. There are hourly guided tours daily at the caves, but these caves are much like any other you may have visited and you might not want to make the effort.

For a spectacular view of Taxco, ride the **cable cars** (gondola) to the Hotel Monte Taxco. Catch them across the street from the state tourism office, left of the arches, near the college campus. Take a combi marked "Los Arcos" and exit just before the arches, turn left, and follow the signs to the cable cars. Daily hours are 8am to 7pm. A round-trip ride is $4.

Spratling Ranch Workshop

6 miles south of town on the Acapulco Hwy. No phone. Free admission. Mon–Sat 9am–5pm.

Spratling's hacienda-style home/workshop on the outskirts of Taxco once again hums with busy hands reproducing his unique designs. A trip here will show you what distinctive Spratling work was all about, for the designs crafted today show the same fine work—even Spratling's workshop foreman is employed again overseeing the development of a new generation of silversmiths. Prices are high, but the designs are unusual and considered collectible. There's no store in Taxco, and unfortunately, most of the display cases hold only samples. With the exception of a few jewelry pieces, most items are by order only. Ask about their U.S. outlets.

Los Castillo

5 miles south of town on the Acapulco Hwy., and in Taxco on Plaza Bernal. ☎ **2-0652** (workshop) or 2-1988 (store). Admission free. Workshop, Mon–Fri 9am–5pm; store, Mon–Fri 9am–6:30pm, Sat 9am–1pm, Sun 10am–3pm.

Castillo was one of hundreds of young men to whom William Spratling taught the silversmithing trade in the 1930s. He was also one of the first to branch out with his own shops and line of designs, which over the years have earned him a fine name. Now his daughter creates her own noteworthy designs, among which are decorative pieces with silver fused into porcelain. Besides Taxco, Castillo has shops in several Mexican cities. You can visit the Castillo workshop, 5 miles south of town, Monday through Friday between 9am and 5pm, but there's no sales outlet at the workshop. His store, Los Castillo, is just off Plaza Borda, reached by walking down the hill beside City Hall; the store is ahead with a big sign. Customers can watch silversmiths here as well. This workshop is near Spratling's (see above for transportation directions).

ACCOMMODATIONS

Compared to Cuernavaca, Taxco is an overnight-stop visitor's dream: charming and picturesque, with a respectable selection of well-kept and delightful hotels. However, hotel prices tend to "bulge" at holiday times (especially Easter week).

EXPENSIVE

Hacienda del Solar

Apdo. Postal 96, Taxco, Gro. 40200. ☎ **762/2-0323.** Fax 762/2-0687. 22 rms. $118–$170 double; $219 double junior suite.

Located on a beautifully landscaped hilltop with magnificent views of the surrounding valleys and the town, this hotel comprises several Mexican-style cottages. The decor is slightly different in each one, but most include bathrooms done in handmade tiles, lots of beautiful handcrafts, hand-painted folk murals, and red-tile floors. Several rooms have Gothic-vaulted tile ceilings and fine private terraces with panoramic views. Standard rooms have no terraces and only showers in the baths; deluxe rooms have sunken tubs (with showers) and terraces. Junior suites are the largest and most luxurious accommodations. The prices I quote here were given to me by the management at the hotel. The rates will be higher if you book rooms through a travel agent.

The hotel is $2^1/_2$ miles south of the town center off Highway 95 to Acapulco; look for signs on the left and go straight down a narrow road until you see the hotel entrance.

Dining/Entertainment: La Ventana de Taxco restaurant overlooking the city, open for lunch and dinner.

Services: Laundry and room service.

Facilities: Heated swimming pool, tennis court.

INEXPENSIVE

Hotel Los Arcos

Juan Ruíz de Alarcón 12, Taxco, Gro. 40200. ☎ **762/2-1836.** 21 rms (all with bath). $20 double.

Los Arcos occupies a converted 1620 monastery. The handsome inner patio is bedecked with Puebla pottery and a gaily dressed restaurant area to the left, all around a central fountain. The rooms are nicely but sparsely furnished, with natural tile floors and colonial-style furniture. You'll be immersed in colonial charm and blissful quiet. To find it from the Plaza Borda, follow the hill down (with Hotel Agua Escondida on your left) and make an immediate right at the bottom of the hill; the hotel is a block down on the left, opposite the Posada de los Castillo (see below).

✪ Hotel Rancho Taxco Victoria

Apdo. Postal 83, Taxco, Gro. 40200. ☎ **762/2-1014** or 2-0010. Fax 762/2-0617. 100 rms (all with bath). $35 double standard room; $44 double deluxe suite; $56 double junior suite.

The Rancho Taxco Victoria clings to the hillside above town, with breathtaking views from its flower-covered verandas. It's a personal favorite partly for the views and partly because it exudes all the charm of old-fashioned Mexico. The furnishings, beautifully kept as if purchased yesterday, whisper comfortably of the hotel's heyday in the 1940s. In the guest rooms—nestled into nooks and crannies of the rambling hillside buildings—are vanities constructed of handmade tiles; local tin-craft reading lamps; old prints of Mexico and Taxco; beamed ceilings; craftwork bedspreads and throw rugs; a plant or two; baths with tubs; and in many cases, small private terraces. Each standard room comes with a bedroom and in front of each is a table and chairs set out on the tiled common walkway. Each deluxe room has a bedroom and private terrace; each junior suite has a bedroom, a nicely furnished large living room, and a spacious private terrace overlooking the city. There's a lovely pool, plus an overpriced restaurant—both with a great view of Taxco. Even if you don't stay here, come for a drink in the comfortable bar/living room, then stroll on the terrace to take in the fabulous view. From Plazuela de San Juan, go up a narrow, winding cobbled street named Carlos J. Nibbi to no. 57 on the hilltop.

Hotel Santa Prisca

Plazuela de San Juan 7, Taxco, Gro. 40200. ☎ **762/2-0080** or 2-0980. Fax 762/2-2938. 34 rms (all with bath). $35 double standard room; $47 double suite; $88 double suites nos. 25 and 26.

The Santa Prisca, one block from Plaza Borda on Plazuela de San Juan, is one of the older and nicer hotels in town. Rooms are small but comfortable, with older baths (showers only), tile floors, wood beams, and a colonial atmosphere. If your stay is long, ask for a room in the adjacent "new addition," where the rooms are sunnier, more spacious, and quieter. There is a reading area in an upstairs salon overlooking Taxco, a lush patio with fountains, and a lovely dining room done in mustard and blue.

Posada de los Castillo

Juan Ruíz de Alarcón 3, Taxco. Gro. 40200. ☎ **762/2-1396.** Fax 762/2–2935. 14 rms (all with bath). $20 double (one or two beds).

The four stories of small rooms here surround a courtyard. Each is simply but beautifully furnished with carved doors and furniture; baths have either tubs or showers. Just off the lobby is a branch of Los Castillo silver store. (The Castillo family owns the hotel.) To find the posada from the Plaza Borda, follow the hill down (the Hotel Escondida will be on your left) and make an immediate right at the bottom; the hotel is a block farther on the right opposite the Hotel Los Arcos (see above).

DINING

Taxco gets a lot of people on day-trips from the capital and Acapulco. There are not enough good restaurants to fill the demand, so prices are high for what you get.

EXPENSIVE

Toni's

In the Hotel Montetaxco. ☎ **762/2-1300.** Reservations recommended. Main courses $25–$40. Tues–Sat 7:30pm–1am. STEAKS/SEAFOOD.

High on a mountaintop, Toni's is an intimate and classy restaurant enclosed in a huge, cone-shaped palapa with a panoramic view of the city below. Eleven candlelit tables sparkle with crystal and crisp linen. The menu of shrimp or beef is limited, but the food is superior. Try the tender, juicy prime roast beef, which comes with Yorkshire pudding, creamed spinach, and baked potato. Lobster is also available. To reach Toni's, take a combi to the convention center/tourist office, then hail a cab from there.

MODERATE

Cielito Lindo

Plaza Borda 14. ☎ **762/2-0603.** Breakfast $3–$5; main courses $7.50–$9. Daily 9am–10pm. MEXICAN/INTERNATIONAL.

Cielito Lindo is probably the most popular place on the plaza for lunch, perhaps more for its visibility and colorful decor than for its food—which is decent, not great. The tables, covered in white and set with blue and white local crockery, are usually packed. You can get anything from soup to roast chicken, enchiladas, tacos, steak, and dessert, as well as frosty margaritas.

Sr. Costilla's ("Mr. Ribs")

Plaza Borda 1. ☎ **762/2-3215.** Main courses $6.75–$12. Daily 1pm–midnight. INTERNATIONAL.

The offbeat decor here includes a ceiling festooned with an assortment of cultural nicknacks. Several tiny balconies hold a few minuscule tables that afford a view of the plaza and church; these fill up long before the large dining room does. The menu is typical of the other Carlos Anderson restaurants you may have encountered in your Mexican travels, with Spanglish jive and a large selection of soups, steaks, sandwiches, spareribs, desserts, and coffee. Wine, beer, and drinks are served. The restaurant is next to the Santa Prisca Church, above Patio de las Artesanías.

La Taberna Restaurant/Bar

Juárez 8. ☎ **762/2-5226.** Main courses $5–$17. Daily 1pm–midnight. ITALIAN/INTERNATIONAL.

La Taberna is the best eatery in town and looks far more expensive than it is. The porch, decked out in turquoise and white napkins and cloths, beckons you into the old stone house. Pass from the bar in the former front sala to the interior plant-filled patio for alfresco dining. The owners, who also run Bora Bora Pizza (see below), serve consistently good food. I enjoyed the fettuccine La Taberna, which comes with ham, bacon, tomatoes, and mushrooms. There are six kinds of crêpes and 14 selections of beef, chicken, and fish, including mustard steak and chicken and beef brochettes.

To get here from Plaza Borda, go down the hill beside the Hotel Agua Escondida, bearing to the left. Then go right to the post office. La Taberna is a few steps farther on your left as you turn the corner.

INEXPENSIVE

Bora Bora Pizza

Callejón de las Delicias 4. ☎ **762/2-1721.** Pizza $4–$16; spaghetti $3.75–$6.25; beer $1.25; wine $2. Daily 1pm–midnight. ITALIAN.

For the best pizza in town, go to Bora Bora Pizza, overlooking Plaza Borda. Without any fanfare, a pair of quiet youths here serve up mouth-wateringly delicious pizza. The crusts are light and chewy, and the ingredients are sparkling fresh—quite an unexpected treat. Tables are festooned in hot pink and purple, and pots of purple petunias decorate the tiny balconies overlooking the plaza.

Restaurante Ethel

Plazuela de San Juan 14. ☎ **762/2-0788.** Soup $2; main courses $4.50–$7; comida corrida $5.75. Daily 9am–10pm (comida corrida served 1–5pm). MEXICAN.

A family-run place opposite the Hotel Santa Prisca on Plazuela de San Juan, one block from Plaza Borda, Restaurante Ethel is kept clean and tidy, with white throws and colorful crumb cloths on the tables and a homey atmosphere. The hearty daily comida corrida consists of soup or pasta, meat (perhaps a small steak), dessert, and coffee.

TAXCO AFTER DARK

Taxco's nighttime action is centered in the luxury hotels. **Paco's** is just about the most popular place overlooking the square for sipping, nibbling, people watching, and people meeting, all of which continues until midnight daily. **La Taberna** (see "Dining," above) stays open until midnight. And finally there's Taxco's dazzling disco, **Windows,** high up the mountain in the Hotel Monte Taxco. The whole city is on view from there, and music runs the gamut from the hit parade to hard rock. For a cover of $8 you can boogie Saturday nights from 9pm to 3am.

Completely different in tone is **Berta's,** next to Santa Prisca Church. Opened in 1930 by a lady named Berta, who made her fame on a drink of the same name (tequila, soda, lime, and honey), Berta's is traditionally the gathering place of the local gentry. Spurs and old swords decorate the walls, and a saddle is casually slung over the banister of the stairs leading to the second-floor room where tin masks leer from the walls. A Berta costs about $3.50; rum, the same. Open daily from 11am to around 10pm.

The Colonial Silver Cities   6

A visitor to Mexico who has not made the rounds of the Silver Cities hasn't seen the country's heart. These cities are among Mexico's finest colonial showpieces, boasting outstanding architectural beauty. **Guanajuato** is almost a fairy-tale town. **Zacatecas** is an architectural gem that lingers in the memory, and **San Miguel de Allende** is a city of fine restored mansions and cobblestone streets. **Querétaro** preserves its charm around its Plaza de la Independencia. And **San Luis Potosí** is a prosperous, picturesque old mining town.

This heartland of Mexico lies between the mountain ranges of the Sierra Madre, spread across a high plateau sculpted by rains and rivers over the eons. Now a maze of highlands, lakes, and valleys called the Valley of Mexico, this was once Anahuac, the center of ancient Mexican civilization.

When the conquistadores subdued Tenochtitlán (where Mexico City would later arise) in the early 1500s, they sent their armies and colonists into the other parts of the Valley of Mexico in search of mineral wealth. They found lead, tin, zinc, iron, antimony, and gold in abundance, but what made the early Spanish governors (and the cities of the northern valley) rich was silver. So rich were the mines here that the Silver Cities of the northern Valley of Mexico became incredibly wealthy and stayed that way for centuries.

EXPLORING THE COLONIAL HEARTLAND

This chapter presents the Silver Cities as you would find them traveling overland from Mexico City. But no matter how you're traveling in Mexico, the Silver Cities are easily accessible, despite their locations in mountain valleys.

If your trip to the Silver Cities begins in Mexico City, the capital is linked to Querétaro by a fast, limited-access toll highway, and from Querétaro you can be in San Miguel de Allende and Guanajuato or any other of the Silver Cities in a few hours' time via good two-lane paved roads.

Bus service in the region is fast, frequent, and comfortable.

As for how to allot your time, much depends on your particular interests. As a bare minimum, I recommend two to three days each in San Miguel de Allende, Zacatecas, and Guanajuato. Querétaro is an easy day-trip from San Miguel de Allende.

1 San Miguel de Allende

180 miles NW of Mexico City, 75 miles E of Guanajuato

San Miguel de Allende, founded in 1542, is one of the prettiest towns in Mexico and, like Taxco, has been declared a national monument. Virtually all the buildings you see date from the colonial era, and newer buildings must conform to existing architecture. Because so much of the city remains as it was during the days of silver mining, many of the hotels, restaurants, and shops along its cobbled streets are housed in beautiful mansions dating from those years.

The iron benches in El Jardín are a good metaphor for life in San Miguel. Mornings find them occupied by resident Americans on their way to and from the post office. By midmorning, tourists who've come for San Miguel's great shopping and dining fill the plaza and the maze of adjoining streets. Language students come with their tutors, and artists sit sketching a slice of San Miguel life. Throughout the day, local residents sell baskets, balloons, and painted pottery. At night, El Jardín spills over with young folks who still practice modern-day courtship rituals. Bands of mariachis wait under the surrounding portals to be hired.

A sizable colony of U.S. students and pensioners has established itself here, although the major portion of this group tends to turn over about twice a year. Apart from relatively well-off retired people, the town's expatriate colony is composed of teachers, writers, painters, and others who have saved up enough to buy themselves six months in the sun.

ESSENTIALS

GETTING THERE & DEPARTING By Plane The nearest international airport is two hours away in León. Querétaro, one hour away, has a small national airport served by **AeroLitoral;** the airline flies once a day from San Antonio, Texas, via Monterrey and San Luis Potosí. Transportation from either León or Querétaro can be arranged in advance through **Viajes Vertiz** (☎ 415/2-1856; fax 415/2-0499). However, the least expensive way to reach San Miguel from the León airport is to take a taxi from the airport to Guanajuato or Silao (both about a 30-minute drive from the airport), then a bus to San Miguel. Colectivo transporation from the León airport direct to San Miguel costs $103 and can be split by up to six or eight people, depending on the amount of luggage. There's also frequent public bus transportation from both León (via Guanajuato) and Querétaro. (For complete plane and ground transportation information, see "Getting There & Departing," below, in Guanajuato.)

By Bus   To/From Mexico City: It's a three- to five-hour trip to San Miguel from Mexico City's Terminal Norte (ticket area 6), depending on whether you take a nonstop directo (with one stop in Querétaro) or a local bus. **Primera Plus** runs four direct deluxe buses a day; **Satelite** has the same service. **Flecha Amarilla** has service every half hour (check to see which is directo) between 5:30am and 7pm. **Herradura de Plata** buses leave every half hour (eight of them operate directo). **Elíte** and **Tres Estrellas de Oro** each has one directo per day, while **Omnibus de México** has one morning local.

To/From Querétaro and Dolores Hidalgo: Satelite buses run to Querétaro and Dolores Hidalgo every half hour; **Flecha Amarilla** serves Dolores Hidalgo every 15 minutes.

   To/From Guanajuato: Flecha Amarilla has nine buses a day to San Miguel, some of which run via Dolores. If you miss the last one, buses run every 20 minutes to Dolores Hidalgo, and buses from there run every 15 minutes to San Miguel. Flecha Amarilla operates buses between San Miguel and Celaya about every 20 minutes from 5:20am to 9pm.

   By Car   From Mexico City: You have a choice of two routes for the three-hour trip—via a Querétaro bypass or via Celaya. The former is shorter—take Highway 57 north, a four-lane freeway toward Querétaro. Past the Tequisquiapan turnoff, there is an exit on the right marked "To San Miguel." This toll road bypasses Querétaro and crosses Highway 57 again north of town. Here it narrows to two lanes and becomes Highway 111. Some 20 miles farther is San Miguel.

   From Guanajuato: The quick route is going south from the city a short distance on Highway 110, then east on a secondary, though paved, road passing near the village of Joconoxtle. The long-but-scenic route is northeast on Highway 110 through Dolores Hidalgo, then south on Highway 51.

   For the Celaya route, follow Highway 57 to Querétaro. As you near Querétaro, watch carefully for signs pointing to Celaya and Highway 45. The signs are almost at the turning point. At Celaya, turn right (north) on Highway 51, a narrow two-lane road, to San Miguel.

   ORIENTATION   Arriving   The bus station is 1 1/2 miles west of town on the westward extension of Calle Canal. Buses to town stop in front. Taxis are generally available at all hours and cost about $2 to $3 for the trip to town.

   Information   The **tourist information office** is on the southeastern corner of the plaza, left of the church (☎ 415/2-1747). The English-speaking staff has maps and information about attractions in San Miguel and the surrounding region. It's open Monday through Friday from 10am to 2:45pm and 5 to 7pm, Saturday from 10am to 1pm. Don't get transportation information here, though, as it may not be current.

   City Layout   San Miguel's beautiful central square, **El Jardín** is shaded by perfectly groomed Indian laurel trees. The center of city life, it's the point of reference for just about all directions and is bounded by Calles Correo (Post Office Street), San Francisco, Hidalgo, and Reloj.

   Getting Around   In San Miguel there are regular inner-city **buses** but no minivans, or colectivos, as in other narrow-street cities in Mexico. Buses to outlying villages (Taboada thermal pool, for example) leave from around the Plaza Cívica. Some **taxis** now have meters. Most of San Miguel's sights are within walking distance of the central Jardín.

FAST FACTS: SAN MIGUEL DE ALLENDE

American Express   The local representative is Viajes Vertiz, Hidalgo 1 (☎ 415/2-1856; fax 415/2-0499), open Monday through Friday from 9am to 2pm and 4 to 6:30pm, and Saturday from 10am to 2pm.

Area Code   The telephone area code is 415.

Communication Services   San Miguel has two unofficial message centers: La Conexión and Pack 'N Mail. For a small monthly charge, residents and visitors can rent post boxes, send and receive faxes, make local or long-distance calls, and have access to both UPS and private messenger and courier services. La Conexión is located at Aldama 1 (☎ and fax 415/2-1599 or 2-1687), where it shares space with a photo store and a small restaurant. Pack 'N Mail has sizable space at Jesús 2-A (☎ and fax 415/2-3191). Both have Laredo addresses and will pack, mail, and transport your gifts. Their hours are generally weekdays from 8am to 5pm and Saturday from 8am to 3pm.

Currency Exchange   Two convenient places near the Jardín change money. Centro Cabiaro, Correo 13, is open Monday through Friday from 8am to 6pm, Saturday from 9am to 5pm, and Sunday from 9am to 2pm. Lloyds, at San Francisco 33, is open Monday through Friday from 9am to 3pm.

Drugstore   For medicine needs try the Farmacia Agundus (☎ 415/1-1198), Canal 26 at Macías. It's open daily from 10am to midnight.

Newspaper   *Atención*, the English-language paper, has local news as well as a full list of what to see and do. If you want to keep up with what's going on in San Miguel even after you leave, a subscription costs $53. Write *Atención*, Biblioteca Pública de San Miguel, Insurgentes 25 (Apdo. Postal 119), San Miguel de Allende, Gto. 37700, México (☎ and fax 415/2-3770).

Parking   San Miguel is congested, and street parking is scarce. White poles and/or signs at the ends of streets mark the stopping point for parking (so that other cars can make a turn). Police are vigilant about parking order and ticket with glee.

Post Office   The post office and telegraph office are at Calle Correo 16, open Monday through Friday from 8am to 7pm and Saturday from 9am to 1pm.

Seasons   Because of the fast freeway access from Mexico City, San Miguel is becoming popular with weekending citizens from the capital. Arrive early on Friday or make a reservation ahead of time if you're there for a weekend. There's also a squeeze on rooms around the Christmas and Easter holidays and around San Miguel's patron saint festival on September 29. October and November are slack months, as are January and February.

EXPLORING SAN MIGUEL

It's difficult to be bored in San Miguel. The shopping is excellent, and you'll run out of time before you can try all the good restaurants. San Miguel is ideally situated for side trips to Dolores Hidalgo, Querétaro, Guanajuato, and San Luis Potosí. This is also one of Mexico's most popular towns for Spanish and arts classes, just in case you find a lull during your vacation.

SPECIAL EVENTS

Holy Week, a movable date in the spring, is special in San Miguel, with numerous processions almost daily beginning the second Saturday before Easter Sunday. On June 13, **Saint Anthony's Day,** children bring decorated animals for a blessing at the Parroquia church—it's quite an event. San Miguel's main festivity, however, is the **Fiesta de San Miguel** on September 29, honoring the town's patron saint. Events center around El Jardín and begin the week prior to the 29th and continue until at least the 31st. For at least two days prior to the 29th, there are almost nonstop parades of colorful regional dancers from all over the country and elaborate nightly fireworks; all of the events are free.

THE TOP ATTRACTIONS

La Parroquía

South side of El Jardín. No phone. Admission free. Daily 6am–9pm.

La Parroquía, the parish church, is an imposing Gothic structure of local sandstone built in the late 19th century by a self-made architect, Ceferino Gutiérrez. The story goes that he had never seen such a church and used a picture to fashion his

San Miguel de Allende

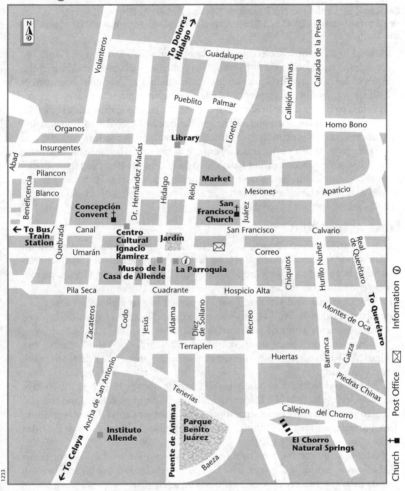

creation. Neoclassical stone altars have replaced the original ones made of gilded wood, but the bell is original. Step inside on any day, and you're likely to find parishioners from surrounding villages carrying on an ancient rite that has both Catholic and pre-Hispanic overtones.

Museo de la Casa de Allende

Southwest corner of El Jardín. No phone. Admission free. Tues–Sun 10am–4:30pm.

The birthplace of the famous independence leader Ignacio Allende has been converted into a museum housing colonial-era furnishings and historical documents. Inside you'll see fossils, pre-Hispanic pottery, and a biography of Allende. Exhibits also detail the fight for independence, which began in nearby Dolores Hidalgo. In 1810, Allende plotted with Padre Miguel Hidalgo of Dolores and Josefa Domínguez of neighboring Querétaro, among others, to organize for independence from Spain. Both Allende and Hidalgo were executed in Chihuahua a year later.

Centro Cultural Ignacio Ramírez (Bellas Artes/El Nigro-Mante)

Hernández Macías 75. ☎ **415/2-0289.** Admission free. Mon–Fri 9am–9pm, Sat 10am–7pm, Sun 10am–2pm.

Housed in the former Convento de la Concepción (1755), between Canal and Insurgentes two blocks west of El Jardín, the center is a branch of the Palacio Bellas Artes of Mexico City. Built on two levels surrounding an enormous courtyard of lush trees, it consists of numerous rooms housing art exhibits and classrooms for drawing, painting, sculpture, lithography, textiles, ceramics, dramatic arts, ballet, regional dance, piano, and guitar. The grand mural by David Alfaro Siqueiros and memorabilia of the artist are worth seeing. A bulletin board lists concerts and lectures given at this institute and elsewhere in the city. The pleasant restaurant, Las Musas, serves Mexican and Italian food daily between 10am and 8pm. Before you leave, notice the magnificent dome behind the convent. It belongs to the Iglesia de la Concepción and was designed by the same unschooled architect who designed the Parroquía (see above).

MORE ATTRACTIONS

The **Centro de Crecimiento,** Zamora Ríos 6, a donation-supported school for handicapped children, conducts regular Saturday tours (usually at 10am) to interesting places in the country around San Miguel. Donations are $15 per person; tickets are available at Casa Maxwell.

The ✪ **House and Garden Tour,** sponsored by the Biblioteca Pública, is a regular attraction in San Miguel. The tour opens the doors of some of the city's most interesting colonial and contemporary homes. Tours leave Sunday at 11:30am from the library at Insurgentes 25 (☎ 415/2-0293) and last about two hours. A $10 donation goes to support various library projects benefiting the youth of San Miguel.

The **Travel Institute of San Miguel,** Cuna de Allende 11 (☎ 415/2-1630 or 2-0078, ext. 4; fax 2-0121), holds walking tours, field trips to colonial and archaeological sites, adventure and nature tours, visits to artisans at work, and workshops in marketing, among other things. The office is open Monday through Saturday from 9am to 2pm and 4 to 7pm.

A couple of the most enjoyable walks in town are to the lookout point **El Mirador,** especially at sunset, which colors the whole town and the lake beyond, and to **Parque Juárez,** a lovely, spacious, and shady park.

The town's **movie theater,** the Aldama, is on San Francisco, in the block between El Jardín and the San Francisco Church. There's another movie theater in the Gigante Shopping Center on the road to Querétaro.

One great way to see the mountains around San Miguel is by **Hire-a-Horse.** For $35 per person, it will provide a horse, a guide, refreshments, and a two- to four-hour outing. Inquire at the Casa Mexas restaurant, Canal 15 Centro, or call 2-3620 for information or reservations.

The **Taboada hot springs** are located just five miles outside San Miguel, about 15 minutes away by car. The Hotel Balneario Taboada is out of budget range, but next door to it is the most popular hot springs/swimming pool in the area, which you can use for about $10. Buses to Taboada leave from Calle San Francisco by the market, supposedly at 9 and 11am and 1 and 3pm. If you should have trouble getting a bus, you can always take a taxi out to any of the three hot springs; it will cost about $10 to $12—not a bad deal if you have several people to split the cost. You can ask the taxi driver to return and pick you up at the end of the day.

Learning at the Source: Going to School in San Miguel

San Miguel is known for its Spanish-language and art schools. These institutions cater to Americans and often provide a list of apartments from which to choose for long-term stays. Rates for language classes are usually by the hour and get lower the more hours you take. If you want a chance to practice, it's best to look for small classes.

Instituto Allende, Calle Ancha de San António 20, San Miguel de Allende, Gto. 37700 (☎ 415/2-0190; fax 415/2-4538), put San Miguel on the map back in the 1930s. It was opened by Enrique Fernández Martínez, the former governor of the state of Guanajuato, and Stirling Dickinson, an American. Today it thrives in the 18th-century home of the former counts of Canal, a beautiful place with big grounds, elegant patios and gardens, art exhibits, and murals. You can wander past classrooms where weavers, sculptors, painters, ceramicists, photographers, and struggling language students are at work. The office maintains a list of local families who rent rooms for stays of a month or more. The institute offers an MFA degree, and the school's credits are transferable to at least 300 colleges and universities in the United States and Canada; noncredit students are also welcome.

Academia Hispano Americana has a reputation for being a comparatively tougher language school with an emphasis on grammar as well as conversation. Classes are limited to 12 people. The work is intensive, and the school is particularly interested in students who plan to use Spanish in their future careers and in people who sincerely feel the need to communicate and understand the other Americas. The school has a continuous program of study of 12 four-week sessions for 35 hours a week. Private lessons cost $10 per hour. It's a member of the International Association of Language Centers. A brochure is available from the Registrar, Academia Hispano Americana, Mesones 4 (Apdo. Postal 150), San Miguel de Allende, Gto. 37700 (☎ 415/2-0349; fax 415/2-2333). Office hours are Monday through Friday from 8am to 1pm and 3:30 to 6:30pm.

Inter/Idiomas primarily uses a conversational method. Classes are small, usually composed of four students and a teacher. Each student's level of Spanish is evaluated before placement in a class. You can begin any time and pay by the hour or week or for private lessons. For information write Inter/Idiomas School of Languages, 20 de Enero Sur #42, Col. San Antonio, San Miguel de Allende, Gto. 37750.

For a delicious change of pace, try **Reyna Polanco de Abrahams' Cooking School** on Fridays from noon to 2pm. You can merely observe or get hands-on experience making everything from tamales in hoja de platano (banana leaves) to chicken in mole sauce. Call 2-1102 for information or reservations.

Also see the **Centro Cultural Ignacio Ramírez,** in "Top Attractions," above.

NEARBY ATTRACTIONS

One of the most pleasant excursions you can make from San Miguel is to **Atotonilco el Grande,** a rural town that contains a wonderful 16th-century *oratorio* (the church of an Augustinian monastery). The imaginative and animated frescoes depicting biblical scenes were used to teach Indians. The trip itself is an introduction to extremely picturesque Mexican country life. By the market, hop an "El Santuario" bus on Calle Humaran and Colegio, which passes every hour on the hour; past Taboada, the route goes left at signs reading MANANTIALES DE LA GRATUA and LA FLOR DEL CORTIJO. The road passes two large mansions that are now spas (see "More Attractions," above), then an aqueduct and a little narrow bridge. In no time you're in the small town square of Atotonilco with the oratorio in front of you.

Querétaro, Guanajuato, and **Dolores Hidalgo** are easy day-trips from San Miguel. See "Getting There & Departing," above, for transportation information, and "Excursions," below.

Two companies use San Miguel as a base for trips to see the **monarch butterflies** in the state of Michoacán west of Mexico City (See Chapter 13, "Tarascan Country"). The **Travel Institute of San Miguel** (see "More Attractions," above) offers this trip between November and March. Another company, **Columbus Travel,** also originates the trip from either San Miguel or Mexico City. Contact them at Rte. 12, Box 382 B, New Braunfels, TX 78132-9701 (☎ 210/885-2000 or 800/843-1060 in the U.S. and Canada).

SHOPPING

In general, stores in San Miguel open at 9am, close between 2 and 4pm, and reopen from 4 to 7pm. Most are closed Sunday. The town is known for its metalwork—brass, bronze, and tin—and for its textiles and pottery, especially Talaveraware (which is also made in Dolores Hidalgo). Shopping, however, is by no means limited to those items. Also, ask to see the charming children's art for sale at the public library; the proceeds help support the children's program.

A **Mercado de Artesanías** is located along the walkway near the entrance to Quinta Loreto; here you can bargain with the vendors during most daylight hours. On the eastern edge of town along the road to Querétaro is a **shopping mall** with food concessions, a grocery store, and shops. The anchor store, Gigante, is a supermarket with everything from folk art to Barbie dolls to barbacoa; it accepts credit cards. For metalwork try **Zacateros,** a street of shops selling pewter, tin, and ironwork.

ART

Galería San Miguel
Plaza Principal 14. ☎ **415/2-1046.**

This is the best local art gallery. It is run by a charming, stylish Mexican-American woman, fluent in English, who is a well-known art dealer. She exhibits the work (in all price ranges) of local residents as well as artists from all over Mexico. The gallery is open Monday through Friday from 10am to 2pm and 4 to 7pm, Saturday from 10am to 2pm and 4 to 8pm, and Sunday from 10am to 2pm.

CRAFTS

Casa Anguiano
Corner of Canal and Macías. ☎ **415/2-0107.**

This is one of the places you will want to return to again and again just to see what's new. The inventory of colorful Michoacán foot-loomed fabric by the bolt is extensive, as is the inventory of blown glass, copper, brass, and Nativity scenes.

It's open Monday through Saturday from 9:30am to 8:30pm and Sunday from 9:30am to 6:30pm.

Casa Cohen
Reloj 12. ☎ 415/2-1434.

Located half a block north of the square, this is the place to find brass and bronze bowls, plates, house numbers, doorknobs, knockers, and drawer pulls, as well as other utilitarian objects made of iron, aluminum, and carved stone. There's also hand-carved wood furniture. It's open the usual San Miguel hours (see the introduction to "Shopping," above).

Casa Maxwell
Canal 14. ☎ 415/2-0247.

This is a beautiful house and garden with every imaginable craft displayed, some high-priced, others fairly reasonable. It's well worth a look around. Hours are Monday through Saturday from 9am to 2pm and 4 to 7pm.

Izcuinapán
Canal 42 at Umaran. ☎ 415/2-0594.

Don't worry about pronouncing the name, but do go here for a very fine display of folk art, particularly Huichol masks and textiles, and an expanding line of furniture. This place offers something for everyone—from those with a limited budget to serious collectors. Look especially for the carved animals with hidden compartments from Michoacán. The store, between Zacateros and Quebrada, is open Monday through Saturday from 10am to 2pm and 4 to 7:30pm.

Mesón de San José
Mesones 38. ☎ 415/2-1367.

This lovely old mansion, across from the market between Juárez and Nuñez, houses a dozen shops and a restaurant. One of the shops, Ono, specializes in children's toys, as well as a smattering of folk art from around Mexico. Another, Talisman, has an outstanding selection of gifts in every price range. All are open daily from 10am to 6pm.

Veryka
Zacateros 6A. ☎ 415/2-9114.

A popular place, this small shop has a very complete collection of folk art from Mexico and the rest of Latin America, as well as fabrics, wall hangings, clothing, and jewelry. The staff is very knowledgeable, and most speak some English. It's open the standard hours (see the introduction to "Shopping," above), plus Sunday from 11am to 3pm.

FURNITURE

Casa María Luisa
Canal 40, at Zacateros. ☎ 415/2-0130.

If your interests are architectural or decorative, you may enjoy browsing here. Among the crowded aisles, you'll find the store's own line of furniture, which might appeal to those who like southwestern decor. Stacked and displayed here and there are decorative ironwork, lamps, masks, pottery, and more. The staff will pack and ship your treasures. Hours are Monday through Saturday from 9am to 2pm and 4 to 7pm, and Sunday from 11am to 5pm.

MASKS

Tonatiu Metztli
Umarán 24, near Zacateros. ☎ **415/2-0869.**

This shop is a must for the mask collector. In addition to the masks hanging all over the shop walls, owner Jorge Guzman has a private collection he shows by appointment. He recently added some fine Huichol art, including figures decorated with exquisite beadwork. It is open the usual San Miguel hours (see the introduction to "Shopping," above) plus Sunday from 9am to 2pm.

ACCOMMODATIONS

There are plenty of accommodations for visitors in San Miguel; for a long stay in San Miguel (more than a month), check at the instituto or the academia (see "Learning at the Source," above) and other bulletin boards around town for lists of apartments or rooms to rent. Most apartments are equipped with kitchens and bedding; some come with maid service. San Miguel is becoming popular as a weekend getaway for residents from the capital, and at least one hotel I checked raised rates on weekends; let's hope this doesn't start a trend. Secured parking is at a premium in San Miguel; if it's not provided by your hotel, you'll pay around $12 to $15 daily in a guarded lot.

VERY EXPENSIVE

Casa de Sierra Nevada
Hospicio 35, San Miguel de Allende, Gto. 36600. ☎ **415/2-0415,** or 800/223-6510 in the U.S. Fax 465/2-2337. 24 rms and suites. TV TEL. $166 standard double; $190–$253 double suite. Free parking.

Four handsome 16th-century townhouses in a row comprise this hotel, which has a restaurant and bar across the street and a fifth house containing the outdoor pool. Each room has its own design; most have private patios or secluded entrances, and all have decorative antiques and beautiful tile floors with area rugs. Guests receive a fruit basket, flowers, and daily paper. The hotel, a member of the Small Luxury Hotels of the World, is one block south of the Jardín between Aldama and Diez de Sollano.

Dining/Entertainment: The elegant restaurant features foods from around the world (jacket and tie recommended evenings); reservations are required for dinner. Patio bar.

Services: Laundry and room service; concierge; tour service; limousine transportation (expensive) from airports in either Mexico City or León.

Facilities: 60-foot heated swimming pool, full-service spa with massage, facials, body scrub, herbal wraps, manicure and pedicure, skin analysis, waxing, and other treatments. Equestrian Center, with supervised trail rides and instruction on the nearby 500-acre ranch belonging to the hotel owner. Guests can go there to walk, hike, jog, or bird-watch. Balloon rides available.

MODERATE

Mi Casa B&B
Canal 58 (Apdo. Postal 496), San Miguel de Allende, Gto. 37700. ☎ **415/2-2492.** 1 rm, 1 junior suite (all with bath). $60 double; $70 suite. Rates include breakfast.

This charming colonial home is professionally decorated, very comfortable, and in a convenient location. The hostess, Carmen McDaniel, is a gracious expatriate and an excellent source of information on San Miguel and the surroundings. Both rooms have a garden-style bath, and the junior suite has a sitting area and fireplace. The flower-filled rooftop patio is a wonderful place for cocktails (honor bar) or morning coffee. This B&B is about three blocks west of the Jardín on Calle Canal, across from Posada de las Monjas.

Pensión Casa Carmen

Correo 31 (Apdo. Postal 152), San Miguel de Allende, Gto. 37700. ☎ and fax **415/2-0844.** 11 rms (all with bath). $60 double; monthly rate $55 daily double. Rates include breakfast.

This small, quiet pension with a friendly, relaxed atmosphere is often booked months in advance. The rooms, all of which have gas heaters, face a lovely colonial courtyard with plants and a fountain; meals are served in a European-style common dining room. You can reserve rooms by the day, week, or month (monthly rates are discounted). You can get here from the Jardín by walking east on Correo past the Parroquía and post office for 2¹/₂ blocks; it's near the corner of Recreo.

Villa Mirasol

Pila Seca 35, San Miguel de Allende, Gto. 37700. ☎ **415/2-1564.** 6 rms (all with bath). $50–$70 double (including breakfast and high tea).

This delightful bed and breakfast, previously known as Casa de Lujo, has individually decorated Mexican-style rooms with bright colors, private entrances, and a patio area. Short-term membership is available at a local country club for swimming, golf, and tennis. To get here, go south from the Jardín one block, then right (west) on Pila Seca for 4¹/₂ blocks. It's between Quebrada and Ladrillera.

INEXPENSIVE

⑨ Casa de Huespedes

Mesones 27, San Miguel de Allende, Gto. 37700. ☎ and fax **415/2-1378.** 7 rms (all with bath). $16 double.

A welcome addition to the inexpensive category, this second-floor hostelry is reached by a stairway from a busy street. Owner Amelia Coglan is usually on hand. The rooms are attractive for this price category, and there is a lovely patio. The staff is friendly, and longer stays are encouraged with a discount and kitchenettes in five units. To get there from the Jardín, go north one block on Reloj then right on Mesones. The casa will be on your left.

Hotel Mansion Virreyes

Canal 19, San Miguel de Allende, Gto. 37700. ☎ **415/2-3355,** or 2-0851. Fax 415/2-3865. 26 rms (all with bath). TV TEL. Weekend $35 double; weekday $26 double. Free parking.

Previously called the Hotel Central, the Mansion Virreyes has lost none of its old charm, and some judicious remodeling has improved the comfort of the 350-year-old building. It was once a private home and became the first hotel in San Miguel following the Mexican Revolution. Located half a block west of the Jardín, it is nestled among shops and restaurants. The rooms are simple but very comfortable, and the pleasant restaurant serves good, moderately priced meals. There is a TV bar behind the restaurant.

Hotel Vianey

Aparacio 18, San Miguel de Allende, Gto. 37700. ☎ **415/2-4559.** 5 rms, 6 suites (all with bath). $15 double; $20 suite for one or two with kitchenette.

This relative newcomer to the San Miguel hotel scene is spotlessly clean, and the rooms with kitchenettes are a good choice for an extended stay. The furniture is new, the place is well lit, and there is a rooftop terrace for sunbathing or stargazing. The location is convenient for those studying at the academia just a block west and across the street, and it's near the Saturday market.

Parador San Sebastián

Mesones 7, San Miguel de Allende, Gto. 37700. ☎ **415/2-0707.** 13 rms (all with bath). $17 double. Parking $3 daily.

The San Sebastián is a colonial-era convent-turned-inn with spacious rooms that face a lovely courtyard and garden. The rooms are simple and comfortable, and the rooftop is great for enjoying morning coffee, sunning, or taking in the city views. They don't take reservations here, so you have to try your luck. From the Jardín, walk east on Correo one block to the post office, then left two blocks to Mesones. Turn right on Mesones, go past the Mercado, and walk another half a block. The hotel is on the north (left) side of the street, across from the academia.

Posada Carmina

Allende 7, San Miguel de Allende, Gto. 37700. ☎ **415/2-0458.** Fax 415/2-0135. 10 rms (all with bath). $28 double.

Located on the south side of the plaza next to the Parroquía is this charming and friendly over-200-year-old colonial-era mansion. Rooms are nicely furnished and built around a central courtyard full of orange trees and flowering vines. Around the upstairs terrace are two comfortable living rooms, chairs, and chaise lounges. A restaurant serving good food is open in the courtyard daily from 8am to 9:30pm.

Quinta Loreto

Calle Loreto 15, San Miguel de Allende, Gto. 37700. ☎ **415/2-0042.** 38 rms (all with bath). $24–$28 double. Weekly and monthly discounts available. Free parking.

This motel is tucked away amid cobblestone lanes and manicured gardens. It has a large pool, a tennis court, a lovely garden, an excellent restaurant, a friendly atmosphere, and simple but pleasant rooms. Meals here are a bargain. Make reservations—the Loreto is very popular and is often booked up months in advance. Outsiders can come for breakfast (which costs $2–$3) and for lunch (which costs $4.50). To get here from the Jardín, walk one block east on Correo. Turn left onto Juárez at the post office, go two blocks to Mesones, then continue for three long blocks (the street curves); the motel is on a small street off Calle Loreto.

DINING

Because of its large expatriate colony and its popularity with Mexican tourists, San Miguel has the best quality and assortment of restaurants of any small city in Mexico. New places open all the time, and eateries only a few years old close down overnight. As in every Mexican town, the **mercado** offers the least expensive food in town.

MODERATE

✪ Casa Mexas

Canal 15 Centro. ☎ **415/2-0044.** Main courses $2.50–$10.50; children's plate $2–$3. Daily noon–11pm. MEXICAN.

A riot of baskets and colorful piñatas hang from the ceiling of this place above white tables and chairs and white napkins stuffed into whimsical papier-mâché napkin rings. As the name suggests, it serves a blend of Mexican food and Tex-Mex, but the fare is much better than standard Tex-Mex. Prices are moderate for the large portions of well-seasoned food. This is a place kids will like, and it offers plate meals with children in mind. It's across from the Casa Maxwell, half a block west of the Jardín on Canal.

Mama Mía
Umarán 8. ☎ **415/2-2063.** Breakfast $1.25–$3; pastas $6.25–$11; main courses $4–$11; coffees $1–$4.50. Daily 9am–11:30pm. ITALIAN.

Casual and hip sums up the atmosphere at this good-quality Italian restaurant in a tree-shaded brick courtyard. You can dine al fresco and enjoy live folkloric South American and flamenco music nightly. In addition to the Italian specialties, there are Mexican and American specials and a large breakfast menu. There's also a nice selection of coffee-based drinks with Kahlúa or brandy. At night it's one of the most popular spots in town (see "After Dark," below). The restaurant is two blocks southwest of El Jardín on Umarán between Jesús and Macías.

✪ Restaurant/Bar Bugambilia
Hidalgo 42. ☎ **415/2-0127.** Antojitos $2.25–$4.50; main courses $5–$8.50. Daily noon–11pm. MEXICAN TRADITIONAL.

Both the food and the atmosphere make this place well worth a long meal. It's delightful, with its tree-filled patio, soft music, good service, and such specialties as pollo en pulque (pulque-marinated chicken) and chiles en nogada (pepper stuffed with meat, raisins, cream, and pomegranates). To find it from the Jardín, walk 2$^1/_2$ blocks north on Hidalgo.

INEXPENSIVE

✪ El Pegaso Café and Deli
Corregidora 6 at Correo. No phone. Breakfast $1.50–$3; soups, salads, sandwiches $2–$4. Mon–Sat 8:30am–10pm. DELICATESSEN/INTERNATIONAL.

You'll notice the full tables at this trendy corner restaurant one block east of the Jardín. Inside, it's cute and cozy with walls of paintings for sale. Meals are light, with soup and salad or sandwich, nachos, sopes, and other deli combinations. Regulars swear they have the best eggs Benedict in town.

La Dolce Vita
Recreo 11. No phone. Coffee $1–$1.50; breakfast $1.50–$2; pastries $1.50–$2; croissants, sandwiches, pizza $1.50–$3.50. Wed–Mon 10am–10pm. PASTRIES/COFFEE.

My favorite place in town for coffee is this cheerful European-style cafe with good, strong brew. It serves excellent light meals and delicious croissant sandwiches. There's a selection of magazines. La Dolce Vita is between Hospicio and Correo.

Villa de Ayala
Ancha de San Antonio 1. ☎ **415/2-3883.** Breakfast $1.75–$3.50; main courses $2–$4; comida corrida $3.75. Daily 8am–10pm (comida corrida served 1–5pm). MEXICAN.

This restaurant is a favorite with families and students from the Instituto de Allende. Reached by a staircase, the place consists of one large room with the kitchen to one side and a video nook in a corner. Piñatas and balloons help dress up the plain tables and brick walls. A specialty of the house, memelas, consists of large thick tortillas with beans, salsa, cheese, and a choice of meat on top. Recorded music during the day is lively but not loud; there is occasional live music on weekends. The restaurant is across the street and a few doors toward town from the instituto; it's a long walk or short taxi ride from the Jardín.

Café del Jardín

Portal Allende 2. ☎ **415/2-5006**. Breakfast $1.75–$3.50; main courses $2–$5.50. Daily 8am–10pm. AMERICAN/MEXICAN.

This new, popular spot in town is, as the name suggests, on the southwest corner of the Jardín. The breakfasts include whole wheat waffles with nuts, raisins, and/ or fruit, as well as egg dishes and scones. There are sandwiches, soups, desserts, and Mexican specialties during the rest of the day. The portals give the eight tables and three counter stools a good view of the "action" in town. Facing the Parroquia, the café is to the right of the Jardín across from the Museo de la Casa de Allende.

⑤ El Correo

Correo 23. ☎ **415/2-1051**. Breakfast $1.50–$3; main courses $2–$5. Thurs–Tues 9am–9:30pm. AMERICAN.

Housed in a colonial-era building opposite the post office half a block east of the Jardín, this place is ideally suited for watching the morning mail ritual among resident Americans. You'll see them lingering over coffee and conversation here—and for that reason, the nine tables are often full, especially around breakfast. Persevere—it's worth it! Walls are stenciled to resemble pale turn-of-the-century wallpaper. For breakfast, the migas natural comes with onions, tomatoes, and chile or ranchero sauce, or you can tank up on apple fritters, orange juice, or fruit with yogurt and granola. For homesick stomachs, at lunch there's fried chicken, stuffed baked potatoes, and soup.

◐ Fonda Mesón de San José

Mesones 38. ☎ **415/2-3848**. Breakfast $1.75–$3; soup $2.50; main courses $4–$6; margarita $1.75. Daily 8am–9pm. MEXICAN/AMERICAN.

Located in the midst of several interesting shops, this open-courtyard restaurant is considered by many locals to be the best restaurant in town. It's an excellent place to just rest (the coffee is excellent) or to have an entire meal. The intriguing menu is so tempting it may be hard to decide between the vegetarian plate with Yucatecan tacos and vegetarian pasta or a main course of chicken curry or the pasta with chicken and spinach in a cream sauce. Everything is fresh and attractively presented.

Olé Olé

Loreto 66. ☎ **415/2-0896**. Main courses $4–$6. Daily 1–8pm. MEXICAN.

Festive and friendly, this small restaurant is a riot of red and yellow banners, colorful streamers, and bullfight memorabilia. The small menu features delicious beef or chicken fajitas, shrimp brochettes, and quesadillas. The place is wildly busy at lunch. To find this restaurant from the San Francisco Plaza, walk north on Juárez and cross Mesonas; jog left then right where the street becomes Loreto and continue for three or four blocks—it's on the left with a small sign.

Restaurant Aquí Es México

Hidalgo 28. ☎ **415/2-0430**. Breakfast $1.50–$2.50; main courses $4.50–$9; comida corrida $3.50. Daily 8am–10pm. MEXICAN REGIONAL CUISINES.

Entered by a narrow stairway next to the owner's office (the owner is a physician), this festively decorated restaurant is a feast for both the eyes and the palate. Family recipes from Michoacán dominate the menu, and many of the decorations are from that area as well. The reasonably priced and filling meals often contain such seasonal specialties as guajalote (turkey), rabbit, or dove, and mixiote de cordero. The restaurant is on Hidalgo two blocks north of the Jardín between Mexones and Insurgentes.

SAN MIGUEL AFTER DARK

Clubs and discos here tend to spring up and die quickly. If you want to have dinner and drinks with live music (including piano, guitar, South American folkloric, and flamenco), see "Dining," above; I've mentioned all the places where there's live music. San Miguel has many such enjoyable restaurants. Be sure also to check San Miguel's English-language paper, *Atención*, for other happenings around town.

La Fragua
Cuna de Allende 3. ☎ **415/2-1144.**

San Miguel's artists and writers drift in and out all afternoon and evening at this popular long-standing gathering spot. Housed in an old colonial home, the restaurant has tables around the courtyard where Mexican musicians perform every evening from 8 to 10:30pm. Several other dining rooms and a comfy bar resembling a living room are off the courtyard. The emphasis here is on standard Mexican fare. Bar hours are daily from noon to 2am, and the restaurant serves from 1pm to midnight.

Mama Mía
Umarán 8. ☎ **415/2-2063.** Cover $3.50.

One of the most popular evening hangouts, there's live jazz and dancing in the courtyard bar every Thursday, Friday, and Saturday from 9pm to 2am. (See "Dining," above, for a review of the restaurant.)

Pancho y Lefty's
Mesones 99. No phone. Cover $5 in high season, free in low season.

Entertainment runs the spectrum here from reggae to rock and country to blues and jazz. It's open from 7pm to 3am Wednesday, Friday, and Saturday. Wednesday night happy hour lasts the whole evening with two drinks for the price of one.

Tío Lucas
Mesones 103 at Macias. ☎ **415/2-4996.** No cover.

Though this is a full restaurant, it's most popular in the evenings when live music—blues, jazz, and bossa nova—is on tap between 8:30pm and midnight. The restaurant opens at 1pm, and there are several cozy, dark dining rooms and a small bar with seating. Happy hour is from 6 to 8pm.

EXCURSIONS FROM SAN MIGUEL DE ALLENDE
DOLORES HIDALGO: BEAUTIFUL, INEXPENSIVE POTTERY

Dolores Hidalgo was made famous when Fr. Miguel Hidalgo de Costilla began the War of Independence on the steps of the parish church. Today, it is famous for its pottery. Only 30 miles from San Miguel, you'll see the factories and store outlets beginning on the outskirts of town and continuing into town almost everywhere you look.

Pottery made here is distinct from the Talaveraware of Tlaxcala and Puebla, although just as colorful and inspired. In fact, the fame of Dolores Hidalgo's ceramics is overtaking that of Tlaxcala's and Puebla's products, primarily because the items produced here are less expensive and produced in greater quantity. Some of Mexico's best hotels turn Dolores ginger jars into lamps and decorate bathrooms with Dolores-made soap dishes and towel and tissue holders. Tiles from Dolores have been popular for years. Prices here are considerably lower than in San Miguel.

It could be daunting to tackle this town without a few recommendations, so I've listed a few factories and shops below. You'll discover even more as you walk the streets. Of course, it's best to go in a car if you plan to purchase much. If you arrive by bus, a box and luggage cart are handy to haul your loot around from store to store.

The stores below are listed in the order you will find them on the road from San Miguel.

Talavera San Gabriel

14 miles from San Miguel on the outskirts of Dolores. ☎ and fax **418/2-0139.**

Here you'll find a large selection of ceramic-framed mirrors and drawer knobs, tiles, sinks, candelabras, casseroles, bowls, platters, anthropomorphic jars and candlestick holders, ginger jars, and tissue holders. If you have the bus let you off here, you'll need a taxi to continue into town. Open Monday through Saturday from 8am to 5pm and Sunday from 8am to 2pm.

Talavera Amora

Farther along the road to Dolores and past the Talavera San Gabriel. ☎ **418/2-0336.** Fax 2-22029.

This is another factory outlet; you will see this signature pottery in many San Miguel stores. Items include dinnerware with a blue and yellow fish motif, chicken and frog planters, and much more. Open daily from 9am to 6pm.

Talavera Cortes

Districto Federal 8, at Tabasco. From the highway, turn left on Veracruz, go three blocks, then go left one block; it's on the corner.

Homeowners in San Miguel patronize this store for sinks, tiles and knobs, towel racks, and paper holders. You can watch craftspeople at work upstairs and browse the large showroom/warehouse downstairs. Open Monday through Friday from 7am to 4:30pm and Saturday from 7am to 1pm.

Azulejos Talavera Vazquez

Puebla at Tamaluipas.

Like the other places I've listed, this is a cornucopia of ceramics, from giant ginger jars to ashtrays and sinks. This store has good prices on colorful ceramic picture frames in many sizes. The store is about two blocks south of the church with the gold and green tile dome. Open Monday through Friday from 7am to 4:30pm and Saturday from 7am to 1pm.

Bazar El Portón

Calz. de los Heroes Km 3.5. ☎ **418/2-2229.** Fax 418/2-0894.

Located on the right side of the road as you enter Dolores, this is the place for architectural antiques and new carved-wood furniture. Among the jumble are horse-head table pedestals, old wooden mining troughs, wagon wheels, rearing stallions, old and new carved doors, and carved sofas. Open Monday through Friday from 7am to 4:30pm and Saturday from 7am to 1pm.

QUERÉTARO: A HISTORIC COLONIAL CITY

If you're driving north from Mexico City, you'll actually pass Querétaro (alt. 5,873 ft.; pop. 455,000; 138 miles north of Mexico City and 63 miles from San Miguel) on your way to San Miguel. It is the capital of the state of Querétaro and a prosperous city with a fascinating history. It was here that Mexico's fight for independence was instigated by Hidalgo in 1810, and it was here that the peace of the

Mexican War was sealed with the Treaty of Guadalupe Hidalgo. Emperor Maximilian was executed here in 1866, and finally, the present Mexican constitution was drafted here in 1916.

The **Dirección de Turismo** is at Av. Constituyentes Ote. 102 (☎ 42/13-8512; fax 42/13-8511), quite a distance from the center of town. A better source is the small **tourism information office** next to the Mesón Santa Rosa on Pasteur at the southwest corner of the Plaza Independencia; it's open Monday through Friday from 9am to 8pm and Saturday and Sunday from 9am to 3pm. From here, the Dirección de Turismo offers a very good $2.50 **guided walking tour** of the city, daily at 10:30am.

Arriving by bus from San Miguel, you'll be at the new bus station, south of town. Catch a bus marked "Centro" or take a taxi for around $5.

Exploring Queretaro

A STROLL AROUND THE HISTORIC CENTER Launch your visit to the city from the pedestrians-only ✪ **Plaza de la Independencia** (also called Plaza de Armas), on 5 de Mayo. It's the historic heart of the city, and the most beautiful plaza, graced by manicured umbrella-shaped trees, a beautiful fountain, and mansions now housing government offices.

Of all the colonial-era buildings surrounding Plaza de la Independencia, the **Casa de la Corregidora/Palacio Municipal** is the most famous. It's a magnificent building, and tourists are welcome to step inside the interior courtyard. On the second floor is the Corregidora's room—where, while under lock and key, she (Doña Josefa Ortíz de Domínguez) managed to send a warning to Father Hidalgo that their conspiracy to declare Mexico's independence from Spain had been discovered. Hidalgo got the message and hurried to publicly shout "independence" in Dolores Hidalgo. The rest is history. Ask the guard if you can see the room and take your camera—the view of the square from here is good.

Across the plaza opposite the Corregidora's house is the **Instituto de las Artesanías, Pasteur 16, at the corner of Libertad** (☎ **12-9100, ext. 215**), a state crafts shop housed in another colonial gem. Walk through the rooms with nicely displayed weavings, regional clothing, pottery, onyx, hand-carved furniture, opals, and jewelry incorporating other semiprecious stones—all from Querétaro and all for sale. There is, as well, a nice quantity of items from other regions of Mexico on its two floors. It's open Monday through Saturday from 10am to 8pm and Sunday from 10am to 5pm.

Left out the front door and across the street from the Instituto is the **Mesón Santa Rosa,** a beautiful hotel and restaurant (see "Dining," below) in a colonial-era building. Leading off this plaza are flower-decorated pedestrians-only brick streets, known as *andadores*, leading to other well-tended plazas and a few shops and restaurants.

Walking two blocks west of the Plaza Independencia on 5 de Mayo is Querétaro's central square, **Plaza Obregón** (recently renamed **Plaza Benito Zenea**). It's bounded by Juárez and Corregidora running north and south and by Madero and 16 de Septiembre running east and west. Across the street is a triangular-looking plaza known as the **Jardín Corregidora,** centered on a graceful statue of the famous Josefa Ortíz de Domínguez and lined with restaurants on the far side.

Plaza Obregón is also flanked by the Templo de San Francisco and the ✪ **Regional Museum,** at Corregidor 3 (☎ 12-2036). This building was originally the Grand Convent of Saint Francis of Assisi, begun in 1540. In 1861, it was used as a fortress by the Imperialists, who backed Maximilian. The structure is one of those palatial edifices the "humble" friars favored, replete with arches and Corinthian columns. The first room you enter holds fascinating memorabilia. Subsequent galleries have artifacts from the pre-Hispanic and contemporary indigenous peoples of the area. Other rooms contain colonial paintings and furniture, and the Sala de Historia holds numerous items of perhaps morbid interest, including Maximilian's coffin and countless period photographs. The museum bookshop sells mostly Spanish-language books. Admission is $3.50; free on Tuesday. It's open Tuesday through Sunday from 10:30am to 6:30pm.

A block beyond the Plaza de la Corregidora and Plaza Obregón, at Juárez and 16 de Septiembre, is the **Teatro de la República,** where Mexico's present constitution was signed in 1917.

Two blocks southwest of the Plaza Obregón, on Allende between Madera and Pino Suárez, is the architecturally fascinating ✪ **Museo de Arte** (☎ 12-2537). Inside this beautiful restored former convent is a fine museum in a fabulous baroque building that was originally an 18th-century Augustinian convent. Construction began in 1731 and was finished in 1745. The building was occupied by soldiers in the 1860s. It was designated a historic monument in 1935, yet it remained neglected, even housing the jail at one time. I saw it years ago when it housed the post office and seemed destined to crumble away chunk by chunk.

What a rebirth it's had! Now visitors are torn between going on an obligatory walk through the museum and gazing at the fabulous interior stonework. (The names of the architects and stonemasons are unknown.) An excellent 15-minute video in Spanish unlocks the mystery of the symbolism in the stone. In case your Spanish is rusty, the video tells that elephants, ducks, horses, and pelicans signify Christ and that each hand sign has a different meaning. Inside is a magnificent collection of 16th- through 18th-century Mexican and European paintings, as well as changing exhibits of contemporary Mexican paintings. Admission is $2; free on Tuesday. The museum is open Tuesday through Sunday from 11am to 7pm.

From the Museo de Arte go right out the front door and right again at the first street, Pino Suárez, and continue for three blocks to E. Montes and turn left. Ahead one block on the left corner at Arteaga is the ✪ **Convent of Santa Rosa de Viterbo.** It was built in the 18th century by Mexico's greatest religious architect, Eduardo Tresguerras. It's known for the unusual inverted flying buttresses on the outside and the magnificent baroque retablos on the inside. It's closed more often than it's open, but try around 4 or 5pm.

Backtracking to the Plaza de la Independencia, take a break in the Mesón Santa Rosa. Then continue straight ahead on 5 de Mayo eight blocks to M. Najera and turn right two blocks to V. Carranza, where you turn left one block to the **Templo y Ex-Convento de la Cruz,** on Avenida Independencia near Carmona. Building began in 1654, with major additions continuing for the next century. A tour through this massive complex will give you some feel for the life of an 18th-century cleric. From these cloisters Fr. Junípero Serra departed for California, and Fr. António de San Buenaventura stopped on his way to found the mission that was to become San Antonio, Texas. Hours are a bit irregular, but ask at the small bookstore about fascinating tours guided by one of the brothers. Nearby is a spectacular view of the aqueduct that supplied the convent and city at that time.

Querétaro

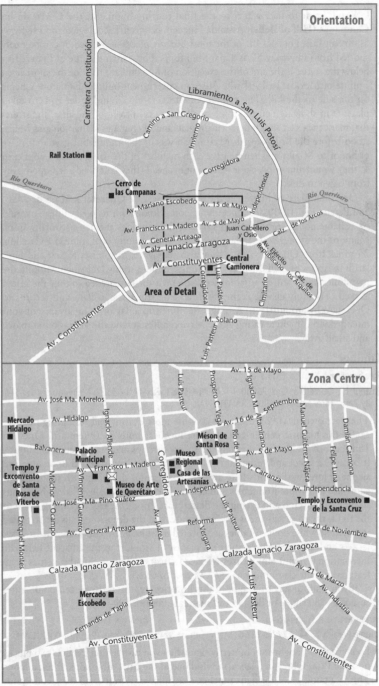

Orientation

Carretera Constitución

Libramiento a San Luis Potosí

Camino a San Gregorio

Invierno

Corregidora

Independencia

Rail Station

Río Querétaro

Río Querétaro

Cerro de
las Campanas

Av. Mariano Escobedo

Av. 15 de Mayo

Av. Francisco I. Madero

Av. 5 de Mayo

Juan Cabellero
y Osio

Calz. de los Arcos

Av. General Arteaga

Calz. Ignacio Zaragoza

Av. Ejército
Republicano

Calz. de
los Árquitos

Av. Constituyentes

Central
Camionera

Corregidora

Luis Pasteur

Cimitario

Area of Detail

Av. Constituyentes

M. Solano

Luis Pasteur

Zona Centro

Av. 15 de Mayo

Luis Pasteur

Prospero C. Vega

Ignacio M. Altamirano

16 de Septiembre

Manuel Gutiérrez Nájera

Damián Carmona

Av. José Ma. Morelos

Av. Hidalgo

Ignacio Allende

Río de la Loza

Av. 16 de Mayo

Felipe Luna

Mercado
Hidalgo

Balvanera

Palacio
Municipal

Méson de
Santa Rosa

V. Carranza

Av. 5 de Mayo

Templo y
Exconvento
de Santa
Rosa de
Viterbo

Melchor Ocampo

Av.
Vicente Guerrero

Francisco I. Madero

Corregidora

Museo
Regional

Casa de las
Artesanías

Av. Independencia

Av. Independencia

Templo y Exconvento
de la Santa Cruz

Museo de Arte
de Querétaro

Av. José Ma. Pino Suárez

Av. General Arteaga

Reforma

Luis Pasteur

Vergara

Av. 20 de Noviembre

Ezequiel Montes

Av. Juárez

Calzada Ignacio Zaragoza

Av. Luis Pasteur

Av. 21 de Marzo

Av. Industria

Calzada Ignacio Zaragoza

Mercado
Escobedo

Japan

Fernando de Tapia

Av. Constituyentes

Av. Constituyentes

1234

You'll want to take a taxi to the final touring highlight, the **Cerro de las Campanas (Hill of Bells),** Avenida Hidalgo, between Técnológico and Highway 57 to San Luis Potosí. One of the most historic places in Mexico, it can be easily spotted from Highway 57 as a giant hill topped by a titanic statue of Juárez. Just below the statue is the site of the execution of Maximilian, ruler of the short-lived Empire of Mexico. In 1901, the Austrian government built an Expiatory Chapel on the side of the hill. The caretaker (who is rarely around to let you in) takes pleasure in showing you the three small columns in front of the altar, the stones that mark the exact spot where Maximilian and his generals, Miramón and Mejia, stood before the firing squad. Maximilian was in the middle but gave that place of honor to Miramón; then he gave each member of the firing squad a gold coin so they would aim at his chest instead of his head (they complied). It's open daily from dawn to dusk.

One final place of interest is the ✪ **Lapidaria de Querétaro,** at 15 de Mayo and Peralta (☎ 12-0030). Since the region is known for its opal mines, it would be a shame not to see the best in stones and mountings at this trustworthy store. Many of the stones you see here come from the family opal mine, La Catalina, 25 miles from Querétaro. But they also sell agate, turquoise, topaz, and lapis lazuli in stones or gold or silver mountings. Besides seeing craftsmen working the raw stones in the store's adjacent workshop, visitors are invited to tour the mines as well. The only charge is for gasoline. The trip starts at 9am and returns to Querétaro by around 1pm. Arrange the mine trip a day or so in advance of your intended visit. If you're eating at the Mariposa Restaurant, the store is only a block and a half away.

Dining

Restaurant Santa Rosa

Pasteur 17, Querétaro, Qro. 76000. ☎ **42/14-5681.** Fax 42/12-5522. Main courses $6–$18. Daily 7am–1am. MEXICAN/INTERNATIONAL.

The state-owned Mesón Santa Rosa is the most elegant and refreshing place to eat in the historic center and also the loveliest hotel in Querétaro. Once an 18th-century stable then quarters for Juárez's troops and later a tenement house, it became a hotel and restaurant in the late 1980s. Iron-studded doors open to sienna-colored walls, and there are two large patios dripping with fuchsia bougainvillea and white-iron tables and chairs. The patio is usually filled with patrons sipping cappuccino and eyeing the dessert cart. Inside the elegant dining room to the right, the color scheme is rose and white, and the deep-rose walls are stenciled to resemble white doilies. Tables are covered in white linen, and waiters wear black jackets and bow ties. Often there's a pianist or violinist in the adjacent bar. The international menu emphasizes Mexican cuisine. (The enchiladas verdes were featured in Patricia Quintana's *The Taste of Mexico*.)

If you want to stay overnight in this historic city, this is the place. Junior suites cost $72–$80 single or double and master suites run $90–$95.

Cafetería La Mariposa

Angela Peralta 7. ☎ **42/12-1166.** Main courses $2–$4. Daily 8am–9:30pm. MEXICAN.

Look for the wrought-iron butterfly sign when you turn left on Peralta (two blocks north of Plaza Obregón [Zenea]) to find one of the city's most popular restaurants. This is a good place for light lunches—enchiladas, a fruit salad, or a club sandwich—or pastries, ice cream, and coffee. Next door is a wickedly tempting sweet shop featuring such irresistibles as candied figs, peaches, bananas, and papaya. You can also order these delicacies in the restaurant, as the two enterprises are under the same management.

✪ A Side Trip: The Fray Junípero Serra Missions

If you're driving, this is a side trip worth taking. Five little-known missions established by Fray Junípero Serra before his journey to California lie in the Sierra Gorda mountain region east of Querétaro. The beautiful buildings have been restored, and the state operates the following three hotels along the route: **Mesón Concá,** near Misión Concá ($50 for a double in the old section of a hacienda); **Mesón de San Joaquín,** at San Joaquín ($20 for a double); and **Mesón de Fray Junípero Serra,** at Jalpan ($30 for a double). Each has a small restaurant. My favorite is the hacienda section of Mesón Concá. The master suite opens to a porch, yard, and steamy thermal water stream. The largest town is **Jalpan,** where an excellent small museum has just opened; the other towns are only small farming villages.

From Querétaro the drive (which begins at the Cadereyta turnoff south of Querétaro on Highway 123) is a winding, mountainous one that takes at least five hours.

En route are two **archaeological sites—Las Ranas,** easily accessible, and **Toluquilla,** reached via a rutted road after which you must climb a mountain to get to the site. Another, less winding route begins far north of Querétaro at the San Luis Potosí turnoff east to Río Verde. From there, go south to Concá and Jalpan.

Whichever route you choose, plan to spend a minimum of two nights in the mission zone. The drive is tiring, and although the missions can be seen in one day, you'd be pushing it to drive out the second afternoon, not to mention rushing through the experience.

2 Guanajuato

221 miles NW of Mexico City, 35 miles E of León, 58 miles W of San Miguel de Allende, 130 miles SW of San Luis Potosí, 102 miles N of Morelia, 175 miles SE of Zacatecas

Guanajuato is one of Mexico's hidden gems; uncovered by relatively few foreign tourists, it's a popular weekend trip for people from Mexico City. Clean and beautifully preserved, Guanajuato should be high on your list of the finest places to visit in Mexico.

It was founded in 1559 around the Río Guanajuato, and its narrow, winding streets reflect the past meanderings of the river. Floods plagued the town, and finally the river was diverted, leaving an excellent bed for what has now become a subterranean highway with cantilevered houses jutting over the roadway. Guanajuato was one of the most important colonial cities (along with Querétaro, Zacatecas, San Miguel, and San Luis Potosí) from the 16th through the 18th centuries. Its mines produced a third of all the silver in the world; and like the gold-rush towns in the United States, it bloomed with elaborate churches and mansions, many in the Moorish style. Today Guanajuato seems like an old Spanish city that has been dumped lock, stock, and barrel into a Mexican river valley.

The name Guanajuato is a Spanish adaptation of the Tarascan word *guanaxuato,* meaning "hill of frogs." To the Tarascans, the rocks above town appeared to be shaped like frogs. This was especially significant since in the Tarascan culture the frog represented the god of wisdom.

ESSENTIALS

GETTING THERE & DEPARTING   By Plane   The León/Bajío airport is 17 miles and about 30 minutes from downtown Guanajuato. Check Chapter 3, "Planning a Trip to Mexico," for carriers serving León from the States. (**American Airlines'** local telephone number is 91-800/9-0460; **Continental's** is 47/18-5254.) **AeroLiterol** (☎ 47/16-6226; 14-0574 at the airport), an Aeroméxico affiliate, flies to León from Guadalajara, Mexico City, Monterrey, and Tijuana. **Mexicana** (☎ 47/14-9500; 13-4550 at the airport) flies in from Guadalajara, Mexico City, and Tijuana. **Taesa** (☎ 47/14-3660 or 12-3621) arrives from Morelia, Mexico City, and Tijuana. From the airport to Guanajuato, a colectivo carrying four people costs around $10 each, or $40 for one person.

There are airline ticket offices in León and at the León/Bajío airport. Flights from Guanajuato can be arranged through **Viajes Frausto,** Plaza de la Paz 10, or other travel agencies in Guanajuato.

By Bus   The bus station in Guanajuato is 3½ miles southwest of town, and frequent buses marked "Central" go between town and the station. From Mexico City's Terminal Norte, the **Flecha Amarilla** line runs buses hourly to Guanajuato. Go to Area 6 ("6 Espera") to find the company's ticket desk and bus platforms. The trip can take as long as six hours if you get a local bus that stops in San Juan del Río, Querétaro, Dolores Hidalgo, and San Miguel de Allende. Ask for the express. From Mexico City, **Estrella Blanca** has four daily express buses to Guanajuato. The first is at 10am and the last at 6:15pm; the trip takes five hours. The deluxe **ETN** coaches go five times daily to Mexico City and also to León and Guadalajara. Primera Plus has seven direct buses to and from Mexico City.

From Guanajuato, **Flecha Amarilla** makes six trips "Vía Presa" (the short route) to San Miguel de Allende; the last is at 2:30pm. The trip takes 1½ hours. Flecha Amarilla has service every 20 minutes to Dolores (a two-hour trip). From Dolores, there's frequent service to San Miguel de Allende—a good thing to know if you've missed the limited service on other lines to San Miguel. Flecha Amarilla also goes to Querétaro, San Luis Potosí, and Mexico City, as well as to Aguascalientes and Guadalajara. Times and itineraries change frequently, so your best bet is to invest 25¢ for a bus ride to the Central and make your choice.

By Car   From Mexico City there are two routes. The faster route, although it may look longer, is Highway 57 north and northwest to Highway 45D at Querétaro, west through Salamanca to Irapuato, where you follow Highway 45 north to Silao and then take Highway 110 east. That route is a four-lane road almost all the way. The other route continues north on Highway 57 past Querétaro, then west on Highway 110 through Dolores Hidalgo and continues to Guanajuato. From San Luis Potosí, the quickest way to Guanajuato is through Dolores Hidalgo.

ORIENTATION   Arriving by Bus   The modern station, about 3½ miles southwest of town on the road to Celaya, opened in February 1990 and has all the latest conveniences—shops, baggage storage, telephone center with fax and long distance, and a caféteria-style fast-food restaurant. If you aren't carting much luggage, take one of the buses marked "Centro" into town. Otherwise, you can take a taxi.

Guanajuato

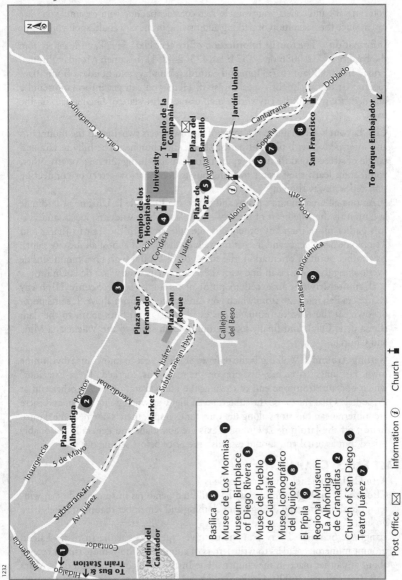

Basílica ❺
Museo de Los Momias ❶
Museum Birthplace of Diego Rivera ❸
Museo del Pueblo de Guanajuato ❹
Museo Iconográfico del Quijote ❽
El Pípila ❾
Regional Museum La Alhóndiga de Granaditas ❷
Church of San Diego ❻
Teatro Juárez ❼

Post Office ☒   Information ⓘ   Church ✚

Arriving by Car   Try not to lose your sanity while finding a place to park. Such a winding, hilly town as Guanajuato defies good verbal or written directions. Just be alert for one-way streets, and after winding around through the subterranean highway a bit, you'll get enough bearings to park. If in doubt, follow the signs TEATRO JUÁREZ or JARDÍN UNIÓN, which will get you to the center of town, where you can park and collect your wits. In fact, consider parking your car until you leave town, since the frustration of parking and driving in the city could spoil your visit.

Information   The **tourist information office** is at Plaza de la Paz 14, across from the basílica (☎ 2-0086 or 2-1574; fax 473/ 2-4251). It's open Monday through Friday from 8:30am to 7:30pm and Saturday, Sunday, and holidays from 10am to 2pm. It has an English-speaking staff. Here, you can get information and a detailed free map of the city with a map of the entire state of Guanajuato on the back.

City Layout   Guanajuato is a town of narrow streets twisting up the mountains and interspersed with pleasant parks, plazas, and churches. The hilly terrain and tangle of streets are difficult to represent on a map—using our map or any other, you'll soon learn they aren't to scale, nor is every narrow street or connecting stairstep walkway shown.

Among all Guanajuato's plazas and parks, the **Plaza de la Unión** (or Jardín de la Unión) is the true heart of the city—the place where students, locals, and visitors gather more than any other. On one side are both the Teatro Juárez and Templo de San Diego, and it's within walking distance of almost all the city sights. As another point of orientation, the statue of **El Pípila,** high on a mountainside overlooking the town, is in line with the Teatro Juárez and Plaza de la Unión.

If you're driving, an excellent point of reference is the **Scenic Highway** (Carretera Panorámica), from which you can see the city from above. It starts north of town off the road to Irapuato, passes El Pípila, continues south to the dam (Presa de la Olla), and finally loops around north again to the Valenciana Mine and Church.

Getting Around   Walking is the only way really to get to know this labyrinthine town. For longer stretches, just hop on the main **bus,** marked "Presa-Estación," which operates from one end of town at the railroad station to the other end at Presa de la Olla. Buses use the subterranean highway when going south, and there are subterranean bus stops along the way; for example, there's one near the Teatro Juárez, off the Jardín de la Unión. **Taxis** are abundant and generally reasonably priced, but as usual you should establish the price before setting out.

FAST FACTS: GUANAJUATO

Area Code   The telephone area code is 473.

Climate   This high-altitude city has mild temperatures in summer, but in winter it can dip to freezing. Bring warm clothing and remember that most hotels have no heat.

Language School   Every year the positive experiences at the Instituto Falcón prompt numerous readers to write letters of commendation—more than I receive about any other place in the country. The Instituto Falcón (Callejón de la Mora 158, Guanajuato 36000, Gto.; ☎ 473/2-3694) is directed by Jorge Barroso, who provides skilled and dedicated tutors for those wishing hourly or intensive studies at all levels. He can also arrange for boarding with local families.

Post Office   The post office (Correo) is located on the corner of Navarro and Carcamanes, near the Templo de la Compañía.

Seasons   Guanajuato has several high seasons during which hotel, and in some cases restaurant, prices go up and unreserved rooms are hard to find. The high seasons are Christmas, Easter Week, all of the Cervantino Festival, and July and August when Mexicans and Europeans vacation.

EXPLORING GUANAJUATO

SPECIAL EVENTS

Every year, from about October 7 to 22, the state of Guanajuato sponsors the
✪ **Festival Cervantino (International Cervantes Festival),** two weeks of
performing arts from all over the world. In recent years, the festival has featured
marionettes from Czechoslovakia, the Elliot Feld Dance Company from New
York, the Kiev Ballet, and a host of Mexican artists. The shows are held in open
plazas and theaters all over town. Book rooms well in advance during the festival; if Guanajuato is full, consider staying in nearby San Miguel de Allende.

For ticket information and a schedule contact Festival Cervantino, Mineral de
Cata s/n (Ex Cava), Guanajuato, Gto. 36060 (☎ 473/2-0959). Once you know
the schedule, you can order tickets through Ticketmaster in Mexico City
(☎ 5/325-9000). Keep your confirmation number; you'll need it to pick up your
tickets in Guanajuato.

THE TOP ATTRACTIONS

✪ Iglesia de San Cayetano (Templo de la Valenciana)
Valenciana. Admission free. Daily 9am–6pm.

The magnificent church, built in 1765 by the first Count of Valencia, is one of
the most beautiful colonial churches in churrigueresque style—a true masterpiece
and one of the finest churches in Mexico. It's absolutely filled with luxurious floor-
to-ceiling carvings in white cedar covered with 18-karat gold. This baroque art
form, unique to Mexico, merged the Spanish artistic style with the abundant gold
of Mexico. You'll also find some beautiful paintings here. If you're lucky, you may
be able to catch a concert of baroque music performed on the large organ.

✪ Teatro Juárez
Jardín de la Unión. ☎ **473/2-0183.** Admission $1.75, 50¢ additional with still camera, $2
additional with video camera. Tues–Sat 9am–1:45pm and 5–7:45pm, Sun 9am–1:45pm.

Built in 1903 during the opulent era of the Porfiriato, this theater is now the venue
for many productions, especially during the Cervantino Festival. Outside are
bronze sculptures of lions and lanterns, and inside the five-story U-shaped theater
is embellished with carved ornamentation in a flurry of red, gold, and blue.

✪ Museum Birthplace of Diego Rivera
Calle Positos 47. ☎ **473/2-1197.** Admission $1.75. Tues–Sat 10am–1:30pm and 4–6:30pm,
Sun 10am–2:30pm.

This is the house where the artist Diego Rivera was born on December 8, 1886.
It has been refurbished and made into a museum. The first floor of this three-story
house is furnished as it might have been in the era of Rivera's birth. Upstairs there's
a fine collection of Rivera's early works. He began painting when he was 10 years
old and eventually moved to Paris, where he became a Marxist during World War
I. The house contains sketches of some of his earlier murals that made his reputation, but most of the works on display are paintings from 1902 to 1956. On the
third floor is a small auditorium where lectures and conferences are held. The
house is north of the Plaza de la Paz, 1 1/2 blocks beyond the Museo del Pueblo.

✪ Museo del Pueblo de Guanajuato
Calle Positos 7. ☎ **473/2-2990.** Admission $1.75. Tues–Sat 10am–2pm and 4–7pm, Sun
10am–2:30pm, open all day during the Cerventino Festival.

North of the Plaza de la Paz and before the Rivera museum (see above) lies this 17th-century mansion that once belonged to the Marqués San Juan Rayas. It holds a priceless collection of more than 1,000 colonial-era civil and religious pieces gathered by local distinguished muralist José Chávez Morado. Chávez murals can be seen in this museum as well as in the Regional Museum La Alhóndiga down the street. In addition to the Chávez collection, contemporary displays upstairs show Mexican artists. Every other year, the museum hosts the Biennial of Diego Rivera, a truly fine exhibit of Mexico's up-and-coming artists.

✪ Regional Museum La Alhóndiga de Granaditas

Mendizabal 6. ☎ 473/2-1112. Admission $4 (50¢ extra with still camera), free for students with ID cards, free for all on Sun. Tues–Sat 10am–2pm and 4–6pm, Sun 10am–2:30pm.

Continuing a long block farther on the same street as the Rivera museum (see above), you'll see the huge Alhóndiga on the left (the entrance is on Positos). The Alhóndiga de Granaditas was built between 1798 and 1809 as the town granary. It was so splendid that it was called El Palacio del Maiz (the Corn Palace). The Spanish took refuge here as El Pípila and company burned down the doors to the Alhóndiga, but they still had not lost the war. A year later, the heads of the revolutionaries Hidalgo, Allende, Aldama, and Jiménez were brought here and hung in iron cages on the four outside corners of the building, where they remained from 1811 to 1821 to remind the populace of what happens to those who rebel. The name plaques below the cornice on the four corners of the building commemorate the four heroes of this stormy period. From 1864 to 1949 the building served as a prison.

The Alhóndinga is now one of the best museums in Mexico. There are two levels with rooms off the courtyard. You'll see numerous pre-Columbian relics, including pots, decorative seals and stamps, terra-cotta figurines, and stone implements. The lower level (on which you enter) has rooms filled with regional crafts and the pre-Hispanic art collection of José Chávez Morado—the artist responsible for the splendid murals on both stairwells (and whose collection is in the important Museo del Pueblo de Guanajuato). Mexico's most complete collection of pre-Hispanic stamps was donated to the museum by American archaeologist Frederick Field. The museum contains Chupícuaro ceramics dating from A.D. 350 to 450 from the southeast part of the state; they were saved when the Solis Dam was constructed in 1949 and are a type of ceramics rarely seen in Mexico. A long corridor contains bronze masks of the revolutionary heroes as well as an eternal flame in their honor.

Upstairs is a Bellas Artes section with exhibits (both temporary and permanent) of national and international artists. There are also several rooms showing the history of the state of Guanajuato, particularly its revolutionary history; there is also an exhibit on the region's dozen mines, the first of which was begun in 1557 on the orders of Charles V. There are some interesting lithographs showing the city in the 18th and 19th centuries, in addition to 20th-century photographs.

✪ El Pípila

Admission free. Daily 24 hours. Go via automobile or bus (marked "Pípila") or on foot along a rugged winding pathway (wear comfortable shoes). Walk up Calle Sopeña from the Jardín de la Unión and turn to the right up Callejón del Calvario. A sign on the wall reads AL PÍPILA (To El Pípila).

High above the town with a great view overlooking the Jardín de la Unión is the city's monument to José de los Reyes Martínez. Nicknamed El Pípila, he was a brave young miner who on Hidalgo's orders set fire to the Alhóndiga de Granaditas, the strategically situated grain warehouse in which the Royalists were hiding during the War of Independence. On September 16, 1810, Hidalgo, a radical priest who had appealed for Mexico's independence from Spain, led an army that captured Guanajuato. In this bloody battle, 600 inhabitants and 2,000 Indians were killed, but the revolution was on its way. Guanajuato became the rebel capital; however, its history was short—10 months later Hidalgo was captured and shot in Chihuahua and his head was sent to Guanajuato to be exhibited.

Today, El Pípila's statue raises a torch high over the city in everlasting vigilance, and the inscription at his feet proclaims AUN HAY OTRAS ALHÓNDIGAS POR INCENDIAR—"There are still other alhóndigas to burn."

From the top of the statue (you can climb inside the statue if you wish), there's a lovely view of the city below. Churches appear everywhere, bronze figures atop the Teatro Juárez, and the massive university unfolds below. It's the best spot in town for photos. There's a little park where kids play ball and families picnic. The atmosphere and view are delightful.

❂ Museo de Los Momias (Mummy Museum)

Calzada del Panteón. ☎ 473/2-0639. Admission $5, $2 extra with still camera or $5 with movie camera. Daily 9am–6pm. It's a steep climb on foot, but the bus labeled "Presa-Estación" runs along the Plaza de la Paz/Sopeña, and this will take you to the foot of the cobbled hill. For this trip, Guanajuato's cab drivers invariably tend to charge what the traffic will bear.

At the northwestern end of town is the Calzada del Panteón, which leads up to the municipal cemetery. Once there, you'll find a building in which the mummies are displayed in tall showcases and glass caskets. Dryness, plus the earth's gases and minerals, have caused decomposition to halt in certain sections of the Panteón. Because of space limitations, people are buried for only five years; then, if the relatives can't continue to pay for the graves, the bodies are exhumed to make room for more. Those on display, however, were exhumed between 1865 and 1985. The mummies stand or recline in glass cases, grinning, choking, or staring. It's impossible to resist the temptation to go up and look at them (everybody does), and this is the only graveyard I've seen with souvenir stands next to the main gate, selling sugar effigies of the mummies.

Museo Iconográfico del Quijote

Manuel Doblado 1. ☎ 473/2-6721. Admission free. Tues–Sat 10am–6:30pm, Sun 10am–2:30pm.

This museum, a long block southeast of the *jardín* and past the Hostería del Frayle, holds a fascinating collection of art based upon Don Quijote. Once you get past the captivating life-size wood carving of the Don and Sancho, you enter (almost physically) into the lives of Cervantes and Don Quixote by way of the wall and ceiling murals that enclose you in the next room and the works of art all around. In the remaining galleries, there are exhibits of artists who found inspiration from the classic tale of Don Quijote such as Salvador Dalí, Picasso, Raul Angiano, José Guadalupe Posada, Daumier, José Moreno Carbonero, and Pedro Coronel.

OTHER ATTRACTIONS

The **Church of San Diego,** on the Jardín de la Unión, stands almost as it did in 1633, when it was built under the direction of Franciscan missionaries. After a 1760 flood that nearly destroyed it, reconstruction was completed in 1786; half the funds were given by the Count of Valenciana. The pink cantera stone facade is a fine example of Mexican baroque (churrigueresque).

The **Plazuela del Baratillo,** just off the Jardín de la Unión, has a beautiful fountain (a gift from Emperor Maximilian) at its center, and you'll always find people sitting around it peacefully, some in the shade and others in the sun; late in the afternoon the plazuela is almost exactly divided between *sol* (sun) and *sombra* (shade). The **Plazuela San Fernando** is larger and has a stone platform where very often there will be local Mexican dances with the younger generation decked out in bright costumes.

The magnificent **university** was founded in 1732, but its entrance was rebuilt in 1945 in a stately manner so the building now dominates the whole town. The university is just behind **Plaza de la Paz,** and it's open every day. Visitors are welcome.

The **Church of the Compañía de Jesús,** next to the university, was built in 1747 by the Jesuit order as the biggest of their churches at that time. It is distinctly churrigueresque on the outside, but the interior, which was restored in the 19th century, is not. This church was built as part of the Jesuit university, founded in 1732 on orders of Philip V on the site of the present university; it's the last of 23 universities built by the Jesuit order in Mexico.

NEARBY ATTRACTIONS

For a suburban outing, hop any bus that says "Presa" (try the bus stop in the Subterranean near Jardín de la Unión) to the **Parque de la Acacias** and the **Presa de la Olla,** the artificial lake. There are several parks and lots of trees—it's a good place for a lazy afternoon.

While in the neighborhood, you might note the **Government Palace** on Paseo de la Presa with its pink-stone front and green-tile interior. The neighborhood around here is residential and will give you another glimpse of Guanajuato away from the bustle of the plazas.

The most famous silver mine is **La Valenciana,** said to have produced a fifth of the silver circulating in the world from 1558 to 1810. It can be reached by taking Route 30, the Dolores Hidalgo road, three miles northeast of town (the bus is "Vallenciana SAHOP"). The mine was closed about 40 years ago but then reopened, and a caretaker is there to show you the eight-sided vertical shaft (1,650 feet deep) and the once-grandiose courtyard. You can take a look down the long mine shaft (but you can't go down) from which silver is still being extracted today, along with about 50 other minerals and metals. Silver products from this mine are sold in the adjoining silver shop. While you're in the area. you may also want to see the Iglesia de San Cayetano described in "Top Attractions," above, and FONART mentioned in "Shopping," below. All through this mountainous area, more than a dozen mines produced silver. Some are now abandoned, and some, like Valenciana, are still functioning.

Also around here there were more than 150 splendid mansions on the haciendas of wealthy colonial mine owners. Most are now either in ruins or restored and privately owned, but you can visit the **Museo Ex-Hacienda San Gabriel de Barrera,** which I certainly recommend. Located about two miles from town on the ancient road to Marfil, the museum is housed in one of the most luxurious of the 18th-century grand haciendas, with a magnificent main house, a gold-adorned chapel, and acres of lovely gardens. You can wander through Italian gardens, English gardens, Chinese gardens, and cactus gardens, all decorated with beautiful statues and fountains from the various countries represented. The hacienda, which had remained in the family for two centuries, was sold to the Mexican government in 1979 and is now a museum furnished with Mexican and European furniture and open to the public. You can visit it any day from 9am to 6:30pm; admission is $2, plus $1 for a still camera or $2.75 for a video camera.

The recommended Hotel San Gabriel de Barrera is also here—see "Expensive" under "Accommodations," below, for information on this and for directions on how to arrive here from town.

SHOPPING

The **Mercado Hidalgo,** housed in a building (1909) that resembles a Victorian railroad station, has a cavernous lower level and an upper balcony that encircles the whole building. It's stacked with lots of stalls that sell pottery and ceramic ware. From this balcony, you can look down onto one of the neatest layouts in Mexico with symmetrical rows of stalls and little eateries providing splashes of orange, green, red, brown, and black—the tones of the fruits and vegetables. The market is open every day from morning to evening.

The **Gorky González Workshop,** Calle Pastita, by the stadium, is a good place to pick up Talavera-style pottery. Hours are irregular, but you may be able to browse through the small showroom Monday through Friday from 9am to 2pm and 4 to 6pm.

Across the street from the Iglesia de San Cayetano, at Valenciana, is the Casa del Conde de la Valenciana, which now houses a fine restaurant by the same name, decorative art galleries, and the government-sponsored **FONART** store (☎ 473/2-2550). Though small, the latter has a selection of the finest crafts from all over Mexico. It's open daily from 10am to 6pm. The Alcocer family, descendants of the count, still own and manage these properties. To get here take the "Valenciana SAHOP" bus by the Alhondiga.

Half a block from the Plaza de la Unión is **Artesanías Vazquez,** Cantarranas 8 (☎ 473/2-5231), an outlet of the family ceramic factory in Dolores Hidalgo. It's small but loaded with the colorful Talavera-style pottery for which Dolores is famous; there are plates, ginger jars, frames, cups and saucers, serving bowls, and the like.

ACCOMMODATIONS

During the International Cervantes Festival held in mid-October, rooms are virtually impossible to find unless you have a reservation, and even then it's good to claim your room early in the day. Some visitors have to stay as far away as Querétaro, León, or San Miguel de Allende and come to Guanajuato for the day.

EXPENSIVE

✪ Casa de Espíritus Alegres B & B

La Ex-Hacienda la Trinidad no. 1, Marfil, Gto. 36250. ☎ **473/3-1013,** or 408/423-0181 in California. 4 rms, 2 suites. $75 double; $90 casita. Rates include breakfast.

Folk art and atmosphere abound in this "house of good spirits," owned and operated by two artists who have incorporated 20th-century comfort into parts of a 16th-century hacienda. Some of the rooms have their own fireplaces, and all are uniquely and colorfully decorated, fulfilling the promise of "a skeleton in every closet." The *casita* has its own kitchen and living room. Breakfasts, overlooking the patio, feature Californian and Mexican cuisine, with generous helpings of fresh fruit. Guest have full use of the living room, decked out in folk art and books as well as paperback novels for loan. The owners also have a small folk art shop downstairs. The facility is sometimes used for workshops and can be rented by groups. Frequent "Marfil" buses run from the highway just outside the grounds into downtown Guanajuato some two miles distant. Get specific directions when you make your reservations.

San Gabriel de Barrera Mision Park Plaza

Camino Antigua a Marfil km 2.5, Guanajuato, Gto. 36050. ☎ **473/2-3980**, or 800/437-7275 in the U.S. Fax 473/2-7460. 139 rms. TV TEL. $78 double. Free parking.

Formerly called Hotel El Presidente Guanajuato, this hotel is two miles from the center of town in a pretty valley next to the beautiful, authentic Hacienda San Gabriel Barrera museum. Rooms are large and attractive and come with either a terrace or balcony. A tidy pool, a restaurant, and a friendly staff round out the services and facilities. The hotel offers free transporation to and from town several times daily between 10am and 8pm. Cabs cost $3 between town and the hotel. If you're driving, follow signs for the Convention Center and then look for Hotel Mision signs.

MODERATE

Hostería del Frayle

Sopeña 3, Guanajuato, Gto. 36000. ☎ **473/2-1179.** Fax 473/2-1179, ext. 38. 37 rms (all with bath). TV TEL. $43 double.

Half a block southeast of the Plaza de la Unión, this hotel is a perfect place to sample accommodations as they might have been in colonial times. Ore was processed here before it went to the mint during the colonial era. Today, the building has been charmingly converted into a hotel. Each room has tall wooden doors, old hardwood floors, and comfortable, cozy furnishings with a hint of yesteryear. It's drafty and nippy in winter, though, so bring your long johns; also be prepared to climb lots of stairs. Housekeeping can be a bit lax, so check your room first. Management is friendly. There's a bar to the left of the lobby.

✪ Hotel Embajadoras

Parque Embajadoras, Guanajuato, Gto. 36000. ☎ **473/2-0081** or 2-4464. Fax 473/2-4760. 27 rms (all with bath). TV TEL. $42 double. Free parking.

This is the best choice out of downtown; it's on the tree-lined street heading toward Paseo Madero. Spread out on shaded grounds, the hotel is attractive, comfortable, and quiet. Rooms, all of which have red-tile floors, are small, clean, and plainly furnished. Covered walkways with chairs link the rooms. There's a patio at the rear with tables, chairs, and a hammock. A good, reasonably priced restaurant/bar takes care of meals. To reach the hotel, take a taxi or the "Paseo de la Presa" bus.

Hotel Santa Fe

Jardín Unión, Guanajuato, Gto. 36050. ☎ **473/2-0084.** Fax 473/2-0084. 50 rms. TEL. $45 double.

Right in the heart of the Jardín Unión, this three-story hotel is almost a re-creation of the 1940s. The beautifully kept, comfortable rooms are furnished in dark wood furniture reminiscent of another era, which befits this historic city. The "minibars" are actually wall cabinets filled with miniature liquor bottles. The tile-filled lobby holds couches perfect for cocktails, and the off-lobby restaurant and outdoor cafe are *the* places to be in Guanajuato.

INEXPENSIVE

❸ Casa Kloster

Alonso 32, Guanajuato, Gto. 36000. ☎ **473/2-0088.** 18 rms (1 with bath). $10–$12 per person.

A European-style pension, this two-story hotel is located on a quiet side street one block northwest of the Jardín de la Unión and Juárez, across from Teléfonos de México. Run by a warm, friendly family, the Kloster has a large central courtyard bursting with birds and flowers; the plain but very clean rooms surround the courtyard. Most rooms have two beds, but several hold three or four. The common baths (two upstairs and one downstairs) are also spotlessly clean. One room for six people has a private bath. No meals are served, but don't be surprised if you're invited to share morning coffee in the family kitchen.

Hotel El Minero

Alhóndiga 12-A, Guanajuato, Gto. 36000. ☎ **473/2-5251.** Fax 473/2-4729. 20 rms (all with bath). TV. $25 double.

Only two blocks beyond the Museo Alhóndiga, this four-story (no elevator) hotel is a good, clean, economical choice. The carpeted rooms have small tile baths with showers, and most have a double and a single bed. The hotel restaurant is next door.

DINING

If you find yourself hungry in the **Mercado Hidalgo** area, stop and try one of the many inexpensive eateries inside or outside to the left of the huge mercado edifice. Observe the sign that says (in Spanish): "Avoid disappointment, ask to see the price list!"

❖ Café El Retiro

Sopeña 14. ☎ **473/2-0622.** Breakfast $1.50–$3; main courses $2–$8; comida corrida $3.50. Daily 8am–11pm (comida corrida served 1–4:30pm). MEXICAN.

Sooner or later everyone—local, student, or visitor—winds up at El Retiro, which recently expanded into the building next door. The best inexpensive lunch in town, consisting of soup, rice with cheese, two or three choices of meat dish, dessert, and coffee, is served here. From the a la carte menu, you can choose from a variety of *antojitos* such as tacos and enchiladas or a quarter chicken. The service is quick and informally friendly. El Retiro is half a block south of the Jardín de la Unión, catercorner to the Teatro Juárez.

Pizza Piazza

Cantarranas at Jardín de la Unión. ☎ **473/2-4259.** Pizza $3.75–$7; main courses $2.50–$3. Daily 2–11pm. ITALIAN.

Young sophisticates and students with a little cash patronize this restaurant just off the Jardín de la Unión. Comfortable booths and plants provide an ambience that promotes easy camaraderie: This is one of the best places in town to meet young Mexicans. Pizzas come in small, medium, and large (which can feed five or six). Beer and sangría are also served, either in the dining room or at the tables under the tree in the plazuela. They serve up lots of spaghetti, hamburgers, sandwiches, and queso fundido.

There are three more Pizza Piazzas, all with the same menu, prices, and hours. One is at the Plaza San Fernando (☎ 2-3094), another is near the Jardín del Cantador at Hidalgo 14 (☎ 2-4259), and the third is on Avenida Juárez, a block before the Mercado Hidalgo Market (☎ 2-6917).

Tasca de Los Santos
Plaza de la Paz 28. ☎ **473/2-2320.** Breakfast $1.25–$3.75; main courses $4–$9. Daily 8am– midnight. MEXICAN/REGIONAL.

This is one of Guanajuato's snazzier restaurants with a completely a la carte menu. The food, service, and heavy Spanish decor will please you. Paella is a house specialty. The restaurant also serves chicken in white-wine sauce and beef à la andaluza. You can order wine by the bottle or glass.

✪ Truco 7
Truco 7. ☎ **473/2-8374.** Breakfast $1.25–$2.50; comida corrida $3.25; main courses $2.50–$6. Daily 8am–11:30pm (comida corrida served 1:30–4pm). MEXICAN.

With its economical prices and warm, colorful atmosphere, this place has quickly established its popularity. The three dining rooms are small and a bit crowded yet nicely decorated with leather *equipal* tables and chairs, paintings by local artists, and photographs taken by the owner. The restaurant is housed in an 18th-century structure originally built for members of the Valenciana silver family. Calle Truco, a short street south of the *basílica*, runs between the Plaza de la Unión and the Plaza de la Paz. You can also reach it from the wide end of the Plaza de la Unión walking towards the Plaza de la Paz.

GUANAJUATO AFTER DARK
If long ago city planners had known the **Plaza de la Unión** was going to be so popular, they might have made it larger. This tiny plaza, shaded by Indian laurel trees, is the true heart and best hangout in the city day and night. No other spot in town rivals its benches and sidewalk restaurants. The quality of the food is less important than the viewing perch, but all the restaurants serve a variety of coffees over which you can linger. Among the best places on the plaza are the living room– type bar and inside/outside restaurant of the **Hotel Santa Fe** and the bar/restau- rant of the **Hotel San Diego** overlooking the plaza. Other nearby gathering spots include the ever-popular **Café El Retiro,** half a block off the Plaza de la Unión, and the cozy **Truco 7** restaurant, at that address a block from the plaza.

Another, more expensive choice is the **Cantarranas Bar** at the Hotel Real de Minas, on the road that leads to Mexico City. A piano player entertains on weekends.

If you don't happen to be in Guanajuato during the Festival Cervantino, you can still catch some worthwhile theater—free—in Plazuela de San Roque at 8pm on any Sunday when the university is in session. These *entremeses* (literally "intermissions") presented by students, are short sketches written to be delivered between performances during the Cervantino Festival. In Guanajuato, they are a very special entertainment during which you can enjoy an evening under the stars in a medieval-style courtyard with about 90 minutes of acting and action by students and faculty of the University of Guanajuato. The show takes place in a real courtyard with galloping horses, water thrown from windows, church bells ringing, gusts of wind blowing out the candles, and people in authentic period costumes looking not too out of place in 20th-century Guanajuato. Don't miss it!

ALONG HIGHWAY 45 FROM GUANAJUATO TO ZACATECAS

On your way to Zacatecas, you'll pass through **León,** Mexico's leather and shoe capital, with thousands of shoe stores lining its streets. Unfortunately, uncontrolled growth has resulted in an ugly city, made more so by the contrast between this city and clean Aguascalientes, beautiful Zacatecas, or historic Guanajuato. There's an international airport in León. From Guanajuato, there are both a fast, inexpensive toll road and a free road to León. The drive takes 15 to 45 minutes depending on which route you take.

Aguascalientes (pop. 514,000), 84 miles south of Zacatecas, means "hot waters," and the city is famous for its hot springs. It was founded by the Spanish in 1575 as a place of protection and rest along the silver highway between Mexico City, Guanajuato, and Zacatecas, as well as a center of food cultivation for the mining region. Today Aguascalientes is known for its copper mining, embroidery, and knitwear. In the streets beside and behind the cathedral and the Plaza Principal, you'll note several stores selling the products of these industries.

With growth, the city has lost some of its colonial charm, although the people here are still friendly and relaxed. The main plaza, around which are several moderately priced hotels and restaurants, dates from the colonial era, and it's a pleasant place to stroll. The main tourist attraction in Aguascalientes is the **José Guadalupe Posada Museum** on the Plaza Encino. Posada was a 19th-century engraver and writer, and his skeleton caricatures of politicians and political events are famous countrywide; the museum has a large collection.

The biggest fair in Mexico, the **Fería de San Marcos,** is held here annually from April 19 to May 10. Festivities include industrial expositions, fireworks, cultural events, rodeos, and bullfights with renowned bullfighters from all over the world. At Aguascalientes, you can choose between the toll or free road to León, which is approximately 85 miles southeast of Aguascalientes. Heavy traffic can make the narrow, two-lane free road frustratingly slow.

3 Zacatecas

392 miles NW of Mexico City, 117 miles NW of San Luis Potosí, 197 miles NE of Guadalajara, 186 miles SE of Durango

A city made rich by silver mines, Zacatecas has magnificently preserved colonial architecture, picturesque brick streets ascending the hillsides, a slew of good museums, and a real dearth of tourists. The fame of the city's fine museums beckons most visitors, who arrive to be thoroughly captivated by the city's unique architectural beauty. It's safe to say that this is Mexico's most beautiful and best preserved colonial city. You can see the town's beauty from the hilltops that dominate the town, most notably from the Cerro de la Bufa.

The capital of the state of the same name, Zacatecas was already an old town when the Spaniards arrived in 1546. The name comes from the Nahuatl words *zacatl* (pasture) and *tecatl* (people)—Zacatecas, then, means "people of the pasture."

ESSENTIALS

GETTING THERE & DEPARTING   By Plane   See "Getting There, By Plane," in Chapter 3, "Planning a Trip to Mexico," for a list of carriers serving Zacatecas from the United States. From points within Mexico, **Mexicana** (☎ 2-7429; at the airport 5-0352) flies nonstop to Zacatecas from Morelia, Mexico City, and Tijuana (the flight from Tijuana is booked months in advance for the Christmas holidays). Nonstop service is also available on **Taesa** (☎ 4-0050 or 2-2555) from Ciudad Juárez, Guadalajara, Mexico City, Morelia, and Tijuana. Transportation from the airport to town is about $18 by taxi, about $6 by minibus.

By Bus   Almost a dozen bus companies provide service in and out of Zacatecas. **Camiones de los Altos** has 11 buses leaving the Central Camionera for Guadalajara daily. There are hourly buses to Fresnillo. **Transportes Chihuahuenses** and **Transportes del Norte** also operate to and from Zacatecas and various cities to the north and west. For those who are just passing through Zacatecas and who want to take the suggested side trip to Guadalupe, **Transportes de Guadalupe** goes there every 15 minutes from the Central Camionera (where you'll be if you arrive by bus) for around 50¢.

By Car   From the south you can take Highway 45D, a toll road in various spots all the way from Querétaro through Irapuato, León, and Aguascalientes. It's fast but expensive. From the north, Highway 54 comes from Saltillo and Monterrey (a five- to six-hour drive), Highway 40/49 from Torreón, Highway 45 from Durango, and Highway 54 from Guadalajara.

ORIENTATION   Arriving   The airport is located about 18 miles north of Zacatecas. **Aero Transportes** (☎ 492/2-5946) provides minibus transportation to and from the airport; allow 30 minutes for the ride. The **Central Camionera** (bus station) is on a hilltop a bit out of town, but a taxi to town costs only $4. Red Ruta 8 buses go to and from the station frequently and can be found in front of the station.

Information   The state of Zacatecas has two tourism offices here. The **Dirección de Turismo** is located in the Esplanade de Ferrocarril s/n (☎ and fax 492/2-9329) and is open Monday through Friday from 9am to 8pm. Downtown on Hidalgo, across from the cathedral, is a one-room **Infotur office;** it's open Monday through Saturday from 9am to 2pm and 4 to 7pm.

City Layout   The touristic heart of Zacatecas is centered on the **Plaza de Armas,** facing Hidalgo, flanked by government buildings and the cathedral, and opposite the tourism office. The late-night *callejoneadas* wind up here with their last burst of singing, dancing, drinking, and band playing.

Getting Around   Zacatecas has excellent inner-city **bus** service. To reach the Central Camionera (bus station), take a Ruta 8 bus at the Plaza de la Independencia. Ruta 7 goes to the Motel del Bosque and teleférico. From the local bus station a block past the Hotel Gallery, buses go to and from Guadalupe every few minutes.

FAST FACTS: ZACATECAS

Altitude   The city is situated at a lofty 8,200 feet. It's very hilly here, and you'll be doing a lot of climbing, which tends to make people winded.

American Express   American Express is handled by Viajes Mazzoco, a travel agent at Enlace 115 (☎ 492/2-5559 or 2-5159; fax 492/2-5559).

Area Code   The telephone area code is 492.

Climate   It's cool enough year-round to require a sweater or other warm wrap. Most hotels aren't heated.

Post Office   The post office (Correos) is at Allende III, half a block down from Avenida Hidalgo.

EXPLORING ZACATECAS

Zacatecas is so picturesque that many travelers regret not having planned at least three nights here—or more if they have come on days when the museums are closed. In addition to its marvelous architecture and museums, Zacatecas is famous among craftspeople for its stone and wood carvings, leatherwork, thread-pulled designs (drawnwork) on textiles, and silver making. Zacatecan handcrafts can be found directly across from the cathedral in the Mercado González Ortega. There are a few other stores on Hidalgo and Tacuba that sell crafts and antiques. Huichol Indians sometimes sell their crafts around the Plaza Independencia.

SPECIAL EVENTS

During Semana Santa, or the **Holy Week** before Easter, Zacatecas hosts an international cultural Festival the town hopes will soon rival the similar Cervantino Festival in Guanajuato. Painters, poets, dancers, musicians, actors, and other artists from around the world converge on the town.

The annual **Fería de Zacatecas,** which celebrates the day the city was founded, begins the Friday before September 8 and lasts for two weeks. Cockfights, bullfights, sporting events, band concerts, and general hoopla prevail. Particularly famous *toreadores* are hired, and bullfight tickets go for around $4; buses leave from downtown for the gigantic Plaza de Toros (and for the nearby cockpit) on days when fights are held. Sports events are held in the Olympic-size sports stadium and in the equally huge gymnasium; there are even car races at the racetrack outside town.

A STROLL AROUND TOWN

The **Plaza de Armas,** the town's main square on Avenida Hidalgo, is where you'll find the **cathedral,** with its fantastically ornate pink stone facade that has earned it the moniker the Parthenon of Mexico Baroque. It took 23 years to build (1729–1752), and the final tower wasn't completed until 1904. The Eucharist is represented on the front facade.

To the left of the cathedral is the 18th-century **Palacio de Gobierno,** where viceregal-era governors lived. By the time of Mexico's revolt against Spain in 1810, it was owned by Don Miguel de Rivera (Count of Santiago de la Laguna). Since 1834 it's been a government building; inside is a modern mural (1970) by António Pintor Rodríguez showing the history of Zacatecas. To the left of this building is the **Residencia de Gobernadores,** with its ornate stone facade; the state governor lived here until 1950. Notice the facade of the building on the corner, to the left of the Radisson Hotel opposite the Palacio de Gobierno. Formerly the building was known as the **Palacio de Mala Noche** (Palace of the Bad Night) after the mine that brought wealth to its original owner—Manuel de Rétegui, a benevolent Spaniard. The Plaza de Armas is a highlight of the fine stone carving and ironwork, a hallmark of Zacatecas, on buildings throughout the downtown. Stone carving is still a major industry in the area.

South of the Palacio de Mala Noche on Avenida Hidalgo, opposite from the right side of the cathedral is the 19th-century **Mercado Jesús González Ortega,** a striking combination of stone and elegant ironwork. Formerly the main market, today it's home to stylish shops. Continuing past the mercado, immediately on the left is the **Plaza Fancisco Goitia,** the venue for frequent open-air artistic performances. On the right you'll pass the **Teatro Calderón** (inaugurated first in 1836 and again in 1891 after a fire), a stately building with lovely stained-glass windows. Scenes from the movie *The Old Gringo* starring Jane Fonda and Gregory Peck were filmed here (the film was adapted from a book by Carlos Fuentes). Opera star Angela Peralta sang here several times in the 1800s, and Plácido Domingo sang here in 1990. The theater is named for a poet/political writer from the state of Jalisco.

Continue on Hidalgo, cross Juárez, and mount the hill to **Sierra de Alica Park** (the street changes names up the hill and becomes Avenida Gral. Jesús González Ortega). The **equestrian statue** (1898) portrays none other than Gen. González Ortega himself, hero of the Battle of Calpulalpan. Behind it is a gazebo with marvelous acoustics and a pleasant, shady park good for a picnic or a romantic stroll. It's also well lit in the evening.

Beginning at Alica Park and extending southward, the famous **Aqueduct of Zacatecas** looms over the street. The wealth of this mining city at the end of the 18th century allowed it to undertake such impressive public works. Water passed along the aqueduct to a large cistern downtown.

To take in the city all at once, climb slowly (remember the altitude) to the Motel del Bosque on the Cerro Grillo hill, west of the cathedral. Here, you can take the **teleférico** (cable car) on a sky ride over Zacatecas to the **Cerro de la Bufa,** a huge knob of a rock on the hilltop (the name, created by a local Basque citizen who was reminded of that part of the animal's anatomy, means "pig's bladder"). When the sun is low in the sky, turning the sandstone town into a golden wonder, and the lights begin to twinkle, Zacatecas seems magical. Watch the time, though, as the teleférico (☎ 492/2-5694 or 2-6013) operates only from 12:30 to 7:30pm, and if it's windy it's not open at all. The cost for a ride is $2 one way or $3 round trip; you can hike up either hill and walk down the other if you wish. Before making that long climb, look to see if the cars are running; they may be in repair or out of service because of winds. A glance will tell you.

Up on Cerro de la Bufa, beside the Museo de la Toma Zacatecas (see below) is the beautiful church **La Capilla de la Virgen del Patrocinio,** patron of Zacatecas. At the very top of the hill is an observatory used for meteorological purposes. Around the far side of the hill is the Mausoleo de los Hombres Ilustres de Zacatecas, where many of the city's important revolutionary fighters still keep watch over their town below.

Churches

Many of Zacateca's churches are notable. **San Agustín** underwent construction in 1613, but its dedication had to wait until 1782. It has been a Catholic church, then a Protestant church (sadly stripped of its elaborate architectural ornamentation), a casino, a hotel, and tenement housing. Today it's an enormous, beautiful shell used for art exhibitions, conferences, and storage and display of pieces of its past glory. The state's **natural history museum** is also housed here. Note the mosaics of carved-stone chunks crammed into the archways and other niches. These pieces formerly decorated the church's ramparts, but now no one knows quite where. Other parts of the interior contain stonework that reveals how beautiful the exterior must have been. The church is five blocks south of the cathedral; walk past the Hotel Posada de la Moneda and turn right on the next street. The church is open Monday through Saturday from 10am to 2pm and 4 to 7pm, and on Sunday from 10am to 5pm. There's no admission.

To the right of the Museo Pedro Coronel is the **temple of Santo Domingo,** completed in 1749, with its characteristic pink-stone facade. It was built by the

Zacatecas

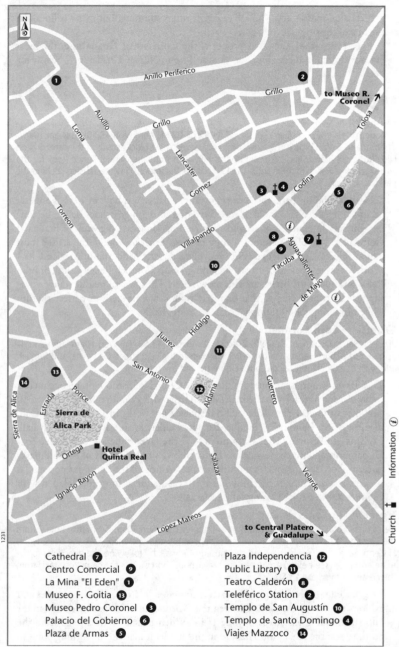

Cathedral ⑦
Centro Comercial ⑨
La Mina "El Eden" ①
Museo F. Goitia ⑬
Museo Pedro Coronel ③
Palacio del Gobierno ⑥
Plaza de Armas ⑤

Plaza Independencia ⑫
Public Library ⑪
Teatro Calderón ⑧
Teleférico Station ②
Templo de San Augustín ⑩
Templo de Santo Domingo ④
Viajes Mazzoco ⑭

Information ⓘ

Church ✝ ■

Jesuits; after their expulsion, the Dominicans assumed responsibility and have taken care of it until today. Inside are stunning gilded altarpieces. During a surge of modernization, the baroque main altarpiece (retable), was replaced with the neo-classical masterpiece you see today. It too is stunning, but many still mourn the loss of the original.

Four miles from Zacatecas proper is the **Convent of Guadalupe,** the most famous church in the region. See "A Side Trip to Nearby Guadalupe," below, for details.

Museums

✪ Museo F. Goitia

Enrique Estrada 102, Col. Sierra de Alica. ☎ **492/2-0211.** Admission $3.50. Tues–Sat 10am–1:30pm and 5–7:30pm; Sun 10am–4pm. Walk seven short blocks south of the cathedral on Hidalgo, cross Juárez, and continue up the hill. Turn right on Manuel Ponce (look for the aqueduct) and walk two more short blocks. Look for the imposing white "palace" behind the park.

Located behind the park, this former governor's palace was built in 1945. Formerly occupied by three governors, it was converted into a high school before becoming this very fine museum. Second-floor exhibits showcase the work of Francisco Goitia (1882–1960), including a copy of *Tata Jesucristo,* one of the artist's most famous pieces. (The original is in the Museo de Arte Moderno in Mexico City.) Works of other Zacatecan artists, including Pedro Coronel, Rafael Coronel, Julio Relas, and José Kuri Breña, are also shown here. The graceful marble stairway was supposedly constructed so that one may walk down its steps in perfect rhythm while humming the "Triumphal March" from *Aïda.*

✪ Museo Pedro Coronel

Plaza de Santo Domingo. ☎ **492/2-8021.** Admission $3.50. Fri–Wed 10am–2pm and 4–7pm. Closed Thurs. Facing the cathedral, walk left to the next street, De Veyna, and turn left and walk one block to Plaza de Santo Domingo and the museum.

This downtown museum, next to the ornate Church of Santo Domingo, contains exhibits from Africa, India, China, Tibet, Thailand, Egypt (even a mummy case!), and ancient Greece and Rome. Also displayed are works of such artists as Dalí, Picasso, Miró, Kandinsky, Braque, Roualt, Calder, Motherwell, Segal, Chagall, Coronel, and others. Especially notable is the large collection of native pre-Hispanic art and masks downstairs, matched by a similar display of African masks directly above it. Coronel's sculptures are placed around the first-floor portals. To the left as you enter is the Biblioteca Elias Amador, a long room laden with volumes devoted to the history of Zacatecas.

Museo de la Toma de Zacatecas

Cerro de la Bufa. ☎ **492/2-8066.** Admission free. Tues–Sun 10am–5pm. Bus: Ruta 7 from the Plaza de la Independencia to the Motel del Bosque and teleférico. Take the teleférico to El Cerro de la Bufa (see above) and the museum or walk by following the directions to the mine entrance (see below) and weaving a few more short streets to the hilltop; taxis from the center of town are $3.50.

The Museum of the Taking of Zacatecas, founded in 1984, displays pictures and exhibits explaining the battle between the *Federales* and the *Revolucionarios* in the hills surrounding Zacatecas in June 1914. When Pancho Villa arrived from the north to seal the fate of the *Federales* in this battle, it marked the turning point in the victory of the Revolution.

La Mina "El Eden"

Cerro Grillo. ☎ **492/2-3002.** Admission $3.50 (includes train and tour). Daily noon–7pm. One entrance is near the teleférico exit and the Motel del Bosque. For the train and tour, take the other entrance a few blocks up Avenida Juárez (which becomes Avenida Torreón). From the cathedral walk down Hidalgo to Juárez (four blocks), turn right on Juárez (which becomes Torreón), and walk about three blocks, passing the long, narrow Alameda (park) and the red Seguro Social building. Turn right at the next street, Dovali Jaime, which leads straight to the mine entrance.

Opened in 1586, this mine was carved by hand by the indigenous population, which was forced into slavery by the Spanish. The Indians (mainly Caxcanes) began working in the mine at the age of 10 or 12 and lived to about 36 years of age. Accidents, tuberculosis, or silicosis caused their early deaths. The mine was extremely rich, yielding gold, copper, zinc, iron, and lead in addition to silver, but it was closed after only 60 years when an attempt to use explosives resulted in an inundation of water in the lower levels. Be sure to take the 40-minute mine tour, beginning with a short ride on the small train 1,720 feet into the mine. A Spanish-speaking guide takes tourists to interesting points in the mine, which is dramatically lit. Visitors can view the special miners' altar by crossing a shaky (but short) suspension bridge over a deep, dark, water-filled crevasse. The tour is worth the time even for those who don't speak Spanish.

✪ Rafael Coronel Museum

Calle Chevano, between Juan de Tolosa and Vergel Nuevo. ☎ **492/2-5661.** Admission $3.50. Thurs–Tues 10am–2pm and 4–7pm. Bus: Ruta 5, 8, or 10. Facing the cathedral, walk left up Hidalgo to the Founder's Fountain (about two blocks), then take the left fork (Calle Abasolo) two more short blocks; at the large yellow-ocher building and traffic triangle, take the right fork. You'll spot the large, old temple ahead.

First stroll through the gorgeous tranquil gardens and ruins of the former Convento de San Francisco, filled with trailing blossoms and verdant foliage and framed by ancient arches and the blue sky. A small wing contains Coronel's drawings on paper.

Once you step inside the mask museum, you'll be dazzled by the sheer number of fantastic masks—4,500 of them—from all over Mexico; they're so exotic they look as if they could be from all over the world. There are entire walls filled with bizarre demons with curling three-foot-long horns and noses; red devils; animals and unidentifiable creatures spitting snakes, pigs, or rats; conquistadores—anything the mind can conjure up. The masks, both antique and contemporary, are festooned with all manner of materials from human hair and animal fur, fabric, plant fibers, and bones to metal screening, steel wool, sequins, plastic, and glitter.

An amazing marionette museum is a great place to bring children. There are entire dioramas showing a bullfight, battling armies, and even a vision of hell. These marionettes are some of the hundreds created during the last century by the famous Rosete-Aranda family of Huamantla, Tlaxcala, where there is also a puppet museum. This superb collection was donated by Rafael Coronel, younger brother of Pedro Coronel, whose work is found in the Museo Pedro Coronel and the Museo Goitia (both in Zacatecas).

Also in the museum, to the left after you enter, is the Ruth Rivera room, where some of Diego Rivera's drawings are on display. Ruth Rivera is the daughter of Diego Rivera and the wife of Rafael Coronel. The museum also has a delightful ground-floor cafe for coffee and pastries and a small gift shop.

A SIDE TRIP TO NEARBY GUADALUPE

The most famous religious edifice in the region, aside from the cathedral, is the Convento de Guadalupe, in Guadalupe, about four miles east of Zacatecas on Highways 45/49. Transportes de Guadalupe buses go to Guadalupe from the

Central Camionera in Zacatecas, or there's a Ruta 13 bus to Guadalupe at López Mateos and Salazar just up from the Hotel Gallery. The bus stops a block from the convent. It leaves about every 15 minutes or so and costs 50¢ for the 20-minute ride. A taxi to Guadalupe will run about $8. If you're driving, look for a red-brick church and steeple and turn right just past it onto Calle Independencia.

✪ Convento de Guadalupe

Calle Independencia, Guadalupe. Museum $5. Tues–Sun 10am–4:30pm.

Dating from 1707, the convent now houses the **Museo de Arte Virreinal de Guadalupe** (☎ 3-2089 or 3-2386). As you enter through a small park/courtyard with stone mosaics, look up at the different domes and doorways of the convent. The museum building is to your right. Inside the convent proper, every wall seems to be covered by paintings; one series of huge paintings describes the life of St. Francis of Assisi on the ground floor and the life of Christ on the floor above.

Remember while touring these holy grounds that they were reserved for men of the cloth; the public was not meant to see the grounds, the paintings, or the sumptuous "cells" where the Franciscan monks spent their spare time. You may catch a glimpse of the brown-robed monks through a slatted wooden door; today part of the building is still in use as a college of instruction in the Franciscan order. The third Franciscan monastery established in the New World, the convent educated missionaries and sent them northward into what is now northern Mexico and the southwestern United States as part of the cultural conquest by the Spaniards. The Dominican order, also important in the Conquest, appears in the artwork of the convent as well, but the brown-robed Franciscans are the more familiar figures. The three knots of their sashes signify their vows of obedience, penitence, and poverty—the occasional fourth knot signifies the additional vow of silence.

The chapel to the left of the main building (as you face the convent from the front court/park) is called the **Capilla de Napoles.** It must have taken a king's ransom in gold to decorate it, with gold ranging in quality from 6 karat on the lower walls up to 22 karat in the dome above. Guides are available for a tour or to open the chapel, which is visible from either the organ loft or the ground floor—be sure to tip the guide for opening the doors and turning on the lights.

✪ Centro Platero de Zacatecas

Ex-Hacienda de Bernardez, Guadalupe. ☎ **2-1007.** Admission free. Mon–Fri 10am–6pm, Sat 10am–2pm.

Since Zacatecas ranks first in Mexico in the production of silver and fourth in gold, it seems only fitting that the art of metalworking is being reborn here. Young silversmiths are learning the trade in an old hacienda that once belonged to the counts of Laguna, located in the Fraccionamiento Lomas near the golf course. The students are trained not only in the art of jewelry making, but also in business so that they'll be capable of opening their own stores. An association of mining engineers and other local groups support the school and students. Most of the unusual jewelry designs are taken from the balconies and other architectural ironwork in Zacatecas; after you've seen them, you'll view Zacatecas's buildings with new eyes. The jewelry is sold at the school, and there's an equally large selection at the Centro Commercial "El Mercado," next to the cathedral in central Zacatecas. The school is about a mile north of the highway, zigzagging past newly constructed upscale homes on streets that don't yet have name signs. You'll be glad you took a cab, which costs about $6 from Guadalupe.

Museo Regional de la Historia

Jardín Juárez, Guadalupe. ☎ **3-2386** or 3-2089. Admission free. Tues–Sun 10am–4:30pm.

This museum is in Guadalupe to right side of the convent. It contains fine examples of carriages and antique cars which were collected from all over Mexico and which formerly belonged to ex-presidents and famous historical figures. Representative forms of transporation from pre-Hispanic times to the present are particularly interesting.

ORGANIZED TOURS

Cantera Tours (☎ 2-9065; fax 2-9121), which has an office located a block south of the cathedral at the far end of the Centro Comercial "El Mercado" on Avenida Hidalgo, has an excellent guided tour that covers Zacatecas, Guadalupe, and the surrounding region (the Convento de Guadalupe, Cerro de la Bufa, the teleférico, and so on). Another five-hour guided tour covers the nearby town of Jerez and the ruins of Chicomostoc (the Zona Arqueológica La Quemada) and is the only way to get directly to Chicomostoc unless you have a car. Prices for these two tours are $17 and $20 per person and require a minimum of two and five people, respectively. The office is open Monday through Saturday from 9am to 2pm and 4 to 7pm.

For a group of ten people or more, Cantera Tours also sponsors the **Calle-joneada Zacatecana,** a traditional walk through the city's *callejones* (the little curv-ing alleys, byways, and plazas) accompanied by music and dancing, on Saturdays beginning around 9pm (8pm in cold weather). Be sure to ask if there will be one while you're in town. Or, if you want a free tour, just join a group as it marches through the streets—they're hard to miss with the drums and horns and a flower-bedecked burro laden with barrels of mescal.

ACCOMMODATIONS
EXPENSIVE

Hotel Quinta Real

Av. Rayón 434, Zacatecas, Zac. 98000. ☎ **492/2-9104** or 91-800/3-6015 in Mexico. 49 suites. Free guarded parking. $140 double master suite; $155 double suite with whirlpool.

I can't think of a more imaginative use of space in Mexico than this gorgeous hotel, built into a former bullfighting ring. Constructed almost directly under Zacateca's ancient aqueduct, the guestrooms and restaurant are handsomely incorporated into the more-than-a-century-old stone bullfighting ring, but half of the stepped edifice remains just as it was when crowds cheered *olé!* Each of the beautifully furnished rooms faces the ring's interior and comes furnished with an armoire concealing the TV, a Queen Anne writing desk, and a couch. Many rooms have balconies overlooking the verdant *plaza de toros.* From the cathedral, walk south on Hidalgo up the hill to the aqueduct, just past where Hidalgo meets Ponce; you'll see the hotel on the left.

Dining/Entertainment: An outdoor restaurant with umbrella-shaded tables uses part of the bleacher section of the old bullfighting ring. The formal indoor restau-rant is plush and sophisticated (see "Dining," below). A bar on the lower level occupies the former bull shoots, and graffiti from this era remains on the rock walls.

Services: Laundry and room service, boutiques, valet parking, tour desk.

Facilities: Whirlpool baths in several rooms.

Mesón de Jobito

Jardín Juárez 143, Zacatecas, Zac. 98000. ☎ and fax **492/4-1722.** 31 suites. MINIBAR TV TEL. $85 standard double; $100–$130 double suite. Parking on street.

A new hotel in a historic edifice, the two-story (no elevator) Mesón de Jobito easily competes in quality with the Paraíso Radisson, but it's more intimate. White-gloved bell boys greet you at the door, and you can check in while comfortably seated. The carpeted rooms are large and nicely furnished with queen or king-size beds, large bathrooms, and in-room safes. Rooms are heated—an important comfort in cold Zacatecas. Like several other old Mexican buildings that have been renovated into beautiful hotels, this one was once a stable and "hotel" for mule drivers and later a tenement apartment building. The hotel is only about four blocks from the cathedral; look for the signs leading to it from the traffic light by the cathedral.

Dining/Entertainment: The elegant Restaurante El Mesonero serves international cuisine at all three meals; there's soft music performed live in the evenings. An adjacent bar is open from 1pm to midnight.

Services: Laundry and room service, concierge, boutique, valet parking, secretarial and fax service.

Facilities: Whirlpool baths in several rooms.

✪ Paraíso Radisson

Av. Hidalgo 703, Col. Centro, Zacatecas, Zac. 98000. ☎ **492/2-6183,** or 800/333-3333 in the U.S. Fax 492/2-6245. 115 rms (all with bath). A/C TV TEL. $75 double. Free parking.

In the heart of historic, beautiful Zacatecas opposite the cathedral, this hotel opened its doors in 1989 behind the facade of a former colonial-era building that most recently housed the Hotel Reina Cristina. The lobby holds a popular bar and good restaurant. The spacious, heated rooms on six floors are fashionably decorated. Rooms facing the plaza have a ringside seat on Zacatecas; from here you can see the mountains; the central plaza; the cathedral; and those exuberant and loud *callejoneadas* that end here anywhere between 11pm and 1 or 2am. Other rooms, facing the interior courtyard, are quieter. All rooms come equipped with TVs broadcasting four U.S. channels; some have king-size beds, and others have two double beds.

INEXPENSIVE

✪ Hotel Colón

López Velarde 508, Zacatecas, Zac. 98000. ☎ **492/2-0464** or 2-8925. Fax 492/2-0464. 37 rms (all with bath). TEL TV. $17 double. Parking on street.

This hotel is basic but well maintained and clean. The beds are good, and the floors are made of terrazzo. It can be noisy, as the hotel sits between two busy streets— López Mateos and Ramón López Velarde. It's a three-story hotel; you enter on the middle level, and there's a floor above and one below. Basement rooms are dark. To reach this hotel, face the cathedral and then walk/wind to the right around to Calle Tacuba. Bearing continuously left, the street first becomes Guerrero, then Ramón López Velarde as you go down the hill; it's a total of about five or six blocks to the hotel.

Hotel del Parque

Paseo González Ortega 302, Zacatecas, Zac. 98000. ☎ **492/2-0479.** 26 rms (all with bath). TV. $12 double.

This budget hotel is Spartan but clean and quiet. It's drafty and cold in winter. The hot water is not so hot sometimes; it goes out altogether in the evening once in a while, but the price is definitely a plus. To find the hotel, walk seven short blocks south of the cathedral on Hidalgo, cross Juárez, and continue up the hill; turn right onto Manuel Ponce (look for the aqueduct) and walk two more short blocks to Sierra de Alica Park; the hotel is a few doors up the hill from the park.

DINING

Between the Plaza de la Independencia and López Mateos runs **Calle Ventura Salazar,** which is lined with taco shops, snack shops, and hole-in-the-wall eateries just fine for a quick bite at ridiculously low prices. The food market is on the north side of the Plaza de la Independencia bounded on the left side of the market by the Callejon del Traffico, a narrow walkway to the left of the market entrance.

EXPENSIVE

✪ La Cuija

Tacuba T-5, Centro Comercial "El Mercado." ☎ **492/2-8275.** Main courses $4–$12. Daily 2pm–midnight. MEXICAN.

When you see LA CUIJA etched into the entry-door glass and the stylishly dressed tables, you'll know that this place is worth a splurge. Appetizers are referred to as "something to open the mouth," and the quesadillas de flor de calabaza are especially good reasons to open up. The succulent lomo zacatecano—broiled pork with a delicate red-chile sauce—is a favorite dish. The pastas are fresh-tasting and an interesting change from Mexican fare. In the evenings, there's often live music.

✪ Hotel Quinta Real

Av. Rayón 434. ☎ **492/2-9104.** Breakfast $5–$8; main courses $8–$14. Daily 7am–11pm. REGIONAL/INTERNATIONAL.

White linen tablecloths, chairs covered with pastel tapestry, high-beamed ceilings, and plants everywhere create an elegant but comfortable ambience at this restaurant. The wraparound dining room faces the center of the former bullring from which this hotel was created. Diners can gaze out at the twinkling lights in the courtyard's potted trees and the illuminated aqueduct which gracefully arches high above. An inventive menu features all sorts of dishes, including red snapper au poblana with poblano peppers on top and chicken breast covered with coconut paste. For dessert, try cajeta (goat's milk candy) crêpes, crêpes Suzette, or chocolate mousse. Even if you don't eat here, drop by for a drink or canapés just to enjoy the unusual setting. To get here, walk seven short blocks south of the cathedral on Hidalgo, cross Juárez, and continue to Manuel Ponce; the hotel is under the aqueduct on the left.

INEXPENSIVE

✪ Café Nevería Acrópolis

Av. Hidalgo and Plazuela Candelario Huzar. ☎ **492/2-1284.** Breakfast $3.50–$4; antojitos $1.80–$5.50; cakes $1.50–$2.50; sandwiches $1.50–$2.50; coffee $1–$3. Daily 8:30am–10pm. MEXICAN/SNACKS.

During the day this is a soda fountain, sweetshop, and ice-cream parlor; it turns into a hip coffeehouse in the evening. Along the wall are photos and signatures of famous people, including Gregory Peck and Jane Fonda, who stayed in Zacatecas for the filming of *The Old Gringo*. This cafe is a great place for a late-afternoon sight-seeing break with tea or coffee and a slab of heavily iced cake, although service can be slow. The cafe is just across the little street to the right of the cathedral.

○ La Cantera Musical Fonda y Bar

Tacuba 2. Centro Comercial "El Mercado." ☎ **492/2-8828.** Breakfast $1.50–$2.50; lunch $2.50–$6; dinner $3–$7. Daily 8am–11pm. MEXICAN/REGIONAL.

Locals consider La Cantera one of the best Zacatecan-style restaurants in town. Against the background of Mexican music, Mexican art, handcrafted tiles, and an arched brick ceiling, colorfully dressed women press and fry masa into tortillas. The flavorful pozole rojo is loaded with chunks of pork and hominy; other dishes are equally filling. The restaurant is below the Mercado González Ortega by the cathedral in the central city.

ZACATECAS AFTER DARK

El Elefante Blanco

Paseo Díaz Ordaz, next to the teleférico station. ☎ **492/2-7104.** Cover $8.

This unusual dance club, whose name means the "White Elephant," is perched on the mountaintop with the Motel del Bosque, right behind the teleférico departure point. The side facing the city is almost round; the floor-to-ceiling windows make for a magnificent panoramic view. The club features a big video section. You might want to call for a reservation, since this is a very popular spot. It's open Thursday through Saturday from 9pm to 2am and Sunday from 6 to 11pm.

El Malacate

Mina El Eden. ☎ **2-3002.** Cover $12.

Have you ever been to a disco located in a silver mine 1,050 feet underground? Call in advance to reserve a table since it's a very popular place. The entrance is at the end of Calle Dovale Jaime, which is the street just past the Seguro Social building on Avenida Torreón. The club is open Thursday through Sunday from 9:30pm to 2am.

AN EXCURSION FROM ZACATECAS

CHICOMOSTOC: 12TH-CENTURY RUINS　About 34 miles south of Zacatecas (about 1¼ miles off Highway 54 en route to Guadalajara), is the **Zona Arqueológica La Quemada,** an archaeological site developed by the 12th-century Nahuatlacas tribe. The pyramids here vaguely resemble those at Mitla and Monte Albán much farther south. The largest pyramid, called the **Temple,** has been restored and offers visitors their first glimpse into this fascinating aspect of Mexico's past. The rest of the site is not very well preserved, but the 11 pillars of granite give you an idea of the size of the grandiose palace that once stood here. Stone-paved avenues and terraces crowded with foundations of houses mark the **Ciudadela,** which is topped by an observatory from which the Nahuatlacas studied the movements of stars and planets and maybe even tracked the course of early extraterrestrial visitors. You can visit the ruins Tuesday through Sunday from 10am to 5pm. Admission is $2.50, free on Sunday.

If you don't have a car, getting to Chicomostoc may present a challenge, since the public bus lets you out only on the highway, leaving you with a walk of a little over a mile to reach the ruins. If you're vigorous, you can make the walk with no trouble. Alternatively, you can take a guided tour through Cantera Tours (see "Organized Tours" in Zacatecas, above).

4 San Luis Potosí

261 miles NW of Mexico City, 216 miles NE of Guadalajara

San Luis Potosí, set more than a mile high in central Mexico's high-plains region, is among the most picturesque and prosperous mining cities of Mexico, and once you visit this bustling city of half a million, you'll see why. It has rich colonial architecture accented by the city's long, momentous history. Capital of the state of the same name, San Luis Potosí was named for Louis, saintly king of France, and "Potosí," the Quechua word for "richness," borrowed from the incredibly rich Potosí mines of Bolivia, which San Luis's mines were thought to rival. San Luis was formally founded in 1583 by Spaniard Fray Magdalena and Captain Caldera on the site of the Chichimec town of Tanga-Manga; the indigenous people had been living on this spot for three centuries before the Spaniards arrived.

The Spaniards came in search of silver and found it, mostly at a small town called San Pedro, 25 miles from San Luis Potosí. But San Luis's mineral springs made it a better place to settle than San Pedro, so this became the mining center. As a state capital, San Luis Potosí exudes prosperity and sophistication, much the way Morelia does. You'll note shady plazas, brick-paved streets, and stunning colonial architecture.

Along with the prospectors came the friars in search of converts: The Franciscans were the first, followed by the Jesuits and the Carmelites. San Luis owes much of its architectural heritage to the vigor—and lavish expenditure—of these groups.

Later, during the Mexican Revolution, the "Plan of San Luis" was proclaimed here. The city has in fact twice been the capital of Mexico—in 1863 and 1867—when Benito Juárez led the fight against European intervention, governing the country from the Palacio de Gobierno (on Plaza de Armas). From this palace he pronounced the death sentence on Maximilian and his two generals.

Today San Luis Potosí lives on industry rather than silver. Everything from automobiles to mezcal is produced in the factories ringing the city, but fortunately the colonial center has been preserved intact.

GETTING THERE & DEPARTING   By Plane   Mexicana (☎ 17-8920 or 17-9020) flies to/from Mexico City daily, as well as Chicago, San Antonio, Monterrey, and Morelia. **Aerolitoral** (☎ 22-2229) flies between Monterrey and Guadalajara. For return transportation to the airport, call **AeroTaxi** (☎ 11-0165 or 11-0167). One way, the fare will be around $12.

By Bus   There are two bus stations here; the large Central Camionera, on the outskirts of town, has the most departures. The old station in town has buses running the 3½ hour route between San Luis Potosí and San Miguel de Allende.

City buses marked "Central" go to the bus station from the Alameda park opposite the train station for around 25¢. The bus station is divided between first- and second-class buses. First-class buses are at the end beyond the restaurant. The **Flecha Amarilla** group has hourly buses to León and Querétaro, 16 buses a day to Mexico City and Morelia, 8 to Guanajuato, 4 to Pátzcuaro. **Estrella Blanca** has direct service to Zacatecas six times a day. **ETN** offers frequent premier service to Querétaro, Mexico City, and Guadalajara. **Del Norte** buses go to Queretaro and

Guadalajara. **Primera Plus** buses go frequently to Morelia, Queretaro, León, and Mexico City. The **Tamaulipas Primera** line goes to Matehuala. **Elite** buses go to Guadalajara, and **Oriente** buses go to León, Guadalajara, Lagos de Moreno, and Querétaro. **Futura** buses run often to Saltillo, Querétaro, and Mexico City. It's an easy 8-hour bus ride from Monterrey or Saltillo and only 3 hours from Zacatecas or Aguascalientes.

By Car   From Mexico City, take Highway 57; from Guadalajara, take Highway 80. There's dramatic scenery on the second half of the trip between Aguascalientes and San Luis Potosí—hair-raising hills and scenic "pueblitos." If you're coming from the north, it takes between 6 and 7 hours to drive the 335 miles from Monterrey to San Luis Potosí.

ORIENTATION   Arriving   The **airport** is about 7 miles from downtown. A taxi to the city center is expensive, but the cost can be shared. A colectivo van is more economical, though don't tarry in the terminal since they leave quickly.

The city's **Central Camionera** (bus station), on Guadalupe Torres at Diagonal Sur, is about 2 miles from the center of town on Highway 57 next to the Motel Potosí. To find city buses to town (50¢) go out the front entrance of the station, turn left, and walk two blocks to the corner of Dolores Jimenez y Muro. There you'll find buses to "Alameda Centro" (the Alameda is a huge park). Get off at the second Alameda stop, which will put you across from the train station. Cabs from the bus station to town cost $3.50 to $4, depending on your bargaining ability.

Information   The **State Tourism Office** is at Carranza 325 (☎ 48/12-9939 or 12-9943; fax 48/12-6769). This is one of the better tourism offices in Mexico, with a helpful staff, excellent maps, and descriptive literature. It's open Monday through Saturday from 9am to 8pm. To find it, from the Jardín Hidalgo walk three blocks west on Carranza. The office is on the south (left) side of the street.

City Layout   The **Jardín Hidalgo** is the historic city center, bounded on all sides by colonial-era buildings and narrow one-way streets—Carranza/Los Bravo, Madero/Othón, Allende/5 de Mayo, and Hidalgo/Zaragoza. It's a delightfully walkable city; most of the museums, restaurants, and hotels are downtown and close to the jardín. Many of the city's historic structures now house museums and restaurants.

FAST FACTS: SAN LUIS POTOSÍ

American Express   The local representative is Grandes Viajes, Av. Carranza 1077 (☎ 48/17-6004; fax 48/11-1166).

Area Code   The telephone area code is 48.

Banks   Banamex, one block off the main plaza (Jardín Hidalgo) to the left of the cathedral, will change traveler's checks or money Monday through Friday from 9am to 1pm.

Climate   It's warm and pleasant year-round here—the average annual temperature is 67°F. Rain is rare, with an average rainfall of 14 inches; the rainy season is from April through November, and the coolest weather is between November and March.

EXPLORING SAN LUIS POTOSÍ
A STROLL AROUND THE HISTORIC CENTER

The center of town is the **Jardín Hidalgo,** a large plaza dating from the mid-1700s and shaded by magnolia and flamboyan trees; before that it was a bullring. After

San Luis Potosí

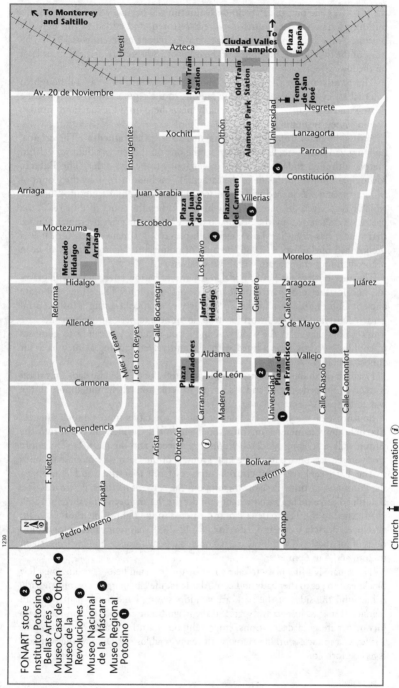

To Monterrey and Saltillo

To Ciudad Valles and Tampico

Plaza España

Uresti

Azteca

New Train Station

Old Train Station

Alameda Park Station

Templo de San José

Av. 20 de Noviembre

Negrete

Lanzagorta

Xochitl

Othón

Universidad

Parrodi

Insurgentes

Constitución

Arriaga

Juan Sarabia

Plazuela del Carmen

Villerias

Moctezuma

Escobedo

Plaza San Juan de Dios

❺

Plaza Arriaga

Los Bravo

❹

Mercado Hidalgo

Morelos

Hidalgo

Calle Bocanegra

Iturbide

Zaragoza

Galeana

Juárez

Reforma

Jardín Hidalgo

Guerrero

Allende

Mier y Teran

5 de Mayo

❸

Aldama

Plaza Fundadores

J. de León

Plaza de San Francisco

Vallejo

Carmona

J. de Los Reyes

Carranza

Madero

❷

Universidad

Calle Abasolo

Calle Comonfort

Independencia

❶

F. Nieto

Arista

Obregón

Bolívar

Zapata

Reforma

Pedro Moreno

Ocampo

FONART store ❷
Instituto Potosino de
  Bellas Artes ❻
Museo Casa de Othón ❹
Museo de la
  Revoluciones ❸
Museo Nacional
  de la Máscara ❺
Museo Regional
  Potosino ❶

Church ✝ ■   Information ⓘ

the plaza was laid out, the **Palacio de Gobierno** was begun. What you see of this building today has been much repaired, restored, and added to through the centuries—the back and the south facade were redone as recently as 1973. The front of the building retains much of the original 18th-century decoration, at least on the lower floors.

The **bandstand** in the center of the plaza was built in 1947 (although in colonial style), using the pink stone famous to the region. You'll see the stone throughout San Luis. The band usually plays here on Thursday and Sunday evenings, free, beginning around 7:30 or 8pm.

Across the plaza from the Government Palace is the **cathedral.** The original building had only a single bell tower, so the one on the left was built in 1910 to match, although today the newer tower looks to be the older. The **Palacio Municipal,** on the north side of the cathedral, was built in 1850 by the Count of Monterrey and was loaded with great wealth—paintings and sculpture—little of which has survived the plaza's stormy history. When the count died in 1890, the palace was taken over by the bishop, and in 1921 by the city government. Since that year it has been San Luis's city hall, peaceful for many years until it was firebombed on January 1, 1986, because of political differences. It has all been restored and functions again with business as usual.

The area south of the Jardín Hidalgo is a grid of narrow streets lined with graceful, and for the most part unmodernized, old mansions. These low, elaborate ancient homes are built in the Spanish style, each containing a lush central garden courtyard. It's well worth a stroll down here to peek through the delicate iron traceries that cover the windows, and if you're lucky you can catch glimpses of cool, aristocratic rooms lined with gilt and velvet, looking as they have for almost a century.

Heading north out of the Jardín Hidalgo, stroll along Calle Hidalgo. This street is reserved for pedestrians, and it's a treat to walk from the jardín almost all the way to the city's Central Market.

Southeast of the Jardín Hidalgo is one of the city's most famous squares, **Plazuela del Carmen,** named for the Templo del Carmen church. From the jardín, walk east along Madero-Othón to Escobedo and the plazuela. The entire area you see was once part of the lush grounds of the Carmelite monastery, built in the 17th century. The church survives from that time and is perhaps the Potosinos' favorite place of worship, but the convent has been destroyed. The beautiful **Teatro de la Paz** now stands on the site, having been built there in 1889.

Attached to the Teatro de la Paz and entered to the right of the theater's main entrance, the **Sala German Gedovius** (☎ 12-2698) has four galleries for exhibitions of international and local art. It's open Tuesday through Sunday from 10am to 2pm and 4 to 6pm.

The square is a fine place to take a rest by the fountain before heading on a few blocks east to get to the shady and cool **Alameda,** the city's largest downtown park. All around the sides of the park are vendors selling handcrafts, fruits, and all manner of snacks. Just across Negrete is the magnificent **Templo de San José,** with lots of ornate gold decorations; huge religious paintings; and *El Señor de los Trabajos,* a miracle-working statue with many retablos testifying to the wonders it has performed.

Plazas

San Luis Potosí has many more plazas than the two most famous ones mentioned above. **Plaza de San Francisco** (also called **Plaza de Guerrero**) is south of the Palacio de Gobierno along Aldama, between Guerrero and Galeana. This shady square—lush with ivy, iris, vine-covered trees, and royal palms—takes its name from the huge monastery of the Franciscan order at the south side of the plaza. The church on the west side, the Church of San Francisco, is dated 1799 and is really worth visiting. It boasts beautiful stained-glass scenes all around the dome; a carved, pink-stone altar; a radiant statue of the Virgin surrounded by angels and golden rays; other lovely statues and paintings; and a spectacular crystal chandelier, shaped like a sailing ship, hanging from the center of the dome.

Another square with a church to visit is **Plaza de los Fundadores,** at the intersection of Obregón and Aldama (northwest of the Jardín Hidalgo). Take a peek through the baroque doorway of the Loreto Chapel, dating from the 16th century, and the neighboring headquarters of the Compañia de Jesús—the Jesuit order. In the chapel is a magnificent golden sunburst over the altar, a reminder of past glories.

It's a ways from downtown, but if you have transportation you might be interested in a visit to **Parque Tangamanga** (☎ 17-6217), one of the largest parks in Mexico, located on Diagonal Sur at the intersection of Tata Nacho. It covers acres and acres, with three lakes; a Hollywood Bowl–type outdoor theater; a planetarium and observatory; a library; a museum; a children's playground; every kind of sports field you can think of; and many picnic sites set up with barbecue pits, tables, and benches, with slatted shelters for shade. The park is open daily from 6am to 6pm (admission free).

Museums

✪ Museo Regional de Arte Popular

Ex-Hacienda de Teneria in Parque Tangamanga. ☎ **17-2926.** Admission free. Tues–Sun 9am–4pm. Bus: Ruta 32 from behind the Del Carmen church.

Near the center of this large and well-kept urban park is the new home of this small gem of a museum housed in a 19th-century hacienda. Previously it was located on the Plaza de San Francisco where FONART, the government crafts store, is now. The exhibits of Potosino crafts are stunning: ceramics, inlaid wood, papier-mâché "sculptures," basketry, musical instruments, masks, lacy altars made of wax, and local designs in weaving and rebozos. After the bus lets you off at the park entrance, it's a long walk to the museum, and roads are poorly marked; I suggest a taxi.

✪ Casa de la Cultura

Av. V. Carranza 1815. ☎ **13-2247.** Admission free. Tues–Fri 10am–2pm and 4–6pm, Sat 10am–2pm and 6–8pm. Transportation: Take a cab or any of the city buses running west on Carranza.

Somewhat removed from the city center, this museum is housed in a splendid neoclassical building constructed at the turn of this century, surrounded by large landscaped gardens. There are works of art, historical pieces, handcrafts, and a collection of archaeological items. Adjoining is the Center of Historical and Geographical Studies. All kinds of national and international cultural events are held here.

✪ Museo Nacional de la Máscara (National Mask Museum)

Villerias 2. ☎ **12-3025.** Admission free. Tues–Fri 10am–2pm and 4–6pm, Sat–Sun 10am–2pm; tours in Spanish are available. From the Jardín Hidalgo (Plaza de Armas), walk east along Madero-Othón to Escobedo and the Plazuela del Carmen. The museum is south, just off the plaza.

Just across from the Teatro de la Paz, the National Mask Museum is the only museum of its kind on the national level in Mexico. It's loaded with regional dance masks from all over the country and is a must-see. In addition to its permanent and temporary exhibits, it offers lectures and workshops on mask making, theater, painting, movies, and history, and it hosts a national mask contest at Carnaval (Mardi Gras) time.

SHOPPING

The best one-stop shopping here is at the ✪ FONART store (☎ 12-7521) on the Plaza de San Francisco. The building was originally part of the Convent of San Francisco, founded in 1590. Today it houses the offices of the Casa de la Cultura, and, on the ground floor, a branch of FONART, the government-operated crafts store. This one is especially well stocked with some of the country's best crafts. It's open Monday through Saturday from 10am to 2pm and 4 to 7pm.

It's several blocks along the pedestrian Calle Hidalgo from the Jardín Hidalgo to the city's **Mercado Hidalgo,** a mammoth building devoted mostly to food but also carrying some baskets, rebozos, and straw furniture. While here, be sure to try some *queso de tuna,* a specialty of the region. Although called a "cheese," it's a sweet paste—something like dried figs or dates with a molasses or burnt-sugar taste—made from the fruit of the prickly-pear cactus. It's delicious and comes in pieces of various sizes, ranging from a taste to a kilo.

But the walk along **Hidalgo** is itself an introduction to the city's commercial life. Hardware stores, craftspeople's shops, shoe stores, groceries, and taverns all crowd the street. Past the Mercado Hidalgo is another big market, the **Mercado República.**

ACCOMMODATIONS

Hotel María Cristina

Juan Sarabia 110, San Luis Potosí, S.L.P. 78000. ☎ **48/12-9408.** Fax 48/12-8823. 75 rms (all with bath). FAN TV TEL. $30 double. Free guarded parking.

This is one of San Luis Potosí's better downtown hotel choices. Furnishings are nondescript but perfectly comfortable, and the carpeted rooms are large. The rooftop pool is a plus after a long drive, and the rooftop restaurant serves a substantial comida corrida. The parking garage is adjacent. You can get here from the Jardín Hidalgo by walking three blocks east on Othón and turning left onto Juan Sarabia; the hotel is on the right, reached by a flight of stairs up to the lobby.

Hotel Plaza

Jardín Hidalgo 22, San Luis Potosí, S.L.P. 78000. ☎ **48/12-4631.** 32 rms (30 with bath). $13–$20 double. Discounts are sometimes available. Free parking (guarded parking for six cars).

If you prefer older buildings with the wistful air of better days, try the small Hotel Plaza, conveniently located on the south side of the Jardín Hidalgo. Rooms are clean, quiet, and old-fashioned with worn bathrooms, old carpets, wallpaper from long ago, chenille bedspreads, and meager furnishings. Higher prices are for rooms that face the plaza. Other rooms face one of two inner courtyards (one covered, the other open) well back from the street. A few rooms have TVs, and there's a TV in the second-floor sitting area.

DINING

Café Florida
Juan Sarabia 230. ☎ **48/12-5669**. Breakfast $1.25–$3; main courses $1.50–$6. Daily 7am–midnight. MEXICAN.

A short walk north of the hotels María Cristina and Principal, and across from the Jardín de San Juan de Díos, this clean and cheerful restaurant offers good value and service in an attractive, color-coordinated setting with stained-glass accents. Besides regional dishes, you can order beer, malts, and desserts—something for everyone, even a separate smoking section. To find it from the Jardín Hidalgo, walk three blocks east on Othón and turn left onto Juan Sarabia; the restaurant is on the right $1^1/_2$ blocks farther.

La Parroquía
Carranza 303. ☎ **48/12-6681**. Breakfast $1.75–$3.25; main courses $3.25–$8; comida corrida $3.50–$5.50. Daily 7am–midnight (comida corrida served 1–4pm). MEXICAN.

At all hours the orange leatherette cafe tables of La Parroquía fill up for conversation, seeing and being seen, and people-watching—the food here is definitely less important than the social life. The menu offers everything from steaks to banana splits. It's two blocks west of the Jardín Hidalgo and across from Plaza Fundadores at the corner of Díaz de León.

✪ Posada del Virrey
Jardín Hidalgo 3. ☎ **48/12-7055**. Breakfast $2–$3; main courses $3.80–$6.25; comida corrida $3.50. Daily 7am–midnight. MEXICAN.

One of the city's most popular restaurants faces the Jardín Hidalgo and is actually three interconnected mansions. It has great atmosphere—a delightful covered courtyard with a bubbling fountain and singing birds—and is the best place to sample local specialties like *enchiladas potosinos* (known elsewhere as empanadas, these come filled with cheese).

5 On the Road from Texas to the Silver Cities

While the easiest way to experience the highlights of colonial Mexico may be to fly into Mexico City or a heartland airport, driving is still the best way to find the real Mexico. Most people who drive into Mexico follow the southward "central route" from Nuevo Laredo at the Texas border through **Monterrey,** a sprawling city that is a gateway to mainland Mexico; **Real de Catorce,** a fascinating ghost town; and on into **San Luis Potosí.** Here are some notes to guide you through the first leg of this journey:

Mexico's third-largest city, **Monterrey** is the first major stop on a southbound drive. Its setting is spectacular, but in reality, it's primarily a commercial and industrial city. The best reason to stop in Monterrey is to see the **Museo de Arte Contemporáneo de Monterrey** (MARCO), Gran Plaza at Zuazua and Ocampo, ☎ 42-4901 or 42-8455.

The touristic heart of the city is centered on both the modern **Gran Plaza** and the adjoining **Zona Rosa,** a pedestrians-only shopping-and-restaurant area between Zaragoza and Morelos. **Avenida Colón** is the main market street.

Since this is one of the three largest cities in Mexico, accommodations are relatively high-priced compared to a provincial town. Your best bets for value are the **Colonial Hotel,** Hidalgo Ote. 475, ☎ 8/343-6791, and **El Paso Autel,** Zaragoza 130 Nte, ☎ 8/340-0690. For meals, check out **La Puntada,** Av. Hidalgo Ote. 123, ☎ 340-6985, which has cheap breakfasts and good Mexican food; **Restaurant Luisiana,** Plaza Hidalgo, ☎ 343-1561, more expensive with lots of beef and seafood dishes; **El Rey del Cabrito,** corner of Dr. Coss and Constitución, ☎ 345-3232, which specializes in roast kid (cabrito), a northern Mexico tradition; or **Sanborn's,** Escobedo 920, ☎ 343-1834, a Mexican chain of variety stores with restaurants that you'll learn to rely on in your Mexican travels.

Taking Highway 40 toward Saltillo, you'll find **Chipinque Mesa** about 13 miles from Monterrey. Turn left at Colonia del Valle, pay a small toll, and drive up the pine-covered slopes of the **Sierra Madre.** The road culminates in a breathtaking view of Monterrey from a 4,200-foot plateau.

Take the bypass around **Saltillo** and barrel on down Highway 57 toward San Luis Potosí. You'll pass through a barren desert of scrubby grass, cactus, and Joshua trees. Fill up your gas tank at every chance.

Matehuala is a tidy town with a good central market and several adequate hotels in town and on the highway. **El Mesquite Restaurant,** on the highway before you enter Matehuala, offers cabrito that's wonderfully flavored, not greasy and not goaty tasting.

There is one fascinating stop along the long, dull road from Saltillo to San Luis Potosí; 140 miles south of Saltillo you'll reach the ghost town of ✪ **Real de Catorce,** one of Mexico's most unusual places—like an 18th-century town preserved in a time capsule and hidden in the mountains. After the discovery of silver in 1773, Real de Catorce became one of Mexico's top three silver-producing towns by the early 1800s, with a population of over 40,000. Streets lined with mansions owned by wealthy mine owners sprouted side by side along with an opera house and a mint. The Mexican Revolution brought the downfall of the town; the mines were flooded, and townspeople fled to safety elsewhere and never returned, although many descendants retain ownership and in recent years a few mines have reopened. Catorce is finally experiencing a renaissance of sorts and many structures are in the process of being restored. The latest population census attributes almost 11,000 people to this town, but locals guess that only around 2,000 people live in the immediate area.

A visit here is a must if you can spare the time. Photographers, historians, lovers of the unusual in Mexico, and people who don't mind uncertainty in their travels will count this among the high points of a trip south of the border. *Important Note:* Fill up with gas in Matehuala—there's no gas in Catorce.

On the northern edge of Matehuala there's a sign on Highway 57 that is the Spanish equivalent of TURN HERE FOR GHOST TOWN. Although it's only 38 miles from the turnoff from Highway 57 to Real de Catorce, it takes 1 to 1 1/2 hours to drive on a well-maintained but teeth-jarring cobblestone road that winds up to 9,000 feet in the mountains, passing an onyx quarry and several tiny, crumbling adobe-walled mining villages. You'll know you've arrived at Catorce when you reach the tunnel, which is 2 miles long and the only entrance into the town. Since it's one way, young men at both ends regulate traffic with walkie-talkies; there's a small fee for this service. Usually there is little traffic, but during past busy festival seasons (October 2) stalled cars and ensuing traffic jams have resulted in a few deaths from fumes. After passing through the tunnel, take the narrow, high street to the right, up into the town.

What travelers find on arrival is a neat mountaintop town of mostly closed-up, crumbling rock-walled and stucco buildings, some of them mansions, with cactus and brush growing on the rooflines; a church that attracts 25,000 penitents every October 2; a mint that is sometimes open for tours; a stone cockfighting arena; a fascinating cemetery; a small museum; and a few stores selling food, mining equipment, and Huichol Indian clothing and folk art. In winter, bring heavy clothes—the hotels have no heat. Hiking boots are useful, and you can inquire about renting a horse.

Although the town is off the beaten track, the small hotels sometimes fill up by nightfall. The **Vista** tries hard, and though each room has a bathroom, rooms are still humble. Find it after driving through town toward the cemetery. It has a restaurant, but no written menu. **El Real,** in a three-story restored townhouse, has pleasingly rustic rooms with private bathrooms and a cozy restaurant with wildly varying food preparation and service. Several people traveling together are often allowed to share a room meant for two to four people; sometimes these are rowdy people. Since the hotel's overnight guard often stays at Real II, there's no control when noisy guests get out of hand. **El Real II** was just being completed when I was there. The facade of an old mansion was preserved, but the interior was gutted to make the stylish rooms and a plant-filled courtyard. The inattentive management is the same as at the El Real. Doubles in these hotels run around $35 to $40 a night. One phone (☎ and fax 488/2-3733) serves the whole town and you can try to make a reservation by fax. Best times to try are around 9am and 5pm weekdays. The phone may be continuously busy since people line up to use it, so keep trying. On weekends Mexico Citians make a mad dash for Catorce, so to beat a possible crowd, arrange to arrive by 3pm on a Thursday or Friday. Sunday through Thursday or Friday morning there should be rooms available. Any day though, if you arrive by 3pm and there are no vacancies, you'll still have time to look around briefly and return to the highway before dark. If you can't arrive by 3pm, spend the night at Matehuala, then get an early start the next day.

From here it's on to the Silver Cities through San Luis Potosí, or blast down Highway 57 all the way to Mexico City.

7

Baja California's Southern Resorts

A peninsula longer than Italy, Baja California stretches 876 miles from Tijuana at its northern edge to Los Cabos at its southern tip. Its desert terrain rises up from both coasts—the Pacific Ocean to the west and the Sea of Cortez to the east—to form a spine of craggy mountains that can change from burnt sienna to vermilion, orange, purple, apricot, or rose, depending on the time of day. Whole forests of majestic cardon cactus, spiky Joshua trees, and spindly ocotillo bushes populate this raw, untamed landscape where volcanoes once roared. Baja's wide-open spaces seem to echo with geological time: It's easy to imagine the toothy Sierras heaving up while seas rolled across the flatlands at their feet.

Georgia O'Keeffe probably would have loved Baja's painted-desert colors and sculpted terrain beside the sea, but others might find it barren. Baja is a place that, depending on your mood, can be boring or breathtakingly beautiful. Its austere but dramatic landscape resembles the American West placed beside a brilliant blue sea. Or it brings to mind a moonscape dotted with palm trees and turquoise bays. Scattered along its coastline and tucked among its mountains are tropical hamlets and little towns planted like oases at the end of a long road.

Baja has always been a land of striking opposites and paradox. It has some of the most beautiful beaches in Mexico, many isolated and blissfully unpopulated, others lined with semipermanent trailers and RVs that have settled in with their satellite dishes on the sand. Though it's the southern playground of America's West Coast, Baja can at times seem like one of the least crowded corners of Mexico. Baja's terrain and climate can be as inviting as a Caribbean isle or as unforgiving as a norther.

Baja is a land of secrets, a place that takes patience to penetrate. Its mountains are riddled with caves painted with bold prehistoric pictures and petroglyphs, but reaching them is an adventure requiring horses, mules, or Jeeps. A wealth of untamed marine life plays beneath the waves: Besides the flying marlin and other game fish that have lured wealthy anglers to this peninsula since the 1950s, there are wave-leaping, cavorting dolphins, colonies of sea lions, giant manta rays, and lagoons full of whales that migrate to Baja's bays in the winter to breed. This land's hidden beauty brings out the explorer in visitors.

The superb sportfishing that is still Baja's main draw has been imperiled by over-zealous commercial fishing, especially from long-liner vessels that cruise the Sea of Cortez with fishing lines dragging thousands of hooks and harvesting tons of sea creatures. Marlin, tuna, dorado, shark, and swordfish are their targets, but dolphins, manta rays, and any other sea creatures caught along the way are destined to die as well. Though the Mexican government is issuing fewer permits to long-liners, patrolling the waters is a difficult task. Environmentalists and sportfishing operators are keeping a close eye on boats they encounter at sea and continue to protest the use of long-liners.

Baja is much more than an angler's paradise. Sailing, kayaking, windsurfing, hiking, whale watching, spelunking to explore ancient cave paintings, and camping on isolated, wild beaches draw more and more visitors to Baja each year. Golf has become a major attraction in Los Cabos, where at least four championship courses are open for play.

Independent travelers may have difficulty organizing many of Baja's best-loved activities. Most can be arranged through local travel agencies. Also keep in mind that many organized trips require a minimum of four to six people; if cost is a consideration, consider traveling with a small group of friends.

Shopping, especially in Cabo San Lucas and La Paz, has become much more varied and interesting in the past few years, as have the dining and lodging options.

1 Los Cabos

Los Cabos means "The Capes" and refers to two resort towns that perch on the southern tip of Baja 22 miles apart: San José del Cabo and Cabo San Lucas. Because each has its own distinctive character and attractions, I have treated them separately. It is possible to stay in one and make day-trips to the other.

The twisting, winding stretch of highway between the two towns, with its drop-dead clifftop vistas, is commonly called the Corridor. The highway has been widened to four lanes and is still being refined. The construction of several large-scale resort developments along the Corridor is drastically changing the wild terrain. Some of the area's most dramatic beaches and coves lie along this road, and the view is outstanding in January and February, when gray whales often spout close to shore. You'll need a car to explore this area thoroughly, so you might consider renting one for a day.

Note: The one airport that serves both towns is 7¹/₂ miles northwest of San José del Cabo and 22 miles northeast of Cabo San Lucas.

SAN JOSÉ DEL CABO

122 miles S of La Paz, 22 miles E of Cabo San Lucas, 1,100 miles S of Tijuana

Despite the *tap-tap-tap* of new construction, San José del Cabo retains the air of a provincial Mexican village, with one- and two-story pastel buildings crowding the narrow streets and a shady plaza, church, and bandstand at its heart. This town of 24,000 seems older and more typically Mexican than Cabo San Lucas, and even though it does have a modest nightlife, San José is the more sedate of the two Cabos.

ESSENTIALS

GETTING THERE & DEPARTING   By Plane   Aero California (☎ 2-0943 at the airport) has nonstop or direct flights from Tijuana; **Mexicana** (☎ 2-0192

or 2-0960) has direct or connecting flights from Guadalajara, Mexico City, Puerto Vallarta, and Mazatlán.

Local numbers: **Alaska Airlines** (☎ 2-1015, 2-1016, or 2-0959 at the airport), **Continental** (☎ 2-3880).

By Bus   The bus station (Terminal de Autobuses) on Valerio González a block east of Highway 1 (☎ 2-1100) is open daily from 5:30am to 9pm—though buses arrive and depart later. The companies **Tres Estrellas de Oro** (first class) and **Aguila** (second class) operate buses which arrive from Cabo San Lucas and La Paz almost hourly from 7am to 8pm and which go to La Paz every hour or two between 6am and 7pm (for points farther north you usually change buses in La Paz). The trip from Cabo San Lucas takes 40 minutes; from La Paz the Vía Corta (short route) buses take 2¹/₂ hours and the other buses 3¹/₂ hours. For La Paz, buy a ticket the day before for the Vía Corta (the shorter route) and request a window seat on the shady side of the bus (depending on the time of day).

By Car   From La Paz take Highway 1 south, a scenic route that winds through foothills and occasionally skirts the eastern coastline; the drive takes three to four hours. From La Paz you can also take Highway 1 south just past the village of San Pedro then take Highway 19 south (a less winding road than Highway 1) through Todos Santos to Cabo San Lucas, where you pick up Highway 1 east to San José del Cabo; this route takes two to three hours. From Cabo San Lucas it's a half-hour drive.

ORIENTATION   Arriving   Upon arriving at the airport, buy a ticket inside the building for a colectivo (a van that takes several passengers to hotels). The fare to San José del Cabo is $7 per person. The taxi fare is $12, which could be shared by four people. It is too far from the bus station to the budget hotels downtown or the beachside hotel zone to walk with luggage. A taxi from the bus station to either area costs $2 to $5.

Information   A new **tourist information office** opened in San José in 1994 in the old post office building on Zaragoza at Mijares (no phone). It's open Monday through Friday from 8am to 3pm.

City Layout   San José del Cabo consists of two zones: **downtown,** where the budget hotels are located, and **Playa Hotelera,** the ritzier hotel zone along the beach.

Zaragoza is the main street leading from the highway into town; **Paseo San José** runs parallel to the beach and is the principal boulevard of the hotel zone. The mile-long **Bulevar Mijares** connects the two areas.

Getting Around   There is no local bus service between downtown and the beach; a **taxi** from one to the other costs $3 to $5.

For day-trips to Cabo San Lucas, catch a **bus** for $2 (see "Getting There & Departing," above) or a cab for $25 one way. **Tourcabos** (☎ 2-0982; fax 2-2050) in the Plaza Los Cabos on Paseo San José offers a day tour to Cabo San Lucas for around $30. The tour leaves at 9am and returns around 4pm. Their office is in the Plaza Los Cabos across from the Fiesta Inn on the Malecón. **Bicycles** rent for $6 an hour and $15 a day from Baja Bicycle Club (☎ 2-2828), at the Brisa del Mar Trailer Park on the highway just south of town.

FAST FACTS: SAN JOSÉ DEL CABO

Area Code   The telephone area code was changed in 1993 from 684 to 114. Calls between San José del Cabo and Cabo San Lucas are toll calls, so you must use the area code.

Banks   Banks exchange currency Monday through Friday from 8:30 to 11am. There are two banks on Zaragoza between Morelos and Degollado.

Post Office   The Correos, on Mijares at Valerio González on the south side of town, is open Monday through Friday from 8am to noon and 2 to 6pm, and Saturday from 8 to 11am.

Telephone   Long-distance calls can be made from the offices on Zaragoza near Morelos and Doblado opposite the hospital; the offices are open daily from 8am to 9pm.

FUN ON AND OFF THE BEACH

San José del Cabo is a fine place to unwind, ride horses across the sand, play golf, shop, and absorb authentic Mexican flavor. Although the area is ideal for water sports, the currents and undertow make swimming risky at Playa Hotelera, the town beach. At the moment San José has no marina, and ecological concerns have halted the construction of one between the town beach and Pueblo La Playa. Beach aficionados who want to explore the beautiful coves and beaches along the 22-mile coast between the two Cabos will have to consider the cost of a rental car ($60 per day and up). Frequent bus service between San José del Cabo and Cabo San Lucas makes it possible to take in the pleasures of both towns (see "Getting There & Departing," above).

Special Events

The festival of the patron saint of San José del Cabo is celebrated on **March 19** with a fair, music, dancing, feasting, horse races, and cockfights. **June 19** is the festival of the patron saint of San Bartolo, a village 62 miles north. **July 25** is the festival of the patron saint of Santiago, a village 34 miles north.

Beaches

The nearest beach safe for swimming is **Pueblo la Playa** (also called "La Playita"), located about 2 miles east of town: From Bulevar Mijares, turn east at the small sign PUEBLO LA PLAYA and follow the dirt road through cane fields and palms to a beach where a number of *pangas* (skiffs) belonging to local fishermen are pulled ashore. A hotel was nearing completion when I last visited here, and there is a small restaurant being remodeled. A taxi to Puebla la Playa beach from San José costs about $5 to $8 one way.

Estero San José, a nature reserve with over 100 species of birds, is located between Pueblo La Playa and the Presidente Inter-Continental Hotel. The estuary is protected as an ecological reserve and was cleaned up in 1994. A building at the edge of the water is gradually being turned into a cultural center.

A fine swimming beach with beautiful rock formations, **Playa Palmilla,** 5 miles west of San José, is located near the Spanish colonial–style Hotel Palmilla—an elegant place to stay or to eat lunch or dinner. To reach Playa Palmilla, take a taxi to the road that leads to the Hotel Palmilla grounds for about $7, then take the fork to the left (without entering the hotel grounds) and follow signs to Pepe's restaurant on the beach.

For a list of other beaches worth exploring if you have a rental car, see "Fun on and off the Beach" in Cabo San Lucas.

Sunset Cruises

Boats depart from Cabo San Lucas; the cruise includes music and open bar for $30 per person. Arrange cruises through a travel agency.

Water Sports

Fishing Several *panga* fleets (a 22-foot skiff used by local fishermen) offer **six-hour** sportfishing trips, usually from 6am to noon, for $160. The cost can be divided between two or three people—weigh the savings against how much elbow room you think you'll need to catch a big one. For information contact **La Playa Sportfishing** (☎ 2-1195) in Pueblo la Playa or **Victor's Aquatics** (☎ 2-1092, or 800/521-2281 in the U.S.) at the Hotel Presidente Inter-Continental and the Hotel Posada Real.

Snorkeling/Diving Trips start around $66 per person and can be arranged through **Tourcabos** (☎ 2-1982), the dive shop at the **Hotel Palmilla** (☎ 2-0582), or **Amigos del Mar** in Cabo San Lucas (☎ 3-0505).

Surfing **Playa Costa Azul,** at km 29 on Highway 1 just south of San José, is the most popular surfing beach in the area. Surfers stay in run-down shacks or camp on the beach; spectators can watch from the highway lookout point at the top of the hill south of Costa Azul.

Whale Watching From January through March, whales congregate offshore. Fishermen at Pueblo la Playa will take small groups out to see the whales; a four-hour trip runs about $40 per person. **Tourcabos** (☎ 2-1982) arranges whale watching for groups of four or more people; the two-hour trip costs $40 per person.

Land Sports

Golf Los Cabos is rapidly becoming a major golf destination, with several new courses open and others under construction. The most economical greens fees are at the nine-hole **Club Campo de Golf Los Cabos** (☎ 2-0905), on Paseo Finisterra across from the Howard Johnson Hotel. The course is open from 7am to 4pm (to 4:30pm in summer). Club guests can use the swimming pool.

New courses have opened along the Corridor between the two towns, including the 27-hole course designed by Jack Nicklaus at the **Palmilla Golf Club** (Palmilla resort, ☎ 2-1701 or 2-1708); the 18-hole Nicklaus course at **Cabo del Sol** (at the Cabo del Sol resort development in the Corridor); and an 18-hole course at **Cabo Real** (by the Melia Cabo Real Hotel in the Corridor, ☎ 114/2-9000, ext. 9205). **Campo de Carlos,** a planned golf resort community in the Corridor close to Cabo San Lucas, is slated to have two 18-hole courses.

Horseback Riding Horses can be rented near the **Presidente Inter-Continental, Fiesta Inn,** and **Palmilla** hotels at $15 to $20 per hour. Most people ride on the beach.

Tennis Tennis is available at the two courts of the **Club Campo de Golf Los Cabos** (☎ 2-0905) for $10 an hour during the day, $12 an hour at night. Club guests can use the swimming pool.

San José del Cabo

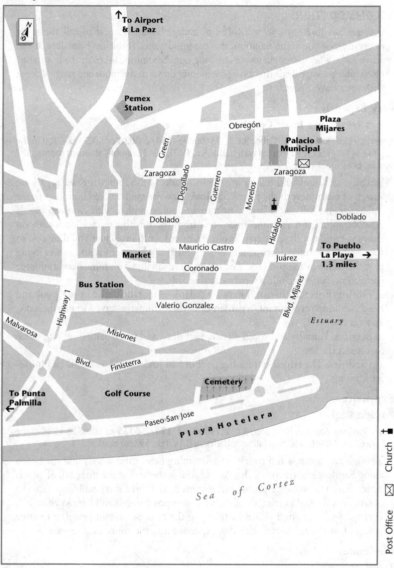

To Airport & La Paz

Pemex Station

Obregón

Plaza Mijares

Palacio Municipal

Green

Zaragoza

Degollado

Guerrero

Morelos

Zaragoza

Doblado

Doblado

Mauricio Castro

Market

Coronado

Hidalgo

Juárez

To Pueblo La Playa
1.3 miles →

Bus Station

Valerio Gonzalez

Highway 1

Blvd. Mijares

Estuary

Malvarosa

Misiones

Blvd. Finisterra

To Punta Palmilla
←

Golf Course

Cemetery

Paseo San Jose

Playa Hotelera

Sea   of   Cortez

† ■ Church

⊠ Post Office

1217

SHOPPING

The town's handful of tourist shops are clustered around **Bulevar Mijares** and **Zaragoza,** the main street. A long line of open-air stalls selling handcrafts and souvenirs line Bulevar Mijares (bargaining is essential). The **municipal market** on Mauricio Castro and Green mainly sells edible and utilitarian wares. For arts, crafts, and jewelry, try **Antigua Los Cabos** (Zaragoza 20; ☎ 2-0233) and **La Casa Vieja Botique** (Mijares 27; ☎ 2-0599). La Botica (Mijares 33; ☎ 2-2727) is a small newsstand and coffeehouse that sells English-language books, magazines, and newspapers.

ACCOMMODATIONS

Because San José has only a handful of budget hotels, it's best to call ahead for reservations if you want economical accommodations. If this isn't possible, try to arrive early, when other guests are checking out. Accommodations in the hotel zone often offer package deals that bring room rates down to the moderate range. Check with your travel agent.

Very Expensive

Hotel Presidente Inter-Continental

Paseo San José, San José del Cabo, B.C.S. 23400. ☎ **114/2-0038** or 800/327-0200 in the U.S. Fax 114/2-0232. 250 rms (all with bath). A/C TV TEL. $132 double, standard room; $187 double, oceanfront room.

Serenity, seclusion, and luxury are the hallmarks of the Presidente, set on a long stretch of beach next to the Estero San José. Low-rise sand-colored buildings frame the beach and San José's largest swimming pool, complete with swim-up bar. If possible, splurge on a ground-floor oceanfront room with a terrace, preferably on the estuary side of the property. From your outdoor lounge chair you'll be able to spot horseback riders trotting along the sand and white herons and egrets flying past the palms as the sun sets. The rooms have satellite TV, mini-bars, and large bathrooms; suites include a separate sitting area.

Dining/Entertainment: There's a palapa restaurant between the pool and beach, an indoor restaurant, a garden cafe where dinner is served under the stars, and a disco.

Services: Laundry and room service, tour desk, and twice-daily shuttle to Cabo San Lucas for $8.

Facilities: The largest swimming pool in San José, as well as tennis and horseback riding.

Expensive

Posada Real

Paseo San José, San José del Cabo, B.C.S. 23400. ☎ **114/2-0155** or 800/528-1234 in the U.S. Fax 114/2-0460. 150 rms (all with bath). A/C TV TEL. $93.50 double.

Though the ocean is too rough for swimming here, three hotels line the beach along San José's hotel zone. The Posada Real is the best of the three (all of which suffer from maintenance problems). Rooms in the three-story buildings face the ocean, pool (heated in winter), or desert landscaped grounds and have satellite TV. Package deals are often available, bringing the rates down and bringing in large groups. Car rentals, horseback riding, sportfishing, and tours are available.

Moderate

Tropicana Inn

Mijares 130, San José del Cabo, B.C.S. 23400. ☎ **114/2-1580.** Fax 114/2-1590. 40 rms (all with bath). A/C TV TEL. Dec 21–April 30 $72 double; May 1–Dec 20 $58 double.

Opened in July 1991, this neo-Spanish-colonial–style hotel frames a courtyard with a graceful arcade bordering the rooms. Each medium-size room in the L-shaped building (which has a two- and a three-story wing) comes with two double beds, a TV with U.S. channels, a window looking out on the courtyard, and a bath with a shower. Amenities include parking, a pool, and room service until 11pm from the adjacent Tropicana Bar & Grill (owned by the hotel). The inn is located behind the restaurant, a block south of the town square.

Inexpensive

Posada Terranova

Degollado, San José del Cabo, B.C.S. 23400. ☎ **114/2-0534.** Fax 114/2-0902. 20 rms (all with bath). A/C TV. $40 double. Extra person $10. Free limited parking.

At the nicest budget hotel in town, each of the bright white rooms has two double beds, tiled counters, a bath with brand new fixtures, a TV, and powerful air-conditioning; one suite even has a small kitchen. The ground-floor restaurant (open daily from 7am to 10pm) has a front patio and an enclosed dining room and serves reasonably priced Mexican and American dishes. The posada is on Degollado, between Zaragoza and Doblado.

DINING

Expensive

✪ Damiana

San José town plaza. ☎ **114/2-0499.** Reservations recommended during the Christmas and Easter holidays. Main courses $5.60–$20. Daily 10:30am–11pm. MEXICAN/SEAFOOD.

This elegant restaurant on the east side of the town plaza is decorated like an 18th-century mansion. Mariachis add to the romantic ambience by playing nightly from 8 to 9pm (mid-December to March) in the tropical courtyard, where candles flicker under the trees and bougainvillea. For an appetizer, try the cheese soup laced with cilantro, poblano peppers, and thick chunks of cheese or the moderately zesty mushrooms diablo. There is an interior dining room, but the courtyard is the most romantic dining spot in Los Cabos.

Tropicana Bar & Grill

Mijares 130. ☎ **114/2-1580.** Breakfasts $3.50–$4.75; burgers $4–$4.75; fajitas for two $15.50; Mexican combination plates $7.50; steaks $10. Daily 8am–midnight. SEAFOOD/MEAT.

The Tropicana remains a popular mainstay for tourists and locals alike. Its bar, Eclipse, has a steady clientele day and night and often features special sporting events on satellite TV. The dining area, where candlelight flickers in the evening, is in a pretty garden with a tiled kitchen at one end. All meats and cheeses are imported, and dinners include thick steaks and shrimp fajitas. Breakfast is the best deal. The restaurant is one block from City Hall.

Inexpensive

Las Hornillas

Calle Manuel Doblado 610. ☎ **114/2-2324.** Half-chickens $3.80; 3 tacos with beans $2.90; chicken fajitas $6. Daily noon–10pm. CHICKEN/MEXICAN.

A true neighborhood eatery, Las Hornillas is the best place in town for chicken roasted on a spit over a wood fire, served with tortillas, beans, and rice. Plants and bird cages hang about the dining room, and there is a sink set to one side so you can wash up after your messy chicken feast. The fajitas can easily feed two moderately hungry adults.

Pescadería El Mercado Del Mar

Blv. Mauricio Castro (also called Highway 1) at Zaragoza. ☎ **114/2-3266.** Seafood cocktails $2–$4.75; main courses $4–$8. Wed–Mon noon–10pm. SEAFOOD.

Opened in 1993, this tiny seafood market/cafe has already become popular. A palapa roof covers the dining area's seven blue-clothed tables. A large wood-burning smoker sits at the far end of the room, and the aroma of smoking fish permeates the restaurant. Start with the *toritos,* small grilled chiles caribe stuffed with smoked marlin, and then move on to marinated oysters, fresh clams, or grilled beer-marinated shrimp. If you catch fish while you're in Los Cabos, consider having it smoked here for a flavorful souvenir. The restaurant is set amid a row of businesses on the east side of Highway 1 at the north end of town.

Zipper's

Playa Costa Azul just south of San José. No phone. Burgers $2.75–$5.75; main courses $4–$6.75. Daily 8am–10pm. BURGERS/MEXICAN.

A popular hangout with surfers, Zipper's sits on a slight rise just above the beach. The burgers, which are given that back-home flavor with imported beef and catsup, are the restaurant's biggest draw. Steaks, lobster, and Mexican combination plates round out the menu. If you're into surfing, this is definitely the place to be, since some of the best waves in the area crash just offshore.

SAN JOSÉ AFTER DARK

San José's nightlife revolves mainly around the restaurants and large hotels. Bulevar Mijares is the town's restaurant row, along which you can amble until you find the restaurant or watering hole with the most appealing music. Several of the hotels have **Mexican Fiestas** and other weekly theme nights that include a buffet (usually all you can eat), drinks, live music, and entertainment for $25 to $35 per person. These can be both fun and a good value for a splurge. For more information, call the Presidente Inter-Continental Hotel (☎ 2-0211), Howard Johnson Hotel (☎ 2-0999), Fiesta Inn (☎ 2-0701), or Hotel Palmilla (☎ 2-0582).

Bones Bar and Disco

Hotel Presidente Inter-Continental, Paseo San José. ☎ **114/2-0211.**

The disco by the Hotel Presidente Inter-Continental has gone through various incarnations but now seems to be the hottest nightspot in San José. Flashing lights, fog machines, and other environmental stimulants keep the dancers moving to a pounding beat. If you're not into dancing, the bar has pool tables and video games. It's open nightly from 8pm to 2am, or until whenever the crowd winds down.

Iguana Bar & Grill

Mijares 24. ☎ **114/2-0266.**

This lively open-air bar and restaurant is sheltered by a broad thatched roof and has a patio under the stars. Live music and dancing on Friday and Saturday get cranking around 9:30pm and can last until 1am. Should hunger strike, the house specialty is barbecued ribs. The place is open daily from 11am to 1am. Drinks run from $2 to $4.50.

Tropicana Bar & Grill

Mijares 30. ☎ **114/5-2684.**

Ensconced in leather barrel chairs in the large bar, guests watch American sports events on the big-screen TV during the day. Come evening, guitarists play from 6 to 11pm. After 9pm on some nights a rock band plays for those inclined to dance. The Tropicana is open daily from 7am to 1am. Drinks go for $3 and up.

AN EXCURSION TO THE CORRIDOR

The Corridor between the towns of San José del Cabo and Cabo San Lucas contains some of Baja's most lavish hotels, designed as self-contained resorts for dream getaways. This area is undergoing considerable development, with three major resort areas—the Palmilla, Cabo Real, and Cabo del Sol—gradually emerging as self-enclosed mini-communities with golf courses, elegant hotels, and million-dollar homes. New hotels are rising here—among the most spectacular still to come is the hacienda-style Hyatt Regency, scheduled to open in 1996 in Cabo del Sol.

If you plan to explore the region while staying at a Corridor hotel, you'll need a rental car for at least a day or two; cars are available at the hotels. Even if you're not staying here, stop by for a look or a meal. All the hotels have excellent restaurants. Hotels are listed as you'll encounter them as you drive from San José to Cabo San Lucas. Rates listed are for the high season and typically are 20 percent lower in the summer. Golf and fishing packages are available at most resorts.

ACCOMMODATIONS

Very Expensive

Hotel Palmilla

Km 27.5 on Hwy. 1, San José del Cabo, B.C.S. 23400. ☎ **114/2-0582,** or 800/637-2226 in the U.S. Fax 114/2-0583. 62 rms, 8 suites, 2 villas. A/C. $205–$350 double.

One of the prettiest hotels in Mexico, the Palmilla consists of a series of white buildings with red-tile roofs, buried palms, and bougainvillea on a cliff top above the sea. Talavera vases, carved dressers and headboards, heavy woven drapes and spreads, and bathrooms walled in hand-painted tiles give the rooms a colonial-Mexican feeling. Standard amenities include bathrobes and fresh juice, coffee, and croissants delivered after your wake-up call. Long isolated, the hotel now sits at the edge of a massive development, and gorgeous private villas are now rising between the hotel and the highway. Lush landscaping, however, adds a sense of privacy. The hotel is scheduled for renovation in 1995.

Dining/Entertainment: The restaurant La Paloma has an outdoor terrace overlooking a small pool, plus a large dining room. The Sunday brunch is as lavish as you could possibly imagine. Friday nights, there's a special fiesta with entertainment and buffet dinner.

Services: Laundry and room service, baby-sitting on request, tour desk, boutiques, hairstyling, car rental.

Facilities: A large palm-shaded pool and 2 miles of beach, 2 tennis courts lit for night play, croquet court, 2 volleyball courts, horseback riding. Across the highway is the resort's championship golf course. The hotel has a small white chapel where weddings take place nearly every weekend. Hotel-owned fishing boats are available for guests. An on-premises dive shop rents equipment and can arrange diving and snorkeling expeditions.

Westin Regina

Km 22.5 on Hwy. 1, Apdo. Postal 145, San José del Cabo, B.C.S. 23400. ☎ **114/2-9000,** or 800/228-3000 in the U.S. Fax 114/2-9010. 243 rms and suites. A/C TV TEL. $207 double with partial ocean view; $240 double with full ocean view.

Architecturally dramatic, the Westin Regina sits at the end of a long paved road atop a seaside cliff. Vivid terra-cotta, yellow, and pink walls rise against a landscape of sandstone, cacti, and palms, with fountains and gardens lining the long pathways from the lobby to the rooms. Electric carts carry guests and their luggage through the vast property. The rooms are gorgeous, with both air-conditioning and ceiling fans (a joy to those who like to leave the windows open), private balconies, satellite TV, in-room safes, and walk-in showers separate from the bathtubs.

Dining/Entertainment: Los Arrecifes restaurant is considered to be one of the most glamorous in Los Cabos. There are five other restaurants and two bars on the property.

Services: Laundry and room service, travel agency, boutique, gift shop, beauty and barber shop, business services.

Facilities: Three swimming pools, a man-made beach, a full fitness center, and two tennis courts provide plenty of distraction. The Palmilla and Cabo Real golf courses are nearby.

Twin Dolphin

Km 11.5 on Hwy. 1, Cabo San Lucas B.C.S. 23410. ☎ **114/3-0256,** or 800/421-8925 in the U.S. Fax 114/3-0496. 44 rms and 6 suites. A/C. $325 double with breakfast; $391 double with three meals.

The hotel's minimalist white-on-white walls, floors, and even beach umbrellas give the Twin Dolphin an austere yet sophisticated feeling. The serene hotel is set on a bluff against a desertscape dotted with cactus. The rooms are in several one-story buildings spread atop the bluff and are simply furnished with pale woods (and without TVs or phones). All have terraces and ocean views. Access to the beach is via stairs down the bluff. Celebrities often stay here and outsiders are discouraged from wandering through the property. It's 6 1/2 miles northeast of Cabo San Lucas.

Dining/Entertainment: One restaurant and bar.

Services: Laundry and room service, concierge, car rental.

Facilities: Swimming pool with swim-up bar, two tennis courts lighted for night play, fitness center with massage, 2-mile marked nature trail suitable for jogging. Three golf courses are nearby. The hotel operates 9 cruisers equipped for diving, snorkeling, and sportfishing. Other water sports include windsurfing, sailing, parasailing, and waterskiing.

Expensive

Hotel Cabo San Lucas

Km 14.5 on Hwy. 1, Cabo San Lucas B.C.S. 23410. ☎ **114/3-3457,** or 800/733-2226 in the U.S. Fax 114/3-0666. 103 rms, suites, and villas. A/C TV TEL. $170–$235 double.

This is a favorite among old-timers who remember Cabo's former wilderness. The hotel, which sits above Chileno Beach, looks and feels like a rugged mountain lodge. The buildings have rock walls and wood-beam ceilings, and the overgrown landscaping shades the pathways and pool. The rooms are comfortable rather than elegant, with heavy wood furnishings and an orange-and-brown color scheme. Hunting and sportfishing excursions are available, along with archery and tennis.

Dining/Entertainment: One restaurant and three bars.

Service: Laundry and room service, gift shop, tour desk.

Facilities: Tri-level swimming pool, a full-service dive shop, two tennis courts, complete line of water sports equipment, massage, several nearby golf courses.

DINING

Da Gorgio

Km 15 on Hwy. 1 at Misiones del Cabo. Breakfast $4–$8; pastas $5.50–$14. Daily 8am–midnight. ITALIAN.

The view surpasses the food at this cliff-top restaurant. Bar tables are set on small platforms scattered down the cliffside beside a rock-strewn waterfall and pond. Get here early if you want a prime sunset-watching spot since demand is high for seats with an incomparable view of the sea and the rock arch at Land's End. Meals are served in an open-air dining room atop the cliff. The pastas and pizzas are good but not exceptional, and there's a lavish salad bar.

AN EXCURSION TO THE EAST CAPE

The coastline of the Sea of Cortez north of San José has long been a favored destination of die-hard anglers, who fly their private planes to airstrips at out-of-the-way lodges. This coastline has experienced considerable development in the past few years, and hotels have expanded their services to please even those who never set foot on a boat. Housing developments are appearing along the main road, but there's still plenty of space for adventurous campers to find secluded beaches.

A rough dirt road called the Coastal Road runs along the East Cape from San José to La Ribera, but it can take up to four hours to complete the 55-mile drive. Along this route you pass by Cabo Pulmo, where Baja's only coral reef lies just offshore. There are no major hotels, restaurants, or dive shops here, and most divers reach the reefs via dive boats from Los Cabos. The more efficient approach to the East Cape is to drive the paved Mexico Highway 1 from San José north to dirt roads leading off the highway to resorts and communities at Punta Colorado, Buena Vista, Los Barriles, and Punta Pescadero. Public buses from San José stop at major intersections, where you'll need to catch a cab to the hotels. Most guests at the hotels take a cab from the airport ($30–$45 per person) and stay put.

ACCOMMODATIONS AND DINING

Hotel Buenavista Beach Resort

Mexico Hwy. 1 at Buena Vista, 35 miles north of San José del Cabo (Apdo. Postal 574, La Paz, B.C.S. 23000). ☎ **112/2-1962** in the U.S. 60 rms. A/C. $96 double without meals; $162 double with three meals daily. For reservations contact 16211 E. Whittier Blv., Whittier, CA 90603. ☎ 310/943-0869 or 800/752-3555. Fax 310/943-4078.

Though the Buenavista has been here for nearly two decades, it's the most modern and luxurious place on the East Cape, thanks to additions, remodeling, and constant care. Tan buildings draped in bougainvillea are scattered down a slight slope toward the beach, with two rooms in each building. The rooms have one king or two double beds, brown-tiled bathrooms with showers, wood tables and chairs, and patios. Adjoining rooms are often used by families, who find the resort the perfect getaway for grown-ups and kids. The excellent sportfishing fleet is a big attraction; there are also two swimming pools with swim-up bars, two hot tubs, volleyball courts, tours to the mountains, and horseback riding. A health and beauty spa was in the planning stages when I visited. The meal plan is a good idea, though there are a few other restaurants in the Buena Vista area.

Rancho Buena Vista

Mexico Hwy. 1 at Buena Vista, 35 miles north of San José del Cabo. No phone. 55 rms. A/C. 156 double. Rates include three daily meals. For reservations contact PO Box 1408, Santa Maria, CA 93456. ☎ 805/928-1719 or 800/258-8200 outside CA. Fax 805/925-2990.

A fishing resort with no pretensions, Rancho Buena Vista has several one-story bungalows spread about the grounds. The simple rooms have red-tiled floors, good showers, double beds, and small patios in front. Hammocks hang under palms and by the swimming pool, and the bar/restaurant is the center of the action. The hotel has an excellent deep-sea fishing fleet with its own dock and a private airstrip.

CABO SAN LUCAS

110 miles S of La Paz, 22 miles W of San José del Cabo, 1,120 miles S of Tijuana

Cabo San Lucas, with a population of 25,000, is the faster growing of the two Cabos. In the past few years, the number of swanky new hotels and condos has nearly doubled around the harbor and amid the steep hills that frame the picturesque blue bay where private American yachts have been dropping anchor since the 1950s. That era marked the beginning of the town's fame as a mecca for hunters of marlin and other big-game fish, and many of its popular watering holes still retain the air of a yacht club mixed with the good-natured silliness of a fraternity party. San Lucas is definitely the party capital of Los Cabos, and its attitude is far flashier than that of San José. It's also the priciest resort in Baja.

ESSENTIALS

GETTING THERE & DEPARTING   By Plane   For arrival and departure information see "Getting There & Departing," above, in San José del Cabo. Local airline numbers are as follows: **Aero California** (☎ 3-0827 or 3-0848; 2-0943 at the airport); **Alaska Airlines** (☎ 2-1015 or 2-1016; 2-0959 at the airport); and **Mexicana** (☎ 3-0411 or 3-0412).

By Bus   The bus terminal (☎ 3-0400) is on Niños Héroes at Morelos; it is open daily from 6am to 9:30pm. **Autotransportes Aguila** buses go to San José del Cabo about every hour between 6:30am and 8:30pm on the Vía Corta (short route). First-class buses to La Paz leave every 90 minutes between 6am and 6pm. Some La Paz–bound buses stop in Todos Santos. On this line, you change buses at La Paz if you're going on to Tijuana. The trip from San José del Cabo takes 40 minutes; from La Paz, the Vía Corta (shorter route) buses take 2¹/₂ hours, and the other buses take four hours.

By Car   From La Paz, take Highway 1 south past the village of San Pedro, then Highway 19 south through Todos Santos to Cabo San Lucas, a two-hour drive. Todos Santos has several restored historic buildings and makes a pleasant stop for a meal—try the Café Santa Fe, which draws diners from Los Cabos with its fresh fish and Italian cuisine.

ORIENTATION   Arriving   Upon arriving at the airport, buy a ticket inside the building for a colectivo. The fare to Cabo San Lucas is $12 per person. The taxi fare is $35, which could be shared by four people. The highway between the airport and Cabo San Lucas was widened to four lanes in 1993.

A taxi from the station to most hotels should be under $5.

Information   A **tourist information office** opened in late 1994 on Avenida Hidalgo at Guerrero (☎ 3-4180; fax 3-2211). The office is open Monday through Friday from 9am to 2pm and 4 to 7pm and on Saturday from 10am to 1pm. For information about boating and other water sports, ask around at the town marina. The *Los Cabos Times*, distributed free at most hotels and shops, has up-to-date information on new restaurants and clubs. *Note:* Beware of "visitor information" booths along the street—they're actually time-share hawkers.

City Layout   The small town spreads out north and west of the harbor of **Cabo San Lucas Bay,** edged by foothills and desert mountains to the west and south. The main street leading into town from the airport and San José del Cabo is **Lázaro Cárdenas**; as it nears the harbor, **Marina Boulevard** branches off from it and becomes the main artery that curves around the waterfront.

Getting Around   Frequent local **buses** run along Lázaro Cárdenas and Morelos, as well as Marina Boulevard, and cost around 50¢. A **taxi** from downtown to the farthest hotels, such as the Solmar near Land's End or the Melia on Medano Beach, should run from $5 to $8.

The quickest new way to get to Medano Beach from downtown is to catch the **water taxi** at the marina by Plaza Las Glorias for $4. For day-trips to San José del Cabo, catch a bus for $2 (see "Getting There & Departing," above) or a cab for $25 one way.

You'll see **car-rental** specials advertised in town, but before signing on, be sure you understand the total price after insurance and taxes have been added to it.

FAST FACTS: CABO SAN LUCAS

Area Code   The telephone area code was changed in 1993 from 684 to 114. Calls between Cabo San Lucas and San José del Cabo are toll calls, so you must use the area code.

Banks   Banks exchange currency Monday through Friday from 9 to 11am.

Post Office   The Correos is at Cárdenas and Francisco Villa, on the highway to San José del Cabo, east of the bar El Squid Roe. It's open Monday through Friday from 9am to 1pm and 3 to 6pm, and Saturday from 9am to noon.

FUN ON AND OFF THE BEACH

Although superb sportfishing put Cabo San Lucas on the map, there's more to do here than dropping in your line and waiting for the Big One. But if that's your fancy, go for it. For most cruises and excursions, try to make reservations at least a day in advance; keep in mind that some trips require a minimum number of people. Fishing and most other sports and outings can be arranged through a travel agency or at the marina.

Special Events

October 12 is the festival of the patron saint of Todos Santos, a town about 60 miles north. **October 18** is the festival of the patron saint of Cabo San Lucas, celebrated with a fair, feasting, music, dancing, and special events.

Sportfishing

Go to the town marina on the south side of the harbor. There, you'll find about two dozen fleet operators with stands alongside the docks. The best deals are offered by the *panga* fleets, which provide five hours of fishing for two or three persons at $150 to $160. To choose a panga, take a stroll around the marina and talk with the captains—you may be able to agree on an economical deal. Try **ABY Charters** (main office at the Giggling Marlin restaurant, ☎ 114/3-0831), **Rafael's Fleet** (☎ 114/3-0018), or **Baja Mar Fleet** (☎ 114/3-2259), all of which are located at the sportfishing dock at the marina. The going rate for a day on a fully equipped cruiser with captain and guide (many of the larger hotels, like the Solmar, have their own fleets) starts at around $300. These cruisers have bathrooms aboard. Divide the price between four persons, and you'll fish for far less.

The fishing really lives up to its reputation: Bringing in a marlin weighing over 100 pounds is commonplace. Angling is good all year, though the catch varies with the season: Sailfish and wahoo are best from June through November; yellow-fin tuna, from May through December; yellowtail, from January through April; black and blue marlin, July through December; and striped marlin are prevalent year-round.

The "catch and release" program is encouraged in Los Cabos. Anglers reel in their fish, which are tagged and released unharmed into the sea. The angler gets a certificate and the knowledge that there will still be billfish in the sea when he or she returns.

Beaches

All along the curving sweep of sand known as **Medano Beach,** on the east side of the bay, you can rent snorkeling gear, boats, waverunners, kayaks, pedalboats, and windsurf boards. You can also take windsurfing lessons. This is the town's main beach and is a great place for safe swimming as well as people watching from one of the many outdoor restaurants along its shore.

Another good beach for swimming and snorkeling is **Playa de Amor (Beach of Love),** south of town near the soaring rock formations that mark Land's End like exclamation points. It costs $30 per hour to rent a *panga* and captain to go to Playa de Amor from the marina. You can also negotiate with someone at the marina to take you and pick you up later for $15 to $20.

Beach aficionados may want to rent a car (see "Getting Around," above) and explore the nearly half dozen out-of-the-way beaches and coves between the two Cabos: **Playas Palmilla, Chileno, Santa María, Barco Varado,** and **Vista del Arcos.** Palmilla, Chileno, and Santa María are generally safe for swimming; the others are worth visiting for the view only or by experienced snorkelers. Always check at a hotel or travel agency for directions and swimming conditions. Although a few travel agencies run snorkeling tours to some of these beaches, there's no public transportation. Your options are renting a car ($60 per day and up) or bus-hiking—catching the bus to San José and asking the driver to drop you off at one of the beach turnoffs (depending on the beach, it can be a long walk from the highway to the beach).

Cruises

Glass-bottom boats leave from the town marina daily from 9am to 4pm. Boat captains bargain with potential passengers on the dock, and when demand is low they will go out when you want for as long as you want. Count on paying about $15 per person for an hour tour past sea lions and pelicans to see the famous "El Arco" (Rock Arch) at Land's End, where the Pacific and the Sea of Cortez meet. Most boats make a brief stop at Playa de Amor or will drop you off there if you ask; you can use your ticket to catch a later boat back (be sure to check what time the last boat departs).

Whale-watching cruises are not to be missed when gray whales migrate to the Los Cabos area between January and March. The sportfishing boats, glass-bottom boats, and cruise catamarans all offer whale-watching trips ranging from $30 to $50 for a half-day trip. You can also spot the whales from shore; good whale-watching spots include the beach by the Solmar Suites hotel on the Pacific and the beaches and cliffs along the Corridor.

A **sunset cruise** on the 42-foot catamaran *Pez Gato* (☎ 114/3-3797 or 3-2458) departs from the Hacienda Hotel dock at 5pm. The two-hour cruise costs $30, which includes margaritas, beer, and sodas. Similar boats leave from the marina and the Plaza las Glorias hotel. Check with travel agencies or hotel tour desks.

Snorkeling/Diving

Several companies offer snorkeling; a two-hour cruise to sites around El Arco costs $25, and a four-hour trip to Santa María costs $45, including gear rental. Among the beaches visited on different trips are Playa de Amor, Santa María, Chileno, and Barco Varado. Snorkeling gear rents for $6 to $10. For scuba diving, contact **Amigos del Mar** (☎ 114/3-0505; fax 3-0887) at the marina. Dives are made along the wall of a canyon in San Lucas Bay, where you can see "sandfalls" that even Jacques Cousteau couldn't figure out—no one knows the source or cause. There are also scuba trips to Santa María Beach and farther places, including the Gordo Banks and Cabo Pulmo. Dives start at $35 for a one-tank dive and $66 for two tanks; trips to the coral outcropping at Cabo Pulmo (said to be the only coral off the coast of Baja) start at $110. The months from April through November are the best times to dive. Reservations can be made in advance.

Surfing

Good surfing can be found from March to November all along the beaches west of town, and there's a famous break right at Chileno Beach, near the Cabo San Lucas Hotel east of town.

Other Sports

Bicycles, boogie boards, snorkels, surfboards, and golf clubs are available for rent at **Cabo Sports Center** in the Plaza Nautica on Boulevard Marina (☎ 114/3-4272); the center is open Monday through Saturday from 9am to 9pm, Sunday from 9am to 5pm. For information about playing **golf** in Los Cabos, see "Fun on and off the Beach" in San José del Cabo, above.

You can rent horses from **Marco's Horse Rentals** at the Hacienda Hotel (☎ 114/3-0123) for around $20 per hour. They have guided beach rides and sunset tours to El Faro Viejo (the Old Lighthouse) for $30 to $40 per person. Marco's is open daily from 7am to 6pm.

Historic Cabo San Lucas

Sports and carousing are Cabo's main attractions, but there are a few cultural and historical points of interest. The stone **Iglesia de San Lucas** (Church of San Lucas), on Calle Cabo San Lucas close to the main plaza, was established in 1730 by Spanish missionary Nicolás Tamaral; a large bell in a stone archway commemorates the completion of the church in 1746. Tamaral was eventually killed by the Pericúe Indians, who reportedly resisted his demands that they practice monogamy. Buildings on the streets facing the main plaza are gradually being renovated to house restaurants and shops, and the picturesque neighborhood promises to have the strongest Mexican ambience of any place in town.

ATV Trips

Expeditions on ATVs (all-terrain vehicles) to visit Cabo Falso, an 1890 lighthouse, and La Candelaría, an Indian pueblo in the mountains, are available through travel agencies. The three-hour tour to Cabo Falso includes a stop at the beach; a look at some sea-turtle nests (without disturbing them) and the remains of a 1912 shipwreck; a ride over 500-foot sand dunes; and a visit to the lighthouse. Tours cost around $50 per person or $60 for two riding on one ATV. The vehicles are also available for rent at $30 for 3 hours.

La Candelaría is an isolated Indian village in the mountains 25 miles north of Cabo San Lucas. Described in *National Geographic*, the old pueblo is known for the white and black witchcraft still practiced here. Lush with palms, mango trees, and bamboo, the settlement is watered by an underground river that emerges at the pueblo. The return trip of the tour travels down a steep canyon, along a beach (giving you time to swim), and past giant sea-turtle nesting grounds. Departing at 9am, the La Candelaría tour costs around $88 per person or $110 for two on the same ATV. A 220-pound weight limit per vehicle applies to both tours.

Day-Trips

Day-trips to La Paz booked through a travel agency cost around $80, including lunch and a tour of the countryside along the way. Usually there's a stop in La Paz at the weaving shop of Fortunato Silva, who spins his own cotton and weaves it into wonderfully textured rugs and textiles.

Shopping

Your first stop should be the open-air market by the marina. Mixed in with T-shirts and touristy junk are some nice crafts and jewelry—be sure to bargain. Most shops are on or within a block or two of Marina Boulevard and the plaza. Several shopping arcades resembling open-air Mexican markets have cropped up around town, offering basically the same selection of blankets, T-shirts, onyx statues, and other souvenirs; bargaining is expected and encouraged at these markets.

For arts and crafts, visit **Mamma Eli's,** one of the nicest shops in Los Cabos (Calle Cabo San Lucas west of the plaza; ☎ 114/3-1616), and **Necri** (Blv. Marina; ☎ 114/3-0283), whose wares are of the best quality. You can design your own cotton or woolen Mexican blanket and have it ready the next day at **Cuca's Blanket Factory** (Cárdenas at Matamoros; ☎ 114/3-1913). **Plaza Bonita** (Marina Boulevard at Lázaro Cárdenas), a large terra-cotta colored plaza on the edge of the marina, is filled with a bookstore and crafts and clothing shops.

Combine shopping, touring, and a look at local culture with a trip to **Glass Factory** (west of Hwy. 1; no phone), a glassblowing factory on the outskirts of town. Glassblowers from Guadalajara and Baja work around enormous gas furnaces and blazing fires. The glassblowers will help you blow your own masterpiece, while a showroom at the front displays more professional work. The tour is free, but visitors are expected to purchase something. Small shot glasses with green glass cacti on the front are about $2 each. The factory is open Monday through Saturday from 8am to 3pm. To get there by car, turn west off Highway 1 north of Cabo San Lucas opposite the post office on Calle Farías or Mendoza, then drive about five dirt blocks inland. A taxi to the factory (your best choice) costs about $4.

ACCOMMODATIONS

All hotel prices listed here are for high season, in effect from November through Easter; summer rates are about 20% less. Several Cabo San Lucas hotels offer package deals that significantly lower the nightly rate; ask your travel agent for information.

Budget accommodations are scarce in Cabo San Lucas. The handful of inexpensive hostelries often have no vacancies, so it's wise to call ahead for reservations or to arrive early when other travelers are checking out.

Very Expensive

Melia San Lucas

Playa Médano, Cabo San Lucas, B.C.S. 23410. ☎ **114/3-1000,** or 800/336-3542 in the U.S. Fax 114/3-0418. 180 rms, 10 suites. A/C MINIBAR TV TEL. $165–$210 double.

By far the most popular hotel in Cabo San Lucas, the Melia sits above Playa Médano within easy walking distance of town. A tall, peaked palapa covers the lobby, with its breathtaking view of El Arco. All rooms, furnished in wicker and

Cabo San Lucas

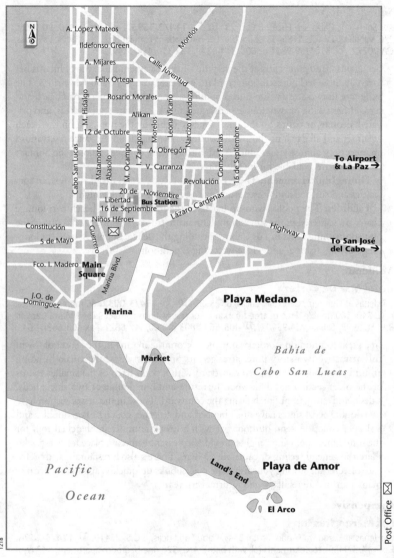

white marble, have balconies with views of the ocean and the landscaped pool area. Satellite TV brings in U.S. channels. Each room has its own safe.

Dining/Entertainment: Three restaurants cover the dining spectrum from haute cuisine (where reservations are required) to seafood by the beach. Two bars, one of them swim-up, keep guests well watered. There's live entertainment nightly in the lobby.

Services: Laundry and room service; boutique; hairstyling; tour desk; car rental; rentals of water sport equipment, bicycles, and motor scooters; nearby golf courses.

Facilities: Pool, heated in winter.

Solmar Suites

Av. Solmar 1, Cabo San Lucas, B.C.S. 23410. ☎ **114/3-3535.** Fax 114/3-0410. 90 suites. A/C MINIBAR TV TEL. $185–$312 double. For reservations contact Box 383, Pacific Palisades, CA 90272. ☎ 310/459-9861 or 800/344-3349. Fax 310/454-3349.

Set against sandstone cliffs at the very tip of the Baja peninsula, the Solmar is beloved by those seeking seclusion, comfort, and easy access to Cabo's diversions. The suites are in two-story white stucco buildings along the edge of a broad beach and have either a king or two double beds, satellite TV, separate seating areas, and private balconies or patios on the sand. Guests gather by the pool and on the beach at sunset and all day long during the winter whale migration. Advance reservations are necessary almost year-round. A small time-share complex adjoins the Solmar; some units are available for nightly stays.

Dining/Entertainment: The restaurant, La Roca, serves excellent Mexican specialties and seafood and presents a Mexican fiesta on Saturday nights.

Facilities: The pool's swim-up bar faces the palapa-covered beach bar; lounge chairs are scattered in the sun and under mature palms. The Solmar has one of the best sportfishing fleets in Los Cabos, including the deluxe Solmar V used for long-range diving, fishing, and whale-watching expeditions.

Moderate

Hotel Mar De Cortez

Cárdenas at Guerrero, Cabo San Lucas, B.C.S. 23410. ☎ **114/3-0032.** 66 rooms, 16 suites. A/C. $40–$60 double. Free guarded parking. For reservations contact 17561 Vierra Canyon Rd., Suite 99, Salinas, CA 93907. ☎ 408/663-5803 or 800/347-8821. Fax 408/663-1904.

In a great location on Cárdenas one block from the marina in the center of town, this attractive two-story hotel arranged its Spanish-style white stucco building around a rambling, landscaped courtyard with a pool. Each of the smaller rooms of the older section has dark-wood furniture and one double or two single beds, a desk, and a tiny front porch facing the courtyard. Those in the newer section have two double beds; suites have one king bed and a sleeper couch or two doubles and a sleeper couch. A semi-outdoor bar with a fireplace under its thatched roof for the sometimes-cool winter nights provides a pleasant gathering place for guests who share the general feeling of camaraderie here. There's also a restaurant with a TV and a freezer for storing your fish. The place books up quickly, apparently because many patrons are regulars who return every year.

Inexpensive

Las Margaritas Inn

Cárdenas at Zaragoza (Apdo. Postal 354), Cabo San Lucas, B.C.S. 23410. ☎ **114/3-1696.** Fax 114/3-0450. 16 apartments (all with bath). A/C. $28 one-bedroom apartment; $47 two-bedroom suite. Free unguarded parking.

Located in Plaza Aramburo in the heart of town across from the marina, this three-story property features 14 one- and two-bedroom apartments which are attractively decorated in white and pastels with contemporary furniture and furnished kitchens. Each bedroom has a double bed, and the living rooms have sleeper sofas. All rooms on the second and third stories open off the balconies overlooking the busy parking lot; when traffic is slow, you can catch a view of the marina across the street. Plaza Aramburo is one of the busiest places in town and has the least expensive grocery store and pharmacy. Noise is a problem here.

Siesta Suites

Zapata at Hidalgo (Apdo. Postal 310), Cabo San Lucas, B.C.S. 23410. ☎ and fax **114/3-2773.** 15 suites (all with bath and kitchenette). A/C or FAN. $30 double; $3.50 extra person.

Reservations are a must at this small inn, which opened in early 1994. The rooms have white tile floors and white walls, kitchenettes with seating areas, refrigerators, and sinks. The mattresses are new and firm and the bathrooms are large and immaculately clean. The proprietors are accommodating. Weekly and monthly rates are available. The hotel is one and a half blocks from the marina, where parking is available.

DINING

Prices, as a rule, decrease the farther inland you walk from the waterfront. For the best dining bargains, walk north along Morelos, heading inland from the sea. Many Los Cabos restaurants have reduced prices in summer; some close for a few weeks or a month if business is really slow.

Expensive

El Galeón

Marina Blv. ☎ **114/3-0443.** Reservations recommended during the Christmas and Easter holidays. Main courses $8–$30; soup $2.50–$8; dessert $3–$5. Daily 4–11pm. ITALIAN.

On a hillside overlooking the town and harbor, this Neapolitan-Italian restaurant serves wonderful Caesar salad, homemade pasta, pizza, and seafood. The night view of lights twinkling around the harbor is especially romantic while the pianist plays in the background. Save room for the chocolate-mousse pie or stop by late in the evening for an espresso by the piano. The restaurant is west of the town marina near the turnoff to the Solmar Suites Hotel.

✪ Mi Casa

Calle Cabo San Lucas. ☎ **114/3-1933.** Main dishes $8–$20. Mon–Sat 2–10pm. MEXICAN.

This is Cabo's finest gourmet Mexican restaurant. The building's vivid cobalt-blue facade is your first clue that this place celebrates Mexico, and the menu confirms your impression. Fresh fish is prepared with delicious seasonings and recipes from throughout Mexico. Especially pleasant at night, the tables, scattered around a large patio, are set with colorful cloths, traditional pottery, and glassware. The restaurant is across from the main plaza.

Moderate

Latitude 22+

Blv. Lázaro Cárdenas. ☎ **114/3-1516.** Tacos $1–$4; burgers $4–$7; main courses $5–$12; New York steak and prime rib $15. Wed–Mon 7am–midnight. MEXICAN/AMERICAN.

You can eat heartily and inexpensively at the taco stand beside the front door of Latitude 22+ or you can feast on prime rib inside. License plates, signs, sports caps, and a 959-pound blue marlin decorate the raffish restaurant/bar. U.S. sports events play on five TVs scattered about, and pool tables, dart boards, and assorted games keep the customers buying more and more beers. Latitude 22+ is located one block north of the town's only traffic light.

Señor Sushi

Blv. Marina at Guerrero. ☎ **114/3-1323.** Tacos $3; main courses $8–$15. Daily 8am–11pm. MEXICAN/AMERICAN.

Despite its name, there's nary a raw fish or seaweed wrapper in sight. Barbecued ribs are the specialty of the house. Drinks are half-priced from 2 to 7pm. Tables are set in a raised dining room above the sidewalk, somewhat removed from the pandemonium of the street. Portions of fajitas, barbecued ribs, and steak are generous, and the ambience is less rowdy than that at neighboring bars and restaurants.

Inexpensive

Tacos Chidos
Zapata s/n. ☎ **114/3-0551.** Breakfast $2; three tacos $2; main courses $2–$4.75. Mon–Sat 7am–10pm. MEXICAN.

At this tiny family-run place with an open kitchen behind the wooden counter, you can sit on a stool and watch the preparation of some of the most delicious cheap eats in Los Cabos. Everything's fresh and homemade, including the corn tortillas and several different salsas. Breakfasts include eggs, rice, beans, and coffee. Fish tacos made with fresh dorado are superb. The place is between Hidalgo and Guerrero, about a block in from Marina Boulevard.

The Fish Company
Av. Guerrero at Zapata. ☎ **114/3-1405.** Three tacos $3.50; grilled fish $5.25; fajitas $3.75. Daily 8:30am–10pm. MEXICAN/SEAFOOD.

Owner Miguel Olvera has a good share of fans among local diners tired of high prices and small portions. His small restaurant has only nine tables covered with white-and-blue cloths, though he has plans for expansion. Fishermen can have their catch prepared with all the fixings (rice or baked potato, beans, and tortillas) for $5. If you're tired of fish, the *carne asada* is great.

CABO SAN LUCAS AFTER DARK

Cabo San Lucas is the nightlife capital of Baja, though after-dark fun is centered around the party ambience and camaraderie found in the casual bars and restaurants rather than around a flashy disco scene. You can easily find a happy hour with live music and a place to dance or a Mexican fiesta with mariachis, and you'll also find discos.

Mexican Fiestas and Theme Nights
Some of the larger hotels have weekly "Fiesta Nights," "Italian Nights," and other buffet-plus-entertainment theme nights that can be fun as well as a good buy. Check travel agencies and the following hotels: the **Solmar** (☎ 114/3-0022), the **Finisterra** (☎ 114/3-0000), the **Hacienda** (☎ 114/3-0123), the **Plaza las Glorias** (☎ 114/3-1220), and the **Melia San Lucas** (☎ 114/3-0420). Prices range from $12 (drinks, tax, and tips are extra) to $30 (which covers everything, including an open bar with national drinks).

Sunset Watching
At twilight time, settle into one of these watering holes on the slender point that leads to Land's End where the two seas meet and watch the sun sink into the Pacific.

El Trebol
In the Solmar Hotel. ☎ **114/3-3535.**

Under a big, round palapa beside a broad beach, you can listen to Pacific rollers thunder in the distance while mariachis play nightly from 6:30 to 7:30pm. As the sun sets, it gilds the high outcropping of sienna rocks behind the hotel. El Trebol is open daily from 7am to 11pm. Beer goes for $2; margaritas cost from $3.50 to $6.

Whale Watcher's Bar
In the Hotel Finisterra. ☎ **114/3-0000** or 3-0100.

The high terrace offers a splendid view of sea and beach, as well as frolicking whales from January to March. Mariachis play on Friday, Saturday, and Sunday from 5 to 8pm. The bar is open daily from noon to 11pm. "Whale margaritas" cost $4; beer, $3. There are two-for-one drinks during happy hour from 4 to 6pm.

Happy Hours
If you shop around, you can usually find an *hora alegre* somewhere in town between noon and 7pm.

Giggling Marlin
On Cárdenas across from the marina. ☎ **114/3-0606.**

Live music alternating with tapes blasts the merry patrons here, who occasionally jump up to dance in front of the band. A contraption of winches, ropes, and pulleys above a mattress provide entertainment as couples literally string each other up by the heels—just like a captured marlin. The food is only fair here; stick with nachos and drinks. There is live music Wednesday through Sunday from 8pm to midnight during high season. The Giggling Marlin is open daily from 8am to midnight; the bar stays open to 1am. Beer runs $2 to $5; schooner margaritas cost $6. There are discounts during happy hour from 2 to 6pm.

Río Grill Restaurant and Bar
Blv. Marina 31-A. ☎ **114/3-1335.**

The curving bar in the middle of the room has a cozy neighborhood feeling, with tourists and locals taking advantage of the two-for-one happy-hour margaritas. Soft music plays during dinner. On Thursday through Sunday live rhythm-and-blues and reggae bands play from 9:30pm to 12:30am. On Thursdays at 8:30pm enthusiastic patrons participate in "Karaoke Kraziness." The Río Grill is open daily from noon to midnight. Margaritas are $3.50 or two for one during happy hour, 3 to 7pm.

El Squid Roe
Blv. Marina. ☎ **114/3-0655.**

El Squid Roe is one of the late Carlos Anderson's inspirations, and it still attracts crowds with its nostalgic decor and eclectic food that's far better than it deserves to be for such a fun party place. As fashionable as blue jeans, this is a place to see and be seen. There's a patio out back for dancing. It's open daily from noon to 2am. Beer costs $2; margaritas cost $3.50. There are two-for-one drinks during happy hour, 2 to 4pm daily.

Dancing

Cabo Wabo Cantina
Guerrero at Cárdenas. ☎ **114/3-1188.** Cover $15 for live shows (includes two drinks); otherwise no cover.

Owned by the band Van Halen and its Mexican and American partners, this "cantina" packs in youthful crowds, especially when rumors fly that a surprise appearance by a vacationing musician is imminent. Live rock bands from the United

States, Mexico, Europe, and Australia perform frequently on the well-equipped stage. When live music is absent, a disco-type sound system blasts out mostly rock and roll; conversations are drowned out by the music. Overstuffed furniture frames the dance floor. For snacks, the Taco-Wabo, just outside the club's entrance, stays up late, too. The cantina is open nightly from 8pm to 4am. Drinks run from $3 to $5.

AN EXCURSION TO TODOS SANTOS

Artists, entrepreneurs, and foreign residents are turning the small town of Todos Santos into one of the most charming spots in Baja. Long the agricultural center of southern Baja, Todos Santos lies 87 miles north of Cabo San Lucas on Mexico Highway 19. The ride up the Pacific Coast passes gorgeous wild beaches, isolated campgrounds, and a few solitary homes. Several farms in the area specialize in organic produce that is shipped to gourmet restaurants in Los Cabos and southern California. The town of 4,000 residents is undergoing a real-estate boom, and entrepreneurs are investing in older mansions around the town plaza for use as private homes, shops, and restaurants. Todos Santos is a good stopover for those traveling between Cabo and La Paz, and the town is well worth a day's excursion, which can be arranged through tour companies in Los Cabos.

ACCOMMODATIONS & DINING

Hotel California

Calle Juárez between Morelos and Marquez de Leon. ☎ **114/4-0002,** or 800/736-8636 in the U.S. Fax 114/5-2333. 16 rms (all with bath). A/C or FAN. $28 double.

This hotel is benefiting from the town's popularity, and reservations are a good idea in high season. Grouped around a courtyard, the rooms face either the street or a courtyard and small pool; most have been refurbished with fresh paint, tiled bathrooms, and new curtains. Parking is available on the street.

Café Santa Fe

Calle Centenario 4. ☎ **114/5-0340.** Main courses $6–$15. Wed–Mon noon–9pm. Closed in October. ITALIAN.

Much of the attention Todos Santos is receiving these days can be directly attributed to this superb cafe. Owners Ezio and Paula Colombo have completely refurbished a large stucco house across from the plaza, creating several dining rooms and a lovely courtyard located near a garden of hibiscus, bougainvillea, papaya trees, and herbs. The Italian cuisine emphasizes local produce and seafood; try the homemade ravioli stuffed with spinach and ricotta in a gorgonzola sauce or the ravioli with lobster and shrimp. In high season the wait for a table at lunch can last for hours; once seated, patrons tend to take their time, lingering over espresso and tiramisu.

2　La Paz

110 miles N of Cabo San Lucas, 122 miles N of San José del Cabo, 980 miles S of Tijuana

La Paz means "Peace," and few things are more peaceful in Baja than relaxing in an open-air cafe along La Paz's palm-fringed seaside boulevard as the sun sets across the saucer-shaped bay. This laid-back yet thriving port city of 180,000 is also the capital of the state of Baja California Sur. Though visitors are welcomed and can find plenty to do, La Paz doesn't have the feeling of a tourist town. Since it's a port, several of its streets bustle with small shops stuffed with foreign goods, including perfumes, high-tech gadgets, and silk pajamas from the Far East.

La Paz is at the center of fine beach country; within a 50-mile radius lie some of the loveliest *playas* in Baja, many accessible by car or bus or through organized tours. While this casual capital is enjoyable anytime, its carefree charm bursts into full bloom during Carnaval, when La Paz is the place to be in Baja for the Mexican version of Mardi Gras.

ESSENTIALS

GETTING THERE & DEPARTING   By Plane   Aero California (☎ 112/5-1023) has flights to La Paz from Los Angeles, Loreto, Tijuana, and Mexico City. **Aeroméxico** (☎ 112/2-0091, 2-0093, or 2-1636) flies in from Ciudad Obregón, Culiacán, Los Mochis, Guaymas, Hermosillo, Mexico City, Guadalajara, Tijuana, Tucson, and Los Angeles.

By Bus   The Central Camionera (main bus station) is at Jalisco and Héroes de la Independencia, about 25 blocks southwest of the center of town; it's open daily from 6am to 10pm. The bus lines—first-class **Tres Estrellas de Oro** (☎ 2-6476), second-class **Aguila** (☎ 2-7094 or 5-7330), and second-class **Transportes de La Paz**—serve La Paz with buses from the south (Los Cabos) and north (as far as Tijuana). From Los Cabos it's $2^{1}/_{2}$ to $3^{1}/_{2}$ hours to La Paz (if you take the short route—the Vía Corta); from Loreto to La Paz it's five hours. Buses leave every two or three hours for Los Cabos (south) and points north (Loreto and beyond). It's best to buy your ticket in person the day before, though Tres Estrellas de Oro says reservations can be made over the phone.

To get to the station, catch the "Ruta INSS" city bus near the corner of Revolucion and Degollado by the market. It's often crowded, so be prepared to stand. The fare is about 50¢. Taxi fare from downtown to the station runs $3 to $3.50.

To get to Pichilingue, the ferry pier, and outlying beaches, the **Aguila** line has a station, sometimes called the "beach bus station," on the Malecón at Independencia (☎ 2-3063 or 2-4270). The station is open daily from 8am to 6pm.

By Car   From San José del Cabo, Highway 1 north is the longer, more scenic route; you can travel a flatter and faster route by taking Highway 1 east to Cabo San Lucas, then Highway 19 north through Todos Santos. A little before San Pedro, Highway 19 rejoins Highway 1 north into La Paz; the trip takes two to three hours. From Loreto to the north, Highway 1 south is the only choice; the trip takes four to five hours.

By Ferry   Two **SEMATUR car ferries** serve La Paz from Topolobampo (the port for Los Mochis) Monday through Saturday at 8pm (a 10-hour trip) and from Mazatlán Sunday through Friday at 3pm. Tickets can be purchased in Topolobampo at the Ferry Pier (☎ 686/2-0141; fax 686/2-0035) and in Mazatlán at the Terminal Transbordadores (☎ 69/81-7020; fax 69/81-7023).

The SEMATUR car ferry departs for Topolobampo Monday and Wednesday through Saturday at 8pm (a 10-hour trip) and for Mazatlán on Sunday through Friday at 3pm (an 18-hour crossing). The dock is at Pichilingue, 11 miles north of La Paz. Passengers pay one fee for themselves and another for their vehicles. The one-way fare per passenger to Topolobampo is $15 in Salón class—about 440 bus-type seats in one or more large rooms on the lower deck. To Mazatlán, one-way fares are $22 for Salón class (which can become very crowded); $43 for Turista class (a tiny room with four bunks, chair, sink, window, and individual baths/

showers down the hall); and $65 for Cabina class (a small room with one bunk, chair, table, window, and private bath).

SEMATUR ferries are usually equipped with a cafeteria and bar. Nevertheless, it's wise to bring some of your own food and bottled water. Also, reserve as early as possible and confirm your reservation 24 hours before departure; you can pick up tickets at the port terminal ticket office as late as the morning of the day you are leaving. Ferry tickets are sold at the office at 5 de Mayo no. 502 at Guillermo Pieta, La Paz, B.C.S. 23000 (☎ 112/5-3833, or 5-4666). Though the office is open daily from 7am to 1pm and 4 to 6pm, you can only purchase tickets between 7 and 10am. Tickets can also be purchased at the SEMATUR office at the Pichilingue ferry dock (☎ 112/2-9485; fax 112/5-6588); it's open daily from 7am to 1pm and 4 to 6pm. Several tour agencies in town book reservations on the ferry, but it is best to buy your ticket in person at the ferry office.

Important note: Those planning to take their cars on the ferry to the Mexican mainland will be required to meet all the requirements listed in "Crossing the Border with Your Car" (see "Getting There" in Chapter 3), and all travelers going to the mainland need tourist cards. Tourism officials in La Paz say it's best to get your car permit and tourist card when you first cross the border at Tijuana, since the system is more efficient there.

The SEMATUR transport to the Pichilingue dock leaves 1½ hours before the ferry departs from the SEMATUR office on 5 de Mayo no. 502; confirm the bus and ferry departure times when you buy your ticket. Buses to Pichilingue also depart from the "beach bus terminal" on the Malecón at Independencia nearly every hour from 8am to 6pm. Bus fare is $1. A taxi from downtown La Paz to the dock will cost around $15.

ORIENTATION   Arriving by Plane   The airport (☎ 2-9386) is 11 miles southwest of town along the highway to Ciudad Constitución and Tijuana. Airport colectivos (minivans) to downtown cost around $10 (they run only from the airport to town, not vice versa). The taxi fare to or from the airport is about $16.

Arriving by Bus   Buses arrive at the **Central Camionera**, about 25 blocks southwest of downtown. A cab from here to hotels into the center of town will run $3 to $3.50.

Arriving by Ferry   Buses line up in front of the ferry dock at Pichilingue to meet every arriving ferry. They charge about $1 for the ride into town, stopping at the "beach bus station" on the Malecón at Independencia—within walking distance of many downtown hotels if you're not encumbered with luggage. A taxi from the ferry into downtown La Paz (11 miles) costs around $15.

Information   The **State Tourist Office** (Secretaría Estatal y Delegación Federal de Turismo de B.C.S.) is headquartered near the Fidepaz Marina at km 5.5 Carretera Nortenorte (☎ 112/4-0100; fax 112/4-0720). The office is open Monday through Friday from 9am to 5pm. More accessible to travelers is the **tourist information office** on the Malecón across from the intersection with Calle 16 de Septiembre (☎ 112/2-1199, 2-7975, or 2-5939). It's open Monday through Friday from 8am to 8pm. The extremely helpful staff speaks English and can supply information on La Paz, Los Cabos, and the rest of the region.

Another source of tourist information is **tourist services in the lobby of the Hotel Los Arcos** (☎ 112/1-5577 or 5-4794), open daily from 9am to 2pm and from 4 to 7pm. Jack and Jackie Velez have been operating this service for years as part of their sportfishing business and are extremely knowledgeable about the area. The English-speaking staff can help with everything from airline schedules to whale-watching trips, not to mention water sports, tours, and cruises.

City Layout   Although La Paz sprawls well inland from the **Malecón** (the seaside boulevard, **Paseo Alvaro Obregón**), you'll probably spend most of your time in the older, more congenial downtown section within a few blocks of the waterfront.

Getting Around   Because most of what you'll need in town is located on the Malecón between the tourist information office and the Hotel Los Arcos or a few blocks inland from the waterfront, it's easy to get around La Paz on foot. There are public **buses** that go to some of the beaches north of town (see "Fun on and off the Beach," below), but to explore the many beaches within 50 miles of La Paz, your best bet is to rent a car. There are several auto-rental agencies on the Malecón.

FAST FACTS: LA PAZ

Area Code   The telephone area code is 112.

Banks   Banks generally exchange currency Monday through Friday from 9am to noon.

Marinas   La Paz has three marinas: Marina de La Paz, at the west end of the Malecón at Legaspi (☎ 112/5-2112 or 5-1646); Marina Palmira, south of town at km 2.5 on the Pichilingue Highway (☎ 112/5-3959); and Marina Fidepaz, scheduled to open in 1995 at km 4.5 Carretera Norte.

Post Office   The Correos is three blocks inland at Constitución and Revolución de 1910 and is open Monday through Friday from 8am to 6pm and Saturday from 8am to 1pm.

FUN ON AND OFF THE BEACH

La Paz combines the unself-conscious bustle of a small capital port city with beautiful beaches not far from town. Everything from whale watching to beach tours to sunset cruises can usually be arranged through travel agencies in major hotels or along the Malecón.

SPECIAL EVENTS

February features the biggest and best **Carnaval/Mardi Gras** in Baja. In March there's the **Festival of the Whale.** May 3 features a **festival celebrating the city's founding** by Cortés in 1535. The annual **marlin-fishing tournament** is in August, with other fishing tournaments scheduled in September and November. And on **November 1–2,** the Day of the Dead, altars are on display at the Anthropology Museum.

BEACHES

Near La Paz lie some of the loveliest beaches in Baja, many rivaling those of the Caribbean with their clear, turquoise water. Don't be surprised if you have a beach or cove to yourself—some isolated shores are accessible only by dirt road or boat. Public buses from the "beach bus station" at Independencia on the Malecón depart almost every hour from 8am to 5 or 6pm for beaches to the north. The buses stop at **Playa Coromuel** (3.1 miles), **Playa Camancito** (5 miles), **Playa Tesorso** (8.9 miles), and **Pichilingue** (10.5 miles; from the ferry stop, walk north to the beach). Both Pichilingue and Coromuel beaches have palapa-shaded bars and restaurants. The last bus back to town leaves the beaches around 6:30pm. The one-way fare is $1. The road is paved as far as **Playa Tecolote** and **Playa Balandra** (13 miles), the prettiest beach, but the buses go only as far as Pichilingue.

The beach at **La Concha Beach Resort,** km 5.5 on the Pichilingue Highway, about six miles north of town (☎ 112/2-6544), rents equipment for snorkeling, waterskiing, diving, fishing, windsurfing, and sailing. Sunset cruises and other nautical adventures are also offered. The beach is open to the public (as are all Mexican beaches), and the hotel has a good poolside restaurant and bar. A taxi from town costs about $10 one way. For more information, call the resort.

For more information about beaches and maps, check at the tourist information office on the malecon.

WHALE WATCHING

Between January and March (and sometimes as early as December), gray whales migrate from the Bering Strait to the Pacific Coast of Baja. The main whale-watching spots are Laguna San Ignacio (on the Pacific near San Ignacio), Magdalena Bay (on the Pacific near Puerto López Mateos—about a two-hour drive from La Paz), and Scammon's Lagoon (near Guerrero Negro).

Though it is located across the peninsula on the Sea of Cortez, La Paz has the only major international airport in the area and thus has become the center of Baja's whale-watching excursions. Most tours originating in La Paz go to Magdalena Bay, where the whales give birth to their calves in calm waters. Several companies arrange whale-watching tours originating either in La Paz or other Baja towns or in the U.S. Most tours from the U.S. begin at $1,000 per person for a week-long trip, including airfare to La Paz.

Baja Expeditions, Sonora 586 (☎ 112/5-3828; fax 112/5-3829), has been operating trips to Baja since 1983 and offers a variety of itineraries with air or ground transportation to the Sea of Cortez, Magdalena Bay, and Laguna San Ignacio. Their whale-watching trips, originating in La Paz, include a boat tour of the whales in the Sea of Cortez, a boat trip around the tip of Baja to Magdalena Bay, and road tours to Magdalena Bay and Laguna San Ignacio. It's best to reserve your spot on a tour through the U.S. office before traveling to La Paz; for reservations and information in the U.S. and Canada contact them at 2625 Garnet Ave., San Diego, CA 92109 (☎ 619/581-3311, or 800/843-6967; fax 619/581-6542).

Baja California Tours (☎ 619/454-7166; fax 619/454-2703 in San Diego, CA) provides information on a variety of tours and offers a motorcoach tour from Tijuana to La Paz with stops at Scammon's Lagoon and Magdalena Bay.

Tour companies in La Paz itself also offer whale-watching trips to Magdalena Bay. The 12-hour excursion starts at around $100 per person, including breakfast, lunch, transportation, and an English-speaking guide. Make reservations at the **Hotel Los Arcos** travel desk (☎ 112/2-2744, ext. 608), **Viajes Buendía Osório** (☎ 112/2-6544 or 5-0467), or **Viajes Coromuel** (☎ 112/2-8006).

You can go whale watching without joining a tour by taking an Aguila bus from La Paz to Puerto López Mateos or San Carlos at Magdalena Bay (a three-hour ride) and hire a boat there. It's a difficult trip to do in one day, but there are a few very modest hotels in San Carlos. Check at the La Paz tourist office for information.

MARINE EXCURSIONS

The most fascinating **cruise** is to Isla Espíritu Santo and Los Islotes to visit the largest sea-lion colony in Baja, stunning rock formations, and remote beaches, with stops for snorkeling, swimming, and lunch. If conditions permit, you may even be able to snorkel beside the sea lions. Both boat and bus tours are available to Puerto Balandra, where pristine coves of crystal-blue water and ivory sand are framed by bold rock formations rising up like humpback whales. **Viajes Coromuel** at the Hotel Los Arcos (☎ 112/2-8006); **Viajes Palmira** (☎ 112/2-4030) on the Malecón across from the Los Arcos; and other travel agencies can arrange these all-day trips, weather permitting, for $40 to $60 per person. Sometimes a minimum of four to six people is required.

Scuba-diving trips, best from June through September, can be arranged through **Fernando Aguilar's Baja Diving and Services** at Independencia 107-A (☎ 112/2-1826; fax 2-8644). Diving sites include the sea-lion colony at Los Islotes; distant Cerralvo Island; the sunken ship *Salvatierra;* a 60-foot wall dive; several sea mounts (underwater mountains) and reefs; and a trip to see hammer-head sharks and manta rays. Rates start at $65 to $75 per person for an all-day excursion and two-tank dive. **Baja Expeditions,** Sonora 586 (☎ 112/5-3828; fax 5-3829) in La Paz (see "Whale Watching," above, for information in the U.S. and Canada), runs live-aboard and single-day dive trips to the above-mentioned locations and other areas in the Sea of Cortez.

Kayaking has become extremely popular in the many bays and coves near La Paz. Many enthusiasts bring their own equipment. Kayaking trips can be arranged in advance with Baja Expeditions (see "Whale Watching," above); **Mar y Aventuras** (☎ 112/2-2744, ext. 608 or 5-4794); or **Baja Outdoor Activities** at the Hotel Yeneka (☎ 112/5-4688).

SPORTFISHING

La Paz is justly famous for its sportfishing and attracts anglers from all over the world; its waters are home to more than 850 species of fish. Here's a list of the most sought-after fish and when you can find them: black marlin, August through November; crevalle, January through October; dorado, June through December; roosterfish, snapper, and grouper, April through October; marlin, May through July; needlefish, May through September; sailfish, June through November; sierra, October through June; wahoo, April though December; yellowfin tuna, April through December; and yellowtail, December through May. The most economical approach is to rent a *panga* (skiff) with guide and equipment for $125 for three hours. Super pangas, which have a shade cover and comfortable seats, start at around $180 for two persons. Larger cruisers with bathrooms start at $240.

Sportfishing trips can be arranged through hotels and tour agencies. One of the best-known operations is Jack Velez's **Dorado Velez Fleet;** call him for reservations at the Hotel Los Arcos Fishing Desk (☎ 112/2-2744, ext. 608) or write to him at Apdo. Postal 402, La Paz, B.C.S. 23000. Other operations include the **Mosquito Fleet** (☎ 112/2-1674) and **Baja Fishing** (☎ 112/2-1313).

HISTORIC LA PAZ

The **Anthropology Museum,** on Altamirano between Constitución and 5 de Mayo (☎ 112/2-0162), features large, though faded, color photos of Baja's pre-historic cave paintings. There are also exhibits on various topics, including the geological history of the peninsula, fossils, missions, colonial history, and daily life. All information is in Spanish. Admission is free (donations are encouraged); it's open Monday through Friday from 8am to 6pm and Saturday from 9am to 2pm.

Our Lady of La Paz Mission (the La Paz cathedral), founded in 1720, is on the main square on Revolución between 5 de Mayo and Independencia. It was part of the chain of California Jesuit missions.

El Teatro de la Ciudad, Av. Navarro 700 (☎ 112/5-0004), is the city's cultural center; there are performances by visiting and local artists.

The **Casa de Gobierno,** across the plaza from the mission church on Madero between 5 de Mayo and Independencia, houses the **Biblioteca de las Californias** (Library of the Californias). The small collection of historical documents and books is the most comprehensive in Baja and is open to the public Monday through Friday from 8am to 8pm. Free international films are sometimes shown in the evenings.

City tours of all the major sights are offered by most tour agencies. Tours last about three hours, include time for shopping, and cost $12 to $15 per person.

A DAY-TRIP

A day-trip by car or guided tour to **Los Cabos** at the southern tip of Baja California, where the Pacific Ocean meets the Sea of Cortez, will take you past dramatic scenery and many photogenic isolated beaches. A guided tour that includes lunch and a glass-bottom-boat tour to El Arco in Cabo San Lucas costs $45 to $60 per person and can be booked through most travel agencies. Most tours last from 7am to 6pm, and some include breakfast.

SHOPPING

La Paz is a shopping mecca for residents of Baja Sur but has little in the way of folk art or other treasures from mainland Mexico. Several large supermarkets display a wide selection of groceries from the United States, and the shops along 16 de Septiembre are stuffed with imported electronic gear and trinkets from China. The dense cluster of streets behind the Hotel Perla between 16 de Septiembre and Degollado is chock-full of small shops, some tacky though others quite upscale. The municipal market at Revolución and Degollado, however, has little of interest to visitors. Stores selling crafts, folk art, clothing, and handmade furniture and accessories lie mostly along the **Malecón (Paseo Obregón)** or a block or two in from the Malecón.

If you like beautiful handwoven tablecloths, place mats, rugs, and other textiles, it's worth the long walk or taxi ride to **Artesanías Cuauhtémoc,** also called "The Weaver" (Abasolo 3315 between Jalisco and Nayarit; ☎ 112/2-4575). Fortunato Silva, an elderly gentleman, weaves wonderfully textured cotton textiles from yarn he spins and dyes himself. He charges far less than what you'd pay for equivalent craftsmanship/artistry in the United States.

ACCOMMODATIONS
EXPENSIVE

Hotel Los Arcos
Paseo Obregón 498 (Apdo. Postal 112), La Paz, B.C.S. 23000. ☎ **112/2-2744** or 2-2150; in the U.S. 714/476-5555 or 800/347-2252. Fax 112/5-4313. 180 rms, 52 in bungalows, 8 suites (all with bath). A/C MINIBAR TV TEL. $89 double; $103 suite. Free guarded parking.

This three-story neocolonial-style hotel at the west end of the Malecón, between Rosales and Allende, is the best place if you want to splurge on downtown accommodations. Los Arcos is decidedly modern in its furnishings and amenities, which include room service, laundry, a cafeteria, an upscale restaurant, a bar with live music, a travel agency, and a desk for fishing information. The hotel's rambling nooks and crannies are filled with fountains, plants, and even rocking chairs that lend lots of old-fashioned charm. Most rooms come with two double beds and a balcony overlooking the pool in the inner courtyard or the waterfront. Bungalows (with fireplaces) in the separate Cabañas de Los Arcos section are nestled into an appealing jungle garden shaded by large trees. This complex also offers two pools (one heated), a sauna, Ping-Pong tables, and a tourist-information booth in the lobby. TVs carry U.S. channels.

La Concha Beach Resort

Km 5 Carretera Pichilingue, La Paz, B.C.S. 23000. ☎ **112/2-6544** or 800/999-2252. Fax 112/2-6218. 107 rms, 12 condos. A/C TEL. $95 double; $140 suite. Free guarded parking.

Though a long distance north of downtown La Paz, the setting of this resort is perfect, on a curving beach ideal for swimming and water sports. All rooms face the water and have double beds, balconies or patios, and small tables and chairs. The only satellite TV available is in a large lounge, where movies are shown every evening. Condos with full kitchens and one or three bedrooms are also available on a nightly basis in the high-rise complex next door. The hotel offers scuba, fishing, and whale-watching packages.

Dining/Entertainment: Two bars. The restaurant and poolside bar often host buffet dinners, brunch, and Mexican fiestas.

Services: Laundry and room service, tour desk, free twice-daily shuttle to town (otherwise, taxis charge around $10 one way).

Facilities: Beachside pool, two tennis courts.

MODERATE

Hotel Perla

Paseo Obregón, 1570 (Apdo. Postal 207), La Paz, B.C.S. 23000. ☎ **112/2-0777.** Fax 112/5-5363. 101 rms (all with bath). A/C TV TEL. $48–$55 double; $60 triple. Extra person $15. Free guarded parking.

Well situated in the center of the Malecón between Callejón La Paz and Arreola, this attractive four-story hotel overlooks the bay. The rooms have white textured walls and chunky, blond-wood furniture, including king-size beds in 10 rooms. Amenities include a pool and sun deck on the second floor, a travel agency, a nightclub, laundry service, and room service daily from 7am to 11pm. A local favorite is the hotel's airy streetside restaurant, La Terraza, a great spot for margaritas and sunsets over the water. Try to get one of the 28 rooms with a sea view.

Hotel Suites Marina

Km 2.5 Carretera a Pichilingue (Apdo. Postal 34), La Paz, B.C.S. 23000. ☎ **112/2-6254** or 800/826-1138 in the U.S. Fax 112/2-6277. 48 rooms and suites (all with bath). A/C TV TEL. $60 double room; $100–$120 double suite. Free guarded parking.

This hotel opened on the road to Pichilingue in 1994 alongside a marina and a time-share complex. The rooms and suites in the four-story building have a blue-and-brown color scheme and balconies facing the water. Regular rooms have two queen-sized beds; studio suites have an additional sofa bed and kitchenette; master suites have a separate bedroom with king-size bed and a full kitchen. A large pool meanders under bridges by the marina.

Mar y Sol

Insurgentes at Margaritas, Apdo. Postal 438, La Paz, B.C.S. 23000. ☎ **112/5-2467** or 415/346-6337 in the U.S. Fax 112/2-0180. 10 suites. AC TV. $308 one-bedroom suite for a week; $594 two-bedroom suite for a week.

More like a private home than a hotel, the Mar y Sol has ten luxurious units with full kitchens and dining areas. A brick wall surrounds the buildings, large swimming pool, and lush landscape of palms and birds of paradise, giving the hotel the look of a private estate. Vivid serape fabrics cover the windows and beds, and the *equipale* and iron furnishings add to the feel of Old Mexico. Many guests return annually for a month or more, becoming friends with owner/manager, Carol Palenzona. Stays longer than a week are discounted. Mar y Sol is two blocks from the beach west of town.

Villas del Mar

Marina Fidepaz (Apdo. Postal 482), La Paz, B.C.S. 23000. ☎ **112/4-0830.** Fax 112/4-0837. 54 suites. A/C TV TEL. $85 junior suite for two persons; $133 two-bedroom suite for up to six persons. Free guarded parking.

After years of construction, the Marina Fidepaz development opened its first hotel rooms in late 1994. The two-story terra-cotta colored buildings sit close to the marina, with a bridge leading over the long swimming pool to the water. All suites have kitchen areas with refrigerators, sinks, and dining tables. The resort complex includes a full gym, convention center, minimarket, and video bar. More suites and a high-rise hotel are in the planning stages.

INEXPENSIVE

El Mesón

Felix Ortega 2330, La Paz, B.C.S. 23000. ☎ **112/5-7454.** Fax 112/5-7464. 8 rms (all with bath). A/C TV TEL. $30 double (including continental breakfast). Free guarded parking.

The sedate decor and courteous clerks make this a regular choice for discerning travelers more interested in a comfortable room than a tourist-oriented location. The handsome rooms have an Asian flair, with large tiled baths, sliding shower doors, double or king-size beds, and verandas. The classy Mexican restaurant, known for its polite service and generous portions, is open daily from 7am to 11pm. A pianist croons romantic ballads Thursday through Sunday from 7 to 11 pm at the piano bar. El Mesón is situated in a quiet residential neighborhood 13 blocks south of the Malecón at the intersection of Ortega and Calle Bravo.

Hotel Aquario's

Ramírez 1665, La Paz, B.C.S. 23000. ☎ **112/2-9266.** Fax 112/5-5713. 60 rms (all with bath). A/C TV TEL. $26 double. Free parking.

This popular, well-maintained three-story motel frames a protected parking lot and pool. Each of the comfortable, neat rooms comes with a small balcony, one or two double beds, a table and two chairs, and a bathroom with a tub as well as a shower. The on-premises restaurant/bar is open daily from 7am to 11pm. Laundry service is available. You'll find the hotel six blocks inland from the Malecón; take Degollado and then make a left on Ramírez.

Hotel Lorimar

Bravo 110, La Paz, B.C.S. 23000. ☎ **112/5-3822.** Fax 112/5-6387. 20 rms (all with bath). A/C. $30.80 double.

This modest hotel is a cheery, peaceful hideaway offering friendly, personal service. The rooms in the two- and three-story buildings are immaculately clean; those facing the back patio are the best choices. The hotel is well known among La Paz regulars; make reservations well in advance during holidays and peak seasons. The upstairs restaurant has a great view from the porch. The hotel may be closed during September; check ahead if you're planning to visit then. The Lorimar is located between Madero and Mutualismo. There are usually parking spaces available on Bravo, which appears safe.

Hotel Mediterrane

Allende 36-B, La Paz, B.C.S. 23000. ☎ and fax **112/5-1195.** 5 rms (all with bath). A/C or FAN. $30–$40 double. Parking on street.

This small inn, on a side street off the Malecón, has become a favorite among European travelers, who settle here for days on end. All rooms have king-size beds, upholstered chairs, pale wood furnishings, and light blue ceilings that meet white walls. The second-story terrace looks out to the waterfront. The owners were putting in a bar on the terrace when I last visited. The hotel sits behind Trattoria La Pazta.

DINING

Although La Paz is not a culinary mecca, it has a growing assortment of small, pleasant restaurants that are good and reasonably priced. In addition to the usual seafood and Mexican dishes, you can find Italian, French, Spanish, Chinese, and even "New Age" vegetarian health food. Restaurants along the seaside Malecón tend to be more expensive than those a few blocks inland.

For baked goods try the **panadería** at Independencia and Domínguez and the **pastelería** at Altamirano and Bravo. Coffee lovers might wish to visit **La Casa del Buen Café** on Serdán near Bravo. Coffee beans (great as souvenir gifts) imported from Guatemala, Cuba, and southern Mexico are sold by the kilo; brewed coffee is free. The shop is open daily from 10am to noon and 4 to 8pm.

EXPENSIVE

El Moro Flair

In the Club El Moro, km 2, Pichilingue Hwy. Breakfast $3–$8; main courses $8–$16. Tues–Sat 8am–10pm. SEAFOOD/CONTINENTAL.

There's no better way to start the day than with a breakfast of orange french toast or huevos motuleños on El Moro's small patio looking out to sea. You might expect the pink-and-gray restaurant at this pseudo-Moorish private club to be outrageously expensive, but the prices are quite reasonable and the setting is extravagant, with such glamorous touches as individual French press coffeepots at each table. For dinner have the Caesar salad mixed tableside, the filet mignon and shrimp or fresh halibut Florentine, and flaming crêpes Suzette. The restaurant is about a 15-minute walk along the waterfront toward Pichilingue.

Trattoria La Pazta

Allende 36. ☎ **112/5-1195.** Main courses $7–$18. Wed–Mon 1–10pm. ITALIAN.

The trendiest restaurant in town, La Pazta gleams with black lacquered tables and white tile; the aroma of garlic and espresso floats in the air. The menu features local fresh seafood such as pasta with squid in wine and cream sauce and crispy fried calamari. The cheese and fruit plate has a nice selection of imported cheeses (depending on what's available at the time). The curried chicken is a pleasant change from traditional Mexican meals.

MODERATE

Bismark 11

Degollado and Altamirano. ☎ **112/2-4854**. Breakfast $2.75–$3.50; main courses $3.50–$13.50. Daily 8am–11pm. MEXICAN/SEAFOOD.

Seafood doesn't get any better than at Bismark, whether you have fish tacos, chile rellenos stuffed with lobster, or a sundae glass filled with ceviche or shrimp. Extremely fresh dorado, halibut, snapper, or whatever is in season can be prepared in many ways. Walk seven blocks inland on Degollado to Altamirano and plan on lingering over a late lunch. The owners will call a cab for you if you wish.

Rosticería California

Serdán 1740. ☎ **112/2-5118**. Main courses $3.50–$9. Mon–Sat 8am–8pm, Sun 8am–6pm. MEXICAN CHICKEN.

Tasty chicken is the main dish here; it comes roasted, fried, and sometimes cooked in soup. Whole- and half-chicken orders are served with salad, french fries, tortillas, and salsa. The decor is cheerful, bright, and airy, with ceiling fans and colorfully embroidered tablecloths from Chiapas. There's also a small patio out back. The Rosticería is five blocks inland from the Malecón on Degollado; turn right on Serdán, and you'll find it not far from the public market.

INEXPENSIVE

Fuente de Sodas Daisy

16 de Septiembre and Paseo Obregón. No phone. Breakfast $2–$3.50; tortas $1.50–$2.50; burgers $2.75–$4; fresh juices 75¢–$1.50. Daily 8am–8pm. MEXICAN/AMERICAN.

You can't miss the bright purple sidewalk tables of this place, just around the corner from the Malecón. The stools at this tiny lunch counter are also a vivid purple, and their occupants are young and hip. The licuados and juices are blessedly refreshing, and the sandwiches and quesadillas hit the spot as a snack or a meal. The few tables under the sidewalk tree are usually occupied, but you may find a seat for a late-afternoon coffee-and-postcard break.

Tacos Hermanos González

Mutualismo and Esquerro. No phone. Tacos $1.15 each. Daily 10am–10pm. FISH TACOS.

Pedestrians literally stop traffic at this busy intersection as they line up for the best tacos in town. Bowls of salsas, cilantro, cabbage, and other condiments sit on the taco carts, where the González brothers wrap chunks of deep-fried fish into warm corn tortillas. You can hardly resist the aroma. Pick up a taco to go or stand on the corner with a cluster of impromptu diners—you'll probably want seconds.

LA PAZ AFTER DARK

A night in La Paz should begin in a cafe along the Malecón as the sun sinks into the sea, often painting a luminous Maxfield Parrish sort of scene with gold-tinged, almost iridescently glowing colors streaking across the broad bay behind the palm trees. Always have your camera ready at sunset.

A favorite ringside seat at dusk is a table at **La Terraza,** next to the Hotel Perla. La Terraza makes good schooner-size margaritas. **Pelicanos Bar,** in the second story of the Hotel Los Arcos, has a good view of the waterfront and a clubby, cozy feel. **La Paz-Lapa** (Obregon at 16 de Septiembre, ☎ 112/2-9290) is swinging most nights and has live music on the weekends. An inexpensive alternative is to stroll along the Malecón and people watch, stopping here and there for a drink or snack or to hear some wandering mariachis.

The Copper Canyon   8

The Copper Canyon (Canyon del Cobre), said to be four times larger than the Grand Canyon, is made up of 20 canyons. Through it runs the famed Chihuahua al Pacífico railway. Acclaimed as an engineering miracle, it covers 390 miles, has 39 bridges and 86 tunnels, and loops down to sea level and up to 9,000 feet through some of Mexico's most majestic pastel-colored, rugged mountain and pine-forest country.

EXPLORING THE COPPER CANYON

With the exception of those in Creel, most of the hotels in the canyon are overly expensive—even considering that rates in most cases include three meals. But you can see the Copper Canyon on a budget. With perseverance, it's possible to plan a trip yourself, balancing train stops with hotels, obtaining your train tickets, and making your reservations—especially if you use Creel as a base. Using a travel agent or one of the tour operators mentioned below can ease the uncertainty of travel, but if you prefer not to you can contact the hotels directly and buy your ticket when you arrive in Los Mochis or Chihuahua (See "Buying a Ticket," below). Or you can travel off-season without hotel reservations and take potluck. **Creel** ("Stop 5," below), with the most budget-priced hotels and some of the best side trips, is the most economical choice as a base for canyon travel. **Batopilas,** while too far away from "civilization" to be considered a "base," does have economical lodgings and it offers a priceless cultural experience of the canyonlands. If you purchase your own train ticket, avoid peak canyon travel times (see below) and try to buy your ticket a day or two in advance, since at times the train is booked to capacity.

    Los Mochis is one terminus into the Copper Canyon aboard the Chihuahua al Pacífico train. **Chihuahua,** on the other side of the canyon, is the other boarding point. Generally speaking, Los Mochis is the preferable starting place for this trip—the most scenic part of the 12- to 15-hour journey is between El Fuerte and Creel, and the chances of seeing it in good daylight are best if the trip begins in Los Mochis. If the train from Chihuahua to Los Mochis runs on schedule (and it has all the times I've taken it), you'll also get daylight during the best part of the trip, but if you don't want to take a chance, start in Los Mochis or El Fuerte. Chihuahua, however, is more interesting than Los Mochis.

A trip on the train with stops to stay at lodges en route is an adventure, fraught with the possibility of uncertainty—sold-out trains, delays, full hotels, being out in the middle of nowhere on an excursion when your Jeep breaks down, and so on—even when you've planned every last detail. Accommodations are comfortable but rustic; most don't have electricity (lanterns provide light), and only in Creel and El Fuerte are there telephones (though a phone line was being installed in Cerocahui when I last visited). Rooms have wood-burning stoves for heat in winter, and most, except where noted, have private bathrooms.

Peak travel times in the canyon are at the end of February, in March, April, and October, and at the beginning of November. Off-season months are June, July, and August (which can be dry, dusty, and extremely hot), January (very cold with snow in the highlands), mid-November, and December. You can pass through the Copper Canyon in one 15-hour day, spending a night in Chihuahua and another in Los Mochis, but you'd miss the essence of the canyon. I'd recommend at least 1 or 2 nights with stops along the way.

The 4-night, 5-day trips often planned by tour companies seem too brief to me. These allow for flying into either Chihuahua or Los Mochis, with 1 night in each city as you begin and end a trip, and 2 nights in the canyon, usually at El Divisadero. This is homogenized canyon travel—everyone has exactly the same limited travel experience. I suggest you begin and end your trip in Chihuahua (taking the train twice), skip Los Mochis, and turn around for the return to Chihuahua from El Fuerte instead. This allows for overnighting at the five stops enroute, or some variation of that. Such a trip would take around 10 days, after which you'll have a real vacation to remember.

If you spend a night en route, you'll have roughly 24 hours at each destination—usually enough time for one or two excursions. Creel, a rustic lumber town, offers the only economical lodgings in the canyon and great hiking and overnight camping—and van tours, too. Every stop is interesting, though Creel and Cerocahui offer the most possibilities.

Drivers from all canyon hotels await trains, and if you don't have a reservation you can ask a driver about room availability. However, the hotels are quite small and groups often fill them up, so it's almost imperative to make reservations in advance, especially in peak season.

An option for those wishing to see the canyons in ultimate comfort and luxury is the **South Orient Express.** It's an independently operated luxury train using vintage passenger cars restored with classic Victorian interiors. Observation and vista-dome cars provide views of the passing scenery; light meals and drinks are available in the dining car.

The train operates in the spring and fall only, with two classes of service. The first includes train travel only and costs $148 one way; the independent tour package, starting at $779 per person for a three-day tour, includes air transport from Tucson, train service, hotel accommodations, and tours in eight different itineraries.

For information and reservations, contact VSP at 713/872-0190 or 800/659-7602; fax 713/872-7123.

1 Los Mochis

126 miles S of Alamos, 50 miles SW of El Fuerte, 193 miles S of Guaymas, 260 miles N of Mazatlán

Los Mochis, in Sinaloa State, is a low-lying city of 350,000 founded in 1703 by an American, Benjamin Johnson of Pennsylvania. It is a wealthy city in a fertile agricultural area and, aside from the enormous sugar mill at the northwestern end of town, there's not much of note. The city's architecture is distinctly American. The town's importance to the tourist is as a boarding point for the Chihuahua al Pacífico train. From the port at Topolobampo Bay nearby, you can take a ferry to La Paz, in Baja California.

ESSENTIALS

GETTING THERE & DEPARTING   By Plane   Aeroméxico (☎ 5-2580; at the airport 2-9272) and its subsidiary **Aerolitoral** have direct service from Chihuahua, Hermosillo, and Mazatlán. **AeroCalifornia** (☎ 5-2250) flies to and from Los Angeles, La Paz, Guadalajara, Mexico City, Culiacán, and Tijuana.

By Train   The **Chihuahua al Pacífico** (Copper Canyon train) runs between Los Mochis and Chihuahua once daily. It leaves Los Mochis at 6am (mountain/Los Mochis time); taxis charge $12 from downtown to the station. From Chihuahua it leaves at 7am and arrives in Los Mochis around 7pm. Complete Copper Canyon train information is in Section 2 of this chapter.

By Bus   Los Mochis is marginally served by buses. Most passing through are de paso. **Tres Estrellas de Oro** is the first-class line, with buses hourly from Mazatlán, Guadalajara, and Mexico City. All buses from Navojoa (the connecting point from Alamos) are de paso. From Navojoa to Alamos is 2¹/₂ hours. Each bus line has its own terminal in this city. Tres Estrellas de Oro, Calle Obregón 61 Pte., at Allende (☎ 2-1757), is in the center of town, though the others are only six blocks away. Tres Estrellas de Oro serves Mexico City (a 24-hour trip), Guadalajara (a 16-hour trip), and Mazatlán hourly. The Expreso de Lujo (luxury express) between Mazatlán and Los Mochis has half the seats of a regular bus, a club section, and video movies. **Transportes Norte de Sonora,** Avenida Morelos 33 Pte., at Zaragoza (☎ 2-0411 or 2-0026), and **Transportes del Pacífico,** Avenida Morelos 337 Pte. (☎ 2-0347 or 2-0341), next door, make the same runs but almost all are de paso. For buses that originate here and pass through Navojoa (crossroads to Alamos), go to the ticket booth in the back of the station. Eleven buses go to Navojoa, the first at 5am and the last at 5pm. There are two places to catch the bus to El Fuerte (1¹/₂ to 2 hours). The first is at the Mercado Independencia, where the bus stops at the corner of Independencia and Degollado. The other is at the corner of Cuahtemoc at Prieto, close to the Hotel America. Ask hotel desk clerks or the tourism office for a schedule. Buses, which run frequently throughout the day, are the school-bus variety, and the purser stows luggage in the back of the bus. Were it not for the numerous stops en route, the trip would take an hour.

By Car   Coastal Highway 15 is well maintained in both directions leading into Los Mochis.

By Ferry   The SEMATUR ferry from La Paz, Baja California, to nearby Topolobampo leaves La Paz daily (except Tuesday) at 8pm and arrives in Los Mochis at 6am—a 10-hour trip.

From Topolobampo the SEMATUR ferry to La Paz, Baja California, leaves Monday through Saturday at 9am and arrives in La Paz at 7pm. For tickets and information, contact **SEMATUR** at the ferry pier in Topolobampo (☎ 686/2-0141; fax 686/2-0035) or **Viajes Paotan** in Los Mochis (☎ 681/5-1914 or 5-8262). Bring your own food and drink. The faster Baja Express ceased operation in 1994.

ORIENTATION   Arriving   The airport is 12 miles north of town. Take a combi (van) from the airport into town for $8; taxi fares are twice that. All bus stations are downtown within walking distance of the hotels. If you arrive by ferry in Topolobampo, you'll have to bargain with waiting taxis for the fare to Los Mochis. The train station is about 3 miles from town, and taxis charge around $14 to take you to the central city.

Information   The **City Tourist Office** is in the State Government building at Ordoñez and Allende (☎ 681/2-6640) and has a helpful staff and usually someone who speaks English. The office is open Monday through Friday from 8am to 3pm.

City Layout   Los Mochis contains no central plaza. To acquaint yourself with this city, use the Tres Estrellas de Oro **bus station,** Calle Obregón 61 Pte., at Allende, as an orientation point. The other bus stations, hotels, and restaurants are within two to six blocks of the station.

Plaza Fiesta Las Palmas, at the corner of Obregón and Rosales, is the shopping mall and the main spot where people of all ages gather, an interesting slice of Mexican life. **Ley,** a large store, sells everything from groceries to clothes to TVs. Hotels, restaurants, and the Plaza Fiesta Las Palmas are all within walking distance of downtown.

FAST FACTS: LOS MOCHIS

American Express   The local representative is Viajes Araceli, Av. Alvaro Obregón 471-A Pte. (☎ 681/5-5780; fax 681/5-8787).

Area Code   The telephone area code is 681.

Time   The entire railroad operates on central time, even though Los Mochis is in the mountain time zone.

EXPLORING LOS MOCHIS

For most travelers, Los Mochis is a stopover en route to somewhere else. There isn't much of importance here, but the town is pleasant, and you can enjoy some of the best seafood in Mexico.

A city tour, hunting and fishing trips, and boat rides around Topolobampo Bay can be arranged through the **Viajes Flamingo** travel agency, on the ground floor of the Hotel Santa Anita (☎ 681/2-1613 or 2-1929); it's open Monday through Saturday from 8:30am to 1pm and 3 to 6:30pm. The boat ride is really just a spin in the bay and not noteworthy, although the bay is pretty.

Topolobampo also has a nice beach, though the town isn't much. To get to Topolobampo, catch the bus at the corner of Obregón and Degollado, across from the Hotel Catalina.

ACCOMMODATIONS
EXPENSIVE

Hotel Santa Anita

Leyva at the corner of Hidalgo (Apdo. Postal 159), Los Mochis, Sin. 81200. ☎ **681/8-7046.** Fax 681/8-7046. 133 rms (all with bath). A/C TV TEL. $80 double. Parking $3 daily.

The Santa Anita is the nicest hotel in Los Mochis. Completely remodeled and well maintained, the rooms are nicely furnished, although some are small. All are carpeted and have comfortable beds, color TVs with U.S. channels, and tap water purified for drinking. The hotel's excellent and popular restaurant is off the lobby. There are two bars, one featuring live music at least one day a week.

Another special feature: Every morning at 5:20 a private hotel bus takes guests to the Chihuahua al Pacífico train, which departs daily at 6am. That spares guests the $12 taxi ride. The hotel also provides pick-up at the train station for a small fee for guests. The lobby travel agency, **Viajes Flamingo** (☎ 681/2-1613 or 2-1929), is about the best in town; you can buy your train tickets here and find out about all the other touristic activities in the area.

To reach the hotel from the Tres Estrellas bus station, turn left on Obregón and walk three blocks, then turn right on Leyva. The hotel is on your left.

INEXPENSIVE

Hotel America

Allende 655 Sur, Los Mochis, Sin. 81200. ☎ **681/2-1355** or 2-1356. Fax 2-5983. 46 rms (all with bath). A/C TEL. $29 double. Free enclosed parking.

The clean marble-floored lobby is an indication of the maintenance of this hotel. The freshly painted rooms have tile floors and large windows facing the street. Rooms away from the Allende side will avoid the noise of the early-morning mufflerless local buses. On the second floor there's a sitting area, purified water, and an ice-making machine. To get here from the Tres Estrellas station turn left on Allende and walk 2¹/₂ short blocks; the hotel is just past Blv. Castro on your right.

DINING

Restaurante Espana

Obregón 526. ☎ **681/2-2221.** Breakfast $2.50–$5, main courses $4.50–$9. Daily 7am–11pm. SPANISH/SEAFOOD

This Spanish-style restaurant is a favorite among downtown professionals, who devour huge bowls of paella at lunchtime. The decor is upscale for Los Mochis, with a splashing fountain in the dining room and heavy, carved-wood tables and chairs.

El Taquito

Leyva at Barrera. ☎ **681/2-8119.** Breakfast $1.50–$6; main courses $2–$9. Daily 24 hours. MEXICAN.

Any time of the day or night, El Taquito has its share of locals enjoying some of the best food in town or lingering over a third cup of coffee. The cafe looks like an American fast-food place with orange Formica tables and booths. The tortilla soup comes in a large bowl, and main-course portions are generous. One and a half blocks left of the Hotel Santa Anita.

2 The Copper Canyon Train

The Chihuahua al Pacífico railway's name conceptualizes the idea of linking arid, desertlike Chihuahua with the natural port of Topolobampo, a few miles west of Los Mochis. American Albert Kinsey Owen, who invested in the project of building the railroad, envisioned it as the shortest route for goods from Kansas City to the Pacific.

Train Departure Times

From Los Mochis		From Chihuahua	
Los Mochis	6am (mountain time)	Chihuahua	7am
El Fuerte	7:25am	Creel	12:25pm
Bahuichivo/Cerocahui	12:15pm	El Divisadero	1:45pm
El Divisadero	1:30pm	Bahuichivo/Cerocahui	3:30pm
Creel	3:15pm	El Fuerte	6:15pm
Chihuahua (arrives)	8:50pm	Los Mochis (arrives)	7:50pm

Note: The railroad runs on central time, although Los Mochis is on mountain time. *This means that if the train is scheduled to depart Los Mochis at 7am railway time, it pulls out at 6am local time.* Be aware of that when reading a printed schedule.

The longest train stop where passengers can see the canyons is the 15-minute stop at El Divisadero—barely enough time to dash to the canyon's edge for a look.

BUYING A TICKET   In Los Mochis, the Ferrocarril Chihuahua al Pacífico station (☎ 681/5-7775) is about 3 miles from the center of town on Av. Onofre Serrano, a half mile past Blv. Gaxiola. This is the station for El Nuevo Chihuahua–Pacífico, which runs between Los Mochis and Chihuahua from both directions simultaneously daily. The ticket window is supposed to be open daily from 5am to 1pm, but it's best to go to the station early in the morning in case the window closes early. A one-way ticket in either direction in Primera Especial costs $25 to $30, or double that if you want a round-trip ticket. There's a 10% extra charge for any stops you make en route.

There are four ways to obtain tickets. The first is from a local travel agency in Los Mochis or Creel. The second is at the train station a day ahead or the same day of your travel (same-day ticket purchase isn't advised since there may be no seats, and if you're traveling with a group it's best to get tickets in advance). A third way is through **Mexico by Train** (see "Getting Around" in Chapter 3). A fourth way, and the most reliable, is through a U.S. travel agency specializing in the Copper Canyon and selling air/train/hotel packages (not tickets alone). The least preferable option is to use a travel agent in Chihuahua because several agencies may sell the same seat more than once, requiring travelers to decide how to share a seat. In Los Mochis I've had good luck using Viajes Flamingo at the Hotel Santa Anita.

If you plan to stop off en route, you must tell the ticket agent at the time you purchase your ticket and know in advance how long you will be staying at the various stopoffs. Once purchased, the ticket is good for those dates only and cannot be changed. A reserved seat is a necessity, but your reserved seat number may be good only until your first stopoff; thereafter, when you reboard you'll have to take what's available. On my last trip, conductors had my name on a list at each stop and had an assigned seat for me—but that's not to say you can count on that efficiency every time. You can buy a ticket for shorter distances along the way, enabling you to spend as much time as you like in any location, but if you're traveling during a peak season, it may mean you'll have to take your chances finding a seat when you reboard the train—or stand in any available space between cars, as many locals do.

Travel Agents   A tour company specializing in the Copper Canyon area can save headaches. I highly recommend the services of **Columbus Travel,** 900 Ridge Creek Lane, Bulverde, TX 78163-2872 (☎ 210/885-2000 or 800/843-1060; fax 210/885-2010), which arranges group tours as well as individualized and special-interest trips in the Copper Canyon.

WHAT TO PACK   While Los Mochis is warm year-round, Chihuahua can be blistering in summer, windy just about any time, and freezing or even snowy in winter. Both cities are wealthy, and Chihuahua in particular can be somewhat on the dressy side.

The canyon is blue-jeans and hiking-boot country, but pay special attention to the climate. From November through March it may snow; even in the tropical bottom of the canyon, you may need a sweater. In the upper elevations, be prepared for freezing temperatures at night, even in spring and fall. Long johns and gloves are a must in winter. Sturdy shoes or hiking boots are essential anytime if you plan even a little walking and hiking.

CONDITIONS OF TRAVEL   The first-class Chihuahua al Pacífico has adjustable cloth-covered seats, air-conditioning in summer (usually), and heating (maybe) in winter. There's no dining car, but food vendors come to the train doors, selling an assortment of pies, tacos, empanadas, fruit, and soft drinks. Toilet paper and water may not be replenished; bring your own along with some snacks.

The train stops many times; the following are stops with hotels:

STOP 1: EL FUERTE

Though not yet in the Copper Canyon proper, the train stops here first. El Fuerte, with cobblestone streets and handsome old colonial mansions, is a former silver-mining town about an hour and a half out of Los Mochis. It's the prettiest town along the train route, well worth visiting for a night. The town has a plaza and bandstand, and historic houses around the square. I prefer to skip Los Mochis and start my train journey here.

The **bus stop** (not really a station) is about 1 1/2 blocks from where the bus from Los Mochis lets you off on the cobblestone street. Ask directions to the plaza and hotel. The train station is several miles from town. Taxis meet each train and cost $7 per taxi into town; get others to share the price in advance so you look like a group together—otherwise the taxi charges per person.

EXPLORING EL FUERTE

Canyon country hasn't begun yet and the main reason for stopping here would be to explore the town, visit nearby villages, go bird-watching, fish for black bass and trout, or hunt for duck and dove. Hotels can arrange guides and all equipment if notified in advance.

ACCOMMODATIONS & DINING

Besides the restaurants at the hotel mentioned here, there are inexpensive restaurants on or near the central plaza.

El Fuerte Lodge

Hidalgo s/n, El Fuerte, Sin. 81820. ☎ **689/3-0242**. 12 rms (all with bath). A/C. $65 double.

Owner Robert Brand and his wife have taken one of the oldest homes in El Fuerte and turned it into a charming inn loaded with antiques and character. The 12 rooms (with 9 more under construction) have double or king beds, tiled baths (with plenty of water pressure for great hot showers), and colonial furnishings that make you feel like you're staying in a museum. An excellent bilingual guide leads trips to nearby villages and knows all about the flora and fauna in the area. The hotel's restaurant menu includes plenty of dishes for those unaccustomed to Mexican food, and is said to be the best in town. The gift shop/gallery has a wonderful display of paintings of the area and a great selection of Casas Grandes pottery. The hotel provides motor transport from the Los Mochis airport for $25 per person one-way, getting you out into the country as soon as you land. Taxis from the El Fuerte bus or train stop cost a high $7.

Hotel Posada Hidalgo

Hidalgo 101, El Fuerte, Sin. 81820. ☎ and fax **689/3-0242** or 8-7046. 38 rms (all with bath). A/C. $80 double. For reservations contact the Hotel Santa Anita, Apdo. Postal 159, Los Mochis, Sin. 81200 (☎ 681/8-7046; fax 681/2-0046).

This delightful hotel four blocks from the bus stop and three miles from the train station has two parts. The mansion section, with open portals around a central patio, belonged to silver grandees in the 18th century; there's even a steep carriage ramp from when it was a stagecoach stop. Rooms in the old section are high-ceilinged and have hardwood floors. New rooms are similarly decorated, each with two double beds; all open onto a shady courtyard with covered walkway. Meals here are expensive.

STOP 2: BAHUICHIVO & CEROCAHUI

This is the first stop in canyon country. Bahuichivo consists mainly of the station and a few humble abodes. Your destination is the village of **Cerocahui** (alt. 5,550 ft.), in a valley about 6 miles from the train stop. Because of the rough, teeth-jarring road, the ride lasts an hour before you see the village, which is home to 600 inhabitants. The Paraíso del Oso is about a mile from the village. Another more expensive hotel, the Misión, is in Cerocahui.

EXPLORING CEROCAHUI

Built around a mission church, Cerocahui consists of little more than rambling unpaved streets and a hundred or so homes. Mountains surround the town, but you have to take an excursion for real canyon vistas. In Cerocahui tourists are besieged by children vying to be their escorts to the **waterfalls.** Both hotels can arrange **horseback riding** to the falls and other lookout points ($6 per hour) and trips by truck to **Cerro Gallego** ($15 to $20 per person), a lookout high in the mountains around the town and worth the trip. It's possible to see the waterfall on arrival and schedule the Gallego trip for the next morning, have lunch, and make the train. The Urique trip (see below) would require another day.

The Paraíso del Oso offers a trip to the mining town of **Urique** at the bottom of the Urique Canyon (one of several canyons that make up the Copper Canyon). You can go down and back in a day or schedule an overnight. The Urique trip costs around $100 and can be split among four to six people.

ACCOMMODATIONS & DINING

Hotel Misión

Cerocahui. No phone. 34 rms (all with bath). $160 double. Rates include meals. For reservations contact the Hotel Santa Anita, Apdo. Postal 159, Los Mochis, Sin. 81200 (☎ 681/8-7046; fax 681/2-0046).

Established years ago in the village of Cerocahui, the Hotel Misión is the only lodging in town. Guest rooms have hot water, as well as electricity until 11pm. The lobby/restaurant area surrounds a large rock fireplace where a local guitarist and singer entertain informally in the evenings. The food is excellent, and the ranch-style rooms, with tile floors, wood-burning stoves, and kerosene lanterns, are comfortable.

Paraíso del Oso

A mile outside Cerocahui. No phone. 15 rms (all with bath). $120 double. Rates include all meals. For reservations contact Columbus Travel, RR 12, Box 382B, New Braunfels, TX 78132; ☎ 210/885-2000, or 800/843-1060.

Opened in 1990, the Paraíso del Oso is slightly more rustic than the Hotel Misión, but its streamside setting is the reason you come to the canyon. And it's at the foot of a toothy mountain with a natural rock profile of an *oso* (bear)—thus its name. The food gets applause from recent guests, who also loved the morning and evening guitar serenades. Each room has two double beds and pine-log furniture. There's no electricity, though there are solar-powered lights in the dining room. Rates include a trip to town, but it's also a nice walk. This is the only area hotel offering Urique Canyon trips by four-wheel-drive vehicle.

STOPS 3 & 4: EL DIVISADERO

Stops 3 and 4 are only 2 miles apart. Stop 3 (coming from Los Mochis) is in front of the Posada Barrancas and opposite the Mansion Tarahumara. Stop 4 is El Divisadero proper (alt. 9,000 ft.), consisting of the Hotel Cabañas Divisadero-Barrancas, taco stands at train time (delicious), and the most spectacular overlook of the canyon that you'll be able to see if you make no overnight stops en route. The train stops for only 15 minutes, long enough for a mad dash to the lookout to see the view and to make some hurried purchases from the Tarahumara Indians who appear at train time to display their beautiful baskets, homemade violins, and wood and cloth dolls.

Hotels can arrange various excursions, including visits to cave-dwelling Tarahumara, hiking, and horseback riding.

ACCOMMODATIONS & DINING

Hotel Cabañas Divisadero-Barrancas

El Divisadero. No phone. 50 rms $122.50 double; $164.50 triple. Rates include three meals. Reservations can be made at Av. Mirador 4516 [Apdo. Postal 31238, Col. Residencial Campestre], Chihuahua, Chih. 31300; ☎ 14/16-5136; fax 14/15-6575.

This hotel's location on the edge of the canyon overlook provides the most spectacular view offered by any hotel in the canyon. It often fills with groups. The restaurant has a large picture window, perfect for sitting and gazing for hours. Each room is beautifully rustic with foot-loomed, brightly colored bedspreads and matching curtains, two double beds, a fireplace, and 24-hour electricity.

Hotel Posada Barrancas Mirador

El Divisadero. No phone. 32 rms (all with bath). $160 double. Rates include meals.

Opened in 1993, the Mirador sits at the edge of the canyon about five minutes up the mountain from its sister hotel, the Rancho (see below). All rooms have heavy wood furnishings, vivid drapes and bedspreads, and individual heaters. Balconies in each room seem to hang right over the cliff's edge. Generous and tasty meals are served in the dining room/lounge by a huge fireplace.

Hotel Posada Barrancas Rancho

El Divisadero. No phone. 36 rms (all with bath). $120 double. Rates include meals. For reservations contact the Hotel Santa Anita, Apdo. Postal 159, Los Mochis, Sin. 81200; ☎ 681/8-7046; fax 681/2-0046.

The train stops right in front of this inn. Rooms are comfortable, each with two double beds and a very warming wood-burning iron stove. Like those in other lodges, meals are a communal affair in the cozy living/restaurant area, and the food is quite good. You can rent horses or hike to the Tarahumara caves and to the rim of the canyon, where a more expensive sister hotel, the Mirador (see above), has a beautiful log-walled enclosed restaurant/bar with a magnificent view.

Mansión Tarahumara

El Divisadero. No phone. 45 rms (all with bath). $105 double. Rates include meals. For reservations contact the Mansion Tarahumara, Calle Juárez 1602-A Col. Centro, Chihuahua, Chih. 31011; ☎ 14/15-4721 or ☎ and fax 14/16-5444.

Built like an enormous stone castle, the Mansión Tarahumara is perched on a hillside opposite the train stop at Posada Barrancas. A van meets the train and carries guests and luggage across the tracks to the hotel. This is among my favorite of the canyon lodges because of the setting, the rooms, and the management's interest in guest comfort. Rock-walled bungalows are behind the castle, and each has a big fireplace and a wall heater and is nicely furnished with two double beds and windows facing the view.

The castle contains the restaurant, boasting a lovely view from its big windows and a large area ideal for dancing or live entertainment, which the hotel sometimes

---

Sierra Madre *Indígenos:* The Tarahumara

Within the Copper Canyon region live the reclusive Tarahumara Indians, in tiny settlements of small log huts in summer and in caves in winter. They have remained aloof from modern civilization, retreating to the rugged canyons and subsisting on corn, tortillas, beans, and herding a few goats and cattle. The men wear sandals, white loincloths, and colorful headbands. Women, who often go barefoot, wear colorful cotton skirts and ruffled blouses. Although they weave fine thick wool blankets, they don't wear wool, even in harsh canyon winters. Social and ritual gatherings are centered around *tesguino,* a fermented corn drink, and because of the frequency of these gatherings, many Tarahumara are alcoholics. They tend to suffer from tuberculosis and other respiratory diseases, but their plight has been addressed by Father Verplancken, a Jesuit missionary based in Creel, and by the Flying Doctors, a group of volunteer U.S. medical professionals who provide health care. Many Tarahumara children attend boarding school in Creel or Cerocahui, returning home on weekends.

sponsors. Most nights a guitarist stops in for a sing-along after dinner. Besides the usual cave tours or horseback riding, the hotel can also arrange guided hiking to the bottom of the canyon or to Batopilas (see Batopilas description in "Stop 5: Creel," below).

STOP 5: CREEL

This rustic logging town (alt. 8,400 ft., pop. 6,000), with paved streets, offers the only economical lodgings in the canyon, as well as some of the best side trips, especially hiking and overnight camping.

ESSENTIALS

GETTING THERE & DEPARTING   By Train   When you're ready to get off the train, keep a lookout for the station because the trains stop here for only a few minutes. When you're ready to reboard, be sure to be at the station before the arrival time of the train. You'll need to be ready to jump on when you see it coming.

By Bus   **Estrella Blanca,** with facilities next to the Hotel Korachi, serves Creel and Chihuahua every 2 hours from 6am to 5:30pm. Direct buses make the trip in 4 hours; de paso buses take 5. (See also buses to Batopilas in "Exploring Creel & Environs," below).

By Car   From Chihuahua, follow the signs to La Junta (but you don't go there), until you see signs to Hermosillo (but you don't go there), and follow those until you see signs to Creel (left) and follow those into Creel; the trip takes about four hours on a paved road. There is now a well-maintained but unpaved road between Creel and El Divisadero; the drive takes about 1 1/2 hours. The road is generally in good condition; however, if you are traveling during or just after rains, it may not be in the best shape. Ask before starting out.

ORIENTATION   The station, opposite the main plaza, is in the heart of the village and within walking distance of all lodgings except the Copper Canyon Sierra Lodge. Look for your hotel's van waiting at the station (unless you're staying at the Casa de Huespedes Margarita, which is close by). There's one main street, López Mateos, and almost everything is on it and within walking distance.

Fast Facts   The telephone **area code** is 145. There's **electricity** 24 hours daily in all Creel hotels. The best sources of **information** are the Mission Store and the hotels. The long-distance **telephone** office is at López Mateos 30, one block east of the plaza. It's open Monday through Saturday from 9am to 1:30pm and 3 to 8pm and on Sunday from 9am to 2pm.

EXPLORING CREEL & ENVIRONS

You'll occasionally see the Tarahumara as you walk around town, but mostly you'll see rugged logging types and tourists from around the world.

There are several stores around Creel that sell Tarahumara arts and crafts. The best is **Artesanías Mission** (Mission Crafts), which has quality merchandise at reasonable prices, with all profits going to the Mission Hospital run by Father Verplancken, a Jesuit priest, and benefiting the Tarahumara. Here you'll find Tarahumara crafts: dolls, pottery, woven purses and belts, drums, violins (a craft inherited from the Spanish), bamboo flutes, bead necklaces, bows and arrows, cassettes of Tarahumara music, wood carvings, baskets, and heavy wool rugs, as well as an excellent supply of books and maps relating to the Tarahumara and the region. It's open Monday through Saturday from 9:30am to 1pm and 3 to 6pm and Sunday from 9:30am to 1pm. It's beside the railroad tracks, on the main plaza.

Nearby Excursions

Close by are several canyons, waterfalls, a lake, hot springs, Tarahumara villages and cave dwellings, and an old Jesuit mission. **Batopilas,** a fascinating 18th-century silver-mining village, is at the bottom of the canyon, an overnight jaunt. You can ask for information about these and other things to do from your hotel.

Whether you go by foot, horseback, bus, or guided tour, if you're planning to do any strenuous hiking, rock climbing, or adventuring, it's strongly recommended you take along someone who knows the area—you're in the wilderness out here, and you can't count on anyone coming along to rescue you should an accident occur.

If you are driving, the new unpaved road between Creel and El Divisadero now makes that village a possible day-trip from Creel (see "Stops 3 & 4," above, for details on El Divisadero). The trip takes around 1 1/2 hours one way. The road is generally in good condition; however, if you are traveling during or just after rains, it may not be in the best shape. Ask about it before starting out.

ORGANIZED TOURS   Hotels offer organized tours. The Motel Parador de la Montaña has 10 different tours, ranging from 2 to 10 hours and priced at $10 to $30 per person (four people minimum); it costs $100 for the Batopilas trip. The Hotel Nuevo and Casa de Huespedes Margarita offer the most economical tours in town, priced around $12 for a day-long canyon and hot-springs tour. All tour availability depends on if a group can be gathered, and your best chance of that is at the Parador de la Montaña, which caters to groups. The Copper Canyon Sierra Lodge arranges packages throughout Tarahumara land.

BATOPILAS   You can make an overnight side trip on your own from Creel to the silver-mining village of Batopilas, founded in 1708. It's 7 to 9 hours from Creel by bus (the school-bus type) along a narrow dirt road winding down through some of the most beautiful scenery in the Copper Canyon. It's unusual to meet any other vehicles, and the mountains rise up on one side of the road and drop precipitously on the other side to a stream that alternately trickles and roars. In Batopilas, which lies beside a river at the bottom of a deep canyon, the weather is tropical, but can be a bit chilly in the evenings. There are a beautiful little church and several walks and a hike to Misión Satevó that you can do from there. The town itself is like something from an 18th-century time warp: The dry goods store has the original shelving and cash register, cobblestone streets twist past whitewashed town homes, miners and ranchers come on horseback, and Tarahumara are frequent visitors. A considerable number of pigs, dogs, and flocks of goats wander at will—this is Chihuahua's goat-raising capital.

Getting to Batopilas   In Creel, take a bus from the unmarked storefront at López Mateos 39 next to D'Flor variety store and opposite the Restaurant Lupita. Buses go to Batopilas on Tuesday, Thursday, and Saturday, leaving Creel at 4am and arriving around noon. From Batopilas, the return bus leaves for Creel on Monday, Wednesday, and Friday at 4am in summer, 6am in winter, supposedly to arrive in Creel around noon, in time to meet the connecting Chihuahua al Pacífico trains leaving for Los Mochis and Chihuahua. In the rainy months of June through August it arrives later. Tickets are supposedly sold between 11am and 8pm the day before; the cost is $6.

Accommodations & Dining in Batopilas   Batopilas has several little restaurants and three hotels, beginning at around $6 per person per night. There are no telephones, though, so you can't make firm reservations. However, the Parador de la Montaña in Creel operates the basic-but-comfortable, 10-room **Parador Batopilas,** and its staff can tell you the likelihood of vacancies. All rooms share the hotel's two baths and cost around $15 for a double per night. There's another nameless hotel with five or six rooms, and if all else fails, you can probably find a family willing to let you stay in an extra room. One night isn't enough for a stay here, since you arrive in late afternoon and must leave at 4 the next morning.

The **Copper Canyon Riverside Lodge,** owned by the Copper Canyon Sierra Lodge in Creel, a mansion-turned-hotel (see below), is booked only on an eight-day package sold by the Copper Canyon Lodges.

Restaurants are informal here, so bring along some snacks and bottled water to tide you over, although most provisions like that are available at the general store. Upon arrival ask for directions to Doña Mica's (everyone knows her). She serves meals on her plant-surrounded front porch, but it's best to let her know in advance when to expect you. On short notice, however, she can probably rustle up some scrambled eggs.

ACCOMMODATIONS

For a small town, Creel has quite a number of places to stay because of its popularity with international tourists and loggers on business. Be sure to have a reservation during high season.

Expensive

Copper Canyon Sierra Lodge

20 rms. $125 per person per night (three-night minimum stay; includes meals and tours). For reservations contact Copper Canyon Lodges, 2741 Paldan Dr., Auburn Hills, MI 48326; ☎ 810/340-7230 or 800/776-3942; fax 810/340-7212.

About 20 minutes (14 miles) southwest of Creel proper, this place has everything you imagine a mountain lodge should—rock walls, beamed ceilings, lantern lights, and wood-burning stoves. In short, it's a charmingly rustic place with no electricity. Its out-of-town location is a great starting point from which to take guided or self-guided hikes and walks in the mountains to the Cusarare Waterfalls, cave paintings, and the present-day Tarahumara cave dwellings. Owner Skip McWilliams has a special reverence for the Tarahumara and has made an effort to become friends with those who live near the lodge. Tarahumara guides conduct tours to villages and into the canyons. Admittedly, there is usually a language barrier with guests and the Tarahumara are shy, but hand gestures and friendliness go a long way. Bilingual guides are also available.

This is one hotel that must be booked ahead of time from the U.S.; drop-ins are likely to find the hotel full. If there is space, drop-ins can sign up for a three-night minimum stay or even the entire eight-night package including Batopilas.

There are several options for getting to the lodge. Guests who fly into Chihuahua by 1pm can take advantage of the hotel's shuttle service by road to the lodge and avoid spending the first night in the city; the ride takes 4 1/2 hours and costs $70. The hotel also offers an air shuttle from Tucson, Arizona, with flights in a small chartered plane over the canyons to Creel's primitive airstrip; the cost is $375. Guests can also opt to arrive by train from Los Mochis or Chihuahua.

The hotel also owns the 15-room Copper Canyon Riverside Lodge in Batopilas. It's available for guests only on the hotel's eight-day package (see "Batopilas," above, and the Riverside description, below).

Copper Canyon Riverside Lodge

No phone. 15 rms (all with bath). Eight-night tours including the Sierra Lodge and Batopilas (including transfers, meals and tours): Oct–Apr, $1300 per person (based on double occupancy); May–Sept, $1100 per person (based on double occupancy). For reservations see Copper Canyon Sierra Lodge, above.

Its owners restored a 19th-century hacienda into this one-of-a-kind lodge set far down into the canyon beside a rushing river. The rooms have large private baths and electrical outlets, as well as kerosene lamps; most have balconies looking out onto the street. Interior courtyards, a parlor filled with antiques, and a library stocked with historical information give the you feeling you've dropped into a time warp. Meals are generous and quite good; guests are free to prepare their own drinks on an honor system. The hotel's rooms are booked as part of a package with the Sierra Lodge, which includes three nights at their lodge in Creel, three nights in Batopilas, two nights (coming and going) in Chihuahua, transfers, and meals at their hotels. Guests can opt to spend additional nights in Batopilas if they wish. Transportation is provided; it's a six-to-eight-hour ride into the remote canyon.

Moderate

Motel Parador de la Montaña

Av. López Mateos s/n, Creel, Chih. 33200. ☎ **145/6-0075.** Fax 145/6-0085. 49 rms (all with bath). $54 double. For reservations in Chihuahua, contact Calle Allende 114, Chihuahua, Chih. 31300; ☎ 14/10-4580; fax 14/15-3468.

The Parador de la Montaña is the largest hotel in town, located two blocks west of the plaza. The comfortable rooms each have two double beds, a high wood-beamed ceiling, central heating, a tiled bath, and very thin walls. Guests congregate in the restaurant, the bar, and the lobby with its roaring fireplace. The bar is the town's evening action spot. Since the motel caters to groups, your best chance of joining one of the 10 area tours is here. The hotel also owns the Parador Batopilas in Batopilas.

Hotel Nuevo

Francisco Villa 121, Creel, Chih. 33200. Fax 145/6-0043. 40 rms (all with bath). $45 double. ☎ 145/6-0022 or 14/17-5539 in Chihuahua for reservations.

There are two hotel sections at the Nuevo—the older one is across the tracks from the train station next to the restaurant and variety store, and new log cabañas are in back. The higher-priced cabañas are carpeted and have TVs. All rooms except six have a heater or fireplace. There is a nice hotel restaurant open from 8:30am to 8pm and a small general store that sells local crafts as well as basic supplies. Ask at the store about rooms.

Inexpensive

Casa de Huespedes Margarita

López Mateos 11, Creel, Chih. 33200. ☎ and fax **145/6-0045.** 23 rms. (all with bath). $2 sleeping bag space (10 spaces); $3 share in four-bed dormitory; $15 double private room; $30 double private cabaña. Rates include breakfast and dinner.

With its youth hostel–type atmosphere, this signless white house between the two churches on the main plaza is the most popular spot in town with international backpacking, student, and minimal-budget travelers. It's also one of the cleanest hotels in the country. Rooms have pine details and tile floors and are decorated with frilly curtains and spreads; there is plenty of hot water and gas heat in each. Meals are taken family style around a big dining table. Nonguests can eat here, too—just let them know in advance; breakfast, lunch, and dinner are $3 each. Margarita is adding more private rooms to the hotel, and has built another more deluxe hotel as well (see below). She's one of the best sources of information in the area and does all she can to help budget travelers enjoy their stays.

Margarita's Plaza Mexicana

Calle Chapultepec s/n, Creel, Chih. 33200. ☎ and fax **145/6-0245.** 26 rms (all with bath). $23 double (without meals); $30 double (including two meals).

Margarita is one of the most popular and enterprising hoteliers in Creel. With this inn she's transformed an old town house into a charming inn filled with Tarahumara folk art. The rooms (including a honeymoon suite) are gaily furnished with wood chairs and dressers from Michoacán and decorated with paintings of Tarahumara scenes. A mural of Semana Santa celebrations covers one wall in the large dining room, where guests have the option of two complete menus at lunch and dinner. Vegetables and salads are prepared with purified water. The hotel is near the Parador Montaña, three blocks west of the plaza.

DINING

El Caballo Bayo

López Mateos 25. ☎ **145/6-0136.** Sandwiches $5; steak dinners $11–$12.50. Daily 2pm–10pm. AMERICAN.

Travelers who've grown weary of Mexican food and are yearning for a taste of home are happy at this bright, clean restaurant with peaked wood ceilings and cheery blue-and-white tablecloths. The menu is primarily American, with burgers and fries, club sandwiches, T-bone steaks from Chihuahua, and shrimp from Los Mochis. The restaurant is across the street from the Parador Montaña hotel.

Restaurant las Rejas

In the Motel Parador de la Montaña, Av. López Mateos. ☎ **145/6-0075.** Breakfast, sandwiches, and hamburgers $2.50–$4; main courses $4.50–$8. Daily 7am–10pm. INTERNATIONAL.

This is easily the largest and most popular restaurant in town for an all-out dinner of soup, salad, steak, dessert, and coffee or just a simple grilled half-chicken dinner. There's full service from the cozy little bar attached, which is open all day and evening until around midnight. With its hanging lanterns, high wood-beamed ceiling, huge fireplace, and friendly atmosphere, Las Rejas is well worth a stop, though the food is less than exceptional. This is *the* gathering place for out-of-towners. It's two blocks west of the plaza.

3 Chihuahua

213 miles S of El Paso, 275 N of Torreón

Chihuahua (alt. 4,700 ft.; pop. 1,000,000), a city of wide boulevards and handsome buildings, is the capital of Chihuahua, the largest and richest state in Mexico. The money comes from mining, timber, cattle raising, many *maquiladoras* (U.S. assembly plants), and tourism—it's one of two major departure points for the Copper Canyon train. Population is booming in Chihuahua largely because of the manufacturing plants, and the city has lost much of its frontier feeling.

Aside from its industry, Chihuahua boasts a modern university and a museum in the house where Pancho Villa lived, but few, if any, of the tiny Chihuahua dogs.

ESSENTIALS

GETTING THERE & DEPARTING **By Plane** **Lone Star Airlines** (☎ 14/ 20-9154, or 800/877-3932 in the U.S.) started daily flights from El Paso and Dallas/Fort Worth to Chihuahua in 1994. (Southwest Airlines, ☎ 800/531-5601, serves El Paso from various U.S. cities.) **Aeroméxico** (☎ 15-6303) and its subsidiary **Aerolitoral** fly direct from El Paso, Guadalajara, Hermosillo, Ciudad Juárez, Mexico City, Monterrey, Torreón, Tijuana, Culiacan, La Paz, Los Mochis, and El Paso, with connecting flights from Los Angeles and San Antonio. **Taesa** has direct flights from Mexico City and connecting flights from Tijuana.

Transportes Aeropuerto (☎ 20-1124) runs colectivo service to and from the airport for $5.50 per person. Taxis charge $16 and up.

By Train The **Chihuahua al Pacífico** (☎ 14/10-9059; fax 14/16-9059) leaves Chihuahua daily for its route through the Copper Canyon to Los Mochis. (The complete train schedule and the train route are in Section 2 of this chapter.) The station in Chihuahua is two blocks behind the prison on 20 de Noviembre, near the intersection with Ocampo. The train is scheduled to leave promptly at 7am daily. To get there from the Plaza Principal and Avenida Juárez, take a bus named "Cerro de la Cruz" or "Ramiro Valles/Penitenaria." It lets you off two blocks from the station.

This public transportation is good to use if you are going to the station to buy tickets. However, for getting to the station for the early-morning train departure, it's best to arrange transportation through one of the travel agencies recommended under "Canyon Arrangements" in "Fast Facts." They pick up clients taking the train each morning; taxis that early can be scarce.

By Bus The Central Camionera (also called the Terminal de Autobuses) is on the outskirts of the city on Av. Juan Pablo II, 5 miles northeast of town, enroute to the airport. Buses leave hourly heading for major points inland and north and south on the coast. **Transportes Chihuahuenses,** the big local line (☎ 29-0242), has deluxe service to Ciudad Juárez at 8am and 2pm.

To travel to Creel, look for the Estrella Blanca line (☎ 15-5404). Buses leave every 2 hours from 6am to 6pm. Direct buses make the trip in 4 hours; de paso buses take 5.

Tres Estrellas de Oro (☎ 16-1408), **Transportes del Norte** (☎ 29-0240), and **Autobuses Estrella Blanca** (☎ 10-4466) also run buses hourly from the border through Chihuahua to points south. **Omnibus de México** has Real Ejecutivo (deluxe) service from Juárez, Mexico City, and Monterrey. **Futura Turistar** (☎ 29-0240 or 29-0218) also has deluxe service to Monterrey and Durango.

By Car Highway 45 leads south from Ciudad Juárez, Highway 16 south from Ojinaga, and Highway 49 north from Torreón. For the drive to Creel, see "Getting There & Departing" in Creel, above.

ORIENTATION **Arriving** From the **airport,** it's a half-hour trip downtown on the express van for $5.50 per person. Airport phone numbers are 20-5104 or 20-0676. Transportes Aeropuerto (☎ 20-1124) runs colectivo service to and from downtown for the same price. Taxis charge $16 for the trip either way. The Central Camionera (bus station) in Chihuahua is 5 miles northeast of the town center and west of the airport. Taxis from the **bus station** to town cost around $7 per person.

Information   For basic tourist information visit the **tourist information center** (☎ 14/10-1077 or 29-3300, ext. 4515 or 1061) on Libertad at Carranza in the Government Palace, just left of the altar and murals dedicated to Father Hidalgo. It's open Monday through Friday from 9am to 7pm, and Saturday and Sunday from 10am to 2pm. There are information booths in the airport and bus station as well.

City Layout   The town center is laid out around the Plaza Principal, bounded by Avenidas Libertad and Victoria (which run northeast-southwest) and Avenida Independencia and Calle 4a (which run northwest-southeast). The cathedral is at the southwest end of the plaza, and the city offices are on the northeast end. Generally, odd-numbered streets are to the northeast, and even-numbered streets are southwest of the plaza.

Getting Around   Local **buses** run along main arteries beginning at the central plaza. **Taxis** can be taken from the town center to most major sights. For early-morning transportation to the train station, it's best to make pickup arrangements with one of the travel agencies, since taxis are scarce at that hour.

FAST FACTS: CHIHUAHUA

American Express   The local representative is Viajes Rojo y Casavantes, with one agent in the Hotel San Francisco and a full office at Vicente Guerrero 1207 (☎ 14/12-5888; fax 15-5384).

Area Code   The telephone area code is 14.

Canyon Arrangements   If you wait to make overnight hotel reservations in the canyon until you are in Chihuahua, consider using a local travel agent. I recommend Turismo Al Mar, Reforma 400, Chihuahua, Chih. 31000 (☎ 10/16-9232; fax 16-6589); Cañon de Urique, Revolución 100, Chihuahua, Chih. 31310 (☎ 14/16-2672). You can buy train tickets yourself at the station, however, but do so before your day of departure.

EXPLORING CHIHUAHUA

To see all the sights of Chihuahua in 1 day, there are 3-hour city tours, with English-speaking guides available. Two recommended agencies are **Turismo Al Mar,** Reforma 400 (☎ 10/16-9232; fax 16-6589), and **Viajes Rojo y Casavantes,** with one agent in the lobby of the Hotel San Francisco and a larger office at Vicente Guerrero 1207 (☎ 14/12-5888). Either agency will pick you up at your hotel for tours. They'll take you to see the museums, the churches, the colonial aqueduct, the state capital building, the state penitentiary, and more. Cost is $12 per person plus admission to the museums. A 7-hour trip to the Mennonite village near Cuauhtémoc costs $30 per person, with a minimum of four people.

SIGHTS IN TOWN

Museum of the Revolution

Calle 10 no. 3014, at the corner of Mendez. ☎ **16-2958**. Admission $1. Daily 9am–1pm and 3–7pm. Bus: "Colonia Dale" heads west down Juárez, turning south onto Ocampo, and will let you off on the corner of Ocampo and Mendez.

Luz Corral de Villa lived in this, Pancho Villa's house, until her death in 1981. Exhibits include Villa's weapons, some personal effects, lots of period photos, and the 1922 Dodge in which he was shot in 1923, complete with bullet holes. It's one of the most interesting museums in the country.

✪ Museo Regional de Chihuahua (Quinta Gameros)

Paseo Bolívar 401. ☎ **16-6684.** Admission $1.50. Tues–Sun 10am–2pm and 4–7pm. Heading away from the Plaza Principal with the cathedral on your right, walk eight blocks on Independencia to Bolívar, turn right, and then walk one more block; it's on the right.

Quinta Gameros is an exact replica of a French Second Empire neoclassical mansion. The mansion was built in 1910 for Manuel Gameros and was converted to a museum in 1961. Pancho Villa used it as a headquarters for a while. Notice the wealth of decorative detail from floor to ceiling, inside and out. There are permanent exhibits of turn-of-the-century art nouveau furnishings and other salons containing exhibits of historical Chihuahuense photographs; an exhibit on the Mennonites of Cuauhtémoc, near Chihuahua; and an exhibit of artifacts from the pre-Hispanic ruins of Paquimé, about 5 hours to the north.

✪ Palacio del Gobierno

Av. Aldama between Guerrero and Carranza. ☎ **10-6324.** Admission free. Daily 8am–10pm. From the Plaza Principal, walk east on Independencia one block, then turn left on Aldama for two long blocks; cross Guerrero and you'll find the entrance on the left.

The Palacio del Gobierno is a magnificently ornate structure dating from 1890. A colorful, expressive mural encompasses the entire first floor of the large central courtyard, telling the history of the area around Chihuahua from the time of the first European visitation up through the Revolution. Note the scene depicting Benito Juárez flanked by Abraham Lincoln and Simón Bolívar, liberator of South America. A plaque and altar commemorate the execution of Miguel Hidalgo, the father of Mexican independence, at 7am on July 30, 1811; the plaque marks the very spot where the hero was killed (it was then a Jesuit convent), and the mural portrays the scene.

Hidalgo's Dungeon

In the Palacio Federal, Av. Juárez at Guerrero. No phone. Admission 50¢. Daily 10am–6pm. From the Plaza Principal, walk north on Libertad for three long blocks, cross Guerrero, and turn left on it to the corner of Juárez; the entrance to the museum is on the right, below the post office.

Father Miguel Hidalgo y Costilla was a priest in Dolores, Guanajuato, when he started the War of Independence on September 15, 1810. Six months later he was captured by the Spanish, brought to Chihuahua, and kept in a dungeon for 98 days, before being shot with his lieutenants, Allende, Aldama, and Jimenez. The four were beheaded, and their heads hung in iron cages for 9 1/2 years on the four corners of the Alhóndiga granary in Guanajuato. It was here in this cell that Hidalgo was kept on bread and water before his execution. The night before his death, he wrote a few words on the wall with a piece of charcoal to thank his guard and the warden for the good treatment they gave him. A bronze plaque commemorates his final message.

ACCOMMODATIONS

EXPENSIVE

Hotel Mision Plaza San Francisco

Victoria 409, Chihuahua, Chih. 31300. ☎ **14/16-7550,** or 800/437-7275 in the U.S. Fax 14/15-3538. 111 rms, 20 suites (all with bath). A/C TEL TV. $105 double.

The excellent location of this modern downtown hotel attracts repeat visitors. Locals and tourists alike use the hotel's lobby and restaurant/bar, Dega, as a meeting place, and the atmosphere is always convivial (see "Dining," below). The nice-size rooms are fashionably furnished, though a bit dimly lit. From the cathedral walk to Victoria and turn right; the hotel is 1¹/₂ blocks down on your right, before Av. Ocampo.

Villa Suites

Escudero 702, Chihuahua, Chih. 31300. ☎ **14/14-3350.** Fax 14/14-3313. 72 suites (all with bath). A/C TEL TV. $72 double. Rates include continental breakfast.

Visitors to Chihuahua rave about the Villa Suites, citing its quiet location and excellent amenities as among the best in the city. All suites have a kitchenette with stove, refrigerator, and coffeemaker and are decorated in a green-and-beige color scheme. The hotel's clubhouse contains an indoor heated swimming pool and fitness center; complimentary breakfast is served here every morning. There's also a full restaurant and room service. Though it's outside the downtown area, this is a good spot to rest up in luxurious surroundings after rugged canyon travels. The hotel is on Escudero between Av. Universidad and Av. de Montes.

INEXPENSIVE

Hotel Bal-Flo

Calle 5a no. 702. Chihuahua, Chih. 31300. ☎ **14/15-4340.** 91 rms (all with bath). A/C TEL. $24.50 double. Free parking.

All rooms at the Bal-Flo are heated and carpeted. Some units have windows on the street; others open onto an air shaft. Rental TVs are extra. The proprietor, Sr. Baltazar Flores, speaks English and is quite helpful. The cafeteria, open daily from 7am to 11pm, serves good, inexpensive food. To get here from the Plaza Principal, walk four long blocks east on Independencia and turn right for two blocks on Niños Héroes; it's on the left at Calle 5.

Hotel Santa Regina

Calle 3a no. 107, Chihuahua, Chih. 31300. ☎ **14/15-3889.** Fax 14/10-1411. 102 rms (all with bath). A/C TV TEL. $29 double. Free parking.

The three-story Santa Regina has carpeted rooms that are heated in winter and TVs that receive U.S. channels. More than half the rooms have windows facing outside; others have windows on the hall. To get here from the Plaza Principal, walk two blocks to Doblado and turn right for two more blocks; the hotel is between Juárez and Doblado.

DINING

For some very inexpensive meals, head for Calle Victoria behind the cathedral to the restaurants of the Hotel Reforma and the Hotel San Juan, mentioned above. Both restaurants are clean, small, and friendly and serve basic Mexican food at low prices. Mi Cafecito, in the Hotel Reforma, serves a comida corrida from 1pm until it runs out and is open daily from 8am to 11pm. The Restaurant San Juan offers one of the least expensive comida corridas in town from 1 to 3pm and is open daily from 8am to 10pm.

EXPENSIVE

Club de los Parados

Av. Juárez 3300. ☎ **15-3509.** Steak dinners $8–$20. Daily noon–11pm. MEXICAN/STEAKS.

Opened by wealthy cattle rancher Tony Vega in the 1950s, the club once hosted a clientele of rugged, rich ranchers who needed a place to drink and dine sumptuously, yet casually. The restaurant is filled with photos of important people from

Chihuahua's history, including actor Anthony Quinn, a local boy who hit the big time in Hollywood. The adobe-style building houses a large dining room with a wood-burning fireplace and a separate private dining room. As might be expected, beef is the big draw here, especially the hefty steaks. The carne asada is served with superb guacamole. Reservations are accepted.

MODERATE

Dega

In the Hotel Mision Plaza San Francisco, Calle Victoria 409. ☎ **16-7550.** Breakfast $2–$6; Sunday buffet $7; menu ejecutivo $7; plato mexicano $7.50. Daily 7am–10:45pm; brunch buffet Sun 10am–1pm; menu ejecutivo Mon–Sat 1–5pm. MEXICAN/INTERNATIONAL.

The restaurant/cafeteria/bar at this popular downtown hotel draws both downtown workers and travelers. The four-course *menu ejecutivo* is served with several choices. The *plato mexicano* comes with a tamale, a chile relleno, beans, chips, and guacamole. Fish, charcoal-grilled chicken, barbecue, and salads are all reasonably priced. American breakfasts and burgers are included in the extensive menu. From the cathedral walk to Victoria and turn right; it's 1 1/2 blocks down on your right, before Av. Ocampo.

Hostería 1900

Independencia 903. ☎ **16-1990.** Crêpes $5–$10; fondue $8–$18. Mon–Thurs 1pm–midnight; Fri–Sun 1pm–2am. INTERNATIONAL.

Cozy and charming in a Greenwich Village way, Hostería 1900 is decorated with black tables and chairs with accents of turquoise, hot pink, and black. Besides fondue and crêpes with several different sauces and fillings, there are meat dishes and soups. There's live music on weekends from 9:30pm to 2am and a happy hour most afternoons when two drinks for the price of one are served with free snacks. At lunch the place is filled with ladies in fashionable dress; at night it's a hangout for the younger set. The Hostería 1900 is three blocks east of the Plaza Principal, and half a block past the Hotel Palacio del Sol.

✪ La Parilla

Calle Victoria 420. ☎ **15-5856.** Steaks $6.50–$12; fajitas $6.50; tacos $2–$8. Daily noon–midnight. STEAKS.

With its ranch-style cafe decor of dark-wood tables and plastic-covered chairs, La Parilla features Chihuahua-bred beef cuts—sirloin, filet mignon, and club. Some meat platters come with consommé, salad, and potato; the *menu turístico* includes salad or soup, steak, and mashed potatos. There are 21 kinds of tacos and lots of side orders, like northern-style pinto beans cooked in beer, hot cheese, tortilla soup, and grilled onions. From the cathedral walk to Victoria and turn right; it's 1 1/2 blocks down on your left, just before Av. Ocampo and just past the Hotel San Francisco, on the left.

CHIHUAHUA AFTER DARK

Most downtown action takes place in hotel lobby bars. At the Hotel Mision Plaza San Francisco, Victoria 409, behind the cathedral, there's live music Monday through Saturday, with happy hour from 5 to 8pm. The Hotel Palacio del Sol, at Independencia 500, has different live entertainment nightly in the lobby bar. The Hostería 1900, at Independencia 902 (see "Dining" above) has live entertainment on weekends from 9:30pm to 2am and is popular with a young crowd, as is Chihuahua Charlie's Bar and Grill at Av. Juárez 3329.

A ROAD TRIP: THE MENNONITE VILLAGE OF CUAUHTÉMOC

Two hours west of Chihuahua, this village makes an unusual side trip. Originally from northern Germany, the Mennonites became an official reformist religious sect under Menno Simons in the early 16th century. With a strict Bible-based philosophy governing their daily lives, prohibiting them from engaging in war and many aspects of popular culture, they immigrated to other lands rather than violate their beliefs.

The group of 5,000 that in 1920 migrated to Cuauhtémoc from Canada petitioned the Mexican government for permission to settle here and maintain their own community traditions; Cuauhtémoc was little more than desert then, and Mexico was trying to develop its lands. The Mennonites transformed this desert into a productive and prosperous farming community. Some still maintain their 16th-century customs, religion, dress, and language (a dialect of Old German). Conservative Mennonites still use the traditional horses and buggies, but some in the community have taken to cars and pickup trucks, and you can even spot an occasional satellite dish. They are especially famous for their delicious cheese, fine woodwork, and embroidery, as well as their agricultural products.

An all-day Mennonite tour to Cuauhtémoc includes a visit to the Mennonite village and agricultural lands and a cheese factory, plus lunch in a Mennonite home, meeting the people and learning about their culture and history. The tour companies mentioned in "Fast Facts" can arrange the tour.

9

Guadalajara

Guadalajara (pronounced "gwa-da-la-HA-ra"), Mexico's second largest city, is also considered by many to be the most authentically Mexican. Much of Mexican tradition developed here or nearby. The jarabe tapatío (the Mexican hat dance) was developed here, and Guadalajara is considered the center for charrarería (Mexican-style rodeo). Mariachi music, the most robust in the country, was born nearby, and tequila, the fiery liquor that's the foundation of the margarita, is produced a few miles south of the city.

In the city's charter, Emperor Charles V called Guadalajara a *muy leal y muy noble ciudad* (most loyal and noble city). As a result of its isolated position southwest of Mexico City, Guadalajara developed into a sophisticated city largely on its own, without a great deal of interference from Spain. Today, it is capital of the state of Jalisco, and 5 million people live here.

As though to emphasize the great things expected from it, Guadalajara's Spanish builders gave the city not one but four beautiful plazas in its center. Today the city's leaders have given it a fifth, the enormous Plaza Tapatía, an ambitious stretch of redevelopment extending for about a mile through the urban landscape. Scattered with trees and monuments and sprinkled with fountains, the superplaza links the city's major colonial buildings and joins the past with the great new buildings of the present.

By the way, *tapatío* (or *tapatía*) is a word you'll come across often in this city. In the early days of the city, people from this area were known to trade in threes (three of this for three of that) called tapatíos. Gradually the people were called tapatíos too, and the word has come to mean "Guadalajaran" in reference to a thing, a person, and even an idea. The way a *charro* (Mexican cowboy) gives his all, or the way a mariachi sings his heart out—that's tapatío!

1 Orientation

ARRIVING & DEPARTING
BY PLANE

Guadalajara's international airport is a 25- to 45-minute ride from the city. Taxi and colectivo (shared ride) tickets to Guadalajara or Chapala are sold outside in front of the airport. Tickets are sold by zone. A shared taxi ride to the heart of Guadalajara costs around $12, and a private taxi costs $16. A taxi to Chapala costs around $30.

On departure from Guadalajara, you'll be required to check in at least 1 1/2 hours before takeoff for international flights, and at least 1 hour before takeoff for domestic flights. Local taxis are the only transport from town to the airport.

MAJOR AIRLINES   See Chapter 3, "Planning a Trip to Mexico," for a list of international airlines serving Mexico. Local numbers for airlines currently flying from Guadalajara to points abroad are: **Alaska Airlines,** ☎ toll free 91/800-426-0333 in Mexico; **American Airlines,** ☎ 616-4090; **Continental Airlines,** ☎ 647-6672 or 647-4605; **Delta,** ☎ 630-3530, and **United,** ☎ toll free 91-800/0-0307 in Mexico.

Aero California (☎ 826-1901 or 826-8850) serves Guadalajara from Tijuana, Mexico City, Los Mochis, La Paz, and Puebla; **Aeroméxico** (☎ 669-0202; at the airport 689-0028) flies from numerous points in the U.S. and Monterrey, Puerto Vallarta, Manzanillo, Mazatlán, Chihuahua, Acapulco, and Tijuana in Mexico; **Mexicana** (☎ 647-2222; at the airport 689-0119) connects with a number of U.S. cities and Cancún, Léon, Los Cabos, Nuevo Laredo, Zihuatanejo, Puerto Vallarta, and Tijuana in Mexico; **Saro** (614-7571; at the airport 688-5876) flies to Mexico City, Monterrey, and Tijuana; **Taesa** (☎ 679-0900) flies from Mexico City, Tijuana, Morelia, some U.S. cities, and seasonally to Puerto Vallarta.

BY BUS

Two bus stations serve Guadalajara—the old one near downtown, and the new one six miles out on the way to Tonala. A convenient place to get bus information is **Servicios Coordinados,** Calzada Independencia 254, a kind of "bus travel agency" located under Plaza Tapatía. There, travelers can make reservations, buy tickets, and receive information on the six main bus lines to all points in Mexico. The **ETN** bus line (☎ 614-8875 or 614-2479) has an office in the Hotel Carlton downtown.

To get from either station to your hotel, look for the **city buses** and white minivans marked "Centro," which pick up passengers in front of each terminal building. These are convenient only if you have a very small suitcase. **Linea Turquesa** (TUR) buses are air-conditioned and offer the most comfortable service since they accept only the number of passengers for whom there are seats. From the bus station, some go to Tonala, and others follow a route along Calzada Tlaquepaque to Tlaquepaque, Revolución, and 16 de Septiembre/Alcalde to the Centro Histórico. Some of these skip Tonala; look for the sign on the front of each bus.

You can also take a **taxi.** Taxi tickets, sold inside each terminal building, are priced by zone. A taxi from the Central Camionera to the downtown Plaza Tapatía area (a 30-minute ride) costs about $7.

THE OLD BUS STATION   For bus trips within a 60-mile radius of Guadalajara, including to **Lake Chapala, Ajijic, Jocotepec, Mazamitla,** and **San Juan Cosalá,** go to the old bus terminal on Niños Héroes off Calzada Independencia Sur and look for **Transportes Guadalajara-Chapala** (☎ 619-5675), which has frequent bus and combi service beginning at 6am to Chapala (also see "Excursions from Guadalajara," Section 8 of this chapter).

THE NEW BUS STATION   The **Central Camionera,** about six miles and a 35-minute ride east of downtown toward Tonala, provides bus service to and from virtually any point in Mexico. None of the buses from here is of the school-bus variety—while the price difference between first and second class is small, the difference in speed, comfort, and convenience is often great. The new terminal resembles an international airport—seven separate buildings are connected by a covered walkway in a U shape, with one-way traffic entering on the right. Each building houses several first- and second-class bus lines. That's the only drawback—you must go to each one to find the line or service that suits you best.

Here is a breakdown of the various parts of the new station, beginning with the first building on the right: **Building 1** holds Primera Plus with deluxe service to Puervo Vallarta (5 hours), Lagos de Moreno, Colima, Manzanillo ($4^1/_2$ hours), and Melaque (5 hours). This building also has the ETN deluxe line to Mexico City (7 hours) and to Aguascalientes (but ETN buses leave from building 2); **Building 2** has many buses to Aguascalientes and Zacatecas. Autotransportes Mazamitla goes to Tuxcueca, La Manzanilla, and Mazamitla hourly between 6am and 6:30pm; these buses don't go through Chapala and Ajijic; instead they pass at the crossroads at Jocotopec. **Building 3** has Primera Plus and Autocamiones Cihuatlan with service to Manzanillo six times daily as well as to Talpa and Macota; **Building 5** has Estrella Blanca with hourly service until 6pm to Puerto Vallarta. Linea Azul Oriente has six buses to San Júan del Lago and Turistar's deluxe buses go to Aguascalientes and Lagos de Moreno; **Building 6** has Omnibus de México buses going to Mexico City and many to Zacatecas and Colima, as well as ETN buses with service to Colima, Manzanillo, Puerto Vallarta, Mexico City, Morelia, and Aguascalientes; **Building 7** has the Expreso Futura line with many buses to Mexico City, the Rojos al Altos line with hourly service to Zacatecas, and Turistar Primera with frequent service to Lagos de Moreno, León, and Puerto Vallarta.

This station is one of the nicest in Mexico, with amenities like shuttle buses, restaurants, gift shops, luggage storage (*guarda equipaje*), book and magazine shops, liquor stores, Ladatel long-distance telephones, and hotel information. There's also a large budget hotel next door (see "Accommodations," below). To get there by bus, take any bus marked "Central" on Avenida 16 de Septiembre/Alcalde opposite the Rotonda de los Ilustres in downtown Guadalajara.

BY CAR

DIRECTIONS   From Nogales on the **California border,** follow Highway 15 south. You can also take a toll road between Guadalajara and Tepic, a 6-hour drive. From **Barra de Navidad** or southeast on the coast, take Highway 80 northeast. A new toll road, running from **Puerto Vallarta** on the Pacific nearly to Tequila (30 miles west of Guadalajara), is scheduled for completion by June 1995. The trip will take four hours. From **Mexico City,** take the free Highway 90 (6 to 8 hours) or the new toll road, which takes $4^1/_2$ hours. Coming from **Colima,** there's another toll road which takes about 4 hours.

VISITOR INFORMATION

The **State of Jalisco Tourist Information Office** is at Calle Morelos 102 (☎ 658-2222 or 658-0305; fax 613-0335) in the Plaza Tapatía at the crossroads of Paseo Degollado and Paraje del Rincón del Diablo. It's open Monday through Friday from 9am to 8pm and Saturday, Sunday, and festival days from 9am to 1pm. This is one of the most efficient and informative tourism offices in the country. They have a supply of maps as well as a monthly calendar of cultural happenings in the city.

Greater Guadalajara

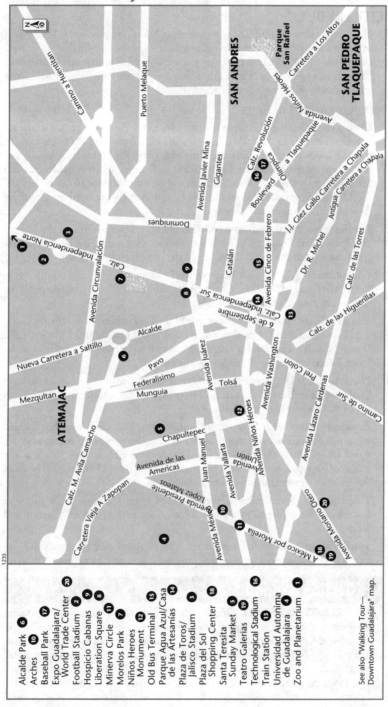

Alcalde Park 6
Arches 10
Baseball Park 17
Expo Guadalajara/World Trade Center 20
Football Stadium 2
Hospicio Cabanas 9
Liberation Square 8
Minerva Circle 11
Morelos Park 7
Niños Heroes Monument 12
Old Bus Terminal 15
Parque Agua Azul/Casa de las Artesanías 14
Plaza de Toros/Jalisco Stadium 3
Plaza del Sol 18
Shopping Center
Santa Teresita 5
Sunday Market 19
Teatro Galerias 16
Technological Stadium 13
Train Station
Universidad Autonima de Guadalajara 4
Zoo and Planetarium 1

See also "Walking Tour—Downtown Guadalajara" map.

1235

CITY LAYOUT

Guadalajara is not a difficult city to negotiate, but it certainly is big. While most of the main attractions are within walking distance of the historic downtown area, others—such as Tonala and Tlaquepaque (which are both nearby) and Lake Chapala and Ajijic (which are both farther away)—are accessible by bus. Street names downtown change at the cathedral.

NEIGHBORHOODS IN BRIEF

Centro Histórico The heart of the city takes in the Plaza de Armas, Plaza de los Laureles, Plaza de los Hombres Ilustres, Plaza Liberación, and Plaza Tapatía. It's the tourist center and contains major museums, theaters, restaurants, hotels, and the largest covered market in Latin America, all linked by wide boulevards and pedestrians-only streets. It's bounded east and west by Avenidas 16 de Septiembre/Alcalde and Prosperidad (across Calzada Independencia) and north and south by Avenida Hidalgo and Calle Morelos.

Parque Agua Azul An enormous city park 20 blocks south of the Centro Histórico, it has a children's area and rubber-wheeled train. Nearby are the state crafts shop, performing-arts theaters, and the anthropology museum.

Chapultepec A fashionable neighborhood with shops and restaurants 25 blocks west of the Centro Histórico, it is reached by Avenida Vallarta. Chapultepec is the main artery through the neighborhood.

Minerva Circle Almost 40 blocks west of the Centro Histórico, Minerva Circle is at the confluence of Avenidas Vallarta and López Mateos and Circunvalación Washington. It's a fashionable neighborhood with several good restaurants and the Hotel Fiesta Americana, all reached by the Par Vial.

Plaza del Sol The largest shopping center in the city, it lies south of Minerva Circle and southwest of the Centro Histórico near the intersection of Avenidas López Mateos and Mariano Otero.

Zapopan Once a separate village founded in 1542, now it's a full-fledged suburb 20 minutes northwest of the Plaza Tapatía via Avenida Ávila Camacho. It's noted for its 18th-century basilica and the revered 16th-century image of the Virgin of Zapopan, made of corn paste and honored every October 12. The city's fashionable country club is just south of Zapopan.

Tlaquepaque Seven miles southeast of the Centro Histórico, it's a village of former mansions turned into shops which front pedestrians-only streets and plazas.

Tonala Four miles from Tlaquepaque, it's a village of over 400 artists working in metal, clay, and paper. A huge street market is held on Thursday and Sunday.

2 Getting Around

BY BUS & TREN LIJERO The city has six kinds of city buses and a rapid transit system called the **Tren Lijero**. Many of the buses run the same routes but offer different kinds of service. **Grey buses with maroon stripes** are better city buses and cost 35¢. **School bus–style buses** cost 25¢. Both of these buses carry seated passengers as well as passengers packed into the aisles. Privately operated **minivans** cost about the same as city buses. Some are numbered and others have their destination written on the windshield. **Linea Turquesa** (turquoise line) buses, colored a pale turquoise, have the distinguishing letters "TUR" on the side and run several routes around the city. These cost $1, are air-conditioned, have padded seats, and best of all, carry only as many passengers as there are seats. Frequent TUR buses also run between the Centro Histórico, Tlaquepaque, Central Caminonera (new bus station), Tonala, and Zapopan. Some of these go to Tonala and not Zapopan, or Zapopan but not Tonala. For information on getting to Tlaquepaque and Tonala by bus, see "Excursions from Guadalajara," below.

Two bus routes of the **"Par Vial"** (electric buses) will satisfy 90% of your intracity transportation needs. Buses bearing the sign "Par Vial" run a rectangular route going east along Independencia/Hidalgo, passing the Mercado Libertad, and going as far west as the Minerva Circle, where they turn back east on Vallarta/Juárez and pass by the Plaza de Armas on their run east.

Many buses run north-south along the Calzada Independencia (not to be confused with Calle Independencia), but the **"San Juan de Dios–Estación"** bus goes between the points you want—San Juan de Dios church, next to the Mercado Libertad, and the railroad station (*estación*) past Parque Agua Azul. This bus is best because most other buses on Calzada Independencia have longer routes (out to the suburbs, for instance) and thus tend to be heavily crowded at all times.

Section 1 of the **Tren Lijero** (rapid transit system) is finished and section 2 should be fully operational when you travel. Section 1 serves a few tourist needs since it runs north-south along Federalismo, curving the distance of Camino de Sur/Prolongación Colón. Section 2 runs east-west along Vallarta/Juárez and Avenida Javier Mina, the eastern extension of Vallarta/Juárez. It takes passengers between the Mercado Liberación and the Parque Revolución (near the restaurants Suehiro and Copenhagen and the Museo de las Artes).

BY COLECTIVO   Colectivos are minivans that run throughout the city day and night, picking up and discharging passengers at fixed and unfixed points. They are often a faster and more convenient way to travel than the bus. There are no printed schedules, and the routes and fixed pick-up points change frequently. However, locals know the routes by heart and can tell you where and how to use them if you tell them where you want to go.

BY CAR   Keep in mind several main arteries. The **Periférico** is a loop around the city that connects with most other highways entering the city. Traffic on the Periférico is slow because it's heavily potholed, filled with trucks, and only a two-lane road. Several important freeway-style thoroughfares crisscross the city. **Gonzalez Gallo** leads south from the town center and connects with the road to Tonala and Tlaquepaque or leads straight to Lake Chapala. **Highway 15** from Tepic intersects with both **Avenida Vallarta** and **Calzada Lázaro Cárdenas.** Vallarta then goes straight to the Plaza Tapatía area. **Cárdenas** crosses the whole city and intersects the road to Chapala and to Tlaquepaque and Tonala.

BY TAXI   Taxis are an expensive way to get around town. A short 10- to 15-minute ride—for example, from the Plaza de Armas to the Zoo and Planetarium—costs an exorbitant $6 or $7, while a bus there costs only 25¢.

BY HORSE-DRAWN CARRIAGE   Take one of the elegant horse-drawn carriages for a spin around town. The cost is about $15, depending on route and length of ride—usually about 45 minutes. Drivers congregate in front of the Museo Regional, near the Mercado Libertad, and also behind the Plaza/Rotonda de los Hombres Ilustres and other spots around town.

FAST FACTS: GUADALAJARA

American Express   The local office is at Av. Vallarta 2440, Plaza Los Arcos (☎ 615-8910); it's open Monday through Friday from 9am to 6pm and Saturday from 9am to noon.

Area Code   The telephone area code is 3.

Climate & Dress   Guadalajara has a mild, pleasant, and dry climate year-round. Bring a sweater for evenings during November through March. The warmest months—April and May—are hot and dry. From June through September, it's rainy and a bit cooler. Guadalajara is as sophisticated and at least as formal as Mexico City. Dress is conservative; resortwear (short shorts, halters, and the like) is out of place here, but knee-length shorts, skirts, slacks, and blouses for women or slacks, bermudas, and shirts for men are fine for all but the few formal restaurants or events.

Consulates   The world's largest American consular offices are here at Progreso 175 (☎ 625-2998 or 625-2700). The offices are open Monday through Friday from 8am to 4:30pm.

Hospitals   For a medical emergency, there's the Hospital México-Americano, Colomos 2110 (☎ 614-0089).

Information   See "Information," above.

Luggage Storage/Lockers   Luggage storage is available in the main bus station, the Central Camionera, and at the Guadalajara airport.

Newspapers/Magazines   The Hotel Fenix, on the corner of Corona and López Cotilla, has English-language newspapers and magazines and maps. It's also a good place to buy Guadalajara's English newspaper, *The Colony Reporter*, published every Saturday, if you don't spot it on the newsstand. Sanborn's, at the corner of Juárez and 16 de Septiembre, has a wide selection of U.S. and Mexican newspapers and magazines.

Post Office   The main post office (Correos) is at the corner of Carranza and Calle Independencia, about four blocks northeast of the cathedral. Standing in the plaza behind the cathedral and facing the Degollada Theater, walk to the left and turn left on Carranza; walk past the Hotel Mendoza, cross Calle Independencia, and look for the post office on the left side.

Safety   As in any large city, don't be careless with your belongings. There are people on the streets at all hours, but to be safe, avoid walking around alone late at night on unlighted streets. As in the rest of Mexico, pedestrians don't have the right of way, so be sure to look left, right, and behind you when crossing any street, even if you cross with the light.

3 Accommodations

DOWNTOWN
EXPENSIVE

Carlton Hotel

Av. Niños Heroes 125 and 16 de Septiembre, Guadalajara, Jal. 44190. ☎ **3/614-7272** or 91-800/3-6200 in Mexico. Fax 3/613-5539. 222 rms and suites. AC MINIBAR TV TEL. $150 standard double; $185 master suite; $195 executive suite. Ask about weekend discounts.

The Carlton is near Agua Azul Park and a short distance from the historic center. The nicely furnished rooms are unusually spacious. All come with hairdryers and remote-control TV with U.S. channels. Master suites have a large living-room area, while junior suites have a small sitting area. Each of the fifth-floor executive suites includes terry robes, continental breakfast, afternoon coffee and pastries, and open bar in the early evening. The 10th floor is reserved for nonsmokers. You'll save money by purchasing a package for this hotel through a travel agent in the United States.

Dining/Entertainment: One indoor/outdoor restaurant, facing the pool, serves all meals. There are two bars, a video disco, and a live-music nightclub.

Services: Laundry, room service, travel agency, purified tap water. For an extra charge guests may use the hotel's fax and copy machine.

Facilities: Large pool. Small, fully equipped fitness center open for men from 7 to 10am and 6 to 9pm and for women all other hours.

Fiesta Americana

Aurello Aceves 225, Glorieta Minerva, Guadalajara, Jal. 44100. ☎ **3/625-3434** or 625-4848, or 800/223-2332 in the U.S. Fax 3/630-3725. 396 rms. A/C MINIBAR TV TEL. $170–$175 double; $190 Fiesta Club.

A 22-story luxury hotel on a grand scale, Fiesta Americana caters to the exacting demands of travelers arriving for both business and pleasure. It's a bustling hotel with a 14-story lobby and popular lobby bar with ongoing live entertainment. Like the public areas of the hotel, the rooms are spacious and beautifully coordinated, all with TV with U.S. channels. The 27 exclusive Fiesta Club rooms and 3 suites on the 12th and 14th floors come with special amenities (see below). One room is handicap-equipped.

Dining/Entertainment: Three restaurants, including the popular and elegant Place de la Concorde, serve all meals. There's a lobby bar. See also "Nightclub/Cabaret" in "Guadalajara After Dark."

Services: Laundry, dry cleaning, room service, travel agency.

Facilities: Heated rooftop swimming pool, two lighted tennis courts, and purified tap water. Fiesta Club guests have key-only access to club floors, separate check-in and checkout, concierge, remote-control TV, continental breakfast and afternoon wine and hors d'oeuvres daily, as well as business services such as secretaries, fax, copy machine, and conference room.

Hyatt Regency

Av. López Mateos Sur y, Moctezuma, Guadalajara, Jal. 45050. ☎ **3/678-1234** or 800/228-9000 in the U.S. and Canada. Fax 3/676-1222. 347 rms and suites. A/C MINIBAR TV TEL. $140–$185 double; $245 suite; $215–$245 Regency Club. Free parking.

The elegant 14-story Hyatt Regency Hotel anchors one end of the Plaza del Sol, the city's largest and most fashionable shopping center. Glass elevators whish up and down the soaring lobby, and guest rooms are as stylish as the hotel's public areas. Rooms vary in size but all are decorated in rose and green with natural wood furniture and all have a tub/shower combination. Four key-only floors are reserved for Regency Club guests who receive special amenities. No-smoking rooms are on the 12th floor.

Dining/Entertainment: Three restaurants meet guests' dining needs, from poolside snacks to fine dining and Mexican specialties. There's also a lobby bar and a cantina.

Services: Laundry, dry cleaning, room service, beauty shop, travel agency, car rental, business center with bilingual secretarial services, and 24-hour doctor. Regency Club guests receive a daily newspaper, continental breakfast, and evening cocktails in the club's separate lounge.

Facilities: Swimming pool on the 12th floor, gym, separate sauna for men and women, ice-skating rink.

Quinta Real

Av. Mexico 2727, Guadalajara, Jal. 44680. ☎ **3/615-0000** or 800/445-4565 in the U.S. and Canada, 91-800/3-6015 in Mexico. Fax 3/630-1797. 78 suites. A/C MINIBAR TV TEL. $215 junior suite; $250 master suite; $275 grand-class suite.

Opened in 1986, this is the city's most intimate hotel. Its casual-but-sophisticated restaurant and bar are the place to be seen if you're climbing any social or political ladder. The hotel hosts many business meetings and is frequently full. Each of the guest rooms is different: Eight have brick cupolas, some have balconies, several have conch-shaped headboards, and four come with whirlpool bath in the bathroom. All have elegant antique decorative touches, remote-control TV with U.S. channels, tub/shower combination, and king-size beds. It's located west of the city center two blocks from the Minerva Circle on Avenida Mexico at López Mateos.

Dining/Entertainment: An elegant off-lobby restaurant has both terrace and indoor dining. The adjacent bar is open till 2am.

Services: Concierge, laundry and dry cleaning, massage by reservation, video players for rent, travel agency.

Facilities: Small heated pool.

MODERATE

✪ Calinda Roma

Juárez 170, Guadalajara, Jal. 14100. ☎ **3/614-8650** or 800/228-5151 in the U.S., 91-800/9-000 in Mexico. Fax 3/613-0557. 172 rms (all with bath). A/C MINIBAR TV TEL. $60–$70 double. Parking $1 daily.

Perfectly situated, this hotel is within walking distance of all downtown sights and restaurants. This quiet and comfortable hotel is one of the best in the city center. For its 100th birthday in 1993, rooms were renovated. Bathrooms will be updated next. Some rooms have exercise bicycles. Higher priced rooms are larger. There's an excellent restaurant and bar in the lobby. The rooftop garden, with a grass putting green and a pool, is a great place to unwind. To find the hotel from the Plaza de Armas, walk two blocks south on Corona. Turn left on Juárez; the hotel is two blocks ahead at the corner of Degollado.

Hotel de Mendoza

Carranza 16, Guadalajara, Jal. 45120. ☎ **3/613-4646** or 800/221-6509 in the U.S. Fax 3/613-7310. 104 rms (all with bath). TV TEL. $90 double.

This restored hotel is popular with foreigners for its quiet, colonial atmosphere and modern conveniences. It's at the corner of Hidalgo, only steps from Liberation Plaza and the Teatro Degollado. Almost all of the large rooms have wall-to-wall carpeting, and some have a tub and a shower. Rooms face either the street or an interior court with a swimming pool. Rates may be higher if you call or reserve from the United States. Walk-in rates are cheaper—get them quoted in pesos. To get there from the Teatro Degollado, go to the left of the theater and look for Carranza, a block down on the left; turn left at the corner church, adjoining the hotel. The hotel has a swimming pool on the first floor and one restaurant, La Forga. El Campañario bar offers dance music. The hotel offers laundry and room service.

INEXPENSIVE

✪ Hotel San Francisco Plaza

Degollado 267, Guadalajara, Jal. 44100. ☎ **3/613-8954** or 613-8971. Fax 3/613/3257. 76 rms (all with bath). A/C TV TEL. $29–$32 double. Free parking.

For a touch of class, try this highly recommended hotel facing a tiny square near Priciliano Sánchez. You get a lot for your money. Stone arches, brick-tile floors, bronze sculptures, and potted plants decorate the four spacious central courtyards. All rooms are large and attractive, and each includes either a double bed, a king-size bed, or two double beds. The English-speaking staff is friendly and helpful. A very good, inexpensive restaurant off the lobby is open daily from 8am to 10pm. To get here from the Plaza de Armas, walk five blocks south on 16 de Septiembre, turn left onto Sánchez, and walk two blocks to Degollado and the hotel.

⑤ Posada Regis

Corona 171, Guadalajara, Jal. 44100. ☎ **3/613-3026** or 614/8633. 19 rms (all with bath). TEL TV. $25 double. Discounts for stays of a week or more.

Opposite the Hotel Fenix, the Posada Regis occupies the second floor of a restored old mansion. The large, carpeted rooms are simply furnished and arranged around a tranquil, covered courtyard, a small restaurant, and potted plants. Rooms with balconies facing the street are quite noisy. Windowless interior rooms are stuffy, so ask for a fan. The mattresses have plastic covers and "nonbreathing" nylon-type sheets. Baths have open ceilings and no doors. I've stayed here and find that it particularly serves my budget and my needs for safety and proximity to downtown. Video movies are shown every evening on the lobby TV. The restaurant serves a very good and inexpensive breakfast ($1.75–$3.15) from 8am to 11am and lunch ($4–$5) from 2 to 4pm. I especially enjoy the good lunch here. Non-guests can take meals too. It's best to call ahead and tell them you're coming, but you can also try dropping in. There's personal laundry service. To find the hotel from the Plaza de Armas, walk 2¹/₂ blocks on Corona. It's on the left almost at the corner of Madero. Enter through a small doorway and go up a flight of stairs to the second-floor hotel and lobby.

A NEARBY SPA

✪ Río Caliente Spa

Primavera Forest, La Primavera, Jal. No phone. 48 rms. Patio area: $161 double. Pool area: $185 double. Rates include all meals. Discounts May 1–Nov 1; 7- and 10-night packages available. For reservations contact Marian Lewis, Spa Vacations Limited Associates, P.O. Box 897 Millbrae, CA 94030; ☎ 415/615-9543; fax 415/615-0601.

Word of mouth keeps this popular and very casual spa busy. Built along the hills of the Primavera forest and on a thermal water river, the setting, at 5,550 feet, is both rugged and serene. Temperatures average 80°F year-round. Individual rooms are clustered in two areas. Those near the activity area are smaller and more simply furnished and cost less than the newer and more stylish rooms with patios near the river and pool. All have one double and one single bed, fireplace, full-length mirror, in-room safety-deposit box, desk, chest, and bedside reading lamps. Water is purified in the pools and kitchen, and jars of fresh purified water are supplied daily in each room. Extra spa programs vary throughout the year and might include special instructors for Spanish and nutrition, and electro-acupuncture face-lifts at an extra cost. A doctor comes daily. Huichol Indians sell crafts on Sunday. Taxi pick-up is available upon request for around $32 one way, or you can take a taxi from the airport for around $40 one way. To save money on transportation from the Guadalajara airport, take one of the airport's colectivo vans to the Fiesta Americana Hotel, then change to a yellow cab. If you're driving, follow Avenida Vallarta west, which becomes Highway 15 with signs to Nogales. Go straight for almost 10^{1}/$_{2}$ miles and pass the village called La Venta del Astillero. Take the next left after La Venta and follow the rough road through the village of La Primavera for almost five miles. Keep bearing left through the forest until you see the hotel's sign on the left. There's no phone at the spa; reservations are through the United States only.

The help-yourself vegetarian meals are served in the cozy dining room. There's an activities room with nightly video movies or satellite TV, plus bingo and honor library.

Guests have a choice of two public-area outdoor thermal pools, and two private pools and sunning areas that are separate for men and women.

Among the services available at extra cost are massage, with a choice of male or female massage therapist, mud wrap, anti-stress and anti-aging therapies, live-cell therapy, horseback riding, sight-seeing and shopping excursions. Included in the cost, besides meals, are daily guided hikes, yoga and pool exercises, use of scented steam room with natural steam from an underground river.

4 Dining

Some travelers find it comforting to know that such U.S. franchise restaurants as Kentucky Fried Chicken, McDonald's, and Dunkin' Donuts are beginning to proliferate in Guadalajara. But as long as you're in Guadalajara, or anywhere in the state of Jalisco for that matter, I urge you to try a local dish called *birria*—a hearty soup of lamb, pork, or goat meat in a tasty chicken-and-tomato broth. Restaurants around El Parian in Tlaquepaque have birria on the menu daily. Another local specialty is the *lonche,* a sandwich made from a scooped-out *bolillo* (a large roll) filled with a variety of meats and topped with sour cream, avocado, onions, and chiles.

On the second floor of the **Mercado Libertad** you can purchase economical meals at any of the seemingly hundreds of little restaurant stands. Some people say you should not eat here. Nonetheless, hundreds of people do eat here every day and seem to be surviving just fine—I've even done it myself. Check it out—it's a fascinating slice of Mexican life. The best time to go is early in the morning, while the food is the freshest. The hotel **Posada Regis** serves a very economical and filling home-style breakfast and lunch (see "Accommodations," above).

EXPENSIVE

Suehiro
La Paz 1701. ☎ **3/826-0094** or 826-3122. Reservations recommended. Main courses $8–$25. Mon–Sat 2–5:30pm and 8–11pm. JAPANESE.

Guadalajarans love this touch of Japan in their city and fill every seat in the several spacious dining rooms. Though not as good as Suntory in Acapulco, the food here is authentically flavored and cooked. Teppanyaki is the specialty, but the menu also offers a wide selection of tempura. You can order a selection of sushi as well, by the plate or piece, or you can dine entirely on sushi in the separate sushi bar, where the selection is large, fresh, delicious, and prepared while you watch. The restaurant is about 13 blocks beyond the Parque de la Revolución and Av. Enrique Díaz de León. To reach it, take the Par Vial from Av Hidalgo to Chapultepec. Get off at Chapultepec and turn left (south) on Chapultepec for three blocks and turn left (east) on La Paz for about three blocks; it's on the right.

MODERATE

Molino Rojo
Hotel Francés, Maestranza 35. ☎ **613-1190.** Main courses $4–$10. Daily 7:30am–10pm. INTERNATIONAL.

I can't recommend the Hotel Francés because of the nightly disco noise, but the off-lobby restaurant of the hotel, with its international offerings, is a pleasant change from more traditional Mexican restaurants downtown. Nice but not elegant, the decor features purple, turquoise, and Mexican pottery accents. Try the spaghetti primavera (natural carrot-and-spinach pasta with fresh vegetables and parmesan cheese), or the tampiqueña plate, or something more American like the club sandwich. From the Plaza de Armas, walk one block east on Moreno to Maestranza and turn right. The hotel and restaurant are on the left.

✪ La Trattoría Pomodoro Ristorante
Niños Héroes 3051. ☎ **3/122-1977.** Pasta $4–$6; chicken, beef, and seafood $6–$11. Mon–Sat 1pm–midnight, Sun 1pm–8pm. ITALIAN.

Sooner or later, visitors learn about the good food at this popular restaurant. Service is friendly and swift, and the newly decorated restaurant is refreshingly appealing with natural wood chairs, cushioned seats, and linen-clad tables. A large span of windows looks out onto Niños Héroes. There's separate seating for smokers and non-smokers. For starters, you might want to sample the antipasto bar or the shrimp in white-wine cream sauce with chiles. As a main course, the fettuccine Alfredo is excellent. The superb salad bar and garlic bread are included in the price of main courses. To find this place, take the Par Vial going west on Independencia/Hidalgo. Get off when the bus turns back at the Minerva Circle. Walk one block farther to Avenida México, cross the street, and get a bus going south to Niños Héroes (about 14 blocks). Cross Avenida México to Niños Héroes and walk about half a block; the restaurant is on the right behind a church.

✪ Recco
Libertad 1981. ☎ **3/625-0724.** Main courses $7–$11. Daily 1–11:30pm. ITALIAN/CONTINENTAL.

Owned by Luigi Cupurro and housed in an old mansion in one of Guadalajara's neighborhoods, this casually fashionable restaurant rates high with the locals. Dining rooms, all decked out in cloth-covered tables and cushioned chairs, are a bit too brightly lit at night to be intimate, but the service and food are good. Starters include small portions of pasta, seafood, and carpaccio or perhaps pâté and prosciutto and cantaloupe. Among the main courses, you'll find pepper steak, charcoal broiled trout, and veal with fettuccine. To find the restaurant from the main plaza, take the Par Vial to Chapultepec and Vallarta. At Vallarta turn left on Chapultepec for two blocks to Libertad and turn left again. You'll see it on the right less than half a block down.

INEXPENSIVE

Acuarius
Prisciliano Sánchez 416. ☎ **3/613-6277.** Breakfast $3; main courses $2.50–$5; soup $2; comida corrida $5. Daily 9:30am–8pm (comida corrida served 1–4pm). VEGETARIAN.

This immaculate, airy little lunch room has soft music playing and shelves of soy sauce and vitamins. The restaurant offers breakfast, an à la carte menu, and comida corrida. For the comida corrida, there's a choice of two main dishes, which you can sample first if you can't make up your mind. When I was here, the choice was zucchini sautéed with mushrooms in tangy tomato sauce or mixed-vegetable stew. Whole-grain bread and whole-grain tortillas come with the meal in addition to soup, fruit, and yogurt or a salad, a tall glass of fruit juice, and dessert. If that's too much food, consider ordering from the menu that offers a daily choice of three main courses made from soy and two of vegetables. From the Plaza de Armas, walk four blocks south on 16 de Septiembre, turn right onto P. Sánchez, and walk 3½ blocks; the restaurant is on the right between D. Guerro and Ocampo.

Café Madrid

Juárez 264. ☎ **3/614-9504.** Breakfast $2–$3; main courses $2–$6. Daily. 7am–11pm. MEXICAN.

Conveniently located, this popular café serves the best coffee in Guadalajara. The aroma wafts outside the café in the morning—americano, espresso, cappuccino, and café con leche are all excellent eye-openers. Signs above the counter advertise chilaquiles and "ricos hot cakes," which are indeed rich and are served with warm syrup. The extra-hearty platillo tapatío includes fried chicken, a taco, an enchilada, and potatoes. From the Plaza de Armas, walk one block on Corona to Juárez and turn right; the café is on the right.

✪ Los Itacates Restaurant

Chapultepec Nte. 110. ☎ **3/825-1106.** Breakfast $1.75–$4; tacos 60¢; main courses $2–$5. Mon–Sat 8am–11pm, Sun 8am–7pm. MEXICAN.

Locals can't say enough about the authenticity and quality of the Mexican food here. The atmosphere is festive with colorfully painted chairs and table coverings. You can choose the sidewalk dining in front or the three interior rooms. Among the specialties are pozole, sopa medula (bone marrow soup), lomo adobado (baked pork), and chiles rellenos. The chicken Itacates comes with a quarter of a chicken, two cheese enchiladas, potatoes, and rice. To find the restaurant, take the Par Vial west on Independence/Hidalgo. Get off at Chapultepec and walk to the right (north) on Chapultepec about three blocks. It's on the right.

Sanborn's

Juárez at 16 de Septiembre. ☎ **3/613-6264.** Breakfast $3–$4; main courses $3–$8. Daily 7:30am–1am. INTERNATIONAL.

Opened in 1992, Sanborn's is filled with patrons at almost any time of day. Like other branches of this Mexican chain, this restaurant features waitresses wearing festive dresses and serving clients swiftly and politely. The varied menu features everything from tacos and hotcakes to steaks and sandwiches. When you're finished eating, the section filled with drug items, English-language books and magazines, and gifts is *the* place to get back in touch with the world; Sanborn's is always well stocked. To find it from the Plaza de Armas, walk one block south on 16 de Septiembre to Juárez; it's on the left corner.

5 Exploring Guadalajara

SPECIAL EVENTS

The Jalisco State Band puts on **free concerts** in the Plaza de Armas usually every Tuesday, Thursday, and Sunday starting at about 7pm.

During September, when Mexicans celebrate their **independence** from Spain, Guadalajara goes all out with a month-long celebration. Look for poster-size calendars listing attractions that include many performances in theaters all over the city. On September 15, the Governor's Palace fills with well-dressed invited guests as they and the massive crowd in the park below await the president's reenactment of the traditional *grito* (shout for independence) at 11pm. The grito commemorates Fr. Miguel Hidalgo de Costilla's pronouncement that began the Mexican War of Independence in 1810. The celebration features live music on a temporary street stage, spontaneous dancing, much shouting of "*Viva México!*," and fireworks. On September 16, there's a parade that lasts an hour or so. For the next couple of days the park in front of the Degollado Theater resembles a country fair and Mexican market. There are games of chance with stuffed-animal prizes and a variety of food, including cotton candy and candied apples. Live entertainment goes on in the park day and night.

October is another month-long celebration called **Fiestas de Octubre** that originally began with the procession of Our Lady of Zapopan. Now the month is a celebration of everything that is notable about Guadalajara and Jalisco. The celebration kicks off with an enormous parade, usually on the Sunday (or possibly the Saturday) nearest the first of the month. Festivities continue all month long with performing arts, rodeos (*charreadas*), bullfights, art exhibits, regional dancing, a food fair, and a Day of Nations involving all the consulates of Guadalajara. Much of the ongoing displays and events take place in the Benito Juárez Auditorium.

On October 12 around dawn, the small, dark figure of **Our Lady of Zapopan** begins her five-hour ride from the Cathedral of Guadalajara to the Cathedral of Zapopan in a suburb. The original figure dates from the mid-1500s, and the tradition of the procession began 200 years later. Crowds spend the night all along the route and vie for position as the Virgin passes by in a new car provided for the occasion. During the months prior to October 12, the figure is carried to churches all over the city. During that time, you may see neighborhoods decorated with paper streamers and banners honoring the passing of the figure to the next church.

The last two weeks in February are marked by a series of **cultural events** before the beginning of Lent.

WALKING TOUR
Downtown Guadalajara

Start: Plaza de Armas.
Finish: Mercado Libertad.
Time: Approximately three hours, not including museum and shopping stops.
Best Times: After 10am, when museums are open.
Worst Times: Mondays or holidays, when the museums are closed.

This walk through downtown Guadalajara will acquaint you with the major historical, cultural, and architectural treasures of the city. Begin the tour in the plaza beside the main cathedral on Avenida Alcalde between Avenida Hidalgo and Calle Morelos in the charming:

1. **Plaza de Armas.** This pleasant plaza has wrought-iron benches and walkways that lead like spokes to the ornate French-made iron central bandstand, directly in front of the:

2. **Palacio del Gobierno.** This eye-catching arched structure dominating the plaza was built in 1774 and combines the Spanish and Moorish influences prevalent at the time. Be sure to go inside to view the spectacular mural of Hidalgo by Clemente Orozco over the beautiful wooden-railed staircase to the right. The panel to the right is called *The Contemporary Circus*, and the one on the left, *The Ghost of Religion in Alliance with Militarism*. The highly esteemed Orozco was a native of Guadalajara.

Going back out the front entrance, turn right and walk to the:

3. **Cathedral.** Begun in 1561, the unusual multispired facade combines several 17th-century Renaissance styles, including a touch of Gothic. An 1818 earthquake destroyed the original large towers; the present ones were designed by architect Manuel Gómez Ibarra. Inside, look over the sacristy to see the painting believed to be the work of renowned 17th-century artist Bartolomé Murillo (1617–82).

Leave the cathedral and turn right out the front doors and walk along Avenida Alcalde to the:

4. **Rotonda de los Hombres Ilustres.** Sixteen gleaming-white columns without bases or capitals stand as monuments to Guadalajara's—and the state of Jalisco's—distinguished sons. To learn who they are, visitors need only to stroll around the flower-filled green park and read the names on the 11 nearly life-size statues of the state's heros. There are 98 burial vaults in the park, only 4 of which are occupied.

East of the plaza, cross Liceo to the:

5. **Regional Museum of Guadalajara.** This building (☎ 3/614-9957), built in 1701 in the churrigueresque style, exhibits some of the region's archaeological finds, fossils, historic objects, and art. Among the highlights is a gigantic reconstructed skeleton of a mammoth and a meteorite weighing 1,715 pounds found in 1792 in Zacatecas. In addition, on the first floor there's a fascinating exhibit of pre-Hispanic pottery featuring unusual pieces that have been in the collection and some exquisite recent pottery and clay figures found near Tequila during the construction of the toll road. On the second floor is a small, interesting ethnography section showing the contemporary dress of the state's indigenous cultures, including the Coras, Huichols, Mexicaneros, Nahuas, and Tepehuanes. It's open Tuesday through Sunday from 9am to 3:45pm. Admission is $4.50 for adults; children enter free.

Outside the museum and to the right is the:

6. **Palacio de Justicia.** Built in 1588 as the first convent in Guadalajara, Santa María de Gracia later became a teachers' college and girls' school. In 1952 it was officially designated as the Palace of Justice. Inside, above the stairway, is a huge mural honoring the law profession in Guadalajara; it depicts historic events, including Benito Juárez with the 1857 constitution and laws of reform.

Outside the palacio and directly to the right, continuing east on Avenida Hidalgo is the:

7. **Church of Santa María de Gracia,** one of Guadalajara's oldest churches which was built along with the convent next door.

Opposite the church is the:

8. **Teatro Degollado** ("Deh-goh-yah-doh"), a beautiful neoclassic 19th-century opera house named for Santos Degollado, a local patriot who fought with Juárez against the French and Maximilian. Notice the seven muses in the theater's triangular facade above the columns. The theater hosts various performances

Walking Tour—Downtown Guadalajara

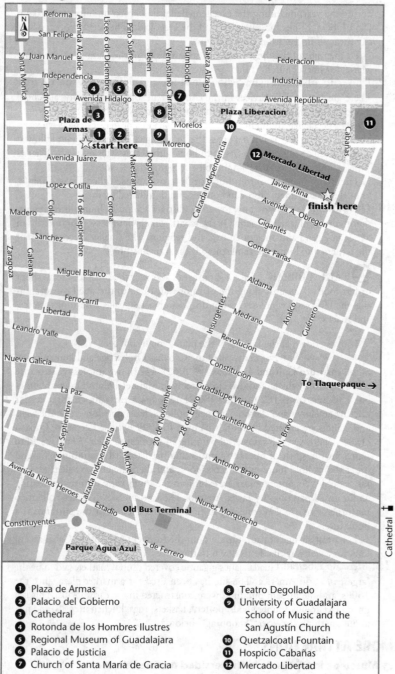

1. Plaza de Armas
2. Palacio del Gobierno
3. Cathedral
4. Rotonda de los Hombres Ilustres
5. Regional Museum of Guadalajara
6. Palacio de Justicia
7. Church of Santa María de Gracia
8. Teatro Degollado
9. University of Guadalajara School of Music and the San Agustín Church
10. Quetzalcoatl Fountain
11. Hospicio Cabañas
12. Mercado Libertad

during the year, including the excellent Ballet Folklórico on Sunday at 10am. Plaza Libertad links the cathedral and the Degollado Theater. It's open Monday through Friday from 10am to 2pm.

To the right of the theater, on the opposite side of the plaza from the Santa María de Gracia church, is the:

9. **University of Guadalajara School of Music and the San Agustín Church.** There are continuous services in the church, and sometimes the music school is open to the public. Continuing east on the plaza, you should be sure to notice the spectacular fountain behind the Degollado Theater; it depicts Mexican history in low relief. You'll next pass the charming children's fountain followed by the unusual sculpture of a tree with lions with nearby slabs of text by Charles V proclaiming Guadalajara's right to be recognized as a city.

The plaza opens up into a huge pedestrian expanse called Plaza Tapatía, framed by department stores and offices and dominated by the:

10. **Quetzalcoatl Fountain.** This towering abstract sculpture/fountain represents the mythical plumed serpent Quetzalcoatl, which figures so prominently in Mexican legend and ancient culture and religion. The smaller pieces represent the serpent and birds; the centerpiece is the serpent's fire.

🍵 **TAKE A BREAK**   Take a short break at one of the small ice-cream shops or fast-food restaurants along the plaza or wait to go to the small cafeteria inside the Hospicio, which serves hot dogs, sandwiches, cake, soft drinks, coffee, and snacks.

Looking down at the far end of the plaza, you'll spot the:

11. **Hospicio Cabañas.** Formerly called the Cabañas Orphanage and known today as the **Instituto Cultural Cabañas** (☎ 3/617-4322), this impressive structure was designed by the famous Mexican architect Manuel Tolsá. It housed homeless children from 1829 until 1980. Today it's a thriving cultural center offering art shows and classes. The main building has a fine dome, and the walls and ceiling are covered by murals painted in 1929 by José Clemente Orozco (1883–1949). Orozco's powerful painting in the dome, *Man of Fire*, is said to represent the spirit of humanity projecting itself toward the infinite. Several other rooms hold more of Orozco's work, and there are also excellent temporary exhibits. A contemporary art exhibit in the south wing features fascinating and unusual paintings by Javier Arevalo. The institute's own Ballet Folklórico performs here every Wednesday at 8:30pm. To the left of the entrance is a bookstore.

For a real change of pace, turn left out the front entrance of the Cabañas and look for a stairway that leads down to the:

12. **Mercado Libertad,** Guadalajara's gigantic covered central market, said to be the largest in Latin America. The site has been used for a market plaza since the 1500s, and the present buildings were constructed in the early 1950s. This is a great place to buy leather goods, pottery, baskets, rugs, kitchen utensils, and just about anything else. (See "Shopping," below.)

MORE ATTRACTIONS

✪ **Museo de las Artes de la Universidad de Guadalajara**

Juárez 975. ☎ **3/625-7553.** Admission $2. Tues–Sat 10am–8pm; Sun and holidays noon–8pm.

Opened in 1994, this museum promises to be one of the most exciting in the country. The excellent opening show featured contemporary artists from all the Americas. Several rooms house the university's collection, mostly of Mexican and Jaliscan artists, and there is always a traveling exhibition. The beautiful building housing the museum was constructed as a primary school in 1914. One wall of the auditorium and the cupola above show two of Orozco's vigorous murals entitled *Man, Creator and Rebel* and *The People and Their False Leaders.*

To reach the museum, take the Par Vial west on Independencia/Hidalgo. Get off after it makes the right turn onto Vallarta/Juárez. From the bus stop on Juárez, walk back (east) two or three blocks; it's on the right opposite the University of Guadalajara. It's also about an 11-block walk from Alcalde/16 de Septiembre, straight west on Juárez; it's four blocks beyond the Parque Revolución, which will be on your left.

✪ Museo de la Ciudad

Independencia 684 at M. Barcena. ☎ **3/658-2531.** Admission $1. Tues–Sat 10am–5pm, Sun 10am–3pm.

Opened in 1992, this fine museum housed in a wonderful old stone convent chronicles Guadalajara's interesting past. The eight *salas,* beginning with the first room to the right and proceeding in chronological order, cover the years just prior to the city's founding by 63 Spanish families to the present. Interesting and unusual artifacts, including rare Spanish armaments and equestrian paraphernalia, give a sense of what day-to-day life was like in Guadalajara's past. As you browse, take time to read the explanations (in Spanish), which give details not otherwise noted in the displays.

Parque Agua Azul

Located near the former bus station at the south end of Calzada Independencia, this park is a perfect refuge from the bustling city. It contains plants, trees, shrubbery, statues, and fountains. Many people come here to exercise early in the morning. The park is open daily from 7am to 6pm. Admission for adults is $1; children 50¢.

Across Independencia, catercorner from a small flower market in a small one-story rock building, is the **Museo Arqueología del Occidente de Mexico.** It houses a fine collection of pre-Hispanic pottery from the states of Jalisco, Nayarit, and Colima and is well worth your time. The museum is open Tuesday through Sunday from 10am to 2pm and 4 to 7pm. There's a small admission charge.

The state-run **Casa de las Artesanías** (☎ 3/619-4664) is just past the park entrance at the crossroads of Calzada Independencia and Gallo (for details, see "Shopping," below).

Plaza de Los Mariachis

Half a block from the Mercado Libertad on Calzada Independencia and Calle Javier Mina beside the San Juan de Dios Church is the Plaza de los Mariachis, actually a short street lined with restaurants and cafes. During the day, small bands of mariachis loaf around or sip drinks, but at night the place is packed with them (see "Guadalajara After Dark," below).

Plaza and Ex-Convento del Carmen

Avenida Juarez. No phone. Tues–Sun 9am–10pm.

The **Ex-Convento del Carmen,** on Avenida Juárez four blocks west of the Centro Histórico, offers a full range of theater, films, and musical events almost nightly.

Tickets are usually sold here just a short while before the performance. Across the street, the **Plaza del Carmen,** with a bubbling fountain, roses, and shade trees, is a nice place to relax. Lovers' embraces may lead to a wedding at the small **Templo del Carmen,** an old church on the plaza. There's usually a mass, wedding, or christening in progress.

ORGANIZED TOURS

Several times daily, **Panoramex** (☎ 3/610-5005 or 610-5109) offers bilingual tours of Guadalajara, Lake Chapala, Tequila, and Zapopan; tours range from $15 to $25. Those without a car might want to consider a tour, especially to the outlying regions. Inquire at the Panoramex office (open Monday through Friday from 9am to 7pm) or at your hotel.

SPECTATOR SPORTS

BULLFIGHTS Many say that Guadalajara and Mexico City host the best bullfights in the country. Every Sunday at 4:30pm (4pm in summer), there's a bullfight at the Plaza de Toros "Nuevo Progreso," across from the football stadium on Calzada Independencia Norte north of town. Tickets range from $4 for seats in the sun to $80 for the best seats in the shade. Buy tickets downtown in the reception area of the Hotel Francés on Thursday from 10am to 2pm or 4 to 7pm or at the Plaza de Toros.

CHARREADA To the east of Agua Azul is the **Aceves Galindo Lienzo,** or rodeo ring, at the corner of Dr. R. Michel and Calzada de las Palmas (☎ 3/19-3232). There's a Mexican rodeo (*charreada*) on Sunday at noon. Mexican rodeos are a special extravaganza with elegant costumes and grand shows of prowess in riding, roping, rope tricks, and a traditional grand promenade. Sometimes there are evening shows.

6 Shopping

The mammoth **Mercado Libertad** (see "Exploring Guadalajara," above) features fresh and cooked food, crafts (including baskets, puppets, wood carvings, pottery, dance costumes), clothing, a great selection of inexpensive watches on the second floor, household wares, and a spectacular glimpse of daily life. Although it opens at 7am, it isn't in full swing until around 10am.

In addition, Guadalajara boasts the largest modern shopping center in Latin America. The **Plaza del Sol** megacomplex sprawls over 120,000 square yards in an area at the junction of Avenidas López Mateos and Mariano Otero, outside the center of town. Here you can buy anything from a taco to a Volkswagen; you can also cash a check, make a plane reservation, or buy a lottery ticket. Hotels and restaurants offer respite for weary shoppers. Take any bus marked "Plaza del Sol" from Calzada Independencia near the Mercado Libertad or on Alcalde in front of the Rotonda de los Ilustres.

There's a convenient **pedestrian passageway** that runs under Avenida Juárez; along this passageway are many stalls selling candied fruits, leather belts, and other goods. A better place to purchase **leather goods,** however, is down on Avenida Pedro Moreno, which runs parallel to Avenida Juárez. For **shoes,** go to E. Alatorre northeast of the Centro Histórico, where there are 70 shoe stores.

One block past the entrance of Agua Azul Park in the direction of the city center (on your right at the crossroads of Calzada Independencia and Gallo) is the

Casa de las Artesanías, Gallo 20 (☎ 3/619-4664). It's an enormous two-story state-run crafts store that sells pottery, silver jewelry, dance masks, and regional clothing from around the state and the country. There's often a great selection of colorful nativity scenes (*natividades*). However, if you're going to the villages, such as Tonala and Tlaquepaque, you may want to postpone buying such items. On the right as you enter are museum displays showing crafts and regional costumes from the state of Jalisco. The craft store is open Monday through Friday from 10am to 6pm, Saturday from 10am to 5pm, and Sunday from 11am to 3pm.

Some of Mexico's best pottery and crafts are made in the suburbs of **Tlaquepaque** and **Tonala.** These two villages are a must, especially on Thursday or Sunday when Tonala spreads out a huge street market. (See "Tlaquepaque & Tonala" under "Excursions from Guadalajara," below.)

7 Guadalajara After Dark

FOLKLORIC BALLET

Ballet Folklórico de la Universidad De Guadalajara

Degollado Theater, Plaza Tapatía. ☎ **3/626-9280** or 614-4773, ext. 144 or 143. Tickets $3–$12.

This wonderful dance company, acclaimed as the best *folklórico* company in all of Mexico, provides light, color, movement, and music that are pure Jalisco. For more than a decade it has been performing at the Degollado Theater. Performances are on Sunday at 10am.

Ballet Folklórico Nacional del Instituto Cultural Cabañas

At the far end of the Plaza Tapatía. ☎ **3/618-6003.** Tickets $6–$8.

Performances are every Wednesday at 8:30pm at the theater of the Instituto Cultural Cabañas.

THE CLUB & MUSIC SCENE

For rousing music and local ambience, go to the **Plaza de los Mariachis,** down by the San Juan de Dios Church and the Mercado Libertad, at the junction of Calzada Independencia and Avenida Juárez/Calle Javier Mina. Every evening the colorfully dressed mariachis, in various states of inebriation, play for money (if they can get it) or for free. Enjoy a meal, a snack, or a soft drink here or just stand around spending nothing but time. It's fun and free; spend at least one evening here. Pickpockets are ever-present, so be careful. It costs nothing to listen as the mariachis belt away around other diners' tables, but if you request a song, ask the price first.

Few places in Guadalajara are more enjoyable to me than **El Parian** in Tlaquepaque, where mariachis serenade diners under the portals (see "Excursions from Guadalajara," below).

Restaurant/Bar Copenhagen 77

Marcos Castellanos 140-Z. ☎ **3/625-2803.** No cover. Restaurant Mon–Sat noon–12:30am; jazz 8:30pm–12:30am.

This dark, cozy jazz club is by the little Parque de la Revolución, on your left as you walk down López Cotilla/Federalismo. There are linen cloths and a red rose on every table. You can come just for a drink or for the restaurant's specialty—the delicious paella Copenhagen al vino. The paella takes a while to prepare, but it's an enjoyable wait as you sip a drink and listen to the jazz.

DANCE CLUBS/DISCOS

Lobby Bar, Hotel Francés

Maestranza 35. ☎ **3/613-1190.**

Though too noisy to recommend as a place to sleep, the stately Hotel Francés is a popular downtown meeting place. Check out the lobby bar, open from 8am to 10:30pm. There's a happy hour from noon to 8pm with two national (not imported) drinks for the price of one. There's often live piano music in the late afternoon and evening.

Maxim's Disco Club

In the Hotel Francés, Maestranza 35. ☎ **3/613-1190.** Mon–Thurs free; Fri–Sun $4. Daily 8pm–midnight.

Despite its name, Maxim's is not a disco but a dance hall with a singer or a live band. There are tables around the dance floor and in the lower bar section.

8 Excursions from Guadalajara

There are a number of interesting places to visit near Guadalajara. Tlaquepaque and Tonala are distant suburbs, and Lake Chapala is a popular vacation spot, especially with foreign visitors.

TLAQUEPAQUE & TONALA: MARIACHIS, MUSEUMS & GREAT SHOPPING

7 & 11 miles S of Guadalajara

ESSENTIALS

GETTING THERE & DEPARTING   By Bus   Two types of buses go to Tlaquepaque and Tonala (a 25-minute ride). Both leave from the corner of Alcalde and Independencia in front of the Cathedral. **Linea Turquesa** buses (numbered 275 A or B) pass every 10 minutes, carry only seated passengers, and cost $1. Linea Turquesa buses pass within a block of Tlaquepaque's main square (it won't be obvious, so tell the driver you want off in Tlaquepaque) and stop several times on the main street going to Tonala (where you'll see the shops and street stalls). Other public buses (also numbered 275 A or B) cover the route, cost 25¢, and are often packed with both standing and seated passengers. On the public buses you'll have to watch for the welcoming arch on the left at Tlaquepaque then get off two stops later and ask for directions to El Parian, Tlaquepaque's central building on the main square. The last stop for this bus is Tonala (another 15 minutes), where it turns around for the return to Guadalajara.

ORIENTATION   Information   The **Tlaquepaque Tourism Office** is in the Presidencia Municipal (opposite El Parian), Calle Guillermo Prieto 80 (☎ 635-1503 or 635-0596); it's open Monday through Friday from 9am to 3pm and Saturday from 9am to 1pm.

The **Tonala Tourism Office** (☎ 683-1740; fax 683-0590) is in the Artesanos building set back a bit from the road at Atonaltecas 140 Sur (the main street leading into Tonala) at Matamoros. Free **walking tours** are held Monday, Tuesday, Wednesday, and Friday at 9am and 2pm and Saturday at 9am and 1pm. They include visits to artisans' workshops (exhibiting ceramics, stoneware, blown glass, papier-mâché, and the like). Tours last between three and four hours and require a minimum of five people. Hours are Monday through Friday from 9am to 3pm and Saturday from 9am to 1pm. Also in Tonala, catercorner from the church, you'll see a small **tourism information kiosk** that's staffed on market days and provides maps and useful information.

Tlaquepaque and Tonala are special treats for shoppers. **Market days** are Sunday and Thursday in Tonala, but on Sunday many of Tlaquepaque's stores are open only from 10:30am to 2:30pm. Thursday is the best day to combine a trip to both villages, about four miles apart. Monday through Saturday, stores in Tlaquepaque usually close between 2:30 and 4pm. A nice day consists of wearing yourself out in Tonala then relaxing at one of Tlaquepaque's pleasant outdoor restaurants for a sunset meal and waiting for the mariachis to warm up at El Parian.

TLAQUEPAQUE

This suburban village is famous for its **fashionable stores** in handsome old stone mansions fronting pedestrians-only streets and for its pottery, furniture, and glass factories. The village is also known for **El Parian,** a circular building dating from the 1800s in the town center, where innumerable mariachis serenade diners in sidewalk cafes. The mariachis are especially plentiful, loud, and entertaining on weekend evenings (Sunday is best), but you'll hear them serenading there just about any time of day. The stores, especially on Calle Independencia, offer the pottery and glass for which the village is famous, plus the best of Mexico's crafts, such as *equipales* furniture, fine wood sculptures, and papier-mâché.

Exploring Tlaquepaque

Tlaquepaque's **Regional Ceramics Museum,** Independencia 237 (☎ 35-5404), is a good place to see what traditional Jalisco pottery is all about. There are high-quality examples dating back several generations. Note the cross-hatch design known as *petatillo* on some of the pieces; it's one of the region's oldest traditional motifs. There are also a wonderful old kitchen and dining room, complete with pots, utensils, and dishes. The museum is open Tuesday through Saturday from 10am to 4pm and Sunday from 10am to 1pm. There is also the National Museum of Ceramics in Tonala (see below.)

Across the street from the museum is **La Rosa Fábrica de Vidrio Soplado,** a glass-blowing factory. From 9:30am to 2:30pm Monday through Friday, the public is invited to go to the rear patio and watch as a dozen scurrying men and boys heat glass bottles and jars on the end of hollow steel poles. Then, blowing furiously, they chase across the room, narrowly missing spectators and fellow workers alike as they swing the red-hot glass within an inch of a man who sits placidly rolling an elaborate jug out of another chunk of cooling glass. Nonchalantly, the old man will leave his own task long enough to clip off the end of the boy's vase at the exact moment at which it comes within reach of his hand. Then he drops the clippers and returns once more to his own task as the youth charges back across the room to reheat the vase in the furnace.

Dining

Read the fine print on menus. The 15% value-added tax may not be included in Tlaquepaque; ask before ordering.

Birrería El Sope

D. Guerra 142. ☎ **35-6338.** Birria $3.50–$6. Mon–Sat 8am–8pm; Sun 8am–10pm. BIRRIA.

This is where locals go for that wonderful Jalisco specialty—birria. Cheery and clean, the restaurant is a long, narrow room in a quiet neighborhood. The decor of cushioned French provincial chairs pulled up to covered tables topped with artificial carnations doesn't quite go along with the country menu, but the food is tasty. Choose your birria by the meat—goat, lamb, or pork—and by the cut—leg, ribs, and so on. An order comes with fresh salsa, chips, and tortillas and beans. Side orders of quesadillas or queso fundido are extra. To find this restaurant from Tlaquepaque's main plaza, walk north on Madero two blocks and turn left on Guerra; it's half a block down on the right.

✪ Mariscos Progreso

Progreso 80. ☎ **657-4995.** Main courses $6–$11. Daily 8am–6pm. SEAFOOD/MEXICAN.

On a cozy tree-shaded patio filled with leather-covered tables and chairs, this restaurant makes an inviting place to take a break from shopping. Charcoal-grilled seafood, Mexican style, is the specialty here. To get here, walk two blocks south on Madero, cross Juárez (one of the streets that borders El Parian), and look for this corner restaurant on the right.

Restaurant with No Name (Sin Nombre)

Madero 80. ☎ **635-4520** or 635-9677. Breakfast $4.75–$10; main courses $8–$13. Sun–Thurs 8:30am–9pm, Fri–Sat 8:30am–midnight. HAUTE MEXICAN.

One of my all-time favorites, this place offers excellent Mexican cuisine with a flair. It's set in a spectacular garden shaded by banana, peach, palm, and other tropical trees and guarded by strutting peacocks. A trio plays music in mid-afternoon. The menu is spoken by the bilingual waiter, not written, so ask for prices as you order. The excellent "no name chicken" is cooked in onions, green peppers, and a buttery sauce and spread around a mound of rice. The quesadillas are outstanding. To get here from the main plaza, face the plaza (with the church to your right) and walk on Madero to the right for 1 1/2 blocks; the restaurant is on the right, between Independencia and Constitución.

TONALA

Tonala is a pleasant, unpretentious village about four miles from Tlaquepaque. You may find Tonala more authentic and easier on the wallet. The streets were paved only recently, but there aren't any pedestrians-only thoroughfares yet. The village has been a center for pottery making since pre-Hispanic times; half of the more than 400 artists who reside here produce high- and low-temperature pottery in different colors of clay with a dozen different finishes. Other local artists also work with forged iron, cantera stone, brass and copper, marble, miniatures, papier-mâché, textiles, blown glass, and gesso.

Exploring Tonala

On Thursday and Sunday **market days,** vendors and street stalls under shade cloths fill the streets; "herb-men" sell multicolored dried medicinal herbs from wheelbarrows; magicians entertain crowds with sleight-of-hand tricks; and craftspeople spread their colorful wares on the plaza's sidewalks. Those who love the hand-blown Mexican glass and folksy ceramics will wish they had a truck to haul the gorgeous and inexpensive handmade items back home. There is certainly greater variety here than in Tlaquepaque—tacky and chic are often side by side.

Tonala is the home of the **National Museum of Ceramics,** Constitución 104, between Hidalgo and Morelos (☎ 683-0494). The museum occupies a huge two-story mansion and displays work from Jalisco as well as pottery from all over the country. There's a large shop in the front on the right as you enter. The museum is open Tuesday through Friday from 10am to 5pm and Saturday and Sunday from 10am to 2pm. A fee of $8.50 per camera will be charged for use of any video or still cameras.

Dining

Los Geranios

Hidalgo 71. ☎ **683-0010.** Fax 683-0700. Main courses $3–$6. Daily 11am–5pm. MEXICAN/ INTERNATIONAL.

This narrow, inviting restaurant next to El Bazar de Sermel offers a cool respite from the blazing sun. Diners can relax in the clean and comfortable white canvas chairs at white-clothed tables or in the small booths. The menu includes Mexican specialties. Try the fish with almonds and mushrooms or the pork baked in orange sauce with baked potato and vegetables or something quick like nachos. To get here, face the church on the plaza, walk to the right turn on that street (Hidalgo) for about half a block; look on the left for a pretty stained-glass sign with red flowers.

LAKE CHAPALA: PICTURE-PERFECT TOWNS, SCENERY & CLIMATE

26 miles S of Guadalajara

Mexico's largest lake and the area surrounding it have long been popular with foreign vacationers because of the near-perfect climate, gorgeous scenery, and several charming little lakeshore towns—Chapala, Ajijic, and Jocotepec among them—each with its own distinct ambience. There's a large permanent expatriate community of around 4,000 people living in settlements along the shoreline and in the villages stretching all the way from Chapala to Jocotepec.

From the mid-1970s until 1991, pollution of the Lerma River, one of the lake's water sources, caused serious concern. During that period, the lake's depth and perimeter diminished dramatically due to its heavy use as a water source by both Mexico City and Guadalajara. Recently Guadalajara developed another source of water and the government intervened to stop pollution of the Lerma. Heavy rains in recent years have raised the lake level so much that it laps the original shore almost as it did in the past, and when you first see it, you'll think it looks like an ocean. It's a stunning sight, ringed by high, forested mountains and fishing villages.

Note: The year-round climate is so agreeable that few hotels offer air-conditioning and only a few have fans; neither is necessary.

ESSENTIALS

GETTING THERE & DEPARTING   By Bus   Buses to Chapala go from Guadalajara's old Central Camionera. **Transportes Guadalajara-Chapala** (☎ 619-5675 in Guadalajara) serves the route. Buses and minibuses run every half hour to Chapala and every hour to Jocotepec.

In Chapala, the bus station (☎ 5-2212) is about seven blocks north of the lake pier. To get to Ajijic and San Juan Cosalá from Chapala, walk toward the lake (left out of the front of the station) and look for the local buses lined up on the opposite side of the street. These buses travel between Chapala and San Juan Cosalá. At San Juan Cosalá change buses to get to Jocotepec or take one of the buses that go directly to Jocotepec from the Chapala bus station every half hour until 8pm. The last bus back to Guadalajara from Chapala is at 9pm.

By Car   Those driving will be able to enjoy the lake and the surrounding towns more fully, but there is intra-village bus service. From Guadalajara, drive to Lake Chapala via the new four-lane Highway 15/80. Leave Guadalajara via Avenida Gonzalez Gallo, which intersects with Calzada Independencia just before Playa Azul Park. Going south on Independencia, turn left onto Gallo and follow it all the way out of town past the airport, where it becomes Highway 15/80 (which may also have signs calling it Highway 44), the main road to Chapala. The first view of the lake isn't until just outside of the town of Chapala.

The highway from Guadalajara leads directly into Chapala and becomes Madero, which leads straight to Chapala's pier, malecón (waterfront walkway and street), and small shopping and restaurant area. The one traffic light in town (a block before the pier) is the turning point (right) to Ajijic, San Antonio, San Juan Cosalá, and Jocotopec. Chapala's **main plaza** is three blocks north of the pier, and the central food **market** flanks the park's back side.

ORIENTATION   Information   The **Jalisco State Information Office** is in Chapala at Aquiles Serdan 26 (☎ 5-3141). Serdan is a narrow side street going toward the lake, one block before the Correo (post office). The office is open Monday through Friday from 9am to 6pm and Saturday and Sunday from 10am to 6pm. The staff is willing to help but doesn't have a lot of information. You may be able to get a map of the area here.

Fast Facts   The **area code** for the whole northern lakeshore (Chapala, Ajijic, San Juan Cosalá, and Jocotopec) is 376. **Currency exchange** can be handled at the local Banamex, located on the right side of Madero just before the light, in Chapala. It's open Monday through Friday from 9am to 5pm; U.S. dollars can be changed all day, and Canadian dollars can be changed between 9am and 1:30pm. There's a Banamex automated teller machine (ATM) for Visa cards to the right of the bank's front door. Just down from Banamex (walking away from the lake), opposite the food market and main plaza, is Lloyds Money Exchange, by Lloyds' front door. It's open Monday through Friday from 9am to 4pm. To the left of the Hotel Nido, Agencias de Cambios is another money exchange office. It's open Monday through Saturday from 9am to 7pm and Sunday from 9am to 2pm.

Several outlets offer **communications services,** including fax, telephone, mail, and messages. Centro de Mensajes Mexicano-Americano is the local affiliate for UPS. They also have 24-hour telephone message and fax receiving service, court-approved translation ability, and secretarial service. It's at Hidalgo 236 (Apdo. Postal 872), Chapala, Jal. 45900 (☎ and fax 376/5-2102), and it's open Monday through Friday from 10am to 6pm and Saturday from 10am to 2pm. Almost next door, Aero Flash, Hidalgo 236 (☎ 376/5-3696; fax 376/5-3063), has a 24-hour fax service and specializes in package mailing. It's the local Federal Express office. The **post office** is on Hidalgo two blocks from the intersection of Madero. Enter down the hill and in back. It's open Monday through Friday from 9am to 1pm and 3 to 6pm and Saturday from 9am to 1pm.

Probably the most convenient **grocery store** is Supergrisa, at the corner of Hidalgo and Madero opposite the Restaurant Superior. It's open daily from 8am, closing most days at 8pm (at 3pm on Thursday and 6pm on Sunday). A good local **bookstore** is Libros y Revistas, at Madero 230 (☎ 5-2021), near the Chamber of Commerce and Lloyds and opposite the plaza; it carries a wide assortment of English-language newspapers, magazines, and books—from the latest paperback novels to *Mirabella, Family Circle, Texas Monthly,* and *Scientific American.* It's open daily from 9am to 4pm.

CHAPALA

Chapala, Jalisco, founded in 1538, is the district's business and administrative center as well as the oldest resort town on Lake Chapala. Much of the town's prosperity comes from the retirees, primarily American and Canadian, who live on the outskirts and come into Chapala to change money, buy groceries, and check the stock ticker. Except on weekends, when throngs of visitors fill the area around the pier and lake's edge, the town of 36,000 can be a pretty sleepy place. There are a couple of hotels in Chapala, but Ajijic is the preferable place to stay in the area. Good restaurants on the lake include Cozumel and Mariscos Guicho.

AJIJIC

Ajijic, another lakeside village, is a quiet place inhabited by fishermen, artists, and retirees. As you reach Ajijic, the highway becomes a wide tree-lined boulevard through **La Floresta,** a wealthy residential district. The La Floresta sign signals you've entered Ajijic, but the central village is about a mile farther on the left. To reach Ajijic's main street, Colón (which changes to Morelos), turn left when you see the SIX (corner grocery) sign on the left. Colón/Morelos leads straight past the main plaza and ends at the lake and the popular Restaurant La Posada Ajijic. The cobblestone streets and arts-and-crafts stores give the town a quaint atmosphere. (See "Essentials," above, for bus information to Ajijic.)

The **Clínica Ajijic** (☎ 376/6-0662; in an emergency 376/6-0875 or 6-0500), on the main highway at the corner of Javier and Mina, has a two-bed emergency section with oxygen and electrocardiogram, ambulance, and five doctors with different specialties. Their 16-bed hospital opened in 1993. The pharmacy there is available after hours for an emergency.

Linea Professional (☎ 6-0187; fax 6-0066) is a locally owned car rental agency in Ajijic. Make reservations as soon as you can—the cars are often all booked.

Exploring Ajijic

In La Floresta, immediately after the modernistic sculpture on the left, you'll see a cluster of buildings, one of which is marked ARTESANÍAS. The **state-owned crafts shop** (☎ 376/6-0548) has a good selection of pottery from all over Mexico as well as locally made crafts such as pottery, glassware, rugs, and wall tapestries. The shop is open Monday though Saturday from 10am to 6pm and Sunday from 10am to 2pm.

Ajijic has long been a center for weavers, but there seem to be fewer now than in the past. Still, it offers moderately good shopping; the best streets are Colón and those leading immediately off of it for a block or so. You'll find designer clothing and decorative accessories such as hand-loomed fabrics made into pillows and bedspreads, furniture, and pottery—but no one item in great abundance.

As for performing arts in the region, productions of **The Lakeside Little Theater** are usually announced in the local paper or the bulletin board at the Nueva Posada Ajijic.

Meeting the local foreign residents is easy; just go to the popular hangouts—the Restaurant Posada Ajijic, La Nueva Posada Ajijic, the Rose Café, and Los Veleros Restaurant and Sports Bar.

Accommodations

La Nueva Posada

Donato Guerra No. 9 (Apdo. Postal 30), Ajijic, Jal. 45900. ☎ **376/6-1444.** Fax 376/6-1344. 16 rms. $47–$50 double. Rates include full breakfast. Free parking.

Ajijic

This new posada (as the name indicates) was built by Michael and Elena Eager, the former owners of the popular Posada Ajijic (now a restaurant and bar under different ownership). Modeled after a gracious, traditional-style hacienda, La Nueva Posada looks a lot more expensive than it is. French doors, marble bathrooms, a wine cellar, and a small swimming pool are some of the amenities—which also include an elegant dining room with a glorious lake view. Original paintings hang in all of the color-coordinated rooms and public areas. Three rooms are equipped for people with disabilities. Some rooms overlook the lake, others have intimate patios, but the former will have less disturbance from the after-hours kitchen crew. A paperback-exchange library is at the reception area, and there's a small pool in the back section of the hotel. The hotel's restaurant, La Rusa, and casual bar (see "Dining" below) are among the most popular meeting places in the village. There's live background music most evenings and some afternoons. The Eagers' new venture is as popular as (but nothing like) their previous hostelry, and La Nueva Posada is often booked up way in advance for holidays. To find the hotel from the plaza walk toward the lake on Colón, then turn left on Independencia/Constitucíon; at Donato Guerro turn right and you'll see the hotel's blue facade on the right by the lake.

✪ Las Artistas

Constitución 105, Ajijic, Jal. 45900. ☎ **376/6-1027.** Fax 376/6-0066. E-mail 74174.1257@.com. 6 rms (all with bath). $40–$60 double. Rates include breakfast.

One of Ajijic's lovely walled-in homes, this inn boasts a beautiful garden setting with a swimming pool. All rooms except one have private entry, and all are colorfully decorated but completely different in size and arrangement. The lowest price is for the smallest room. Guests have use of the pool and run of the downstairs, which includes a comfortable living room with TV, video, and stereo; kitchen; and dining room. Breakfast is served inside or out by the pool and patio. To find Las Artistas from the intersection of Colón/Morelos and Constitución,

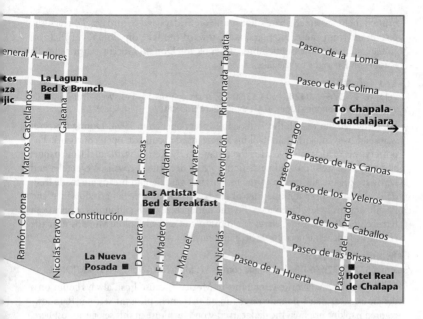

turn left on Constitución and walk five blocks; it's on the left, and its name is on a small tile plaque on the brick wall beside the iron gate.

La Laguna Bed and Brunch

Zaragoza 29, Ajijic, Jal. 45900. ☎ **376/6-1174** or 6-1186. Fax 376/6-1188. 4 rms (all with bath). $25 double (including brunch).

The rooms in this small inn are handsomely furnished with king-size beds covered in bright loomed bedspreads, thick tile floors, and fireplaces. Breakfast/brunch is served Monday through Friday from 8:30am to noon, Sunday 9am to noon. As you dine in a lovely glassed-in dining room facing the back patio, your meal begins with fruit and apple-bran muffins which are followed by a choice of eggs as you like them. Nonguests can also partake of brunch for $3–$4.50. To find La Laguna from the main highway, turn left on Colón and left again on the first street. It's 1¹/₂ blocks down on the left behind the Laguna Ajijic Real Estate Office (which faces the main highway).

Dining

La Rusa

Donato Guerra no. 9. ☎ **376/6-1444.** Reservations recommended. Dec–Apr. Breakfast $3–$5; lunch $5–$7; dinner main courses $7–$12; Sun brunch $5.50–$7; garden grill $6–$9. Mon–Sat 8am–9pm, Sun 9am–8pm (Sun brunch served 9am–1pm; grill in the garden Mon–Fri 5–10pm). INTERNATIONAL.

Once you step inside the dining/drinking area of the La Nueva Posada Ajijic, you'll know the setting is right, whether you're in the *equipales*-furnished bar, the elegant dining room with garden and lake view, or the garden. La Rusa continues to be a popular dining spot with locals and *tapatíos* alike. The lunch menu is simple—crêpes, sandwiches, and salads. The dinner menu, printed on a large poster, has a dozen meat, seafood, and chicken main courses, plus soup, salad, and dessert. The Sunday brunch offers an entirely different selection. The higher-priced brunch includes wine. There's live music on Fridays and Saturdays. To reach the restaurant from the Ajijic plaza, walk toward the lake on Colón, turn left on Independencia/16 de Septiembre, and look for Donato Guerra. Turn right; La Rusa is on the right by the lake.

✪ Los Telares

Morelos 6. ☎ **376/6-0428.** Pasta $3.50–$5; main courses $5–$11. Wed–Thurs and Sun noon–9pm; Fri–Sat noon–10pm. ITALIAN/INTERNATIONAL.

Sophisticated but casual, this fashionable eatery opened in 1994. Dining tables set with handwoven cloths and napkins are arranged around an open courtyard. The pottery was made exclusively for the restaurant by Ken Edwards of Tlaquepaque, and works of well-known international artists decorate the walls. Vegetables and herbs are organically grown in the restaurant's garden, and breads are made fresh daily. Main courses include filet of sea bass in a smooth tamarindo sauce and Pacific prawns in key lime sauce. Try the outrageously rich and unforgettably fresh fettuccine Alfredo. Los Telares is almost at the end of Colón/Morelos near the corner of Independencia/16 de Septiembre.

✪ Manix Restaurant

Ocampo 57. ☎ **376/6-0061.** Comida corrida $7. Mon–Sat 1–9pm. INTERNATIONAL.

This is one of my favorite restaurants in Mexico because I can always count on a delicious meal that's politely served in an extremely pleasant setting. Rainbow-colored napkins brighten the dark carved-wood furniture in this serene atmosphere. There are usually two different international *comidas* daily. Seafood, beef, and sometimes chicken Cordon Bleu, ossu bucco, or chicken parmesan are served. Servings are generous and each comida comes with soup and dessert. To get here from the plaza, turn your back to the church, walk straight ahead on Colón for two blocks, and turn right on Ocampo; the restaurant is down the street on the right, but the sign is obscured by the lone tree on the street.

Restaurant La Posada Ajijic

Morelos and Independencia. ☎ **376/6-0744.** Sandwiches $3–$6; main courses $5–$10; Sunday brunch $5–$6. Mon–Thurs and Sun noon–10pm; Fri–Sat 10am–11pm; Sun brunch 9am–1pm. MEXICAN/INTERNATIONAL.

Formerly under the management of the owners of La Nueva Posada Ajijic, this restaurant facing the lake has reopened with graceful Mexican-inspired decor and good service. The menu covers traditional fare, including soups, salads, sandwiches, and more filling Mexican specialties, as well as imaginatively prepared beef, chicken, and seafood main courses. Sunday brunch is served on the patio facing the gardens. The bar, opposite the restaurant, is a favorite Ajijic hangout. The restaurant is at the end of Colón/Morelos; you enter through the back by the lake, where there's parking.

⑤ Rose Café

Carretera Poniente 26. ☎ **376/6-1599.** Breakfast $2–$3.50; lunch special $3.50–$4. Tues–Sun 9am–4:30. VEGETARIAN.

Everyone enjoys the Rose Café, both for its food and for its casual and friendly atmosphere. Tables are set outside under the pink awning and inside back a bit from the highway. Among the best breakfast selections are fresh banana and chocolate muffins, delicious hot cakes, waffles with apple-raisin sauce, fruit salad, yogurt, and a variety of omelettes and fritatas. The daily lunch special might include calzones, salad, and a grapefruit drink. The cafe is beside the Second Hand Rose thrift shop on the outskirts of town on the highway going west.

Puerto Vallarta & the Central Pacific Coast

Mazatlán, Puerto Vallarta, and Manzanillo—the modern resort cities of Mexico's Central Pacific Coast—have come of age. They are linked to major cities by air and are guarded from the sea by towering walls of high-rise luxury hotels. Although the resorts advertise somewhat homogeneous beach holidays, each city possesses its own distinctive Mexican *ambiente*.

The budget-conscious tourist does not need to hang a hammock alongside the luxury hotels. There are still inexpensive hotels and restaurants in the older downtown sections of most cities along the Pacific coast. The high-rises on the beaches offer some good values, and the villages near each of cities are generally less expensive.

This chapter describes the central section of Mexico's Pacific coast and its sparkling resort cities, which, from north to south, are Mazatlán, in the state of Sinaloa; Puerto Vallarta, in the state of Jalisco; and Manzanillo, in the state of Colima. The route south from the U.S. border along Mexico's 2,000-mile-long Pacific coast, with its hazy desert pinnacles, makes for scenic meandering. The northern reaches of the coast edge the Sonoran Desert, but once you get south of Culiacán, the lush tropical climate is perfect for beach resorts.

EXPLORING THE CENTRAL PACIFIC COAST

Mexico's central Pacific coast caters to so many kinds of vacationers it's impossible to suggest one resort city over another. Mazatlán, with a loyal following of repeat visitors, is also a mecca for sportfishing, and like Manzanillo, it's less expensive overall than Puerto Vallarta. Puerto Vallarta is very picturesque and sophisticated, with excellent restaurants, shopping, and nightlife. Manzanillo is all about good food, good sunsets, and relaxation. Along this section of coast, villages such as San Blas, Bucerías, Barra de Navidad, and Melaque are still laid-back, almost undiscovered, and relatively inexpensive. Inland, Colima (the capital of the state of Colima) offers a beautiful and slow-paced colonial-style alternative to a beachside vacation. Excursions to these smaller villages make easy day-trips or extended stays and offer an altogether different kind of experience. Several are so close together that you can easily try them all out before heading home.

1 Mazatlán

674 miles NW of Mexico City, 314 miles NW of Guadalajara, 976 miles S of Mexicali

Mazatlán was once best known as a resort for sportfishermen who came to catch sailfish and marlin. You can still hire a boat for big-game fishing or guns and a guide for a hunting expedition to the countryside at some of the most reasonable prices in Mexico. But nowadays, Mazatlán is better known as a world-class beach resort, and with good reason—17 miles of inviting sandy beaches extend northward from the original old city. Hotels, restaurants, shops, and clubs now cozy up those beaches as this city of 500,000 grows to accommodate its yearly influx of a million visitors.

Compared to many Mexican cities, Mazatlán is a mere child, barely 200 years old. The city has no ancient ruins and very few great legends. It does, however, possess an interesting 20-block historic area called Old Mazatlán, which dates back to the 19th century (see "Architecture," below).

ESSENTIALS

GETTING THERE & DEPARTING   **By Plane**   There are some direct or nonstop flights to Mazatlán, most from the west coast of the U.S. See Chapter 3, "Planning a Trip to Mexico," for a list of international carriers serving Mexico. (**Alaska Airlines'** local telephone number is 85-2730 at the airport or toll free 95-800/426-0333 in Mexico; **Delta's** is 13-2709.) From elsewhere in Mexico, **Aero California** (at the airport, ☎ 13-2042, 16-2190, or 16-2191) flies in from Tijuana, Guadalajara, and Mexico City. **Aeroméxico** (☎ 13-1111 or 13-1621) has flights to Mazatlán from Mexico City, Los Mochis, Durango, Tijuana, and León. **Mexicana** (☎ 82-7722) offers service from, Mexico City, Guadalajara, and Los Cabos. The regional carrier **Noroeste** (at the airport, ☎ 14-1455) flies from Ciudad Obregón, Culiacán, Hermosillo, Durango, Chihuahua, and Mexicali. Check with a travel agent for the latest **charter flights.**

By Bus   First-class and deluxe **Tres Estrellas de Oro** and **Elite** buses (☎ 81-5308) depart almost hourly for Guadalajara and Mexico City; Tres Estrellas also has service to Guaymas, Mexicali, and Los Mochis. **Transportes Norte de Sonora** (☎ 81-3684 or 81-3846) has daily service to San Blas, Nogales, and Agua Prieta. **Transportes del Norte** (☎ 81-2335) serves Durango and Monterrey. **Transportes del Pacífico** (☎ 82-0577) goes to Mexico City, Tijuana, Nogales, Los Mochis, Tepic, and Escuinapa.

The second-class bus station is located directly behind the first-class station across the lot where the buses park. The best way to figure out which line serves your desired destination is to check the names posted on the buses; drivers also call out their destinations as they're getting ready to depart. From this station **Autotransportes Concordia** has 12 buses daily to Concordia and one bus to Copala; **Autotransportes Escuinapa** has several daily buses to Escuinapa; from there you can transfer to Teacapán. Taking a public bus to Copala and Concordia is less expensive than the tour price. Traveling for the day to Concordia is no problem; just make sure you verify the time of the last bus back. Copala presents a different dilemma; there is only one daily bus to and from there, and the town offers few places to stay overnight, so check the schedule carefully before departing. Bus fare to Concordia is $2 and $3.50 to Copala.

By Car Take International Highway 15 from Nogales, Arizona, to Culiacán. In Culiacán you may want to change to the four-lane tollway that makes Mazatlán only a 10-hour drive from the United States. But get ready for a shock to your budget—the tollway costs about $70. Because of the high cost, the road is little traveled and motorists on it find themselves somewhat isolated. The paucity of traffic has made it appealing to robbers, and there have been a few reports of motorists being robbed along the tollway. Ask about conditions before traveling. Gas up in Culiacán, too, in case the gas stations on the tollway are closed.

By Ferry Passenger ferries operated by **SEMATUR** run between Mazatlán and La Paz, Baja California. The ferry leaves Friday through Wednesday at 3pm and arrives in La Paz at 9am. Costs vary depending on if you want a seat, a bed, or a private cabin. Tickets for the ferry must be purchased in advance at the ferry office on Carnaval or through travel agents. To find the ferry office, go south on Olas Altas and turn left on Alemán; Carnaval is the second street; turn right and you'll find the office in the middle of the block. Ferries return from La Paz to Mazatlán Thursday through Tuesday.

ORIENTATION Arriving The **airport** is about 10 miles south of town. **Transportes Terrestres** colectivo minivans from the airport to hotels charge $8 per person; a taxi from the airport will cost $15. The **Central de Autobuses** (main bus terminal) is at Río Tamazula and Chachalacas. To get there from Avenida del Mar, walk three blocks inland on Río Tamazula; the station is on your right. A taxi from the bus station to most hotels will cost around $3. You can catch a local bus for 50¢, but you may have to change buses en route.

Information The **City and State Tourism Office** is on Olas Altas at the corner of Escobedo, near Old Mazatlán (☎ 69/81-5837; fax 69/81-5835). This is one of the most helpful tourist offices in the country with a friendly English speaking staff. It's open Monday through Friday from 8am to 3pm and Saturday from 9am to 1pm.

City Layout Mazatlán extends north from the port area on the peninsula along **Avenida Leyva** and **Avenida Barragan,** where the cruise ships, sportfishing boats, and ferries dock. The downtown begins with the historic area of **Old Mazatlán** and **Olas Altas Beach** to the south. The waterfront drive continues north for 17 miles, changing names often. Traveling north, it begins as **Avenida Olas Altas** then becomes **Paseo Claussen** parallel to the commercial downtown area. The name changes to **Avenida del Mar** at the beginning of the **North Beach** area, where several moderately priced hotels are located. The curving seaside boulevard, or **Malecón,** runs all the way from Olas Altas to North Beach.

About 4 miles north of downtown lies the Sábalo traffic circle in the Golden Zone near Punta Camarón rocky outcropping over the water. The **Zona Dorada,** or Golden Zone, begins here as **Avenida del Mar** intersects **Avenida Rafael Buelna** and becomes **Avenida Camarón Sábalo,** which leads north through the abundant hotels and fast-food restaurants of the tourist zone. From here, the resort hotels, including the huge El Cid Resort complex, continue to spread northward along and beyond **Sábalo Beach.** The new **Marina Mazatlán** development has changed the landscape considerably north of the Golden Zone, as hotels, condo complexes, and private residences rise around the new marina. North of here is **Los Cerritos** (Little Hills), the northern limit of Mazatlán.

Keep in mind that Mazatlán is fully 17 miles long. Use the landmarks of downtown, the Sábalo traffic circle, El Cid Resort, Marina Mazatlán, and Los Cerritos to find your way.

GETTING AROUND   The downtown transportation center for buses, taxis, and pulmonías is on the central plaza facing the cathedral.

By Bus: Lumbering buses, some with air-conditioning and tinted windows, cover most of the city and make getting around this long resort relatively easy. The "Sábalo Centro" buses run from the Golden Zone along the waterfront, then turn into downtown near the market and central plaza, and then go on to Avenida Miguel Alemán before heading south at Olas Altas. The "Cerritos-Juárez" line starts near the train station, cuts across town to the Malecón beside the Golden Zone, and heads north to Cerritos and back. The "Sábalo Cocos" line runs through the Golden Zone, heads inland to the bus station and on to downtown by a back route (instead of the waterfront), also stopping at the market. The "Playa Sur" line goes to the area where the sportfishing and tour boats depart. The buses run daily from 6am to 11pm and charge around 25¢.

By Pulmonía: These Jeep-type open-air vehicles carry up to three passengers. Pulmonías (literally "pneumonias") have surreylike tops and open sides to let in the breezes. As a rule they're cheaper than taxis, but you should still settle on a price before boarding.

By Taxi: In 1994 Mazatlán began a new taxi service called **Eco Taxi.** The green-and-white cabs have set fares which are posted.

FAST FACTS: MAZATLÁN

American Express   The office is on Camarón Sábalo in the Centro Comercial Balboa shopping center, Loc. 4 and 16 (☎ 13-0600), between the traffic circle and El Cid Resort; it's open Monday through Friday from 9am to 5pm and Saturday from 9am to noon.

Area Code   The telephone area code is 69.

Banks   Foreign currency is exchanged at most banks Monday through Friday from 9 to 11am.

Climate   As the northernmost major beach resort on the mainland, Mazatlán can be cooler in summer than the resorts farther south. The wettest month is September.

Post Office   The Correo is downtown on the east side of the main plaza, on Juárez just off Angel Flores.

Spanish Classes   Classes in Spanish, with a maximum of six students, begin every Monday at the **Centro de Idiomas,** three blocks west of the cathedral near 21 de Marzo and Canizales. In addition to small-group and individual instruction, the language center offers a homestay program and a person-to-person program that matches students with local people of similar interests and vocations. On Friday at 7pm the center holds free Spanish and English conversation groups open to both visitors and locals. The school also offers special tours for those enrolled in its programs, including a once-a-month walking tour of Old Mazatlán. For more information, call or write Dixie Davis, Belisario Domínguez 1908, Mazatlán, Sin. (☎ 69/82-2053; fax 69/85-5606).

Telephones   Most telephone numbers for the Golden Zone, from the Camino Real hotel south to the Playa Mazatlán Hotel, begin with a 1, except those at the Los Sabalos Hotel and at the retail complex housing the El Sheik restaurant and Valentino's disco. Numbers in downtown and along Avenida de Mar begin with an 8.

Mazatlán Area

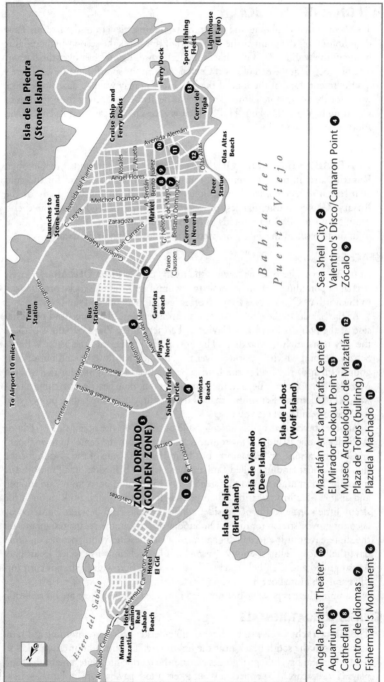

Isla de la Piedra (Stone Island)

Bahía del Puerto Viejo

Isla de Lobos (Wolf Island)

Isla de Venado (Deer Island)

Isla de Pajaros (Bird Island)

ZONA DORADO (GOLDEN ZONE) ③

To Airport 10 miles →

Estero del Sabalo

Marina Mazatlán, Hotel Camino Real, Hotel El Cid, Sabalo Beach

Av. Sabalo Cerritos

Gaviotas, Camaron, Sabalo, R.T. Loaiza, Garzas

Sabalo Traffic Circle ④

Gaviotas Beach

Playa Norte

Bus Station

Train Station

Carretera Internacional, Avenida Rafael Buelna, Revolucion, Reforma

Avenida del Mar

Gutierrez Najera, Juan Carrasco

G. Leyva, Avenida del Puerto

Rosales, Angel Flores, Melchor Ocampo, Zaragoza

T. Azueta, Benito Juárez, Av. Serdán, Market, 5 de Mayo, G. Nelson, Belisario Domínguez

Avenida Alemán

Olas Altas

Cerro de la Neveria

Paseo Claussen

Deer Statue

Olas Altas Beach

Cerro del Vigia

Ferry Dock

Cruise Ship and Ferry Docks

Launches to Stone Island

Sport Fishing Fleets

Lighthouse (El Faro)

Angela Peralta Theater ⑩
Aquarium ⑤
Cathedral ⑧
Centro de Idiomas ⑦
Fisherman's Monument ⑥

Mazatlán Arts and Crafts Center ①
El Mirador Lookout Point ⑬
Museo Arqueológico de Mazatlán ⑫
Plaza de Toros (bullring) ③
Plazuela Machado ⑪

Sea Shell City ②
Valentino's Disco/Camaron Point ④
Zócalo ⑨

1220

FUN ON & OFF THE BEACH

To orient yourself, hike up and enjoy the panoramic view from the famous **Faro** (lighthouse), on the point at the south end of town. It's the second-highest lighthouse in the world (only Gibraltar is higher), towering 447 feet over the harbor. The hike begins at the end of Paseo Centenario near the sportfishing docks. There's a refreshment stand at the foot of the hill, but you may want to take along some water for the 45-minute climb. The view is nearly as spectacular from the top of **Cerro de la Vigía** (Lookout Hill), which is accessible by car from Avenida Olas Altas.

SPECIAL EVENTS

IN NEARBY VILLAGES On the weekend of the first Sunday in October, **Rosario,** a small town 45 minutes south on Highway 15 known for the gold altar screen of its colonial church, holds a **festival honoring Our Lady of the Rosary.** Games, music, dances, processions, and festive foods mark the event. From May 1 to 10, Rosario holds its **Spring Festival.**

In mid-October, the village of **Escuinapa** holds a **Mango Festival.**

BEACHES

At the western edge of downtown is the rocky, pebbly **Playa Olas Altas,** a lovely stretch of pounding surf not suitable for swimming. Around a rocky promontory to the north of Olas Altas is **Playa Norte,** several miles of good sand beach.

At the Sábalo traffic circle, Punta Camarón juts into the water, and on either side of the point is **Playa Las Gaviotas.** Farther north, **Playa Sábalo** is perhaps the very best beach in Mazatlán. The next point jutting into the water is Punta Sábalo, beyond which is a bridge over the channel that flows in and out of a lagoon. North of the bridge the landscape has been redesigned for the Marina Mazatlán development. Beyond the marina lie even more beaches stretching all the way to Los Cerritos. Remember that all beaches in Mexico are public property, so feel free to wander where you like.

Another beach that makes an enjoyable outing is on the ocean side of **Isla de la Piedra** (Stone Island) on the southeast of town. From the center of town, board a "Circunvalación" or "Playa Sur" bus from the north side of the Zócalo for the ride to the boat landing, called Embarcadero Isla de la Piedra. Small motorboats make the five-minute trip to the island every 15 minutes or so from 7am to 7pm and charge $1.25 round trip. When you alight on the island, walk through the sleepy little village to the ocean side, where the pale-sand beaches, bordered by coconut groves, stretch for miles. On Sunday afternoon, the palapa restaurants on the shore have music and dancing, attracting families and young people; on other days the beach is almost empty. Carmelita's has delicious fish called lisamacho, served grilled and slightly blackened (over an open fire) with fresh, hot corn tortillas and salsa for about $10 a kilo ($2^{1}/_{5}$ lb.).

Camping here is possible but not recommended because there are no facilities.

CRUISES & BOAT RENTALS

The **Fiesta Yacht Cruise** runs a large double-decker boat every morning at 11am, leaving from the south beach near the lighthouse. The three-hour cruise takes in the harbor and bay; bilingual guides explain the marine life while a marimba band plays. Tickets cost $12 per person (youngsters 5 to 8 pay half price). Purchase tickets through a major hotel or travel agency.

A Week-Long Bender: Mazatlán's *Carnaval*

The week before Lent (usually in February) is Mazatlán's famous **Carnaval,** or Mardi Gras. People come from all over the country and abroad for this flamboyant celebration. Parades, special shows, the coronation of the Carnaval Queen, and many other extravaganzas take place all over town (for event information, check at major hotels or the Tourism Office and look for posters). Every night during Carnaval week, all along the Olas Altas oceanfront drive in the southern part of town, music fills the street with roving mariachi groups, the local traditional *bandas sinaloenses* (lots of brass instruments), and electrified bands set up under tarpaulin shades. Everyone dances, laughs, and mills about. The crowd increases each day, until on the last night (Shrove Tuesday), the Malecón is packed with musicians, dancers, and people out for a good time. The following day, Ash Wednesday, the party is over. People receive crosses of ashes on their foreheads at church, and Lent begins.

Amphibious boats heading for Isla de Venados (Deer Island), one of three big islands off the coast, leave from the beaches of the **El Cid Resort** (☎ 69/13-5611) throughout the day for $6.50 round trip. When you buy your ticket, you can rent snorkeling gear for an additional $5.

DEEP-SEA FISHING

It's slightly cheaper to enjoy deep-sea fishing in Mazatlán than in other parts of Mexico. Rates are $170 per day for a 24-foot *panga* for up to three persons; $265 per day for a 38-foot cruiser for up to four persons; and $292 per day for a 36-foot cruiser for up to 10 passengers; rates do not include fishing licenses and gratuities. Try the **Star Fleet** (☎ 69/82-2665; fax 82-5155), the **Aries Fleet** (☎ 69/16-3468 or 800/633-3085 in the U.S. and Canada); or **Mike Mexemins' Faro Fleet** (☎ 69/81-2824 or 82-4977). Locals suggest making fishing reservations for October through January at least a month in advance; at the very least, do it the minute you arrive in town.

WATER SPORTS

Among the best places to rent water-sports equipment—from snorkeling gear to Hobie Cats—are the Aqua Sport Center at the **El Cid Resort** (☎ 69/13-3333) and the Ocean Sport Center at the **Camino Real Hotel** (☎ 69/13-1111).

TENNIS, GOLF & OTHER OUTDOOR SPORTS

Mazatlán has more than 100 **tennis** courts. Try the courts at the **El Cid Resort,** Camarón Sábalo (☎ 69/13-3333), though hotel guests have priority; the **Racquet Club Gaviotas, Ibis** and **Río Bravo** in the Golden Zone (☎ 69/13-5939); and **Club Deportivo Reforma,** on Rafael Buelna (☎ 69/83-1200). Many larger hotels in Mazatlán also have courts.

As for **golf,** try the 18-hole course at the **El Cid Resort** (☎ 69/13-3333), mainly used by hotel guests; or the 9-hole course at the **Club Campestre Mazatlán** (open to the public), on Highway 15 on the outskirts of downtown (☎ 69/84-7494).

In addition to its worldwide reputation for year-round sportfishing (especially for sailfish and marlin), Mazatlán is known for good **hunting,** principally duck and dove. For information about transportation, guides, equipment, and licenses, call the **Aviles Brothers** (☎ 69/81-3728) or the **Tourism Office** (☎ 69/81-5837 or 81-5838).

You can rent horses for **horseback riding** on Isla Piedra for $10 per hour.

SPECTATOR SPORTS

There's a bullring on Rafael Buelna, about a mile from the Golden Zone (take the "Sábalo-Cocos" bus). From December through early April, **bullfights** are held every Sunday and on holidays at 4pm; locals recommend arriving by 2pm. Tickets range from $10 for general admission (ask for the shady side—*la sombra*) to $30 for the front of the shaded section; tickets can be purchased in advance at most travel agencies and tour desks.

Mexican **rodeos**, or *charreadas,* are held at the Lienzo Charro (ring) of the **Association of Charros of Mazatlán** (☎ 69/83-3154). Tickets are available through most major hotels and travel agencies.

At Playa Olas Altas, daring **cliff divers** take to the rock ledges of El Mirador and plunge into the shallow, pounding surf below. The divers perform sporadically during the day as tour buses arrive near their perch and sometimes dive with torches at 7pm. After the dive they collect donations from spectators. The public buses don't travel along this section of the waterfront; your closest stop is the Shrimp Bucket restaurant. From here walk north along the water about two blocks; El Mirador is on your left.

MUSEUMS

Museo Arqeológico de Mazatlán

Sixto Osuna 76, a block in from Paseo Olas Altas. ☎ **69/85-3502.** Admission $2. Tues–Sun 10am–1pm and 4–7pm.

This small but attractive museum exhibits both pre-Columbian artifacts and occasional contemporary artists. To get here from Olas Altas, walk inland on Sixto Osuna 1 1/2 blocks; the museum is on your right. Art exhibits are also sometimes held in the Casa de la Cultura across the street from the museum.

Acuario Mazatlán Aquarium

Av. de los Deportes 111, half a block off Av. del Mar. ☎ **69/81-7815** or 81-7817. Admission $4 adults, $2 children 3-14. Daily 9:30am–6:30pm; sea lion-, bird-, and fish-feeding shows almost hourly 10:30am–5pm.

Children and adults alike interested in the sea will love this aquarium, one of the largest and best in Mexico. To find the aquarium from Avenida del Mar heading toward the Golden Zone, turn right on Avenida de los Deportes; it's one block down on your left.

Museo De Conchas (Sea Shell Museum)

Rodolfo Loaiza 407, in the Golden Zone. ☎ **69/13-1301.** Admission free. Daily 9am–7pm.

Shell collectors and kids will enjoy this vast, fascinating collection of shells and shell art, much of which is for sale. To reach the museum from the Hotel Playa Mazatlán, turn left on Loaiza and walk two long blocks; it's on your right.

ARCHITECTURE

Two blocks south of the plaza stands the lovely and historic **Angela Peralta Theater** (☎ 69/82-4447), which in 1989 celebrated its first full season since the initiation of its renovation four years earlier. The theater was named for one of the world's great divas, who, along with the director and 30 members of the opera, died in Mazatlán of cholera in the 1863 epidemic. Some city tours make a stop at the theater; if you're visiting on your own, ask the guard if you can go in. The theater is open daily from 8:30am to 7pm; the fee for touring the building is 75¢. For information on scheduled performances call or check at the box office at the theater.

The 20-block historic area near the theater, including the small square **Plazuela Machado** (bordered by Frías, Constitución, Carnaval, and Sixto Osuna), is packed with beautiful old buildings and rows of colorful town houses trimmed with wrought iron and carved stone; many buildings have recently been restored as part of a city project. Small galleries are beginning to appear in these houses as the neighborhood becomes the center of Mazatlán's artistic community. Check out the **town houses** on Libertad between Domínguez and Carnaval and the two lavish **mansions** on Ocampo at Domínguez and at Carnaval. For a rest stop, try the Café Pacífico (decorated with historic pictures of Mazatlán) on Plazuela Machado.

The **Plaza Principal,** also called Plaza Revolución, is the heart of the city, filled with vendors, shoeshine stands, and people of all ages out for a stroll. At its center is a Victorian-style wrought-iron bandstand with a diner-type restaurant underneath. Be sure to take a look at the **cathedral** with its unusual yellow-tiled twin steeples and partially tiled facade. It's on the corner of Calle 21 de Marzo and Nelson.

ORGANIZED TOURS

In addition to twice-daily **city tours** (for $12), there are excursions to many colorful and interesting villages nearby, such as Concordia or Copala (see below). Some towns date back to the Spanish conquest during the 16th century; others are modest farming or fishing villages. Information and reservations are available at any travel agency or major hotel. Several tours are detailed below:

Copala-Concordia: This popular countryside tour stops at several mountain villages where furniture and other items are crafted. Copala has a pretty Spanish-colonial church. Lunch is included in the $35 tour. To go on your own see "By Bus" under "Getting There & Departing," above. For more about Copala see "Excursions from Mazatlán," below.

Mazatlán Jungle Tour: Some might say that David Perez's "Jungle Tour" is misnamed, but it's still worth doing. It consists of a 1¹/₂-hour boat ride past a Mexican navy base, Mazatlán's shrimp fleet and packing plants, and into the mangrove swamps to Stone Island. There's a three-hour stop at a pristine beach where the sand dollars may be the world's largest. Horseback rides on the beach are $6 for a half-hour ride. After the beach stop, feast on pescado zarandeado (fish cooked over coconut husks, green mangrove, and charcoal). Tours last from 9am to 3:30pm and cost $30 per person. Days vary, so call 14-2400 (☎ and fax) for dates and reservations.

SHOPPING

Most stores are open Monday through Saturday from 9 or 10am to 6 or 8pm. Very few close for lunch, and some stores are open on Sunday afternoon.

The **Golden Zone** is the place to shop. For a huge selection of handicrafts from all over Mexico, visit the **Mazatlán Arts and Crafts Center,** at Calle Gaviotas and Loaiza (☎ 69/13-5423). Streets throughout the Golden Zone have a good selection of clothing, fabrics, silver jewelry, leather, art, and other Mexican crafts.

The **Centro Mercado** in Old Mazatlán is another kind of shopping experience. Here you'll find women selling freshly gathered shrimp under colorful umbrellas; open-air food stalls; and indoor shops stacked with pottery, clothing, and crafts (mostly of lesser quality). Small galleries and shops are beginning to appear in Old Mazatlán; one of the nicest is **NidArt Galleria,** on Av. Libertad (☎ 69/81-0002).

La Gran Plaza is a large shopping mall just three blocks inland from the waterfront on Avenida de los Deportes. The plaza has a large supermarket, department stores, and specialty shops and is a good place for buying basic supplies.

ACCOMMODATIONS

The hotels in downtown Mazatlán are generally older and cheaper than those along the beachfront heading north. As a rule, room rates rise the farther north you go from downtown. The three major areas to stay are Olas Altas and downtown, the North Beach, and the Golden Zone (Zona Dorada).

Important note: Mazatlán hotels fill up quickly during Carnival and Easter week; some of the choicest rooms are reserved a year in advance, and room rates generally rise 30 to 40%.

THE GOLDEN ZONE

The Golden Zone is an elegant arc of golden sand serviced by a palm-lined boulevard and bordered by flashy hotels and a sprinkling of elaborate beach houses with high walls and watchdogs. A bonus here is the sunset view, unique because of the three islands just offshore, which seem to melt gradually into the fading colors of evening. In summer as well as May and September, many hotels along this beach cut their prices.

✪ Camino Real

Punta de Sábalo s/n, Mazatlán, Sin. 82100. ☎ **69/13-1111** or 800/722-6466. Fax 69/14-0311. 169 rms. A/C MINIBAR TV TEL. $121 double standard room; $132 double junior suite.

Long considered the grande dame of Mazatlán's hotels, the Camino Real continues to be the best choice for those seeking seclusion amid luxurious surroundings. A purple, pink, and green color scheme covers the marble-floored hallways and carpeted rooms, which have bathtubs and showers, large closets, and vanity tables. Junior suites have king-sized beds and comfy couches. The hotel is about a 10-minute drive from the heart of the Golden Zone.

Dining/Entertainment: Two restaurants serve all three meals.

Services: Room service, travel agency, boutique, beauty shop.

Facilities: The pool is very small, but the beach edges a small cove perfect for swimming. There are two tennis courts.

Pueblo Bonito

Av. Camarón Sábalo 2121 (Apdo 6), Mazatlán, Sin. 82000. ☎ **69/14-3700** or 800/ 262-4500. Fax 69/14-1723. 250 suites. A/C TV TEL. $137.50 double junior suite; $165 one-bedroom suite for 2 adults and 2 children. Free guarded parking. For reservations contact Mexico Condo Reservations, 5801 Soledad Mountain Rd., La Jolla, CA 92037. ☎ 619/ 275-4500, or 800/262-4500 in the U.S.

Many regard the Pueblo Bonito as the best hotel in Mazatlán—with good reason. All suites have kitchens and seating areas and such nice architectural touches as curving ceilings, arched windows, and tiled floors. The grounds are gorgeous—peacocks and flamingos stroll over lush lawns, a waterfall cascades into a large pool, and a row of palapas lines the beach. The suites are available as timeshares or hotel rooms, but be forewarned—the timeshare hustle can be intrusive.

Dining/Entertainment: Two good restaurants on the property.
Services: Room and laundry service, sightseeing desk, boutiques, hair dressers.
Facilities: Large pool, equipped gym, sauna, massage.

PLAYA NORTE

The waterfront between the downtown and the Golden Zone is Mazatlán's original tourist strip. Moderately priced hotels and motels line the street across from the beach, where taco and souvenir vendors set up shop on weekends. Señor Frog's, Mazatlán's most famous restaurant, is in this neighborhood, as is the bus station (though those with heavy luggage might still want to take a cab). In summer as well as May and September, many hotels along this beach cut their prices.

Expensive

Hotel Playa Mazatlán

Av. Rodolfo Loaiza 202 (Apdo. 207), Mazatlán, Sin. 82110. ☎ **69/13-1120** or 13-4455, 800/762-5816 in the U.S. Fax 69/14-0366. 423 rms. A/C TV TEL. $84 double with garden view; $102 double with ocean view. Free guarded parking.

The most happening place on the beginning stretch of the Golden Zone, the Playa Mazatlán is enduringly popular with families, tour groups, and dozens of regulars who return annually for winter vacations or spring break. The quietest rooms are in the three-story section around an interior lawn; those by the terrace restaurant and beach can be very noisy. The hotel hosts Mexican fiestas and fireworks displays and has several fast-food stands on the grounds.

Dining/Entertainment: Two restaurants serve the hotel in high season; one is open during the remainder of the year. There's a bar near the main restaurant.
Services: Laundry and room service, boutique, small gift shop/pharmacy, and tour desk.
Facilities: Two pools and two outdoor whirlpools.

Moderate

Costa de Oro

Av. Camarón Sábalo, Mazatlán, Sin. 82110. ☎ **69/13-5444** or 800/351-1612 in the U.S. Fax 69/14-4209. 310 rms and suites. A/C TV TEL. $60 double standard room without ocean view; $102 one-bedroom ocean-view suite for up to four persons. Free guarded parking.

You can't miss this terra-cotta colored complex spreading along both sides of the avenue. The rooms away from the beach are the least expensive and have the feeling of a motel. Those in the main complex and in the tower by the beach are far more pleasant. Suites have arched ceilings, handpainted porcelain sinks, and kitchenettes with full refrigerators and stove-top burners. The beds, set above the living area, can be shut off from the rest of the room with shutters.

El Quijote Inn

Av. Camarón Sábalo (Apdo. 934-966), Mazatlán, Sin. 82000. ☎ **69/14-1134.** Fax 69/14-3344. 67 rms and suites (all with bath). A/C TEL TV. $48 double studio without ocean view; $63 studio with ocean view for up to four persons; $97 one-bedroom suite for up to four persons; $122 for a two-bedroom suite for up to six persons. Free guarded parking.

The brown, pink, and orange color scheme may be outdated, but the suites at El Quijote are some of the best values in town. Most have a murphy bed that folds into the wall and that is far more comfortable than the couches provided at similar establishments. All rooms, except the studios, have full kitchens with a bar and dining table; those with ocean views have arched windows and balconies. A fair-size pool and a hot tub are set beside the beach; the hotel does not have a restaurant.

✪ Fiesta Inn

Av. Camarón Sábalo 1927, Mazatlán, Sin. 82110. ☎ **69/89-0100** or 800/FIESTA1 in the U.S. Fax 69/89-0130. 117 rms. A/C FAN TV TEL. $49.50–$60.50 double standard room; $82.50 junior suite for four persons. Free guarded parking.

Opened in 1994, the Fiesta Inn is one of the nicest hotels on the tourist strip. All rooms have oceanfront balconies, large bathrooms with both tubs and showers, satellite TV, small tables and chairs, and sliding glass doors to block the ocean breeze. The restaurant serves a reasonably priced brunch every morning, and the pool is long enough for lap swimming. There's a tour desk with very helpful personnel; a large, popular lobby bar; and an excellent fitness center. The Fiesta Inn is on Sábalo Beach, almost equidistant between the El Cid resort and the Hotel Camino Real at the entrance to the estuary.

Inexpensive

Apartments Fiesta

Ibis 502 at Río de la Plata, Mazatlán, Sin. 82110. ☎ **69/13-5355.** 7 apts (all with bath). A/C or FAN. $200–$400 per month; $70–$100 per week; $20 double per night.

A real find for long-term stays, the bright-blue-and-orange Fiesta has one- and two-bedroom apartments, all with kitchens, clustered around a small courtyard. Each apartment is decorated differently with a variety of wooden tables, chairs, and beds. The proprietors, Yolanda and Francisco Olivera, are very accommodating hosts. They don't take reservations far in advance and prefer that you call a week before you plan to visit. The complex is two blocks inland from Camarón Sábalo, an easy walk from the beach.

✪ Hotel Suites Don Pelayo

Av. del Mar 1111 (Apdo. Postal 1088), Mazatlán, Sin. 82000. ☎ **69/83-1888.** Fax 69/84-0799. 96 rms, 72 junior suites (all with bath). A/C TV TEL. $40 double; $46 double suite. Free enclosed parking.

Following a total refurbishing in 1994 and 1995, the Don Pelayo is the top choice on North Beach. The waterfront rooms have small balconies; all rooms have a king-size bed or two double beds, satellite TV, and central air-conditioning (without individual controls). The lighting and furnishings are gradually being improved. Suites have minibars and kitchenettes. Facilities include a restaurant, bar, two pools, and tennis courts. The hotel is very popular with families.

Plaza Gaviotas

Bugambilias 100 (Apdo. 970), Mazatlán, Sin. 82110. ☎ **69/13-4322.** Fax 69/13-6685. 67 rms (all with bath). A/C TEL TV. $32 double.

This small, friendly inn is a haven among the busier hotels in this neighborhood. It attracts guests who stay for several weeks and even months. The three-story building frames a courtyard and swimming pool. The brown-and-peach decor makes the small rooms somewhat dark; on the plus side, the sink is located outside the bathroom. To get here from the Tropicana Hotel turn right, then right again on Bugambilias; the hotel is a half block up on your left. The beach at the Playa Mazatlán Hotel is just a block away.

Racquet Club Las Gaviotas

Calle Ibis at Río de la Plata (Apdo 173), Mazatlán, Sin. 82110. ☎ and fax **69/13-5939.** 15 condos (all with bath). A/C. $700 per month for a two-bedroom condo. Some free parking.

The big plus at this small complex is the tennis center, where members and guests at the condos do not pay fees to play on the six courts. The complex includes bungalows and condos in several yellow buildings. The condos, some of which are available for monthly stays, have two bedrooms and two bathrooms, balconies overlooking the gardens and pool, and full kitchens. Advance reservations are essential, especially in the winter.

DOWNTOWN SEAFRONT/PLAYA OLAS ALTAS

The old section of Mazatlán is spread around a picturesque beach a short walk from downtown. It was here that the movie stars of the past came to frolic in the sun and surf; the hotels where they stayed are still here, seeming to whisper of their former glory. All the hotels are right on the waterfront, and their seaside rooms have private balconies with beautiful views of the cove and the sunset. There are a few nice seafront restaurants along here, too, which are open from early until late, making it easy to dine near your hotel.

✪ Hotel La Siesta

Av. Olas Altas 11, Mazatlán, Sin. 82000. ☎ **69/81-2640.** 57 rms (all with bath). A/C TEL. $15.50 double; $18 triple.

A fresh coat of tan paint makes the Siesta blend into its surroundings among the old mansions of Mazatlán. Inside, three levels of green-and-white railings surround a central courtyard. The rooms facing the ocean have balconies opening to sea breezes and pounding waves and the roar of traffic. Those at the back of the hotel are quieter but less charming. All have two beds, white walls with arched ceilings, a small table and chair, good lighting, and dependably hot water. There's a jug of purified water on each level. TVs cost extra. The courtyard houses the popular El Shrimp Bucket restaurant, where live marimbas and recorded music play until 10pm. This is the nicest hotel in old Mazatlán and fills up quickly. Reservations are strongly advised. To get here from the deer statue on Olas Altas, go right one block.

DINING

Mazatlán, boasting one of the largest shrimp fleets in the world, is a great town for tasty seafood. Yet seafood here is not cheap, and often Mexican plates are the best bargain.

An alternative to eating in a restaurant is to stop at one of the many **loncherías** scattered throughout the downtown area. At these, a torta or lonche (a sandwich on a small French roll) stuffed with a variety of meats, cheeses, tomatoes, onions, and chiles generally costs $1 to $1.50.

DOWNTOWN, NORTHBEACH & THE GOLDEN ZONE

Expensive

Señor Frog's

North Beach Malecón, Av. del Mar. ☎ **69/85-1110,** or 82-1925. Main courses $7–$15. Daily noon–1:30am. MEXICAN.

A sign over the door says JUST ANOTHER BAR & GRILL, but the line waiting to get in indicates just the opposite. The decor is delightfully silly, the food and loud music are great, and the atmosphere is friendly and lively. Revelers have been known to dance on the tables late into the night. The food is among the best in town. Try the tasty ribs, Caesar salad, or mango crêpes. The restaurant is on the waterfront drive at Playa Norte next to the Frankie Oh! disco.

El Shrimp Bucket

Av. Olas Altas 11 at Escobedo in the Hotel La Siesta. ☎ **69/81-6350** or 82-8019. Reservations recommended during major holidays. Mexican plates $3.50–$8; seafood and steak $7–$15. Daily 6am–11pm. MEXICAN/SEAFOOD.

A total remodeling in 1994 has rejuvenated the somewhat weary El Shrimp Bucket, making it once again one of the most popular restaurants in town. You can sample great shrimp in the air-conditioned dining room or under umbrellas in the center courtyard. The marimbas start up around 7pm. For wining, dining, and dancing, this is a great place for a splurge. El Shrimp Bucket is on Olas Altas at the corner of Escobedo.

Moderate

Bahía Mariscos

Mariano Escobedo 203. ☎ **69/81-2645.** Main courses $5.50–$14. Daily 11am–5pm. SEAFOOD.

A charming old mansion in Olas Altas has been transformed into this delightful restaurant specializing in bountiful seafood lunches. The campechana bahía is a delicious medley of shrimp, octopus, oysters, and calamari, and the fried whole fish is the best you'll find in the city. To get here from El Shrimp Bucket (at M. Escobedo and Olas Altas), walk south one block and turn left on Escobedo; the restaurant is on your left.

✪ Copa de Leche

Olas Altas 33 Sur. ☎ **69/82-5753.** Breakfast $1.50–$4.50; main courses $4–$10; soup $2–$4.50. Daily 7am–11pm. MEXICAN.

This shaded sidewalk cafe on the waterfront at Playa Olas Altas has the feeling of Mazatlán in the 1930s. The food is consistently as good as the ocean view. The menu includes alambre barbecue (beef cooked with onion, peppers, mushrooms, ham, and bacon); wonderful seafood soup loaded with squid, shrimp, and chunks of fish; and great shrimp with chipotle sauce. Inside the cafe, the bar is an old wooden boat, and the dining tables are covered with linen cloths. To get here from El Shrimp Bucket (at M. Escobedo and Olas Altas), turn south and walk ¹/₂ block down Olas Altas; the cafe is on your left.

✪ Doney's

Mariano Escobedo 610. ☎ **69/81-2651.** Soup or salad $1.50–$8; main courses $4.50–$12; Mexican plate $2.50–$6. Daily 8am–10pm (comida corrida served noon–4pm). MEXICAN.

This tried-and-true favorite, in a converted colonial home immediately south of the plaza, is regarded by many locals as the best moderately priced restaurant downtown. The mood is serene under the brick domes covering the interior courtyard. Inside, stained glass, handsome woodwork, and old sepia photographs add a turn-of-the-century flavor, especially when piano music fills the air. The large bilingual menu includes what some claim is the best apple pie in town. From the plaza with the city hall on your left, walk one block down Angel Flores then turn left on Cinco de Mayo; the restaurant is at the end of the block at Escobedo.

✪ Pastelería Panamá

Juárez and Canizales. ☎ **69/85-1853.** Breakfast $1.80–$3.60; sandwiches $2–$4; coffee 75¢. Daily 7am–10pm. FAST FOOD.

Busy, busy, busy describes all five locations of this successful chain. Everyone in Mazatlán must visit one location at least once a day for a leisurely coffee, a quick sandwich, a sweet roll, or piece of chocolate cake. To reach the place from the cathedral, walk straight (with the plaza behind you) one block on Juárez to Canizales; the restaurant is across the street on your right. The branch in the Golden Zone on Camarón Sábalo is the largest in the chain and is constantly busy. Going north on Loaiza, the Pastelería Panamá in the Golden Zone is on the right at Las Garzas, almost equidistant between the Sábalo traffic circle and the Mazatlán Arts and Crafts Center.

THE GOLDEN ZONE

Expensive

✪ Angelo's

Pueblo Bonito Hotel, Camarón Sábalo 2121. ☎ **69/14-3700.** Main courses $10–$36. Daily 6pm–midnight. ITALIAN.

Even locals consider this hotel restaurant one of the best in town, as much for its ambience as for its food. Beveled glass doors open to a soothing dining room gleaming with brass, polished wood, and crystal chandeliers. A pianist plays in the background as formally dressed waiters present menus featuring homemade pastas, shrimp dishes including a superb scampi, and a large selection of imported wines. Reservations are a must during high season.

✪ Sr. Pepper's

Av. Camarón Sábalo 2121. ☎ **69/14-3700.** Main courses $8–$30; specials $10. Daily 6pm– midnight; bar open daily 6pm–2am. INTERNATIONAL.

The best steaks in Mazatlán are served at this swanky restaurant, which manages to be both elegant and casual. Potted plants, candlelight, and lots of polished crystal, silver, and brass give the dining room a romantic feeling, and some nights it seems as if all the diners are old friends. The Sonoran beef steaks are grilled over mesquite and served in staggering portions; lobster and shrimp are also big hits. The restaurant has a nightly special including appetizer, steak or seafood, vegetables, soup or salad, and a complimentary appetizer at the bar on Friday and Saturday nights.

Moderate

Terraza Playa

In the Hotel Playa Mazatlán, R. T. Loaiza 202. ☎ **69/13-4455.** Breakfast $2.50–$5; Mexican plates $5.50–$12; seafood and meat $8–$22. Daily 6am–midnight. MEXICAN/SEAFOOD.

During the day, diners view the sea, beach, swimmers, sunbathers, and Isla de Venados (Deer Island). After sundown, they must be content with the stars overhead (in the completely open section) and the surging sounds of the waves as a backdrop to the live music presented nightly from 7pm to midnight. There's a floor for dancing, too. Splurge here on Sunday and enjoy front-row seats to the hotel's weekly free fireworks show.

Inexpensive

Jungle Juice

Las Garzas and Laguna. ☎ **69/13-3315.** Breakfast $2–$4; main courses $4.50–$12. Restaurant, daily 7am–1am. Bar, daily 4pm–1am. MEXICAN.

A front patio surrounded by lattice and an upstairs bar hung with piñatas give this semi-open-air restaurant a festive touch. Smoothies and many kinds of juices are its specialties, as are vegetarian plates and meat dishes grilled over mesquite on the patio. This casual spot also serves good breakfasts and makes a nice stop after shopping in the Golden Zone. Look for daily specials on the blackboard. To get here from Pastelería Panamá on Sábalo, turn right on Las Garzas; it's a block down on your right. (Heading north on Loaiza, Las Garzas and the Pastelería Panamá are on the right after the Sábalo traffic circle but before the Mazatlán Arts and Crafts Center.)

Pura Vida

Calle Laguna. ☎ **69/16-5815.** Breakfast $1–$3; sandwiches and salads $2.50–$4. Mon–Sat 8am–10pm. VEGETARIAN/HEALTH FOOD.

Nearly hidden behind thick plants, Pura Vida has several small seating sections with green wooden picnic tables and a central lunch counter. Fabulous veggie and white chicken sandwiches are served on whole wheat rolls, and though there are plenty of meat substitute dishes like soy burgers, you're better off sticking with the vegetable selections. There are plenty of juice and smoothie combos to choose from as well. To get here from Pastelería Panamá on Sábalo, turn right on Las Garzas, then left one block down onto Laguna. The cafe is on your right. (Going north on Loaiza, the Pastelería Panamá and Las Garzas are on the right almost equidistant between the Sábalo traffic circle and the Mazatlán Arts and Crafts Center.)

MAZATLÁN AFTER DARK

There's a free **fireworks show** every Sunday, beginning at 8pm, on the beach fronting the Hotel Playa Mazatlán, R. T. Loaiza 202, in the Golden Zone (☎ 69/13-4444 or 13-5320). The display is visible from the beach or from the hotel's Terraza Playa restaurant.

This hotel also presents an excellent **Fiesta Mexicana,** complete with buffet, open bar, folkloric dancing, and live music. Fiestas are presented on Tuesday, Thursday, and Saturday year-round beginning at 7pm; try to arrive by 6pm to get a good table. Tickets are $25.

DISCOS & BARS

Café Pacífico

Frías and Constitución. ☎ **69/81-3972.** No cover.

If you're staying downtown or would prefer a quiet atmosphere, this bodega-like bar in a restored historic building on Plazuela Machado is a pleasant place to spend some time. The doors are inset with stained glass, and the thick roof beams and walls are decorated with braided garlic, dried peppers, and old photographs. Another room contains a pool table. Beer is $1.50; margaritas cost $2. Open daily from 11am to midnight. There's a second, newer, cafe that is open the same hours on Loaiza in the Golden Zone by the artisans market.

Joe's Oyster Bar

Loaiza 100, on the beachfront at Los Sabalos Hotel. ☎ **69/83-5333.** No cover.

Beer, burgers, fresh oysters, and loud music are the house specialties at this casual open-air disco. Beer costs $2, and margaritas go for $3. Open daily from 11am to 2am.

Valentino's

Punta Camarón, near the Camarón Sábalo traffic circle. ☎ **69/83-6212.** Cover $5.

Dramatically perched on a rocky outcropping overlooking the sea, this all-white, Moorish-looking building houses one of the area's most popular discos. There's a good high-tech light show complete with green laser beams. For a break from the pulsating dance floor there are pool tables in another room and some quiet (relatively) areas for talking. Drinks run $1.50 to $5. Open daily from 9pm to 4am.

EXCURSIONS FROM MAZATLÁN
THE RUSTIC VILLAGE OF TEACAPÁN

Teacapán is the quintessential Mexican fishing village. It's just two hours south of Mazatlán (82 miles) at the tip of an isolated peninsula which extends 18 miles down a coastline of pristine beaches. Mangrove lagoons and canals border its other side. Palm and mango groves, cattle ranches, and an occasional cluster of houses dot the peninsula, which ends at the Boca de Teacapán, a natural marina separating the states of Sinaloa and Nayarit. Shrimping boats line the beach at the edge of this marina, backed by the worn houses and dirt streets of town.

Birdwatchers hire local fishermen to take them out around the lagoons, where they can see herons, flamingos, Canadian ducks, and countless other species of birds. Inland, the sparsely populated land is a haven for deer, ocelot, and wild boars. There's talk of making the entire peninsula into an ecological preserve, and thus far, residents have resisted attempts by developers to turn the area into a large-scale resort. For now, visitors are treated to the ultimate peaceful refuge.

Note to drivers: To reach Teacapán, drive south from Mazatlán on the highway to Escuinapa. There are no signs marking the right turn for the road to Teacapán; ask for directions in Escuinapa.

Accommodations
Rancho Los Angeles

Km 25 Carretera Escuinapa-Teacapán. No phone. 14 rms, 1 bungalow (all with bath). A/C or FAN. $33 double on the waterfront; $27.50 double in the bungalow; $22 double by the main street. For reservations contact Palmas 1-B, Colonia Los Pinos, Mazatlán, Sin. 82000; ☎ and fax 69/81-7867.

Dr. Ernesto Rivera Gúzman and his sons have created this small resort at the edge of the sea in the midst of coconut groves. The best rooms are in the hacienda-style building with terraces and a clean blue pool beside a long beach. The single rustic bungalow is a few feet from the main building, while other rooms are in a motel-like structure beside the main road to town. Boat tours and horseback riding are available. The hotel's small restaurant serves meals on the patio by the pool.

COPALA: AN OLD SILVER TOWN

Popular tours from Mazatlán stop here for lunch only, but Copala is well worth an overnight stay. The town was founded in 1565; from the late 1880s to the early 1900s, it was the center of the region's silver mining boom. When the mines closed, the town became nearly deserted. Today, it's a National Historic Landmark, with 600 full-time residents and a part-time community of retired Canadians and U.S. citizens devoted to Copala's picturesque solitude. In fact, some residents were less than pleased when the area received electricity in 1979.

Every building in town is painted white, and most have red-tile roofs splashed with fuschia-colored bougainvillea. Cobblestone streets wind from the entrance to town up slight hills at the main plaza and the Cathedral of San José, built in 1610. The town bustles around noon, when the tour buses arrive and visitors stroll the streets surrounded by small boys selling geodes extracted from the local hills. By

3pm, most of the outsiders have left, and you can wander the streets in peace and visit the century-old cemetery, the ruins of old haciendas, and the neighborhoods of white villas. The town's burros, roosters, and dogs provide the main background noise, and few cars clatter up the streets.

Note: Copala is an easy two-hour drive from Mazatlán, but it is only served by one bus a day (see "By Bus" under "Getting There & Departing," above, at the beginning of the Mazatlán section). You may be able to talk one of the tour bus drivers into giving you a lift back to Mazatlán for a small fee.

Accommodations & Dining

Daniel's

At the entrance to town. ☎ **69/86-5736.** 10 rms (all with bath). FAN. $25 double (including breakfast).

Daniel's restaurant is Copala's best-known landmark, revered for the sublime banana-cream coconut pie served with nearly every meal. Owner Daniel Garrison restored his uncle's turn-of-the-century home into the restaurant, set against the backdrop of the Sierra Madre foothills. The restaurant fills with guests at lunch time, and later in the day becomes the favored hangout of local expatriates. To the side of the restaurant is a small hotel housing large guest rooms with bathrooms, comfortable beds, and windows looking out to the countryside. Daniel's also offers Copala tours from Mazatlán; call the number listed above or check at the Hotel San Diego in Mazatlán for information. Daniel's is less than a 10-minute walk to town.

2 Puerto Vallarta

620 miles W of Mexico City, 260 miles W of Guadalajara, 175 miles N of Manzanillo, 300 miles S of Mazatlán, 112 miles S of Tepic

The gorgeous village of Puerto Vallarta boasts tropical mountains right beside the sea, coves and beaches, white buildings with red-tile roofs, and streets of brick and cobblestone. The construction of luxury hotels and shopping centers—mostly on the outskirts of the original town—has developed the town into a city of 250,000 people without destroying its charm. With miles of high-rise hotels flanking the picturesque village center, Puerto Vallarta does a better job than any other coastal city to balance Mexico's sophisticated resort environment with captivating colonial-era charm. In fact, I always recommend this city as the spot for a Mexican coastal vacation to people who want a taste of inland Mexico combined with the best of Mexico's hotel and restaurant services, shopping, and sports.

Once an agricultural village on the Bay of Banderas, Puerto Vallarta ceased to be a secret when a film of Tennessee Williams's *Night of the Iguana*, starring Richard Burton, Ava Gardner, and Deborah Kerr, was made here. Elizabeth Taylor came along for the filming, and the romance between Burton and Taylor became headline news, throwing Puerto Vallarta into the world's limelight. After Taylor's love affair, the tiny seaside village grew into a booming resort with a good highway and airport. Restaurants, shops, and hotels here are some of the country's best.

Puerto Vallarta has captivated so many foreigners that a considerable colony of Americans and Canadians has taken up permanent residence here.

ESSENTIALS

GETTING THERE & DEPARTING **By Plane** For a list of international carriers serving Mexico, see Chapter 3, "Planning a Trip to Mexico." Some local numbers of international carriers: **Alaska Airlines,** ☎ 1-1350 or 1-1352; **American Airlines,** ☎ 1-1972, 1-1799, or 1-1032; **Continental,** 1-1025 or 1-1096; and **Delta,** ☎ 1-1919 or 1-1032.

From other points in Mexico, **Aeroméxico** (☎ 4-2777, or 1-1055) flies from Aguascalientes, Guadalajara, La Paz, León, Mexico City, and Tijuana. **Mexicana** (☎ 4-8900, 1-1266, or 1-0243) has direct or nonstop flights from Guadalajara, Mazatlán, Los Cabos, and Mexico City.

By Bus **Elite,** at the corner of Basillio Badillo and Constitución, has many first-class buses to Guadalajara.

The deluxe-class **ETN** shares a space with the first-class **Primera Plus** and the second-class **Servicios Coordinados** (☎ 2-6986) at Cardenas 258, near Vallarta. ETN has several buses to Mexico City and Guadalajara. Primera Plus buses go to Guadalajara. Servicios Coordinados buses have the most frequent service to Manzanillo, Barra de Navidad, and Melaque/San Patricio.

The second-class **Autotransportes del Cihuatlan,** at the corner of Constitución and Madero (☎ 2-3436), has hourly buses to Manzanillo from 5am to 6pm (a six-hour trip) and almost as frequent service to Melaque (a 4½-hour trip). **Transportes Norte de Sonora,** at Caranza 322, near Insurgentes (☎ 2-6666), has two daily buses via the short route to San Blas (a three-hour trip); the route through Tepic takes at least five hours to reach San Blas. **Transportes del Pacífico,** Insurgentes 282 at Carranza (☎ 2-1015), has both first- and second-class service to Guadalajara traveling the short route (Vía Corta), which takes 6½ hours, and to Mexico City, which takes 14 hours. If you intend to head north, for instance to Mazatlán, you'll need to go to Tepic first and then catch a direct bus from there.

By Car The coastal Highway 200 is the only choice between Mazatlán to the north (six hours away) or Manzanillo to the south (3½ hours). The eight-hour journey from Guadalajara through Tepic can be shortened to six hours by taking Highway 15A from Chapalilla to Compostela (this bypasses Tepic and saves two hours), then continuing south on Highway 200 to Puerto Vallarta. A new toll highway between Guadalajara and Puerto Vallarta was about to be constructed when I checked and may be finished by the time you travel. With the new highway, the trip should take about four hours.

ORIENTATION **Arriving by Plane** The airport is close to the north end of town near the Marina Vallarta, only about six miles from downtown. You'll have a choice of transport from the airport: the **Transportes Terrestres** minivan (colectivo) or taxis called **Areomovil.** The cost of taxi or colectivo-minivans accrue according to the number of zones they have traversed. The closest zone to the airport is the Marina Vallarta; the next zone is anything before the Río Cuale; beyond the Río Cuale in the downtown area constitutes the next zone; and the farthest is the southern hotel zone. Be sure you know the area of your hotel and double-check what you are charged—the drivers make mistakes. A shared ride in the minivan costs $3.50 to the Marina Vallarta or downtown before the Río Cuale and $6 beyond it. A private ride by Aeromovil taxi costs $8.50 to the Marina

Vallarta, $10 to downtown before the river, $16.75 beyond the river, and $20 to the southern hotel zone.

Important note: Colectivos run only when they fill up after flights arrive, so avoid tarrying in the arrivals hall or you'll miss the colectivos. Between such times, only Aeromovil taxis operate. Another option is to walk about a block to the highway and hail a passing taxi; this option is cheaper than Aeromovil but more expensive than the colectivo. City buses also pass on the highway on their way to town and are useful if you have only a small bag. Coming in from the airport north of town, you'll pass (on your right) the **Terminal Maritima** (Cruiseline Pier), the **Marina Vallarta** development, and many luxury hotels; the Malecón, downtown in the village proper, is lined with restaurants, and shops, and a few hotels. However, most downtown hotels are off the Malecón.

Arriving by Bus If you arrive by bus, you'll be south of the river on Madero, Insurgentes, or Constitución and close to all of the hotels I have recommended below. Most of the bus "stations" are small offices or waiting rooms for the various lines. The city has planned a central bus station away from this downtown area for years, but so far, there's no movement on this idea.

Information The **State Tourism Office,** at Juárez and Independencia (☎ 322/ 2-0242, 3-0844, or 3-0744; fax 322/2-0243), is in a corner of the white Presidencia Municipal building on the corner of the main square. This is also the office of the tourist police. It's open Monday through Friday from 9am to 9pm and Saturday from 9am to 1pm.

City Layout The seaside promenade, or **Malecón** (also known as **Paseo Díaz Ordaz**), follows the rim of the bay from north to south in the village, and the town stretches back into the hills a half a dozen blocks. The area north of the **Río Cuale** is the oldest part of town—the original Puerto Vallarta. The area south of the river, once only beach, has become as built-up as the old town in the last decade, although it's less sophisticated and more rustic. Today the best budget lodgings, as well as the bus "stations," are here.

Once you're in the center of town, you'll find nearly everything within walking distance. Puerto Vallarta has grown to the north and south of the original village along the beach. **Marina Vallarta,** a resort-city-within-a-city, is at the northern edge of the hotel zone not far from the airport—you pass it on the right as you come into town from the airport. It boasts luxury hotels and condominium projects, a huge marina with 300 yacht slips, a golf course, restaurants and bars, an office park, and a shopping plaza. Between it and downtown are many more luxury hotels, such as the Krystal and Fiesta Americana. **Nuevo Vallarta,** another planned resort, is just north of Marina Vallarta across the Ameca River in the state of Nayarit (about eight miles north of downtown). It also has hotels, condominiums, a yacht marina, and a convention center. For now, though, Nueva Vallarta is too difficult to reach by public transportation, and all the hotels here are out of budget range. **Bucerías,** a village of cobblestone streets, villas behind walls, and small hotels is on the far side of Banderas Bay 19 miles beyond the Puerto Vallarta airport. **Punta de Mita,** at the northern end of the bay, has always been a daytime beach hangout with palapa-style restaurants. A new resort is under construction there now, and access to Punta Mita isn't available now.

Going in the opposite direction, south of the original village about six miles on **Mismaloya Beach** (where *Night of the Iguana* was filmed) lies the Jolla de

Puerto Vallarta Area

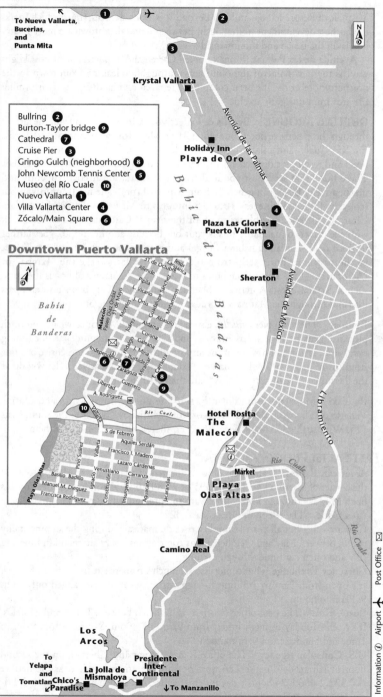

To Nueva Vallarta,
Bucerias,
and
Punta Mita

Krystal Vallarta

Bullring ❷
Burton-Taylor bridge ❾
Cathedral ❼
Cruise Pier ❸
Gringo Gulch (neighborhood) ❽
John Newcomb Tennis Center ❺
Museo del Río Cuale ❿
Nuevo Vallarta ❶
Villa Vallarta Center ❹
Zócalo/Main Square ❻

Holiday Inn
Playa de Oro

Plaza Las Glorias
Puerto Vallarta

Sheraton

Downtown Puerto Vallarta

Bahía
de
Banderas

31 de Octubre
Lángarica
Jesús
Allende
Pipila
L. Vicario
J. Ortiz
Guadalupe Sánchez
Matamoros
Morelos
Juárez
Abasolo
Hidalgo
Aldama
Galeana
Corona
Independencia
J. Mina
Iturbide
E. Carranza
Miramar
Zaragoza
Guerrero
Libertad
A. Rodriguez

Río Cuale

S de Febrero
Aquiles Serdán
Francisco I. Madero
Lazaro Cárdenas
Pino Suárez
Vallarta
Ignacio
Venustiano Carranza
Basilio Badillo
Manuel M. Diéguez
Constitución
Intsurgentes
Aguacate
Jacarandas
Francisca Rodríguez

Playa Olas Altas

Malecón
Paseo Díaz Ordaz
31 de Mayo

Bahía

de

Banderas

Avenida de las Palmas

Avenida de México

Libramiento

Hotel Rosita
The
Malecón

Río Cuale

Market

Playa
Olas Altas

Río Cuale

Camino Real

Los
Arcos

To
Yelapa
and
Tomatlan Chico's
Paradise

La Jolla de
Mismaloya

Presidente
Inter-
Continental

↓ To Manzanillo

Information ⓘ   Airport ✈   Post Office ✉

1221

Mismaloya Resort & Spa, and just beyond it is **Boca de Tomatlán,** which marks the farthest development to the south. Between it and downtown are more luxury hotels on the beach and mountainside.

Avenida de las Palmas (formerly called Carretera Aeropuerto, or Airport Highway) is the new name of the multilane thoroughfare leading from town to the northern hotel zone. It's been completely repaved and landscaped, transforming the area from unsightly to chic.

GETTING AROUND   By Bus & Colectivo   City buses run from the airport through the expensive hotel zone along 31 de Mayo (the waterfront street), across the Río Cuale, and inland on Vallarta, looping back through the downtown hotel and restaurant districts on Insurgentes and several other downtown streets. These buses will serve just about all your transportation needs frequently and inexpensively. Buses run generally from 6am to 11pm. The no. 02 **minivan** bus (colectivo) goes south every 10 to 15 minutes to Mismaloya Beach from Plaza Lázaro Cárdenas, a few blocks south of the river at Cárdenas and Suárez. Check with the driver to make sure this is your bus because another no. 02 goes farther to Boca de Tomatlán (a fishing village) and may not stop at Mismaloya. To get to the northern hotel strip from old Puerto Vallarta, take the "Ixtapa" or "Aeropuerto" bus. These same buses may also post the names of hotels they pass such as Krystal, Fiesta Americana, Sheraton, and others. City buses now also pass into and through the Marina Vallarta area, where they were once prohibited.

By Boat   The town pier (*muelle*), also called Terminal Maritima, where you catch pleasure boats to Yelapa, Las Animas, and Quimixto and you depart for fishing excursions, is north of town near the airport and a convenient, inexpensive bus ride from town. Just take any bus marked "Ixtapa" and tell the driver to let you off at the Terminal Maritima (ter-MEEN-ahl mah-REE-tee-mah).

By Taxi   Most trips from downtown to the northern hotel strip and Marina Vallarta cost between $4 and $5; to or from Mismaloya Beach to the south costs $15. With such good bus service, however, there's little reason to use them.

FAST FACTS: PUERTO VALLARTA

American Express   The local office is located in the village at Morelos 660, at the corner of Abasolo (☎ 322/3-2995 or 91-800/0-0555 toll free in Mexico). It's open Monday through Friday from 9am to 6pm and Saturday from 9am to 1pm.

Area Code   The telephone area code is 322.

Climate   It's hot all year. Humidity rises dramatically during the summer rainy season between May and October. Rains come almost every afternoon in June and July and often continue through evening.

Currency Exchange   Bancomer has a branch on Juárez at the corner of Mina. It's open from 9am to 1:30pm; foreign currency can be exchanged only from 9:30am to noon.

Post Office   The post office (Correo) is on Mina between Juárez and Morelos. It's open Monday through Friday from 9am to 7:30pm, Saturday from 9 am to 1pm, and Sunday from 9am to noon.

U.S. Consular Agency   The office is at Miramar and Libertad, on the second floor of Parian del Puente 12A, just north of the river bridge near the market (☎ 322/2-0069, 24 hours a day for emergencies). It's open Monday through Friday from 9am to 1pm.

FUN ON & OFF THE BEACH

Travel agencies can provide information on what to see and do in Puerto Vallarta and can arrange tours, fishing, and other activities.

Note: Beware of "tourist information" booths, especially along Ordaz and the Malecón—they are usually time-share hawkers offering "free" or cheap Jeep rentals, cruises, breakfasts, and so forth as bait. If you're suckered in, you may or may not get what is offered, and the experience will cost at least half a day of your vacation.

SPECIAL EVENTS

Santa Cecilia, the patron saint of mariachis, is honored for a solid 24 hours on **November 22.** Beginning at midnight on the 22nd until midnight of the 23rd, different mariachi groups take turns playing in the cathedral. That evening mariachis parade and fireworks are set off in the central plaza. The week leading up to **December 12**—the "birthday" of Mexico's patron saint, the Virgin of Guadalupe—there are processions of las peregrinas (religious pilgrims) and much merrymaking.

THE BEACHES

Its beaches are Puerto Vallarta's main attraction. They start well north of town, out by the airport, with **Playa de Oro** and extend all around the broad Bay of Banderas. The easiest to reach is **Playa Olas Altas,** also known as **Playa Muertos** or **Playa del Sol,** just off Calle Olas Altas, south of the Río Cuale. The water is polluted here so the beach is good for sunning but not for swimming.

Playa Mismaloya is in a beautiful sheltered cover about six miles south of town along Highway 200. The water is clear and beautiful. Entrance to the public beach is just to the left of the Mismaloya hotel. Colorful palapa restaurants dot the small beach and will rent you a beach chair for sunning, or you can stake out a table under a palapa for the day. Using a restaurant's table and palapa is a reciprocal arrangement—they let you be comfortable, and you buy your drinks, snacks, lunch there. Before choosing your spot, be sure you'll want to eat and drink there too by briefly inspecting the set-up they have. The *Night of the Iguana* was filmed at Mismaloya. You can still see and hike up to the stone buildings that were constructed for the movie, on the point framing the south side of the cove. The Jolla de Mismaloya Resort is to the right of the public beach and restaurants there are available to outsiders as well This and all beaches in Mexico are public.

Animas and **Yelapa** beaches are very good but are reached only by boat. These are larger than Mismaloya and are similarly set up with restaurants fronting a wide beach. If you aren't keen on taking an expensive boat trip see how to do it less expensively in "Boat Trips," below.

BOAT TRIPS

Puerto Vallarta offers a number of different boat trips, including **sunset cruises** and excursions to **Yelapa** (a tiny town on a lovely cove), **Las Animas Beach,** and **Quimixto Falls.** Most of these make a stop at **Los Arcos** for snorkeling; some include lunch; and most provide music and an open bar on board. Most leave around 9:30am, stop for 45 minutes at Los Arcos, and arrive at the beach destination around noon for a $2^{1}/_{2}$-hour stay before returning around 3pm. These beaches have many colorful restaurants where you can take a table under a shady umbrella on the beach while you sun, eat, and buy drinks. It's customary to make your food and drink purchases at the restaurant whose table you occupy, so on arrival visitors are besieged by restaurant representatives to take a seat at many of them. Pick one that suits you and enjoy your time there. At Quimixto, where the shoreline is rocky and there's no beach, visitors can take the half-hour hike to the falls or rent a horse for a ride to the falls. Prices range from $20 for a sunset cruise or a trip to one of the beaches with open bar to $35 for an all-day outing with open bar and meals. Travel agencies have tickets and information.

If you prefer to spend a longer time at Yelapa or Las Animas without taking time for snorkeling and cruise entertainment, then try the **water taxi** south of the Río Cuale by the Hotel Marsol on Francisco Rodriguez. For around $15 round trip, boatmen advertise direct trips to Las Animas, Yelapa, or Quimixto. Supposedly, this water taxi takes off at 10:30 and 11am and returns at 3:30pm. In reality, however, the operators of this service would rather sell the lengthy tour and don't seem too enthusiastic about the direct trips, which take 40 minutes each way; a direct trip from these folks costs only slightly less than an excursion with all the trimmings. There's also another water taxi next to the Hotel Rosita (north of the river at Diaz Ordaz and 31 de Octubre) which advertises direct trips daily at 11am for $7.

WATER SPORTS

Puerto Vallarta offers good diving and snorkeling; there's a **national underwater park** at Los Arcos, an island rock formation. Underwater enthusiasts from beginner to expert can arrange scuba diving at **Chico's Dive Shop**, Díaz Ordaz 770–5 by Carlos Obrien's (☎ 322/2-1895). Chico's also has branches at the Marriott, Vidafel, Vila del Palmar, Camino Real, and Continental Plaza hotels. **Vallarta Divers**, in the Marina del Rey Condominium at Marina Vallarta (☎ 322/1-0492), also offers scuba outings, as well as resort courses and PADI and NAUI certification courses. Dives cost around $35–$60 with equipment; the price varies depending on how far you go. Snorkeling trips cost around $35.

Waterskiing, parasailing, and other water sports are available at many beaches along the Bay of Banderas.

FISHING

A fishing trip can be arranged through travel agencies or through the **Cooperativo de Pescadores** (Fishing Cooperative) on the Malecón, north of the Río Cuale next door to the Rosita Hotel and across from McDonald's (☎ 322/2-1202). Fishing charters cost $200–$300 a day for four to eight people. Price varies with the size of the boat. Although the posted price at the fishing cooperative is the same as through travel agencies, you may be able to negotiate a lower price at the cooperative. It's open Monday through Saturday from 7am to 2pm, but make arrangements a day ahead.

Note: Most fishing trips include equipment and bait but not drinks or snacks, so arrange to bring refreshments with you.

GOLF

Puerto Vallarta has two golf courses. The one nearest town is the 18-hole private course at the Marina Vallarta (☎ 322/1-0171), for members only. Most of the luxury hotels have memberships which their guests can use. North of town about 10 miles is the 18-hole Los Flamingos Club de Golf (☎ 329/8-0606), a few miles beyond the Nuevo Vallarta development. It's open from 7am to 5pm daily, with a bar (no restaurant) and full pro shop. The greens fee is $30, plus $15 for club rental and $25 for a motorized cart or $5 for a pull cart.

BULLFIGHTS

Bullfights are held from December through April on Wednesday afternoon at the bullring "La Paloma," across the highway from the town pier. Tickets can be arranged through travel agencies and cost around $25.

ESCORTED TOURS

Hotel travel desks and travel agencies can arrange a **Tropical Tour** ($20) or a **jungle tour** ($20). What's called the "Tropical Tour" is really an expanded city tour and includes the workers village of Pitallal, the posh neighborhood of Conchas Chinas, the cathedral, the market, the Taylor-Burton houses, and lunch at Chino's Paradise.

Horseback-riding trips can be arranged through travel agents or by going to the horse owners who gather at the end of Basilio Badillo, south of the Río Cuale by the Restaurant Corral. Rides cost around $8 an hour. Horsemen arrive about 9am, and rides take off around 9:30am and return around 1:30pm. Ask for Fernando Peña, one of the horsemen who can also take riders from his house on the outskirts of town and into the mountains. Arrange this with him a day ahead.

Or for a unique getaway, try **Horseback on Mexico's Hacienda Trail from Sea to Sierra Madre,** several week-long journeys by horseback into the mountains. They include camping en route to stays in centuries-old haciendas. For details, contact Pam Aguirre or Ann Sherman, Rancho El Charro, Av. Francisco Villa 895, Puerto Vallarta, Jal. (☎ 322/4-1014).

Mountain Bike Tours, Badillo 381 (☎ 322/2-0080), offers **mountain-bike trips** to outlying areas. Trips cost around $30 for four hours and include bike, helmet, gloves, water, and an English-speaking guide. Trips start at around 8am. Make arrangements a day ahead.

You can also tour the **Taylor/Burton villas** (Casa Kimberley; ☎ 322/2-1336), the two houses owned by Elizabeth Taylor and Richard Burton, located at 445 Calle Zaragoza. Tours cost $5, and proceeds go toward cleft-palate operations for area youngsters.

A **house-and-garden tour** of four private homes in town is offered every Thursday and Saturday during high season by the **International Friendship Club** (☎ 322/2-6060), for a donation of $20 per person. The tour bus departs from the main plaza by the tourism office (which has information about this event) at 11am. Proceeds are donated to local charities.

Sierra Madre, D. Ordaz 732-B, at Vicario (☎ 322/3-0661), may be a sophisticated cover for time-share sales of the Westin Reginas in Mexico, huge photos of which cover the back wall. The trendy storefront features a safari theme, as well as ecologically oriented books, tee shirts, postcards—and trips. Supposedly, funds generated by trips go toward several government and privately sponsored ecological reserves and studies. Among the trips they offer are treks to the mountain foothills $1^1/_5$ hours away, an "Artistic Mexico" trip featuring nearby villages and artisans, mountain-bike tours, whale watching, and horseback riding, all conducted by ecologically oriented leaders who point out local flora and fauna. Prices range from $15 to $45 depending on the trip. It's open daily from 9am to 10pm.

A Stroll Through Town

Puerto Vallarta's tightly knit cobblestone streets are a delight to explore (with good walking shoes!); they are full of tiny shops, rows of windows edged with curling wrought iron, and vistas of red-tile roofs and the sea. Start with a walk up and down the Malecón, the seafront boulevard.

Among the sights you shouldn't miss is the **municipal building,** on the main square (next to the tourism office), which has a large Manuel Lepe mural inside in its stairwell. Nearby, up Independencia sits the **cathedral,** topped with its curious crown; on its steps women sell colorful herbs and spices to cure common ailments. Here Richard Burton and Elizabeth Taylor were married the first time—she in a Mexican wedding dress, he in a Mexican *charro* outfit.

Three blocks south of the church, head uphill on **Libertad,** lined with small shops and pretty upper windows; it brings you to the **public market** on the river. After exploring the market, cross the bridge to the **island in the river;** sometimes a painter is at work on its banks. Walk down the center of the island toward the sea, and you'll come to the tiny **Museo del Cuale,** which exhibits pre-Columbian ceramics and works by local artists; it's open Monday through Saturday from 10am to 4pm. Admission is free.

Retrace your steps back to the market and Libertad and climb up steep Miramar to **Zaragoza.** At the top is a magnificent view over rooftops to the sea. Up Zaragoza to the right two blocks is the famous pink arched bridge that once connected Richard Burton's and Elizabeth Taylor's houses. This area, known as **Gringo Gulch,** is where many Americans have houses.

SHOPPING

Excellent-quality merchandise is brought to Puerto Vallarta from all over Mexico. Prices are higher than those in the places where the goods originated, and if you're planning to visit other parts of Mexico, you might want to wait and make your purchases at the source. In Tonala and Tlaquepaque (suburbs of Guadalajara), six hours away by bus, prices are considerably lower.

Puerto Vallarta's **municipal market** is just north of the Río Cuale where Libertad and A. Rodríguez meet. The *mercado* sells clothes, jewelry, serapes, shawls, leather accessories and suitcases, papier-mâché parrots, stuffed frogs and armadillos, and of course T-shirts. Be sure to do some comparison shopping before buying. The market is open daily from 8am to 8pm.

The **Río Cuale** under the bridge is lined with a variety of shops selling crafts, gifts, art, and clothing.

Calle Libertad, next to the market, is the place to buy *huaraches*—comfortable, practical sandals made of leather strips and rubber-tire soles. Buy a pair that fits a little tightly—they stretch out quickly and can become too floppy.

CRAFTS & FOLK ART   South of the Río Cuale   The **Olinala Gallery,** Cárdenas 274 (☎ 2-4995), has two floors of fine indigenous Mexican crafts and folk art, including an impressive collection of authentic masks and Huichol beaded art. It's open Monday through Saturday from 10am to 2pm and 5 to 9pm.

Pirámide Galeria, Badillo 272 (☎ 2-3161), offers an enormous selection of Huichol Indian art and contemporary art. It's open Monday through Saturday from 10am to 2pm and 6pm to 10pm.

La Rosa de Cristal Vidrio Soplado Artesanías, Insurgentes 272, between Cárdenas and Madero (☎ 2-5698), has the best prices and greatest selection in

Puerto Vallarta of Mexican blown-glass objects in all colors. It all comes from their factory in Tlaquepaque near Guadalajara; seconds are in the back. The shop is open Monday through Saturday from 10am to 8pm.

North of the Río Cuale The **Sergio Bustamante Gallery,** Juárez 275 near Zaragoza (☎ 2-1129), is open Monday through Saturday from 10am to 9pm. Bustamante's fantastic creatures emerging from eggs and other surreal and colorful images are his trademarks. His gold and silver jewelry is for sale in abundance. Two more Busatmante stores are at Ordaz 546 and Ordaz 700.

Gallery Indígena, Juárez 270, between Guerrero and Zaragoza (☎ and fax 2-3007), is a large shop featuring silver, Oaxaca pottery and wood carvings, lacquer chests, dance masks, pre-Hispanic pottery reproductions, and Huichol Indian art. Owner Ignacio Jacobo is usually on hand. Ask about shipping items to the United States and delivery to Puerto Vallarta hotels. It's open Monday through Saturday from 10am to 3pm and 5 to 9pm.

La Reja, Juárez 501 (☎ 2-2272), next to Querubines, has a great selection of Mexican ceramics and some lovely Guatemalan fabrics; it's open Monday through Saturday from 9am to 2pm and 4 to 8pm. **Querubines,** Juárez 501A (☎ 2-3475), offers Guatemalan and Mexican wares, including embroidered and handwoven clothing, bolts of foot-loomed fabric, wool rugs, jewelry, straw bags, and Panama hats. It's open Monday through Saturday from 9am to 9pm and Sunday 10am to 6pm. It's at the corner of Galeana.

Arte Mágico Huichol, Corona 178 (☎ 2-3077), has several rooms of Huichol Indian art. It carries very fine large and small yarn paintings by recognized Huichol artists, as well as intricately beaded masks, bowls, and ceremonial objects. The gallery is open Monday through Saturday from 10am to 9pm.

Sucesos, at the corner of Libertad and Hidalgo, specializes in unique, expensive hand-painted clothing. It's open Monday through Saturday from 10am to 8pm and Sunday from 11am to 3pm. **Nacho's,** Libertad 160A (☎ 2-3007), sells beautifully made silver jewelry from Taxco and lacquerware from Olinala. Nacho's is open Monday through Saturday from 10am to 2pm and 5 to 8pm.

El Baúl, Juárez 512, inside Las Margaritas between Corona and Galeana (☎ 3-2580), has fine decorative objects, colorful furniture, pottery, glass, and pewter; it's open Monday through Saturday from 10am to 2pm and 4:30 to 8pm.

Casa Bombay, Morelos 527 near Corona (☎ 3-0723), specializes in Asian furniture, clothing, tribal jewelry, silks, and other textiles. It's open Monday through Saturday from 10am to 9pm. Next door, **El Souk,** Morelos 533 (☎ 3-1340), features textiles, furniture, rugs, jewelry, and masks from Morocco, Tunisia, and Egypt. It's open Monday through Saturday from 10am to 9pm. **Nevaj,** Morelos at Libertad (☎ 2-6959), has quality folk art from Central and South America and Mexico; it's open Monday through Saturday from 10am to 2pm and 5 to 9pm.

Instituto de la Jalisciense, Juárez 284 (☎ 2-1301), is the state-operated store, featuring crafts from Jalisco as well as a few other states. It's at Zaragoza catercorner from the zócalo; hours are Monday through Saturday from 10am to 2pm and 4 to 8pm.

CONTEMPORARY ART The following galleries carry contemporary Mexican and/or foreign artists: **Galería Uno,** Morelos 561 at Zaragoza (☎ 2-0908), is the leading art gallery, open Monday through Saturday from 10am to 8pm; **Galeria**

Pacífico, Río Cuale opposite Le Bistro Jazz Café (☎ 2-2748), is open Monday through Saturday from 10am to 9pm.

ACCOMMODATIONS

MARINA VALLARTA

The Marina Vallarta is the northern extension of the "Hotel Zone" and is located just before the airport. The hotels below are built around the new 400-slip marina and 18-hole golf course designed by Joe Finger. All except the Bel-Air Resort are on the beach.

Bel-Air Resort Puerto Vallarta

Pelicanos 311, Marina Vallarta, Puerto Vallarta, Jal. 48300. ☎ **322/1-0800** or 800/457-7676 in the U.S. and Canada, 91-800/3-2832 in Mexico. Fax 322/1-0801. 67 suites and villas. A/C TV TEL. High season $170–$240 double suite; $280–$400 villa. Low season $125–$225 double suite; $225–$325 villa.

This stylish inn is located in the heart of the Marina Vallarta development squarely between the first and 18th holes of the golf course. Few Mexican hotels can claim such masterful use of elegant Mexican furniture—many of the gorgeous pieces are replicas of furniture found in the Museo Alfenique in Puebla—a kind of Mexican Chippendale. The suites combine those designs with sculpted faces prepared especially for the hotel by the renowned Mexican sculptor Sergio Bustamante. Spacious junior suites all have balconies (some have two). Master suites all have balconies with bubbling whirlpools overlooking the golf course. Deluxe suites have a balcony, whirlpool bath for two, and living-room area. The two-story villas have small bar areas, living rooms, dining rooms, and from one to three bedrooms and private pools.

Dining/Entertainment: The multilevel, excellent, Restaurant El Candil overlooks the golf course, wide outdoor patio, and pool through a wide expanse of windows and is open from 7am to 11pm. Live harp or piano music accompanies all meals. Another restaurant/bar by the pool serves snacks during the day. The terrace bar features live nightly entertainment.

Services: Laundry, room service, car rental, concierge, transportation to the beach. Guests receive champagne and fresh juice on arrival, have separate check-in and access to the hotel's fax and secretarial services.

Facilities: Large gorgeous pool facing the golf course; golf privileges at the Marina Vallarta Golf Course at reduced rates with pickup and drop-off at the hotel; 2 tennis courts; 46 private pools; fitness center with no fee for guests. A fully staffed private beach club will open in 1995 with a restaurant and water sports.

Marriott Casamagna

Marina Vallarta, Puerto Vallarta, Jal. ☎ **322/1-0004** or 800/228-9290 in the U.S. 433 rms and suites (all with bath). A/C MINIBAR TV TEL. High season $190 double sunset view; $156 double ocean view; $330–$480 suite.

You'll first be impressed by the splendid openness of this grand hotel which debuted in 1990; the enormous lobby soars and baronial hallways lead to the rooms and beach; from the lobby to the beach you cross a small artificial pond. The sound of fountains is ever present throughout the hotel. Rooms are accented in pale sienna and pale ocher and all have ocean views and balconies, ironing boards and irons, and in-room safety-deposit boxes. Rooms with king-size beds have a couch; those with two double beds have an easy chair and game table.

Dining/Entertainment: Two indoor restaurants serve all three meals; one restaurant open evenings features Japanese cuisine. The poolside restaurant is open for breakfast and lunch. A lobby lounge opens at 11am, and 60's Disco Bar is open evenings.

Services: Laundry, room service, travel agency, car rental, beauty salon, barber shop, gift shop, summer children's program (ages 5 to 12) at extra cost, 14 security cameras.

Facilities: Huge oceanside pool, coed gym, five tennis courts (three lighted for night play), volleyball court.

HOTEL ZONE

The main street from town and fronting the hotel zone has recently been renamed Paseo de las Palmas but locals may still refer to it as Avenida de las Garzas, or the airport road—a handy piece of information to keep in mind when reading or hearing addresses.

Fiesta Americana Puerto Vallarta

Av. de las Palmas s/n, Puerto Vallarta, Jal. 48300. ☎ **322/4-2010** or 800/223-2332 in the U.S. 363 rms and suites. A/C MINIBAR TV TEL. High season $230–$300 double superior or deluxe room. Low season $115–$155 double. Free parking.

The Fiesta Americana's enormous thatched palapa lobby is a landmark in hotel row. With lots of plants, splashing fountains, breezes, and sitting areas, the lobby has a casual South-Seas feel to it. The nine-story building embraces a large plaza with pool facing the beach. Marble-trimmed rooms in neutral tones with pastel accents come with pretty, carved headboards and comfortable furniture. All have private balconies with sea views.

Dining/Entertainment: The hotel's three restaurants include two for casual dining and one for fine dining. There's live music nightly in the lobby bar. Friday López is the popular disco, open from 10:30pm to 3am.

Services: Laundry, room service, travel agency, beauty shop.

Facilities: Pool, six tennis courts, tennis privileges at the Fiesta Americana Plaza Vallarta, health club with sauna and massage, pool activities, and children's activities in high season.

✪ Krystal Vallarta

Av. de las Palmas s/n, Puerto Vallarta, Jal. 48300. ☎ **322/4-1041** or 800/231-9860 in the U.S. and Canada. Fax 322/4-0150. 368 rms, suites, and villas. A/C MINIBAR TV TEL. High season $180 deluxe room or double villa; $210–$460 double suite. Low season $130–$190 deluxe room or villa double; $170–$320 suite double.

Built to resemble a Mexican village with cobblestone streets, this completely self-contained resort oasis is spread out over 37 plant- and fountain-filled acres with a prime beachfront location. Interwoven into this setting are the accommodations in one- and two-story buildings. Although the resort is large, it's very quiet, and there is still a sense of seclusion, with many shaded interior walkways linking the various pool areas and restaurants. In fact, with seven restaurants and numerous bars, you can dine and drink without ever leaving the place, should that be your choice. All the guest rooms were completely refurnished and renewed in 1991. The four varieties of accommodations include 38 three-bedroom villas with private pools, 22 suites with spacious living rooms, 48 junior suites, and 251 deluxe rooms. Trios of villas share a private pool. All come with tile floors, area rugs, in-room security boxes, and remote-control TVs with cable channels. Some rooms have a patio or balcony. Electric carts take guests to and from their rooms, for, depending on where your room is, it can be a long walk within the grounds. The hotel is not far from the main pier and airport. City buses stop right in front of the hotel.

Dining/Entertainment: The hotel's has seven restaurants, including Bogart's, one of the finest restaurants in Puerto Vallarta, open evenings. Kamakura, an excellent Japanese restaurant, is also open evenings; another restaurant features steaks. Among the six bars, the lobby bar has live music nightly. For evening entertainment there's Christine's disco, open from 10:30pm to 3am; Le Café in the lobby for special coffees, tea, and pastries. There is a Mexican Fiesta every Tuesday and Saturday.

Services: Laundry, room service, travel agency, shops, babysitting with 12 hours' advance notice, wedding arrangements with advance notice, car rental.

Facilities: Olympic-size pool, 2 free-form pools, 38 private pools, 2 tennis courts, racquetball court.

NORTH OF THE RÍO CUALE

This is the real center of town, where the market, principal plazas, church, and town hall all lie. Budget lodgings are scarce here, although most of the hotels are moderately priced.

Moderate

Hacienda Buenaventura

Paseo de la Palma, Apdo. Postal 95-B, Puerto Vallarta, Jal. 48310. ☎ **322/4-6667** or 800/307-1847 in the U. S. Fax 322/4-6400. 155 rms. A/C TEL. High season $57–$69 double. Low season $36–$44 double. (In low season ask about a free fourth night.)

You can stay right on the hotel strip and skip the high prices at this congenial hotel, which offers a real Mexican colonial atmosphere, inside and out. Hacienda-style rooms have soft colors on stucco walls, alcove-type windows, and are built around tropical gardens that include a functioning aqueduct. The far end of the gigantic pool encircles a large palapa-roofed swim-up bar and the other end fronts the restaurant La Cascada. Although the Hacienda has no beachfront of its own, guests are provided passes for use of the beach and facilities next door at the luxury Krystal Vallarta.

Inexpensive

Hotel Rosita

Ordaz 90. (Apdo. Postal 32), Puerto Vallarta, Jal. 48300. ☎ and fax **322/2-1033.** 103 rms, 9 suites. A/C FAN. $20–$22 double with A/C or poolside; $23–$26 double suite. Discounts Sept., Nov., May, June.

Vacationers have been flocking to the Rosita for decades, both for its ideal location on the beach and for its prices. Rooms, with dated but coordinated furnishings, are well kept. Some are carpeted, and some have tile floors. Those with air-conditioning are on the street side. A palm-shaded pool and restaurant open for all meals are by the beach. The Rosita is nine blocks north of the main plaza at the corner of Diaz Ordaz and 31 de Octubre, opposite McDonald's.

✪ Los Cuatro Vientos

Matamoros 520, Puerto Vallarta, Jal. 48350. ☎ **322/2-0161.** Fàx 322/2-2831. 13 rms (all with bath). FAN. $40 double (including continental breakfast). Low-season discounts.

A quiet, cozy, and secluded inn set on a hillside overlooking Banderas Bay, Los Cuatro Vientos features rooms built around a small central patio and pool. A flight of stairs takes you to the second-floor patio, pool, and the cozy Chez Elena restaurant, which is open evenings. The cheerful, spotless, and differently colored rooms have small tiled baths, brick ceilings, red-tile floors, and glass-louvered windows facing outdoors. Each is decorated with simple Mexican furnishings and accented with local crafts. The whole rooftop, with a panoramic view of the city, is great for sunning, and it's the best place in the city for drinks at sunset. Continental breakfast is served on the terrace for guests only from 8 to 10:30am.

The friendly owner, Gloria Whiting, and the equally helpful manager, Lola Bravo, can offer many suggestions for sightseeing. The hotel is affiliated with the University of Guadalajara's language school in Puerto Vallarta and offers special packages for students attending the school. Also ask about the week-long Women's Getaway offered several times a year. The program includes cultural discussions; exercise classes; hikes; some meals; and optional massages, facials, manicures, and pedicures. From the central plaza, walk two blocks east on Iturbide; turn left at Matamoros and walk up Matamoros (the hill gets very steep) for three blocks; the hotel is on the right just before the corner of Corona.

SOUTH OF THE RÍO CUALE
Moderate

Hotel Fontana del Mar
Dieguez 171, Puerto Vallarta, Jal. 48380. ☎ **322/2-0583** or 2-0712 or 800/221-6509 in the U.S. Fax 322/2-2418. 27 rms, 15 suites (all with bath). A/C MINIBAR TV TEL. High season $38 double. $5–$7 more for suite. Low season $34 double.

One of the best budget hotels in the area, this place is on a quiet street in downtown Vallarta, only two blocks from the Playa del Sol. The inviting decor includes curly white ironwork and royal-blue trim. The clean, comfortable rooms overlook the plant-filled courtyard, with more frilly iron ornamentation. Rooms have showers or bathtubs, and the suites come with balconies or kitchenettes. Guests can use the small rooftop pool or the pool and beach-club facilities at the Hotel Playa Los Arcos, a block away. The Fontana del Mar is eight blocks south of the Vallarta Bridge, near the corner of Olas Altas.

Hotel Molino de Agua
Vallarta 130 (Apdo. Postal 54), Puerto Vallarta, Jal. 48380. ☎ **322/2-1907** or 2-1957 or 800/826-9408 in the U.S., 800/423-5512 in California. Fax 322/2-6056. 12 rms, 4 suites, 25 cabins (all with bath). A/C. High season $65–$100 double. Low season $50–$97 double. Free protected parking.

This complex of cabins and small buildings reached by winding walkways is nestled into lush tropical gardens beside the river and sea; it's half a block south of the river on Vallarta at Serdán. Although the hotel centrally located on a main street, it's a completely tranquil oasis with big trees and open space. Some units are individual bungalows with private patios, and there's a small three-story building near the beach. Amenities include a whirlpool beside the pool and a restaurant/bar, the Aquarena, as well as its offshoot, the Lion's Court, in the garden. The hotel is on the right immediately after you cross the Vallarta Bridge going south.

Inexpensive

Hotel Azteca
Madero 473, Puerto Vallarta, Jal. 48300. ☎ **322/2-2750.** 46 rms (all with bath). FAN. $8 double. Discounts available for stays of a week or more.

This four-story (no elevator) hotel is one of the best buys in town. Many wintering Northerners return to this hotel year after year. Though the rooms are very plain and basically furnished with a bed and crude table and chairs, the Villa Señor family keeps the place clean, well maintained, and safe. No visitors are allowed after 10:30pm. Rooms face the interior walkway and courtyard and are brighter than most hotels with this architectural arrangement. The hotel is 5¹/₂ blocks west of the beach between Jacarandas and Naranjo.

Hotel Yasmin

Badillo 168, Puerto Vallarta, Jal. 48380. ☎ **322/2-0087.** 27 rms (all with bath). FAN. $14 double.

The Yasmin is a great budget choice located only about a block from the beach. The hotel is a neat, hidden retreat with three stories of rooms (no elevator) built around a shady garden courtyard. The freshly painted rooms are clean and come with tile floors, firm beds with nice plaid bedspreads, small baths, and full-length mirrors. The popular Café de Olla is just off the reception/patio area. Noise created by restaurant patrons—and the delightful strolling musicians catering to them—lasts until about 11pm. The hotel is five blocks south of the river on Vallarta between Olas Altas and Pino Suárez.

SOUTH TO MISMALOYA

Camino Real

Hwy. 200 south to Mismaloya, km 3.2. ☎ **322/2-5000** or 800/722-6466. 337 rms and suites. A/C MINIBAR TV TEL. Low season $143–$170 double standard and superior rooms; $215–240 double Camino Real Club.

Not so long ago, the Camino Real, 2¹/₂ miles south of town, was the most remote hotel or establishment of any kind. Though it has neighbors now, down the highway, it's still set apart with a lush mountain backdrop and retains the exclusivity that made it popular from the beginning. The hotel actually consists of two buildings: the 250-room main hotel curving gently with the shape of the Playa Las Estacas and the new 11-story, 87-room Camino Real Club, also on the beach. Rooms in the main building are large, some with sliding doors facing the bay and others with balconies. Royal Beach Club rooms from the sixth floor up have balconies with whirlpool spas. The top floor is divided among six two-bedroom Fiesta Suites with whirlpool spas on the balcony, and each has a private swimming pool. All rooms are accented with the vibrant colors of Mexico and come with remote-control TVs (with U.S. channels) and in-room safe-deposit boxes. Royal Beach Club rooms have robes besides other amenities mentioned below.

Dining/Entertainment: Three restaurants serving Mexican, French, seafood and international food are open for all meals, plus there's a beachside eatery. Live bands frequently entertain evenings in the lobby bar with dancing on weekends.

Services: Laundry; room service; travel agency; car rental; children's program December, June, July, and August.

Facilities: Two swimming pools; two lighted tennis courts; health club with weights, sauna, steam room, and weekday aerobic classes; boutiques, and convenience store. Royal Beach Club guests enjoy separate check-in and concierge, daily complimentary continental breakfast, and evening cocktails and hors d'oeuvres.

Presidente Inter-Continental

Hwy. 200, km 8.5 (Apdo. Postal 448), Puerto Vallarta, Jal. 48300. ☎ **322/8-0507** or 800/ 327-0200. Fax 322/8-0116. 120 suites. A/C MINIBAR TV TEL. High season $195–$220 double; $270–$925 double suite. Low season $185–$210 double; $235–$825 double suite.

On a beautiful beach five miles south of town, this 10-story white hotel (formerly the Hyatt Coral Grand) has window boxes spilling over with vines and bougain-villea. The open-air lobby is accessed from a bridge that connects it to the street four stories above the beach. There's a serene, intimate ambience here, with spacious suites done in white with pastel accents, tasteful art, comfortable furniture, and queen or double beds. Each suite has a living room with a couch that makes into a bed, and small balconies provide a view of the ocean. Deluxe suites have whirlpool baths, king-size beds, and robes. Master suites have two bedrooms and a whirlpool. There are two handicap-equipped rooms on the first floor and wheel-chair access to the pool.

Dining/Entertainment: There are two indoor restaurants, plus a swim-up bar open for lunch and a poolside bar open daylight hours. There's often live enter-tainment in the lobby bar during evening hours.

Services: Laundry, room service, travel agency, concierge, babysitting.

Facilities: One large pool, children's pool, one tennis court lighted at night, table tennis and pool tables, plus other board games, children's game room, water sports, gym with massage service and steam baths.

DINING

Although eating out in Puerto Vallarta has become more expensive, some bargains and good values remain.

HOTEL ZONE

Bogart's

Krystal Vallarta Hotel, Av. de las Garzas s/n. ☎ **322/4-0202.** Full meal $30–$40. Daily 6pm– midnight. CONTINENTAL/ECLECTIC.

Pointed Moorish arches, murmuring fountains, a silky tent ceiling, and high-backed peacock chairs create the mysterious mood of Casablanca in this softly lighted, sumptuous restaurant. A pianist plays in the background while waiters out of *Arabian Nights* serve such delicacies as Persian Crêpes (sour cream, cheese, and caviar), escargots, sorbet between courses, and flambéed Shrimp Krystal. For a big splurge or a special occasion, a dinner in this fantasy place is unforgettable. It's north of town near the main pier; take the "Muelle" bus. Bogart's is on the front of the hotel property, facing the main boulevard.

NORTH OF THE RÍO CUALE

Expensive

Café des Artistes

Guadalupe Sánchez 740. ☎ **322/2-3228.** Main courses $12–$25. Daily 7–11pm. INTERNA-TIONAL.

The Café des Artistes, located at the corner of Vicario three blocks from the malecón, is slightly off the beaten path—it's easy to miss this charming indoor/ outdoor eatery. Opened in 1990, it's a sophisticated little place with lots of light, a black-and-white decor, and an interesting menu. Among the appetizers you'll find crêpes, quiche, chilled cream of prawns, and pumpkin soup. The seafood menu is extensive and includes sautéed shrimp with mushroom and chile guajillo salsa served with pasta. There's an interesting spring chicken flambé, stuffed with prunes and dates. It's worth a trip just to read the menu. The unusual combinations are enough to make you order something even if you're not hungry.

Chef Roger

A. Rodriguez 267. ☎ **322/2-5900.** Reservations recommended. Main courses $7–$15. Daily 6:30–11pm. NOUVELLE MEXICAN/SWISS.

This sophisticated little dinner-only restaurant has developed quite a following since it opened in 1989, a success that owes something to owner Roger Dreir's prior reputation as a caterer in the city. A European-trained chef, he's combined elements of the cuisines of Europe, the American Southwest, and Mexico and created a highly personal style of cooking. Guests enjoy their meals on the patio or in one of the adjoining half open-air dining rooms. There are five or six daily specials using whatever is fresh; these might include steaks and lobster and such interesting combinations as pasta with crêpes huitlacoche. The restaurant is catercorner from the craft market between Matamoros and Hidalgo.

Inexpensive

✪ Café San Cristóbal

Corona 172. ☎ **322/3-2551.** Coffee $1–$2; pastries 65¢–$1.25; sandwiches $3; kilo of fresh-ground coffee $7. Daily 8am–9pm. COFFEE/PASTRIES/SANDWICHES.

This comfortable cafe is a great spot for coffee, pastries, sandwiches, and conversation. The brew, which features Mexican coffees from the states of Veracruz, Nayarit, and Chiapas, comes most any way imaginable—over ice, hot, or with milk. You can also get latte, cappuccino, or espresso, and there's Mexican chocolate as well. There are fresh cheese and pâté, quiche, bread, cheese and fruit plates, lemonade, and liquados. The cream cheese, cucumber, tomato, and bean sprout sandwich on fresh homemade bread is delicious. Bags of whole or ground coffee are sold by the half or full kilo. This cafe is three blocks north of the main plaza between Morelos and Juárez.

✪ Papaya 3

Abasolo 169. ☎ **322/2-0303.** Breakfast $2–$2.75; soups, salads, and sandwiches $2.50–$3.50; main courses $3.50–$5.35. Mon–Sat 8am–10pm. VEGETARIAN.

Opened in 1991, this fine, small restaurant serves innovative and delicious meals. Juice and fruit drinks include such tropical shakes as the Cancún—a blend of guayaba, coconut, melon milk, or rompope. Yogurt shakes come with fruit. The Shanghai salad is a large plate of steamed vegetables. Pastas are topped with imaginative sauces, and many entrees feature chicken or fish. Papaya 3 is north of the river between Morelos and Juárez.

Tutifruti

Morelos 552. ☎ **322/2-1068.** Breakfast $2.75–$3.25; cinnamon coffee 65¢; fresh juices or licuados $1.35–$1.75; sandwiches $1.50–$2.50. Mon–Sat 8am–10pm. VEGETARIAN/AMERICAN.

This small, clean corner eatery is a good spot for a quick snack on stools that pull up to three narrow counters. The menu includes hot or cold sandwiches and hamburgers with all the trimmings, as well as fruit plates and yogurt. Eat at the counter or take your meal out. To get here from the main plaza, walk four blocks north on Morelos; it's on the right corner at Corona.

SOUTH OF THE RÍO CUALE

South of the river is the most condensed restaurant area. Here, you can find places in all price categories. Some restaurants now close during the low season. You can purchase inexpensive fruit, vegetables, and picnic fixings at the **municipal market,** beside the Río Cuale where Libertad and Rodríguez meet. The **Supermercado Gutierrez Ruiz,** Serdán and Constitución, has an especially large bakery and cold cut and cheese selection, as does **Gigante,** on the northern hotel strip fronting Avenida de las Palmas.

Expensive

Le Bistro Jazz Café

Río Cuale. ☎ **322/2-0283.** Breakfast $3–$7.50; main courses $6–$9; wine and mixed drinks $2.50–$7. Mon–Sat 9am–11pm. INTERNATIONAL.

Of all Puerto Vallarta's restaurants, this is the best at combining good food, a serene and sophisticated environment, attentive service, and entertainment. The black-and-white dining area spreads out on decks overlooking the river. The cozy bar, with couches and sitting areas, is also outdoors. At breakfast, the appealing menu includes omelets, crêpes, and eggs Benedict. Lunch, light and casual, features sandwiches as well as chicken and steak. The evening menu has both Mexican and international offerings, mostly fish, seafood, and steaks. Many varieties of coffee are available. A great collection of recorded jazz plays in the background all day. The bistro is below the Insurgentes bridge on the left if you're arriving from the main plaza.

✪ Restaurant Argentino Los Pibes

Badillo 261. ☎ **322/2-1507.** Grilled meat $10–$15; pasta $5–$6. Daily 6pm–midnight. ARGENTINIAN GRILLED MEAT.

The food is so authentic and delicious here you may later dream of your meal, and you certainly won't forget it. Argentinian Cristina Juhas, along with her *pibes* (kids)— daughter Vanina and son Nicolás (the chef)—opened this restaurant in 1994. You select your meat cut from a tray of fresh meat (portions are huge). While it's being prepared, you can try one of the wonderful empanadas filled with meat, corn, or ham and cheese or savor an order of alubias, which are marinated beans eaten with bread. The homemade sausage is delicious, and you won't find better chimchuri sauce anywhere. In addition to beef, there are baby pig, lamb, and chicken fixed several Italian ways. Try the crêpes Los Pibes (cooked with apples and orange liqueur) for dessert. This slice of Argentina is 5$^{1}/_{2}$ blocks south of the Vallarta bridge between Vallarta and Constitución.

Moderate

Café Adobe

Badillo 283. ☎ **322/2-6720.** Main courses $7–$13. Wed–Mon 6–11pm. Closed Aug–Sept. INTERNATIONAL.

The Café Adobe is casually chic with a trendy southwestern flair. Waiters wearing jeans and chambray shirts serve imaginative food, including "Adobe-style" fettuccine with shrimp and pesto, red snapper with a mango hollandaise sauce, and chicken with chipotle chiles—to name just a few specialties. Owner Rudolfo

Choperena is almost always on hand, which accounts for the consistently fine food and service. Café Adobe is located at the corner of Badillo and Vallarta opposite the Restaurant Argentino Los Pibes.

Puerto Nuevo

Badillo 284. ☎ **322/2-6210.** Main courses $7–$11. Daily 12:30–11pm. MEXICAN/SEA-FOOD.

Owner and chef Roberto Castellon presents seafood with inventive flair. Try the crab enchiladas, shrimp with lobster sauce, or smoked marlin. Salads are particularly fresh and delicious, with house vinaigrette dressing. The selection of after-dinner coffees could serve as dessert. Dine inside or in the roofed, open-air sidewalk area hung with plants for a jungly effect. You'll find it five blocks south of the river off Vallarta, one-half block left on Badillo.

Inexpensive

Café de Olla

Badillo 168. ☎ **322/3-1626.** Main courses $2.50–$5.75. High season Tues–Sun 10am–11pm. Low season Tues–Sun noon–11pm. MEXICAN.

This small, inviting place gets high marks from both locals and tourists. It's almost always full in the evening. You'll find large portions of New York steak, fish and shrimp, American-style barbecue ribs and chicken, Oaxaca-style tamales, and a great Plato Mexicana. It's six blocks south of the Vallarta bridge near the corner of Olas Altas.

✪ El Dorado

Pulpito 102. ☎ **322/2-1511.** Breakfast $2.50–$6; main courses $3–$8; salad or sandwiches $3–$6. Daily 8am–9pm. MEXICAN.

This open-air palapa-roofed restaurant on the beach is a decades-old local favorite, especially for a hearty breakfast by the sea. Try the huevos motuleños—Yucatan-style eggs on tortillas with black beans, cheese, and tangy salsa. In the late afternoon, sip a cool drink as you watch the surfers and parasailors. Seafood is another specialty here, and iced tea is always available. To get here, walk nine blocks south of the river on Vallarta, then turn right onto Pulpito to its end at the beach.

✪ Memo's La Casa de Hotcakes (The Pancake House)

Badillo 289. ☎ **322/2-6272.** Breakfast $2.50–$5. Low season, daily 8am–2pm. AMERICAN/MEXICAN/BREAKFAST.

Owner Memo Barroso hosts the village's best, most popular breakfast eatery, where patrons receive true value and good food. The menu, while definitely not limited to pancakes, features mouth-watering pancakes and waffles imaginatively mixed with apples, caramel, raisins, granola, chocolate, nuts, and even peanut butter. You can also enjoy great eggs Benedict, eggs Florentine, cheese blintzes, breakfast burritos, and huge omelets. Egg dishes come with delicious hash browns. There's a wide assortment of healthy dishes, including fruit, yogurt, granola, whole-wheat pancakes, and waffles and egg dishes made with egg whites. The coffee keeps coming, but you only pay for it once. Memo's is six blocks south of the Vallarta bridge between I. Vallarta and Constitución.

✪ Pie in the Sky Bakery

Badillo 278. ☎ **322/2-5099.** $1.75–$25. Mon–Fri 9am–9pm, Sat–Sun 10:30am–8:30pm. PASTRIES.

This is a good place to have dessert after a meal on Badillo or to pick up some scrumptious goodies to nibble on in your room. Owners Don and Teri Murray turn out *besos* (kisses)—out-of-this-world confections that are crosses between brownies and muffins—and a variety of cheesecake, carrot cake, chocolate cake, almond cake, and mint cream tarts. There are two tables where you can eat while sipping Italian dark roast coffee. This location is six blocks south of the river, on Badillo's "restaurant row" between Constitución and Vallarta. There are two other locations—one in the Villa Vallarta shopping center, by the Continental Plaza Hotel, and one north of town at the entrance to Bucerías, with a big sign on the right side of the highway.

JUNGLE RESTAURANTS

One of the unique attractions of Puerto Vallarta is its "jungle restaurants," located to the south, toward Mismaloya. Each offers open-air dining in a magnificent tropical setting by the sea or beside a mountain river. Determine the distance from town by the kilometer in the address. For minivan transportation see "Getting Around" in Chapter 3.

Chino's Paraiso

Hwy. 200, km 6.5. ☎ **322/3-0102.** Main courses $12–$30. Daily noon–5pm. GRILLED SEAFOOD/STEAK.

Tucked into some rock formations, this shady, cool jungle restaurant offers five open-air terraces overlooking a green river flanked by giant boulders under grand palapas. Guests often take a dip in the swimming holes and waterfalls before or after eating. Marimbas usually play from 1 to 3pm. To get there take a cab or minivan as far as the entrance to La Jolla de Mismaloya Resort, then hike or hire a taxi about a mile on the dirt road on the landward side of the highway, you'll see the road and Chino's sign opposite La Jolla Resort.

El Edén

Off Hwy. 200, km 6.5. No phone. Main courses $15–$30. Daily 11am–6pm. GRILLED SEAFOOD/STEAK/CHICKEN.

With just enough jungle cleared in this luxuriant spot beside a clear river to set up movie cameras, a crew shot scenes here for *The Predator,* starring Arnold Schwarzenegger. Then the set became a restaurant. Guests can dine while watching other guests dropping into the inviting green river Tarzan-style from a rope swing. It's three miles off the highway on the mountain side farther on the same road to Chino's Paraiso(see above). There's a small fee to stay without eating. It has no phone, so check first with a travel agent or at the tourist office to confirm it is open.

PUERTO VALLARTA AFTER DARK

Wander down the malecón after dark, and you'll hear music pouring out from a dozen inviting restaurant/bars with their windows open to the sea.

RESTAURANT/BARS

Ándale

Olas Altas, 425 at A. Rodriguez. ☎ **322/2-1054.**

South of the river, Ándale can be one of the wildest watering holes in town for all ages. The restaurant upstairs is a bit quieter, with tables overlooking the street. Margaritas cost $1.75, and beer is $2. It's open daily from 10am to 4am or later.

Carlos O'Brian's

Paseo Díaz Ordaz 786 (the Malecón), at Pipila. ☎ **322/2-1444** or 2-0356.

Eager patrons form a long line out front in the evening as they wait to join the party inside. Late at night, the scene resembles a rowdy college party. During the day, this place serves just good food. Drinks run $2 to $5. It's open daily from 11am to 2am. Happy hour is from 6 to 8pm.

Roxy's Music Bar & Coffee House

Vallarta 217. ☎ **322/3-2404.** No cover.

Settle in here for live rhythm and blues between 10pm and 1am and for happy hour between 6 and 9pm, when the drinks are two for the price of one. It's south of the river between Madero and Cárdenas. Hours are Monday through Saturday from 6pm to 1am.

Mariachi Loco

Cárdenas at Vallarta. ☎ **322/3-2205.** Cover $2.

Musicians start warming up in the early evening, but around 10pm, it really gets going with rancho music. At 11pm the mariachi show begins, with 10 vibrant mariachis. Afterward, the mariachis stroll and play as guests join in impromptu singing. After midnight the mariachis play for pay, which is around $8.50 for each song. There are a set-price meal and an a la carte menu, plus lots of drinks. It's open daily from 3pm to 2am. Food is served from 3pm to 10pm, and music is continuous from 10pm to 2am.

Mogambo

Paseo Díaz Ordaz 644 (the malecón). ☎ **322/2-3476.** No cover.

Live jazz lures in passersby to sit beneath the crocodiles and other stuffed creatures on the walls of this African-theme bar/restaurant, which looks across the street to the ocean. Drinks are $2.50 and up; specialty coffee is $3.50. It's open daily from 8am to 2am, with live jazz nightly from 9pm to 2am.

Restaurant/Bar Zapata

Upstairs at Paseo Díaz Ordaz 522 (the malecón). ☎ **322/2-4748.** No cover.

Photographs and memorabilia from the Mexican Revolution surround you as you listen to live South American music at this restaurant/bar. National (as opposed to imported) drinks cost $2.50 and up. It's open from noon to midnight, with music until midnight. Happy hour runs from noon to midnight.

SPORTS BARS & DISCOS

The discos in Puerto Vallarta are loud and expensive but a lot of fun. Admission is $4 to $16, and you'll generally pay $3 for a margarita, $2 for a beer, more for a whiskey and mixed drinks. Keep an eye out for the free disco passes that are frequently available in hotels, restaurants, and other tourist spots. Most discos are open from 10pm to 4am.

The malecón now has competition for the after-dark crowd. The new hip area, the south side of old Puerto Vallarta, contains parts of Vallarta, Cárdenas, Carranza, and Badillo. Some of the newer places heavily frequented by tourists are **La Esquina** (the Corner), Vallarta and Cárdenas, for televised sports, drinks, and fun; and **Diva Disco,** on Vallarta, where Friday night is ladies night.

Cristine

In the Krystal Vallarta Hotel, Av. de las Palmas, north of downtown off the airport road. ☎ **322/2-1459.** Cover $10.

The interior of this place is a cross between an octagonal jewelbox and a turn-of-the-century gazebo.—When the opening light show starts, however, the stage fogs up, lights swing down and start flashing, and suddenly you're enveloped in booming classical music like you've never heard before. After the show, video screens and disco sounds take over. Drinks go for $2.50 to $7. The disco is open nightly from 10pm to 4am; the opening light show begins at 11pm. *Note:* No shorts (for men), tennis shoes, or thongs.

Friday Lopez

In the Hotel Fiesta Americana Puerto Vallarta, north of downtown off Av. de las Palmas. ☎ **322/4-2010.** Cover $5; women free on Wed.

Live bands keep everyone hopping in this festive nightspot. Classic rock-and-roll is the music of choice. Drinks run $2.50 to $6. This place is open nightly from 10pm to 4am.

MEXICAN FIESTAS & HOTEL EVENTS

La Iguana

Cárdenas 311, between Constitución and Insurgentes. ☎ **322/2-0105.** Cover $20 per person.

La Iguana offers an evening of entertainment that includes an open bar and an all-you-can-eat buffet. The eclectic show features Mexican folkloric dancing, mariachis, rope-twirling, piñatas, fireworks, and music for dancing. The show goes on Thursday and Sunday from 7 to 11pm.

Krystal Vallarta Hotel

Av. de las Garzas, north of downtown off the airport road. ☎ **322/2-1459.** Cover $30.

Mexican fiestas are held just about every night at major hotels around town and generally include a Mexican buffet, open bar, and live music and entertainment. Shows are usually held outdoors but move indoors when necessary. One of the best is hosted by the Krystal Vallarta on Tuesday and Saturday at 7pm.

EXCURSIONS FROM PUERTO VALLARTA
PLAYA YELAPA

To visit a cove out of a tropical fantasy, you only have to take two-hour trip by boat down the coast. Go to the town marina and catch the 9am boat, the *Serape*, to Yelapa for $15–$20 round trip; the return is at around 4pm. The fare includes two drinks on board, but you need to bring your own lunch or buy it in Yelapa. Several other boats and cruises go to Yelapa and include lunch and open bar for $40–$50. Travel agencies can provide tickets and information, but get reservations two or three days in advance in high season.

Once you're in Yelapa, you can lie in the sun, swim, and eat fresh grilled crayfish or seafood at a restaurant right on the beach. You can also have your picture taken with an iguana (for $1 a shot!), let local "guides" take you on a tour of the town or up the river to see the waterfall, and hike up to visit Rita Tillet's crafts shop on the edge of the mountain. *Note:* If you use a local guide, agree on a price before you start out!

For inexpensive accommodations, ask around to see if residents are renting rooms.

BUCERÍAS: A QUIET COASTAL VILLAGE

Only 11 miles north from the Puerto Vallarta airport, Bucerías (pronounced Boo-sah-REE-ahs) is a small coastal fishing village of 8,000 people in Nayarit state on

Banderas Bay. It's beginning to catch on as an inexpensive alternative to Puerto Vallarta.

Before you reach the town center in Bucerías, turn left when you see all the cook stands. You'll see cobblestone streets leading from the highway to the beach and hints of the villas and town homes behind high walls. Bucerías has already been discovered by second-home owners and by about 1,000 transplanted Americans as a peaceful getaway; casual tourists are beginning to discover its relaxed pace as well.

To get here from Puerto Vallarta, take a minivan or city bus to the stop opposite the entrance to the airport; then catch a minivan marked BUCERÍAS (they run from 6am to midnight and cost $1.15 one way).The last stop is Bucería's town square, where it departs for the return to Puerto Vallarta.

Exploring Bucerías

Come here for a day-trip from Puerto Vallarta just to enjoy the uncrowded beach and good seafood at the restaurants on the beach. If you are inclined to stay a few days, you can relax inexpensively and explore more of Bucerías while staking out an appealing place for a return trip. Sunday is street-market day, but it doesn't get going until around noon, in keeping with Bucería's casual pace.

Accommodations

Several small hotels and condominiums rent rooms here. Listed below is an inn where you can get situated while you poke around in search of a place that suits you. **Los Pericos Travel** in Bucerías (☎ 329/8-0601 or 8-0061; fax 329/8-0601) will book accommodations, including villas, houses, and condos. Call ahead or ask in Bucerías for directions to their office, open Monday through Friday from 9am to 2pm and 4 to 7pm and Saturday from 9am to 2pm.

Posada Olas Altas

Calle Héroes de Nacozari s/n, Bucerías, Nay. 63732. ☎ **329/8-0407.** 22 rms (all with bath). FAN. $12 two beds; $18 king–size bed. Free parking on the street.

Fronting the highway and just down (left) from the cook shops, this is the ideal inexpensive place to stay while getting to know the area. Owners Arnulfo Sánchez and his wife Rosalina Ortega have created cheery and clean rooms with scored concrete floors and blue-iron doors and window frames. Bathrooms have doors and walls but no ceiling separating them from the rest of the room. Most rooms have a single and double bed or two doubles, and one room on the roof has both a king-size bed and a double bed. There's no hot water unless you ask for it (the room price is the same with or without it). A fine inexpensive lobby restaurant is open Monday through Saturday from 7am to 7pm and Sunday from 7am to 2pm.

Dining

In addition to the seafood restaurants near the town square and the beach, there are inexpensive outdoor kitchens on the street fronting the highway that serve delicious grilled chicken marinated in orange juice.

Adriano's

Av. Pacífico 2. ☎ **329/8-0088.** Breakfast $2.25–$3.75; seafood $6–$10; beer 85¢. Daily 8am–11pm. SEAFOOD.

Just off Bucerías's main square (on the far left) on the beach, Adriano's is an inviting place to eat while spending the day on the beach. (They have a shower and bathroom just for their beach clientele). The extensive menu includes french toast and shrimp omelets at breakfast, seafood, and nachos. Though large, this restaurant isn't on the bus tour route, so you won't be abandoned in favor of a busload of foreign tourists.

Mark's

Lázaro Cárdenas 56. ☎ **329/8-0303.** Pasta $6–$7; other main courses $7; nightly specials $8–$10. Wed–Mon 5:30–11pm. PASTA/STEAK/SEAFOOD

It's worth a special trip to Bucerías just to eat at this evening-only covered-patio restaurant. The most popular American hangout, Mark's offers a great assortment of whole-wheat pizzas seasoned with fresh herbs grown in the garden. In fact, everything from the shrimp in angel-hair pasta to the shrimp cakes to the delicious Caesar salad has a wonderfully fresh taste. Mark's is only a half a block from the beach, so you can take a dip before dining. The restaurant has a boutique and live music some evenings.

From the highway, turn left just after the bridge where there's a small sign for Mark's. Then double back left at the next street (it's immediately after you turn left) and turn right at the next corner. Follow that street almost to the end, where you'll see the ocean ahead and Mark's on the right.

SAN BLAS: FOR BIRDWATCHERS & SURFERS

San Blas is a rather ugly Pacific coast fishing village of 10,000 people in Nayarit State. Upon your arrival, the dirt streets and ragtag central square will make you wonder "Is this it?" The uninviting wide beaches with hard-packed, thick-grained, grayish-colored sand sport few palm trees. At night, especially during the rainy season, the whole town is infested with "no-see-ums" that require an armor of insect repellent to ward off. Were it not for its reputation as a birders' mecca and surfers' delight, the town would likely languish as an undesirable outpost. Still, most of the year it attracts an assortment of tourists, some of whom are looking for an inexpensive retreat on this increasingly expensive coast and others who come just to see the birds or to surf. The few hotels are often full, especially on major Mexican holidays.

Essentials

Transportes Norte de Sonora buses from Puerto Vallarta take the short route, but be sure to specify which route you want since the long route through Tepic takes five hours. As an alternative, you can take a **Pacífico bus** to Las Varas and change buses to San Blas; there may, however, be a wait—try to get to Las Varas before noon.

Only 150 miles from Puerto Vallarta, San Blas is an easy 3¹/₂-hour trip, now that the new non-toll highway bypasses Tepic. This new two-lane paved highway, which starts at Las Varas off Highway 200 (a sign announces Las Varas), goes through the villages of Santa Cruz and Aticama before connecting with the two-lane highway into San Blas. Signs are few, so if you're driving, keep asking directions.

As you enter the village, you'll be on **Avenida Juárez,** the principal street, which leads to the main plaza on the right. At its far end sits the old church, with a new church next to it. Across the street from the church is the bus station, and on the other side of the churches is the *mercado* (market). After you pass the square, the first one-way street to your left is **Batallón,** an important street that passes a bakery, a medical clinic, several hotels, and Los Cocos Trailer Park and ends up at **Borrego Beach,** with its many outdoor fish restaurants. Nearly everything is within walking distance, and there are public buses that go to the farther beaches—Matanchen and Los Cocos—on their way to Santa Cruz, the next village to the south.

The **Tourist Office,** next door to McDonald's restaurant on Avenida Juárez, is open Monday through Friday from 9am to 3pm.

As for the **climate**, October is the wettest month of the rainy season, which runs from May through October and witnesses the worst of the "no-see-um" attacks. Summer is hot and steamy.

Exploring San Blas

After you've walked around the town and taken the river cruise, there's not a lot to do besides relax, swim, read, walk the beach, and eat fish—unless you're a serious birdwatcher or surfer. During the winter, however, you can also look for **whales** off the coast of San Blas.

PORT OF SAN BLAS   Like Acapulco, San Blas was once a very important port for New Spain's trade with the Philippines, and the town was fortified against pirates. Ruins of the fortifications, complete with cannons, the old church, and houses all overgrown with jungle, are still visible atop the hill **La Contadura.** The fort settlement was destroyed during the struggle for independence in 1811 and has been in ruins ever since. Also, it was from San Blas that Fr. Junípero Serra set out to establish missions in California in the 18th century.

The view from La Contadura is definitely worth the trouble to get there. The entire surrounding area stretches out before you, a panorama of coconut plantations, coastline, town, and lighthouse at Playa del Rey. To reach the ruins from San Blas, head east on Avenida Juárez about half a mile, as if going out of town. Just before the bridge, take the stone path that winds up the hill to your right.

BEACHES & WATER SPORTS   One of the closest beaches is **Borrego Beach,** south from the town plaza on Batallón until it ends. This is a gray sand beach edged with palapa restaurants selling fish. For a more secluded place to swim, pay a fisherman to take you across Estuary El Pozo at the southwest edge of town to the "island," actually **El Rey Beach.** Walk to the other side of the island and you might have it all to yourself, or try the beach on the other side of the lighthouse on this island. Bring your own shade, as there are no trees. The fisherman "ferry" charges about $1 one way and operates from 6am to 6pm. Canoes and small boats can also be rented at the harbor on the west side of town, following Avenida Juárez.

About three miles south of San Blas is **Matanchen Bay.** If you're driving, head out Avenida Juárez toward Tepic, cross the bridge, and turn right at the sign to Matanchen. A bus also stops there on its way south to the village of Santa Cruz; it departs from the bus station on the main square at 9 and 11am and 3 and 5pm. Check on the return stops at Matanchen Bay, which are generally an hour later. There's a little settlement here where you can have a snack or a meal or rent a boat and guide for the jungle-river cruise.

Half a mile past the settlement is a dirt road to **Las Islitas Beach,** a magnificent swath of sand stretching for miles with a few beach-shack eateries. This is a famous surfing beach with mile-long waves, and real and would-be surfing champions come from Mexico and the United States to test their mettle here, especially during September and October, when storms create the biggest waves. If you don't have a surfboard, you can usually rent one from one of the local surfers. The bodysurfing at Islitas and Matanchen is good, too. A taxi to Islitas will cost about $6 from downtown San Blas.

Farther south from Matanchen is beautiful **Playa Los Cocos,** lined with coconut palms. It's also on the bus route to Santa Cruz, but double-check on stops and schedules before boarding in San Blas.

JUNGLE CRUISE TO TOVARA SPRINGS   Almost the moment you hit San Blas, you'll be approached by a "guide" who offers "a boat ride into the jungle." This is one of Mexico's unique tropical experiences, and to make the most of it, find a guide who will leave at 6:30 or 7am. The first boat on the river encounters the most birds, and the Tovara River is like glass early in the morning, unruffled by breezes. Around 9am the boatloads of tour groups start arriving, and the serenity evaporates like the morning mist.

The cost is about $40 for a boatload of one to four people for the three- to four-hour trip from the bridge at the edge of town on Juárez. It's less (about $30) for the shorter, two-hour trip from the embarcadero near Matanchen Bay, out of town. Either way, you won't regret taking the early-morning cruise through shady mangrove mazes and tunnels past tropical birds and cane fields to the beautiful natural springs, La Tovara, where you can swim. There's a restaurant here, too, but stick to soft drinks or beer.

Note: The guide may also offer to take you to "The Plantation," which refers to pineapple and banana plantations on a hill outside of town. The additional cost of this trip is not worth it for most people.

BIRDWATCHING   Birding is best from mid-October to April. As many as 300 species of birds have been sighted here, one of the highest counts in the Western Hemisphere. Birders and hikers should go to the Hotel Las Brisas Resort in San Blas (see "Accommodations," below) to buy a copy of the booklet *Where to Find Birds in San Blas, Nayarit,* by Rosalind Novick and Lan Sing Wu. With maps and directions, it details all the best birding spots and walks, including hikes to some lovely waterfalls where you can swim. Ask the staff at Las Brisas Motel (☎ 321/5-0307 or 5-0558) which bilingual guide they currently recommend, and they'll put you in touch with this person. A day's tour will cost around $100, which can be divided among the participants.

Accommodations

Hotel Las Brisas Resort

Calle Paredes Sur s/n, San Blas, Nay. 63740. ☎ **321/5-0480** or 5-0307. Fax 321/5-0308 or 5-0112. 42 units, 5 minisuites. A/C FAN TV. $70 double; $80 suite (including breakfast). Free parking.

A block inland from the waterfront and nestled among pretty gardens of palms, hibiscus, and other tropical plants are the cottagelike fourplexes and other buildings of this oasislike resort. You'll find a tranquil ambience, two pools (one for toddlers), and one of the best restaurant/bars in town—just a few of the details that make this the nicest place to stay in San Blas. Rooms are modern, bright, airy, and immaculate, with well-screened windows and fans and air-conditioning. Several rooms have a kitchen and come with king-size beds; otherwise, most have two double beds, and a few have an extra single bed. Each room has an in-room safety deposit box. The manager, María Josefina Vazquez, is one of the most knowledgeable and helpful people I've met on the Pacific coast.

To get here, walk south from the square on Batallón about six blocks, turn right on Campeche across from the Marino Inn, then turn left on the next street, Paredes Sur.

Hotel Los Bucaneros

Av. Juárez 75 Pte., San Blas, Nay. 63740. ☎ **321/5-0101.** 33 rms (all with bath). FAN. $20 double.

A six-foot-long stuffed crocodile smiles with open jaws at visitors in the lobby of this hotel. The neat and freshly painted rooms are arranged around a courtyard, and guests enjoy the pool and patio. The hotel is on the main street one block west of the town plaza.

Motel Posada Del Rey

Calle Campeche 10, San Blas, Nay. 63740. ☎ **321/5-0123.** 12 rms (all with bath). FAN. $22 double.

Rooms at the Posada del Rey are arranged around a tiny courtyard entirely taken up by a little pool; six rooms have air-conditioning. An open-air bar on the third floor provides a lovely view of the ocean and palms. The motel is one block inland from the waterfront at El Pozo Estuary, five blocks south of the town plaza. Turn right at the Marino Inn, and you'll find the hotel straight ahead two blocks on the right.

Dining

For an inexpensive meal, in high season on or on weekends, try fresh grilled fish from one of the little shacks on the beach. The prices are the same at all these places. From town, take Avenida Batallón south from he plaza—follow your nose when you smell the fish being grilled. There are several restaurants near the main plaza.

✪ Restaurant El Delfín

In the Hotel Las Brisas Resort, Calle Paredes Sur s/n. ☎ **321/5-0112.** Main courses $6–$13. Daily 8am–9:30pm. INTERNATIONAL.

This hotel restaurant serves the best food in San Blas in a beautiful air-conditioned dining room with marble floors and a pink-and-green decor. Soft light, soft music, and comfortable captain's chairs add to the serene ambience. The chef masterfully draws from a wide repertoire of sauces. Try the exquisite shrimp or chicken with creamy chipotle pepper sauce. The spaghetti dishes include seafood marinara and spaghetti Alfredo with seafood. The homemade soups and desserts also deserve encores.

3 Manzanillo

160 miles S of Puerto Vallarta, 167 SW of Guadalajara, 40 miles S of Barra de Navidad

Outsiders think of Manzanillo, Colima State, as a resort community, but this city of 90,000 is today Mexico's foremost Pacific port. Sea traffic, as well as fishing and iron-ore mining, generate more income than the tourist business. Manzanillo remains one of the Pacific coast's hidden retreats; it lacks major air links and is over 150 miles from both Puerto Vallarta and Guadalajara. Tourists don't come in droves, as they do to those cities.

Manzanillo first began to attract foreigners seeking relief from north-of-the-border winters in the 1970s; condominiums were built on hillsides and on the beaches. Today, lots of their little private enclaves on some of the most prime bay property are strung out for more than 20 miles from town center toward the airport. There are few hotels relative to private dwellings and to other Mexican resort cities, and the hotels are just as scattered as the condominiums.

Manzanillo still isn't much to look at; its town center faces the port and railroad tracks, and outlying roadways are veiled in a swirl of dust. Recently the city has begun a long-overdue program to beautify itself, widening and resurfacing its streets and planting palms and flowers in the center medians. The deficiencies in the appearance of the town and its main boulevards are compensated for by the beauty of the bays, the excellent climate, the few good beaches, and the town's relaxing pace. Manzanillo has a delightfully laid-back ambience as well as some very good restaurants, and it's the ideal point from which to launch further explorations north to the coastal villages of Barra de Navidad and Melaque and inland to Colima, the state capital.

ESSENTIALS

GETTING THERE & DEPARTING   By Plane   The airport is 45 minutes northwest of town at Playa de Oro. The colectivo airport service, **Transportes Terrestres** (☎ 4-1555), picks up passengers at hotels. Call a day ahead for reservations. One way, the cost is $7–$11; by taxi it costs $20. **Aeroméxico** (at the airport, ☎ 333/3-2424) and **Mexicana** (at the airport, ☎ 333/3-2323) offer flights to and from Mexico City and Guadalajara. There are connecting flights several times a week from Monterrey, and a few from cold weather cities in the U.S. and Canada. Ask a travel agent about the numerous charters that operate in winter from the States.

By Bus   Manzanillo's Central Camionera (bus station) is about 12 long blocks east of town. If you follow Hidalgo east, the Camionera will be on your right. **Autotransportes Colima** (also known as Los Altos; no phone) goes to Colima every 30 minutes. On a Directo the trip takes 1 1/2 hours with two stops. An Ordinario leaves every 15 minutes and takes two hours, stopping frequently. Both types of bus drop off passengers within two blocks of Colima's main square rather than Colima's outlying Central Camionera. To Barra de Navidad (1 1/2 hours north) and to Puerto Vallarta (five hours north) the company with the most frequent service is **Auto Camiones de Pacífico** and **Cihuatlan** (☎ 2-0515). It offers deluxe service (de paso), which they call "Primera Plus" (not to be confused with a line by the same name) six times a day and 10 daily second-class buses. **La Línea** (☎ 2-0123) has Plus (first-class) service to Colima (1 1/2 hours) and Guadalajara (4 1/2 hours) seven times daily. **Servicios Coordinados** (☎ 2-0210) has frequent first-class buses to Guadalajara. **Primera Plus** (☎ 2-0210) has deluxe buses with video movies and air-conditioning hourly to Guadalajara and Puerto Vallarta.

By Car   Coastal Highway 200 leads from Acapulco and Puerto Vallarta. From Guadalajara, take Highway 54 through Colima (outside Colima you can switch to a toll road, which is faster but less scenic, into Manzanillo).

Motorists' advisory: Motorists planning to follow Highway 200 south from Manzanillo toward Lázaro Cárdenas and Ixtapa should be aware of recent reports of random car and motorist hijackings on that route, especially around Playa Azul. Before heading in that direction, ask locals and the tourism office about the current state of affairs.

ORIENTATION   Arriving   Manzanillo's **Central Camionera** (bus station) is about 12 long blocks east of town. Here you can buy a sandwich, send a fax, make a long-distance call, or store luggage (look for the *guarda equipaje*). Taxis to town line up out front and cost around $6 to the town center.

Information   The **tourism office** (☎ 3-2277 or 3-2264) in Manzanillo is on the Costera Miguel de la Madrid 4960, km 8.5. It's open Monday through Friday from 9am to 3:30pm.

City Layout   The town is at the end of a seven-mile-long beach, **Playa Azul,** whose northern terminus is the **Santiago Peninsula.** Santiago is seven miles from downtown; it's the site of many beautiful homes and the best hotel in the area, Las Hadas. There are two lagoons; one, **Laguna de Cuyutlán,** is almost behind the city, and the other, **Laguna de San Pedrito,** lurks behind the beach. Both are good sites for birdwatching. There are also two bays. **Manzanillo Bay** encompasses the harbor, town, and beaches; it's separated by the Santiago Peninsula from the second bay—**Santiago.**

Downtown activity centers around the **plaza,** officially known as the Jardín Alvaro Obregón, which is separated from the waterfront by railroad and shipyards. The plaza has a brilliant poinciana tree with red blossoms, a fountain, kiosk, and a view of the bay. Large ships dock at the pier nearby. **Avenida México,** the street leading out from the plaza's central gazebo, is the town's principal commercial thoroughfare. Walking along here you will find a few shops, small eateries, and juice stands.

GETTING AROUND   By Bus   The local buses (*camionetas*) make a circuit from downtown in front of the train station. They go out along the lagoon opposite Playa Azul and then along the Bay of Manzanillo to the Santiago Peninsula and the Bay of Santiago to the north. The main buses are "Las Brisas," which goes to the Las Brisas crossroads then to the Las Brisas Peninsula and back to town; "Miramar," "Santiago," and "Salahua" buses go to outlying settlements along the bays and to most restaurants mentioned below. Buses marked "Las Hadas" go to the peninsula and make a circuit by the Las Hadas resort and the Sierra Manzanillo and Plaza las Glorias hotels. This is an inexpensive way to see the coast as far as Santiago and to take a tour of the Santiago Peninsula.

By Taxi   Taxis in Manzanillo supposedly have fixed rates for trips within town, as well as to more distant points, but they aren't posted; ask your hotel staff what a ride should cost to get a feel for what's right, and then bargain. A taxi from the Central Camionera to the Salahua area costs around $7; a taxi to town center costs about $5.

FAST FACTS: MANZANILLO

American Express   The local representative is Bahías Gemelas Travel Agency, Costera M. Madrid, km 10 (☎ 333/3-1000 or 3-1053; fax 333/3-0649).
Area Code   The telephone area code is 333.
Bank   Banamex downtown is just off the plaza on Avenida México; it's open Monday through Friday from 9:30am to 1:30pm but changes foreign currency only until 12:30pm.

EXPLORING MANZANILLO

Activities in Manzanillo depend on where you stay. Most of the resort hotels here are completely self-contained, and they have restaurants and sports on the premises. This isn't necessarily true of my hotel recommendations, however, since several of them do not have pools and are not on the beach.

BEACHES   La Audiencia Beach, on the way to Santiago, offers the best swimming, but **San Pedrito,** shallow for a long way out, is the most popular because

Manzanillo Area

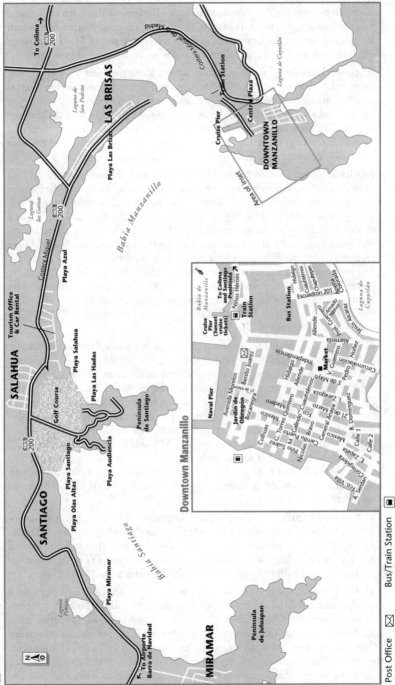

To Colima →
MEX 200

LAS BRISAS

Costera Manuel de Madrid

Laguna de San Pedrito

Playa Las Brisas

Laguna las Garzas

MEX 200

Playa Azul

Costera Manuel

Bahía Manzanillo

Tourism Office & Car Rental

SALAHUA

Playa Salahua

Playa Las Hadas

Península de Santiago

Golf Course

Playa Olas Altas

Playa Santiago

SANTIAGO

Playa Audiencia

MEX 200

Bahía Santiago

Laguna Peña

Playa Miramar

To Aeropuerto Barra de Navidad ←

Península de Juluapan

MIRAMAR

Train Station

Cruise Pier

Central Plaza

DOWNTOWN MANZANILLO

Area of Inset

Laguna de Cuyutlán

N

Downtown Manzanillo

Bahía de Manzanillo

To Colima and Santiago Peninsula ↑

Cruise Pier (Sunset cruise tickets)

Train Station

Bus Station

Niños Héroes

Escuadrón 201

Hidalgo

Cuauhtémoc

Chapultepec

Avenida Colonia

Laguna de Cuyutlán

Naval Pier

Jardín de Obregón

Avenida Morelos

21 de Marzo

Benito Juárez

Bocanegra

Independencia

Hidalgo

Market

5 de Mayo

V. Guerrero

Pedro Núñez

Allende

Allende

Jesús

Prol. Carillo

Cruz Amado Nervo

Alameda

Circunvalación

Colhuas

Pino Suárez

G. Torres Quintero

M. Galindo

Camino Puerto

Nicolás Bravo

México

Fco. Madero

Cuauhtémoc

General Núñez

Allende

L. Zaragoza

21 de Marzo

México

Corregidora

A. Serdán

Fco. Villa

M. Suárez

E. Zapata

Calle 1

B. Domínguez

Calle 2

Post Office ⊠   Bus/Train Station ◾

1222

it's much closer to the downtown area. **Playa Miramar,** on the Bahía de Santiago past the Santiago Peninsula, is another of the town's popular beaches, well worth the ride out here on the local bus from town. The major part of **Playa Azul** drops off a little too steeply for safe swimming and is not recommended for waders.

BIRDWATCHING   There are many lagoons along the coast. As you go from Manzanillo up past Las Brisas to Santiago, you'll pass **Laguna de Las Garzas** (Lagoon of the Herons), also known as **Laguna de San Pedrito,** where you can see many white pelicans and huge herons fishing in the water. They nest here in December and January. Back of town, on the road leading to Colima (the capital), is the **Laguna de Cuyutlán** (follow the signs to Cuyutlán), where birds can usually be found in abundance; species vary between summer and winter.

DIVING   Susan Dearing pioneered diving in Manzanillo and has come up with some unusually intriguing underwater scenery. Many locations are so close to shore there's no need for a boat; such dives are less expensive than those using a boat. Close-in dives include the jetty with coral growing on the rocks at 45 feet, and a closeby sunken frigate downed in 1959 at 28 feet . Divers can see abundant sea life, including coral reefs, sea horses, giant puffer fish, and moray eels. Dives requiring a boat cost $65 each with a three-person minimum. Off-shore dives cost $50 per person. Susan Dearing is certified in scuba (YMCA and CMAS) and life saving and CPR by the Red Cross, and she offers divers certification in very intensive courses of various durations. For reservations contact her at the Hotel La Posada (☎ and fax 333/3-1899), at the spa at the Hotel Sierra (☎ 333/3-200 ext. 250), or by cellular phone (90-335-80327).

FISHING   Manzanillo is also famous for its fishing, particularly sailfish. Marlin and sailfish are abundant year-round. Winter is best for dolphinfish and dorado (mahi mahi), and in summer wahoo and roosterfish are in greater supply. The international sailfish competition is held around the November 20 holiday, and the national sailfish competition is in November before Thanksgiving. Fishing can be arranged through travel agencies or directly at the **fishermen's cooperative** (☎ 2-1031), downtown where the fishing boats are moored.

I can recommend **Gerardo Montes** (☎ 333/2-0817 or 2-5085), whose boats, the *Albatros I* and *II* are generally docked by the Naval Station. Fishing costs $35 per hour in a 28-foot boat and $45 per hour in a 38-foot boat with a five-hour minimum. The cost can be shared by up to seven people in the larger boat and up to four in the smaller boat.

SUNSET CRUISES   For a sunset cruise, buy tickets from travel agents, or downtown at La Perlita Dock (across from the train station) fronting the harbor. Tickets go on sale at La Perlita daily from 10am to 2pm and 4 to 7pm and cost around $15 for the La Perlita cruise. The trip is a peaceful one; there's no music or entertainment, but both cruises include two drinks. Cruises last $1^{1}/_{2}$ to 2 hours.

TOURS   Because Manzanillo is so spread out, you might consider a city tour. I highly recommend the services of Luís Jorge Alvarez at **Viajes Lujo,** Av. México 143-2, Manzanillo, Col. 28200 (☎ 333/2-2919; fax 333/2-4075). Office hours are Monday through Friday from 9am to 2pm and 4 to 7pm and Saturday from 9am to noon, but tours can take place at any time. A half-day city tour costs around $20. Other tours include one to Colima ($40) and to Barra de Navidad ($40), which includes a stop at a banana and coconut plantation. Luís uses air-conditioned vehicles and speaks English.

SHOPPING   Only a few shops carry Mexican crafts and clothing, and almost all are downtown on the streets near the central plaza. You can also try exploring the new American-style malls on the road to Santiago.

ACCOMMODATIONS

The strip of coastline on which Manzanillo is located can be divided into three areas: **downtown,** with its shops, markets, and continual activity; **Las Brisas,** the hotel-lined beach area immediately to the north of the city; and **Santiago,** both the name of a town and peninsula which is virtually a suburb situated even farther north at the end of Playa Azul. Transportation by either bus or taxi make all three areas fairly convenient to each other. Reservations are recommended for hotels during the Christmas and New Year's holidays.

DOWNTOWN

Hotel Colonial

Av. México 100 and Gonzales Bocanegra, Manzanillo, Col. 28200. ☎ and fax **333/2-1080** or 2-1134. 40 rms (all with bath). A/C (25 rms) FAN (15 rms). $18–$20 double.

An old favorite, this three-story colonial-style hotel changes little from year to year, It still offers the same beautiful blue-and-yellow tile, colonial-style carved doors, and windows in the lobby and restaurant. Rooms are decorated with the same minimal furniture, red-tile floors, and basic comforts. In the central courtyard there is a restaurant/bar. The highest rates are for rooms with air-conditioning. With your back to the plaza, walk one block inland on Juárez to the corner of Galindo; the hotel is on the right corner.

LAS BRISAS

Buses run out to Las Brisas from downtown. Look for "Brisas Direc" on the signboard. It's a six-mile trundle around Manzanillo Bay, ultimately curving southward. Most hotels, bungalows, and condominiums are on the single main road.

Hotel La Posada

Av. Lázaro Cárdenas 201, Las Brisas (Apdo. Postal 135), Manzanillo, Col. 28200. ☎ and fax **333/3-1899.** 24 rms. FAN. High season $79 double. Low season $60 double. All rates include breakfast.

Another longtime favorite of traveling cognoscenti, this small inn has a shocking-pink stucco facade with a large arch that leads to a broad tiled patio right on the beautiful beach. The rooms have exposed brick walls and simple furnishings with Mexican decorative accents. The atmosphere here is casual and informal—you can help yourself to beer and soft drinks all day long, and at the end of your stay, owner Bart Varelmann (a native of Ohio) counts the bottle caps you deposited in a bowl with your room number. All three meals are served in the dining room or out by the pool. If you want to come for a meal, breakfast, served between 8 and 11am, costs around $7; lunch and dinner (sandwiches), served between 1:30 and 8pm, cost about the same. During low season the restaurant is open only from 8am to 3pm. Or just come for a drink at sunset; the bar's open until 9pm all year. It's at the far end of Las Brisas Peninsula—the end closest to downtown. From the town center take the "Las Brisas" bus.

ⓢ Hotel Star

Lázaro Cárdenas 1313, Manzanillo, Col. 28200. ☎ **333/3-2560** or 3-1980. 39 rms, 2 suites. A/C FAN. $18–$25 double; $35 double suite.

In a row of modest hotels, the Hotel Star stands out for its tidy appearance and careful management. It features a two-story sunny complex facing a courtyard and a pool by the beach. The color scheme combines red tile floors with orange bedspreads and curtains. Rooms are comfortable but sparsely decorated with rattan furniture. The higher prices are for rooms with air-conditioning and television. Both suites have air-conditioning and televisions, and one has a kitchen.

SANTIAGO

Three miles north of Las Brisas is the wide Santiago Peninsula. The settlement of Salahua is on the highway at one end where you enter the peninsula to reach the hotels Las Hadas, Plaza las Glorias, and Sierra Manzanillo, as well as the Mantarraya Golf Course. Buses from town marked "Las Hadas" go every 20 minutes into the interior of the peninsula and pass by these hotels. Past the Salahua turnoff and at the end of the settlement of Santiago, an obscure road on the left is marked "Zona de Playas" and leads to the hotels on the other side of the peninsula, including Hotels Marlyn and Playa de Santiago. To get to the latter hotels, take a bus to the main Santiago bus stop. Get off there and transfer to a taxi (available at all hours).

Very Expensive

Camino Real Las Hadas

Santiago Peninsula, Manzanillo, Col. 28200. ☎ **333/3-0000** or 800/722-6466 in the U.S. and Canada. 220 rms and suites. A/C MINIBAR TV TEL. High season $260–$295 double; $355–$420 Camino Real Club. Low season $182–$205 double; $305–$370 Royal Beach Club.

Anyone who has ever heard of Manzanillo has heard of Las Hadas; say Las Hadas and a lot of people think that *is* Manzanillo. You may remember it from the movie *10* which featured Bo Derek and Las Hadas. The self-contained Eden that put Manzanillo on the map was the brainchild of the Bolivian entrepreneur Antenor Patino, featuring Moorish-style architecture that started a trend in Mexico. Built on the beach and up a half-moon shaped curve of the peninsula, the elegant white resort hotel is one of the most famous, popular, and exclusive in Mexico; it's among the exclusive "Leading Hotels of the World." The rooms, built around the hillside overlooking the bay, are connected by cobbled lanes lined with colorful flowers and palms. Covered, motorized carts are on call for transportation within the property. Though it's a large resort, it maintains an air of seclusion since rooms are large, spread out, and tucked here and there in short rows among the landscaped grounds. The six categories of accommodations are roughly divided among those with views of partial views and by room size and those with extra amenities. The understated, elegant, and spacious rooms have white-marble floors, sitting areas, and comfortably furnished balconies. Robes, in-room security boxes, and remote-control TVs are standard in all rooms. Royal Beach Club guests have rooms on the upper tier with great bay views, and nine rooms have private pools. Room 804 in the Camino Real Club has a whirlpool on the patio with a fabulous view of the bay.

To find the hotel from the Costera, turn left at the golf course and follow the signs to Las Hadas. Entry, through a guarded gate, is to hotel guests occupants of condominiums on an adjacent hill, patrons with restaurant reservations, or to bearers of tickets for the sunset cruise that takes off from here.

Dining/Entertainment: Of this resort's four restaurants, the most famous is elegant Legazpi Restaurant and Lounge, open in high season 6pm to midnight (see "Dining," below). Special theme nights feature patio dining; Italian, Mexican, and Japanese cuisine; and mariachis at a cost of $45 per person. There are five lounges and bars with live entertainment somewhere on the property almost every evening, plus the disco, Le Cartouche, open nightly in high season from 10pm to 2am. Hours and restaurants may vary during low season.

Services: Laundry, room service, shopping arcade, travel agency, beauty and barber shops, child care (special children's activities in high season). Camino Real Club guests have rapid check-in, continental breakfast, cocktails, concierge, preferred restaurant reservations, and late checkout.

Facilities: Club Las Hadas includes La Mantarraya, the hotel's 18-hole, 71-par golf course designed by Roy Dye; two pools; beach with shade tents; 10 tennis courts (8 hard-surface, 2 clay); marina for 70 vessels; and water sports—scuba diving, snorkeling, sailing, and trimaran cruises. Camino Real Club guests have an exclusive pool and reserved lounge chairs at the pool and beach.

Expensive

Hotel Plaza Las Glorias

Av. de Tesoro s/n, Santiago Peninsula. Manzanillo, Jal. 28200. ☎ **333/3-0812** or 3-0622; 800/342-2644 in the U.S., 91-800/3-6566 in Guadalajara. Fax 333/3-1395. 86 rms, 17 Beach Club suites. A/C TV TEL. High season $125–$185 double. Low season $100–$165 double. (Prices may vary with season or holiday.)

The deep burnt-orange-colored walls of this pueblo-like hotel ramble over a hillside on Santiago Peninsula. From the restaurant on top and from most rooms is a broad vista of other red-tiled rooftops and either the palm-filled golf course or bay. It's one of Manzanillo's hidden resorts, known more to wealthy Mexicans than to Americans. Originally conceived as private condominiums, the quarters were designed for living; each accommodation is spacious, stylishly furnished, and very comfortable. Each unit has a huge living room; a small kitchen/bar open to the living room; one, two, or three large bedrooms with Saltillo-tile or brick floors; large Mexican tiled bathrooms; huge closets; and large furnished private patios with views. A few of the rooms can be partitioned off and rented by the bedroom room only. Water is purified in the tap and each room has a key-locked security box. Try to get a room on the restaurant and pool level—otherwise there'll be a lot of stairs to climb. However, there's a hillside rail elevator that goes from top to bottom, but doesn't stop in between. The less luxurious Beach Club suites are at another location on Las Brisas Beach, several miles from the main hotel. Standard Beach Club suites have two bedrooms, two bathrooms, a fully equipped kitchen, and a separate dining area open to the sunken living room (off of which there is a terrace or balcony). Penthouse suites at the Beach Club are two stories with the living and kitchen/dining area and a bedroom and bathroom downstairs, two bedrooms and a bathroom upstairs, and balconies on both levels. The hotel is often full weekends and holidays, so make reservations early. Package rates can cut the cost of your stay.

Dining/Entertainment: La Plazuela restaurant a casual and informal restaurant shaped like a half-moon, is beside the pool and fronts the bay side to capture both the views and breezes. It's open for all three meals. Live musicians often serenade diners.

Services: Laundry, room service, elevator from bottom of property to top, babysitters arranged with advance notice.

Facilities: One pool on the restaurant level; Beach Club on Las Brisas beach, where there's a pool and small restaurant; transportation to the Beach Club from the main hotel in the morning with return transportation in the afternoon.

Hotel Sierra Plaza Manzanillo

Av. La Audiencia 1, Los Riscos, Manzanillo, Col. 28200. ☎ **333/3-2000** or 800/333-3333 or 800/544-4686 in the U.S. Fax 333/3-2272. 333 rms and suites. A/C MINIBAR TV TEL. Low season $120–$130 standard double; $210–$370 double suite.

Opened in 1990, this hotel boasts 21 floors overlooking La Audiencia beach. Architecturally it mimics the white Moorish style that has become so popular in Manzanillo. Inside it's palatial in scale and covered in a sea of pale grey marble. Room decor picks up the pale grey theme with washed grey armoires that conceal the TV and minibar. Most standard rooms have two double beds or a king-size bed plus a small table, chairs, and desk. Several rooms at the end of most floors are small, with one double bed, small port-hole-size windows, no balcony, and no view. Most rooms, however, have balconies and either ocean or hillside views. The 10 gorgeous honeymoon suites are carpeted and have sculpted shell-shaped headboards, king-size beds, and chaise lounge. Junior suites have a sitting area with couch and large bathrooms.

Dining/Entertainment: Four restaurants cover all meals and styles from casual to elegant. During high season, weekends, and holiday evenings from 8pm to 2am there's live music for dancing in Bar Sierra, which is open daily from 1pm to midnight.

Services: Laundry, room service, ice machine on each floor, hairdryers, beauty salon with massage available, travel agency, 24-hour currency exchange.

Facilities: Grand pool on the beach; children's pool; four lighted tennis courts; extra cost health spa with exercise equipment, scheduled aerobics, hot tub, and separate sauna and steam rooms for men and women. Scuba-diving lessons are given in the pool, and excellent scuba-diving sites are within swimming distance of shore.

Inexpensive

Hotel Playa de Santiago

Santiago Peninsula (Apdo. Postal 147), Manzanillo, Col. 28860. ☎ **333/3-0055** or 3-0270. Fax 333/3-0344. 105 rms, 24 bungalows (all with bath). FAN TEL. $35 double; $38 bungalow. Free parking.

This is one of those 1960s-era hotels aimed at the jet set who've since migrated around the peninsula to Plaza Las Glorias and Las Hadas. You get the essence of glamour at a fraction of the price, and the hotel is on a small beach. Rooms in the main hotel building are small and clean with nearly up-to-date furnishings, tile floors, tiny closets, and balconies facing the ocean. Most have two double beds. Bungalows are in a separate building next door and are rather dreary with dark-green bedspreads, old furniture, small baths, and walls that need painting. Some bungalows have kitchenettes, and all have nice-size patios but no patio furniture. The restaurant/bar is positioned for its views, and there are a pool and tennis court.

DINING

For picnic fixings, there's a big supermarket, the **Centro Comercial Conasuper,** on the road leading into town, half a block from the plaza at Morelos. The huge store sells food, produce, household goods, clothes, hardware, and more. It's open daily from 8am to 8pm.

DOWNTOWN

Restaurant Roca del Mar

21 de Marzo 204. ☎ **333/2-0302** or 2-0424. Breakfast $1.50–$2.50, main courses $1.50–$6. Daily 7:30am–10:30pm. MEXICAN.

Cool, friendly, and open to the breeze, this popular restaurant is one of the best meeting places downtown. The large menu includes salads of chicken, fruit, seafood, and fresh vegetables, plus sandwiches, Mexican food, and seafood. It faces the main plaza, between Morelos and Juárez on the same side of the street as Helados Bing and Bar Social.

Botaneros

Botaneros are a tradition almost exclusive to Manzanillo. For the price of a beer or soft drink, they serve complimentary delicious snacks—ceviche, soup, shark stew, pickled pigs' feet, tacos—the list goes on. The more you drink, the more the food appears. Bring a group of four or more and platters really arrive. It's customary to order at least two drinks and to tip the waitress well. She puts a box for your empties at your table and tallies the tab from its contents when you're ready to leave. Sometimes roving musicians come in to serenade; you pay per song, so settle on the price in advance. And most botaneros have a form of betting game, which you'll have to get a local to explain. Besides those below, there's also El Menudazo on the way to Santiago. Most are open daily from noon to 8pm and all charge about the same for a beer or soft drink.

El Último Tren

Niños Heroes. ☎ **333/2-3144.** Beer or soft drink $2. Daily noon–8pm. DRINKS/SNACKS.

Among the cheeriest of the botaneros, El Último Tren (the last train), is covered by a grand high palapa with ceiling fans to stir up the breeze. There's enough of a family feel to the place to bring older children, although technically they aren't allowed. It's not far from downtown proper, on the right, several blocks past the train station. Just in case—women's rest rooms are named *máquinas* (cars) and the men's room is a *garrotero* (signalman).

SANTIAGO ROAD

The restaurants below are on the Costera Madrid between downtown and the Santiago Peninsula and includes an area known as Salahua.

Expensive

Manolo's Bistro

Costera Madrid, km 11.5. ☎ **333/3-2140.** Main courses $8–$18. Mon–Sat 6–11pm. INTERNATIONAL/STEAK/SEAFOOD.

Manolo's offers refined dining with cloth-covered tables set with a single fresh flower and handsome wood-backed chairs with a patina reminiscent of a European dining room. Owners Manuel and Juanita López and family serve diners. They cater to American tastes with a "safe" salad that is included with dinner. Among the popular entrées are filet of fish Manolo on a bed of spinach with melted cheese Florentine style and frogs' legs in brandy batter. Most people can't leave without first being tempted by the fresh coconut or homemade pecan pie. Coming from downtown, Manolo's is on the right about three blocks before the turn to Las

Hadas, its yellow-colored walls almost dwarfed by the sprawling burnt-orange walls of El Vaquero Campestre next door. From the town center, take a "Miramar," "Salahua," or "Santiago" bus and return on an "Estación" bus.

Osteria Bugatti

Santiago and Las Brisas crossroads. ☎ **333/3-2999.** Reservations recommended after 8pm. Sonora steaks and seafood $10.75–$17; pasta $7–$8.50. Daily 1pm–1am. Closed Sept 15–27. STEAKS/SEAFOOD.

One of the best restaurants in town, this place is in a dark, vaulted cellar with a brick ceiling and soft lighting. Your English-speaking waiter arrives bearing a platter laden with quality Sonora beef, plus pork and seafood. Your selection is cooked to your specifications. There's a small selection of pastas. Air-conditioning, plus a complete international bar, help to make this a popular place. It's at the Las Brisas crossroads, several miles north of the town center. Take a "Las Brisas," "Salahua," "Santiago," or "Miramar" bus from the town center and get off at the Las Brisas crossroads; the restaurant is across the busy boulevard. Take the "Estación" bus back to town.

Moderate

Benedetti's Pizza

Las Brisas. ☎ **333/4-0141.** Pizza $5–$9; main courses $3.75–$11. Daily 10am–6pm. PIZZA.

Since there are several branches in town (some called Giovanni's Pizza), you'll probably find a Benedetti's not too far from where you are staying. The variety isn't extensive, but the pies taste quite good; add some chimichurri sauce to add flavor. In addition to pizza, you can select from pastas, sandwiches, burgers, fajitas, salads, Mexican soups, cheesecake, and apple pie. This branch is on the Costera de la Madrid, on the left just after the Las Brisas turn; it's next to Goodyear Tire. Another branch is at the Las Hadas marina (☎ 333/3-2350).

Bigotes III

Puesta del Sol 3. ☎ **333/3-1236.** Main courses $6–$15. Daily noon–1am. SEAFOOD.

Good food and a festive atmosphere make locals flock to this large, breezy restaurant by the water. Strolling singers serenade diners, who satisfy themselves with large portions of grilled seafood. To find Bigotes, follow the Costera de la Madrid from downtown past the Las Brisas turnoff. Look for Portofino restaurant on the right; the left turn (and a sign pointing to Bigotes) is across the street opposite Portofino's.

El Vaquero Campestre

Km 11.5, Salahua. ☎ **333/3-0475.** Main courses $5–$7; beer $1.75; wine $2.50. Daily 1–11:30pm. GRILLED MEATS.

It's hard to miss the sprawling burnt-orange stucco wall and wagon wheels along the iron work and over the door of this restaurant. Cloth-covered plastic tables and chairs are set under a couple of grand thatched palapas. The specialty here is Sonora beef cut just about any way you can think of on either side of the border—T-bone, mignon, ribeye, tampiqueña. The arrachera is similar to the tampiqueña (a long, thin cut), but the meat is softer. The churrasco is a filet for two people, charcoal-grilled then sliced and served with potatoes, beans, and tortillas. Most meats are served with grilled onions, beans, and tortillas. Prices on the menu are for four people; I've listed what the prices would be for one person. Most cuts are also available by the kilo for two or more people. To get here take the "Santiago," "Salahua," or "Miramar" bus.

LAS BRISAS

In addition to Willy's, below, the **Hotel La Posada** (see "Accommodations," above) offers breakfast to nonguests at its beachside restaurant; it's a great place to mingle with other tourists and enjoy sunset and cocktails.

✪ Willy's

Las Brisas crossroads. ☎ **333/3-1794.** Reservations required. Main courses $7–$13. Daily 7pm–midnight. SEAFOOD/INTERNATIONAL.

You're in for a treat at Willy's, one of Manzanillo's most popular restaurants. It's breezy, casual, and small, with perhaps 13 tables inside and 10 more on the narrow balcony over the bay. Among the grilled specialties are shrimp filet imperial wrapped in bacon; red snapper tarragon; dorado basil; robalo with mango and ginger; homemade pâté; and coconut flan. The food has flair and wins over locals and tourists alike.

If you double back left at the Las Brisas crossroads, you'll find Willy's on the right down a short side street that leads to the ocean. From the train station, take a "Las Brisas" bus and ask the driver to let you off at Willy's; then walk half a block toward the ocean.

SANTIAGO PENINSULA

Legazpi

Camino Real Las Hadas hotel, Santiago Peninsula. ☎ **333/4-0000.** Main courses $25–$45. Every other day in high season 6pm–midnight. INTERNATIONAL.

For sheer elegance, gracious service, and outstanding food, dining here is a must. The candlelit room allows for dining in tranquillity: Tables, covered in pale pink and white, are set with silver and flowers, and a pianist plays softly in the background. Enormous bell-shaped windows on two sides show off the sparkling bay below. Meals begin with a basket of warm breads, and courses are interspersed with servings of fresh-fruit sorbet. The sophisticated menu includes prosciutto with melon marinated in port wine, crayfish bisque, broiled salmon, roast duck, lobster, or veal, and flaming desserts from crêpes to Irish coffee. It's an unforgettable dining experience.

MANZANILLO AFTER DARK

Nightlife in Manzanillo consists mainly of finding a splendid sunset and dining spot, followed by a good night's sleep. However, for the more active tourist, **Carlos 'n' Charlies, Costera Madrid, km 5 (☎ 3-1150),** is always a good choice for both food and fun. Reservations are recommended after 6pm. In the evening during high season, there may be a required minimum order/cover if you come just to drink, but the "cover" includes three drinks. On weekends and during high season they open the dance area. **Le Cartouche Disco,** at Las Hadas resort, opens at 10pm and has a cover charge of around $16. **El Bar de Felix,** between Salahua and Las Brisas by the Avis rental-car office, is open Tuesday through Sunday from 9pm to 2am; there's no cover charge. Next door and open the same days, **VOC Disco** opens from 10pm to 4am and charges a $12 cover. The 11pm light show splatters light beams over the waterfall, rock walls, and large central dance floor. **Jalapeños Restaurant** (by the Ford agency on the Costera) entertains patrons with live Mexican music from 9:30 to 11pm on Friday and Saturday nights. Most of these establishments have a dress code that prohibits patrons wearing *huaraches* (sandals) or shorts, but the prohibition generally applies to males rather than females.

EXCURSIONS FROM MANZANILLO
COLIMA: A COLONIAL CITY WITH FINE MUSEUMS

Colima, the attractive capital of the state of Colima, boasts a colonial-era town center and a number of interesting museums. It is a balmy metropolis that dates back to 1523; its founder was the conquistador Gonzalo de Sandoval, the youngest member of Cortés's band. Hotels and restaurants are on or near the main plaza.

From Manzanillo, you can reach Colima in an hour by taking a picturesque road that skirts the 12,870-foot Volcano de Colima, which last erupted in 1991. Also visible on this trip is the 14,000-foot Nevado de Colima, which actually lies in the state of Jalisco. Colima can also be reached by frequent bus service from the central bus station in Manzanillo. See "By Bus" under "Getting There & Departing," above, for exact information on reaching Colima from Manzanillo.

Note: Policemen are abundant in this city and seem overly eager to hand out citations for speeding and other minor infractions such as driving the wrong way on a street—so beware!

Exploring Colima

Of the city's several museums, two are standouts. *Important note:* Colima's museums are closed on Sunday.

Museo de Occidente de Gobierno de Estado (Museum of Western Cultures)

Galvan at Ejército Nacional. No phone. Admission free. Daily 9am–7:30pm.

Also known as the Museum of Anthropology, this is one of my favorite museums in the country. It has many pre-Hispanic pieces, including the famous clay dancing dogs of Colima. There are fine examples of clay, shell, and bone jewelry; exquisite human and animal figures; and diagrams of tombs showing unusual funeral customs.

Museo de la Cultura Popular María Teresa Pomar (Museum of Popular Culture)

University of Colima, 27 de Septiembre and Manuel Gallardo Zamora. ☎ 333/2-5140. Admission free. Mon–Sat 9am–2pm and 4–7pm. From the Museum of Western Cultures, go left out the front door and walk five blocks to the wide Avenida Galvan, at Ejército; cross the street, and the museum will be on your right. (The front wall says INSTITUTO UNIVERSITARIO DE BELLAS ARTES.)

One of the city's most interesting museums, this attraction contains regional costumes and musical instruments from all over Mexico. There are also photographs showing the day-to-day use of costumes and masks and folk art from Oaxaca, Guerrero, and elsewhere. The section devoted to Mexican sweet bread (*pan dulce*) is set up like an authentic bakery, with each bread labeled. At the entrance is a shop selling Mexican folk art.

BARRA DE NAVIDAD & MELAQUE: A QUIET BEACH GETAWAY

Only 1¹/₂ hours north of Manzanillo (65 miles), this pair of modest beach villages (only three miles apart from each other) has been attracting vacationers for decades. Barra has cobbled streets, good budget hotels and restaurants, and funky beach charm, while Melaque has a lineup of hotels both on and off the beach, fewer restaurants, and no funky charm, though the beach is as wide and beautiful as Barra's. Both villages appeal to those looking less for expensive, modern, and sophisticated destinations and more for quaint, quiet, and inexpensive hideaways. From

Manzanillo, the highway twists through some of the Pacific coast's most beautiful mountains covered in oak and coconut palm and acres of banana plantations.

Buses from Manzanillo run the route up the coast frequently on their way to Puerto Vallarta and Guadalajara. Most stop in the central villages of both Barra de Navidad and Melaque. From here Puerto Vallarta is a five-hour bus ride. By car, take coastal Highway 200 north; it takes three to four hours from Manzanillo.

In the 17th century, Barra de Navidad was a harbor for the Spanish fleet, and it was from here that galleons set off in 1564 to find China. Located on a gorgeous crescent-shaped bay with curious rock outcroppings, Barra de Navidad and neighboring Melaque (both are on the same wide bay) boast a perfect beach and a peaceful ambience. So far only Barra has been "discovered," primarily by a small number of people who come from December through Easter and on Mexican holidays. Other times it's a quiet getaway, with lots of empty hotel rooms and an easy pace.

Now that the first phase of the long-awaited **Isla Navidad Resort** project is nearing completion across the water from Barra's main pier, the area's pace may quicken. The 18-hole golf course is complete, and the first hotel was nearly completed when I last visited here. Hillside homes and condominiums are planned to follow.

The **tourism office** for both Barra de Navidad and Melaque is in Barra at the end of Legazpi (heading out of town) in the DIF building complex (☎ and fax 335/5-5100). The office is open Monday through Friday from 9am to 7pm and Saturday from 9am to 1pm.

In Barra, the main beachfront street, **Legazpi,** is lined with hotels and restaurants. From the bus station, beachfront hotels are two blocks straight ahead across the central plaza. Two blocks behind the bus station and to the right is the lagoon side, with its main street, **Morelos/Veracruz,** and more hotels and restaurants. Few streets are marked, but 10 minutes of wandering will acquaint you with the village's entire layout.

A special request: If you have any good used clothing or toys, you can deposit them with Philomena Garcia at Los Pelicanos Restaurant in Melaque (See "A Side Trip to Melaque," below). She'll distribute them among needy children in the area.

Exploring Barra de Navidad

Swimming and enjoying the lovely beach and bay view take up most tourists' time. Renting a small boat can be done in two ways. Go toward the Malecón on Calle Veracruz until you reach the tiny boatmen's cooperative with fixed prices posted on the wall. You can also walk a short bit farther to the thatched gazebo at the end of the Malecón itself. Prices are the same. A round-trip to the village of **Colimilla,** just across the lagoon and popular for its many pleasant restaurants, costs $7 for up to eight people, and you stay as long as you like; a 30-minute **tour around the lagoon** costs $12; out on the sea, it costs $25. **Sportfishing** is $15 per hour for up to six people. **Waterskiing** costs $15 per hour.

Unusual **area tours, house and apartment rentals,** and **sports equipment rental** can be arranged through **The Crazy Cactus**, Legazpi 138 A (☎ 335/5-5910; fax 335/5-5349), a gift shop operated by Trayce Blackstone and Mari Blanca Perez. Besides gifts for sale, you'll find bicycles, boogie boards, snorkeling equipment, and life jackets to rent. Among the unique tours is one along the coast to lagoons and mangroves and another to nearby small towns for market days and shopping. **El Medico,** Av. Veracruz 230 (☎ 5-5008 and fax 5-5807), rents yachts, camping and fishing equipment; they also organize fishing tournaments and sell fishing lures and yacht parts. **Beer Bob's Books,** Av. Mazatlán 61, between Sinaloa and Guanajuato, is a booklovers' institution in Barra and sort of a community service Bob does for fun. His policy of "leave a book if you take one" means vacationers can select from thousands of neatly shelved trade paperbacks. When beer was cheap, he kept a cooler stocked and browsers could sip and read. When the price of beer went up, Bob put the cooler away, but he's still called Beer Bob.

Accommodations

During low season (May through November) it doesn't hurt to ask for a discount, even on rates already lowered.

✪ Hotel Barra de Navidad

Legazpi 250, Barra de Navidad, Jal. 58987. ☎ **335/5-5122.** Fax 335/5-5303. 60 rms (all with bath). FAN. High season $35–$40 double. Low season $22–$25 double.

At the northern end of Legazpi, this popular, comfortable hotel on the beach has a friendly management and fine balconies overlooking the beach and bay. Rooms with a street view cost the least in each category. A second-floor terrace restaurant overlooks the bay and swimming pool. Hotel patrons rave about the food; the restaurant is open for all meals.

Hotel Bogavante

Legazpi s/n, Barra de Navidad, Jal. 48987. ☎ **335/5-5384.** Fax 335/5-5808. 20 rms (all with bath). FAN. Low season $25 double; $30 triple.

Although it was once shabby, this newly renovated hotel sports fresh paint and new tile throughout, making it a good value right on the beach. First-floor rooms come with a single and double bed, and second-floor rooms hold from four to eight people. Third-floor rooms all have kitchens and living areas. About half of the rooms have ocean views. The hotel is near the north end of Legazpi.

✪ Hotel Delfín

Morelos 23, Barra de Navidad, Jal. 48987. ☎ **335/5-5068.** Fax 335/5-8020 or 5-6020. 25 rms, 3 apts (all with bath). FAN. High season $22 double. Low season $17 double. Free parking in front.

One of Barra's better-maintained hotels, the three-story Delfín, on the landward side of the lagoon, is my personal favorite. It offers nice, well-cared-for rooms, each of which has a red-tile floor and either a double or two single beds (no elevator). Outside each room are tables and chairs on the covered walkways. The tiny courtyard with a small pool and lounge chairs is shaded by an enormous tree. A small but humdinger of a breakfast buffet is served from 8:30 to 10:30am in the lovely second-level breakfast terrace.

Hotel Sands

Morelos 24, Barra de Navidad, Jal. 48987. ☎ **335/5-5018.** 43 rms (all with bath). FAN. High season $30 double. Low season $20 double.

The colonial-style Sands, catercorner from the Hotel Delfín (see above) on the lagoon side at Jalisco, offers small but homey rooms, which have red-tile floors and windows with both screens and glass. Lower rooms look onto a public walkway and wide courtyard; upstairs rooms are brighter. Three rooms have air-conditioning. In back there is a beautiful pool by the lagoon. The hotel is known for its high-season happy hour from 2 to 6pm at the pool terrace bar. After 6pm, the hotel is quiet again.

Dining

Don't overlook the marvelous breakfast-only restaurant in the Hotel Delfín—it's the best place in Barra to start the day.

Panchos

López de Legazpi 53. No phone. Breakfast $2–$3; main courses $4–$10. High season, daily 9am–10pm. Low season, daily 8am–7pm. SEAFOOD.

Pancho's is on the beach, toward the far end of Legazpi. The most popular place in town, it's where locals hang out for food and conversation. Pull up a chair on the sand floor and join them. The spicy deviled shrimp was invented here, and the ground marlin ceviche, in a sauce of tomatoes and mildly hot peppers, is fabulous.

Café y Restaurant Ambar

Av. Veracruz 101-A. No phone. Breakfast $2–$4; crêpes $2–$8. Daily 8am–11pm (happy hour 1pm–midnight). Closed Sept. CRÊPES/VEGETARIAN/MEXICAN.

At the corner of Veracruz and Jalisco opposite the Restaurant y Ceñaduría Patty, you'll find this cozy thatched-roof upstairs restaurant open to the breezes. The crêpes are named after towns in France; the delicious crêpe Paris, for example, is filled with chicken, potatoes, spinach, and green sauce. Mexican specialties include tortas and quesadillas. For something lighter, try a seafood or fruit salad. This highly recommended restaurant lies one block inland from the Hotel Tropical on Legazpi.

○ Veleros

Veracruz 64. ☎ **335/5-5838.** Main courses $4–$9. High season, daily 8am–11pm. Low season, daily noon–11pm. SEAFOOD/BEEF.

Watch the small boats glide across the glassy lagoon in this clean and casual restaurant at the water's edge. Decorated with striped-cloth-covered tables, it is a tranquil spot for a lengthy meal. Depend on impeccable service and consistently good food. Seafood specialties include shrimp brochette and fish filet, but there are also steak and chicken.

Barra de Navidad After Dark

During high season there is always happy hour from 2 to 6pm at the **Hotel Sands** poolside/lagoonside bar.

At the **Disco El Galleón,** in the Hotel Sands on Calle Morelos, cushioned benches and cement tables encircle the round dance floor. It's all open air, but garden walls restrict air flow and there are few fans so you can really work up a sweat dancing the night away. It serves drinks only, no snacks. Admission is $4, and it's open on Friday and Saturday from 9pm to 2am. The beachside **Capricho Disco Club,** on Legazpi (by the Pacífico Restaurant), is the favorite sunset gathering place between 6 and 8pm when drinks are two for the price of one.

A Side Trip to Melaque (San Patricio)

For a change of scenery, you may want to wander over to Melaque (also known as San Patricio), three miles from Barra on the same bay. You can walk on the beach from Barra or take one of the frequent local buses from the bus station near the main square in Barra for 50¢. The bus is marked "Melaque." To return to Barra, take the bus marked "Cihuatlán."

Melaque's pace is even more laid-back than Barra's, and though it's a larger village, it seems smaller. It has fewer restaurants and less to do. It has more hotels or "bungalows," as they are usually called here, but none with the charm of those in Barra. If Barra hotels are full on a holiday weekend, then Melaque would be a second choice for accommodations. The paved road ends where the town begins. A few yachts bob in the harbor, and the palm-lined beach is gorgeous.

If you come by bus from Barra, you can exit the bus anywhere in town or stay on until the last stop, which is the bus station in the middle of town, a block from the beach. Restaurants and hotels line the beach, and it's impossible to get lost, but some orientation will help. Coming into town from the main road, you'll be on the town's main street, **Avenida López Mateos.** You'll pass the main square and come down to the waterfront, where there's a trailer park. The street going left (southeast) along the bay is **Avenida Gómez Farías;** the one going right (northwest) is **Avenida Miguel Ochoa López.**

DINING   In addition to the restaurants below, there are many rustic palapa restaurants in town on the beach and farther along the bay at the end of the beach. You can settle in on the beach and use one of the restaurants as your base for drinking and dining.

✪ Los Pelicanos

North end of Melaque beach. Breakfast $2.25–$3; main courses $5–$12; lobster for 2 persons $30. High season, daily 9am–10pm. Low season, daily 9am–7pm. INTERNATIONAL.

Friendly ex-Pennsylvanian Phil Garcia, along with her spouse, Trine, prepares meals like you might find at home. During high season there might be pork roast and mashed potatoes along with her usual seafood specialties. Year-round you can find burritos, nachos, and hamburgers. The tender fried squid is delectable with one of Phil's savory sauces. Order lobster 24 hours in advance. Many Barra guests come here to stake a place on the beach and use the restaurant as a day-long headquarters for sipping and nipping. It's peaceful to watch the pelicans bobbing just in front of this restaurant. The restaurant is at the far end of the bay before the Hotel Legazpi.

EL TAMARINDO

After Barra de Navidad, and about 25 miles north of the Manzanillo airport, you'll see a sign pointing left to El Tamarindo; turn and follow the narrow road seven miles through the dense forest to this new and *very* exclusive resort nestled in a dense forest beside the ocean. It's part of a larger plan that eventually will include private residences; most of the mountain lots, costing in the millions of dollars, have been sold. When I was last here, nine holes of the projected **18-hole golf course** were complete. The course has a spectacular setting on mountain tops overlooking jagged cliffs that meet the crashing ocean; it is like courses you may have experienced in Ireland.

Hotel Bel-Air El Tamarindo

Km 7.5, Carretera Manzanillo-Barra de Navidad. ☎ **332/1-0071** or 800/457-7676 in the U.S. 40 villas. A/C TV. $316 one-bedroom villa; $490 two-bedroom villa; $450 junior suite; $460 ranch suite; $550 one-bedroom grand suite; $575 one-bedroom mountain villa; $590-1030 beach villa. Rates include breakfast and dinner.

Set on 860 secluded acres stretching nine miles along the ocean, the 40 individual stucco villas are spread under palms and huge oaks and pines facing the beach. The villas, decorated with brightly colored Mexican and Guatemalan textiles, are one-story units with spacious open-air patios and living rooms with ceiling fans. The large bedrooms have fans and air-conditioning. Rates include two daily meals, use of the tennis courts, non-motor water sports, and a jungle tour. You are miles from "civilization," so you'll need a car if you want to explore the area. If you are a bird or nature lover, you will appreciate the amazingly beautiful forest, "untouched" until now, surrounding the hotel. The resort is a member of the Small Luxury Hotels of the World.

Dining/Entertainment: One restaurant serves all meals.

Services: Helicopter transfer service 10 minutes from the Manzanillo airport, laundry, room service, concierge. Airport pickup can be arranged.

Facilities: Pool, tennis courts, water sports, boat excursions, fishing, and turtle watching. The 18-hole golf course should be completed when you travel; 9 holes were in use in 1994. Guests also have full privileges at the Hotel Bel-Air Costa Careyes, 25 miles north, where there's an equestrian center.

COSTA CAREYES

After El Tamarindo (see above), the next development is Costa Careyes (which means "turtle coast") with two resorts—the Hotel Bel-Air Costa Careyes (formerly the Hotel Costa Careyes), part of a 2,500-acre development, and Club Med Playa Blanca. Each resort has its own beaches, amenities, and a small, beautiful bay all to itself. The two bays adjoin but are completely separated by bluffs.

The two resorts are roughly 50 miles north of Manzanillo and 100 miles south of Puerto Vallarta. They're about a $1^1/_2$ hour drive north of Manzanillo on Highway 200 but only about a one-hour drive from the Manzanillo airport. If you haven't arranged for transportation through either hotel, taxis from the Manzanillo airport charge around $90 one way for the trip. There are car rentals at both the Manzanillo and Puerto Vallarta airports. While these resorts are completely self-contained, a car is useful for exploring the coast—Barra de Navidad and other resorts, for example—but the hotels can also make such touring arrangements.

Hotel Bel-Air Costa Careyes

Hwy 200 km 53, Careyes, Jal. ☎ **335/1-0000** or 800/457-7676 or 800/525-4800 in the U.S. Fax 335/1-0100. TV TEL. High season $190–$375 double. Low season $140–$300 double.

The old Hotel Costa Careyes was gutted to create this totally luxurious lodging, in a secluded setting facing the ocean. The first thing you see as you step into the breezy, open "lobby" is the expansive, palm-shaded lawn leading to the ocean and free-form pool. The hotel is both rustic and sophisticated, with scrubbed, pastel room facades forming a U around the center lawn. Rooms, with colony shutters, white tile floors, handsome loomed bedspreads, and colorful pillows, are dramatically luxurious. Some rooms have balconies, and all have ocean views; robes and hairdryers; and small refrigerators. Twenty rooms have private pools. The hotel is a member of the Small Luxury Hotels of the World.

The hotel runs a number of special-interest activities for guests. Named after the hawksbill turtle (*carey* in Spanish), the hotel (which has a staff biologist) sponsors a "save the turtle" program in which guests can participate from July through December. Pacific ridley, leatherback, black, and hawksbill turtles, all in danger of extinction, nest in nearby Playa Teopa. You can also arrange a birding expedition to nearby Bird Island, a natural habitat for nesting boobies from July through September. The dry months from November through May are good for birding on the mainland since birds fly over during migration. There are no official birding walks; you're on your own. Boat tours to other nearby beaches; fishing; horseback excursions; and riding lessons are available at the equestrian center. Polo clubs from around the world converge here for polo season, December through April.

Dining/Entertainment: Two restaurants/bars, both casually chic and with international menus, serve all meals in an open setting beside the beach and pool. "Just for Kids" is a program of activities for children. A movie theater provides evening entertainment, and the library has an assortment of reading material.

Services: Laundry, purified tap water, and room service. Helicopter or limo transportation from the Manzanillo airport can be arranged for an additional fee.

Facilities: A fully equipped, state-of-the-art spa with massage; loofa scrub; wax; hot and cold plunge; steam and sauna; and weight equipment. Large free-form pool by the ocean. Guests also have privileges at the super-exclusive Hotel Bel-Air El Tamarindo (see above), 25 miles south, where there's a fabulous golf course.

LAS ALAMANDAS

About 45 minutes beyond Careyes and almost equidistant between Manzanillo (1¹/₂ hours) and Puerto Vallarta (1³/₄ hours), a small sign points in the direction of the ocean to Las Alamandas. The dirt road winds for about a mile through a poor village to the guardhouse of Las Alamandas.

Las Alamandas

Hwy 200 Manzanillo-Puerto Vallarta. ☎ **328/5-5500.** Fax 328/5-5027. Information and reservations: ☎ 800/223-6510 in the U.S. 5 multi-room villas. $500–$1000 for one room; $1,800–$2,500 whole villa. Rates include some meals.

Part of a 1,500-acre estate set on 70 acres against a low hill, the small cluster of buildings in this resort almost spreads to the wide, clean beach. The most exclusive resort in Mexico, its architecture, a blend of Mediterranean, Mexican, and Southwestern U.S., has been featured in *Architectural Digest, Condé Nast Traveler*, and *Vogue*. The furnishings are a stunning blend of Mexican handcrafted furniture, pottery and folk art, and sofas beds and pillows covered in bright textiles from Mexico and Guatemala. Though exquisite, the furnishings give the rooms a relaxed feel. Only 20 guests can be accommodated at any one time, and the threat of crowds is nonexistent.

All of the villas are spacious and have high-pitched tiled roofs, cool tiled floors, and tiled verandas with ocean views. The villas have several bedrooms (each with its own bath), which can be rented separately or as a whole house; preference for reservations is given to guests who rent whole villas. Some villas are on the beach, while some are set back from the beach across a cobblestone plaza.

Dining/Entertainment: One restaurant serves all meals. There's an honor bar and selection of video movies. All rooms have TVs with VCRs, but there's no television reception from the outside.

Services: Room service; massage. Transportation in the hotel's van to and from Manzanillo ($250 one way) and Puerto Vallarta ($230 one way) can be arranged when you reserve your room.

Facilities: Weight room; 60-foot swimming pool; lighted tennis court; horses; hiking trails; fishing; boat tours to Río San Nicolás for birding; mountain bikes, boogie boards. Private, 3,000-foot, paved landing strip capable of accommodating a King Air turbo prop; make advance arrangements for landing.

11

Acapulco & the Southern Pacific Coast

This southern part of Mexico's Pacific coast encompasses its oldest resort, Acapulco; its newest, the Bahías de Huatulco (Bays of Huatulco); and its best pair, modern Ixtapa and its neighbor, Zihuatanejo, a centuries-old oceanfront fishing village. Between Acapulco and Huatulco lie the small laid-back coastal villages of Puerto Escondido and Puerto Angel, both of which front beautiful bays.

Only a four-hour drive north of Acapulco, the resort city of Ixtapa opened in the mid-1970s beside the seaside village of Zihuatanejo. Here you can experience the best of Mexico—sophisticated high-rise hotels in Ixtapa alongside the colorful village of Zihuatanejo—and you'll pay less overall for a vacation than you would in Acapulco.

Acapulco, on the other hand, has historical glamour. The largest and most colorful resort of them all, Acapulco caught the world's attention in the late 1930s when Hollywood stars began arriving. Behind them came a groundswell of tourists, and the city became internationally known as the place to see and be seen. It has retained this exciting edge even into the mid-1990s. South of Acapulco, the Bahías de Huatulco megaproject began in 1986 when the first of nine planned bays opened on an undeveloped portion of Oaxaca's coast.

This chapter encompasses two states, Guerrero and Oaxaca, both of which contain stunning coastlines and lush mountainous terrain. Outside the urban centers, roads are few, and both states are still poor despite decades of tourism.

EXPLORING THE SOUTHERN PACIFIC COAST

Most people traveling to this part of Mexico have sun, surf, and sand firmly entrenched in their imaginations, and tend to camp themselves in a single destination and relax. Each of these beach towns—from Ixtapa and Zihuatanejo in the north to Acapulco and on through the Oaxacan resorts of Puerto Escondido and Huatulco—stands alone as a holiday resort worth enjoying for a few days, or for a week or more. If you've got a little more time and some wanderlust, several of the coastal resorts covered in this chapter could be combined into a single peripatetic trip.

Each has a distinct personality—your choices range from a city that offers every luxury to sleepy towns offering only basic-but-charming seaside relaxation.

Acapulco City offers the best airline connections, the broadest range of all-night entertainment, some very sophisticated dining, and a wide range of accommodations, from hillside villas and luxury resort hotels to modest inns on the beach and in old Acapulco. Beaches are wide, clean, and numerous, but the ocean is polluted—though cleaner than in the past. It's a good launching pad for side trips to colonial Taxco (Mexico's "Silver Capital"), only 2 1/2 hours away using the toll road, and to Ixtapa/Zihuatanejo.

The latter offers all that Acapulco has but on a smaller, newer, less hectic scale, plus excellent beaches and clean ocean waters. Since the two are only a four- to five-hour drive apart, many people fly into Acapulco (where air service is better), spend a few days there and go on to Ixtapa/Zihuatanejo by bus or rental car.

Puerto Escondido is a six-hour drive south of Acapulco on coastal Highway 200. Most people don't drive or take a bus from Acapulco to Puerto Escondido, though that's easy enough to do. Usually Puerto Escondido, noted for its surfing waves, laid-back beachside village, inexpensive inns, and nearby nature excursions, is a destination on its own. But many travelers combine it with a trip to or from the inland city of Oaxaca. The two are six hours apart by serpentine highway, or less than an hour by air.

The small village of Puerto Angel, only 50 miles south of Puerto Escondido or 30 miles north of the Bays of Huatulco, could be a day trip from either of those destinations, or a quiet place to vacation for several days providing you aren't big on nightlife and grand hotels of which there are none in Puerto Angel. A couple of hotels serve very good food, and there are beachside restaurants serving fresh fish, but otherwise dining is limited. However, visiting nearly unoccupied beaches near Puerto Angel can be a prime activity.

Huatulco, 80 miles south of Puerto Escondido, with its 18-hole golf course and a few resort hotels, was built to appeal to the luxury traveler. Besides golf, boat tours of the nine Huatulco Bays, and a couple of nature excursions that are actually nearer Puerto Escondido, there's not a lot to do. But the setting is beautiful and relaxing. The few budget-priced hotels in Huatulco cost more than budget hotels of similar quality almost anywhere on the Pacific coast.

1 Zihuatanejo & Ixtapa

360 miles SW of Mexico City, 353 miles SE of Manzanillo, 158 miles NW of Acapulco

As Mexico develops, the secluded hideaways that made the Pacific coast an intrepid traveler's dream come true are being discovered by hordes of tourists. Such is the fate of Ixtapa and Zihuatanejo (pronounced "ees-TA-pa" and "see-wa-ta-NAY-ho). Before the opening of Ixtapa, the government-planned resort four miles from Zihuatanejo in 1976, Zihuatanejo had a population of about 4,000; now the population of the municipality (including outlying towns) is over 85,000.

Despite the rapid development, Zihuatanejo, a picturesque, authentically Mexican seaside village, complements Ixtapa, a tranquil, sophisticated ocean-front resort. The pair is also developing some of the vibrancy of Puerto Vallarta, including excellent restaurants, shopping, and nightlife. In comparison to both Puerto Vallarta and Acapulco, food and lodging are still reasonably priced—if you know where to look. Ixtapa is my favorite of all Mexico's planned resorts, primarily because it has retained its tranquillity while offering the visitor a taste of both village life and modern Mexico.

ESSENTIALS

GETTING THERE & DEPARTING By Plane See Chapter 3, "Planning a Trip to Mexico," for information on flying to Ixtapa/Zihuatanejo from the United States and Canada. Here are the local numbers of some international carriers: **Aeroméxico,** ☎ 4-2018, 4-2022, or 4-2019; **Delta,** ☎ 4-3386, or in Mexico 91-800/9-0221; **Mexicana,** ☎ 3-2208, 3-2209, or 4-2227; **Northwest,** ☎ 5/202-4444 in Mexico City.

Ask your travel agent about **charter flights,** which are becoming the most efficient and least expensive way to get here.

If you're flying in from elsewhere in Mexico, **Mexicana** has nonstop or direct flights from Guadalajara and Mexico City, and **Aeroméxico** flies in from Mexico City.

Taxis are the only option for returning to the airport from town and charge around $5.50–$10 one way.

By Bus There are two bus terminals in Zihuatanejo: the **Central de Autobuses,** from which most lines operate, and the **Estrella de Oro station,** on Paseo del Palmar near the market and within walking distance of downtown hotels.

At the **Central de Autobuses,** several companies offer service to Acapulco and other cities, including first-class **Estrella Blanca** (☎ 4-3478) and second-class **Flecha Roja** (☎ 4-3477 or 4-3483). Estrella Blanca's buses are air-conditioned—most of the time—and depart for Acapulco hourly from 6am to 10pm; the cost is $8.50 one way. Keep in mind, however, that the Estrella Blanca station in Acapulco is far from the hotels I've recommended in that city and means a costly taxi ride on arrival. Flecha Roja buses to Acapulco run every hour or so; these stop in Zihuatanejo and take on passengers as space permits. En route they stop frequently and take longer to reach Acapulco so choose them only if there's no other way. **Frontera** has buses to Puerto Escondido and Huatulco daily at 6:30 and 9pm.

To go north to Manzanillo or Puerto Vallarta, you must buy a ticket for Lázaro Cárdenas (Estrella Blanca has service every 30 minutes) and change buses there.

First-class **Estrella de Oro** (☎ 4-2175) runs five first-class and three deluxe daily buses to Acapulco between 7am and 10pm. You can purchase advance tickets with seat assignments in Ixtapa at **Turismo Caleta** in the La Puerta shopping center next to the tourism office (☎ 3-0044, fax 3-2024). In Acapulco the Estrella de Oro station is near many budget hotels.

The trip from Mexico City to Zihuatanejo takes five hours (bypassing Acapulco); from Acapulco, four to five hours. From Mexico City, Tres Estrellas de Oro buses to Zihuatanejo depart from the Terminal Central de Autobuses del Sur (South Bus Station) near the Tasqueña Metro line.

From Zihuatanejo, it's three or four hours to Lázaro Cárdenas, another six or seven to Manzanillo, and an additional six to Puerto Vallarta, which doesn't include time spent waiting for buses.

By Car From Mexico City, the shortest route is to take Highway 15 to Toluca then Highway 130/134 the rest of the way, though on the latter highway gas stations are few and far between. The other route is Highway 95D (four lanes) to Iguala then Highway 51 west to Highway 134.

From Acapulco or Manzanillo, the only choice is the coastal highway, Highway 200. The ocean views along the winding, mountain-edged drive from Manzanillo are spectacular.

Motorists' advisory: Motorists planning to follow Highway 200 north from Ixtapa or Zihuatanejo toward Lázaro Cárdenas and Manzanillo should be aware of reports of car and motorist hijackings on that route, especially around Playa Azul. Before heading in that direction, ask locals and the tourism office about the status of the route when you are there, and don't drive at night. According to tourism officials, police patrols of the highway have been increased and the number of crime incidents has decreased dramatically.

ORIENTATION   Arriving by Plane   The Ixtapa-Zihuatanejo airport is 20 minutes (about 10 miles) south of Zihuatanejo. **Transportes Terrestres** minivans (called "colectivos") transport travelers to hotels in Zihuatanejo for $3.75, to Ixtapa for $4.50, and to Club Med for $5.60; colectivo tickets are sold just outside the baggage-claim area. A taxi will cost $13.50 to Zihuatanejo, $16.75 to Ixtapa, and $20 to Club Med.

Arriving by Bus   In Zihuatanejo, the **Estrella de Oro bus station,** on Paseo del Palmar at Morelos, is a few blocks beyond the market and is within walking distance of some of the downtown hotels I have suggested. The clean, warehouse-like **Central de Autobuses,** the main terminal serviced by all other buses, is a mile or so farther out, opposite the Pemex station and IMSS Hospital on Paseo Zihuatanejo at Paseo la Boquita. A taxi from either bus station to most Zihuatanejo hotels costs $1.60; continuing to Ixtapa adds another $2.50 or so to the fare.

Information   The **State Tourism Office,** in La Puerta shopping center in Ixtapa across from the Presidente-Inter-Continental Hotel (☎ and fax 755/3-1967), is open Monday through Friday from 9am to 2pm and 4 to 7pm and on Saturday from 9am to 2pm. The **Zihuatanejo Tourism Office,** on the main square by the basketball court, at Alvarez (☎ and fax 4-2001, ext. 120), is open Monday through Friday from 9am to 3pm and 6 to 8pm.

Time-share booths in both towns formerly masqueraded as information booths, but the State of Guerrero clamped down on their deceptive practices. Booths must be clearly marked by their business names and cannot carry signs claiming to be tourist information centers. Time-share employees must wear uniforms and may not leave their stands to accost passers-by. If you encounter any problems or false claims from the time-share operators, contact the tourist office.

City Layout   The fishing village and resort **Zihuatanejo** spreads out around the beautiful Bay of Zihuatanejo, framed by downtown to the north and a beautiful long beach and the Sierra foothills to the east. Beaches line the perimeter and boats bob at anchor. The heart of Zihuatanejo is the waterfront walkway **Paseo del Pescador** (also called the **Malecón**), bordering the Municipal Beach. Rather than a plaza as in most Mexican villages, Zihuatanejo's centerpiece is the **town basketball court,** which fronts the beach; I use it as a point of reference for directions. The main thoroughfare for cars, however, is **Juan Álvarez,** a block behind the Malecón. Sections of several of the main streets are designated as "zona peatonal" (pedestrian zone). The area is zigzagged and seems to block parts of streets haphazardly.

A cement-and-sand **walkway** runs from the Malecón in downtown Zihuatanejo along the water to Playa Madera, making it much easier to walk between the two points. The walkway is lit at night. Access to Playa la Ropa is via the main road, **Camino a Playa la Ropa,** about a half-hour walk from downtown. A road is under construction between Playa La Ropa and Playa Las Gatas; until it's finished the only access is by boat.

Zihuatanejo & Ixtapa Area

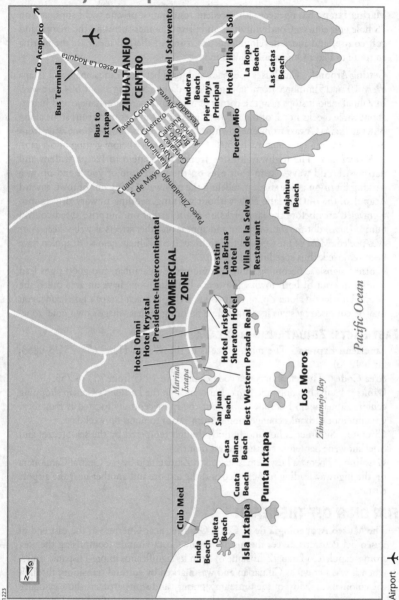

Zihuatanejo & Ixtapa Area

To Acapulco

Bus Terminal

Paseo La Ropita

ZIHUATANEJO CENTRO

Bus to Ixtapa

Paseo Cocotal

Guerrero

Galeana

Ejido

González

Nava

Alamillano

Cuauhtémoc

5 de Mayo

paseo Zihuatanejo

Ascencio Alvarez

Bravo

pescador-Alvarez

Hotel Sotavento

Madera Beach

Pier Playa Principal

Hotel Villa del Sol

La Ropa Beach

Las Gatas Beach

Puerto Mío

Majahua Beach

Presidente-Intercontinental

COMMERCIAL ZONE

Hotel Omni
Hotel Krystal

Hotel Aristos
Sheraton Hotel

Westin Las Brisas Hotel

Villa de la Selva Restaurant

Marina Ixtapa

Best Western Posada Real

San Juan Beach

Casa Blanca Beach

Cuata Beach

Punta Ixtapa

Club Med

Quieta Beach

Linda Beach

Isla Ixtapa

Los Moros

Zihuatanejo Bay

Pacific Ocean

Airport

N

1223

A good highway connects "Zihua" to **Ixtapa,** 4 miles to the northwest. The 18-hole Ixtapa Golf Club marks the beginning of the inland side of Ixtapa. Tall hotels line Ixtapa's wide beach, **Playa Palmar,** against a backdrop of lush palm groves and mountains. It's accessed by the main street, **Bulevar Ixtapa.** On the opposite side of the main boulevard lies a huge area of small shopping plazas (many of the shops are air-conditioned) and restaurants. At the far end of Bulevar Ixtapa,

Marina Ixtapa has opened with excellent restaurants, private yacht slips, and an 18-hole golf course. Condominiums and private homes surround the marina and golf course, and more developments are rising in the hillsides past the marina en route to Playa Quieta and Playa Linda.

Getting Around   City **buses** goes back and forth between Zihuatanejo and Ixtapa every 10 or 15 minutes from 5am to 11pm daily, charging about 50¢ one way. In Zihuatanejo it stops near the corner of Morelos/Paseo Zihuatanejo and Juárez, about three blocks north of the market. In Ixtapa it makes numerous stops along Bulevar Ixtapa. A taxi from one town to the other costs about $4 one way; from midnight to 5am rates increase by 50% (agree on a price before getting into a cab).

Special note: The highway leading from Zihuatanejo to Ixtapa widens and narrows in odd ways—keep your eyes on the white line or you'll end up in a parking lot or on a side street paralleling the highway. Going out of town toward Acapulco, the outside lane ends without warning, sending unwary drivers into a graveled area before the lane picks up again farther on. Surprise speed-control bumps (*topes*) dot the thoroughfare and appear on other streets as well—keep your eyes peeled. Most of the *topes* on the highway from Zihuatanejo to Acapulco have been removed, thus speeding up the trip.

Street signs are becoming more common in Zihuatanejo, and good signs lead you in and out of both towns. However, both locations have an area called the "Zona Hotelera" (Hotel Zone), so if you're trying to reach Ixtapa's hotel zone, you may be confused by signs in Zihuatanejo pointing to that village's own hotel zone.

FAST FACTS: ZIHUATANEJO & IXTAPA

American Express   The main office is in the Westin Hotel (☎ 755/3-0853; fax 3-1206).

Area Code   The telephone area code changed in 1995 from 753 to 755.

Banks   Ixtapa has only one bank, Bancomer, in the La Puerta Centro shopping center. Zihuatanejo has four banks, but the most centrally located is Banamex, Cuauhtémoc 4. Banks change money from 10am to noon on weekdays.

Climate   Summer is hot and humid, though tempered by the sea breezes and brief showers; September is the wettest month.

Gasoline   There's a busy Pemex station in Zihuatanejo by the Central Camionera on the highway leading to Acapulco and the airport and another near the airport entrance.

FUN ON & OFF THE BEACH

The **Museo Arqueología de la Costa Grande,** near Guerrero at the east end of Paseo del Pescador, traces the history of the Costa Grande (comprising the area from Acapulco to Ixtapa/Zihuatanejo) from its significance in pre-Hispanic times, when it was known as Cihuatlán and was marked by cultural transition, through the colonial era. Most of the museum's pottery and stone artifacts show evidence of extensive trade with other far-off cultures and regions, including the Toltec and Teotihuacán cultures near Mexico City; the Olmec culture on both the Pacific and Gulf coasts; and areas known today as the states of Nayarit, Michoacán, and San Luis Potosí. Some items are from a site found several years ago near the airport. Among the tribute items indigenous groups from this area paid the Aztecs were cotton *tilmas* (capes) and *cacao* (chocolate). The museum is well done and worth the half an hour or less it takes to stroll through; information is given in Spanish. Admission is $1, and it's open Tuesday through Sunday from 10am to 5pm.

Downtown Zihuatanejo

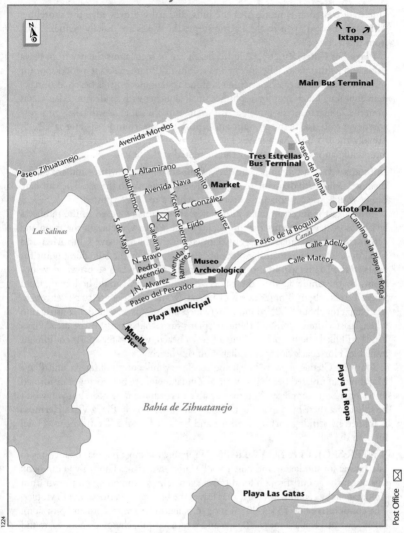

THE BEACHES In Zihuatanejo At Zihuatanejo's town beach, **Playa Municipal,** the local fishermen pull up their colorful boats onto the sand. Small shops and restaurants line the waterfront, making this a great spot for people watching and for absorbing the flavor of daily village life. This beach is protected from the main surge of the Pacific.

Besides the peaceful Playa Municipal, Zihuatanejo has three other beaches (*playas*): Madera, La Ropa, and Las Gatas. **Playa Madera,** just east of Playa Municipal, is open to the surf but generally tranquil. Many attractive budget lodgings overlook this area from the hillside.

South of Playa Madera is Zihuatanejo's largest and most beautiful beach, **Playa La Ropa,** a long sweep of sand with a great view of the sunset. Some lovely, small hotels and restaurants nestle into the hills, and palm groves edge the shoreline. Although it's also open to the Pacific surge, the waves are usually gentle. A taxi from town costs $1.75.

Playa Las Gatas, a pretty, secluded beach can be seen across the bay from Playa Ropa and Zihuatanejo. The small coral reef just offshore makes it a good spot for snorkeling and diving. The open-air seafood restaurants on this beach also make it an appealing lunch spot for a splurge. Small launches with shade run to Las Gatas from the Zihuatanejo town pier, a 10-minute trip; the captains will take you across whenever you ask between 8am and 4pm, and the round-trip fare is $2.25. Usually the last boat back leaves Las Gatas at 4:30pm; be sure to double-check! Snorkeling and water-sports gear can be rented at the beach.

In Ixtapa Ixtapa's main beach, **Playa Palmar,** is a lovely white-sand arc edging the hotel zone, with dramatic rock formations silhouetted in the sea. The surf here can be rough; use caution and never swim when a red flag is posted.

Several of the nicest beaches in the area are essentially closed to the public as lavish resort developments rise and claim them. **Playa Quieta,** on the mainland across from Isla Ixtapa, is largely claimed by the all-inclusive Club Med and Qualton Club. The remaining piece of beach used to be the launching point for boats to the Isla Ixtapa, but it is gradually being taken over by a private development. By the time you visit, the Isla Ixtapa-bound boats should be leaving from **Playa Linda,** about 8 miles north of Ixtapa. Water taxis here ferry passengers to Isla Ixtapa for about $2.25 round trip. Concession stands were under construction when I last visited here, and there are plans for a trailer park in the area. Playa Linda will likely be the primary out-of-town beach, with water-sports equipment available. Horseback riding is available on this beach.

Playa las Cuatas, a pretty beach and cove a few miles north of Ixtapa, and **Playa Majahua,** an isolated beach just west of Zihuatanejo, are both being transformed into large resort complexes. You may be able to reach them by boat, but you won't be able to get there by land as the building continues. Lovely **Playa Vista Hermosa** is framed by striking rock formations and bordered by the Westin Brisas Hotel high on the hill.

WATER SPORTS & BOAT TRIPS Probably the most popular boat trip is to **Isla Ixtapa** for snorkeling and lunch at El Marlin restaurant. Though you can book this outing as a tour through local travel agencies, you can go on your own from Zihuatanejo by catching the boat that leaves the boat cooperative at the town pier. The **cooperative** (☎ 755/4-2056) is open daily from 9am to 2pm and 3 to 7pm. Boats leave at 11:30am for Isla Ixtapa and return at 4pm, charging about $7 round trip. Along the way, you'll pass dramatic rock formations and the Los Moros de Los Péricos islands, known for the great variety of birds that nest on the rocky points jutting out into the blue Pacific. On Isla Ixtapa you'll find good snorkeling and a nature trail through an unfenced area with a few birds and animals. Snorkeling, diving, and other water-sports gear is available for rent on the island. Be sure to catch the last water taxi back at 4pm.

Separate excursions to **Los Moros de Los Péricos islands** for **birdwatching** can usually be arranged through local travel agencies, though it would probably be less expensive to rent a boat with a guide at the town pier in Zihuatanejo. The islands are offshore from Ixtapa's main beach.

Sunset cruises on the trimaran *TriStar,* arranged through **Yates del Sol** (☎ 755/4-3589), depart from the pier at Puerto Mío. A taxi to the pier from

Zihuatanejo will cost $1.60; from Ixtapa, $4. The sunset cruise costs $35 and includes an open bar. An all-day trip to Isla Ixtapa on this yacht begins at 10:30am, costs $55, and includes an open bar and lunch. Schedules vary, so call for current information and about special trips.

Fishing trips can be arranged with the boat cooperative at the Zihuatanejo town pier (☎ 755/4-2056) and cost $100 to $200, depending on the size of the boat, how long the trip lasts, and other factors; most trips are six hours. The cost is higher for a trip arranged through a local travel agency; the least expensive trips are on small launches called *pangas*; most have shade. Both small-game and deep-sea fishing are offered, and the fishing here rivals that found in Mazatlán or Baja. Trips that combine fishing with a visit to near-deserted ocean beaches extending for miles along the coast from Zihuatanejo can also be arranged. Sportfishing packages including air transportation and hotels can be arranged through Stan Lushinsky at **Ixtapa Sportfishing Charters,** 33 Olde Mill Run, Stroudsburg, PA 18360 (☎ 717/424-8323; fax 717/424-1016).

Boating and fishing expeditions from the new **Marina Ixtapa,** a bit north of the Ixtapa hotel zone, can also be arranged.

Sailboats, Windsurfers, and other water-sports equipment rentals are usually available at various stands on Playa la Ropa, Playa las Gatas, Isla Ixtapa, and at the main beach, Playa Palmar, in Ixtapa. **Parasailing** is also available at La Ropa and Palmar. **Kayaks** are available for rent at the **Zihuatanejo Scuba Center** (see below), hotels in Ixtapa, and some water-sports operations on Playa La Ropa. The rate is about $5 per hour.

Scuba-diving trips are arranged through the **Zihuatanejo Scuba Center,** on Cuauhtémoc 3 (☎ and fax 755/4-2147). Fees start at around $70 for two dives, including all equipment and lunch. Marine biologist and dive instructor Juan Barnard speaks excellent English , is extremely helpful, and is very knowledgeable about the area, which has nearly 30 different dive sites, including walls and caves. Diving is done year-round, though the water is clearest May through December, when there is 100-foot visibility or better. The nearest decompression chamber is in Acapulco, though local divers are hopeful that the one in Zihuatanejo will be repaired soon. Advance reservations for dives are advised during Christmas and Easter; make them by contacting the Scuba Center or **Dive Discovery,** 155 Montgomery St. Suite 508, San Francisco, CA 94104 (☎ 415/274-8926 or 800/886-7321; fax 415/781-0213).

Surfing is choice at Petacalco Beach north of Ixtapa.

GOLF, TENNIS & TOURS   In Ixtapa, the **Club de Golf Ixtapa** (☎ 755/3-1062 or 3-1163) has an 18-hole course designed by Robert Trent Jones, Jr. Bring your own clubs or rent them here. The greens fee is $50; caddies cost $17; and electric carts cost $33. Call for reservations. The **Marina Ixtapa Golf Course** (☎ 755/3-1410; fax 755/3-0825), designed by Robert von Hagge, has 18 challenging holes. Fees are $55 for green fees and cart, or $45 without cart. Call for reservations.

To polish your **tennis** serve in Zihuatanejo, try the **Hotel Villa del Sol** at Playa la Ropa (☎ 755/4-2239 or 4-3239). In Ixtapa, the **Club de Golf Ixtapa** (☎ 755/3-1062 or 3-1163) and the **Marina Ixtapa Golf Course** (☎ 755/3-1410, fax 755/3-0825) both have courts that are lit at night and both rent equipment. Fees are $7 per hour, $10 per hour at night. Call for reservations. In addition, the **Dorado Pacífico** and several other hotels on the main beach of Ixtapa have courts.

For **horseback riding, Rancho Playa Linda** (☎ 755/4-3085) offers guided trail rides from the Playa Linda beach (about 8 miles north of Ixtapa).Guided rides begin at 8:30, 9:45, and 11am and 3:30 and 5pm. Groups of three or more riders can arrange their own tour, which is especially nice a little later in the evening for sunset (though you'll need mosquito repellant in the evening). Riders can chose to go along the beach to the mouth of the river and back through coconut plantations or stay along the beach for the whole ride (which usually lasts 1 to 1¹/₂ hours). The fee is $20. Travel agencies in either town can arrange your trip but will charge a bit more for transportation. Reservations are suggested in the high season.

A **countryside tour** of fishing villages; coconut and mango plantations; and the Barra de Potosí Lagoon, which is 14 miles south of Zihuatanejo and known for its tropical birds, is available through local travel agencies for $25. The tour typically lasts 5¹/₂ hours and includes lunch and time for swimming.

For **off-the-beaten-track tours,** contact Alex León Pineda, the knowledgeable owner of **Fw4 Tours** in the Los Patios Center in Ixtapa (☎ 755/3-1442; fax 3-2014). His countryside tour goes to coconut and banana plantations, small villages where brickmakers work in the traditional fashion and residents live in palm thatch huts, and finally to the beach at La Saladita, where fisherman and the tour clients prepare a lunch of fresh lobster, dorado, or snapper. When I last visited, Fw4 Tours was in the process of putting together a cultural tour to include the town of Petatlán and the small archeological site of La Chole.

SHOPPING
ZIHUATANEJO

Like other resorts in Mexico, Zihuatanejo has its quota of T-shirt and souvenir shops. But it's becoming a better place to buy Mexican crafts, folk art, and jewelry. The **artisan's market** on Calle 5 de Mayo is a good place to start a shopping spree before moving on to specialty shops. The **municipal market** on Avenida Benito Juárez (about five blocks inland from the waterfront) is also good, especially the stands specializing in huaraches, hammocks, and baskets. The market area sprawls over several blocks and is well worth an early morning visit. Spreading inland from the waterfront three or four blocks are numerous small shops worth exploring. Besides the places listed below, check out **Alberto's** at Cuauhtémoc 15 and **Ruby's** at Cuauhtémoc 7 for jewelry.

Shops are generally open Monday through Saturday from 10am to 2pm and 4 to 8pm; many of the better shops close on Sunday, but some smaller souvenir stands stay open, though hours vary.

Boutique D'Xochitl
Ejido at Cuauhtémoc. ☎ **755/4-2131.**

This is my favorite place to pick up light crinkle cotton clothing that's perfect for tropical climes. Hours are Monday through Saturday from 9am to 9pm, Sunday from 2 to 9pm.

Casa Marina
Paseo del Pescador 9. ☎ **755/4-2373.**

This small complex extends from the waterfront to Álvarez near 5 de Mayo and houses four shops, each specializing in hand-crafted wares from Mexico and

Guatemala. Items include rugs, textiles, masks, papier-mâché, wood carvings, and silver jewelry. Café Marina, the small coffee shop in the complex, has shelves and shelves of used paperback books in several languages for sale. It's open daily from 9am to 9pm during the high season and from 10am to 2pm and 4 to 8pm during the rest of the year.

Coco Cabaña Collectibles
Guerrero and Álvarez. ☎ **755/4-2518.**

Located next to Coconuts Restaurant, this gorgeous shop is crammed with carefully selected crafts and folk art from all over the country, including fine Oaxaca wood carvings. Owner Pat Cummings once ran a gallery in New York, and the inventory reveals her discriminating eye. If you purchase something, she'll cash your dollars at the going rate. It's opposite the Hotel Citali. It's open Monday through Saturday from 10am to 2pm and 6 to 10pm; it's closed during September and October.

Galería Maya
Bravo 31. ☎ **755/4-3606.**

This small folk art store is packed with Guatemalan jackets, *santos,* silver, painted wooden fish from Guerrero, tin mirror frames, masks, lacquered gourds, rain sticks, and embroidered T-shirts. The store is open Monday through Saturday from 10am to 2pm and 6 to 9pm.

Mueblart
Álvarez 13-B. ☎ **755/3-2530.**

You'll wish you owned a nearby beach house after browsing through this handsome collection of handcrafted furniture or you can simply ship your purchases back home if you'd prefer. Smaller items include wooden and gourd masks and wicker baskets in bright colors. The store is across the street from the Hotel Avila. It's open Monday through Saturday from 11am to 2:30pm and 5 to 9pm.

IXTAPA

Shopping gets better in Ixtapa every year as several fine folk art shops become established. There are several plazas with air-conditioned shops carrying fashionable resort wear and contemporary art, as well as T-shirts and jewelry. Brand-name sportswear is sold at **Ferroni, Bye-Bye, Aca Joe,** and **Navale.** All of these shops are within the same area on Bulevar Ixtapa, across from the beachside hotels. Most of the shops are open from 9am to 2pm and 4 to 9pm, including Sundays.

La Fuente
Los Patios Center on Bulevar Ixtapa. ☎ **755/3-0812.**

This terrific shop carries gorgeous talavera pottery; wicker tables in the form of jaguars; handblown glassware; masks; tin mirrors and frames; and wood and papier-mâché miniatures. It's open daily from 9am to 2pm and 4 to 9pm.

Mic-Mac
La Puerta Center on Bulevar Ixtapa. ☎ **755/3-1733.**

The owners of La Fuente created a second shop featuring embroidered and appliquéd clothing from Guatemala and Mexico; textile wall hangings; and ceramic and brass home accessories. Mic-Mac is open daily from 9am to 2pm and 4 to 9pm.

ACCOMMODATIONS

Ixtapa and Playa Madera have the most expensive hotels, with a couple of choices in the budget to moderate price ranges. Central Zihuatanejo has the most choices in the budget range.

IXTAPA

Very Expensive

✪ Westin Brisas Resort

Bulevar Ixtapa, Ixtapa, Gro. 40880. ☎ **755/3-2121** or 800/228-3000 in the U.S. Fax 755/3-0751. 428 rms, 19 suites. A/C MINIBAR TV TEL. High season $235 single or double, $272 Royal Beach Club, $481–$1,250 suite. Low season $162 single or double, $200 Royal Beach Club, $375–$1,138 suite. Free parking.

Sitting above the high-rise hotels of Ixtapa on its own rocky promontory, the Westin is both literally and figuratively a cut above the others. The austere yet luxurious public areas, all in stone and stucco, are bathed in sweeping breezes and announce that this is a special hotel. The spare luxury carries into the rooms with Mexican tile floors, and grand-but-private, half-shaded and plant-decorated patios with hammocks and lounges. All rooms face the hotel's cove and private beach. The six master suites come with private pools. Water is purified in your tap and there's an ice machine on each floor. The 16th floor is reserved as a no-smoking floor and three rooms on the 18th floor are equipped for disabled travelers.

Dining/Entertainment: From elegant indoor dining to casual open air restaurants this hotel's five restaurants mean you can stay put and just relax without going out for good food. The airy lobby bar is one of the most popular places to enjoy sunset cocktails while a soothing trio croons romantic songs of Mexico.

Services: Laundry and room service, travel agency, car rental, massage, babysitting.

Facilities: Shopping arcade, barber and beauty shop, four swimming pools (one for children), four lighted tennis courts with pro on request, elevator to secluded beach.

Expensive

Krystal

Bulevar Ixtapa s/n, Ixtapa, Gro. 40880. ☎ **755/3-0333** or 800/231-9860 in the U.S. Fax 753/3-0216. 245 rms, 19 suites. A/C MINIBAR TV TEL. High season $165 single or double, $305–$683 suite. Free parking.

Krystal hotels are known in Mexico for the high quality of service and well-maintained rooms. This one is no exception. The multistoried V-shaped building encloses the grounds and pool area. Each spacious, nicely furnished and carpeted room has a balcony with an ocean view, game table, tile bathrooms, and either two double beds or a king-size bed. Master suites have large, furnished triangular-shaped balconies. Ask it the daily buffet breakfast is included in your daily rate. Two children under age 12 can stay free in their parent's room. The eighth floor is no-smoking, and there's one handicapped-equipped room.

Dining/Entertainment: Among the hotel's five restaurants is the evening-only Bogart's (see "Dining" below). There's live music nightly in the lobby bar. The Krystal's famous Cristine Club, born in Cancún, is reincarnated here with the best disco flash around.

Services: Laundry and room service, travel agency, auto rental, beauty and barber shop, massage.

Facilities: swimming pool, two tennis courts, racquetball court, gym with sauna. Ice machines on floors 2, 5, 8, and 11.

Sheraton Ixtapa

Bulevar Ixtapa, Ixtapa, Gro. 40880. ☎ **755/3-1858** or 3-4858, or 800/325-3535 in the U.S. and Canada, 91-800/90-325-MEX in Mexico. Fax 755/3-2438. 322 rms, 12 suites. A/C MINIBAR TV TEL. Low season $176 single or double; $231 junior suite; $357.50 master suite. Free parking.

This grand, resort-style hotel has large, handsomely furnished and open public areas facing the beach; it's a very inviting place to come for a drink and to people-watch. Rooms are as nice as the public areas. Most have balconies with views of either the ocean or the mountains. Thirty-six rooms on the fifth floor are no-smoking. Rooms equipped for the disabled are available.

Dining/Entertainment: Four restaurants; nightclub; Wednesday night Mexican fiesta with buffet and live entertainment outdoors.

Services: Room and laundry service, travel agency, concierge, car rental.

Facilities: There's one beachside pool, four tennis courts, a fitness room, ice machine on each floor, beauty and barber shop, boutiques, pharmacy/gift shop.

Villa del Lago

Retorno Alondras 244,(Apdo. Postal 127) Ixtapa, Gro. 40880. ☎ **755/3-1482.** Fax 755/3-1422. 6 rms. A/C TEL. High season $126–$176 single or double. Low season $93.50–$143 single or double. Rates include breakfast. Street parking available.

Architect Raul Esponda has transformed his private villa into a luxurious, secluded bed and breakfast overlooking Ixtapa's golf course. The best room is the tri-level master suite, with a sunken tiled shower, huge bedroom with great views of the golf course, and a large living room and private terrace. Other rooms are smaller but still delightful, decorated with fine folk art and carved furnishings. Breakfast is served on the terrace; get up early enough and you'll probably spot the two resident alligators sunning in the golf course's lake, or a giant gray heron perched in a nearby palm. The lounge chairs by the swimming pool are a perfect spot for reading a novel from the well-stocked library or just watching the golfers cast envious glances your way. The staff of five keeps a watchful eye over the guests, predicting their whims and needs. Reasonable golf, tennis and meal packages are available. Advance reservations are a good idea, since regular guests sometimes claim the entire villa for weeks at a time.

Dining/Entertainment: Formal dining room for breakfast; lunch and dinner are available on request for both guests and non-guests. TV room with satellite service and a good video library. Family room stocked with games and books. Well-stocked honor bar by the pool.

Services: Transportation to Ixtapa's hotel zone.

Facilities: Swimming pool.

Moderate

Hotel Aristos

Bulevar Ixtapa, Ixtapa, Gro. 40380. ☎ **755/3-0011** or 800/527-4786 in the U.S. Fax 755/3-2031. 250 rms. A/C TV TEL. $60–$80 single or double (including breakfast); $85–$115 single or double (including all three meals). Free parking.

The decor at the bright pink Aristos might be called "Moorish modern," mixing pointed arches with contemporary lines. The standard rooms are in need of renovation and are medium-sized with a sea view (some have balconies) and come with two double beds, marble-trimmed bath, contemporary furniture, and satellite TV with U.S. channels. Check out a few rooms before settling on one; some are in much better condition than others. Parking is in an open lot off Bulevar Ixtapa. The Aristos has an all-inclusive program covering all meals and most activities. This hotel often offers cut-rate deals, and since it's on the same beach as other more expensive hotels, you can enjoy the setting at a fraction of the price. Two restaurants serve buffets only, either included in your all-inclusive package or for a set fee. The one coffee shop has a regular menu. The hotel offers laundry, babysitting, and secretarial and business services, and has a swimming pool, travel agency, shops, two tennis courts, and exercise and water-sports equipment.

ZIHUATANEJO

The term "bungalow" is used loosely in Zihuatanejo, as it is elsewhere in Mexico. A bungalow may be an individual unit with a kitchen and bedroom, or a bedroom only; it also may be two stories high or in a building with multiple units, some of which have kitchens. It may be attractive or rather rustic, and there may or may not be a patio or balcony. Beware of vanishing belongings if your room has a balcony.

Playa Madera and Playa La Ropa, separated from each other only by a craggy shoreline, are both accessible by road. Prices here tend to be higher than those in town. The town is just 5 to 20 minutes away, depending on whether you walk or take a taxi. The most economical hotels are in Zihuatanejo rather than in Ixtapa.

Many long-term guests in Ixtapa and Zihuatanejo search out apartments and condos for rent. Information on rentals, as well as hotel reservations and personalized service, are available from Julia Ortíz Bautista at **Job Representatives,** Villas del Pacífico, Edificio C, Dept. 01, Zihuatanejo, Gro. 40880 (☎ and fax 755/4-4374).

In Town

Apartamentos Amueblados Valle

Vincente Guerrero 14, Zihuatanejo, Gro. 40880. ☎ **755/4-2084.** Fax 753/4-3220. 8 apts. FAN. High season $40 one-bedroom apt, $65 two-bedroom apt. Low season $31 one-bedroom apt, $50 two-bedroom apt.

You can rent a well-furnished apartment for a little more than the price of a hotel room. The five one-bedroom apartments accommodate up to three people; the three two-bedroom apartments can fit four comfortably. Each apartment is different, but all are clean and airy, with ceiling fans, private balconies, and kitchenettes. Maid service is provided daily. There's a paperback-book exchange in the office. Luís Valle, the owner, can often find cheaper apartments elsewhere for guests who want to stay several months. Reserve well in advance during high season. It's on Guerrero about two blocks in from the waterfront between Ejido and N. Bravo.

Hotel Ávila

Juan Álvarez 8, Zihuatanejo, Gro. 40880. ☎ **755/4-2010.** Fax 755/4-3299. 27 rms. A/C or FAN TV. High season $55–$66 single or double. Low season $44–$55 single or double. Street parking is available.

This hotel offers overly expensive rooms conveniently located on the beach—you're paying for location. Eighteen rooms have private balconies facing town, but no ocean view. The rest share a terrace facing the sea. Rooms with ceiling fan or air conditioning cost the same. Ocean-view rooms are the highest priced in each category. There's a restaurant bar off the lobby, with tables spreading across the sidewalk and onto the beach. With your back to the water at the basketball court turn right; the Ávila is on your left.

✪ Hotel Imelda

González 11, Zihuatanejo, Gro. 40880. ☎ **755/4-7662.** Fax 755/4-3199. 45 rms (all with bath). A/C or FAN TV. High season $40 single or double with fan; $45 single or double with A/C. Low season $25 single or double with fan; $28 single or double with A/C. Free enclosed parking.

Despite its proximity to the market area, this hotel is well maintained and remarkably quiet. Each room has a tile floor and tile bath (no shower curtain), a large closet, louvered windows without screens, and two or three double beds. There's a long lap pool and a cheerful restaurant, Rancho Grande, which offers an inexpensive comida corrida. To get here from the museum, walk inland four blocks and turn left on González; the Imelda is on your right between Cuauhtémoc and Vicente Guerrero.

Hotel Susy

Juan Álvarez 3 (at Guerrero), Zihuatanejo, Gro. 40880. ☎ **755/4-2339.** 20 rms (all with bath). FAN. High season $25 single or double. Low season $20 single or double.

Consistently clean, with lots of plants along a shaded walkway set back from the street, this two-story hotel offers small rooms with louvered glass windows with screens. Upper-floor rooms have balconies overlooking the street. Facing away from the water at the basketball court on the Malecón, turn right and walk two blocks; the hotel is on your left at the corner of Guerrero.

✪ Posada Citlali

Vicente Guerrero 3, Zihuatanejo, Gro. 40880. ☎ **755/4-2043.** 17 rms (all with bath). FAN. $22 double.

The small rooms in this pleasant three-story hotel are arranged around a shaded plant-filled courtyard decked out with comfortable rockers and *equipale* (leather-covered) chairs. Bottled water is in help-yourself containers on the patio. Furnishings in each room include an orange chenille bedspread and a large wall mirror with a shelf beneath it. The stairway to the top two floors is narrow and steep. The hotel is near the corner of Álvarez and Guerrero.

Playa Madera

Madera Beach is a 15-minute walk or a $3 taxi ride from town. Most of the accommodations are on the road, Calle Eva S. de López Mateos, that overlooks Madera Beach. If you walk 15 minutes east of town beside the canal, crossing a footbridge and following the road running uphill, you will intersect Mateos.

✪ Bungalows Ley

Calle Eva S. de López Mateos s/n, Playa Madera (Apdo. Postal 466), Zihuatanejo, Gro. 40880. ☎ **755/4-4563** or 4-4087. 6 rms (all with bath). A/C or FAN. $34 double with fan; $40 double with A/C; $56 for two-bedroom suite with kitchen and fan for up to 4 persons, $90 with A/C; $111 for up to six persons.

No two suites are the same at this small complex, one of the nicest on Playa Madera. If you're traveling with a group, you may want to splurge on the most expensive suite (called Club Madero), which comes with a rooftop terrace with tiled hot tub, outdoor bar and grill, and a spectacular view. All the rooms are immaculately clean; the simplest are studios with one bed and a kitchen in the same room. Most rooms have terraces or balconies just above the beach. Clients praise the management. To find the complex, follow Mateos to the right up a slight hill; it's on your left.

✪ Bungalows Pacíficos

Calle Eva S. de López Mateos, Playa Madera (Apdo. Postal 12), Zihuatanejo, Gro. 40880. ☎ and fax **755/4-2112.** 6 rms (all with bath). FAN. High season $50 single or double. Low season $45 single or double.

Tranquil and comfortable, each room in this hotel has a bedroom and a narrow alcove with two additional beds. All the rooms have fully equipped (though humble) kitchens with a small dining table; and the rooms open onto large terraces with a table and chairs, a hammock, flowering plants, and magnificent views. The owner, Anita Hahner, can answer all your questions in four languages, including English, and seems to know everyone in town. The three-story building is arranged in tiers on the steep hillside, and the beach is just a five-minute walk away. Birdwatchers will be delighted here; over 74 species of birds have been spotted and catalogued by guests. Facing Mateos, take the road to the right until you reach its terminus overlooking town; the hotel is on the left.

Hotel Irma

Calle Adelita, Playa Madera (Apdo. Postal 4), Zihuatanejo, Gro. 40880. ☎ **755/4-2101** or 4-2025. Fax 4-3738. 72 rms (all with bath). A/C FAN TV TEL. $50–$70 single or double.

The rooms atop this multi-level hotel have a spectacular view of the bay; some on the lower level face the hallways or sunny terraces. The rooms are gradually being remodeled and the dark wood stripped to its lighter, natural state. Not all rooms have screens and only 44 have air-conditioning, but all are very clean and have two double or one king-size bed (6 rooms have three beds), large bathrooms, TVs with Mexican stations, and plentiful hot water. The staff members are very friendly and helpful. The hotel has a small shop, a travel agency, two pools on a terrace overlooking the beach, and a good restaurant. There's a 58-step stairway from the hotel down to the beach, but guests can also use the beach and pool facilities at the Fiesta Mexicana Hotel on Playa la Ropa. Many of the clients return annually to claim their favorite rooms, usually those with large terraces. From the intersection of Mateos and Adelita turn left and climb a steep hill; the Irma is on your right at the top.

Villas Miramar

Calle Adelita, Playa Madera (Apdo. Postal 211), Zihuatanejo, Gro. 40880. ☎ **755/4-2106** or 4-2616. Fax 753/4-2149. 18 suites. A/C FAN TEL. High season $79 suite for one or two, $89 with ocean view; $115 two-bedroom suite. Low season $50 suite for one or two, $55 with ocean view. Free parking.

Some of these elegant suites are built around a beautiful shady patio that doubles as a restaurant. Those across the street center around a lovely pool and have private balconies and sea views. Parking is enclosed. To find Villas Miramar, follow the road leading south out of town towards Playa La Ropa, then take the first right after the traffic circle, then left on Adelita.

Playa La Ropa

Some travelers consider Playa La Ropa the most beautiful of Zihuatanejo's beaches. It's a 20- to 25-minute walk south of town on the east side of the bay, or a $2 taxi ride.

La Casa Que Canta

Camino Escénico a la Playa La Ropa, Zihuatanejo, Gro. 40880. ☎ **755/4-2722** or 4-2782 or 800/432-6075 or 800/448-8355 in the U.S. 18 suites. A/C. High season $260–$400 single or double. Low season $215–$315 single or double.

La Casa Que Canta (The House that Sings) opened in 1992, and in looks alone it's one of those very special hotels. Meandering down a mountainside overlooking Zihuatanejo Bay, it was designed with striking molded-adobe architecture. Rooms, all with handsome natural-tile floors, are individually decorated in unusual painted Michoacán furniture, antiques, and stretched-leather equipales. Handloomed fabrics are used throughout. All units have large, beautifully furnished terraces with bay views. Hammocks under the thatched roof terraces, supported by rough-hewn vigas, are perfectly placed for watching yachts sail in and out of the harbor. The four categories of rooms, all spacious, get larger as you go up the price scale. Beginning with the smallest, there are three terrace suites, four deluxe suites, nine grand suites, and two private pool suites. Rooms meander up and down the hillside, and while no stairs are extensive, there are no elevators. La Casa Que Canta is a member of the Small Luxury Hotels of the World. Technically it's not on Playa La Ropa; it's on the road leading there. The closest stretch of beach (still not yet Playa La Ropa) is down a steep hill. Children under 18 aren't allowed.

Dining/Entertainment: There's a small restaurant/bar on a shaded terrace overlooking the bay.

Services: Laundry and room service.

Facilities: Freshwater pool on the main terrace; saltwater pool on the bottom level.

Hotel Catalina and Hotel Sotavento

Playa La Ropa, Zihuatanejo, Gro. 40880. ☎ **755/4-2032;** 604/652-0456 in Canada. Fax 753/4-2975; 604/652-3571 in Canada. 85 rms, 24 bungalows. $40–$75 standard room; $82–$87 bungalow or terrace room.

Perched high on the hill close to each other and managed together by the same owners, these two attractive hotels were among the first in the area and retain the slow-paced, gracious mood of Zihuatanejo in its early days as a little-known hideaway. The spectacular panoramic views of Playa La Ropa below alone are worth the price of staying here. The terrace rooms of the Sotavento are quite large and decorated with wood furniture that evokes the 1950s and 1960s, including one double and one single bed. Best of all is the large, shared ocean-view terrace, equipped with hammocks and a chaise lounge for each room—great for sunning and sunset-watching. The Catalina has recently remodeled many of its rooms with Mexican tile, wrought iron, and other handcrafted touches; these also have lovely terraces with ocean views and come with two queen-size beds. Between them the two hotels cover eight stories climbing the slope and two restaurants and bars. Do ask to see at least a couple of rooms first, as they can vary quite a bit in furnishings and price. Also keep in mind the hike down many steps to the beach (depending on the room level) and the lack of air conditioning, compensated for by the ceiling fans and sea breezes. Nor is there a swimming pool. To get here, take the highway south of Zihuatanejo about a mile, turn right at the hotels' sign, and follow the road to the hotels.

Villa del Sol

Playa La Ropa (Apdo. Postal Box 84), Ixtapa/Zihuatanejo, Gro. 40880. ☎ **755/4-2239** or 800/223-6510 in the U.S., 800/422-5500 in Canada. Fax 753/4-2758. 22 standard mini-suites, 8 deluxe suites, 6 master suites, 11 condominiums. A/C. High season $275–$580 single or double. Low season $150–$365 single or double. Breakfast and either lunch or dinner, $50 per person, is mandatory in high season. 10% gratuity added to everything.

Few inns in Mexico compare to this one for luxury, attention to quality, service, and tranquillity. This beachfront hotel is one of two in Mexico to meet the tough standards of the French Relais & Châteaux. It's also a member of Small Luxury Hotels of the World. Units lie along the beachfront in a U-shape anchored by immaculately kept grounds and the oceanside restaurant and bar. Each spacious, split-level suite (with either one or two bedrooms) comes with a living room facing a private patio and is tastefully furnished with tile floors, Mexican decorative objects, and a king-size bed draped in white netting. Standard rooms are smaller and don't have TV or telephone. All have fans in addition to air conditioning, plus hairdryers and luxurious bathrobes in the rooms. Some suites have TV, telephone, minibar, in-room safety-deposit boxes, and a small pool on the patio. Eleven of the 18 condominiums are included in the rental pool. June and September are slow months and last-minute reservations have a better chance then. Children under 14 aren't allowed during high season.

Dining/Entertainment: Open-air restaurant by the beach with classical music and a beachside bar. Friday night Mexican fiesta for $30 at the beachside restaurant. Nonguests pay $25 each to use the beach and restaurant and $15 of the cost goes toward the purchase of a meal in the hotel's restaurant.

Services: Room service, laundry, beauty shop, travel agency, Tane jewelry store.

Facilities: Two pools, two tennis courts (reserve courts in advance), beauty shop, massage service, paperback lending library.

DINING
IXTAPA
Very Expensive

Villa de la Selva
Paseo de la Roca. ☎ **755/3-0362.** Reservations recommended during high season. Main courses $15–$31. Daily 6–11pm. MEXICAN/CONTINENTAL.

Set on the edge of a cliff overlooking the sea, this elegant restaurant enjoys the most spectacular sea and sunset view in Ixtapa. The elegant candlelit tables are arranged on three terraces; try to come early in hopes of getting one of the best vistas, especially on the lower terrace. The cuisine is delicious and classically rich: Filet Villa de la Selva is red snapper topped with shrimp and hollandaise sauce. The cold avocado soup or hot lobster bisque makes a good beginning; finish with chocolate mousse or bananas Singapore.

Expensive

✪ Beccofino
Marina Ixtapa. ☎ **755/3-1770.** Breakfast $2.75–$3.75; pastas $6.50–$11; main courses $8–$14. Daily 9:30am–midnight. NORTHERN ITALIAN.

If you like Italian food, try this casual but classy restaurant early in your stay since you'll probably want to return again and again. Owner Angelo Rolly Pavia provides his guests with the flavorful northern Italian specialties he grew up with. Once seated at the breezy marina location, diners peruse a menu that includes dishes with rice and with short, long, and wide pastas. Ravioli, a house specialty, comes stuffed with the seafood in season. The garlic bread is terrific, and there's an extensive wine list. This place is highly recommended.

Moderate

✪ Golden Cookie Shop
Los Patios Center. ☎ **755/3-0310.** Breakfast $3.60–$4.50; sandwiches $3.60–$5.50; main courses $5–$9. Mon–Sat 8am–3pm and 6–10pm. PASTRIES/INTERNATIONAL.

Although the name is misleading—there are more than cookies here—Golden Cookie's freshly baked cookies and pastries are worthy of a detour, and the coffee menu is the most extensive in town. The large sandwiches, made with fresh soft bread, come with a choice of sliced deli meats. Chicken curry is among the other specialty items. To get to the shop, walk to the rear of the shopping center as you face Mac's Prime Rib; walk up the stairs; turn left and you'll see the restaurant on your right.

✪ Mamma Norma

La Puerta Center, Bulevar Ixtapa. ☎ **755/3-0274.** Breakfast $2.75–$3; main courses $5.50–$8.50; pizza $6.75–$9. Daily 8am–11pm (deliveries made 3–11pm). ITALIAN/AMERICAN.

At one of the most popular restaurants in Ixtapa, you can choose from 17 kinds of pizza (they also deliver), 8 different pasta dishes (including a spicy putanesca), and regional Mexican dishes including cochinita pibil. You'll also find a generous antipasto, burgers, sandwiches, and ice cream. To get to Mamma Norma from the tourist office, walk to the back of the La Puerta Center and look for the sidewalk tables covered with red cloths.

ZIHUATANEJO

Zihuatanejo's **central market,** located on Avenida Benito Juárez (about five blocks inland from the waterfront), offers cheap, tasty food. The food is best at breakfast and lunch because the market activity winds down in the afternoon. The market area is one of the best on this coast for shopping and people watching.

Expensive

El Patio

5 de Mayo 3 at Álvarez. ☎ **755/4-3019.** Breakfast $4–$7; Mexican platters $7.50–$30; seafood $12–$25. Daily 9am–2pm and 3–11pm. SEAFOOD/MEXICAN.

Casually elegant, this patio restaurant is decorated with baskets and at night flickering candles create a romantic atmosphere. Whatever you're a fan of it's likely you'll find it here. There are fajitas and steak, chicken, chiles rellenos, green or red enchiladas, and lobster in garlic sauce. The breakfast menu is typical, but you can also order hamburgers and salads. In the evenings musicians often play Latin American favorites. It's one block inland from Álvarez and next to the church.

Moderate

✪ Casa Elvira

Paseo del Pescador. ☎ **755/4-2061.** Main courses $4.50–$16. Daily noon–10:30pm. MEXICAN/SEAFOOD.

Casa Elvira almost always has a crowd, drawn in by its neat, clean atmosphere and by the wide selection of inexpensive lunches and dinners on its bilingual menu. House specialties are snapper (or whatever fish is in season) and lobster; the restaurant also serves meat dishes and chicken mole. The most expensive seafood platter includes lobster, red snapper, and jumbo butterfly shrimp. Facing the water and the basketball court, turn right; Casa Elvira is on the west end of the waterfront near the town pier.

Garrobos

Álvarez 52. ☎ **755/4-2977.** Main courses $3.50–$13.50. Tues–Sun 2–10pm. MEXICAN/SEAFOOD.

This very popular, roomy restaurant offers large meat and seafood dishes attractively presented with rice and two vegetables. It also serves paella and the local specialty tiritas de pescado—little strips of marinated fish (as with ceviche, the fish is "cooked" by the lemon or lime juice). In the evening trios often serenade diners. To reach Garrobos, turn left on Alvarez with your back to the basketball court; the restaurant is on your right beneath the Hotel Raúl Tres Marías Centro.

La Bocana

Álvarez 13. ☎ **755/4-3545.** Breakfast $4–$6.75; main courses $7.75–$23. Daily 8am–11pm. MEXICAN/SEAFOOD.

One of Zihuatanejo's finest seafood restaurants, La Bocana is known for its huge *plato de mariscos*—a seafood platter that feeds two to four people. It comes heaped with lobster, crayfish, shrimp, fish filet, rice, and salad. Mariachis and marimba bands come and go on Sunday. It's on the main street near the town plaza.

✪ Restaurant Paul's

5 de Mayo s/n. ☎ **755/4-2188.** Main courses $9–$15. Daily 6–10pm. INTERNATIONAL/SEAFOOD.

It's hard to find a seat after 7pm at this small open-air restaurant, where the Swiss chef has attained a fanatical following. It must be the only place in town that serves fresh artichokes as an appetizer, and the ubiquitous fish filet is covered with a smooth, delicately flavored shrimp and dill sauce. The pasta comes topped with a pile of shrimp and fish in a light cream sauce, and the pork chops and beef medallions are thick and juicy. To get to Paul's from the main pier, turn right on Álvarez and walk one block, then turn left onto 5 de Mayo; Paul's is on your right before the church.

Inexpensive

Casa Puntarenas

Calle Noria, Colonia Lázaro Cárdenas. No phone. Soup $1.35; main courses $2.25–$5. 6:30–9pm. MEXICAN/SEAFOOD.

A modest spot with a tin roof and nine wooden tables, Puntarenas is one of the best spots in town for fried whole fish served with toasted bolillos, sliced tomatoes, onions, and avocado. The chilis rellenos are mild and stuffed with plenty of cheese; the meat dishes are less flavorful. To get to Puntarenas from the pier, turn left on Álvarez and cross the footbridge on your left. Turn right after you cross the bridge; the restaurant is on your left.

Nueva Zelanda

Cuauhtémoc 23 at Ejido. ☎ **755/4-2340.** Tortas $2.50–$4.75; enchiladas $3.50–$4.75; fruit-and-milk licuados $1.50; cappuccinos $1.80. Daily 8am–10pm. MEXICAN.

One of the most popular places in town, this clean open-air snack shop welcomes diners with rich cappuccinos sprinkled with cinnamon and pancakes with real maple syrup. The mainstays of the menu are tortas and enchiladas. For only 5¢ more, you can order a cappuccino to go (say "para llevar") and get twice as much coffee. You'll find Nueva Zelanda by walking three blocks inland from the waterfront on Cuauhtémoc; the restaurant is on your right.

Ruben's

Calle Adelita s/n. ☎ **755/4-4617.** Burgers $2.75–$3.50; vegetables $1.60; ice cream $1.40. Daily 6–11pm. BURGERS/VEGETABLES.

The choices are easy here—you can order either a big sloppy burger made from top sirloin beef grilled over mesquite or a foil-wrapped packet of baked potatoes, chayote, zucchini, or sweet corn. Homemade ice cream , beer, and soda fills out the menu, which is posted on the wall by the kitchen. Guests snag a waitress and rattle off their orders, grab their own drinks from the cooler, and tally their own tabs. Rolls of paper towels hang over the tables on the open porch and shaded terrace. Ruben's is a popular fixture in the Playa Madera neighborhood—though the customers come from all over town. To get here from Mateos, turn right on Adelita; Ruben's is on your right.

La Sirena Gorda

Paseo del Pescador. ☎ **755/4-2687.** Breakfast $2.50–$2.75; main courses $3.25–$5.50. Thurs–Tues 7am–10pm. MEXICAN.

For the best inexpensive breakfast in town, head to La Sirena Gorda for a variety of eggs and omelets, hotcakes with bacon, as well as fruit with granola and yogurt. For lunch or dinner try the house specialty—seafood tacos with fish prepared to taste like machaca or carnitas or covered with mole. There's always a short list of daily specials, such as blackened red snapper, steak, or fish kebabs. Patrons enjoy the casual sidewalk-cafe atmosphere. To get here from the basketball court, face the water and walk to the right; La Sirena Gorda is on your right just before the town pier.

Bakeries

El Buen Gusto

Guerrero 4. ☎ **755/4-3231.** All items 25¢–$2.25. Mon–Sat 7:30am–10pm. BAKED GOODS.

Small but packed with goodies, this pastry shop offers what's usually found in a Mexican bakery—then goes beyond expectations by offering banana bread, French bread, doughnuts, and cakes. To get here from the museum, walk a half a block up Guerrero; the bakery is on your left.

PLAYA MADERA & PLAYA LA ROPA

Kon-Tiki

Camino a Playa La Ropa. ☎ **755/4-2471.** Pizza $9–$25. Daily 1pm–midnight; happy hour 6–7pm. PIZZA.

In the air-conditioned dining room on a cliff overlooking the bay, enjoy 13 types of pizzas in three different sizes. The vegetarian is topped with beans, peanuts, onion, mushroom, bell pepper, garlic, pineapple, and avocado. There's also a big-screen sports-video bar, open the same hours.

La Perla

Playa La Ropa. ☎ **755/4-2700.** Breakfast $2.50–$6.50; main courses $8–$16. Daily 10am–10pm; breakfast served 10am–noon. SEAFOOD.

There are many palapa-style restaurants on Playa La Ropa, but La Perla is one of the best. Cloth-covered tables under the trees and thatched roof make for pleasant dining. Plus the long swath of pale sand stretching out in either direction and an array of wooden chairs under palapas combine with good food to make La Perla a favorite with visitors. The "filet of fish La Perla" is cooked deliciously, wrapped in foil with tomatoes, onions, and cheese. Around sunset, visitors gather in the bar to watch the news on the TV, which shows American channels. It's near the southern end of La Ropa Beach. Take the right fork in the road; there's a sign in the parking lot.

Rossy

Playa La Ropa. No phone. Breakfast $3.25–$4; tacos $2.50–$4; seafood $2.50–$16; beer $1.50; margarita $3.50. Daily 9am–10pm. SEAFOOD/SANDWICHES/TACOS.

Another locally favorite beachside restaurant, this one too is casual with orange and yellow cloth-covered tables and peach and orange chairs and lounges near the water. The menu emphasizes seafood with a short beef and taco section. Seafood includes ceviche, breaded lobster, and river crawfish during the rainy season. It's at the far end of La Ropa Beach. Take the left fork in the road and follow it to the end.

ZIHUATANEJO & IXTAPA AFTER DARK

With an exception or two, Zihuatanejo nightlife dies down around 11pm or midnight. For a good selection of clubs, hotel fiestas, special events, and watering holes with live music and dancing, head for Ixtapa. But keep in mind that the shuttle bus stops at 11pm, and a taxi ride back to Zihuatanejo after midnight costs 50% more than the regular price. During off-season (after Easter or before Christmas) hours vary: Some places open only on weekends, while others are closed completely.

THE CLUB & MUSIC SCENE

Many discos and dance clubs stay open until the last customers leave, so closing hours vary. Most discos have a ladies' night at least once a week when women are admitted free and drink free. Call to check the day.

The Bay Club And Samba Café

Camino a Playa La Ropa, Zihuatanejo. ☎ 755/4-4844. No cover.

It's fun to dance under the stars on the beautifully lit patio surrounded by tropical plants. The restaurant/bar is perched on a hillside with a splendid view of the town lights and bay. Live music ranges from jazz to soft rock. The mesquite-grilled dinners are expensive, but come after dinner to enjoy the music with an appetizer or dessert. Drinks cost between $1.50 and $3.50, and snacks from $3.50 to $8. A full dinner goes for $12.25 and up. The club is open daily during high season from 9:30pm to midnight; happy hour is 5 to 7pm. Closed in the off season.

Carlos 'n' Charlie's

Bulevar Ixtapa (just north of the Best Western Posada Real), Ixtapa. ☎ 755/3-0085. Cover (including drink tokens) after 9pm for dancing $2.50.

Decorated with all sorts of bric-a-brac, silly sayings, and photos from the Mexican Revolution, this restaurant/nightclub offers party ambience and good food. The eclectic menu includes iguana in season (Alka-Seltzer and aspirin are on the house). Out back by the beach is an open-air section (part of it shaded) with a raised wooden platform called the "pier" for dancing at night, thus mixing the sound of the surf with recorded rock and roll. The restaurant is open daily from noon to midnight; pier dancing is nightly from 9pm to 3am.

Cristine

In the Hotel Krystal, Bulevar Ixtapa, Ixtapa. ☎ 755/3-0456. Cover $4.50.

This flashy streetside disco is famous for its midnight light show, which features classical music played on a megasound system. A semicircle of tables in tiers overlooks the dance floor. No tennis shoes, sandals, shorts, or jeans are allowed, and reservations are advised during high season. Drinks cost $1.50 to $5. It's open daily during high season from 10:30pm to the wee hours; the light show is at midnight. (Off-season hours vary.)

Euforia Disco
Bulevar Ixtapa, Ixtapa. ☎ **755/3-1190.** Cover $4.50.

You can't miss the Euforia Disco, next to the Lighthouse Restaurant and in front of the Best Western Posada Real at the turnoff to Carlos 'n' Charlie's. Levels of tables rise on one side of the circular dance floor, behind which is a volcano that actually erupts. Go early in time to see the sound-and-light show. No shorts are allowed. Drinks cost between $1.50 and $4. Ask about seasonal discounts on the admission. It's open daily during high season and on holidays from 10pm to the wee hours, and is closed in the off season.

Señor Frog's
Bulevar Ixtapa in the La Puerta Center, Ixtapa. ☎ **755/3-0272.** Cover (including drink tokens) after 9pm for dancing $3–$5.

A companion of Carlos 'n' Charlie's, Señor Frog's has several dining sections and a warehouse-like bar with raised dance floors. Rock 'n' roll blares from large speakers, and even those stopping by for dinner sometimes dance by their tables between courses. The restaurant is open daily from 6pm to midnight; the bar is open until 3am.

HOTEL FIESTAS & THEME NIGHTS

Many hotels hold Mexican fiestas and other special events that usually include dinner, drinks, live music, and entertainment for a fixed price ($30 to $40). The **Sheraton Ixtapa** (☎ 755/3-1858) is famous for its Wednesday-night fiesta; good Mexican fiestas are also held by the **Krystal Hotel** (☎ 755/3-0333) and **Dorado Pacífico** (☎ 755/3-2025) in Ixtapa and the **Villa del Sol** (☎ 755/4-2239) on Playa La Ropa in Zihuatanejo. The Sheraton Ixtapa is the only one that offers these in the off season. The **Westin Brisas Ixtapa** (☎ 755/3-2121) and the **Sheraton Ixtapa** also put on theme nights featuring the cuisine and music of different countries. Call to make reservations (travel agencies also sell the tickets) and be sure you understand what the fixed price covers (drinks, tax, and tip are not always included).

A TRIP TO TRONCONES, A SLEEPY FISHING VILLAGE

The tiny fishing settlement of Troncones, with its long beaches, has become a favorite escape from Ixtapa and Zihuatanejo. There's nothing much to do but stroll the empty beach, swim in the sea (if the surf is not high), and have a seafood feast at one of the fishermen's-shack restaurants or at Casa de la Tortuga (see below). Unfortunately, no public buses serve this area, and you'll have to join a tour or hire a taxi to take you there. For about $16, the driver will take you and return at the hour you request to bring you back to town.

ACCOMMODATIONS & DINING

Casa de la Tortuga and El Burro Boracho
Troncones, 6 miles north of Ixtapa on Highway 200. Fax 755/4-3296. 6 suites, 1 master suite, 3 rms, 5 RV spaces. $35–$50 double. For reservations write Apdo. Postal 37, Zihuatanejo, Gro. 40880.

Dewey and Karolyn MacMillan, a young American couple, have created an isolated paradise on the beach at Troncones. Casa Tortuga is a four-bedroom home with a separate guesthouse; you can rent room separately or as an entire vacation home. El Burro Boracho has six suites in three rustic stone bungalows; each room has a private bath, a king-size bed, and a hammock on the porch. The MacMillans invite day-trippers to the patio of their modest beachfront bungalow for a home-cooked lunch of lobster, shrimp, or other fish. It's very casual and comfortable, and the meal is among the best I've ever eaten. If you have difficulty reaching the McMillans, call Anita Hahner at Bungalows Pacíficos (see "Accommodations," above) on Playa La Ropa in Zihuatanejo and she may be able to help.

2 Acapulco

262 miles S of Mexico City, 170 miles S of Taxco, 612 miles SE of Guadalajara; 158 miles SE of Ixtapa/Zihuatanejo, 470 miles NW of Huatulco

To the world, Acapulco has a perennially romantic reputation and a jet-set image. Acapulco first grabbed the world's attention in the 1960s when it was the stomping ground of Hollywood celebrities, and it is still growing. A plethora of new villas and condominiums have appeared seemingly overnight on the mountain slopes. The latest development is the enormous Acapulco Diamante project running along the coast from Puerto Marqués almost to the airport. It includes the new Sheraton, Camino Real, and Vidafel resort hotels, and even more hotels are on the drawing board.

Acapulco's nightlife never dims; the vibrant variety of this city's discos and clubs is hard to top in Mexico. The view of Acapulco Bay at night, spangled with twinkling lights, is also beyond compare.

Acapulco, however, is a real city of about 1 million now, rather than simply a resort. It has its share of grit along with glitz. There are slums as well as villas, and some of the hotels could use a facelift. The city continues to work hard to maintain the glamour that originally put it on the map. A program called "ACA-Limpia" ("Clean Acapulco") has cleaned up the bay, where whales have been sighted recently for the first time in years, and has spruced up the Costera. And the itinerant vendors that hawk their wares to tourists on the beaches and sidewalks have been moved to newly created market areas, such as the Diana traffic circle on the Costera.

ESSENTIALS

GETTING THERE & DEPARTING   By Plane   See Chapter 3, "Planning a Trip to Mexico," for information on flying from the United States or Canada to Acapulco. Local numbers for major airlines that have nonstop or direct service to Acapulco are: **Aeroméxico,** ☎ 85-1600 for reservations, or 66-9104 at the airport; **American,** ☎ 84-1244 or 84-1179 for reservations, or 84-0372 at the airport; **Continental,** ☎ 66-9063 or 66-9064 at the airport; **Delta,** ☎ 84-0716 or 84-0717 at the airport, or 91-800/9-0221 in Mexico; **Mexicana,** ☎ 84-6943 or 84-6890, or 84-1815 at the airport; and **Taesa,** ☎ 66-9067 for reservations, or 86-4576; or 81-1214 at the airport.

Within Mexico, Aeroméxico flies from Guadalajara, Mexico City, Toluca, and Tijuana; Mexicana flies from Mexico City; and Taesa flies from Laredo, Mexico City, and Guadalajara. Regional carriers include **AeroLibertad,** flying from Ixtapa/

Zihuatanejo and Oaxaca, and **AeroMorelos,** flying from Cuernavaca and Puebla. Check with a travel agent about charter flights.

Transportes Terrestres (☎ 83-6500) has colectivo service to and from the airport. Call the day before your departure for a reservation. The one-way trip costs $7 per person. The service picks you up 1 1/2 hours (for flights within Mexico) to two hours (international flights) before your departure time. **Taxis** cost about $20.

By Bus   To/From Mexico City: Buses to Acapulco leave from the **Terminal Central de Autobuses del Sur** (Tasqueña Metro line) for the four-to six-hour trip. Travel time depends on the number of stops. **Estrella de Oro** and **Estrella Blanca** have hourly service from Mexico City to Acapulco, but try to reserve your seat a few days in advance. There's little difference in quality between express and deluxe service, but get a directo if you want to arrive without a lot of stops in between.

From Acapulco, **Estrella de Oro** (☎ 85-8705 or 85-5282) has frequent direct buses to Mexico City. **Oro Plus** has service to Mexico City daily at 7:45, 10, and 11am; 10:15pm; and 1am. All Oro passengers must check luggage that is over one foot long. The baggage-check counter is to the right of ticket sales. **Turistar Plus** buses to Mexico City cost roughly double those of Estrella Blanca.

To/From Ixtapa & Zihuatanejo: Estrella Blanca has several direct buses daily, and **Turistar** has Plus service daily at 6:30am and 5pm. From Acapulco, **Estrella de Oro** runs several daily buses to Ixtapa/Zihuatanejo.

To/From other Points in Mexico: Estrella Blanca (☎ 83-0802) has service to Monterrey, Zacatecas, Guadalajara, the region around San Luis Potosí, Taxco, Chilpancingo, Mexico City, Puerto Escondido, and Huatulco. **Estrella de Oro** offers three daily buses to Taxco (at 7 and 9am and 4:30pm).

By Car   From Mexico City, you can take Highway 95 south or the curvy toll-free highway (six hours). You can also take Highway 95 D, the toll highway (3 1/2 to four hours), which costs around $80 one way. The free road from Taxco is in good condition, so it's worth taking to save around $40 in tolls from there through Chilpancingo to Acapulco. From points north or south along the coast, the only choice is Highway 200.

ORIENTATION   Arriving by Plane   The **airport** is 14 miles southeast of town near Puerto Marqués, over the hills east of the bay. **Transportes Terrestre** has desks at the front of the airport where you can buy tickets for minivan colectivo transportation into town ($7 per person); you can also go by taxi ($20).

Arriving by Bus   The **Estrella de Oro** bus station is a distance from downtown at Cuauhtémoc 1490 and Massieu, within walking distance of some budget-range accommodations. Local buses pass the terminal going both directions on Cuauhtémoc. The relatively new (1990) **Estrella Blanca** terminal at Ejido 47 is north of downtown and farthest from the hotels I have recommended below. The station has a hotel-reservation service, **Sendetur,** open 24 hours. Just before you exit you'll see a taxi ticket booth where rates are set for every hotel.

Information   The **State of Guerrero Tourism Office** operates the **Procuraduria del Turista** on street level in front of the Convention Center (☎ 84-4583 or 84-7050, ext. 165 or 175). It offers maps and information about the city and state and is open daily from 9am to 9pm.

Acapulco Bay Area

**To Pie de la Cuesta
Ixtapa - Zihuatanejo**

La Quebrada

**Plaza
Las Glorias/
El Mirador**

Playa
Langosta

Market

5

Zócalo

6

Av. Constituyentes

Escudero Serdán

Mendoza

Av. Cuauhtémoc

Vasco Nuñez

Ria Camaron

**Parqu
Papag**

Hotel Paraíso
Radisson

Playa Hornos

Playa
Horn

Commercial Wharfs

**Downtown Acapulco
(See Inset)**

Bahía de Acapulco

Costera M. Alemán

La Pinzona

Playa Larga

Av. de la Aguada

Gran Via Tropical

3

2

Av. A. López Mateo

4

Playa Caletilla

Playa Caleta

Playa Roqueta

Isla La Roqueta

Acapulco Region

Rio Coyuca

200

*Laguna de
Coyuca*

Bahía de Coyuca

● Pie de la Cuesta

95

Acapulco

200

*Laguna de
Tres Palos*

✈ **Aeropuerto**

Bahía de Acapulco

Barra Vieja

1225

Centro Internacional de Convivencia Infantil (CICI) **8**	Mágico Mundo Marino **4**
Cliff divers **1**	Plaza de Toros **2**
Convention Center **7**	Zócalo/Plaza Alvarez **5**
Fort San Diego/Museo Histórico de Acapulco **6**	
Jai Alai Fronton/Stadium **3**	

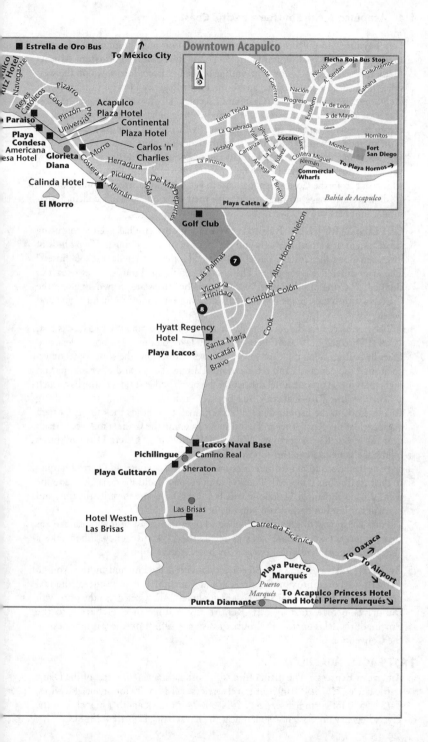

Estrella de Oro Bus

To México City

Downtown Acapulco

Flecha Roja Bus Stop

Nación
Progreso

Vicente Guerrero
Nicolás
A. Serdán
Cuauhtémoc
Galeana

Escudero
V. de León
5 de Mayo

Lerdo Tejada
La Quebrada
Iglesias
Valle
Hidalgo
Carranza
La Paz
B. Juárez
Arteaga
A. Bretón
La Pinzona

Zócalo

Morelos
Hornitos

Fort
San Diego

Costera Miguel
Alemán
To Playa Hornos →

Commercial
Wharfs

Playa Caleta ↙

Bahía de Acapulco

Acapulco
Plaza Hotel

Continental
Plaza Hotel

Carlos 'n'
Charlies

Navegante
Reyes
Católicos
Pizarro
Cosa
Pinzón
Universidad

Paraíso

**Playa
Condesa**
Americana
esa Hotel

**Glorieta
Diana**

Morro
Herradura
Picuda
Del Mar
Sola
Deportes

Calinda Hotel

Costera M. Alemán

El Morro

Golf Club

Las Palmas

7

Cristóbal Colón

Victoria
Trinidad

8

Cook

Av. Alm. Horacio Nelson

Hyatt Regency
Hotel

Santa María
Yucatán
Bravo

Playa Icacos

Icacos Naval Base

Pichilingue

Camino Real

Playa Guittarón

Sheraton

Las Brisas

Hotel Westin
Las Brisas

Carretera Escénica

To Oaxaca →
To Airport ↘

**Playa Puerto
Marqués**

Puerto
Marqués

Punta Diamante

To Acapulco Princess Hotel
and Hotel Pierre Marqués ↘

City Layout   Acapulco stretches for more than four miles around the huge bay, so walking to see it all is impractical. The main boulevard, **Costera Miguel Alemán** (the Costera), follows the outline of the bay from downtown on the west side, where "Old Acapulco" began, to the Hyatt Regency Hotel on the east side. It continues by another name **(Carretera Escenica)** all the way to the airport. Most hotels are either on the Costera and the beach or a block or two away; as you go east from downtown they become increasingly luxurious. **Avenida Cuauhtémoc** is the major artery inland and runs roughly parallel to the Costera.

Street names and numbers in this city can be confusing and hard to find—many streets are not well marked or change names unexpectedly. Fortunately, you're seldom far from the Costera, so it's hard to get really lost. Street numbers on the Costera seem to have nothing to do with their location, so don't conclude that similar numbers will necessarily be close together.

GETTING AROUND   By Bus   Even though the city has such a confusing street system, it's amazingly easy and inexpensive to use city buses. Two kinds of buses run along the Costera: pastel color-coded buses and regular "school buses." The main difference is the price. The new air-conditioned tourist buses **(Aca Tur Bus)** are 75¢; the old buses are 40¢. Covered bus stops are located all along the Costera, with handy maps on the walls showing bus routes to major sights and hotels.

The best place near the zócalo to catch a bus is beside Sanborn's, two blocks east. **"Caleta Directo"** or **"Base-Caleta"** buses will take you to the Hornos, Caleta, and Caletilla beaches along the Costera. Some buses return along the same route; others go around the peninsula and return to the Costera. To get to the restaurants and nightspots in the upscale hotel district on the north and east sides of the bay, catch a **"Base–Cine Río–Caleta"** bus beside Sanborn's. It runs inland along Cuauhtémoc to the Estrella de Oro bus terminal, then heads back to the Costera and beach at the Ritz Hotel and continues east along the Costera to Icacos Beach near the Hyatt Regency Hotel. **"Zócalo Directo"** and **"Caleta Directo"** buses follow the same route in the opposite direction.

For expeditions to more distant destinations, there are buses to Puerto Marqués to the east (the bus is marked "Puerto Marqués–Base") and Pie de la Cuesta to the west (the bus is marked "Zócalo–Pie de la Cuesta"). Be sure to verify the time and place of the last bus back if you hop one of these!

For a cheap way to get to the discos and restaurants east of town near the Las Brisas Hotel, take a "Base" bus as far as the Hyatt Regency. Then take a "Las Brisas" bus the rest of the way. City buses stop at 10pm.

By Taxi   Taxis charge $2 to $8 for a ride within the city and more if you go farther out. For approximate prices, ask at your hotel or scan one of the taxi tariff lists found in the lobbies of most major hotels. Always establish the price with the driver before starting out. Report any trouble or overcharges to the Procuraduria del Turista—the tourist assistance Office on the Costera next to the Convention Center (☎ 74/84-4416).

FAST FACTS: ACAPULCO

American Express   The main office is at Costera Alemán 709, east of the Diana traffic circle (☎ 74/84-1095 for travel services, 74/84-5200 for financial services, 74/84-5550 for customer service, 74/84-6060 for tours); another branch is at the Hyatt Regency on Costera Alemán near the naval base (☎ 74/84-2888).

Climate   June through October is the rainy season; June, September, and October are the wettest months, while July and August are relatively dry.

Consular Agents   The United States has an agent at the Hotel Club del Sol on Costera Alemán at R. Católicos (☎ 74/85-6600), across from the Hotel Acapulco Plaza; it's open Monday through Friday from 10am to 2pm. The agent of Canada is also at the Hotel Club del Sol (☎ 74/85-6621), open Monday through Friday from 9am to 1pm. The agent of the United Kingdom is at the Las Brisas Hotel on Carretera Escénica near the airport (☎ 74/84-6605); it's open Monday through Friday from 9am to 6pm.

Currency Exchange   Banks along the Costera are open Monday through Friday from 9am to 1 or 1:30pm (though hours for exchanging money may be shorter) and generally have the best rates. Casas de cambio (currency-exchange booths) along the street may have better exchange rates than hotels.

Parking   It is illegal to park on the Costera at any time.

Post Office   The central post office (correo) is on the Costera near the zócalo and Sanborn's. Other branches are located in the Estrella de Oro bus station on Cuauhtémoc, inland from the Acapulco Ritz Hotel, and on the Costera near Caleta Beach.

Safety   Pay careful attention to warning flags posted on Acapulco beaches! Riptides claim a few lives every year. Red or black flags mean stay out of the water, yellow flags signify caution, and white or green flags mean it's safe to swim. Don't swim on any beach that fronts an open sea. But don't let down your guard on the bays either. It's difficult to imagine how powerful an undertow can be.

As always, tourists are vulnerable to thieves. This is especially true when you're shopping in a market; lying on the beach; wearing jewelry; or carrying a camera, purse, or bulging wallet. Tourists out for a morning walk on the beach should be especially alert. Pay attention to joggers coming from both directions—one knocks you down, then they rob you. To remove temptation from would-be thieves, purchase a waterproof plastic tube on a string to wear around your neck at the beach— it's big enough for a few bills and your room key. Street vendors and hotel variety shops sell them.

Telephone Numbers   The area code for Acapulco is 74, a recent change from the old code, which was 748. Be aware that now all Acapulco numbers begin with "8," but many people have not made the transition and still give their numbers without the "8" or still print the area code as 748.

Tourist Police   If you see policemen in uniforms of white and light blue, they're from a special corps of English-speaking police who assist tourists.

FUN ON & OFF THE BEACH

Great beaches and water sports abound in Acapulco. It's also pleasant to take a walk early in the day (before it gets too hot) around the **zócalo,** called Plaza Álvarez. Visit the **cathedral**—the bulbous blue onion domes make it look more like a Russian Orthodox church, and it was actually designed as a movie theater! From the church, turn east along the side street going off at a right angle (Calle Carranza, which doesn't have a marker), where there's an arcade with newsstands and shops.

A fabulous view of Acapulco awaits you from the top of the hill behind the cathedral. Take a taxi up the hill from the main plaza, following the signs leading to **La Mira.**

City tours, day-trips to Taxco, cruises, and other excursions and activities are offered through local travel agencies.

THE BEACHES

Here's the rundown, from west to east around the bay. **Playa la Angosta** is a small, sheltered, and often-deserted cove just around the bend from **La Quebrada** (where the cliff divers perform).

South of downtown on the Peninsula de las Playas lie **Caleta Beach** and **Caletilla Beach.** They are separated by a small outcropping of land containing the new aquarium and water park, Mágico Mundo Marino. Here you'll find thatch-roofed restaurants, water-sports equipment for rent, and the brightly painted boats that ferry passengers to Roqueta Island. You can rent beach chairs and umbrellas for $6 per day. Mexican families favor these beaches because they're close to several inexpensive hotels. In the late afternoon, fishermen pull their colorful boats up on the sand and sell their catch and sometimes oysters on the half shell.

The pleasure boats dock at **Playa Larga,** also south of the zócalo. Charter fishing trips sail from here. In the old days, these downtown beaches—Larga, Caleta, and Caletilla—were what Acapulco was all about. Nowadays the beaches and the resort development stretch the entire four-mile length of the bay's shore.

Going east from the zócalo, the major beaches are **Hornos** (near Papagayo Park), **Hornitos, Condesa,** and **Icacos,** followed by the naval base (La Base) and **Punta del Guitarrón.** After Punta del Guitarrón, the road climbs to the legendary hotel Las Brisas, where many of the 300 casitas (bungalow-type rooms) have their own swimming pools (there are 250 pools in all) and start at $200 per day in winter, $125 in the off-season. Past Las Brisas, the road continues to **Puerto Marqués** and **Punta Diamante,** about 12 miles from the zócalo. The fabulous Acapulco Princess and Pierre Marqués hotels dominate the landscape.

The bay of Puerto Marqués is an attractive area for **swimming**. The water is calm, the bay sheltered, and waterskiing available. Past the bay lies **Revolcadero Beach** and a fascinating jungle lagoon.

Warning: Each year in Acapulco at least one or two unwary swimmers drown because of deadly rip tides and undertow (see "Safety" in "Fast Facts," above). Swim only in Acapulco Bay or Puerto Marqués Bay—but be careful of the undertow no matter where you go!

Other beaches are difficult to reach without a car. **La Pie de la Cuesta** is eight miles west of town (buses leave town every five or 10 minutes). You can't swim here, but it's a great spot for watching big waves and the sunset, especially over coco locos (refreshments made with a fresh coconut with the top whacked off) at one of the rustic beachfront restaurants hung with hammocks. If boys try to collect money from you for sitting under the thatched palapas on the public beach, you don't have to pay them.

If you are driving, continue west along the peninsula, passing Coyuca Lagoon on your right, until you have almost reached the small air base at the tip. Along the way, you'll be invited to drive into different sections of beach by various private entrepreneurs, mostly small boys.

BAY CRUISES & ROQUETA ISLAND

The deck of a boat is a wonderful place from which to view the whole bay, and Acapulco has a variety of them to choose from—yachts, huge catamarans and trimarans, single- and double-decker—you name it. Cruises are offered morning, afternoon, and evening. Some offer buffets, open bars, and live music; others have snacks, drinks, and taped music. (The music, by the way, may be loud enough to preclude talking.) Prices range from around $20 to $60. The operators of these cruises come and go, and their phone numbers change so frequently from year to year that it's pointless to list them here; to find out what cruises are currently operated, contact any Acapulco travel agency or hotel tour desk. They usually have a scrapbook with pictures and brochures so you can get a good idea about what a cruise entails before booking it.

Boats from Caletilla Beach to **Roqueta Island**—a delightful place to snorkel, sunbathe, hike to a lighthouse, visit a small zoo, or eat lunch—leave every half hour from 10am until the last one returns at 5pm. The cost is $5 round trip or $7.75 on a glass-bottom boat (use the same ticket to return on any launch). You may disagree, but I don't think the glass-bottom boat ride is worth the bucks; you circle the bay looking down at a few fish, then a diver swims down to a statue of a madonna. Purchase tickets directly from any boat that's loading or from the **information booth** on Caletilla Beach (☎ 74/82-2389). The booth also rents inner tubes, small boats, canoes, paddleboats, and beach chairs; it can also arrange waterskiing and scuba diving.

WATER SPORTS & BOAT RENTALS

An hour of **waterskiing** can cost as little as $30 or as much as $60. Caletilla Beach, Puerto Marqués Bay, and Coyuca Lagoon have waterskiing facilities.

Scuba diving costs $40 for $1\frac{1}{2}$ hours of instruction if you book directly with the instructor on Caleta Beach. It costs $45 to $55 if you make arrangements through a hotel or travel agency. Dive trips start around $50 per person for one dive.

Boat rentals are the least expensive on Caletilla Beach, where an information booth rents inner tubes, small boats, canoes, paddleboats, and beach chairs; it can also arrange waterskiing and scuba diving (see "Bay Cruises & Roqueta Island," above).

For **deep-sea fishing** excursions, go to the pale-pink building of the boat cooperative opposite the zócalo. Charter fishing trips from here run from $100 to $150 for seven hours, arranged through the **boat cooperative** (☎ 74/82-1099). Booked through a travel agent or hotel, fishing trips start around $150 to $200 for four people. The fishing license, food, and drink are extra.

Parasailing, though not without risks (like landing on a palm tree or a building), can be a fantastic thrill. The pleasure of floating high over the bay hanging from a parachute towed by a motorboat is yours for $45. Most of the parachute rides operate on Condesa Beach.

GOLF, TENNIS, RIDING & BULLFIGHTS

A round of 18 holes of **golf** at the **Acapulco Princess Hotel** (☎ 74/84-3100) costs $107 for nonguests and $70 for guests. At the **Club de Golf Acapulco,** off the Costera next to the Convention Center (☎ 74/84-0781 or 84-0782), you can play nine holes for $35 or 18 holes for $46.

Tennis at one of the tennis clubs open to the public costs around $11 per hour. Try the **Club de Golf Acapulco** (☎ 74/84-4824 or 84-0782), open daily from 7am to 7pm. Singles cost $11 per hour; doubles, $16.

Horseback-riding tours on the beach are available through the **Lienzo Charro "México Real,"** near the Acapulco Princess Hotel (☎ 74/85-0331). The two-hour rides depart at 9:30 and 11:30am and 3:30pm daily and cost $40, including two beers or soft drinks.

Traditionally termed the Fiesta Brava, the **bullfights** are held during Acapulco's winter season at a ring up the hill from Caletilla Beach. Tickets purchased through travel agencies cost around $40 and usually include transportation to and from your hotel. The festivities begin each Sunday in winter at 5:30pm.

MUSEUMS & WATER PARKS

Centro Cultural de Acapulco
Costera Alemán. ☎ **74/84-4004.** Admission free. Daily 9am–2pm and 5–8pm.

The State of Guerrero's Instituto Guerrerense de la Cultura sponsors this cultural center. It's located one block east of CICI in a complex of small buildings in a shady grove across from the Acapulco Dolphins Hotel and Fersato's Restaurant, near the eastern end of the Costera. The archeological museum has a compelling collection of pre-Columbian artifacts. Other buildings contain crafts exhibits (many crafts are for sale) or host classes in painting or guitar, poetry readings, and performances of music and dance.

Fuerte De San Diego
Costera Alemán, east of the zócalo. Admission $4.50; free Sun. Tues–Sun 10:30am–4:40pm. The best time is in the morning, since the "air-conditioning" is minimal. Follow Costera Alemán past old Acapulco and the zócalo; the fort is on a hill on the right.
Note: You can reach the fort by a road through a military zone; coming from the main plaza, look for the road on the left (landward) side of the Costera. If you're in good shape, you can climb a cascade of stairs opposite the cargo docks.

The original Fort San Diego was built in 1616 to protect the town from pirate attacks. At that time, the port was wealthy from its trade with the Philippine Islands, which like Mexico were part of Spain's enormous empire. The fort you see was rebuilt after extensive damage by an earthquake in 1776. Today the structure houses the **Museo Histórico de Acapulco** (Acapulco Historical Museum), filled with exhibits that tell the fascinating story of Acapulco, beginning with its role as a port for conquest of the Americas and going through the conversion of the natives to Catholicism and the city's trade with the Orient. The first room has changing shows. Recently, it displayed artifacts from the Aztec Templo Mayor excavation in Mexico City. Other rooms chronicle Acapulco's pre-Hispanic past and the coming of the conquistadores, complete with Spanish armor. There are also displays about the Spanish imperial conquest of the South Seas, for which Acapulco was a base, and a six-foot-tall model of a *Manila Galeón*, one of the famous ships that sailed back laden with treasures from the Orient. Artifacts from the China trade, including fine chests, vases, textiles, and furniture, are also on exhibit.

Centro Internacional de Convivencia Infantil (CICI)
Costera Alemán, at Colón. ☎ **74/84-1970.** Admission $9 adults, $6 children (under 2, free). Daily 10am–6pm.

This sea life and water park east of the Convention Center offers a variety of swimming pools with waves, water slides, and water toboggans. Dolphin shows at noon and 2:30 and 5pm are in English and Spanish. Bird shows are at 11:15am and 1:15 and 3:45pm. Amenities include a cafeteria and restrooms.

SHOPPING

Acapulco is not the best place to buy Mexican crafts, but there are a few interesting shops. The best places are at the **Mercado Parazal** (often called the **Mercado de Artesanías**) on Calle Velásquez de León near 5 de Mayo in the downtown zócalo area (when you see Sanborn's, turn right and walk behind it for several blocks). Stall after covered stall of curios from all over the country are here, including silver, embroidered cotton clothing, rugs, pottery, and papier-mâché. Artists paint ceramics with village folk scenes while waiting for patrons. It's a pleasant place to spend a morning or afternoon.

Shopkeepers are vigilant and not too pushy, but they'll test your bargaining mettle. The starting price will be astronomical, and getting the price down may take more time than you have. But as always, acting uninterested often brings down prices in a hurry. Before buying silver here, examine it carefully and be sure it has ".925" stamped on the back (this signifies that the silver is 92.5% pure). The market is open daily from 9am to 8pm.

For a familiar, brightly lit department store with fixed prices, try **Artesanías Finas de Acapulco** (☎ 74/84-8039), called AFA-ACA for short. To find it, go east on the Costera until you see the Hotel Romano Days Inn on the seaward side and Baby-O disco on the landward side. Take Avenida Horacio Nelson, the street between Baby-O and the Hotel El Tropicana. On the right, half a block up, is AFA-ACA, a huge air-conditioned store that's popular with tour groups. The merchandise includes clothes, marble-top furniture, saddles, luggage, jewelry, pottery, papier-mâché, and more. The store is open Monday through Saturday from 9am to 7:30pm and Sunday from 9am to 2pm. **Sanborn's** is another good department store.

The **Costera Alemán** is crowded with boutiques selling resort wear. These stores have an abundance of attractive summer clothing at prices lower than those you generally find in the United States. If they have a sale, that's the time to stock up on some incredible bargains. Pay close attention to the quality of zippers; sometimes Mexican zippers are not up to the task. One of the nicest air-conditioned shopping centers on the Coserta is **Plaza Bahía,** Costera Alemán 125 (☎ 74/86-2452), which has two stories of shops and small fast-food restaurants, including a tempting pastry shop—Café Paris. The center is located just west of the Fiesta Americana Acapulco Plaza Hotel. In front of the hotel there is a fine silver shop called **Fini.**

ACCOMMODATIONS

The descriptions below begin with the very expensive resorts south of town (nearest the airport) and continue along the famous main avenue, Costera Miguel Alemán, to those less expensive hotels north of town in what is considered the zócalo, downtown, or "Old Acapulco" part of the city. Rather than pay the rates quoted here at the Very Expensive and Expensive hotels, inquire first about promotional rates or check airlines to see what air and hotel packages are available.

If you need a room upon arrival, both the Estrella de Oro and Estrella Blanca bus stations have **hotel-reservation services,** operated by the Hotel and Motel Association. The staff here will either call a member hotel of your choice or try to find one to suit your requirements. If they make the reservation, you pay them for one night in advance (they'll give you a voucher for the hotel).

If you plan to make reservations before leaving home, be aware that the hotel may quote you a higher price than if you walked in off the street and asked for a room. The quote might be as much as $60 as opposed to $25! This practice seems to be waning in favor of more honesty, but be aware that it could happen. During Christmas and Easter weeks, some hotels double their normal rates.

Private, very secluded villas are available for rent all over the hills south of town; renting one of these luxurious and palatial homes makes an unforgettable Acapulco vacation alternative. See Chapter 3, Section 9 for U.S. companies handling Acapulco villa rentals.

SOUTH OF TOWN

The steep forested hillsides south of town between the naval base and Puerto Marquéz hold some of Acapulco's most exclusive hotels, restaurants, and villas for which Acapulco is justly famous. The new **Hotel Camino Real** on Playa Guitarrón and the enormous **Vidafel** resort, next to the Acapulco Princess Hotel, just opened as this book went to press.

Very Expensive

Acapulco Princess

El Revolcadero Beach, Acapulco, Gro. 39868. ☎ **74/84-3100** or 800/223-1818 in the U.S. Fax 74/84-7185. 916 rms, 92 suites, 11 penthouses. A/C MINIBAR TV TEL. High season (including breakfast and dinner) $320–$600 single or double. Free parking.

The first luxury hotel most people see on arriving in Acapulco is the 480-acre Acapulco Princess on El Revolcadero Beach just off the road to the airport. Set apart from the Manhattan of skyscraper hotels downtown, the Princess complex, framed by the fabulously groomed and palm-dotted golf course, reminds one of a great Aztec ceremonial center. Its pyramidlike buildings dominate the flat surrounding land.

Within the spacious and gracious complex of buildings at the Acapulco Princess is a self-contained tropical-paradise world: a system of waterfalls, fountains, and pools set amid tropical trees, flowers, and shrubs, with swans, peacocks, and flamingos. Though the beach is long, inviting, and beautifully kept, there is no bay and therefore swimming in the open here is unsafe; look but don't go in. The dramatic lobby is enormous, and other public spaces are bold and striking in the best Mexican fashion. Guest rooms at the Acapulco Princess are big, bright, and luxurious, with marble floors and balconies. Room rates vary from selection of standard, superior, and deluxe rooms, and two types of suites, with the highest prices for the one- and two-bedroom penthouses.

During high season, prices include two meals. During low season children within these age groups may share a room with two adults at no extra charge. Ask about special packages which may include unlimited golf and daytime tennis, free use of the fitness center and other perks, and, during high season, perhaps a seven-night stay for the price of five nights.

Next door is the older, more sedate **Hotel Pierre Marqués,** open during high season only and offering Princess amenities and privileges at a fraction of Princess prices.

Dining/Entertainment: Seven restaurants in all (some subject to seasonal closings); in general all are excellent and you may find no reason to go elsewhere to eat. Fine dining, sheltered outdoor dining. Bars include Laguna and La Cascada, where mariachis often entertain; La Palma and La Palapa by the beach; and Grotto, the swim-up bar. Tiffany's is the trendy disco that gets going late and stays open until the wee hours of the morning. Garden theme parties, with regional music and dancing, are often offered.

Services: Laundry and room service, travel agency, babysitter, cribs, wheelchairs.

Facilities: Five free-form swimming pools, a saltwater lagoon with water slide, two 18-hole golf courses, and nine outdoor tennis courts (all lit for night play) and two indoor courts with stadium seating. Fishing and other water sports can be arranged with the hotel's travel agency. There's also a barber and beauty shop with massage available, a fitness center with aerobic classes, boutiques, a flower shop, and an ice machine on each floor.

Camino Real Diamante

Carretera Escénica Km 14, Calle Bajacatitia 18, Pichilinque, Puerto Marquéz, Acapulco, Gro. 39887. Tel and fax **74/81-2010** or 800/7-CAMINO in the U.S. and Canada. 156 rms. A/C MINIBAR TV TEL. High season $170–$240. Ask about low season and midweek discounts.

One of Acapulco's finest, this hotel opened in 1993 in a secluded location on 81 acres as part of the enormous Acapulco Diamante project. From the Carretera Escénica, you wind down, down, down a handsome brick road to the hotel's location beside and overlooking Puerto Marquéz Bay. Reception is gracious in the expansive lobby, which offers a sitting area and an enormous terrace facing the water. Elevators whisk you to all but the outside terrace levels. The spacious rooms, each with a small sitting area, have cool marble floors, and are furnished in an elegantly austere way. Televisions and minibars are sequestered within lightly hued wooden armoires. Each room has a ceiling fan in addition to air conditioning and a safety deposit box in the closet.

It's secluded here in this relaxing, completely self-contained resort. And it's an ideal choice for accommodations if you already know Acapulco and don't need to explore much, since a taxi to town costs $6 or more one way.

Dining/Entertainment: Outdoor seafood grill overlooking the bay. Cabo Diamante features both Mexican and international food. The open-air lobby bar facing the bay is the place to be for evening cocktails.

Services: Room and laundry service, travel agency, car rental.

Facilities: Tri-level pool, tennis courts, beauty and barber shops, and shopping arcade. The health club offers aerobics, massage, and complete workout equipment.

Westin Las Brisas

Apdo. Postal 281, Carretera Escénica, Las Brisas, Acapulco, Gro. 39868. ☎ **74/84-1580** or 800/228-3000 in the U.S. Fax 74/84-2269. 300 units. A/C MINIBAR TV TEL. High season (including continental breakfast) Nov–Apr $285–$540 double; $15 per day service charge extra (in lieu of all tips).

Some consider this the ultimate hostelry in Acapulco. Perched in tiers on a hillside overlooking the bay, it presents a pink stucco facade that is a traditional trademark in Acapulco. The pink theme is carried on to the 175 pink Jeeps rented exclusively to Las Brisas guests. The hotel is a community unto itself: The elegantly simple, marble-floored rooms are like separate little villas built into a terraced hillside, and each has a private (or semiprivate) swimming pool with a panoramic bay view. Spacious Regency Club rooms are at the top of the property and all have private pools and fabulous commanding views of the bay. Altogether, there are 300 casitas and 250 swimming pools. Although its location on the airport road southeast of the bay means that Las Brisas is a long way from the center of town, guests tend to find this an advantage rather than a drawback. Outsiders aren't permitted on the property without an invitation.

Prices for this luxury (wait till you see the lights of all Acapulco twinkling across the bay) depend on the number of bedrooms you want, whether you want a room with a private or shared pool, and whether you choose to be a Regency Club guest.

Dining/Entertainment: Complimentary breakfast of fruit, rolls, and coffee served to each room daily. Bella Vista is the reservation-only (and now open to the public) panoramic-view restaurant, open 7 to 11pm daily. El Mexicano Restaurant on a starlit terrace is open Saturday to Thursday evenings. La Concha Beach Club offers seafood daily from 12:30 to 4:30pm. The Deli Shop is open from 11am to 7pm daily.

Services: Travel agency and gas station, express checkout with advance notice, 24-hour shuttle transportation around the resort, laundry and room service, beauty and barber shops.

Facilities: Private or shared pools with each room with fresh floating flowers daily; private La Concha Beach Club at the bottom of the hill has both fresh and saltwater pools; five tennis courts; pink Jeeps rent for $85 each a day and include tax, gas, mileage, and insurance.

Expensive

Acapulco Sheraton Resort

Costera Guitarrón 110, Acapulco, Gro. 39300. ☎ **74/84-3737** or 800/325-3535 in the U.S. Fax 74/84-3760. 226 rms, 8 suites. A/C MINIBAR TV TEL. High season "Sure Saver" rate (14-day advance booking)$126 double. Parking $5 daily.

Opened in 1992, this is one of the newest resort hotels north of town. Secluded and tranquil, and completely invisible from the scenic highway, it's nestled in a landscaped ravine with a waterfall and wonderful bay view. The 17 multistoried units descend to a small beach beside the pool. Each building unit has an elevator, making it possible to come and go from the lobby to the rooms without climbing stairs—though you may need a trail of rice to remember your route. Rooms have travertine tile floors and rattan furniture and come with a private or shared balcony, purified tap water, and in-room safety-deposit boxes. Some have separate living room and kitchenette. The 32 Sheraton Club rooms have extra amenities. All rooms have remote-control TV, alarm clocks, and tub/shower combinations. It's located between La Base and Las Brisas, off the Carretera Escénica at Playa Guitarrón at the eastern end of the bay. A small sign marks the turnoff.

Dining/Entertainment: Besides a restaurant with kosher service, an ocean view restaurant, there's La Bahía Restaurant, with a magnificent semicircular bay view, elegantly set tables, and international cuisine. The Lobby Bar offers live piano music nightly and a bay view. The famous Jorongo Bar of the Sheraton María Cristina in Mexico City is re-created here with its cantina atmosphere, live trio music, and regional food specialties. Restaurants and bars are seasonal and all may not be open during low season.

Services: Laundry and room service, travel agency, car rental; scheduled shuttle service to and from town may be offered.

Facilities: Beach, two swimming pools, two handicapped-equipped rooms, 20 no-smoking guest rooms, boutiques, beauty shops, small gym with sauna, steam room, and massage. The hotel has a tennis membership at the Club Brittanica and provides guests with free transportation.

CONVENTION CENTER & ICACOS BEACH AREA

These hotels are all on the far eastern side of the bay, near the Convention Center (Centro Acapulco) and CICI *(Centro Internacional de Convivencia Infantil)*, Acapulco's fabulous children's water amusement park.

Very Expensive

Villa Vera Racquet Club

Lomas del Mar 35, Acapulco, Gro. 39690. ☎ **74/84-0333** or 800/223-6510 in the U.S. Fax 74/84-7479. 80 rms, suites, and villas. A/C MINIBAR TV TEL. High season $175 single or double superior room; $210–$380 single or double suite; $290 single or double villa. No children under age 16 are accepted. Free parking.

What began as a private home with villas for visiting friends in the 1950s has become one of Acapulco's most exclusive inns. Pat and Richard Nixon celebrated their 25th wedding anniversary here, and President Eisenhower and Elvis Presley were booked at the same time when Elvis filmed *Fun in Acapulco.* Elizabeth Taylor and Mike Todd tied the knot here with Debbie Reynolds and Eddie Fisher as attendants. The roster of who's who in guests doesn't stop even today, and the inn remains as captivating as ever for the rich and/or famous of our present era.

Spread out inland on a secluded 15-acre hillside with a spectacular view of Acapulco Bay, there's a range of choices in accommodations, all handsomely furnished. Private villas, called Las Casas de Villa Vera, include the Casa Lisa and Casa Alanda with four bedrooms. Both are sumptuously outfitted, luxury Mexican-style homes and come with 24-hour security, cook, servant, two maids, and gardeners. Casa Lisa, however, is not air-conditioned.

Spacious two-bedroom villas (there are three) include the Villa Laurel (the largest) with a private pool; Villa Teddy, also with private pool; and the Penthouse, with a spectacular view—but no private pool. Spacious one-bedroom villas (there are five of these) come with a private pool and terrace, separate living area, and huge bedrooms and baths. Suites (seven in all) have large living and bedroom areas and share a pool. Most of these have a terrace or patio and great bay views. Superior deluxe suites (there are eight of these), scattered throughout the grounds, have a large bedroom and sitting area and most have a shared pool. Most of the largish superior rooms (38 of these) are in one building and share a pool. Though there are many pools here, guests discover the place to see and be seen is at the main pool and other pools are practically empty during the day.

Dining/Entertainment: The dining terrace by the pool and overlooking the grounds and Acapulco Bay serves daily from 7:30am to 11pm.

Services: Room and laundry service, beauty shop with sauna and massage. Front desk will make car-rental and golf arrangements.

Facilities: One large pool by the outdoor dining terrace and 19 private pools; three lighted clay tennis courts with tennis pro and pro shop. Guests pay $17 per hour for tennis and nonguests pay $25.

Expensive

Hotel Elcano

Costera Alemán 75, Acapulco, Gro. 39690. ☎ **74/84-1950** or 800/222-7692 in the U.S. Fax 74/84-2230. 144 rms. A/C TV TEL. $165 studio and standard room; $180 junior suite. Ask about promotional discounts.

If you knew the old El Cano, you'll see that this completely new one is nothing like it. Completely gutted during two years of renovation, it reopened without showing even a hint of its former frumpy self. The lobby is a sea of Caribbean blue and white and the rooms are themed around trendy navy-and-white tile. All have tub/shower combinations, and ceiling fans in addition to the central air conditioning; all except studio rooms have balconies. The very large junior suites, all located on corners, have two queen-size beds and huge closets. Standard rooms are a little smaller than suites. Studios are quite small, with king-size beds and small sinks outside the bathroom area. In the studios a small portion of the TV armoire serves as a closet. The studios don't have balconies, but full sliding doors open to let in the breezes. All rooms have purified tap water and in-room safety-deposit boxes.

Dining/Entertainment: The informal Bambuco restaurant is by the pool and beach and is open from 9am to 11pm daily. The more formal Victoria is on an outdoor terrace overlooking the pool and beach and is open from 6 to 11pm daily.

Services: Room and laundry service, travel agency.

Facilities: One beachside pool, workout room, gift shop, boutiques, travel agency, beauty shop, massages, video-game room, an ice machine on each floor.

Moderate

Acapulco Dolphins Hotel

Costera Alemán 50, Acapulco, Gro. 39300. ☎ **74/84-4441** or 84-6678. Fax 74/84-3072. 255 rms. A/C TV TEL. High season $75 single or double. Low season $65 single or double.

A young and lively clientele that includes many French-speaking Canadians is attracted to this hotel. The rooms are tidy, modern, and comfortably furnished. There's a swimming pool in an interior courtyard. You'll find it south of CICI next to Fersato's restaurant.

Hotel La Palapa

Playa Icacos, Fracc. Costa Azul, Fragata Yucatán 210, Acapulco, Gro. 39850. ☎ **74/84-5363** or 91/800-10-9777 in Mexico. Fax 74/84-8399. 333 rms. A/C TEL. High season $80 single or double (including breakfast). Two children stay free in parents' room. Free parking.

Between the naval base and the Convention Center, you can't fail to see this hotel's 30 stories towering over the beach. While not in the luxury category, with white Formica furniture, every room has an ocean view and balcony. Some rooms are smaller than others but all are suites, with living area separate from the bedroom, many have small bars and a dining table, and all have in-room safety-deposit boxes. The palm-lined beachside pool is the hotel's relaxing focal point. Mariscos is the poolside restaurant, open 7:30am to 11pm daily. La Nouvell is off the lobby and open for all three meals. El Muelle Pizzaria, with seafood specialties, is open daily in high season only from 1 to 11pm. There's a travel agency in the lobby, and the hotel offers laundry and room service.

CONDESA BEACH & DIANA CIRCLE AREA

The row of gigantic hotels along the northern shore of Acapulco Bay has been photographed over and over for travel brochures and posters, and at dusk as the lights twinkle on, these giants certainly do offer a romantic vista.

Expensive

Calinda Acapulco Quality Inn

Costera Miguel Alemán 1260, Acapulco, Gro. 39300. ☎ **74/84-0410** or 800/228-5151 in the U.S. Fax 74/84-4676. 358 rms. A/C TV TEL. Year-round $115 double.

You can't miss this tall cylindrical tower rising at the eastern edge of Condesa Beach. The design allows each room to have a view, usually of the bay. The guest rooms, though not strikingly furnished, are large and comfortable and most come with two double beds. Remodeling in recent years has given it a modern face-lift.

A package price will reduce the rates listed above, which otherwise are too high for the quality of accommodations. Numerous discount rates apply to senior citizens, government and military employees, corporations, and travel clubs such as AAA, Allstate, and Quest.

Dining/Entertainment: Three restaurants from snacks by the pool to indoor informal dining cover most guests' needs. For cocktails, the Lobby Bar gets going around 6pm and stops at 1am, with a happy hour from 4 to 9pm when drinks are two for the price of one and live music between 9pm and 1am.

Services: Laundry and room service, travel agency.

Facilities: There's one swimming pool, several lobby boutiques, a pharmacy, beauty shop, ice machine on the third floor, two handicapped-equipped rooms, and four no-smoking floors.

Fiesta Americana Condesa Acapulco

Costera Miguel Alemán 1220, Acapulco, Gro. 39300. ☎ **74/84-2355** or 800/223-2332 in the U.S. Fax 74/84-1828. 475 rms, 13 suites. A/C MINIBAR TV TEL. High season $150–$175 single or double.

Once called the Condesa del Mar, the Fiesta Americana Condesa Acapulco is among Acapulco's long-standing favorite luxury hotels. The 18-story hotel towers above Condesa Beach, just east up the hill from the Glorieta Diana. The attractive and very comfortable rooms are furnished in soft pastels. Each has a private terrace with an ocean view. The more expensive rooms have the best bay views and all rooms have purified tap water.

Dining/Entertainment: Coffee shop, poolside restaurant, 18th-floor fine-dining restaurant. Latter has marvelous panoramic view of the town and the bay and live (but soft) music for dining most evenings. Lobby bar with live entertainment most nights.

Services: Laundry and room service, travel agency.

Facilities: Dramatic adults-only swimming pool perched atop a hill with the land dropping off toward the bay, affording swimmers the best view of Acapulco from any pool in the city. Smaller pool for children. Two handicapped-equipped rooms, beauty shop, boutiques, and pharmacy.

Moderate

Hotel Acapulco Tortuga

Costera Miguel Alemán 132, Acapulco, Gro. 39300. ☎ **74/84-8889** or 800/832-7491 in the U.S. Fax 74/84-7385. 250 rms. A/C TV TEL. High season $80 single or double.

The Acapulco Tortuga is a modern eight-story hotel on the landward side of the Costera Alemán near Condesa Beach, almost across the street from the Fiesta Americana Condesa hotel and Beto's Safari Restaurant. You enter the hotel to find a cavernous atrium lobby, in the midst of which are the restaurants Los Portales and La Fonda. Despite its modern construction, the decor in the atrium is theatrical Spanish colonial, with lots of greenery. The reception desk is at the left-rear side of the cavernous atrium. The rooms have wall-to-wall carpeting, cable color TVs, and radios, though upkeep could be better. At the very back of the hotel is a nice little swimming pool with a shady palapa (thatched shelter). By the way, the toll-free number (which you dial in the U.S.) rings in Mexico and those who answer may not speak English if you call before 9am, midafternoon, or late evening.

PAPAGAYO PARK TO DIANA CIRCLE

Hotel Howard Johnson Maralisa

Calle Alemania s/n, Acapulco, Gro. 39670. ☎ **74/85-6677** or 800/446-4656 in the U.S. Fax 74/85-9228. 90 rms. A/C TV TEL. High season $95–$207 single or double.

Of the smaller hotels in the row of giants, this, the former Hotel Maralisa, is one of the most congenial. It's got all the things the huge hotels have without the tremendous size: a fine palm-shaded swimming pool, plus a smaller pool, a private stretch of beach, La Mar bar between the beach and the swimming pool, and a dining room overlooking the bay. Lower-priced rooms have two twin beds and higher-priced ones have two double beds and balconies. Whichever accommodation you choose, you'll have a comfortable, modern, air-conditioned room with sliding glass doors (in most cases) opening onto a balcony or back interior walkway—the latter are the least expensive rooms. Besides standard rooms there are three handicapped-equipped rooms, a travel agency, and pharmacy/gift shop. It's just off the Costera at Alemania; turn when you see the Baskin-Robbins, and it's on the side street going toward the beach. It's also near the Hotel Acapulco Ritz.

Paraíso Acapulco Hotel

Costera Miguel Alemán 163, Acapulco, Gro. 39300. ☎ **74/85-5596.** Fax 74/85-5543. 422 rms. A/C TV TEL. High season $130–$150 single or double.

The Paraíso stands right at the eastern end of Papagayo Park on Hornos Beach. Though it's among the resort's older hotels, it has been well maintained. The lofty lobby is an expanse of gleaming black marble leading to large windows overlooking the beach, dotted with little palapas. The hotel's attractive sun deck next to the beach is set with comfy lounge chairs. The guest rooms are spacious, with nice tiled bathrooms, marble vanities, and little balconies. More expensive rooms are those with a sea view. Land-view rooms can be a bit noisy because of the busy traffic along the Costera.

Dining/Entertainment: Beachside informal restaurant, rooftop restaurant with fabulous view of the bay, a dance floor, and live piano music.

Services: Laundry and room service, travel agency.

Facilities: Oceanside pool, ice machine on each floor, one handicapped-equipped guest room; floors 2 and 17 are no-smoking.

DOWNTOWN—ON LA QUEBRADA

Numerous budget-quality hotels dot the streets fanning out from the zócalo (Acapulco's official and original downtown) and they are among the best buys in Acapulco if you aren't looking for luxury. Be sure to check your room first to see that it has the basic comforts you expect.

Expensive

Plaza Las Glorias/El Mirador

Quebrada 74, Acapulco, Gro. 39300. ☎ **74/83-1221** or 800/342-2644 in the U.S. 91/ 800-9-0027 in Mexico. Fax 74/82-4564. 100 rms. A/C TV TEL. High season $115 single or double. Parking on street.

One of the landmarks of "Old Acapulco," the former El Mirador Hotel overlooks the famous cove where the cliff divers perform. Renovated with lush tropical landscaping and lots of handsome Mexican tile, this romantic hotel offers attractively furnished rooms with double or queen-size beds, mini-fridge and wet bar, and large bathrooms with marble counters. Most have a separate living room area and all are accented with handsome Saltillo tile and other Mexican decorative touches. Ask for a room with a balcony (there are 42) and ocean view (95 rooms).

To get there, follow the Costera past the Club de Esquies (on the left), the Pemex station (on the right). Turn right at the Hotel Avenida and follow the street right around the mountain. You'll see the Quebrada and the hotel across the small, deep cove on the left.

Dining/Entertainment: Evening buffet ($35 to $45) in setting offering great views of the cliff-diving show. Coffee Shop with mediocre food and slow service. Large comfortable and breezy lobby bar is a favorite spot to watch day fade into night on the beautiful cove and bay.

Services: Room service for breakfast and lunch, laundry service, travel agency.

Facilities: Three pools, protected cove with good snorkeling, saltwater pool accessed by mountainside elevator.

Inexpensive

⑨ Hotel Asturias

Quebrada 45, Acapulco, Gro. 39300. ☎ **74/83-6548.** 15 rms (all with bath). FAN. $9 per person.

This little charming budget hotel gets high marks for cleanliness and friendly management. There's also a nice pool which is just big enough to cool off. Rooms are clean and airy, with tile floors and small tile baths (no toilet seats). Louvered glass windows in each room face the open common walkways of the hotel's interior, letting in light and air—as well as mosquitoes. Each room has either two double beds, and some also have a single. To find the hotel from the zócalo, walk up Quebrada three blocks; the hotel is on the left opposite the Secretaría de Finanzas. You will notice it by its blue columns flanking a wide stucco arch over the front porch.

⑨ Hotel Misión

Felipe Valle 112, Acapulco, Gro. 39300. ☎ **74/82-3643.** 27 rms. (all with bath). FAN. $16 single or double.

Enter this hotel's plant-filled brick courtyard, shaded by an enormous mango tree, and you'll step back to an earlier Acapulco. This tranquil 19th-century hotel lies two blocks inland from the Costera and the zócalo. The original L-shaped building is at least 100 years old. The rooms have colonial touches such as colorful tile and wrought iron and come simply furnished with one or two beds. Breakfast and lunch are served on the patio. Soft drinks and beer are usually available all day.

ON PLAYA LA ANGOSTA

If you stand on the zócalo and face the water, to your right the Costera leads to hotels on the hilly peninsula that curves back into the bay. Their location gives some of these hotels great views of the city and bay; luxury hotels were built here in the 1950s. On the back side of the peninsula is Playa la Angosta. To get there, take any bus along the Costera, which runs along the base of the peninsula, and get off at the Hotel Avenida. Walk a block to Playa la Angosta; the hotels are on the left facing the bay.

Hotel Villa Romana

Av. López Mateos 185, Fracc. Las Playas, Acapulco, Gro. 39300. ☎ **74/82-3995.** 9 rms (all with bath). A/C. High season $32 double. Low season $27 double.

With terraces facing the sparkling Playa la Angosta, this is one of the most comfortable inns in the area, ideal for a long stay. Some rooms are tiled and others carpeted, and all have small kitchens with refrigerators. There are a small plant-filled terrace on the second floor with tables and chairs and a fourth-floor pool with a splendid view of the bay.

NEAR PLAYAS CALETA & CALETILLA

The layout of streets on the peninsula that separates the two beaches is confusing, and the disorganized street names and numbers is enough to drive one to tears. A street will be named Avenida López Mateos, but so will the street meeting it at a 90° angle. Some streets have two names, while others have none; many buildings have two street numbers.

The following hotels are easy to find. Simply take a "Caleta" bus to Mágico Mundo Marino, a popular local tourist attraction, and you'll be within walking distance (one to four blocks) of any of the hotels.

Hotel Belmar

Gran Vía Tropical and Av. de las Cumbres, Acapulco, Gro. 39360. ☎ **74/82-1525** or 82-1526. 80 rms (all with bath). A/C or FAN MINIBAR. Year-round $28 double.

Two pools and shady patios fill the grassy lawn in front of this hotel. Built in the 1950s, it's immaculately kept, with large, breezy rooms, enormous balconies, and relaxing views; 70 rooms are air-conditioned. It's an ideal place to spread out and unwind. There's a comfortable restaurant/bar. To get here, put your back to the Hotel de la Playa (a very large hotel two blocks from Mágico Mundo Marino), and you'll see the Belmar sign. Take the street to your left up and up and up the hill about 1¹/₂ blocks.

Hotel Lindavista

Playa Caleta, s/n (Apdo. Postal 3), Acapulco, Gro. 39300. ☎ **74/82-5414.** Fax 74/82-2783. 43 rms. A/C or FAN. $26 single or double with fan; $33 single or double with A/C. Free parking.

The old-fashioned Lindavista snuggles into the hillside above Caleta Beach. Older American and Mexican couples are drawn to the well-kept rooms, beautiful views, and slow pace of the area here. Most of the rooms have air-conditioning, and those that don't have fans. There are a small pool and a terrace restaurant/bar. Coming from Caleta Beach, you'll find the hotel up the hill to the left of the Hotel Caleta.

DINING

Dining out in Acapulco can be one of the best experiences you'll ever have in Mexico—whether you're clad in a bathing suit and munching a hamburger on the beach, or whether you're seated at a candlelit table with the glittering bay spreading out before you.

The price of a meal in a deluxe establishment in Acapulco may not be much higher than what you'd pay for something of inferior quality at a mass market restaurant. The proliferation of U.S. franchise restaurants (McDonald's, Subway, Shakey's Pizza, Baskin-Robbins, Tony Roma's, etc.), has increased competition in Acapulco and more expensive places have reduced prices in response; the quality of their food is much better, offering more value for the money than supposedly budget restaurants.

The restaurants I've taste-tested below reflect a mixture of both value and good food. And if it's a romantic place you're looking for, you won't have to look far, since Acapulco fairly brims over with such inviting places.

SOUTH OF TOWN: LAS BRISAS AREA

Very Expensive

Restaurant Miramar

Plaza La Vista, Carretera Escénica. ☎ **74/84-7874**. Reservations required. Main courses $22–$31; desserts $4–$12. Daily 6:30pm–midnight. ITALIAN/FRENCH/MEXICAN.

The Miramar is about as formal as an Acapulco restaurant gets, and with the view of the bay and outstanding food, the dining experience is something not soon forgotten. Waiters wearing black suits and ties are quietly solicitous as you make your selection and ponder the view between courses. The menu, as refined as the service, offers familiar continental classics such as duck in orange sauce, coq au vin, and tournedos Rossini, all exquisitely presented. But save room for a dessert, all as memorable as the main courses. Dress up a bit for dining here, but as lightly as possible, since bay breezes are few and the fans aren't quite adequate. When the tab for your wonderful meal comes, check it carefully; I don't know if they get busy and make mistakes or what exactly happens, but sometimes unordered items appear on the bill, or the total is more than the sum of the prices. The Miramar is in the La Vista complex near the Hotel La Brisas.

Spicey

Carretera Escénica. ☎ **74/81-1380**, or 81-0470. Reservations recommended on weekends. Main courses $16–$40. Mon–Fri 1:30–5pm; daily 7–11:30pm. INTERNATIONAL.

For original food with a flair, you can't beat this trendy new restaurant in the Las Brisas area, next to Kookaburas. Diners (in cool attire that's on the dressy side of casual) can enjoy the air conditioning indoors or the completely open rooftop terrace, with its sweeping view of the bay. To begin, try the shrimp Spicey, in a fresh coconut batter with an orange marmalade and mustard sauce. Among the main courses, the grilled veal chop in pineapple and papaya chutney is a good choice, as is the beef tenderloin—prepared with the flavors of Thailand, or Santa Fe style, or blackened á la Louisiana. The chiles rellenos in mango sauce win raves.

Expensive

✪ Madeiras

Carretera Escénica 33. ☎ **74/84-4378**. Reservations required. Fixed-price dinner $35. Daily 7–11pm (two seatings: 7–8:30pm and 9–11pm). MEXICAN/CONTINENTAL.

Enjoy an elegant meal and a fabulous view of glittering Acapulco Bay at night at Madeiras, east of town on the scenic highway before the Las Brisas Hotel. The several small dining areas have ceiling fans and are open to the evening breezes. If you arrive before your table is ready, have a drink in the comfortable lounge. Selections might include tamal al chipotle (corn tamale made with tangy chipotle sauce); roast quail stuffed with tropical fruits; or fish cooked in orange sauce. There are such old favorites as filet mignon, beef Stroganoff, and frogs' legs in garlic and white wine. Wines are reasonably priced if you stick to the Mexican labels.

THE COSTERA: ICACOS BEACH TO PAPAGAYO PARK

Very Expensive

✪ Suntory

Costera Alemán at Maury. ☎ **74/84-8088** or 84-8766. Reservations recommended. Suntory course $15; Midori course $25; Imperial course $43; sushi plates $17–$30; à la carte meals $9–$40. Daily 2pm–midnight. JAPANESE.

For a refreshingly cool and serene respite from Acapulco's heat, sand, and zooming Costera, try this touch of Japan in Mexico. Though prices are expensive, the food is outstanding. The extensive menu includes the Suntory course, a teppanyaki with a choice of U.S. ribeye, chicken, or fish, all with vegetables, crisp salad, small bowl of soup, and a heaping main platter (bring a big appetite), most of which is cooked at your table. The more expensive Midori course includes much of the Suntory course plus an appetizer, pickled vegetables, and dessert. The extensive Imperial course, for which you'll need a huge appetite, incorporates those items already mentioned but with shrimp salad, lobster soup, and a teppanyaki that includes lobster, and fresh fruit. The à la carte menu includes grilled and fried main courses, tempuras, and sushi. The delicious sushi platters come with between 16 and 22 beautifully prepared and presented pieces, and include a glass of wine and misoshiro soup; either platter is enough for two or three people to share. Drinks to try besides the traditional hot or cold sake include the jarra Suntory, a mixture of white wine with mango and peach flavorings, and Midori, a melon-based liqueur. There's also a full list of imported and domestic wines and liquors. Highly recommended.

Expensive

Dino's

Costera Alemán s/n. ☎ **74/84-0037**. Reservations recommended. Main courses $10–$20. Daily 4pm–midnight. NORTHERN ITALIAN.

A popular dining spot for years, Dino's continues with its combination of good food and service at respectable prices for what you get. Plus from its second story dining room there's a modest bay view between high-rise hotels. The restaurant is famous for its fettuccine Alfredo and waiters prepare it with fanfare, often tableside. Other main courses include broiled seafood and steak, all of which come with baked potato, vegetables, and Dino's special oven-baked bread. It's on the landward side of the Costera beside the Tortuga Hotel and opposite the Langosta Loca.

✪ Su Casa/La Margarita

Av. Anahuac 110. ☎ **74/84-4350** or 84-1261. Reservations recommended. Main courses $10–$20. Daily 6pm–midnight. INTERNATIONAL.

Su Casa (Your House) is one of the most delightful restaurants for dining with a view while enjoying some of the best food in the city. Owners Shelly and Angel Herrera opened this restaurant on the patio of their hillside home. Both are aficionados in the kitchen and both are on hand nightly to greet guests to their patio. The menu changes often, so that each time you go, there's something new to try. But some things are standard, such as the unusual chile con carne, which is served both as a main dish and as an appetizer; shrimp à la patrona in garlic; and marinated and grilled chicken Su Casa, grilled fish and steak, delicious barbecue chicken, and enchiladas in green sauce. The flaming filet al Madrazo, a delightful brochette, is first marinated in tropical juices. Those are just a few of the unusual main courses. Most come with refreshing garnishes of cooked banana or pineapple, often a baked potato or rice, plus there are off-the-menu specials to ask about. The margaritas are big and delicious. Su Casa is on a hillside above the Convention Center. Highly recommended.

Moderate

El Cabrito

Costera Alemán 1480. ☎ **74/84-7711.** Breakfast $4–$9; main courses $5–$12. Daily 8am–1am. NORTHERN MEXICAN.

With its arched adobe decor and waitresses in embroidered dresses and location in the heart of the Costera, this restaurant is aimed at the tourist trade. But its authentic and well-prepared specialties attract Mexicans in the know—a stamp of approval I find comforting. Among its specialties are *cabrito al pastor* (roasted goat), charro beans, northern-style steaks, and burritos de machaca. Regional specialties from other areas include Jalisco-style birria and mole Oaxaca-style. Dine inside or outside on the patio facing the Costera. It's on the ocean side of the Costera opposite the Hard Rock Cafe, and south of the Convention Center.

100% Natural

Costera Alemán at Yucatán. ☎ **74/84-4462.** Breakfast $2–$3.50; main courses $4–$6; fruit and vegetable drinks $2–$3; sandwiches $2.50–$4. Daily 7am–11pm. MEXICAN/VEGETARIAN.

You'll see branches of 100% Natural in just about every area of Acapulco, some with green awnings and others with yellow. Actually those with green signs are rival chains of those with yellow signs, but their menus are quite similar. They both feature soups, salads, sandwiches, fruit, yogurt, shakes, and pasta dishes that please vegetarians and carnivores alike. Although each restaurant is part of a franchise, they're individually owned, so the hours vary; some stay open 24 hours. This branch is on the east end of the Costera between the Roman Days Inn and the Magic Disco.

Restaurant Cocula

Costera Alemán 10. ☎ **74/84-5079.** Breakfast $3–$5; main courses $3–$11. Daily 7am–1am; happy hour 6pm until closing. MEXICAN.

You can dine on the patio out front or on one of the two levels of terraces. Appetizers include guacamole, black-bean soup, and watercress salad. Grilled meats are the specialty, and you can choose from among red snapper, shrimp, broiled chicken, quail, spiced pork sausage, ribs, shish kebab, and mixed grill. The restaurant is on the inland side of the east end of the Costera, across from Acapulco 2000.

Sanborn's

Costera at Condesa Beach near the El Presidente Hotel. ☎ **74/84-4465.** Breakfast $3.50–$5; main courses $3.50–$10. Daily 7:30am–11pm. AMERICAN/MEXICAN.

The best of the American-style restaurants, Sanborn's offers a cool dining area. Reminiscent of upscale dining rooms of the 1950s, it features American colonial decor, brass light fixtures, and well-padded booths. It's especially good for breakfast, though it also has good enchiladas, club sandwiches, burgers, sincronizadas (ham and cheese melted between corn tortillas), pastas, and fancier fare such as fish and steaks. Beer, wine, and cocktails are served. For an inexpensive snack, buy pastries to go at the store's bakery. Upstairs are clean bathrooms. You'll find this branch two blocks east of the zócalo on the Costera.

The other Sanborn's is in old acapulco near the zócalo at Costera Alemán and Escudero (☎ 82-6167).

DOWNTOWN: THE ZÓCALO AREA

The old downtown area of Acapulco is packed with simple, inexpensive eateries serving up tasty food. It's easy to pay more elsewhere in Acapulco and not get such consistently good food as what you'll find at the restaurants in this part of town. To explore this area, start right at the zócalo and stroll west along Juárez. After about three blocks you'll come to Azueta, lined with small seafood cafes and streetside stands.

Moderate

Mariscos Pipo

Almirante Breton 3. ☎ **74/83-8801** or 82-2237. Main courses $3.75–$15. Daily 11am–8pm. SEAFOOD.

Diners can look at photographs of Old Acapulco on the walls while sitting in the airy dining room of this place, decorated with hanging nets, fish, glass buoys, and shell lanterns. The English-language menu lists a wide array of seafood, including ceviche, lobster, octopus, crayfish, and baby-shark quesadillas. This local favorite is five blocks west of the zócalo on Breton, just off the Costera, behind the large curved building boasting in sky-high green letters EDIFÍCIO STIBADORES. Another branch, open daily from 1 to 9pm, is at Costera M.Aleman and Canadá (☎ 74/84-0165).

Inexpensive

La Granja del Pingue

Juárez 10. ☎ **74/83-5339.** Breakfast $2.50; main courses $2–$4; lunch special $3.50. Daily 7am–10pm. ECLECTIC/PASTRIES/ICE CREAM.

Specializing in ice cream and French/Viennese pastries, this restaurant offers an eclectic menu that includes burgers and fries, Tex-Mex chili, and a lunch special usually in the American home-cooking genre. It also claims to have the best coffee in town, with free refills. The dining area is an attractive shaded patio hung with piñatas. Bring your paperback novels to exchange here. This place is two blocks west of the zócalo.

San Carlos

Juárez 5. ☎ **74/82-6459.** Breakfast special $3; main courses $2.50–$6; comida corrida $3. Daily 7:30am–11pm (comida corrida served 1–6pm.) MEXICAN.

Western-style food such as charcoal-broiled chicken and fish is served at chuck-wagon prices on the front patio of this place or in its open, fan-cooled dining room. Colorful tablecloths brighten this cheery cafe a few steps west of the zócalo. On Sunday one of the many specialties is chicken mole. There are at least 11 main-course choices for the comida corrida.

DINING WITH A VIEW

Among the pleasures of vacationing in Acapulco is dining with a fabulous view of the city spread out before you. Good places for this include **Madeiras, Grazziel, Miramar, Trebeca,** and **Kookabura,** all in the Las Brisas area; **Su Casa** on a hill above the Convention Center; **La Bahía Restaurant** at the Sheraton Hotel; the **Bella Vista Restaurant** (now open to the public) at the Hotel Las Brisas; the rooftop **Fraggata Restaurant** at the Paraíso Radisson Hotel; and the 18th-floor

Techo del Mar (Roof of the Sea), the fine-dining restaurant at the Hotel Fiesta Americana Condesa.

BREAKFAST/BRUNCH

Among the good places for an economical breakfast and brunch is a strip of competing little restaurants, including **100% Natural,** on the Costera just before the Romano Days Inn and south of the Convention Center. Another option includes the breakfast buffet at the **Hotel Continental Plaza.**

EATING ON THE BEACH

The area around Caleta and Caletilla beaches have nice shady palapas and beach chairs, clean sand, and fine palm trees. Three buildings have been built to house *vestidores, regarderas* (changing rooms, showers, and lockers), and restaurants. Little dining places line the outer periphery of the buildings. To find a good meal, wander along the rows of restaurants, looking for busy spots where people are eating (and not just sipping drinks). Study menus, which will either be displayed or handed to you on request. Although the restaurants may tend to look all the same, you'll be surprised at the difference in prices. *Filete de pescado* (fish filet) might be $4 at one place, and twice as much at another; beer can cost anywhere from $1.50 to $3. Stick with cooked seafood rather than ceviche which is made with raw fish and seafood.

ACAPULCO AFTER DARK

The **"Gran Noche Mexicana"** given by the **Acapulco Ballet Folklórico** is held in the plaza of the Convention Center every Tuesday, Thursday, and Saturday night at 8pm. With dinner and open bar the show costs $50; general admission (including three drinks) is $24. Call for reservations (☎ 74/84-7050) or consult a local travel agency.

Another excellent **Mexican fiesta/folkloric dance show,** which includes *voladores* (flying pole dancers) from Papantla, is held at Marbella Plaza near the Continental Plaza Hotel on the Costera on Monday, Wednesday, and Friday at 7pm. The $42 fee covers the show, buffet, open bar, taxes, and gratuities. Make reservations through a travel agency.

Many major hotels also host Mexican fiestas and other theme nights that include dinner and entertainment. Consult a travel agency for information.

NIGHTCLUBS & DISCOS

Acapulco is more famous for its nightclubs than for its beaches. The clubs open and close with shocking regularity, though, so others may be open when you travel and some of these may be closed. Every club seems to have a cover charge around $28 in high season, $14 in low season, and drinks can cost anywhere from $2.50 to $9.

Many periodically waive their cover charge or offer some other promotion to attract customers. Another trend is to have a big cover charge with an open bar. Call the disco or look for promotional material around hotel reception areas, at travel desks or concierge booths, and in local publications.

In addition, the high-rise hotels have their own bars and sometimes discos. Informal lobby or poolside cocktail bars often offer live entertainment to enjoy for the price of drinks.

Note: When the managers of local discos say no shorts, they mean no shorts for men; they welcome women in them.

Death-Defying Divers

High divers perform at La Quebrada each day at 12:45, 7:30, 8:30, 9:30, and 10:30pm for $4 admission. From a spotlit ledge on the cliffs in view of the lobby bar and restaurant terraces of the Hotel Plaza Las Glorias/El Mirador, each solitary diver plunges into the roaring surf 130 feet below after praying at a small shrine nearby. To the applause of the crowd that has gathered, he then climbs up the rocks and accepts congratulations and gifts of money from onlookers. The best show is at 10:30pm, when they dive with torches.

You can watch from the hotel's terraces for a cover charge in the form of an obligatory drink for $9.50. However, you might try arriving at the lobby bar 30 minutes before a performance and ordering less expensive drinks; they don't always collect the cover charge from people who are already there. You could also get around the cover by having dinner at the hotel's La Perla restaurant. The buffet is $35. Reservations (☎ 83-1155) are recommended during the high season.

Acapulco also has its own spectacular cultural and convention center, the **Centro Acapulco,** on the eastern reaches of the bay between Condesa and Icacos beaches. Within the modern center are several forms of entertainment, including a mariachi bar, a piano bar, a disco, a movie theater, a live theater, a cafe, a nightclub, several restaurants, and outdoor performance areas.

Afro Antillanos
Costera Alemán at Cuando la Cosa 32. ☎ **74/84-7235.** Cover $15–$20.

Live tropical salsa music is the specialty of the house at this relatively new disco not far from the Continental Plaza Hotel. Shorts are a no-no. It's open nightly from 9:30pm to 4am; open bar closes at 3am.

Baby-O
Costera Alemán. ☎ **74/84-7474.** Cover $15–$20.

Baby-O's can be very selective about who they let in when it's crowded. Your chances of getting in here increase greatly if you're young, pretty, and female. Your next best shot is to be older, affluent looking, and male. Across from the Romano Days Inn, this intimate disco has a small dance floor surrounded by several tiers of tables and sculpted, cavelike walls. It even has a hot tub and breakfast area. Drinks run $5 to $6.

Carlos 'n' Charlie's
Costera Alemán 999. ☎ **74/84-1285** or 84-0039. Nightly 6:30pm–midnight.

For fun, high-decibel music, *and* good food all at the same time, you can't go wrong with this branch of the Carlos Anderson chain. It's always packed, an indication that people like what they get for the price they pay. Come early and get a seat on the terrace overlooking the Costera. It's east of the Diana traffic circle and across the street from the El Presidente Hotel and the Fiesta Americana Condesa.

Extravaganzza
Carretera Escénica. ☎ **74/84-7154** or 84-7164. Cover $15–$20.

If you have something trendy and dressy to wear, you might venture into this snazzy neo-deco chrome-and-neon extravaganza, perched on the side of the mountain between Los Rancheros Restaurant and La Vista Shopping Center. You can't miss the neon lights. The plush, dimly lit interior dazzles patrons with a sunken dance floor and panoramic view of Acapulco Bay. The door attendants wear tuxedos, so don't expect to get in wearing shorts, jeans, T-shirts, sneakers, or sandals. It opens nightly at 10:30pm; fireworks blast off at 3am. Call to find out if reservations are needed. National (as opposed to imported) drinks run $5 to $6.

Fantasy
Carretera Escénica. ☎ **74/84-6727** or 84-6764. Cover $15–$20.

This club has a fantastic bay view and sometimes waives the cover charge as a promotion. Periodically during the evening it puts on a good show with green lasers, which it also shoots out across the bay. The dress code does not permit shorts, jeans, T-shirts, or sandals. Reservations are recommended. Located in the La Vista Shopping Center, it's open nightly 10:30pm to 4am. Drinks go for $6.

Hard Rock Cafe
Costera Alemán 37. ☎ **74/84-0077.** Cover for live music. Daily noon–2am; live music Wed–Mon 11:30pm–1:30am.

If you like your music loud and your food trendy, dip into this cool and interestingly decorated place. The decor is a combination of nostalgia and museum, all with a modern twist. Elvis memorabilia greets you in the entry area, and among other numerous framed or encased mementos is the Beatles' gold record for "Can't Buy Me Love." Naturally there's a bandstand for the live music and a small dance floor. It's on the seaward side towards the southern end of the Costera, south of the Convention Center and opposite El Cabrito.

Magic
Costera Alemán at Yucatán. ☎ **74/84-8816** or 84-8815. Cover $15–$20.

Magic draws a youthful crowd to its pyramid-shaped building with a waterfall in front. It lies on the east end of the Costera near the Romano Days Inn. The dress code frowns on shorts, tennis shoes, and sandals. It opens nightly at 10:30pm.

News
Costera Alemán. ☎ **74/84-5902.** Cover (including open bar) $15–20.

The booths and love seats ringing the vast dance floor can seat 1,200, so this disco can double as a concert hall. But while high-tech in style, it's laid-back and user-friendly. It doesn't even have a dress code! Across the street from the Hyatt Regency, it opens at 10:30pm nightly.

3 Puerto Escondido

230 miles SE of Acapulco, 150 miles W of Salina Cruz, 50 miles W of Puerto Angel

Puerto Escondido (pronounced "PWER-toe es-con-DEE-do") translates to "Hidden Port"; although this town of 50,000 has been "discovered," touristic development here hasn't yet transformed it. Anyone who wandered into Acapulco half a century ago might have found a similar scene and a similar ambience. So catch Puerto Escondido before it's gone forever. The lush palm-lined beach off the town center is one of the most beautiful in the country, with colorful boats pulled up on the sand—it makes for the kind of scene long since gone from more developed resorts.

When looking out on the Bahía Principal and its beach, you'll see to your left the eastern end of the bay, consisting of a small beach, Playa Marinero, followed by rocks jutting into the sea. Beyond this is Playa Zicatela, which attracts surfers like a magnet. By way of contrast, the western side of the bay, to your right, is about a mile long with low green hills (and a lighthouse) descending to meet a long stretch of fine sand. The coastline is slowly being developed. Where there was once nothing, Zicatela Beach now has restaurants, bungalows, surf shops and hotels, although the construction there is well back from the shoreline. Westward, the beaches are not quite as accessible by land, but hotels are overcoming this by constructing beach clubs reached by steep private roads and jeep shuttles.

Laziness is a state of mind here—sipping a cool bottle of something refreshing, feeling the sea breeze, watching the pelicans soar and wheel and then come down to race across the surface of the water. Duck into a fan-cooled restaurant by day or return in the cool evening and find informal groups discussing the day's events.

GETTING THERE & DEPARTING   By Plane   AeroMorelos has several daily flights between Oaxaca and Puerto Escondido flying a 40-passenger turbo-prop. **Aerovega** also serves the route to and from Oaxaca with one, and sometimes 2 daily morning flights using a 5-passenger AeroCommander. Tickets for both these lines are handled by Turismo Rodimar (see below). **Mexicana** (☎ 2-0098) flies from Mexico City to Puerto Escondido five days per week.

If space on flights to Puerto Escondido is booked solid, you have the option of flying Aeroméxico into the Huatulco airport six days per week. This is an especially viable option if your destination is Puerto Angel, which lies between Puerto Escondido and Huatulco but is closer to the Huatulco airport. There is frequent bus service between the three destinations.

Aerotransportes Terrestres sells colectivo transportation tickets to the airport through **Turismo Rodimar** near the east end of the pedestrians-only zone (☎ 958/2-0734 or tel/fax. 2-0737). The price is $2.25 one way and includes pickup at your hotel.

By Bus   Buses are frequent between Acapulco, Oaxaca, and south along the coast to and from Huatulco and Pochutla, the transit hub for Puerto Angel. Puerto Escondido's several bus stations are all within a three-block area. For **Gacela** and **Estrella Blanca,** the station is just north of the coastal highway where Perez Gasga crosses it. First-class buses go from here to Pochutla and Huatulco hourly, and almost hourly to Acapulco and Zihuatanejo. Five daily direct buses with assigned seats go to Acapulco, one to Zihuatanejo and two to Mexico City. The most comfortable bus to Mexico City (12 hours) is the deluxe Futuro de Lujo bus leaving at 7 and 10pm.

A block north at Hidalgo and Primera Poniente is **Transportes Oaxaca Istmo.** The office is in a small restaurant. Several buses daily leave for Pochutla (1 hour), Salina Cruz (5 hours), or Oaxaca (10 hours via Salina Cruz). **Autotransportes Turisticas** has twice daily first-class service to Oaxaca, via Pochutla (7 hours). The terminal for **Lineas Unidas, Estrella del Valle,** and **Oaxaca Pacífico** is two blocks farther down on Hidalgo, just past 3rd Oriente. All buses go to Oaxaca via Pochutla; four are ordinario and three are directo buses, leaving at 8:15am, and 10:15 and 10:45pm.

Cristóbal Colón buses, Primera Norte 207, serve Salina Cruz, Tuxtla Gutiérrez, and San Cristóbal de las Casas. It also has two first-class buses to Oaxaca, via Salina Cruz, at 4 and 9pm. Here you can enjoy an air conditioned waiting room.

By Car   From Oaxaca, Highway 175 via Pochutla is the least bumpy road. The 150-mile trip takes five to six hours. Highway 200 from Acapulco is also a good road. Don't attempt to come from Oaxaca via Zimatlán—about 100 miles of it is unpaved and in poor condition.

From Salina Cruz to Puerto Escondido is a four-hour drive, past the Bahías de Huatulco and the turnoff for Puerto Angel. The road is paved but can be rutty in the rainy season.

ORIENTATION   Arriving   The airport is about $2^1/2$ miles from the center of town near Playa Bacocho. Prices for the Aerotransportes Terrestres minibus to hotels are posted: $3.25 per person. Arriving by bus, you will be deposited at one of the terminals described above. Minibuses from Pochutla or Huatulco will let you off anywhere en route, including the spot where Perez Gasga leads down to the pedestrians-only zone.

Information   The **State Tourist Office, SEDETUR** (☎ 958/2-0175), is about a half mile from the airport, at the corner of Carretera Costera and Bulevar Benito Juárez. It's open Monday through Friday from 9am to 2pm and 5 to 8pm and Saturday from 10am to 1pm. A kiosk at the airport is open for incoming flights, and another, near the west end of the paved tourist zone is open Monday through Saturday from 9am to 2pm and 5 to 8pm.

City Layout   Puerto Escondido is oriented roughly east-west, with the long Zicatela Beach turning sharply southeast. Residential areas lying behind (east of) Zicatela Beach tend to have unpaved streets, while the older town (with paved streets) lies north of the Carretera Costera (Highway 200). The town streets were recently numbered, with Avenida Oaxaca the dividing line between east (oriente) and west (poniente), and Avenida Hidalgo the divider between north (norte) and south (sur). Formerly they were named after historic dates and famous people. But the streets are not marked, so finding your way involves a bit of guesswork and asking directions.

South of this is the tourist zone, through which Avenida Perez Gasga makes a loop. Part of this loop is a paved pedestrian-only zone (or PZ) along which are found many hotels, shops, restaurants, travel agencies and other services. Actually, in the morning, taxis, delivery trucks and private vehicles are allowed. But at noon it becomes a closed zone, and chains are fastened at each end. However, motorbikes and bicycles get in, so don't become complacent.

Avenida Perez Gasga angles down from the Highway at the east end, and on the west, where the PZ terminates, it climbs in a wide northward curve to cross the Highway, after which it becomes Av. Oaxaca.

The **beaches,** Playa Principal in the center of town and Marinero and Zicatela, southeast of the town center, are interconnected and it's easy to walk from one to the other, crossing behind the separating rocks. Puerto Angelito, Carrizalillo and Bacocho beaches are west of town and can be reached by road or boat. Surfers find Zicatela Beach's big curling waves are the best for board surfing. Playa Bacocho hosts most of the expensive hotels.

Getting Around Almost everything is within walking distance of the pedestrian zone. Taxis cost no more than $1.50 to $4.50 to beaches or anywhere in town. Mountain bikes ($9/day or $2.25/hour) and Honda motor bikes ($33.50/day or $7.75/hour) can be rented at Mango Club, Av. Perez Gasga 605-E, on your right just as you enter the PZ on the east. For intrepid walkers, it is now possible to walk beside the sea from the Playa Principal to the tiny beach of Puerto Angelito. However, I recommend the hike only for the hardy because it's rather arduous and the sun beats down unrelentingly. Carry water and wear a hat!

FAST FACTS: PUERTO ESCONDIDO

Area Code The telephone area code is 958.

Currency Exchange Near the middle of the PZ is a money-exchange office, Puerto Bahias, open Monday through Saturday from 9am to 2pm and 5 to 8pm.

Safety Crime in Puerto Escondido is on the rise, and beach muggings are not unknown. Don't leave your belongings unattended on the beach and deposit other valuables in the hotel safe. Positively do not take a midnight stroll down the deserted beach. And respect the power of waves and undertow. Drownings occur all too frequently.

Seasons Seasons vary from business to business. Most, however, consider high season to be mid-December through January, then again before, during and after Easter week. A third high season occurs in July and August, during school and business vacations.

Telephone There are numerous businesses offering long-distance telephone service, and several offer credit card convenience. One is several doors west of the Hotel Las Palmas (near the center of the PZ) and is open daily from 9am to 10pm. Another is at the west end of the PZ (beach side) and is open daily from 7:30am to 10pm.

SWIMMING, SURFING & OTHER THINGS TO DO
BEACHES

Playa Principal and Playa Marinero, both adjacent to the town center and on a deep bay, are the best swimming beaches. Zicatela beach adjoins Playa Marinero and extends southeasterly for several miles. The surfing part of Zicatela, with large curling waves, is about $1^1/2$ miles from the town center.

Barter with one of the fishermen on the main beach for a ride to **Puerto Angelito** and other small coves just west of town, where the swimming is safe and the pace decidedly calmer than in town. Both places have palapas and hammock rentals for $1 per day. Both also boast clear blue water excellent for snorkeling and can provide equipment. After you've worked up an appetite, enjoy fresh fish, tamales, and other Mexican dishes cooked right at the beach by local entrepreneurs. **Playa Bacocho** is on a shallow cove farther to the northwest and is best reached by taxi or boat rather than walking.

Warning: Swimming at a beach that fronts on open sea is a risk to your life. The waves (and undertow) are unpredictable—you're floating peacefully in shoulder-deep water when suddenly the water sinks to knee level and before you can blink it's crashing over your head. Don't follow the surfers' example; they have surfboards to cling to, and they know waves and tides. Despite big warning signs, there are several drownings every year. Swim at the beach in town or at other sheltered beaches in bays and coves.

SURFING

Zicatela Beach, 1¹/₂ miles southeast of Puerto Escondido's town center, is a world-class surf spot. A **surfing competition** in August, and **Fiesta Puerto Escondido,** held for at least 10 days each November, feature Puerto Escondido's well-known surfing waves. The tourism office can supply exact dates and details.

SEEING NESTING RIDLEY TURTLES

The beaches around Puerto Escondido and Puerto Angel are nesting grounds for the endangered Ridley turtle. Tourists can sometimes see the turtles laying eggs or observe the hatchlings trekking to the sea.

Escobilla beach near Puerto Escondido and another near Barra de la Cruz beach near Puerto Angel seem to be favored among other nesting grounds for ridley turtle. Furthermore, in 1991 the Mexican government established the **Centro Mexicano la Tortuga,** known locally as the Turtle Museum, for the study and life-enhancement of the turtle. Present are examples of all species of marine turtles living in Mexico, plus six species of fresh water turtles and two species of land turtles. The center is located on Mazunte Beach, near the town of the same name. Hours are 9am–5pm daily, and entry is $2.25. Buses go to Mazunte from Puerto Angel (50¢) about every half hour, and a taxi will take you there for $3.50–$4.50. You can fit this in with a trip to Zipolite Beach, the next one closer to Puerto Angel.

SHOPPING

The PZ sports a row of tourist shops selling straw hats, post-cards and Puerto Escondido T-shirts plus a few stores featuring Guatemalan and Oaxacan clothing as well as art and souvenirs from various parts of the country. Interspersed among the hotels, restaurants, and shops are pharmacies and minimarkets selling basic necessities.

ACCOMMODATIONS

Note: Even the more expensive hotels have their share of mosquitos, so come armed with a small container of your favorite insect repellent.

MODERATE

Hotel Santa Fe

Calle del Morro (Apdo. Postal 96), Puerto Escondido, Oax. 71980. ☎ **958/2-0170.** Fax 958/2-0260. 51 rms, 8 bungalows (all with bath). A/C. High season $74 double; $85 bungalow. Low season $55.50 double. Free parking.

This very good hotel is about half a mile southeast of the town center off Highway 200. It is located just where Marinero and Zicatela Beaches join, and overlooks a rock outcropping that's a prime sunset-watching spot. The hacienda-style buildings have tiled stairs and archways laden with blooming bougainvillea. The ample rooms have large tile baths, colonial furnishings, hand woven fabrics, Guerrero pottery lamps, and both air-conditioning and ceiling fans. There's a small pool in the central patio. Some rooms don't have telephones, but who are you going to call anyway? Bungalows are next to the hotel, and each comes equipped with a living room, a kitchen, and a bedroom with two double beds. Park in front of the hotel entrance.

Hotel Suites Villasol

Loma Bonita s/n, Fracc. Bacocho, Puerto Escondido, Oax. 71980. ☎ **958/2-0061.** Fax. 958/2-0451. 72 rms, 24 Jr. Suites, 12 Suites (all with bath). A/C TV TEL. High season $85.50 single or double. Low season $61 single or double.

Only five minutes from the airport, and about the same from Puerto Escondido's tourist zone, this four story hotel offers a great deal for the money. It's built around a large courtyard with a swimming pool and palapa bar/snack bar, restaurant and bakery at ground level. All rooms open onto this courtyard. The nice-size standard rooms have one double and one single bed and moderate size bathrooms. Although the hotel is away from the bluff on the top of the hill, a shuttle service whisks you either to town or to the beach club (on Bacocho Beach) where another restaurant and bar tends to your after-swim needs.

INEXPENSIVE

Castillo de los Reyes

Av. Perez Gasga s/n, Puerto Escondido, Oax. 71980. ☎ **958/2-0442.** 16 rms (all with bath). FAN. High season $21 double. Low season $13.50 double.

Don Fernando, the proprietor at Castillo de los Reyes, has a gift for making his guests feel at home. Guests converse around tables on a shady patio near the office. Your white-walled room may have a special touch—perhaps a gourd mask or carved coconut hanging over the bed. There's hot water, and the rooms are shaded from the sun by aging palms. It's on your left as you go up the hill on Perez Gasga after leaving the pedestrian zone (you can also enter Perez Gasga off Highway 200).

✪ Hotel Flor de María

Playa Marinero, Puerto Escondido, Oax. 71980. ☎ and fax **958/2-0536.** 24 rms (all with bath). FAN. $31 double.

This is a real find. Canadians María and Lino Francato built their cheery three-story hotel facing the ocean, which you can see from the rooftop and common walkways linking rooms in the upper stories. Built around a garden courtyard, each room is colorfully decorated with beautiful *trompe l'oeil* still-lifes and landscapes painted by Lino, some of which are headboards. All rooms have windows facing the outdoors, double beds with orthopedic mattresses, and small safes. On the roof you'll find great views, a small pool, shaded hammock terrace, and an open-air bar (open 5–9pm) with evening happy hour specials and a TV that receives American channels. This is a great place to be for sunset. The first floor restaurant is highly recommended (see "Dining," below). Ask about off season discounts for long-term guests. The hotel is a third of a mile from the PZ and 200 feet up a sandy road from Marinero Beach on an unnamed street at the eastern end of the beach.

Hotel Loren

Av. Gasga 507, Puerto Escondido, Oax. 71980. ☎ **958/2-0057.** Fax 958/2-0591. 23 rms (all with bath). FAN. High season $23 double. Low season $15.50 double. Free enclosed parking.

This four-story hotel is tucked in a shady bend of Avenida Perez Gasga past the west end of the pedestrian zone (it can also be reached off Highway 200), around the corner from both the Hotel Nayar and the Hotel Paraíso Escondido. It faces an open interior patio with an inviting pool. The best views are from small private balconies on the upper levels (no elevators). Rooms are immaculate but sparsely furnished, each with two double beds, a chair, and a table.

Hotel Las Palmas

Av. Perez Gasga s/n, Puerto Escondido, Oax. 71980. ☎ **958/2-0230** or 2-0303. 38 rms (all with bath). FAN. High season $27 double. Low season $22.50 double.

This traditional favorite has an overgrown courtyard surrounded by a three-story U-shaped building in the center of the tourist zone facing the ocean and the beach. Each nicely furnished room has a double and a twin bed covered with tasteful foot-loomed bedspreads and matching drapes. The windows and glass doors offer two choices: You either shut all the curtains for privacy (no natural light) or leave them open and have natural light but no privacy. The louvered windows are screenless. The best rooms are on the second and third floors, facing the sea. While the food isn't particularly outstanding, the hotel's beachfront restaurant location is a comfortable place to dawdle away the hours watching the beach scene. Beside the restaurant is a comfy shaded bar with lounge chairs where guests become engrossed in thick novels.

Hotel Rincón del Pacífico

Av. Perez Gasga 900, Puerto Escondido, Oax. 71980. ☎ **958/2-0056.** Fax 958/2-0101. 28 rms, 5 suites (all with bath). FAN. Year round $30 double; $39–$48 suite.

This two-story, U-shaped hotel surrounds a patch of sand shaded by a few tremendous palms. It's opposite Bancomer, close to the center of the PZ and to the Hotel Las Palmas, facing the Pacific. In fact, the rooms are similar to those at Las Palmas, with a glass wall and doors, although the decor is from the 1960s. All except two rooms have a double and one twin bed. The suites have a living room, a minibar, air conditioning, a TV, and a small patio overlooking the beach. The beach-level restaurant, Danny's Terrace, is open daily from 7am to 10pm, with two drinks for the price of one Happy Hour from 4 to 6pm.

DINING
MODERATE

✪ Art & Harry's Bar and Grill

Av. Morro s/n. No phone. Seafood $2.25–$6.75; steaks $9–$13.50. Daily 10am–10pm. SEAFOOD/STEAKS.

Located about $^3/_4$ mile southeast of the Hotel Santa Fe on the road fronting Zicatela Beach, is the robust watering hole where the sun seems to go down in a more spectacular fashion if you are eating one of their monster shrimp cocktails, or savoring fork-tender pieces of budget- and diet-busting grilled beef. A few hours spent here in the late afternoon and early evening watching the surfers and tourists, the sun as it sinks, and the resident cat (no dogs allowed) will give you a sense of Puerto Escondido.

Nautilus

Av. Perez Gasga. No phone. Breakfast $1.75–$2.75; main courses $4.50–$10; comida corrida $6. Daily 8am–midnight. INTERNATIONAL/SEAFOOD.

Here at the west end of the pedestrian zone, you may hear exhilarating mariachi music, Billie Holiday, or Patsy Cline coming from the tape player. From the second-story dining room there's a fabulous bay view for watching fishermen and brown pelicans. Breakfast selections include German and continental dishes. Usually there are several tourist specials featuring soup through dessert in various price ranges. For splurge specialties, try huachinango or vegetarian dishes Hindu style with fruit, wine, and curry. Pastas are more moderately priced, as well as chicken and a small selection of vegetarian dishes.

Eco-Tours & Other Unusual Explorations

The Turismo Rodimar Travel Agency, on the landward side just inside the PZ (☎ 2-0734 or 2-0737; open daily 7:30am–10pm), is an excellent source of information and can arrange all types of tours and travel. Manager Gaudencio Díaz speaks English. He can arrange individualized tours or formal ones such as **Michael Malone's Hidden Voyages Ecotours.** Malone, a Canadian ornithologist, takes you on a dawn or sunset trip to **Manialtepec Lagoon,** a bird-filled mangrove lagoon about 12 miles northwest of Puerto Escondido. The cost is $25 to $30 and includes a stop on a secluded beach for a swim. Probably the best all day tour is to **Chacahua Lagoon National Park** about 42 miles west at a cost of $30. These are true ecotours—small groups touching the environment lightly. You visit a beautiful sandy spit of beach, and the lagoon with incredible birdlife and flowers including black orchids. Locals can provide fresh barbecued fish on the beach. If you know Spanish, and get information from the tourism office, it's possible to stay overnight under a small palapa, but bring plenty of insect repellant. If no agency led tour is available, ask at the tourism office for the names of a couple of locals who also lead these trips.

An interesting and slightly out-of-the-ordinary endeavor is **Jorge Perez' Aventura Submarina,** located "on the strip" (Zicatela Beach, Calle del Morro s/n, in the Acuario building near the Cafecito; ☎ 958/2-1026). Jorge, who speaks fluent English and is a certified scuba dive instructor, guides individuals or small groups of qualified divers along the Coco trench, just offshore. He also arranges surface activities such as deep sea fishing, surfing, trips to lesser known yet nearby swimming beaches, and dirt bike tours into the mountains. If you want to write ahead, contact him at Apdo. Postal 159, Puerto Escondido, Oax., 71980.

Fishermen keep their colorful *pangas* (small boats) on the beach beside the PZ. A **fisherman's tour** around the coastline in his boat will cost about $35, but a ride to Zicatela or Puerto Angelito Beaches will cost only $3. Most hotels offer or will gladly arrange tours to meet your needs.

Restaurant Santa Fe

In the Hotel Santa Fe, Calle del Morro s/n. ☎ **958/2-0170.** Breakfast $2–$4; main courses $4–$12.50. Daily 7am–10:30pm. INTERNATIONAL

The atmosphere here is cool and breezy, with great views of the sunset and the waves on Zicatela Beach. The seafood dishes are a little expensive, but the vegetarian and pasta dishes are reasonably priced and creative, adapting traditional Mexican and Italian dishes. One of my favorites is the house specialty, chiles rellenos: mild green peppers stuffed with cheese, raisins, and nuts; baked in a mild red-chile sauce; and served with brown rice, beans, and salad. My other favorite is the tostada special—big crispy tortillas heaped high with beans, lettuce, cheese, avocado, and salsa. The restaurant is across the street from the beach about half a mile southeast of the town center.

INEXPENSIVE

✪ Carmen's La Patisserie

Playa Marinero. ☎ **958/2-0005.** Pastries 50¢–$1.25; sandwiches $1.50–$2. Daily 7am–7pm. FRENCH PASTRY/SANDWICHES/COFFEE.

Dan and Carmen are the proprietors of this tiny-but- excellent cafe/bakery which has a steady and loyal clientele. Carmen's baked goods are positively unforgettable. By 8am on one weekday there was only one mango creme roll left, and other items were disappearing fast. The coffee, perhaps the best in town, has a flavor and full-ness which keeps you asking for re-fills. Taped international music provides a soothing background, and a paperback exchange creates another reason to linger. Fruit, granola and sandwiches (croissant or whole wheat) round out the menu. Dan and Carmen also provide space for an English-speaking AA group here.

La Patisserie is across the street from the Hotel Flor de María. A second shop, El Cafecito (open 6am) is on Zicatela Beach, near Bruno's Surf Shop. Surfers and observers gather here to critique each other.

✪ María's Restaurant

In the Hotel Flor de María, Playa Marinero. ☎ **958/2-0536.** Breakfast $2.25; main courses $4.50–$5.50. Daily, 8–11am; noon–3pm; 6–10pm. INTERNATIONAL.

Probably the best restaurant in Puerto Escondido, meals are served in the first floor open-air dining room of this hotel near the beach. The menu changes daily and includes specials that include María Francato's homemade pasta dishes. ingredients based on what's fresh that day. María's is a third of a mile from the PZ and 200 feet up a sandy road from Marinero Beach on an unnamed street at the eastern end of the beach.

Restaurant Alicia

Av. Perez Gasga. ☎ **958/2-0690.** Breakfast $1.50–$3.50; main courses $1.75–$4.50. Daily 8am–11pm. MEXICAN.

Here in the middle of the pedestrian zone, a few doors from the Hotel Las Palmas, is Puerto Escondido's honorary United Nations. Visitors from all over wait in line to enjoy the inexpensive meals and good service here. Decor is simple; half a dozen cloth-covered tables look onto Perez Gasga's passing scene. The menu is posted on a large board facing the street and features fish, chicken, and beef dishes as well as tacos and enchiladas served with small salads. Drink specialties are licuados and fruit milk shakes.

Taquería Fiord

Av. Perez Gasga. No phone. Tacos, quesadillas, and sandwiches $1.25–$4.50. High season, daily 7am–midnight. Low season daily 3–11pm. MEXICAN.

Take a seat on a backless chair at one of the uncovered wooden tables here and try the food. Chances are you'll forget what the place looks like once you've tried an inexpensive taco de pollo on a whole-wheat tortilla with it generous portion of chicken, sliced onion, fresh cilantro, lime, and salsa. The restaurant is at the east end of the PZ, on the landward side.

PUERTO ESCONDIDO AFTER DARK

Sunset-watching is a ritual you won't tire of since there are many good lookout points. Watch the surfers at Zicatela from the **Los Tres Osos restaurant** or mingle with them at **Art and Harry's Bar and Grill,** both about a quarter of the way down the beach near the end of current development. For another great sunset view, go to the **Hotel Santa Fe** at the junction of Zicatela and Marinero Beaches or the rooftop bar of **Hotel Flor de María.** Dedicated sun worshipers might want to spring for a cab (about $1.75) or walk half an hour or so west to the **Hotel Posada Real,** overlooking Playa Bacocho. The hotel's clifftop lawn is a perfect sunset-watching perch. Or you might climb down the cliff side (or take the hotel's shuttle bus) to the pool-and-restaurant complex on the beach below. The food isn't great, but the restaurant is an amazing sight, with an artificial tropical lagoon in the middle and leopard-skin swings at the bar.

There are several choices for after-dark entertainment in Puerto Escondido. **El Tubo** is an open-air beachside disco just west of Restaurant Alicia on the PZ. **Son y la Rumba** features live Latin music and dancing, across and up the hill from Las Palmas. **Cocos,** near the east end of the PZ, and **Tío Mac,** also near the east end, feature live music during high season and have happy hours from 6 to 8pm. Both the **Posada Real and Villa Sol,** on Bacocho Beach, have Beach Clubs where one can dance the night away. Most nightspots are open until 3am or until the customers leave.

AN EXCURSION TO PUERTO ANGEL: LAID-BACK SUN & SAND

Fifty miles southeast of Puerto Escondido and 30 miles southwest of the Bays of Huatulco is the tiny fishing port of Puerto Angel (pronounced "PWER-toe on-HEL"). Once known only to a handful of vacationers who came here regularly (mostly from Mexico City and Oaxaca), Puerto Angel today is very popular with the international backpacking set and others looking for an inexpensive and restful vacation. A small, beautiful bay and several inlets provide peaceful swimming and good snorkeling, and the village's out-of-the-way position assures a sleepy, tranquil atmosphere. The population of Puerto Angel is listed as 15,000, but the figure is a misleading because it includes the surrounding farming area. On any given day you'll see very few people in the village, and many of these are tourists. Fishermen leave very early in the morning and return with their catch by late forenoon. Taxis make up most of the traffic, although the bus from Pochutla passes every half hour or so.

ESSENTIALS

GETTING THERE & DEPARTING   There are no direct **buses** from Puerto Escondido or Huatulco to Puerto Angel; however, numerous buses leave Puerto Escondido and Huatulco for **Pochutla,** 7 miles north of Puerto Angel, where you can transfer for the short ride to the village. If you arrive at Pochutla from either Huatulco or Puerto Escondido, you may be dropped at one of several bus stations that line the main street; if so, walk one or two blocks toward the large sign that says POSADA DON JOSÉ. The buses to Puerto Angel are in the lot just before the sign. Ask for the "amarillos" buses (to Puerto Angel). That's what the locals call them—they're yellow—although the name of the line is Estrella del Valle. Estrella del Valle buses originating in Huatulco (about every hour, $1.50) drop passengers at their station in Pochutla. Buses depart from Pochutla for Puerto Angel every 20 or 30 minutes and cost 50¢. Pochutla has many taxis, and they will be glad to take you to Puerto Angel or Zipolite Beach for $3.50 to $4.50, or to the Huatulco airport ($18) or Puerto Escondido ($23).

The bus will let you off in Puerto Angel near the small market in the central part of town. The town center is only about four blocks long, oriented more or less east–west. There are few signs in the village giving directions, and off the main street much of Puerto Angel is a narrow sand-and-dirt path. The navy base is toward the far (west) end of town, just before the creek-crossing toward Playa Panteón (Cemetery Beach).

If you're traveling **by car,** take coastal Highway 175 to Puerto Angel.

ORIENTATION   Puerto Angel now has several **public telephones.** Primary of these is a TelMex office, just past the turn-off to La Buena Vista, and across from the Casa de Huespedes Anahi. It's open daily from 7am to 10pm. Their numbers are 958/4-3055 and 4-3063, and they will accept messages to be picked up (Spanish only). Another public long distance phone is available at the small restaurant next to Gambusino's Travel Agency and near the entrance to the Hotel Soraya. The office is open daily from 7pm to 10pm.

If you want to stash your luggage while you look for lodgings, Gambusino's Travel Agency offers **luggage storage** for $1.25 during their office hours (Monday through Saturday from 10:30am to 2pm and 4 to 6pm). It's about half a block up the street opposite the pier.

The closest **bank** is Bancomer in Pochutla, which will change money Monday through Friday from 9 to 10:30am; however, it's not uncommon for it to run out of cash. It may be hard to change foreign currency with locals in Puerto Angel. Your best bet is simply to come with enough pesos for your stay.

The **post office** (correo), open Monday through Friday from 9am to 3:30pm, is on the curve as you enter town.

BEACHES, WATER SPORTS & BOAT TRIPS

The golden sands of Puerto Angel and the peaceful village life are the attractions here, so in the "where to soak" category let's begin with **Playa Principal** in the central village. You can't miss it, as the beach lies between the pier from which the bulk of the local fishing fleet works and the Mexican navy base. On one end near the pier, fishermen pull their colorful boats on the beach and unload their catch in the late morning while trucks wait to haul it off to processing plants in Veracruz. The rest of the beach is for enjoyment, and except on Mexican holidays, it's relatively deserted. It's important to note that Pacific coast currents deposit trash on Puerto Angel beaches. The townsfolk do a fairly good job of keeping it picked up, but those currents are constant.

Playa Panteón is the main **swimming** and **snorkeling** beach. It's about a 15-minute walk from the town center, straight through town on the main street that skirts the beach. Just before you reach Playa Panteón you pass the panteón (cemetery), on the right, for which the beach is named.

The 3.7 miles of paved road to the village of **Playa Zipolite** (that's "SEE-poh-lee-teh") is walkable but only for the hardy in the midday sun. Taxis charge around $4.50 for single passenger (taxis are expensive here), or you can catch a taxi colectivo on the main street in the town center and share the cost. If you walk, the heat can sap the last bit of your energy, so at least wear a hat and, better still, carry drinking water.

Zipolite is a beach without protection from the open sea. Consequently, swimming can be very dangerous. One of the beach's claim to fame is surfing, with many surfers ensconced in hammocks under numerous palapas along the beach. Beyond a large rock outcropping at the far end of the beach is an area where nude bathing has been tolerated for several years. One caveat: Police could roust au naturel bathers at any time, as they are technically breaking the law. Even more serious is the possibility of drug busts. Mexican jails are not as pleasant as those in the U.S. In Mexico you are under Mexican law.

In Playa Panteón some of the palapa restaurants and a few of the hotels rent **snorkeling** and **scuba** gear and can arrange **boat trips,** but all tends to be quite expensive. And above all, be cautious about the gear—particularly scuba gear. Often the chaps who rent from the beach have rusted and worn equipment, and are hardly interested in either your capability or safety. One reliable boatman, **Mateo López,** at the Posada Cañon Devata (See "Accommodations," below), will take you fishing or snorkeling. He emphasizes that aside from being a life-long fisherman, he is also fully insured.

ACCOMMODATIONS

Two areas in Puerto Angel have accommodations: **Playa Principal** in the tiny town and **Playa Panteón,** the pretty beach area beyond the village center. The bus will let you out at either place—but in Playa Panteón you'll be stuck with your luggage while you look for lodging. A taxi to Playa Panteón from town is $1.75.

Between Playa Panteón and town are numerous bungalow and guesthouse setups with budget accommodations.

Most hotels now receive mail in Puerto Angel, although some still maintain a P.O. Box in Pochutla. During the high season—December, January, around Easter, and July and August—rates can go up and you should reserve well in advance.

✪ La Buena Vista

Apdo. Postal 48, Puerto Angel, Oax. 70902. ☎ and fax **958/4-3104**. 18 rms (all with bath). FAN. All year $20 double.

To find La Buena Vista, follow the road through town and shortly you'll see a sign on the right pointing to the hotel. It's on a hillside, so to get to the lobby/patio you follow the sign, taking a left at Casa de Huespedes Alex, after which you climb a formidable flight of stairs. This will take you to the lobby, where you'll discover why this hotel's name means "good view," with the bay and village in the distance. The rooms, each with a natural tile floor, one or two double beds, and well-screened windows, are tastefully furnished with Mexican accents. On the upper floor is a wonderful little reasonably priced restaurant with bay views. It's open for breakfast from 7:30 to 11am and for dinner from 6 to 10pm.

Hotel La Cabaña De Puerto Angel

Apdo. Postal 22, Pochutla, Oax. 70902. ☎ **958/4-0026.** 23 rms (all with bath). FAN. All year $18 single or double.

Covered in vines and plants, with lots of shade, this hacienda-style hotel is efficient and accommodating, with a friendly, helpful staff; owner Diego Oropeza is truly gracious. The clean, sunny rooms have louvered windows and screens, ceiling fans, and double beds. The rooftop patio is a nice place to sunbathe peacefully, and a hot pot of free coffee awaits guests every morning at 7am in the lobby. The hotel is on Playa Panteón on the landward side of the road, just steps from the beach and several restaurants.

✪ Posada Cañon DeVata

Calle Canyon del Vata (Apdo. Postal 10), Puerto Angel, Oax. 70902. ☎ **958/4-3048.** 10 rms, 4 bungalows (13 with bath). $22.25 double; $26.75 bungalow for two. Closed May–June.

One of the most inviting places in Puerto Angel is a three-minute walk almost straight up from Playa Panteón. Americans Suzanne and Mateo López run this ecologically sound, homey, cool, green and wooded oasis in a narrow canyon. All water is recycled for the benefit of the resident plants and critters. Rooms are agreeably rustic-chic, with fans, beds covered in Guatemalan tie-died cloth, and

Mateo's paintings hanging from the walls (the paintings can be bought). The patio restaurant serves delicious food featuring home-baked bread and the posada's own organically grown vegetables. Don't miss climbing to the appropriately named El Cielo to see the bay bathed in the light of the setting sun, and to enjoy the Happy Hour from 5pm until dark. Mateo also offers fishing and snorkeling trips (see "What to See and Do" above).

To find it, walk just past the Hotel Cabaña del Puerto Angel to where the road more or less ends; turn right and go down the sandy path to an area with a few parked cars. Walk across the tiny bridge on your right and follow the stairs on the left until you reach the restaurant, where someone is around to rent rooms and serve food.

DINING

In addition to the restaurants below and those mentioned under hotels above, there are four or five palapa-topped restaurants on the main beach in town as well as on Playa Panteón. Hawkers from these various establishments implore you to try their restaurants, but they're all similar in price, menu, and service. Breakfasts generally cost $2.25 to $4.50, and meat or seafood plates run $4.50 to $11.25. Watch for overbilling in these restaurants.

✪ Restaurant Cañon DeVata

At Posada Cañon Devata, Calle Cañon Devata. ☎ **958/4-3048.** Breakfast $1.75–$4.50; sandwiches $3.50; dinner $6. Daily 7:30am–4pm and 7–8:30pm. Closed May–June. VEGETARIAN.

It's always a few degrees cooler under the thatched palapa in the middle of the canyon area. Fresh flowers centered on the thick wooden tables set the mood. Guests partake of some of the healthiest cooking around, mainly vegetarian dishes with occasional fish specialties. The restaurant is in the hotel by the same name, on the right, past the Hotel Cabaña de Puerto Angel.

✪ Villa Florencia

Bulevar Virgilio Uribe. ☎ **958/4-3044.** Breakfast $1.15–$2.25; pasta dishes $2.25–$6.75; pizzas $4–$5. Daily 7am–11pm. ITALIAN.

One of the best restaurants in town is Lulu and Walter Pelliconi's delightful slice of Italy. Their generous servings are prepared in a spotlessly clean kitchen that contains a purifier for all water used on the premises. Pasta products are imported from Italy, and the chefs use only extra virgin olive oil. The restaurant is located near the pier and the bus drop-off in the central village.

4 Bahías de Huatulco

40 miles E of Puerto Angel, 425 miles SE of Acapulco

"The next Cancún!" trumpets the tourist literature—but it's going to be a while before this statement is true. Oaxaca's coastline is one of the last undeveloped stretches of pure white sands and isolated coves in Mexico, and it's a joy to see. Birds and tropical blossoms abound. The sea is crystal clear and bathwater warm, the air blessedly free of gasoline fumes.

The FONATUR development of the Bahías de Huatulco, a government megaresort on the nine pristine bays of Huatulco, is an ambitious project that will sprawl across 124,000 acres of land, most still undeveloped. The small communities of locals have been transplanted away from the coast into Crucecita, and corporate giants are vying for the rights to huge parcels of prime, pristine bayfront jungle.

It's unlikely that the developers' ambitious original projections of a million visitors annually by the year 2000 will be realized. Huatulco's growth pace has (for some) been painfully slow and measured. Perhaps this leisurely development will help spare Huatulco from thoughtless overdevelopment and from the ruination of the unspoiled beauty of its setting. Right now, the area is distinctly divided into three sections—Santa Cruz, Crucecita, and Tangolunda (see "City Layout," below).

ESSENTIALS

GETTING THERE & DEPARTING   **By Plane**   Three times daily **Mexicana** (☎ 958/7-0243, or 1-0208 at the airport), connects Huatulco with Cancún, Guadalajara, and Los Angeles by way of Mexico City. **Aeroméxico** (☎ 958/1-0336 or 1-0329, or 91-800/9-0999), offers service from Mexico City once daily Monday through Saturday. **AeroVega** arrives daily from Oaxaca. **AeroMorelos** (through Servicios Turísticos del Sur, ☎ 958/1-0055) has direct flights from Oaxaca five days per week, and via Puerto Escondido three days per week. **Club Med charter flights** originate at the Dallas/Fort Worth Airport.

Transportes Terrestres minibuses to the hotels from Huatulco's international airport, about 13 miles northwest of the Bahías de Huatulco, cost $4.50 per person. It's $8–$10 by taxi to Santa Cruz/Tangolunda.

By Bus   Reaching Huatulco by bus has become easier. There are three bus stations in Crucecita, but none in Santa Cruz or Tangolunda, so a bus trip to any destination begins and ends in Crucecita. The stations in Crucecita are all within a few blocks of one another. The **Gacela and Estrella Blanca** station (☎ 958/7-0103), is at the corner of Gardenia and Palma Real. Here you'll find ten daily buses traveling semi-direct to Acapulco, as well as one direct service to Mexico City. Others go to hourly to Puerto Escondido and to Pochutla. Gacela and **Oaxaca Pacífico** have several buses daily to Puerto Escondido.

The **Cristóbal Colón** station (☎ 958/7-0261) is at the corner of Gardenia and Ocotillo, four blocks from the Plaza Principal. Most of these buses go east to Salina Cruz, Tehuantepec and Juchitan, and then either across the Isthmus to Acayucan, or on to Tuxtla Gutiérrez and San Cristóbal de las Casas. But there are also several to Oaxaca (via Salina Cruz), Puerto Escondido (9 trips), and Pochutla. There's also service to Huatulco from Acapulco. If you come from tiny Puerto Angel you must change buses in Pochutla. The fare is 50¢ for the 30-minute ride to Pochutla and $1.50 for the hour ride into Huatulco. Any bus going to Huatulco will drop you off at Crucecita. To avoid confusion, read the "City Layout" section, below.

To get to the **Estrella del Valle** station (☎ 958/7-0193), start from the corner of Guanacostle and Gardenia. Go eight blocks on Gardenia (passing the Colón station) to Palo Verde, then left one block to Jasmin, then right ¹/₂ block to the station (it is between Sabali and Carrizal). From here, three buses leave for Oaxaca daily.

The stations in Crucecita are all within a few blocks of one another.

By Car   The coastal Highway 200 leads to Huatulco (via Pochutla) from the west and is generally in good condition. Allow at least eight hours for the trip from Oaxaca City on mountainous Highway 175.

ORIENTATION   Arriving   The airport is 13 miles from town, and the trip costs $4.50 by Transporte Terrestre to Santa Cruz or Crucecita and $8–$10 to Tangolunda. If you arrive by bus you'll be dropped off in Crucecita.

Information   The closest thing to a **tourist office** the area has is a quasitourism office located in Crucecita on Guamuchil, near the corner of Bugambilia, just off the Plaza Principal. It is run by the tourist publication *Huatulco Espacio 2000* (☎ 958/7-0027), though they speak little English and are seldom there. Best to go to Sunrise Tours (Plaza Gardenia #2-B, across Calle Flamboyan from the Plaza Principal). Here Lic. Miguel Gonzaléz will provide you with maps of Puerto Angel and Puerto Escondido and advice on everything in the area. They're open Monday through Saturday from 9am to 10:30pm and Sunday 4 to 10:30pm.

The **State Tourism Office** (Oficina del Turismo) once again is said to be open in the shopping center area of Tangolunda Bay. It's always offered erratic service and uncertain hours, so don't count on it. Supposedly it's open Monday through Saturday from 9am to 3pm and 6 to 8pm.

City Layout   Just naming where you want to go in Huatulco can be confusing. The resort area is called Bahías de Huatulco and includes all nine bays. It shouldn't be confused with Santa María de Huatulco, 17 miles inland. **Santa Cruz Huatulco,** normally called just Santa Cruz, is the original coastal settlement on the bay. It has a pretty central park with a bandstand kiosk, an artisans' market by the park, a few hotels and restaurants, and a marina where bay tours and fishing trips set sail. **Juárez** is Santa Cruz's main street, about only four blocks long in all, anchored at one end by the Hotel Castillo Huatulco and at the other by the Posada Binniguenda. Opposite the Hotel Castillo is the marina, and beyond it are restaurants housed in new colonial-style buildings facing the beach. The area's banks and a couple of convenience stores are on Juárez. It's impossible to get lost—you can see almost everything at a glance.

A mile and a half inland from Santa Cruz is **Crucecita,** a planned city that sprang up in 1985 centered on a lovely grassy plaza edged with flowering hedges. It's the residential area for the resorts, with neighborhoods of new stucco homes mixed with makeshift wooden ones and small apartment complexes. Most of the area's less expensive hotels and restaurants are here.

Until other bays are developed **Tangolunda Bay,** 3 miles east, is the focal point of development for the nine bays. Gradually, half the bays will have resorts, places where guests will arrive on a shuttle from the airport and then stay put. For now, Tangolunda has the 18-hole golf course, as well as the Club Med, Sheraton Huatulco, Royal Maeva, Holiday Inn Crowne Plaza, Casa del Mar, and Omni Zaachila hotels. Small strip centers with a few restaurants occupy each end of Tangolunda Bay. Chahue Bay, between Tangolunda and Santa Cruz, is a small bay with a marina under construction as well as houses and hotels.

Getting Around   It's too far to walk between any of the three destinations of Crucecita, Santa Cruz, and Tangolunda, but there are minibus services between the towns. In Santa Cruz, catch the bus across the street from Castillo Huatulco; in Tangolunda, in front of the Holiday Inn; and in Crucecita, catercorner from the Hotel Grifer.

FAST FACTS: BAHÍAS DE HUATULCO

Area Code   The telephone area code is 958.

Banks   Santa Cruz has banks; there are two and both are on Juárez (Banamex and Bancomer). Their hours for changing money are generally 9am to noon weekdays.

Taxis   In Crucecita there's a taxi stand opposite the Hotel Grifer, and another on the Plaza Principal. To or from Santa Cruz, Crucecita, or Tangolunda Bay, the cost is $2.25 to $3.50, but you can often share a cab for 50¢ per person.

Telephones   The long-distance telephone office is on Calle Flamboyan near the corner of Bugambilia in Crucecita. It's open Monday through Saturday from 7:30am to 9:30pm and Sunday and holidays from 8am to 1pm.

BEACHES, WATER SPORTS & OTHER THINGS TO DO

BEACHES   A portion of the beach at **Santa Cruz** (away from the small boats) can be inviting as a sunning spot. Several restaurants are on the beach, and palapa umbrellas are found down to the waters edge. Jet skis can be rented for about $35/ hour. **Tangolunda Bay** beach, fronting the best hotels, is wide and beautiful. Theoretically all beaches in Mexico are public, however, non-guests at Tangolunda hotels may have difficulty being allowed to enter the hotel to get to the beach. At other beach locations in Mexico hotels are so busy that an outsider doesn't stand out, but that's not so at the luxury hotels in Huatulco and outsiders may be escorted back out. For about $5 one way, pangas from the marina in Santa Cruz will ferry you to **La Entrega Beach,** one bay over from Santa Cruz. There you'll find a row of palapa restaurants, all with beach chairs out front. Find an empty one and use that restaurant for your refreshment needs in return. A snorkel equipment-rental booth is about midway down the beach, and there's some fairly good snorkeling on the end away from where the boats arrive; be careful of wave action pushing you against the rocks.

BAY CRUISES/TOURS   Huatulco's major attraction is the coastline, that magnificent stretch of pristine bays. The only way to really grasp the beauty of the place is by taking a cruise of the bays, stopping at Chahue or Maguey Bay for a dip in the crystal-clear water and a fish lunch from one of the palapas on the beach.

The best way to arrange a bay tour is to go to the boat owners' cooperative in the red-and-yellow tin shack at the entrance to the marina. Prices are posted here, and you can buy tickets for definite times for sightseeing, snorkeling, or fishing. Prices start at $11 per person for a round-trip to La Entrega Beach and go to $17 per person, or $110 for a private all-day cruise. (La Entrega Beach, by the way, is remembered in Mexican history as the place where President Vicente Guerrero was put ashore as a prisoner after he was kidnapped in Acapulco.) Besides La Entrega Beach, there are other beaches farther away that are noted for good off-shore snorkeling. These beaches, however, have no food or toilet facilities, so bring your own provisions. Boatmen at the cooperative will arrange to return to get you at an appointed time. Round-trip boat transportation to these outer beaches costs from $40–$85; a trip to see all the bays costs around $50 for about an hour without stops.

A third approach is to consult a travel agency. In Crucecita, **Sunrise Tours** (Plaza Oaxaca, Local #11, ☎ 958/7-0892) offers bay tours (7 bays, $20), Puerto Angel, Puerto Escondido and associated beaches ($33.50), an ecotour on the Río Copalito (7 hours, $33.50), or an all day tour to a coffee plantation. **Servicios Turísticos del Sur**, in both the Hotel Castillo in Santa Cruz and the Sheraton Hotel in Tangolunda (☎ 958/1-0055, ext. 784 or 788), offers similar tours.

BIRDING   Although there are no formal birding walks or tours, if birds are your interest, Huatulco will be rewarding. Before setting out, be sure to wear protective clothing (against the sun, not the birds) and sturdy shoes.

GOLF & TENNIS   The 18-hole Campo de Golf Tangolunda is adjacent to Tangolunda Bay and has tennis courts as well. The Greens fee is $35 and carts cost about the same.

SHOPPING   There's a good **folk-art store** in the Sheraton Hotel, but for the most part shopping is confined to the Santa Cruz market, by the marina in Santa Cruz, and the Crucecita market, on Guamuchil half a block from the plaza in Crucecita.

ACCOMMODATIONS

Moderate and budget-priced hotels in Santa Cruz and Crucecita hotels are generally overpriced compared to similar hotels in other Mexican beach locations. The luxury beach hotels are priced at rates that are comparable to Mexico's other beach locations. Low season here is considered September, October, February, and June. During other months hoteliers may invoke high-season prices.

EXPENSIVE

Omni Zaashila

Rincón Sabroso, Bahía de Tangolunda Hualtuco. Oax. 70989. ☎ **958/1-0460.** Fax. 958/1-0461. in USA: 800/325-3535. 120 rms (all with bath). A/C TEL TV. High season $178 double. Low season $112 double.

The white stucco facade of this luxurious mediterranean-style hotel stands out from it's more stately looking neighbors, and seems to fit perfectly in it's beach side location. The spacious rooms are beautifully furnished with a Mediterranean flair, cool tile floors, and TV with remote control concealed in an armoire. Most have balconies and a view facing the ocean or pool.

   Dining/Entertainment: The restaurant serves delicious seafood, steaks and Oaxacan dishes. A kiosk bar/snack bar sits between it and the beach.

   Services: Laundry and room service, tour desk.

   Facilities: The large freeform swimming pool on the beach, extends in curves and narrows some 50 yards.

MODERATE

Club Med

Tangolunda Bay, Santa Cruz de Huatulco, Oax. 70900. ☎ **958/1-0033** or 800/258-2633 in the U.S. Fax 958/1-0101. 500 rms (all with bath). A/C. High season $652 per person per week, double occupancy (includes all meals and activities); $93 per person per night. Ask about air-inclusive packages, low-season discounts, and kids free weeks.

Considering that all meals and a slew of activities are included in one price, Club Med is value-packed splurge experience in Huatulco. The best time to come is in low season, when prices are lower. Everything is included in one price except excursions, deep-sea fishing, horseback riding, massage, and use of the public 18-hole golf course. It caters to all adult ages (married and single), with an atmosphere like a country club for the sports- or relaxation-minded. In summer there's a teen club for ages 12 to 17 has special supervised sports and activities. The setting has a spectacular view of Tangolunda Bay and lineup of hotels on the opposite side of the bay. Each room has a private patio with hammock, and all rooms have sea views. Rooms have both air-conditioning and fans, and you need both—the air-conditioning isn't very effective.

Five restaurants feature different cuisines, with an emphasis on fresh seafood, French, and Moroccan specialties (but not all may be open in low season). There's a nightly disco, water sports (sailing, kayaking, windsurfing, snorkeling), three swimming pools, an air-conditioned workout room with aerobics classes, three air-conditioned squash courts, a practice golf course, archery, volleyball, basketball, soccer, softball, bocce ball, billiards, ping pong, a circus area with trapeze instruction, arts and crafts, massage, horseback riding, and very popular activities for teens. The snorkeling is quite good on a coral reef on one of the club's beaches. Seven of the 12 tennis courts are lighted for night play. Deep-sea fishing costs extra. Unlike other Club Meds in Mexico, where you're a long distance from town, at this one you're no farther from town than the hotels across the bay; it's easy to call a taxi and go off to Crucecita on your own or to enjoy the beach and restaurants at the hotels on the bay. A taxi to town for shopping is cheaper than the hotel's boat excursion to the shopping area. However, there's so much to do here (and not so much to do in town) that most people stay within the Club Med boundaries; a stay here might mean never having to know you're in Mexico, but you'll sure enjoy the gorgeous bay and coastal setting.

Hotel Binniguenda

Blv. Santa Cruz s/n (Apdo. Postal 175), Santa Cruz de Huatulco, Oax. 70989. ☎ **958/ 7-0077.** Fax 958/7-0284. 74 rms (all with bath). A/C TV TEL. High season $78.50 single or double. Low season $44.50 single or double.

This was Huatulco's first hotel, and it retains the Mexican charm and comfort that made it memorable. Rooms have Mexican tile floors, foot-loomed bedspreads, colonial-style furniture, and French doors opening onto tiny wrought-iron balconies overlooking Juárez. The TV receives Mexican channels plus HBO. There's a nice shady area around the hotel's beautiful pool in back of the lobby. The restaurant is only fair. The hotel is away from the marina at the far end of Juárez, only a few blocks from the water. They offer free transportation to a beach club at Chahue Bay.

INEXPENSIVE

Suites Begonias

Bugambilia No. 503, between Flamboyan and Chacah, Crucecita, Bahías de Huatulco, Oax. 70989. ☎ **958/7-0018.** 12 rms (all with bath). FAN TV. High season $40 single or double. Low season $22.25 single or double.

The smallish suites at the Begonias are open and airy, with orange-and-black bedspreads and festive Talavera-style lamps. Two large rooms overlook Guamuchil and have table and chairs and a small balcony. It's on Bugambilia, just off the Plaza Principal.

DINING

Outside of the hotels, the best choices are in Crucecita and on the beach in Santa Cruz.

Restaurant Avalos Doña Celia

Santa Cruz Bay. ☎ **958/7-0128.** Breakfast $3.50–$9.75; seafood $5.75–$11.25. Daily 8:30am–10pm. SEAFOOD.

Doña Celia, an original Huatulco resident, chose to stay in business in the same area where she started her little thatch-roofed restaurant years ago. Now she's in a new building at the end of Santa Cruz's beach, serving the same good food. Among her specialties are filete empapelado, a foil-wrapped fish baked with tomato, onion, and cilantro, and filete almendrado, a fish fillet covered with a hotcake batter, beer and almonds. The ceviche is terrific (one order is plenty for two). The Platillo a la Huatulqueño (shrimp and young octopus fried in olive oil with chile and onion and served over white rice) should satisfy any seafood lover.

✪ Restaurant Juquilita
Calle Palo Verde at Gardenia, Crucecita. No phone. Fixed price meal $2.75. Daily 6am–9pm. OAXACAN.

Don't come here if you are not hungry, or if you must have traditional eggs for breakfast. Do come here if you want something that will hold you till late afternoon! Simmering on the stove in the back, and tended by the owner/cook (an ample and jovial motherly type from Juchitan), are chocolate, guisado (stew), black beans, chicken, and mole. Plus there are tamales and stacks of tortillas. You can tell from the clientele that they come here not because it's chic, but because of good food at the right price.

✪ Restaurante María Sabina
Flamboyan 15, Crucecita. ☎ **958/7-1039.** Main courses $2.25–$23; regional $3.50–$10; seafood $5.50–$13.50. Daily 1pm–midnight. SEAFOOD/OAXACAN.

This popular restaurant, which is probably the best in town, is on the far side of the Plaza Principal. The staff is super attentive and owner Jaime Negrete presides over the big open grill where the tantalizing aroma of grilled steak, ribs, chicken, and fresh fish drift throughout the cafe. Almost always full, this is where carnivores gather. The lengthy menu also features Oaxacan dishes.

BAHÍAS DE HUATULCO AFTER DARK

Bring a supply of books—Huatulco is short on entertainment. Besides the disco below, a lot of people finish off an evening at one of the eateries on Santa Cruz Bay or at **Carlos 'n' Charlie's** in Crucecita a block from the Hotel Grifer. The food is good and it's open for dinner and dancing to mega-loud music nightly from 5pm to midnight

Disco Magic Circus, Santa Cruz Bay (☎ 958/7-0017 or 7-0037), is across the street and a block away from the Posada Binniguenda, going toward the marina. The music is a mix of salsa and rock. Admission is $9 (women free on Sunday, more often in low season). It's open daily from 10pm to 3am.

12

Veracruz & the Gulf Coast

One of the least-traveled parts of Mexico, the Gulf Coast is also one of the most interesting—and economical. Friendly and gracious, the Gulf Coast is like the Mexico of many years ago, and its prices are like those of bygone times as well—an immensely appealing discovery in this country filled with costly and contrived resorts. Your money will go farther here than anywhere else in the country.

The region is studded with archaeological ruins left by indigenous groups. The **Huastec** occupied the area running from the north of the Cazones River to Soto la Marina, which includes portions of Veracruz, Tamaulipas, and San Luis Potosí; the **Totonac** lived from the south of the Cazones River to the Papaloapan River, in mid- to upper Veracruz; and the **Olmec,** a civilization dating back 3,000 years, lived from Río Papaloapan to La Venta in southern Veracruz and northern Tabasco. Pyramidal sites dot the coast, some of which, like El Tajín and Zempoala, make for excellent off-the-beaten-track travel. First-rate museums along the way are devoted to explaining these cultures and their impact on Mexico. At least 15% of the people speak Indian languages: Otomi is spoken around Puebla spilling into Veracruz; Huasteco, a Maya-linked language, is spoken in Tamaulipas and San Luis Potosí; and Nauahtl and Totonaco are used in both Puebla and Veracruz.

EXPLORING THE GULF COAST

The real highlights of the Gulf coast—Veracruz and the Zempoala ruins, the ruins of El Tajín, Jalapa, and Lake Catemaco—are clustered within an hour or so of the city of Veracruz. Many people fly directly to Veracruz from the States and base their exploration of the Gulf coast from that exuberant city. And Veracruz can be easily reached from Mexico City by plane, bus, or car.

Veracruz is a natural base for side trips to Jalapa, the capital of Veracruz, and to the ruins of Zempoala, but allow 3 days. Getting to and seeing Papantla and El Tajín requires around 3 days. Don't plan to spend less than 2 nights in Catemaco and two in the Tuxtlas.

In Veracruz state, Veracruz has the most flights from the United States, but if you want to fly from Mexico City to Minatitlán (south of Catemaco), it's very easy to work your way north from there by bus.

1 Veracruz City

145 miles E of Mexico City, 68 miles SE of Jalapa

Veracruz (Bay-rah-CROOS), today a delightfully raucous port town, boasts an intriguing combination of European and African influences and a clean and impressive shoreline. Despite its reputation as a good-time town—especially during Carnaval, just before Lent—there's a refreshingly relaxed atmosphere in this city of 328,000 residents, more like the Mexico of many years ago.

No trip to Veracruz is complete without indulging in two local customs: drinking coffee at La Parroquia, just off Plaza de Armas, and listening to marimba music beneath the portals of Plaza de Armas.

Veracruz has been Mexico's principal port almost since Hernán Cortés landed here on Good Friday in 1519. Within 3 months, however, he moved his forces 45 miles north to a place called Quiauixtlan, a small Indian settlement known today as Villa Rica. Six years later, in 1525, Cortés's forces re-settled near the mouth of the Río Huitzilapan at what is now Antigua (about 14 miles north of modern Veracruz). This move was somewhat more permanent—the ruins of several massive stone houses such as the House of Cortés (La Casa de Cortés) still stand there. Then, in 1599, the settlement was moved south to the original landing site, and Villa Rica de la Vera Cruz ("the Rich Town of the True Cross")—Cortés's name for the town—became permanent.

The Spaniards once shipped most of their gold and silver out of the port, and looting pirates periodically corralled the townfolk in the parish church or abandoned them on an island in the bay while they methodically ransacked the town. The citizens in turn built a high wall around the old town (around Plaza de Armas) and constructed a massive fort, San Juan de Ulúa, on what was then an island in the harbor (now connected to the mainland by a curving pier). Despite these formidable precautions, the pirates pillaged the port in 1654 and again in 1712. Later the French invaded in 1832 and 1861, and the Americans attacked in 1847 and 1914.

ESSENTIALS

GETTING THERE & DEPARTING   By Plane Mexicana (☎ 32-2242; at the airport 21-4020) flies to Veracruz from Mexico City five times daily and from Mérida twice daily. **AeroLitoral** (☎ 35-0701), an Aeroméxico affiliate, flies from Ciudad Juárez, McAllen and San Antonio (Texas), Minatitlán, Monterrey, Tampico, and Villahermosa. **Aeroméxico** (☎ 35-0142; at the airport 34-3428, or toll free 91-800/3-6202), flies from in Mexico City. **Continental** (☎ 38-2255, or toll free 91-800/9-0050) has service from Houston. **Aerocaribe/Aerocozumel** (☎ 37-0260; at the airport 34-5888) arrives from various locations in the Yucatán, Guatemala, Belize, and Cuba.

The airport is 2^1/$_2$ miles from the town center. Minibuses of **Transportación Terrestre Aeropuerto** (☎ 37-8719) go out for every departing flight and cost $10.50.

By Bus   There are frequent buses from Jalapa, Orizaba, Córdoba, and Mexico City to Veracruz. From Veracruz's ADO station, **ADO** (☎ 37-5744) buses leave frequently for Orizaba, Córdoba, and San Andrés Tuxtla; buses to Jalapa leave every 30 minutes.

From the **Central Camionera** (☎ 29/37-6790), frequent buses head from Veracruz to Mexico City—a 7-hour trip. Six buses daily go directly to Catemaco.

By Car Veracruz is less than 2 hours away from Jalapa via Highway 140 to the coastal Highway 180 and the toll road into Veracruz, or cut off before the coast at Puente Nacional and go south to Veracruz on toll-free Highway 146.

From Mexico City, Córdoba, or Orizaba, take Highway 150 to the coast and then drive north on Highway 180 to Veracruz; it's less than a 2-hour drive from the latter two cities.

ORIENTATION   Arriving   If you arrive **by plane,** don't tarry long in the airport before getting to the colectivo minivans that await each flight and cost $3: They fill up and leave rapidly and don't return until the next expected flight. The **bus station** is many blocks south of the Plaza on Díaz Mirón (between Orizaba and Molina). Since the bus station is a good distance from downtown, try to make your onward reservations when you arrive in Veracruz.

The **Central Camionera** (main bus station) is 20 or so blocks south of the town center on Diaz Mirón between Orizaba and Molina. Taxis cost around $1.75 to Plaza de Armas. "Díaz Mirón" buses go to and from the town center. Catch the outbound on Avenida 5 de Mayo (two blocks west of the Plaza de Armas).

Information   The **tourism office** (☎ 29/32-1999), with its enthusiastic staff, is right downtown on Plaza de Armas. The office is on the ground floor of the Palacio Municipal (Town Hall), on the east side of the square; it's open daily from 9am to 9pm, although sparsely staffed from 1 to 4pm.

City Layout   Parallel to the shoreline, **Paseo del Malecón/Bulevar Camacho** runs north and south; it goes into the town center and out to the beaches and resorts south of town. (Technically, the malecón is named Insurgentes, but that name is seldom used.) City life gravitates around **Plaza de Armas,** one block west of Malecón. It's bounded by Lerdo and Zamora going east and west and by Independencia and Morelos going north and south. Most museums, restaurants, and hotels are either here or within a short walk.

Getting Around   **City buses** are inexpensive (around 25¢ to 40¢) and easy to use. I have mentioned those that get you to and from the most important places in town. **Taxis** are incredibly cheap compared to those in other cities in Mexico; you pay around $1.75 to get almost anywhere in the downtown area, including the bus station.

FAST FACTS: VERACRUZ

American Express   Viajes Olymar represents American Express. They have offices in Plaza Mocambo, Local A-18 (☎ 29/21-9923), as well as on Bulevar Camacho 2221, Col. Zaragoza (☎ 29/31-4636; fax 29/31-3169).

Area Code   The telephone area code is 29.

Impressions

A chronic complaint along the coast of Veracruz is the blast of Boreas called the "Norther." It swoops down upon the sea like a bird of prey, sending ships ashore, and laying low many a forest monarch and many a residence on land.

—Fredrick A. Ober, *Travels in Mexico and Life Among the Mexicans,* 1884

Downtown Veracruz

Climate   You'll find it hot and sultry in summer and mild in spring, fall, and winter, with windy, sand-blowing *nortes* (northers) from November to March.

Consulate   The U.S. Consultate is located on Víctimas del 25 de Junio, no. 384, almost at the corner of Gómez Farías (☎ 29/31-0142). It's open Monday through Friday from 9am to 1pm.

High Season   The peak tourist season falls in June, July, and August and then December through March.

Post Office   The correo (post office), located on Avenida de la República, near the Maritime Customs House, is open Monday through Friday from 8am to 8pm.

EXPLORING VERACRUZ

More than anything else, you'll remember the liveliness of Veracruz after you visit here. There is a certain carefree spirit about this bustling seaport. From 1 or 2pm until the early morning, you'll hear **mariachi** and **marimba** bands playing in and around Plaza de Armas, and on Tuesday, Thursday, and Saturday from 8 to 10pm, the city band plays in front of the **Palacio Municipal,** where local couples often dance a unique form of the waltz known as **danzón.** Up and down the **Malecón** and in the square, people gather to socialize, listen to the music, or sell trinkets. It's a lively town, especially on a Sunday, which seems to be the big socializing day, and Parque Zamora hosts evening dancing.

Sightseeing trolleys—open-air, rubber-wheeled trolleys, replicas of those that ran on rails in Veracruz until the early 1980s—leave from Insurgentes (corner of 16 de Septiembre, on the Malecón) every hour daily (unless the weather is bad) from 10am to 11:30pm, making an hour-long tour through town. The cost is $3.25 round-trip.

The **Ballet Tradicional de México** (☎ 29/31-0574 or 32-6693 for reservations) performs at the Teatro J. Clavijero. Tickets cost $3.50 to $7. Check with the tourism office (see "Information," above).

For the 3 days before Ash Wednesday, **Carnaval** takes place in Veracruz, and it's one of the best in Mexico. Visitors from Mexico City pack the streets and hotels; those without rooms live out of their cars. Indians, who've walked a day's journey from their villages, spread their crafts on the sidewalks. Even the townspeople, normally attentive to their own affairs, join the crowds in the music-filled streets.

There are fabulous floats (in Spanish, *carros alegóricos*, "allegorical cars") made with true Mexican flair—bright colors, papier-mâché figures (even the Muppets showed up on one float), large flowers, and live entertainment. Groups from the neighboring villages don their peacock- and pheasant-feathered headdresses in preparation for the dances they will perform during the festivities. There are costumed Draculas and drag queens and women in sparkling dresses parading down the streets. Most of the other activities center in Plaza de Armas and begin around noon, lasting well into the night.

If you plan to be in Veracruz for the 3 days of Carnaval, reserve hotel space months in advance, as everything's jammed full at this time. On the Sunday before Ash Wednesday, the longest and most lavish of the Carnaval parades takes place on the Malecón. Parades on Monday and Tuesday are scaled-down versions of the Sunday parade (ask at the tourist office about the parade routes on Monday and Tuesday), and by Wednesday, it's all over.

MUSEUMS & AN AQUARIUM

San Juan de Ulua

☎ **29/38-5151.** Admission $4.50. Tues–Sun 9am–5pm. Drive across the bridge that heads north out of Plaza de Armas between Avenida de la República and Avenida Morelos, then turn right past the box storage and piers. Bus: "San Juan de Ulua" from the *parada* (stop) across from Calle Juárez on Avenida de la República.

Built as a limestone-rock fortress against pirate invasion, the structure became infamous instead as a prison noted for extreme cruelty and for the famous people who were incarcerated there, among them Benito Juárez. He later led the Reform Movement from the fort and became one of the country's most revered presidents. English-speaking guides charge for tours at the entrance or you can go on your own.

Baluarte Santiago

At the corner of Rayón and Gómez Farías. ☎ **29/31-1059.** Admission $4.50. Tues–Sun 10am–4:30pm. From Plaza de Armas, walk five blocks south on Independencia, then turn left (east) onto Rayón and walk for two more blocks.

This bulwark was built in 1636 as part of the city's fortifications against the pirates, but this bastion is all that's left of the old city walls and the original nine forts. It's remarkable to see the type of construction that was used in those days— it's solid, to say the least. A collection of pre-Hispanic gold jewelry, recovered several years ago by a fisherman along the coast some miles north of Veracruz, is on permanent display.

City Museum

Zaragoza 397. ☎ **29/31-8410.** Admission $1. Tues–Sun 9am–3pm. From the Palacio Municipal, walk 4½ blocks south on Zaragoza; the museum is on the right.

Recently restored, this 120-year-old building was converted into the City Museum years ago. Twelve rooms on two levels off the beautiful interior courtyard house archaeological relics from pre-Columbian Gulf Coast sites. The collection is small compared to those of the museums in Jalapa and Villahermosa, but the displays are attractive. The Indian cultures represented here are the Olmec, the Totonac, and the Huastec. Several rooms display regional costumes and crafts.

El Acuario

Plaza Acuario Veracruz, Blv. M. Ávila Camacho at Playón de Hornos. ☎ **29/37-4422.** Admission $5 adults; $1.75 children ages 2–12. Daily 10am–7pm. The Plaza Acuario Veracruazana is at the eastern edge of downtown where Bulevar Ávila Camacho meets Xiconténcatl. Walking along the Malecón, you'll find it about 15 blocks from the corner of Insurgentes (Malecón) and Camacho. Buses marked "Mocambo-Boca del Río" stop here.

Opened in the fall of 1992, the aquarium has become a major attraction in the state. Located in a shopping center, the aquarium is one of the largest of its kind in Latin America, with 9 freshwater and 15 saltwater tanks featuring the marine life of the area and all of Mexico. The circular *gran pecera* (large tank) gives the illusion of being surrounded by the ocean and its inhabitants—including sharks.

Venustiano Carranza Museum

Malecón between Xicoténcatl and Hernandez. No Phone. Free admission. Tues–Sun 9am–4pm. The Faro (lighthouse) is a block west of the Pemex Tower on the Malecón, next to the Hotel Emporio.

Located on the second floor of the headquarters of the 3rd Naval Military Zone and the site of the port's second lighthouse, this small museum is dedicated to Venustiano Carranza, who became president of Mexico in 1917. A leading figure in Mexico during the Revolutionary period, Carranza served as First Chief of the Constitutionalistic Army. He was assassinated in 1920 by killers vaguely linked to Álvaro Obregón, who sought to overthrow him. The museum consists of four rooms: Carranza's office/bedroom; two rooms of photographs showing Carranza at various stages of his life (including a facsimile of his autopsy report); and a room with a copy of the Constitution, a portrait of Carranza, and a diagram of the trajectory of the bullets that killed him.

MORE ATTRACTIONS

GUIDED BOAT TRIPS   Guided boat tours of the harbor (most in Spanish only) pass many of the sights listed above, as well as many of the international tankers and ships docked in the port. Launches leave sporadically (depending on the weather and demand) from the dock in front of the Hotel Emporio. The cost is $3.50 for adults and $1.75 for children 2 to 8, plus a tip for the guide. If the group is small, the price may go up to $5 per adult.

BEACHES   Veracruz has beaches, but none of them is very good because the grayish sand is hard-packed and the gulf water tends to be shallow. There are points all along the waterfront downtown where people swim, but the nearest legitimate beach is at the **Villa del Mar,** an open-air terrace and palm-lined promenade with changing rooms and showers at the southern end of town. To get there, take the "Playa V. del Mar" bus, which travels south on Zaragoza. The trip takes 15 minutes.

About 5 miles south of Veracruz along the Gulf Coast is the beach of **Mocambo,** where boats, snorkeling equipment, and waterskis can be rented. There are **public pools** at both Villa del Mar (entrance $1.50) and Mocambo (entrance $2) beaches.

A little farther past Mocambo at the mouth of the Jamapa River is **Boca del Río.** Both places can easily be reached by taking the buses that leave every 30 minutes (on the hour and half hour) from the corner of Serdán and Zaragoza near the municipal fish market. The bus stop is marked with the sign costa verde or boca del río; the trip takes 30 minutes.

SHOPPING

The Veracruz **market** (near the corner of Madero and Gonzales Pages) is one of the most interesting in Mexico—it's possible to find just about anything from caged parrots to live iguanas with tethered feet and tied tails. You can shop for curios in little shops along the **Malecón** opposite the Hotel Oriente and around the corner toward the pier. Here, the wares include more typical beachside junk—full shark's jaws, tacky shell art, ships in a jar, and the like.

ACCOMMODATIONS

Veracruz has a good assortment of hotels, but be careful of noise in this town—auto and truck noise combines with marimba and mariachi noise, for this is a festive town whose residents stay up until the early-morning hours. High season is June, July, August and the period from December through March.

Note: Veracruz is a favorite weekending spot for tourists from the capital city, and they fill every means of transportation on Friday. The flood of people traveling back up into the mountains is reversed on Sunday. Importers and exporters fill hotel rooms on weekdays. Arrive as early in the week and as early in the day as possible.

EXPENSIVE

Hotel Mocambo

Boca del Río (Apdo. Postal 263), Veracruz, Ver. 91700. ☎ **29/22-0205** or 407/367-9306 in the U.S. Fax 29/37-1660. 125 rms, 4 suites (all with bath). A/C TV TEL. $83–$100 single or double. Free parking.

The Mocambo, built in 1932, is nine miles southeast of the town center on one of Veracruz's best stretches of beach. One of the city's first and best hotels, it has hosted presidents, movie stars, and governors. Never out of fashion, it has become a comfortable, stylish hotel with the right amount of old-fashioned touches. The palatial hotel contains 129 rooms, wide halls, terraces, a sauna, a Jacuzzi and four pools (two indoor), a tennis court, Ping-Pong tables, and a restaurant; it's definitely a splurge hotel. Most rooms have sea views, but the cost of rooms varies depending on quality of view and the size of the room. At least 32 rooms have balconies, and 30 rooms are carpeted. Inquire about the cheaper (standard) rooms, since that might not be the first price you are quoted. Even if you don't decide to stay here, you might want to come out for a look, a meal, or a swim. The beach is public—you needn't stay at the hotel. If you're not driving, take the bus marked

"Mocambo" from Zaragoza and Serdán by La Prosperidad restaurant; buses stopping at the hotel's front gate go into town.

INEXPENSIVE

✪ Hotel Baluarte

Canal 265, Veracruz, Ver. 91700. ☎ **29/32-6042**. Fax. 29/32-5486. 81 rms (all with bath). A/C TV TEL. $28–$40 double. Free parking.

This is an excellent choice for comfort and value. Five stories tall, the hotel is modern and attractive and in a quiet location. The rooms are clean and comfortable. Guests can use the hotel's own parking lot across the street, and a small air-conditioned restaurant off the lobby is good for breakfast or a light meal. To get here from Plaza de Armas, walk five blocks south on Independencia, then turn left (east) on Canal toward the Gulf for five blocks to 16 de Septiembre; the hotel is on the left, catercorner from the Baluarte Santiago. It is also five blocks west of the Malecón.

✪ Hotel Colonial

Plaza de la Constitución, Veracruz, Ver. 91700. ☎ **29/32-0193**. Fax 29/32-2465. 182 rms (all with bath). A/C TV TEL. $34–$40 double. Parking $4.25 daily.

The pleasant and ideally located Colonial has two sections; the older has centrally controlled air-conditioning, and the newer has individually controlled air-conditioning. Rooms are very comfortable, and all the expensive hotel services are here, including private covered parking and an indoor pool on the second floor. The Colonial faces the Plaza de Armas; there's an entrance on the plaza and another through the garage.

Hotel Prendes

Independencia 1064, Veracruz, Ver. 91700. ☎ **29/31-0241**. Fax 29/31-0491. 34 rms (all with bath). A/C TV TEL. $26 single or double. Free parking.

The Prendes faces the action on Plaza de Armas, but the entrance is on Independencia. An elevator takes you to the three floors of nicely furnished, spacious guest rooms, all of which have good beds. Exterior rooms have balconies and wood-louvered French doors; interior rooms are much quieter but have no windows.

⑤ Hotel Villa Rica

Camacho 165, Veracruz, Ver. 91700. ☎ **29/32-4854**. 32 rms (all with bath). FAN. $21 double; $26 triple. Parking nearby $3.50.

Right at the northern (beginning) end of Bulevar Manuel Ávila Camacho, the four-story Villa Rica attracts Mexican families and young people on vacation who want to stay near the beach but not that far from downtown. The rooms are adequate, with fans and stenciled wall decoration. To get here from the market, walk 10 blocks east toward the Gulf; the hotel is on the corner of Figueroa and Doblado.

DINING

The restaurants under the portals that surround Plaza de Armas are the best places for eating, drinking, and merrymaking. While they're more expensive than places a few blocks away, their prices are not outrageous.

On Landero y Coss between Arista and Serdán is the **municipal fish market,** its street level chockablock with little *ostionerías* (oyster bars) and shrimp stands. Take a stool, ask the price, and order. Look upstairs for more good places.

The **Paris** is a *panadería* and *pastelería* (bakery and pastry shop) that sells a very wide selection of Mexican rolls and pastries for 5¢ to 50¢. You can't miss the assortment and the smell at Av. 5 de Mayo at the corner of Molina.

MODERATE

La Paella

Zamora 138. ☎ **29/32-0322**. Breakfast $1.25–$3; main courses $3–$8; comida corrida $4. Daily 8:30am–10pm (comida corrida served 1–4pm). SPANISH.

Devotees of Spanish food will undoubtedly like La Paella, where the four-course comida corrida is popular but portions are small. Three of the courses include such internationally known Spanish specialties as crema bretona, paella valenciana, and tortilla española (potato omelet). The walls are festooned with bullfight posters. La Paella is right at the southeast corner of Plaza de Armas, near the tourism office and next door to KFC—look for its very colonial-tiled facade.

Pizzaría Piro Piro Da Liuseppe

Arista 692. ☎ **29/31-6144**. Pizza $8–$13; spaghetti $4.50. Daily 9am–1am. ITALIAN.

Piro Piro, decorated like a cozy Italian trattoria, serves 18 different kinds of medium-size pizza, as well as spaghetti made in seven different ways. In a town full of seafood restaurants, it's a nice break. To get here from Plaza de Armas, walk three blocks south on Independencia and then turn left on Arista; the restaurant is on the right. Other locations are at Washington no. 146 (☎ 29/35-1775) and Cuautémoc no. 1118 (no phone).

INEXPENSIVE

✪ Café Andrade

Calle Hernández y Hernández 541. No phone. Desserts $1–$2.50; sandwiches $1.50–$2.50. 10am–8pm. COFFEE/SNACKS.

If you want to take a break from touring, this is a great place for coffee and a light snack. The local brew is served up six ways hot and three ways cold. You can also buy it in bean form or ground by the kilo ($3 to $5). Light snacks include sandwiches, croissants, pies, and wonderful cookies from the village of Xico. It's 2 1/2 blocks east of the Balvarte Santiago.

✪ Gran Café de la Parroquia

Av. Insurgentes s/n. No phone. Breakfast $2–$4; coffee $1–$1.50; main courses $2.50–$8. Daily 7am–1am. MEXICAN/COFFEE.

A trip to Veracruz without eating at La Parroquia is like going to New Orleans without eating beignets. In 1994, the original La Parroquia moved from its longtime location opposite the Plaza de Armas to it current spot; almost next-door is a second branch facing the harbor two blocks before the Hotel Emporio. Bright and always busy, with music (usually marimba) at almost any hour, this restaurant has customers who ritualistically occupy the same tables at the same time every day. Novice Parroquia patrons can catch onto the ritual quickly. Two waiters scurry about with big aluminum kettles, one with thick black coffee and the other with hot milk. Order the rich café lechera, and you'll get a few fingers of coffee in the bottom of your glass. Then pick up your spoon and bang on the glass to call the waiter with the milk—La Parroquia is filled with the constant chime of banging spoons. If there's too much coffee in your glass, pour the excess into the waiter's coffee kettle, then he'll pour the milk. Though the cafe is known for coffee and pastries, its main courses are also quite good.

2 Exploring North of Veracruz

THE RUINS OF ZEMPOALA

On Highway 180, about 14 miles north of Veracruz, is the village of **Antigua,** on the Río Antigua. It's not well known today, but for 75 years, beginning in 1525, it was a seat of Spanish power. The village, situated on the banks of the river, is small and primitive. Beside the old church on the main plaza are the ruins of several massive stone structures, one of which is said to be the **House of Cortés** (La Casa de Cortés). In ruins now with trees growing up from the interior and thick vines rooted to the rock walls, it's still interesting to see. An ancient cypress tree is said to have been used to tie up Cortés's ships. The village is well known for its seafood restaurants and is especially festive on weekends.

About 25 miles north of Veracruz, past Antigua on the way to Jalapa, are the ruins at **Zempoala** (or Cempoala), surrounded by lush foliage and rich agricultural land. Though not as large as the site of El Tajín, it's still noteworthy.

Zempoala is a pre-Columbian ruin of the Totonacs. Both cities flourished during the Classic Period (A.D. 300 to 900); although Tajín was later abandoned in the 13th century, Zempoala continued to thrive and was the capital of the Totonacs during the Spanish Conquest. Zempoala, which means "place of the twenty waters," was named for the many rivers that converged at the site. When the conquerors saw Zempoala for the first time, the whitewashed stuccoed walls glimmered like silver in the tropical sun—which naturally drew the Spaniards closer. Though disappointed, the Spaniards still made friends, and this city of Totonac Indians became Cortés's first ally. The Spaniards spent considerable time here, learning about the Totonacs' hatred of the Aztecs and about the Aztec Emperor Moctezuma, before heading overland to the Aztec capital of Tenochtitlán.

Most buildings at Zempoala date from the 14th and 15th centuries—quite late for pre-Columbian structures. It was, however, inhabited before the time of Jesus Christ. The **Great Temple** resembles the Temple of the Sun in Tenochtitlán, probably as a result of Aztec influence during the 15th century. The **Temple of the Little Faces** has stuccoed faces set into the walls, along with hieroglyphs painted on the lower sections. The **Temple of Quetzalcoatl,** the feathered serpent god, is square, and the **Temple of Ehecatl,** god of the wind, is, as usual, round.

Admission to the archaeological site is $3.50; it's open daily from 9am to 6pm. A permit for use of a video camera costs $8.50. You can get to the archaeological site on buses of the TRV (Transportes Regionales Veracruzianas), which run hourly from Veracruz; the trip takes 1¹/₂ hours and is truly a beautiful journey through tropical forests. If you're going by car, driving time is 40 minutes north on Highway 180 through Cardel; the ruins of Zempoala are just north of Cardel.

JALAPA: A PRETTY TOWN WITH A GREAT MUSEUM

Capital of the state of Veracruz, Jalapa (65 miles NW of Veracruz; pronounced "ha-LAP-a" and spelled "Xalapa" by its residents), is an interesting town to explore for a day or more. Although modern, the city is riddled with old, narrow streets that wind up and down. In addition to being the jalapeño-pepper capital of

Mexico, Jalapa is the hometown of António López de Santa Anna, whose various terms as president of Mexico spanned 22 years; his hacienda is now a museum southeast of town.

Earlier in the city's history, Cortés and his troops passed through nearby Xico on their way from the Gulf Coast to the Aztec capital of Tenochtitlán for the first time. Chroniclers of the Conquest described the hazards of the trip and particularly noted the *chipi chipi*, a fine but pelting rain that is a frequent part of Jalapa life. Coffee plantations surround the city for miles around, so take time out for a cup of the excellent local brew.

ESSENTIALS

GETTING THERE & DEPARTING   Veracruz, 2 hours south of Jalapa, has the closest major **airport,** although some charter flights use the small Jalapa airport. Both ADO and AU **buses** have much the same routes, with frequent service to and from Mexico City and Veracruz. Three ADO buses from Zempoala leave at very odd hours. If you're coming from or going to the north, the trip by bus to or from Papantla takes about 6 hours over the long route through Perote (with an incredible number of rest stops but also an incredible number of alpine views); if you're in a hurry, be sure to ask for one of the 10 daily buses going the short route (4 hours) via Cardel or take a bus going directly to or from Poza Rica, where you can change to a bus to or from Papantla.

If you're **driving** from Veracruz, take Highway 180 to Cardel and then turn left (west) onto Highway 140 past the coffee plantations. From Mexico City, Puebla, Tlaxcala, or Papantla, there is danger of dense fog between Perote and Jalapa. Reckless drivers pass even when they can't see ahead on the narrow two-lane highway. On a clear day this drive will remind you of Switzerland, with spotted cows grazing on verdant hillside pastures.

ORIENTATION   Arriving   The bus station, **Caxa,** is about a mile and a half east of the town center just off Calle 20 de Noviembre. It resembles a sophisticated airport, with arrivals upstairs and departures downstairs and an overhanging roof for protection from the elements. Inside it's sleek, with shops, telephone and fax service, car rental, guarded luggage, and a fast-food cafeteria in the center. A **tourist booth** is open daily from 7am to 10:30pm. Taxis are downstairs; prices here are controlled, so there is no haggling. Buy your ticket at the kiosk. Tickets to the center of town cost around $1.75.

Information   The **State Tourism Office** is some 12 blocks (about a mile) northwest of the town center on Av. Camacho 191 at Bravo (☎ 28/14-4622). Little English is spoken, but they have maps and literature. Hours are Monday through Friday from 9am to 3pm and 6 to 9pm and Saturday from 9am to 1pm.

City Layout   Jalapa is a hilly town with streets seemingly without much order, which is very confusing to the visitor. The center of town is the beautiful **Plaza Juárez,** where on a clear day the Pico de Orizaba is visible to the southwest. Facing and across the street (north) from the plaza is the **Palacio Municipal** (city hall), while just east is the **Palacio del Gobierno** (state offices). Across (north) from this is the **cathedral**. A tunnel runs under the park and connects **Avenidas Zaragoza** and **Ávila Camacho,** two of the main arteries which cross the city, randomly changing name and direction in the process.

Getting Around   The hotels and restaurants I have recommended (see "Accommodations" and "Dining," below) are within easy walking distance of the central

Jalapa Orientation

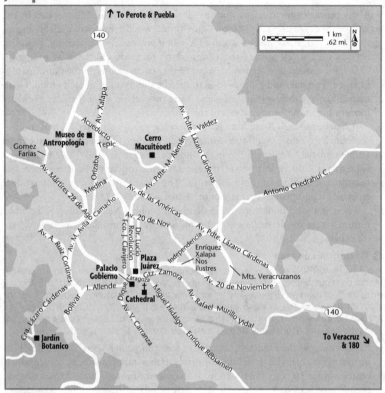

↑ To Perote & Puebla

140

0 ▬▬▬▬ 1 km
.62 mi.

N

Av. Xalapa
Acueducto
Museo de Antropología
Gomez Farias
Av. Mártires 28 de AGO
Tepic
Cerro Macuiltéoetl
Av. Pdte. Lázaro Cárdenas
Valdez
Av. Pdte. M. Alemán
Antonio Chedrahuí C.
Orizaba
Medina
Av. de las Américas
Av. M. Ávila Camacho
Av. 20 de Nov
Dr. Lucio
Revolución
Fco. J. Clavijero
Independencia
Enríquez
Xalapa
Nos
Ilustres
Av. Pdte. Lázaro Cárdenas
Plaza Juárez
Gtz. Zamora
Mts. Veracruzanos
Av. 20 de Noviembre
Av. A. Ruiz Cortines
Palacio Gobierno
Zaragoza
I. Allende
Dique
Miguel Hidalgo
Av. Rafael Murillo Vidal
Gra. Lázaro Cárdenas
Bolívar
Cathedral
Av. V. Carranza
Enrique Rébsamen
Jardín Botanico
140
To Veracruz & 180

1260

Plaza Juárez. Taxis in Jalapa are inexpensive—around $1.25 to $1.75 to most places in the city. City buses are 20¢.

Fast Facts   The **telephone area code** is 28. The **climate** is humid and warm in summer and humid and chilly in winter. Year-round, be prepared for the *chipi chipi* (chee-pee chee-pee) rain that comes and goes.

EXPLORING JALAPA

Take a look at the murals by José Chávez Morado in the **Palacio de Gobierno** and glance into the massive **cathedral**, with its disconcerting floor which inclines upward toward the altar. Walk through the streets and admire the bougainvillea, fruit trees, and flowers. Jalapa is halfway between the mountains and the tropics, so it has both coffee plantations and sultry breezes.

The Agora, a hangout for artists, students, and other cosmopolitan types, is just off the main park. For books, records, films, conversation, and concerts look here first. Then, check out the **Teatro del Estado,** at Manuel Ávila Camacho and Ignacio de la Llave. This is Jalapa's official cultural center and home of the Jalapa Symphony Orchestra. There's always something going on.

✪ Museo de Antropología de Jalapa

Av. Jalapa at Av. Aqueducto. ☎ **28/15-0920** or 15-4952. Admission $2.50. Museum, Tues–Sun 9:30am–5pm; shop, Tues–Sun 10am–4:30pm. Bus: "Museo" from Plaza Juárez or on Avenida Jalapa or Avenida Americas.

Many people come to Jalapa just to visit this suburban museum operated by the University of Veracruz. It's second only to the world-renowned anthropological museum in Mexico City and worth a the visit if you're anywhere nearby. Designed by Edward Durrell Stone (who designed the Kennedy Center in Washington, D.C.), it's divided into sections devoted to the Indian groups on the Gulf Coast—Huastec, Totonac, and Olmec—and to specific sites relating to each group. Good maps illustrate the regions and sites. An ethnographic section shows the daily modern life of these groups (except the Olmec).

A signature giant Olmec head is the first thing you see on entering, and you will see four more before you finish. Although the gigantic Olmec pieces are the most visible and the Olmec culture is the oldest (it began around 1500 B.C.), each subsequent culture left powerful artifacts—it's unlikely you'll see pieces as magnificent as these in other museums. The museum is highly recommended, especially if you plan to visit any of the actual sites in your travels.

There is a shop/bookstore to the right of the lobby. Near the shop is the auditorium where music recitals at noon on Sunday ("Domingos Culturales") are often held.

✪ Hacienda Lencero

Km 9 on Hwy. 140 toward Veracruz. No phone. Admission $3.25; free Spanish-speaking guides on request. Tues–Sun 10am–5pm. Drive or take a taxi ($18.50 round trip) about 9 miles south of town on Highway 140 toward Veracruz, past the country club; watch for the signs on the right. You can also catch a bus marked "Banderilla-P. Crystal-Lencero" on Avenida Lázaro Cárdenas. The bus will stop either in the village of Lencero or at a nearby spot along the highway. From either stop it's a walkable distance to the hacienda.

Known today as the Hacienda Lencero, or sometimes the Museo de Muebles (Furniture Museum), this fabulous country estate 9 miles southeast of the town center was for 14 years (1842–1856) the home of António López de Santa Anna, president of Mexico 11 times. Here he retreated from the world, but on occasion he opened his doors to receive countless notable visitors. Purchased by the state of Veracruz in 1981, the hacienda is one of the best museums of its kind in the country.

Rooms in the sprawling mansion are filled with furniture from Mexico, Europe, and Asia, depicting a type of elegance found in Mexico during the 19th century. Among them is Santa Anna's bed with the national emblem of an eagle holding a snake in its beak. The carefully tended grounds are awash with flowers and shaded by centuries-old trees. Next to the grand house, the spacious servants' quarters, with a gracious, wide covered patio facing a lake fed by a natural spring, has been converted into a restaurant serving light snacks, pastries, and soft drinks.

SHOPPING

At the **Casa de Artesanías,** Paseo de la Laguna (☎ 28/17-0804), the quantity and quality of crafts varies from time to time, but you can usually pick up packaged Veracruz coffee, cans of jalapeño peppers, baskets from Papantla, and pottery from San Miguel Aguasuelos—all local products. The store is open Monday through Friday from 9am to 1pm and 4 to 7pm and on Saturday from 9am to 3pm. It's on Calle Dique, off Zaragoza, six blocks south of Plaza Juárez and near a lakeside park.

A good place to pick something for yourself or for a gift that is typical of the region is **Café Colón,** downtown at Primo Verdad 15. The staff roasts, grinds, and packages coffee here, and it's available for purchase ground or *en grano* (whole bean) by the kilo or partial kilo. Walk two blocks east from the Parque Juárez on Zaragoza, then north half a block on Primo Verdad. Café Colón is on the right.

ACCOMMODATIONS

✪ Mesón de Alférez

Sabastiano Camacho 2, Jalapa, Ver. 91000. ☎ **28/18-6351.** Fax 28/14-9665. 9 rms, 11 suites (all with bath). TV TEL. $34 double; $46–$51 suite. Free secure parking nearby.

The owners of the lovely Posada del Cafeto (see below) also own this wonderful hotel in the 1808 home of the former Spanish viceroy's representative. Rooms, named after historic Jalapa streets, are furnished in colonial style; bright accents of color warm the colonial-era stone. Some rooms feature a cozy loft bedroom overlooking a living room. The dining room, Hostería La Candela, is located in what had been the private chapel. The dining room is open from 7:30am to 8:30pm, and meals are accompanied by pleasant music and attentive service. To find the Mesón from the Plaza, go one block east on Zaragoza to the corner of Sabastiano Camacho; it's close to the Hotel Monroy. The entrance is actually on Zaragoza.

✪ Posada del Cafeto

Canovas 12, Jalapa, Ver. 91000. ☎ **28/17-0023.** 23 rms (all with bath). $17 double. Free secure parking nearby.

What a treat it is to discover this colorful and comfortable town-house-turned-hotel, opened in 1987. It was named for the coffee industry in the region, so there's coffee available morning and evening, and guests can help themselves. The owners gave the rooms colorful Mexican style, with bright bedspreads, royal-blue metal doors and window frames, white walls with painted flower designs, and Mexican tile accents. Windows let in plenty of light. Each room is slightly different; some are small and have two single or two double beds or a single and a double. From the Plaza Juárez, walk four blocks east on Zaragoza, then one block south where it bends. Canovas is the first street on your right, and the Posada is further down on the right.

DINING

Walk almost any block in the downtown area and you'll find restaurants of all kinds. **Callejón del Diamante** is a narrow pedestrians-only street 1½ blocks from Plaza Juárez with half a dozen restaurants—La Fonda and La Sopa El Mayab among them. Prices are reasonable and most are open Monday through Saturday from 8am to 10pm. To find them, turn your back to the cathedral and walk left on Enríquez across Lucio one block; the callejón will be on the left.

Restaurant La Casona del Beaterio

Zaragoza 20. ☎ **28/18-2119.** Breakfast $3–$5: main courses $2–$9; comida corrida $4.75. Daily 8:30am–10:30pm. MEXICAN.

This delightful place near the zócalo supplies good food and service in a charming atmosphere. Tables and chairs are plain, but there are high-beamed ceilings, plants, and photos of old Jalapa on the walls. The menu lists a variety of chicken dishes, such as *pechuga maguey* (chicken breast in rich liquor). You can find La Casona on Zaragoza, two blocks east from Parque Juárez on the south side of the street; it's at the end of a row of restaurants.

Salon Don Quijote (in the Hotel Mexico)

Lucio 4. ☎ **28/17-3365.** Breakfast $2.50–$4.50; main courses $4.50–$8.25; comida corrida $4.75; paella (Sun only) $7. Daily 7am–10pm (comida corrida served 1–5:30pm). MEXICAN.

For years this restaurant, far back in the parking lot of the Hotel Mexico, has been serving the best comida corrida downtown. It begins with fruit, then soup, vegetables, meat, rice, dessert, and coffee. You can't go wrong here. It's half a block east of Plaza Juárez, facing the left side of the cathedral, and has lovely stained-glass windows.

PAPANTLA & THE RUINS OF EL TAJÍN

The best reasons to visit Papantla, a city of 159,000 140 miles northwest of Veracruz, include its proximity to the impressive ruins of **El Tajín** (el ta-HEEN), the frequent shows of the *voladores* (flying pole dancers), and its festivities around **Corpus Christi Day.** El Tajín is one of Mexico's most important, but still mysterious, archaeological sites. Vast excavation in recent years has revealed more unusual buildings and more of its history.

Papantla is the former vanilla capital of the world. The hybrid symbol of the community, displayed at both entrances to the city, is a very large concrete vanilla bean with inscribed hieroglyphs. Vanilla extract can be purchased here for about half of what it costs in the States. The long, slender, almost-black vanilla beans are also for sale, but more than likely you'll see them fashioned into figures, flowers, or a dozen different designs.

ESSENTIALS

GETTING THERE & DEPARTING   Wherever you're coming from, it's often easier to take one of the frequent **buses** to Poza Rica and change there for a bus to Papantla. There are two bus stations in Papantla. The first-class **ADO station** (☎ 784/2-0218) is downhill north of the plaza, at the corner of Venustiana Carranza and Benito Juárez. From here, four deluxe buses leave daily for Poza Rica, two to Tuxpan, seven to Jalapa, and two to Veracruz. Frequent de paso buses also go to Poza Rica, Jalapa, Veracruz, Minatitlan, and Villahermosa.

From the **second-class station** at 20 de Noviembre no. 200, buses (mostly the school-bus type) depart for Poza Rica every 10 to 15 minutes (watch out for pickpockets!) and to Tecolutla every 40 minutes. There are also eight departures daily to Jalapa and 12 to Veracruz.

If you're **driving** up from the south, Papantla is a 4- to 5-hour mountainous drive (if there is no fog) from Jalapa, via Misantla, Martínez de la Torre, and finally Highway 180 on the coast. From Veracruz, Papantla is about 5 hours away along Highway 180.

ORIENTATION   Arriving   If you arrive by a Transportes Papantla bus you'll be six blocks from the center of town, which is at the top of the hill. To get to town center, walk out the front door of the bus station, turn left, and go up Juárez six blocks to the central park, cathedral, and Hotel El Tajín. You'll be at the bottom of the hill if you arrive at the ADO station.

City Layout   Coming into town, you'll most likely arrive at the bottom of the hill. Fix your eyes on the cathedral and blue facade of the Hotel El Tajín at the top of the hill. That's the center of town, with a shady zócalo (main square), hotels, markets, plaza, and restaurants.

Getting Around   City buses go to the ruins of El Tajín (see below), and taxis are available around the central plaza. Almost everything worth seeing is within easy walking distance of the central plaza.

Fast Facts   The **telephone area code** is 784. The **climate** is sultry, rainy, and hot in summer, cold and rainy in winter; hotels are unheated.

EXPLORING PAPANTLA & EL TAJÍN

In Papantla, you might want to visit the lovely, shady, ceramic tile **zócalo** (main square), where couples and families sit while gray squirrels with rust-red under-bellies beg for food. The cathedral wall facing the square is covered with an artist's impression of El Tajín done in concrete. On top of a hill overlooking the city is an enormous statue of a *volador* (flying pole dancer).

SPECIAL EVENTS   The **Feast of Corpus Christi,** the ninth Sunday after Easter, is surrounded by a very special week in Papantla. Well-known Mexican entertainers perform. Also the native *voladores* (see "The Ruins of El Tajín," below) make special appearances. Lodging is scarce during this week, so be sure to book ahead.

THE RUINS OF EL TAJÍN   The major attraction is the nearby ruins of El Tajín, which are definitely worth seeing. Of the 150 buildings identified at the site, 20 have been excavated and conserved, transforming them from essentially grass-covered mounds into a semblance of their original form. At least 17 ball courts have been found, though only 5 are visible. Mural fragments led archaeologists to discover a Teotihuacán-influenced mural at the top of Building 11, which has been restored.

The ruins at Tajín are divided into the old section (Tajín Viejo) and the new section (Tajín Chico). The most impressive structure, which is in the old section, is the **Pyramid of the Niches.** The pyramid, made of stone and adobe, has 365 recesses on all four sides of the building. The pyramid was once covered in red-painted stucco, with the niches painted black. It is one of the most unusual pre-Columbian structures in Mesoamerica, though there is a similar one near Cuetzalan, Puebla. Near the Pyramid of the Niches is a restored **ball court** with beautiful carved reliefs on the vertical playing sides depicting religious scenes and sacrifices.

The **Temple of the Columns** is in the new section. A stairway divides the columns, three on either side and each decorated with reliefs of priests and warriors and hieroglyphic dates. Many mounds are still unexcavated, but with the reconstruction that has been done so far, it's increasingly easier to see the ruins as a city. The view from atop one of the pyramids, overlooking the rich, green forests dotted with mounds and excavated buildings, is very impressive.

The *voladores* (fliers) are an additional attraction; they are local Totonac Indians who perform their flying upside-down pole dance in a clearing near the museum. There's no set schedule for performances, so when you hear the sounds of a drum and flute, the voladores are ready. Five of them, dressed in satin pants, vests, and cone-shaped hats with ribbons and small round mirrors, climb the tall pole (donated by Pemex) to the top, where there is a square revolving platform. One dancer stands beating a drum and playing a flute while the four others perch on the four sides of the platform and attach themselves by their waists to a rope. When the time is right, the four lean over backward and fall off, suspended by the rope, revolving 13 times before they reach the ground. The number 13 corresponds to the number of months in the Aztec calendar.

A small but impressive **museum** greets you as you approach the esplanade. In-side are selected pieces from the site, including two burials, some lovely pots, and two restored wall paintings. Perhaps most interesting are two large models of the area, giving you the effect of seeing the site from the air; this is helpful, as the entire archaeological zone covers about 4 square miles.

Across from the museum is a small snack/gift shop, as well as a small restaurant. In a semicircle facing the volador pole are several more gift shops. Admission to the site and museum is $2; it is free to all on Sunday. The fee for a personal video camera is $8.50. Use of a tripod requires a permit from INAH (the Instituto Nacional de Antropologia y Historia) in Mexico City. If you watch a performance of the voladores, one of them will collect an additional $4 from each spectator. The site is open daily from 9am to 5pm; the voladores fly around Friday through Sunday at 11am and 4pm, although any time a tour bus arrives they tend to suit up.

To get to El Tajín from Papantla, look for buses marked "Chote/Tajín," which run to El Tajín from beside the Juárez market (opposite the front of the church, at the corner of Reforma and 20 de Noviembre) every hour beginning at 7am—but don't count on always finding these buses. As an alternative, buses marked "Chote" pass more frequently and will leave you at the Chote crossroads; from there, wait for a bus for the short distance to El Tajín or take a taxi from there for around $5. From Veracruz, take Highway 180 to Papantla; from there, take Route 127, which is a back road to Poza Rica, going through Tajín.

SHOPPING   There are two principal markets in Papantla, both near the central plaza. **Mercado Juárez** is opposite the front door of the church. **Mercado Hidalgo** is a block or two down Reforma on the left, away from the plaza. The latter has a better selection of locally made baskets and regional clothing. Besides vanilla, **Xanath,** a popular local liqueur, makes a good gift and costs around $13; **Vreez,** another type, costs $11: Embroidered blouses and dresses, typical attire of the region's Indians, are sold in the market.

ACCOMMODATIONS

Hotel Premier

Enríquez 103, Papantla, Ver. 93400. ☎ **784/2-1645** or 2-0080. 20 rms (all with bath). A/C TV TEL. $40 double. Free secure parking a half block away.

The Premier's second-floor lobby is reached through a mirror-lined hallway. Opened in 1990, this hotel is a fine alternative to Papantla's otherwise meager selection of hotels. Rooms are nicely furnished and have tile floors, baths with showers, and some have small balconies overlooking the zócalo. Others toward the back are windowlesss and quiet and are reached through a tunnel-like hallway.

El Tajín Hotel

Nuñez 104, Papantla, Ver. 93400. ☎ **784/2-0121,** 2-1623, or 2-0734. Fax 784/2-1062. 60 rms (all with bath). A/C or FAN TV TEL. $30–$35 double. Free secure parking a half block away.

Walk along the cathedral wall up the hill to the thriving El Tajín Hotel, the building with the bright-blue facade near the top. The rooms here are small and tidy; some have king-size beds. The Restaurant Tajín in the hotel is clean and inexpensive (but the coffee is terrible).

DINING

Mercado Juárez has numerous cookshops that in the morning bring in some outstandingly delicious *zacahuil* (the huge tamal cooked in a banana leaf). Look around until you see a cook with a line of patrons—that's where you'll get the best zacahuil. Outside the market, rolling cart vendors sell steamy hot atole.

Besides zacahuil, be sure to try delicious molotes, small football-shaped creations of fried masa that are served as appetizers.

⑤ Cenaduría M.Y.R.

16 de Septiembre no. 117. No phone. Molotes $1; tostadas 80¢–$1.50; main courses $2–$3. Daily 6–11pm. REGIONAL.

Cenadurías are dinner places, so don't come for lunch. A "Formica and folding chair" sort of place, the M.Y.R. is short on atmosphere but makes up for it in taste. This is the best place to try *molotes*. And you may want to top off any meal with fresh bananas and cream. This cenaduría is across from the church on the uphill side.

✪ Plaza Pardo

Enriquez 105. ☎ **784/2-0059.** Breakfast $2.50–$4.25; sandwiches $2–$4.25; main courses $2.25–$5.50. Daily 7:30am–10:30pm. MEXICAN/AMERICAN.

This cheerful place, located across from the main plaza, has the look of an old-fashioned ice-cream parlor. Try the coconut (*coco*) or pecan (*nuez*) ice cream; the strawberry malts (malteadas de fresa) are so fresh and frothy you'll be certain you're having something healthy! You can also get a full meal morning to night.

3   Exploring South of Veracruz

Highway 180 southeast from Veracruz is a good and uneventful road with numerous glimpses of the Gulf and deserted beaches as you drive along the bar separating the Gulf from the Alvarado Lagoon. The fishing village of **Alvarado,** founded in 1518 and celebrated locally for successfully warding off an attack by the U.S. Fleet in 1846, is an excellent spot for a fresh seafood lunch at one of the many small restaurants lining the lagoon shore.

Some 30 miles farther along, the 5000-foot extinct volcano **San Martín** begins to show through the haze on the horizon, and soon the road starts climbing into the lush, green foothills. You are now entering Olmec country.

LAKE CATEMACO & LOS TUXTLAS

The beautiful and interesting region around Lake Catemaco, 99 miles southeast of Veracruz, includes two Tuxtlas—San Andrés Tuxtla and Santiago Tuxtla. The area offers natural beauty and the remains of the Olmec culture.

About 6¹/₂ miles long and almost 5 miles wide, **Lake Catemaco,** dotted with islands, was formed by the long-ago eruption of volcanoes and is one of the most beautiful lakes in Mexico. Ringed by lush forested mountains and two volcanoes, it resembles Lake Atitlán in Guatemala. At least 556 species of birds live or migrate here. Between Catemaco and **San Andrés Tuxtla** is tobacco country; broad green fields are awash in the tall leggy plant between July and October. The region is dotted with enormous barns for drying the aromatic leaves and with smaller facilities where the leaves are sorted and sold. Just over the mountain from San Andrés is **Santiago Tuxtla,** a handsome colonial town with one of the most beautiful palm-studded plazas in Mexico. On one side of the plaza is the Museo Regional containing Olmec artifacts, and the on-site Museum of Tres Zapotes is 12 miles away. The entire region lies only a few miles from undeveloped beaches on the Gulf of Mexico and within reach of the 500-acre Balzapotes Scientific Station to the northeast near the coast.

ESSENTIALS

GETTING THERE & DEPARTING   By Bus   From Veracruz, there are approximately 18 daily departures, but most of these go only as far as the cigar-making town of San Andrés Tuxtla, 7 miles short of Catemaco. You can take one of the five daily first-class buses which go directly to Catemaco from Veracruz. You can also go to San Andrés Tuxtla and catch a local bus or hire a taxi for the last short leg. First-class service out of Lake Catemaco is limited, so check departure times when you arrive in town. Reserve tickets as far in advance as possible.

Second-class service from Catemaco is more frequent on **Autotransportes Los Tuxtlas.** Buses make the run to Veracruz throughout the day. They go to San Andrés and Santiago Tuxtla every 10 minutes from midnight to 6pm and every hour in the evening. The terminal is located on Calle Cuauhtémoc (though this won't help you much, as the streets aren't marked), a short walk from the main plaza; ask for directions.

By Car   Whether you're driving south from Veracruz or west from Villahermosa, you'll take Highway 180 to Catemaco.

ORIENTATION   Arriving   The first-class **ADO bus station** in Catemaco is located behind the church, on the corner of Aldama and Bravo. The lake is a block or so behind the station. The cathedral and main plaza are left up the hill, and the Hotel Koniapan and the southern end of town facing the lake are to the right.

Fast Facts   The **telephone area code** is 294. As for the **climate,** Lake Catemaco is a balmy oasis in a region where the rule is muggy heat. Free from extremes of heat and cold, it's more like year-round eternal spring. It's hottest from March through May. A jacket is handy December through February. Always be prepared for rain—there are only 150 days of sun on average. The **high season** in this area is July, August, Christmas, and Easter week.

EXPLORING THE LAKE CATEMACO AREA

The lake region is located between the only mountains on the steaming coastal plain that reaches from Tampico to the Yucatán. Two volcanic peaks— **San Martín** and **Santa Marta**—reach to nearly 5,600 feet. North of Catemaco is **Monte Cerro Blanco,** where it is rumored that wizards (*brujos*) meet each March. Brujos have been known to put out signs in Catemaco the way doctors do in other towns.

Many artifacts have been found in the area, once the site of a pre-Hispanic village. Townsfolk who were children when Catemaco's streets were prepared for paving remember playing with pre-Hispanic artifacts unearthed by bulldozers. **Isla Agaltepec,** one of four large islands in the lake, was an Olmec ceremonial site.

SPECIAL EVENTS   The El Carmen Church on the zócalo is visited by thousands of pilgrims each year around July 16, the **Feast of El Carmen.** Look for testimonial drawings around the portals. The interior walls are stenciled with a pattern of golden-yellow and white flowers, while the ceiling is laced with gilded arches. There's also a blessing of the fleet during the festival, and decorated boats sail up and down the shore giving free rides.

ECO-TOURS   The forests in the area of Los Tuxtlas represent the northernmost tropical rain forest on the continent. Some of the more than 500 varieties of migratory and local bird life are apparent even on a brief walk along the lake.

Mammals and reptiles are represented by around 100 species each, along with almost 50 species of amphibians. More than 1,000 types of bromeliads have been identified in the region, and they are still being counted. Many area hunters supplement their diets by taking squirrels, armadillos, iguanas, and wild pigs. A serious education and preservation effort has been mounted on the part of both public and private interests in the area. For information on educational and scientific expeditions and summer camps, contact Operadora Turística de Los Tuxtlas at the Hotel Playa Azul (☎ 294/3-0761); see "Accommodations," below.

BOAT TRIPS If you're sports-minded, boats are available for **waterskiing** or **fishing**. If sightseeing is your pleasure, you can just about tailor the trip to fit your budget.

You can also take a **tour** of the lake by boat, passing the black-sand lake beaches, the river, a shrine honoring the local miraculous Virgin, numerous flocks of white herons, a mineral spring called Arroyo Agrio (literally "Sour Brook") for its acid content, and another spring called Coyamé—you may have seen its water bottled and on your dinner table.

The most interesting part of the tour is the two **monkey islands.** In an experiment to readapt monkeys to the wild, the University of Veracruz brought several families of macaco monkeys from Thailand to two small islands on the lake. One group has learned to swim between the two islands, while the other group has not. Because the university sends out food each day, the monkeys line up in hopeful expectation when they see approaching boats; have your cameras ready, for as soon as they discover there's no food, they disperse.

In April and May, hundreds of **herons** nest on a tiny island called **Isla de las Garzas** (Heron Island), and the tour boats pass by for a look.

Another stop may be **Nanciyaga,** a rather touristy private nature reserve ($2 entrance). Guides lead you across the jungle stream, wind through the woods to a mud-facial house (optional; $2 donation suggested), then travel back by a pond reserved for nesting crocodiles (it's defunct now since something was making the crocs sick). The cost of the 1$^{1}/_{2}$-hour lake tour is about $6.25 per person for a boatload of up to six people; a private boat for up to six people ranges from $25 to $37. Two **boat cooperatives** operate from the Malecón. Look for posted prices.

BEACHES The cheapest way to get to two volcanic-sand beaches—**Playa Azul** and **Playa Hermosa**—is by bus. Take the "Monte Pio" bus (one leaves every 1$^{1}/_{2}$ hours) from the second-class bus terminal or look for the "La Margarita" bus from the town square (though the latter runs only about three times a day). You can also walk or hitch the 1$^{1}/_{4}$ miles. Be forewarned that these "beaches" are more aptly described as narrow spits of dirt. For real beaches, you have to go to the ocean (reached by the "Monte Pio" bus in about 1$^{1}/_{4}$ hours). The "La Margarita" bus goes out to the Cuetzalapan River on the opposite side of the lake, known for its cold, transparently clear waters; flowers; bird life; and interesting rock formations.

ACCOMMODATIONS

Cabañas Don Armando

Carretera Sontecomapan km. 2.5, Catemaco, Ver. 95870. 9 rms, 1 suite (all with bath). FAN. $21 single or double ($25 in high season). $38–$43 suite. Free parking. For reservations contact Cabañas Zazil Kin Don Armando in Tulum, Quintana Roo; ☎ 987/4-4539.

Somewhat removed from town but only a three-minute downhill walk from the shore, this delightful retreat has a stunning view of the lake and its environs. Beds are firm and the rooms spotless. The suite is a second-floor mini-penthouse that sleeps up to five people, while the other rooms are all on the ground floor. Fans and the breeze keep you cool. With the small restaurant/bar and an attractive pool, there's no need to go into town. There is also a Don Armando's in Tulum (which is nothing like this branch); contact the branch in Tulum to make reservations for either place.

Hotel Los Arcos

Madero 7, Catemaco, Ver. 95870. ☎ **294/3-0003.** Fax 294/3-0250. 35 rms (all with bath). FAN TV TEL. $23 double. Free parking.

The three-story Los Arcos has nice, well-kept rooms with red-tile floors, louvered glass windows, and ceiling fans; there's also good cross-ventilation. All rooms come with TVs, but only one has air-conditioning. To reach the rooms you pass through motel-style walkways that also serve as balconies with either street or lake views. To get here from the ADO bus station, turn left out the front door, go around the church, and then walk one block past the church.

Posada (Motel) Koniapan

Malecón and Revolución, Catemaco, Ver. 95870. ☎ **294/3-0063**. Fax 294/3-0939. 21 rms (all with bath). A/C or FAN TEL. $25.50–$27.50 double. Free parking.

This motel is a favorite place to stay in Catemaco; it's located across the street from the lakeshore. Rooms are bright and clean and come with screened windows, small tile baths, neocolonial furniture, and two double beds. Upstairs rooms have private balconies and views of the lake. There's a clean pool in the front yard; the open-air restaurant next to it is sometimes open. Room prices may be a bit higher in July and August. To get here from the ADO bus station, turn right out the front door and go straight for two blocks; the hotel is on the right facing the lake.

DINING

Although the lake is famed for its whitefish (*mojarra*), fare in Catemaco is not always of the highest quality. In addition to whitefish, smoked pork is a specialty and is quite good. *Pelliscadas* are salted tortillas fried in lard and topped with various sauces or cheese, and local clams are made into ceviche.

When the **street market** is in operation around the Hotel Los Arcos, little cookshops are set up. The market is the cheapest, most colorful place to sample the lake's mojarra or dozens of other kinds of food. Prices, which are not set, depend on how the fishing season's going, how much money has been made that day, and how prosperous you seem to be. (Ask the price before you order!)

Hotel Catemaco

Carranza 8. ☎ **294/3-0203.** Breakfast $2–$3; main courses $5–$9. Daily 8am–11pm. MEXICAN.

Perhaps the best all-around restaurant, Hotel Catemaco offers indoor and outdoor dining for breakfast, lunch, and dinner. A view of the town's busy plaza adds to the most refined, pleasant decor in town. The specialty is steak, and to help you know which cut to order, there's a lighted diagram of a cow with cuts marked in Spanish and English.

La Luna

Malecón. ☎ **294/3-0050.** Breakfast $1.50–$3; main courses $3.50–$6. Daily 8am–9pm. MEXICAN.

Facing the lake across the street and a few doors west of La Ola, La Luna offers tasty meals. A good-sized mojarra can be cooked one of eight deliciously different ways, and the *carne ahumado* (smoked pork) will make you want to return for more. The food compensates for the less-than-stellar view of the lake.

EXCURSIONS FROM CATEMACO

San Andrés Tuxtla: Part Colonial, Part Caribbean

Seven miles northwest of Catemaco, San Andrés Tuxtla (pop. 125,000) is the administrative center of the region. Along the way there, you'll pass fields of tobacco between July and October, alternating with corn in the off-months. At Sihuapan, about halfway between Catemaco and San Andrés, you'll see signs to **El Salto Eyipantla,** a 150-foot waterfall with 244 steps leading down to it. There's no charge to enter the area (but many "volunteer" guides vie for tips), and there's a good restaurant at the top of the stairs.

San Andrés, a lovely, prosperous town with an interesting mix of colonial, Caribbean, and 1960s architecture, is centered around a pretty square with a frilly white-iron kiosk and church. If you arrive by bus, you'll be by the market packed with locally grown fruits. The town center is up the hill.

This is such a clean, inviting town that you may want to do what the locals do—pull up a chair at the Hotel del Parque (catercorner from the main plaza), order café con leche, and watch the town saunter by.

While here, you might like to go by the **Tabacos de San Andrés** factory, a large and poorly lit barnlike building where some 20 workers ferment, process, cut, roll, and pack La Prueba and Ejecutivo brand cigars. Visitors are welcome Monday through Friday from 9am to 1pm and 3 to 7pm. It is a fascinating procedure even for a nonsmoker. The factory is on the road toward Catemaco, on the right just past the turn-off into San Andrés.

The ✪ **Hotel del Parque,** Madero 5, ☎ 294/2-0198, is catercorner across the main plaza, and offers comfortable rooms and a pleasant management. The restaurant, which is both indoors and outdoors under the portals facing the street, is the social center of downtown San Andrés. The menu lists a wide assortment of inexpensive Mexican dishes, including regional specialties of *enfrijoladas* with chicken, fried bananas with black beans, and dishes from the Yucatán and Oaxaca. Coffee comes four ways, all inexpensive, and there's an extensive cocktail list.

Santiago Tuxtla: A Colonial Town with a Lovely Plaza

Some 13 miles from Lake Catemaco and 8 miles from San Andrés Tuxtla, thriving Santiago Tuxtla (pop. 50,000) is reached by a winding drive over hill and dale. Along the way, you'll pass herds of grazing cattle and green rolling hills planted with sugarcane, corn, oranges, bananas, and mangoes, much of it for sale in neatly arranged roadside stands.

The **Museo Tuxteco** (formerly the Regional Museum of Anthropology), facing the beautiful main square, is the reason most tourists seek out this picturesque town. In addition to a small but important selection of mostly Olmec artifacts, there are articles from the Huasteca and Totonac cultures. The museum is open Tuesday through Saturday from 9am to 7pm, Sunday from 9am to 3pm. Admission is $3.25. On Sunday it is free.

On the plaza opposite the museum is a 45-ton **Olmec head** with a scowling face. The **market,** next to the museum, has several good small cookshops, and there's a hotel, Los Castellanos, with a decent restaurant/bar across the park.

13 Tarascan Country

Perennially off the beaten tourist track, Tarascan Country offers a distinctive, unusual taste of Mexico without the bad aftertaste of high prices. The area is situated northwest of Mexico City, in Michoacán (Meech-oh-ah-kahn), Mexico's sixth-largest state. Its best-known towns are Morelia, Pátzcuaro, and Uruapan. All of them are old colonial towns with their own unique charms, and they're all within range of Michoacán's seemingly timeless fascinations: trips through the countryside to see volcanoes or millions of monarch butterflies, to wander through Purépecha ruins, or to visit the area's many small, colorful villages—where centuries-old craft traditions are alive today.

The land of the Tarascans has maintained a special place in the country's history since before the Spanish Conquest of Mexico. Unconquered by the Aztecs, the proud and courageous Tarascan people held themselves and their land apart in majestic forested mountains dotted with misty lakes. Their language and influence were known as far north as the present-day states of Querétaro, Guerrero, Colima, Jalisco, and Guanajuato. Even the name Guanajuato is a Spanish corruption of the Tarascan word *guanaxuato*, meaning "hill of the frogs." Their pyramids, connecting half circles and rectangles, were called *ycatas*, the most visible of which are at Tzintzuntzán, near Pátzcuaro. Good examples of their pottery, stonework, and metalwork are displayed at the Museo del Estado in Morelia, at La Huatapera in Uruapan, and at the Museo de Arte Regional y Popular in Pátzcuaro.

The true name of the indigenous people here, and their language, is not Tarascan but *Purépecha* (sometimes spelled Purápecha), a word heard often in the region. When Spaniards married into Indian families, the Indians called them *tarasco*, which means "son-in-law" in Purépecha. The Spaniards heard the name so often they named the people Tarascans—and it stuck. The Purépecha language is still spoken by more than 200,000 people; according to the Cultural Atlas of Mexico, it's remotely linked to the Mixe and Zoque languages in Mexico and to the Quecha language of Peru. But even from village to village, there are differences in pronunciation within the language.

Two very different leaders stand out in the colonial history of Pátzcuaro. Conquistador Nuño de Guzman is remembered for his infamous greed and brutality; he terrorized the Tarascan population and burned their chief alive because he wouldn't—or couldn't—disclose the location of gold deposits. After Guzman was arrested, a humane bishop named Vasco de Quiroga was sent to reconstruct the area. De Quiroga taught the Indians several trades, a different one in each village. As a result, today the region is well known for its crafts, including handsome hand-loomed fabrics made in Pátzcuaro; pottery and straw weavings in Tzintzuntzán and Ihuatzio; and hand-carved furniture and wood sculptures in Quiroga, Tzintzuntzán, Cuanaja, Tocuaro, and Pátzcuaro. Santa Clara del Cobre's shops shimmer with copper, and both Pátzcuaro and Uruapan are known for distinctive lacquerware. The bishop became so revered that he is still honored today. Streets and hotels are named after him, and his statue stands in the main plaza of Pátzcuaro.

Although most Tarascans have given up truly distinctive regional dress, women still wear their hair braided and interlaced with satin ribbons in the traditional manner, don embroidered blouses and hand-loomed skirts, and wrap themselves in rebozos. In remote villages, older men (more often than young men or boys) wear traditional white cotton homespun pants and shirts.

While the region is completely integrated into the commerce of mainstream Mexico—through agriculture (avocados and coffee) and industry (furniture and lumber)—it is still culturally set apart, primarily because of the beautiful but mountainous terrain. Architecturally, it's almost unchanged from colonial times. Its unique culture makes it one of the most enjoyable regions in Mexico to visit.

EXPLORING TARASCAN COUNTRY

The time required to travel between any of the three major cities is no more than an hour or two, and public transportation is frequent. Plan no less than a day (2 nights) in Morelia and a minimum of 2 days (3 nights) in Pátzcuaro. Uruapan is an easy day-trip, but you may want to stay longer for a visit to the Paricutín volcano. During Easter week or the Day of the Dead (actually 2 days, November 1–2), the plazas in Pátzcuaro and Uruapan are loaded with regional crafts. Processions and other traditional customs make Easter week exceptional in Pátzcuaro. Reserve rooms well in advance for these holidays.

1 Morelia

195 miles W of Mexico City, 228 miles SE of Guadalajara

Morelia, the capital of the wildly beautiful state of Michoacán, is a lovely colonial city. Over the years, it has earned a reputation as one of Mexico's intellectual and artistic centers. As with much of Mexico, there is layer upon layer of fascinating history here. The area was inhabited first by the indigenous peoples, notably the Tarascans. Founded by the Spanish in 1541, the city was originally named Valladolid and was changed later to honor the revolutionary hero José María Morelos, who once lived here.

Morelia's many original colonial buildings add a special touch of ancient Mexican/Spanish elegance. To preserve the architectural harmony, the city government long ago decreed that all new major construction continue the same style and be built no taller than the existing structures.

ESSENTIALS

GETTING THERE & DEPARTING By Plane Aerolitoral (3-6202, or 91-800/9-0999 toll free in Mexico), an Aeromexico affiliate, flies from Guadalajara, Mexico City, León, and Tijuana. **Aero SudPacífico** (☎ 15-8952) flies daily to Lázaro Cárdenas and Zihuatanejo. **Taesa** (☎ 15-7463) has flights to Mexico City, Tijuana, and Guadalajara.

By Bus The **Central Camionera** is at Eduardo Ruíz and Valentín Gómez Farías, seven blocks northwest of the cathedral. To and from Mexico City, **Flecha Amarilla** runs 42 daily buses (including 14 deluxe), while **Tres Estrellas** has 10 daily buses, and the deluxe line **ETN** also has frequent service. In Mexico City, Flecha Amarilla buses leave from both the Norte and Poniente (Observatorio) stations. From Morelia, Flecha buses also go hourly to Querétaro, Pátzcuaro and Uruapan, and to León (4-hour trip) every 20 minutes. ETN also runs 9 daily buses to Guadalajara.

By Car With the new toll highway running between Mexico City and Guadalajara, the trip to Morelia from either city now only takes 2 to 3 hours (formerly a tedious 4- to 5-hour trip). From Mexico City it goes to Toluca then north to Atlacomulco, Marvatio, and Zinapecuaro. From Guadalajara it goes direct to La Barca (northeast of Lake Chapala), passing just south of Lake Cuitzeo. From either direction, the turnoff to Morelia is Highway 43. The new, free, four-lane Highway 120 (which, on a map, looks like an extension of Highway 43) links Morelia to Pátzcuaro; the trip takes about 40 minutes. (The left turnoff from Highway 120 to Tupátaro and Guanajo, covered in "Excursions from Pátzcuaro," below, is about midway between Morelia and Pátzcuaro.) Highway 15 (the long route) runs west and north from Mexico City and east and south from Guadalajara. Both sections of Highway 15 are mountainous and have hairpin curves. Highway 43 north is a fairly direct and noncurvy route from San Miguel de Allende through Celaya (2 hours) and Guanajuato (4 hours).

ORIENTATION Arriving Aeropuerto **Francisco J. Mugica** is a 45-minute drive from the city center on the Carretera Morelia-Zinepecuaro, km 27 (☎ 13-6074, 13-6177, or 13-6178). Taxis meet each flight and cost around $17 to town; return by taxi costs the same. The bus station is seven blocks northwest of the cathedral. Taxis line up out front to collect passengers. A ride to hotels around the central plaza should cost around $3.

Information The **State Tourism Office** is in a former Jesuit monastery, the Palacio Clavijero, at the corner of Madero and Nigromante (☎ 43/13-2654; fax 43/12-9816) Members of the helpful staff usually speak English and can provide excellent maps and information on Morelia and Michoacán. The office is open daily from 9am to 9pm.

City Layout The heart of the city is the pretty **central plaza,** bounded north and south by **Madero** and **Allende/Valladolid** and east and west by **Abasolo, Hidalgo,** and the **cathedral.** Streets change directions at the plaza. Most of the major attractions and the hotels I recommend are in this historic central zone anchored by the plaza.

GETTING AROUND Taxis are a fairly good bargain here. Although there are no meters, cab drivers are supposed to charge 50¢ per kilometer, or about $1.80 between various points downtown. Here, as anywhere in Mexico, settle the fare before you enter the cab.

Morelia

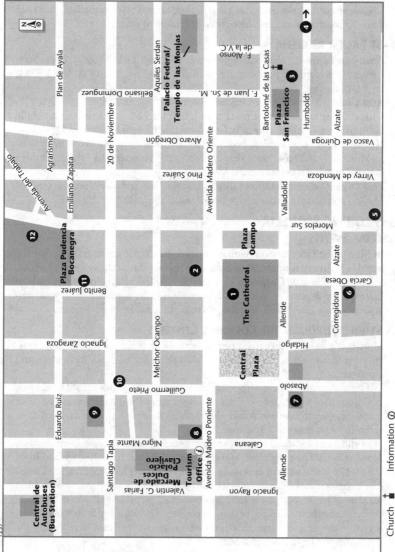

Church ✝ ■   Information ⓘ

Combis, at 35¢ per ticket, are cheaper than taxis. These customized vans hold up to 15 passengers and are color-coded according to route.

FAST FACTS: MORELIA

American Express   The local representative is Lopsa Travel Agency, in the Servi Center, Avenida del Campestre and Artilleros del 47 no. 1520 (☎ 43/15-3211; fax 43/14-7716).

Area Code   The telephone area code is 43.

Climate   At an altitude of more than 6,000 feet, Morelia can be a bit chilly mornings and evenings, especially from November through February.

Newspapers   The local paper, *La Voz de Michoacán*, has a "What's New in Morelia This Week" page that appears every Monday and lists all kinds of interesting cultural events around Morelia.

Post Office/Telegraph Office   Both are in the Palacio Federal, on the corner of Madero and Serapio Rendón, five blocks east of the cathedral.

EXPLORING MORELIA

SPECIAL EVENTS

In March, the **International Guitar Festival** attracts musicians from all over the world. The **International Organ Festival** is held in May at the cathedral. In June, there is the **Fiesta de Corpus,** with a special cathedral lighting ceremony and the International Festival of Music. In September, for the **birthday of Revolutionary hero Don José María Morelos,** there are independence celebrations.

A STROLL THROUGH THE COLONIAL CENTER

Morelia is a beautiful city that's perfect for walking, since most of the museums, restaurants, and shops are all within strolling distance of downtown hotels and restaurants.

The walk outlined below begins at the cathedral and winds up at the Casa de la Cultura. Set aside a whole day to do it, or spread it out over two days. The museums open at 9am; you'll find a lot of places are closed on Mondays, holidays, and other days between 2 and 4pm.

In the heart of Morelia, on Madero between Ignacio Zaragoza and Avenida Morelos Norte, past the plaza, is the **Cathedral,** which took 104 years to build (1640–1744) and has two impressive spires over 220 feet high that can be climbed (the doors are locked, but the man with the key is usually hanging around at midday). The interior of the church is awesome, particularly if you're fortunate enough to be there when the organist is playing. The organ, with its 4,600 pipes, is one of the best in Latin America. Great organists perform here during the International Organ Festival in May.

Across the street (Madero) from the cathedral, is the **Government Palace,** built in 1732 as a seminary. It now contains grand, colorful murals depicting the history of the state of Michoacán and of Mexico. Some of them were done by a well-known local artist named Alfredo Zalce. Notice the building's lovely arches.

If you wish to visit one of the best regional museums of art and showrooms of crafts, walk two blocks east on Madero (turn left out the door of the government Palace), then turn south (right) onto Vasco de Quiroga for one block to the **Casa de las Artesanías de Michoacán,** across Plaza de San Francisco in the colonial building attached to the church of the same name. Outside, rows of crafts vendors have set up semi-permanent stalls. Inside, high-quality traditional-style crafts of all sorts are displayed in both a museum and large sales outlet upstairs and downstairs. (See "Shopping," below). It's open daily from 9am to 8pm; admission is free.

Leaving the Artesanías, turn left to the first street (Humboldt), turn left again to Calle Vicente Santa María (it runs north-south behind the Artesanías), then turn right (south) for five blocks to the huge **Mercado Independencia,** which is open daily. Browse and enjoy the wonders of the Mexican street market—everything from clothing to cookware to flowers is sold here.

From the market, walk three blocks west to Avenida Morelos Sur and two blocks north to visit the **Casa Museo de Morelos,** Morelos Sur 323 (☎ 43/13-2651), where the city's namesake José María Morelos lived as an adult. It's a pleasant house with an authentically preserved kitchen, in addition to furniture and personal effects of the hero. It's open daily from 9am to 7pm; admission costs $3.50. For those who still want to learn more about Morelos, walk another block west to García Obesa, turn right, and on the corner of Corregidora is the **Casa Natal de Morelos (Birthplace of Morelos),** at Corregidora and Obeso (☎ 43/12-2793). There's more memorabilia, including historical documents, old posters, and modern murals depicting the Revolution. A terrific bookstore selling local and national historic and ethnographic literature is on the right as you enter. The house is open daily from 9am to 7pm.

From here, turn left out the front door and go half a block to Hidalgo and turn right, then turn left again for another block to Allende and the **Museo Michoacano,** Allende and Abasolo (☎ 43/12-0407). This is a good introduction to the history of the state from prehistoric times to Mexico's Cardenist period of the 1930s. The building, finished in 1775, was originally owned by Isidor Huarte, father of Ana Huarte (Emperor Iturbide's wife).

To the right as you enter, a great bookstore features literature on Mexico's archaeology as well as pottery reproductions from the Museum of Anthropology in Mexico City. The museum is open Tuesday through Saturday from 9am to 7pm and Sunday from 9am to 2pm. Admission is $4.

Head north across the park to Madero for a rest stop. Back on Madero in front of the cathedral is a choice of cafes, beginning with El Paraíso, across from the cathedral on the corner of Benito Juárez, and running down past the Café Catedral and Hotel Casino to Prieto.

Continue west on Madero one block to the corner of Nigromante, where, on the right corner, you'll find the **College of San Nicolás de Hidalgo,** a beautiful colonial-era university that claims to be the "oldest in the western hemisphere." Founded in Pátzcuaro in 1540, it was moved to Valladolid (present-day Morelia) in 1580 and incorporated into the University of Michoacán in 1917. Turn north (right) on Nigromante and walk three short blocks to Santiago Tapia and turn right; on the left side is the **Conservatorio de Música,** in the former Convento de Las Rosas, established as a convent for Dominican nuns in 1500. In 1785, it became a school for boys with musical skill, and it is now the home of the internationally acclaimed Morelia Boys Choir. Don't miss them if there's a practice or performance while you're in town; you can listen and observe quietly.

Catercorner across the street is the **Museo del Estado,** at the corner of Tapia and Guillermo Prieto (☎ 43/13-0629), a delightfully well done free museum with information about Michoacán from cavemen and fossils to an on-site, intact 19th-century apothecary shop, to contemporary art on the second floor. This was the childhood home of Ana Huerta, first empress of Mexico and wife of Emperor

Agustin de Iturbide. The museum is open Monday through Friday from 10am to 2pm and 4 to 8pm and Saturday, Sunday, and holidays from 10am to 7pm.

For another interesting museum, continue east on Santiago Tapia two blocks to Benito Juárez and turn north (left) to the **Museo de Arte Colonial,** Av. Benito Juárez 240 (☎ 43/13-9260). It's filled with religious art from the 16th to the 18th century, housed in another old town house with a central courtyard. It's open Tuesday through Sunday from 10am to 2pm and 5 to 8pm.

To find out about local cultural events, cross the small street to the north (around the corner to the right from the museum) and turn left onto the next street (Avenida Morelos Norte). Follow the high wrought-iron fence enclosing whimsical, contemporary sculpture made from machine parts to reach the entrance of the **Casa de la Cultura.** This cultural complex (☎ 43/13-1320) includes a mask museum, an open-air cafe, and several art galleries. It's open daily from 10am to 8pm, and there's no admission charge. Posters in the entryway announce events taking place here and at other locations in town.

SHOPPING

✪ Casa de Artesanías
Plaza de San Francisco. ☎ **43/12-1248.**

This is one of the best crafts shops in the country. In the showroom, to the right as you enter on the first floor, you'll find fantastic carved wooden furniture; people-size ceramic pots; beautiful handwoven clothing; embroidered scenes of daily life, wooden masks, lacquerware from Pátzcuaro and Uruapan, cross-stitch embroidery from Taracuato; waist-loomed table runners (they use them for mufflers) and carved pine furniture from Cuanajo; woodwork and guitars from Paracho; and close-woven hats from the Isla de Jaracuaro. Straight ahead in the fabulous interior courtyard of this monumental structure are showcases laden with the best regional crafts. Upstairs individual villages have sales outlets for fabric, wood carving, weaving, copper, and the like. Everything on display is for sale at reasonable prices. Upstairs is a living crafts museum where workers create and display their art. The shop is open daily from 9am to 8pm; admission is free.

Mercado de Dulces
Beside the Palacio Clavijero, along Valentín Gómez Farías.

This delightful jumble of shops, west on Madero from the cathedral and north on Nigromante, sells *cubitos de ate* (candied fruit wedges), jelly candies, honey, goat's milk, strawberry jam, and *chongos* (a combination of milk, sugar, cinnamon, and honey). Upstairs is a shop with all kinds of regional *artesanías* and hundreds of picture postcards from all over Michoacán. The mercado is open daily from 7am to 10pm.

MORE ATTRACTIONS
The **Templo de las Monjas** is a lovely old church a few blocks down Madero, east of the cathedral and beside the massive **Palacio Federal,** which houses, among many other official bureaus, the post and telegraph offices.

ACCOMMODATIONS
EXPENSIVE

Hotel Virrey de Mendoza
Madero Pte. 310, Morelia, Mich. 58000. ☎ **43/12-4940.** Fax 43/12-6719. 55 rms (all with bath). TV TEL. $66 double; $75–$195 suite. Free parking nearby.

Overlooking the main plaza, this recently renovated hotel exudes colonial elegance. Almost a museum, the hotel has a fabulous collection of antiques and an impressive stained-glass canopy. The lobby is exquisite, with huge fresh-flower arrangements, fine antiques, and an inviting sitting area. Each guest room is uniquely decorated with antique furniture and wall ornaments. All rooms have bathtubs, a hard-to-find luxury in Mexico, and many have fine writing desks. Oriental carpets and armoires that disguise TVs add to the charm. The only drawback here is the noise. Exterior rooms contend with street noise at this busy intersection. Interior rooms, which have shuttered windows (the only ventilation), are subject to taped music in the lobby in the afternoons and live piano entertainment drifting up between 8 and 10pm. Cable TV helps drown out some of the noise, but bring earplugs. The Virrey de Mendoza is on the northwest side of the Plaza de Armas.

Dining/Entertainment: The restaurant on the first floor serves all three meals, and the bar off the lobby is open in the afternoons and evenings.

Services: Laundry and room service, concierge.

Villa Montaña

Patzimba 201 (Apdo Postal 233) Morelia, Mich. 58090. ☎ **43/14-0231** or 14-0179 or 800/223-6510 in the U. S. or 800/44-UTELI in Canada. Fax 43/15-1423. 12 rms 24 suites. TV TEL. $132 double standard; $165–$200 double suite.

Set in the Santa Anna Hills overlooking Morelia, this small inn is truly one of Mexico's finest. One glance at the carefully selected exquisite antiques, lustrous patina of tiled floors, the setting and food, and it's obvious why it's a member of the Small Luxury Hotels of the World. Guests receive attentive service. Rooms, sequestered behind exuberant foliage and patios, are each unique, but each is furnished with antiques, carefully coordinated textiles, and comfortable sitting areas. This hotel is so popular among repeat guests that it's almost always full around the Days of the Dead (November 1–2), Christmas, and most of February.

Dining/Entertainment: One handsome restaurant serves delicious meals facing an inner courtyard with views of the city. The bar adjoins the restaurant and overlooks the Morelia. Romantic soloist or guitarists perform most evenings. It's open daily from 7:30am to 11pm.

Services: Laundry and room service, tour desk (for seeing monarch butterflies or other regional sights), concierge, lending library, boutique. In-room massage and hairstyling.

Facilities: Heated swimming pool, tennis court.

INEXPENSIVE

Hotel Casino

Portal Hidalgo 229, Morelia, Mich. 58000. ☎ **43/13-1003.** Fax 43/12-1252. 50 rms (all with bath). TV TEL. $40 double.

This fine old hotel boasts several nice touches—beams, chandeliers, and columns—along with an excellent location practically across the street from the cathedral. The immaculate rooms have wall-to-wall carpeting. The restaurant, located in the covered courtyard on the first floor and outside under the portals, is one of the best in town.

Posada de la Soledad

Ignacio Zaragoza 90, Morelia, Mich. 58000. ☎ **43/12-1888.** 58 rms, 9 suites (all with bath). TV TEL. $45–$50 double. Free parking.

A tranquil, beautiful hacienda-style manor, the hotel was built in 1719 as the home and carriage house of a rich Spaniard. Old carriages are handsomely placed around the first floor. Some of the rooms have a fireplace, a tub as well as a shower, and a small balcony. Standard rooms are small, and most are plainly furnished with one or two double beds and colonial-style furniture. The hotel restaurant/bar, one of the most inviting in Mexico, is open daily from 7:30am to 10:30pm, with tables set under the portals. To reach the hotel from the cathedral, walk one block west on Madero to Zaragoza; turn right and you'll find the hotel on the right, near Ocampo.

DINING

✪ Las Mercedes Restaurant
León Gúzman 47. ☎ **43/2-6113.** Main courses $5–$9. Mon–Sat 1:30–11:30pm. MEXICAN/INTERNATIONAL.

If you eat only one meal in Morelia take it here, in a stone-arched inner courtyard filled with palms, flowers, and succulents in tubs and pots. One wall is lined with colorful birds in cages and others with exotic murals. At night, small spotlights illuminate each table's colorful, fresh bouquet. Pastel-clothed tables are set with handpainted ceramic plates bearing charming scenes, and wine is presented in a translucent, hand-blown fluted green glass. A plate of small tacos is automatically brought while diners make their choices. Homemade bread also arrives with a small tub of herb-flavored butter. The menu includes pasta; crêpes with piñons and pistachios; beef brochette; and various seafood and meat offerings. To get here from the cathedral, walk six short blocks west on Madero. Turn right on León Guzman and look for a small sign on the left over the door.

✪ Las Viandas de San José
Alvaro Obregón 263 at Emilano Zapata. ☎ **43/2-3728.** Breakfast $2–$2.50; main courses $4–$7; comida corrida $5.50. Daily 8am–11pm. REGIONAL/INTERNATIONAL.

Dining is a pleasure under the arcades or adjacent rooms of this mansion, built around an open interior patio. Service is gracious, and the menu offers intriguing regional specialties such as *uchepos*; *corrundas*; bone-marrow soup; rabbit in wine sauce; chicken placero with enchiladas; and 11 different fish dishes, including Pátzcuaro whitefish. Beef and chicken prepared home-style round out the menu. You can't go wrong with the huge comida corrida. This is a sibling of Los Comensales at Zaragoza 148, a block and a half from the main plaza. The menus are almost the same, but Las Viandas has superior service. To find Las Viandas from the cathedral, walk three blocks east on Madero Oriente and turn left on Alvaro Obregón. Walk straight for three blocks; it's on the corner opposite the Iglesia San José.

INEXPENSIVE

Restaurante El Paraíso
Portal Galeana 103, at the corner of Juárez. ☎ **43/2-0374.** Breakfast $2.25–$3; main courses $2–$4; comida corrida $3.75; buffet $3–$4.50. Daily 7:30am–11pm (comida corrida served noon–3:30 or 4pm). MEXICAN.

This simple, pleasant restaurant is always crowded with people who enjoy the good prices and the casual ambience of a sidewalk cafe. Inexpensive breakfast combinations come with juice, coffee, and toast; dinner choices come with salad, beans, and french-fried potatoes. The comida corrida, surprisingly ample, includes a salad, soup, rice, beans, a dish of the day, a dessert, and coffee.

FOR COFFEE AND DESSERT

Across from the main plaza and cathedral, on the same side of the street as the Hotel Casino and the Restaurant El Paraíso, is an entire block replete with **sidewalk cafes.** This is local life on parade—people linger for hours sipping coffee in its many varieties or downing whole meals. All the restaurants here are popular, so pick one that's appealing.

MORELIA AFTER DARK

Morelia's cafes (see "For Coffee & Dessert," above) become its nightspots after dark. Hot coffee and cold beer are served to a lively college crowd. Another nice cafe and nightspot is **Colibri,** Galeana 36, a block behind Hotel Virrey de Mendoza (go two blocks west of the cathedral then turn left on Galeana; Colibri is on the right side). Softly strumming his guitar, a singer entertains patrons with a variety of lovely ballads, mostly Mexican and Latin American. On winter evenings around Christmas, the owner personally serves complimentary cups of the traditional hot fruit punch.

AN EXCURSION TO SEE MICHOACÁN'S MONARCH BUTTERFLIES

Visiting the winter nesting grounds of the monarch butterfly in the mountains of Michoacán—a very long day-trip from Morelia—is an awesome experience. The monarchs wing down from Canada for the winter, so the best time to see them is from November through February. Take one of the tours offered by a number of travel agents in Morelia or rough it going by bus on your own. Having done the latter, I recommend the former, since in the long run the tour involves less time, money, and effort.

On an Organized Tour   Tour companies in Morelia offer this trip frequently during peak months for about $30 to $45. The tour takes about 10 to 12 hours by van. The **Wagon-Lits travel agent** (☎ 43/ 12-7766; fax 43/12-7660), in the lobby of the Hotel Alemeda on the corner of Madero and G. Prieto (just west of the cathedral), handles this and other tours through Auto Turismo de Michoacán (☎ 43/2-4987 or 2-6810). You might also try **Viajes Flamingo,** Zaragoza 93 (☎ 43/12-0059 or 12-4833; fax 12-4833). Monarch tours generally leave at 10am and return at 7:30pm; tours require a minimum of five people.

In the tiny, unpaved village of El Rosario, the brilliant butterflies welcome visitors with a blizzard of orange and black. At the nearby **El Rosario Sanctuary** (admission $3; open daily from 10am to 5 or 6pm), a guide (who should be tipped a few dollars) accompanies each group of visitors along the loop trail (about an hour's steep walk at high altitude). It's worth the time, effort, and expense to get here to be surrounded by the magic of millions of monarchs. Be quiet and you'll hear almost a billion wings—this is one of the few places in the world where one can hear the soft sound of butterflies flying.

At the high point of the trail, the branches of the tall pine trees bow under their burden of butterflies. For folks unable to tackle the walk, monarchs are visible around the car park. There's also a comprehensive video show at the nearby information center, as well as snacks, soft drinks, and toilets.

By Car   To drive your own car, just follow the main roads to the towns described above. Zitácuaro is on Highway 15 between Toluca and Morelia. A Volkswagen Beetle carried me up the final dirt road from Ocampo to El Rosario.

Tours from Elsewhere Travel agencies from San Miguel de Allende often have monarch tours. See the section on San Miguel in Chapter 6 for details. **Columbus Travel** (☎ 800/843-1060 in the U.S. and Canada) has frequent trips to the butterflies via Mexico City.

2 Pátzcuaro

231 Miles W of Mexico City, 178 miles SE of Guadalajara, 43 miles SW of Morelia

Pátzcuaro is a well-preserved colonial town with low overhanging red-tile roofs, whitewashed buildings, two plazas, and no traffic lights. Coming from Morelia, you'll immediately notice the difference between that city's regal colonial architecture and Pátzcuaro's rural colonial-era structures. No new buildings interfere with the timeworn harmony of Pátzcuaro's colonial roofline.

Except for its paved streets, little has changed about Pátzcuaro's appearance since colonial times. Here, as in San Miguel de Allende, you have the feeling of traveling centuries back in time. More than San Miguel or even Morelia, Pátzcuaro has Indian roots that still run deep. Though distinct regional costumes are seldom seen, Indian women still braid their hair with ribbons and wear bright blue rebozos, and women from several villages wear a distinctive cross-point stitched apron—a new kind of costume. The ancient Tarascan language is heard frequently, especially in the central market. The town is known for its lake, one of the world's highest at 7,250 feet, where fishermen catch delicious whitefish with nets of such delicate texture and wide-winged shape that they've been compared to butterflies. If there is any drawback to Pátzcuaro, it is that its lovely stone park benches aren't scrubbed and that the unkempt appearance of both plazas obscures their beauty.

ESSENTIALS

GETTING THERE & DEPARTING By Bus The bus station is on the outskirts of Pátzcuaro, about a 20-minute bus ride to town or 10 minutes by taxi. **From Mexico City:** Service is more frequent to Morelia than directly to Pátzcuaro. It may therefore be more efficient to take a bus first to Morelia and then one of the frequent buses running from there to Pátzcuaro. **Flecha Amarilla** and **Autobuses de Occidente** have two buses from Mexico City to Pátzcuaro that cost about $12. **From Morelia: Autotransportes Galeana** runs between Pátzcuaro and Morelia every 15 minutes; the 40-minute to 1-hour trip costs $1.50 to $2. The same line has buses to and from Uruapan every 20 minutes, and the one-hour trip costs $1.50 to $2. **ETN** has 10 daily buses to Morelia. **Parhikuni** buses run every few minutes between Pátzcuaro and Morelia. **To Tocuaro and Erongaricaro: Occidente** buses make the 30- to 40-minute trip every 20 minutes. **To Tupátaro and Cuanajo:** Buses of the **Herradura de Plata** line run hourly between 7am and 9pm. **To Tzintzuntzn:** Frequent buses of the Galeana and Occidente lines labeled "Quiroga" go frequently to Tzintzuntzn (40 minutes). **To Santa Clara del Cobre:** Frequent buses labeled "Ario de Rosales" pass first through Santa Clara del Cobre (the so-called "Copper Capital" of Mexico), a 30-minute drive from Pátzcuaro. Occidente or Galeana buses are among the several buses that go there. **To Ihuatzio:** Frequent minivans and buses pass by the Plaza Chica in Pátzcuaro en route to Ihuatzio. **To San Miguel de Allende: Flecha Amarilla** has four daily buses making the 4- to 5-hour trip.

By Car See "Getting There & Departing: By Car" in Morelia, above, for information from Mexico City, Guadalajara, San Miguel de Allende, and Morelia.

Pátzcuaro

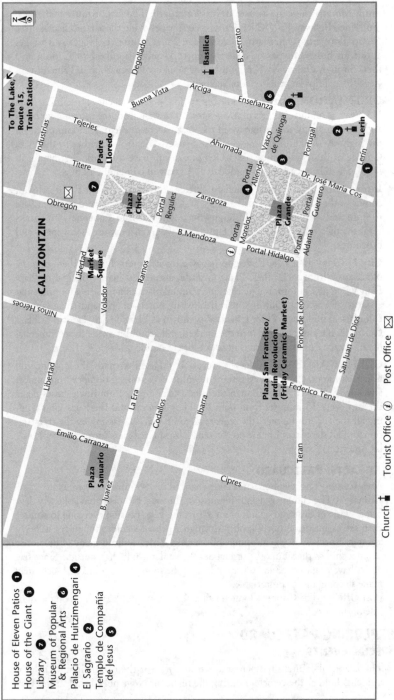

To The Lake,
Route 15,
Train Station

CALTZONTZIN

Basilica

Degollado
B. Serrato
Buena Vista
Arciga
Enseñanza
Industrias
Tejeries
Ahumada
Vasco de Quiroga
Portugal
Lerín
Titere
Padre Lloredo
Zaragoza
Portal Allende
Dr. José Maria Cos
Obregón
Plaza Chica
Portal Regules
Portal Guerrero
B. Mendoza
Portal Morelos
Plaza Grande
Portal Aldama
Portal Hidalgo
Libertad
Market Square
Ramos
Volador
Niños Héroes
Ponce de León
San Juan de Dios
Libertad
La Era
Codallos
Ibarra
**Plaza San Francisco/
Jardin Revolucion
(Friday Ceramics Market)**
Federico Tena
Teran
Emilio Carranza
B. Juarez
Plaza Sanuario
Cipres

Church ✝■   Tourist Office 🛈   Post Office ✉

House of Eleven Patios ❶
House of the Giant ❸
Library ❼
Museum of Popular
 & Regional Arts ❻
Palacio de Huitzimengari ❹
El Sagrario ❷
Templo de Compañia
 de Jesus ❺

1258

From Morelia there are two routes to Pátzcuaro: The fastest route is the new four-lane Highway 120, which passes near Tiripetío and Tupátaro/Cuanajo (see "Road Trips from Pátzcuaro," below). The longer route via Highway 15 takes about an hour and passes near the pottery-making village of Capula and then through Quiroga, where you follow signs to Pátzcuaro and Tzintzuntzán (see "Road Trips from Pátzcuaro," below).

ORIENTATION **Arriving** The bus station, on Libramiento Ignacio Zaragoza Highway, is on the outskirts of town—too far to walk from the center. City buses and minivans (15¢ to 25¢) arrive in the lot adjacent to the bus station or out on the highway (half a block away). Those marked "Centro" go either to the Plaza Grande or the Plaza Chica; ask which one if you have a specific destination in mind. Small bags can be accommodated. A taxi will cost about $2.50.

Information The **State Tourism Office,** catercorner from the northwest corner of the Plaza Grande at Ibarra 3 (☎ 434/2-1214), is open daily from 9am to 2pm and 4 to 7:30pm. Although you might not find someone who speaks English, the staff will try to be helpful, and you can pick up useful maps and brochures.

City Layout In a way, Pátzcuaro has two town centers, both of them plazas a block apart from each other. **Plaza Grande,** also called Plaza Principal or Plaza Don Vasco de Quiroga, is a picturesque tranquil plaza centered on a fountain and a statue of Vasco de Quiroga. It is flanked by hotels, shops, and restaurants in colonial-era buildings. **Plaza Chica,** also known as Plaza de San Agustín or Plaza Gertrudis Bocanegra, flows into the market, and around it swirls the commercial life of Pátzcuaro. Plaza Chica is north of Plaza Grande

GETTING AROUND With the exception of Lake Pátzcuaro, the lookout, and hotels on Lázaro Cárdenas, everything is within easy walking distance from almost any hotel in Pátzcuaro. Although the lake is over a mile from town, buses make the run every 15 minutes from both the Plaza Grande and the Plaza Chica, going all the way to the pier (the embarcadero or *muelle*), passing by the train station and all the places I name on Avenida Lázaro Cárdenas (formerly Avenida de las Américas).

FAST FACTS: PÁTZCUARO

Area Code The telephone area code changed in 1994 from 454 to 434.

Climate The climate is delightful most of the year, but occasional blustery days bring swirls of dust and a chill of air across the lake, causing everyone to shutter themselves inside. From October through April, it's cold enough for a heavy sweater, especially in the morning and evening. Thick walls in many of the hotels retain a chill so that it may be several degrees cooler inside than outside. Since few hotels have fireplaces or any source of heat in the rooms, long johns and socks may make sleeping more comfortable.

Post Office The Correo is located half a block north of Plaza Chica, on the right side of the street.

EXPLORING PÁTZCUARO
SPECIAL EVENTS

The island of Janitzio has achieved world fame for the candlelight vigil local residents hold at the cemetery during the nights of November 1 and 2, the **Day**

of the Dead. Tzintzuntzán also hosts very popular festivities, including folkloric dances in the main plaza and in the nearby *yácatas* (pre-Hispanic ruins), concerts in the church, and decorations in the cemetery. If you wish to avoid crowds, however, skip Janitzio and Tzintzuntzán and go to one of the smaller lakeside villages or other islands on the lake that also have extraordinary rituals. The Tourism Office (see "Information," above) has a schedule of events for the entire area and publishes an explanatory booklet "Día de los Muertos."

Easter week, beginning the Friday before Palm Sunday, is special here, too. Most activity centers around the basílica. There are processions involving the surrounding villages almost nightly, and in Tzintzuntzán there's a reenactment of the betrayal of Christ and a ceremonial washing of the feet. Although written in 1947, Frances Toor's description of Holy Week in Pátzcuaro, in *A Treasury of Mexican Folkways* (Crown), is still accurate and a good preparation for a visit at that time.

During both events, the Plaza Grande is loaded with regional crafts.

Important note: Make hotel reservations months in advance for either event. Most hotels require a 3-night minimum stay during Holy Week and Days of the Dead.

A STROLL AROUND TOWN

Pátzcuaro is a beautiful town, worthy of leisurely strolls through its ancient, unchanged streets and plazas. The **Plaza Chica,** crisscrossed by walkways, has a statue of Gertrudis Bocanegra, heroine of Mexican independence, in the middle. Immediately west of and across the street from the Plaza Chica, the **market** and large market plaza has myriad stalls where vendors sell pottery, copper, rebozos, serapes, and food. North of the market across the street, facing the Plaza Chica, is the **public library,** also named for Doña Bocanegra. Occupying the former monastery of San Agustín, the library contains a huge mural painted by Juan O'Gorman (the artist's first mural), depicting the history of the area from the Tarascan legends up to the Revolution. The former living quarters of the monks, next door, were converted into the Teatro Emperador Caltzontzin.

Just one long block south is the splendid **Plaza Grande,** surrounded by colonial-era buildings. It's a vast tree-shaded expanse of roughly kept lawns; in the center is an elaborate stone fountain with a large figure of beloved Vasco de Quiroga, "Tata Vasco," in a benevolent posture. On the north side of the plaza is the **Palacio de Huitzimengari,** built by the Spaniards for the Tarascan emperor—one of the few instances in colonial Mexico of respect and equitable treatment for the indigenous people. Local Indian artisans now occupy the slowly deteriorating building.

One of the oldest buildings in Pátzcuaro is the **House of the Giant,** on the east side of Plaza Grande at Portal de Matamoros 40. It was named after the 12-foot-high painted statue that supports one of the arches around the patio. This residence was built in 1663 by a Spanish count and represents the colonial taste of that period—carved stone panels, thick columns, and open courtyards.

The **basílica,** east of the small plaza on top of a small hill, was built in the 16th century at the prompting of Bishop Don Vasco and designated a basílica by papal decree in 1907. It opened in 1554, but Don Vasco died before it was completed. Now reconstructed, it has been through many catastrophes from earthquakes to the civil war of the mid-19th century. Be sure to go to the main altar to see the Virgin, which is made of "corn-stalk pulp and a mucilage obtained from a prized orchid of the region." She is a very sacred figure to the Indians of this area, and on the eighth day of each month they come from the villages to pay homage to her, particularly for her miraculous healing power.

Two blocks to the south of the basílica is the **Museum of Popular and Regional Arts** (☎ 434/2-1029). It's yet another beautiful colonial building (1540), originally Don Vasco's College of San Nicolás. The rooms, filled with fine examples of regional crafts and costumes, are located off the central courtyard. The museum is open Tuesday through Saturday from 9am to 7pm and Sunday from 9am to 3pm. Admission is $4; free on Sunday.

Of the many old churches in Pátzcuaro, one of the most interesting is the **Temple of the Compañía de Jesús,** just south of the museum. This church was Don Vasco's cathedral before the basílica and afterward was given to the Jesuits. The buildings across the street from the church were once part of the complex, containing the hospital, soup kitchen, and living quarters for religious scholars.

The **House of the Eleven Patios,** located between José María Cos and Enseñanza, is one of the most outstanding architectural achievements of the colonial period. Formerly a convent of the Catherine nuns, today it houses the **Casa de las Artesanías de Michoacán,** with every type of local artistry for sale. (See "Shopping," below.)

A NEARBY ATTRACTION

No visit to Pátzcuaro is complete without a trip on the lake, preferably across to the isolated island village of **Janitzio,** dominated by a hilltop statue of José María Morelos. The village church is famous for the annual ceremony on the Day of the Dead, held at midnight on November 1, when villagers climb to the churchyard carrying lighted candles in memory of their dead relatives and then spend the night in graveside vigil. It begins October 30 and lasts through November 2.

The most economical way to get to Janitzio is by colectivo launch, which makes the trip when enough people have gathered to go—about every 20 to 30 minutes from about 7:30am to 6pm. Round-trip fare is $2 for those 5 years and older; a private boat costs $33 round trip; a trip to three islands costs $35. The **ticket office** (☎ 434/2-0681) is open daily from 7am to 5pm.

At the ticket office on the pier (embarcadero), a map of the lake posted on the wall shows all the boat trips possible around the lake to various islands and lakeshore towns. Launches will take you wherever you want to go. Though prices are high (see above) up to 20 people can split the cost.

SHOPPING

Pátzcuaro is one of Mexico's best shopping towns because of the textiles, copper, wood carving, lacquer work, and straw weavings made in the region. Most shops

---

Impressions

I like Mexico, I like its color, its violence, its raw tumbling mountains, green checker-board valleys, dizzy trails, purple blue sky and stabbing sun. I like its crumbling mon-asteries and cathedrals with cactus growing from their roofs, and even more its ancient pyramids rising earth-covered and defiant from jungle plain and mountain top.
　　　　　　　　　　　　　　　　—Stuart Chase, Mexico: *A Study of Two Americas,* 1931

are on the Plaza Grande and the streets leading from it to the Plaza Chica, the place of choice for copper vendors. There are also a couple of shops on the street facing the basílica. In addition to the shops in Pátzcuaro, nearby Tzintzuntzán, Ihuatzio, Cuanaja, Tupátaro, and Santa Clara del Cobre are must-stops for shoppers (see "Road Trips from Pátzcuaro," below).

✪ Casa de las Artesanías de Michoacán/House of the Eleven Patios
Calle Lerin between José Cos and Enseñanza. No phone.

Housed in a former convent (see "A Stroll Around Town," above), this is the best one-stop shopping in the village. Much of what's produced in the region is for sale here—textile arts, pottery and ceramic dishes, lacquerwork, paintings, wood carvings, jewelry, copperwork, and musical instruments, including the famous Paracho guitars. Most of the shops are open daily from 9am to 2pm and 4 to 7pm.

✪ Comunidad de Santa Cruz
José María Cos 3. No phone.

Berta Servin Barriga is the helpful powerhouse behind this cooperative. Women of the farming community of nearby Santa Cruz, where she lives, send their embroidery work to be sold here. Scenes of village life are embroidered on colorful cloth panels ranging from 3 by 5 inches to 20 by 40 inches, plus tablecloths and clothing. Ask Berta or her daughter Esther to explain the events in each festive scene. The delightful panels are fabulous framed or as pillows. There's no sign, but it's next to Mantas Típicas (see below), near the corner of Lerin. The shop is open Monday through Friday from 10am to 8pm and Saturday and Sunday from 10am to 5pm.

Diseño Artesana
José Cos 1. No phone.

Owner Esperanza Sepulveda designs one-of-a-kind clothing using locally made fabrics. It's on the west side of the Plaza Grande and open daily from 10am to 3pm and 4:30 to 8pm.

✪ Friday Pottery Market
Plaza San Franciso, Ponce de León at Federico Tena. No phone.

Early each Friday morning this plaza, one block west of the Plaza Grande, fills with sellers of various styles of regionally made pottery, most of it not for sale in Pátzcuaro on other days. This is a market for the locals, and few tourists seem to know about it. Prices are incredibly cheap.

Galería del Arcangel
Corner of Enseñanza and Vasco de Quiroga. ☎ and fax **434/2-0172.**

Catercorner from the basílica and a block east of the Plaza Grande, this store offers a fine collection of quality regional pottery and handcarved furniture, plus some of the best crafts from other parts of Mexico. It's open daily from 10am to 7pm.

✪ Galeria de Arte Iturbe
Portal Morelos 59. ☎ **434/2-0368.**

If you are an art afficionado, this powerful collection of works by Michoacán artists will impress you. There's also a small selection of folk art from Ocumichu and Michoacán and books on Mexican art. Enter either through the Hotel Iturbe (go all the way to the back) or on Ahumada off the Plaza Grande. The gallery is open daily from 10am to 8pm.

Herrajes Artísticos

José Cos 36. ☎ **434/2-0674.**

Beautiful "drawn-work" (fabric threads pulled apart to make elaborate designs) is a diminishing art in the region. This store still carries some of the best-made drawn-work, including elegant jackets and tableware. The shop is on the west side of the Plaza Grande and is open Monday through Saturday from 10am to 8pm and Sunday from 10am to 6pm.

Mantas Típicas

José Cos 5. ☎ **434/2-1324.** Fax 2-0522.

A factory outlet for the company's textile mill, this is one of several textile outlets on the Plaza Grande. Shelves are laden with colorful foot-loomed tablecloths, napkins, bedspreads, and bolts of fabric. It's at the corner of Lerin. Open daily from 9am to 7pm.

Market Plaza

West of Plaza Chica

The House of the Eleven Patios (above) should be your first stop, and this should be your second. The entire plaza fronting the food market is filled with covered stalls selling crafts, clothing, rugs, rebozos, and more. Locally knitted sweaters are a good buy. Streets surrounding the plaza churn with exuberant sellers of fresh vegetables and caged birds.

ACCOMMODATIONS

All the hotels mentioned below are within walking distance of the two central village plazas, restaurants, and shopping. All are charming hostelries which would cost a lot more if they were located in one of the country's beach resorts.

MODERATE

Hostería de San Felipe

Av. Lázaro Cárdenas 321 (Apdo. Postal 209), Pátzcuaro, Mich. 61600. ☎ **434/2-1298.** 11 rms (all with bath). $32 double. Free parking.

Located off Highway 14 as you come into town, this hotel is very clean, quiet, and comfortable. Rooms are in back and arranged around a green lawn; each has a fireplace, wall-to-wall carpeting, and dark-wood ceilings. Its tranquillity makes this place ideal for a long-term stay.

Hotel Los Escudos

Portal Hidalgo 73, Pátzcuaro, Mich. 61600. ☎ **434/2-0138** or 2-1290. Fax 434/2-0207. 30 rms (all with bath). TV. $29 double. Parking: $2 daily.

The rooms in this handsome colonial-style hotel on the west side of Plaza Grande are decorated with lush red or blue carpeting, red drapes, lace curtains, and scenes of an earlier Pátzcuaro painted on the walls. Some of the rooms have fireplaces, while others have private balconies overlooking the plaza. There's an excellent restaurant off the lobby.

✪ Hotel Fiesta Plaza

Plaza Bocanegra 24, Pátzcuaro, Mich. 61600. ☎ **434/2-2515** or 2-2516. Fax 434/2-2515. 60 rms (all with bath). TV TEL. $27 double. Free parking.

When you enter the Fiesta Plaza's inviting courtyard, you're surrounded by three tiers of rooms (no elevator) with richly lustrous pine columns and wrought-iron banisters. The comfortable rooms have pine furniture, carpets, and small tile baths.

Each has windows opening onto covered walkways, which are furnished with tables and chairs. A restaurant/bar is on the open patio as you enter. It faces the north side of the Plaza Chica/Bocanegra at the corner of Libertad/Padre Lloreda.

✪ Hotel Mansión Iturbe Bed and Breakfast

Portal Morelos 59, Pátzcuaro, Mich. 61600. ☎ **434/2-0368**. 15 rms (all with bath). $40 double; $52 suite. Rates include breakfast. Free parking.

Located on the north side of the Plaza Grande, this 17th-century building was formerly a combination home (upstairs), commercial outlet (first floor), and stable (in back) for muleteers traversing Mexico's mountains with trade goods. Today the ground floor (where the shops once were) holds Doña Paca, the hotel's excellent restaurant (see "Dining," below), and the Viejo Gaucho (see "Pátzcuaro After Dark," below), the local venue for evening music, is located in the stable area. The hotel also houses the fine Galería de Arte Iturbe, featuring Michoacán artists. Music from Viejo Gaucho can't be heard in the front guestrooms. Rooms are on the second floor and have original plank flooring; heavy, dark Spanish-style wooden furniture; deep-red drapes; and plaid bedspreads.

The bathrooms are large. The hot water is slow to arrive, but it eventually gets really hot. Though there are bedside lights, lighting in general in this hotel is on the dim side. Rates include a welcome drink, full breakfast with delicious cappuccino or coffee, 2 hour's use of a bicycle, and a free daily paper; in addition, the fourth night is free. Instant coffee and hot water are in the lobby early in the morning before the restaurant opens. This deal is hard to beat in Pátzcuaro.

Posada San Rafael

Plaza Grande, Pátzcuaro, Mich. 61600. ☎ **434/2-0770**, or 2-0779. 103 rms (all with bath). $23–$30 double. Free parking in courtyard.

This comfortable, colonial-style inn on the south side of Plaza Grande has rooms that open onto a sunny, central courtyard filled with lush potted plants and a fountain. Rooms are small and traditionally furnished; some are carpeted. The higher price in each category is for remodeled rooms, but the difference in room quality is not worth the extra price. Note that the rooms can be quite cold in winter, and desk clerks have been known to be stingy with blankets. The second-story restaurant is open daily from 8am to 9pm.

INEXPENSIVE

Ⓢ Hotel Posada de la Basílica

Arciga 6, Pátzcuaro, Mich. 61600. ☎ **434/2-1108**. 11 rms (all with bath). TV. $20 double. Children under 12 stay free in parents' room. Free enclosed parking.

A mansion-turned-hotel, this appealing colonial-style inn across from the basílica is built around a lovely patio. The sunny rooms have wonderful views, red curtains, heavy Spanish-style furniture, and little brick fireplaces. The hotel's restaurant, whose tables are decorated with regional pottery, is open for breakfast and lunch. Service is slow, but there's a fabulous view of the village while you wait. The hotel is opposite the basílica, at the corner of Arciga and La Paz.

✪ Posada de la Salud

Serrato 9, Pátzcuaro, Mich. 61600. ☎ **434/2-0058**. 15 rms (all with bath). $15 double. Street parking available.

This posada offers two tiers of exceptionally quiet rooms built around an attractive courtyard. All rooms have beautiful beds with carved wooden headboards and matching desks. Two rooms have fireplaces. To get here from the Plaza Grande, walk one block east on P. Allende/V. De Quiroga and turn left on Arciga; walk a block and turn right onto Serrato (not marked, but on the right side of the basílica). The hotel is a long half- block up on the right.

DINING

Restaurants open late and close early in Pátzcuaro, so don't plan on hot coffee if you're up early, and plan ahead for late-evening hunger pangs. For inexpensive food, try the tamal and atole vendors in front of the basílica and by the market. Even more prolific are the pushcart taco stands that line up near Plaza Chica and the market in the mornings to sell tacos containing meat from different parts of the cow (don't ask which parts; they simply taste good); there are also steamy cups of atole, hot *corrundas* (little triangular-shaped tamales with hot sauce and cream), and huge tamales sold by housewives. Breakfast will cost $1 or less here.

In the afternoons, different vendors show up to sell other parts of the cow. In the evenings, **Plaza Chica** is filled with small sidewalk restaurants selling another specialty—Pátzcuaro chicken with enchiladas (tortillas with sauce) and heaps of fried potatoes and carrots. *Buñelos* come dripping with honey. **Café Botafumeiro,** a coffee shop on the southwest corner of Plaza Grande, dispenses a variety of excellent Uruapan coffees by the cup or kilo and chocolate steaming hot or by the kilo.

✪ El Patio

Plaza Grande 19. ☎ **434/2-0484.** Breakfast $2.50–$5; main courses $4.50–$8; comida corrida $4.50–$5. Daily 8am–8pm (comida corrida served 1:30–4pm). MEXICAN.

Wood-beamed ceilings, charming chandeliers woven in basketry, and paintings of local scenes make this a very pleasant restaurant. Be sure to notice the unusual bar made of bottles and a gun embedded in the stucco. El Patio, on the south side of Plaza Grande, offers delicious, inexpensive meals. Hot bread and butter are served with dishes like *carne asada*. The three-course comida corrida is delicious and plentiful.

✪ Restaurant Doña Paca

Hotel Iturbe, Portal Morelos 59. ☎ **434/2-0366.** Main courses $3–$6. Daily 8am–9pm. MEXICAN REGIONAL.

This is one of the best places for regional Michoacán cuisine. Warmly inviting, with leather *equipal* chairs, beamed ceilings, French doors facing the *portales* and Plaza Grande, and photos of old Pátzcuaro decorating the walls, it's a good place to linger. Try the corrundas or the trout served *al gusto* (as you like it) with a choice of cilantro (marvelous), garlic, or other herbs. This is one of the few places featuring *churipo*, a regional beef and vegetable stew served with corrundas—ask to see if it's prepared before promising your tastebuds. For a tasty encore try a buñelo topped with delicious coconut yogurt. Margarita Arriaga, the English-speaking owner, prides herself on the coffee she serves—and with good reason. The cappuccino is the best in Mexico. The wonderful hot chocolate comes in a big cup frothed to a puffy frenzy. The food is worthwhile, but the service is slow—don't expect to dine in a hurry.

NEARBY DINING

The traditional place to dine on whitefish is at one of the many restaurants lining the road to the lake. For an economical meal, wander down to the little

The Dance of the Little Old Men

The **Danza de los Viejitos** (Dance of the Little Old Men) is an ancient mask dance created by the Tarascans to ridicule the Spaniards during the Conquest. Dancers in traditional regional costume, including comical pink masks with hooked noses and big red smiles, perform a skillful dance. Clacking on the floor with wooden sandals, they are bent over all the while like old men hobbling on wooden canes—but, oh, do their feet fly! The dance is still performed each Saturday night at 8pm at the reasonably priced Restaurant Los Escudos in the patio of the Hotel Escudos on the Plaza Grande (see "Accommodations," above).

The dance is also performed every Wednesday and Saturday at 9pm in the restaurant of the Hotel Posada de Don Vasco, on Avenida de Lázaro Cárdenas going toward the lake. A full dinner costs around $12, but you can dine for much less. After the dancers, an eight-piece mariachi group performs. You can reserve a table if you wish on the day of the performance. There's no admission charge for people dining during the performance in either place.

open-air restaurants on the wharf (embarcadero), where señoras fry up the delicious fish while you watch. Fish, garnishes, and a soft drink cost $7 to $10. The restaurants are open daily from 8am to 6pm.

Camino Real
Carretera Patz-Tzurumutaro. No phone. Main courses $4–$9; comida corrida $4. Daily 7am–midnight. MEXICAN.

Locals claim that this hard-to-find restaurant serves the best food in town. The *chilaquiles,* cooked with eggs or potatoes, will keep you going for hours. The chicken and fish dishes are also delicious, and the comida corrida is a three-course feast. Service is good even when the restaurant is full. Camino Real is about a mile outside of town on the road to Morelia (Highway 14), shortly before the turnoff to Tzintzuntzán-Quiroga and beside the Pemex station.

Restaurant Las Redes
Av. Lázaro Cárdenas 6. ☎ **434/2-1275.** Main courses $3–$7; comida corrida $4.50–$5. Daily 9am–8pm (comida corrida served 1–8pm). Bus: On the road to the wharf. MEXICAN.

Local residents gather at this rustic restaurant on the road to the wharf for the comida corrida, which comes with soup, rice, fish or meat, frijoles, and coffee. The restaurant is famous for its *pescado blanco* (whitefish).

PÁTZCUARO AFTER DARK

Generally speaking, Pátzcuaro closes down before 10pm, so bring a good book or plan to rest up for the remainder of your travels.

Late-night music lovers flock to the **Viejo Gaucho** for performances that include Mexican trios, Peruvian music, and jazz. The small restaurant serves empanadas, steaks, hamburgers, beer, and mixed drinks. It's in the Hotel Iturbe, Portal Morelos 59. (☎ 434/2-0366), but the entry is on Ahumada. It's open Thursday through Sunday from 6pm to 2am. Music starts between 8:30 and 9pm. After the music starts there's a cover charge of $2.50–$5.

ROAD TRIPS FROM PÁTZCUARO
EL ESTRIBO: A SCENIC OVERLOOK

For a good view of the town and the lake, head for the **lookout** at El Estribo, 2 miles from town on the hill to the west. Driving from the main square on Calle Ponce de León, following the signs, will take 10 to 15 minutes. Walking will take you about 45 minutes since it's up a continuously steep hill. Once you reach the gazebo, you can climb the more than 400 steps to the very summit of the hill for a bird's-eye view. The gazebo area is great for a picnic; there are barbecue pits and sometimes a couple selling soft drinks and beer.

TZINTZUNTZÁN: TARASCAN RUINS, STRAW HANDCRAFTS, CERAMICS, & WOVEN GOODS

Tzintzuntzán (zeent-ZUNT-zahn) is an ancient village 10 miles from Pátzcuaro on the road to Quiroga (see "Getting There & Departing: By Bus," above). In earlier centuries, Tzintzuntzán was the capital of a Tarascan empire that controlled over a hundred other towns and villages. On a hill on the right before you enter town, pyramids upon pyramids still remind visitors of the glorious (and bloody) past. Today the village is known for its straw handcrafts—mobiles, baskets, and figures (skeletons, airplanes, reindeer, turkeys, and the like)—as well as for its pottery and woven goods. The old market is now housed in a neocolonial building. Across from the **basket market** are several open-air wood-carving workshops full of photogenic life-size wooden saints and other figures. There is a footpath along the shore of Lake Pátzcuaro.

During the week of February 1, the whole village honors **Nuestro Señor del Rescate** (Our Lord of the Rescue) with religious processions. The village also takes part in Holy Week celebrations.

SANTA CLARA DEL COBRE: COPPER CRAFTS

Although the copper mines that existed here during pre-Conquest times have been lost forever, local artisans still make copper vessels using the age-old method by which each piece is pounded out by hand. The streets of the village (also known as Villa Escalante) are lined with shops, and little boys pounce on every visitor to direct them to stores (where they get a commission). The **Museo del Cobre** (Copper Museum), half a block from the main plaza, at Morelos and Pino Suárez, is a fine introduction to the quality and styles of local work. A sales showroom to the left as you enter features the work of 77 local craftsmen. There's no admission; the museum is open daily from 10am to 3pm and 5 to 7pm.

The **National Copper Fair** is held here each August, which coincides on August 12 with the Festival of Our Lady of Santa Clara de Asis, and on August 15 with the Festival of the Virgin of the Sacred Patroness, with folk dancing and parades.

To get here from Pátzcuaro, take a bus from the Central Camionera (see "Getting There & Departing: By Bus," above). Buses back to Pátzcuaro run approximately every few minutes (or more) from the plaza. Cabs crammed full of people head back to Pátzcuaro for the same price as the bus.

During Easter Week and Days of the Dead, when Pátzcuaro's hotels fill up, it may be useful to know of two inexpensive hotels that face Santa Clara's main plaza: The **Hotel Oasis,** Portal Allende 144 (☎ 434/3-0040), the better of the two; and **Hotel Real del Cobre,** Portal Hidalgo 19 (☎ 343/3-0205), which has a restaurant.

TOCUARO & ERONGARICARO: MASKS & ONE-OF-A-KIND FURNITURE

Tocuaro, a village of mask carvers, and Erongaricaro, noted for its colonial center and furniture factory, are both easy jaunts from Pátzcuaro. Both are on the same road skirting the lake.

To find Tocuaro, walk the equivalent of three or four blocks from the highway where the bus lets you off. As you stroll the streets, villagers will ask you if you're interested in masks and invite you to their homes. When you want to return, go back to the highway and flag down a bus.

A few miles farther is Erongaricaro, formerly known for its textiles. Today its most famous factory, **Muebles Finos Artesanales Erongarícaro** (MFA/ ERONGA) (☎ and fax 434/4-0017), is the creator of whimsical folk-art-style furniture, some of which is copied by regional furniture makers. There's nothing quite like the fine furniture here, decorated with the likeness of Frida Kahlo, plump Botero-inspired figures, and forms that recall Gauguin or Picasso, among others. Their fine furniture designs are featured in the luxury Casa Que Canta hotel in the Pacific Coast village of Zihuatanejo, among other upscale places in Mexico and the States. Each piece is unique and expensive. This is a working factory and there's no showroom, so the owners, Maureen and Steve Rosenthal, kindly ask that only serious buyers arrive for a look around. The factory is open Monday through Friday from 9am to 2pm and 4 to 6pm. Their wholesale warehouse in Tucson, Arizona (☎ 602/798-1086) has a catalog.

TUPÁTARO & CUANAJO: A HISTORIC CHURCH & HAND-CARVED FURNITURE

The turnoff into these two colonial-era villages is approximately 20 miles northwest of Pátzcuaro off Highway 120 going to Morelia (see "Getting There & Departing," above). Each town possesses a unique attraction.

The narrow paved road passes first through tiny Tupátaro (pop. 600), which in Tarascan means "place of tule of Chuspata" ("tule" is a reed).

Just opposite the small main plaza is the Templo del Señor Santiago Tupátaro, unique in Mexico for its 18th-century painted ceiling. Restored in 1994 under a civilian program, it's still a parish church but is overseen by the Institute of Anthropology and History (INAH). The church was built in 1775 after the miraculous discovery of a crucifix formed in a pine tree. Indian artists, whose names are unknown today, brilliantly painted the entire wood-plank ceiling with scenes of the life and death of Christ and Mary. The magnificent gilt retablo, still intact, behind the altar features Solomonic columns and paintings. In the center of the retablo is Santiago (St. James), above which appears the face of the Eternal Father; above all is the sign of the dove.

When visitors arrive at the church, electric lights are turned on to illuminate the fabulous colors of the ceiling and the retablo. There's no admission charge and no photos are permitted. The church is open daily from 8am to 8pm. Days of religious significance here include the Tuesday of Carnaval week and July 25, which honors Santiago (St. James). Across the plaza a small cafe serves soft drinks and snacks and sells regional crafts.

Five miles farther is Cuanajo (pop. 8,000), a village devoted to hand-carved pine furniture and weaving. On the road as you enter and around the pleasant, tree-shaded main plaza, you'll see storefronts with colorful furniture inside and on the street. Parrots, plants, the sun, moon, and faces are among the myriad subjects carved into furniture, which is then painted with a fabulous combination of colors. Furniture is also sold at a cooperative on the main plaza. Here too you'll find softspoken women who weave exquisite tapestries and thin belts on waist looms. Motifs in their handsome tapestries include birds, people, and plants. Everything is for sale. It's open daily from 9am to 6pm.

Festival days in Cuanajo include **March 8** and **September 8,** both of which honor the patron saint Virgin María de la Natividad. These are solemn occasions when neighboring villages make processions carrying figures of the holy virgin.

IHUATZIO: TULE FIGURES & PRE-HISPANIC ARCHITECTURE

This little lakeside village is noted for its weavers of tule figures—fanciful animals such as elephants, pigs, and bulls made from a reed that grows on the edge of the lake—and for a rather spread-out group of pre-Hispanic buildings. The turnoff to Ihuatzio is on a paved road a short distance from the outskirts of Pátzcuaro on the road to Tzintzuntzán (see "Getting There & Departing: By Bus," above).

ZIRAHUÉN: A PRISTINE LAKE

To see one of the few lakes in Mexico that remains more or less in its natural state, visit Zirahuén, about 7 miles west of Pátzcuaro on the road to Uruapan. Since there are no regular buses, it's difficult to get to Zirahuén without a car. A taxi costs about $12 one way. Lakeside restaurants serve fish (inspect fish carefully for cleanliness by look and by smell).

URUAPAN: CRAFTS, A VISIT TO A VOLCANO & OTHER SIDE TRIPS

Uruapan, Michoacán, 38 miles west of Pátzcuaro and an hour away, has long been known for its lacquered boxes and trays. Although this city of 217,000 people has few tourist attractions of its own, it makes a good base for several interesting side trips, the most famous of which is to the Paricutín volcano and the lava-covered church and village near Angahuán. If you leave Pátzcuaro early and change buses in Uruapan for Angahuán, you can see Uruapan and Angahuán in a day. Otherwise you may wish to spend the night in Uruapan and start for Angahuán early the next day.

ESSENTIALS   The **tourist office** (☎ 542/3-6172), is in the shopping area below the Hotel Plaza, just off the main plaza. It's open Monday through Saturday from 9am to 2pm and 4 to 7pm.

The main plaza, **Jardín Morelos,** is actually a very long rectangle running east to west, with the churches and La Huatapera Museum on the north side and the Hotel Victoria on the south. Everything you need is within a block or two of the square, including the market, which is behind the churches.

Uruapan's main square is 20 blocks from the bus station. Minivans labeled "Centro" and "Central" (central bus station), circulate from the street in front of the bus station to the south side of the main plaza all day.

Be prepared for cold mornings and evenings from October through April; bring a heavy sweater and gloves. Few hotels have heat.

ACCOMMODATIONS   If you want to spend the night in Uruapan, consider three hotels by the main plaza: The inexpensive but neat **Hotel Villa de Flores,** Emiliano Carranza 15 (☎ 452/4-2800),and the slightly more expensive **Hotel Nuevo Hotel Alameda,** Av. 5 de Febrero 11 (452/3-3635). The best hotel in downtown and also by the plaza is the **Hotel Plaza Uruapan,** Ocampo 64

(☎ 452/3-3980). All have restaurants, and there are numerous good restaurants on or near the plaza.

EXPLORING URUAPAN   Uruapan's main plaza fills with craftspeople from around the state during the week before and after the **Day of the Dead** (November 1 and 2) and before and during **Easter week.** It's an unbelievable array of wares, all neatly displayed.

The **antojitos market,** opposite the monument in the middle of the main square, has copper, crosspoint blouses and tablecloths, hats, huaraches, caged birds, fresh vegetables, and lots of cookshops.

✪ **La Huatapera,** attached to the cathedral on the main square, is a fabulous museum of regional crafts. It is housed in a former hospital built in 1533 by Fray Juan de San Miguel, a Franciscan. It's open Tuesday through Sunday from 9:30am to 1:30pm and 3:30 to 6pm. Admission is free.

For the finest in foot-loomed tablecloths, napkins, and other beautifully made textiles, take a taxi to ✪ **Tellares Uruapan** (☎ 4-0677 or 4-6135), in the Antigua Fabrica de San Pedro. Call in advance, and the English-speaking owners may give you a tour of the factory, which contains fascinating turn-of-the-century machinery.

When you enter the **Parque Nacional Eduardo Ruíz,** a botanical garden eight blocks west of the main plaza, you'll feel like you're deep in the tropics. This multi-acre semitropical paradise includes jungle paths, deep ravines, rushing water, and clear waterfalls. Children pester visitors, offering to be their guides, but you'll enjoy touring more with only a map (25¢). The garden is open daily from 8am to 6pm, and there is a small admission fee. Buses marked "Parque" leave from in front of the telegraph office on the main square and stop at the park.

OUTSIDE URUAPAN   A Waterfall   A bus marked "Tzaráracua" goes to the impressive **A Waterfall at Tzaráracua,** 6 miles from the main plaza. The Río Cupatitzio originates as a bubbling spring in the national park and then forms a cascade on its way to the Pacific. A trip to Tzaráracua and to the national park can be made in a day, even in an afternoon. The falls are reached down a steep pathway.

Handmade Guitars   Often called Mexico's "Guitar Capital" for its fine hand-made guitars, **Paracho** is a 30-minute bus ride from Uruapan's Central Camionera. Take the Flecha Amarilla or Servicios Coordinados lines.

Angahuán & Paricutín Volcano   Twenty-one miles away from Uruapan, Angahuán is the village from which to launch trips to **Paricutín Volcano,** which began an extended eruption in 1943 that would eventually cover portions of this village under lava. Autotransportes Galeana buses leave every 30 minutes from Uruapan's Central Camionera for the hour-long trip.

If you don't know the story of how Paricutín appeared, stop by the plaza in Angahuán and take a look at the carved wooden door of a nearby house which faces the church, around the stone fence to the right, two doors down. The story of the volcano, carved in pictures and words, shows how a local man was plowing his cornfield in the valley on February 20, 1943, when at 3pm, the ground began to boil. At first he tried to stop it up; when that proved impossible, he decided to run. By that evening, rocks, smoke, and fire were flying up out of the ground. Some villagers fled that same night; others days later. The volcano was active for 9 years, growing larger and larger, until finally it breathed its last breath on March 6, 1952, stopping as suddenly as it had begun.

On arrival in Angahuán, tourists are besieged by guides ready to take them on horseback to see the half-buried **Church of San Juan Parangaricutiro,** looming silently up out of the lava, and to the crater of the volcano. Though a horse is not necessary, a guide is advisable.

The road to the volcano—not at all obvious (or marked) in the village—is a few blocks to the left of the plaza, with the church to the right. About half a mile down the road from Angahuán toward old San Juan and the lava flow is a state-run lodge/restaurant with bathrooms (the only ones in the area) and a stone patio with a good view of the church and volcanic cone. Unless there's an abundance of hikers or riders headed for the church, orient yourself here; once you're down in the woods, the church is not visible and there is a maze of unmarked trails in every direction. The walk to the church takes about an hour or so. There you can climb over the lava to the bell tower and see the mighty gray volcano in the distance.

Those who want to climb the volcano should allow at least 8 hours from Angahuán. The round-trip is about 14 miles. Take plenty of food and water because there's none along the way. The hike is mostly flat, with some steeper rises toward the end. Climbing the steep crater itself takes only about 40 minutes for those who exercise regularly, but count on more time to walk around the crater's rim on top (1 to 2 miles) to enjoy the spectacular view.

By horse, the trip to the church and volcano takes about 6 or 7 hours and costs $20 to $30, plus tip. The asking price for a horse to the volcano is $15 to $20 per horse—and you must also pay that amount for the guide's horse. It's possible to bargain the price down to a total of $25 (for two horses and a guide). However, don't be surprised when, a few kilometers into the ride, the guide asks for a tip to be paid at the end of the trip. My guide climbed to the top of the crater with me; pointed out various interesting features, including steaming *fumeroles*; and provided riding instructions and a good history of the area. Acting as a guide to the volcano is one of the few opportunities to earn money for the obviously poor Angahuán villagers. Just don't pay until the ride is over and the services were delivered as promised.

Plan to spend an entire day for the trip from Uruapan, the ride to the foot of the volcano, the short climb, the return to Angahuán, and the trip back to Uruapan.

The Southernmost States: Oaxaca, Chiapas & Tabasco

These three neighboring Mexican states span the distance from the Gulf of Mexico to the Pacific Ocean. **Oaxaca** is one of the country's poorest states but is richly endowed with tradition and culture. The state's handsome colonial-era capital city (also named Oaxaca) and the vast archaeological sites, Indian populations, and markets that surround it have drawn increasing numbers of tourists over the last 10 or so years. (See Chapter 11 for information about Oaxaca's Pacific coast resorts.) **Tabasco** and its cities have profited from the oil trade along its coast; the state is also noted for its production of tobacco and cacao. **Chiapas,** which is hemmed in by majestic mountains and an undeveloped coast, produces some of the best coffee in Mexico.

All three states boast important indigenous influences, evident even now in the everyday clothing, costumes, customs, and festivals of their peoples. The famous Olmec site, La Venta, is in Tabasco state; museums in Villahermosa, the capital, hold Olmec sculpture and artifacts. Numerous Indian groups in the state still speak Maya-related languages. Villahermosa is also a main route to the ruins of Palenque and an important gateway to San Cristóbal de las Casas, Chiapas, which is surrounded by indigenous villages. Each of these villages has unique language, cultural, and craft traditions. And finally, Oaxaca city is sandwiched between Mitla and Monte Albán, two important archeological sites; several lesser but still fascinating sites are nearby.

EXPLORING OAXACA, CHIAPAS & TABASCO

Many people who travel to this southernmost part of Mexico want to hit the highlights of all three states in one visit. Improved airline and bus service makes doing so easier than ever before. Some people arrive by bus or air in Villahermosa and continue inland by bus to Palenque and San Cristóbal, then on to Tuxtla Gutiérrez, flying from Tuxtla to Oaxaca. Others take the opposite approach, beginning at Oaxaca, flying to Tuxtla Gutiérrez, and from there traveling by bus to San Cristóbal, Palenque, and Villahermosa. This works well if you'll be moving on to the Yucatán Peninsula.

Palenque and San Cristóbal de las Casas are the two stellar attractions in the Tabasco-Chiapas area. You might budget your time in the following manner: Spend one day in Villahermosa and no less than a day (two nights) at Palenque. You'll want at least two days amid San Cristóbal's captivating culture and another two days to visit the outlying villages— try to spend at least four days there, but eight days would be even better. Oaxaca can be so engrossing that five days won't be nearly enough, particularly if you go during Christmas or the Day of the Dead. Try to plan on no less than four days there, allowing at least two days for seeing the ruins, at least a day in the city itself, and a day at craft villages and markets.

1 Oaxaca City

325 miles S of Mexico City, 144 miles S of Tehuacán, 168 miles N of Puerto Escondido

Oaxaca (pronounced "Wa-HAH-kah") is a booming commercial and industrial center located in a secluded valley 5,070 feet high in the rugged mountains. Although prosperity has given the city a cosmopolitan touch, its 800,000 residents, called Oaxaqueños (pronounced "Wah-HAH-kehn-yos"), have carefully preserved the colonial beauty of the central city so most visitors are almost unaware of the modern industry on the outskirts.

The Zapotecs came to this high valley about 800 B.C. and soon built a beautiful city and a flourishing culture at Monte Albán, six miles from the modern city. Evidence from White Cave, near Mitla, indicates the presence of primitive inhabitants in the valley as early as 10,000 B.C. Some authorities consider that Olmec influence reached the Oaxaca valley around 1200 B.C. However, it was the Zapotecs who created the city and a high-level culture, building monuments visible at the site today.

After this flowering of Zapotec culture (ca. A.D. 300–700), another tribe, the Mixtecs, built a rival center at Mitla, 36 miles away on the other side of what is today Oaxaca, and the two tribes struggled for control of the valley until the Aztec threat united them against the common enemy. However, even the two tribes united were no match for the Aztecs, and in the late 1400s and the early 1500s Aztec influence predominated.

The local tribes didn't have to worry about the Aztecs for long, however—an even more formidable enemy appeared in 1521. After the Spanish subdued the valley, they set up a military post called Antequera here; six years later the town of Oaxaca was founded. Hernán Cortés was later given the title of Marqués del Valle de Oaxaca by the Hapsburg emperor Charles V, and with the title came grants of land, some of which were controlled by Cortés's descendants until the Mexican Revolution in 1910.

Two of Mexico's presidents, Porfirio Díaz and Benito Juárez, were born near Oaxaca. Nobody does much to remember Díaz these days, but monuments to Juárez are everywhere: statues, murals, streets named for him, even a Benito Juárez University. In fact, the city's official name is Oaxaca de Juárez. A Zapotec, Juárez was born in the nearby village of Guelatao and "adopted" by a wealthy Oaxacan family who clothed, educated, and taught him Spanish in return for his services as a houseboy. He fell in love with the daughter of the household and promised he would become rich and famous and return to marry her. He managed all three, and Oaxaca adores him for it. Juárez attended law school, was the governor of the state of Oaxaca (1847–52), and later became a resistance leader and president of the republic. He is a national hero.

Oaxaca has become the destination of choice for travelers seeking colonial surroundings, archaeological sites, and indigenous creativity. The city is a

Oaxaca Area

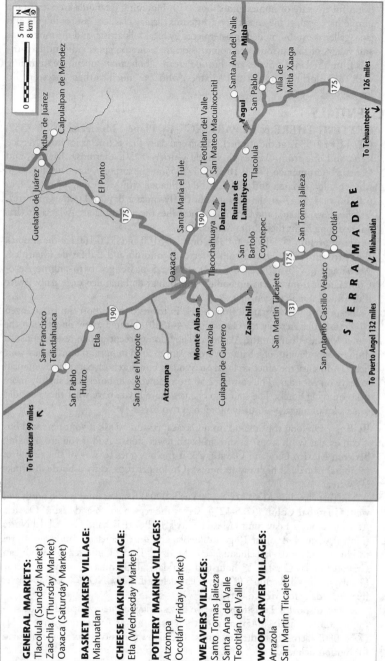

GENERAL MARKETS:
Tlacolula (Sunday Market)
Zaachila (Thursday Market)
Oaxaca (Saturday Market)

BASKET MAKERS VILLAGE:
Miahuatlan

CHEESE MAKING VILLAGE:
Etla (Wednesday Market)

POTTERY MAKING VILLAGES:
Atzompa
Ocotlán (Friday Market)

WEAVERS VILLAGES:
Santo Tomas Jalieza
Santa Ana del Valle
Teotitlán del Valle

WOOD CARVER VILLAGES:
Arrazola
San Martin Tilcajete

beautiful treasure of homes and shops, with blooming jacaranda trees casting a purple haze against the cobalt sky. Museums display classic treasures in gold and jade, galleries exhibit modern masterpieces by local folk artists, and the mountains and valleys of the surrounding countryside are a photographer's dream. Expatriates from the United States and Europe create a bohemian subculture, mingling with the colorful Zapotecs and Mixtecs, who live much as their ancestors did long ago.

ESSENTIALS

GETTING THERE & DEPARTING **By Plane** **Mexicana** (☎ 6-7352, 6-8414, or 1-5337 at the airport), has several daily flights to Oaxaca from Mexico City, and one from Oaxaca to Tuxtla Gutiérrez, Villahermosa, Mérida, and Cancún. **Aeroméxico** (☎ 6-1066 or 1-5055 at the airport), has daily flights to Mexico City. **Aviacsa and AeroCaribe** (affiliated with Mexicana, ☎ 6-0229, or 6-0266 or 1-5247 at the airport), both fly once a day to Tuxtla Gutiérrez, Villahermosa, Mérida and Cancún; Aviacsa flies the newer planes. Aviacsa also has an incoming night flight from Mexico City.

Aeromorelos (☎ 6-0974, 6-0975, or ☎ 1-5100 and fax 6-1002 at the airport), flies turboprop to Oaxaca from Puerto Escondido and Bahías de Huatulco. **AeroVega** (☎ 6-6294 or 6-2777), flies a 5-passenger twin-engine Aero-Commander from Puerto Escondido and Bahías de Huatulco once daily (twice if there are enough passengers).

Inexpensive transportation from hotels in town to the airport can be arranged by Transportes Aeropuerto Oaxaca (☎ 4-4350), located a few doors from the Hotel Monte Albán on the Alameda. They don't accept phone reservations, so drop by Monday through Saturday from 9am to 2pm or 5pm to 8pm to buy your ticket. And since the office is closed on Sunday, buy tickets on Saturday if you plan to leave on Monday. The cost is $2.50 from downtown hotels and slightly more from outlying hotels. The staff also charges more if you have what they consider to be a lot of luggage—usually more than two bags.

By Bus On long trips to and from Oaxaca, be sure to ask if your potential bus is con escalas (with stops) or directo (with fewer stops). And if you are traveling between Mexico City and Oaxaca, ask if the bus goes by way of the autopista (5 hours) or federal highway (9 hours). On longer trips, carry a bottle of drinking water.

The first class line **ADO** (☎ 5-1703 or 5-0903) handles most traffic north and west; **Cristóbal Colón** (☎ 5-1214) serves the region south and east of Oaxaca. At least 50 buses a day run to Mexico City's TAPO (East) and Central del Norte (North) stations. Another 10 go to Puebla, and 4 to Tehuacán. Buses also travel to Huatulco (1 a day); Tehuantepec (12 a day); Tuxtla Gutiérrez (5 a day); San Cristóbal de las Casas, a 13-hour trip (2 a day); Tapachula (1 a day); Veracruz (3 a day); and Villahermosa (2 a day). The deluxe **Linea UNO** (☎ 3-3550) leaves five times daily for Mexico City.

Autotransportes Turísticos has two buses a day to Puerto Escondido, departing at 8:30am and 10:45pm from their terminal at Armenta y López 721, (☎ 4-0806) across from the Red Cross. The highway is curvaceous, so be prepared for motion sickness.

Fletes y Pasajes, at the second-class station, has frequent departures for most of the villages surrounding the city. Buses for Guelatao (birthplace of Benito

Juárez) leave from the second-class station several times daily. Buy your tickets a day in advance to be sure of space and a good seat.

By Car   It's an easy 5-hour drive from Mexico City, via the toll road. About 50 miles east of Puebla the new toll road, opened in late 1994, goes south to terminate in Oaxaca. For adventurous souls, the old federal highway still winds through the mountains and offers spectacular views for some 9 or 10 hours.

ORIENTATION   Arriving by Plane   The airport is south of town, about a 20-minute (and $10) cab ride. Transportes Aeropuerto Oaxaca, Alameda de León 1A (☎ 4-4350), operates an airport minibus service between the hotels in the center of town and the airport at a cost of $2.50 each way.

Arriving by Bus   The Central Camionera first-class bus station is north of the center of town on the main highway (Calzada Niños Héroes de Chapultepec). Taxis between here and the zócalo cost about $2.50. City bus transportation must be caught several blocks down the street. Turn right as you leave the station to get to the intersection of Niños Héroes and Vasconcelos (look for buses marked "Col. América" and "Col. Reforma." Or turn left for two blocks to Juárez ("Centro" buses go to the zócalo, "Central" buses go to the second class terminal.) But remember that large suitcases or backpacks are not totally compatible with a crowded city bus.

The Central Camionera de Segunda Clase (second-class bus terminal) is near the Abastos market buildings; walk eight blocks west (the cathedral faces west) from the zócalo on Trujano (across the railroad tracks). Or take an "Estación" bus along Hidalgo. Buses from the second-class station go to such outlying villages as Guelatao, Mitla, and Teotitlán del Valle.

Information   The municipal Tourist Office (Oficina de Turismo) is at the corner of Morelos and Cinco de Mayo (☎ 951/6-4828; fax 951/6-1550); it's open daily from 8am to 8pm. The well staffed and extremely helpful State Tourist office is located across from the Alameda at Independencia 607, (corner of García Vigil; ☎ 6-0984). It's open daily from 9am to 3pm and 6 to 8pm.

City Layout   Oaxaca's central historic section was laid out on a north-south and east-west grid. The cathedral faces west toward the Alameda Park, and the Palacio del Gobierno faces north overlooking the zócalo. Do not confuse the Plaza Alameda with the zócalo. Oaxaca's **zócalo** is one of the prettiest main plazas in Mexico. The city streets change names here. North-south streets change at Independencia, while east-west streets change at Alcalá/Bustamante. Alcalá is closed to all but cross-street traffic from Avenida Independencia to Avenida Gurrión (at the Santo Domingo church), forming a pedestrian mall. Most of the more expensive hotels, restaurants, and galleries are located north of the zócalo; the market and inexpensive hotels are south.

North, near the first-class bus station, is **Parque Paseo Juárez,** also known as El Llano. This is where families, children, teens and lovers congregate both by day and by night: groups practicing dance steps, children learning to skate, joggers running or stretching, they are all there. Here you see the life of the city.

GETTING AROUND   By Bus   Buses to the outlying villages of Guelatao, Teotitlán del Valle, and Mitla leave from the second-class station just north of the Abastos Market. City buses run along Juárez and Pino Suárez, Tinoco y Palacios and Porfirio Díaz, and others.

By Taxi   Colectivo taxis depart to the villages from Calle Mercadores, on the south side of the Abastos Market. You can negotiate rides to the ruins based on the number of people in your group. The average cost is around $10 per hour, which can be shared with up to five people. A regular taxi stand is along Independencia at the north side of the Alameda, while another is on Calle Murguía just south of the Hotel Camino Real. An honest, careful, and dependable English-speaking driver, **Tomás Ramírez,** can be found here, or reached at his home (☎ 1-5061).

FAST FACTS: OAXACA

American Express   The office, in Viajes Misca, is at Valdivieso and Hidalgo (northeast corner of the zócalo; ☎ 951/6-2700; fax 951/6-7475). Office hours are Monday through Friday from 9am to 2pm and 4 to 6pm and on Saturday from 9am to 1pm. Here you will find both their travel agency and financial services office.

Area Code   The telephone area code is 951.

Consulates   Several consulates can be contacted through Grupo Consular, upstairs at Hidalgo 817 #4 (☎ 951/4-2744). The U.S. Consular Agency is at Alcalá 201 (☎ and fax 951/6-4272 or 4-3054). Hours are Monday through Friday from 9am to 1pm.

Currency Exchange   Banks change dollars only from Monday through Friday, from 9am to 12:30pm. Look for a window saying COMPRA Y VENTA DE DIVISAS. Most banks charge a commission for cashing travelers checks, and Banpaís charges a small fee for changing dollars. There are several casas de cambio (money-changing storefronts) around the plaza, most of which offer a slightly lesser exchange rate than the banks. Most require a Tourist Card or passport as identification.

One such storefront is Interdisa (☎ 951/6-3399 or 4-3098) near the corner of Valdivieso and the zócalo, just around the corner (right) from the Hotel Marqués del Valle. It's open Monday through Saturday from 8am to 8pm and Sunday from 9am to 5pm.

Canadian visitors can exchange money at Banamex, Bancomer, Comermex and others.

Newspapers/Magazines   The English newspaper *The News,* published in Mexico City, is sold for $1 at newsstands ($1.50 on Sunday). There is a supply of English language magazines at the Biblioteca Circulante. The monthly give-away *Oaxaca Times,* published in English, is available at the Tourist Offices and many hotels. Another monthly, *OAXACA,* is tri-lingual (English, Spanish and French) and is widely available.

Post Office   The Correos (main post office) is at the corner of Independencia and the Alameda Park. It is open Monday to Friday from 9am to 7pm and Saturday 9am to 1pm.

Safety   Petty crime is increasing in Oaxaca. Take normal precautions and you should have no trouble: park your car in a lot overnight, don't leave anything in the car within view, watch your property at all times when you're waiting in the bus station, and be especially careful of very professional pickpockets in the markets and buses—they can take your wallet out of your back or front pocket, handbag, or knapsack and you won't know it until the time comes to pay for dinner. Luckily, violent crime (including mugging) is still very rare here. In most cases, the police are of little help.

Shipping   Oaxaca is a shoppers' delight, and it's hard to keep from accumulating huge quantities of pottery, rugs, and other heavy goods that must be sent home. Many of the better shops can arrange shipping, but if your goods have come from the markets and villages you'll need to ship them yourself. The first rule of shipping is this: you must have a receipt. That means carrying a notebook and asking merchants to write out a receipt for you when you shop. All shipped items must be stamped HECHO EN MÉXICO (Made in Mexico). Mexicana airlines has a cargo office at Libres 617 (☎ 951/5-3711), open Monday through Saturday from 9am to 8pm, and it can ship your goods to any gateway cities in the United States that have U.S. customs offices. Mexicana requires eight copies of your receipts and charges a minimum of $120 for 1 to 20 kilos (2 to 44 lbs.) to send a package to, for example, Los Angeles. To avoid shipping, however, remember you're allowed two suitcases on a flight.

EXPLORING OAXACA

There are several very good museums, convents, and colonial buildings in Oaxaca, as well as a wonderful zócalo where the band plays every other night, and sidewalk cafes provide the perfect place for travelers and locals to watch the action. There are also many interesting excursions—to nearby ruins at Monte Albán and Mitla, or to the outlying Indian villages for pottery, wood carving, and textiles. You'll want to visit Oaxaca's market and the various popular art shops around town; the craft work of this state is some of the finest in Mexico. Remember that Oaxaqueños observe the siesta from 2 to 4pm and most shops and museums will be closed.

The life of the city centers around the zócalo, bordered by Avenidas Hidalgo, Trujano, Magón, and Valdivieso. Calle Magón becomes García Vigil to the north and Cabrera to the south, while Valdivieso becomes Alcalá to the north and Bustamante to the south. The white wrought-iron gazebo in the center and several fountains along the pathways make it a delightful place to walk or sit. This is the place from which to orient yourself.

To get a feel for this lovely city, I recommend walking around town to see the churches and monuments, and then (mañana) a visit to the Regional Museum and the Rufino Tamayo Museum of pre-Hispanic art.

SPECIAL EVENTS

Oaxaca is famous for its festivals, filled with the color and exuberance of traditional life. The most important ones are during Holy Week at Easter, the Guelaguetza in July, Días de los Muertos in November, and the Radish Festival in December. Make hotel reservations well in advance if you plan to visit during these times.

During **Holy Week** (the principal activities of which begin the Thursday before Easter Sunday), figurines made of palm leaves are made and sold on the streets by village families. On Palm Sunday (the Sunday before Easter) there are colorful parades, and on the following Thursday, Oaxaca residents follow the Procession of the Seven Churches. Hundreds of the pious move from church to church, taking communion in each one to ensure a prosperous year. The next day, Good Friday, many of the barrios have "Encuentros," where groups depart separately from the church, carrying relics through the neighborhoods, then "encountering" each other back at the church. Throughout the week each church sponsors concerts, fireworks, fairs, and other entertainment.

On the Mondays following the last two weekends in July you can witness the **Fiesta Guelaguetza,** or Feast of Monday of the Hill. In the villages, a guelaguetza is held by a family needing to acquire the means of holding a wedding or other obligatory community celebration. Gifts are catalogued and will be repaid in kind at other guelaguetzas. In Oaxaca it has been a civic celebration since 1974, when the stadium was built.

During these last two weeks in July there are fairs and exhibits, and regional dances are performed in the stadium on the Cerro del Fortín each Monday (about 10am to 1pm). It's a marvelous spectacle of color, costumes, music, and dance. Some 350 different huipils and dresses can be seen during the performance as the villages of the seven regions of Oaxaca present their traditional dances. Admission ranges from free (in Section C) to $50–$75 (in Section A), and tickets must be reserved in advance through the State Tourism office (no later than May). A travel agency may be able to help you. I recommend Sections 5 and 6 in Palco A for the best seating in the Cerro del Fortín stadium. The color of your ticket matches the color of your seat. You will be sitting in strong sunlight, so wear a hat and long sleeves. At about 7:30 in the evening, following the Guelaguetza dances, a free performance of the Legend of Donají is presented in the stadium.

On the Sunday nights before the Guelaguetza, university students present an excellent program in the Plaza de la Danza at the Soledad church. The production is called the Bani Stui Gulal, and is an abbreviated history of the Oaxaca valley. The program begins at 9pm, but since the event is free and seating is limited, you should get there quite early.

The **Días de los Muertos** (Days of the Dead), November 1 and 2, are next to Easter in importance and blend Indian and Hispanic customs. Markets brim with marigolds and offerings for altars built to honor the dead. Be sure to take one of the night cemetery tours offered around this time. An excellent one is offered out of Casa Arnel (☎ 951/5-2856, fax 3-6285). They leave for Xoxo (pronounced "ho-ho") around 10pm on October 31, taking flowers and candles to be placed on tombs that have no visitors, and return about 1:30am. Cost is $15.50. Viajes Mitla, in the Hotel Mesón del Angel (☎ and fax 951/6-6175) goes to a different village each night and the cost ranges for $16 to $19.

Xoxo is the most traditional on Oct. 31, but other villages have different kinds of festivities on the next two nights, some of them quite carnival-like with masked street dancers and no cemetery vigil.

The **December Festivals** begin on the 12th, with the festival of the Virgen de Guadalupe, and continue on the 16th with a *calenda,* or procession, to many of the older churches in the barrios, all accompanied by dancing and costumes. Festivities continue on the 18th with the Fiesta de la Soledad in honor of the Virgen de la Soledad, patroness of Oaxaca state. On that night there is a cascade of fire from a "castle" erected for the occasion in Plaza de la Soledad. December 23 is **the Night of the Radishes,** when the Oaxaqueños build fantastic sculptures out of radishes (the most prized vegetable cultivated during the colonial period), as well as flowers, leaves, and fruits. They are on display in the Alameda, just off the zócalo. On December 24 each Oaxacan church organizes a procession with music, floats, and crowds bearing candles.

New Year's Eve is celebrated with the Petition of the Cross, where villagers from all over come to a forlorn chapel on the hill beyond Tlacolula (about 22 miles southeast of Oaxaca, near Mitla) to light candles and express their wishes for the coming new year. Mock bargaining, with sticks and stones to represent livestock

Downtown Oaxaca

Basílica de
la Soledad **5**
Cathedral **8**
Church of
San Felipe Neri **12**
House of Benito
Juárez **2**
Instituto de Artes
Gráficas **1**
Mercado de
Artesanias **11**
Museo del Arte
Contemporanea
(MACO) **7**
Regional Museum
of Oaxaca **3**
Rufino Tamayo
Museum of Pre-
Hispanic Art **6**
San Juan de Dios **10**
Santo Domingo
Church **4**
Teatro Macedonio
de Alcalá **9**

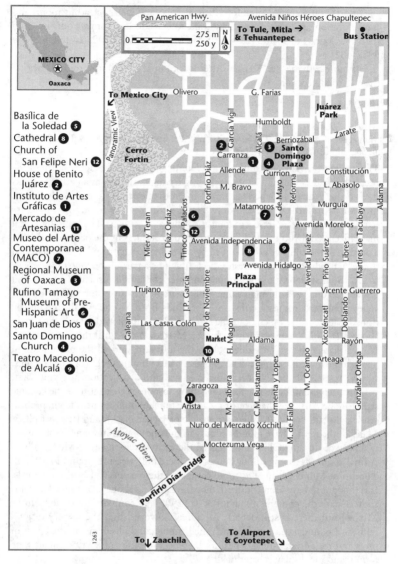

and produce, is part of the traditional way of expressing hopes for the new year. Tiny symbolic farms and fields are built in the hope for real prosperity.

At festival time in Oaxaca, sidewalk stands are set up in the market areas and near the cathedral to sell buñuelos, the Mexican equivalent of a papadum (a delicacy from India), only sweet. You'll be served your buñuelo in a cracked or otherwise flawed dish or bowl, and after you're finished you smash the crockery on the sidewalk for good luck. Don't be timid! After a while, you may find yourself buying more and more buñuelos—about 90¢ each—just for the fun of smashing plates.

Note: If you want to come for Christmas or the Guelaguetza but rooms and transportation are booked, you may want to consider Sanborn's Tours for both festivals. Contact them at 2015 S. 10th St., McAllen, TX 78502 (☎ toll free 800/ 395-8482).

For more activities see "Oaxaca After Dark" and "Road Trips from Oaxaca" at the end of this section.

MUSEUMS

Regional Museum of Oaxaca

Gurrión at Alcalá. ☎ **951/6-2991.** Admission $3.25; free Sun and holidays. Tues–Fri 10am– 6pm. Sat, Sun & holidays 10am–5pm.

This former convent next to the Santo Domingo Church six blocks north of the zócalo has had a colorful history, including having been used as an army barracks during the War of Independence. All the rooms open onto the lovely arched interior courtyard, where the only sound is that of the fountain. There are remnants of elaborate frescoes along the walls and ceilings. The building is still magnificent, and you can feel the pervasive peacefulness of the place. Until 1994 a portion of the convent was occupied by the military. That area has been returned to the state which has begun restoration. It will be a part of the museum.

On the first floor, the first room you enter contains a display of objects and artifacts leading you through some 8000 years of human history in the Oaxaca valley. The next rooms are dedicated to finds from Monte Albán, the nearby ruined Zapotec city, which flourished from 600 B.C. until its decline beginning in about A.D. 800. Later occupation by the Mixtecs lasted until the 15th century. Unfortunately there's no guidebook to the museum, and all the plaques are in Spanish. Here are a few hints: The Zapotecs had a number system of bars and dots, similar to that of the Olmecs and the Maya, and a collection of glyphs that, perhaps, represent a calendar; another thing to note is that most of the ceramic sculpture here has the characteristic Zapotec touches of prominent teeth, proboscises, elaborate headgear (often as an eagle or jaguar mask), and large ear plugs. Many of the figures have mouths similar to the ones found in Olmec sculpture— it's thought that the Olmecs influenced the early development of Monte Albán. A final room on the first floor houses the incredible treasures found in 1932 in Tomb 7 at Monte Albán. The tomb contained the remains of 12–14 individuals. It is thought to have been constructed by the Zapotecs about A.D. 500, while some sources date the contents to about A.D. 1250. The contents are thought to be Mixtec, but there is still debate. All agree, however, that the jewelry in gold (almost 8 pounds), turquoise, conch shell, amber, and obsidian and the bowls of onyx and rock crystal are very beautiful. Some 500 pieces of jewelry and art were found, and the display is breathtaking.

On the upper floor are rooms devoted to an ethnographic exhibit of regional crafts and costumes; mannequins dressed in authentic regional dress portray facets of religious, social, and cultural life. This, and the exhibit of items from the Dominican presence in Oaxaca, are not always open. But the gallery of Oaxacan history is, and is worth a visit.

Rufino Tamayo Museum of Pre-Hispanic Art

Av. Morelos 503. ☎ **951/6-4750.** Admission $2.25. Mon and Wed–Sat 10am–2pm and 4–7pm, Sun 10am–3pm. Closed Tuesday and holidays.

The artifacts displayed in this unique museum were chosen "solely for the aesthetic rank of the works, their beauty, power, and originality." The result is one of the most beautiful museums in all Mexico. The collection was amassed over a 20-year period by artist Rufino Tamayo, born in Oaxaca. The artifacts range from the Pre-Classical Period up to the Aztecs: terra-cotta figurines, scenes of daily life, lots of female fertility figures, Olmecan and Totonac sculpture from the Gulf Coast, and Zapotec long-nosed god figures. Plaques in Spanish give the period, culture, and location of each find, but you'll find yourself ignoring this information and just admiring the works and displays. The rooms are beautiful in themselves and are painted pink, blue, lavender, green, and orange in succession. To get to the museum, walk two blocks north of the zócalo on Alcalá to Morelos, then left two and a half blocks. It's between Tinoco y Palacios and Porfirio Díaz.

Oaxaca Museum of Contemporary Art

Alcalá 202, between Matamoros and Morelos. ☎ **951/6-8499.** Admission free (donation requested). Daily 9am–9pm.

Also known as the House of Cortés (and formerly the Museum of the City of Oaxaca), this museum is 2½ blocks north of the zócalo. It exhibits the work of contemporary artists, primarily from Oaxaca state. The museum also hosts international exhibits. If there's an opening night, join the crowd; concerts and other cultural events are also held in the main patio. A second patio has a cafe and cine club. A fine small bookstore is to your right as you enter. The beautifully restored 16th-century building housing the museum was supposedly built on the order of conqueror Hernán Cortés after receiving the title of Marqués of the Valley of Oaxaca (he died in Spain without seeing it).

Institute of Graphic Arts

Alcalá 507. ☎ **951/6-6980.** Admission free (donation requested). Wed–Mon 10:30am–8pm. Closed Tues.

Also known simply as IAGO, the Institute features an outstanding national and international graphic arts collection, which contains the works of Goya, Posada, Tamayo, Toledo and others. Prints, drawings and posters comprise the collection and there is a fine library of over 6,000 volumes (including videos) spread over several rooms. The front gallery features traveling exhibits and there is a small bookstore. Housed in the former residence of the Toledo family, the Institute was inaugurated in late 1988, and is located across from the front of the Santo Domingo church.

CHURCHES

Cathedral of Oaxaca

Fronting the Parque Alameda. No phone. Admission free. Daily 7am–9pm.

Anchoring the east end of the Alameda is the cathedral, originally built in 1553 and reconstructed in 1773. It has an elaborate 18th-century baroque facade and a glittering interior with three naves and many side chapels. It contains a bronze sculpture above the altar, a huge pipe organ, stained-glass windows and fine etched-glass doors.

Basílica de la Soledad

Independencia at Galeana. No phone. Admission to museum 25¢. Museum, Mon–Sat 10am–2pm and 4–6pm. Sun 11am–2pm. Basílica, daily 7am–2pm and 4–9pm.

The basílica, the most important religious center in Oaxaca, is seven blocks west of the zócalo. Here is where you'll find a representation of the Virgen de la Soledad sculpted in black stone and resting high on the west wall (around to the left as you face the church). The basílica is actually a huge complex of buildings, including a garden, convent, and museum. A small outdoor patio/theater (Plaza de la Danza), with stone and concrete step/seats lies just in front of the church grounds; here spectators can witness the famous Bani Stui Gulal (see "Special Events," above). The original church, begun in 1582, was much damaged by the many earthquakes which occurred during the early years of the Conquest, and was rebuilt in 1682–90. The Basílica has four levels on the outside, each decorated with carvings of saints. The interior is an overpowering array of chandeliers, angels, gilt ceiling, paintings, and statues. The figure of La Virgen de la Soledad (patroness of the State of Oaxaca) is above the altar in the basílica. A copy is in the museum at the back of the church, to your right as you exit. Both statues are draped in black velvet and the copy resides in a chapel filled with white wedding regalia made of glass, pearl, and plastic. Other items of interest include a 3-foot-square case containing innumerable miniature glass figurines (birds, angels, animals, and flowers) surrounding the Christ Child, many 18th century retablos expressing thanks for favors granted, and a four panel stained-glass representation of the legend of the finding of the Virgen's carved head and hands. The garden outside the museum has a life-size metal sculpture of the legendary mule train in which the mysterious chest was found.

✪ Santo Domingo Church

Corner of Gurrión and Alcalá. No phone. Admission free. Daily 7am–2pm and 4–11pm.

There are 27 churches in Oaxaca, but you should make a special effort to see this one next to the Regional Museum of Oaxaca, six blocks north of the zócalo. Don't judge a church by its facade. Started in the 1550s by Dominican friars and finished a century later, it contains the work of all the best artists of that period. The walls and ceiling are covered with ornate plaster statues and flowers, most of them gilded. The sun shines through the yellow stained-glass window, casting a golden glow over the whole interior. There is a large gilded rosary chapel to the right as you enter. Also, be sure to notice the genealogical tree of the Guzman family in the apse (Don Felíz de Guzman founded the church). If you are there around 11am Mon–Sat, you are likely to hear the lovely sound of the gift shop operator singing her devotions in the Rosario chapel. It is worth timing your visit for this.

Church of San Felipe

Tinoco y Palacios at Independencia. No phone. Admission free. Daily 8am–11pm.

This church 2¹/₂ blocks northeast of the zócalo was built in 1636 and displays all the architectural opulence of that period: the altar and nave are covered with ornately carved and gilded wood, and the walls are frescoed—ornate but not overpowering. In the west transept/chapel is a small figure of St. Martha and the dragon; the faithful have bedecked her with ribbons, praying that she assist them in vanquishing their woes (often a spouse).

San Juan de Dios

20 de Noviembre s/n, corner Aldama and Arteaga. No phone. Admission free. Daily 6am–11pm.

This is the earliest church in Oaxaca, built in 1521 or 1522 of adobe and thatch. The present structure was begun during the mid-1600s, and included a convent and hospital (where the 20 de Noviembre market is now). The exterior is nothing special but the interior has an ornate altar and paintings on the ceiling by Urbano Olivera. A glass shrine to the Virgen near the entrance and one to Christ (off to the right) are especially revered by Oaxaqueños. Because it's by the market, one block west and two blocks south of the zócalo, many of the people who visit the church are villagers who've come in to buy and sell. There's an interesting guitar mass on Sunday at 1pm.

SPANISH, ART & COOKING CLASSES

The **Instituto Cultural Oaxaca A.C.,** Av. Juárez 909 (Apdo. Postal 340), Oaxaca, Oax. 68000, Mexico (☎ 951/5-3404; fax 951/5–3728), offers Spanish classes for foreigners, as well as workshops with Mexican artisans such as weavers, potters, and cooks. There are also lectures emphasizing Oaxaca's history, archeology, anthropology, and botany. Although the normal course length is four weeks, arrangements can be made for as short a period as a week, and the Institute will arrange inexpensive housing with local families. The Institute itself is housed in a lovely old hacienda next to the Pan American Highway. Even a short time at the Institute will give you a better understanding of both the language and Oaxaca.

The **Instituto de Comunicación y Cultura,** Alcalá 307-12, Oaxaca, Oax. 68000 (☎/fax 951/6-3443), provides group or private Spanish instruction to many satisfied students. They can also arrange for home-stays with a Mexican family.

Seasons of My Heart Cooking School chef Susana Trilling offers professional instruction in the creation of the mole of Oaxaca. Available are Day classes, Long Weekend classes, Week-long Group classes (twice per year), and Group Market and Ruin Tours. Raw materials used are purchased in the markets or are gathered wild, and emphasis is placed on "hands-on" experience rather than mere observation. Classes are held in Susana's kitchen at Rancho Aurora, a half hour from downtown Oaxaca. Students stay in the city, and are transported to the school daily. There's also a small bed-and-breakfast at Rancho Aurora. For information, contact Susana at Apartado Postal 42, Admon. 3, Oaxaca, Oax., 68101 Mexico (fax 951/6-5280).

OTHER ATTRACTIONS

Teatro Macedonio de Alcalá
Independencia at Armenta y López. No phone. Open only for events.

This beautiful 1903 belle époque theater, two blocks east of the zócalo, holds 1,300 people and is still used for concerts and performances in the evening. Peek through the doors to see the marble stairway and Louis XV vestibule. A list of events is sometimes posted on the doors.

Cerro del Fortín
Díaz Ordaz at Calle Delmonte. No phone.

To take all this sightseeing in at a glance, those with cars can drive to this hill at the west of town from which you can get a panoramic view of the city, especially good just before sunset. Recognize the hill by a statue of—who else?—Benito Juárez and a stadium built to hold 15,000 spectators. The annual Fiesta Guelaguetza is held here.

You can walk to the hill as well. Head up Díaz Ordaz/Crespo and look for the Escaleras del Fortín (Stairway to the Fortress) shortly after you cross Calle

Delmonte; the 180 plus steps (interrupted by risers) are a challenge, but the view is worth it.

SHOPPING

It's a toss-up as to what tourists do first in Oaxaca: see the nearby ruins or shop. Oaxaca and the surrounding villages have some of the country's best buys in locally hand-crafted pottery, wood carvings, and textiles. It's easy to buy more than you ever imagined, so come prepared with extra suitcases. Note: Before you load down with tons of pottery, wood carvings, and weavings, however, keep in mind that your luggage is weighed at flight check-in. You'll be charged a fee for bags over 25 kilos (slightly over 55 lbs.). The transport bus to the airport also charges extra for passengers with overly bulky or excess baggage.

ARTS & CRAFTS

Several of the stores mentioned below are on the pedestrians-only Alcalá (but watch out for motorbikes), which has been closed to traffic from Independencia to Gurrión, making it a most pleasant place to browse. The Benito Juárez Market (see "City Markets," below) mainly features meat, produce and household needs. The 20 de Noviembre Market, a block further south, has a huge crafts section. Both markets can be accessed from either Cabrera or 20 de Noviembre streets, both of which are open to traffic.

Artesanías y Industrias Populares del Estado de Oaxaca (ARIPO)
García Vigil 809. ☎ **951/6-9211.**

The State of Oaxaca runs ARIPO, which includes a workshop and store. It is located two blocks farther up the hill beyond the Benito Juárez house. You can hear looms working in the back as you browse through the handicrafts expertly displayed in the many rooms. ARIPO has possibly the widest selection of black pottery in the city. There's also a good supply of masks, clothing, and cutlery. Open Monday through Saturday from 9am to 7:30pm to 7pm, at the corner of Vigil and Cosijopi.

Arte y Tradición
García Vigil 406. ☎ **951/6-3552.**

Four blocks north of the zócalo and just around the corner from the FONART store, a brightly painted doorway leads one into this attractive arcade of shops with an open patio in the center. Each shop functions as a cooperative, with articles on consignment from the various villages, such as Teotitlán del Valle, Arrazola, etc. Individuals from these villages are on hand to explain the crafts (weaving, wood-carving, etc.) as practiced by their townspeople. You'll also find an excellent restaurant serving authentic Oaxacan cuisine, the Belaguetza Travel Agency and a small bookstore. The English-speaking manager, Judith Reyes, is a real dynamo and has tremendous pride in her Mixtec heritage. The store is open daily 9am to 8pm, although the individual shop hours may vary.

FONART
M. Bravo 116. ☎ **951/6-5764.**

Oaxaca's branch of this government-supported chain is on M. Bravo at García Vigil. The name stands for Fondo Nacional para el Fomento de las Artesanías. Prices are fixed. Featuring a wide selection of native crafts from all over Mexico, the store is open Monday through Saturday from 9am to 2pm and 4 to 7pm.

Galería Arte de Oaxaca
Murgía 105. ☎ and fax **951/4-0910** or 4-1532.

Owner Nancy Mayagoitia has made this the city's best showcase for the state's lead-ing contemporary artists. There's always something artistically exciting happening here. Open Monday through Friday from 11am to 3pm and 5 to 9pm.; Saturday 11am to 3pm. You'll find it two blocks north and one block east of the zócalo.

La Mano Mágica
Alcalá 203. ☎ **951/6-4275.**

This gallery of contemporary and popular art is across from the city museum. The name means "magic hand," and it's a true celebration of Oaxacan artistic crea-tivity. Fine exhibits of paintings by local artists occupy the front room. The back rooms are full of regional folk art by the area's best artisans, folk who carry on an inherited artistic tradition in their village homes. Pieces are personally selected by owners Mary Jane and Arnulfo Mendoza (don't miss his weavings). They can help you ship purchases anywhere in the world via DHL courier service. Located between Morelos and Matamoros opposite the Museum of Contemporary Art/MACO (House of Cortés), it's open Monday through Saturday from 10am to 1:30pm and 4 to 7:30pm.

Mercado de Artesanías
J. P. García at Zaragoza.

If the crafts section of the Benito Juárez market mentioned under "City Markets," below, leaves you wanting, this is a good place to get an overview of Oaxaca's folk arts, particularly textiles. Women and men weave rugs, belts, huipils, serapes, and bags on looms and display their finest work. Ask the artisans where they're from and you'll get an idea of which villages you'd like to visit. Located one block south and one block west of the 20 de Noviembre Market and four blocks south and two blocks west of the zócalo, it's open daily from 10am to 4pm.

Victor's
Porfirio Díaz 111. ☎ **951/6-1174.**

This art shop in a 17th-century monastery is managed by Sr. Ramón Fosado, who goes to the villages himself in search of the best native art. He speaks English and is very pleasant. If you're shopping for serapes and blankets, be sure to stop at Victor's to do a little research. The quality of these goods varies, but the friendly staff here are willing to tell you about the differences in materials (wool vs. synthetic), dyes (natural and chemical), and designs. You should also scout around and compare the various products in the open markets. Open Monday through Saturday from 9am to 2pm and 4 to 8pm.

Yalalag de Oaxaca
Alcalá 104. ☎ **951/6-2108.**

This old mansion near the corner of Alcalá and Morelos displays a multifarious but affordable collection of art. Black pottery, Talavera ceramics, terra-cotta figurines, tin sculpture, table linens, apparel, papier-mâché sculpture, and other quality crafts from all over Mexico can be found here. Open Monday through Saturday from 9:30am to 1:30pm and 4:30 to 8pm.

CHOCOLATE & MOLE

Although Oaxaca produces some chocolate, most that is processed here comes from Tabasco and Chiapas. The state is better known for its 20 (more or less) varieties of mole (pronounced "moh-lay"), of which chocolate is often an ingredient; it comes in colors of red, yellow, black, brown, and green. Mole is used to make a sauce usually served over turkey or chicken but also as a flavoring in regional tamales. In the market area, strolling vendors sell chocolate in thick half-dollar–size cakes usually six or eight to the package. However, you'll have more choices (and more fun deciding) if you buy it in a store specializing in chocolate. Establishments that sell fresh chocolate often also grind and mix the ingredients for mole and sell it in a paste. Mole can be found in heaps in both the Abastos and Benito Juárez markets (see "City Markets," below), at grinders on Mina, or at the Chocolate Mayordomo mentioned below. Mole keeps for a year if stored in a refrigerator.

Chocolate Mayordomo

20 de Noviembre at Mina. ☎ **951/6-1619** or 6-0246.

This corner store is actually a huge operation with another outlet across the street on Mina and several others throughout the city. All sell chocolate and mole, their mix or ground to your specifications. Here you'll find shelves of boxed chocolate either amargo (unsweetened) or semidulce (semisweet), with or without almonds and/or cinnamon, in small, hard cakes or in a soft paste. Either is used in cooking or for making hot chocolate. A half-kilo of chocolate costs around $1.50; gift boxes of plastic-wrapped fresh black or red mole are also found here for $3.50 per kilo. They make excellent gifts for friends back home. Ask General Manager Salvador Flores about chocolate—you'll learn a lot! The store is open daily from 8am to 8:30pm.

CITY MARKETS

Abastos Market

Across the railroad tracks and just south of the second-class bus station.

The Abastos Market is open daily but is most active on Saturday, when Indians from the villages come to town to sell and shop. You'll see huge mounds of dried chilies, herbs, vegetables, crafts, bread, and even burros for sale at this bustling market.

Benito Juárez Market

Bordered by Las Casas, Cabrera, Aldama and 20 de Noviembre.

One block south of the zócalo, this covered market is big and busy every day, but especially on Saturday. The area around it is then an open street market, teeming with vendors of chilies, string, parrots, talismans, food, spices, cloth, dresses, blankets—one of the most exciting markets in Mexico, because the people who come to sell their wares are so colorful. The bulk of the produce trade has been relocated to a new building called the Abastos Market (see above), where the local color is even more profound.

20 de Noviembre Market

Bordered by Las Casas, Cabrera, Mina and 20 de Noviembre.

Anchored on the northwest corner by the San Juan de Dios church and immediately south of, and truly a continuation of, the Juárez market, this one has its own separate name. It occupies the area where once stood the convent and hospital of the San Juan de Dios church. In addition to many food products, there are innumerable cookshops offering juices and complete meals.

SHOPPING IN THE OUTLYING VILLAGES

One of the main reasons many people come to Oaxaca is to visit the markets and crafts villages nearby. For market days in outlying villages and directions to the wood-carvers and other crafts villages of importance, see "Road Trips from Oaxaca," below.

ACCOMMODATIONS

Oaxaca is in the midst of a tourism boom—and a shortage of hotel rooms. You can generally arrive and find a room easily enough, but in the high tourist periods of Easter, July, November, and December, it's best to have reservations for at least your first two nights in town.

VERY EXPENSIVE

✪ Hotel Camino Real

5 de Mayo no. 300, Oaxaca, Oax. 68000. ☎ **951/6-0611** or 800/722-6466 in the U.S. Fax 951/6-0732. 91 rms (all with bath). FAN TV TEL. $189 double. Children under 12 stay free in parents' room.

Converted from the four-centuries-old former Convent of Santa Catalina (if you listen carefully in the morning, you can hear monks chanting), this hotel is one of the most beautiful of its kind in Mexico. Through the centuries it has been used as the city municipal office, a government palace, a jail, a movie theater, and a school twice. Since becoming a hotel (as such it was first known as the Presidente), the building has been designated a "national treasure."

The hotel's two floors are decorated with frescoes and colonial relics. The rooms are adorned with Mexican textiles and local pottery. Interior rooms are quieter—those with windows on the street echo with passing traffic until the wee hours. The hotel is three blocks north and one block east of the zócalo, between Murgía and Abasolo.

Dining/Entertainment: The dining room spills onto the portals in the interior courtyard and is one of the city's most pleasant places to dine. On Sundays there's a lavish brunch. The breakfast buffet changes daily but always includes Oaxacan specialties. On Friday evenings the hotel hosts a Guelaquetza—a great regional dance show and dinner buffet.

Services: Laundry and room service, travel agency.

Facilities: Swimming pool.

MODERATE

Calesa Real

García Vigil 306, Oaxaca, Oax. 68000. ☎ **951/6-5544.** Fax 951/6-7232. 77 rms (all with bath). FAN TV TEL. $49 double. Free parking.

The Calesa Real, in a colonial building $3^{1}/_{2}$ blocks north of the zócalo, is a traditional favorite. One of the nicest features here is a small kidney-shaped pool in a cool courtyard. Eight of the rooms on the first floor have French doors opening to the pool area; others on the second and third floors have small balconies. There is a second-story terrace and restaurant overlooking the pool. The large rooms have blue-tile baths and double beds. The hotel is between Bravo and Matamoros.

Casa Colonial Bed & Breakfast

División Oriente, corner Negrete (Apartado 640), Oaxaca, Oax. 68000. ☎/fax **951/6-5280.** Fax 951/6-7232. 15 rms (all with bath). $81 double (including breakfast). Free parking.

You'll feel at home in this casa if your Spanish is limited. Owners Jane and Thornton Robison are very knowledgeable about Oaxaca and lead specialty tours to surrounding villages. Formerly a mansion, the Casa Colonial has been a private guest house for more than 20 years. Each room is individually decorated with comfortable antique furniture. There is a sala, or living room, full of books about Mexico, and the dining room has both a large family-style table and smaller individual tables. To reach the hotel from the zócalo, walk one block north on García Vigil then turn left on Independencia for six blocks. Just pass La Soledad church, angle right for a couple of blocks; the Casa will be on your left.

Hotel Misión de Los Angeles

Porfirio Díaz 102, Col. Reforma, Oaxaca, Oax. 68050. ☎ **951/5-1500.** Fax 951/5-1680. 173 rms (all with bath). AC TV TEL. $69 double; $119 junior suite.

Situated in a garden, this two-story hotel is more like a country club set on immaculate grounds. Most of the comfortable rooms look out on the large swimming pool and highly manicured lawns. The restaurant is a delight. Seated by the pool, you face the tough decision of whether to move to the palapa bar or walk the half mile to the zócalo.

INEXPENSIVE

Hotel Antonio's

Independencia 601, Oaxaca, Oax. 68000 ☎ **951/6-7227.** Fax 951/6-3672. 15 rms (all with bath). TV. $23.50 double; $26.75 triple.

Opened in 1991, this comfortable and conveniently located hotel was converted from an old two-story townhouse, with an interior patio surrounded by an arcaded walkway. There is a small restaurant on the patio. Each room has a tile floor, colonial-style pine furniture, some with two double beds, and a small tile bath. Wall hooks solve the storage problem in rooms without closets. It's located a block and a half west of the cathedral, at the corner of Porfirio Díaz and Independencia.

⑤ Hotel Casa Arnel

Aldama 404, Col. Jalatlaco, Oaxaca, Oax. 68080. ☎ **951/5-2856.** Fax 951/3-6285. 30 rms (22 with bath).$12.25 double without bath; $16.75 double with bath. Parking $1.25 daily.

This favorite budget hotel is slightly removed from the city center but still within walking distance of most sights. The casa is a U-shaped two-story building constructed around a cool tropical garden behind the Cruz family home. Sooner or later, you'll meet a member of this large family. The rooms are plain but clean and comfortable; some share a bath among four rooms. Across the street in the new wing are three additional rooms with double beds and private baths, plus four furnished apartments with fully equipped kitchens. In the apartments, stays of 15 days are allowed at half the monthly rate. Breakfast and dinner are served on the family patio.

To get to the hotel, turn right out the front door of the first-class bus station, go two blocks, and turn right onto Aldama. The casa is seven blocks ahead on your left across from the Iglesia San Matías Jalatlaco.

Hotel Las Rosas

Trujano 112, Oaxaca, Oax. 68000. ☎ **951/4-2217.** 29 rms (all with bath). $34 double.

Las Rosas, formerly the Plaza Hotel, has been renovated and painted bright white. A narrow flight of stairs leads up from the street to the second-story lobby and colonial courtyard. Rooms open onto the courtyard, and some have windows; those without windows are claustrophobic. Rooms are cheerily decorated with a few regional crafts and colorful tile work; in some you'll find a turquoise wall and coordinated bedspreads. Some rooms have floor fans. The hotel is situated one half block west of the zócalo, between Magón and 20 de Noviembre. Ten of the 29 rooms are across the street in the Annex.

Hotel Principal

Cinco de Mayo no. 208, Oaxaca, Oax. 68000. ☎ and fax **951/6-2535.** 17 rms (all with bath). $20.50 double; $24 triple.

The Principal, one block east and 2¹/₂ blocks north of zócalo, is a longtime favorite of budget travelers, for good reason. The courtyard is one of the prettiest in town, and the rooms are clean and filled with sunlight. Six upstairs rooms have balconies. Travelers congregate in the courtyard to share information, and the staff is most helpful. Make reservations in advance if you can.

✪ Las Golondrinas

Tinoco y Palacios 411, Oaxaca, Oax. 68000. ☎ **951/6-8726.** Fax 951/4-2126. 24 rms (all with bath). $21.25 double; $24.50 triple.

Owned and personally managed by Guillermina and Jorge Velasco, Las Golondrinas (which means "The Swallows") has been growing more popular every year. This charming one-story hotel is situated amid rambling patios with roses, fuchsia, bougainvillea, and mature banana trees. The 24 simply furnished rooms, with windows and doors opening onto courtyards, are individually accented with Mexican crafts; all have tile floors and a small desk and chairs. Breakfast (nonguests welcome) is served between 8 and 10am in a small tile-covered cafe in a garden setting. To reach the hotel, go two blocks west of the zócalo, then turn right for four and a half blocks. It's between Allende and Bravo.

Marqués del Valle

Portal Clavería s/n, Oaxaca, Oax. 68000. ☎ **951/6-3677** or 6-6294. Fax 951/6-9961. 95 rms (all with bath). TV TEL. $41.25 double.

One of the most charming traditional hotels in Oaxaca, the Marqués del Valle has large rooms built around an inner courtyard. It's across from the zócalo next to the cathedral, yet this side of the plaza isn't very noisy (except for Sunday afternoon band concerts). Rooms with French doors facing the plaza have a grand view. Be sure to try one of the coffees in the cafe under the colonnade in front of the hotel. Service is slow, but the coffee is the best in town. Walk-in customers get lower hotel rates than those who reserve ahead.

DINING

Oaxaca's regional foods are among the best in Mexico. The state is known for its varieties of mole, cheese, tamales, peppers, tortillas, bread, and chocolate. To see a magnificent array of these foods, walk through the Abastos Market on Saturday; the quantity and variety are unforgettable. When you hear women shouting "*tlayuda, tlayuda,*" take a look at the 12-inch tortillas they're selling. Oaxaca is also known for pozole Mixteco, a delightfully different version of this hearty soup that includes chicken and red mole sauce. Restaurants in the city often feature mole, tamales, and Oaxaca cheese. Fortunately, and at last, good restaurants are becoming easier to find in Oaxaca and the prices here are better than in almost any other city in Mexico.

For a snack or light breakfast, pick up your fill of pastries, cookies, sweet rolls, and breads from the large **Panificadora Bamby,** at the corner of Morelos and García Vigil, two blocks north of the zócalo. It's open daily from 7am to 9pm.

EXPENSIVE

Restaurant del Vitral

Guerrero 201. ☎ **951/6-3124.** Breakfast $3.50–$5.75; soup/salad $3.50–$6; main courses $8–$10.50. Daily 8am–11pm. MEXICAN/REGIONAL.

As soon as you pass from the courtyard fountain to the wide stairway, you know you're in a fine restaurant. This feeling is reinforced as you reach your white cloth-covered table with crystal glasses. The interesting menu features cold cucumber and avocado soup; brochette of beef, shrimp, and chicken; and the botana oaxaqueño—a selection of regional sausage, cecina, chile relleno, molotes, quesadilla, memelitas, guacamole, and grilled onions. This is not just a place to eat; it is a place to savor the food and atmosphere. The restaurant is only a block east of the zócalo, at the corner of Armenta y López.

MODERATE

La Casa de la Abuela

Av. Hidalgo 616. ☎ **951/6-3544.** Main courses $8.25–$13. Daily 1–11pm. MEXICAN/REGIONAL.

This upstairs restaurant overlooks both the zócalo and the Alameda. Wood plank floors, yellow-ochre stucco walls, and dark-green cloths on chairs and tables create a rich, cozy setting in which to taste the region's foods. "Grandmother's house," as the name translates, offers chapulines (fried grasshoppers); huge tlayuda tortillas; empanadas with many local sauces; black bean soup; tamales; mole; caldo de gato (cat's stew) made with beef and pork; and much more. The entrance is just west of the zócalo.

Restaurant/Bar Catedral

García Vigil 105. ☎ **951/6-3285.** Breakfast $1.75–$2.75; main courses $5–$10. Daily 8am–2am. MEXICAN/REGIONAL.

Two blocks north of the zócalo, at the corner of Morelos, is this cool place to enjoy a leisurely meal. A few tables are near the fountain in the small courtyard, while others are in two large interior rooms. One can sense the elegance here: cloth napkins dress the tables and waiters wear jackets and ties. The restaurant is known for its excellent cuts of beef.

INEXPENSIVE

Cafetería Bamby

García Vigil 205. ☎ **951/6-3285.** Breakfast $1.50–$3; soups/salads $1.50–$2; main courses $3.50–$5.50; comida corrida $3.50. Daily 8am–8pm. MEXICAN.

Two and one half blocks north of the zócalo is this bright, clean U.S.-type cafe. When you're feel a bit homesick for homestyle food, this is the place to come. Service is courteous and prompt, and the nice selection of dishes attracts both local and tourist clientele. And the bathrooms are way above average!

✪ Doña Elpidia

Miguel Cabrera 413. ☎ **951/6-4292.** Fixed-price lunch $5.25. Daily 8:30–10am, 1–5pm. MEXICAN.

This restaurant is virtually an institution in Oaxaca; Doña Elpidia and her family have been catering to a refined, selective local clientele for more than 40 years. Inside the deceptively shabby-looking door is a beautiful and heavily shaded courtyard filled with birds and plants. Five tables are set out in the arcade, and there are a dozen more in the indoor dining rooms. The five-course comida corrida includes an appetizer, vegetable or pasta soup, a meat or enchilada course, a dessert, and Mexican coffee. Doña Elpidia's also serves a different mole daily. The place is a bit hard to find since the sign says only "RESTAURANT," but it's 5¹/₂ blocks south of the zócalo, between Arista and Nuño del Mercado.

✪ Gecko Coffee Shop

5 de Mayo 412. ☎ **951/4-8024.** Sandwiches $1.25; desserts $1–$1.25; coffee 75¢; chocolate $1.25. Mon–Sat 7am–8pm. SANDWICHES/CHOCOLATE/COFFEE.

Less than half a block from the Santo Domingo church is this little habit-forming gem. A variety of delicious sandwiches and pastries are served either in a small dining room or in the more ample patio. Here you have peace and quiet to sip, snack, and read or write the ever-necessary postcards. And when you finally tear yourself away, a gallery, small bookstore, and the wonderful Instituto Welte are just off the patio.

✪ Restaurant El Mesón

Av. Hidalgo #805 at Valdivieso. ☎ **951/6-2729.** Breakfast and lunch buffet $3.25; comida corrida $2; tacos $1.50–$3.50; Mexican specialties $1.50–$5. Daily 8am–1am (breakfast buffet 8am–noon; lunch buffet and comida corrida noon–8pm). MEXICAN.

This clean, attractive restaurant is a pleasure to return to year after year. The food is good and reasonably priced, and it's a great place to try regional specialties. What's more, the location is excellent and it's a popular meeting place for fellow travelers and locals alike. You see señoritas patting out fresh tortillas as you enter, and if you sit at the counter you can watch all the kitchen preparations. The menu and prices are printed on a sheet the waitress gives you; just check off what you want and present the waitress with your selection. Taco prices are per order (usually 2 tacos). Besides the large range of tacos, they serve some "especialidades" such as tamal Oaxaqueño (for which Oaxaca is known), pozole, and puntas de filete albañil (bricklayers' beef tips). There's the regular assortment of beer and soft drinks, but this is a good place to try the chocolate with water or milk (so hot and good on a chilly morning) or the equally delicious atole.

Restaurant Flor de Loto

Plaza Gourmet, Morelos 509. ☎ **951/6-9146.** Breakfast $1.50–$3.50; crêpes $3.25; vegetable plate $2–$3.25; comida corrida $3.50. Mon–Sat 8am–10pm, Sun 8am–9pm. MEXICAN/REGIONAL/VEGETARIAN.

Impressions

In Mexico there is always a brooding sense of the past. Turn off the highway, and the rutted road leads you over humpbacked bridges, past the gates of old haciendas, through the villages where the church stands on the plaza as it always has. The high mesa blossoms pink with cosmos in late August, and far away on the edge of the hills shine the tile domes. Farther up the hills are markets where not everyone speaks Spanish, where women are still wearing garments which they weave for themselves.

—Elizabeth Wilder Weismann, *Art and Time in Mexico*, 1985

This "Lotus Flower," with a colorful and clean decor, serves good basic food for vegetarians and meat eaters alike. The menu might include freshly baked whole-wheat bread and butter, pizza, a fruit plate, soup, crêpes with cheese, squash with mushrooms or vegetables, spaghetti, papaya water, and baked guava for dessert. It's four blocks north and 1 1/2 blocks west of the zócalo, near the corner of Morelos and P. Díaz.

○ Restaurant Las Quince Letras
Abasolo 300. ☎ **951/6-9016.** Breakfast $1.75–$5.25; botana Oaxaqueño $6; soups/salads $1.75–$3.25; main courses $4–$6.75; comida corrida $4. Daily 8am–9pm. MEXICAN/ REGIONAL.

You have to look hard to find this outstanding small restaurant and even harder to find one better! Look for a purple entry-way with the word RESTAURANT painted vertically in white on it. You are not actually sure of the name until you receive the menu. But from then on you don't care. While you make the hard decision of what to order, you will munch on complementary memelitas, a masa creation similar to a sope. If you order the filling botana Oaxaqueña, the dozen different enticements leave barely enough room for a light dessert. To find it from the zócalo, walk north on Alcalá 4 blocks to Abasolo, then right 3 1/4 blocks.

○ Restaurant T.L.C.
J. P. García at Aldama. ☎ **951/6-4331.** Breakfast $1.25–$2.75; main courses $2.25; burgers $1.25–$4. Daily 8am–2am. MEXICAN.

Should you find yourself on Mina in the chocolate part of town at lunch time, walk two blocks for a treat. Well prepared food served by a pleasant staff at tables in front or in a small patio will be your reward. That is the T.L.C. (Tacos, Liquados, Comida), and it is unique in this part of town. It is a block west of the markets on Aldama, and two blocks south and two blocks west of the zócalo.

OAXACA AFTER DARK
Among the best entertainments in Oaxaca are the **band concerts** in the zócalo— and they're free, too! The State band plays on Tuesday, Thursday, and Sunday, while Monday, Wednesday, Friday and Saturday the marimbas take over. Oaxaca has the jolliest and most active zócalo in all of Mexico, enjoyed by everyone in town, young and old, rich and poor, citizen or tourist.

A smaller version of the **Guelaguetza,** the famous regional dance of Oaxaca, is performed at the Hotel Camino Real on Friday from 7 to 10pm by a group of highly professional dancers. The cost of $28 per person includes a buffet and elaborate show. The Hotel Monte Albán presents more reasonably priced folk dances daily from 8:30 to 10pm for $4.50 for the show alone. Dinner and drinks are extra. Buy your ticket the day before; then when you enter, you'll find your name card placed at your reserved seat.

Concerts and dance programs are offered all year long at the **Teatro Macedonio de Alcalá,** at Independencia and Armenta y López. Schedules are often posted by the front doors of the theater. The **Casa de la Cultura** (ex-convent of the Seven Princes), at the corner of Colón and G. Ortega, offers exhibits, lectures, films, and various art and music classes, as does the **Centro Cultural Ricardo Flores Magón** (Alcalá 302).

One of Oaxaca's hottest **discos** is in the Hotel Victoria, on the Cerro del Fortín, northwest of the center of town (☎ 5-2633). It's active from 10pm till 2am on Friday and Saturday. You'll need a taxi to get there, or at least to get home. In town at the Disco Eclipse (Calle Porfirio Díaz 219, between Matamoros and Morelos, ☎ 951/6-4236) you'll find another "get down" crowd gathered Thursday through Sunday (10pm until the crowd decides to leave). For night owls who are not up to the disco scene, there's **live music** at El Sagrario (Valdivieso 120, behind the cathedral; ☎ 951/4-0303) the club provides food and beverages while (from 8pm on) you listen to salsa, guitar, and Andean pan pipes. Also there is the Terranova, at Portal Benito Juárez 116. (☎ 951/4-0533), a restaurant with live music between 8pm and 11pm. And near Santo Domingo Church is La Candela, Allende 211, a block and a half west of Santo Domingo (☎ 951/6-7933). It's a good enough restaurant in its own right, but it's a popular night spot with live salsa, reggae, etc., and dancing from about 9:30pm till 1:30am Tuesday through Saturday.

ROAD TRIPS FROM OAXACA

Monte Albán and Mitla are the two most important archeological sites near Oaxaca, but there are several smaller ruins that are also interesting. I've also mentioned a few day-trips to the more interesting villages outside Oaxaca. (For Puerto Escondido, Huatulco, and San Angel, see Chapter 11, "Acapulco & the Southern Pacific Coast.") The tourist office will give you a map showing the nearby villages where beautiful handicrafts are made. It's a fun excursion by car or bus.

MONTE ALBÁN: FABLED MOUNTAINTOP CEREMONIAL CENTER

For some 1500 years prior to 500 B.C., the Oaxaca valleys were inhabited by more or less sedentary village dwelling peoples, whose origins are mysterious. Then, between 800 and 500 B.C., a new ceramic style appeared, presumably produced by an influx of new peoples, now called Zapotec. Around 500 B.C. these peoples began to level the top of a mountain upon which to build the magnificent city we know as Monte Albán ("MON-teh al-BAN").

Very little of the original structures remain—they were either built over or their stones reused. However, the Danzantes friezes are of this period, and their subject matter has inspired many theories, some a bit far-fetched.

Monte Albán was an elite center of Zapotec culture, although affected by contemporary cultures outside the valley of Mexico. You can see Olmec influence in the early sculptures; later masks and sculptures reflect contact with the Maya. When Monte Albán was at its zenith in A.D. 300, architectural ideas were borrowed from Teotihuacán. By around A.D. 800, the significance of Monte Albán in the Zapotec cosmos began to decline. Although probably never totally abandoned, it became a mere shell of its former grandeur. Then, around the beginning of the 13th century, the remnants of this star of the valley were appropriated by the Mixtecs. The Mixtecs, who had long coexisted in the area with the Zapotecs, now imposed their own, by now more highly developed, culture. At Monte Albán, they did very little building of their own, but are renowned for the treasure they left in Tomb 7.

Monte Albán covers about 15 square miles and is centered on the Great Plaza, a large grassy area that was once a mountain top. From this plaza, aligned north-south, you can overlook the lush Oaxacan valley, a gorgeous setting for any civilization. The excavations at Monte Albán have revealed more than 170 tombs, numerous ceremonial altars, stelae, pyramids, and palaces.

Begin your tour of the ruins on the eastern side of the **Great Plaza** at the I-shaped **ball court.** This ball court differs slightly from Maya and Toltec ball courts in that there are no goal rings and the sides of the court are sloped. Also on the east side of the plaza are several altars and pyramids that were once covered with stucco. Note the sloping walls and the wide stairs and the ramps, which are typical of Zapotec architecture and resemble the architecture of Teotihuacán. The building slightly out of line with the plaza (not on the north-south axis) is thought by some to have been an **observatory** and was probably aligned with the heavenly bodies rather than with the points of the compass.

The south side of the plaza has a large platform that bore several stelae, most of which are now in the National Museum of Anthropology in Mexico City. There's a good view of the surrounding area from the top of this platform.

The west side has more ceremonial platforms and pyramids. On top of the pyramid substructure are four columns that probably held the roof of the temple at one time.

The famous **building of the Dancers (Danzantes)** is on the west side of the plaza, and is the earliest known structure at Monte Albán. This building is covered with large stone slabs carved into distorted naked figures (these are copies; the originals are protected in the site museum). There is speculation as to who carved these figures and what they represent. There is certainly a distinct resemblance to the Olmec "baby faces" seen at La Venta. The distorted bodies and pained expressions of the faces perhaps imply disease. There are clear examples of figures representing childbirth, dwarfism, and infantilism. Because of the fluidity of the figures, they became known as the Danzantes, but this is only a modern label for these ancient and mysterious carvings.

The **Northern Platform** is a maze of temples and palaces interwoven with subterranean tunnels and sanctuaries. Wander around here, for there are numerous reliefs, glyphs, paintings, and friezes along the lintels and jambs as well as the walls.

Leaving the Great Plaza, head north to the cemetery and tombs. Of the tombs so far excavated, the most famous is Tomb 7, to the east of the cemetery. Inside were found some 500 pieces of jewelry made of gold, amber, and turquoise, as well as art objects made of silver, alabaster, and bone. This amazing collection is on display at the Regional Museum of Oaxaca.

If you have more than one day to spend at Monte Albán, be sure to visit some of the tombs, for they contain some really magnificent glyphs, paintings, and stone carvings of gods, goddesses, birds, and serpents. Two tombs that are especially absorbing, Tombs 104 and 105, are guarded and can be entered via ladders; the guards are usually helpful about pointing out areas of special interest. Ignore the vendors hawking "original" artifacts, supposedly found at the site—if they were real, these guys would hardly need to wander around in the midday sun trying to sell them!

As you enter the site you'll see an on-site museum, a shop selling guide-books to the ruins, a cafe, and a crafts shop. I recommend you purchase one of the guidebooks.

Admission to the ruins is $3.25; free on Sunday and holidays. The site is open daily from 8am to 5pm. Licensed guides charge $13.50 per person for a walking tour. Video camera permits cost $5.50.

To get to Monte Albán, take a bus from the Hotel Mesón del Angel, Mina 518, at Mier y Terán. Autobuses Turísticos makes seven runs daily, leaving at 8:30, 9:30, 10:30 and 11:30am and 12:30, 1:30 and 3:30pm. Return service leaves the ruins at 11am, noon, and 1, 2, 3, 4, and 5:30pm. The round-trip fare is $1.75. The ride takes half an hour, and your scheduled return time is two hours after your arrival. It's possible to take a later return for an additional $1; inform the driver of your intent (but you won't be guaranteed a seat). During high season there are usually additional buses.

THE ROAD TO MITLA: RUINS, MARKETS & CRAFTS VILLAGES

East of Oaxaca, the Pan American Highway to Mitla rolls past several important archeological sites, markets, and crafts villages. En route you can visit the famous El Tule tree; the church at Tlacochahuaya; the ruins at Dainzú, Lambityeco, and Yagul; the weaver's village of Teotitlán del Valle; and Saturday market village of Tlacolula.

Without a car, it's impossible to cover all these destinations in one day, and by car the route takes a very long day. On a Sunday you could combine the Tlacolula market with all the archeological sites, which have free admission on Sunday. Save the weaving village of Teotitlán del Valle and the church of Tlacochahuaya for another day.

The **Fletes y Pasajes** bus line (☎ 6-2270) runs buses every 20 minutes from 6am to 8pm to Mitla from the second-class terminal. The terminal is eight long blocks west of the zócalo on Trujano. The trip takes an hour and 15 minutes and costs $1 each way. The driver will stop at any point along the way; let him know in advance.

The SEDETUR Tourist Office in Oaxaca (across from the Alameda; ☎ 951/6-0123 or 6-4828, fax 951/6-0984) has a hand in maintaining small **one-bedroom houses** for tourists in nine Zapotec villages in the Oaxaca valley. They are called "Tourist Yu'u" (*Yu'u* means house in Zapotec), and are equipped with bare kitchen necessities, bathrooms, etc., and rent for $6.75 per person. They are located on the outskirts of the villages, but within walking distance. Contact SEDETUR for reservations or more information.

Santa María del Tule: Home of a 2,000-Year-Old Tree

Santa María del Tule is a small town (eight miles outside Oaxaca) that's filled with turkeys, children, and rug vendors. The town is famous for the immense **El Tule Tree,** or *ahuehuete* tree (Montezuma cypress), in a churchyard just off the main road. The ancient tree is still growing today, as is evidenced by the foliage, but pollution and a lowering ground water level are posing a serious threat. This whole region around Santa María del Tule was once very marshy; in fact, the word tule means "reed." A private foundation has been established in an effort to provide protection for this survivor. Beyond El Tule is agricultural country, and at siesta time you'll see whole families resting in the shade of giant cacti.

The **Church of San Jerónimo Tlacochahuaya** is a fine example of how the Spanish borrowed from Zapotec architectural design. Inside you'll see how the church leaders artistically melded the two cultures. Note the elaborately carved altar and the crucified Christ fashioned from ground dried corn cobs. Also, don't miss the still functional organ (dated 1620) in the choir loft. The church is open from 10am to 2pm and 4 to 6pm. It's on the right side of the road, past El Tule Tree, and 14 miles from Oaxaca.

The Mitla bus will drop you off at the road leading into town. You can either hitch a ride with locals or walk the distance.

Shopping at the Source: Oaxaca's Splendid Market Villages

You could spend a full week in Oaxaca just visiting the various markets held in nearby villages. Each has its specialty—cheese, produce, livestock, weaving, and pottery—and its unique character. Market days in the villages are as follows:

- **Wednesday: Etla,** known for its cheese; 9¹/₂ miles north.
- **Thursday: Zaachila,** ruins and agriculture; 11 miles southwest. **Ejutla,** agriculture; 40 miles south.
- **Friday: Ocotlán,** pottery, textiles, and food; 18¹/₂ miles south.
- **Saturday: Oaxaca,** Abastos Market.
- **Sunday: Tlacolula,** agriculture and crafts (visit the chapel as well); 19¹/₂ miles southeast.

You can get to any of these crafts villages by taking a bus from the second-class bus station, eight blocks west of the zócalo on Trujano. On market days these buses are crammed with passengers. If you get off a bus between destinations—say, at Dainzú on the way to Mitla or at Cuilapan on the way to Zaachila—but want to continue to the next place, return to the highway and hail a passing bus.

It's also possible to take a colectivo taxi to the villages that don't have bus service. To find a colectivo, head to the south end of the Abastos Market. On Calle Mercaderos you'll see dozens of parked maroon-and-white colectivo taxis. The town each one serves is written on the door, trunk, or windshield. There are also posted metal signs for destinations. They fill up relatively fast and are an economical way to reach the villages. Be sure to go early; by afternoon the colectivos don't fill up as fast and you'll have to wait.

Tours to all the markets as well as the crafts villages and ruins can easily be arranged through **Tours Arnel,** at Hotel Casa Arnel, Aldama 404 (☎ 951/5-2856), or **Belaguetza,** at Arte y Tradición, García Vigil 406, (☎ 951/6-3552). There are, of course, many tour agencies in Oaxaca, but these both offer friendly, personal, English-speaking guide service at competitive prices. Three- to four- hour tours to Monte Albán or Mitla will cost about $9 per person (plus site entry). Other villages can be included at minimal cost.

Many of these historical and/or craft villages have, in the past several years, developed some truly fine small municipal museums. **San José El Mogote,** site of one of the very earliest pre-Hispanic village dweller groups, has a display of carvings and statues found in and around the town and a display model of an old hacienda and details of its produce and social organization. **Teotitlán del Valle** is another with such a municipal museum; it features displays on the weaving process. Ask at the State Tourism Office (north side of the Alameda on Independencia) for more information on these and others.

Dainzú: Zapotec Ruins

Sixteen miles from Oaxaca, this site (first excavated in the 1960s), dates to sometime between 700–600 B.C. Increasingly sophisticated building continued until about A.D. 300. One of the major buildings was constructed against a west-facing hill; incorporated into the lower portion of this building were found some

35 carvings resembling the Danzantes seen in Monte Albán. These carvings are now housed in a protective shed which a caretaker will unlock for interested parties. There is a partially reconstructed ball court. The site provides an outstanding view of the valley. Admission is $1.50.

Dainzú ("dine-ZOO"), beautiful in the afternoon sun, lies less than a mile south of Highway 190, at the end of a mostly paved road. Look for a sign 16 miles from Oaxaca.

Lambityeco: Another Archaeological Site

On the south side of Highway 190, a few miles east of the turnoff to Dainzú, is the small site of Lambityeco. Part of a much larger site containing over 200 mounds, it is thought to have been inhabited from about 600 B.C., although the fully studied part belongs to the period following the decline of Monte Albán. Of particular interest are the two beautifully executed and preserved stucco masks of the rain god Cocijo. A product of Lambityeco was salt, distilled from saline ground waters nearby. Admission is $1.50; $5.50 is charged for your video camera.

Teotitlán del Valle: Beautiful Blankets & Serapes

This town is famous for weaving; its products can be found in the shops in Oaxaca, but you might enjoy buying them from the source. Many of the weavers sell out of their homes, and give demonstrations. The prices are slightly lower than in Oaxaca.

Entering Teotitlán, you'll see a sign for LA GRANA. Here you can see all the elements involved in the dyeing process. The rugs displayed are expensive, but real works of art. The church in town is well worth a visit, as is the community museum; there is an artisan's market adjacent to both. And for a real treat, plan to include **Restaurant Tlaminalli,** run by six lovely Zapotec sisters. Their comida seems a bit steep at $13.50, but after you have finished you realize that you got a bargain. It's one of the most renowned restaurants in the country, widely known for its authentic regional cuisine. It's open Tuesday through Sunday from 1 to 6pm.

Direct buses make the run between Oaxaca and Teotitlán from the second-class bus station. If you're coming from or going to Mitla, you'll have to hitch or walk from the highway crossroads.

Tlacolula: A Fine Market & Unique Chapel

Located about 19 miles from Oaxaca, southeast on the road to Mitla, Tlacolula is famous for its market and **Dominican chapel,** which is considered by many to be the most beautiful of the Dominican churches in the Americas. The wrought-iron gates, choir loft, and the wrought iron pulpit, considered to be unique in Mexico, are worth a look, as well as the frescoes and paintings in relief. A few years ago a secret passage was found, leading to a room that contained valuable silver religious pieces. The silver was hidden during the Revolution of 1916 when there was a tide of anti-religious sentiment; the articles are now back in the church.

Sunday is market day in Tlacolula, with rows of textiles fluttering in the breeze, and aisle after aisle of pottery and baskets.

Yagul: Ruins of a Zapotec Fortress

This was a fortress city on a hill overlooking the valley. It's 20 miles southeast of Oaxaca, about half a mile off the road to Mitla. There's a small sign indicating the turnoff to the left; go up the paved road to the site. The setting is absolutely gorgeous, and because the ruins are not as fully reconstructed as those at Monte Albán, you're likely to have the place to yourself. It's a good place for a picnic lunch.

The city was divided into two sections: the fortress at the top of a hill and the area of palaces lower down. The center of the palace complex is the plaza, surrounded by four temples. In the center is a ceremonial platform, under which is the Triple Tomb. The door of the tomb is a large stone slab decorated on both sides with beautiful hieroglyphs. The tomb may or may not be open for viewing.

Look for the beautifully restored ball court, typical of Zapotec ball courts (which are without goal rings). North of the plaza is the incredible palace structure built for the chiefs of the city. It's a maze of huge rooms with six patios, decorated with painted stucco and stone mosaics. Here and there you can see ceremonial mounds and tombs decorated in the same geometric patterns that are found in Mitla. This is one of the most interesting palaces in the area. The panoramic view of the valley from the fortress is worth the rather exhausting climb.

Admission is $1.50; free on Sunday and holidays. Still cameras are free, but use of a video camera, will cost you $5.50. Save your receipt—it will serve for any other sites visited the same day. The site is open daily from 8am to 5:30pm, but be prepared to blow 13¢ for parking.

It's just a few miles farther southeast to Mitla. The turnoff comes at a very obvious fork in the road.

Mitla: Large Zapotec and Mixtec Site

Mitla is 2³/₄ miles from the highway, and the turnoff terminates at the ruins by the church. If you've come here by bus, it's about half a mile up the road from the dusty town square to the ruins; if you want to hire a cab, there are some available in the square.

Mitla was settled by the Zapotecs around 600 B.C., but became a Mixtec bastion in the late 10th century. This city of the Mixtecs was still flourishing at the time of the Spanish Conquest, and many of the buildings were used through the 16th century.

The town of Mitla (pop. 10,000) is often bypassed by the tour groups but is worth a visit. The University of the Americas maintains the **Museum of Zapotec Art** (previously known as the Frissell collection) in town. It contains some outstanding Zapotec and Mixtec relics. Admission is free (a donation is requested) after signing in. Be sure to look at the Leigh collection, which contains some real treasures. The museum is housed in the restful **Restaurant La Sorpresa,** Av. Juárez #2 (☎ 8-0194), an old hacienda. You can dine inside or out on the patio daily between 9am and 5pm. Breakfast costs from $3.50; the daily lunch special costs $5.75 and includes soup, salad, a main course, and dessert.

You can easily see the most important buildings in an hour. Mixtec architecture is based on a quadrangle surrounded on three or four sides by patios and chambers, usually rectangular in shape. The chambers have a low roof, which is excellent for defense but which makes the rooms dark and close. The stone buildings are inlaid mosaic-like with small cut stones to form geometric patterns.

There are five groups of buildings divided by the Mitla River. The most important buildings are on the east side of the ravine. The Group of the Columns consists of two quadrangles, connected at the corners with palaces. The building to the north has a long chamber with six columns and many rooms decorated with geometric designs. The most common motif is the zigzag pattern, the same one seen repeatedly on the Mitla blankets. Human or animal images are rare in Mixtec art. In fact, only one frieze has been found (in the Group of the Church, in the north patio). Here you'll see a series of figures painted with their name glyphs.

Admission to the site is $2.25; free on Sunday and holidays. Use of a video camera costs $5.50. It's open daily from 8am to 5pm.

Outside the ruins you'll be bombarded by vendors. The moment you step out of a car or taxi, every able-bodied woman and child for 10 miles around will come charging over with shrill cries and a basket full of bargains—heavily embroidered belts, small pieces of pottery, fake archeological relics, cheap earrings. Offer to pay half the price the vendors ask. There's a modern handicrafts market near the ruins, but prices are lower in town.

In Mitla and on the highway going south, you'll find **mezcal outlets** (expendios de mezcal), which are factory outlets for little distilleries that produce the fiery cactus aguardiente. To be authentic, a bottle of mezcal must have a worm floating in it. The liquor is surprisingly cheap, the bottle labels are surprisingly colorful, and the taste is quite different. It is not unlike tequila—mix a shot of mezcal with a glass of grapefruit or pomegranate juice and you've got a cocktail that will make you forget the heat, even in Mitla. Watch out for the worm!

SOUTH OF MONTE ALBAN: ARRAZOLA, CUILAPAN & ZAACHILA

Arrazola: Wood-Carving Capital

Arrazola ("ar-a-ZO-la") is in the foothills of Monte Albán, about 15 miles southwest of Oaxaca. The tiny town's most famous resident is **Manuel Jimenez,** the septuagenarian grandfather of the resurgence in wood carving as a folk art. Jimenez's polar bears, anteaters, and rabbits carved from copal wood are shown in galleries throughout the world; his home is a Mecca of sorts for folk-art collectors. Now the town is full of other carvers, all making fanciful creatures painted in bright, festive colors. Among those who should be sought out are Antonio and Ramiro Aragon; their delicate and imaginative work should rank them with Jimenez. Little boys will greet you at the outskirts of town offering to guide you to individual homes for a small tip. Following them is a good way to know the town, and after a bit you can dismiss them.

If you're driving to Arrazola, take the road out of Oaxaca city that goes to Monte Albán, then take the left fork after crossing the Atoyac River and follow the signs for Zaachila. Turn right after the town of Xoxo and you will soon be there. There are no road signs, but other travelers along the way will direct you. The bus from the second-class station in Oaxaca will let you off at the side road to Arrazola where it meets the highway. From there it's a pleasant 3¹/₂-mile walk to the town, past a few homes, the occupants of which are wood carvers who will invite you in for a look at their work. To return, colectivo taxis make the run to Zaachila and Oaxaca for around $2, which can be shared—it's worth it.

Cuilapan: A Dominican Monastery

Cuilapan ("kwi-LAP-an") is located about 10 miles southwest of Oaxaca. The Dominican friars began their second monastery here in 1550. However, parts of the convent and church were never completed due to political machinations of the late 16th century. The roof of the monastery has fallen, but the cloister and the church remain. The church is being restored and is still used today. There are three naves with lofty arches, large stone columns, and many frescoes. It is open daily from 10am till 6pm; entry is $5.50, plus $8.50 for a video camera. The monastery is visible on the right a short distance from the main road to Zaachila, and there's a sign as well. The bus from the second-class station stops within a few hundred feet of the church.

Zaachila: Market Town with Mixtec Tombs

Farther on from Cuilapan, 15 miles southwest of Oaxaca, Zaachila ("Za-CHEE-la") has a Thursday market; baskets and pottery are sold for local household use, and the produce market is always full. Also take note of the interesting livestock section and a mercado de madera (wood market) just as you enter town.

Near and behind the church is the entrance to a small archeological site containing several mounds and platforms and two quite interesting tombs. Artifacts found there now reside in the National Museum of Anthropology in Mexico City, but Tomb 1 contains carvings worth seeing.

At the time of the Spanish Conquest, Zaachila was the last surviving city of the Zapotec rulers. When Cortés marched on the city, the Zapotecs did not resist and instead formed an alliance with him, which outraged the Mixtecs, who invaded Zaachila shortly afterward. The site and the tombs are open daily from 9am till 4pm, and the entrance fee is $1.50.

To return to Oaxaca, you have a choice of walking several blocks back to the second-class bus station near the animal market or lining up with the locals for one of the colectivo taxis on the main street across from the market. I prefer the taxi.

SOUTH ALONG HIGHWAY 175

San Bartolo Coyotepec: Black Pottery

San Bartolo is the home of the black pottery you've seen in all the stores in Oaxaca. It's also one of several little villages named Coyotepec in the area. Buses frequently operate between Oaxaca and this village, 23 miles south on Highway 175. In 1953, a native woman named Doña Rosa invented the technique of smoking the pottery to make it black during firing and rubbing the fired pieces with a piece of quartz to produce a sheen. Doña Rosa died in 1979, but her son, Valente Nieto Real, carries on the tradition. It is an almost spiritual experience to watch Valente change a lump of coarse clay into a work of living art with only two crude plates used as a potter's wheel. The family's home/factory is a few blocks off the main road; you'll see the sign as you enter town. It's open daily from 9am to 5:30pm.

Black pottery is sold at many shops on the little plaza or in the artists' homes. Villagers who make pottery often place a piece of their work near their front door, by the gate, or on the street. It's their way of inviting prospective buyers to come in.

San Martín Tilcajete: Another Wood-Carving Center

San Martín Tilcajete is a recent addition to the tour of folk-art towns. Located about 10 miles south of San Bartolo Coyotepec, San Martín is noted, as is Arrazola, for its wood carvers and their fantastical, brightly painted animals and dragons. The Sosa and Hernández families are especially prolific, and you can easily spend half a day wandering from house to house to see the amazing collections of hot-pink rabbits, 4-foot-long bright-blue twisting snakes, and two-headed dalmatians.

Ocotlán: Market Town & the Aguilar Potters

One of the best markets in the area is held on Friday in Ocotlán de Morelos, 35 miles south of Oaxaca on Highway 175. The variety of goods includes modern dishware and cutlery, hand-molded earthenware jugs, polyester dresses, finely woven cotton or wool rebozos (scarves), hand-dyed and tooled leather, and electronics, as well as produce. You won't find a more varied selection except in Oaxaca. On other than market day, you can always visit Ocotlán's most famous potters, the noted Aguilar family—Josephina, Guillermina, and Irena. On the right, just at the outskirts of Ocotlán, their row of home-workshops is distinguished by pottery pieces stuck up on the fence and the roof. Their work, often figures of daily life, is colorful, sometimes humorous, and highly prized by collectors. Visitors are welcome daily.

NORTH OF OAXACA

Guelatao: Birthplace of Benito Juárez

Set high in the mountains north of Oaxaca, this town has become a living monument to its favorite son, Benito Juárez. Although usually peaceful, this lovely town comes to life on Juárez's birthday (March 21). The museum, statues, and plaza all attest to the town's obvious devotion to the patriot.

To get here, a second-class bus departs from Oaxaca's first-class station six times daily. There are also several departures from the second-class station. The trip will take at least two hours, through gorgeous mountain scenery. Buses return to Oaxaca every two hours until 8pm.

EN ROUTE TO SAN CRISTÓBAL DE LAS CASAS

Tuxtla Gutiérrez, the boomtown capital of the wild, mountainous state of Chiapas, is a necessary crossroads for getting to San Cristóbal from the west along Highway 190. If you need to stop for a night's rest, the large, comfortable **Hotel Bonampak Tuxtla** (Blv. Dominguez 180; ☎ 961/3-2050) on the outskirts of town, or the less expensive but sometimes loud **Gran Hotel Humberto** (Av. Central 180; ☎ 961/2-2080) right downtown, will both do nicely. And no trip to Tuxtla is complete without a meal at **Las Pichanchas** (Av. Central Ote. 837; ☎ 961/2-5351), a colorful restaurant that's devoted to the regional food and drink of Chiapas. If you've got some time to spare, check out Tuxtla's fine zoo (**ZOOMAT**), or the awesome, sheer-walled **El Sumidero Canyon.** Trips to the latter can be arranged by Transportes al Cañon (☎ 3-3584) in Tuxtla.

2 San Cristóbal de las Casas

143 miles SW of Palenque, 50 miles E of Tuxtla Gutiérrez, 46 miles NW of Comitán, 104 miles NW of Cuauhtémoc, 282 miles E of Oaxaca

San Cristóbal is a colonial town set in a lovely valley—still nearly 7,000 feet high—where the centuries-old Maya civilization continues to flourish. Part of the town's name is derived from the 16th-century bishop Fray Bartolome de las Casas, who sought to protect native peoples from exploitation. Nearly all the Indians in the immediate area speak languages such as Tzotzil or Tzeltal which are derived from the ancient Maya. The town of 90,000 is the major market center for Maya Indians of various groups who trek down from the surrounding mountains, but some groups, such as the Lacandóns (who number only about 450) don't come into town at all; they live so far off in the forests of eastern Chiapas that it takes six days on horseback to get to their territory.

Probably the most visible among the local indigenous groups are the Chamula. The men wear baggy thigh-length trousers and white or black serapes, while the women wear blue rebozos, gathered white blouses with embroidered trim, and black wool wraparound skirts.

San Cristóbal de las Casas

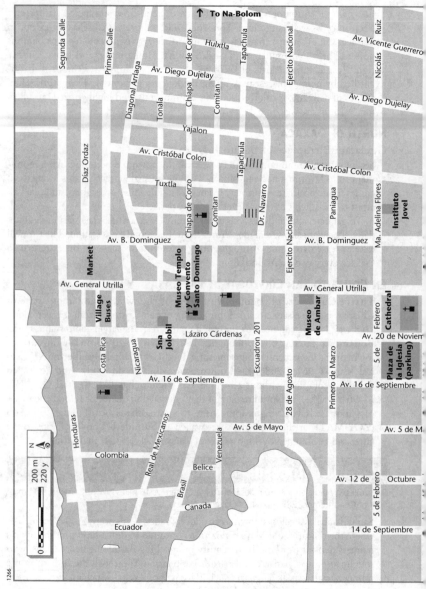

Another local Indian group is the Zinacantecan, whose male population dresses in light-pink overshirts with colorful trim and tassels and sometimes short pants. Hat ribbons (now a rare sight) are tied on married men, while ribbons dangle loosely from the hats of bachelors and community leaders. The Zinacantecan women wear beautiful, brightly colored woven shawls along with black wool skirts. You may also see Tenejapa men clad in knee-length black tunics and flat straw hats and Tenejapa women dressed in beautiful reddish and rust-colored huipils.

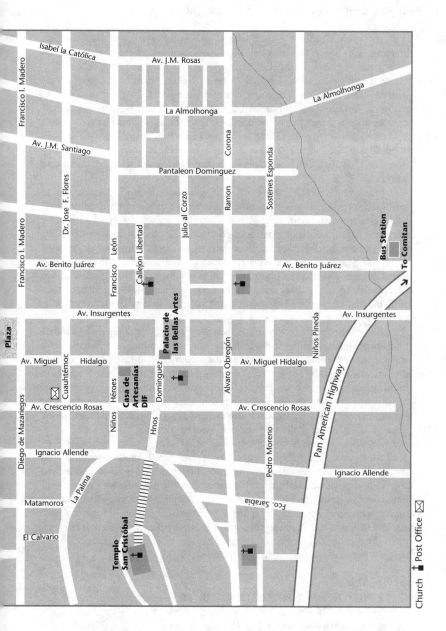

Church ■   Post Office ⊠

Women of all groups are barefooted, while men wear handmade sandals or cowboy boots.

There are several Indian villages within access of San Cristóbal by road—Chamula, with its weavers and non-Christian church; Zinacantán, whose residents practice a unique religion and wear brilliantly colored clothing; Tenejapa, San Andrés, and Magdalena, known for brocaded textiles; Amatenango del Valle, a town of potters; and Aguacatenango, known for embroidery. Most of these "villages" consist of little more than a church and the municipal government building, with homes scattered for miles around and a general gathering only for church and market days (usually Sunday).

You'll hear the word *ladino* here—it refers to non-Indian Mexicans or people who have taken up modern ways, changed their dress, dropped their Indian traditions and language, and decided to live in town. It may be used derogatorily or descriptively, depending on who is using the term and how it's used.

Other local lingo you should know about includes *Jovel*, San Cristóbal's original name, used often by businesses, and *coleto*, meaning someone or something from San Cristóbal. You'll see signs for tamales coletos, coleto bread, and coleto breakfast.

In recent years, San Cristóbal has become more popular with Mexicans, not to mention North Americans and Europeans in search of a charming, "unspoiled" traditional town to visit. Evangelical Protestant missionaries recently have converted large numbers of indigenous peoples, and in some villages new converts find themselves expelled from their homelands—in Chamula, for example, as many as 30,000 people have been expelled. Many of these people, called *expulsados* (expelled ones), have taken up residence in new villages on the outskirts of San Cristóbal de las Casas. They still wear their traditional dress. Other villages, such as Tenejapa, allow the Protestant church to exist, and villagers to attend it without prejudice.

Although the influx of tourists is increasing and the influence of outsiders (including Mexicans) is inevitably chipping away at the culture, the Indians aren't really interested in being or looking like the foreigners in their midst. They may steal glances at tourists or even stare curiously, but mainly they pay little attention to outsiders. Just in case we think they are envious of our clothing, possessions, or culture, I'll repeat an interesting comment made one night during dinner at Na-Bolom with a Maya specialist living in San Cristóbal: "They think we are the remains of a left-over civilization and that we eat our babies."

Important note: In January 1994, Indians from this area led a revolt against the *ladino*-led towns and Mexican government over health care, education, land distribution, and representative government. Though the issues are still unresolved and news of uprisings continues to be reported, while traveling for this edition I found tourists, primarily Europeans, filling hotels almost to capacity. Polite armed military personnel were stopping traffic at several roadblocks on all highways leading to San Cristóbal. At these stops, travelers were required to present personal travel documents such as tourist permits, passports, or other identification and to state the purpose of their travel. Some vehicles were searched.

ESSENTIALS

GETTING THERE & DEPARTING   By Plane   A new airport near San Cristóbal may be open by the time you travel. Initially it will be for small aircraft seating ten to twelve passengers. For the status of services, check with the Municipal Tourism Office (see "Information," below). Until the new airport is open, there are no commercial flights to San Cristóbal—only charter flights to Comitán. Tour agencies in Palenque and San Cristóbal can arrange charter flights between the two cities for a minimum of four people, but the flights are costly.

Charter-flight arrangements or flight changes on any airline in another city can be made through ATC Tours and Travel, across from El Fogón de Jovel Restaurant in San Cristóbal (☎ 967/8-2550; fax 967/8-3145).

By Bus   The **Autotransportes Tuxtla Gutiérrez** (☎ 8-4867) second-class bus station is a half block north of Highway 190 on Avenida Allende. Use this station only if all first-class transportation is full. Buses go to Palenque, Tuxtla, and Comitán. There are two distinct bus lines at this station, and you cannot make reservations on them. **Autotransportes Lacandonia** (☎ 8-1455) second-class buses (also second-rate) leave from their station, located one-half block east of the corner of Highway 190 and Crecencio Rojas. Buses go to Palenque and Villahermosa.

To/From Palenque: From both Tuxtla Gutiérrez and Palenque, **Transportes Rudolfo Figueroa, Mundo Maya**, and **Autotransportes Cristóbal Colón** all have deluxe service several times a day. Three first-class Cristóbal Colón buses go to Palenque daily at 9:30am, and 4:45 and 5:15pm. In either city, buy your ticket the day before your planned departure to ensure a seat.

To/From Tuxtla Gutiérrez: The best way to get to San Cristóbal from Tuxtla Gutiérrez is to hop on one of the 12 direct buses from the first-class Cristóbal Colón bus station for the 1$^{1}/_{2}$-hour trip or to take one of the deluxe Autotransportes Cristóbal Colón or Transportes Rudolfo Figueroa buses. The road between Tuxtla and San Cristóbal is curvy and the buses cover it rapidly, so motion sickness is a consideration. The highway climbs to almost 7,000 feet in a matter of 50 miles, and the scenery is spectacular. To Tuxtla, **Cristóbal Colón** (☎ 8-0291) has hourly first-class buses (called locales) from 6:30am to 9:30pm originating in San Cristóbal; nine others pass through (de paso). There are deluxe "plus" Cristóbal Colón buses departing for Tuxtla daily at 4 and 5:30pm.

To/From Villahermosa: One daily Cristóbal Colón bus leaves for Villahermosa at 10am and takes seven to eight hours.

To/From Oaxaca: There's daily service on Cristóbal Colón to Oaxaca at 10am and 5:15pm; be prepared for a 12-hour trip.

To/From Mérida: Deluxe "plus" Cristóbal Colón buses leave for Mérida at 9am and 8pm (a 14-hour trip). Purchase your ticket a day or two in advance.

By Taxi   Taxis from Tuxtla Gutiérrez to San Cristóbal leave from both the airport and the Cristóbal Colón bus station. See "Getting There & Departing" in Tuxtla Gutiérrez for details.

By Car   From Tuxtla, a 1$^{1}/_{2}$-hour trip, the road winds through beautiful mountain country. The road between Palenque and San Cristóbal de las Casas is adventurous and provides jungle scenery, but portions of it may be heavily potholed, washed out, or have dangerous dips. The trip takes about five hours.

ORIENTATION   Arriving   The **first-class Cristóbal Colón bus station** is on Highway 190, which runs on the southern outskirts of San Cristóbal. The street that intersects the highway in front of the bus station is Avenida de los Insurgentes. From the station, the main plaza is nine blocks north along Insurgentes (a 10- or 15-minute walk).

Deluxe **Rudolfo Figueroa** buses traveling between Palenque and Tuxtla drop passengers on the side of the highway near the first-class bus station. To catch a cab or minibus, walk over to the station.

Urbano minibuses (see "Getting Around," below) pass by the station on Utrilla headed toward the central plaza. Use these if you have only a small bag; if you have heftier luggage, take one of the taxis from in front of the station.

Information   The **Municipal Tourism Office** (☎ 967/8-0660, ext. 126), on the main square in the town hall, across the street from the cathedral, is well organized and has a friendly, helpful staff. The office keeps especially convenient hours: Monday through Saturday from 9am to 8pm and Sunday from 9am to 2pm. Check the bulletin board here for apartments, shared rides, cultural events, and local tours.

City Layout   The cathedral marks the main plaza, where Avenida de los Insurgentes becomes Utrilla. All streets crossing the plaza change their names here. The market is nine blocks north along Utrilla, while the bus station is south. From the market, minibuses (colectivos) trundle to outlying villages.

Take note that this town has at least three streets named "Domínguez." There's Hermanos Domínguez, Belisário Domínguez, and Pantaleón Domínguez.

GETTING AROUND   Most of the sights and shopping in San Cristóbal are within walking distance of the plaza.

Urbano buses are minibuses that take residents to and from town and the outlying neighborhoods. All buses pass by the market and central plaza on their way through town. Utrilla and Avenida 16 de Septiembre are the two main arteries; all buses use the market area as the last stop. Utrilla is one way going toward the market, and any bus on that street will take you to the market. "María Auxiliadora" buses pass by all the bus stations on the way to the distant barrio of the same name.

Colectivo buses to outlying villages depart from the public market at Avenida General Utrilla. Buses late in the day are usually very crowded. Always check to see when the last or next-to-last bus returns from wherever you're going, then take the one before that—those last buses sometimes don't materialize, and you'll be stranded. I speak from experience!

As traffic increases in the city, it often seems quicker to walk to your destination than to grab a taxi. Rides from the plaza to most parts of the city are less than $2. There is a taxi stand on the east side of the plaza.

Rental cars come in handy for trips to the outlying villages and may be worth the expense when shared by a group, but keep in mind that insurance is invalid on unpaved roads. There's a **Budget** rental-car office here at Av. Mazariegos 36 (☎ 967/8-3100). You'll save money by arranging the rental from your home country; otherwise, a day's rental with insurance will cost $62 for a VW Beetle with manual transmission, the cheapest car for rent. Office hours are from 8am to 1pm and 5 to 8pm Monday through Sunday.

Rental bicycles are another option for getting around the city; a day's rental is about $10. Bikes are available at **Rent a Bike,** Av. Insurgentes 57 (☎ 967/ 8-4157), and at some hotels.

FAST FACTS: SAN CRISTÓBAL DE LAS CASAS

Area Code   The telephone area code is 967.

Books   *Living Maya* (Abrams) by Walter Morris with photography by Jeffrey Fox, is the best book to read to understand the culture around San Cristóbal de las Casas. *The People of the Bat: Mayan Tales and Dreams from Zinacantán* (Smithsonian) by Robert M. Laughlin is a priceless collection of beliefs from that village near San Cristóbal.

Bookstore   For a good selection of books about local Indians and crafts, go to Librería Soluna, Real de Guadalupe 13B and Insurgentes 27. Another good bookstore is La Pared de Las Casas, located in the Centro Cultural El Puente (Real de Guadalupe #55). Here you'll find a selection of both new and used books, as well as a collection of travel guides and postcards.

Climate   San Cristóbal can be very cold day or night year-round, especially during the winter. Most hotels are not heated, although some have fireplaces. Come prepared to bundle up in layers that can be peeled off. I always bring heavy socks, gloves, longjohns, and a wool jacket, except in June, July, and August, when I take only heavy socks and a medium-weight jacket or sweater. Some sort of rain gear is handy year-round as well, especially in summer, when rains can be torrential.

Currency Exchange   Banamex is on the main plaza opposite the municipal palace; it's open Monday through Friday from 9:30am to 1pm. However, the most convenient place to exchange money is the Lacantún Money Exchange on Real de Guadalupe 12A, half a block from the plaza and next to the Real del Valle Hotel. It's open Monday through Saturday from 9am to 2pm and 4 to 8pm and Sunday from 9am to 1pm.

Parking   If your hotel does not have parking, use the underground public lot (*estacionamiento*) located in front of the cathedral, just off the main square on 16 de Septiembre. Entry is from Calle 5 de Febrero. They charge $1.50 for 12 hours, $3 for 24 hours.

Photography Warning   Photographers should be very cautious about when, where, and at whom or what they point their cameras. In San Cristóbal, taking a photograph of even a chile pepper can be a risky undertaking, partly because of the native belief that a photograph endangers the soul and partly because the native people are tired of being photographed. Especially in the San Cristóbal market, people who think they or their possessions are being photographed may angrily pelt photographers with whatever object is at hand. Be respectful and ask first. You might even try offering a small amount of money in exchange for taking a picture. Young handcraft vendors will sometimes offer to be photographed for money.

Important note: In villages outside of San Cristóbal, there are strict rules about photography. To ensure proper respect by outsiders, villages around San Cristóbal, especially Chamula and Zinacantán, require visitors to go to the municipal building upon arrival and sign an agreement (written in Spanish) not to take photographs. The penalty for disobeying these regulations is stiff—confiscation of your camera and perhaps even a lengthy stay in jail. They mean it!

Post Office   The post office (Correo) is at Crecencio Rosas and Cuauhtémoc, half a block south of the main square. It's open Monday through Friday from 8am to 7pm for purchasing stamps and mailing letters, 9am to 1pm and 4 to 5pm for mailing packages, and Saturday and holidays from 9am to 1pm.

Spanish Classes   The **Centro Bilingue,** at the Centro Cultural El Puente, Real de Guadalupe 55, San Cristóbal de las Casas, Chi. 29250 (☎/fax 967/8-3723 or 800-303-4983 in the U.S.), offers classes in Spanish. The Director, Roberto Rivas, customizes instruction, be it one-on-one or in a small group, and strongly recommends that students expand their study by lodging with a local family. The **Instituto Jovel,** María Adelina Flores 21 (Apdo. Postal 62), San Cristóbal de las Casas, Chi. 29250 (☎/fax 967/8-4069) is another well-regarded center for learning Spanish. Living with a local family is also part of the learning experience.

EXPLORING SAN CRISTÓBAL

Although San Cristóbal, a mountain town, is hard to get to, it continues to draw more and more visitors who come to enjoy the scenery, air, and hikes in the mountains. The town's biggest attraction is its colorful, centuries-old indigenous culture.

The Chiapan Maya, attired in their beautifully crafted native garb, surround tourists in San Cristóbal, but most travelers take at least one trip to the outlying villages for a truer vision of Maya life

SPECIAL EVENTS

In nearby Chamula, **Carnaval,** the big annual festival which takes place three days before Lent, is a fascinating mingling of the Christian pre-Lenten ceremonies and the ancient Maya celebration of the five "lost days" at the end of the 360-day Maya agricultural cycle. Around noon on Shrove Tuesday, groups of village elders run across patches of burning grass as a purification rite, and then macho residents run through the streets with a bull. During Carnaval, roads are closed in town and buses drop visitors at the outskirts.

Warning: No photography of any kind is allowed during the Chamula Carnaval celebrations.

Nearby villages (except Zinacantán) also have celebrations during this time, although they're perhaps not as dramatic. Visiting these villages, especially on the Sunday before Lent, will round out your impression of Carnaval in all its regional varieties. In Tenejapa, the celebrants are still active during the Thursday market after Ash Wednesday.

San Cristóbal explodes with lights, excitement, and hordes of visitors during the week after Easter, when the annual **Feria de Primavera** (Spring Festival) is held. Activities, which fill an entire week, include carnival rides, food stalls, handcraft shops, parades, and band concerts. Hotel rooms are scarce, and room prices rise accordingly.

Another spectacle is staged July 22–25, the dates of the annual **Fiesta of San Cristóbal,** the town's patron saint. The steps up to San Cristóbal church are lit with torches at night. Pilgrimages to the church begin several days earlier, and on the night of the 24th, there's an all-night vigil.

ATTRACTIONS IN TOWN

✪ Na-Bolom

Av. Vicente Guerrero 3, San Cristóbal de las Casas, Chi. 29200. ☎ and fax **967/8-5586** for the cultural center; tel and fax 8-1418 for hotel reservations. Admission $2 individual tours; $3 group tour and film *La Reina de la Selva*. Individual tours (in Spanish) are available daily 9am–1:30pm. The group tour and film *La Reina de la Selva* (in English) is offered Tues–Sun 4:30–7:30pm. Leave the square on Real de Guadalupe, walk 4 blocks to Avenida Vicente Guerrero, and turn left; Na-Bolom is 5^1/$_2$ blocks up Guerrero, just past the intersection with Comitán.

If you're interested in the anthropology of this region, you'll want to visit this house-cum-museum and stay here if you can. The house, built as a seminary in 1891, became the headquarters of anthropologists Frans and Trudy Blom in 1951 and the gathering place of outsiders interested in studying the region. Frans Blom led many early archaeological studies in Mexico, and Trudy was noted for her photographs of the Lacandón Indians and her efforts to save them and their forest homeland. Postcards of her Lacandón photographs are on sale in Na-Bolom, and a room showcases a selection of them. A tour of the home includes the displays of pre-Hispanic artifacts collected by Frans Blom, the cozy library with its numerous volumes about the region and the Maya, and the gardens Trudy Blom started for the ongoing reforestation of the Lacandón jungle. The tour ends with an excellent 50-minute film on the Bloms, the Lacandóns, and Na-Bolom.

Another film, *La Reina de la Selva* (The Queen of the Selva), about Trudy and the Lacandóns, is shown after the tour. Trudy Blom died in 1993, but Na-Bolom continues to operate as a nonprofit public trust.

The 13 guest rooms, named for surrounding villages, are decorated with local objects and textiles. All rooms have fireplaces. Guests are allowed to use the extensive library devoted to Maya literature. Prices for rooms (including breakfast) are $45 single and $50 double.

Even if you're not a guest here you can come for a meal, usually a delicious assortment of vegetarian dishes. Just be sure to make a reservation and be on time. The colorful dining room has one large table; it's a gathering place for scholars, anthropologists, archeologists, and the like, and the eclectic mix can make for interesting conversation. After dinner, if there's interest, a host will light a fire in the library, and guests can gather there for coffee and conversation amidst more of the Blom's pre-Hispanic artifacts. Breakfast costs $5, lunch and dinner $8 each. Following breakfast at 9am, tours to San Juan Chamula and Zinacantán are offered.

Museo Templo y Convento Santo Domingo
Av. 20 de Noviembre. ☎ **967/8-1600.** Admission free to church. Museum, Mon–Sat $3; Sun and holidays free. Museum, Tues–Sun 10am–5pm.

Inside the front door of the carved-stone plateresque facade, there's a beautiful gilded wooden altarpiece built in 1560, walls with saints, and gilt-framed paintings. Attached to the church is the former Convent of Santo Domingo, which houses a small museum about San Cristóbal and Chiapas. The museum, housed on three floors, has changing exhibits and often shows cultural films. It's five blocks north of the zócalo.

Cathedral
20 de Noviembre at Guadalupe Victoria. No phone. Admission free. Daily 7am–6pm.

San Cristóbal's main cathedral was built in the 1500s and boasts fine timberwork and a very fancy pulpit.

Palacio de las Bellas Artes
Av. Hidalgo, four blocks south of the plaza. No phone.

Be sure to check out this building four blocks south of the plaza if you are interested in the arts. It periodically hosts dance events, art shows, and other performances. The schedule of events is usually posted on the door if the Bellas Artes is not open. There's a public library next door.

Templo de San Cristóbal
For the best view of San Cristóbal, climb the seemingly endless steps to this church and *mirador* (lookout point). Leave the zócalo on Avenida Hidalgo and turn right onto the third street (Hermanos Domínguez); at the end of the street are the steps you've got to climb. A visit here requires stamina. By the way, there are 22 more churches in town, some of which also require a strenuous climb.

Museo de Ambar
Plaza Sivan, Utrilla 10. ☎ **967/8-3507.** Admission free. Daily 9:30am–7pm. From the plaza, walk 2¹/₂ blocks north on Utrilla (going toward the market); the museum will be on your left.

Seen from the street, this place looks like just another store selling Guatemalan clothing, but pass through the small shop area and you'll find the long, narrow museum — a fascinating place to browse. It's the only museum in Mexico devoted to amber, a vegetable-fossil resin thousands of years old mined in Chiapas near Simojovel. Owner José Luís Coria Torres has assembled more than 250 sculpted amber pieces as well as a rare collection of amber with insects trapped inside and amber fused with fossils. Amber jewelry and other objects are also for sale.

HORSEBACK RIDING

The **Casa de Huespedes Margarita** and **Hotel Real del Valle** (see "Accommodations," below) can arrange horseback rides for around $15 for a day, including a guide. Reserve your steed at least a day in advance. A horse-riding excursion might go to San Juan Chamula, to nearby caves, or just up into the hills.

THE NEARBY MAYA VILLAGES & COUNTRYSIDE

I highly recommend taking a tour of local villages. One tour is led by a very opinionated mestiza woman, **Mercedes Hernández Gómez.** Mercedes, a largely self-trained ethnographer, is extremely well informed about the history and folkways of the villages. She explains (in English) the religious significance of what you see in the churches, where shamans try to cure Indian patients of various maladies. She also facilitates tourists' firsthand contact with Indians. Her group goes by minivan to the village or villages she has selected; normally the return to the plaza is at about 2:30pm. You can meet her near the kiosk in the main plaza at 9am (she will be carrying an umbrella). The tour is worth every peso of the $10-per-person charge.

Important note: Do not take photographs in the villages around San Cristóbal (see the "Photography Warning" in "Fast Facts," above). During Carnaval in 1990, I met a French photographer who took one picture from a hill above Chamula, after which villagers hiding in the bushes wrestled him to the ground and seized his Nikon.

For excursions farther afield, see "Road Trips from San Cristóbal" at the end of this section.

CHAMULA & ZINACANTÁN   A side trip to the village of San Juan Chamula will really get you into the spirit of life around San Cristóbal. Sunday, when the market is in full swing, is the best day to go shopping, but other days, when you'll be unimpeded by anxious children selling their crafts, are better for seeing the village and church. Colectivos (minibuses) to San Juan Chamula leave the municipal market in San Cristóbal about every half an hour and charge 75¢. Don't expect anyone in these vans to speak English or Spanish.

The village, five miles northeast of San Cristóbal, is the Chamula cultural and ceremonial center. Activity centers on the huge church, the plaza, and the muni-cipal building. Each year, a new group of citizens is chosen to live in the municipal center as caretakers of the saints, settlers of disputes, and enforcers of village rules. As in other nearby villages on Sunday, local leaders wear their leadership costumes with beautifully woven straw hats loaded with colorful ribbons befitting their high position. They solemnly sit together in a long line somewhere around the central square. Chamula is typical of other villages in that men are often away working in the "hot lands" harvesting coffee or cacao, while women stay home to tend the sheep, the children, the cornfields, and the fires. It's almost always the women's and children's work to gather sticks for fires, and you see them along roadsides bent against the weight.

I don't want to spoil your experience of the interior of the Chamula church for the first time by describing it too much. Just don't leave Chamula without seeing it. As you step from bright sunlight into the candlelit interior, it will take a few minutes for your eyes to adjust. The tile floor is covered in pine needles scattered amid a meandering sea of lighted candles. Saints line the walls, and before them people are often kneeling and praying aloud while passing around bottles of soft drinks. Shamans are often on hand, passing eggs over sick people or using live or dead chickens in a curing ritual. The statues of saints are similar to those you might see in any Mexican Catholic church, but they take on another meaning to the Chamulas that has no similarity to the traditional Catholic saints other than in name. Visitors can walk carefully through the church to see the saints or stand quietly in the background and observe.

Carnaval, which takes place just before Lent, is the big annual festival. The Chamulas are not a very wealthy people as their economy is based on agriculture, but the women are the region's best wool weavers, producing finished pieces for themselves and for other villages.

In Zinacantán, a wealthier village than Chamula, you must sign a rigid form promising not to take any photographs before you are allowed to see the two side-by-side sanctuaries. Once permission is granted and you have paid a small fee, an escort will usually show you the church, or you may be allowed to see it on your own. Floors may be covered in pine needles here, too, and the rooms are brightly sunlit. The experience is an altogether different one from that of Chamula.

AMATENANGO DEL VALLE   About an hour's ride south of San Cristóbal is Amatenango, a town known mostly for its women potters. You'll see their work in San Cristóbal—small animals, jars, and large water jugs—but in the village, you can visit the potters in their homes. All you have to do is arrive and walk down the dirt streets. Villagers will lean over the walls of family compounds and invite you in to select from their inventory. You may even see them firing the pieces under piles of wood in the open courtyard or painting them with color derived from rusty iron water. The women wear beautiful red-and-yellow huipils, but if you want to take a photograph, you'll have to pay.

To get here, take a colectivo from the market in San Cristóbal, but before it lets you off, be sure to ask about the return-trip schedule.

AGUACATENANGO   Located 10 miles south of Amatenango, this village is known for its embroidery. If you've been in San Cristóbal shops before arriving here, you'll recognize the white-on-white or black-on-black floral patterns on dresses and blouses for sale. The locals' own regional blouses, however, are quite different.

TENEJAPA   The weavers of Tenejapa make some of the most beautiful and expensive work you'll see in the region. The best time to visit is on market day (Sunday and Thursday, though Sunday is best). The weavers of Tenejapa taught the weavers of San Andrés and Magdalena, which accounts for the similarity in their designs and colors. To get to Tenejapa, try to find a colectivo in the very last row of colectivos by the market or hire a taxi for around $30. On Tenejapa's main street, several stores sell locally woven regional clothing, and you can bargain for the price.

THE HUITEPEC CLOUD FOREST   **Pronatura,** a private nonprofit ecological organization, offers environmentally sensitive tours of the cloud forest. The forest is a haven for migratory birds, and over 100 bird species and 600 plant species have been discovered here. In the past, tours have been offered Tuesday,

Thursday, and Saturday at 9:30am at a cost $6 per person; these tours have been temporarily suspended because Pronatura has moved their office. Inquire for their address and phone number at the Municipal Tourism Office in San Cristóbal (see "Information," above). To reach the reserve on your own, drive on the road to Chamula; the turnoff is at km 3.5. The reserve is open Tuesday through Saturday from 9am to 5pm.

SHOPPING

Many Indian villages near San Cristóbal are noted for their weaving, embroidery, brocade work, leather, and pottery, making the area one of the best in the country for shopping. The craftspeople make and sell beautiful serapes, colorful native shirts, magnificently woven huipils (women's long overblouses), all of which often come in vivid geometric patterns. In leather they are artisans of the highest rating, making sandals and men's handbags. There's a proliferation of tie-dyed jaspe from Guatemala, which comes in bolts and is made into clothing, as well as other textiles from that country. There are numerous shops up and down the streets leading to the market. Calle Real de Guadalupe houses more shops than any other street.

Crafts

La Albarrada, Centro Desarrollo Comunitario Dif
Barrio María Auxiliadora. No phone.

At this government-sponsored school, young men and women from surrounding villages come to learn how to hook Persian-style rugs, weave fabric on footlooms, sew, make furniture, construct a house, cook, make leather shoes and bags, forge iron, and grow vegetables and trees for reforestation. Probably the most interesting crafts for the general tourist are the rug making and weaving. Artisans from Temoaya in Mexico State learned rugmaking from Persians, who came to teach this skill in the 1970s. The Temoaya artisans in turn traveled to San Cristóbal to teach the craft to area students, who have since taught others. The beautiful rug designs are taken from brocaded and woven designs used to decorate regional costumes. Visitors should stop at the entrance and ask for an escort. You can visit all the various areas and see students at work or simply go straight to the weavers. There's a small sales outlet at the entrance selling newly loomed fabric by the meter, leather bags, rugs, and baskets made at another school in the highlands. The rug selection is best here, but the Casa de Artesanías DIF in the town center (see "Textile Shops," below) features these crafts and more from around Mexico. La Albarrada is in a far southern suburb of the city off the highway to Comitán, to the right. To get here take the "María Auxiliadora" urbano bus from the market. Ask the driver to let you off at La Albarrada. The same bus makes the return trip, passing through town center and ending its route at the market.

Central Market
Av. Utrilla. No phone.

The market buildings and the streets surrounding them offer just about anything you need. The market in San Cristóbal is open every morning except Sunday (when each village has its own local market), and you'll probably enjoy observing the sellers as much as at the things they sell. See the "Photography Warning" in "Fast Facts," above, regarding photography here. The mercado is north of the Santo Domingo church, about nine blocks from the zócalo.

El Encuentro

Calle Real de Guadalupe 63-A. ☎ **967/8-3698.**

This place is tended by a pair of *dueñas muy simpáticas*, and you'll find some of your best bargains here—or at least you'll think the price is fair. The shop carries many regional ritual items, such as new and used men's ceremonial hats, false saints, and iron rooftop adornments, plus many huipils and other textiles. It's open Monday through Saturday from 9am to 8pm. It's between Dujelay and Guerrero.

La Galería

Hidalgo 3. ☎ **967/8-1547.**

This lovely shop beneath a great cafe has a wonderful selection of paintings and greeting cards by Kiki, a German artist who has found her niche in San Cristóbal. There is also an extensive selection of Oaxacan rugs and pottery, plus unusual silver jewelry. Open daily from 10am to 9pm.

Textile Shops

Casa de Artesanías Dif

Niños Héroes at Hidalgo. ☎ **967/8-1180.**

Crafts made under the sponsorship of DIF (a governmental agency that assists families) are sold in a fine showroom in one of the city's old houses. Here you'll find such quality products as lined wool vests and jackets, bolts of foot-loomed fabrics, Persian-style rugs made at La Albarrada (see "Crafts," above), pillow covers, amber jewelry, and more. In back is a fine little museum showing costumes worn by villagers who live near San Cristóbal. Open Monday through Saturday from 9am to 2pm and 5 to 8pm.

Plaza de Santo Domingo

Av. Utrilla.

The plazas around this church and the nearby Templo de Caridad are filled with women in native garb selling their wares. Here you'll find women from Chamula weaving belts or embroidering, surrounded by piles of loomed woolen textiles from their village. More and more Guatemalan shawls, belts, and bags are included in their inventory. There are also some excellent buys in Chiapan-made wool vests, jackets, rugs, and shawls similar to those in Sna Jolobil (see below), if you take the time to look and bargain. Vendors arrive between 9 and 10am and begin to leave around 3pm.

Sna Jolobil

Av. 20 de Noviembre. No phone.

Meaning "weaver's house" in the Maya language, this place is located in the former convent (monastery) of Santo Domingo, next to the Templo de Santo Domingo between Navarro and Nicaragua. This cooperative store is operated by groups of Tzotzil and Tzeltal craftspeople and has about 3,000 members who contribute products, help in running the store, and share in the moderate profits. Their works are simply beautiful; prices, which are set and high—as is the quality. Be sure to take a look. Open Monday through Saturday from 9am to 2pm and 4 to 6pm; credit cards are accepted.

Tzontehuitz

Real de Guadalupe 74. ☎ and fax **967/8-3158.**

About 3¹/₂ blocks from the plaza, this shop is one of the best on Calle Real de Guadalupe, near the corner of Diego Dujelay. Owner Janet Giacobone specializes in her own textile designs and weavings. Some of her work is loomed in Guatemala, but you can also watch weavers using foot looms in the courtyard. Hours are Monday through Saturday from 9am to 2pm and 4 to 7pm.

Unión Regional de Artesanías de los Altos
Av. Utrilla 43. ☎ **967/8-2848.**

Another cooperative of weavers, this one is smaller than Sna Jolobil (see above) but not necessarily any cheaper and not as sophisticated in its approach to potential shoppers. Also known as J'pas Joloviletic, it's worth looking around, and credit cards are accepted (though they weren't in the past). Open Monday through Saturday from 9am to 2pm and 4 to 7pm and Sunday from 9am to 1pm.

ACCOMMODATIONS

Keep in mind that among the most interesting places to stay in San Cristóbal is an anthropologist's dream—the house/museum of **Na-Bolom.** See "Attractions in Town," above, for details.

If you're interested in a very cheap hospedaje, ask around in a restaurant or cafe, and you're sure to find one, or go to the tourist office, which often displays notices of new hospedajes on the metal flip rack in the office.

Some of the best economical offerings are on Calle Real de Guadalupe, east of the main square.

Important note about hotel prices: The prices quoted below are the highest rates hotels charge and usually apply only during July, August, Easter week, and Christmas. In the past, *rates were 20% lower at all other times*, but with the peso devaluation, this could change.

MODERATE

Hotel Casa Mexicana
28 de Agosto No. 1, San Cristóbal de las Casas, Chi. 29200. ☎ **967/8-0698.** Fax 967/8-2627. 31 rms (all with bath). TV TEL. $62.50 double. Free secure parking.

This lovely new hotel is a luxurious addition to the San Cristóbal scene. Tastefully designed, decorated, and furnished, the hotel has a colonial feel enhanced by two courtyards. Rooms have electric heaters for chilly mornings and either one or two double beds. There's a reasonably priced restaurant as well. To find the hotel from the Museo de Ambar, walk one-half block north on Utrilla and turn left on Agosto/Eje Nacional; the hotel is on the right.

✪ Hotel Casavieja
Ma. Adelina Flores 27, San Cristóbal de las Casas, Chi. 29200. ☎ and fax **967/8-5253** or 967/8-0385. 36 rms (all with bath). TV TEL. $45 double. Free parking.

The Casavieja, originally built in 1740, is undoubtedly one of the choice hotels in Mexico. Restoration and new construction have faithfully replicated the original design and detail. The large size and beautiful furnishings of the rooms make you want to stay in rather than going out sightseeing. The hotel's restaurant, Doña Rita, offers delicious authentic Mexican dishes at reasonable prices.

✪ Hotel Rincón del Arco
Ejército Nacional 66, San Cristóbal de las Casas, Chi. 29200. ☎ **967/8-1313.** Fax 967/8-1568. 36 rms (all with bath). TV TEL. $45 double. Free parking.

The original section of this former colonial-era home, dating from 1650, is built around a small interior patio. Rooms in this part exude charm, with tall ceilings and carpet over hardwood floors. Those in the adjacent new section face a large grassy inner yard and are clean and sizable. Each room in this section is distinct: some are furnished in antiques and others in colonial style. Some have small balconies; all have fireplaces. Throughout the hotel, there are coordinated drapes and bedspreads loomed in the family factory. Owner José António Hernánz is eager to make your stay pleasant. There's an excellent restaurant just behind the lobby. The hotel offers special discounted prices to students (make arrangements in advance and be able to show university identification). To find the hotel from the plaza, walk three blocks north on Utrilla to Ejército Nacional, then turn right and walk five blocks; the hotel is on the corner of Avenida V. Guerrero.

Hotel Posada de Los Angeles
Calle Francisco Madero 17, San Cristóbal de las Casas, Chi. 29200. ☎ **967/8-1173** or 8-4371. Fax 967/8-2581. 20 rms (all with bath). TV TEL. $50 double.

With beautiful etched-glass doors opening to the street, this inn, which opened in 1991, deserves your attention. The vaulted ceilings and skylights make the three-story hotel seem much larger and brighter than many others in the city. Rooms have either two single or two double beds, and the baths are large, modern, and immaculately clean. Windows open onto a pretty courtyard with a fountain. The rooftop sun deck is a great siesta spot. The hotel is a half a block east of the plaza between Insurgentes and Juárez.

INEXPENSIVE

Hotel Don Quijote
Colón 7, San Cristóbal de las Casas, Chi. 29230. ☎ and fax **967/8-0346.** 22 rms (all with bath). TV. $22.50 double; $27 triple. Free secure parking.

Upon entering this three-story hotel in a former residence built around a small patio, you'll see walls decorated with costumes from area villages. Throughout the hotel there are photos of old San Cristóbal and murals depicting Don Quixote. The small rooms are crowded with furniture and closets are small, but the rooms are carpeted and coordinated with warm, beautiful textiles foot-loomed in the family factory. All have two double beds with lamps over them, private tiled baths, and plenty of hot water. To find the hotel from the plaza, walk two blocks east on Real de Guadelupe then left on Colón; the hotel is on the right.

Hotel Fray Bartolomé de las Casas
Niños Héroes 2, San Cristóbal de las Casas, Chi. 29200. ☎ **967/8-0932.** Fax 967/8-3510. 26 rms (all with bath). $22.50 double.

This clean, quiet old colonial inn makes a beautiful impression with its low, sloping red-tile roof supported by dark-wood columns around a beautiful red-tile court-yard. The plain rooms are in fair condition. In some the carpets are stained, and

Impressions

No other race that I can call to mind allowed so wide a disparity between the simple bread with which they feed their bodies and the arts by which they nourished their souls. . . . Even today, Mexican Indians have only a rudimentary development of the so-called instinct of acquisition, and a very sophisticated development of artistic appreciation as reflected in their craftsmanship.
—Stuart Chase, Mexico: A Study of Two Americas, 1931

some showers drip constantly; other rooms are entirely satisfactory. The courtyard has planters, wrought-iron furniture, and lots of flowers. Breakfast is served in the small dining room. To find it from the plaza, walk two blocks south on Insurgentes; the hotel is on the right at the corner of Insurgentes and Niños Heroes.

⚫ Hotel Palacio de Moctezuma

Juárez 16, San Cristóbal de las Casas, Chi. 29200. ☎ **967/8-0352** or 8-1142. Fax 967/8-1536. 42 rms (all with bath). TV TEL. $27 double. Free limited parking.

An excellent choice near the plaza, this three-story hotel is delightfully filled with bougainvillea and geraniums. Fresh-cut flowers tucked around tile fountains are a hallmark of this hotel. The rooms have lace curtains on French windows, handsome coordinated drapes and bedspreads, red carpeting, and modern tiled showers. Two suites have a TV and refrigerator. Overstuffed couches face a large fireplace in the lobby bar, and the cozy restaurant looks out on the interior courtyard. On the third floor is a solarium with comfortable tables and chairs and great city views. To find the hotel from the plaza, walk two blocks south on Insurgentes and turn left on León; the hotel is on the next corner on the left.

Hotel Plaza Santo Domingo

Utrilla 35, San Cristóbal de las Casas, Chi. 29200. ☎ and fax **967/8-1927**. 29 rms (all with bath). TV TEL. $24 double. Limited parking.

New in 1992, this hotel is ideally situated close to the Santo Domingo Church, near the bustling market area. Behind the lobby and plant-filled entry courtyard are the nicely furnished, carpeted rooms. Each comes with a small closet and small desk below the TV, which is set high on the wall. Baths are trimmed in blue-and-white tile, and the sink area is conveniently placed outside the shower area. A large pleasant indoor dining room is off the lobby, along with a smaller patio dining area and a large bar. This is one of the few places near Santo Domingo and the market where you can get a good meal and use clean restrooms.

⚫ Hotel Real de Valle

Real de Guadalupe 14, San Cristóbal de las Casas, Chi. 29200. ☎ **967/8-0680**. Fax 967/8-3955. 36 rms (all with bath). $16.50 double.

The helpful staff at the Real de Valle is quick to help guests in any way possible. The 24 new rooms in the back three-story section have new baths, big closets, and a brown-and-cream decor. In addition to a rooftop solarium with chaise lounges, you'll find a small cafeteria and an upstairs dining room with a big double fireplace. Services include a travel agency offering personally guided tours, horse rental, laundry, Spanish-language study, and use of a fax and photocopy machine. To find the hotel from the plaza, walk a half block east of the central plaza on Real de Guadalupe.

⑤ Posada Jovel

Flavio Paniagua 28, San Cristóbal de las Casas, Chi. 29200. ☎ **967/8-1734**. 18 rms (9 with bath). $10.50 double without bath; $13.50 double with bath.

If you're low on funds and want to stay a while in cheery surroundings, then you may find this modest two-story inn to your liking. The bright, freshly painted rooms have tile floors and colorful blanket/bedspreads and *ixtle* (basket) lamps. Shelves and hooks hold belongings, and beds are firm. This place belongs to an association of posadas, so they'll recommend another budget lodging if they're full. The posada is between the market and main plaza, 2¹/₂ very long blocks east of Utrilla.

Posada San Cristóbal

Insurgentes 3, San Cristóbal de las Casas, Chi. 29200. ☎ **967/8-4238.** 10 rms (all with bath). $22.50 double.

This small, quiet hotel, fashioned from a two-story town house, is built around a lovely central courtyard. The small rooms are immaculately clean and have wood floors, simple wooden beds and dressers, no heat, and no toilet seats. The showers tend to flood the bathroom floors. While not fancy, the hotel has charm, convenience, and comfort. The reasonably priced hotel restaurant Kukulkán in back offers a view of the street and courtyard. To find the hotel from the plaza, walk one block south on Insurgentes; it's on the right.

DINING

San Cristóbal is one of the country's best dining-out towns because of the sheer quality of its food. In addition to the establishments mentioned below, most hotels have their own restaurants and serve good meals. Be sure to look for regional Chiapan food like large tamales, butifarra (a delicious sausage), and posh (a local firewater similar to aguardiente). Remember that you're about a mile and a half high here, and therefore you digest your food more slowly.

MODERATE

✪ El Fogón de Jovel

16 de Septiembre no. 11. ☎ **967/8-1153.** Corn soup $2.75; Chiapan tamales $4.25 for 5; main courses $5–$7.50. Daily 1–5pm, 7–11pm. CHIAPAN.

If word-of-mouth doesn't lead you here, the lively sounds of marimba music will. Chiapan food is served at this handsome old town house, with dining under the portals and rooms built around a central courtyard. The waiters wear local costumes. Walls are hung with Guatemalan and Chiapan prints and folk art. Each dish and regional drink such as posh (a distilled sugar-and-corn drink) is explained on the menu, which is available in English. I highly recommend the Chiapan tamales, the corn soup, and the beef-stuffed chiles rellenos. A basket of steaming warm tortillas with six condiments arrives before the meal. The restaurant is only a block northwest of the plaza at the corner of Guadalupe Victoria/Real de Guadalupe.

La Parrilla

Belisario Domínguez 32. ☎ **967/8-2220.** Tacos $3.50–$4.25; grilled meat plates $3.50–$9; side dishes $1.75–$3.50. Mon–Sat 6:30pm–midnight; Sun noon–midnight. GRILLED MEAT.

If you're hungering for a rib-sticking meat-and-potatoes meal, La Parrilla is your place. Guests check off their orders on a printed list of selections, available in English and Spanish. Meats are grilled over a wood fire in the main dining room. Side dishes are ordered separately; don't miss the ranch-style beans and grilled whole onion or the queso fundido served several ways. There are also several varieties of tacos, quesadillas, and pizzas. To find La Parrilla from the plaza, walk four blocks north on Utrilla and turn right on Dr. Navarro for one block until you reach B. Domínguez.

Restaurant El Faisan

Madero 2. ☎ **967/8-2000.** Breakfast $2.50–$4.50; main courses $3.50–$8.50; comida corrida $5. Daily 7am–11pm (comida corrida served 2–6pm). MEXICAN/REGIONAL.

Low lighting, clay lanterns, glass-top tables, and native embroidery draw a romantic dinner crowd to this small restaurant. The menu includes delicious pollo a la plancha, cochinita guisado, and quesadillas with sliced red peppers. Wine is served, and there are free coffee refills at breakfast. The restaurant is two doors east of the plaza.

INEXPENSIVE

⊜ Café El Puente

Real de Guadalupe 55. ☎ **967/8-2250.** Breakfast $1.75–$3; soups and salads $1–$3; pastries 50¢–$2. Mon–Sat 8am–10:30pm. MEXICAN.

Ex-Californian Bill English has turned a huge old mansion into a cafe/cultural center where tourists and locals can converse. The café takes up the main part of the building; there are a weaver's shop and travel agency to the side. The Centro Bilingue language school is headquartered here as well, and movies, plays, and lectures are presented nightly in an interior patio and meeting room. It's the kind of place you return to often, for fresh waffles and coffee in the morning, for an inexpensive lunch or dinner of brown rice and veggies, or for good conversation at any time of day. Guests are welcome to post notices, messages, and advertisements on the long bulletin board, which is well worth checking out if you're looking for a ride, a place to stay, or information on out-of-the-way destinations. It's 2$^1/_2$ blocks east of the plaza.

✪ Madre Tierra

Insurgentes 19. ☎ **967/8-4297.** Main courses $2–$5.50; comida corrida $7.25. Restaurant, daily 8am–9:45pm (comida corrida served 1–5pm); bakery, Mon–Sat 9am–8pm, Sun 9am–noon. MEXICAN/VEGETARIAN.

This restaurant satisfies the cravings of meat lovers and vegetarians alike. The bakery specializes in whole-wheat breads, pastries, pizza by the slice, quiche, grains, granola, and dried fruit. The restaurant serves the bakery's goods and other delicious fare in an old mansion with wood-plank floors, long windows looking onto the street, and tables covered in colorful Guatemalan jaspe. Classical music plays softly in the background. It's a good place for a cappuccino and pastry or an entire meal; the comida corrida is very filling, and I also recommend the chicken curry, lasagna, and fresh salads. Madre Tierra is on Insurgentes, 3$^1/_2$ blocks south of the plaza.

✪ Paris-Mexico Restaurant

Madero 20. ☎ **967/8-0695.** Crêpes $1.75–$3.50; pizzas $4.75–$6; comida corrida $4.75–$5.50. Daily 7am–11pm. MEXICAN/FRENCH/ITALIAN.

Decorated with plain, nicely finished wood tables and chairs, the Paris-Mexico resembles a cozy neighborhood café. The food is wonderfully prepared. The comida corrida might consist of salad, grilled chicken breast, potatoes or rice, fruit salad, and coffee or tea. You can also choose from an endless list of crêpes for breakfast, lunch, dinner, or dessert; pizza served 10 ways; five variations on spaghetti; or a small selection of beef and chicken dishes. The Paris-Mexico is on Madero, a half block east of the plaza.

✪ Restaurant Tuluc

Insurgentes 5. ☎ **967/8-2090.** Breakfast $1.75–$3.50; main course $3–$6; comida corrida $4.50. Daily 7am–10pm (comida corrida served 1–5pm). MEXICAN.

This warm and inviting restaurant has lustrous wooden booths and tables with Guatemalan fabric. It's a cozy place for a cup of hot chocolate or espresso, but above all, the comida corrida is an exceptional value here. The evening menu is equally popular. The house specialty is the filete Tuluc, a beef filet wrapped around spinach and cheese served with fried potatoes and green beans. The Chiapaneco breakfast is a filling quartet of juice, toast, two Chiapan tamales, and your choice of tea, coffee, cappuccino, or hot chocolate. The owner speaks seven languages. Tuluc is 1½ blocks south of the plaza between Cuauhtémoc and F. Leon.

COFFEEHOUSES

Since Chiapan-grown coffee is highly regarded, it's natural to find a proliferation of coffeehouses here. Most are concealed in the nooks and crannies of San Cristóbal's side streets.

Café Altura and Casa Naturista

Primero de Marzo #6C. ☎ **967/8-4038.** Soy burgers $2; salads $2; coffee 75¢–$1.25. Daily 7am–9pm. VEGETARIAN.

Café Altura specializes in organic vegetarian meals. Breakfasts include granola, yogurt, fruit, and whole-wheat breads, and a variety of coffees is available all day. Grains, granola, teas, and coffee beans are sold in bulk. The cafe is three blocks north of the plaza near the corner of Primero de Marzo and 16 de Noviembre.

Café San Cristóbal

Cuauhtémoc 1. ☎ **967/8-3861.** Coffee 50¢–$1; cake $1.25–$2.50. Mon–Sat 9am–10pm, Sun 10am–2pm and 5–10pm. COFFEE/CAKE.

Not only is this a cafe, but it also sells coffee beans by the kilogram (2.2 lb.) for $4. Chess is the game of choice at the few tables and booths; men hunker over their chessboards for hours, drinking coffee and visiting with friends. A cup of coffee here provides a respite from the rush outside. The restaurant is one block south of the plaza near the corner of Cuauhtémoc and Insurgentes.

A BAKERY

Panadería Mercantil

Mazariego 17. ☎ **967/8-0307.** 15¢–$3. Mon–Sat 8am–9:30pm, Sun 9am–9pm. BAKERY.

This bakery has shelves laden with freshly baked bread, cookies, and rolls. The restaurant is 1½ blocks west of the plaza between 16 de Septiembre and 5 de Mayo.

ROAD TRIPS FROM SAN CRISTÓBAL

Several travel agencies in town offer excursions to nearby villages and those farther away. Strangely, ex-cept where noted otherwise, the cost of the trip includes a driver but does not necessarily include either a bilingual guide or guided informa-tion of any kind. You pay extra for those services, so if you want to be informed while taking a tour, be sure to ask if the tour is merely transportation or if it in-cludes a knowledgeable guide as well.

RUINS OF TONINÁ The Maya ruins of Toniná (which means "house of rocks") are two hours from San Cristóbal and 8½ miles east of Ocosingo. Dating from the Classic Period, the terraced site covers an area of at least nine square miles. Extensive excavations are under way here during the dry season.

As early as A.D. 350, Toniná emerged as a separate dynastic center from the Maya and has the distinction of having the last recorded date of the long count yet found (A.D. 909) on a small stone monument. Another stone, dated A.D. 711, discovered here depicts the captured King Kan-Xul of Palenque (the younger brother of Chan-Bahlum and the son of King Pacal); the portrait shows him with his arm tied by a rope but still wearing his royal headdress. Recently a huge stucco panel was unearthed picturing the Lord of Death holding Kan-Xul's head, confirming long-held suspicions that the king died at Toniná.

At the moment there are no signs to guide visitors through the site, so you're on your own. The caretaker can also show you around (in Spanish), after which a tip is appreciated. Ask at the Casa Margarita in San Cristóbal (see "Accommodations," above) about guided trips to Toniná for $18 per person, with a four-person minimum. The trip includes the services of a bilingual driver, a tour of the site, lunch, and a swim in the river. From November through February you'll see thousands of swallows swarming near the ruins.

You can go on your own by bus to Ocosingo and from there take a taxi to the ruins, but have the taxi wait for your return. The ruins are open daily from 8am to 5pm; admission is $3.

PALENQUE, BONAMPAK & YAXCHILÁN Many visitors to San Cristóbal want to visit the ruins of Palenque near Villahermosa and the Bonampak and Yaxchilán ruins on Mexico's border with Guatemala. A trip to Palenque can be accomplished in a long day-trip from San Cristóbal, but I don't recommend it because Palenque should be savored. Bonampak and Yaxchilán are easier to see from Palenque.

For arranging these trips from San Cristóbal, I highly recommend **ATC Tours and Travel,** located across from El Fogón restaurant, Calle 5 de Febrero no. 15 at the corner of 16 de Septiembre (☎ 967/8-2550; fax 967/8-3145). The agency has bilingual guides and good vehicles. There's also a branch in Palenque. See the Palenque section, below, for details on Bonampak and camping overnight at Yaxchilán; see "Outdoor Sports, Adventure Travel & Wilderness Trips" in Chapter 3 for other ATC regional tours focusing on birds and orchids, textiles, hiking, and camping.

If you're considering a day-trip to the archaeological site of Palenque using ATC (mentioned above) or a similar travel agency, here's how your tour will be arranged. You starting at 7 or 8am and within three hours reach the Agua Azul waterfalls, where there's a 1 1/2-hour stop to swim. From there it's another 1 1/2-hour drive to Palenque. You'll have about 2 hours to see the site. If your group agrees, you can skip the swim and have more time at Palenque. It'll be a minimum 16-hour day and costs about $80 per person with a minimum of four people traveling.

CHINCULTIC RUINS, COMITÁN & MONTEBELLO NATIONAL PARK Almost 100 miles southeast of San Cristóbal, near the border of Guatemala, is the Chincultic archeological site and Montebello National Park, with 16 multicolored lakes and exuberant pine-forest vegetation. Forty-six miles from San Cristóbal is Comitán, a pretty hillside town of 40,000 inhabitants known for its flower cultivation and a sugarcane-based firewater called *comitecho*. It's also the last big town along the Pan American Highway before the Guatemalan border, and it's the location of the nearest airport to San Cristóbal.

The Chincultic ruins, a Late-Classic site, have barely been excavated, but the main acropolis, set high up against a cliff, is magnificent to see from below and worth the walk up for the vista. After passing through the gate, you'll see the trail ahead; it passes ruins on both sides. Steep stairs leading up the mountain to the acropolis are flanked by more unexcavated tree-covered ruins. From there, you can gaze upon distant Montebello Lakes and miles of cornfields and forest. The paved road to the lakes passes six lakes, all different colors and sizes ringed by cool pine forests; most have car parks and lookouts. The paved road ends at a small restaurant. The lakes are best seen on a sunny day, when their famous brilliant colors are optimal.

Most travel agencies in San Cristóbal offer a day-long trip that includes the lakes, the ruins, lunch in Comitán, and a stop in the pottery-making village of Amatenango del Valle. If you're driving, follow Highway 190 south from San Cristóbal through the pretty village of Teopisca and then through Comitán; turn left at La Trintaria, where there's a sign to the lakes. After the Trintaria turnoff and before you reach the lakes, there's a sign pointing left down a narrow dirt road to the Chincultic ruins.

3 Palenque

89 miles SE of Villahermosa, 143 miles NE of San Cristóbal

The ruins of Palenque are one of the most spectacular of the Maya archeological sites, with roof-combed temples ensconced in lush vegetation high above the savannas. The ruins, located on the edge of the jungle in the state of Chiapas, are part of a reserve known as the Parque Nacional Palenque. The flora of the surrounding countryside continues to encroach on the park, and it takes a team of machete wielders to hold the jungle back.

Were it not for the local ruins, the town of Palenque (pop. 16,000) would hardly exist. This slow-paced, somnolent village is accustomed to visitors passing through, but it pays them little heed.

ESSENTIALS

GETTING THERE & DEPARTING   By Plane   A new airport at San Cristóbal de las Casas should be open by the time you travel to handle smaller private and charter aircraft. Check with travel agencies in Villahermosa, Tuxtla Gutiérrez, and San Cristóbal de las Casas for information. Until the new airport was slated to open in San Cristóbal, the airport at Comitán (about 50 miles southeast of San Cristóbal de las Casas) served all Palenque charter flights; however, it was closed when I checked.

By Bus   Four bus stations serve Palenque, and all are within three blocks of the hospital on Avenida Juárez. Of these, the Transportes Cristóbal Colón and Transportes Rudolfo Figueroa (which share a building) should be the first choice when looking for transportation. ADO and Autotransportes Tuxtla Gutiérrez offer limited service.

From Tuxtla Gutiérrez, with stops in San Cristóbal, both **Omnibus Cristóbal Colón**   (☎ 934/5-0140) and **Transportes Rudolfo Figueroa** (☎ 934/5-0369) run several deluxe buses to Palenque. The trip from Palenque to San Cristóbal takes around six hours. When TRF buses reach San Cristóbal, passengers are only dropped off on the highway near the bus station and cannot board for a return to ride to Palenque or Tuxtla. TRF buses are the most deluxe buses traveling this route, with movies, curtained windows, air-conditioning, and heat. The bathroom is never unlocked. If you tend toward claustrophobia or nausea, however, be forewarned that the windows do not open. From Mérida, the trip to Palenque takes around nine hours. Twice daily, deluxe Cristóbal Colón buses make the trip with onboard bathroom, movies, snacks, and soft drinks.

From Villahermosa's first-class **ADO** station (☎ 934/5-0400), there are eight buses to Palenque daily; the trip takes 1¹/₂ to 3 hours. From San Cristóbal there are three buses which leave at 9am, 7 and 8pm for the three-hour run. Three buses run to Mérida at 8am and 8 and 9:30pm, eight to Villahermosa, one to Chetumal at 10:30pm, and three to Escárcega at 8am and 8 and 8:30pm.

Autotransportes Tuxtla Gutiérrez (☎ 934/5-0369) is on your left (north) about a block beyond the Pemex station as you enter town from the ruins. These buses, going to Tuxtla and San Cristóbal are second class and should be considered only if other lines are full. The line also has buses to Agua Azul at 8 and 11:30am; tickets can be purchased only 30 minutes in advance.

Almost directly across the street from the Pemex station is the **Terminal de Transportes Dag Dug** (no phone). It's known locally as the **Mérida station,** although only one bus daily goes to Mérida. There are so few buses operating from here that this should be a choice only when all other lines are full.

By Car   The 143-mile trip from San Cristóbal to Palenque takes five to six hours and passes through lush jungle and mountain scenery. Take it easy since potholes and other hindrances occur. Highway 186 from Villahermosa is in good condition, and the trip from there and on the Palenque turnoff should take about 1 1/2 hours.

ORIENTATION   Arriving   Most travelers reach Palenque on buses, which arrive four or five blocks from the zócalo. Taxis from the bus stations to most hotels cost less than $1.50; only those hotels surrounding the zócalo are within walking distance if you're carrying heavy luggage.

Information   The **State Tourism Office** (☎ 934/5-0760 or 5-0828) is located a block west of the zócalo on Juárez at the corner of Abasolo (north side of the street). The office is open Monday through Saturday from 8am to 9pm.

City Layout   The **ruins** are about 5 miles southwest of town. The road from Villahermosa forks just west of town at the impossible-to-miss Maya statue; the ruins are southwest of the statue, and the town lies to the east.

Palenque has three separate areas where tourists tend to congregate. The most central area is around the **main plaza,** bordered by Avenidas Hidalgo, 20 de Noviembre, Independencia, and Jiménez. **La Cañada** is a pleasant area located five very long blocks west of the main plaza on Merle Green, a partially paved road that runs through a tropical forest. Here, you'll find a few small hotels and restaurants and stands of artists who carve and paint. Aside from the main plaza area, this is the best location for travelers without cars, since the town is within a few blocks and the buses that run to the ruins pass by La Cañada. The third tourist zone is along the **road to the ruins,** where small hotels, RV parks, and campgrounds are tucked into the surrounding jungle. This is an ideal location for those with cars.

GETTING AROUND   The cheapest way to get back and forth from the ruins is on the Chambalu colectivo buses, which depart from the terminal at Avenidas Juárez and Allende every 10 minutes from 6am to 6pm; the fare is 50¢. Chambalu also runs buses five times daily to Misol Ha and Agua Azul; the fare is $6. The buses pass La Cañada and hotels along the road to the ruins, but they may not stop if they're full.

Taxis from town to the ruins cost $3 to $4.50; drivers may charge more from the ruins back to town.

FAST FACTS   The **telephone area code** is 934. As for the **climate,** Palenque's constant humidity is downright oppressive in the summer, especially after rain showers. During the winter, the damp air can be chilly, especially in the evenings, so a jacket is a good idea. Rain gear is important any time of year. For **books** regarding background on the region, two important works will significantly enhance your visit: John Stephen's two volumes of *Incidents of Travel in Central America, Chiapas and Yucatán* (Dover Press, 1963) written in 1841 and 1843; and *A Forest of Kings: An Untold Story of the Ancient Maya* (William Morrow, 1990) by Linda Schele and David Friedel.

EXPLORING PALENQUE

The real reason for being here is the ruins, which can be toured in a morning; but many people like to savor Palenque. Despite the fame of the ruins, the village of Palenque remains rather uncommercialized, though more shops are opening and new hotel construction has started on the road into town. There are no must-see sights in the town; if you have time to spare, sit on the main plaza and observe the goings-on. The La Cañada area west of town (see "City Layout," above) is a pleasant spot for a leisurely lunch and for browsing through Maya reproductions made by local artists.

PARQUE NACIONAL PALENQUE

The archaeological site of Palenque underwent several changes in 1994, which culminated in the opening of a new museum/visitors' center on the highway to the ruins. The complex includes a large parking lot; a refreshment stand serving snacks and drinks; and two shops with an impressive display of quality folk art from throughout Chiapas. The **museum,** although not large, is worth an additional entrance fee and the time it takes to see it. Inside are well-chosen and artistically displayed exhibits. Explanatory texts, in both Spanish and English, explain the life and times of the magnificent city of Palenque. New pieces are constantly being added as they are uncovered in ongoing excavations. The **main entrance,** about a mile beyond the museum, is still at the top of a hill at the end of the paved highway. There, you'll find a large parking lot, a refreshment stand, a ticket booth, and two shops displaying folk art. Among the vendors selling souvenirs by the parking lot are Lacandón Indians wearing white tunics and hawking bows and arrows.

Admission to the ruins is $4.75; free on Sunday. There's a $7.50 charge for each video camera used. Parking at the main entrance and at the visitors' center is free. The site and visitors' center shops are open daily from 8am to 5pm; the crypt is open daily from 10am to 4pm. Admission to the museum is an additional $4.75; it's open Tuesday through Sunday from 10am to 5pm.

TOURING THE RUINS Pottery found during the excavations shows that people lived in this area as early as 300 B.C. During the Classic Period (A.D. 300–900), the ancient Maya city of Palenque was a ceremonial center for the high priests; the civilization peaked at around 600 to 700.

When John Stephens visited the site in the 1840s, the cleared ruins you see today were buried under centuries of accumulated earth and a thick canopy of jungle. The dense jungle surrounding the cleared portion still covers yet unexplored temples, which are easily discernible even to the untrained eye. Of all the ruins in Mexico open to the public, this is the most haunting because of its majesty and sense of the past. Scholars have unearthed names of the rulers and their family histories, putting visitors on a first-name basis with these ancient people etched in stone.

King Pacal's Tomb

The great stone hieroglyphic panels found inside the Temple of the Inscriptions contain the dynastic family tree of King Pacal (most of the panels are in the National Anthropological Museum in Mexico City). The temple is famous for the tomb, or crypt, of Pacal that archaeologist Alberto Ruz Lhuller discovered in its depths in 1952. This is the only pyramid in Mexico built specifically as a tomb. (Ruz's own gravesite is opposite the Temple of the Inscriptions, on the left as you enter the park.)

Pacal began building the temple less than a decade before he died at age 80 in A.D. 683. It took Ruz and his crew four seasons of digging to clear out the rubble that was put there to conceal the crypt containing the remains of King Pacal. Ascending to the throne at age 12, Pacal reigned for 67 years. The crypt itself is 80 feet below the floor of the temple and was covered by a monolithic sepulchral slab 12$^1/_2$ feet long and 7 feet wide, engraved with a depiction of Pacal falling backwards from the land of the living into the underworld. A plaster tube running the length of the stairs to the crypt was meant to bring air to the five natives (four men and a woman) who were killed and left at the entrance to the crypt when it was sealed. They were supposed to accompany Pacal on his journey through the underworld. Unless you're claustrophobic, you should definitely visit the tomb. The way down is lighted, but the steps can be slippery due to condensed humidity. Carved inscriptions on the sides of the crypt (which visitors can't see) show the ritual of the funerary rites carried out at the time of Pacal's death and portray the lineage of Pacal's ancestors, complete with family portraits. Read about it in *A Forest of Kings* (see "Fast Facts," above).

As you enter the ruins from the entrance, the building on your right is the **Temple of the Inscriptions,** named for the great stone hieroglyphic panels found inside.

Just to your right as you face the Temple of the Inscriptions is **Temple XIII,** which is receiving considerable attention from archeologists. Recently, the burial of another important male personage was discovered here. He was richly adorned and was accompanied in death by an adult female and an adolescent. These remains are still being studied.

When you're back on the main pathway, the building directly in front of you will be the **Palace,** with its unique watchtower. A new pathway between the Palace and the Temple of the Inscriptions leads to the **Temple of the Sun,** the **Temple of the Foliated Cross,** the **Temple of the Cross,** and **Temple XIV.** This group of temples—now cleared and in various stages of reconstruction—was built by Pacal's son, Chan-Bahlum, who is usually shown on inscriptions as having six toes. Chan-Bahlum's plaster mask was found in Temple XIV next to the Temple of the Sun. Archeologists have recently begun probing the depths of the Temple of the Sun in search of Chan-Bahlum's tomb. Little remains of this temple's exterior carving. Inside, however, behind a fence, a carving of Chan-Bahlum shows him ascending the throne in A.D. 690. The panels, which are still in place, depict Chan-Bahlum's version of his historic link to the throne.

The Northern Group, to the left of the Palace, is also undergoing restoration. Included in this area are the **Ball Court** and the **Temple of the Count,** so named because Count Waldeck camped there in the 19th century. Explorer John Stephens camped in the Palace when it was completely tree- and vine-covered, spending sleepless nights fighting off mosquitoes. At least three tombs, complete with offerings for the underworld journey, have been found here. The lineage of at least 12 kings has been deciphered from inscriptions left at this marvelous site.

Just past the Northern Group is a small building (once a museum) now used for storing the artifacts found during the restorations. It is closed to the public. To the right of the building, a stone bridge crosses the river, leading to a pathway down the hillside to the new museum. The path is lined with rocks and has steps in the steepest areas, leading past the **Cascada Motiepa,** a beautiful waterfall that creates a series of pools perfect for cooling weary feet. Benches are placed along the way as rest areas, and some small temples have been reconstructed near the base of the trail. In early morning and evening, you may hear monkeys crashing through the thick foliage by the path; if you keep noise to a minimum, you may spot wild parrots as well. Walking downhill (by far the best way to go), it will take you about 20 minutes to reach the main highway. The path ends at the paved road across from the museum. The colectivos going back to the village will stop here if you wave them down.

ACCOMMODATIONS

The main hotel zones are near the fork in the road at La Cañada; in the village; and on the road to the ruins.

IN LA CAÑADA

Hotel La Cañada

Calle Merle Green, Palenque, Chi. 29960. ☎ **934/5-0102.** Fax 934/5-0392. 10 rms (all with bath). FAN. $29 double. Free parking.

This secluded group of cottages is surrounded by dense woods. Carlos Morales Márquez built the hotel in the 1960s, and his sons, who inherited it, now run the place. Some of the rooms are now part of the Hotel Xibalba (see below), run by another of the Morales brothers. La Cañada's palapa restaurant is one of the best in this area. The hotel is on the dirt-and-gravel road in La Cañada, about 100 yards north of the Maya statue. The noise from the nightclub just down the road can be significant on weekend nights; choose a room as far away from it as possible.

Hotel Maya Tulipanes

Calle Merle Green No. 6, Palenque, Chi. 29960. ☎ **934/5-0201.** Fax 934/5-1004. 34 rms (all with bath). A/C or FAN. $36.50–$52.50 double; $43–$62 triple. Free parking.

Maya statues, carvings, and paintings fill the hallways and public areas in this rambling, overgrown, but comfortable two-story hotel. Some of the windows are even shaped like the Maya corbeled arch. You definitely feel as if you're in the jungle here, and the dark shade is a cool respite from the sun's glare. The hotel is one long block north of the Maya statue in La Cañada.

Hotel Xibalba

Calle Merle Green, Palenque, Chi. 29960. ☎ **934/ 5-0411.** Fax 934/5-0392. 8 rms (all with bath). A/C FAN. $27 double. Free parking.

Marco Morales Fimbres, one of the sons of the original owner of the Hotel La Cañada (see above), has taken over some of that hotel's best rooms and created his own small inn. The four rooms in a modern building are the nicest in the area, with air-conditioning and ceiling fans, lots of space, and bathtubs (a rarity in these parts). Four more rooms are located over the owner's Shivalva travel agency and have showers and fans. The hotel also features Mero Lec, the most attractive new restaurant in the area.

IN TOWN
Expensive
Hotel Misión Park Inn Palenque
Domicilio Conocido, Rancho San Martín de Porres, Palenque, Chi. 29960. ☎ **934/5-0241.** Fax 934/5-0300. $100 double.

Palenque's most luxurious hotel, this place is a 20-minute walk from the first-class bus station or a $2–$3 taxi ride. The views of the surrounding peaceful country-side—encompassing mountains and jungle—are beautiful. The spacious rooms, with high-beamed ceilings and cobalt-blue and white walls, are in long, two-story buildings overlooking the gardens; rooms near the restaurant must bear hearing music until 10pm. The beds are enormous and the bathrooms sparkling clean, but the air-conditioners are the noisiest I've ever heard. The pool is a blessing after a morning of pyramid climbing or playing tennis on the hotel's courts; there's a hot springs nearby for soaking your weary feet. The restaurant is remarkably good for one that serves busloads of European tour groups. The hotel's free shuttle goes to and from the ruins six times a day. The hotel is at the far eastern edge of town; go left at the end of Cinco de Mayo.

Inexpensive
Hotel Casa de Pakal
Av. Juárez 10, Palenque, Chi. 29960. ☎ **934/ 5-0393.** 15 rms (all with bath). A/C. $29.75 double; $36 triple.

This bright, relatively new four-story hotel far surpasses most others on Juárez. Air-conditioning is a big plus here. The rooms are small but far brighter and cleaner than those at nearby establishments, and they come with either one double or one single bed covered with chenille spreads. A good restaurant is on premises. The hotel is one-half block east of the main plaza.

Hotel Kashlan
5 de Mayo no. 105, Palenque, Chi. 29960. ☎ **934/5-0297.** Fax 934/5-0399. 58 rms (all with bath). A/C (28 rms) FAN (30 rms). $22.50–$34.50 double.

You'll be well located if you lodge in the Kashlan. The spiffily clean rooms have interior windows opening onto the hall, marble-square floors, nice bedspreads, tile baths, small vanities, and luggage racks. Your *Frommer's* book may get you a discount. To find this hotel from the main plaza, walk west on 5 de Mayo (towards the bus stations); it's 1 1/2 blocks down on the right.

ON THE ROAD TO THE RUINS
Chan-Kah Ruinas
Carretera Palenque Km 31, Palenque, Chi 29960. ☎ **934/5-0318.** Fax 934/5-0820. 30 rms. FAN. $90 double

These comfortable, little wood-and-stone bungalows are spread out in a beautiful jungle setting. Sliding glass doors in the rooms open onto small patios facing the jungle. Facilities include a large swimming pool and a nice restaurant with decent food. Taxis are hard to come by here and charge extra for picking you up at the hotel; instead, walk to the main road and flag down a colectivo or taxi to town. Christmas prices may be higher than those quoted here, and you may be quoted a higher price if you reserve a room in advance from the U. S. The hotel is on the left side of the road to the ruins, 2½ miles northwest of the ruins.

DINING

Avenida Juárez is lined with many small eateries, none of which is exceptional. Good options are the many markets and *panaderías* (bakeries) along Juárez. **Panificadora La Tehuanita,** near the bus stations, has fresh cookies firm enough to withstand hours in the bottom of a purse, and **La Bodeguita** has a beautiful display of fresh fruit—just stick with those you can peel.

Chan-Kah Centro

Av. Independencia s/n. ☎ **934/5-0318.** Breakfast buffet (7–11am) $3.50; comida corrida $4; quesadillas $2.50. Daily 7am–11pm. MEXICAN.

This attractive hotel restaurant, on the east side of the main plaza at the corner of Independencia, is the most peaceful place to eat. The waiters are extremely attentive, and the food is fairly well prepared (avoid the tough beef though). The second-story bar overlooks the main plaza and has live music on some weekend nights.

✪ La Chiapaneca

Carretera Palenque. ☎ **934/5-0363.** Main courses $8.50–$12. Daily 11am–10pm. MEXICAN.

Palenque's traditional "best" restaurant continues to serve top-notch regional cuisine in a pleasant tropical setting. Though it has a thatched roof, the dining room is large and refined. The pollo Palenque (chicken with potatoes in a tomato-and-onion sauce) is a soothing choice; save room for the flan. Mexican wines are served by the bottle. La Chiapaneca is about a 20-minute walk from the Maya statue toward the ruins.

Girasoles

Juárez 189. ☎ **934/5-0383.** Comida del día $4; main courses $3–$5. Daily 7am–11pm. MEXICAN.

There's always a smattering of locals and foreigners here taking advantage of the good prices. The simple decor boasts cloth-covered tables, wicker lampshades on ceiling lights, and fans. It's a good place for resting your feet and watching the action, in addition to getting a good deal on the food. The menu covers the basics and has fish, poultry, and Mexican specialties, including decent tacos that are more like flautas. The freshly brewed coffee comes from Chiapas, and you can buy it ground by the kilo. Girasoles is on 5 de Mayo across from the ADO bus station.

✪ Restaurant Maya

Av. Independencia s/n. No phone. Breakfast $2.25–$4.25; main courses $3.50–$7.50. Daily 7am–10pm. MEXICAN.

The most popular place in town among tourists and locals, Restaurant Maya is opposite the northeast corner of the main plaza near the post office. Breezy and open, it's managed by a solicitous family. At breakfast, there are free refills of very good coffee. Try the tamales.

EXCURSIONS FROM PALENQUE

AGUA AZUL & CASCADA DE MISOL HA: SPECTACULAR WATERFALLS

The most popular excursion from Palenque is a day-trip to the Agua Azul cascades. Trips can be arranged through Shivalva Tours and ATC Tours and Travel (see "Bonampak & Yakchilán," below). Minivans from the Chambalu Colectivo Service make the trip to Agua Azul and the Cascada de Misol Ha every day with two round-trips beginning at 10am; the last van departs Agua Azul for Palenque at 6:30pm. They may wait until six or eight people want to go, so check a day or two in advance of your proposed trip. Several new travel agencies have popped up in town, most offering the same tours and services. Prices have become a bit more competitive, so it's worth checking out a few of the agencies along Avenida Juárez. Be sure to ask if private or public transportation is used for the tours.

BONAMPAK & YAXCHILÁN: RUINS & RUGGED ADVENTURE

Intrepid travelers might consider the two-day excursion to the Maya ruins of Bonampak and Yaxchilán. The ruins of Bonampak, southeast of Palenque on the Guatemalan border, were discovered in 1946. The mural discovered on the interior walls of one of the buildings is the greatest battle painting of pre-Hispanic Mexico. Reproductions of the vivid murals found here are on view in the Regional Archeology Museum in Villahermosa.

You can fly or drive to Bonampak. Several tour companies offer a two-day (minimum) tour by four-wheel-drive vehicle to within $4^1/2$ miles of Bonampak. You must walk the rest of the way to the ruins. After camping overnight, you continue by river to the extensive ruins of the great Maya city, Yaxchilán, famous for its highly ornamented buildings. Bring rain gear, boots, a flashlight, and bug repellent. All tours include meals but vary in price ($80 to $120 per person); some take far too many people for comfort (the seven-hour road trip can be unbearable).

Among the most reputable tour operators is **Viajes Shivalva,** Calle Merle Green 1 (Apdo. Postal 237), Palenque, Chi. 29960 (☎ 934/5-0411; fax 934/5-0392). Office hours are Monday through Friday from 7am to 3pm. A branch office is now open a block from the zócalo at the corner of Juárez and Abasolo (across the hall from the Tourism office). Their phone is 934/5-0822, and they are open Monday through Saturday from 9am to 9pm.

Information about **ATC Tours and Travel** (☎ and fax 934/5-0297) can be obtained at the Hotel Kashlan, 5 de Mayo and Allende (see "Accommodations," above, in Palenque). This agency has a large number of clients (and thus the best chance of making a group) and offers a large number of tours. Among its offerings is a one-day trip to the ruins of Tikal in Guatemala for five people; another tour takes in Yaxchilán, Bonampak, and Tikal with a minimum of four people. Though rustic, they have the only permanent overnight accommodations at Yaxchilán at their Posada del Río Usumacinta. Their headquarters are in San Cristóbal (see "San Cristóbal de las Casas," above), so you can make arrangements there as well.

An alternative way to reach Bonampak and Yaxchilán is via tours run by the **Chambalu Colectivo Service** at Juárez and Allende. A minimum of five people is needed to make the trip. The Palenque-Bonampak portion takes five hours by road and another $2^1/2$ hours to hike, and then there's an overnight stay in rustic huts with wood-slat beds and no meals or mosquito netting, another two-hour bus ride, a river trip to Yaxchilán, and the long ride back to Palenque. It's a strenuous, no-frills trip that can be absolutely wonderful if you don't expect great service and if you bring plenty of food and drink, a hammock and net, and a great deal of patience. The two-day trip costs about $75 to $85 per person.

When negotiating the deal, be sure to ask how many will be in the bus, or you may not have a place to sit for hours on bumpy dirt roads. Recent road improvements should shorten the trip and may alter tour arrangements considerably.

VILLAHERMOSA: WAY STATION ON PALENQUE-YUCATÁN ROUTE

Villahermosa is a growing oil town and capital of the state of Tabasco, but it's the city's proximity to Palenque that makes it of interest to tourists. You can't go wrong staying at the comfortable, busy **Best Western Hotel Maya Tabasco** (Av. Ruíz Cortínez 907; ☎ 93/12-1111) or the downtown **Hotel Madan** (Pino Suárez 105; ☎ 93/12-1650). Adjacent is **Galerías Madan,** a mainstay of Mexican homestyle cooking; for a more elegant meal, try **Los Tulipanes** (in the CICOM Center; ☎ 93/12-9217).

15 Cancún

Say the word "Cancún" to most people, and they'll think of fine sandy beaches, limpid, incredibly blue Caribbean waters, and expensive luxury resorts—these images are all true. Isla Cancún is lined with shopping centers and upscale resort hotels, many of which are luxurious by any world standard. Ciudad Cancún, on the mainland, grew up with hotels more for the budget-minded traveler and boasts a downtown area chockablock with restaurants, each trying to outdo the others to attract clientele. Many travelers who select an island hotel as a base never get to explore the more funky mainland establishments.

Twenty years ago, the name Cancún meant little to anyone, but these days Cancún is the magic word in Mexican vacations. A hook-shaped island on the Caribbean side of the Yucatecan coast, Cancún opened for business in 1974 with one hotel and a lot of promotion, after being judged the best spot in the country for a new jet-age resort. Meanwhile, Ciudad Cancún popped up to house the working populace that flocked to support the resort.

Cancún *is* a perfect resort site: the long island's powdery limestone sand beaches; air and water temperatures that are just right. Further-more, Cancún can be a starting point for exploration of other Yucatecan lures. The older, less expensive island resorts of Isla Mujeres and Cozumel are close at hand. The Maya ruins at Tulum, Chichén-Itzá, and Cobá are within driving distance, as are the snorkeling reserves of Xcaret and Xel-Ha. And along the coast south of Cancún, in places such as Playa del Carmen, new resorts in all price ranges are popping up.

Cancún today is a city of 450,000 people and boasts more than 18,000 hotel rooms between the mainland city and the resort-filled island. The 14-mile-long island's resorts together make for quite a variegated display of modern architectural style; they seem to get grander and more lavish each year.

Fans of Cancún see its similarity to U.S. resorts as a plus—a foreign vacation without foreign inconveniences. Cancún is a good place to ease into Mexican culture, though it's not at all like the rest of the country. But if you like beaches, Cancún and the coast to its south have the best beaches in Mexico. Food and drinks are just one sybaritic step from your lounge chair.

If you're beginning your Yucatecan adventure in Cancún, you should read up on the history of the Yucatán in Chapter 17.

1 Orientation

ARRIVING & DEPARTING

BY PLANE   See Chapter 3, "Planning a Trip to Mexico," for a list of airlines (and their toll-free telephone numbers) that fly to Cancún from points in the United States and Canada.

Several airlines connect Cancún with other Mexican and Central American cities. **Mexicana** (☎ 87-4444 or 87-2769 in Cancún) flies in from Guadalajara, Mexico City, and Flores, Guatemala. **Aeroméxico** (☎ 84-3571 or 84-1186) offers service from Mexico City, Mérida, and Tijuana. **Taesa** (☎ 87-4314), has flights from Tijuana, Chetumal, Mérida, and other cities within Mexico. Regional carriers **Aerocozumel** and **Aerocaribe** (☎ 84-2000, both affiliated with Mexicana) fly from Cozumel, Havana, Mexico City, Tuxtla Gutiérrez, Villahermosa, Mérida, Oaxaca, Veracruz, and Cuidad del Carmen. The regional airline **Aviateca** (☎ 84-3938 or 87-1386) flies from Cancún to Mérida, Villahermosa, Tuxtla Gutiérrez, Guatemala City, and Flores (near Tikal).

You'll want to confirm departure times for flights back to the States; here are the Cancún airport numbers of the major international carriers: **American** (☎ 86-0151), **Continental** (☎ 86-0005 or 86-0006), **Northwest** (☎ 86-0188 or 86-0044), and **United** (☎ 86-0158).

Special vans run from Cancún's international airport into town for $9 per person. Rates for a cab from the airport to the Zona Hotelera range from around $25 to Club Med to $40 to downtown and the northern part of the island. There's no minibus transportation to the Puerto Juárez passenger ferry to Isla Mujeres. The least expensive way to get there is to take the minibus to the bus station in downtown Cancún and from there bargain for a taxi, which should cost around $6–$8. Most major rental-car firms have outlets at the airport, so if you're renting a car, consider picking it up on arrival and dropping it off when you leave at the airport to save on these exorbitant airport-transportation prices.

There is no colectivo service returning to the airport from Ciudad Cancún or the Zona Hotelera, so you'll have to hire a taxi. From Ciudad Cancún the fare's around $12 to $18; from the Zona Hotelera it's around $10 to $18.

BY BUS   The bus station is in downtown Ciudad Cancún at the intersection of Avenidas Tulum and Uxmal, within walking distance of several of my hotel suggestions. All out-of-town buses arrive there. Cancún's bus terminals and the streets around them were being renovated when I last visited; some lines may have moved to other buildings by the time you read this.

The most frequent buses to Cancún and Playa del Carmen are the **Autotransportes Playa Express** minibuses (☎ 84-1984) which run almost every half hour between 6am and 9pm from the corner of Avenida Tulum and Pino (at one end of the bus station). Purchase your tickets on board. The line with the most frequent service to Mérida (3¹/₂ hours), Valladolid, and Chichén-Itzá is **Autotransportes del Caribe** with 24 daily departures. Deluxe Caribe Express buses also go to Mérida, Campeche (5 hours), and Chetumal (5 hours).Buy tickets at least a day in advance from the air-conditioned office at the station. **Expreso de**

Oriente (☎ 84-5542),in the ADO terminal, runs 11 daily deluxe departures to Mérida.

Primera Clase (☎ 84-1378) offers buses to Tizimin, Chichén-Itzá, Valladolid, Playa del Carmen, Tulum, and Chetumal.

BY FERRY   For ferry service to Cozumel or to Isla Mujeres, see Chapter 16.

VISITOR INFORMATION

The **State Tourism Office** (☎ 98/84-8073) is centrally located downtown on the east side of Avenida Tulum between the Ayuntamiento Benito Juárez building and Comermex Bank, between Avenidas Cobá and Uxmal. The office was closed when I last visited, but was scheduled to reopen by the time you travel. A second tourist information office (☎ 98/84-3238 or 84-3438) is located on Avenida Cobá at Avenida Tulum, next to Pizza Rolandi and is open daily from 9am to 9pm. Hotels and their rates are listed here, as well as ferry schedules.

Many people (the "friendliest" in town) offer information in exchange for listening to a spiel about the wonders of a Cancún time-sharing or condo purchase. If you get suckered in by these sales professionals you will spend no less than half a day of your vacation listening to them; you may not receive the gift they'll promise.

Pick up free copies of the monthly *Cancún Tips* booklet and a seasonal tabloid of the some name. Both are useful and have fine maps. The publishers have connections with time-share properties and restaurants.

CITY LAYOUT

There are two Cancúns: **Isla Cancún** (Cancún Island) and **Ciudad Cancún** (Cancún City). The latter, on the mainland, has restaurants, shops, and less expensive hotels, as well as all the other establishments that make life function—pharmacies, dentists, automotive shops, banks, travel and airline agencies, car-rental firms—all within an area about nine blocks square. The city's main thoroughfare is **Avenida Tulum.** Heading south, Avenida Tulum becomes the highway to the airport, as well as to the south to Tulum and Chetumal; heading north, it intersects the highway to Mérida and the road to Puerto Juárez and the Isla Mujeres ferries.

The famed **Zona Hotelera** (alternately called the **Zona Turística**) stretches out along Isla Cancún, a sandy strip 14 miles long, shaped like a "7." It's now joined by bridges to the mainland at the north and south ends. **Avenida Cobá** from Cancún city becomes **Paseo Kukulkán,** the island's main traffic artery. Cancún's international airport is just inland from the south end of the island.

FINDING AN ADDRESS   The street-numbering system is left over from Cancún's early days. Addresses are still given by the number of the building lot and by the *manzana* (block) or *super-manzana* (group of city blocks). The city is still relatively small, and the downtown section can easily be covered on foot.

On the island, addresses are given by kilometer number on Paseo Kukulkán or by reference to some well-known location.

2 Getting Around

BY BUS   In town, almost everything is within walking distance. **Ruta 1** and **Ruta 2** ("Hoteles") city buses travel frequently from the mainland to the beaches along Avenida Tulum (the main street) and all the way to Punta Nizuc at the far end of the Zona Hotelera on Isla Cancún. **Ruta 8** buses go to Puerto Juárez/Punta Sam for ferries to Isla Mujeres. They stop on the east side of Avenida Tulum. Both these city buses operate between 6am and midnight daily. Beware of private buses plying the same route they charge far more than the public ones! The public buses have the fare amount painted on the front; when last I checked it was 2.5 pesos.

BY TAXI　Settle on a price in advance. The trip from Ciudad Cancún to the Hotel Camino Real, for example, should cost $6.50; from Ciudad Cancún to the airport, $10 to $12; within Cancún proper, $3 to $5.

BY MOPED　Mopeds are a dangerous way to cruise around through the very congested traffic. Rentals start at $25 for a day. A credit-card voucher is required as security for the moped. You should receive a crash helmet (it's the law) and instructions on how to lock the wheels when you park. Read the fine print on the back of the rental agreement regarding liability for repairs or replacement in case of accident, theft, or vandalism. You rent at considerable risk.

BY RENTAL CAR　There's really no need to have a car in Cancún, since bus service is good, taxis on the mainland are relatively inexpensive, and most things in Ciudad Cancún are within walking distance. For seeing the rest of the Yucatán or taking a couple of days down the coast toward Tulum, I do recommend renting a car, since public transportation is sparse. But if you do rent, the cheapest way is to arrange for the rental before you leave your home country. Cars rented after you arrive begin at $55 a day and can go as high as $75 certain times of the year. For more details, see "Getting Around" in Chapter 3.

Important Note: Observe all speed zones on the island and the mainland. Police give tickets to speeders!

FAST FACTS: CANCÚN

American Express　The local office is at Av. Tulum 208 and Agua (☎ 84-1999, 84-4243, or 87-0831), open Monday through Friday from 9am to 2pm and 4 to 6pm and Saturday from 9am to 1pm. It's one block past the Plaza México.

Area Code　The telephone area code is 98.

Climate　It's hot but not overwhelmingly humid. The rainy season is May through October. August through October is the hurricane season, which brings erratic weather. November through February can be cloudy, windy, somewhat rainy, and even cool, so a sweater is handy, as is rain protection.

Consulates　The U.S. Consular Agent is in the Maruelos Building at Av. Nader 40 (☎ 98/84-2411). The office is open Monday through Friday from 9am to 2pm and 3 to 6pm. In an emergency, call the U.S. Consulate in Mérida (☎ 99/47-2285).

Crime　Car break-ins are just about the only crime, and they happen frequently, especially around the shopping centers in the Zona Hotelera. VW Beetles and Golfs are frequent targets. Don't leave valuables in plain sight.

Currency Exchange　Most banks are downtown along Avenida Tulum and are usually open Monday through Friday from 9:30am to 1:30pm. There are also a few *casas de cambio* (exchange houses). Downtown merchants are eager to change cash dollars, but island stores don't offer good exchange rates. Avoid changing money at the airport as you arrive, especially at the first exchange you see—its rates are less favorable than any in town or others farther inside the airport concourse.

Drugstores　Next to the Hotel Caribe Internacional, Farmacia Canto, at Avenida Yaxchilán 36, at Sunyaxchen (☎ 98/84-4083 or 84-9330), is open 24 hours.

Downtown Cancún

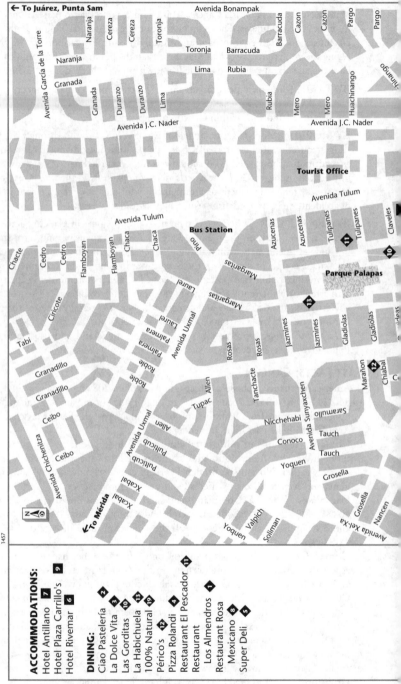

ACCOMMODATIONS:
Hotel Antillano 7
Hotel Plaza Carrillo's 9
Hotel Rivemar 6

DINING:
Ciao Pastelería 2
La Dolce Vita 3
Las Gorditas 10
La Habichuela 13
100% Natural 12
Périco's 12
Pizza Rolandi 4
Restaurant El Pescador 11
Restaurant
Los Almendros 1
Restaurant Rosa
Mexicano 8
Super Deli 5

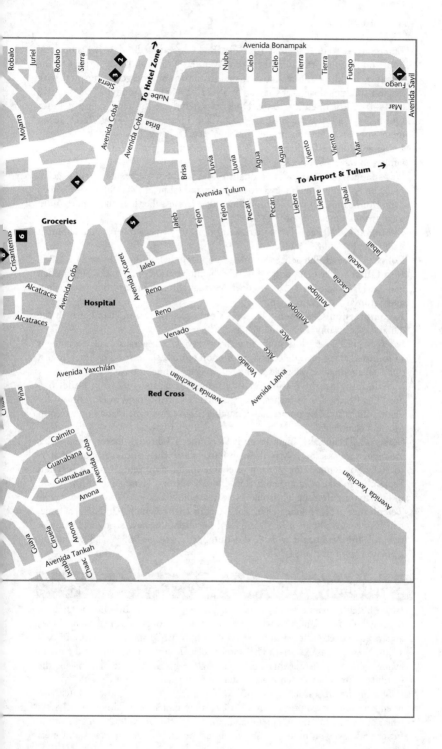

Emergencies For first aid, Cruz Roja (Red Cross; ☎ 98/84-1616) is open 24 hours on Avenida Yaxchilán between Avenidas Xcaret and Labná, next to the Telemex building. Total Assist, a small nine-room emergency hospital with English-speaking doctors at Claveles 5, SM22, at Avenida Tulum (☎ 98/84-1058 or 84-1092), is open 24 hours. Desk staff may have limited English. Clínica Quirurgica del Caribe, at SM63, Mz Q, Calle 3 inte. no. 36 (☎ 98/84-2516), is open 24 hours. *Urgencias* means "Emergencies."

Luggage Storage/Lockers Hotels will generally tag and store excess luggage while you travel elsewhere.

Newspapers/Magazines For English-language newspapers and books, go to Fama on Avenida Tulum between Tulipanes and Claveles (☎ 98/84-6586), open daily from 8am to 10pm. (Avoid filling out a contest flier here that will result in a call from a time-share promoter.)

Photographic Needs For batteries and film, try Omega on Avenida Tulum at Tulipanes (☎ 98/84-3860).

Police To reach the police (Seguridad Pública), dial 98/84-1913 or 84-2342.

Post Office The main post office is at the intersection of Avenidas Sunyaxchen and Xel-Ha (☎ 98/84-1418). It's open Monday through Friday from 8am to 7pm and Saturday from 9am to 1pm.

Recompression Chamber The area's only recompression chamber is in the Total Assist hospital (see "Emergencies," above).

Safety There is very little crime in Cancún. People in general are safe late at night in touristed areas; just use ordinary common sense. As at any other beach resort, don't take money or valuables to the beach. See "Crime," above.

Swimming on the Caribbean side presents real dangers from undertow. See "The Beaches" in "Beaches, Water Sports & Other Things to Do," below, for flag warnings and "Recompression Chamber" above about the island's only recompression chamber.

Seasons Technically, high season is December 15 through Easter, when prices are higher; low season is May through November, when prices are reduced 10% to 30%. Some hotels are starting to charge high-season rates between July and September to take advantage of school-holiday visitors. There's a mini-low season in January just after the Christmas-New Year's holiday.

Telephones The phone system for Cancún changed in 1992. The area code, which once was 988, is now 98. All local numbers now have six digits instead of five; all numbers begin with 8. If a number is written 988/4-1234, when in Cancún you must dial 84-1234.

3 Accommodations

Island hotels run almost the gamut, but extravagance is the byword in the more recently built hotels, most of which are awash in a sea of marble, mahogany, brass, and white-gloved bellmen in waistcoats. Others, while sporting a more relaxed attitude, are just as exclusive. The water is placid on the upper end of the island facing Bahía de Mujeres, while beaches lining the long side of the island facing the Caribbean are subject to choppier water on windy days.

During the off-season (from April to November), prices go down. Hotels also often have discounted prices from February up to Easter week. Although rack rates (the hotel's rate to the public) are high, a package that includes hotel and airline ticket may save you money. Also ask about special promotional rates and meal credits. Note that the price quoted to you when you call a hotel's reservation number from the U.S. doesn't include Cancún's 10 percent tax. When I checked for this edition, prices at some hotels were up over 40% from last year, while other hotels quoted rates that were 20% to 50% lower—it pays to shop around.

The hotel listings in this chapter begin on Cancún Island, the most expensive place to stay, and finish in Cancún City, where bargain lodgings abound.

CANCÚN ISLAND
VERY EXPENSIVE

Camino Real Cancún

Paseo Kukulkán, Punta Cancún (Apdo. Postal 14), Cancún, Q. Roo 77500. ☎ **98/83-0100** or 800/722-6466 in the U.S. Fax 98/83-1730. 381 rms and suites. A/C MINIBAR TV TEL. High season $190–$215 double; low season $110–$215 double. Package deals provide the best value. Daily fee for guarded parking adjacent to hotel.

On four acres right at the tip of Punta Cancún, the Camino Real, a member of Leading Hotels of the World, is among the island's most appealing places to stay. The rooms are elegantly outfitted with pink breccia-marble floors, tropical high-backed raffia easy chairs, and drapes and spreads in soft pastel colors. Some rooms in the new 18-story Camino Real Club have elegant Mexican decor, while standard rooms in this section are much like rooms in the rest of the resort. Master suites have expansive views, swivel TVs, large dining tables with four chairs, and hot tubs on the balconies. Camino Real Club guests receive a complimentary continental breakfast daily in the Beach Club lobby, as well as complimentary cocktails and snacks there each evening. Lower priced rooms have lagoon views.

Dining/Entertainment: Three restaurants serve all meals and include a beach and pool-side snack with seafood specialties; indoor casual dining with flame-broiled meat; and an elegant evening-only restaurant featuring Chinese cuisine. There's a children's menu at the more casual restaurants. A Mexican fiesta takes place on Saturday nights. The lobby bar features Mexican music nightly from 5:30 to 7:30pm, and the oceanview Azucar Disco swings into action Monday through Saturday at 9:30pm.

Services: Laundry and room service, travel agency, car rental, in-room safety boxes, babysitting (with advance notice).

Facilities: Freshwater pool; private saltwater lagoon with sea turtles and tropical fish; private beach; sailing pier; water-sports center. There are also three lighted tennis courts, beach volleyball, boutiques, and barber and beauty shops.

Cancún Sheraton Resort

Paseo Kukulkán km 13.5, Cancún, Q. Roo 77500. ☎ **98/83-1988** or 800/325-3535 in the U.S. Fax 98/85-0974. 748 rms and suites. A/C MINIBAR TV TEL. High season $290–$330 double; low season $105–$230 double. (Ask about summer "Temptation" packages.) Free parking.

These three lavish, pyramid-style buildings are set on their own vast stretch of beach. The impressive lobby has large expanses of green tiles and a dramatic stainless-steel sculpture of birds in flight. Emerald lawns extend in every direction from the main buildings, and a small reconstructed Maya ruin crowns a craggy limestone hillock. Rooms and suites are luxurious, with views of the Caribbean (to the east) or of the lagoon (to the west). In the V-shaped tower section, all units have in-room security boxes, and guests enjoy the services of a personal butler who attends to a variety of tasks from shoe shines to snack service. There's a no-smoking floor, and rooms are available for guests with disabilities.

Dining/Entertainment: At least four restaurants cover every aspect of eating from grilled food by the beach to lavish breakfast buffets to Italian feasts to Mexican food. There are five bars, including the lobby bar where there's live music from noon to midnight.

Services: Laundry and room service, travel agency, car rental, massage, and babysitting.

Facilities: Three swimming pools; six lighted tennis courts with tennis pro on duty; beach; fitness center with sauna, steam bath, and whirlpool; mini-golf; aerobics, swimnastics; arts and crafts; Spanish classes; children's playground; basketball court; table games; pharmacy; beauty and barber shop; business center; flower shop; and boutiques.

Fiesta Americana Cancún

Paseo Kukulkán km 7.5, Cancún, Q. Roo 77500. ☎ **98/83-1400** or 800/223-2332 in the U.S. Fax 98/83-2502. 281 rms. A/C MINIBAR TV TEL. High season $240–$270 double; low season $170–$253 double. (Ask about summer "Fiesta" packages.) Free parking.

With colorful stucco walls and oddly placed balconies and windows, the Fiesta Americana has old-world charm. Originally built with honeymooners in mind, it's smaller than most island accommodations and is Cancún's most intimate hotel. On a nice beach and calm bay, the quiet rooms are beautifully furnished with balconies facing the ocean. Some rooms have in-room safety-deposit boxes. The location is ideal—it's right across the street from shopping malls and restaurants near the Convention Center.

Dining/Entertainment: The hotel's three restaurants cover your dining needs, from formal dining to light meals at poolside (where there's a swim-up bar). The lobby bar, open most of the day, features piano entertainment in the evening between 8 and 11 pm. Caliente Sports/TV Betting Bar has big-screen TVs for viewing sporting events.

Services: Laundry and room service, travel agency, and wedding arrangements.

Facilities: One swimming pool, water-sports rental on the beach, boutiques, wheelchairs.

Fiesta Americana Coral Beach

Paseo Kukulkán km 9.5, Cancún, Q. Roo 77500. ☎ **98/83-2900** or 800/223-2332 in the U.S. Fax 98/83-3173. 602 suites. A/C MINIBAR TV TEL. High season $340 double. Low season $265 double.

This enormous, spectacular hotel, which opened in 1991, has a lot to recommend it: perfect location; gracious service; grand public areas; the full gamut of water sports and beach activities; and beautiful guest rooms decorated with marble, area rugs, tasteful use of Mexican decorative arts, and balconies facing the ocean, plus remote-control TVs and hairdryers. Master suites have double vanities, dressing room, bathrobes, whirlpool baths, and large terraces. Two concierge floors feature daily continental breakfast and evening cocktails, and a 24-hour reception-cashier. Two junior suites are equipped for handicapped guests.

The hotel's great Punta Cancún location (opposite the Convention Center, and within walking distance of shopping centers and restaurants) has the advantage of north-facing beach, meaning the surf is calm and just perfect for swimming.

Dining/Entertainment: Elegant seafood and Mexican restaurants for dinner; a café-style restaurant with international food and an ocean view serving a breakfast buffet and lunch; a snack bar and stylish outdoor palapa restaurant serve the beach and pool. Five bars.

Isla Cancún (Zona Hotelera)

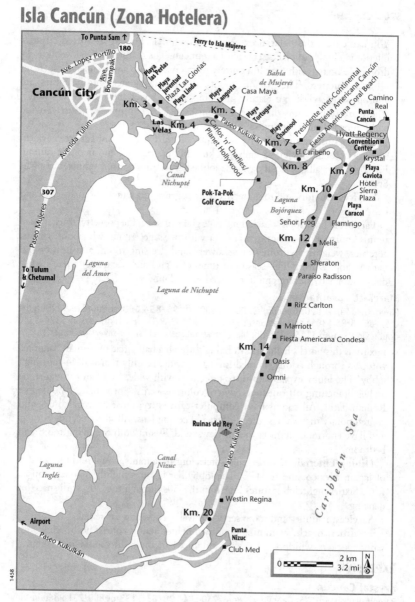

Services: Laundry and room service, travel agency, car rental, and massage.

Facilities: A 660-foot-long free-form swimming pool; swim-up bars; 1,000 feet of beach; three indoor tennis courts with stadium seating; gymnasium with weights, sauna, and massage; water-sport rentals on the beach; business center; tennis pro shop; fashion and spa boutiques; and beauty and barber shops.

Hotel Melia Cancún

Paseo Kukulkán km 14, Cancún, Q. Roo 77500. ☎ **98/85-1114** or 800/336-3542 in the U.S., 91-800/2-1779 in Mexico. Fax 98/85-1263. 450 rms and suites. A/C MINIBAR TV TEL. High season $330–$365 double; low season $190–$220 double.

You can't miss the palatial exterior of this hotel. The eight-storied circular interior is a jungle of plants set against a fountain. The marble-and-teakwood backdrop is decorated with majolica pottery from Guanajuato and lacquer chests from Olinalá, Guerrero. The spacious rooms, all with sitting areas and balconies, are appropriately stylish and feature in-room security boxes and purified tap water. There are four rooms on the first floor especially equipped with extra-wide bathrooms for guests with disabilities.

Dining/Entertainment: Five restaurants feature foods from France, Mexico, and the U.S. and include a daily breakfast buffet, seafood, and poolside dining. Five bars serve all guests all day. The lobby bar features Latin rhythms starting at 8pm.

Services: Laundry and room service, travel agency, car rental, and baby cribs and babysitters.

Facilities: Two pools; beach; nine-hole golf course on the property; three lighted tennis courts; Ping-Pong; gymnasium with massage, sauna, whirlpool, facials, aerobics, weights, hydromassage showers, and dressing room; and beauty and barber shop. During high season or times of high hotel occupancy there's a full daily list of activities for children posted in the lobby.

Marriott Casamagna

Paseo Kukulkán km 20, Cancún, Q. Roo 77500. ☎ 98/85-2000 or 800/228-9290 in the U.S. Fax 98/85-1385. 450 rms and suites. A/C MINIBAR TV TEL. High season $324–$360 double; low season $155–$185 double. (Ask about seasonal "super-saver" packages.)

Luxury is this hotel's hallmark. Entering through a half-circle of Roman columns, you pass through a long, domed foyer to a wide, lavishly marbled 44-foot-high lobby. The lobby expands in three directions with wide, Mexican cantera-stone arches branching off outdoors, where columns vanish into shallow pools like Roman baths. All rooms have computer-card entry; most have balconies and contemporary furnishings, tiled floors, and ceiling fans. All suites occupy corners and have enormous terraces, ocean views, and TVs in both the living room and bedroom.

Dining/Entertainment: At this hotel's four restaurants, you'll find the cuisines of Japan, Mexico, and the U.S. The lobby bar features nightly mariachi music, while Sixties nightclub features hits from the '50s through the '70s, with space for dancing.

Services: Laundry and room service, travel agency, and car rental.

Facilities: Beach; swimming pool; two lighted tennis courts; health club with saunas, lockers, whirlpool, aerobics, and juice bar; and beauty and barber shop.

EXPENSIVE

Krystal Cancún

Paseo Kukulkán km 7.5, Cancún, Q. Roo 77500. ☎ 98/83-1133 or 800/231-9860 in the U.S. Fax 98/83-1790. 316 rms. A/C MINIBAR TV TEL. Low season $135–$165 double. Free parking.

The Krystal Cancún lies on Punta Cancún with the Camino Real and Hyatt Regency, near the Convention Center, shops, restaurants, and clubs. The Krystal uses lots of cool marble in its decor. The guest rooms, in two buildings, have bamboo furniture, drapes and spreads in earthy tones, two double beds, and water views. The hotel's tap water is purified, and there are ice machines on every floor. The presidential suites have private pools. Club Krystal rooms come with in-room safety boxes, complimentary continental breakfast, and evening canapés and drinks; guests in those rooms also have access to the Club Lounge, a rooftop sun lounge with a whirlpool and concierge service.

Dining/Entertainment: Among the hotel's five restaurants are two that have gained countrywide recognition for fine cuisine—Bogart's, a chic dining room with a Moroccan "Casablanca" theme, and the luxurious Hacienda El Mortero, a replica of a colonial hacienda featuring Mexican cuisine. The hotel also hosts theme nights throughout the week. In the evening there's live entertainment in the lobby bar. Christine's, one of the most popular discos in town, is open nightly from 10pm to 4am.

Services: Laundry, room service, travel agency, and car and moped rental.

Facilities: Swimming pool complex overlooking the Caribbean and a beach with fairly safe swimming; pharmacy; barber and beauty shop; boutiques and a silver shop; two tennis courts with an on-duty tennis pro; a racquetball court; a dive shop; and a fitness club with whirlpool, sauna, and massage facilities.

Radisson Sierra Plaza

Paseo Kukulkán, Cancún, Q. Roo 77500. ☎ **98/83-2444** or 83-3655 or 800/333-3333 in the U.S. and Canada. Fax 98/83-3486. 260 rms. A/C MINIBAR TV TEL. High season $190–$300 double; low season $160–$190 double. Free parking.

There's a luxurious South Seas feel here; the interior is decorated with lots of potted palms, rattan furniture, brass, hot-pink and purple area rugs, and wood louvered doors in the guest rooms. The hotel has its own marina and lagoon in front and both lagoonview and oceanview pools. Each standard room has a balcony, sitting area, combination bathtub/shower, and ceiling fan. Master suites have standard amenities and lots of extras like Berber carpets, large living/dining areas, and kitchens with their own private entries. In the junior suites, the living and sleeping areas are divided by handsome dresser/TV consoles, and there are separate bathtubs and showers. The lowest-priced rooms have lagoon views; more expensive ones are either oceanfront or oceanview.

Dining/Entertainment: Three restaurants cover all your needs and include poolside dining. The lobby bar has trio music nightly.

Services: Room and laundry service, travel agency, and car rental.

Facilities: Swimming pools, two lighted tennis courts, health club, beach, marina, and water-sports rental.

MODERATE

Calinda Cancún Viva

Paseo Kukulkán km 8.5, Cancún, Q. Roo 77500. ☎ **98/83-0800** or 800/228-5151 in the U.S. Fax 98/83-2087. 210 rms. A/C TV TEL. High season $140 double; low season $105 double. Free parking.

From the street, this hotel looks like a blockhouse, but on the ocean side you'll find a small but pretty patio garden and a beach that is safe for swimming. You have a choice of rooms with either lagoon or ocean view . At least 162 rooms have refrigerators and 64 have kitchenettes.

Dining/Entertainment: The main restaurant, La Fuente, serves all three meals. La Palapa and La Parilla, both beside the pool, serve drinks and light meals; Bar La Terraza is in the lobby.

Services: Laundry and room service, travel agency.

Facilities: Swimming pool for adults and one for children, one lighted tennis court, water-sports equipment rental, marina, pharmacy, and gift shop.

Flamingo Cancún

Paseo Kukulkán km 11.5, Cancún, Q. Roo 77500. Tel **98/83-1544.** Fax 98/83-1029. 162 rms. A/C MINIBAR TV TEL. High season $140 double; low season $95 double. Free unguarded parking across the street in the Plaza Flamingo.

The Flamingo seems to have been inspired by the dramatic, slope-sided architecture of the Camino Real, but the Flamingo is considerably smaller. Guest rooms form a quadrangle or courtyard with the swimming pool. The Flamingo is in the heart of the island hotel district, opposite the Flamingo Shopping Center and close to other hotels, shopping centers, and restaurants.

Dining/Entertainment: La Joya Restaurant and Don Francisco Restaurant are both open daily from 7am to 11pm. El Coral is the lobby bar.

Services: Laundry and room service, travel agency, and car rental.

Facilities: Swimming pool and beach.

Misión Miramar Park Inn

Paseo Kukulkán km 9.5, Cancún, Q. Roo 77500. ☎ **98/83-1755.** Fax 98/83-1136. 189 rms. A/C MINIBAR TV TEL. High season $175–$190 double; low season $115–$150 double.

Each of the ingeniously designed rooms has views of both the lagoon and ocean. Public spaces throughout the hotel have lots of dark wood, cream-beige stucco, red tile, and pastel accents. The big swimming pool is next to the beach. Rooms are on the small side but comfortable, with bamboo furniture offset by pastel-colored cushions and bedspreads; bathrooms have polished limestone vanities.

Dining/Entertainment: Two restaurants serve cuisine of Mexico and the U.S. There's live music nightly in the lobby bar, and the bar by the pool serves guests during pool hours. Batacha also has live music for dancing from 9pm to 4am Tuesday through Sunday.

Services: Laundry and room service, travel agency, and car rental.

Facilities: Pool, beach, pharmacy, and gift shop.

Presidente Inter-Continental Cancún

Paseo Kukulkán km 7, Cancún, Q. Roo 77500. ☎ **98/83-0200** or 800/327-0200 in the U.S. Fax 98/83-0200. 292 rms. A/C MINIBAR TV TEL. High season $155–$300 double; low season $155–$255 double. Free parking.

Elegant and spacious, the Presidente sports a modern design with lavish marble and wicker accents. Rooms have king-size beds, private balconies, tastefully simple unfinished pine furniture, and in-room safes. Sixteen rooms on the first floor have patios with outdoor whirlpool tubs. The club floors offer robes, magnified makeup mirrors, complimentary continental breakfast, evening drinks and canapés, and use of a private key-activated elevator. Two rooms are available for guests with disabilities and two floors are reserved for nonsmokers. Coming from Cancún City, you'll reach the Presidente on the left side of the street before you get to Punta Cancún—it's behind the golf course and next to million-dollar homes.

Dining/Entertainment: The fine-dining restaurant features foods from France, Greece, Italy, Spain, and Morocco. El Caribeño, a three-level palapa restaurant by the beach and pool, serves all meals (see "Dining," below).

Services: Room and laundry service, travel agency, car rental.

Facilities: Two landscaped swimming pools with a waterfall; whirlpools; fitness center; a great beach fronting the calm Bahía Mujeres; lighted tennis courts; water-sports equipment rental; and marina.

CANCÚN CITY

Hotel Antillano

Claveles 37, Cancún, Q. Roo 77500. ☎ **98/84-1532.** Fax 98/84-1878. 46 rms, 2 suites (all with bath). A/C TV TEL. High season $50 double; low season $35 double. Free guarded parking.

This modern wood-and-stucco hotel is one of the nicer downtown establishments. There's a small bar to one side of the reception area. Rooms overlook Avenida Tulum, the side streets, and the interior pool. Each room has one or two double beds, a sink area separate from the bath, and red-tile floors. To find the hotel, walk west from Tulum on Claveles for a half a block; the hotel is opposite the Restaurant Rosa Mexicana.

Hotel Plaza Carrillo's

Claveles 5, Cancún, Q. Roo 77500. ☎ **98/84-1227.** Fax 98/84-2371. 43 rms (all with bath). A/C TV TEL. High season $33 double; low season $30 double. Parking spaces available around the Parque Palapas.

Rooms at this excellently located hotel are very comfortable and well kept with fresh paint and tile floors. Beds are on concrete platforms that are a little too low to the floor. The pool is in the center behind the streetside restaurant. Guests have privileges at the Club de Playa by the Verano Beat Hotel on the island, and the hotel provides free transportation to the club at 10am, noon, and 2pm. From Avenida Tulum, the hotel is ¹/₂ block west on Claveles.

Hotel Rivemar

Tulum 49–51, Cancún, Q. Roo 77500. ☎ **98/84-1199.** 36 rms (all with bath). A/C TV TEL. $23 double; $33 triple.

Right in the heart of downtown Cancún, this hotel is perfectly located. Rooms are clean; each has tile floors, two double beds, and small baths. All rooms have windows, some with street views and some with hall view. The hotel is at the corner of Crisantemas, 1¹/₂ blocks north of the corner of Avenidas Cobá and Uxmal.

4 Dining

Restaurants change names with amazing rapidity in Cancún, so the restaurants I've chosen are a mix of those with dependable quality and staying power and those that were new or newly thriving when I checked them for this edition.

One of the first things you'll notice on arrival in Cancún is the invasion of U.S. franchise restaurants. You'll see them almost everywhere you look, including Wendy's, Subway, McDonalds, Pizza Hut, Tony Roma's, Ruth's Chris Steak House, KFC, and Burger King. Among the most economical chains are Vips and Denny's, which are also in several locations.

ON CANCÚN ISLAND
VERY EXPENSIVE

Captain's Cove

Paseo Kukulkán km 15, ☎ **98/85-0016.** Breakfast buffet $7–$10; seafood dishes $18–$40; children's menu $4–$5. INTERNATIONAL

Though it sits almost at the end of Paseo Kukulkán far from everything, the Captain's Cove continues to pack customers in on its several dining levels.

Diners face big open windows overlooking the lagoon and Royal Yacht Club Marina. During breakfast there's an all-you-can-eat buffet. Lunch and dinner main courses of steak and seafood are the norm, and there's a menu catering especially to children. For dessert there are flaming coffees, crêpes, and key lime pie. The restaurant is on the lagoon side opposite the Omni Hotel.

El Caribeño

In the Presidente Inter-Continental Hotel, Paseo Kukulkán, km 7.5. ☎ **98/83-0200.** Breakfast buffet $10; main courses $9–$17. Daily 7am–11pm. MEDITERRANEAN.

Especially nice for breakfast or lunch, El Caribeño sits on the beach with a stunning view of the water and Isla Mujeres in the distance. The breakfast buffet is a sumptuous affair including made-to-order omelets and a gorgeous array of tropical fruits and fresh sweet rolls. Lunch is a good choice since you'll be able to see the sea and will pay a bit less for your main courses. Despite the added expense, dinner is romantic and charming; you can order from the lunch menu at dinner, even though there's a less extensive and more expensive dinner menu. Try the fresh fish prepared Yucatecan style in achiote sauce. The restaurant is on the grounds of the Presidente Inter-Continental, on your left as you face toward the Convention Center on Paseo Kukulkán.

CANCÚN CITY
VERY EXPENSIVE

La Dolce Vita

Av. Cobá 87, near Av. Nader. ☎ **98/84-1384.** Reservations required. Main courses $10–$19. Mon–Fri 1pm–midnight; Sat—Sun 5pm–midnight. ITALIAN.

Try this place early in your stay, for you may want to return more than once. La Dolce Vita is among the most pleasant, popular, and casually elegant small downtown restaurants. Appetizers include p‰oté of quail liver and sautéed shrimp in garlic and herbs. You can order such pastas as green tagliolini with lobster médallions; linguine with clams or seafood; or rigatoni Mexican style (with chorizo, mushrooms, and chives), as an appetizer for half price or as a main course for full price. Other main courses include veal with morels, fresh salmon with cream sauce, scampi, and various fish dishes. To find La Dolce Vita from the corner of Tulum and Cobá, walk 2^1/2 blocks east toward the island Zona Hotelera; it's on the left (north) side of Cobá, almost next to Ciao Pastelería.

✪ La Habichuela

Margaritas 25. ☎ **98/84-3158.** Reservations recommended in high season. Seafood and steaks $10–$30; Mexican dishes $6–$20. Daily 1–11:30 pm. GOURMET SEAFOOD/BEEF/MEXICAN.

In a garden setting with tables covered in pink-and-white linens and soft music in the background, this restaurant is an ideal setting for romance and gourmet dining. For an all-out culinary adventure, try Habichuela (string bean) soup; huitlacoche crêpes; shrimp with tomatoes, yellow peppers, olives, and capers; and the Maya coffee with Xtabentun. The grilled seafood and steaks are excellent as well. The restaurant is a few steps from the northwest end of the Parque Palapas on Margaritas.

Restaurant Rosa Mexicano

Claveles 4. ☎ **98/84-6313.** Reservations recommended for parties of six or more. Main courses $14–$18; lobster $30. Daily 5—11pm. MEXICAN HAUTE.

For a nice evening out, try this beautiful little place that has candlelit tables and a plant-filled patio in back. Colorful paper banners and piñatas hang from the ceiling, efficient waiters wear bow ties and cumberbunds color-themed to the Mexican flag, and a trio plays romantic Mexican music nightly. The menu features "refined" Mexican specialties. Try the pollo almendro—chicken covered in a cream sauce and sprinkled with ground almonds, served with rice and vegetables. The steak tampiqueño is a huge platter that comes with guacamole salad, quesadillas, beans, salad, and rice. The restaurant is a half a block west of Tulum.

EXPENSIVE

Restaurant El Pescador

Tulipanes 28, off Av. Tulum. ☎ **98/84-2673.** Seafood $19–$29; Mexican plates $8.50–$10. Daily 11am–10:30pm. SEAFOOD.

There's often a line at this restaurant, which serves well-prepared and moderate-to high-priced fresh seafood. You can sit on the streetside patio, in an interior dining room, or upstairs. Feast on cocktails of shrimp, conch, fish, or octopus; Créole-style shrimp (camarones a la criolla); charcoal-broiled lobster; and stone crab. There's a Mexican specialty meal as well. El Pescador is one block west of Tulum.

MODERATE

✪ Restaurant Los Almendros

Av. Bonampak and Sayil. ☎ **98/84-0807.** Main courses $4–$10. Daily 10:30am–11pm. YUCATECAN.

The illustrated menu shows color pictures of the typical Yucatecan dishes served at this place. Some of the regional specialties include lime soup, poc-chuc, and chicken or pork pibil. The combinado Yucateco is a sampler of four typically Yucatecan main courses—pollo (chicken), poc-chuc, sausage, and escabeche. A second location opened in 1994 on Paseo Kulkulkán across from the convention center. To find the downtown location, go to the corner of Tulum and Cobá and walk toward Cancún island (east) two long blocks and turn right on Avenida Bonampak; it's opposite the bullring 7 short blocks ahead.

100% Natural

Av. Sunyaxchen 6. ☎ **98/84-1617.** Breakfast $3.50–$4; spaghetti $5–$9; fruit or vegetable shakes $3–$4; sandwiches and Mexican plates $5.25–$9; coffee $1.50. Daily 7am–11pm. SEMI-VEGETARIAN.

For great mixed-fruit shakes and salads, the ever-popular 100% Natural is *the* place. Coffee is expensive but comes with several refills. Full meals include large portions of chicken or fish, spaghetti, or soup and sandwiches. Dine on the pretty patio in back to avoid the roar of Sunyaxchen. The restaurant is near the corner of Avenidas Yaxchilán and Sunyaxchen opposite the Hotel Caribe Internacional. Two other locations are in the Zona Hotelera at Plaza Terramar (open 24 hours) and Plaza Kukulkán (open 8am–midnight).

Périco's

Av. Yaxchilán 71. ☎ **98/84-3152.** Main courses $4.50–$15. Daily 1pm–1am. MEXICAN/SEAFOOD.

Made of sticks to resemble a large Maya house, the always-booming Périco's is decorated with baskets, old musical instruments, photos, and dance masks. The extensive menu offers well-prepared steak, seafood, and traditional Mexican dishes for moderate rates (the lobster is more expensive). Witty waiters are part of the fun, and don't be surprised if everybody dons huge Mexican sombreros to bob and snake in a conga dance. There's marimba music from 7:30 to 10:30pm, followed by mariachis until midnight. To find this place, go west of Avenida Tulum to the Parque Palapas. Cross the middle of the park and continue west one block on Gladiolas to Yaxchilán. Périco's is across Yaxchilán at the corner of Chiabal.

Pizza Rolandi

Cobá 12. ☎ **98/84-4047.** Pasta $4.50–$6; pizza and main courses $4.50–$9.50. Mon–Sat 1pm–midnight; Sun 1pm–11pm. ITALIAN.

The outdoor patio of this restaurant is usually very crowded, so elbow your way in. It serves a hearty, wood-oven cheese-and-tomato pizza, and a full selection of spaghetti, calzones, and desserts, as well as beer and mixed drinks. To find it from the corner of Tulum and Cobá, walk east (towards the island) a few steps; Rolandi's is on the left.

✪ Restaurant El Pescador

Tulipanes 28, off Av. Tulum. ☎ **98/84-2673.** Seafood $16–$25; Mexican plates $7–$9; beef and chicken $7.50–$12. Daily 11am–10:30pm. SEAFOOD.

There's often a line at this restaurant, which serves well-prepared fresh seafood in lovely surroundings. Feast on shrimp cocktails, conch, fish, octopus, Créole-style shrimp (camarones à la criolla), charcoal-broiled lobster, and stone crabs. There's a Mexican-specialty menu as well. The restaurant is a half a block east of Avenida Tulum.

INEXPENSIVE

Las Gorditas

Alcatraces at Claveles. ☎ **98/84-0270.** Burritos and gorditas $3–$4.50; sandwiches $2–$3. Mon–Sat 8:30am–10pm. MEXICAN.

Las Gorditas is a pretty open-air cafe with a few tables and a simple, authentically Mexican menu. Gorditas, the main feature, are thick corn tortillas stuffed with a choice of such fillings as tinga (a stew of pork or chicken and vegetables), pollo mole, potatoes, and cheese. Other selections include fruit salads. There's a second location in the Los Portales commercial center on Avenida Sunyaxchen near the main post office. To get to the first location from Tulum, turn west on the second Claveles; its a block ahead at Alactraces.

COFFEE AND PASTRIES

✪ Ciao Pastelería

Cobá 30. ☎ **98/84-1216.** Pastries $1–$2; special coffees $3–$5.75. Mon–Sat Noon–10pm. PASTRIES/COFFEE.

Resembling a little French cafe with half-curtain windows, a few wood tables and chairs, and a display case of delightful pastries, this place looks like it belongs in Georgetown or Greenwich Village. Try the croissant plain with butter or filled with chocolate or jam. There's a full menu of mixed drinks, plus hot and cold coffees with many innovative mixtures. To find it from the corner of Tulum and Cobá, walk 2¹/₂ blocks east toward the Zona Hotelera; it's on the left (north) side of Cobá, almost next to La Dolce Vita.

A DELICATESSEN

Super Deli

Tulum at Xcaret/Cobá. ☎ **98/84-1412.** Breakfast $2–$7.50; sandwiches $5–$7.50; pizzas $5.75–$8. Daily 24 hours. DELICATESSEN.

You can't miss the trendy awning and outdoor restaurant here. It's very popular for light meals any time, and inside is a well-stocked, medium-size grocery store with an excellent delicatessen. There's another branch (smaller) on the island in the Plaza Nautilus. This Cancún City location is on the west side of Tulum just past the intersection of Tulum and Xcaret, almost next to the Hotel Handall.

5 Beaches, Water Sports & Other Things to Do

Although most people come to Cancún to kick back and relax on the beach, options for exploring beyond your selected beach chair are numerous.

The first thing to do is explore the Zona Hotelera on Isla Cancún, just to see the fabulous resort itself and to get your bearings. Frequent **Ruta 1** or **Ruta 2 buses** marked "Hoteles" and those marked "Turismo" run from the mainland city along the full 12 miles to the end of the island and cost around 75¢ per ride. You can get on and off anywhere to visit hotels, shopping centers, and beaches. The best stretches of beach are dominated by the big hotels.

THE BEACHES

All of Mexico's beaches are public property. Be especially careful on beaches fronting the open Caribbean, where the undertow can be deadly. Swim where there's a lifeguard. By contrast, the waters of Mujeres Bay (Bahía Mujeres) at the north end of the island, are usually calm. Get to know Cancún's water-safety pennant system, and make sure to check the flag at any beach or hotel before entering the water. Here's how it goes:

White	Excellent
Green	Normal conditions (safe)
Yellow	Changeable, uncertain (use caution)
Black or Red	Unsafe—use the swimming pool instead!

Here in the Caribbean, storms can arrive and conditions can change from safe to unsafe in a matter of minutes, so be alert: If you see dark clouds heading your way, make your way to shore and wait until the storm passes and the green flag is displayed again.

Playa Tortuga (Turtle Beach) is the public beach. Besides swimming, you can rent a sailboard and take lessons there. Shuttle boats to Isla Mujeres also depart from here along with some tour boats.

WATER SPORTS

Many beachside hotels offer water-sports concessions that include rental of rubber rafts, kayaks, and snorkeling equipment. On the calm Nichupte Lagoon are outlets for renting sailboats, water jets, and water skis. Prices vary and are often negotiable, so check around.

Besides **snorkeling** at Garrafón National Park (see "Boating Excursions," below), travel agencies offer an all-day excursion to the natural wildlife habitat of Isla

Contoy, which usually includes time for snorkeling. It costs more than doing it on your own from Isla Mujeres (see Chapter 20 for details).

You can arrange a day of **deep-sea fishing** at one of the numerous piers or travel agencies for around $150 to $200 for four hours for up to four people.

Scuba trips run around $66 and include two tanks. **Scuba Cancún,** Paseo Kukulkán, km 5, on the lagoon side (☎ 98/83-1011; fax 84-2336, open 9am to 2pm, phone reservations also available in the evenings from 7;30-10:30pm), offers a four-hour resort course for $100. Full certification takes four to five days and costs around $350. Scuba Cancún also offers diving trips to 12 nearby reefs, including Cuevones at 30 feet, and the open ocean at 54 to 56 feet (offered in good weather only). The average dive is around 35 feet. One-tank dives cost $45, and two-tank dives cost $66.

For windsurfing, go to the Playa Tortuga public beach, where there's a **Windsurfing School** (☎ 84-2023) with equipment for rent.

BOATING EXCURSIONS

The island of Isla Mujeres, just 10 miles offshore, is one of the most pleasant day-trips from Cancún. At one end is **El Garrafón National Underwater Park,** which is excellent for snorkeling. And at the other end is the delightful village with small shops, restaurants, and hotels, and Playa Norte, the island's best beach. (See Chapter 16 for more on Isla Mujeres.) If you're looking for relaxation and can spare the time, Isla Mujeres is worth several days.

There are three ways to get there: by public ferry from Puerto Juárez, which takes around 45 minutes, by a shuttle boat from Playa Linda or Playa Tortuga (a one-hour ride) and by one of the day-long pleasure boats.

It's easy to go on your own. The Puerto Juárez **public ferries** are just a few miles from downtown Cancún. From Cancún city, take the Ruta 8 bus on Avenida Tulum to Puerto Juárez; the ferry docks in downtown Isla Mujeres. You'll need a taxi to go Garrafón Park at the other end of the island. You can stay as long as you like and return by ferry, but be sure to ask about the time of the last returning ferry—don't depend on the posted hours. Taxi fare from downtown Cancún to the pier will cost around $8. The ferry costs $1.50 to $3.50 one way. (For more details see Chapter 16.) The Isla Mujeres Shuttle departs from Playa Linda and Playa Tortuga in the Zona Hotelera. The round-trip fare is $13.50 and the trip takes about one hour. (For more details and a shuttle schedule see Chapter 16.)

Pleasure boat cruises to Isla Mujeres are a favorite pastime here. Modern motor yachts, catamarans, trimarans, and even old-time sloops take swimmers, sunners, snorkelers, and shoppers out into the limpid waters. Some tours include a snorkeling stop at Garrafón, lunch on the beach, and a short time for shopping in downtown Isla Mujeres. Most leave at 9:30 or 10am; last about five or six hours; and include continental breakfast, lunch, and rental of snorkel gear. Others, particularly the sunset and night cruises, go to beaches away from town for pseudo-pirate shows and include a lobster dinner or Mexican buffet. If you want to actually see Isla Mujeres, go on a morning cruise, or go on your own and return on the public ferry.

Tour companies are also beginning to offer cruises that emphasize Cancún's natural attributes. The **lagoons** along the Zona Hotelera are ideal for spotting herons, egrets, and crabs in the mangroves. Often billed as **jungle cruises,** they don't go to a jungle but they usually include time for lagoon snorkeling. Other

On the Road in the Yucatán

The most economical way to see the Yucatán is by bus. Although service is still best between the major cities, since 1992 it has improved considerably to other parts of the peninsula as well. There are more deluxe buses. You can sometimes purchase tickets in advance—often selecting your seat on a computer screen. However, using buses as the primary means of transportation, will add more days to your trip. On highways, you can still flag down buses that are going your way and hop aboard, though you'll spend a lot of time waiting at intersections, particularly near Uxmal and Kabah and along the Caribbean coast. If you're waiting on a busy route—say between Cancún and Tulum—many full buses will pass you by. Distances are deceiving. For example, a bus trip using the new highway from Mérida to Cancún takes 4 hours; bus travel between Mérida and Palenque takes 9 hours. To find the fastest bus, get in the habit of asking if a bus goes *sin escalas* or *directo* (nonstop or direct); either may mean no stops or only a couple of stops as opposed to many stops on a regular bus.

The best way to see the Yucatán is by car. It's one of the most pleasant parts of the country for a driving vacation. The jungle- and beach-lined roads, while narrow and without shoulders, are generally in good condition and have little traffic. And they are straight, except in the southern part of Yucatán state and west to Campeche, where they undulate through the Yucatán "Alps."

The four-lane toll road between Cancún and Mérida is complete but actually ends short of either city. Costing around $30 one-way, it cuts the trip from 5 to around 4 hours. The old two-lane free road is still in fine shape and passes through numerous villages with many speed-control bumps (topes)—this route is much more interesting. New directional signs seem to lead motorists to the toll road (cuota) and don't mention the free road (libre), so if you want to use it, ask locals for directions. A new four-lane stretch of road is finished from Cancún almost to Puerto Morelos. Originally it was to extend to Chetumal, but the local rumor is that a new toll road instead will parallel the existing two-lane road and connect Cancún and Chetumal; construction hasn't yet begun. Meanwhile, traffic on the remaining two-lane road has increased substantially. See important information in Chapter 18 on how to use local driving customs to travel this stretch with safety.

Be aware of the long distances in the Yucatán. Mérida, for instance, is 400 miles from Villahermosa, 125 miles from Campeche, and 200 miles from Cancún. Leaded gas (Nova) is readily available in the Yucatán; unleaded gas (Magna Sin) is available at most stations. Many stations close early in the evening. If you're planning to rent a car to travel the area, see Chapter 3 "Car Rentals."

excursions go to the **reefs** in glass-bottom boats, so you can have a near-scuba-diving experience and see many colorful fish. However, the reefs are a distance from shore and impossible to reach on windy days with choppy seas. They've also suffered through overuse and their condition is far from pristine. Still other boat excursions visit Isla Contoy, a **national bird sanctuary** that's well worth the time. If you are planning to spend time in Isla Mujeres, the Contoy trip is easier and more pleasurable to take from there.

The operators and names of boats offering excursions change often. To find out what's available when you're there, check with a local travel agent or hotel tour desk, for they should have a wide range of options. You can also go to the Playa Linda Pier either a day ahead or the day of your intended outing and buy your own ticket. If you go on the day of your trip, arrive at the pier around 8:45am since most boats leave around 9 or 9:30am.

RUINAS EL REY

Cancún has its own Maya ruins. It's a small site and not impressive compared to ruins at Tulum, Cobá, or Chichén-Itzá. The Maya fishermen built this small ceremonial center and settlement very early in the history of Maya culture. It was then abandoned, to be resettled later near the end of the post-Classic Period, not long before the arrival of the conquistadores. The platforms of numerous small temples are visible amid the banana plants, papayas, and wildflowers. A new golf course has been built around the ruins, but there is a separate entrance for sightseers. You'll find the ruins about 13 miles from town, at the southern reaches of the Zona Hotelera, almost to Punta Nizuc. Look for the Caesar's Palace hotel on the left (east), then the ruins on the right (west). Admission is $4.50 (free on Sundays and holidays); the hours are daily from 8am to 5pm.

A MUSEUM

The Cancún Convention Center has a small museum with relics from archeological sites around the state. Admission is $3.50 (free on Sundays and holidays); the hours are Tuesday to Saturday from 9am to 7pm, Sunday from 9am to 5pm.

BULLFIGHTS

Cancún has a small bullring (☎ 98/84-8372) near the northern (town) end of Paseo Kukulkán opposite the Restaurant Los Almendros. Bullfights are held every Wednesday at 3:30pm during the winter tourist season. There are usually four bulls. Travel agencies in Cancún sell tickets: $45 for adults and $25 for children.

6 Shopping

Although shops in Cancún are more expensive than their equivalents in any other Mexican city, most visitors spend a portion of their time browsing.

There are several open-air **crafts markets** easily visible on Avenida Tulum in Cancún city and near the convention center in the hotel zone.

Malls on Cancún Island are air-conditioned, sleek, and sophisticated. Most of these are located one after another on Paseo Kukulkán between km 7 and km 12—Plaza Lagunas, Costa Brava, La Mansión, Mayfair, Plaza Terramar, Plaza Caracol, Plaza Flamingo and Plaza Kulkucán. These malls offer shops selling anything from fine crystal and silver to designer clothing and decorative objects. Numerous restaurants are interspersed among the shops, many with prices higher than their branches on the mainland. Stores are generally open daily from 10am to 8 or 10pm. Stores in malls near the convention center generally stay open all day, but some, and especially in malls farther out, close between 2 and 5pm.

Cancún's **"people market"** selling food, spices, housewares, piñatas, party supplies, and the like is behind the post office at Sunyaxchen and Xelha. It's open Monday through Saturday from 9am to 1pm and 4 to 9pm and Sunday from 9am to 2pm. There you can also find **Disco Tinhorot II** (☎ 84-3728), with a large selection of Mexican tapes and CDs. It's open the same hours as the market.

7 Cancún After Dark

One of Cancún's draws is its active nightlife. Sometimes there's entertainment enough just strolling along thriving Avenida Tulum, where restaurant employees show off enticing sample plates to lure in passersby. But there are also snazzy discos and a variety of lobby entertainment at island hotels.

A THEME PARK   Cancún's answer to an entertainment theme park may be **Mexico Magico,** an outrageously colorful multiacre operation on Bulevar Kukulkán. Inside are variety shows—from folkloric, flamingo, and pre-Hispanic dancing to mariachis and Mexican-style comedy. A printed nightly schedule, with a map, tells you what's showing when and where, and you can pick any shows that interest you. Three or four dinner shows vary nightly and cost extra—around $30 per person. Each program usually offers two or three seatings per evening, at 6:30 and 8pm or at 7, 9, and 11pm. Outside the entertainment pavilions are shops selling imported crafts. Several eateries sell fast food and soft drinks.

General admission is $20 per person. However, many hotel tour and concierge desks have coupons good for free admission, so look around before paying full fare. One caveat: Few of the entertainment pavilions are covered, so during the rainy season shows may be rained out, or you may spend lots of time waiting for the rain to clear so the shows can start again. Since there's no drainage, the streets inside Mexico Magico become rivers.

CONVENTION CENTER   The long-awaited convention center is open with slick (and I mean slick) marble floors, arcades of fashionable shops and restaurants, entertainment, meeting rooms, and an auditorium.

THE PERFORMING ARTS   Several hotels host **Mexican fiesta nights,** including a buffet dinner and a folkloric dance show; admission, including dinner, ranges from $30 to $50. The **Ballet Folklórico de Mexico** appears Monday through Saturday nights in a two-hour show at the Continental Villas Plaza (☎ 98/ 85-1444, ext. 5690). The Hyatt Regency Cancún (☎ 98/83-1234) has a dinner, folkloric, and mariachi fiesta, Tuesday through Sunday nights during the high season, as does the Camino Real (☎ 98/83-1200). El Mexicano restaurant (☎ 98/84-4207) in the Costa Blanca shopping center hosts a tropical **dinner show** every night except Sunday as well as live music for dancing.

On Fridays at 7:30pm the downtown Parque de las Palapas hosts Noches Caribeños with tropical music and dancing.

THE CLUB & MUSIC SCENE   Almost all the **island hotels** included in this book have live bands in their lobby bars in the evenings; many have dance floors. Before going, however, call to be sure there's entertainment that night and inquire about the type of music, which can change nightly. At discos cover charges run $14 to $20 per person, and drinks cost $5 to $9. Most feature rock in all its variations or other hip music as long as it's loud, fast, and "in." *Note:* It goes without saying that the disco dress code is no shorts or jeans. Most discos open late and stay open until the crowds start to dwindle, usually between 2:30am and dawn. Perico's, on the mainland, offers nightlife for the price of a meal (see "Dining," above).

Christine's at the Hotel Krystal on the island (☎ 98/83-1793), is one of the most popular discos. It's open at 9:30pm nightly.

Dady'O, Paseo Kukulkán, km 9.5. is another of the island's flashiest discos—at last visit it was certainly drawing the biggest crowds. It opens at 9:30pm nightly.

La Boom, Bulevar Kukulkán, km 3.5 (☎ 98/83-1152), has two sections: On one side is a video bar, and on the other is a bilevel disco with the required cranium-cracking music. There's blessed air conditioning in both places. Each night there may be a special client-getting attraction like no cover, free bar, ladies' night, or bikini night. It's open nightly from 8pm to 6am. A sound and light show begins at 11:30pm in the disco.

Azucar Bar Caribeño, adjacent to the Hotel Camino Real (☎ 98/83-0441), offers spicy tropical dancing of the salsa, merengue, and bolero kind, with bands from Cuba, Jamaica, and the Dominican Republic; it's open Monday to Saturday from 9:30pm to 4am.

Tequila Sunrise Grill Bar & Fiesta, in the Mayfair Shopping Center, is a restaurant, but it's also a lively dancing spot popular with the twentysomething crowd; there's no cover, and it's open daily from 7pm to 4am.

Planet Hollywood, Flamingo Shopping Center, Paseo Kukulkán km 11 (☎ 98/85-3022), is the trendy brainchild of Sylvester Stallone, Bruce Willis, and Arnold Schwarzenegger. It's a restaurant and nighttime music/dance spot with mega-decible live music. It's open daily from 11am to 2am.

Carlos 'n' Charlies, and **Señor Frog,** Paseo Kukulkán km 4.5 (☎ 98/83-0846), two restaurants that are also popular night spots, are located side by side opposite the Hotel Casa Magna. Señor Frog's features a live band nightly—reggae music was playing the last time I was here—and both have dance floors. Live music starts around 9pm, when the cover charge is also implemented if you're not planning to eat. If you're eating, there's no cover. They're open daily from noon to 2am.

SPORTS WAGERING This form of entertainment seems to be sweeping Mexico's resorts. TV screens mounted around the room at **LF Caliente** (☎ 98/83-3704), at the Fiesta Americana Hotel, show all the action in racetrack, football, soccer, and so on in a bar/lounge setting. **Espactaculos Deportivas de Cancún** (☎ 98/83-3900 or 83-3901), is a huge building on Paseo Kukulkán, km 4.5, next to the Playa Linda Pier. Inside is the **Super Book,** with 12 satellite dishes poised to capture major U.S. sporting events, as well as horse and dog races. Action begins here daily at 1pm and runs until midnight. There's a restaurant/bar as well. Admission is free, and bets begin at $2. The jai alai court next door is closed, but may reopen as a theater for live stage performances.

8 Excursions from Cancún

Outside of Cancún are all the many wonders of the Yucatán Peninsula; you'll find the details in Chapters 16 and 17. Cancún can be a perfect base for day- or overnight trips or the starting point for a longer exploration. Any travel agency or hotel tour desk in Cancún can book these tours, or you can elect to do them on your own via local bus or rental car. The Maya ruins to the south at **Tulum** or **Cobá** should be your first goal, then perhaps the *caleta* (cove) of **Xel-ha** or the new lagoon day-trip to **Xcaret**. And if you're going south, consider staying a night or two on the island of **Cozumel** or at one of the budget resorts on the **Tulum coast** or **Punta Allen,** south of the Tulum ruins. **Isla Mujeres** is an easy day-trip off mainland Cancún (see Chapter 16).

About 80 miles south of Cancún begins the **Sian Ka'an Biosphere Reserve,** a 1.3-million-acre area set aside in 1986 to preserve a region of tropical forests, savannas, mangroves, canals, lagoons, bays, cenotes, and coral reefs, all of which are home to hundreds of birds and land and marine animals (see Chapter 21 for details). The Friends of Sian Ka'an, a nonprofit group based in Cancún, offers biologist-escorted day-trips from Cancún daily (weather permitting) at $115 per person. The price includes lunch, round-trip van transportation to the reserve, a guided boat/birding trip through one of the reserve's lagoons, and use of binoculars. For reservations, contact Amigos de Sian Ka'an, Plaza America (☎ 84-9583; fax 87-3080), or make reservations through a Cancún travel agent.

Although I don't recommend it, by driving fast or catching the right buses, you can go inland to **Chichén-Itzá,** explore the ruins, and return in a day, but it's much better to spend at least two days seeing Chichén-Itzá, Mérida, and Uxmal. See Chapter 17 for transportation details and further information on these destinations.

16

Isla Mujeres, Cozumel & the Caribbean Coast

Once obscured by Cancún's glitter, Mexico's other Caribbean vacation spots have shouldered their way into the tourist spotlight. **Isla Mujeres,** just a short ferry ride from Cancún, offers low-priced and low-key Caribbean relaxation. The island of **Cozumel,** somewhere on the spectrum between Isla Mujeres' slow pace and Cancún's fast-lane bustle, has scuba and snorkeling possibilities that compare with any in the world. And the Quintana Roo coast, dubbed the **Costa Turquesa** (Turquoise Coast), stretches south from Cancún all the way to Chetumal—230 miles of powdery white-sand beaches, lush jungle, crystal-clear lagoons full of coral and colorful fish, flashy new resorts, and inexpensive hideaways.

Chapter 17 supplies full information on points west of Cancún, such as Chichén-Itzá and Mérida. Let's look now at the islands off the peninsula, and the mainland coast south of Cancún.

EXPLORING MEXICO'S CARIBBEAN

Isla Mujeres Many people enjoy a brief day-trip to Isla Mujeres on a party boat from Cancún, which is fine if you don't have much time. However, most of those trips provide little time in the village, and you get no sense of what island life is like. I recommend at least two nights in Isla Mujeres, and you could even spend a whole week relaxing here.

Passenger ferries go to Isla Mujeres from Puerto Juárez near Cancún, and car-ferries to Isla Mujeres leave from Punta Sam, also near Cancún.

Cozumel This truly laid-back island getaway is a perfect place to relax for a week or more, with opportunities for the best diving in Mexico, good fishing, and excursions to villages and ruins only a ferry ride away on the mainland. If you're considering a package (usually offered for three or four nights) remember that you'll spend a day coming and going. Buy a longer package if you can, but remember that there are many inexpensive places to stay that won't be part of a package deal and you can still do all the diving and sightseeing you want.

A car/passenger ferry runs between Puerto Morelos (south of Cancún) and Cozumel. Passenger ferries also run between Playa del Carmen and Cozumel—the preferred way to go.

The Costa Turquesa Signs pointing to brand-new, expensive resort developments are sprouting up all along Highway 307 from Cancún south to Tulum, a stretch known as the "Tulum Corridor." Some are actually under construction and others may never progress further than a big sign and a pipe dream. This frenzy of construction is changing the character of Corridor, but there are still plenty of small, inexpensive beachfront hideaways as well as luxury places, just a short distance from the highway. And south of Tulum, almost 100 miles of this coast have been saved from developers and set aside as the Sian Ka'an Biosphere Reserve.

A trip down the coast is a great way to spend a day of a vacation centered in Cancún. The most popular agency-led tour out of Cancún is to the ruins of Tulum, followed by a stop at Xel-Ha for a swim and/or snorkeling in the beautiful clear lagoon. Once a placid and little-known spot, Xcaret Lagoon opened in 1991 as a full-blown tourist attraction for people who plan to spend the day.

Though Chetumal is the capital of Quintana Roo state, it has little to recommend it. It's best to think of it as a gateway to Guatemala, Belize, the several ruins near the city, and the excellent diving and fishing to be had off the Xcalak Peninsula. The reexcavation of many of the ruins near Chetumal may be a reason for a detour there, but Lago Bacalar is the preferred place to stay near Chetumal.

The Costa Turquesa is best experienced in a car. (See Chapter 15, "Cancún," for information on rentals.) It's not impossible to get about by bus, but doing so requires careful planning, more time, and lots of patience. Besides Cancún, Playa del Carmen has the best selection of bus services. There are frequent buses between Cancún and Chetumal that stop at the more populous towns—Playa del Carmen, Tulum, and Felipe Carrillo Puerto. These buses will also let you off on the highway if you want to go to Xel-Ha, Xcaret, Pamul, or other spots, but you'll have to walk the mile or so from the highway to your destination. On your return you'll have to walk back and wait on a sweltering highway along with hordes of ravenous mosquitos to flag a passing bus—and be prepared to watch buses pass you by if they're full. Hitching a ride with other travelers is another possibility, though I don't recommend hitchhiking on the highway. You can always hire a taxi for the return to Cancún.

Highway 307 south of Cancún is flanked by jungle on both sides, except where there are beaches and beach settlements. Traffic, which was once scarce, can be dangerously dense. (See the "Traveler's Advisory" box, below.)

Here are some drive-times from Cancún: Puerto Morelos (port for the car-ferry to Cozumel), 45 minutes; Playa del Carmen (a laid-back beachside village) 1 hour; Xcaret lagoon and Pamul, $1^1/4$ hours; Akumal, $1^3/4$ hours; Xel-Ha and Tulum, around 2 hours; and Chetumal, about 5 hours.

1 Isla Mujeres

10 miles N of Cancún

For total, laid-back, inexpensive Caribbean relaxation, it's hard to beat Isla Mujeres. Once called the "poor man's Cancún," Isla Mujeres has gotten more expensive in the last several years, though the rise in prices seems to have slowed down a bit recently. It may not be quite the deal it once was, but it's still a bargain compared to Cancún—and I much prefer it. The sand streets have been bricked, and Hurricane Gilbert provided an unexpected blessing; lots of painting and refurbishing have given the island a fresh face. This is not a place for restless night owls: the relaxed, suntanned visitors hang out in open-air cafes, talking and trading paperback novels until about 10pm, when restaurants and shop owners start to yawn and the whole island beds down.

There are two versions of how Isla Mujeres ("Island of Women") got its name. The more popular story claims that pirates parked their women here for safe-keeping while they were marauding the Spanish Main. The other account attributes the name to conquistador Francisco Hernández de Córdoba, who was reportedly impressed by the large number of female terra-cotta figurines he found in temples on the island.

ESSENTIALS

GETTING THERE & DEPARTING   Puerto Juárez, just north of Cancún, is the dock for the passenger ferries to Isla Mujeres. The *Caribbean Queen* makes the trip many times daily; it takes 45 minutes and fare is $1.50. The newer *Caribbean Express* makes the trip in 15 minutes; the cost is $3.50. There is no ticket office; pay as you board. Baggage may be stored at a counter at the foot of the pier, near the tourism office, which is open sporadically. Taxi fares are now posted at the lot where the taxis park. The fare to the Cancún airport is $15; to downtown Cancún, $6; and to the Hotel Zone, $5.45 to $15.

Isla Mujeres is so small that a vehicle isn't necessary. But, if you're taking a ve-hicle to Isla Mujeres, you'll use the Punta Sam port a little farther past Puerto Juárez. The ferry runs the 40-minute trip five or six times daily all year except in bad weather (check with the tourist office in Cancún for a current schedule).

There are also boats from the Playa Linda pier in Cancún; though they're less frequent and more expensive than those from Puerto Juárez, they do save you some time. The *Isla Mujeres Shuttle* departs from Playa Linda four times daily, and costs $13.50 round trip. However, if there aren't enough passengers it won't go. Overall, it's more reliable (and a more interesting cultural experience) to use the public ferries from Puerto Juárez.

To get to either Puerto Juárez or Punta Sam from Cancún, take any Ruta 8 city bus from Avenida Tulum. If you're coming from Mérida, you can either fly to Cancún and then proceed by bus to Puerto Juárez, or you can take a first- or second-class bus directly from the Mérida bus station to Puerto Juárez; they leave several times a day. From Cozumel, you can either fly to Cancún (there are daily flights) or take a ferry to Playa del Carmen (see the Cozumel section below for details), where you can catch a bus to Puerto Juárez.

 ORIENTATION   Arriving   Ferries arrive at the dock in the center of town. Taxis are always lined up in front and ask around $2 to take you to almost any hotel. The price gets lower if you wait until all passengers have left the area. Un-less you're loaded with luggage, you don't need transportation since most hotels (except those on Playa Norte) are within walking distance.

Visitor Information   The **City Tourist Office** is on Hidalgo in a white wooden building facing the Plaza Principal and next to the Palacio Municipal (☎ and fax 987/7-0316). It's open Monday through Friday from 9am to 2:30pm and 7 to 9pm.

Island Layout   Isla Mujeres is about 5 miles long and 2¹/₂ miles wide. The **ferry docks** are right at the center of town, within walking distance of most hotels. The street running along the waterfront is **Rueda Medina,** commonly called the **malecón.** The **market** (Mercado Municipal) is by the post office on **Calle**

Guerrero, an inland street at the north edge of town, which, like most streets in the town, is unmarked.

Getting Around   The best and most efficient way to see the island is to rent a moto, the local sobriquet for motorized bikes and scooters. If you don't want to fool with gears and shifts, rent a fully automatic one for around $30 per day or $6 per hour. They come with seats for one person, but some are large enough for two. Take time to get familiar with how the scooters work and be careful on the road as you approach blind corners and hills where visibility is poor. There's only one main road with a couple of offshoots, so you won't get lost. Be aware that the rental price does not include insurance, and any injury to yourself or the scooter will come out of your pocket. Electric golf carts, ideal for getting around, are available for rent at many hotels for $10 per hour or $50 per day. Keep in mind they don't go more than 20 miles per hour. Bicycles are also available for rent at some hotels for $5 per day.

FAST FACTS: ISLA MUJERES

Area Code   The area code of Isla Mujeres is 987. The first digit for all telephone numbers on the island has been changed from 2 to 7.

Hospital   The Hospital de la Armada, on Medina at Ojon P. Blanco (☎ 7-0001), has the island's only decompression chamber. It's half a mile south of the town center.

Post Office/Telegraph Office   The correo is on Calle Guerrero, by the market.

Telephone   There's a long-distance telephone office in the lobby of the Hotel María José, Avenida Madero at Medina, open Monday through Saturday from 9am to 1pm and 4 to 8pm. There are Ladatel phones accepting coins and pre-paid phone cards at the plaza.

Tourist Seasons   Isla Mujeres' tourist season (when hotel rates are higher) is a bit different from that of other places in Mexico. High season runs December through May, a month longer than in Cancún; some hotels raise their rates in August and some hotels raise their rates beginning in mid-November. Low season is June through mid-November.

BEACHES, WATER SPORTS & OTHER ATTRACTIONS

THE BEACHES

The most popular beach in town used to be called Playa Cocoteros (Coco for short). Then, in 1988, Hurricane Gilbert destroyed the coconut palms on the beach. Gradually, the name has been changed to **Playa Norte,** referring to the long stretch of beach that extends around the northern tip of the island, to your left as you get off the boat. This is a truly splendid beach—a wide swath of fine white sand and calm, lucidly clear, turquoise-blue water. Topless sunbathing is okay here. The beach is easily reached on foot from the ferry and from all downtown hotels. Water-sports equipment, beach umbrellas, and lounge chairs are available for rent.

Impressions

It becomes a virtue, almost a necessity, to do some loafing. The art of leisure is therefore one of Mexico's most stubbornly defended practises [sic] and one of her subtle appeals; a lesson in civilization which we of the hectic north need very badly to learn.
— Anita Brenner, *Your Mexican Holiday*, 1932

Garrafón National Park is known best as a snorkeling area, but there is a nice stretch of beach on either side of the park. **Playa Lancheros** is on the Caribbean side of Laguna Makax. Local buses go to Lancheros, then turn inland and return downtown. The beach at Playa Lancheros is nice, but the few restaurants there are high-priced.

WATER SPORTS

SWIMMING   Wide Playa Norte is the best swimming beach, with Playa Lancheros second. There are no lifeguards on duty on Isla Mujeres, and the system of water-safety flags used in Cancún and Cozumel isn't used here either. Be very careful!

SNORKELING   By far the most popular place to snorkel is **Garrafón National Park,** at the southern end of the island, where you'll see numerous schools of colorful fish. The well-equipped park has beach chairs, changing rooms, lockers, showers, and a snack bar. Taxis from the central village cost around $3.50 one way. Admission is $2; lockers rent for $1.50.

Another excellent location is around the lighthouse in the **Bahía de Mujeres** (bay) opposite downtown, where the water is about 6 feet deep. Boatmen will take you for around $10 per person if you have your own snorkeling equipment or $15 more if you use theirs.

DIVING   Several dive shops have opened on the island, most offering the same trips. The traditional dive center is **Buzos de México,** on Rueda Medina at Morelos (☎ 987/7-0274), next to the boat cooperative. Dive master Carlos Gutiérrez offers certification and resort courses, and makes sure all courses are led by certified dive masters. **Bahia Dive Shop,** on Rueda Medina 166 across from the car-ferry dock (☎ and fax 987/7-0340), is a full-service shop with dive equipment for sale and rent and resort and certification classes. The most popular reefs are Manchones, Banderas, and Cuevones. All 30- to 40-foot dives cost $40 to $65 for a two-tank trip; equipment rental costs $15. Cuevas de los Tiburones ("Caves of the Sleeping Sharks") is Isla's most famous dive site and costs $60 to $80 for a two-tank dive. Your chance of actually seeing sharks, by the way, is less than 50%. The best season for diving is from June through August, when the water is calm.

FISHING   To arrange a day of fishing, ask at the **Sociedad Cooperativa Turística** (boatmen's cooperative; ☎ 987/7-0274) or the travel agency mentioned below, under Isla Contoy. The cost can be shared with four to six others and includes lunch and drinks. All year you'll find bonito, mackerel, kingfish, and amberjack. Sailfish and sharks (hammerhead, bull, nurse, lemon, and tiger) are in good supply in April and May. In winter, larger grouper and jewfish are prevalent. Four hours of fishing costs around $120, with 8 hours for $240. The cooperative is open Monday through Saturday from 8am to 1pm and 5 to 8pm and Sunday from 7:30 to 10am and 6 to 8pm.

OTHER ATTRACTIONS

A MAYA RUIN   Just beyond the lighthouse, at the southern end of the island, is a pile of stones that formed a small Maya pyramid before Hurricane Gilbert struck. Believed to have been an observatory built to the moon goddess Ixchel, now it's reduced to a rocky heap. The location, on a lofty bluff overlooking the sea, is still worth seeing. If you're at Garrafón National Park and want to walk, it's not too far. Turn right from Garrafón. When you see the lighthouse, turn toward it down the rocky path.

Isla Mujeres

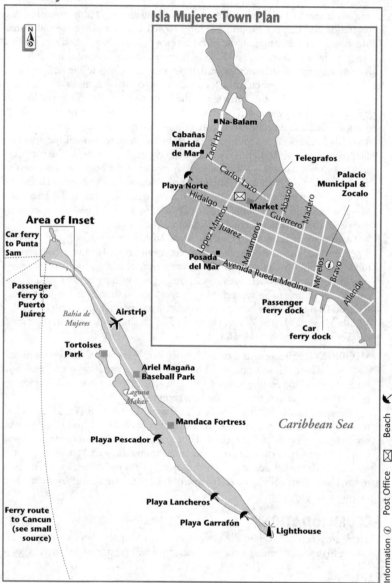

Isla Mujeres Town Plan

N

Area of Inset

Car ferry to Punta Sam

Passenger ferry to Puerto Juárez

Bahia de Mujeres

Airstrip

Tortoises Park

Ariel Magaña Baseball Park

Laguna Makax

Mandaca Fortress

Playa Pescador

Caribbean Sea

Ferry route to Cancun (see small source)

Playa Lancheros

Playa Garrafón

Lighthouse

Na-Balam

Cabañas Marida de Mar

Zacil Ha

Telegrafos

Carlos Lazo

Palacio Municipal & Zocalo

Playa Norte

Hidalgo

Market

Abasolo

López Mateos

Juarez

Guerrero

Madero

Matamoros

Posada del Mar

Avenida Rueda Medina

Morelos

Bravo

Allende

Passenger ferry dock

Car ferry dock

Information ⓘ Post Office ⊠ Beach

1277

A PIRATE'S FORTRESS   The Fortress of Mundaca is about $2^{1}/_{2}$ miles in the same direction as Garrafón, about half a mile to the left. The fortress was built by the pirate Mundaca Marecheaga, who in the early 19th century arrived at Isla Mujeres and proceeded to set up a blissful paradise in a pretty, shady spot while making money from selling slaves to Cuba and Belize.

A VISIT TO ISLA CONTOY   If at all possible, plan to visit this pristine unin-habited island, 19 miles by boat from Isla Mujeres, that was set aside as a national wildlife reserve in 1981. The oddly shaped 3.8-mile-long island is covered in lush vegetation and harbors 70 species of birds as well as a host of marine and animal life. Bird species that nest on the island include pelicans, brown boobies, frigates, egrets, terns, and cormorants. Flocks of flamingos arrive in April. June, July, and August are good months to spot turtles who bury their eggs in the sand at night. Most excursions anchor en route for a snorkeling expedition, and skirt the island at a leisurely pace for close viewing of the birds without disturbing the habitat. Visitors are no longer allowed to walk on the island, and must be content to check out the wildlife from offshore, but that could change so be sure to ask. The trip from Isla Mujeres takes a minimum of $1^1/_2$ hours one way, more if the waves are choppy. Because of the tight-knit boatmen's cooperative, prices for this excursion are the same everywhere—$30. You can buy a ticket at the **Sociedad Cooperativa Turística** (☎ 987/7-0274) on Avenida Rueda Medina, next to Mexico Divers and Las Brisas restaurant, or at one of several travel agencies, such as **La Isleña**, on Morelos between Medina and Juárez (☎ 987/7-0578). La Isleña is open daily from 7am to 6pm and is a good source for tourist information.

Three types of boats go to Contoy. Small boats have one motor and seat 8 or 9 people. Medium-size boats have two motors and hold 10. Large boats have a toilet and hold 16. Some boats have a sun cover; others do not. Boat captains should respect the cooperative's regulations regarding capacity and should have enough life jackets to go around. I highly recommend the services of boat owner **Ricardo Gaitan.** Ask for him at the cooperative or write to him directly: P.O. Box 42, Isla Mujeres, Q. Roo 77400. He speaks English, and his large boat, the *Estrella del Norte,* comfortably holds 16 seated.

SHOPPING   Shopping is a casual activity here—few glittery, sleek shops and none of the hard sell you find in the big resorts. Prices are also lower. You'll find silver, fine jewelry, Saltillo serapes, Oaxacan rugs, masks, Guatemalan clothing, pottery, blown glassware, and T-shirts in abundance.

One store stands out from the rest: **La Loma,** Guerrero 6 (☎ 987/7-0223), stocks a great variety of good folk art, including Huichol yarn "paintings," masks, silver chains and coins, a good selection of textiles, Oaxacan wood carvings, Olinalá lacquer objects, and colorful clay candelabras from Izúcar de Matamoros. You'll see it opposite the left side of the church beside La Peña restaurant, and almost next to the Hotel Perla del Caribe II. It's open Monday through Saturday from 10am to 3pm and 5 to 8pm.

ACCOMMODATIONS

There are plenty of hotels in all price ranges on Isla Mujeres. Rates are at their peak during high season, which is the most expensive and most crowded time to go.

EXPENSIVE

Hotel Cabañas María del Mar

Av. Carelos Lazo 1, Isla Mujeres, Q. Roo 77400. ☎ **987/7-0179.** Fax 987/7-0213. 52 rms. A/C. High season $85 double; $75 bungalow; new "castle" section $85–$90 double. Low season $45–$66 double; "castle" $45–$75 double. Rates include continental breakfast.

A good choice, the Cabañas María del Mar is located on Playa Norte, a half block from the Hotel Nabalam. There are three completely different sections to this hotel. The two-story section behind the reception area and beyond the garden offers nicely outfitted rooms facing the beach, all with two single or double beds, refrigerators, and balconies with ocean views. Eleven single-story cabañas closer to the reception and pool are rather dark. The newest addition, El Castillo, is across the street and built over and beside Buho's restaurant. It contains all "deluxe" rooms, but some are larger than others; the five rooms on the ground floor all have large patios. Upstairs rooms have small balconies. Most have one double bed. All have ocean views, blue-and-white tile floors, and tile lavatories and are outfitted in cool cotton bedspreads and natural-toned neocolonial furniture. There's a small, unkempt pool in the garden. The owners also have a bus for tours and a boat for rental, as well as car and moto rental.

To get here from the pier walk left one block, then turn right on Matamoros. After four blocks, turn left on Lazo, the last street. The hotel is at the end of the block.

✪ Hotel Na Balam

Zacil Ha 118, Isla Mujeres, Q. Roo 77400. ☎ **987/7-0279** or 7-0593. Fax 987/7-0446. 19 suites (all with bath). A/C FAN. High season $85 standard suite (double), $105 master suite (double). Low season $65 standard suite, $95 master suite. Free unguarded parking.

This two-story hotel near the end of Playa Norte Beach is my favorite lodging on the island. Its comfortable rooms are on a quiet, ideally located portion of the beach in a palm grove. All rooms have either a patio or balcony facing the ocean. Each nicely furnished and spacious suite contains two double beds, a seating area, and folk-art decorations. The restaurant, Zacil-Ha, is one of the island's most popular.

To find the hotel from the pier, walk five blocks to López Mateos; turn right and walk four blocks to Lazo (the last street). Turn left and walk to the sandy road parallel to the beach and turn right. The hotel is a half a block farther.

MODERATE

Hotel Posada del Mar

Av. Rueda Medina 15, Isla Mujeres, Q. Roo 77400. ☎ **987/7-0300.** Fax 987/7-0266. 40 rms (all with bath). A/C TEL. High season $50 double. Low season $40 double.

Attractively furnished, this long-established hotel faces the water and a wide beach three blocks north of the ferry pier. The rooms, all with a fresh coat of white paint, are in a large garden palm grove in a three-story building. Some rooms are in one-story bungalow units. Given the spaciousness of the rooms and the location, this hotel is one of the best buys on the island. A wide, seldom-used but appealing stretch of Playa Norte is across the street. A casual palapa-style bar and a pool are set on the back lawn, and the restaurant Pinguino is by the sidewalk at the front of the property. Ask about specials—four nights for the price of three and seven nights for the price of five. From the pier, go left for four blocks; the hotel is on the right.

INEXPENSIVE

Hotel Belmar

Av. Hidalgo, Isla Mujeres, Q. Roo 77400. ☎ **987/7-0430.** Fax 987/7-0429. 10 rms (all with bath). A/C FAN TV TEL. High season $35 double. Low season $30 double.

Situated above Pizza Rolandi (which generates noise), this hotel is run by the same people who serve up those wood-oven pizzas. Each of the simple but stylish rooms comes with two twin or double beds and handsome tile accents. Prices are high considering there are no views, but the rooms are very pleasant. A satellite dish brings in U.S. TV channels.

To find the hotel from the pier, walk left half a block, then turn right on Abasolo; go straight for two blocks and turn left on Hidalgo; the hotel is half a block down on the right.

✪ Hotel Francis Arlene

Guerrero 7, Isla Mujeres, Q. Roo 77400. ☎ and fax **987/7-0310**, in Cancún 98/84-3302. 12 rms (all with bath). A/C or FAN. High season $30–$35 double. Low season $22–$27 double.

The Magaña family operates this neat little two-story inn behind the family home, which is built around a small shady courtyard. You'll notice the tidy cream-and-white facade of the building from the street. Rooms are clean and comfortable, with tile floors and all-tile baths. Each downstairs room has a refrigerator and stove; each upstairs room comes with a refrigerator and toaster. All rooms have either a balcony or a patio.

To get here from the ferry dock, turn left, then right on Madero for three blocks; turn left again on Guerrero; the hotel is on the right.

DINING

The Municipal Market, next door to the telegraph office and post office on Avenida Guerrero, has several little cookshops operated by hard-working señoras and enjoyed by numbers of tourists. On Sunday, Nacho Beh, El Rey del Taco (The King of the Taco), prepares sublime cochinita pibil tacos. Get there early!

MODERATE

Las Palapas Chimbo's

Norte Beach. No phone. Breakfast $3–$5; sandwiches and fruit $2–$6; seafood $5.50–$9. Daily 8am–6pm (bar open to 1am or so). SEAFOOD.

If you're looking for the best beachside palapa-covered restaurant where you can wiggle your toes in the sand while savoring fresh seafood, this is the place. Locals recommend it as their favorite restaurant on Norte Beach. Try the delicious fried whole fish, which comes with rice, beans, and tortillas.

If you're feeling restless late at night in Isla Mujeres you'll inevitably wind up here—Chimbo's becomes a very modest but game disco at night, and draws a motley crew of drinkers and dancers.

From the pier, walk left to the end of the Malecón, then right onto the Playa Norte beach; this restaurant is on the right about half a block down.

Pinguino

In the Hotel Posada del Mar, Av. Rueda Medina 15. ☎ **987/7-0300.** Breakfast $2–$5; main dishes $5–$10. Daily 7am–9pm; bar open to midnight. MEXICAN/SEAFOOD.

The best seats on the waterfront are on the deck of this restaurant/bar, especially in late evening when islanders and tourists arrive to dance and party. This is the place to splurge on lobster; though you'll pay dearly, you'll get a large, sublimely fresh lobster tail with a choice of butter, garlic, and secret sauces. Breakfasts include fresh fruit, yogurt, and granola or healthy platters of eggs, served with homemade wheat bread. The manager, Miguel, whips up some potent concoctions at the bar, and the band, playing nightly from 9pm to midnight, is superb. Pinguino is in front of the hotel, three blocks west of the ferry pier.

⑤ Pizza Rolandi

Av. Hidalgo. ☎ **987/7-0429.** Main courses $3.25–$27; pizza $6–$18. Daily 1–11pm. ITALIAN.

Pizza Rolandi, the chain that saves the day with dependably good, reasonably priced food amid other expensive resorts, comes through in Isla Mujeres as well. In the casual dining room, in an open courtyard of the Hotel Belmar, you can munch on plate-size pizzas, pastas, and calzones cooked in a wood oven. There's also a more expensive menu with fish, beef, and chicken dishes. Guitarists often perform in the evenings. It's 3¹/₂ blocks inland from the pier, between Madero and Abasolo.

INEXPENSIVE

Cafecito

Calle Juárez. No phone. Coffee drinks $1–$3; crêpes $3–$6; breakfast $3–$5; main courses $5.50–$9.75. Fri–Wed 8am–noon and 6–10pm. CRÊPES/ICE CREAM/COFFEES.

Begin the day with a croissant and cream cheese or end it with a hot fudge sundae, and stop by any time for the most flavorful cup of coffee on the island. Crêpes are served with yogurt, ice cream, fresh fruit, or chocolate sauces, as well as ham and cheese; eggs are served with fresh croissants. Dinners include fish and curried shrimp. From the pier turn left on Medina and right on Matamoros; it's on your left.

Estrellita Marinera

Hidalgo 103. No phone. Breakfast $2.50–$4; soup $3–$5; main courses $4–$8.50. Daily 8am–8pm. MEXICAN.

One of the most popular inexpensive eateries in town these days, Estrellita has a front porch that fills up with young Europeans at meal times. The best deal is the full meal (similar to a comida corrida), which consists of fried fish or another main course, rice, beans, and tortillas. Beer is expensive, but that may be to discourage lounging on the porch. From the pier walk straight inland on Abasalo and left on Madero; it's on your left.

2 Cozumel

44 miles S of Cancún

Cozumel, 12 miles from Playa del Carmen, comes from the Maya word *Cuzamil*, meaning "land of the swallows." It's Mexico's largest Caribbean island, 28 miles long and 11 miles wide, but it's only 3% developed, leaving vast stretches of jungle and uninhabited shoreline. The only town is San Miguel de Cozumel, usually called just San Miguel.

Today Cozumel is one of the Yucatán's top resort destinations as well as the country's scuba-diving capital. If Cancún is the jet-set's port of call and Isla Mujeres is the poor man's Cancún, Cozumel is a little bit of both. More remote than the other two, this island (pop. 60,000) is a place where people come to get away from the day-tripping atmosphere of Isla Mujeres or the megadevelopment of Cancún.

All the necessaries for a good vacation are here: excellent snorkeling and scuba places, sailing and water sports, expensive resorts and modest hotels, elegant restaurants and taco shops, even a Maya ruin or two. If, after a while, you do get restless, the ancient Maya city of Tulum, the lagoons of Xel-Ha and Xcaret, or the nearby village of Playa del Carmen provide convenient and interesting excursions.

During pre-Hispanic times the island was one of three important ceremonial centers (Izamal and Chichén-Itzá were the other two). Salt and honey, trade products produced on the island, further linked Cuzamil with the mainland; they were brought ashore at the ruins we know today as Tulum. The site was occupied when Hernán Cortés landed here in 1519. Before his own boat docked, Cortés's men sacked the town and took the chief's wife and children captive. According to Bernal Díaz del Castillo's account, everything was returned. Diego de Landa's account says Cortés converted the Indians and replaced their sacred Maya figures with a cross and a statue of Mary in the main temple at Cozumel. After the Spanish Conquest the island was an important port; however, diseases brought by the foreigners decimated the population, and by 1570 it was almost uninhabited.

The inhabitants returned later, but the War of the Castes in the 1800s severely curtailed Cozumel's trade. Cozumel continued on its economic roller coaster, and after the Caste War it again took its place as a commercial seaport. Merchants exported henequén, coconuts, sugarcane, bananas, chicle, pineapples, honey, and wood products, though in 1955 Hurricane Janet all but demolished the coconut palm plantations. In the mid-1950s Cozumel's fame as a diving destination began to grow, and real development of the island as the site for a vacation resort evolved along with Cancún beginning in the mid-1970s.

ESSENTIALS

GETTING THERE & DEPARTING   By Plane   Aero Cozumel, a Mexicana affiliate, has numerous flights to and from Cancún and Mérida. **Mexicana** flies from Mexico City. **Taesa** flies from Cancún, Chetumal, and Mérida.

Here are some telephone numbers for confirming departures to and from Cozumel: Aero Cozumel (☎ 987/2-3456 or 988/4-2002 in Cancún; fax 987/2-0877 in Cozumel); Continental (☎ 987/2-0847 in Cozumel); Mexicana (☎ 987/2-0157 or 2-2945 at the airport; fax 987/2-2945); and Taesa (☎ 987/2-4420).

Cozumel has no colectivo vans, but taxis go to the airport for $6 to $8.

By Ferry   Passenger ferries to Cozumel depart from Playa del Carmen on the mainland; there is also a car ferry from Puerto Morelos. You can catch a bus to Playa del Carmen from Cancún.

The Car Ferry from Puerto Morelos: The first thing to know is that you're better off without a car in Cozumel; parking is difficult. A solution is to drive to Playa del Carmen, find a reliable place to leave your car, and take the passenger ferry. If you do want to take your car over, the terminus in Puerto Morelos (☎ 987/1-0008), the largest establishment in town, is very easy to find. The car-ferry schedule is complicated and may change, so double-check it before arriving in Puerto Morelos. On Monday, the ferry leaves at 7pm; on Tuesday at 11am; on Wednesday through Sunday at 6am. The crossing takes approximately three hours.

Cargo takes precedence over cars. Officials suggest that camper drivers stay overnight in the parking lot to be first in line for tickets. In any case, *always arrive at least three hours in advance of the ferry's departure to purchase a ticket and to get in line.*

Since passenger-boat service between Playa del Carmen and Cozumel is quite frequent now, I don't recommend that foot passengers bother with this boat.

When returning to Puerto Morelos from Cozumel, the ferry departs from the international cruise-ship pier daily. Get in line about three hours before departure, and double-check the schedule by calling 987/2-0950. The fare is $35 for a car and $6 per passenger.

The Passenger Ferry from Playa del Carmen: There are several passenger ferries running between Cozumel and Playa del Carmen. The WJ *México,* a modern water jet, makes the trip in 45 minutes compared to 60 on the *Cozumeleño.* The WJ *México* costs $10 round-trip and is enclosed, usually air-conditioned, with cushioned seats and video entertainment. The *Cozumeleño* runs an open-air vessel with canopies for $6 round trip. In Playa del Carmen, the ferry dock is 1 1/2 blocks from the main square. Both companies have ticket booths at the main pier in Cozumel. Since schedules change frequently, be sure to double-check them at the docks—especially the time of the last ferry back, if that's the one you intend to use. Be prepared for seasickness on windy days.

From Playa del Carmen to Cozumel, The WJ *Mexico* runs every hour or every two hours between 5:30am and 8:45pm. The *Cozumeleño* runs five times between 9:30am and 6:30pm.

From Cozumel to Playa del Carmen, the WJ *Mexico* runs approximately every hour or hour and a half between 4am and 8pm. The *Cozumeleño* runs four times, between 8am and 5:30pm.

ORIENTATION **Arriving** Cozumel's airport is near downtown. Aero Transportes colectivo vans at the airport provide transportation into town for $3 and to either the north or south hotel zone for $5 to $7.50.

Information The **State Tourism Office** (☎ and fax 987/2-0972) is on the second floor of the Plaza del Sol commercial building facing the central plaza and is open from Monday through Friday from 8:30am to 3pm.

City Layout San Miguel's main waterfront street is called **Avenida Rafael Melgar,** running along the western shore of the island. Passenger ferries dock right in the center, opposite the main plaza and Melgar. Car-ferries dock south of town near the hotels Sol Caribe, La Ceiba, and Fiesta Inn.

The town is laid out on a grid, with avenidas running north and south, calles running east and west. The exception is **Avenida Juárez,** which runs right from the passenger-ferry dock through the main square and inland. Juárez divides the town into northern and southern halves.

Heading inland from the dock along Juárez, you'll find that the avenidas you cross are numbered by fives: 5a av., 10a av., 15a av. If you turn left and head north, calles are numbered evenly: 2a Norte, 4a Norte, 6a Norte. Turning right from Juárez heads you south, where the streets are numbered: 1a Sur (also called Adolfo Salas), 3a Sur, 5a Sur.

Island Layout The island is cut in half by one road, which runs past the airport and the ruins of San Gervasio to the almost uninhabited southern coast of the island. The northern part of the island has no paved roads. It's scattered with small badly ruined Maya sites, from the age when "Cuzamil" was a land sacred to the moon goddess Ixchel. San Gervasio is accessible by motor scooter and car.

Most inexpensive hotels are in the town of San Miguel. Moderate to expensive accommodations are north and south of town. Many cater to divers. Beyond the hotels to the south is **Chankanaab National Park,** centered on the beautiful lagoon of the same name. Beyond Chankanaab are **Playa Palancar** and, offshore, the **Palancar Reef** (arrecife). At the southern tip of the island are **Punta Celarain** and the lighthouse.

The eastern, seaward shore of the island is mostly surf beach, beautiful for walking but dangerous for swimming.

Getting Around   You can walk to most destinations in town. The trip from town to the Chankanaab Lagoon by taxi costs around $6. For a day at the beach, finding some like-minded fellow travelers and sharing the cost of a cab is the most economical way to go. Taxis should charge no more than $6 from the town center to the farthest hotels.

Car rentals are as expensive here as in other parts of Mexico. Open-top jeeps are popular for rental, but be aware they roll over easily and many tourists have been injured or killed using them. See "By Car" under "Getting Around" in Chapter 3 for specifics.

Moped rentals are all over the village and cost about $25 for 24 hours, but terms and prices vary. Carefully inspect the actual moped you'll be renting to see that all the gizmos are in good shape: horn, light, starter, seat, mirror. And be sure to note all damage to the moped on the rental agreement. Most important, read the fine print on the back of the rental agreement, which states that you are not insured, are responsible for paying any damage to the bike (or for all of it if it's stolen or demolished), and must stay on paved roads. It's illegal to ride a moped without a helmet. *Important Note*: North/south streets have the right of way, and these drivers don't slow down.

FAST FACTS: COZUMEL

American Express   The local representative is Fiesta Cozumel, Calle 11 no. 598 (☎ 987/2-0725 or 987/2-0433; fax 987/2-1044).

Area Code   The telephone area code is 987.

Climate   From October through December there can be strong winds all over the Yucatán, as well as some rain. In Cozumel, wind conditions in November and December make diving dangerous. May through September is the rainy season.

Parking   Since many of the downtown hotels are on streets closed to traffic, parking space and parking lots are scarce. There is a public lot, Estacionamiento Cozumel, behind the church on Avenida 10 Sur. Parking is 50¢ per hour or $5 overnight.

Post Office   The post office (correo) is on Avenida Rafael Melgar at Calle 7 Sur, at the southern edge of town; it's open Monday through Friday from 9am to 6pm and Saturday from 9am to noon.

Recompression Chamber   The recompression chamber (cámara de recompreción) is on Calle 5 Sur one block off Melgar between Melgar and Avenida 5 Sur (☎ 987/2-2387; fax 987/2-1430). Normal hours are 8am to 1pm and 4 to 8pm.

Seasons   High season is Christmas through Easter, and in August.

Telephone   Long-distance telephones are on Salas between Avenidas 5 Sur and 10 Sur on the exterior of the telephone building. Use a credit card to get an American operator, or push the star button twice, then push 01 for the United States and Hawaii, wait for an operator, give your area code and number and credit-card number; or make it collect; or have a pile of coins ready to feed the phone. The calling station on Melgar at Calle 3 Sur is a full-service phone center with air-conditioned booths, no surcharges, fax services and a bulletin board where you can leave messages for friends. It's open Monday through Saturday from 8am to 11pm, and Sunday from 9am to 10pm. You can also make collect calls from the Sports Page restaurant.

Cozumel Island

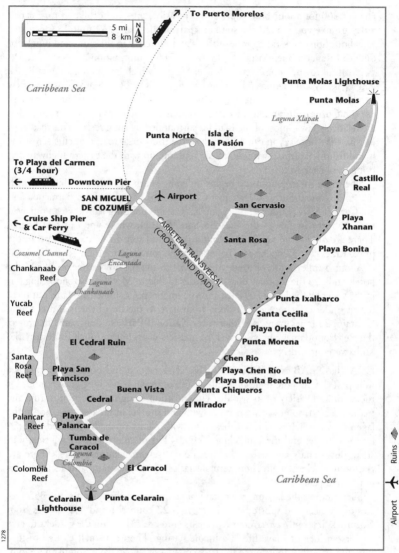

Cozumel Island map

To Puerto Morelos

Caribbean Sea

Punta Molas Lighthouse
Punta Molas
Laguna Xlapak

Punta Norte   Isla de
               la Pasión

To Playa del Carmen
(3/4 hour)
← Downtown Pier

SAN MIGUEL
DE COZUMEL   ✈ Airport

Castillo
Real

Playa
Xhanan

San Gervasio

Playa Bonita

← Cruise Ship Pier
& Car Ferry

Santa Rosa

Cozumel Channel

CARRETERA TRANSVERSAL (CROSS ISLAND ROAD)

Chankanaab
Reef

Laguna
Encantada

Laguna
Chankanaab

Punta Ixalbarco

Yucab
Reef

Santa Cecilia

Playa Oriente

Punta Morena

El Cedral Ruin

Chen Rio

Santa
Rosa
Reef

Playa San
Francisco

Playa Chen Río
Playa Bonita Beach Club
Punta Chiqueros

Buena Vista

Cedral

El Mirador

Palancar
Reef

Playa
Palancar

Tumba de
Caracol

Laguna
Colombia

Colombia
Reef

El Caracol

Caribbean Sea

Celarain
Lighthouse   Punta Celarain

Ruins
Airport

1278

DIVING, EXPLORING THE ISLAND & OTHER THINGS TO SEE & DO
SPECIAL EVENTS

Carnaval/Mardi Gras is Cozumel's most colorful fiesta. It begins the Thursday before Ash Wednesday with daytime street dancing and nighttime parades on Thursday, Saturday, and Monday (the best).

TOURING THE ISLAND

Travel agencies can book you on a group tour of the island for around $30, depending on whether the tour includes lunch and a stop for snorkeling. A taxi driver charges $60 for a four-hour tour. You can easily rent a motorbike or car for half a day to take you around the southern part of the island (42 miles). Or, take a four-hour horseback riding tour of the island's interior to the ruins and jungle for $60; call Rancho Buenavista (☎ 987/2-1537) for information.

North of town, along Avenida Rafael Melgar (which becomes Carretera Pilar), you'll pass a yacht marina and a string of Cozumel's first hotels as well as some new condominiums. A few of the hotels have nice beaches, which you are welcome to use (on Cozumel this public ownership is more important than ever, since beaches are relatively few—most of the island is surrounded by coral reefs). This road ends just past the hotels; you can backtrack to the transversal road that cuts across the island from west (the town side) to east and link up with the eastern highway that brings you back to town.

The more interesting route begins by going south of town on Melgar (which becomes Costera Sur or Carretera a Chankanaab) past the Hotel Barracuda and Sol Caribe. After about 3¹/₂ miles you'll see a sign pointing left down an unpaved road a short distance to the **Rancho San Manuel,** where you can rent horses. There are only seven horses here, but a guide and soft drink are included in the price. Rides cost $25 per hour. It's open daily from 8am to 4pm.

About 5 miles south of town you'll come to the big Sol Caribe and La Ceiba hotels and also the car-ferry dock for ferries to Puerto Morelos. Go snorkeling out in the water by the Hotel La Ceiba and you might spot a sunken airplane, put there for an underwater movie. Offshore, from here to the tip of the island at Punta Celarain, 20 miles away, is **Underwater National Park,** so designated to protect the reef from damage by visitors. Dive masters warn not to touch or destroy the underwater growth.

CHANKANAAB NATIONAL PARK   This lagoon and botanical garden is a mile past the big hotels and 5¹/₂ miles south of town. It has long been famous for the color and variety of its sea life. The intrusion of sightseers began to ruin the marine habitat, so now visitors must swim and snorkel in the open sea, not in the lagoon. The beach is wide and beautiful, with plenty of shady thatched umbrellas to sit under and the snorkeling is good—lots of colorful fish. Arrive early to stake out a chair and palapa before the cruise-ship visitors arrive. There are restrooms, lockers, a gift shop, several snack huts, a restaurant, and a snorkeling-gear-rental palapa.

Surrounding the lagoon, the botanical garden, with shady paths, has 352 species of tropical and subtropical plants from 22 countries and 451 species from Cozumel. Several Maya structures have been re-created within the gardens to give visitors an idea of Maya life in a jungle setting. There's a small natural-history museum as well. Admission to the park costs $4; it's open daily from 8am to 5pm.

BEACHES   After another 10 miles, you'll come to **Playa San Francisco** and, south of it, **Playa Palancar.** Besides the beach at Chankanaab Lagoon, they're the best on Cozumel. Food (usually overpriced) and equipment rentals are available.

The **Playa Bonita Beach Club** near Playa Chiqueros has water sports and windsurfing-equipment rentals. The restaurant is open daily from 10am to 5pm.

THE EASTERN SHORE   The road along the east coast of the island is wonderful. There are views of the sea, the rocky shore, and the pounding surf. On the land side are little farms and forests. Exotic birds take flight as you approach, and monstrous (but harmless) iguanas skitter off into the undergrowth.

Most of the east coast is unsafe for swimming because the surf can create a deadly undertow that will pull you far out to sea in a matter of minutes. There are always cars pulled off along the road here, with the occupants spending the day on the beach, but not in the churning waters. Three restaurants catering to tourists are along this part of the coast, complete with sombrero-clad iguanas for a picture companion.

Halfway up the east coast, the paved eastern road meets the paved transversal road (which passes the ruins of San Gervasio) back to town, 9 1/2 miles away. The east-coast road ends when it turns into the transversal, petering out to a narrow track of sandy road by a nice restaurant in front of the Chen Río beach; vehicles, even motorbikes, will get stuck on the sand road. If you're a birdwatcher, leave your vehicle on the highway here and walk straight down the sandy road. Go slowly and quietly and at the least you'll spot many herons and egrets in the lagoon on the left that parallels the path. Much farther on are Maya ruins.

MAYA RUINS One of the most popular trips is to **San Gervasio** (100 B.C.–A.D. 1600). A road leads there from the airport, or you can continue on the eastern part of the island following the paved transversal road. The worn sign to the ruins is easy to miss, but the turnoff (left) is about halfway between town and the eastern coast. Stop at the entry gate and pay the $1 road-use fee. Go straight ahead over the potholed road to the ruins about two miles farther and pay the $3.50 to enter; camera permits cost $8.50 for each still or video camera you want to bring in. A small tourist center at the entrance has cold drinks and snacks for sale.

When it comes to Cozumel's Maya remains, getting there is most of the fun, and you should do it for the trip, not for the ruins. The buildings, though preserved, are crudely made and would not be much of a tourist attraction if they were not the island's only cleared and accessible ruins. More significant than beautiful, the site was once an important ceremonial center where the Maya gathered, coming even from the mainland. The important deity here was Ixchel, known as the goddess of weaving, women, childbirth, pilgrims, the moon, and medicine. Although you won't see any representations of her at San Gervasio today, Bruce Hunter, in his *Guide to Ancient Maya Ruins*, writes that priests hid behind a large pottery statue of her and became the voice of the goddess speaking to pilgrims and answering their petitions. She was the wife of Itzamná, Maya god above all, who invented corn, cacao, writing, and reading.

Tour guides charge $12 for a tour for one to six people, but it's not worth it. Seeing it takes 30 minutes.

PARQUE ARQUEOLÓGICA This park contains reproductions of many of Mexico's important archeological treasures, including the 4-foot-high Olmec head and the Chaac-Mool seen in Chichén-Itzá. A Maya couple demonstrate the lifestyle of the Maya in a na, or thatch-roofed oval home. The park is a nice addition to the island's cultural attractions and is well worth visiting—but lather on the bug repellent before you begin exploring. The park is open daily from 8am to 6pm; admission is $3. To get there, turn left on the unmarked road across from the International Pier, off Costera Sur just south of the La Ceiba hotel, then left on Avenida 65 Sur and follow the signs.

A History Museum

The **Museo de la Isla de Cozumel,** on Avenida Melgar between Calles 4 and 6 Norte, is more than just a nice place to spend a rainy hour. On the first floor an excellent exhibit showcases endangered species, the origin of the island, and its present-day topography and plant and animal life, including an explanation of coral formation. Upstairs, showrooms feature the history of the town; artifacts from the island's pre-Hispanic sites; and colonial-era cannons, swords, and ship paraphernalia. It's open daily from 10am to 6pm. Admission is $3; guided tours in English are free. During the summer months check at the museum for possible tours to watch the sea turtles laying their eggs on the beach. There's an overpriced rooftop restaurant open long hours.

ON AND UNDER THE WATERS

SNORKELING Anyone who can swim can go snorkeling. Rental of the snorkel (breathing pipe), goggles, and flippers should cost only about $5 for half a day; a snorkeling trip costs $30 to $40. The brilliantly colored tropical fish provide a dazzling show. Chankanaab Park is one of the best places to go on your own for an abundant fish show.

SCUBA DIVING Cozumel is Mexico's dive capital. Various establishments on the island rent scuba gear—tanks, regulator with pressure gauge, buoyancy compensator, weight belts, mask, snorkel, and fins. Many will also arrange a half-day expedition in a boat, complete with lunch, for a set price. Sign up the day before if you're interested. A two-tank morning dive costs around $45; some shops are now offering an additional afternoon one-tank dive for $9 for those who took the morning dives, or $25 for those who are diving only in the afternoon. However, if you're a dedicated diver, you'll save many dollars by buying a diving package that includes air transportation, hotel, and usually two dives a day. There's a recompression chamber on the island (see "Fast Facts," above).

The underwater wonders of the famous **Palancar Reef** are offshore from the beach of the same name. From the car-ferry south to Punta Celarain is more than 20 miles of offshore reefs. In the famous blue depths, divers find caves and canyons, small and large colorful fish, and an enormous variety of sea coral. The **Santa Rosa Reef** is famous for its depth, sea life, coral, and sponges. **San Francisco Reef,** off the beach by the same name south of town, has a drop-off wall, but it's still fairly shallow and the sea life is fascinating. The **Chankanaab Reef,** where divers are joined by schools of tropical fish, is close to the shore by the national park of the same name. It's shallow and good for novice divers, as is **Paradise Reef** by the La Ceiba hotel. Next after Chankanaab going south on the eastern road, **Yucab Reef** has beautiful coral.

Numerous vessels on the island operate daily diving and snorkeling tours, so if you aren't traveling on a prearranged dive package, the best plan is to shop around and sign up for one of those. Of Cozumel's many dive shops, two are among the top: **Aqua Safari,** next to the Vista del Mar Hotel at Melgar at Avenida 5 (☎ 987/2-0101, fax 987/2-0661) and in the Hotel Plaza Las Glorias (☎ 987/2-3362 or 2-2422); and **Deportes Aquáticas,** at Avenida Melgar and Calle 8 Norte (☎ and fax 987/2-0460).

You can save money by renting your gear at a beach shop and diving from shore. The shops at the Plaza Las Glorias and La Ceiba hotels are good for shore diving—you'll find plenty to see as soon as you enter the water. It costs about $5 to rent one tank and weights.

WINDSURFING One of Mexico's top windsurfing champions, Raul de Lille, offers windsurfing classes and equipment rentals at the beach in front of Sol

San Miguel de Cozumel

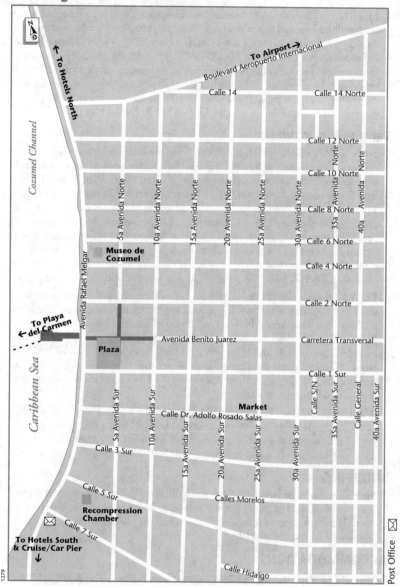

Cabañas del Caribe, on the north side. For information call 987/2-0017; fax 987/2-1942.

BOAT TRIPS Boat trips are another popular pastime at Cozumel. Some excursions include snorkeling and scuba diving or a stop at a beach with lunch. Various types of tours are offered, including rides in glass-bottom boats, a mock submarine, or a Catamaran; tours range from $15 or an hour to $49 for a full day.

FISHING　The best months for fishing are April through September, when the catch will be blue and white marlin, sailfish, tarpon, swordfish, dorado, wahoo, tuna, and red snapper. Half a day of fishing costs $250. **Viajes Internacionales Palancar,** Avenida 10 Sur no. 124 (☎ 987/2-2259, fax 987/2-2348), can arrange fishing trips. The Cozumel Angler's Fleet at the marina north of town offers a variety of fishing options, including half-day, full-day, and two- and four-day fishing packages, even a package including hotel. For advance reservations, contact them at Apdo. Postal 341, Cozumel, Q. Roo 77600 (☎ and fax 987/2-1135).

TRIPS TO THE MAINLAND

SIAN KA'AN BIOSPHERE RESERVE　On the mainland south of Cozumel is the Sian Ka'an Biosphere Reserve, 1.3 million acres set aside to protect hundreds of species of birds, animals, and plants (see "Tulum, Punta Allen & Sian Ka'an," later in this chapter, for details). **Viajes Internacionales Palancar,** Av. 10 Sur no. 124, Cozumel, Q. Roo 77600 (☎ 987/2-2259; fax 987/2-2348), offers day-long excursions to the reserve from Cozumel for $125 per person. A minimum of four people is required for the trip, which leaves at 8am, returns at 7pm, and includes a guided boat tour of the reserve with an English-speaking guide, a box lunch, and drinks. **Viajes Turquesa** (Calle 1 Sur in the Plaza Villa Mar behind Las Palmeras restaurant, ☎ 987/2-3609 or 987/2-3710) has a similar tour for $130 per person.

PLAYA DEL CARMEN & XCARET　One of the easiest do-it-yourself excursions from Cozumel is to Playa del Carmen, a laid-back mainland resort village just a 25- to 45-minute ferry ride away (see "Playa del Carmen," later in this chapter). From there it's a short taxi ride to the Xcaret underwater park. Xcaret may be crowded, but both it and Playa offer fine beaches and are ideal for a day of lazing. Cozumel travel agencies offer an Xcaret tour that includes the ferry fee, transportation to the park and the admission fee for $45 (only about $6 more than it costs to do the trip on your own).

TULUM & COBÁ　**Fiesta Cozumel Tours** (Calle 11 no. 598, ☎ 987/2-0725 or 987/2-0433; fax 987/2-1044 or at several hotels) offers a tour to the ruins of both Tulum and Cobá with a stop afterward for swimming at Akumal for $79. They also offer a Tulum and Xel-Ha tour for $69.

SHOPPING

Shopping has improved beyond the ubiquitous T-shirt shops into expensive resortwear, silver, and better decorative and folk art. Most of the stores are on Avenida Melgar. Prices for serapes, T-shirts, and the like are normally less expensive on the side streets off Melgar.

ACCOMMODATIONS

Cozumel's hotels are in three separate locations: The oldest resorts, most of which are expensive, line beaches and coral and limestone outcroppings north of town; the more budget-oriented inns are in the central village; and other expensive hotels lie south of town. *Note:* There's one **central reservations number** for many (not all) of the island's hotels—☎ 800/327-2254 in the U.S. and Canada or 305/670-9439 in Miami.

NORTH OF TOWN

I'll start with the northernmost hotels going through town, and move onward to the end of the southern hotel zone. Like beaches south of town, those along the northern shore appear sporadically and some hotels have enclosed them with re-taining walls. **Carretera Santa Pilar** is the name of Melgar's northern extension, so just take Melgar north and all the hotels are lined up in close proximity to each other on the beach a short distance from town and the airport.

Very Expensive

Hotel Melia Mayan Plaza

Carretera Santa Pilar km 3.5 (Apdo. Postal 9), Cozumel, Q. Roo 77600. ☎ **987/2-0411** or 800/336-3542 in the U.S. Fax 987/2-1599. 220 rms. A/C MINIBAR TV. High season $395 double. Low season $295 double. (Prices vary depending on when you travel.) Free parking.

The low-key, elegant lobby, with pale-gray marble floors and rose and pale-green accents, is a welcome respite. Since it's such a comfortable lobby, and there's a small bar at one end, guests frequently congregate on the inviting couches. The spacious and beautifully furnished rooms all have ocean views from either a bal-cony or patio. Some of the standard rooms are right on the beach. If you want a quiet, secluded getaway removed from traffic (what little there is in Cozumel) and the town, this is the place. It's at the end of the paved northern shore road.

Dining/Entertainment: All meals are included in the price of the room. La Isla Restaurant is open daily for all meals; a poolside restaurant and a snackbar are open during daylight hours. Ask about special once-or-twice-a-week fiestas featuring regional dancing and buffet dining.

Services: Travel agency; room and laundry service; motorcycle, car, and bicycle rental.

Facilities: Two swimming pools, one of the longest stretches of beach on the island, two tennis courts, water-sports equipment.

Expensive

Cabañas del Caribe

Carretera Santa Pilar km 4.5 (Apdo. Postal 9), Cozumel, Q. Roo 77600. ☎ **987/2-0017** or 987/2-0072 or 800/336-3542 in the U.S. Fax 987/2-1599. 48 rms. A/C. High season $125–$135 double. Low season $90–$110 double. Free parking.

Built in two sections, the hotel gives you two choices of room styles. Standard rooms in the two-story section adjacent to the lobby are smallish (but very nice) and decorated in southwest shades of apricot and blue. All have small sitting areas and either a porch or balcony facing the beach and pool. The one-story bungalow/cabaña section has a similar decor, but rooms are larger and have patios on the beach.

Dining/Entertainment: The main restaurant is in a glassed-in terrace on the beach, and there's a poolside spot for snacks.

Services: Travel agency.

Facilities: Swimming pool; water-sports equipment for rent including sailboats, jet skis, and diving, snorkeling, and windsurfing equipment; pharmacy; gift shop.

Moderate

Hotel Fontan

Carretera Santa Pilar km 2.5, Cozumel, Q. Roo 77600. ☎ **987/2-0300.** Fax 987/2-0105. 48 rms. A/C TV TEL. High season $80 double. Low season $60 double. Free unguarded parking.

Rooms on all four floors of this bright-yellow hotel are well maintained and have private balconies; most have ocean views. Baths all have showers. There's a nice pool by the beach (held up by a retaining wall) that's surrounded by lounge chairs.

There's a restaurant/bar, plus a dock for water sports. The hotel is an excellent value for your money.

HOTELS IN TOWN
Moderate
Hotel Barracuda

Av. Rafael Melgar 628 (Apdo. Postal 163), Cozumel, Q. Roo 77600. ☎ **987/2-0002** or 987/2-1243. Fax 987/2-0884 or 987/2-3633. 50 rms (all with bath). A/C FAN. High season $62 double. Low season $43 double. Parking on the street.

You won't think much of this plain pink building a short walk south of town, but the view from the interior is outstanding. Rustic carved-wood furnishings decorate the cozy rooms, all with balconies looking out to sea. There's a refrigerator in each room as well. An inner hallway leading to the rooms blocks out the noise from the road. There's no pool, but lounge chairs are lined up on an elevated strip of sand, and stairs lead down to a good snorkeling area. There is a small oceanfront café serving breakfast and snacks, as well as a good dive shop. The hotel is on Costera Sur, a 10-minute walk from town; from the pier walk right, and the hotel is on your right.

Inexpensive
Hotel El Marqués

Av. 5 Sur no. 180, Cozumel, Q. Roo 77600. ☎ **987/2-0677.** Fax 987/2-0537. 40 rms all with bath). A/C. High season $22 double; $26 junior suite; $41 full suite. Low season $20 double; $23 junior suite; $27 full suite.

Each of the sunny rooms here has gold trim and Formica-marble countertops, gray-and-white tile floors, and two double beds. The junior suites have refrigerators; full suites have refrigerators, stoves, and sitting areas. Third-floor rooms have good views. The staff is friendly and attentive. From the plaza, turn right (south) on Av. 5 Sur; the hotel is on the right up the stairs next to Cocos restaurant.

Hotel Mary-Carmen

Av. 5 Sur no. 4 (Apdo. Postal 14), Cozumel, Q. Roo 77600. ☎ **987/2-0581.** 30 rms (all with bath). A/C or FAN. High season $25 double. Low season $21 double.

Watched over by eagle-eyed señoras, the two stories of rooms at the Mary-Carmen surround an interior courtyard shaded by a large mamey tree. Rooms are clean and carpeted, with well-screened windows facing the courtyard. Most have two double beds. It's a half a block south of the zócalo on the right.

Hotel Safari Inn

Av. Melgar at Calle 5 Sur (Apdo. Postal 41), Cozumel, Q. Roo 77600. ☎ **987/2-0101.** Fax 987/2-0661. 12 rms (all with bath). A/C. High season $45 double. Low season $35 double.

The nicest budget hotel in town, the Safari is located above and behind the Aqua Dive Shop. Natural colors and stucco pervade the interior of this three-story establishment. The huge rooms come with firm beds, built-in sofas, and tiled floors. The hotel caters to divers and offers some good dive packages. From the pier turn right (south) and walk $3^1/2$ blocks on Melgar; the hotel is on your left facing the Caribbean at the corner of Calle 5 Sur.

Hotel Vista del Mar

Av. Rafael Melgar 45, Cozumel, Q. Roo 77600. ☎ **987/2-0545.** Fax 987/2-0445. 26 rms (all with bath). A/C. High season $30–$35 double without ocean view. Low season $25–$30 double. Free guarded parking.

An older family-run hotel right across from the Malecón, the Vista del Mar has 17 rooms facing the sea; the rest of the rooms look out to the pool and courtyard in back. The rooms have fresh white paint, two double beds, small refrigerators, and gold-and-orange spreads and drapes. The highest rates are for oceanview rooms. One of Cozumel's best restaurants is right in front of the hotel; the best dive shop is next door. From the pier, turn right (south) on Melgar and walk 4¹/₂ blocks; the hotel is on your left behind the Waffle House.

HOTELS SOUTH OF TOWN

The best beaches are south of town, but not all the best ones have hotels on them. Each hotel has either a swimming pool, a tiny cove, a dock, or all three. You'll be able to swim, sun, and relax at any of these hotels and most are diver-oriented. **Costera Sur,** also called **Carretera a Chankanab,** is the southern extension of Melgar, so just follow Melgar south through town to reach these hotels, which are, generally speaking, farther apart than those north of town.

Very Expensive

Presidente Inter-Continental Cozumel

Costera Sur km 6.0, Cozumel, Q. Roo 77600. ☎ **987/2-0322** or 800/327-0200 in the U.S. Fax 987/2-1360. 253 rms. A/C MINIBAR TV TEL. High season $130–$365 double. Low season $130–$265 double. Discounts and packages available. Free parking.

The first thing you'll notice here is the palatial scale of the place and the masterful, stylishly grand combination of marble with hot-pink stucco and stone as you enter. Near the Chancanab Lagoon, the hotel, surrounded by shady palms, spreads out on a beautiful beach with no close neighbors. Rates vary widely depending on your view and time of year you travel even within seasons. There are four categories of rooms—some have balconies and garden views, while very spacious rooms come with balconies and ocean views. Deluxe beachfront rooms have comfortable patios and direct access to the beach on the ground floor; on the second floor there are balconies with ocean views. The no-smoking rooms are all on the fourth level, and two rooms are set aside for guests with disabilities. Naturally each category of room has a different price. Absolutely ask about discounts and packages.

Dining/Entertainment: The Arrecife restaurant serves international specialties and is open daily from 6pm to midnight. Caribeño, by the pool and beach, is open from 7am to 7pm.

Services: Room and laundry service; travel agency; car and motorbike rental.

Facilities: Swimming pool; two tennis courts; water-sports equipment rental; dive shop and dive-boat pier; pharmacy; boutiques.

Expensive

La Ceiba Beach Hotel

Costera Sur km 4.5 (Apdo. Postal 284), Cozumel, Q. Roo 77600. ☎ **987/2-0815** or 800/437-9609. Fax 800/235-5892. 113 rms. A/C MINIBAR TV TEL. High season $160–$200 double. Low season $115 double. Diving packages available. Free parking.

Across from the Sol Caribe, on the beach side of the road, La Ceiba is named for the lofty and majestic tree, sacred to the Maya, which grows in the tropics. It's a popular hotel, and the large lobby seems to always be abustle with guests. Rooms all have ocean views and balconies, and bathrooms have combination tubs and showers. The swimming pool is only steps from the beach.

The emphasis here is on water sports, particularly scuba diving, and if this is your passion, be sure to ask about the special dive packages when you call for reservations.

Dining/Entertainment: The Galleon Bar/Restaurant, off the lobby, has walls shaped like an old ship and is open for all meals. Chopaloca, by the beach, is open daily from early morning until almost midnight.

Services: Laundry and room service, travel agency.

Facilities: Large, free-form swimming pool by the beach, tennis court, water sports, dive shop and dive-boat pier, roped-off area for snorkeling.

Moderate

Galápagos Inn

Costera Sur km 1.5 (Apdo. Postal 289), Cozumel, Q. Roo 77600. ☎ **987/2-0663** or 2-1133, or call Aqua-Sub Tours 800/847-5708 in the U.S. or 713/783-3305 in Texas. 54 rms. A/C. High season three-night package $342 per person. Low season $323 per person (includes all meals and two days diving). Longer diving packages and lower rates for nondivers available.

Homey, shady, and done in colonial style with white stucco and red-brick accents, this older inn is usually peopled by divers who have signed up for one of the several money-saving three-, five-, and seven-night package deals. The inn, located a mile south of the main square, has its own small swimming pool and a bit of walled-in beach. A row of hammocks swings under a long thatched roof by the ocean where there's nothing but the sound of surf and breezes. Some rooms have balconies or terraces on the beach. All have ocean views. One restaurant serves all meals with specific meal times. The bar, with drinks only, is open daily from 7 to 11pm. There's a fully equipped dive shop; dives take off from the hotel's pier.

DINING

Zermatt, a terrific little bakery, is on Av. 5 at Calle 4 Norte. On Calle 2 Norte, half a block in from the waterfront, is the **Panificadora Cozumel,** excellent for a do-it-yourself breakfast, or for picnic supplies. It's open from 6am to 9pm daily. **Frutas Selectas,** at Salas and Calle 20, has great fruit drinks, coffee, and pastries. It's closed on Sunday.

Very Expensive

Pepe's Grill

Av. Rafael Melgar at Salas. ☎ **987/2-0213.** Reservations recommended. Main courses $10–$30; children's menu $10. Daily 5–11:30pm. GRILLED SPECIALTIES.

Pepe's started the grilled-food tradition in Cozumel and continues as a popular trendsetter with low lights, soft music, solicitous waiters, and excellent food; the perpetual crowd is here for a reason. The menu is extensive, with flame-broiled specialties such as beef filet Singapore and shrimp Bahamas. The children's menu offers breaded shrimp and fried chicken. For dessert try the cajeta crêpes.

Expensive

✪ D'Pub

Calle 4 Norte. ☎ **987/2-4132.** Reservations recommended in high season. Main courses $7–$16. Daily 5pm–midnight. Closed Sun in low season. SEAFOOD/INTERNATIONAL.

Though the building is new, this Caribbean-style house, with its front porch and cut-out wood trim, looks like the few remaining wooden houses from Cozumel's past. Inside it's a handsome combination of English pub and gracious garden dining establishment. In the main room as you enter, casual couches and conversational areas are conducive to leisurely drinking, chatting, playing cards or backgammon, or watching low-volume CNN or sporting events. Farther on there's dining inside or outside on the patio fronting the manicured inner courtyard. The eclectic menu includes great fish and chips, barbecue chicken, dip roast-beef sandwiches, fajitas, stir-fried vegetables, rack of lamb, seafood, steaks, and an enormous Mexican combo including roasted chicken, rice, beans, guacamole, an enchilada and a quesadilla. From the plaza, turn left (north) on Av. 5 Norte, walk two blocks, and turn right on Calle 4 Norte; it's on your right midway up the block.

Moderate

✪ Pizza Prima

Calle Salas 109. ☎ **987/2-4242.** Small pizzas $5.50–$8; large pizzas $8.80–$12; pastas $4–$12; subs $3–$4. Tues–Sun 3–11pm. ITALIAN.

This is one of the few good Italian restaurants in Mexico. Everything is fresh—the pastas, calzones, and sourdough pizza. Owner Albert Domínguez grows most of the vegetables in his hydroponic garden on the island. The menu changes daily and might include shrimp scampi, fettuccine with pesto, and crab ravioli with cream sauce. The fettuccine Alfredo is wonderful, as are the puff-pastry garlic "bread" and crispy house salad. The submarine sandwiches are big and varied, and the large pizza easily feeds three adults. Dining is upstairs on the breezy terrace. From the pier, turn right (south) on Melgar and walk two blocks to Calle 5 Sur and turn left. Pizza Prima's bright-orange building is visible on your left between Calles 5 and 10 Sur. Hotel delivery is available.

Pizza Rolandi

Av. Melgar, between Calles 6 and 8 Norte. ☎ **987/2-0946.** Main courses $6–$12; pizza $6–$11. Mon–Sat 11am–11pm; Sun 5–11pm. ITALIAN.

Deck chairs and glossy wood tables make the inviting interior garden of this restaurant a restful place in the daytime, and at night, it becomes romantic with candlelight. The specialty here (as in their branches in Isla Mujeres and Cancún) is wood-oven-baked pizzas. But for a change, look for pasta prepared five ways and the weekly specials, which may be a special appetizer of sea bass carpaccio, pizza, pasta, or fish with an Italian twist. From the pier, turn left (north) on Melgar and walk four blocks; the restaurant is on your right.

Inexpensive

✪ Café Caribe

Av. 10 Sur 215. ☎ **987/2-3621.** Coffee and pastries $1–$3. Mon–Sat 8am–1pm and 6–9:30pm. PASTRIES & COFFEE.

This cute little eatery behind a facade of fuchsia and dark green may become your favorite place to start or finish the day or for a snack in between. You'll find ice cream, milk shakes, freshly-made cheesecake and carrot cake, waffles, bagels, croissants, and biscuits. Nine different coffees are served, including Cuban, cappuccino, espresso, and Irish. From the plaza turn right (south) on Av. 5 Sur, walk one block, and turn left on Calle Salas then right on Av. 10; the café is on your left.

✪ The Waffle House

Av. Melgar. ☎ **987/2-0545,** or 987/2-3065. Waffles $2.50–$5; breakfast $3–$6; main courses $4–$8. Daily 8am–1pm and 6–9pm. BREAKFAST/DESSERTS/MEXICAN.

In the past, the Waffle House was one of Cozumel's hidden gems, tucked away past the tourist zone. Now it's moved to the waterfront and become a full-scale restaurant. Jeanie De Lille, the island's premier pastry chef, bakes crisp, light waffles and serves them in many ways, including the waffle ranchero with eggs and salsa. Hash browns, homemade breads, and great coffee are other reasons to drop in for breakfast whether it's morning or evening. The menu has been expanded to include tamales, carne asada tampiqueña, and several pasta dishes, and there is a full bar. From the pier turn right (south) on Melgar and walk 4^1/$_2$ blocks; this place is on your left between the Aqua Safari and the Hotel Vista del Mar.

COZUMEL AFTER DARK

Cozumel is a town frequented by sports-minded visitors who play hard all day and wind down early at night. People sit in outdoor cafes around the zócalo enjoying the cool night breezes until the restaurants close. **Carlos 'n' Charlie's,** at Av. Melgar 1, and the **Hard Rock,** at Av. Melgar 2A, are always the liveliest places in town.

Popular discos include **Scaramouche** and **Neptuno** on Avenida Melgar, both open nightly from 10pm to 3am. The cover charge varies.

3 Puerto Morelos

21 miles S of Cancún

Most people come here to take the car-ferry to Cozumel, several hours away. Puerto Morelos has begun to resume the building boom that was beginning when Hurricane Gilbert came through. It's still fairly a somnolent village, with almost no traffic. Tourism is also fairly undeveloped, but innkeepers can tell you whom to contact for diving and fishing. The sand is nice but fairly littered with seaweed. There are several restaurants and small hotels here in various price levels.

Buses from Cancún's to Tulum and Playa del Carmen usually stop here, but be sure to ask in Cancún if your bus makes the Puerto Morelos stop. If you are driving, take Highway 307 south from Cancún to the km 36 marker. **Croco Cun,** a zoological park where crocodiles are raised. one of the most interesting attractions in the area—don't be put off by the comical name. Though far from grand, the park has exhibits of crocodiles in all stages of development, as well as animals of nearly all the species that once roamed the Yucatán Peninsula. The snake exhibit is fascinating, though it may make you think twice about roaming in the jungle. The rattlesnakes and boa constrictors are particularly intimidating, and the tarantulas are downright enormous. Children enjoy the guides' enthusiastic tours and are entranced by the spider monkeys and wild pigs. Wear plenty of bug repellent and allow an hour or two for the tour, followed by a cool drink in the restaurant. Croco Cun is open daily from 8am to dark. Admission is $5, and free for children under 6. The park is at km 33 on Highway 307.

About half a mile before Puerto Morelos is the 150-acre **Jardín Botánico,** opened in 1990 and named after Dr. Alfredo Barrera, a biologist who studied the selva (tropical evergreen broadleaf forest). A natural, protected showcase for native plants and animals, it's open Tuesday through Sunday from 9am to 4pm. Admission is $3; it's worth the money—and every minute of the hour or more it will take to see it. Slather on the mosquito repellent, though.

The park is divided into six parts: an epiphyte area (plants that grow on others); Maya ruins; an ethnographic area, with a furnished hut and typical garden;

Traveler's Advisory

Highway 307 has four lanes from Cancún nearly to Puerto Morelos. Traffic is quite heavy from Cancún to Tulum, and drivers go too fast. A stalled or stopped car is hard to see, and there are no shoulders for pulling off the roadway. Follow these precautions for a safe journey: Never turn left while on the highway (it's against Mexican law anyway). Always go to the next road on the right and turn around and come back to the turnoff you want. Occasionally, a specially constructed right-hand turnoff, such as at Xcaret, allows motorists to pull off to the right in order to cross the road when traffic has passed. Don't speed and don't follow the car in front of you too closely. There have been many accidents and fatalities on this road lately, and these precautions could save your life. After Tulum, traffic is much lighter, but follow these precautions anyway—especially about turning left.

Except in Cancún, Isla Mujeres, Playa del Carmen, and Cozumel, exchanging money is difficult along this coast.

Gas stations are found in all major towns, but they're only open from around 8am to around 7pm; most stations have regular (Nova) and unleaded gas (Magna Sin).

Except in Isla Mujeres and Cozumel, mosquitoes are numerous and fierce on this coast, so bring plenty of mosquito repellent that has DEET as the main ingredient. (Avon's Skin So Soft, a bath oil that's acquired quite a reputation in the States for its unexpected effectiveness as a pleasant-smelling mosquito repellent, is almost useless here.)

a chiclero camp, about the once-thriving chicle (chewing gum) industry; a nature park, where wild vegetation is preserved; and mangroves. Wandering along the marked paths, you'll see that the dense jungle of plants and trees are named and labeled in English and Spanish. Each sign has the plant's scientific and common names, use of the plants, and the geographic areas where they are found in the wild. It's rich in bird and animal life, too, but to catch a glimpse of something you'll have to move quietly and listen carefully.

The ferry dock (☎ 987/1-0008), the largest establishment in town, is very easy to find. Look to the Cozumel section below for details on the car-ferry schedule, but several points bear repeating here: The car-ferry schedule is complicated and may change, so double-check it before arriving. And always arrive at least three hours in advance of the ferry's departure to purchase a ticket and to get in line.

EN ROUTE TO PLAYA DEL CARMEN

Heading south on Highway 307 from Puerto Morelos, you'll find the village of Muchi to be the next landmark. It's only 20 miles from Puerto Morelos to Playa del Carmen, so you'll be there in half an hour or less. However, you'll pass several small beach resorts en route. Less than three miles before Playa del Carmen, you'll pass several roads that head out to the very relaxed, isolated resorts at **Punta Bete,** which is the name of a fine beach—not a town.

If you come here between July and October, you can walk the beach at night to watch for **turtles** lumbering ashore to lay their eggs, or watch the eggs hatch and the tiny vulnerable turtles scurry to the ocean in the last two months.

However, turtles will not lay eggs where there is too much light, so as development continues (and more lights are installed) we'll see fewer turtles nesting.

ACCOMMODATIONS & DINING
Expensive

✪ KaiLuum Camp-Tel

Carretera Cancún-Tulum km 62, Playa del Carmen, Q. Roo. No phone. 40 tents (shared baths). High season $110 double, low season $99 double (includes breakfast and lunch; three-night minimum stay). For reservations Turquoise Reef Group, Box 2664, Evergreen, CO 80439; ☎ 303/674-9615 or 800/538-6802 in the U.S.

Of the three excellent Turquoise Reef Group resorts just north of Playa del Carmen, KaiLuum is the most unusual. At KaiLuum one lives outside in what is truly a bit of paradise on earth—but with none of the chores, inconveniences, and headaches of primitive camping. Its palapa-sheltered tents are ranged along an unspoiled, absolutely idyllic stretch of palm-studded beach; at night the sand pathways are illuminated marvelously by torchlight (there's no electricity here). The tents, which are big enough to stand up and walk around in, have either a full double bed or two twin beds (there's daily maid service), bottles of purified water, and hammocks strung up in front facing the Caribbean. Guests share a bathhouse that has hot showers, jugs of purified water, and amusing signs that will leave no doubt as to how to pronounce the Maya "X."

The sand-floored dining room is beneath a giant palapa on the beach—the food is consistently delicious, and you'll take your meals seated at large family-style tables with other guests. It's a nice way to make friends with your neighbors, who are mostly youngish couples, hip enough to prefer this setting over Cancún and to enjoy midnight strolls in search of nesting turtles. (Many return year after year—during high season rooms are usually booked well in advance.) Sometimes there's live music at dinner, and there's always a cold one at hand in the fully stocked honor bar.

April through July are the best months for fishing; the Camp-Tel promotes a tag and release program. Some unusual snorkeling trips and dives to nearby coral reefs can be arranged next door at the excellent dive shop shared with the Posada del Capitán Lafitte (KaiLuum's sibling property, an equally laid-back if more traditional beach resort).

Very occasionally the staff and return guests at KaiLuum can be overbearing about green politics, those horrible big cities in the States, and the KaiLuum way of vacationing (the traditions and protocols of the place are zealously guarded). Some here seemed convinced that their way is the right way, but I'm really not inclined to argue: romantic, relaxed, and a perfect base for exploring the coast in a rental car, KaiLuum is really an idealized vision of Mexico as laid-back paradise.

Turquoise Reef offers a shuttle service from the Cancún airport, but if you're driving yourself, turn left into the drive for La Posada del Capitán Lafitte (there's a huge sign); when you reach the Lafitte, turn left on the sandy path and continue the short distance to the giant hut on the right at the end.

Shangri-La Caribe

Carretera Cancún-Tulum km 69.5 (Apdo. Postal 116), Playa del Carmen, Q. Roo 77710. ☎ **987/2-2888.** Fax 987/3-0500. 50 oceanview bungalows, 5 beachfront cabañas. High season $165 oceanview double, $209 beachfront double, $352 family unit; low season $114 oceanview double, $150 beachfront double, $245 family unit (book well in advance during high season). FAN. Free parking. For reservations Turquoise Reef Group, Box 2664, Evergreen, CO 80439; ☎ 303/674-9615 or 800/538-6802 in the U.S.

Only a mile or so before you reach Playa del Carmen on Highway 307 you'll see the huge sign for the Shangri-La Caribe and another resort called Las Palapas. Turn left and you'll find the Shangri-La a mile down a semipaved road. The two-story, high-domed, palapa-topped bungalows meander to the ocean linked by sidewalks and edged by tropical vegetation. All come with two double beds, nice tile baths, and a hammock strung on the patio or balcony. Prices get higher the closer you get to the beach and are higher for two-bedroom casas.

Dining/Entertainment: One restaurant serves all three meals, and the bar is open long hours.

Services: Car rental and taxi tours to nearby lagoons and ruins.

Facilities: The large inviting pool is surrounded by a sun deck, and there are horses for rent at $40 an hour. The Cyan-Ha Diving Center on the premises offers diving, snorkeling, and fishing trips, and equipment rental for these sports. May and June are best for fishing with abundant marlin, sailfish, and dorado.

Inexpensive

Cabañas Xcalacoco

Carretera Cancún-Tulum km 52 (Apdo. Postal 176), Playa del Carmen, Q. Roo 77710. No phone. 7 cabañas (all with bath). $40 for cabaña with two beds; RVs and campers $4 per person. Discounts available in low season. Free parking.

A little further south beyond the sign for the Posada del Capitan Lafitte you'll see a road on your left with a small sign that reads PUNTA BETE. The narrow, over-grown road isn't much, but have faith and keep bearing right. Soon you'll reach the beach and a compound with cabañas facing the ocean. Though close to Playa del Carmen, you might as well be a thousand miles from civilization given the secluded feeling. It's a real hideaway. The cabañas are tidy white-washed buildings with small porches, all right on the beach. All have baths; five have king-size beds, and the others have two double beds each. Since there's no electricity, kerosene lamps light rooms in the evenings. Camping facilities are available for those in recreational vehicles and others wishing to hang a hammock under a thatched-roof covering. For these folks there's a shower and bathroom but no electricity. An excellent, small restaurant serves guests, but it's always a good idea to bring along packaged and canned snacks, water, and soft drinks. The home-style cooking at the restaurant is so good that many people drive over from Playa del Carmen just to eat here. Owners Ricardo and Rosa Novelo can arrange snorkeling and fishing trips for up to four people.

4 Playa del Carmen

20 miles S of Puerto Morelos, 44 miles S of Cancún

This rapidly expanding Caribbean village grew up around the mainland terminus of the passenger-boat service to Cozumel. Travelers soon discovered that Playa del Carmen's long stretches of white beach were far better than those on Cozumel and it has developed quite a tourist trade of its own. The tide of progress is rolling on with the appearance of the all-inclusive Diamond Resort and the Hotel Continental Plaza Playacar, both new resorts south of the center of town; new sewage and water lines; telephone service; and more brick paved streets. Playa del Carmen severed its political apron strings from Cozumel and now has its own mayor, and is contained in its own separate *municipio* (like a county). The town doubled in size in 1993 is preparing for 50,000 inhabitants by the year 2000.

Time-share hawkers ply their same fake friendly ways in Playa, but not in the numbers present in Puerto Vallarta or Cancún. Topless sunbathing, though against the law in Mexico, seems condoned here—including leisurely topless strolling anywhere there's a beach. It's so casually topless, in fact, that there was a sign in the post office to the effect of NO TOPLESS IN HERE. Nightlife consists of pleasant strolling and sitting at streetside cafes, listening to music until 10 or 11pm (although there are a few places where you can party into the wee hours).

Avenida Juárez (also known as Avenida Principal) leads into town and has always been considered "main street," but the four-lane Avenida 30, five blocks from the beach, has been paved and is positioned as another "main street."

Playa del Carmen is something of a fork in the road for southbound travelers—you can go by ferry east to Cozumel or continue south to Akumal, Tulum, Cobá, Punta Allen, and Chetumal on Highway 307.

Though Playa has lost its innocence, it's still a peaceful place where you can hang out on the beach for hours without feeling the need to explore. However, get there quickly—it's changing fast.

ESSENTIALS

GETTING THERE & DEPARTING **By Bus** There are three bus stations in Playa del Carmen, all on Avenida Principal (the main street): **Transportes de Oriente, Playa Express,** and **Inter-Caribe** are ½ block north of the main square and Avenida 5 on Avenida Principal; **Expreso Oriente** is on the corner of Avenida 5 and Avenida Principal; and the **ADO** station is 4 blocks north of the ferry dock and 2 blocks north of the plaza.

Playa Express has minibus service from Cancún every half hour from 4am to 9pm. From Cancún, Transportes de Oriente runs one confirmed-seat bus. Eight de paso ADO buses pass through Playa del Carmen on the way to Cancún, the first at 6:45am. Seven ADO buses go to Valladolid, Chichén-Itzá, and Mérida. ADO also goes to Villahermosa and Mexico City from here.

Inter-Caribe has seven deluxe express buses to Chetumal daily, five express buses to Mérida and eight de paso buses to Cancún, and frequent service to Xel-Ha, Tulum, and Felipe Carrillo Puerto. Transportes de Oriente runs five buses to Cancún with continuing service to Valladolid and Mérida, the first at 5:50am and the last at 9pm, as well as buses to Tulum, Valladolid, and Cobá. Several second-class buses run the same routes. Expreso Oriente goes to Villahermosa, Mérida, Tulum, Cancún, Felipe Carrillo Puerto, and Chetumal.

By Car The turnoff to Playa del Carmen from Highway 307 is plainly marked, and you'll arrive on the town's widest street, Avenida Principal, also known as Avenida Benito Juárez (not that there's a street sign to that effect).

By the Playa del Carmen–Cozumel Passenger Ferry See the Cozumel section above for the details on the passenger ferry service between Playa del Carmen and Cozumel.

By Taxi Taxi fares to the Cancún airport are prohibitively high, but there is a service offering shared taxi rides for $10 per person. Check at your hotel or at the Caribe Maya restaurant on Avenida 5 at Calle 8 for information and reservations.

ORIENTATION **Arriving** The ferry dock in Playa del Carmen is 1½ blocks from the main square and within walking distance of hotels. Buses are along Avenida Principal, a short distance from hotels, restaurants, and the ferry pier.

City Layout   Villagers know and use street names, but few street signs exist. The main street, **Avenida Principal,** also known as **Avenida Benito Juárez,** leads into town from Highway 307, crossing Avenida 5 one block before it ends at the beach next to the main plaza or zócalo. Traffic is diverted from Avenida Principal at Calle 10. The other main artery (closed to traffic from Avenida Principal to Calle 8), **Avenida 5,** leads to the ferry dock, two blocks from the zócalo; most restaurants and hotels are either on Avenida 5, or a block or two off of it. The village's beautiful beach parallels Avenida 5 and is only a block from it.

FAST FACTS: PLAYA DEL CARMEN

Area Code   The telephone area code is 987.

Money Exchange   There are two branches of the Cicsa Money exchange, one at the foot of the pier and the other at the Rincón del Sol plaza on Av. 5 at Calle 8. Both are open from Monday through Friday from 7:30am to 7:30pm and Saturday from 7:30am to 1pm and 3:30-6:30pm.

Parking   Because of the pedestrians-only blocks and increasing population and popularity of Playa, parking close to hotels has become more difficult. There was talk of prohibiting vehicular traffic inside the village by corralling all vehicles into a pay lot, which would be serviced by special taxis. For now, the most accessible parking lot is the Estacionamiento Mexico at the corner of Avenida Principal and Avenida 10, open daily 24 hours; the fee is $1.25 per hour and $8 per day.

Post Office   The post office is on Avenida Principal three blocks north of the plaza, on the right past the Hotel Playa del Carmen and the launderette.

Seasons   High season is December through Easter and August. Low season is all other months, but November is becoming very popular.

Spanish Lessons   The Centro Bilingue de Playa del Carmen (☎ and fax 987/3-0558), offers informal classes in conversational Spanish as well as Spanish geared toward government and business. For a reasonable fee they'll arrange transport to the Cancún airport and confirm airline tickets. The school is on Avenida 5 between Calles 4 and 6 above the Panadería Caribe.

Telephones   Many hotels have phones and faxes now; often both are on the same phone line. So, to send a fax call and ask for the fax tone: "Por favor, dar me el tono por el fax."   Public phones are available at the Hotel Playa del Carmen on Avenida Principal, on the plaza by the church, and at some shops along Avenida 5.

WHAT TO DO

Playa is for relaxing. But beyond that, the island of Cozumel is an quick ferry ride away; Tulum, Xel-Ha, Xcaret and Xcalacolco are easy excursions. Reef diving can be arranged through **Tank-Ha Dive Shop** (☎ 987/3-0302), at the Hotel Maya Bric. Snorkeling trips cost $25 and include soft drinks and equipment. Two-tank dive trips are $60; resort courses are available.

WHERE TO STAY
VERY EXPENSIVE

Continental Plaza Playacar
Frac. Playacar km 62.5, Playa del Carmen, Q. Roo 77710. ☎ **987/3-0100** or 800/882-6684 in the U.S. Fax 987/3-0105. 204 rms. A/C TEL. High season $150–$450 double. Low season $90–$330 double.

Playa del Carmen's most lavish and comfortable hotel, the Continental Plaza Playacar opened in 1991 on 308 acres spreading out along the beach beyond the ferry pier. Almost 200 Maya ruins were found during development of the resort. The entry leads through a sunny, wide marble lobby beyond which you see the pool and beach. The large, beautifully furnished rooms all have in-room safety boxes, purified tap water, tile floors, large baths, wet bars with refrigerators, and balconies. Rates vary depending on your view—garden, ocean, parking lot, or brick wall—and on whether you have one or two bedrooms. To find it from the ferry pier, turn left when you get off the ferry and follow the road a short distance until you see the Playacar sign.

Dining/Entertainment: La Pergola, with pool, beach, and ocean view, serves international food daily from 7 to 11am and 6 to 11pm. La Sirena, the poolside restaurant, is open from 7am to 6pm daily. The stylish and welcoming lobby bar is open between 11am and 1am daily with live music in the evenings.

Services: Room and laundry service, babysitting, gift shop and boutiques, travel agency, and tours to nearby archeological zones and lagoons.

Facilities: Oceanside pool, water-sports equipment, one lighted tennis court.

MODERATE

✪ Albatros Royale

Calle 8 (Apdo. Postal 31), Playa del Carmen, Q. Roo 77710. ☎ **987/3-0001,** or 800/ 538-6802 in the U.S. and Canada. 31 rms (all with bath). FAN. High season $45–$65 double. Low season $35–$50 double.

Next door to the Cabañas Albatros (see below), this "deluxe" sister hotel rises up on a narrow bit of land facing the beach. The two stories of rooms all have tile floors, tile baths with marble vanities and showers; balconies or porches. Most rooms have ocean views. Most have two double beds, but seven have queen-size beds. From the corner of Avenida 5 and Calle 8 (where you'll see the Rincón del Sol center), turn toward the water on Calle 8; the hotel is midway down the block on your left. Street parking is scarce.

Bungalows Yax Ha

Apdo. Postal 84, Playa del Carmen, Q. Roo 77710. No phone. 4 rms. FAN. $40–$80 double large bungalow; $30–$60 double small bungalow.

This little grouping of rustically comfortable bungalows is in an idyllic setting of shady sand pathways edged by tropical plants and conch shells. No two are alike inside although each one has a covered porch and kitchen. For example, the thatch-roofed Casa Alta has a single bed downstairs with the living room and kitchen. A ladder goes to the loft sleeping area with a double bed. Casa Rodonda sleeps four people in two separate rooms. The other two cottages have concrete roofs—a plus considering the mosquitoes—and a single cot and double bed in one bedroom.

It's right on the beach at the corner of Calle 10 between Calles 8 and 10.

INEXPENSIVE

Cuevo Pargo

Calle 8 s/n, Playa del Carmen, Q. Roo 77710. ☎ and fax **987/3-0351.** 8 rms (all with bath). FAN. High season $30–$50 double. Low season $25–$45 double.

Owners Sandy and Bill Dillon have given the Cuevo Pargo a splendid cleaning and revamp. Set in a small patch of undisturbed jungle, with bungalows linked by stone pathways, this place is cooler than any in town and comes complete with its own *cenote* (well). Rooms are rustic but comfortable and have unusual architecture—no two are alike. Four rooms have kitchens. One room has a loft bed overlook-

The Yucatán´s Upper Caribbean Coast

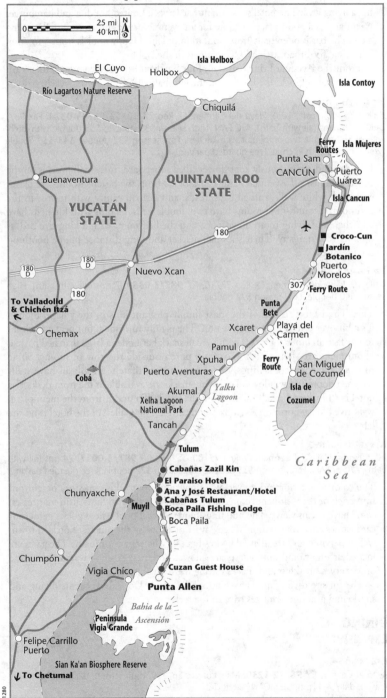

0 |⎯⎯⎯⎯⎯⎯| 25 mi
         40 km

N

El Cuyo

Holbox

Isla Holbox

Isla Contoy

Río Lagartos Nature Reserve

Chiquilá

Buenaventura

QUINTANA ROO STATE

Ferry Routes

Punta Sam

CANCÚN

Isla Mujeres

Puerto Juárez

YUCATÁN STATE

Isla Cancun

180

■ **Croco-Cun**

■ **Jardín Botanico**

Nuevo Xcan

Puerto Morelos

180
D

180
D

307 **Ferry Route**

To Valladolid & Chichén Itzá

180

Punta Bete

Chemax

Xcaret

Playa del Carmen

Pamul

Xpuha

Ferry Route

San Miguel de Cozumel

Cobá

Puerto Aventuras

Akumal

Yalku Lagoon

Isla de Cozumel

Xelha Lagoon National Park

Tancah

Tulum

Caribbean Sea

● **Cabañas Zazil Kin**
● **El Paraiso Hotel**
● **Ana y José Restaurant/Hotel**
● **Cabañas Tulum**
● **Boca Paila Fishing Lodge**

Chunyaxche

Muyil

● **Boca Paila**

Chumpón

● **Cuzan Guest House**

Vigia Chíco

Punta Allen

Bahia de la Ascensión

Peninsula Vigia Grande

Felipe Carrillo Puerto

Sian Ka'an Biosphere Reserve

↓ **To Chetumal**

Airport ✈   Reef |||||

1280

ing a living area. The hotel's restaurant/bar serves a limited hot dog and hamburger menu and is a good place to come for an evening drink and to meet fellow travelers. The bar is open daily from 3pm to midnight. Happy hour is from 5 to 7pm. There's a TV broadcasting U.S. channels in the "lobby."

From the Avenida Principal, walk four blocks north on Avenida 5, then turn right for half a block; the hotel is on the left, half a block from the beach.

Hotel Alejari

Calle 6 (Apdo. Postal 166), Playa del Carmen, Q. Roo 77710. ☎ **987/3-0374.** Fax 987/3-0005. 15 rms (all with bath). A/C FAN. High season $35 double; $55 double with kitchenette; $60 double two-story unit with kitchen. Low season $32 double; $43–$50 double two-story unit with kitchen. Free guarded parking.

Built around a fastidiously kept flower-filled inner yard, this small hotel is on the beach side just off Avenida 5 and half a block from the beach. Rooms are clean, each with white walls, ruffled bedspreads, and a small vanity with mirror in the bedroom. Ground-level rooms have two double beds. Rooms with kitchens have a kitchen and living room downstairs, and the bedroom, with a king-size bed, is up a narrow stairway. There's a small market and long-distance phone booth on the premises.

La Rana Cansada

Calle 10, Playa del Carmen, Q. Roo 77710. ☎ **987/3-0389.** 7 rms (all with bath). High season $40 double. Low season $22 double.

The "Tired Frog" is one of the most simply pleasant inns in the village, though it's a bit over priced in the high season. The plainly furnished, but neat and clean, rooms face an inner courtyard with a small snack bar under a large thatched palapa. Hammocks are strung on the covered porch outside the row of rooms. Some rooms have concrete ceilings, and others have a thatched roof; all have well-screened doors and windows. Trade paperbacks are available at the front desk. The hotel is a block and a half inland from the beach. To find it from the main plaza, walk five blocks north on Avenida 5 and turn left on Calle 10; the hotel is on the left.

Maya-Bric Hotel

Av. 5 Norte, Playa del Carmen, Q. Roo 77100. ☎ and fax **987/3-0011.** 24 rms (all with bath). A/C or FAN. High season $35 double. Low season $22 double. Free guarded parking.

The colorful exterior and flowers will draw your eye to this two-story beachfront inn. Each of the well-kept rooms has two double beds with fairly firm mattresses; some have ocean views. The buildings frame a small pool where guests gather for card games and conversation. The Maya-Bric is one of the quietest hotels in town, well supervised and frequented by loyal guests who return annually. The gates are locked at night, and only guests are allowed to enter. A small restaurant by the office serves breakfast and snacks during the high season.

The on-site dive shop, Tank-Ha (See "What to Do," above) rents diving and snorkeling gear and arranges trips to the reefs.

DINING
EXPENSIVE

Chicago

Av. 5 at Calle 6. ☎ **987/2-1230.** Main courses $6–$16. High season, daily 3–11pm. Low season, daily 7–11pm. MEXICAN/AMERICAN.

Playa del Carmen

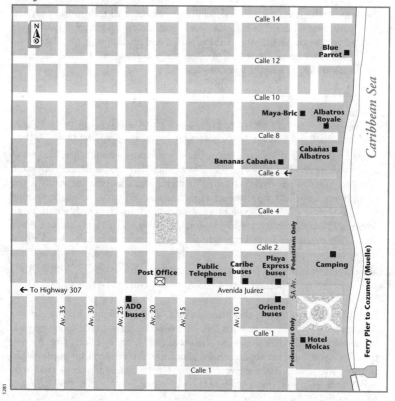

The menu is constantly being revamped at this popular restaurant, and now it emphasizes Mexican dishes, including chimichangas, chilis releno, and shrimp fajitas. Many regulars stop in for the beef, imported from the U.S. The burgers, steak sandwiches, and flambéed filet mignon are all very good; all foods are prepared with purified water, and the bar has an amazingly extensive selection of imported liquors. Diners have a choice of ground-floor, second-story, and deck dining areas; Chicago is still the only restaurant on Avenida 5 with a sea view. There's a fresh orange juice stand open in front of the restaurant in the morning.

Flippers

Av. 5 at Calle 4. No phone. Grilled specialties $5–$15; seafood platter $25. Daily 3–10:30pm. MEXICAN/GRILLED MEAT.

There's almost always a crowd at Flippers, which is noticeable from the street for its nautical theme, created by fishnets and ropes under a thatched palapa. There's an extensive bar list as well as a varied menu that includes hamburgers, poc-chuc, beef tampiqueña, and grilled seafood.

La Parrilla

Av. 5 at Av. 8. No phone. Fajitas $5–$7; main courses $5–$15. Daily noon–1am. MEXICAN/MEATS.

The Rincón del Sol plaza is one of the prettiest buildings in Playa, and now it houses one of the most popular restaurants in town. The dining room is set in two levels above the street with the open kitchen in back, and the aroma of grilling meat permeates the air. The huge chicken fajitas come with plenty of homemade tortillas and beans, and if you want to splurge on lobster, this is the place to do it. The tables fill quickly in the evening, but there are smaller bar tables set out in the plaza's courtyards, where you can wait.

MODERATE

Cabañas Albatros

On the beach, at Calle 6. ☎ **987/3-0001.** Breakfast $2–$6; main courses $4–$9. Daily 7–11am, 12:30–3pm, and 6–10pm (happy hour noon–1pm and 4–6pm). MEXICAN/ITALIAN.

On the beach, this is a good place to meet Americans who live here and while away some hours munching and people-watching. The food is dependably good. The lunch menu has nachos (loaded or plain), fruit, submarine sandwiches, hamburgers, ceviche, soup, seafood, fajitas, salads, and tacos, while the evening menu in season offers seafood and a few offerings from the lunch menu. From Avenida Principal, walk three blocks north on Avenida 5, turn right one block on Calle 6 to the beach, and turn left; the hotel/restaurant is half a block down the beach.

Restaurant El Chino

Calle 4 at Av. 15, No phone. Breakfast $1.25–$3; main courses $4–$6. Daily 8am–11pm. YUCATÁN/MEXICAN.

Locals highly recommend this place, as do I. Though slightly off the popular Avenida 5 row of restaurants, it has its own cool ambience with tile floors and plastic-covered tables set below a huge palapa roof with whirring ceiling fans. Among the offerings at breakfast are cornflakes, pancakes, and blended fruit drinks. Main courses include such regional favorites as poc-chuc, chicken pibil, and Ticul-style fish. Other selections are lobster and shrimp crêpes; brochettes of beef, chicken, or shrimp; fajitas; and ceviche.

INEXPENSIVE

Daily Doughnuts

Av. 5, between Calles 8 and 10. ☎ **987/3-0396.** Doughnuts 75¢; doughnut centers 30¢; sandwiches $2–$3; molletes $1; coffee 75¢. Mon–Sat 7am–9pm. DOUGHNUTS/CROISSANT SANDWICHES.

Paulino and Federico Suárez, a pair of enterprising Mexico City youths, opened this delicious doughnut shop in 1993. The variety is mouthwatering—50 kinds in all, with terrific toppings of glaze, chocolate, or nuts or combined flavorings of coffee, almonds, cream, blueberries, strawberries, peanut butter, and more. The Chiapan blend they use makes the best cup of coffee in town.

Deli Cafe

Av. 5. No phone. Breakfast $1–$3.50; sandwiches $2.50–$3.50. Daily 24 hours. SANDWICHES/BREAKFAST/FRUIT DRINKS.

Featuring cafe tables with orange and white umbrellas set outside a small juice stand, this has become one of the most popular places to hang out along the pedestrian walkway. Breakfast is served all day—try the burritos sureñas, filled with ham and melted cheese, or the regional huevos motuleños. Baguette submarine sandwiches are served in two sizes, and the juice selection is extensive. A 10% service charge is added to all bills.

La Hueva de Coronado

Av. 5 between Calles 4 and 6. No phone. Breakfast $3–$5; main courses $4–$12. Daily 9am–midnight. MEXICAN.

Another of Playa's popular restaurants with a breezy nautical decor and tables set out on the pedestrian walkway, this place is especially popular at breakfast. The menu also offers beef, chicken, and fish as main courses. Try the filling and well-prepared plate lunch special.

5 Highway 307 from Xcaret to Xel-Ha

This section of the mainland coast—between Playa del Carmen and Tulum—is right on the front lines of the Caribbean coast's transformation from idyllic backwater to developing tourist destination. South of Playa del Carmen along Highway 307 are a succession of brand-new planned resorts and nature parks, commercially developed beaches, and—for now, anyway—a few rustic beach hideaways and unspoiled coves. From north to south, this section will cover Xcaret, Pamul, Xpuha, Puerto Aventuras, Akumal, and Xel-Ha.

Of the fledgling resorts south of Playa del Carmen, **Akumal** is one of the most developed, with moderately priced hotels and bungalows scattered among the graceful palms that line the beautiful, soft beach and gorgeous bay. **Puerto Aventuras** is a privately developed, growing resort city aimed at the well-heeled traveler and private-condo owner. **Pamul** and **Xpuha** offer inexpensive inns on gorgeous beaches 2^1/2 miles apart. If the offbeat beach life is what you're after, grab it now before it disappears. (Other little-known and inexpensive getaways can be found on the Punta Allen Peninsula south of Tulum; see the next section for details.) You'll also enjoy a swim in the nearby lagoon of **Xel-Ha,** one of the coast's prettiest spots. And the new parklike development of **Xcaret** will appeal to some for an all-day excursion.

EN ROUTE SOUTH FROM PLAYA DEL CARMEN   Bus transportation from Playa del Carmen south is no longer as chancy as it used to be, but it's still not great. There are four bus companies in Playa; buses depart fairly frequently for Chetumal, stopping at every point of interest along the way. There's even bus service to and from Cobá three times a day. Though buses originate here, you may be told you can't buy tickets ahead of time. If you choose to hire a car and driver, be sure to find a driver you like; remember, you'll be with him all day.

XCARET: A DEVELOPED NATURE PARK

Three miles south of Playa del Carmen is the turnoff to Xcaret ("ISH-car-et"), a heavily commercialized, specially built tourist destination that promotes itself as a 150-acre ecological park. Meant as a place to spend the day, it's open daily from 9am to 5:30pm.

Xcaret may celebrate mother nature, but its builders rearranged quite a bit of her handiwork in completing it. If you're looking for a place to escape the commercialism of Cancún, this may not be it; it's expensive and contrived and may even be very crowded, thus diminishing the advertised "natural" experience. Children, however, seem to love it, and the palm-lined beaches are beautiful. Once past the entry booths (built to resemble small Maya temples) you'll find pathways that meander around bathing coves, the snorkeling lagoon, and the remains of a group of Maya temples. You'll have access to swimming beaches with canoes and pedal boats; limestone tunnels to snorkel through; marked palm-lined pathways; and a visitor's center with lockers, first aid, and gifts. There's also a museum, a "farm," and a botanical garden. Visitors aren't allowed to bring in food or drinks, so you're at the mercy of the high-priced restaurants. Personal radios are a no-no, as is use of suntan lotion if you swim in the lagoon; chemicals in lotion will poison the lagoon habitat.

The price of $25 per person entitles you to all the facilities—boats, life jacket and snorkeling equipment for the underwater tunnel and lagoon, and lounge chairs and other facilities. However, there are often more visitors than equipment (such as beach chairs), so bring a beach towel and your own snorkeling gear. Travel agencies in Cancún offer Xcaret as a day-trip that includes transportation and admission. You'll also see Xcaret's colorfully painted buses hauling people from Cancún.

PAMUL: A BEACH HIDEAWAY

About 10 miles south of Xcaret, 60 miles south of Cancún, and half a mile east of the highway is Pamul, which in Maya means "a destroyed ruin." Here you can enjoy a beautiful beach and a safe cove for swimming; it's a delightful place to leave the world behind.

A PADI- and SSI-certified American dive instructor moved to Pamul a few years ago and opened **Scuba Max** (☎ and fax 987/4-1729), a fully equipped dive shop

---

Sea Turtles of the Yucatán

At least four of Mexico's nine species of marine turtles nest on the beaches of Quintana Roo—the loggerhead, green, hawksbill, and leatherback varieties. Of these, the leatherback is almost nonexistent, and the loggerhead is the most abundant—but all are endangered.

Most turtles lay eggs on the same beach year after year, and as often as three times in a season. You'll have to be very lucky to actually see the event occur, but strolling along the beach late at night in search of giant turtles (prime egg-laying hours are between 10pm and 3am) is a special experience that will make you feel closer to the Yucatán's environment. It may take you a while to get used to the darkness, but try not to use your flashlight—lights of any kind repel the turtles. Laying the eggs is tough work—a female will dig nonstop with back flippers for more than an hour; the exercise leaves its head and legs flushed. Depositing the 100 or more eggs takes only minutes, then she makes the nest invisible by laboriously covering it with sand, and disappears into the sea. Each soft-shelled egg looks like a ping-pong ball.

Hatchlings scurry to the sea 45 days later, but successful incubation depends on the temperature and depth of the nest. When conditions are right, the hatch rates of fertile eggs are high; however, only 5% of those that do make it to the sea escape predators long enough to return.

Despite recent efforts to protect Mexico's turtles, the eggs are still considered an aphrodisiac and there's a market for them; turtles are killed for their shells and meat as well. Since turtle life expectancy is more than 50 years, killing one turtle kills thousands more. Costly protection programs include tagging the female and catching the eggs as they are deposited and removing them to a protected area and nest of identical size and temperature.

next to the cabañas. Using three 38-foot boats, he takes guests on dives 5 miles in either direction. If it's too choppy, the reefs in front of the hotel are also excellent. The cost per dive is $45 if you have your own equipment or $65 if you rent. There's another branch in the Hotel Costa del Mar in Playa del Carmen.

The snorkeling is excellent in this protected bay and the one next to it.

ACCOMMODATIONS & DINING

✪ Cabañas Pamul

Carretera Cancún-Tulum, km 85 (Apdo. Postal 83), Playa del Carmen, Q. Roo 77710. ☎ 987/4-3240 or 99/25-9422 in Mérida. 7 bungalows (all with bath); 76 trailer spaces (all with full hookups). FAN. Dec–Feb $50 double. March–June, Sept–Nov $30 double. July–Aug $40 double. RV space with hookups $15 per day, $92 per week. Tent camping $3 per person.

When you reach this isolated, relaxing hotel, you'll see coral-and-white beachfront bungalows with covered porches steps away from the Caribbean. Each cabaña contains two double beds, tile floors, rattan furniture, ceiling fans, hot water, and 24-hour electricity. A new, large palapa restaurant was under construction when I last visited and will be open year-round; until it's finished, meals are served in a small dining room in the main building. There's a small market by the main entrance where you can get drinks and snacks. For stays longer than a week, ask for a discount, which can sometimes be as much as 10% to 20%. Trailer guests have six showers and separate baths for men and women. Laundry service is available. Turtles nest here June through September. The Pamul turnoff is clearly marked on the highway; then it's almost a mile on a straight, narrow, paved but rutted road to the cabañas. Visitors not staying here are welcome to use the beach, though the owners request that they not bring in drinks and food and use the restaurant instead.

PUERTO AVENTURAS: A RESORT COMMUNITY

About 2¹/₂ miles south of Pamul (65 miles south of Cancún), you'll come to the new city-size development of Puerto Aventuras on Chakalal Bay. Though it's on 900 oceanfront acres, you don't see the ocean unless you walk through one of the three hotels. A complete resort, it includes a state-of-the-art marina, hotels, several restaurants, and multitudes of fashionable condominiums winding about the grounds and around the marina. The golf course has nine holes open for play.

Even if you don't stay here, the **Museo CEDAM** on the grounds is worth a stop. CEDAM means Center for the Study of Aquatic Sports in Mexico, and the museum houses displays on the history of diving on this coast from pre-Hispanic times to the present. Besides dive-related memorabilia, there are displays of pre-Hispanic pottery, figures, and copper bells found in the cenote of Chichén-Itzá, shell fossils, and sunken ship contents. It's supposed to be open daily from 10am to 1pm and 2 to 6pm. Donations are requested.

If you're hungry, there's a restaurant opposite the museum.

ACCOMMODATIONS & DINING

Hotel Oasis Puerto Aventuras

Carretera Puerto Juárez–Chetumal km 295, Puerto Aventuras, Q. Roo 77710. ☎ 987/2-3000 or 800/446-2747. Fax 987/3-5051. 309 rms and suites. A/C TV TEL. High season $350–$800 one- to three-bedroom unit, low season $225–$550 one- to three-bedroom unit.

Built on a grand scale, the Hotel Oasis makes lavish use of space and travertine marble both in the open and flowing public areas and in the guest rooms. The seven stories are built in a U-shape, facing Chakalal Bay. Suites come with one bedroom, two double beds, and a Murphy bed. Junior suites have a large sitting area and two bedrooms; and master suites have three bedrooms, large separate living and dining areas, and two balconies. Some master suites have a jet tub on the balcony. Rooms have either an ocean view or overlook the marina.

Dining/Entertainment: There are two restaurants, a disco, and lobby bar.

Services: Room and laundry service, travel agency, mini-cart transportation within the development. Package prices may include transportation from Cancún.

Facilities: Two pools, beach, one tennis court, super deli/market, gift shop, pharmacy, use of sports facilities and rental equipment at Hotel Club de Playa.

XPUJA: ANOTHER BEACH HIDEAWAY

Almost three miles beyond Pamul, east of the highway, is an area known as Xpuja (pronounced "ISH-poo-hah").

When I was there, it was marked by three separate crude signs pointing to rough narrow roads cutting through the jungle. Any of the roads will lead to the three separate places, nicely spaced apart in a row, that face an incredibly beautiful beach. This area was once owned by *cocoteros* (coconut growers), and two of their descendants have opened budget inns in this gorgeous setting. Aside from the two inns, there's also a for-pay day beach, where guests are charged a price to spend the day.

Though they call these inns "villas," that word implies much more than the reality of these simply furnished, painted cinder-block buildings. The **restaurant** of the Villas Xpuja offers excellent home-style cooking (great fresh-fish platters) daily from 7am to 8pm. It's ideal for day-trippers who want to spend the day on the beach and have restaurant facilities, too; they request that visitors not bring food. As long as you use the restaurant of the Villas Xpuja, there's no charge for the two public baths and showers. Within walking distance is a huge lagoon, and the reef is not far offshore.

ACCOMMODATIONS & DINING

Villas Xpuja and Restaurant
Carretera Cancún-Tulum, km 88 (Apdo. Postal 115), Playa del Carmen, Q. Roo 77710. No phone. 5 rms (all with bath). FAN. High season $40 double. Low season $32 double.

The five rooms here line up in a row of blue buildings; four have a porch area on the beach and ocean, and one is an island-style wooden structure. The rooms are plain but clean, each with nice tile floors, two windows, two single beds, two plastic chairs, hammock hooks, and a place for a suitcase—but no closet. A single bare bulb in the center of each ceiling provides light. Count on 24-hour electricity and hot water. The hotel has a dive shop offering diving and snorkeling trips and kayak rentals.

AKUMAL: RESORT ON A LAGOON

Continuing south on Highway 307 a short distance, you'll come to Akumal, a resort development built around and named after a beautiful lagoon. Signs point the way in from the highway, and the white arched Akumal gateway is less than half a mile toward the sea. The resort complex here consists of five distinct establishments sharing the same wonderful, smooth palm-lined beach and the adjacent Half

Moon Bay and Yalku Lagoon. The hotel's signs and white entry arches are clearly visible from Highway 307.

You don't have to be a guest to enjoy the **beach,** swim in the beautiful clear bay, and eat at the restaurants. It's an excellent place to spend the day while on a trip down the coast. Besides the excellent snorkeling, ask at the reception desk about **horseback rides** to Chemuyil ($30) and a tour of the Sian Ka'an Biosphere Reserve ($140). For **scuba diving,** two completely equipped dive shops with PADI-certified instructors serve the hotels and bungalows in this area. Both are located between the two hotels. There are almost 30 dive sites in the region (from 30 to 80 feet), and two-tank dives cost around $45. Both shops offer resort courses as well as complete certification. **Fishing trips** can also be arranged through the dive shops. You're only 15 minutes from good fishing. Two hours (the minimum period) costs $75, and each additional hour is $25 for up to four people with two fishing lines.

Hotel-Club Akumal Caribe Villas Maya

Carretera Cancún-Tulum (Hwy. 307) km 63. ☎ **987/2-2532.** 73 rms. A/C TEL. High season $85 bungalow, $100 hotel room, $155–$375 villa; low season $75 bungalow, $90 hotel room, $145–$210 villa. For reservations P.O. Box 13326, El Paso, TX 79950; ☎ 915/584-3552, or 800/351-1622 in the U.S. outside Texas, 800/343-1440 in Canada.

The white arches you drive under and the entry are not impressive, but the lodging varieties here are. The 48 spacious **Villas Maya Bungalows** have beautiful tile floors and comfortable, nice furniture, all with fully equipped kitchens. The 21 rooms in the new three-story **beachfront hotel** are similarly furnished but with small kitchens (no stove), a king-size or two queen-size beds, pale tile floors, and stylish Mexican accents. The **Villas Flamingo** are four exquisitely designed and luxuriously (but comfortably) furnished two-story homes facing Half Moon Bay. Each has one, two, or three bedrooms; large living, dining, and kitchen areas; and a lovely furnished patio just steps from the beach. The hotel has its own pool separate from other facilities on the grounds. Akumal's setting is truly relaxing and there's a restaurant facing the beach and lagoon.

XEL-HA: SNORKELING & SWIMMING

The Caribbean coast of the Yucatán is carved by the sea into hundreds of small *caletas* (coves) that form the perfect habitat for tropical marine life, both flora and fauna. Many caletas remain undiscovered and pristine along the coast, but Xel-Ha, 8 miles south of Akumal, is enjoyed daily by throngs of snorkelers and scuba divers who come to luxuriate in its warm waters, and swim among its brilliant fish. Xel-Ha (pronounced "Shell-hah") is a swimmers' paradise, with no threat of undertow or pollution. It's a beautiful, completely calm cove that's a perfect place to bring kids for their first snorkeling experience (experienced snorkelers may be disappointed—the crowds here seem to have driven out the living coral and a lot of the fish, and you can find more abundant marine life and avoid an admission charge at Akumal, among other spots).

The entrance to Xel-Ha is half a mile in from the highway. You'll be asked to pay a $5 per-person "contribution" to the upkeep and preservation of the site. Children under 12 are admitted free. It's open daily from 8am to 4:30pm.

Once in the park, you can rent snorkeling equipment and an underwater camera—but it's much cheaper to bring your own. You can also buy an outrageously priced drink or a meal, change clothes, take showers, and count lizards—the place is teeming with iguanas and other species. When you swim, be careful to observe the SWIM HERE and NO SWIMMING signs. (The greatest variety of fish can be seen right near the ropes marking off the NO SWIMMING areas and near any groups of rocks.)

Just south of the Xel-Ha turnoff on the west side of the highway, don't miss the **Maya ruins** of ancient Xel-Ha. You'll likely be the only one there as you walk over limestone rocks and through the tangle of trees, vines, and palms. There are a huge, deep, and dark cenote to one side and a temple palace with tumbled-down columns, a jaguar group, and a conserved temple group. A covered palapa on one pyramid guards a partially preserved mural. Admission is $2.50.

Xel-Ha is close to the ruins at Tulum—it's a good place for a dip when you've finished clambering around the Maya castles. You can make the short 8-mile hop north from Tulum to Xel-Ha by bus. When you get off at the junction for Tulum, ask the restaurant owner when the next buses come by—otherwise you may have to wait as much as two hours on the highway. Most tour companies in Cancún and Cozumel include a trip to Tulum and a swim at Xel-Ha in the same journey.

6 Tulum, Punta Allen & Sian Ka'an

Tulum (80 miles south of Cancún) and the Punta Allen Peninsula (the southern tip of which is 110 miles south of Cancún) are the southernmost points many travelers reach in their wanderings down the Caribbean coast (although there is more to discover farther down the coast). The walled Maya city of Tulum—a large Post-Classic Maya site that dramatically overlooks the Caribbean—is a natural beacon to visitors to Quintana Roo, and from Cancún it's within a two-hour drive. Tour companies and public buses make the trip regularly from Cancún and Playa del Carmen. And for those who want to leave the modern world a long, long way behind, the village of Punta Allen (between 1¹/₂ and 3 hours' drive from Tulum, depending on road conditions) may be the ultimate. It's a place without the crowds, frenetic pace, or the creature comforts of the resorts to the north—down here, the generator shuts down at 10pm (if there is one). What you will find is great fishing and snorkeling, the natural and archeological riches of the Sian Ka'an Biosphere Reserve, and a chance to rest up at what truly feels like the end of the road. A few beach cabañas now offer reliable power, telephones, and hot showers.

ESSENTIALS

ORIENTATION When traveling south of Highway 307, get your bearings on **Tulum** by thinking of it as several distinct areas: First, there's the junction of Highway 307 and the **old access road** to the Tulum ruins (it no longer provides access); here you'll find two small hotels, two restaurants, and a Pemex gas station. Next, a few feet south of the old road on Highway 307 is the **new Tulum ruins access road,** leading to a large parking lot. And a few feet farther along 307 is the road leading to the hotels and campgrounds south of the ruins.

This is the road south along the narrow **Punta Allen Peninsula** to **Boca Paila,** a portion of the **Sian Ka'an Biosphere Reserve,** and **Punta Allen,** a lobstering/fishing village at the tip's end. Though most of this 30-mile-long peninsular stretch of sandy, potholed road is uninhabited, there are several rustic inns along a fabulous beach south of the ruins.

(Across the highway from the turnoff to the Punta Allen Peninsula on Highway 307 is the road to Cobá, another fascinating Maya city 40 miles inland. See "Cobá," below, for details.)

Finally, south of the Punta Allen road on Highway 307 is the **village of Tulum.** The highway here is lined with businesses, including the bus stations, auto repair shops, markets, and pharmacies.

EXPLORING THE TULUM ARCHAEOLOGICAL SITE

Located 8 miles south of Xel-Ha, Tulum is a Maya fortress overlooking the Caribbean. At the end of the Classic Period, in A.D. 900, Maya civilization began to decline and most of the large ceremonial centers were deserted. During the post-Classic Period (A.D. 900 to the Spanish Conquest), small rival states developed with a few imported traditions from the Mexicans. Tulum is one such walled city-state; built in the 10th century, it functioned as a seaport. Aside from the spectacular setting, Tulum is not an impressive city when compared to Chichén-Itzá or Uxmal. There are no magnificent pyramidal structures as are found in the Classic Maya ruins. The stone carving is crude, and the site looks as though it was put together in a hurry or by novice apprentices rather than skilled masters. The primary god here was the diving god, depicted on several buildings as an upside-down figure above doorways. Seen at the Palace at Sayil and Cobá, this curious, almost comical figure is also known as the bee god.

The most imposing building in Tulum is the large stone structure on the cliff called the **Castillo** (castle), actually a temple as well as a fortress, once covered with stucco and painted. In front of the Castillo are several unrestored palacelike buildings partially covered with stucco. And on the beach below, where the Maya once came ashore, tourists frolic, combining a visit to the ruins with a dip in the Caribbean.

The **Temple of the Frescoes,** directly in front of the Castillo, contains interesting 13th-century wall paintings inside the temple, but entrance is no longer permitted. Distinctly Maya, they represent the rain god Chaac and Ixchel, the goddess of weaving, women, the moon, and medicine. On the cornice of this temple is a relief of the head of the rain god. If you get a slight distance from the building you'll see the eyes, nose, mouth, and chin. Notice the remains of the red-painted stucco on this building—at one time all the buildings at Tulum were painted a bright red.

Much of what we know of Tulum at the time of the Spanish Conquest comes from the writings of Diego de Landa, third bishop of the Yucatán. He wrote that Tulum was a small city inhabited by about 600 people, who lived in dwellings situated on platforms along a street and who supervised the trade traffic from Honduras to the Yucatán. Though it was a walled city, most of the inhabitants probably lived outside the walls, leaving the interior for priestly hierarchy and religious ceremonies. Tulum survived about 70 years after the Conquest, when it was finally abandoned.

Because of the excessive amount of visitors this site receives, it is no longer possible to climb the ruins. Visitors are asked to remain behind roped-off areas to view them.

In late 1994 a new entrance to the ruins was constructed about a 10-minute walk from the archeological site. Cars and buses enter a large parking lot; some of the public buses from Playa del Carmen go directly to the visitor's center. A large visitors' center was still under construction when I visited; when completed it will house over 50 artisans' stands, book stores, and a museum. Open when I visited were a restaurant, several large restrooms, and a ticket booth for Inter-Playa buses, which depart for Playa del Carmen and Cancún frequently between 7:40am and

4:40pm. After walking through the center, visitors pay the admission fee to the ruins, and another fee ($1.50 round trip) to ride an open-air shuttle to the ruins. You can easily walk, however. Admission is $5; free on Sunday. There's an additional charge of $8.50 for a permit to use a video camera at the site. Parking costs $1.55. Licensed guides have a stand by the path to the ruins and charge $20 for a 45-minute tour in English, French, or Spanish for up to four persons. They will point out many architectural details you might otherwise miss, but their history information may not be up-to-date

EN ROUTE TO FELIPE CARRILLO PUERTO

If you continue along the main Highway 307 past the Cobá turnoff, it heads southwest through Tulum village. About 14 miles south of Tulum village are the ruins of **Muyil** (ca. A.D. 1–1540) at the settlement of **Chunyaxche**, on the left side. Although archaeologists have done extensive mapping and studies of the ruins, only a few of the more than 100 or so buildings, caves, and subterranean temples have been excavated; it's actually more historically significant than it is interesting, and for most people it may not be worth the time or admission price. Birding in the early morning, however, is quite worthwhile. New excavations take place off and on, so keep checking the progress. One of the objects of this research is to find evidence of an inland port, since canals link the site to the Caribbean 9 miles east of the Boca Paila cut.

The Friends of Sian Ka'an in Cancún (see "Sian Ka'an Biosphere Reserve," below) organizes trips through the canals from Boca Paila. The Cuzan Guest House in Punta Allen and the Cabañas Ana y José south of the Tulum ruins (see listings below) also guide visitors here through the lagoons and canals. *Note:* The mosquito and dive-bombing fly population is fierce, but this is one of the best places along the coast for birding—go early in the morning.

Admission is $3; free for children under 12 and free for everyone on Sunday and festival days. It's open daily from 8am to 5pm.

After Muyil and Chunyaxche, Highway 307 cuts through 45 miles of jungle to Felipe Carrillo Puerto (see below).

THE PUNTA ALLEN PENINSULA

About 3 miles south of the Tulum ruins on the Punta Allen Road, the pavement ends and the road becomes narrow and sandy, with many potholes during the rainy season. Beyond this point is a 30-mile-long peninsula called Punta Allen, split in two at a cut called Boca Paila, where a bridge connects the two parts of the peninsula and the Caribbean enters a large lagoon on the right. From Tulum it takes at least one to 1 1/2 hours to reach the village of Punta Allen; a Volkswagen Beetle will make the trip. It's part of the far eastern edge of the 1.3-million-acre Sian Ka'an Biosphere Reserve (see below). Along this road you'll find several cabaña-type inns, all on beautiful beaches facing the Caribbean. Taxis from the ruins can take you to most of these; then you can find a ride back to the junction at the end of your stay.

EXPLORING THE PUNTA ALLEN PENINSULA

The natural environment is the peninsula's marquee attraction, whether your tastes run to relaxing on the beaches or going on bird-watching expeditions (these are available between June and August, with July being best). Sea turtles nest on the beaches along here. Alfonso Herrera and wife María Guadalupe Breseño, local

Tulum Ruins

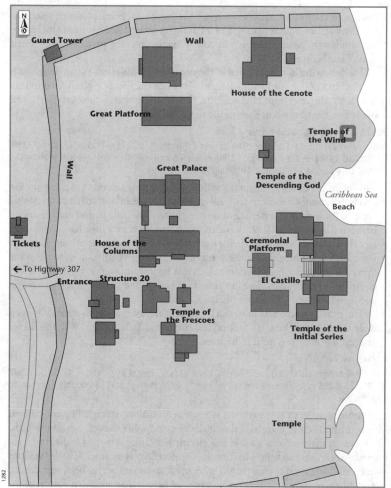

residents who live at Rancho Kan Zuul, next to the Cabañas Tulum, are hired by the state to protect the nests (*nidos* in Spanish) and see that, 45 days later, the hatchlings have a safe journey to the sea. They protect around 1,500 nests of three different species of turtles a season, with an average of 90 to 170 eggs in each nest. It takes the turtles about 90 exhausting minutes to dig their nests with their back flippers, and tourists can watch. But please, no flash pictures or flashlights—light disorients the turtles, making them switch directions and upsetting the laborious nesting process. The turtles lumber ashore at night, usually between 10pm and 3am. If you participate, a tip to the family would be courteous.

ACCOMMODATIONS & DINING

Lodgings here vary in quality—some are simple but quite comfortable, while others are a lot like camping out. One or two have electricity for a few hours in the evening; most don't have hot water. The first one is half a mile south of the ruins, and the farthest is 30 miles down the peninsula. Bring plenty of mosquito repellent and mosquito netting and a flashlight. From October through December winds may be accompanied by nippy nights, so come prepared—the hotels don't have blankets.

The following hotels are listed in the order you'll find them as you drive south on the Punta Allen road (from Tulum). To reach the first one you'll need to take the Punta Allen exit from Highway 307, then turn left when it intersects the coastal road. The rest of the hotels are to the right.

Restaurant y Cabañas Ana y José

Punta Allen Peninsula, Carretera Tulum, km 7 (Apdo. Postal 15), Tulum, Q. Roo 77780. ☎ **98/80-6021** in Cancún. Fax 98/80-6022. 16 rms (all with bath). High season $55 double. Low season $42 double. Free, unguarded parking.

This place started as a restaurant and blossomed into a comfortable inn on the beach. It is somewhat overpriced. All cabañas have tiled floors, one or two double beds, baths with cold-water showers (in eight rooms), little patios, and electricity between 6 and 10pm. The rock-walled cabañas in front are a little larger, and some face the beautiful wide beach just a few yards off. New rooms have been added on a second level. The only drawback is the lack of cross ventilation in some of the lower rooms in the back section, which can be uncomfortable at night without electricity to power fans. The inn also offers bicycle and kayak rentals, snorkeling and dive trips, and a boat tour of Sian Ka'an for $50.

The excellent, screened-in restaurant, with sand floors under the palapa, is open daily from 8am to 9pm. It's four miles south of the Tulum ruins. Write ahead for reservations; they're a must in high season.

Cabañas Tulum

Punta Allen Peninsula, Carretera Tulum, km 7 (Apdo. Postal 10), Tulum, Q. Roo 77780. ☎ **98/25-8295** in Mérida. 18 rms (all with bath). FAN. High season $34 double. Low season $23 double.

Next door to Ana y José's (above) is a row of bungalows facing a heavenly stretch of ocean and beach. Each bungalow includes a cold-water shower, two double beds, screens on the windows, a table, one electric light, nice-size tiled baths, and a veranda where you can hang a hammock. The electricity is on from 5:30 to 10:30pm only, so bring candles or a flashlight. A small restaurant serves beer, soft drinks, and all three meals for reasonable prices. The cabañas are often full between December 15 and Easter and July and August, so make reservations. It's four miles south of the ruins.

Boca Paila Fishing Lodge

Apdo. Postal 59, Cozumel, Q. Roo 77600. ☎ and fax **987/872-0053** or 987/872-1176. 8 cabañas. FAN. High season (Dec 3–June 2) $2,050 per person double. Low season $1,630 per person double. Rates for six days and seven nights, including all meals and a private boat and bonefishing guide for each cabaña. Ask about prices for nonangler sharing a double with an angler. Nonfishing drop-in prices July–Sept, $200 per person double with three meals; $275 one or two people for day of fishing with lunch but no overnight. For reservations contact Frontiers, P.O. Box 959, 100 Logan Rd., Wexford, PA 15090; ☎ 412/935-1577, or 800/245-1950 in the U.S.; fax 412/935-5388.

Easily a top contender for the nicest spot along this road, the white stucco cabañas offer a friendly beachside comfort that makes it an ideal choice. Spread out on the beach and linked by a nice walkway, each individual unit has a mosquito-proof palapa roof, large tiled rooms comfortably furnished with two double beds, rattan furniture, hot water in the bathrooms, wall fans, 24-hour electricity, and

The Sian Ka'an Biosphere Reserve

Down the peninsula a few miles south of the Tulum ruins, you'll pass the guard house of the Sian Ka'an Biosphere Reserve, 1.3 million acres set aside in 1986 to preserve tropical forests, savannas, mangroves, coastal and marine habitats, and 70 miles of coastal reefs. The area is home to jaguars, pumas, ocelots, margays, jaguarundis, spider and howler monkeys, tapirs, white-lipped and collared peccaries, manatees, brocket and white-tailed deer, crocodiles, and green, loggerhead, hawksbill, and leatherback sea turtles. It also protects 366 species of birds—you might catch a glimpse of an ocellated turkey; a great curassow; a brilliantly colored parrot; a toucan or trogon; a white ibis; a roseate spoonbill; a jabiru or wood stork; a flamingo; or one of 15 species of herons, egrets, and bitterns.

The park is separated into three parts: a "core zone," restricted to research; a "buffer zone," where visitors and families already living there have restricted use; and a "cooperation zone," outside the reserve but vital to its preservation. If you drive on Highway 307 from Tulum to an imaginary line just below the Bahía (bay) of Espíritu Santo, all you see on the Caribbean side is the reserve; but except at the ruins of Muyil/Chunyaxche (see "En Route to Felipe Carrillo Puerto" in "Cobá," below), there's no access. At least 22 archaeological sites have been charted within Sian Ka'an. The best place to sample the reserve is the Punta Allen Peninsula, part of the "buffer zone." The inns were already in place when the reserve was created. Of these, only the Cuzan Guest House (see "Accommodations & Dining" below) offers trips for birding. But bring your own binoculars and birding books and have at it—the birdlife anywhere here is rich. At the Boca Paila bridge you can often find fishermen who'll take you into the lagoon on the landward side, where you can fish and see plenty of birdlife; but it's unlikely the boatman will know bird names in English or Spanish. Birding is best just after dawn, especially during the April through July nesting season.

Day-trips to the Sian Ka'an are led from Cozumel (see "Cozumel," earlier in this chapter) and by a biologist from the **Friends of Sian Ka'an** in Cancún. For more information about the reserve or trip reservations, contact them at Plaza América, Av. Cobá 5, 3a Piso, Suite 48–50, Cancún, Q. Roo 77500 (☎ 98/84-9583; fax 98/87-3080). From Cozumel, **Viajes Internacionales Palancar,** Av. 10 Sur no. 124, Cozumel, Q. Roo 77600 (☎ 987/2-2259; fax 987/2-2348), offers day-long excursions to the reserve.

comfortable screened porch. The Boca Paila attracts a clientele that comes for saltwater flyfishing in the flats, mostly for bone fish. Prime fishing months are March through June. But when occupancy is low, nonfishing guests can be accommodated with advance notice. Overnight non-fishing rates are priced high as a discouragement to drop-ins. The lodge is about midway down the Punta Allen Peninsula, just before the Boca Paila bridge.

Cuzan Guest House

Punta Allen. 12 rms (6 with bath). $25–$60 double. All inclusive seven-day fly-fishing package $1,499.

About 30 miles from the Tulum ruins is the end of the peninsula and Punta Allen, the Yucatán's best-known lobstering and fishing village planted on a palm-studded beach. Isolated and rustic, it's part Indiana Jones, part Robinson Crusoe, and certainly the most laid-back end of the line you'll find for a while. The small town has a lobster cooperative, a few streets with modest homes, and a lighthouse at the end of a narrow sand road dense with coconut palms and jungle on both sides. So it's a welcome sight to see the beachside Cuzan Guest House and its sign in English that reads STOP HERE FOR TOURIST INFORMATION. A stay here could well be the highlight of your trip, provided you're a flexible traveler.

Two rooms are Maya-style oval stucco buildings with concrete floors and private baths. Three comfortable spacious huts with thatched roofs and bathrooms are at the water's edge and have a fabulous view of the water. The remainder of the accommodations are very comfortable teepee-shaped thatched palapa huts with concrete floors and double beds, all sharing two very clean bathrooms. Everything is solar powered. The real charmer here is the sand-floored restaurant run by co-owner Sonja Lillvik, a Californian who makes you feel right at home. If it's lobster season you may have lobster at every meal, always prepared with a deliciously different recipe. But you might also be treated to a pile of heavenly stone crabs or some other gift from the sea.

Sonja arranges fly-fishing trips for bone, permit, snook, and tarpon to the nearby saltwater flats and lagoons of Ascension Bay. The $25-per-person boat tour of the coastline that she offers is a fascinating half day of snorkeling, slipping in and out of mangrove-filled canals for birdwatching, and skirting the edge of an island rookery loaded with frigate birds. November through March is frigate-mating season and the male frigate shows off his big billowy red breast pouch to impress potential mates. The overnight Robinson Crusoe Tour costs $150 per person and includes an overnight boat excursion to remote islands, beaches, reefs, ruins (Muyil/Chunyaxche), jungles, lagoons, and birdwatching areas. Or you can simply relax in a hammock on the beach or in your room or go kayaking along the coast.

For reservations contact Apdo. Postal 24, Felipe Carrillo Puerto, Q. Roo 77200 (☎ 983/4-0358 and fax 983/4-0383 in Felipe Carrillo Puerto).

7 Cobá

105 miles S of Cancún

The impressive Maya ruins at Cobá, deep in the jungle, are a worthy detour from your route south. You don't need to stay overnight to see the ruins, but there are a few hotels. The village is small and poor, gaining little from the visitors who pass through to see the ruins. Used clothing (especially for children) would be a welcome gift.

ESSENTIALS

GETTING THERE & DEPARTING   By Bus   From Playa del Carmen there are three buses to Cobá. Two buses leave Valladolid for Cobá, but they may fill early, so buy tickets as soon as possible.

Several buses a day leave Cobá: At 6:30am and 3pm a bus goes to Tulum and Playa del Carmen, and at noon and 7pm there's a bus to Valladolid.

By Car   The road to Cobá begins in Tulum, across Highway 307 from the turn-off to the Punta Allen Peninsula. Turn right when you see the signs to Cobá and continue on that road for 40 miles. When you reach the village, proceed straight until you see the lake; when the road curves right, turn left. The entrance to the ruins is at the end of that road past some small restaurants. Cobá is also about a three-hour drive south from Cancún.

ORIENTATION   The highway into Cobá becomes one main paved street through town, which passes El Bocadito restaurant and hotel on the right (see "Accommodations & Dining," below) and goes a block to the lake. If you turn right at the lake you reach the Villas Arqueológicas a block farther. Turning left will lead past a couple of informal/primitive restaurants on the left facing the lake, and to the ruins, straight ahead, the equivalent of a block.

EXPLORING THE COBÁ RUINS

The Maya built many breathtaking cities in the Yucatán, but few were grander in scope than Cobá. However, much of the 42-square-mile site, on the shores of two lakes, is unexcavated. A 60-mile-long *sacbe* (a pre-Hispanic raised road or causeway) through the jungle linked Cobá to Yaxuná, once a large and important Maya center 30 miles south of Chichén-Itzá. It's the Maya's longest-known sacbe, and there are at least 50 or more shorter ones from here. An important city-state, Cobá, which means "water stirred by the wind," flourished between A.D. 632 (the oldest carved date found here) until after the founding of Chichén-Itzá, around 800. Then Cobá slowly faded in importance and population until it was finally abandoned. Scholars believe Cobá was an important trade link between the Yucatán Caribbean coast and inland cities.

Once in the site, keep your bearings—it's very easy to get lost on the maze of dirt roads in the jungle. Bring your bird and butterfly books; this is one of the best places to see both. Branching off from every labeled path you'll notice unofficial narrow paths into the jungle, used by locals as shortcuts through the ruins. These are good for scouting for birds, but be careful to remember the way back.

The **Grupo Cobá** boasts a large, impressive pyramid, the **Temple of the Church** (La Iglesia), which you'll find if you take the path bearing right after the entry gate. Walking to it, notice the unexcavated mounds on the left. Though the urge to climb the temple is great, the view is better from El Castillo in the Nohoc Mul group farther back at the site.

From here, return back to the main path and turn right. You'll pass a sign pointing right to the ruined *juego de pelota* (ball court), but the path is obscure.

Continuing straight ahead on this path for 5 to 10 minutes, you'll come to a fork in the road. To the left and right you'll notice jungle-covered, unexcavated pyramids, and at one point you'll cross a raised portion crossing the pathway—this is the visible remains of the sacbe to Yaxuná. Throughout the area, intricately carved stelae stand by pathways, or lie forlornly in the jungle underbrush. Though protected by crude thatched roofs, most are so weatherworn as to be indiscernible.

The left fork leads to the **Nohoc Mul Group,** which contains El Castillo, the tallest pyramid in the Yucatán (rising even higher than the great El Castillo at Chichén-Itzá and the Pyramid of the Magician at Uxmal). So far, visitors are still permitted to climb to the top. From the magnificent lofty position you can see unexcavated jungle-covered pyramidal structures poking up through the forest all around. The right fork (more or less straight on) goes to the **Conjunto Las Pinturas.** Here, the main attraction is the **Pyramid of the Painted Lintel,** a small structure with traces of the original bright colors above the door. You can climb up to get a close look. Though maps of Cobá show ruins around two lakes, there are really only two excavated buildings to see after you enter the site.

Note: Because of the heat, visit Cobá in the morning or after the heat of the day has passed. Mosquito repellent, drinking water, and comfortable shoes are imperative.

Admission is $5; children under 12 enter free daily, and Sunday and holidays it's free to everyone. Camera permits are $8.50 for each video. The site is open daily from 8am to 5pm.

ACCOMMODATIONS & DINING

✪ El Bocadito

Calle Principal, Cobá, Q. Roo. No phone. 8 rms (all with bath). FAN. $10–$13 double. Free unguarded parking. For reservations contact Apdo. Postal 56, Valladolid, Yuc. 97780.

El Bocadito, on the right as you enter town, could take advantage of being the only game in town besides the much more expensive Villas Arqueológicas—but it doesn't. Next to the hotel's restaurant of the same name, the rooms are arranged in two rows facing an open patio. They're simple, each with tile floors, two double beds, no bedspreads, a ceiling fan, and a washbasin separate from the toilet and cold-water shower cubicle. It's agreeable enough and always full by nightfall, so to secure a room, arrive no later than 3pm.

The clean open-air restaurant offers good meals at reasonable prices, served by a friendly, efficient staff. Busloads of tour groups stop here at lunch (always a sign of approval). I enjoy the casual atmosphere of El Bocadito, and there's a bookstore and gift shop adjacent to the restaurant.

Villas Arqueológicas Cobá

Cobá, Q. Roo. ☎ **5/203-3086** in Mexico City, or 800/258-2633 in the U.S. 44 rms (all with bath). A/C. Rates include all charges and taxes. $75 double. Free guarded parking.

Operated by Club Med but nothing like a Club Med village, this lovely lakeside hotel is a five-minute walk from the ruins. The hotel has a French polish, and the restaurant is top-notch, though expensive. Breakfast costs $10; lunch and dinner cost $25. A room rate including meals is available. The rooms, built around a plant-filled courtyard and beautiful pool, are stylish and soothingly comfortable. The hotel also has a library on Mesoamerican archeology (with books in French, English, and Spanish). Make reservations—this hotel fills with touring groups.

To find it, drive through town and turn right at the lake; the hotel is straight ahead on the right.

8 Felipe Carrillo Puerto

134 miles S of Cancún

Felipe Carrillo Puerto (pop. 47,000) is a busy crossroads in the jungle along the road to Ciudad Chetumal. It has gas stations, a market, a small ice plant, a bus terminal, and a few modest hotels and restaurants.

Since the main road intersects the road back to Mérida, Carrillo Puerto is the turning point for those making a "short circuit" of the Yucatán Peninsula. Highway 184 heads west from here to Ticul, Uxmal, Campeche, and Mérida.

As you pass through, consider its strange history: This was where the rebels in the War of the Castes took their stand, guided by the "Talking Crosses." Some remnants of that town (named Chan Santa Cruz) are still extant. Look for signs in town pointing the way. For the full story, see the features on Yucatecan history in Chapter 17.

ESSENTIALS

GETTING THERE   By Bus   There's frequent bus service south from Cancún and Playa del Carmen.

By Car   Coastal Highway 307 from Cancún leads directly here.

ORIENTATION   The highway goes right through the town, becoming **Avenida Benito Juárez** in town. Driving in from the north, you'll pass a traffic circle with a bust of the great Juárez. The town **market** is here.

The directions given above assume you'll be driving. If you arrive by bus, the **bus station** is right on the plaza. From there it's a 10-minute walk east down Calle 67, past the cathedral and banks, to Avenida Juárez. Turn left onto Juárez to find restaurants and hotels and the traffic circle I use as a reference point.

Fast Facts   The telephone **area code** is 983. **Banks** here don't exchange foreign currency. This is the only place to buy **gasoline** between Tulum and Chetumal.

ACCOMMODATIONS

Small hotels and good restaurants are located on the highway (Av. Juárez) as it goes through town.

9 Majahual, Xcalak & the Chinchorro Reef

Continuing south from Felipe Carrillo Puerto, you'll come to the turnoff (left) onto Highway 10, 1^1/$_2$ miles after Limones, to the coastal settlements of Majahual and Xcalak. If you're sampling this coast's offbeat offerings, if you're a diver looking for new underwater conquests, and if you're a roll-with-the-punches kind of traveler, you won't want to miss this remote and relatively undeveloped (for the moment) area. Bird lovers will find an abundance of colorful birdlife. Your destination is the Cabañas Costa de Cocos diving resort and the nearby fishing village of Xcalak near the end of the peninsula. Offshore reefs and the little-known Chinchorro reef offer great diving possibilities. The village of Xcalak once had a population as large as 1,200 before the 1958 hurricane; now has only 200 inhabitants. You'll pass many down-and-out places on the way, so the clean Costa de Coco's will stand out when you see it.

The **Chinchorro Reef Underwater National Park** is a 24-mile-long, eight-mile-wide oval-shaped reef with a depth of three feet on the reef's interior to 3,000 feet on the exterior. Locals claim it's the last virgin reef system in the Caribbean. It's invisible from the ocean side, so one of its diving attractions is the number of shipwrecks—at least 30 of them—along the reef's eastern side. One is on top of the reef. Divers have counted 40 cannon at one wreck site. On the west side are walls and coral gardens, but it's too rough to dive there.

Just to orient yourself, the turnoff from Highway 307 is 163 miles southeast of Cancún, 88 miles southeast of Tulum and just south of the small village of Limones.

Important notes: Bring large quantity of strong mosquito repellent with deet as a main ingredient—the mosquitos are undaunted by anything else. Your last chance for gas is at Felipe Carrillo Puerto, although if you're desperate, the tire repairman's family in Limones might sell you a liter or two. Look for the big tire leaning against the fence. Driving from the turnoff at Highway 307 to Xcalak (65 miles) takes around two hours. Go straight (no turns) to the end of the road, where you'll find the Caribbean and small military guard station of Mahajual. Tell the guard your destination and continue on the sandy, sometimes potholed road for 35 more miles—about an hour. *Slow down at settlements. Residents aren't expecting much traffic, and dogs and children play on the road.*

ACCOMMODATIONS & DINING

Costa de Cocos Dive Resort

Carretera Majahual-Xcalak km 52. Q. Roo. 8 cabañas. FANS. Rates include breakfast and dinner. $35 double with one bed, $40 double with two beds; $30 triple. Dive package (daily rate including dives, breakfast, and dinner) $105 double with one bed, $95 triple. Three-night minimum stay with dive package. For reservations ☎ 708/529-4473 or 800/443-1123; fax 813/488-4505).

Far and away the most sophisticated hostelry along this route, this place will seem a welcome respite in a palm grove just before the fishing village of Xcalak, which is a half mile farther at the end of the peninsula. The beautifully constructed thatch-roofed cabañas are fashioned after Maya huts but with sophisticated details like limestone walls halfway up, followed by handsomely crafted mahogany-louvered and screened windows, beautiful wood plank floors in the bedroom, large tile bathrooms, comfortable furnishings, and shelves of paperback books. Hot water and mosquito netting were being added to each room when I was there. Nice as it is, it still won't hurt to inspect your shoes daily for hidden critters—this is the jungle, after all. All dive equipment is available and included in dive packages or rented separately for day guests. The resort operates a 40-foot dive boat for diving Chinchorro. Water-sports equipment for rent includes an ocean kayak and windsurf board. PADI open-water certification can be arranged also at an additional cost. Beer and soft drinks are sold at the resort, but bring your own liquor and snacks. Besides the rates quoted above there are separate diving rates for individuals without package arrangements.

Anytime the sea gets choppy your planned dive at Chinchorro Reef (22 miles offshore) may be grounded. However, the diving five minutes offshore from the Costa de Cocos Resort is highly rewarding when weather prohibits Chinchorro diving.

10 Lago Bacalar

65 miles S of Felipe Carrillo Puerto, 23 miles N of Chetumal

If you can arrange it, staying in Bacalar sure beats staying in Chetumal or Carrillo Puerto. The crystal-clear spring-fed waters of Lake Bacalar, which is slightly over 65 miles long, empty into the Caribbean. Spaniards fleeing coastal pirates used Maya pyramid stones to build a fort in Bacalar, which is now a modest museum. The area is very quiet—the perfect place to swim and relax. At least 130 species of birds have been counted in the area. From here it's a 30-minute drive to Chetumal and to the Corozol Airport in Belize.

ESSENTIALS

GETTING THERE   By Bus   Buses going south from Cancún and Playa del Carmen stop here.

By Car   Signs into Bacalar are plainly visible from Highway 307.

ACCOMMODATIONS

✪ Rancho Encantado

Carretera Felipe Carrillo Puerto-Chetumal (Apdo. Postal 233), Chetumal, Q. Roo 77000. ☎ and fax **983/8-0427.** 8 casitas. FAN. Rates include continental breakfast and dinner. Nov–April, $86–$120 double; May–Oct, $70–$96 double ($17.50 per person less without food). For reservations contact P.O. Box 1256, Taos, NM 87571 (☎ 800/505-6292 in the U.S.; fax 505/776-5878).

Rancho Encantado's immaculate tile-roofed stucco casitas are spread out on a shady manicured lawn beside Lago Bacalar. Each spacious and beautifully kept room has mahogany-louvered windows, a cedar ceiling, a shiny red-tile floor, a handsome blue-tile kitchenette, dining table and chairs, a living room, a porch with chairs, and hammocks strung between trees. Casita 8 sleeps five, and casita 1 sleeps four. The large palapa-topped restaurant overlooks the lake and serves all three meals; the food is excellent. You can swim from the hotel's dock. The on-staff massage therapist charges $40 per session.

Managers here keep abreast of developments at the nearby archeological sites and are the only source of current information before you reach the ruins. Special packages and excursions can be arranged in advance from the hotel's U.S. office. Among them are day-trips to the Río Bec ruin route, an extended visit to Calakmul, a Yucatecan-style cookout, outings along the coast and lake, and trips to Belize. Groups interested in birding, yoga, archeology, and the like are invited to bring a leader and use Rancho Encantado as a base. To find it, look for the hotel's sign on the left about 1 1/2 miles before Bacalar.

DINING

Besides the excellent lakeside restaurant of Rancho Encantado (see "Accommodations," above), you may enjoy the **Restaurant Cenote Azul,** a comfortable open-air thatched-roof restaurant on the edge of the beautiful Cenote Azul. In both places, entrees cost from $5 to $10. To get there, follow the highway to the south edge of town and turn left at the restaurant's sign; follow that road around to the restaurant. At Rancho Encantado you can swim in Lago Bacalar, and at the Restaurant Cenote you can take a dip in placid Cenote Azul—but without skin lotion of any kind because it poisons the cenote.

17

Mérida & the Maya Cities

Mérida and its environs in Campeche and the Yucatán states in the western Yucatán are abundantly endowed with the qualities that can make a Mexican vacation something to remember. The area is rich in living pre-Hispanic traditions—you'll find clothing, crafts, and village life that hearkens back to Maya ways of 10 centuries ago. And there are plenty of the more traditional reminders of the past—the ruins of spectacular Maya cities such as Chichén-Itzá, Uxmal, and others, along with walled Spanish colonial cities like Campeche. The western half of the Yucatán also offers the budget-minded traveler a wide choice of economical lodgings, and you'll enjoy the relaxed pace of Yucatecan life and warm, friendly people.

Maya village women wear cool, embroidered cotton shifts and go about village life oblivious to the peninsula's fame as a premier resort destination. Their day-to-day cultural and belief system holds many elements that can be traced to pre-Hispanic times.

Though shy, the Maya are immensely courteous and helpful, and they eagerly chat with strangers even when there's a language barrier. More than 350,000 Maya living in the Yucatán peninsula's three states speak a Maya dialect, and many, particularly men, speak Spanish, too. Many, especially those serving tourists, slip easily between Maya, Spanish, and English. You'll get along even if English is your only language.

EXPLORING THE YUCATÁN'S MAYA HEARTLAND

The cultural center of the Yucatán, beautiful Mérida is a natural launching pad for trips to the Yucatán's major archaeological sites, to the Gulf coast, and to the Yucatán's northern coast. This part of the Yucatán Peninsula is among the best places in Mexico to take a driving tour—there are no mountains, roads, though only two-lane, are fairly well maintained, traffic is light, and stops in the many rock-walled villages are delightful.

Celestún National Wildlife Refuge: A Wetlands Reserve   This flamingo sanctuary and offbeat sand-street fishing village on the Gulf coast is a 1¹/₂-hour drive from Mérida. Plan a long day—with a very early start—for the 7am flamingo trip. However, people looking for solitude might find this a welcome respite for a week.

Dzibilchaltún: Maya Ruins   This Maya site, now a national park is located 9 miles north of Mérida along the Progreso road. Here you'll find a number of pre-Hispanic structures, nature trails, and the new Museum of the Maya. Make this one-half-day trip in the cool of the morning.

Uxmal: Spectacular Maya Ruins   The best way to visit the splendid archaeological zone of Uxmal ("Oosh-mahl"; it's about 50 miles to the south of Mérida) is to rent a car, stay two nights in a hotel at Uxmal or a less expensive hotel in Ticul, and allow for two to three full days of sightseeing. It's also possible—though a bit rushed—to see Uxmal and the quartet of ruins south of there on a day trip by special excursion bus from Mérida. Sunday is a good day to go, since admission is free to the archaeological sites.

Campeche: Walled Colonial City   A pretty colonial city with a relaxed pace, Campeche is also somewhat off the main tourist path. It's about 3 hours southwest of Mérida. Two nights and a full day should give you enough time to see Campeche's architectural highlights and museums.

Don't miss the **Museo Regional de Campeche,** especially the clay and jade objects taken from the freshly excavated southern Campeche ruins of Calakmul. You can stay at either the handsome, oceanfront **Ramada Inn** (Av. Ruíz Cortínez 51; ☎ 981/6-2233) or the much cheaper **Posada del Angel** (Calle 10 no. 307; ☎ 981/6-7718). For meals try either the classic **Parroquia** (Calle 55 no. 9) or **La Pigua** (Av. Miguel Alemán no. 197A), which is a good place to spend a leisurely afternoon.

Chichén-Itzá & Valladolid   From Mérida, it's 75 miles to the famed ruins of **Chichén-Itzá.** The ruins at Chichén-Itzá are so vast that you'll want to spend the better part of two days, taking your time in the heat, to see this site.

1 Mérida: Gateway to the Maya Heartland

900 miles E of Mexico City, 200 miles SW of Cancún

Mérida, capital of the state of Yucatán, has been the major city in the area since the mid-1500s, when the Spanish founded it on the site of the defeated Maya city of Tihó. Although it's a major touristic crossroads—within range of both the peninsula's archaeological ruins and its glitzy coasts—this modern city is easygoing, and the friendliness of its people remains its trademark.

Downtown Mérida is full of fine examples of colonial-style architecture. Vestiges of the opulent 19th-century era of the Yucatán's henequen boom remain in the ornate mansions sprinkled throughout the city. In the market and elsewhere, you'll notice items woven of a sisal fiber from the henequen plant; it's used to make hammocks, baskets, purses, shoes, tablemats, twine, rope, and packing material.

ESSENTIALS

GETTING THERE & DEPARTING   By Plane   For carriers serving Mérida from the United States, see Chapter 3, "Planning a Trip to Mexico." **Mexicana** (☎ 24-6633, 24-7421, or 23-0508; 46-1332 at the airport), flies in from Mexico City. **Aeroméxico** (☎ 27-9000; 46-1305 at the airport) flies to and from Cancún and Mexico City. **AeroCaribe,** a Mexicana affiliate (☎ 28-6786; 28-6790 at the airport), provides service to and from Cozumel, Cancún, Oaxaca, Tuxtla Gutierrez, Veracruz, Villahermosa, and points in Central America. **Taesa** (☎ 46-1826 at the airport) flies in from Monterrey and Mexico City. **Aviateca** (☎ 24-4354) flies in from Guatemala City. **Aviacsa** (at the airport ☎ 46-1344) provides service from

Cancún, Monterrey, Villahermosa, Tuxtla Gutiérrez, Tapachula, Oaxaca, and Mexico City. Taxis to and from the city to the airport cost nearly $10.

By Bus The second-class **Central Camionera** is seven blocks southwest of Plaza Mayor at Calle 68, between Calles 69 and 71. The new-first class station, **CAME,** is directly behind it on Calle 70, between Calles 69 and 71. A separate station for travelers to **Progresso** is at Calle 62 no. 524, between Calles 65 and 67.

To/From Uxmal: Autotransportes del Sur (☎ 24-9374) buses depart at 6 and 9am, noon, and 2:30pm; return trips are at 2:30, 3:30, and 7:30pm. The same company also offers one bus daily on the Mérida-Uxmal-Kabah-Sayil-Labná-Xlapak route. The trip costs $11; it departs Mérida at 8am and returns at 4pm. The driver allows passengers to spend around two hours at Uxmal and 30 minutes at each of the other archaeological sites before returning. There is no evening departure for the sound-and-light show at Uxmal.

To/From Chichén-Itzá: There are first-class **ADO** (☎ 24-8391) buses at 7:30am and 3:30pm, leaving from the CAME. If you're planning a day-trip (something I don't recommend because you'll want more time to see the impressive ruins), take the 7:30am bus and reserve a seat on the 3:30pm return bus.

To/From Pisté: Autotransportes de Oriente (☎ 22-2387) runs second-class buses every hour from 5am till midnight, and a luxury bus at 11am.

To/From Valladolid and Cancún: Expresso de Oriente (☎ 22-2387) offers deluxe service—video, restroom, and refreshments—to Cancún (a four- to five-hour trip) 19 times daily between 6am and 11:15pm. The line also has eight deluxe buses daily to Valladolid between 6am and 11:45pm. **Caribe Express** (☎ 24-4275) runs nine deluxe buses daily to Cancún between 7:15am and 10pm. **Autotransportes del Caribe** goes to Cancún at 6:30am and 5:30 and 11:45pm, and **ADO** runs three buses to Valladolid.

To/From Playa del Carmen, Tulum, and Chetumal: Three deluxe **ADO** buses go to Valladolid and on to Playa del Carmen between 7:30am and midnight. ADO also has deluxe buses to Chetumal at 10:10am and 5:30pm. **Caribe Express** buses to Playa del Carmen and Tulum depart at 6:15am and 11pm; Caribe Express buses to Chetumal depart at 7:30 and 10:30am and 1, 10, and 11pm. **Autotransportes Peninsulares** (☎ 24-1844) offers Servicio Plus deluxe service to Chetumal at 8:30am and 6pm.

To/From Campeche: Autotransportes Peninsulares offers deluxe service to Campeche at 8am and 3pm. **ADO** has first-class service to Campeche every half hour between 6am and 10pm; **Autotransportes del Sur** (☎ 24-9374) buses leave every 45 minutes from 6am to 11:30pm.

To/From Palenque and San Cristóbal de las Casas: ADO has first-class service to Palenque at 8am and 10pm. **Autotransportes del Sureste** offers second-class service to Palenque and San Cristóbal de las Casas at 6pm.

To/From Progreso, Dzibilchaltún, and Celestún: Buses depart from the Progreso Station at Calle 62 no. 524, between Calles 65 and 67.

By Car Highway 180 from Cancún, Chichén-Itzá, or Valladolid leads into Calle 65 past the market and within one block of the Plaza Mayor. Highway 281 from Uxmal (via Muna and Uman) becomes Avenida Itzáes (if you arrive by that route, turn right on Calle 63 to reach the Plaza Mayor). From Uxmal (via Ticul and the ruins of Mayapán) the road passes through Kanasín before joining Highway 180 from Valladolid into Mérida.

A traffic loop encircles Mérida, making it possible to skirt the city and head for a nearby city or site. Directional signs are generally good into the city, but going around the city on the loop requires constant vigilance.

The eight-lane toll highway (autopista) between Mérida and Cancún was completed in 1993 and cuts the driving between the two cities by about one hour. The highway begins about 35 miles east of Mérida at Kantuníl, intersecting with Highway 180. It ends at Nuevo Xcan, which is about 50 miles before Cancún. One-way tolls cost about $30.

See "En Route to Uxmal," below, at the end of the Mérida section for suggested routes from Mérida.

ORIENTATION   Arriving by Plane   Mérida's airport is eight miles from the city center on the southwestern outskirts of town where Highway 180 enters the city. The airport has desks for renting a car, reserving a hotel room, and getting tourist information. **Taxi tickets** to town are sold outside the airport doors under the covered walkway. A colectivo ticket costs $6 per person, but you have to wait for a group of five to assemble. Private taxis cost $10.

City bus no. 79 ("Aviación") operates between the town center and the airport (40¢), but the buses do not have frequent service. Other city buses run along Avenida Itzáes, just out of the airport precincts, heading for downtown.

Arriving by Bus   From Mérida's main bus station you're only six blocks from the Plaza Mayor and within walking distance of several hotels. Buses to town stop on the corner to the left of the bus station's front door.

Information   The most convenient source of information is the downtown branch of the **State of Yucatán Tourist Information Office,** in the hulking edifice known as the Teatro Peón Contreras, on Calle 60 between Calles 57 and 59 (☎ 24-9290 or 24-9389). It's open Monday through Sunday from 8am to 8pm, as are the information booths at the **airport** (☎ 24-6764), the bus station, and on Calle 62 next to the Palacio Municipal. **Yucatán Information Office,** Apdo. Postal 343, Administración 1, Mérida, Yuc. (☎ 99/27-7254), is non-profit service of the Mesoamerica Foundation. They offer helpful information about the Yucatán, such as the current cost of admission to archaeological sites and new museums.

City Layout   As in most colonial Mexican cities, Mérida's streets were originally laid out in a grid: **Even-numbered streets** run north-south; **odd-numbered streets** run east-west. In the last few decades the city has expanded well beyond the grid, and several grand boulevards have been added on the outskirts to ease traffic flow.

When looking for an address, you'll notice that street numbers progress very slowly because of the many unnumbered dwellings and -A, -B, and -C additions. For example, the distance between 504 to 615D on Calle 59 is 12 blocks.

The center of town is the very pretty **Plaza Mayor** (sometimes called the Plaza Principal), with its shady trees, benches, vendors, and a social life all its own. Around the Plaza Mayor are the massive cathedral, the Palacio de Gobierno (state government headquarters), the Palacio Municipal, and the Casa de Montejo. Within a few blocks are several smaller plazas, the University of Yucatán, and the sprawling market district.

Mérida's most fashionable address is the broad tree-lined boulevard called **Paseo de Montejo** and the surrounding neighborhood. The Paseo de Montejo begins seven blocks northwest of the Plaza Mayor and is home to Yucatán's anthropological museum, several upscale hotels, and the U.S. consulate. New high-rise deluxe hotels are opening just off the Paseo on **Avenida Colón,** another shaded boulevard containing some of the city's finest old mansions. Within the next few years, this neighborhood will become Mérida's more exclusive tourism zone, with fine restaurants and boutiques catering to the travelers drawn to the new hotels.

GETTING AROUND   By Bus   A ride on a city bus costs only 40¢. You can take a bus to the large, shady Parque Centenario on the western outskirts of town. Look for a bus of the same name ("Centenario") on Calle 64. Most buses on Calle 59 go to the zoo or to the Museum of Natural History. "Central" buses stop at the bus station, and any bus marked "Mercado" or "Correo" (post office) will take you to the market district.

By Taxi   Taxi drivers are beginning to overcharge tourists in Mérida the way they do in Mexico City. Taxi meters start at $3.50.

By Car   Cars are handy for your explorations of Mayapán, Uxmal, and Kabah, but you don't need one to get around Mérida or to reach Chichén-Itzá or Cancún. Rental cars are expensive, averaging $45 to $75 per day for a VW Beetle. **Mexico Rent-A-Car,** at Calle 60 #495 (☎ 27-4916), quoted a Beetle for $36 (high season $60) with unlimited mileage and a $600 deductible. For more detailed rental-car information see "Getting Around" in Chapter 3.

By Horse-Drawn Carriage   Look for a line of *coches de caleta* near the cathedral and in front of the Hotel Casa del Balam. Haggle for a good price; a one-hour tour of the city costs around $8.

On Foot   Most tourist attractions are within walking distance of the Plaza Mayor.

FAST FACTS: MÉRIDA

Area Code   The telephone area code is 99.

Bookstore   The Librería Dante, Calle 60 at Calle 57 (☎ 99/24-9522), has a selection of English-language cultural-history books on Mexico. It's open Monday through Friday from 8am to 9:30pm, Saturday from 8am to 2pm and 5 to 9pm, and Sunday from 10am to 2pm and 4 to 8pm.

Climate   From November through February the weather can be chilly, windy, and rainy. You'll need a light jacket or sweater for occasional cool winter weather and thin, light clothes for summer days. Light rain gear is suggested for the brief showers in late May, June, and July, but there's a chance of rain year-round in the Yucatán.

Consulates   The U.S. Consulate is at Paseo de Montejo 453, at the corner of Avenida Colón (☎ 99/25-5011), near the Holiday Inn. It's open Monday through Friday from 7:30am to 4pm. Visa matters are dealt with only on Monday, Tuesday, Wednesday, and Friday from 7:30 to 11am; other kinds of problems are considered the same days from noon to 3:30pm and Thursday until 4pm. The telephone number of a duty officer is posted at the entrance. The British Vice-Consulate is at Calle 58 no. 498 (☎ 99/28-6152). Though in theory it's open Monday through Friday from 9:30am to 1pm, you may find no one there. The vice-consul fields questions about travel to Belize as well as British matters.

Currency Exchange   Banamex, in the Palacio Montejo on the Plaza Mayor, usually provides a better rate of exchange than other banks, but the lines are often maddeningly long. Exchange hours are Monday through Friday from 9:30am to 1:30pm. Another option is the money-exchange office just as you enter the bank gates, and more banks are located on and off Calle 65 between Calles 62 and 60.

Hospitals   Hospital O'Horan is on Avenida Itzáes at Calle 59A (☎ 99/24-8711), north of the Parque Centenario.

Post Office   Mérida's main post office (correo) is located in the midst of the market at the corner of Calles 65 and 56. A branch office is located at the airport. Both are open Monday through Friday from 8am to 5pm and Saturday from 8am to 2pm.

Seasons   There are two high seasons—one in July and August when the weather is very hot and humid and when Mexicans most commonly take their vacations, and one between November 15 and Easter Sunday when the northerners flock to the Yucatán to escape winter weather and when weather in the Yucatán is cooler.

Spanish Classes   Maya scholars, Spanish teachers, and archaeologists from the United States are among the students at the **Centro Idiomas del Sureste,** Calle 14 no. 106 at Calle 25, Colonia México, Mérida, Yucatán, 97000 (☎ 99/26-1155; fax 99/26-9020). The school has two locations: in the Colonia México, a northern residential district, and on Calle 66 at Calle 57 in the downtown area. Students live with local families or in hotels; sessions running two weeks or longer are available for all levels of proficiency and areas of interest. For brochures and applications, contact Chloe Conaway de Pacheco, directora.

Telephones   There are long-distance *casetas* at the airport and the bus station. Look also for the blue-and-silver Ladatel phones appearing in public places all over Mexico. Also see "Telephones" in Chapter 1. *Important note:* Telephone numbers are being changed throughout the city, so if you have difficulty reaching a number, ask the telephone operator for assistance.

EXPLORING MÉRIDA

Most of the city's attractions are within walking distance of each other in the downtown area.

SPECIAL EVENTS

On the evening of the **first Friday** of each month, Dennis LaFoy of the Yucatán Trails Travel Agency (☎ 99/28-2582) invites the English-speaking community to a casual get-together. They usually gather at the Hotel Mérida Misión Park Plaza on Calle 60, across from the Hotel Casa del Balam, but call Dennis to confirm the location.

Many Mexican cities offer weekend concerts in the park, but Mérida surpasses them with almost-daily high-quality public events, most of which are free.

Sunday   Each Sunday from 9am to 9pm there's a fair called **Domingo en Mérida** (Sunday in Mérida). The downtown area, blocked off from traffic for the day, bustles with activity; there are children's art classes, antiques vendors, and food stands, as well as concerts of all kinds. At 11am in front of the Palacio del Gobierno, musicians play everything from jazz to classical and folk music. Also at 11am the police orchestra performs Yucatecan tunes at the Santa Lucía park. At 11:30am, marimba music brightens the Parque Cepeda Peraza (Parque Hidalgo) on Calle 60 at Calle 59. At 1pm in front of the Palacio Municipal on the Plaza Mayor, folk ballet dancers reenact a typical Yucatecan wedding. All events are free.

Monday   The **City Hall Folklore Ballet** and the **Police Jaranera Band** perform at 8pm in front of the Palacio Municipal. The music and dancing celebrate the Vaquerías feast, which occurs after the branding of cattle on Yucatecan haciendas.

Among the featured performers are dancers with trays of bottles or filled glasses on their heads—a sight to see. Admission is free.

Tuesday The theme for the Tuesday entertainment, held at 9pm in Parque Santiago, on Calle 59 at Calle 72, is **Musical Memories.** Tunes range from South American and Mexican to North American. Admission is free. Also at 9pm in the Teatro Peón Contreras on Calle 60 at Calle 57 the **University of Yucatán Folklore Ballet** presents "Yucatán and Its Roots." Admission is $5.

Wednesday The **University of Yucatán Folklore Ballet,** along with guitarists and poets, performs at 8pm at the Mayab Culture House on Calle 63, between Calles 64 and 66. Admission is free.

Thursday Typical Yucatecan music and dance are presented at the **Serenata** in Parque Santa Lucía at 9pm; admission is free.

Friday At 9pm in the patio of the University of Yucatán, Calle 60 at Calle 57, the **University of Yucatán Folklore Ballet** often performs typical regional dances from the Yucatán. Admission is free.

WALKING TOUR
Mérida

Start: Plaza Mayor.
Finish: Palacio Cantón.
Time: Allow approximately two hours, not counting time for browsing or refreshment.
Best Times: Tuesday through Sunday before noon.
Worst Times: Monday, when the Anthropology Museum is closed.

Downtown Mérida is a visitor's visual delight, with several tree-shaded parks and most of the finest examples of both colonial and late-19th-century architecture the city has to offer. The downtown is within an easy stroll of the:

1. **Plaza Mayor.** Flanked east and west by Calles 61 and 63 and north and south by Calles 60 and 62, the plaza began its history as the Plaza de Armas—a training field for Montejo's troops. It was renamed Plaza de la Constitución in 1812 and then Plaza de la Independencia in 1821 before assuming its current name. Other common names for it include Plaza Grande, Plaza Principal, and the zócalo. Today this beautiful town square, shaded by topiary laurel trees, is decked out in manicured shrubs and lawns with iron benches. Numerous entertainment events open to the public take place here throughout the year. On the east side of the plaza stands the:

2. **Cathedral.** Built between 1561 and 1598, it looks like a fortress, as do many other early churches in the Yucatán. (For several centuries, defense was actually one of the functions of such churches, as the Maya did not take kindly to European domination.) Much of the stone in the cathedral's walls came from the ruined buildings of Tihó, the former Maya city. Inside, decoration is sparse, with altars draped in fabric colorfully embroidered like a Maya woman's shift. The most notable feature is a picture over the right side door of Ah Kukum Tutul Xiú visiting the Montejo camp. (For more information on the Montejos and the Spanish Conquest of the Yucatán, see the box below, "Centuries of Conflict: Spanish & Maya in the Yucatán.")

Walking Tour—Mérida

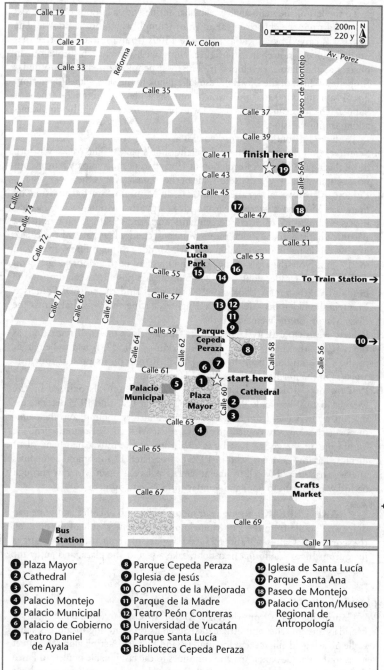

1. Plaza Mayor
2. Cathedral
3. Seminary
4. Palacio Montejo
5. Palacio Municipal
6. Palacio de Gobierno
7. Teatro Daniel de Ayala
8. Parque Cepeda Peraza
9. Iglesia de Jesús
10. Convento de la Mejorada
11. Parque de la Madre
12. Teatro Peón Contreras
13. Universidad de Yucatán
14. Parque Santa Lucía
15. Biblioteca Cepeda Peraza
16. Iglesia de Santa Lucía
17. Parque Santa Ana
18. Paseo de Montejo
19. Palacio Canton/Museo Regional de Antropología

To the left of the main altar is a smaller shrine with a curious charred cross recovered from the church in the town of Ichmul, which burned down. The figure was carved by a local artist in the 1500s from a miraculous tree that burned but did not char. The figure, along with the church, broke out in blisters as the flames enveloped it. The local people named it Cristo de las Ampollas (Christ of the Blisters). Also take a look in the side chapel (open from 8 to 11am and 4:30 to 7pm), which contains a life-size diorama of the Last Supper. The Mexican Jesus is covered with prayer crosses brought by supplicants asking for intercession.

To the right (south) of the cathedral is a:

3. **Seminary** and the former site of the archbishop's palace. The palace was torn down during the Mexican Revolution in 1915; part of the seminary remains but now contains shops. On the south side of the Plaza Mayor is the:

4. **Palacio Montejo,** also called the Casa de Montejo. Started in 1542 by Francisco Montejo *el mozo* (the Younger, i.e., the first Montejo's natural son) it was occupied by Montejo descendants until the 1970s. It now houses a Banamex bank branch, which means you can get a look at parts of the palace just by wandering in during banking hours: Monday through Friday from 9am to 1:30pm. Note the arms of the Spanish kings and of the Montejo family on the plateresque facade, along with figures of the conquistadores standing on the heads of "barbarians." Look closely and you'll find the bust of Francisco Montejo the Elder, his wife, and his daughter. Facing the cathedral across the Plaza Mayor (on the west side) is the:

5. **Palacio Municipal** (City Hall) with its familiar clock tower. It started out as the *cabildo*—the colonial town hall and lockup—in 1542. It had to be rebuilt in the 1730s and again in the 1850s, when it took on its present romantic aspect. On the north side of the Plaza Mayor is the:

6. **Palacio de Gobierno,** dating from 1892. Large murals painted by the Meridiano artist Fernando Pacheco Castro between 1971 and 1973 decorate the interior walls. Scenes from Maya and Mexican history abound, and the painting over the stairway depicts the Maya spirit with ears of sacred corn, the "sunbeams of the gods." Nearby is a painting of the mustached benevolent dictator Lázaro Cárdenas, who in 1938 expropriated 17 foreign oil companies and was hailed as a Mexican liberator. The palace is open Monday through Saturday from 8am to 8pm and Sunday from 9am to 5pm.

> ☕ **TAKE A BREAK** Revive your motor with a cup of coffee and some pan dulce or a bolillo from the Pan Montejo on the southwest side of the plaza on the corner of Calles 63 and 62. Add a glass of fresh orange or papaya juice from Jugos California next door, take a seat at the plaza, and enjoy the morning sun.

Exploring Calle 60

Continuing north from the Plaza Mayor up Calle 60, you'll see many of Mérida's old churches and little parks. Several stores catering to tourists along Calle 60 sell gold-filigree jewelry, pottery, and folk art. A stroll along this street leads to the Parque Santa Ana and continues to the fashionable boulevard Paseo de Montejo and its Museo Regional de Antropología. On your left as you leave the northeast corner of the Plaza Mayor, the:

7. Teatro Daniel de Ayala offers a continuous schedule of performing artists from around the world. A few steps beyond and across the street is the:

8. Parque Cepeda Peraza (also called the Parque Hidalgo), named for the 19th-century General Manual Cepeda Peraza, was part of Montejo's original city plan. Small outdoor restaurants front hotels on the *parque*, making it a popular stopping-off place at any time of day.

⚫ **TAKE A BREAK**   Any of the several outdoor restaurants on the Parque Cepeda Peraza makes an inviting respite. My favorite is **Giorgio,** where you can claim a table and write postcards while bartering for hammocks, amber jewelry, and baskets displayed by wandering artisans. It's in front of the Gran Hotel.

Bordering Parque Cepeda Peraza across Calle 59 is the:

9. Iglesia de Jesús, or El Tercer Ordén (the Third Order), built by the Jesuit order in 1618. The entire city block on which the church stands was part of the Jesuit establishment, and the early schools developed into the Universidad de Yucatán. Walk east on Calle 59, five blocks past the Parque Cepeda Peraza and the church, and you'll see the former:

10. Convento de la Mejorada, a late-1600s work by the Franciscans. While here, go half a block farther on Calle 59 to the **Museo Regional de Artes Populares.** Backtrack to Calle 60 and turn north. Just beyond the church (Iglesia de Jesús) is the:

11. Parque de la Madre (also called the Parque Morelos), which contains a modern statue of the Madonna and Child. The statue is a copy of the work by Lenoir that stands in the Luxembourg Gardens in Paris. Beyond the Parque de la Madre and across the pedestrian way is:

12. Teatro Peón Contreras, an enormous beige edifice designed by Italian architect Enrico Deserti in the early years of this century. In one corner you'll see a branch of the state tourist information office facing the Parque de la Madre. The main theater entrance, with its Carrara marble staircase and frescoed dome, is a few steps farther. Domestic and international performers appear here frequently. On the west side of Calle 60, at the corner of Calle 57, is the:

13. Universidad de Yucatán, founded in the 19th century by Felipe Carrillo Puerto with the help of General Cepeda Peraza. The founding is illustrated by a fresco (1961) by Manuel Lizama.

A block farther on your left, past the Hotel Mérida Misión Park Inn, is the:

14. Parque Santa Lucía. Surrounded by an arcade on the north and west sides, the *parque* once was where visitors first alighted in Mérida after arriving in their stagecoaches. On Sunday, Parque Santa Lucía holds a used-book sale and small swapmeet, and several evenings a week it hosts popular entertainment. On Thursday nights performers present Yucatecan songs and poems. A block west from the *parque* on Calle 55 at the corner of Calle 62 is:

15. Biblioteca Cepeda Peraza, a library founded by the general in 1867. Back to the Parque Santa Lucia and facing it is the ancient:

16. Iglesia de Santa Lucía (1575). To reach Paseo de Montejo, continue walking north on Calle 60 to the:

17. Parque Santa Ana, four blocks up Calle 60 from the Parque Santa Lucía. Turn right here on Calle 47 for $1^1/_2$ blocks; then turn left onto the broad, busy boulevard known as the:

18. **Paseo de Montejo,** a broad tree-lined thoroughfare with imposing banks, hotels, and several 19th-century mansions erected by henequen barons, generals, and other Yucatecan potentates. It's Mexico's humble version of the Champs-Elysées.

☕ **TAKE A BREAK** Before or after tackling the Palacio Cantón (see below), stop for break at the **Dulcería y Sorbetería Colón,** on Paseo de Montejo one block north of the Palacio between Calles 39 and 41. Far grander than its sister café at the Plaza Mayor, this bakery/ice-cream shop/candy shop has a long glass counter displaying sweet treats. Unfortunately, coffee and tea are not available.

At the corner of Calle 43 is the:

19. **Palacio Cantón** (entrance on Calle 43), which houses the **Museo Regional de Antropología** (Anthropology Museum; ☎ 99/23-0557). Designed and built by Enrico Deserti, the architect who designed the Teatro Peón Contreras, this is the most impressive mansion on Paseo de Montejo and the only one open to the public. It was constructed between 1909 and 1911 during the last years of the Porfiriato as the home of General Francisco Cantón Rosado. The general enjoyed his palace for only six years before he died in 1917. The house was converted into a school and later became the official residence of the governor of the Yucatán.

This is an interregional museum covering not only the state but also the rest of the peninsula and Mexico. Its exhibits include cosmology, pre-Hispanic time computation and comparative timeline, musical instruments, weaving examples and designs, and stone carving from all over the country.

On the right as you enter is a room used for changing exhibits, usually featuring "the piece of the month." After that are the permanent exhibits with captions mostly in Spanish. Starting with fossil mastodon teeth, the exhibits take you through the Yucatán's history, paying special attention to the daily life of its inhabitants. You'll see how the Maya tied boards to babies' skulls in order to reshape their heads, giving them the slanting forehead that was then a mark of great beauty, and how they filed teeth to sharpen them or drilled teeth to implant jewels. Enlarged photos show the archaeological sites, and drawings illustrate the various styles of Maya houses and how they were constructed. The one of Mayapán, for instance, clearly shows the city's ancient walls. Even if you know only a little Spanish, the museum provides a good background for explorations of Maya sites. The museum is open Tuesday through Saturday from 8am to 8pm and Sunday from 8am to 2pm. Admission is $4.50; free on Sunday. There's a museum bookstore on the left as you enter.

ECO-TOURS & ADVENTURE TRIPS

Companies that organize nature and adventure tours of the Yucatán Peninsula are just beginning to establish themselves. **Ecoturismo Yucatán,** Calle 3 no. 235, Col. Pensiones, Mérida, Yuc. 97219 (☎ 99/25-2187; fax 99/25-9047), is run by Alfonso and Roberta Escobedo. Alfonso has been guiding adventure tours for more than a dozen years, and Roberta runs the office with professional efficiency. The various tours emphasize remote ruin sites and culture in the Yucatán, Campeche, Chiapas, Tabasco, Oaxaca, Belize, and Guatemala. Customized tours are available.

Another specialty tour agency is **Yucatán Trails,** Calle 62 #482 (☎ 99/28-2582). Canadian Dennis LaFoy, well known and active in the English-speaking community, is a font of information and can arrange a variety of individualized tours.

Roger Lynn at **Casa Mexilio Guest House** (☎ 99/28-2505), mentioned in "Accommodations," below, arranges a variety of specialized trips. Concentrating on nature, Yucatán train trips, and haciendas, these are among the most unique trips in the area. Roger is operations manager for the Turquoise Reef Group, so you can request information through them at P.O. Box 2664, Evergreen, CO 80439 (☎ 800-538-6802).

SHOPPING

Mérida is known for hammocks, guayaberas (short-sleeve, lightweight men's shirts that are worn untucked), and Panama hats. And there are good buys in baskets made in the Yucatán and pottery, as well as crafts from all over Mexico, especially at the central market. Mérida is also the place to pick up prepared achiote—a mixture of ground achiote, oregano, garlic, masa, and other spices used in Yucatecan cuisine, especially on grilled meat and fish. I don't leave the Yucatán without some achiote.

Mérida's bustling **market district,** bounded by Calles 63 to 69 and Calles 62 to 54, is a few blocks southeast of the Plaza Mayor. The streets surrounding the market can be as interesting and crowded as the market itself. Heaps of prepared achiote are sold in the food section. On occasion, achiote is also found bottled and already mixed with juice of the sour orange. Buy the prepared achiote only if you're heading directly home from Mérida since it needs refrigeration. Mix it with vinegar to a soupy consistency for a marinade for fish and chicken.

CRAFTS

Casa del Las Artesanías
Calle 63 no. 513, between Calles 64 and 66. ☎ **99/23-5392.**

This beautiful restored monastery houses an impressive selection of crafts from throughout Mexico. Stop by here before going to the various crafts markets to see what high-quality work looks like. The monastery's back courtyard is used as a gallery, with rotating exhibits on folk and fine arts. It's open Monday through Saturday from 8am to 8pm.

Crafts Market
In a separate building of the main market, Calle 67 at Calle 56.

Look for a large pale-green building behind the post office. Climb the steps and wade into the clamor and activity while browsing for leather goods, hammocks, Panama hats, Maya embroidered dresses, men's formal guayabera shirts, and craft items of all kinds.

Museo Regional de Artes Populares
Call 59 no. 441, between Calles 50 and 48. No phone.

A branch of the Museo Nacional de Artes y Industrías Populares in Mexico City, this museum displays regional costumes and crafts in the front rooms. Upstairs is a large room full of crafts from all over Mexico, including filigree jewelry from Mérida, folk pottery, baskets, and wood carving from the Yucatán. Open Tuesday through Saturday from 8am to 8pm and Sunday from 9am to 2pm. Admission is free.

GUAYABERAS

T-shirts, polo shirts, dress shirts, and the like can be horrendously hot and uncomfortable in Mérida's soaking humidity. For this reason, businessmen, politicians, bankers, and bus drivers alike don the guayabera—a loose-fitting button-down shirt worn outside pants. Mérida could well be called the hotbed of guayaberas, which can be purchased for under $10 at the market or for over $50 custom-made by a tailor. A guayabera made of Japanese linen can set you back about $65. The most comfortable shirts are made of light, breathable cotton, though polyester is surprisingly common, despite its tendency to seal in perspiration against the skin. Several guayabera shops are located along Calle 59; most display ready-to-wear shirts in several price ranges.

Jack Guayaberas
Calle 59 no. 507A. ☎ **99/28-6002.**

The tailors at Jack's, known for their craftsmanship since the mid 1950s, can make you the guayabera of your dreams in three hours. Connoisseurs have very definite opinions on color, the type of tucks that will run down the front, and the embroidery that will swirl around the buttons. Check out the shirts on the racks for your first guayabera or perhaps a blouse or dress. The shop is open daily from 9am to 1pm and 4 to 8pm.

HAMMOCKS

The comfortable Yucatecan fine-mesh hammocks (*hamacas*) are made of string woven from silk, nylon, or cotton. Silk is extremely expensive and only for truly serious hammock sleepers. Nylon is long-lasting. Cotton is attractive, fairly strong, and inexpensive, but it wears out sooner than nylon. Here's how to select a hammock: Hold the hammock loosely and make sure the space between the weave is no larger than the size of your little finger. Grasp the hammock at the point where the wide part and the end strings meet and hold your hand level with the top of your head. The body should touch the floor; if not, the hammock is too short for you.

Hammocks are sold as *sencillo* (single, about $15); *doble* (double, $20); and *matrimonial* (larger than double, about $25). The biggest hammock of all is called *matrimonial especial.* Buy the biggest hammock you can afford—the bigger ones take up no more room than smaller ones and are more comfortable, even for just one person.

Street vendors selling hammocks will approach you at every turn, *"¿Hamacas, señor, señorita?"* Their prices will be low, but so is the quality of their merchandise. If you buy from these vendors, be sure to examine the hammock carefully. Booths in the market have a larger selection and offer hammocks at only slightly higher prices.

La Poblana
S.A., Calle 65 no. 492, between Calles 60 and 58. No phone.

La Poblana has been well recommended for years. Prices are marked, so don't try to bargain. Upstairs there's a room hung wall-to-wall with hammocks where you can give your prospective purchase a test-drive. La Poblana sells ropes and mosquito nets for hammocks, as well as Maya women's dresses and men's guayaberas. The store is open Monday through Saturday from 8am to 7pm.

MAQUECH—THE LEGENDARY MAYA BEETLE

One of the most unusual items for sale in the Yucatán is the live maquech beetle. Storekeepers display bowls of the large dusty-brown insects with long black legs and backs sprinkled with multicolored glass "jewels" attached to a small gold chain. The chain hooks to a small safety pin and behold—you have a living brooch to wear.

One version of the maquech legend goes that a Maya princess became the forbidden love object of a Maya prince. Without her knowledge, he crept into her garden one night, and just as they met, he was captured by the princess's guards. To save the prince, a sorceress turned him into a beetle and put him on a decaying tree near where he was captured. When the princess recovered from her faint, she looked for the prince where she had last seen him and found the bejeweled beetle instead; in an instant she knew it was the prince. Using a few strands of her long hair, she harnessed the beetle and kept it over her heart forever. Another version has it that the prince asked a sorceress to put him close to the heart of his beloved princess, and because he was very rich, she turned him into a bejeweled beetle pin.

No matter which legend you believe, putting a beetle close to your heart costs $7 to $10 and comes with a piece of its favorite wood, a nice little box with air holes to carry it in, and a chain and safety pin. U.S. customs, however, doesn't permit the beetle to cross the border, so plan to find it a home before you leave Mexico.

PANAMA HATS

Another very popular item are these soft, pliable hats made from the palm fibers of the jipijapa in several towns along Highway 180, especially Becal, in the neighboring state of Campeche. There's no need to journey all the way to Campeche, however, as Mérida sells the hats in abundance. Just the thing to shade you from the fierce Yucatecan sun, the hats can be rolled up and carried in a suitcase for the trip home. They retain their shape quite well.

Jipi hats come in three grades determined by the quality (pliability and fineness) of the fibers and closeness of the weave. Hats with the coarser, more open weave of fairly large fibers cost a few dollars (street vendors in Cancún and Cozumel charge up to $10). The middle grade—a fairly fine, close weave of good fibers—should cost about $15 in a respectable shop. The finest weave, truly a beautiful hat, can cost more than $50.

ACCOMMODATIONS

Mérida is easier on the budget than other Yucatán cities, and a few of the economical places even have pools. You may find every room taken in July and August, when Mexicans vacation in Mérida.

VERY EXPENSIVE

Casa del Balam

Calle 60 no. 48, Mérida, Yuc. 97000. ☎ **99/24-8844** or 800/624-8451 in the U.S. Fax 99/24-5011. 54 rms, 2 suites. A/C MINIBAR TV TEL. $80 double; $110 suite. Free parking.

One of Mérida's most popular and centrally located hotels, the Casa del Balam is built around a lush interior courtyard. In two sections of three and six stories respectively, the colonial-style rooms are accented with Mexican textiles, folk art, dark furniture, iron headboards, and tile floors with area rugs. It's hard to top this place for location and comfort. There's a travel agency and a rental-car agency in the lobby, as well as a popular restaurant and bar with trio entertainment in the evenings. The tables scattered around the courtyard have become a favorite romantic spot for evening cocktails and appetizers.

The owners also run the Hacienda Chichén-Itzá hotel, at the entrance of the ruins of Chichén-Itzá, so you can make arrangements here to stay there. To find the hotel, walk three blocks north of the Plaza Mayor.

Hyatt Regency Mérida

Calle 60 no. 344, Mérida, Yuc 97000. ☎ **99/25-6722** or 800/228-9000 in the U.S. Fax 99/25-7002. 300 rms and suites. A/C MINIBAR TV TEL. High season $165–$200 double. Low season $117 double. Ask about "super saver rates."

The most luxurious place in town, this 17-story hotel far surpasses the services and style to which Mérida is accustomed. The large, modern rooms have channels on satellite TV, 24-hour room service, direct-dial long-distance phone service, and personal safes. Regency Club rooms take up two floors of the hotel; guests here receive complimentary continental breakfast, evening cocktails, and hors d'oeuvres; special concierge service; and private lounges and board rooms. The hotel is at the intersection of Calle 60 and Avenida Colón.

Dining/Entertainment: Several restaurants and bars.

Services: Complete business center, travel agency, and shops.

Facilities: Pool with swim-up bar.

EXPENSIVE

Hotel Misión Park Inn

Calle 60 no. 491, Mérida, Yuc. 97000. ☎ **99/23-9500** or 800/448-8355. Fax 99/23-7665. 73 rms. A/C TV TEL. $82 double; $90–$150 suite.

The Misión Park Inn is actually a large modern addition grafted onto a gracious older hotel. The location is excellent—right across the street from the university and the Teatro Peón Contreras, at the corner of Calle 57 and only two short blocks from the Plaza Mayor. Enter the hotel's cool lobby from the noisy street, and you'll find yourself in an oasis complete with bubbling fountain, high ceilings, and a nice little swimming pool. Though the public rooms are colonial in style, the guest units are Spartan in a modern way with blond furniture, tile floors, drapes and shutters, and two double beds in most rooms. Some of the suites have small kitchens and separate living-room areas.

One restaurant serves all meals. La Trova Bar has live piano entertainment Monday through Saturday evenings. There's also laundry and room service and a travel agency.

MODERATE

✪ Casa Mexilio Guest House

Calle 68 no. 495, Mérida, Yuc. 97000. ☎ and fax **99/28-2505** or 800/538-6802 in the U.S. 7 rms, 1 suite (all with bath). $39 double (including breakfast). Parking on street.

Roger Lynn, part owner and host, has created the atmosphere of a private home rather than that of a hotel in this 19th-century town house. Guests have the run of this three-story home built around indoor and outdoor patios. Each room is unique, and Mexican crafts are used as decoration throughout the house. On the back patio are a small pool and whirlpool. The hotel is connected with the Turquoise Reef Group, which runs inns on Mexico's Caribbean coast between Cancún and Chetumal. You can make reservations here for those inns and sign up for a variety of trips in the Yucatán (see "Eco-Tours & Adventure Trips," above).

To find the hotel from the Plaza Mayor, walk one block north on Calle 62. Turn left on Calle 59 and walk for three blocks. Turn right on Calle 68; the hotel is one-half block down on the left.

✪ Hotel Caribe

Calle 59 no. 500, Mérida, Yuc. 97000. ☎ **99/24-9022** or 800/826-6842 in the U.S. Fax 99/24-8733. 18 rms, 38 suites (all with bath). A/C (2) or FAN (16) TV TEL. $26–$31 double; $40 suite for two with A/C. Free guarded parking.

Step inside the entry of this small two-story central hotel and discover a jewel. Well-coordinated colonial-style furnishings accent new pastel-colored tile floors. Comfortable sitting areas along the three stories of covered open-air walkways are like extended living rooms offering a cozy respite at any time of day. On the top floor are a small pool, a sun deck, and great views of the cathedral and town. Rooms with air-conditioning are the most expensive. The interior restaurant is arranged around a quiet central courtyard, while the hotel's sidewalk cafe, El Mesón, is set out in front in the shady Parque Cepada Peraza. From the Plaza Mayor, walk one-half block to the Parque Cepeda Peraza. The hotel is in the right back corner of the park.

INEXPENSIVE

✪ Hotel Mucuy

Calle 57 no. 481, Mérida, Yuc. 97000. ☎ **99/21-5193.** Fax 99/23-7801. 22 rooms (all with bath). FAN. $14 double; $16.50 triple.

One of the most hospitable budget hotels in the country, the Mucuy is named for a small dove said to bring good luck to places where it alights. You'll see doves fluttering about the flower-filled interior courtyard. Owners Alfredo and Ofelia Comin strive to make guests feel welcome with conveniences like a communal refrigerator in the lobby and laundry and clothesline facilities for guest use. Outside there are comfortable tables and chairs. Inside, two floors of freshly painted rooms with window screens, showers, and ceiling fans face the courtyard. Señora Comin speaks English. To find the hotel from the Plaza Mayor walk two blocks north on Calle 60, then turn right on Calle 57 and go a block and a half; it's between Calles 56 and 58.

DINING

To make your own breakfast, try the **Panificadora Montejo,** at the corner of Calles 62 and 63 on the southwest corner of the Plaza Mayor, where you can choose from a number of delectable treats. **Juice bars** have sprouted up all over Mérida; several are on or near the Plaza Mayor.

EXPENSIVE

Alberto's Continental

Calle 64 no. 482. ☎ **99/28-5367.** Reservations recommended. Main courses $9–$18. Daily 11am–11pm. LEBANESE/YUCATECAN/ITALIAN.

Created from a fine old town house, the large elegantly furnished rooms, are built around a plant- and tree-filled patio that's framed in Moorish arches. Cuban floor tiles from a bygone era and antique furniture and sideboards create an Old World mood. The eclectic menu features Lebanese, Yucatecan, and Italian specialties. There's a sampler plate of four Lebanese favorites, plus traditional Yucatecan specialties such as pollo pibil and fish Celéstun (bass stuffed with shrimp). Polish off your selections with Turkish coffee. Alberto's is at the corner of Calle 57.

La Casona

Calle 60 no. 434. ☎ **99/23-8348.** Reservations recommended. Pasta courses $5–$9; meat courses $7–$14. Daily 1pm–midnight. CONTINENTAL/ITALIAN.

A gracious old Mérida house and its lush interior garden make a charming, romantic restaurant. The cuisine is Yucatecan and continental, especially Italian, so you can choose among such dishes as pollo pibil, filet mignon with brandy and cream, linguine with mushrooms, and lasagna. It's also a fine place to wind up the day sipping espresso or cappuccino. From the Plaza Mayor, walk north on Calle 60 six blocks; it's at the corner of Calle 47.

MODERATE

✪ Restaurante Portico del Peregrino

Calle 57 no. 501. ☎ **99/28-6163.** Reservations recommended. Main courses $5–$8. Daily noon–11pm. MEXICAN/INTERNATIONAL.

This romantic restaurant captures the spirit of 19th-century Mexico with its patio dining. Inside is an air-conditioned dining room decorated with antique mirrors and elegant sideboards. The extensive menu offers soup, fish filet, grilled gulf shrimp, spaghetti, pollo pibil, baked eggplant with chicken and cheese, and coconut ice cream topped with Kahlúa. From the Plaza Mayor, walk $2^{1}/_{2}$ blocks north on Calle 60 and turn left on Calle 57; it's one-half block down on the right before Calle 62.

Los Almendros

Calle 50A no. 493. ☎ **99/28-5459.** Main courses $5–$8; daily special $6–$9. Daily 9am–11pm. YUCATECAN.

The original Los Almendros is located in Ticul, deep in the Maya hinterland, but the branch in Mérida has become a favorite spot to sample local delicacies. The colorful chairs and tables will put you into a festive mood. Ask to see the menu with color photographs of the offerings accompanied by descriptions in English. It's worth trying the famous poc-chuc— marinated and grilled pork created at the original restaurant in Ticul some years ago. From the Parque Cepeda Peraza, walk east on Calle 59 for five blocks, then left on Calle 50A; the restaurant is half a block down on the left facing the Parque de Mejorada.

INEXPENSIVE

Café Alameda

Calle 58 no. 474. ☎ **99/28-3635.** Breakfast $2.25–$2.50; main courses $3–$6. Mon–Sat 8am–10pm. YUCATECAN/MIDDLE EASTERN.

At about 10am on weekdays, the Alameda is filled with businesspeople all eating the same late breakfast—a shish kebab of marinated beef, a basket of warm pita bread, and coffee. If eggs are more your style, order them with beans; otherwise, you'll get a small plate with a little pile of eggs. Vegetarians can choose from tabbouleh, hummus, cauliflower, eggplant or spinach casseroles, and veggie tamales. The umbrella-shaded tables on the back patio are pleasant places to eat. To find the cafe from the Plaza Mayor, walk east on Calle 61 for one block, then turn left on Calle 58 and walk three blocks north, near the corner of Calle 55.

⑤ Restaurante Los Amigos

Calle 62 no. 497. ☎ **99/23-1957.** Comida corrida $2.50. Tues–Sun noon–midnight. MEXICAN.

This place serves a comida corrida of Yucatecan specialties which includes soup, entree, and dessert. It's not classy, but the price is right. To find it from the Palacio Municipal (which faces the Plaza Mayor), walk north on Calle 62 a half a block; it's on the left between Calles 61 and 59.

✪ Vito Corleone

Calle 59 at Calle 60. ☎ **99/28-5777.** Pizza $3–$10; beer $1; soda 65¢. Daily 9:30am–11:30pm. PIZZA.

Aside from the food (the thin-crusted pizzas taste smoky and savory), the most impressive aspect of this tiny pizza parlor is the interesting use of *ollas* (clay pots) embedded in the wall above the hand-painted tile oven. The oven's golden yellow tiles are as handsome as those that decorate church domes. The tables by the sidewalk are the only bearable places to sit when its warm, since the oven casts off incredible heat. Another section upstairs in the back is also tolerable. To find it from the Plaza Mayor, walk north on Calle 60 one block and turn left on Calle 59; it's a half a block ahead.

MÉRIDA AFTER DARK

For a full range of free or low-cost evening entertainment, as well as daily public events, in Mérida, see "Special Events," above.

Teatro Peón Contreras, at Calles 60 and 57, and the **Teatro Ayala,** on Calle 60 at Calle 61, both feature a wide range of performing artists from around the world. Stop in and see what's showing.

The scenes at the hotel bars, lounges, and discos depends on the crowd of customers presently staying at each hotel. Most of Mérida's downtown hotels, however, are filled with tour groups whose members prefer to rest after an exhausting day.

ROAD TRIPS FROM MÉRIDA

CELESTÚN NATIONAL WILDLIFE REFUGE: FLAMINGOS & OTHER WATERFOWL

This flamingo sanctuary and offbeat sand-street fishing village on the Gulf coast is a 1½-hour drive from Mérida. To get here, take Highway 281 (a two-lane road) past numerous old henequen haciendas. Around 10 **Autobuses de Occidente** buses leave Mérida for Celestún from the terminal at Calles 50 and 67 daily between 6am and 6:30pm.

One **telephone** at the Hotel Gutiérrez (☎ 99/28-0419) serves as the public phone for the entire village. You'll find a bank, two gas stations (but no unleaded gas), and a grocery store. Bus tickets are purchased at the end of the row of market stalls on the left side of the church. Celestún hotels don't furnish drinking water, so bring your own or buy it in town.

December 8 is the Feast Day of the Virgen de Concepción, the patron saint of the village. On the Sunday that falls nearest to **July 15,** a colorful procession carries Celestún's venerated figure of the Virgen de Concepción to meet the sacred figure of the Virgen de Asunción on the highway leading to Celestún. Returning to Celestún, they float away on decorated boats and later return to be ensconced at the church during a mass and celebration.

Seeing the Waterfowl

The town is on a narrow strip of land separated from the mainland by a lagoon. Crossing over the lagoon bridge, you'll find the 14,611-acre **wildlife refuge** spreading out on both sides without visible boundaries. You'll notice the small boats moored on both sides waiting to take visitors to see the flamingos. In addition to flamingos, you may see frigate birds, pelicans, cranes, egrets, sandpipers, and other waterfowl feeding on shallow sandbars at any time of year. Of the 175 bird species that come here, 99 are permanent residents. At least 15 duck species have also been counted. Flamingos are found here all year; some nonbreeding flamingos remain year round even though the larger group takes off around April to nest on the upper Yucatán Peninsula east of Río Lagartos.

A 1½- to 2-hour **flamingo-sighting trip** costs around $30 for four persons or twice that much if you stay half a day. The best time to go is around 7am, and the worst is midafternoon, when sudden storms come up. Be sure not to allow the boatmen to get close enough to frighten the birds; they've been known to do it for photographers, but it will eventually cause the birds to abandon the habitat permanently. Your tour will take you a short distance into the massive mangroves that line the lagoon to a sulfur pool, where the boatman kills the motor and poles in so you can experience the stillness and density of the jungle, feel the sultry air, and see other birds.

ACCOMMODATIONS

To find restaurants and hotels, follow the bridge road a few blocks to the end. On the last street, Calle 12, paralleling the oceanfront, you'll find a few restaurants and hotels, all of which have decent rooms but marginal housekeeping standards. Always try to bargain for lower rates, which can go down by as much as 30% in the off-season.

Hotel María del Carmen

Calle 12 no. 111, Celestún, Yuc. 97367. ☎ **99/28-0152.** 9 rms (all with bath). FAN. $15 double.

New in 1992, this three-story hotel on the beach is a welcome addition to Celestún's modest accommodations lineup. Spare but clean and large, each room has terrazzo floors, two double beds with sheets but no bedspread, screened windows (check screens for holes), and a small balcony or patio facing the ocean. Best of all, there's hot water in the baths (not necessarily a hallmark of other Celestún hotels) but not always toilet seats. Lorenzo Saul Rodríguez and María del Carmen Gutiérrez own the hotel and are actively involved in local conservation efforts, particularly in protecting the sea turtles that nest on the beach in early summer. Look for the sign for Villa del Mar, the hotel's restaurant; the rooms are behind it across the parking area.

DINING

Calle 12 is home to several rustic seafood restaurants aside from the place listed below. All have irregular hours of operation.

Restaurant Celestún

Calle 12, on the waterfront. No phone. Main courses $3–$8; soft drinks $1; beer $1.50. Daily 10am–6pm (sometimes). SEAFOOD/MEXICAN.

I highly recommend this ocean-view restaurant, owned by Elda Cauich and Wenseslao Ojeda; the service is friendly and swift. Tables and chairs fill a long room that stretches from Calle 12 to the beach. The house specialty is a super-delicious shrimp, crab, and squid omelet (called a "torta"). But if you're a fan of stone crabs ("manitas de cangrejo" on the menu), this is definitely the place to chow down. Trapped in the gulf by Celestún fishermen, they come freshly cooked and seasoned with lime juice. Also popular during the fall season is pulpo (octopus). Other local specialties include mullet (liza) and caviar de Celestún (mullet eggs). To find the restaurant, follow the bridge road to the waterfront (Calle 12); turn left and the restaurant is immediately on the right.

DZIBILCHALTÚN: MAYA RUINS

This Maya site, now a national park located 9 miles north of Mérida along the Progreso road and 4^1/$_2$ miles east off the highway, is worth a stop. Though it was founded about 500 B.C. and flourished around A.D. 750, Dzibilchaltún was in decline long before the coming of the conquistadores but may have been occupied until A.D. 1600—almost a hundred years after the arrival of the Spaniards. Since its discovery in 1941, more than 8,000 buildings have been mapped. The site, which was probably a center of commerce and religion, covers an area of almost 10 square miles with a central core of almost 65 acres. At least 12 sacbeob (causeways), the longest of which is 4,200 feet, have been unearthed. Dzibilchaltún means "place of the stone writing," and at least 25 stelae have been found, many of them reused in buildings constructed after the original ones were covered or destroyed.

Today, the most interesting buildings are grouped around the **Cenote Xlacah,** the sacred well, and include a complex of buildings around Structure 38; the **Central Group** of temples; the raised **causeways;** and the **Seven Dolls Group,** centered on the **Temple of the Seven Dolls.** It was beneath the floor of the temple that those seven weird little dolls (now in the museum) showing a variety of diseases and birth defects were discovered. The Yucatán State Department of Ecology has added nature trails and published a booklet (in Spanish) of birds and plants seen at various points along the mapped trail. The booklet tells where in the park you are likely to see specific plants and birds.

The new **Museum of the Maya** on the grounds of Dzibilchaltún should be open by the time you travel. The museum will be a replica of a Maya village of houses, called nas, staffed by Maya demonstrating traditional cooking, gardening, and folk-art techniques.

To get to Dzibilchaltún by bus from Mérida, go to the Progreso bus station at Calle 62 no. 524, between Calles 65 and 67. There are five buses per day on Monday through Saturday at 7:10 and 9am and 1, 2, and 3:20pm to the pueblo of Chanculob; it's a 1-kilometer walk to the ruins from there. On Sunday there are only three buses to Chanculob—at 5:40 and 9am and 2pm. The return bus schedule is posted at the ticket window by the ruins. The last bus is at 4:15pm.

The site and nature trails are open daily from 8am to 5pm. Admission is $3.50, free on Sunday; video camera use costs $8. Parking costs $1, and a guided tour costs about $17 for a small group.

EN ROUTE TO UXMAL

There are three routes to Uxmal, about 50 miles south of Mérida. The most direct is Highway 261 via Uman and Muna. A second possibility is to follow

The Mysteries of the Maya's Beginnings

Ever since New York lawyer and amateur anthropologist John L. Stephens recorded his adventures traveling in the Yucatán, Chiapas, and Central America in a fascinating series of travel book adventures, foreigners have been touring the Yucatán to view its vast crumbling cities and ponder the fall of the great Maya civilization, which developed mathematical theories far in advance of European thought and perfected an extremely accurate calendar.

For a detailed list of suggested background reading, see "Recommended Books" in Chapter 2.

The Olmec civilization took shape between 1500 B.C. and A.D. 300 (the **pre-Classic Period**) on the Gulf coast of Mexico. Historians speculate that the Maya were descended from the mysterious Olmecs, but a definitive link in the cultures is missing, except for a few archaeological finds like Izapa, a huge site found almost intact on the Pacific coast of Chiapas. Izapa is considered a transitional culture between the Olmec and the Maya that arose between 400 B.C. and A.D. 400.

Other than conclusions drawn from the stone carvings and historic significance of Izapa, the development of the Maya culture remains a mystery. Somewhere along the way the Maya perfected the Olmec calendar and refined and developed their ornate system of hieroglyphic writing and their early architecture. The Maya religion, with its 166 deities, was also being shaped in these early centuries, which were contemporaneous with the Roman Empire. The Maya guided their lives by using a number of interwoven and complex calendars (see below).

The great years of Maya culture (the so-called **Classic Period**), lasted from A.D. 320 to 925, when Rome was falling to the barbarians and the Dark Ages were spreading over Europe. The finest examples of Maya architecture date from these years, well before the Gothic style made its appearance in Europe. These supreme achievements of Maya art can be seen at Palenque (near Villahermosa), at Copán in Honduras, and at Quirigua in Guatemala. All these sites flourished during the last part of the 700s.

The Classic Period ended with a century of degradation and collapse, roughly equivalent to the A.D. 800s. By the early 900s the great ceremonial centers were abandoned and the jungle took them over, but why classic Maya culture collapsed so quickly is still something of a mystery.

After the Classic Period, the Maya migrated from their original home in Guatemala and Chiapas into the northern lowlands of the Yucatán (roughly the modern states of Yucatán and Campeche), where they spent six centuries (A.D. 900–1500) trying to recover their former greatness.

During this **Post-Classic Period,** the cities near the Yucatán's low western Puuc hills were built. The architecture of the region, called Puuc style, is generally characterized by elaborate exterior stonework appearing above door frames and extending to the roofline. Examples of this architecture can be seen in Kabah, Sayil, Labná, and Xlapak. Even though Maya architecture never regained the heights achieved at Palenque or Tikal, the Puuc buildings, such as the Codz Poop at Kabah and the palaces at Sayil and Labná, are quite beautiful and impressive.

The Putún Maya   The Yucatán was also profoundly affected by a strong influence from central Mexico. Some theories claim that a distantly related branch of the Maya people, the Putún Maya, came from the borders of the peninsula and crowded into the Yucatán during the post-Classic Period. The Putún Maya were traders and navigators who had controlled the trade routes along the coast and rivers between mainland Mexico and the classic Maya lands in Petén and Chiapas. They spoke the Maya language poorly and used many Náhuatl (Aztec) words.

The Itzáes   When the Putún Maya left their ships and moved inland, they became known as the Itzáes because, after unsuccessfully trying to conquer Yaxuná, they settled 12 miles north in what eventually became known as **Chichén-Itzá** (Well of the Itzá), a perfect place because of its access to water and its proximity to population centers ripe for conquering. They brought with them years of experience in trading far and wide (thus explaining the influence of the Toltecs that shows up so strongly at Chichén-Itzá). Eventually they were successful in conquering other peninsular kingdoms and creating the vast city of Chichén-Itzá.

The Toltec Invasion Theory   Research revealed in Linda Schele and David Freidel's *A Forest of Kings* shows that the bas-relief history found at Chichén-Itzá does not support a Toltec invasion theory. They believe Chichén-Itzá's adoption of Toltec architecture demonstrates it was a cosmopolitan city that absorbed elements brought by the Itzáes from another region; the continuity of buildings and bas-relief figures show it was a continuous Maya site.

The Legend of Kukulkán   Legend has it that when the great man-god Quetzalcoatl fled Tula in central Mexico in shame after succumbing to a series of temptations, he took refuge first on the east coast of Mexico and later in the Yucatán, where he became known as Kukulkán. Scholars once placed him leading the invasion of Chichén-Itzá or establishing Mayapán, which came after Chichén-Itzá. Now the jury is out again. That Kukulkán existed is not in doubt, but precisely how he fit in is being reexamined.

The Xiú   According to some authorities, Uxmal was inhabited during this same period (around A.D. 1000) by a tribe known as the Tutul Xiú, who came from the region of Oaxaca and Tabasco. Some scholars think the Xiú took the city from earlier builders because evidence shows the region around Uxmal was inhabited as early as 800 B.C.

The three great centers—Chichén-Itzá, Mayapán, and Uxmal—lived in peace under a confederation: The Itzá ruled in Chichén-Itzá, the Cocom tribe in Mayapán, and the Xiú in Uxmal. Authorities don't agree on the exact year, but sometime during the 12th century the people of Mayapán overthrew the confederation, sacked Chichén-Itzá, conquered Uxmal, and captured the leaders of the Itzá and the Xiú. Held in Mayapán, the Itzá and the Xiú princes reigned over, but did not rule, their former cities. Mayapán remained the seat of the confederation for over 200 years.

The Xiú took their revenge in 1441 when they marched from Uxmal on Mayapán, capturing and destroying the city and killing the Cocom rulers. They founded a new city at Maní. Battles and skirmishes continued to plague the Maya territory until it was conquered by the Spanish conquistadores.

Highway 180 through Uman, turn east onto Highway 184, then at Muna rejoin Highway 261 South to Uxmal. And your third choice is a scenic but meandering trip down State Highway 18. Additional details on this last route are provided below.

HIGHWAY 261: YAXCOPOIL & MUNA   Ten miles beyond Uman along Highway 261 is Yaxcopoil, the tongue-twisting Maya name of a fascinating 19th-century hacienda on the right side of the road between Mérida and Uxmal. It's difficult to reach by bus.

This hacienda, dating from 1864, was originally a cattle ranch comprising over 23,000 acres. Around 1900, it was converted to growing henequen (for the manu-facture of rope). Take half an hour to tour the house (which boasts 18-foot ceilings and original furniture), factory, outbuildings, and museum. You'll see that such haciendas were the administrative, commercial, and social centers of vast private domains; they were almost little principalities carved out of the Yucatecan jungle. It's open Monday through Saturday from 8am to 6pm and Sunday from 9am to 1pm.

From Mérida via Uman, it's 20 miles to the Hacienda Yaxcopoil ("Yash-ko-poe-EEL") and 40 miles to Muna on Highway 261. Uxmal is 10 miles from Muna.

HIGHWAY 18: KANASIN, ACANCEH, MAYAPÁN & TICUL   Taking Calle 67 east, head out of Mérida toward Kanasin ("Kahn-AH-seen") and Acanceh ("Ah-KAHN-keh"), for about 12 miles. When Calle 67 ends, bear right, then go left at the next big intersection. Follow the wide divided highway with speed bumps. At Mérida's periférico (the road that circles the city), you'll see signs to Cancún. You can either cross the periférico and go straight into Kanasin or turn and follow the Cancún signs for a short distance and then follow the signs into Kanasin. In **Kanasin,** watch for signs that say "circulación" or "desviación." As in many Yucatán towns, you're being redirected to follow a one-way street through the urban area. Go past the market, church, and the main square on your left and continue straight out of town. The next village you come to, at km 10, is **San António Tehuit,** an old henequen hacienda. At km 13 is **Tepich,** another hacienda-centered village, with those funny little henequen-cart tracks criss-crossing the main road. After Tepich comes **Petectunich** and finally Acanceh.

Across the street from and overlooking **Acanceh's** church is a partially restored pyramid. From Acanceh's main square, turn right (around the statue of a smiling deer) and head for **Tecoh** with its huge crumbling church (5^1/$_2$ miles farther along Highway 18) and **Telchaquillo** (7 miles farther). This route takes you past several old Yucatecan haciendas, each with a big house, chapel, factory with smoke-stack, and workers' houses.

Shortly after the village of Telchaquillo, a sign on the right side of the road will point to the entrance of the ruins of Mayapán.

2   The Ruins of Mayapán & Village of Ticul

THE RUINS OF MAYAPÁN

30 miles S of Mérida; 25 miles NE of Ticul; 37 miles NE of Uxmal

Founded by the man-god Quetzalcoatl (Kukulkán in Maya) in about A.D. 1007, Mayapán ranked in importance with Chichén-Itzá and Uxmal and covered at least 2^1/$_2$ square miles. For more than two centuries, it was the capital of a Maya confederation of city-states that included Chichén and Uxmal. But before the year

1200 the rulers of Mayapán ended the confederation by attacking and conquering Chichén and by forcing the rulers of Uxmal to live as vassals in Mayapán. Eventually a successful revolt by the captive Maya rulers brought down Mayapán, which was abandoned during the mid-1400s.

Though ruined, the main pyramid is still impressive. Jungle paths lead to other small temples, including El Caracol, with its circular tower. These piles of stones do not reflect the grandeur of the walled city of Mayapán in its heyday. Supplied with water from 20 cenotes, it had over 3,000 buildings in its enclosed boundaries of several square miles. Today, all is covered in dense jungle.

The site is open daily from 8am to 5pm. Admission is $2.25; free on Sunday; use of a personal video camera is $8.

FROM MAYAPÁN TO TICUL   The road is a good one, but directional signs through the villages are almost nonexistent. Stop and ask directions frequently. From Mayapán, continue along Highway 18 to **Tekit** (5 miles), turn right and go to **Mama** on a road as thrilling as a roller-coaster ride (4$^1/_3$ miles), then turn right again for **Chapab** (8 miles).

After Chapab you reach **Ticul** (6$^1/_4$ miles), the largest town in the region.

TICUL

12 miles NE of Uxmal, 53 miles S of Mérida

Many of the 27,000 inhabitants of this sprawling town make their living embroidering huipiles (the Maya women's shiftlike dress), weaving straw hats, making shoes and gold-filigree jewelry, and shaping pottery. Workshops and stores featuring most of these items are easy to find, especially in the market area.

ESSENTIALS

GETTING THERE & DEPARTING   There are frequent buses from Mérida. The Ticul bus station is near the town center on Calle 24 between Calles 25 and 25A. Buses return to Mérida daily at 7 and 10am and 5:30 and 7pm. Also check with the drivers of the minivans that line up across from the bus station. Buses run twice hourly to Muna, where you can change for a bus to Uxmal. For car information, see "En Route to Uxmal," above.

ORIENTATION   The market, most hotels, and Los Almendros, Ticul's best-known restaurant, are on the main street, **Calle 23,** also called Calle Principal. The **telephone area code** is 997. Since cars, buses, trucks, bicycles, and tricycles all compete for space on the narrow potholed streets, **parking and driving** have become difficult. Consider parking several streets away from the center of town and walking around from there. Directional signs that allow drivers to bypass the most congested part of town are beginning to appear.

EXPLORING TICUL

Special Events

Ticul's **annual festival,** complete with bullfights, dancing, and carnival games, is held during the first few days of April.

Shopping

Ticul is best known for the cottage industry of huipil embroidery and for the manufacture of ladies' dress shoes. It's also a center for large-size commercially produced pottery. Most of the widely sold sienna-colored pottery painted with Maya designs comes from Ticul.

Centuries of Conflict: Spanish & Maya in the Yucatán

The conquest of the Yucatán took 20 years and was achieved by three men all with the same name: Francisco de Montejo, the Elder (also called El Adelantado, the pioneer), who started the process; his son Francisco Montejo, the Younger (known as El Mozo, the lad); and a cousin. Montejo the Elder sailed from Spain in 1527 with 400 soldiers and landed at Cozumel but was forced to relaunch his campaign from the western coast, where he could more easily receive supplies from New Spain (Mexico).

From Mexico, he conquered what is now the state of Tabasco (1530), pushing onward to the Yucatán. But after four difficult years (1531–35) he was forced to return to Mexico penniless and exhausted. In 1540, Montejo the Younger and his cousin (another Francisco de Montejo) took over the cause, successfully establishing a town at Campeche and another at Mérida (1542); by 1546, virtually all of the peninsula was under his control.

A few weeks after the founding of Mérida, the greatest of the several Maya leaders, Ah Kukum Xiú, head of the Xiú people, offered himself as Montejo's vassal and was baptized, giving himself the name Francisco de Montejo Xiú. With the help of Montejo's troops, Montejo the Younger and his cousin then accomplished their objective, the defeat of the Cocoms. By allying his people with the Spaniards, Xiú triumphed over the Cocoms but surrendered the freedom of the Yucatecan Maya. In later centuries warfare, disease, slavery, and emigration all led to the decline of the peninsula's population. Fray Diego de Landa, second bishop of Yucatán, destroyed much of the history of the Maya culture when he ordered the mass destruction of the priceless Maya codices, or "painted books," at Maní in 1562; only three survived.

The Yucatán struggled along under the heavy yoke of Spanish colonial administration until the War of Independence (begun in 1810) liberated Mexico and the Yucatán in 1821. In that same year, the Spanish governor of the Yucatán resigned, and the Yucatán, too, became an independent country. Though the Yucatán decided to join in a union with Mexico two years later, this period of sovereignty is testimony to the Yucatecan spirit of independence. That same spirit arose again in 1846 when the Yucatán seceded from Mexico.

Arte Maya, Calle 23 No. 301, Carretera Ticul Muna (☎ 997/2-1095; fax 997/2-0334) is owned and operated by Luis Echeverria and Lourdes Castillo, this shop and gallery produces museum-quality art in alabaster, stone, jade, and ceramics! Much of the work is done as it was in Maya times; soft stone or ceramic is smoothed with the leaf of the siricote tree, and colors are derived from plant sources. If you buy from them, guard their written description—some of their reproductions have caused the U.S customs to delay entry of people carrying their wares, which seem so authentic.

ACCOMMODATIONS & DINING

Only 12 miles northeast of Uxmal, Ticul is an ideal spot from which to launch regional sightseeing trips and to avoid the high cost of hotels in Uxmal. Decent restaurants are few. The busy market on Calle 23 is a good place to mingle with

After the war, sugarcane and henequén cultivation were introduced on a large scale, organized around vast landed estates called haciendas, each employing hundreds of Maya virtually as slaves. During the war for secession, weapons were issued to the Maya to defend independent Yucatán against attack from Mexico or the United States. The Maya turned these same weapons on their local oppressors, setting off the **War of the Castes** in 1847.

The Maya ruthlessly attacked and sacked Valladolid and strengthened their forces with guns and ammunition bought from British merchants in Belize (British Honduras). By June 1848, they held virtually all the Yucatán except Mérida and Campeche—and Mérida's governor had already decided to abandon the city.

Then followed one of the strangest occurrences in Yucatecan history. It was time to plant the corn, and the Maya fighters dropped their weapons and went off to tend the fields. Meanwhile, Mexico sent reinforcements in exchange for the Yucatán's resubmission to Mexican authority. Government troops took the offensive, driving many of the Maya to the wilds of Quintana Roo, in the southeastern reaches of the peninsula.

Massed in southern Quintana Roo, the Maya, seeking inspiration in their war effort, followed the cult of the Talking Crosses, which was started in 1850 by a Maya ventriloquist and a mestizo "priest," who carried on a tradition of "talking idols" that had flourished for centuries in several places, includ-ing Cozumel. The "talking cross" first appeared at Chan Santa Cruz (today's Felipe Carrillo Puerto), and soon several crosses were talking and inspiring the Maya.

The Yucatecan authorities seemed content to let the rebels and their talking crosses rule the southern Caribbean coast, which they did with only minor skirmishes until the late 1800s. The rebel government received arms from the British in Belize, and in return allowed the British to cut lumber in rebel territory.

At the turn of the century, Mexican troops with modern weapons penetrated the rebel territory, soon putting an end to this bizarre, if romantic, episode of Yucatecan history. The town of Chan Santa Cruz was renamed in honor of a Yucatecan governor, Felipe Carrillo Puerto, and the Yucatán was finally a full and integral part of Mexico.

chatting Maya women while you select fresh fruit or grab a bite at one of the little eateries.

Hotel Bougambillias Familiar

Calle 23 no. 291A, Ticul, Yuc. 97860. ☎ **997/2-0761.** 20 rms (all with bath). FAN. $12 double, one bed; $17 double, two beds. Free secure parking.

Ticul's nicest inn is more like a motel, with parking outside the rooms. The half-circle drive into the arched entrance is lined with plants and pottery from the owner's local factory. Ceiling-height windows don't let in much light, the rooms have saggy beds, and bathrooms come without shower curtains and toilet seats. But the cool tile floors and ready hot water are attractions. In back is the hotel's pretty restaurant, Xux-Cab. To find the hotel, follow Calle 23 through Ticul on the road to Muna. It's on the right before you leave town, past the Santa Elena turnoff.

✪ Los Almendros

Calle 23 no. 207. ☎ **997/2-0021.** Main courses $5–$7. Daily 9am–7pm. YUCATECAN.

Set in a big old Andalusian-style house with interior-courtyard parking, this is the first of a chain that now has branches in Mérida and Cancún. The Maya specialties include papadzules (sauce-covered, egg-filled tortillas) poc chuc (which originated here), and the spicy pollo ticuleño; as in Mérida, the quality of the food can vary. Ask for the illustrated menu in English (also Spanish and French) that explains the dishes in detail. To find it, walk one and a half blocks west of the plaza/church on Calle 23; it's on the left.

From Ticul to Uxmal

From Ticul to Uxmal, follow the main street (Calle 23) west through town. Turn left at the sign to **Santa Elena.** It's 10 miles to Santa Elena; then, at Highway 261, cut back right for about 2 miles to Uxmal. The easiest route to follow is via Muna, but it's also longer and less picturesque. Drive straight through Ticul 14 miles to Muna. At Muna, turn left and head south on Highway 261 to Uxmal, 10 miles away.

3 The Ruins of Uxmal

50 miles S of Mérida, 12 miles SW of Ticul, 12 miles S of Muna

One of the highlights of a vacation in the Yucatán, the ruins of Uxmal, noted for their rich geometric stone facades, are the most beautiful on the peninsula. Remains of an agricultural society indicate that the area was occupied possibly as early as 800 B.C. However, the great building period took place a thousand years later, between A.D. 700 and 1000, during which time the population probably reached 25,000. Then Uxmal fell under the sway of the Xiú princes (who may have come from the Valley of Mexico) after the year 1000. In the 1440s, the Xiú conquered Mayapán, and not long afterward the glories of the Maya ended when the Spanish conquistadores arrived.

Close to Uxmal, four other sites—Sayil, Kabah, Xlapak, and Labná—are worth visiting. With Uxmal, these ruins are collectively known as the Puuc route, for the Puuc Hills of this part of the Yucatán.

ESSENTIALS

GETTING THERE & DEPARTING   By Bus   See "Getting There & Departing" in Mérida, above, for information about bus service between Mérida and Uxmal. To return, wait for the bus on the highway at the entrance to the ruins. There is no evening departure from Mérida for the sound-and-light show at Uxmal.

By Car   Three routes to Uxmal from Mérida—via Highway 261, via Highways 180 and 184, or via State Highway 18—are described in "En Route to Uxmal," at the end of the Mérida section, above. *Note:* There's no gasoline at Uxmal, so top off the tank in Mérida, Muna, or Ticul before continuing.

ORIENTATION   Uxmal consists of the archaeological site and its visitor center, four hotels, and a highway restaurant. The visitor center—open daily from 8am to 9pm—has a restaurant (with good coffee); toilets; a first-aid station; and shops selling soft drinks, ice cream, film, batteries, and books. There are no phones except at the hotels. Restaurants at hotels near Uxmal and at the visitor center are expensive, so if you're coming for the day, bring a lunch. Most public buses pick up and let off passengers on the highway at the entrance to the ruins. The site itself is open daily from 8am to 5pm. Admission to the archaeological site of Uxmal is $6.75, but a Sunday visit will save money since admission is free to Uxmal and other recommended sites nearby. *There's an $8 charge for each video camera you bring in (save your receipt; it's good for other area sites on the same day). Parking costs $1.*

Guides at the entrance of Uxmal give tours in a variety of languages and charge $25 for one person or a group. The guides frown on an unrelated individual joining a group (presumably a group is people traveling together). They'd rather you pay as a single entity, but you can hang around the entrance and ask other English speakers if they would like to join you in a tour and split the cost. As at other sites, the guides' information is not up-to-date, but you'll see areas and architectural details you might otherwise miss.

A 45-minute **sound-and-light show** is staged each evening in Spanish for $3 at 7pm and in English for $4 at 9pm. The bus from Mérida is scheduled to leave near the end of the Spanish show; confirm the exact time with the driver. If you stay for the English show, the only return to Mérida is via an expensive taxi. After the impressive show, the chant "*Chaaac, Chaaac*" will echo in your mind for weeks.

A TOUR OF THE RUINS

The Pyramid of the Magician   As you enter the ruins, note the *chultún* (cistern) inside the entrance to the right. Besides the natural underground cisterns (such as cenotes) formed in the porous limestone, chultúnes were the principal source of water for the Maya.

Just beyond the chultún, Uxmal's dominant building, the Pyramid of the Magician (also called the Soothsayer's Temple) with its unique rounded sides, looms majestically on the right as you enter. The name comes from a legend about a mystical dwarf who reached adulthood rapidly after being hatched from an egg and who built this pyramid in one night. Beneath it are five temples, since it was common practice for the Maya to build new structures atop old ones as part of a prescribed ritual.

The pyramid is unique because of its oval shape, height, steepness, and odd doorway on the opposite (west) side near the top. The doorway's heavy ornamentation, a characteristic of the Chenes style, features 12 stylized masks of the rain god Chaac, and the doorway itself is a huge open-mouthed Chaac mask.

The tiring and even dangerous climb to the top is worth it for the view. From on top you can see Uxmal's entire layout. Next to the Pyramid of the Magician, to the west, is the Nunnery Quadrangle, and left of it is a conserved ball court, south of which are several large complexes. The biggest building among them is the Governor's Palace, and behind it lies the partially restored Great Pyramid. In the distance is the Dovecote, a palace with a lacy roofcomb (false front) that looks like the perfect apartment complex for pigeons. From this vantage point, note how Uxmal is special among Maya sites for its use of broad terraces or platforms constructed to support the buildings; look closely and you'll see that the Governor's Palace is not on a natural hill or rise but on a huge square terrace, as is the Nunnery Quadrangle.

The Nunnery   The 16th-century Spanish historian Fray Diego López de Cogullado gave the building its name because it resembled a Spanish monastery. Possibly it was a military academy or a training school for princes, who may have lived in the 70-odd rooms. The buildings were constructed at different times: The northern one was first, then the southern, then the eastern, then the western. The western building has the most richly decorated facade, composed of intertwined stone snakes and numerous masks of the hook-nosed rain god Chaac.

The corbeled archway on the south was once the main entrance to the Nunnery complex; as you head toward it out of the quadrangle to the south, look above each doorway in that section for the motif of a Maya cottage, or *na,* looking just like any number of cottages you'd see throughout the Yucatán today. All this wonderful decoration has been restored, of course—it didn't look this good when the archaeologists discovered it.

The Ball Court   The unimpressive ball court is conserved to prevent further decay, but keep it in mind to compare with the magnificent restored court at Chichén-Itzá.

The Turtle House   Up on the terrace south of the ball court is a little temple decorated with colonnade motif on the facade and a border of turtles. Though it's small and simple, its harmony is one of the gems of Uxmal.

The Governor's Palace   In size and intricate stonework, this is Uxmal's masterwork—an imposing three-level edifice with a 320-foot-long mosaic facade done in the Puuc style. Puuc means "hilly country," the name given to the hills nearby and thus to the predominant style of pre-Hispanic architecture found here. Uxmal has many examples of Puuc decoration, characterized by elaborate stonework from door tops to the roofline. Fray Cogullado, who named the Nunnery, also gave this building its name. The Governor's Palace may have been just that—the administrative center of the Xiú principality, which included the region around Uxmal. It probably had astrological significance as well. For years, scholars pondered why this building was constructed slightly turned from adjacent buildings. Originally they thought the strange alignment was because of the *sacbe* (ceremonial road) that starts at this building and ends 11 miles distant at the ancient city of Kabah. But recently scholars of archaeoastronomy (a relatively new science) discovered that the central doorway, which is larger than the others, is in perfect alignment with Venus.

Before you leave the Governor's Palace, note the elaborately stylized headdress patterned in stone over the central doorway. As you stand back from the building on the east side, note how the 103 stone masks of Chaac undulate across the facade like a serpent and end at the corners where there are columns of masks.

The Great Pyramid   A massive, partially restored nine-level structure, it has interesting motifs of birds, probably macaws, on its facade, as well as a huge mask. The view from the top is wonderful.

The Dovecote   It wasn't built to house doves, but it could well do the job in its lacy roofcomb—a kind of false front on a rooftop. The building is remarkable in that roofcombs weren't a common feature of temples in the Puuc hills, although you'll see one (of a very different style) on El Mirador at Sayil.

ACCOMMODATIONS

Unlike Chichén-Itzá, which has several classes of hotels from which to choose, Uxmal has (with one exception) only one type: comfortable but expensive. Less expensive rooms are also available in nearby Ticul.

EXPENSIVE

Hotel Hacienda Uxmal

Km 80 Carretera Mérida-Uxmal, Uxmal, Yuc. 97840. ☎ and fax **99/49-4754.** 75 rms (all with bath). A/C (21) or FAN (54). $114 double. $121 suite. Free guarded parking. For reservations contact Mayaland Resorts, Hotel Casa del Balam, Calle 60 at Calle 57 (Apdo. Postal 407), Av. Mérida, Yuc. 97000; ☎ 99/23-685 or 800/235-4079 in the U.S.; fax 99/ 24-6290.

One of my favorites, this is also the oldest hotel in Uxmal. Located on the highway across from the ruins, it was built as the headquarters for the archaeological staff years ago. Rooms are large and airy, exuding an impression of a well-kept yesteryear, with patterned tile floors, heavy furniture, and well-screened windows. All rooms have ceiling fans, and TVs are being added. Guest rooms surround a handsome central garden courtyard with towering royal palms, a bar, and a pool. Other facilities include a dining room and gift shop. Meals are expensive here: Breakfast costs $4 to $6; lunch $7 to $11; dinner, $9 to $15. A guitar trio usually plays on the open patio in the evenings. Checkout time is 1pm, so you can spend the morning at the ruins and take a swim before you hit the road again. It's on the highway opposite the road entrance to the ruins.

Mayaland Resorts, owners of the hotel, offers tour packages that include free car rentals for the nights you spend in its hotels. Car rental is free, but there's a daily insurance charge, which for a Volkswagen Beetle is $18 per day. They also have Ford Escorts at a higher price. Mayaland also has a transfer service between the hotel and Mérida for about $30 one way.

Villa Arqueológica

Ruinas Uxmal, Uxmal. Yuc. 97844. ☎ **99/49-6284** or 800/258-2633 in the U.S. Fax 99/ 49-5961. 40 rms and 3 suites. A/C. $102 double. Free guarded parking.

A Club Med operation, the Villa Arqueológica boasts a beautiful two-story layout around a plant-filled patio and a pool. It also offers a tennis court, a library, and an audiovisual show on the ruins in English, French, and Spanish. Each of the serene rooms has two oversize single beds. French-inspired meals are a la carte only and cost $6–$8 for breakfast and $5.75–$10 for lunch or dinner. It's easy to find— follow the signs to the Uxmal ruins, then turn left to the hotel just before the parking lot at the Uxmal ruins.

INEXPENSIVE

Rancho Uxmal

Km 70 Carretera Mérida-Uxmal, Uxmal, Yuc. 97840. No local phone. 20 rms (all with bath). A/C or FAN. $18–$24 double; $4 per person campsite. Free guarded parking. For reservations contact Sr. Macario Cach Cabrera, Calle 26 #156, Ticul, Yuc. 97860; ☎ 997/ 2-0277 or 99/23-1576.

This modest little hotel is an exception to the high-priced places near Uxmal, and it gets better every year. Air-conditioning has been added to ten of the rooms, all of which have good screens, hot-water showers, and 24-hour electricity. The restaurant is good; a full meal of poc chuc, rice, beans, and tortillas costs about $5.75, and breakfast is $2.25–$3. It's a long hike to the ruins from here, but the manager will help you flag down a passing bus or combi or even drive you himself if he has time. A primitive campground out back offers electrical hookups and use of a shower. The hotel is 2¼ miles north of the ruins on Highway 261.

DINING

Besides the hotel restaurants mentioned above and the restaurant at the visitor's center, there are few other dining choices.

Café-Bar Nicte-Ha

In the Hotel Hacienda Uxmal, across the highway from the turnoff to the ruins. ☎ 99/24-7142. Soups and salads $2–$4; pizzas and enchiladas $6; main courses $7–8; fixed-price lunch $9. Daily 1–8pm. MEXICAN.

This small restaurant attached to the Hotel Hacienda Uxmal is visible from the crossroads entrance to the ruins. The food is decent, though the prices tend to be high. If you eat here, take full advantage of the experience and spend a few hours by the pool near the café—use is free to customers. This is a favorite spot for bus tours, so come early.

EXCURSIONS: THE PUUC MAYA ROUTE & VILLAGE OF OXKUTZCAB

South and east of Uxmal are several other Maya cities worth exploring. Though smaller in scale than either Uxmal or Chichén-Itzá, each has gems of Maya architecture. The facade of masks on the Palace of Masks at **Kabah,** the enormous palace at **Sayil,** and the fantastic caverns of **Loltún** may be among the high points of your trip. Also along the way are the **Xlapak** and **Labná** ruins, and the pretty village of **Oxkutzcab.**

Note: All these sites are currently undergoing excavation and reconstruction, and some buildings may be roped off when you visit. And for photographers: You'll find afternoon light the best.

Kabah is 17 miles southeast of Uxmal. From there it's only a few miles to Sayil. Xlapak is almost walking distance (through the jungle) from Sayil, and Labná is just a bit farther east. A short drive beyond Labná brings you to the caves of Loltún. And Oxkutzcab is at the road's intersection with Highway 184, which can be followed west to Ticul or east all the way to Felipe Carillo Puerto.

If you are driving, between Labná and Loltún you'll find a road and a sign pointing north to Tabi. A few feet west of this road is a narrow dry-weather track leading into the seemingly impenetrable jungle. A bit over a mile up this track, the jungle opens to remains of the fabulous old henequen-producing **Hacienda Tabí.** The hewn-rock, two-story main house extends almost the length of a city block, with the living quarters above and storage and space for carriages below. In places it looks ready to collapse. Besides the house, you'll see the ruined chapel, remnants of tall chimneys, and broken machinery. Though not a formal public site, the caretaker will ask you to sign a guestbook and allow you to wander around the hulking ruins—without climbing to the second story.

If you aren't driving, a daily bus from Mérida goes to all these sites, with the exception of Loltún and Tabí. (See "By Bus" under "Getting There & Departing," in Mérida, above, for more details.)

KABAH If you're off to Kabah, head southwest on Highway 261 to Santa Elena (8¹/₂ miles), then south to Kabah (8 miles). The ancient city of Kabah is on both sides along the highway. Make a right turn into the parking lot.

The most outstanding building at Kabah is the huge **Palace of Masks,** or Codz Poop ("rolled-up mat"), named for a motif in its decoration. You'll notice it first on the right up on a terrace. Its outstanding feature is the Chenes-style facade, completely covered in a repeated pattern of 250 masks of the rain god Chaac, each one with curling remnants of Chaac's elephant-trunk-like nose. There's nothing like this facade in all of Maya architecture. For years stone-carved parts of this building lay lined up in the weeds like pieces of a puzzle awaiting the master puzzlemaker to put them into place. Now workers are positioning the parts, including the broken roofcomb, in place. Sculptures from this building are in the museums of anthropology in Mérida and Mexico City.

Once you've seen the Palace of Masks, you've seen the best of Kabah. But you should take a look at the other buildings. Just behind and to the left of the Codz Poop is the **Palace Group** (also called the East Group), with a fine Puuc-style colonnaded facade. Originally it had 32 rooms. On the front you see seven doors, two divided by columns, a common feature of Puuc architecture. Recent restoration has added a beautiful L-shaped colonnaded extension to the left front. Further restoration is underway at Kabah, so there may be more to see when you arrive.

Across the highway, a large, conical dirt-and-rubble mound (on your right) was once the **Great Temple,** or Teocalli. Past it is a **great arch,** which was much wider at one time and may have been a monumental gate into the city. A sacbe linked this arch to a point at Uxmal. Compare this corbeled arch to the one at Labná (below), which is in much better shape.

The site is open daily from 8am to 5pm. Admission is $3.25, free on Sunday; use of a video camera at any time costs $8.

SAYIL Just about 3 miles south of Kabah is the turnoff (left, which is east) to Sayil, Xlapak, Labná, Loltún, and Oxkutzcab. And 2¹/₂ miles along this road are the ruins of Sayil (which means "place of the ants").

Sayil is famous for **El Palacio,** the tremendous 100-plus-room palace that's a masterpiece of Maya architecture. Impressive for its simplistic grandeur, the building's facade, stretching three terraced levels, is breathtaking. Its rows of columns and colonettes give it a Minoan appearance. On the second level, notice the upside-down stone figure of the diving god of bees and honey over the doorway; the same motif was used at Tulum several centuries later. From the top of El Palacio there is a great view of the Puuc hills. Sometimes it's difficult to tell which are hills and which are unrestored pyramids, since little temples peep out at unlikely places from the jungle. The large circular basin on the ground below the palace is an artificial catch basin for a chultún (cistern) because this region has no natural cenotes (wells) to catch rainwater.

In the jungle past El Palacio is **El Mirador,** a small temple with an oddly slotted roofcomb. Beyond El Mirador, a crude **stele** has a phallic idol carved on it in greatly exaggerated proportions.

The site is open daily from 8am to 5pm. Admission is $3.50, free on Sunday. Video camera use is $8.

XLAPAK Xlapak (pronounced "Shla-pahk") is a small site with one building; it's 3¹/₂ miles down the road from Sayil. The **Palace at Xlapak** bears the masks of the rain god Chaac. It's open daily from 8am to 5pm, and the admission is $2.25 (free on Sunday); use of your video camera costs an additional $8.

LABNÁ   Labná, which dates to between A.D. 600 and 900, is 18 miles from Uxmal and only $1^3/_4$ miles past Xlapak. Like other archaeological sites in the Yucatán, it's also undergoing significant restoration and conservation. Descriptive placards fronting the main buildings are in Spanish, English, and German.

The first thing you see on the left as you enter is **El Palacio,** a magnificent Puuc-style building much like the one at Sayil but in poorer condition. There is an enormous mask of Chaac over a doorway with big banded eyes, a huge snout nose, and jagged teeth around a small mouth that seems on the verge of speaking. Jutting out on one corner is a highly stylized serpent's mouth out of which pops a human head with a completely calm expression. From the front you can gaze out to the enormous grassy interior grounds flanked by vestiges of unrestored buildings and jungle.

From El Palacio you can walk across the interior grounds on a newly reconstructed sacbe leading to Labná's **corbeled arch,** famed for its ornamental beauty and for its representation of what many such arches must have looked like at other sites. This one has been extensively restored, although only remnants of the roofcomb can be seen, and it was part of a more elaborate structure which is completely gone. Chaac's face is on the corners of one facade, and stylized Maya huts are fashioned in stone above the doorways.

You pass through the arch to **El Mirador,** or **El Castillo,** as the rubble-formed, pyramid-shaped structure is called. Towering on the top is a singular room crowned with a roofcomb etched against the sky.

There's a refreshment/gift stand with restrooms at the entrance. The site is open daily from 8am to 5pm. Admission is $3 (free on Sunday); use of a personal video or still camera is $8.

LOLTÚN   The caverns of Loltún are $18^1/_2$ miles past Labná on the way to Oxkutzcab, on the left side of the road. The fascinating caves, home of ancient Maya, were also used as a refuge and fortress during the War of the Castes (1847-1901). Inside, examine statuary, wall carvings and paintings, chultúnes (cisterns), and other signs of Maya habitation, but the grandeur and beauty of the caverns alone are impressive. In front of the entrance is an enormous stone phallus. The cult of the phallic symbol originated south of Veracruz and appeared in the Yucatán between A.D. 200 and 500.

The entrance fee is $5.25 Monday to Saturday and $2 on Sunday; $1^1/_2$-hour tours in Spanish are given daily at 9:30 and 11am and 12:30, 2, and 3pm and are included in the price. Before going on a tour, confirm these times at the information desk at Uxmal.

Impressions

The architects of pre-Columbian America were more fortunate than most of those of Europe. Their masterpieces were never condemned to invisibility, but stood magnificently isolated, displaying their three dimensions to all beholders. European cathedrals were built within the walls of cities; the temples of the aboriginal American seem, in most cases, to have stood outside.

—Aldous Huxley, *Beyond the Mexique Bay,* 1934

To return to Mérida from Loltún, drive the $4^1/_2$ miles to Oxkutzcab and from there go northwest on Highway 184. It's 12 miles to Ticul, and (turning north onto Highway 261 at Muna) 65 miles to Mérida.

OXKUTZCAB

Oxkutzcab (pronounced "Ohsh-kootz-KAHB"), seven miles from Loltún, is the heartland of the Yucatán's fruit-growing region, particularly oranges. The tidy village of 21,000, centered around a beautiful 16th-century church and the market, is worth a stop if for no other reason than to eat at Su Cabaña Suiza (see below) before heading back to Mérida, Uxmal, or Ticul.

During the last week in October and first week in November is the **Orange Festival,** when the village goes nuts with a carnival and orange displays in and around the central plaza.

Dining
Su Cabaña Suiza
Calle 54 no. 101. ☎ **997/5-0457.** Main dishes $3; soft drinks or orange juice 75¢. Daily 7:30am–6:30pm. CHARCOAL-GRILLED MEAT/MEXICAN.

It's worth a trip from Loltún, Ticul, or Uxmal just to taste the delicious charcoal-grilled meat at this unpretentious eatery dripping with colorful plants. Park in the gravel courtyard, then take a seat at one of the metal tables either under the palapa roof or outdoors where caged birds sing. Señora María Antónia Puerto de Pacho runs the spotless place with an iron hand, and family members provide swift, friendly service. The primary menu items include filling portions of charcoal-grilled beef, pork, or chicken served with salad, rice, tortillas, and a bowl of delicious bean soup. But you can also find a few Yucatecan specialties, such as costillos entomatados, escabeche, queso relleno, and pollo pibil. The restaurant is between Calles 49 and 51 in a quiet neighborhood three blocks south of the main square.

4 The Ruins of Chichén-Itzá & Village of Pisté

112 miles SW of Cancún, 75 miles SE of Mérida

The fabled pyramids and temples of Chichén-Itzá are the Yucatán's best-known ancient monuments. You must go, since you can't say you've *really* seen the Yucatán until you've gazed at the towering El Castillo, seen the sun from the Maya observatory called El Caracol, or shivered on the brink of the gaping cenote that may have served as the sacrificial well.

This Maya city was established by Itzáes perhaps sometime during the ninth century A.D. Linda Schele and David Friedel, in *A Forest of Kings* (Morrow, 1990), have cast doubt on the legend that Kukulkán (called Quetzalcoatl by the Toltecs—a name also associated with a legendary god) came here from the Toltec capital of Tula, and, along with Putún Maya coastal traders, built a magnificent metropolis that combined the Maya Puuc style with Toltec motifs (the feathered serpent, warriors, eagles, and jaguars). Not so, say Schele and Friedel. Readings of Chichén's bas-reliefs and hieroglyphs fail to support that legend and instead shows that Chichén-Itzá was a continuous Maya site which was influenced by association with the Toltecs but not by an invasion. Kukulkán's role in the Yucatán is once again in question.

Though it's possible to make a round trip from Mérida to Chichén-Itzá in one day, it will be a long, tiring, and very rushed day.

Try to spend at least one night at Chichén-Itzá (you'll actually stay in the nearby village of Pisté) or two if you can and take your time seeing the ruins in the cool of the morning or the afternoon after 3pm; take a siesta during the midday heat. The next morning, get to the ruins early; when the heat of the day approaches, catch a bus to your next destination. This may involve paying the admission fee more than once (unless you're there on a Sunday, when it's free), but the experience is worth it. Day-trip groups generally arrive when it's beginning to get hot, rushing through this marvelous ancient city in order to catch another bus or have lunch.

ESSENTIALS

GETTING THERE & DEPARTING **By Plane** Day-trips on charter flights from Cancún and Cozumel can be arranged by travel agents in the U.S. or in Cancún.

By Bus From Mérida, first-class **ADO buses** leave at 7:30am and 3:30pm. If you go round trip in a day (a 2¹/₂-hour trip one way), take the 8:45am bus and reserve a seat on the return bus. There are direct buses to Cancún at 11:15am and 6pm and to Mérida at 3pm. De paso buses to Mérida leave hourly day and night, as do those to Valladolid and Cancún.

By Car Chichén-Itzá is on the main Highway 180 between Mérida and Cancún.

ORIENTATION **Arriving** You'll arrive in the village of Pisté, at the bus station next to the Pirámide Inn. From Pisté there's a sidewalk to the archaeological zone, which is a mile or so east of the bus station.

City Layout The small town of **Pisté,** where most hotels and restaurants are located, is about a mile and a half from the ruins of Chichén-Itzá. Public buses from Mérida, Cancún, Valladolid and elsewhere discharge passengers here. A few hotels are at the edge of the ruins, and one, the **Hotel Dolores Alba** (see "Accommodations," below), is out of town about 1¹/₂ miles from the ruins on the road to Valladolid.

Fast Facts The **telephone area code** is 985.

EXPLORING THE RUINS

The site occupies four square miles, and it takes a strenuous full day (from 8am to noon and 2 to 5pm) to see all the ruins, which are open daily from 8am to 5pm. Service areas are open from 8am to 10pm. Admission is $6, free for children under 12 and free for all on Sunday and holidays. A permit to use your own video costs an additional $8. Parking costs $1. *You can use your ticket to reenter on the same day, but you'll have to pay again for another day.*

The huge visitor center, at the main entrance where you pay the admission charge, is beside the parking lot and consists of a museum, an auditorium, a restaurant, a bookstore, and restrooms. You can see the site on your own or with a licensed guide who speaks either English or Spanish. These guides are usually waiting at the entrance and charge around $30 for one to six people. Although the guides frown on it, there's nothing wrong with your approaching a group of people who speak the same language and asking if they would like to share a guide with you. The guide, of course, would like to get $30 from you alone and $30 each from other individuals who don't know one another and still form a group. Don't believe all the history they spout—some of it is just plain out-of-date, but the architectural details they point out are enlightening.

Chichén-Itzá Archeological Site

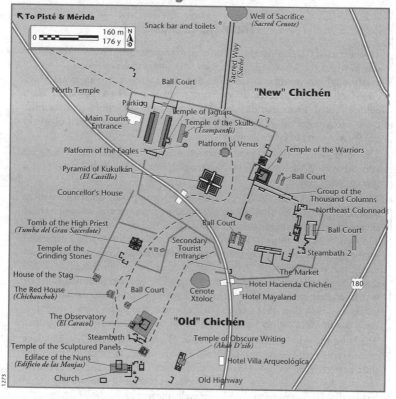

Chichén-Itzá's light-and-sound show was completely revamped in 1993, and is well worth seeing. The Spanish version is shown nightly at 7pm and costs $2.50; the English version is at 9pm and costs $3. The show may be offered in French and German as well. Ask at your hotel.

There are actually two parts of Chichén-Itzá (which dates from around A.D. 600 to 900). There's the northern (new) zone, which shows distinct Toltec influence, and the southern (old) zone, which is mostly Puuc architecture.

El Castillo   As you enter from the tourist center, the beautiful 75-foot El Castillo pyramid will be straight ahead across a large open area. It was built with the Maya calendar in mind. There are 364 stairs plus a platform to equal 365 (days of the year), 52 panels on each side (which represent the 52-year cycle of the Maya calendar), and 9 terraces on each side of the stairways (for a total of 18 terraces, which represents the 18-month Maya solar calendar). If this isn't proof enough of the mathematical precision of this temple, come for the spring or fall equinox (March 21 or September 21 between 3 and 5pm). On those days, the seven stairs of the northern stairway and the serpent-head carving at the base are touched with sunlight and become a "serpent" formed by the play of light and shadow. It appears to descend into the earth as the sun hits each stair from the top, ending with the serpent head. To the Maya this was a fertility symbol: The golden sun had entered the earth, meaning it was time to plant the corn.

The Maya Calendar

To understand Chichén-Itzá fully, you need to know something about the unique way in which the Maya kept time on several simultaneous calendars.

Although not more accurate than our own calendar, the intricate Maya calendar systems begin, according to many scholars, in 3114 B.C.—before Maya culture existed. From that date, the Maya could measure time—and their life cycle—to a point 90 million years in the future! They conceived of world history as a series of cycles moving within cycles.

The Solar Year　The Maya solar year measured 365.24 days. Within that solar year there were 18 "months" of 20 days each, for a total of 360 days, plus a special 5-day period.

The Ceremonial Year　A ceremonial calendar, completely different from the solar calendar, ran its "annual" cycle at the same time, but this was not a crude system like the Gregorian calendar, which has saints' days, some fixed feast days, and some movable feasts. It was so intricate that the ordinary Maya depended on the priests to keep track of it. Complex and ingenious, the ceremonial calendar system consisted of 13 "months" of 20 days; but within that cycle of 260 days was another of 20 "weeks" of 13 days. The Maya ceremonial calendar interlaced exactly with the solar calendar. Each date of the solar calendar had a name, and each date of the ceremonial calendar also had a name; therefore, every day in Maya history has two names, which were always quoted together.

The Double Cycle　After 52 solar years and 73 ceremonial "years," during which each day had its unique, unduplicated double name, these calendars ended their respective cycles simultaneously on the very same day, and a brand-new, identical double cycle began. Thus, in the longer scheme of things, a day would be identified by the name of the 52-year cycle, the name of the solar day, and the name of the ceremonial day.

Mystic Numbers　As you can see, several numbers were of great significance to the system. The number 20 was perhaps most important, as calendar calculations were done with a number system with base 20. There were 20 "suns" (days) to a "month," 20 years to a katun, and 20 katuns (20 times 20, or 400 years) to a baktun.

The number 52 was of tremendous importance, for it signified, literally, the "end of time," the end of the double cycle of solar and ceremonial calendars. At the beginning of a new cycle, temples were rebuilt for the "new age," which is why so many Maya temples and pyramids hold within them the structures of earlier, smaller temples and pyramids.

The Maya Concept of Time　The Maya considered time not as "progress" but as the wheel of fate, spinning endlessly, determining one's destiny by the combinations of attributes given to days in the solar and ceremonial calendars. The rains came on schedule, the corn was planted on schedule, and the celestial bodies moved in their great dance under the watchful eye of Maya astronomers and astrologers.

As evidence of the Maya obsession with time, Chichén's most impressive structure, El Castillo, is an enormous "timepiece."

El Castillo, also called the Pyramid of Kukulkán, was built over an earlier structure. A narrow stairway entered at the western edge of the north staircase leads into the structure, where there is a sacrificial altar-throne—a red jaguar encrusted with jade. The stairway is open at 11am and 3pm and is claustrophobic, usually crowded, humid, and uncomfortable. A visit early in the day is best. No photos of the figure are allowed.

Main Ball Court (Juego de Pelota)   Northwest of El Castillo is Chichén's main ball court, the largest and best preserved anywhere, and only one of nine ball courts built in this city. Carved on both walls of the ball court are scenes showing Maya figures dressed as ball players decked out in heavy protective padding. The carved scene also shows a headless player kneeling with blood shooting from the neck; the player is looked upon by another player holding the head.

Players on two teams tried to knock a hard rubber ball through one or the other of the two stone rings placed high on either wall, using only their elbows, knees, and hips (no hands). According to legend, the losing players paid for defeat with their lives. However, some experts say the victors were the only appropriate sacrifices for the gods. Either way, the game must have been exciting, heightened by the marvelous acoustics of the ball court.

The North Temple   Temples are at both ends of the ball court. The North Temple has sculptured pillars and more sculptures inside, as well as badly ruined murals. The acoustics of the ball court are so good that from the North Temple a person speaking can be heard clearly at the opposite end about 450 feet away.

Temple of Jaguars   Near the southeastern corner of the main ball court is a small temple with serpent columns and carved panels showing warriors and jaguars. Up the flight of steps and inside the temple, a mural was found that chronicles a battle in a Maya village.

Temple of the Skulls (Tzompantli)   To the right of the ball court is the Temple of the Skulls with rows of skulls carved into the stone platform. When a sacrificial victim's head was cut off, it was stuck on a pole and displayed in a tidy row with others. As a symbol of the building's purpose, the architects provided these rows of skulls. Also carved into the stone are pictures of eagles tearing hearts from human victims. The word "Tzompantli" is not Maya but came from central Mexico. Reconstruction using scattered fragments may add a level to this platform and change the look of this structure by the time you visit.

Platform of the Eagles   Next to the Tzompantli, this small platform has reliefs showing eagles and jaguars clutching human hearts in their talons and claws, as well as a head coming out of the mouth of a serpent.

Platform of Venus   East of the Tzompantli and north of El Castillo near the road to the Sacred Cenote is the Platform of Venus. In Maya-Toltec lore, Venus was represented by a feathered monster or a feathered serpent with a human head in its mouth. It's also called the tomb of Chaac-Mool because a Chaac-Mool figure was discovered "buried" within the structure.

Sacred Cenote   Follow the dirt road (actually an ancient sacbe) that heads north from the Platform of Venus, and after five minutes you'll come to the great natural well that may have given Chichén-Itzá (the Well of the Itzáes) its name. This well was used for ceremonial purposes, not for drinking water, and according to legend, sacrificial victims were drowned in this pool to honor the rain god Chaac.

Anatomical research done early this century by Ernest A. Hooten showed that bones of both children and adults were found in the well. Judging from Hooten's evidence, they may have been outcasts, diseased, or feeble-minded.

Edward Thompson, American consul in Mérida and a Harvard professor, bought the ruins of Chichén early this century, explored the cenote with dredges and divers, and exposed a fortune in gold and jade. Most of the riches wound up in Harvard's Peabody Museum of Archeology and Ethnology. Later excavations in the 1960s brought up more treasure, and studies of the recovered objects show offerings from throughout the Yucatán and even farther away.

Temple of the Warriors (Templo de los Guerreros) Due east of El Castillo is one of the most impressive structures at Chichén—the Temple of the Warriors—named for the carvings of warriors marching along its walls. It's also called the **Group of the Thousand Columns** for the many columns flanking it. During the recent restoration, hundreds more of the columns were rescued from the rubble and put in place, setting off the temple more magnificently than ever. Climb up the steep stairs at the front to reach a figure of Chaac-Mool and several impressive columns carved in relief to look like enormous feathered serpents. South of the temple was a square building called by archaeologists the market (mercado). Its central court is surrounded by a colonnade. Beyond the temple and the market in the jungle are mounds of rubble, parts of which are being reconstructed.

The main Mérida-Cancún highway used to run straight through the ruins of Chichén, and though it has now been diverted, you can still see the great swath it cut. South and west of the old highway's path are more impressive ruined buildings.

Tomb of the High Priest (Tumba del Gran Sacerdote) Past the refreshment stand to the right of the path is the Tomb of the High Priest, which stood atop a natural limestone cave in which skeletons and offerings were found, giving the temple its name.

This building is being reconstructed, and workers are unearthing other smaller temples in the area. As the work progresses, some buildings may be roped off and others will open to the public for the first time.

House of Metates (Casa de los Metates) This building, the next one on your right, is named after the concave corn-grinding stones used by the Maya.

Temple of the Deer (Templo del Venado) Past the House of Metates is this fairly tall though ruined building. The relief of a stag that gave the temple its name is long gone.

Little Holes (Chichan-chob) This next temple has a roofcomb with little holes, three masks of the rain god Chaac, three rooms, and a good view of the surrounding structures. It's one of the older buildings at Chichén, built in the Puuc style during the Late Classic Period.

Observatory (El Caracol) Construction of the Observatory, a complex building with a circular tower, was carried out over a long period of time. Without a doubt, the additions and modifications reflected the Maya's increasing knowledge of celestial movements and their need for increasingly exact measurements. Through slits in the tower's walls, Maya astronomers could observe the cardinal directions and the approach of the all-important spring and autumn equinoxes, as well as the summer solstice. The temple's name, which means "snail," comes from a spiral staircase, now closed off, within the structure.

On the east side of El Caracol, a path leads north into the bush to the **Cenote Xtoloc,** a natural limestone well that provided the city's daily water supply. If you see any lizards sunning there, they may well be *xtoloc,* the lizard for which the cenote is named.

Temple of Panels (Templo de los Tableros)   Just to the south of El Caracol are the ruins of a **steambath** (Temazcalli) and the Temple of Panels, named for the carved panels on top. This temple was once covered by a much larger structure, only traces of which remain.

Edifice of the Nuns (Edificio de las Monjas)   If you've visited the Puuc sites of Kabah, Sayil, Labná, or Xlapak, the enormous nunnery here will remind you at once of the "palaces" at the other sites. Built in the Late Classic Period, the new edifice was constructed over an older one. Suspecting that this was so, Le Plongeon, an archaeologist working earlier in this century, put dynamite in between the two and blew part of the newer building to smithereens, thereby revealing part of the old. You can still see the results of Le Plongeon's indelicate exploratory methods.

On the eastern side of the Edifice of the Nuns is an annex (Anexo Este) constructed in highly ornate Chenes style with Chaac masks and serpents.

The Church (La Iglesia)   Next to the annex is one of the oldest buildings at Chichén, ridiculously named The Church. Masks of Chaac decorate two upper stories. Look closely and you'll see among the crowd of Chaacs an armadillo, a crab, a snail, and a tortoise. These represent the Maya gods called bacab, whose job it was to hold up the sky.

Temple of Obscure Writing (Akab Dzib)   This temple is along a path east of the Edifice of the Nuns. Above a door in one of the rooms are some Maya glyphs which gave the temple its name, since the writings have yet to be deciphered. In other rooms, traces of red handprints are still visible. Reconstructed and expanded over the centuries, this building has parts that are very old; it may well be the oldest building at Chichén.

Old Chichén (Chichén Viejo)   For a look at more of Chichén's oldest buildings, constructed well before the time of Toltec influence, follow signs from the Edifice of the Nuns southwest into the bush to Old Chichén, about half a mile away. Be prepared for this trek with long trousers, insect repellent, and a local guide. The attractions here are the **Temple of the First Inscriptions** (Templo de los Inscripciones Iniciales), with the oldest inscriptions discovered at Chichén, and the restored **Temple of the Lintels** (Templo de los Dinteles), a fine Puuc building.

ACCOMMODATIONS
EXPENSIVE

Hacienda Chichén-Itzá

Zona Arqueológica, Chichén-Itzá, Yuc. 97751. ☎ **985/6-2513** or 6-2462. 18 rms (all with bath). FAN. $66 double. Closed off-season. For reservations contact Casa del Balam, Calle 60 no. 48, Mérida, Yuc. 97000; ☎ 99/24-8844 or 800/624-8451 in the U.S.; fax 99/24-5011.

A romantic hotel a short walk from the back entrance to the ruins, the Hacienda Chichén-Itzá consists of bungalows built years ago for those who were excavating the ruins. Each cottage is named for an early archeologist working at Chichén. There's a pool open to those who drop in for lunch. The dining room is outside under the hacienda portals overlooking the grounds. But any meal is expensive: Breakfast is $7, lunch around $14, and dinner $20.

The hacienda is closed from May through October, though the owners were reconsidering this policy and it may be open year-round. It's often booked solid in the high season; advance reservations are strongly recommended.

Hotel Mayaland

Zona Arqueológica, Chichén-Itzá, Yuc. 97751. ☎ **985/6-2777.** 164 rms (all with bath). A/C or FAN TV. High season $125 double. Low season $90–$100 double. Free guarded parking. For reservations contact Mayaland Resorts, Av. Colón 502, Mérida, Yuc. 97000; ☎ 99/25-2122 or 800/235-4079 in the U.S.; fax 99/25-7022.

In operation since the 1930s, this is a long-time favorite by the ruins. No other hotel quite captures the feel of a ruins experience with the front doorway framing El Caracol (the observatory) as you walk outside from the lobby. Rooms in the main building, connected by a wide, tiled veranda, have air-conditioning and TV, tiled baths (with tubs), and colonial-style furnishings. Romantic oval-shaped Maya huts with beautifully carved furniture, palapa roofs, and mosquito netting, are tucked around the wooded grounds. The grounds are gorgeous, with huge trees and blossoming ginger plants. There's a long pool and lounge area, and a restaurant that serves only fair meals at fixed prices, about $20 for a full lunch or dinner. You're better off ordering light meals and snacks by the pool or in the bar. Mayaland has a shuttle service between the hotel and Mérida for about $35 each way.

The Hotel Mayaland is a great bargain if you take advantage of their rental-car deal. If you stay at one of their hotels and rent a car through their office in Mérida or Cancún, your car rental is free with no minimum stay. There is a charge for car insurance, however.

Hotel Villa Arqueológica

Zona Arqueológica, Chichén-Itzá, Yuc. 97751. ☎ **985/6-2830** or 800/258-2633 in the U.S. 32 rms. A/C. $123 double.

Operated by Club Med, the Villa Arqueológica is almost next to the ruins and built around a swimming pool. The very comfortable rooms are like those at Uxmal and Cobá, each with two oversized single beds. There are tennis courts, and the hotel's rather expensive restaurant features French and Yucatecan food (breakfast is $15, lunch and dinner are $25 each).

MODERATE

Pirámide Inn

Carretera Mérida-Valladolid km 117, Pisté, Yuc. 97751. ☎ Caseta Pisté **985/6-2462** (leave a message). Fax 985/6-2671. 44 rms. A/C. $45 double.

Less than a mile from the ruins at the edge of Pisté, this hospitable inn has large motellike rooms equipped with two double beds or one king-size bed; but do check your mattress for its sag factor before accepting the room. Hot water comes on between 5 and 9am and 5 and 9pm. Water is purified in the tap for drinking. There is a pool in the midst of landscaped gardens, which include the remains of a pyramid wall. Try to get a room in the back if street noise bothers you. If you're coming from Valladolid it's on the left, and from Mérida look for it on the right.

INEXPENSIVE

✪ Hotel Dolores Alba

Km 122 Carretera Mérida-Valladolid, Yuc. 97751. No phone. 18 rms (all with bath). A/C or FAN. $16–$22 double. Free unguarded parking. For reservations contact Hotel Dolores Alba, Calle 63 no. 464, Mérida, Yuc. 97000; ☎ 99/28-5650; fax 99/28-3163.

You'll be a mile from the back entrance to the ruins and about two miles from Pisté if you stay at the Dolores Alba. The nice rooms are clean with matching furniture, tile floors and showers, and well-screened windows. There's a pool with palapa in front of the restaurant. The restaurant serves good meals at moderate prices. Breakfast (served between 7 and 9am) runs $2–$4, and main courses at dinner (7–9pm) are around $6–$8. But you should realize that when it comes to dining you have little choice—the nearest alternative restaurant or tienda where you can buy your own supplies is several miles away. Free transportation is provided to the ruins during visiting hours, but you'll have to get back on your own (about a 30-minute walk). A taxi from the ruins to the hotel costs about $6. The Dolores Alba in Mérida, also recommended, is owned by the same family, so either hotel will help you make reservations. The hotel is 1 1/2 miles past the ruins on the road going east to Cancún and Valladolid.

DINING

Reasonably priced meals are available at the restaurant in the visitor's center at the ruins. Hotels restaurants near the ruins are more expensive than the few in Pisté. In Pisté, however, most of the better spots cater to large groups, which converge on them for lunch after 1pm.

Puebla Maya

Carretera Mérida-Valladolid, Pisté. No phone. Fixed-price lunch buffet $9. Daily 1–5pm. MEXICAN.

Opposite the Pirámide Inn, the Puebla Maya looks just like its name, a Maya town with small white huts flanking a large open-walled palapa-topped center. Inside, however, you cross an artificial lagoon, planters drip with greenery, and live musicians play to the hundreds of tourists filling the tables. Service through the huge buffet is quick, so if you've been huffing around the ruins all morning, you have time to eat and relax before boarding the bus to wherever you're going. You can even swim in a lovely landscaped pool.

Restaurant Bar "Poxil"

Calle 15 s/n, Carretera Mérida-Valladolid, Pisté. ☎ 985/1-0123. Breakfast $3; main courses $3.50. Daily 7am–8pm. MEXICAN/REGIONAL.

A poxil is a Mayan fruit somewhat akin to a guayabana. Although this places doesn't actually serve them, what is on the menu is good, though not gourmet, and the price is right. You will find the Poxil near the west entrance to town on the south side of the street.

5 Valladolid

25 miles E of Chichén-Itzá & Pisté, 100 miles SW of Cancún

The somewhat sleepy town of Valladolid (pronounced "BYE-ah-doh-LEET"), 25 miles east of Pisté/Chichén-Itzá, is an inexpensive alternative to staying in Pisté near the ruins of Chichén. You can get an early bus from Mérida, spend the day at the ruins, then travel another hour to Valladolid to overnight.

ESSENTIALS

GETTING THERE & DEPARTING   By Bus   Buses leave almost hourly from Mérida, passing through Pisté and Chichén-Itzá on the way to Valladolid and Cancún. There are also regular buses from Cancún and at least six daily buses from

Playa del Carmen. Because of the frequency of buses to Mérida and Cancún, advance purchase of tickets isn't usually necessary.

Autotransportes Oriente (☎ 985/6-3449) offers de paso buses to Pisté (the town nearest the Chichén-Itzá ruins) every hour from 2am to midnight; these same buses go on to Mérida. De paso buses on this same line go to Cobá at 4:30am and 1pm. Buses to Tizimin leave every hour from 5am to 10pm. **Expresso de Oriente** buses (☎ 6-3630) go to Mérida six times daily, to Playa del Carmen six times daily, and to Cancún five times daily. **Autobuses del Centro del Estado** offers five daily buses to Tinum and several other small towns on the way to Mérida.

By Car From Valladolid, there are frequent signs directing you via the toll road (*cuota*) to Mérida ($11.50), Chichén-Itzá, or Cancún ($21). No signs point you to the free (*libre*) road, but don't despair. To take the free road to Pisté/Chichén-Itzá and Mérida, take Calle 39, a one-way street going west on the north side of the Parque Cantón (the main plaza); this becomes the free Highway 180. Calle 41, a one-way east-bound street on the south side of the zócalo, becomes the free highway to Cancún.

Highway 180 links Valladolid with both Cancún and Mérida. It's a good, well-marked road and goes right past the main square in town. If you come from the toll road, the exit road leads to the Parque Cantón (the main plaza).

ORIENTATION Information There is a small tourism office in the Palacio Municipal which will furnish you with some good information and maps. Señora Tete Mendoza B. is extremely helpful and knows her city and its history.

City Layout All hotels and restaurants are within walking distance of Valladolid's pretty **main square**, the **Parque Francisco Cantón Rosado**. The Valladolid **bus station** is at the corner of Calles 37 and 57, ten very long blocks from the parque and too far to haul heavy luggage. Taxis are usually in front of the station.

EXPLORING VALLADOLID

Valladolid was founded in 1543 on the shore of a lagoon near the coast. As it lacked good agricultural land, two years later it was moved to its present location on the site of a Maya religious center called Zací (meaning White Hawk). The Franciscans built an impressive monastery here, the **Convento de San Bernardino de Siena** (1552); the town boasts another half-dozen colonial churches, including the Templo de Santa Ana built in the 1500s originally for the exclusive use of the Maya. Two cenotes, one only two blocks east of the Parque Cantón, supplied water during colonial times. A small park, with a restaurant, a small bowl for the performing arts, and three Mayan-style stick-and-thatched-roof houses, has been created around the cenote Zací. These houses are meant to depict a typical Mayan settlement, and inside are some old photographs of Valladolid and a few arts and crafts for sale. **El Parroquia de San Servasio** (1545), the parish church, is on the south side of the main square, and the **Palacio Municipal** (Town Hall) is on the east.

SHOPPING Embroidered Maya dresses can be purchased at the **Mercado de Artesanías de Valladolid** at the corner of Calles 39 and 44 and from women around the main square. The latter also sell—of all things—Barbie-doll-size Maya dresses! Just ask "¿Vestidos para Barbie?" and out they come.

The **food market** is on Calle 32 between Calles 35 and 37. Though it's open other days, the main market time is Sunday morning, when it's most active.

ACCOMMODATIONS

Hotels (and restaurants) here are less crowded and less expensive than the competition in Chichén.

✪ Hotel El Mesón del Marqués

Calle 39 no. 203, Valladolid, Yuc. 97780. ☎ **985/6-3042** or 6-2073. Fax 985/6-2280. 38 rms (all with bath). A/C TV TEL. $28 double; $50 double, suite. Free interior, secure parking.

This comfortable colonial-era mansion-turned-hotel on the north side of the Parque Cantón opposite the church offers rooms in both the original 200-year-old mansion and a new addition built around a pool in back. There is always hot water, and most of the rooms are sheltered from city noise. On the first floor there's a travel agency, gift shop, and restaurant (see "Dining," below).

Hotel María de la Luz

Calle 42 no. 195, Valladolid, Yuc. 97780. ☎ and fax **985/6-2071**. 33 rms (all with bath). A/C FAN TV. $18 double. Free secure parking.

The two stories at the María de la Luz are built around an inner pool. The freshly painted rooms have been refurbished with new tile floors and baths and new mattresses. A couple of rooms have balconies overlooking the square. The wide interior covered walkway to the rooms is a nice place to relax in comfortable chairs. The hotel is on the west side of the Parque Francisco Cantón Rosado (the main square) between Calles 39 and 41.

Tinum: A Homestay in a Maya Village

Adventurous travelers should consider staying in Tinum, a 30-minute drive from Valladolid, to experience more authentic Maya life. Some years ago, Ms. Bettina McMakin Erdman left Miami to settle in the tiny village of Tinum. She learned the Maya language, became acquainted with the villagers, and soon hosted visitors interested in discovering exactly what it's like to live as the Maya still do.

Her 18-year tradition of hospitality continues, now carried on by Jacinto Pool Tuz, whom everyone knows as Don Chivo. He will arrange for you to board with a Maya family in their *na* (house of sticks with a thatched roof) and to eat with them and share their daily life. The cost, paid directly to the family, is about $10 per day. You'll need to bring a hammock to sleep on, or since nearly everyone here makes their own hammocks, you can write ahead to have one made and waiting for you in Tinum. A double-size hammock is best even for one person and costs $17 to $28 a piece. Be sure you realize that this is the real thing—you sleep in your hammock in a na with a dirt floor, cook on a fire, and use one of the two bathrooms in Doña Bettina's house. You're welcome for two or three nights.

To get to Tinum, take one of the five daily buses from Valladolid. The trip takes 40 minutes and costs 95¢. By car from Valladolid, head out toward Chichén-Itzá; just at the edge of town the road splits (straight ahead to Chichén, right to Tinum). The bus from Mérida leaves from the Progreso bus station.

When you arrive in town ask for directions to the home of Don Chivo; everyone knows him. Advance reservations are necessary; to make them, write Sr. Jacinto Pool "Don Chivo," Calle 24 no. 102A, Tinum, Yuc. 97750.

DINING

The lowest restaurant prices are found in the Bazar Municipal, a little arcade of shops beside the Hotel El Mesón del Marqués right on the main square.

Casa de Los Arcos Restaurant

Calle 39 no. 200A. ☎ **985/6-2467.** Breakfast $3; antojitos $3.50–$4.50; main courses $3.50–$7.50; comida corrida $5. Daily 7am–10pm (comida corrida served 1–4pm). MEXI-CAN/YUCATECAN.

A lovely, breezy courtyard with a black-and-white tiled floor makes this restaurant especially appealing. The hearty comida corrida might feature a choice of meat and include red beans, tortillas, and coffee. There's also a full menu of beef, chicken, seafood, and a few Mexican specialties, one of which is the delicious longaniza à la Valladolid. To reach the restaurant from the main square (with the Hotel El Mesón del Marqués on your left), take Calle 39 two blocks; the restaurant is on the right across from the Hotel Don Luís.

Hostería del Marqués

Calle 39 no. 203. ☎ **6-2073.** Breakfast $2–$4; Mexican plates $2–$3; main courses $4–$9; sandwiches $2–$3. Daily 7am–10:30pm. MEXICAN/YUCATECAN.

This place is part of the Hotel El Mesón del Marqués facing the main square. Its patrons often spill out of the air-conditioned dining room onto the hotel's open *portales* on the interior courtyard, where tables have fresh flowers and are festively decorated in hot pink and turquoise. It's definitely a popular place, often crowded at lunch. The guacamole is great.

EXCURSIONS FROM VALLADOLID

EKBALAM: NEWLY EXCAVATED MAYA RUINS   About 21 miles northeast of Valladolid is Ekbalam (which in Maya means "star jaguar"), a newly opened archaeological site. Excavations of these ruins, which date from 100 B.C. to A.D. 1200, are ongoing.

To get here from Valladolid, go north on Highway 259 for 11 miles. Watch for the sign pointing right to the village of **Hunuku** and turn right there, following the road for 8¹⁄₂ miles. When you reach Hunuku, a small village, ask someone to point to the dirt road that leads about 1¹⁄₂ miles to the ruins. Caretaker Felipe Tuz Cohuo or willing young children can point out the highlights (the children have absorbed a lot of information during the years the ruins have been excavated). A tip to the caretaker is greatly appreciated. Pencils or ballpoint pens are good gifts for the children.

To really get a lot out of this site, you should be prepared to climb up the mountainlike pyramids with sides made of loose dirt and even looser rocks. Some of the important parts can also be seen from the pathway, but climbing is much more rewarding.

You can park at the entry sign and walk from there. Located on 2,500 wooded acres, the buildings are grouped closely around a large central area; along 350 feet of the perimeter are the remains of two low walls. The largest building, called **Structure 1** or **The Tower,** is impressive for its dimensions—it's 100 feet high, 517 feet long, and 200 feet wide. From the top you can see the tallest building of Cobá, 30 miles southeast as the crow flies. Scholars believe that Ekbalam was the center of a vast agricultural region. From this lofty vantage point, all around you can see fertile land that still produces corn, cotton, and honey.

Structure 3, also called **The Palace of the Nuns,** has a row of corbel-arched rooms. Though greatly destroyed, this architecture resembles the Puuc style of other Yucatecan sites. A few badly weathered stelae fragments are on display under flimsy thatched coverings. Structures show partial walls, some made of irregular rocks and others of carefully fitted and cut rock. Sacbeob (causeways) fan out in several directions, but so far none is thought to go farther than a mile or so. If you do any climbing at all, seeing the area will take a minimum of two hours.

The site is open daily from 8am to 5pm. Admission is $3, free on Sunday. A video-camera permit costs $8.

RÍO LAGARTOS WILDLIFE REFUGE: NESTING FLAMINGOS   Some 50 miles north of Valladolid (25 miles north of Tizimin) on Highway 295 is Río Lagartos, a 118,000-acre refuge established in 1979 to protect the largest nesting population of flamingos in North America. Found in the park's dunes, mangrove swamps, and tropical forests are jaguars, ocelots, sea turtles, and at least 212 bird species (141 of which are permanent residents).

You can make the trip in one long day from Valladolid, but you'll have to leave by at least 5am to get to Río Lagartos by 7am, in time to arrange a trip to see the flamingos with one of the local boatmen. There's one poor-quality hotel in Río Lagartos, which I don't recommend. If you prefer to overnight closer to the refuge, then a good choice is **Tizimin** (pop. 50,000), 35 miles north of Valladolid. This pleasant city is the agricultural hub of the region. From Tizimin to Río Lagartos is about a 30-minute drive. Inexpensive hotels and restaurants are on or around Tizimin's main square.

Seeing the Río Lagartos Refuge   Río Lagartos is a small fishing village of around 3,000 people who make their living from the sea and from the occasional tourist who shows up to see the flamingos. Colorfully painted homes face the Malecón (the oceanfront street), and brightly painted boats dock along the same half-moon-shaped port. While Río Lagartos is interesting, if you have time for only one flamingo foray, make it in Celestún (west of Mérida). I've seen more flamingos and other kinds of birds at Celestún.

Plan to arrive in Río Lagartos around 7am and go straight to the dock area. There, boatmen will offer to take you on an hour-long trip to the flamingo lagoons for around $40 for up to six people in a motor-powered wooden boat. Ask around for Filiberto Pat Zem, a reliable boatman who takes the time to give a good tour.

Although thousands of flamingos nest near here from April to August, it is prohibited by law to visit their nesting grounds. Flamingos need mud with particular ingredients (including a high salt content) in order to multiply, and this area's mud does the trick. On your boat tour you'll probably see flamingos wading in the waters next to Mexico's second-largest salt-producing plant—the muddy bottom is plenty salty here. Flamingos use their special bills to suck up the mud, and they have the ability to screen the special contents they need from it. What you see on the boat trip is a mixture of flamingos, frigates, pelicans, herons in several colors, and ducks. Don't allow the boatman to frighten the birds into flight for your photographs; it causes the birds to eventually leave the habitat permanently.

Appendix

USING THE TELEPHONES

Area codes and city exchanges are being changed all over the country. If you have difficulty reaching a number, ask an operator for assistance. Mexico does not have helpful recordings to inform you of changes or new numbers.

Most **public pay phones** in the country have been converted to Ladatel phones, many of which are both coin and card operated. Instructions on the phones tell you how to use them. When your time limit for local calls is about to end (about three minutes), you'll hear three odd sounding beeps, and then you'll be cut off unless you deposit more coins. Ladatel cards come in denominations of 10, 20, and 30 New Pesos. If you're planning to make many calls, purchase the 30 New Peso card; it takes no time at all to use up a 10 peso card (about $1.65). They're sold at pharmacies, bookstores, and grocery stores near Ladatel phones. You insert the card, dial your number, and start talking, all the while watching a digital counter tick away your money.

Next is the *caseta de larga distancia* (long-distance telephone office), found all over Mexico. Most bus stations and airports now have specially staffed rooms exclusively for making long-distance calls and sending faxes. Often they are efficient and inexpensive, providing the client with a computer printout of the time and charges. In other places, often pharmacies, the clerk will place the call for you, then you step into a private booth to take the call. Whether it's a special long-distance office or a pharmacy, there's usually a service charge of around $3.50 to make the call, which you pay in addition to any call costs if you didn't call collect.

For **long-distance calls** you can access an English-speaking ATT operator by pushing the star button twice then 09. If that fails, try dialing 09 for an international operator. To call the United States or Canada tell the operator that you want a collect call (*una llamada por cobrar*) or station-to-station (*teléfono a teléfono*), or person-to-person (*persona a persona*). Collect calls are the least expensive of all, but sometimes caseta offices won't make them, so you'll have to pay on the spot.

To make a long-distance call from Mexico to another country, first dial 95 for the United States and Canada, or 98 for anywhere else in the world. Then, dial the area code and the number you are calling.

To call long distance (abbreviated "lada") within Mexico, dial 91, the area code, then the number. Mexico's area codes (claves) may be one, two, or three numbers and are usually listed in the front of telephone directories. In this book the area code is listed under "Fast Facts" for each town. (Area codes, however, are changing throughout the country.)

To place a phone call to Mexico from your home country, dial the international service (011), Mexico's country code (52), then the Mexican area code (for Cancún, for example, that would be 98), then the local number. Keep in mind that calls to Mexico are quite expensive, even if dialed direct from your home phone.

Better hotels, which have more sophisticated tracking equipment, may charge for each local call made from your room. Budget or moderately priced hotels often don't charge, since they can't keep track. To avoid check-out shock, it's best to ask in advance if you'll be charged for local calls. These cost between 50¢ and $1 per call. In addition, if you make a long-distance call from your hotel room, there is usually a hefty service charge added to the cost of the call.

POSTAL GLOSSARY

Airmail   Correo Aereo
Customs   Aduana
General Delivery   Lista de Correos
Insurance (insured mail)   Seguros
Mailbox   Buzón
Money Order   Giro Postale
Parcel   Paquete
Post Office   Oficina de Correos
Post Office Box (abbreviation)   Apdo. Postal
Postal Service   Correos
Registered Mail   Registrado
Rubber Stamp   Sello
Special Delivery, Express   Entrega Inmediata
Stamp   Estampilla or Timbre

B Basic Vocabulary

Most Mexicans are very patient with foreigners who try to speak their language; it helps a lot to know a few basic phrases.

I've included a list of certain simple phrases for expressing basic needs, followed by some common menu items.

ENGLISH-SPANISH PHRASES

English	Spanish	Pronunciation
Good Day	**Buenos días**	*bway*-nohss-*dee*-ahss
How are you?	**¿Cómo esta usted?**	*koh*-moh *ess*-tah oo-*sted*
Very well	**Muy bien**	mwee byen
Thank you	**Gracias**	*grah*-see-ahss
You're welcome	**De nada**	day *nah*-dah
Goodbye	**Adios**	ah-dyohss

Please	**Por favor**	pohr fah-*bohr*
Yes	**Sí**	see
No	**No**	noh
Excuse me	**Perdóneme**	pehr-*doh*-ney-may
Give me	**Déme**	*day*-may
Where is . . . ?	**¿Dónde esta . . . ?**	*dohn*-day *ess*-tah
the station	**la estación**	la ess-tah-see-*own*
a hotel	**un hotel**	oon oh-*tel*
a gas station	**una gasolinera**	oon-nuh gah-so-lee-nay-rah
a restaurant	**un restaurante**	oon res-tow-*rahn*-tay
the toilet	**el baño**	el *bahn*-yoh
a good doctor	**un buen médico**	oon bwayn *may*-dee-co
the road to	**el camino a . . .**	el cah-*mee*-noh ah
To the right	**A la derecha**	ah lah day-*ray*-chuh
To the left	**A la izquierda**	ah lah ees-ky-*ehr*-dah
Straight ahead	**Derecho**	day-*ray*-cho
I would like	**Quisiera**	keyh-see-*air*-ah
I want	**Quiero**	*kyehr*-oh
to eat	**comer**	*ko*-mayr
a room	**una habitación**	oon-nuh ha-bee tah-see-*own*
Do you have?	**¿Tiene usted?**	tyah-nay oos-*ted*
a book	**un libro**	oon *lee*-bro
a dictionary	**un diccionario**	oon deek-see-own-ar-eo
How much is it?	**¿Cuanto cuesta?**	*kwah*-to *kwess*-tah
When?	**¿Cuando?**	*kwah*-doh
What?	**¿Que?**	kay
There is (Is there?)	**¿Hay . . .**	eye
Yesterday	**Ayer**	ah-*yer*
Today	**Hoy**	oy
Tomorrow	**Mañana**	mahn-*yawn*-ah
Good	**Bueño**	*bway*-no
Bad	**Malo**	*mah*-lo
Better (best)	**(Lo) Mejor**	(loh) meh-*hor*
More	**Más**	mahs
Less	**Menos**	may-noss
No Smoking	**Se prohibe fumar**	seh pro-*hee*-beh foo-*mahr*
Postcard	**Tarjeta postal**	tahr-*hay*-ta pohs-*tahl*
Insect repellent	**Rapellante contra insectos**	rah-pey-*yahn*-te *cohn*-trah een-sehk-tos

MORE USEFUL PHRASES

Do you speak English? **¿Habla usted inglés?**

Is there anyone here who speaks English? **¿Hay alguien aquí qué hable inglés?**

I speak a little Spanish. **Hablo un poco de español.**

I don't understand Spanish very well. **No lo entiendo muy bien el español.**

The meal is good. **Me gusta la comida.**

What time is it? **¿Qué hora es?**

May I see your menu? **¿Puedo ver su menu?**

The check please. **La cuenta por favor.**

What do I owe you?. **¿Cuanto lo debo?**

What did you say?   **¿Mande? (colloquial expression for American "Eh?")**
I want (to see) a room   **Quiero (ver) un cuarto (una habitación)** ...
for two persons   **para dos personas**
with (without) bath.   **con (sin) baño.**
We are staying here only   **Nos quedaremos aqui solamente** ...
one night   **una noche**
one week.   **una semana.**
We are leaving tomorrow.   **Partimos mañana.**
Do you accept traveler's checks?   **¿Acepta usted cheques de viajero?**
Is there a laundromat near here?   **¿Hay una lavandería cerca de aquí?**
Please send these clothes to the laundry.   **Hágame el favor de mandar esta ropa a la lavandería.**

NUMBERS

1	**uno** (*ooh*-noh)		16	**dieciseis** (de-*ess*-ee-sayss)
2	**dos** (dohs)		17	**diecisiete** (de-*ess*-ee-*syeh*-tay)
3	**tres** (trayss)		18	**dieciocho** (dee-*ess*-ee-*oh*-choh)
4	**cuatro** (*kwah*-troh)		19	**diecinueve** (dee-*ess*-ee-*nway*-bay)
5	**cinco** (*seen*-koh)		20	**veinte** (*bayn*-tay)
6	**seis** (sayss)		30	**treinta** (*trayn*-tah)
7	**siete** (*syeh*-tay)		40	**cuarenta** (kwah-*ren*-tah)
8	**ocho** (*oh*-choh)		50	**cincuenta** (seen-*kwen*-tah)
9	**nueve** (*nway*-bay)		60	**sesenta** (say-*sen*-tah)
10	**diez** (dee-ess)		70	**setenta** (say-*ten*-tah)
11	**once** (*ohn*-say)		80	**ochenta** (oh-*chen*-tah)
12	**doce** (*doh*-say)		90	**noventa** (noh-*ben*-tah)
13	**trece** (*tray*-say)		100	**cien** (see-en)
14	**catorce** (kah-*tor*-say)		200	**doscientos** (*dos*-se-en-tos)
15	**quince** (*keen*-say)		500	**quinientos** (*keen*-ee-ehn-tos)
			1000	**mil** (meal)

BUS TERMS

Bus   **Autobus**
Bus or truck   **Camion**
Lane   **Carril**
Nonstop   **Directo**
Baggage (claim area)   **Equipajes**
Intercity   **Foraneo**
Luggage storage area   **Guarda equipaje**
Gates   **Llegadas**
Originates at this station   **Local**
Originates elsewhere; stops if seats available   **De Paso**
First class   **Primera**
Second class   **Segunda**
Nonstop   **Sin Escala**
Baggage claim area   **Recibo de Equipajes**
Waiting room   **Sala de Espera**
Toilets   **Sanitarios**
Ticket window   **Taquilla**

C Menu Glossary

Achiote   Small red seed of the annatto tree.

Achiote preparada   A prepared paste found in Yucatán markets made of ground achiote, wheat and corn flour, cumin, cinnamon, salt, onion, garlic, and oregano. Mixed with juice of a sour orange or vinegar and put on broiled or charcoaled fish (tikin chick) and chicken.

Agua fresca   Fruit-flavored water, usually watermelon, canteloupe, chia seed with lemon, hibiscus flour, or ground melon seed mixture.

Antojito   A Mexican snack, usually masa-based with a variety of toppings such as sausage, cheese, beans, onions; also refers to tostadas, sopes, and garnachas.

Atole   A thick, lightly sweet, warm drink made with finely ground rice or corn and usually flavored with vanilla.

Birria   Lamb or goat meat cooked in a tomato broth, spiced with garlic, chiles, cumin, ginger, oregano, cloves, cinnamon, and thyme and garnished with onions, cilantro, and fresh lime juice to taste; a specialty of Jalisco state.

Botana   A light snack—an antojito.

Buñelos   Round, thin, deep-fried crispy fritters dipped in sugar.

Cabrito   Grilled kid; a northern Mexican delicacy.

Carnitas   Pork that's been deep-cooked (not fried) in lard, then steamed and served with corn tortillas for tacos.

Ceviche   Fresh raw seafood marinated in fresh lime juice and garnished with chopped tomatoes, onions, chiles, and sometimes cilantro and served with crispy, fried whole corn tortillas.

Chiles rellenos   Poblano peppers usually stuffed with cheese, rolled in a batter and baked; other stuffings include ground beef spiced with raisins.

Choyote   Vegetable pear or merleton, a type of spiny squash boiled and served as an accompaniment to meat dishes.

Churro   Tube-shaped, bread-like fritter, dipped in sugar and sometimes filled with cajeta or chocolate.

Cochinita pibil   Pig wrapped in banana leaves, flavored with pibil sauce and pit-baked; common in Yucatán.

Corunda   A triangular tamal wrapped in a corn leaf, a Michoacan specialty.

Enchilada   Tortilla dipped in a sauce and usually filled with chicken or white cheese and sometimes topped with tomato sauce and sour cream (enchiladas Suizas—Swiss enchiladas), or covered in a green sauce (enchiladas verdes), or topped with onions, sour cream, and guacamole (enchiladas Potosiños).

Epazote   Leaf of the wormseed plant, used in black beans and with cheese in quesadillas.

Escabeche   A lightly pickled sauce used in Yucatecan chicken stew.

Frijoles charros   Beans flavored with beer, a northern Mexican specialty.

Frijoles refritos   Pinto beans mashed and cooked with lard.

Garnachas   A thickish small circle of fried masa with pinched sides, topped with pork or chicken, onions, and avocado or sometimes chopped potatoes, and tomatoes, typical as a botana in Veracruz and Yucatán.

Gorditas   Thickish fried-corn tortillas, slit and stuffed with choice of cheese, beans, beef, chicken, with or without lettuce, tomato, and onion garnish.

Gusanos de maguey   Maguey worms, considered a delicacy, and delicious when charbroiled to a crisp and served with corn tortillas for tacos.

Horchata Refreshing drink made of ground rice or melon seeds, ground almonds, and lightly sweetened.

Huevos Mexicanos Eggs with onions, hot peppers, tomatoes.

Huevos Motulenos Eggs atop a tortilla, garnished with beans, peas, ham, sausage, and grated cheese, a Yucatecan specialty.

Huevos rancheros Fried egg on top of a fried corn tortilla covered in a tomato sauce.

Huitlacoche Sometimes spelled "cuitlacoche," mushroom-flavored black fungus that appears on corn in the rainy season; considered a delicacy.

Machaca Shredded dried beef scrambled with eggs or as salad topping; a specialty of Northern Mexico.

Manchamantel Translated means "tablecloth stainer," a stew of chicken or pork with chiles, tomatoes, pineapple, bananas, and jícama.

Masa Ground corn soaked in lime used as basis for tamales, corn tortillas, and soups.

Mixiote Lamb baked in a chile sauce or chicken with carrots and potatoes both baked in parchment paper made from the maguey leaf.

Mole Pronounced "*moh*-lay," a sauce made with 20 ingredients including chocolate, peppers, ground tortillas, sesame seeds, cinnamon, tomatoes, onion, garlic, peanuts, pumpkin seeds, cloves, and tomatillos; developed by colonial nuns in Puebla, usually served over chicken or turkey; especially served in Puebla, State of Mexico, and Oaxaca with sauces varying from red, to black and brown.

Molletes A bolillo cut in half and topped with refried beans and cheese, then broiled; popular at breakfast.

Pan de Muerto Sweet or plain bread made around the Days of the Dead (Nov.1–2), in the form of mummies, dolls, or round with bone designs.

Pan dulce Lightly sweetened bread in many configurations usually served at breakfast or bought at any bakery.

Papadzules Tortillas are stuffed with hard-boiled eggs and seeds (cucumber or sunflower) in a tomato sauce.

Pavo relleno negro Stuffed turkey Yucatán-style, filled with chopped pork and beef, cooked in a rich, dark sauce.

Pibil Pit-baked pork or chicken in a sauce of tomato, onion, mild red pepper, cilantro, and vinegar.

Pipian Sauce made with ground pumpkin seeds, nuts, and mild peppers.

Poc-chuc Slices of pork with onion marinated in a tangy sour orange sauce and charcoal broiled; a Yucatecan specialty.

Pollo Calpulalpan Chicken cooked in pulque, a specialty of Tlaxcala.

Pozole A soup made with hominy and pork or chicken, in either a tomato-based broth Jalisco-style, or a white broth Nayarit-style, or green chile sauce Guerrero-style, and topped with choice of chopped white onion, lettuce or cabbage, radishes, oregano, red pepper, and cilantro.

Pulque Drink made of fermented sap of the maguey plant; best in state of Hidalgo and around Mexico City.

Quesadilla Four tortillas stuffed with melted white cheese and lightly fried.

Queso relleno "Stuffed cheese" is a mild yellow cheese stuffed with minced meat and spices, a Yucatecan specialty.

Rompope Delicious Mexican eggnog, invented in Puebla, made with eggs, vanilla, sugar, and rum.

Salsa verde   A cooked sauce using the green tomatillo and pureed with mildly hot peppers, onions, garlic, and cilantro; on tables countrywide.

Sopa de calabaza   Soup made of chopped squash or pumpkin blossoms.

Sopa de lima   A tangy soup made with chicken broth and accented with fresh lime; popular in Yucatán.

Sopa Tlalpeña   A hearty soup made with chunks of chicken, chopped carrots, zucchini, corn, onions, garlic, and cilantro.

Sopa Tlaxcalteca   A hearty tomato-based soup filled with cooked nopal cactus, cheese, cream, and avocado with crispy tortilla strips floating on top.

Sopa tortilla   A traditional chicken broth-based soup, seasoned with chiles, tomatoes, onion, and garlic, bobbing with crisp fried strips of corn tortillas.

Sopa Tarascan   A rib sticking pinto-bean based soup, flavored with onions, garlic, tomatoes, chiles, and chicken broth and garnished with sour cream, white cheese, avocado chunks and fried tortilla strips; a specialty of Michoacán state.

Sopa seca   Not a soup at all, but a seasoned rice which translated means "dry soup."

Sope   Pronounced "*soh*-pay," a botana similar to a garnacha, except spread with refried beans and topped with crumbled cheese and onions.

Tacos al pastor   Thin slices of flavored pork roasted on a revolving cylinder dripping with onion slices and juice of fresh pineapple slices.

Tamal   Incorrectly called tamale (tamal singular, tamales plural), meat or sweet filling rolled with fresh masa, then wrapped in a corn husk or banana leaf and steamed; many varieties and sizes throughout the country.

Tepache   Drink made of fermented pineapple peelings and brown sugar.

Tikin Xic   Also seen on menus as "tikin chick," char-broiled fish brushed with achiote sauce.

Tinga   A stew made with pork tenderloin, sausage, onions, garlic, tomatoes, chiles, and potatoes; popular on menus in Puebla and Hidalgo states.

Torta   A sandwich, usually on bolillo bread, usually with sliced avocado, onions, tomatoes, with a choice of meat and often cheese.

Torta Ahogado   A specialty of Lake Chapala is made with scooped out roll, filled with beans and beef strips and seasoned with a tomato or chile sauce.

Tostadas   Crispy fried corn tortillas topped with meat, onions, lettuce, tomatoes, cheese, avocados, and sometimes sour cream.

Venado   Venison (deer) served perhaps as pipian de venado, steamed in banana leaves and served with a sauce of ground squash seeds.

Xtabentun   (pronounced "Shtah-ben-*toon*") A Yucatán liquor made of fermented honey and flavored with anise. It comes *seco* (dry) or *crema* (sweet).

Zacahuil   Pork leg tamal, packed in thick masa, wrapped in banana leaves, and pit baked; sometimes pot-made with tomato and masa; specialty of mid-to-upper Veracruz.

Index